더 얇게, 더 쉽게 20일 만에 700+ 달성하는

정재현 토익 똑똑한 기본서

LC + RC

SMART

정재현

D 영단기

정재현 토익
똑똑한 기본서 LC+RC

대표저자	정재현
저자	조대호 송다영
연구원	우중민 정수현 김다현 엄혜원 Michael Putlack Julie Tofflemire
기획 총괄	김영일
기획·편집	정유상
마케팅·영업	손지한 김정현 양윤화 김보경
표지 디자인	김보라
내지 디자인	남보라
펴낸날	2판 1쇄 2020년 8월 1일
	4쇄 2024년 10월 20일
펴낸이	김정택
펴낸곳	㈜에스티유니타스
등록번호	제25100-2022-000072호
홈페이지	eng.conects.com
고객센터	카카오톡 플러스 친구 [영단기] / 커넥츠 영단기 1:1 게시판
주소	서울시 구로구 경인로 662 타워동 30층/31층
ISBN	979-11-6576-058-8 (13740)

잘못 만들어진 책은 구입처에서 바꿔 드립니다.
가격은 뒤표지에 있습니다.
이 책에 실린 모든 글과 사진, 일러스트를 포함한 디자인 및 편집 형태, 배포에 대한 권리는
㈜에스티유니타스에 있으므로 무단으로 전재하거나 복제, 배포, 전송할 수 없습니다.

저자의 말

기본 개념과 실전유형을 모두 담은 제대로 된 '기본서', 그러나 몇 년에 한번 출제되는 내용까지 모두 다루느라 두껍고 부담스러운 기본서가 아니라, 필요한 내용만 알차게 담은 '똑똑한 기본서'를 오랫동안 고민하고 준비해 왔습니다. 특히, 요즘 700-800점을 필요로 하는 토익 수험생들이 많기에, LC와 RC를 한 권으로 끝낼 수 있는 <정재현 토익 똑똑한 기본서 LC+RC>를 출간하게 되어 정말 기쁜 마음입니다.

<정재현 토익 똑똑한 기본서 LC+RC>는 저의 주관적인 판단을 배제하고 철저하게 데이터 분석을 통한 출제빈도를 반영하여 본문 내용을 구성하였습니다. 750점 달성 기준인 정답 개수 LC 85개, RC 75개 이상을 충분히 맞힐 수 있도록 반드시 학습해야 할 필수적인 내용들만 교재에 포함시켰기 때문에 학습자 여러분들은 방대한 내용을 학습하느라 시간을 낭비할 필요없이 최소한의 학습과 시간으로 목표 점수에 도달할 수 있을 것입니다.

토익 초·중급자들을 위해, 길고 어려운 이론 설명보다는 핵심 설명으로 기본기를 익히게 한 뒤 많은 연습문제 풀이를 통해 실제 시험에 적용할 수 있도록 교재를 구성했습니다. 따라서 <정재현 토익 똑똑한 기본서 LC+RC>는 각 DAY별로 충분한 연습문제 및 실전문제를 담고 있으며, '기출 연습하기' 코너에서는 각 유형별로 가장 출제 빈도가 높은 문제를 담아, 시중의 그 어떤 경쟁서보다 학습 내용에 대한 확실한 정리 및 이해가 가능하도록 하였습니다. 또한 실전 시험과 동일한 난이도의 문제들로 구성된 모의고사를 1회 제공하여, 효율적인 마무리를 할 수 있게 하였습니다.

최고의 교재를 만들기 위해, 기획부터 방대한 자료의 분석 및 집필까지 그 모든 단계에서 저와 함께 머리를 맞대고 고민해온 정재현어학연구소 연구원들과 커넥츠영단기 출판본부 직원분들께 진심으로 감사드리며 이번 <정재현 토익 똑똑한 기본서 LC+RC> 교재를 통해 여러분들이 '토익'이라는 도전을 빠르고 자신감 있게 끝낼 수 있기를 소망합니다.

여러분을 온 마음으로 응원합니다.

여러분의 토익 선생님,
정재현 드림

TOEIC 시험 정보의 모든 것

토익 소개

TOEIC 시험이란?
TEST OF ENGLISH FOR INTERNATIONAL COMMUNICATION의 약자로, 모국어가 영어가 아닌 사람이 일상적인 생활 또는 업무에서 의사소통이 가능한지를 평가하는 시험입니다.

시험 구성
듣기(LC) 4개 파트 100문제와 읽기(RC) 3개 파트 100문제로 총 7개 파트에 걸쳐 200문제가 출제됩니다. 200문제 모두 선택지 중에서 정답을 찾는 객관식 문제로 출제됩니다.

구성	PART 구성	출제 내용	문항수	시간	점수
LC (Listening Comprehension)	PART 1	사진 묘사 (사진 보고 문제 풀기)	6	45분 내외	495점
	PART 2	질문-대답 (질문 듣고 답변 고르기)	25		
	PART 3	짧은 대화 (두세 사람의 대화를 듣고 질문에 답하기)	39		
	PART 4	설명문 (전화 메시지, 연설문, 안내방송, 일기예보 등을 듣고 질문에 답하기)	30		
RC (Reading Comprehension)	PART 5	문장 빈칸 채우기 (하나의 문장 안에 있는 빈칸에 알맞은 말(문법 & 어휘) 고르기)	30	75분	495점
	PART 6	지문 빈칸 채우기 (짧은 지문 안에 있는 빈칸에 알맞은 말(문법 & 어휘 & 문장) 고르기)	16		
	PART 7	싱글 지문 (1개의 지문을 읽고 질문에 답하기)	29		
		더블 지문 (2개의 지문을 읽고 질문에 답하기)	10		
		트리플 지문 (3개의 지문을 읽고 질문에 답하기)	15		
총계			200	약 120분	990점

출제 범위 및 주제
일상생활 및 업무에 대한 영어 의사소통 능력을 평가하기 때문에 특정 분야의 전문 지식 또는 이와 관련된 어휘는 출제하지 않습니다. 국제 업무 환경에 맞게 다양한 국가의 지명과 성명이 등장하며, 듣기 평가에서는 미국, 영국, 호주 발음이 고르게 섞여 출제됩니다. 다음의 주제를 참고해 봅시다.

기업 일반	이사회, 편지, 공지, 전화, 팩스, 이메일, 사무실 장비 및 가구, 사무실 규정, 계약, 협상, 합병 및 인수, 판매, 보증, 사업계획, 회의, 노사관계
공식 연회	식사 및 연회, 장소 예약
엔터테인먼트	영화, 공연, 전시
재무	은행업무, 투자, 세금, 회계, 청구
의료	건강보험, 병원 방문 및 예약
부동산	건설 및 보수 내역, 부동산 구매 및 임대, 기타 설비
제조	제품 조립, 공장 경영, 품질 관리
채용	모집, 고용, 퇴임, 승진, 급여, 일자리 지원서, 구인광고, 연금, 시상
구매	쇼핑, 주문, 배송, 송장
기술	전자장비, 기술지원, 컴퓨터, 연구실과 관련 장비
여행	교통 관련 일정, 교통 관련 각종 공지, 렌터카, 호텔 예약, 연착 및 취소

세상에서 가장 친절한 토익 시험 가이드

1 토익 접수 방법
- 토익 시험의 인터넷 접수 기간을 한국 TOEIC 위원회 사이트(www.toeic.co.kr)에서 확인합니다.
- 사이트에서 인터넷 접수를 선택하고 시험일, 고사장, 수험정보 등의 정보를 입력합니다.
- 시험 접수 시 최근 6개월 이내 사진(JPG 형식)이 필요하오니 미리 준비합니다.

TIP 시험 D-30부터는 특별 추가 접수에 해당하여 약 5천원 정도의 추가 비용이 발생합니다. 미리 시험을 접수하는 것이 좋습니다.

2 시험 당일 꼭! 챙겨야 할 준비물
- **규정 신분증**
  성인의 경우, 주민등록증, 운전면허증, 기간 만료 전 여권, 공무원증 등이 인정됩니다. 중고등학생에 한하여 학생증(국내 학생증만 허용)도 신분증으로 인정됩니다.
- **연필 (볼펜, 사인펜은 No!)**
  연필 끝을 뭉뚝하게 만들어 준비하면 답안 마킹을 더 쉽게 할 수 있습니다.
- **지우개**
- **아날로그 손목시계 (전자식 시계는 No!)**

3 입실 전 유의사항
- 시험 시간이 오전일 경우, 오전 9:20까지, 시험 시간이 오후일 경우 오후 2:20까지 입실합니다.

TIP 오전 시험은 오전 9:50 이후, 오후 시험은 오후 2:50 이후로는 절대 입실할 수 없으니 꼭 시간을 지켜 미리 입실합니다.
TIP 시험 시간 직전에는 독해 문제를 풀기보다는 듣기 연습을 충분히 하여 귀를 훈련시키는 게 더 효과적입니다.

4 시험 진행 안내

오전 시험	오후 시험	시험 진행
9:30~9:45 (15분)	2:30~2:45 (15분)	답안지 작성 오리엔테이션
9:45~9:50 (5분)	2:45~2:50 (5분)	쉬는 시간
9:50~10:05 (15분)	2:50~3:05 (15분)	신분증 확인
10:05~10:10 (5분)	3:05~3:10 (5분)	문제지 배부, 파본 확인
10:10~10:55 (45분)	3:10~3:55 (45분)	듣기 평가 (LC)
10:55~12:10 (75분)	3:55~5:10 (75분)	독해 평가 (RC)

5 성적 확인 및 성적표 발급 방법 알아보기
- 시험일로부터 10일 후 낮 12시에 한국 TOEIC 위원회 사이트(www.toeic.co.kr)에서 성적 확인이 가능합니다.
  (토요일 시행 시험 등 일부 회차 시험은 11일 후에 발표될 수 있습니다.)
- 성적 수령은 온라인 출력이나 우편 수령을 택할 수 있습니다.
- 온라인 출력 시, 성적 유효 기간 내 홈페이지에서 출력할 수 있습니다.
- 우편 수령 시, 성적 발표 후 접수 시 기입한 주소로 성적표가 우편 발송됩니다. (약 7~10일 소요)
- 온라인 출력과 우편 수령은 1회 발급만 무료이며, 이후에는 유료로 발급됩니다.

이 책의 **구성과 특징**

빠른 700+점 달성을 위한 전략

본격적으로 학습을 시작하기 앞서, [빠른 700+점 달성을 위한 전략]을 먼저 살펴보세요. 700점 목표라면 과감히 버려도 되는 문제를 확인하면 최소한의 학습과 시간으로 목표 점수에 도달할 수 있습니다.

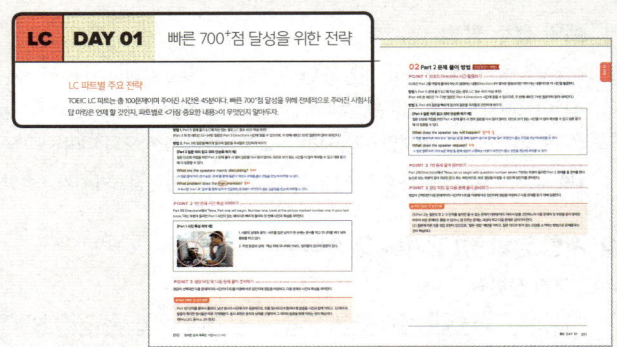

기본기 익히기 & 출제 포인트

이론이 필요한 부분은 [기본기 익히기]로 기초부터 탄탄히 하고, 각 Day별로 깔끔하게 정리된 [출제 포인트]로 핵심 내용만 학습하세요.

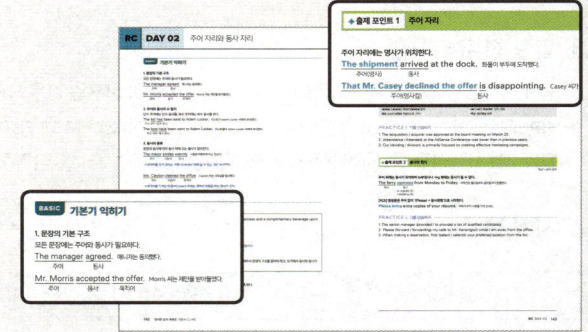

기출 유형 맛보기 & 기출 연습하기

어떻게 문제를 푸는지 단계별로 보여주는 [기출 유형 맛보기]로 기출 문제를 푸는 방법을 익히고, [기출 연습하기]를 통해 적용해보세요.

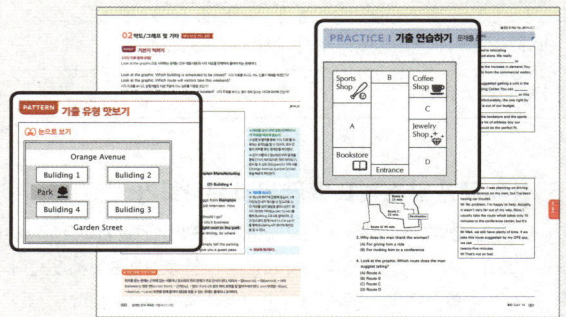

기출 표현 익히기
& 패러프레이징 연습

다양한 어휘가 필수적인 LC에는 [기출 표현 익히기] 코너가, 본문의 내용이 다른 말로 바뀌어서 정답으로 출제되는 RC에는 [패러프레이징 연습] 코너를 수록했습니다.

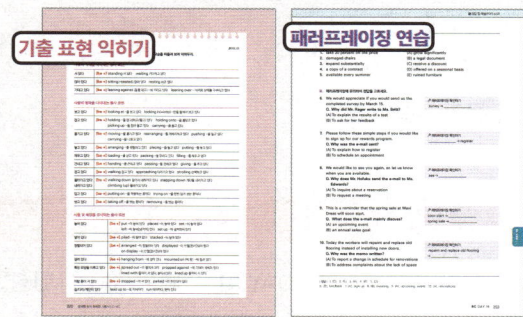

출제 포인트별 출제빈도 수록
& 실전문제

철저히 분석한 데이터를 바탕으로 실제 토익 시험의 출제 빈도를 출제 포인트별로 정리했습니다. 빈도수가 높은 출제 포인트는 더 주의 깊게 살펴보세요.
또한 실전 시험과 동일한 난이도의 문제들로만 구성된 실전 문제를 통해 각 day가 끝날 때마다 학습한 내용을 적용해 문제를 풀어볼 수 있습니다.

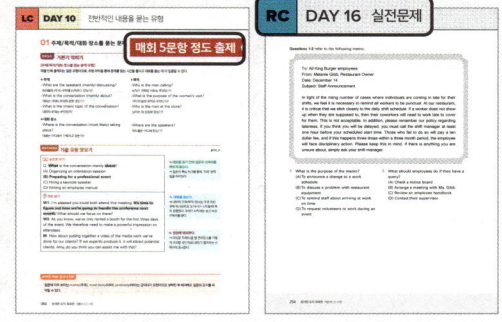

친절하고 자세한 해설집(책 속의 책)
& 무료 MP3 다운로드

정답의 단서가 되는 부분은 별도의 색으로 표시하여 한눈에 파악할 수 있고, 자세한 해설을 수록하여 풀이 방식 및 정답의 이유를 명확하게 이해할 수 있습니다.
다양한 버전의 MP3 음원을 커넥츠 영단기 홈페이지에서 로그인 없이도 무료로 다운로드 받을 수 있습니다.

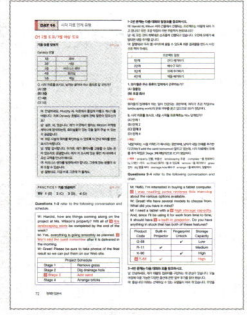
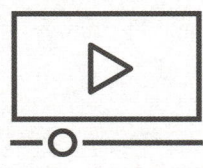

MP3 다운로드 경로
▶ [eng.conects.com] – [교재구매] – [MP3/해설집 다운] – [정재현 토익 똑똑한 기본서 LC+RC]

목차

저자의 말		001
TOEIC 시험 소개		002
이 책의 구성과 특징		004

LC

	DAY 01	빠른 700⁺점 달성을 위한 전략	010

PART 1

DAY 02	시제·태/오답 유형	016
DAY 03	1인·2인 사진/다인·사물·풍경 사진	022

PART 2

DAY 04	의문사 의문문 (1) – Who/What/Which	028
DAY 05	의문사 의문문 (2) – When/Where	034
DAY 06	의문사 의문문 (3) – How/Why	040
DAY 07	비 의문사 의문문 (1)	046
DAY 08	비 의문사 의문문 (2)	052
DAY 09	비 의문사 의문문 (3)	058

PART 3

DAY 10	전반적인 내용을 묻는 유형	064
DAY 11	세부적인 내용을 묻는 유형 (1)	070
DAY 12	세부적인 내용을 묻는 유형 (2)	076
DAY 13	세부적인 내용을 묻는 유형 (3)	082
DAY 14	시각 자료 연계 유형	088

PART 4

DAY 15	전반적인 내용을 묻는 유형	094
DAY 16	세부적인 내용을 묻는 유형 (1)	100
DAY 17	세부적인 내용을 묻는 유형 (2)	106
DAY 18	담화 유형_전화 메시지/광고	112
DAY 19	담화 유형_회의 발췌록/투어 정보	120
DAY 20	담화 유형_안내 방송/방송/뉴스	128

RC

	DAY 01	빠른 700⁺점 달성을 위한 전략	138

PART 5&6

	DAY 02	주어 자리와 동사 자리	148
	DAY 03	태 / 시제 / 가정법	156
	DAY 04	명사	162
	DAY 05	대명사	168
	DAY 06	형용사 / 부사	174
	DAY 07	to부정사 / 동명사	182
	DAY 08	분사	190
	DAY 09	전치사	196
	DAY 10	부사절 접속사 / 등위·상관 접속사	202
	DAY 11	명사절 접속사 / 형용사절 접속사(=관계 대명사)	208
	DAY 12	비교	214
	DAY 13	어휘 – 동사 / 형용사 / 부사	220
	DAY 14	어휘 – 명사 / 전치사	228
	DAY 15	Part 6	236

PART 7

	DAY 16	주제, 목적 및 대상을 묻는 유형	250
	DAY 17	세부 사항을 묻는 유형	258
	DAY 18	진위 확인 유형	266
	DAY 19	문장 넣기 / 의도 파악 / 동의어 찾기 유형	274
	DAY 20	다중 지문 연계 유형	284

ACTUAL TEST 294

해설집 (책 속의 책)

PART 1

DAY 01 빠른 700⁺점 달성을 위한 전략
DAY 02 시제·태/오답 유형
DAY 03 1인·2인 사진/다인·사물·풍경 사진

PART 2

DAY 04 의문사 의문문 (1) – Who/What/Which
DAY 05 의문사 의문문 (2) – When/Where
DAY 06 의문사 의문문 (3) – How/Why
DAY 07 비 의문사 의문문 (1)
DAY 08 비 의문사 의문문 (2)
DAY 09 비 의문사 의문문 (3)

정재현 토익
똑똑한 기본서
LC+RC

PART 3

DAY 10 전반적인 내용을 묻는 유형
DAY 11 세부적인 내용을 묻는 유형 (1)
DAY 12 세부적인 내용을 묻는 유형 (2)
DAY 13 세부적인 내용을 묻는 유형 (3)
DAY 14 시각 자료 연계 유형

PART 4

DAY 15 전반적인 내용을 묻는 유형
DAY 16 세부적인 내용을 묻는 유형 (1)
DAY 17 세부적인 내용을 묻는 유형 (2)
DAY 18 담화 유형_전화 메시지/광고
DAY 19 담화 유형_회의 발췌록/투어 정보
DAY 20 담화 유형_안내 방송/방송/뉴스

LC | DAY 01 빠른 700⁺점 달성을 위한 전략

LC 파트별 주요 전략
TOEIC LC 파트는 총 100문제이며 주어진 시간은 45분이다. 빠른 700⁺점 달성을 위해 전체적으로 주어진 시험시간을 어떻게 활용할 것인지, 정답 마킹은 언제 할 것인지, 파트별로 <가장 중요한 내용>이 무엇인지 알아두자.

01 Part 1 문제 풀이 방법 6문항 (1~6번)

POINT 1 1분 30초의 Directions 시간 활용하기
90초간 Part 1 예제와 함께 문제를 어떻게 풀어야 하는지 설명하는 내용(Directions)이 영어로 방송되지만 듣지 않고 이 시간을 활용한다.

방법 1. Part 5 문제 풀기 (LC에 자신 있는 경우, LC 점수 400 이상 추천)

방법 2. Part 3의 질문을 빠르게 읽으며 질문을 우리말로 간단하게 바꾸기
(Part 3 의 첫 세트인 32~34번 질문은 Part 3 Directions 시간에 읽을 수 있으므로, 두 번째 세트인 35번 질문부터 읽어 내려간다.)

> **[Part 3 질문 미리 읽고 의미 단순화 하기 예]**
> 질문 단순화 작업을 하면 Part 3 문제 풀이 시 영어 질문을 다시 읽지 않아도 되므로 보기 읽는 시간을 더 많이 확보할 수 있고 대화 듣기에 더 집중할 수 있다.
>
> **What** are the speakers mainly **discussing**? 주제
> → 영문 옆에 미리 적어 놓은 '주제'를 통해 질문이 대화의 주제를 묻는 것임을 한눈에 파악할 수 있다.
>
> **What problem** does the (man) mention? 문제
> → 표시된 'man'과 '문제'를 통해 남자가 언급하는 문제점이 무엇인지 묻는 질문임을 한눈에 파악할 수 있다.

POINT 2 1번 문제 사진 특성 파악하기
Part 1의 Directions에서 "Now, Part one will begin. Number one. Look at the picture marked number one in your test book."라는 부분이 들리면 Part 1 사진이 있는 페이지로 빠르게 돌아와 첫 번째 사진의 특성을 파악한다.

> **[Part 1 사진 특성 파악 예]**
>
>
>
> 1. 사람의 상태와 동작 : 셔츠를 입은 남자가 한 손에는 문서를 쥐고 모니터를 쳐다 보며 통화를 하고 있다.
> 2. 주변 환경의 상태 : 책상 위에 모니터와 키보드, 정리함이 있으며 창문이 있다.

POINT 3 정답 마킹 및 다음 문제 풀이 준비하기
정답이 선택되면 다음 문제까지의 시간(약 5초)을 이용해 바로 답안지에 정답을 마킹하고, 다음 문제의 사진의 특성을 파악한다.

> 📌 **빠른 700⁺점 달성 TIP**
> Part 1은 단어를 몰라서 틀린다. 낯선 명사가 사진에 자주 등장하므로, 빈출 명사의 단수형/복수형 발음을 사진과 함께 익히고, 단/복수의 발음이 특이한 명사들은 따로 기억해둔다. 동사 표현은 동작과 상태를 구별하여 그 의미와 발음을 함께 익히는 것이 핵심이다.
> (명사 p.26, 동사 p. 20 참조)

02 Part 2 문제 풀이 방법 〔25문항 (7~31번)〕

POINT 1   30초의 Directions 시간 활용하기

30초간 Part 2를 어떻게 풀어야 하는지 설명하는 내용(Directions)이 영어로 방송되지만 듣지 않고 이 시간을 활용한다.

방법 1. Part 5 문제 풀기 (LC에 자신 있는 경우, LC 점수 400 이상 추천)

방법 2. Part 4의 질문을 빠르게 읽으며 질문을 우리말로 간단하게 바꾸기
(Part 4의 첫 세트인 71~73번 질문은 Part 4 Directions 시간에 읽을 수 있으므로, 두 번째 세트인 74번 질문부터 읽어 내려간다.)

> **[Part 4 질문 미리 읽고 의미 단순화 하기 예]**
> 질문 단순화 작업을 하면 Part 4 문제 풀이 시 영어 질문을 다시 읽지 않아도 되므로 보기 읽는 시간을 더 많이 확보할 수 있고 담화 듣기에 더 집중할 수 있다.
>
> What does the speaker say will happen? 일어날 일
> → 영문 옆에 미리 적어 놓은 '일어날 일'을 통해 질문이 앞으로 일어날 일이 무엇인지 묻는 것임을 한눈에 파악할 수 있다.
>
> What does the speaker request? 요청
> → 영문 옆에 미리 적어 놓은 '요청'을 통해 질문이 요청하는 내용이 무엇인지 묻는 것임을 한눈에 파악할 수 있다.

POINT 2   7번 문제 풀이 준비하기

Part 2의 Directions에서 "Now, let us begin with question number seven."이라는 부분이 들리면 Part 2 문제를 풀 준비를 한다. 눈으로 보는 부분이 없이 귀로만 듣고 푸는 파트이므로, 바로 정답을 마킹할 수 있도록 답안지를 준비한다.

POINT 3   정답 마킹 및 다음 문제 풀이 준비하기

정답이 선택되면 다음 문제까지의 시간(약 5초)을 이용해 바로 답안지에 정답을 마킹하고 다음 문제를 듣기 위해 집중한다.

> 🔖 **빠른 700⁺점 달성 TIP**
>
> (1) Part 2는 질문의 첫 2~3 단어를 놓치면 풀 수 없는 문제가 대부분이다. 따라서 답을 고민하느라 다음 문제의 첫 부분을 듣지 못하면 아무리 쉬운 문제라도 틀릴 수 있으니, 잘 모르는 문제는 과감히 찍고 다음 문제로 넘어가야 한다.
> (2) 질문에 따른 빈출 정답 표현이 있으므로, '질문-정답' 패턴을 익히고, 질문 의도와 맞지 않는 오답을 소거하는 방법으로 문제를 푸는 것이 핵심이다.

03 Part 3 문제 풀이 방법 39문항 (32~70번)

POINT 1 30초의 Directions 시간 활용하기

30초간 Part 3를 어떻게 풀어야 하는지 설명하는 내용(Directions)이 영어로 방송되지만 듣지 않고 이 시간을 활용한다.
1단계 Part 3의 첫 세트인 32~34번 질문을 빠르게 읽으며 질문을 우리말로 간단하게 바꾸기
2단계 • 세 문제 보기 중 가장 긴 보기부터 먼저 읽기
 • 보기의 명사에 동그라미 하기
 → 대화에서 단서로 제시된 단어가 정답 보기에 그대로 나오는 경우가 많으며, 그 중 명사의 비중이 가장 높다.

[Part 3의 첫 3문제 예]

32. Who most likely is the woman? 직업
 (A) An investor
 (B) An intern
 (C) A job applicant
 (D) A supervisor

33. What does the man request that the woman do? 요청
 (A) Download a program
 (B) Sign a form
 (C) Write an e-mail
 (D) Share her opinions

34. What did the man recently do? 최근 한 일
 (A) He registered for a conference.
 (B) He published a book.
 (C) He purchased some furniture.
 (D) He reviewed customer feedback.

1단계. 적어도 질문의 내용을 미리 알아야 대화의 어떤 부분에 집중해서 들어야 하는지 알 수 있다.

2단계. 세 문제 보기 중 가장 길이가 긴 보기이므로 먼저 읽은 후, 각 문제 보기의 명사에 빠르게 동그라미 한다.

POINT 2 32번 문제 풀이 준비하기

Part 3 Directions에서 "Questions thirty two through thirty four refer to the following conversation."라는 부분이 들리면 32~33번 첫 두 질문의 요지를 빠르게 확인한 후, 대화에 집중하여 듣는다.
→ 두 번째 질문이 전반적인 내용 혹은 문제점을 묻는 내용이라면, 대화의 초반부에 첫 두 문제의 단서가 겹쳐서 제시될 수 있으므로, 두 질문의 요지를 기억하고 대화를 듣는 것이 좋다.

[Part 3 대화에서 단서가 겹쳐서 제시되는 문제 유형 예]
32. Where are the speakers? 장소
33. What problem does the man mention? 문제점
 → 두 번째 문제가 문제점을 묻는 유형이므로, '장소'와 '남자의 문제점' 둘 다 기억하며 대화를 듣는다.

POINT 3 정답 마킹 및 다음 문제 풀이 준비하기

대화를 들으며 정답이 들리는 순간 문제지에 빠르게 마킹한 후, 다음 대화가 시작 될 때까지의 시간(약 37초)을 이용해 바로 다음 세 문제의 질문과 보기를 빠르게 파악한다.

[Part 1 Directions 시간에 질문을 미리 읽어 놓은 세트]
- 보기를 빠르게 읽기. 이 때 세 문제 중 가장 긴 보기부터 먼저 읽기 시작하기

[질문을 미리 읽어 놓지 않은 세트]
- 질문 먼저 읽으며 의미를 간단히 적은 후, 가장 긴 보기부터 읽기 시작하기

→ Part 3 정답 마킹은 LC 파트가 모두 끝난 후에 한다.

빠른 700⁺점 달성 TIP

Part 3은 대화를 듣기 전 질문 내용을 먼저 파악해야 정답을 맞힐 수 있다. 특히 LC 초보자의 경우, 대화를 들으면서 동시에 질문이나 선택지를 읽는 것은 불가능하다. 따라서 질문의 요지가 한눈에 들어올 수 있도록 평소에 질문의 요지를 간단히 우리말로 적고, 선택지의 의미를 빠르게 해석하는 연습을 해야 빠른 점수 상승이 가능하다. 또한 문제 유형별로 자주 반복되는 단서 표현을 알아두면 정답 찾기가 쉬워진다.

04 Part 4 문제 풀이 방법 30문항 (71~100번)

POINT 1 30초의 Directions 시간 활용하기

30초간 Part 4를 어떻게 풀어야 하는지 설명하는 내용(Directions)이 영어로 방송되지만 듣지 않고 이 시간을 활용한다.

1단계 Part 4의 첫 세트인 71~73번 질문을 빠르게 읽으며 질문을 우리말로 간단하게 바꾸기

2단계
- 세 문제 보기 중 가장 긴 보기부터 먼저 읽기
- 보기의 명사에 동그라미 하기

→ 담화에서 단서로 제시된 단어가 정답 보기에 그대로 나오는 경우가 많으며, 그 중 명사의 비중이 가장 높다.

[Part 4의 첫 3문제 예]

71. What is the purpose of the message? 목적
    (A) To complain about parking
    (B) To request an estimate
    (C) To report a broken machine
    (D) To arrange a meeting

1단계. 적어도 질문의 내용을 미리 알아야 담화의 어떤 부분에 집중해서 들어야 하는지 알 수 있다.

72. What problem does the speaker report? 문제
    (A) A worker has been absent.
    (B) Some equipment has been damaged.
    (C) Some materials are unavailable.
    (D) Production costs have increased.

2단계. 세 문제 보기 중 가장 길이가 긴 보기이므로 먼저 읽은 후, 보기의 명사에 빠르게 동그라미 한다.

73. What will the speaker most likely do next? 다음 할 일
    (A) Show a video
    (B) Respond to inquiries
    (C) Pass out samples
    (D) Give a demonstration

POINT 2 71번 문제 풀이 준비하기

Part 4 Directions에서 "Questions seventy one through seventy three refer to the following ~~." 라는 부분이 들리면 71~72번 질문의 요지를 빠르게 확인한 후, 담화에 집중해서 듣는다.

→ 담화에서 두 번째 질문의 내용이 전반적인 내용 혹은 문제점을 묻는 내용이라면, 담화의 초반부에 첫 두 문제의 단서가 겹쳐서 제시될 수 있으므로, 두 질문의 요지를 기억하고 담화를 듣는 것이 좋다.

[Part 4 담화에서 단서가 겹쳐서 제시되는 문제 유형 예]
71. What kind of business does the speaker work for? 화자 직장
72. What is the speaker announcing? 발표 내용
→ 두 번째 문제가 전반적인 내용을 묻는 유형이므로, '화자 직장'과 '발표 내용' 둘 다 기억하며 담화를 듣는다.

POINT 3 정답 마킹 및 다음 문제 풀이 준비하기

담화를 들으며 정답이 들리는 순간 문제지에 빠르게 마킹한 후, 다음 담화가 시작 될 때까지의 시간(약 37초)을 이용해 바로 다음 세 문제의 질문과 보기를 빠르게 파악한다.

[Part 2 Directions 시간에 질문을 미리 읽어 놓은 세트]
• 보기를 빠르게 읽기. 이 때 세 문제 중 가장 긴 보기부터 먼저 읽기 시작하기

[질문을 미리 읽어 놓지 않은 세트]
• 질문을 먼저 읽으며 의미를 간단히 적은 후, 가장 긴 보기부터 읽기 시작하기

→ LC 파트가 모두 끝난 후, Part 3과 Part4의 정답을 답안지에 옮겨 적는다.

> **빠른 700⁺점 달성 TIP**
>
> Part 4는 담화를 듣기 전 질문 내용을 먼저 파악해야 정답을 맞힐 확률이 높아진다. 특히 LC 초보자의 경우, 담화를 들으면서 동시에 질문이나 선택지를 읽는 것은 불가능하다. 따라서 질문과 선택지의 요지가 한눈에 들어올 수 있도록 평소에 질문과 길이가 긴 보기를 빠르게 읽으며 간단히 우리말로 요지를 적는 연습을 하는 것이 중요한데, 이는 문제 풀이시 영문을 다시 읽지 않아도 되어 담화에 더 집중하여 들을 수 있기 때문이다. 또한 문제 유형별, 담화 유형별로 자주 반복되는 단서 표현을 알아두면 정답 찾기가 쉬워진다.

700⁺점 목표라면 과감히 버려도 되는 문제

TOEIC 700점을 목표로 한다면, 일반적으로 RC 보다 LC가 점수를 올리기 용이하므로 LC 점수는 350-400점을 목표로 하는 것이 좋다. LC 점수 350-400점을 위해서는 대략적으로 100문제 중 16~23개 정도 틀리면 되는데, 어떤 유형이 고난도 문제인지 알아둔다면, 풀어서 맞힐 수 있는 문제에 좀 더 집중할 수 있다.

01 Part 3~4의 의도 파악 문제 유형

의도 파악 문제는 Part 3에서는 매회 2-3문항, Part 4에서는 매회 2-3문항으로 매회 총 5문항 정도 출제된다. 의도 파악 문제는 단서가 의도 파악 문장보다 먼저 나오는 경우가 대부분이며 대화나 담화의 흐름을 파악하며 들어야 한다. 또한 보기의 길이가 긴 편이므로 쉽게 답을 찾을 수 없는 경우가 많으며 그럴 경우 고민하지 말고 바로 다음 문제로 넘어가야 한다.

> [의도 파악 문제의 형태]
> What does the man **mean** when he says, "It took such a long time"?
> Why does the woman **say**, "I attended the conference last year"?
> What does the speaker **imply** when she says, "Please check your schedule"?

→ 질문에 mean/say/imply 동사가 쓰이며 모두 대화나 담화 속에 쓰인 표현이 "~" 형태로 들어가 있다.

02 Part 4의 시각 자료 연계 유형

Part 4 시각 자료 연계 유형은 매회 2-3문항이 출제되며 Part 3의 시각 자료 연계 유형은 명확한 단서가 주어지고 함정이 없는 문제가 많은 반면, Part 4의 시각 자료 연계 유형은 단서 이외에도 함정이 주어지는 문제가 많다. 따라서 쉽게 답을 찾을 수 없는 경우가 많으므로 그럴 경우 고민하지 말고 바로 다음 문제로 넘어가야 한다.

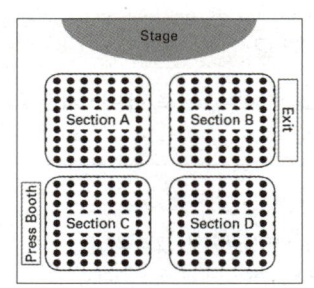 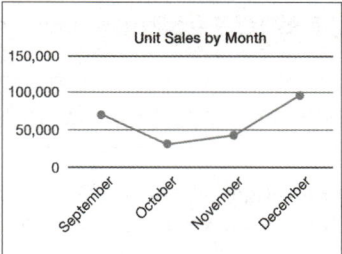

Employee Business Expenses: Walter Bennett		
DATE	AMOUNT	BUSINESS
August 1	$ 25	Mahlon Café
August 9	$ 40	Groton Inc.
August 24	$ 15	Jacobs Taxis
August 25	$130	Deleo Hotel

Look at the graphic. Where can the listeners find empty seats?
Look at the graphic. When did the company run some advertisements?
Look at the graphic. Which business does the speaker inquire about?

→ 위와 같은 시각 정보가 제공되며 "Look at the graphic ~"으로 시작하는 문제는 모두 시각 자료 연계 문제이다.

LC DAY 02 시제·태/오답 유형

01 문장의 시제와 태

♪ D02_01

Part 1에는 다양한 시제와 태로 된 동사가 출제되며, 동사의 시제와 태에 따라 문장의 의미가 달라지므로 가장 많이 출제되는 4가지 시제·태 유형을 알아두자.

◆ 출제 포인트 1   현재 진행 능동태(is/are V-ing) & 현재 진행 수동태(is/are being p.p.)

is/are V-ing(~하고 있는 중이다)는 Part 1에서 가장 많이 출제되는 동사 형태로, 주로 사람의 동작을 나타내지만 사람이나 사물의 상태를 나타내기도 한다. is/are being p.p.(~되고 있다)는 대부분 사물이 당하는 동작을 나타낸다.

Some workers **are repairing** a roof. (O)   몇몇 일꾼들이 지붕을 수리하고 있다. [사람의 동작]
= A roof **is being repaired**. (O)   지붕이 수리되고 있다. [사물이 당하는 동작]
→ 사람의 동작은 현재 진행(is/are + V-ing)과 현재 진행 수동태(is/are + being + p.p.)로 나타낸다.

A man **is wearing** a shirt. (O)   남자가 셔츠를 입은 상태이다. (이미 착용한 상태) [사람의 상태]
A painting **is hanging** on the wall. (O)   그림이 벽에 걸려 있다. [사물의 상태]
→ 현재 진행(is/are + V-ing)은 사람과 사물의 상태도 나타낼 수 있다.

◆ 출제 포인트 2   현재 수동태(is/are p.p.) & 현재 완료 수동태(has/have been p.p.)

is/are p.p.(~되어 있다)는 주로 사물의 상태나 위치를 나타낸다. has/have been p.p.(지금까지 ~인 상태이다)도 주로 사물을 묘사할 때 쓰며, 과거에 일어난 일이 현재까지 지속되고 있다는 의미이므로 현재 수동태와 같은 상황을 묘사할 수 있다.

The chairs **are arranged** in a circle. (O)
= The chairs **have been arranged** in a circle. (O)   의자들이 원형으로 놓여 있다.
→ 사물의 상태는 현재 수동태(is/are + p.p.)와 현재 완료 수동태(has/have + been + p.p.)로 나타낸다.

The boxes **are stacked**. (O)
= The boxes **have been stacked**. (O)   상자들이 쌓여 있다.
The boxes are being stacked. (X)   상자들이 쌓이는 중이다.
→ 현재 수동태와 현재 완료 수동태는 '쌓여 있는 상태'를 나타내며 현재 진행 수동태는 '쌓이는 동작'을 나타내므로 그 의미를 구별할 수 있어야 한다.

> 🔖 **빠른 700⁺점 달성 TIP**
>
> 사물의 상태나 위치를 묘사하는 표현으로 'There + is/are + 명사(~가 있다)'도 자주 정답으로 출제되므로 알아두자.
> ex) <u>There is</u> a book on the table.   테이블 위에 책 한 권이 있다.

PRACTICE | 기출 연습하기

보기가 사진과 일치하면 O, 다르면 X, 헷갈리면 △ 표기하며 문제를 푼 후, 빈칸을 채워보세요.

받아쓰기를 위해 보기는 두 번씩 들려줍니다.

1

(A) A man is _____ into a bag.
(B) A man is _____ some merchandise.
(C) A man is _____ a shopping cart.
(D) A man is _____ his shirt.

2

(A) The woman is _____ a glass.
(B) The woman is _____.
(C) The man is _____.
(D) The man is _____ a serving _____.

3

(A) There's some _____ on the _____.
(B) Passengers are _____ a train.
(C) The train is _____ the station.
(D) Some tracks are _____.

4

(A) Some chairs have _____ the table.
(B) Some _____ have been _____ a corner.
(C) A rug is _____.
(D) A _____ is being _____.

02 오답 유형

Part 1은 사진을 빠르게 판독한 후, 선택지를 들으며 순발력 있게 오답을 소거해 나갈 수 있어야 한다. Part 1의 대표적인 4가지 오답 유형을 알아두자.

◆ 출제 포인트 1 명사·동사 오류

문장의 동사는 사진을 제대로 묘사하지만 사진에 없는 명사가 들어있거나, 문장의 명사는 사진에 있으나 동사 표현이 적절하지 않은 경우가 Part 1의 가장 대표적인 오답 유형이다.

A ~~pedestrian~~ is crossing the street. (✗)
보행자가 길을 건너고 있다. [사진에 없는 명사 오류]
→ 보행자가 없으므로 오답이다.
Some cars are parked in a ~~garage~~. (✗)
몇몇 자동차들이 차고에 주차되어 있다. [사진에 없는 명사 오류]
→ 차고가 없으므로 오답이다.

A woman is ~~replacing~~ her phone. (✗)
여자가 전화기를 교체하고 있다. [사진에 없는 동사 오류]
→ 전화기를 교체하는 동작이 없으므로 오답이다.
A woman is ~~watering~~ a plant. (✗)
여자가 식물에 물을 주고 있다. [사진에 없는 동사 오류]
→ 물을 주는 동작이 없으므로 오답이다.

◆ 출제 포인트 2 동작·상태/배열·위치·장소 오류

이미 입고 있는 상태인데 입고 있는 동작으로 묘사하거나, 다른 표현은 모두 적절한데 장소나 배열 상태가 사진과 다른 경우도 자주 오답으로 출제된다.

She is ~~putting on~~ a sweater. (✗)
여자가 스웨터를 착용하는 중이다. [동작·상태 오류]
→ 입는 동작이 없으므로 오답이다.
[비교] She is wearing a sweater. (O)
여자가 스웨터를 착용한 상태이다.
→ 입은 상태를 나타내므로 정답이다.

A bag has been placed ~~on her lap~~. (✗)
가방이 여자의 무릎 위에 있다. [배열·위치·장소 오류]
→ 가방이 무릎 위에 놓인 것이 아니므로 오답이다.
A woman is taking a photo ~~indoors~~. (✗)
여자가 실내에서 사진을 찍고 있다. [배열·위치·장소 오류]
→ 실내가 아니므로 오답이다.

> 🚀 빠른 700⁺점 달성 TIP
>
> Part 1에 출제되는 동사는 익숙한 것이 많지만, 명사는 entryway(건물 입구의 통로), handrail(난간), silverware(은식기류), patio(테라스) 등과 같이 생소한 경우가 많다. 따라서 자주 출제되는 사물 명사를 익혀두는 것이 필요하다.

PRACTICE | 기출 연습하기

보기가 사진과 일치하면 O, 다르면 X, 헷갈리면 △ 표기하며 문제를 푼 후, 빈칸을 채워보세요.

받아쓰기를 위해 보기는 두 번씩 들려줍니다.

1

(A) He is _____ his sweater.
(B) He is _____ a staircase.
(C) The stairs are _____.
(D) Some artwork is _____ the railing.

2

(A) Some people are _____ a truck.
(B) One of the men is _____ a hat.
(C) Some people are _____ boxes _____.
(D) A truck is being _____.

3

(A) A man is _____ a laptop.
(B) A man is _____ his shirt.
(C) The table is _____.
(D) Some documents are _____ a desk.

4

(A) Some artwork has _____ the wall.
(B) Some furniture is _____.
(C) There is a desk _____.
(D) A drawer has _____.

PART 1 기출 표현 익히기

♪ D02_03

Part 1에는 반복적으로 출제되는 동사 표현이 있다. 사진 속 모습을 떠올려 보며 익혀두자.

사람의 자세를 나타내는 동사 표현

서 있다	**[be +]** standing 서 있다 waiting 기다리고 있다
앉아 있다	**[be +]** sitting(=seated) 앉아 있다 resting 쉬고 있다
기대고 있다	**[be +]** leaning against (등을 대고) ~에 기대고 있다 leaning over ~ 너머로 상체를 구부리고 있다

사람의 동작을 나타내는 동사 표현

보고 있다	**[be +]** looking at ~을 보고 있다 looking in(=into) ~안을 들여다 보고 있다
잡고 있다	**[be +]** holding ~을 잡고(쥐고/들고) 있다 holding onto ~을 붙잡고 있다 picking up ~을 집어 들고 있다 carrying ~을 들고 있다
옮기고 있다	**[be +]** moving ~을 옮기고 있다 rearranging ~을 재배치하고 있다 pushing ~을 밀고 있다 carrying ~을 나르고 있다
놓고 있다	**[be +]** arranging ~을 정렬하고 있다 placing ~을 놓고 있다 putting ~을 놓고 있다
채우고 있다	**[be +]** loading ~을 싣고 있다 packing ~을 꾸리고 있다 filling ~을 채우고 있다
건네고 있다	**[be +]** handing ~을 건네고 있다 passing ~을 건네고 있다 giving ~을 주고 있다
걷고 있다	**[be +]** walking 걷고 있다 approaching 다가가고 있다 strolling 산책하고 있다
올라가고 있다 내려가고 있다	**[be +]** walking down 걸어서 내려가고 있다 stepping down 계단을 내려가고 있다 climbing (up) 올라가고 있다
입고 있다	**[be +]** putting on ~을 착용하는 중이다 trying on ~을 한번 입어 보는 중이다
벗고 있다	**[be +]** taking off ~을 벗는 중이다 removing ~을 벗는 중이다

사물 및 배경을 묘사하는 동사 표현

놓여 있다	**[be +]** put ~이 놓여 있다 placed ~이 놓여 있다 set ~이 놓여 있다 left ~이 놓여[남겨져] 있다 set up ~이 설치되어 있다
쌓여 있다	**[be +]** piled ~이 쌓여 있다 stacked ~이 쌓여 있다
정렬되어 있다	**[be +]** arranged ~이 정렬되어 있다 displayed ~이 진열[전시]되어 있다 on display ~이 진열[전시]되어 있다
걸려 있다	**[be +]** hanging from ~에 걸려 있다 mounted on (벽 등) ~에 걸려 있다
특정 모양을 이루고 있다	**[be +]** spread out ~이 펼쳐져 있다 propped against ~에 기대어 세워져 있다 lined with 줄지어 서 있다, 늘어서 있다 lined up 줄지어 서 있다
차량 등이 서 있다	**[be +]** stopped ~가 서 있다 parked ~이 주차되어 있다
길/다리/계단이 있다	lead up to ~로 이어지다 run 이어지다, 뻗어 있다

DAY 02 실전문제

ACTUAL TEST
D02_Test

1

2

3
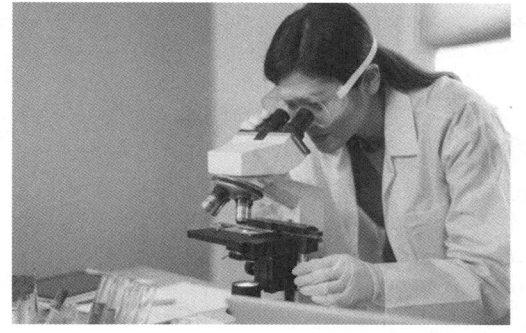

4

5

6

LC DAY 03 — 1인·2인 사진 / 다인·사물·풍경 사진

01 1인·2인 사진

♪ D03_01

Part 1의 6문제 중, 사진 속에 인물이 한 명 있는 1인 사진은 보통 2~4문제가 출제되며, 인물이 두 명 있는 사진은 보통 1~2문제가 출제된다. 1인 사진은 인물의 동작과 배경 및 사물의 특징을 잘 살피고, 2인 사진은 개인별 동작과 상태뿐만 아니라 두 명의 공통 동작과 상태도 확인해야 한다.

◆ 출제 포인트 1   1인 사진

👀 눈으로 보기

1. 사진을 판독한다.
① 인물의 상태와 동작
- 셔츠를 입은 여자 한 명이 의자에 앉아 서랍을 들여다 보고 있다.
② 배경 및 사물의 특징
- 책상 위에 컴퓨터와 키보드, 마우스가 있다.
- 여자 옆에 빈 의자가 하나 있다.

🎧 귀로 듣기

(A) The woman is <u>typing</u> on a keyboard.
(B) The chairs <u>are being stacked</u>.
(C) The woman's looking in a drawer.
(D) There is <u>a plant</u> on the desk.

→ (✗) 키보드를 두드리는 동작이 없다.
→ (✗) 의자가 쌓이는 동작이 없다.
→ (○) 정답
→ (✗) 책상 위에 화분이 없다.

2. 선택지를 들으며 오답 보기를 소거하고 정답을 선택한다.

◆ 출제 포인트 2   2인 사진

👀 눈으로 보기

1. 사진을 판독한다.
① 인물의 상태와 동작
- 한 여자가 사다리 위로 연결된 텐트 안에 앉아, 잔디에 앉아 있는 다른 여자를 보고 있다.
② 배경 및 사물의 특징
- 야외 테이블 위에 물건들이 놓여 있다.
- 차량 위에 텐트가 설치되어 있고, 텐트에 사다리가 연결되어 있다.

🎧 귀로 듣기

(A) They are <u>shaking hands</u>.
(B) A table has been set up outdoors.
(C) One of the women is <u>putting up</u> a tent.
(D) A ladder is <u>being moved</u>.

→ (✗) 악수하는 동작이 없다.
→ (○) 정답
→ (✗) 텐트를 설치하는 동작이 없다.
→ (✗) 사다리를 옮기는 동작이 없다.

2. 선택지를 들으며 오답 보기를 소거하고 정답을 선택한다.

> 🚀 **빠른 700⁺점 달성 TIP**
>
> 인물이 중심에 위치하는 사진이라도 인물의 동작이 아닌 주변 배경이나 사물을 묘사하는 표현이 정답이 될 수 있으므로 항상 사물의 종류와 위치 관계 등도 함께 파악해 둬야 한다.

PRACTICE | 기출 연습하기

보기가 사진과 일치하면 O, 다르면 X, 헷갈리면 △ 표기하며 문제를 푼 후, 빈칸을 채워보세요.
받아쓰기를 위해 보기는 두 번씩 들려줍니다.

1

(A) The man is _____ a mug.
(B) The man is _____.
(C) The man is _____ a notepad.
(D) The man is _____ a laptop computer.

2

(A) A man is _____.
(B) A man is _____.
(C) A copy machine is _____.
(D) Some equipment is _____ the room.

3

(A) The man is _____ the handrail.
(B) The man is _____ the woman.
(C) The woman is _____ the steps.
(D) The woman is _____ some food.

4

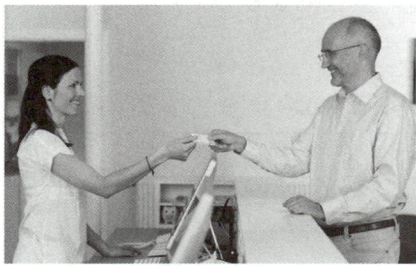

(A) They are _____.
(B) They are _____ the counter.
(C) The man is _____ his glasses _____.
(D) The counter has _____ items.

02 다인/사물·풍경 사진

🎵 D03_02

Part 1의 6문제 중, 사진 속에 인물이 3명 이상 있는 다인 사진은 보통 1~2문제가 출제되며, 인물 없이 사물이나 풍경만 있는 사진은 보통 1문제 출제된다. 다인 사진은 사진 속 사람들의 공통점을 묘사한 표현이 정답으로 나오기도 하지만, 한 명 혹은 일부에 대해 묘사한 표현이 정답으로 출제되기도 한다. 사물·풍경 사진은 배열이나 위치에 대한 묘사가 사진과 맞는지 확인하는 것이 중요하다.

✚ 출제 포인트 1　다인 사진

👀 눈으로 보기

1. 사진을 판독한다.
① 인물의 상태와 동작
- 여자 2명과 남자 1명이 계단에서 난간을 잡고 서로 마주보고 이야기하고 있다.
② 배경 및 사물의 특징
- 인물들 뒤로 건물 벽이 보인다.

👂 귀로 듣기

(A) A man is leaning against the wall.
(B) Some people are holding onto the handrail.
(C) Some people are getting out of the building.
(D) The staircase is being fixed.

2. 선택지를 들으며 오답 보기를 소거하고 정답을 선택한다.
→ (✘) 남자가 벽에 기대고 있지 않다.
→ (○) 정답
→ (✘) 건물 밖으로 나오는 동작이 없다.
→ (✘) 계단이 수리되는 동작이 없다.

✚ 출제 포인트 2　사물·풍경 사진

👀 눈으로 보기

1. 사진을 판독한다.
① 배경 및 사물의 특징
- 중앙에 있는 큰 테이블 위에 꽃병이 놓여 있다.
- 중앙에 있는 큰 테이블과 창문 사이에 소파가 놓여 있다.
- 소파 양 옆으로 전등이 있고, 불이 켜져 있다.
- 전등 하나는 작은 테이블 위에 놓여 있다.
- 뒤쪽에 창문이 있고 블라인드가 설치되어 있다.

👂 귀로 듣기

(A) There is a lamp hanging from the ceiling.
(B) There is a floral arrangement on a table.
(C) A sofa is being assembled.
(D) A rug is being unrolled on the floor.

2. 선택지를 들으며 오답 보기를 소거하고 정답을 선택한다.
→ (✘) 천장에 매달려 있는 전등이 없다.
→ (○) 정답
→ (✘) 소파가 조립되는 동작이 없다.
→ (✘) 깔개가 펼쳐지는 동작이 없다.

🖊 빠른 700⁺점 달성 TIP

'be + being + p.p.' 동사 표현은 대부분 사람의 동작을 나타내므로, 사람 없이 사물이나 풍경만 있는 사진에서 이 표현이 들리면 오답으로 소거하면 된다. 단, 예외적으로 is[are] being displayed는 '사물이 진열되어 있는 상태' 표현으로 출제되었으니 알아두자.

PRACTICE | 기출 연습하기

보기가 사진과 일치하면 O, 다르면 X, 헷갈리면 △ 표기하며 문제를 푼 후, 빈칸을 채워보세요.

받아쓰기를 위해 보기는 두 번씩 들려줍니다.

1

(A) Some people are _____.
(B) Some people are _____ a waiting area.
(C) One of the people is _____.
(D) One of the people is _____.

2

(A) A streetlamp is _____.
(B) Some _____ are _____ the sidewalk.
(C) A car _____ to the _____.
(D) Some people are _____.

3

(A) The beach is _____ bathers.
(B) A boat is _____ the shore.
(C) Some umbrellas are _____.
(D) Some chairs are _____.

4

(A) Some doors _____.
(B) The pavement _____.
(C) Some tables _____ outdoors.
(D) The chairs are _____.

PART 1 기출 표현 익히기

♪ D03_03

Part 1에는 반복적으로 출제되는 명사 표현이 있다. 사진 속 모습을 떠올려 보며 익혀두자.

① intersection 교차로
② streetlamp 가로등
③ traffic light 신호등
④ pedestrians 보행자들
⑤ crosswalk 횡단보도
⑥ sidewalk 인도, 보도
⑦ curb 연석, 도로 경계석
⑧ cyclist 자전거 타는 사람
⑨ pavement 포장된 도로, 포장된 인도

① light fixture 조명, 전등
② drawer 서랍
③ brick wall 벽돌로 된 벽
④ artwork 미술품
⑤ ceiling 천장
⑥ vase 꽃병
⑦ pillow 쿠션
⑧ briefcase 서류 가방
⑨ staircase 계단
⑩ entryway 출입구, 입구의 통로
⑪ railing(= handrail) (계단 등의) 난간, 손잡이

① display case 진열장, 진열대
② silverware 은식기류
③ cookware 조리 기구
④ pot 냄비, 용기
⑤ merchandise 상품
⑥ counter 계산대

① column 기둥
② walkway 통로, 보도
③ archway 아치형 입구, 아치형 통로

DAY 03 실전문제

ACTUAL TEST

1

2

3

4

5
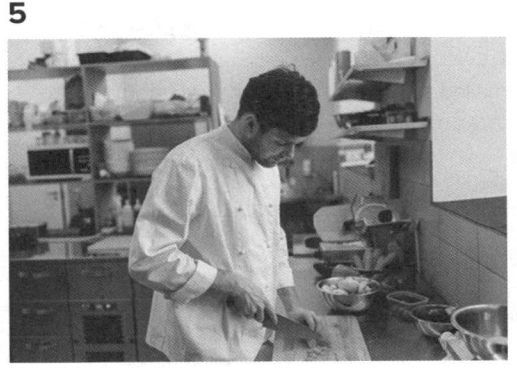

6

LC DAY 04   의문사 의문문(1) – Who/What/Which

✓ Who 의문문은 매회 1~2문항, What/Which 의문문은 매회 1~2문항 정도 출제되며, 각각 Part 2 문제의 6.5%, 6.5%를 차지한다.

01 Who 의문문

♪ D04_01

Who로 시작하는 의문문은 문제의 60% 이상이 의문사만 듣고도 정답을 맞힐 수 있는 유형으로 출제되며, who 뒤의 동사까지 들을 수 있다면 대부분 정답을 맞힐 수 있다.

◆ 출제 포인트 1   Who + 책임/담당을 나타내는 동사

책임, 담당을 묻는 'Who + be in charge of[head, manage, lead](누가 ~을 맡고 있는가)'와 'Who + ask/call/speak[talk] to[with]/contact(누구에게[와] 질문/전화/대화/연락해야 하는가)'는 덩어리 표현으로 들을 수 있어야 한다.

대표 질문 유형	대표 정답 유형		대표 오답 유형
	직접적인 응답	간접적인 응답	
Who's in charge of the renovation project? 누가 개조 공사 프로젝트를 책임지고 있나요?	Lisa Goldman is. (O) Lisa Goldman 씨요.	We are still deciding. (O) 아직 결정 중입니다.	Charge it to my credit card. (X) 제 신용카드로 청구해 주세요. → [오답type] charge와 같은 단어를 활용한 오답
Who will manage the design team after Mr. Ando retires? Ando 씨가 은퇴하면 누가 디자인 팀을 총괄하나요?	I heard it was Mr. Perez. (O) Perez 씨였다고 들었어요.	I thought he would be working a few more years. (O) 그분이 몇 년 더 일하신다고 생각했어요.	In the fashion magazine. (X) 패션 잡지에서요. → [오답type] Where의 정답 / design에서 연상되는 단어
Who should I speak[talk] to[with] about the roof repair? 지붕 수리 공사와 관련해 누구와 얘기해야 하나요?	The maintenance department. (O) 시설 관리부요.	Mr. Ortega has that information. (O) Ortega 씨가 그 정보를 갖고 있어요.	Yes, I fixed it yesterday. (X) 네, 제가 어제 고쳤어요. → [오답type] 의문사 의문문은 Yes/No로 응답 불가

◆ 출제 포인트 2   Who + 기타 동사

'Who + 동사(누가 ~하는가)'는 who 뒤의 동사를 잘 듣는 것이 중요하다.

대표 질문 유형	대표 정답 유형		대표 오답 유형
	직접적인 응답	간접적인 응답	
Who called the Mester Hotel this morning? 누가 오늘 아침에 Mester 호텔에 전화했나요?	The manager did. (O) 부장님이 했어요.	I e-mailed them. (O) 제가 그쪽에 이메일을 보냈습니다.	For three nights. (X) 3박이요. → [오답type] How long의 정답 / Hotel에서 연상되는 단어

빠른 700⁺점 달성 TIP

직접적인 정답으로 사람 이름이 제시되기도 하지만, 그 사람이 속한 부서명이나 업체명, 혹은 그 사람의 직책도 정답이 될 수 있으므로 이에 유의한다.

♪ D04_01_T

PRACTICE | 기출 연습하기 문제를 푼 후, 질문과 정답을 2번씩 들으며 받아쓰기 해보세요.

1. (A) (B) (C)   1. _____'s _____ the reservation for the retirement party?
   [정답] Lucy is _____.

2. (A) (B) (C)   2. _____ should I _____ to return this oven?
   [정답] I'll get the _____ for you.

3. (A) (B) (C)   3. _____ up the summary of the new tax regulations?
   [정답] _____ on the accounting _____.

4. (A) (B) (C)   4. _____ are you currently _____?
   [정답] A _____ in the robotics industry.

5. (A) (B) (C)   5. _____ was selected to _____ our firm at the conference?
   [정답] _____ has _____ anything yet.

6. (A) (B) (C)   6. _____'s _____ for correcting errors in the document?
   [정답] Did you _____?

02 What/Which 의문문

What/Which로 시작하는 의문문은 What/Which의 의미가 '무엇/어느 것'인 경우뿐만 아니라 '어느'의 의미로 뒤의 명사를 수식하는 'What/Which+명사'의 형태로도 많이 출제되므로, 'What/Which+명사'를 한 덩어리로 들을 수 있는 것이 중요하다.

◆ 출제 포인트 1   What/Which + 명사

'What(무슨 ~) + 명사'와 'Which(어느 ~) + 명사'는 what/which 뒤의 명사를 잘 듣는 것이 중요하다.

대표 질문 유형	대표 정답 유형		대표 오답 유형
	직접적인 응답	간접적인 응답	
What time does your train depart? 당신 기차가 몇 시에 떠나나요?	In 20 minutes. (O) 20분 후에요.	I'm taking the bus this time. (O) 이번에는 버스를 탈 겁니다.	On platform 7. (✗) 7번 승강장에서요. → [오답type] Where의 정답 / train에서 연상되는 단어
Which hotel is Lauren staying at? Lauren이 어느 호텔에 머무르고 있나요?	The one on Oakland Avenue. (O) Oakland 가에 있는 곳이요.	You'd have to ask Ms. Yoon. (O) Yoon 씨에게 물어보셔야 할 겁니다.	I will stay for three days. (✗) 저는 3일 동안 머무를 거예요. → [오답type] How long의 정답 / staying과 소리가 비슷한 단어

◆ 출제 포인트 2   What ~ think of[about]

'What ~ think of[about](~에 대해 어떻게 생각하는가)'는 덩어리 표현으로 들을 수 있어야 한다.

대표 질문 유형	대표 정답 유형		대표 오답 유형
	직접적인 응답	간접적인 응답	
What did you think of the finance seminar? 금융 세미나에 대해서 어떻게 생각하셨나요?	It was informative. (O) 유익했어요.	I attended a different one. (O) 저는 다른 세미나에 참석했어요.	In the finance department. (✗) 재무 부서에서요. → [오답type] Where의 정답 / 같은 단어를 활용한 오답

◆ 출제 포인트 3   What + 조동사 + 주어 + 본동사

'What + 조동사 + 주어 + 본동사(무엇을 ~하는가)'는 본동사를 잘 듣는 것이 중요하다.

대표 질문 유형	대표 정답 유형		대표 오답 유형
	직접적인 응답	간접적인 응답	
What are you going to **bring** to Jenny's party? Jenny의 파티에 무엇을 가져갈 거예요?	A bottle of wine. (O) 와인 한 병이요.	Actually, I have other plans. (O) 사실은, 저는 다른 계획이 있어요.	It is not my part. (✗) 제가 맡은 부분이 아닙니다. → [오답type] Why의 정답 / party와 소리가 비슷한 단어

> **빠른 700⁺점 달성 TIP**
>
> What으로 시작하는 의문문은 '모른다/물어봐/확인해봐' 등의 회피성 응답도 많이 출제되며, the+(형용사)+one은 Which 의문문의 정답으로 자주 출제되므로 기억해두자.

♪ D04_02_T

PRACTICE | 기출 연습하기 문제를 푼 후, 질문과 정답을 2번씩 들으며 받아쓰기 해보세요.

1. (A) (B) (C)   1. _____ should we subscribe to this year?
   [정답] I'm interested in _____.

2. (A) (B) (C)   2. _____ is creating the posters for the upcoming performance?
   [정답] The _____ we hired in spring.

3. (A) (B) (C)   3. _____ are you planning to book a seat on?
   [정답] It _____ the price.

4. (A) (B) (C)   4. _____ does the train for Milan leave?
   [정답] _____ thirty _____.

5. (A) (B) (C)   5. _____'s the delivery _____ for this carpet?
   [정답] It might be _____.

6. (A) (B) (C)   6. _____ did you _____ of the marketing workshop?
   [정답] I attended a _____.

LC | DAY 04 실전문제

1. Mark your answer on your answer sheet. (A) (B) (C)

2. Mark your answer on your answer sheet. (A) (B) (C)

3. Mark your answer on your answer sheet. (A) (B) (C)

4. Mark your answer on your answer sheet. (A) (B) (C)

5. Mark your answer on your answer sheet. (A) (B) (C)

6. Mark your answer on your answer sheet. (A) (B) (C)

7. Mark your answer on your answer sheet. (A) (B) (C)

8. Mark your answer on your answer sheet. (A) (B) (C)

9. Mark your answer on your answer sheet. (A) (B) (C)

10. Mark your answer on your answer sheet. (A) (B) (C)

11. Mark your answer on your answer sheet. (A) (B) (C)

12. Mark your answer on your answer sheet. (A) (B) (C)

13. Mark your answer on your answer sheet. (A) (B) (C)

14. Mark your answer on your answer sheet. (A) (B) (C)

15. Mark your answer on your answer sheet. (A) (B) (C)

16. Mark your answer on your answer sheet. (A) (B) (C)

17. Mark your answer on your answer sheet. (A) (B) (C)

18. Mark your answer on your answer sheet. (A) (B) (C)

19. Mark your answer on your answer sheet. (A) (B) (C)

20. Mark your answer on your answer sheet. (A) (B) (C)

21. Mark your answer on your answer sheet. (A) (B) (C)

22. Mark your answer on your answer sheet. (A) (B) (C)

23. Mark your answer on your answer sheet. (A) (B) (C)

24. Mark your answer on your answer sheet. (A) (B) (C)

25. Mark your answer on your answer sheet. (A) (B) (C)

LC DAY 05 의문사 의문문(2) –When/Where

> When 의문문은 매회 2문항, Where 의문문은 매회 2문항 정도 출제되며, 각각 Part 2 문제의 7.5%, 8%를 차지한다.

01 When 의문문

♪ D05_01

When으로 시작하는 의문문은 when만 들어도 풀 수 있는 문제의 비율이 75% 정도로 높고, this Friday(이번 주 금요일), 3 o'clock(3시 정각)과 같은 직접적인 시점 표현이 정답이 되는 경우가 70% 이상이다.

◆ 출제 포인트 1 When + 현재/미래 동사

'When + 현재/미래 동사' 의문문은 시각/요일/월 표현 외에 next/by (the end of)/not until+시점, in+기간 등의 미래를 나타내는 표현이 자주 정답으로 출제된다.

대표 질문 유형	대표 정답 유형		대표 오답 유형
	직접적인 응답	간접적인 응답	
When will the lease on our office expire? 우리 사무실 임대 계약이 언제 만료되나요?	Probably next June. (O) 아마 내년 6월일 겁니다.	I'll look for the paperwork. (O) 서류를 찾아볼게요.	At least two offices. (✗) 최소한 두 곳의 사무실이요. → [오답type] How many의 정답 / 같은 단어를 활용한 오답
When can I have the test results? 제가 언제 테스트 결과를 받을 수 있나요?	By the end of this week. (O) 이번 주말까지요.	It's written on your calendar. (O) 당신 달력에 쓰여 있어요.	I took the exam last week. (✗) 저는 지난주에 시험을 봤어요. → [오답type] 미래(앞으로의 가능성)로 물었으나 과거로 대답
When is our first meeting this week? 이번 주에 언제 우리의 첫 회의가 있죠?	Not until Tuesday. (O) 화요일이나 되어야 해요.	All were canceled. (O) 모두 취소되었어요.	No, I don't think so. (✗) 아뇨, 저는 그렇게 생각하지 않아요. → [오답type] 의문사 의문문은 Yes/No로 응답 불가

◆ 출제 포인트 2 When + 과거 동사

'When + 과거 동사' 의문문은 ~ago/after+과거동사/last+시점 등의 과거를 나타내는 표현이 자주 정답으로 출제된다.

대표 질문 유형	대표 정답 유형		대표 오답 유형
	직접적인 응답	간접적인 응답	
When did Mr. Wang start working as a nurse? Wang 씨는 언제 간호사로 일하기 시작하셨나요?	About three years ago. (O) 약 3년 전에요.	Didn't he tell you? (O) 그가 얘기해 주지 않았나요?	A medical school. (✗) 의과 대학이요. → [오답type] What의 정답 / nurse에서 연상되는 단어
When did Ms. Martinez visit the Tokyo office? Martinez 씨가 언제 도쿄 사무실을 방문했나요?	Sometime last month. (O) 지난달 중에요.	She actually went to the New York office. (O) 그분은 사실 뉴욕 사무실로 가셨어요.	It has been relocated. (✗) 그곳은 이전되었습니다. → [오답type] Why의 정답 / office에서 연상되는 단어

빠른 700⁺점 달성 TIP

'at / on / in / by / before / after / not until / this / next / by the end of + 시점 표현'이 자주 정답으로 출제되므로 해당 표현을 정리해두는 것이 좋다.

♪ D05_01_T

PRACTICE | 기출 연습하기 문제를 푼 후, 질문과 정답을 2번씩 들으며 받아쓰기 해보세요.

1. (A) (B) (C)   1. _____ the deadline for application for the position?
   [정답] A couple of _____.

2. (A) (B) (C)   2. _____ Mr. Weber assign next week's work shifts?
   [정답] No later than _____.

3. (A) (B) (C)   3. _____ I return this library book?
   [정답] _____ at the latest.

4. (A) (B) (C)   4. _____ you have time to review the budget?
   [정답] How about _____?

5. (A) (B) (C)   5. _____ the new office furniture be delivered?
   [정답] _____ two _____.

6. (A) (B) (C)   6. _____ the first day of the biotechnology conference?
   [정답] I _____ it on your _____.

02 Where 의문문

🎵 D05_02

Where로 시작하는 의문문은 where만 들어도 풀 수 있는 문제의 비율이 75% 정도로 높고, on your desk(당신의 책상 위에), in Barcelona(바르셀로나에서)처럼 직접적인 장소 표현이 정답이 되는 경우가 70%이상이다.

◆ 출제 포인트 1   Where + 외부 장소/문서[물품]

Where 의문문 중 최빈출 유형은 외부 장소의 위치를 묻는 문제로, 자주 정답으로 출제되는 ~Street/~Avenue 등의 거리명이나 길 안내 표현을 알아두는 것이 중요하다.

대표 질문 유형	대표 정답 유형		대표 오답 유형
	직접적인 응답	간접적인 응답	
Where is Ms. Monroe's office located? Monroe 씨의 사무실이 어디에 위치해 있나요?	Down the hall and to the right. (O) 복도를 따라 가시다가 오른쪽에 있어요.	There's the building directory behind you. (O) 당신 뒤에 건물 안내 목록이 있습니다.	No, she is not here. (✗) 아뇨, 그분은 여기 없어요. → [오답type] 의문사 의문문은 Yes/No로 응답 불가
Where can I buy a stapler? 스테이플러를 어디에서 살 수 있나요?	Try the store on 10th Street. (O) 10번가에 있는 매장에 가 보세요.	You can use mine. (O) 제 것을 쓰셔도 됩니다.	About 5 dollars each. (✗) 각각 약 5달러요. → [오답type] How much의 정답
Where did you leave the travel reimbursement forms? 출장 경비 환급 양식을 어디에 두셨나요?	On your desk. (O) 당신 책상 위에요.	Mr. Rivera has them. (O) Rivera 씨가 갖고 있어요.	A new itinerary. (✗) 새 여행 일정표요. → [오답type] What의 정답 / travel에서 연상되는 단어
Where should I put the office supplies? 사무용품을 어디에 둘까요?	In the storage room, near Mr. Oh's office. (O) Oh 씨의 사무실 근처에 있는 창고에요.	There's no space here. (O) 여기에는 둘 공간이 없어요.	I ordered them three weeks ago. (✗) 3주 전에 주문했어요. → [오답type] When의 정답 / office supplies에서 연상되는 단어

◆ 출제 포인트 2   Where + 행사

행사가 열리는 장소를 묻는 문제는 'in+도시명/나라명'이 자주 정답으로 출제된다.

대표 질문 유형	대표 정답 유형		대표 오답 유형
	직접적인 응답	간접적인 응답	
Where will the conference be held? 컨퍼런스가 어디에서 열리나요?	It's in Barcelona, I think. (O) 바르셀로나 같아요.	It hasn't been decided yet. (O) 아직 결정되지 않았어요.	Monday or Tuesday. (✗) 월요일 또는 화요일이요. → [오답type] When의 정답

빠른 700⁺점 달성 TIP

'in / on / at / near / next to / by + 장소' 등의 '전치사+장소 표현'이 정답으로 가장 많이 출제되므로 해당 표현을 정리해 두는 것이 좋으며, 직접적인 장소/이동 표현 외에 장소로 찾아가는 방법을 알려 주는 답변도 종종 정답으로 제시되므로 이와 같은 답변에 함께 대비하면서 들어야 한다. 또한 where의 영국식 발음과 when 발음이 혼동될 수 있으므로 유의한다.

♪ D05_02_T

PRACTICE | 기출 연습하기 문제를 푼 후, 질문과 정답을 2번씩 들으며 받아쓰기 해보세요.

1. (A) (B) (C)   1. _____ is a good place to get my car _____?
   [정답] Try the shop _____ the _____.

2. (A) (B) (C)   2. _____ did the delivery man leave the _____?
   [정답] On your _____.

3. (A) (B) (C)   3. _____ can I find out about employee _____?
   [정답] On the _____'s _____.

4. (A) (B) (C)   4. _____'s the duty-free _____?
   [정답] On the _____.

5. (A) (B) (C)   5. _____ is the journalism _____ scheduled to take place?
   [정답] _____ in New York.

6. (A) (B) (C)   6. _____ should we put these potted _____?
   [정답] This _____ is already _____.

LC | DAY 05 실전문제

1. Mark your answer on your answer sheet.   (A) (B) (C)

2. Mark your answer on your answer sheet.   (A) (B) (C)

3. Mark your answer on your answer sheet.   (A) (B) (C)

4. Mark your answer on your answer sheet.   (A) (B) (C)

5. Mark your answer on your answer sheet.   (A) (B) (C)

6. Mark your answer on your answer sheet.   (A) (B) (C)

7. Mark your answer on your answer sheet.   (A) (B) (C)

8. Mark your answer on your answer sheet.   (A) (B) (C)

9. Mark your answer on your answer sheet.   (A) (B) (C)

10. Mark your answer on your answer sheet.   (A) (B) (C)

11. Mark your answer on your answer sheet.   (A) (B) (C)

12. Mark your answer on your answer sheet.   (A) (B) (C)

13. Mark your answer on your answer sheet.   (A) (B) (C)

14. Mark your answer on your answer sheet.　　(A)　(B)　(C)

15. Mark your answer on your answer sheet.　　(A)　(B)　(C)

16. Mark your answer on your answer sheet.　　(A)　(B)　(C)

17. Mark your answer on your answer sheet.　　(A)　(B)　(C)

18. Mark your answer on your answer sheet.　　(A)　(B)　(C)

19. Mark your answer on your answer sheet.　　(A)　(B)　(C)

20. Mark your answer on your answer sheet.　　(A)　(B)　(C)

21. Mark your answer on your answer sheet.　　(A)　(B)　(C)

22. Mark your answer on your answer sheet.　　(A)　(B)　(C)

23. Mark your answer on your answer sheet.　　(A)　(B)　(C)

24. Mark your answer on your answer sheet.　　(A)　(B)　(C)

25. Mark your answer on your answer sheet.　　(A)　(B)　(C)

LC | DAY 06 | 의문사 의문문(3) - How/Why

How 의문문은 매회 2~3문항, Why 의문문은 매회 2문항 정도 출제되며, 각각 Part 2 문제의 9%, 7.5%를 차지한다.

01 How 의문문

How로 시작하는 의문문은 how만 듣고 풀 수 있는 문제의 비율은 5% 미만으로 매우 낮으며, 거의 대부분의 문제가 'how+형/부'나 'how+본동사'까지 들어야 풀 수 있다.

◆ 출제 포인트 1   방법을 묻는 How

'How + 조동사 + 주어 + 본동사(어떻게~하는가)'는 How 뒤의 본동사를 잘 듣는 것이 중요하다.

대표 질문 유형	대표 정답 유형		대표 오답 유형
	직접적인 응답	간접적인 응답	
How can we **get to** the conference site? 우리가 컨퍼런스 장소에 어떻게 갈 수 있나요?	You can take the bus from here. (O) 여기서 버스를 타면 됩니다.	The information is on our Web site. (O) 그 정보는 우리 웹 사이트에 있어요.	At the Fenix Center. (✗) Fenix Center에서요. → **[오답type]** Where의 정답 / conference에서 연상되는 단어

◆ 출제 포인트 2   의견을 묻는 How~like[enjoy]/How + be + 명사

'How~ like[enjoy](~를 어떻게 생각하는가)'와, 'How + be + 명사(~가 어떤가)'는 덩어리 표현으로 들을 수 있어야 한다.

대표 질문 유형	대표 정답 유형		대표 오답 유형
	직접적인 응답	간접적인 응답	
How did you like the ice cream? 아이스크림이 어떠셨나요?	We really enjoyed it. (O) 저희는 정말 맛있게 먹었어요.	One more scoop, please. Thanks. (O) 한 숟갈 더 주세요. 고맙습니다.	A birthday party. (✗) 생일 파티요. → **[오답type]** What의 정답 / ice cream에서 연상되는 단어
How was the restaurant? 그 레스토랑 어땠나요?	It was very busy. (O) 정말 붐비던데요.	I haven't tried it yet. (O) 아직 거기 안 가봤어요.	The vegetarian pizza, please. (✗) 채식 피자 주세요. → **[오답type]** What의 정답 / restaurant에서 연상되는 단어

◆ 출제 포인트 3   How + 형용사/부사

'How + 형용사/부사(얼마나 ~한/하게)는 How 뒤의 형용사/부사를 잘 듣는 것이 중요하다.

대표 질문 유형	대표 정답 유형		대표 오답 유형
	직접적인 응답	간접적인 응답	
How long does it take to complete the on-line course? 그 온라인 과정을 수료하는 데 얼마나 오래 걸리나요?	About 6 months. (O) 약 6개월이요.	Let's check the brochure. (O) 안내 책자를 확인해 봅시다.	Around 4:30. (✗) 4시 30분쯤이요. → **[오답type]** When의 정답

빠른 700⁺점 달성 TIP

'How + 형용사/부사' 유형은 How 뒤의 형용사나 부사가 바뀐 질문의 정답이 오답으로 자주 제시되기 때문에 특별히 주의해야 한다. 예를 들어 How long(기간)으로 물었는데 오답이 3 dollars(how much(금액)에 대한 응답)로 제시되는 경우다. 따라서 How long(기간, 분량), How much(금액), How often(빈도), How many(인원, 개수), How soon(미래 시점), How far(거리)을 하나의 덩어리로 익히고, 각 질문 형태에 대한 응답을 정리해 두는 것이 필요하다.

♪ D06_01_T

PRACTICE | 기출 연습하기   문제를 푼 후, 질문과 정답을 2번씩 들으며 받아쓰기 해보세요.

1. (A) (B) (C)　　1. _____ will you be gone this time?
　　　　　　　　　[정답] I'm _____.

2. (A) (B) (C)　　2. _____ would it be to repair this cracked window?
　　　　　　　　　[정답] Approximately two hundred fifty _____.

3. (A) (B) (C)　　3. _____ does the company hire new employees?
　　　　　　　　　[정답] At least _____ a year.

4. (A) (B) (C)　　4. _____ will you _____ while visiting Berlin?
　　　　　　　　　[정답] Mostly by _____.

5. (A) (B) (C)　　5. _____ the International Science Symposium?
　　　　　　　　　[정답] I _____ a lot.

6. (A) (B) (C)　　6. _____ can I _____ this machinery?
　　　　　　　　　[정답] Didn't you _____ the _____ session?

02 Why 의문문

Why로 시작되는 의문문을 들을 때는 이유를 묻는 것인지 제안/권유를 하는 것인지부터 빠르게 파악할 수 있어야 한다.

◆ 출제 포인트 1 이유를 묻는 Why

'Why~(왜 ~인가)'인지 'Why haven't/didn't/wasn't/can't~(왜 아닌가)'인지 구별하는 것이 중요하다.

대표 질문 유형	대표 정답 유형		대표 오답 유형
	직접적인 응답	간접적인 응답	
Why did Moa Publishing **cancel** the meeting? Moa Publishing 사가 왜 회의를 취소한 거죠?	Because of a scheduling conflict. (O) 일정이 겹쳐서요.	Mr. Gibbons will find out. (O) Gibbons 씨가 알아볼 겁니다.	Last Monday at 4 P.M. (✗) 지난 월요일 오후 4시에요. → [오답type] What time의 정답 / meeting에서 연상되는 단어
Why is the restaurant **closed** today? 그 식당이 왜 오늘 문을 닫은 건가요?	For renovations. (O) 보수 공사 때문에요.	You'd better ask Rosa. (O) Rosa 씨에게 물어보시는 게 나을 겁니다.	On Monday nights. (✗) 매주 월요일 밤에요. → [오답type] When의 정답 / closed에서 연상되는 단어
Why **hasn't** the monthly expense report been finished yet? 월간 지출 보고서가 왜 아직 완료되지 않은 건가요?	Because some receipts have not been submitted. (O) 일부 영수증이 제출되지 않았기 때문입니다.	You haven't received it? (O) 아직 못 받으셨어요?	She's a news reporter. (✗) 그분은 뉴스 기자입니다. → [오답type] Who나 What의 정답 / report와 소리가 비슷한 단어

◆ 출제 포인트 2 제안, 권유의 Why don't we[you] ~

'Why don't we/you/I~(우리가/당신이/내가 ~하는 게 어떨까)'는 덩어리 표현으로 들을 수 있어야 한다.

대표 질문 유형	대표 정답 유형		대표 오답 유형
	직접적인 응답	간접적인 응답	
Why don't we hire more people for sales? 영업에 필요한 사람을 추가로 고용하는 건 어떨까요?	Yes, that's a really good idea. (O) 네, 정말 좋은 생각입니다.	We need to recruit for the personnel department first. (O) 인사부에 먼저 사람을 모집해야 해요.	To submit a sales report. (✗) 영업 보고서를 제출하기 위해서요. → [오답type] Why의 정답 / 같은 단어를 활용한 오답
Why don't you join us for dinner? 저희와 함께 저녁 식사하시는 건 어떠세요?	Thanks, I will. (O) 고마워요, 그럴게요.	I already had dinner. (O) 저는 이미 저녁 식사했어요.	A membership discount. (✗) 회원 할인이요. → [오답type] What의 정답 / join에서 연상되는 단어

빠른 700⁺점 달성 TIP

'이유'를 물어보는 의문문의 약 50%정도는 why만 들어도 정답을 맞힐 수 있는 유형으로 출제되므로 보기를 들으며 오답 표현을 소거하는 것이 중요하다. 대표적인 오답 표현으로는 Yes/No, sure 등의 거절이나 수락을 나타내는 표현, thanks 등의 감사를 나타내는 표현, 명령문이 있다.

♪ D06_02_T

PRACTICE | 기출 연습하기
문제를 푼 후, 질문과 정답을 2번씩 들으며 받아쓰기 해보세요.

1. (A) (B) (C)   1. _____ request extra funding this quarter?
   [정답] What a _____!

2. (A) (B) (C)   2. _____ agree to give a speech at the convention?
   [정답] I _____ have _____ to attend.

3. (A) (B) (C)   3. _____ did you submit the budget report so _____?
   [정답] _____ my heavy workload.

4. (A) (B) (C)   4. _____ the invitations been _____ yet?
   [정답] We're _____ addresses.

5. (A) (B) (C)   5. _____ are you _____ to Toronto?
   [정답] _____ an _____.

6. (A) (B) (C)   6. _____ I _____ to my company account?
   [정답] Did you _____ the _____?

LC | DAY 06 실전문제

1. Mark your answer on your answer sheet.   (A) (B) (C)

2. Mark your answer on your answer sheet.   (A) (B) (C)

3. Mark your answer on your answer sheet.   (A) (B) (C)

4. Mark your answer on your answer sheet.   (A) (B) (C)

5. Mark your answer on your answer sheet.   (A) (B) (C)

6. Mark your answer on your answer sheet.   (A) (B) (C)

7. Mark your answer on your answer sheet.   (A) (B) (C)

8. Mark your answer on your answer sheet.   (A) (B) (C)

9. Mark your answer on your answer sheet.   (A) (B) (C)

10. Mark your answer on your answer sheet.   (A) (B) (C)

11. Mark your answer on your answer sheet.   (A) (B) (C)

12. Mark your answer on your answer sheet.   (A) (B) (C)

13. Mark your answer on your answer sheet.   (A) (B) (C)

14. Mark your answer on your answer sheet.   (A) (B) (C)

15. Mark your answer on your answer sheet.   (A) (B) (C)

16. Mark your answer on your answer sheet.   (A) (B) (C)

17. Mark your answer on your answer sheet.   (A) (B) (C)

18. Mark your answer on your answer sheet.   (A) (B) (C)

19. Mark your answer on your answer sheet.   (A) (B) (C)

20. Mark your answer on your answer sheet.   (A) (B) (C)

21. Mark your answer on your answer sheet.   (A) (B) (C)

22. Mark your answer on your answer sheet.   (A) (B) (C)

23. Mark your answer on your answer sheet.   (A) (B) (C)

24. Mark your answer on your answer sheet.   (A) (B) (C)

25. Mark your answer on your answer sheet.   (A) (B) (C)

LC | DAY 07 | 비 의문사 의문문(1)

> Do/Be/Have동사로 시작하는 의문문은 매회 3문항, can/could등의 조동사로 시작하는 의문문은 매회 2문항 정도 출제되며, 각각 Part 2 문제의 11%, 8%를 차지한다.

01 Do/Be/Have 동사로 시작하는 의문문

♪ D07_01

Do/Be/Have로 시작되는 의문문은 대부분 사실 확인이 목적이므로 Yes/No로 시작되는 응답을 기대하기 쉬우나, Yes/No가 없는 응답이 더 많이 정답으로 출제되므로 유의한다.

◆ 출제 포인트 1   Do/Does/Did 의문문

'Do/Does/Did + 주어 + 본동사(~가 하는가/했는가)'는 본동사를 잘 듣는 것이 중요하다.

대표 질문 유형	대표 정답 유형		대표 오답 유형
	직접적인 응답	간접적인 응답	
Do you want to go to the festival? 축제에 가고 싶으신가요?	(Yes,) I'd love to. (O) (네,) 꼭 그렇게 하고 싶어요.	Let me check my schedule. (O) 제 일정을 확인해 볼게요.	The dancers were great. (✗) 댄서들이 훌륭했어요. → [오답type] festival에서 연상되는 단어
Did you attend the social media seminar yesterday? 어제 소셜 미디어 세미나에 참석하셨나요?	(No,) I didn't have time. (O) (아뇨,) 시간이 없었어요.	I thought it had been postponed. (O) 연기되었다고 생각했는데요.	No, all participants. (✗) 아뇨, 모든 참가자들이요. → [오답type] seminar에서 연상되는 단어

◆ 출제 포인트 2   Is/Are/Was/Were 의문문

'Is/Are/Was/Were + 주어 + 보어(~가 ~인가/~였는가)'는 주어와 보어를 잘 듣는 것이 중요하다.

대표 질문 유형	대표 정답 유형		대표 오답 유형
	직접적인 응답	간접적인 응답	
Is this office big enough for all the employees? 이 사무실이 모든 직원을 위해 충분히 큰가요?	Well, I haven't heard any complaints. (O) 글쎄요, 불평은 듣지 못했어요.	There are only 10 workers here. (O) 이곳에는 겨우 10명의 직원들만 있어요.	On the fifth floor. (✗) 5층에요. → [오답type] Where의 정답 / office에서 연상되는 표현
Are you available for lunch this afternoon? 오늘 오후에 점심 식사할 시간 있으세요?	(Yes,) I'd be happy to join you. (O) (네,) 기꺼이 합류할게요.	Are you coming? (O) 당신도 오시나요?	Let me check the label. (✗) 라벨을 확인해 볼게요. → [오답type] Available과 소리가 비슷한 단어

◆ 출제 포인트 3   Have/Has 의문문

'Have/Has + 주어 + p.p.(~가 했는가)'는 주어와 p.p.를 잘 듣는 것이 중요하다.

대표 질문 유형	대표 정답 유형		대표 오답 유형
	직접적인 응답	간접적인 응답	
Have you **tried** the new headphones? 새로 나온 헤드폰 사용해 보셨어요?	(No,) Not yet. (O) (아뇨,) 아직이요.	Which ones?(O) 어느 것이요?	They all love music. (X) 그들은 모두 음악을 사랑해요. → [오답type] headphones에서 연상되는 단어

🚀 빠른 700⁺점 달성 TIP

Do/Be/Have 동사로 시작하는 의문문에 대한 응답의 경우, 정답이 Yes/No로 시작하지 않는 경우도 많으므로, '질문-Yes/No가 없는 문장'을 반복 청취하여, 적절한 질문-응답 패턴에 익숙해지는 것이 핵심이다.

🎵 D07_01_T

PRACTICE | 기출 연습하기   문제를 푼 후, 질문과 정답을 2번씩 들으며 받아쓰기 해보세요.

1. (A) (B) (C)   1. Did _____ remember to _____ that memo we talked about?
[정답] No, but I'll _____.

2. (A) (B) (C)   2. Have you _____ of the pamphlet?
[정답] Yes, at yesterday's _____.

3. (A) (B) (C)   3. Excuse me. Are _____ for a _____?
[정답] Yes, we'll _____ for four.

4. (A) (B) (C)   4. Do _____ to _____ these performance evaluations today?
[정답] I have several _____.

5. (A) (B) (C)   5. Do you _____ I can get more staples?
[정답] Probably in the _____.

6. (A) (B) (C)   6. Is the monthly utility _____ today?
[정답] It's _____ been _____.

02 Can/Could/Would/Should로 시작하는 의문문

♪ D07_02

Can/Could/Would/Will로 시작하는 의문문은 '사실 확인'을 묻는 경우도 있지만 대부분 '요청/부탁/허락/의향'을 묻는 문제로 출제된다.

◆ 출제 포인트 1 Can/Could 의문문

'Can/Could you + 본동사(당신이 ~해 주시겠어요)'는 요청의 의미로, Can/Could I + 본동사(제가 ~해도 될까요)'는 허락을 구하거나 제안하는 의미로 이해하며 듣는 것이 중요하다.

대표 질문 유형	대표 정답 유형		대표 오답 유형
	직접적인 응답	간접적인 응답	
Can[Could] you give me a ride to the city center after work? 퇴근 후에 도심까지 저를 차로 데려다 주실 수 있으세요?	(Sure,) I'd be happy to. (O) (그럼요,) 기꺼이 그렇게 해 드릴게요.	I took the subway to work today. (O) 저는 오늘 지하철을 타고 출근했어요.	At the shopping center. (X) 쇼핑 센터에서요. → [오답type] Where의 정답 / 같은 단어를 활용한 오답
Can[Could] I use this business lounge? 이 비즈니스 라운지를 이용할 수 있을까요?	Only for two hours. (O) 오직 두 시간 동안만 가능합니다.	There will be an extra charge. (O) 추가 청구 비용이 있습니다.	A new tablet computer. (X) 새로운 태블릿 컴퓨터요. → [오답type] What의 정답 / business lounge에서 연상되는 단어

◆ 출제 포인트 2 Would/Should 의문문

의향/부탁을 나타내는 'Would you like/mind~ (당신이 ~하시겠어요)'는 덩어리 표현으로 들을 수 있어야 하며, 당위성을 묻는 Should I/we+본동사(제가/우리가 ~해야 할까요)'는 본동사를 잘 듣는 것이 중요하다.

대표 질문 유형	대표 정답 유형		대표 오답 유형
	직접적인 응답	간접적인 응답	
Would you like to come to the party tonight? 오늘 밤 파티에 오시겠어요?	(Yes,) At what time? (O) (네,) 몇 시죠?	I was planning to visit the night market. (O) 저는 야시장을 방문할 계획이었어요.	Sure, a new caterer. (X) 물론이죠. 새로운 출장 요리 업체요. → [오답type] party에서 연상되는 단어
Would you mind doing the night shifts next week? 다음 주에 야간 근무조로 일해 주시겠어요?	(Sure,) I can do that. (O) (물론이죠,) 그렇게 할 수 있어요.	I will be on my vacation. (O) 저는 휴가를 가 있을 겁니다.	They are shifting community programs. (X) 그들이 지역 사회 프로그램들을 바꾸고 있어요. → [오답type] shifts와 소리가 비슷한 단어
Should I turn on the air conditioner? 에어컨을 틀어야 할까요?	(Yes,) It is quite hot in here. (O) (네,) 이 안이 꽤 덥네요.	Please open a window. (O) 창문을 열어 주세요.	Please take a left turn. (X) 좌회전 하십시오. → [오답type] 같은 단어를 활용한 오답

🔑 빠른 700⁺점 달성 TIP

Part 2에 출제되는 Can/Could/Would/Will로 시작하는 의문문은 '요청/부탁/허락/의향'을 묻는 문제의 출제 빈도가 절대적으로 높으며, 이에 대한 응답으로 'Sure, here it is(물론이죠, 여기 있어요)'와 같이 수락을 나타내는 표현이나, 'No, I have another appointment(다른 일정이 있어요)'와 같이 거절의 이유를 나타내는 표현도 자주 정답으로 출제되므로 정리해두는 것이 필요하다.

🎵 D07_02_T

PRACTICE | 기출 연습하기   문제를 푼 후, 질문과 정답을 2번씩 들으며 받아쓰기 해보세요.

1. (A) (B) (C)   1. Can you _____ me that _____, please?
   [정답] Sure. _____.

2. (A) (B) (C)   2. Would you like to _____ a _____ to Europe?
   [정답] Yes, _____?

3. (A) (B) (C)   3. Could you double-_____ these sales _____ for me?
   [정답] I'll _____ them _____ this afternoon.

4. (A) (B) (C)   4. _____ the new interns?
   [정답] OK, I'll _____.

5. (A) (B) (C)   5. Can I _____ an _____ on the merger?
   [정답] I'm on my _____.

6. (A) (B) (C)   6. Should I _____ my _____ in the conference room?
   [정답] We _____ be coming back _____.

LC | DAY 07 실전문제

1. Mark your answer on your answer sheet. (A) (B) (C)

2. Mark your answer on your answer sheet. (A) (B) (C)

3. Mark your answer on your answer sheet. (A) (B) (C)

4. Mark your answer on your answer sheet. (A) (B) (C)

5. Mark your answer on your answer sheet. (A) (B) (C)

6. Mark your answer on your answer sheet. (A) (B) (C)

7. Mark your answer on your answer sheet. (A) (B) (C)

8. Mark your answer on your answer sheet. (A) (B) (C)

9. Mark your answer on your answer sheet. (A) (B) (C)

10. Mark your answer on your answer sheet. (A) (B) (C)

11. Mark your answer on your answer sheet. (A) (B) (C)

12. Mark your answer on your answer sheet. (A) (B) (C)

13. Mark your answer on your answer sheet. (A) (B) (C)

14. Mark your answer on your answer sheet. (A) (B) (C)

15. Mark your answer on your answer sheet. (A) (B) (C)

16. Mark your answer on your answer sheet. (A) (B) (C)

17. Mark your answer on your answer sheet. (A) (B) (C)

18. Mark your answer on your answer sheet. (A) (B) (C)

19. Mark your answer on your answer sheet. (A) (B) (C)

20. Mark your answer on your answer sheet. (A) (B) (C)

21. Mark your answer on your answer sheet. (A) (B) (C)

22. Mark your answer on your answer sheet. (A) (B) (C)

23. Mark your answer on your answer sheet. (A) (B) (C)

24. Mark your answer on your answer sheet. (A) (B) (C)

25. Mark your answer on your answer sheet. (A) (B) (C)

LC DAY 08 비 의문사 의문문(2)

> 부정 의문문은 매회 1~2문항, 부가 의문문은 매회 2~3문항 정도 출제되며, 각각 Part 2 문제의 7%, 9%를 차지한다.

01 부정 의문문

🎵 D08_01

부정 의문문은 Do/Be/Have동사에 not을 붙여 Don't/Isn't/Haven't 등의 축약 형태로 시작하는 의문문 유형이다.

◆ 출제 포인트 1 Don't/Doesn't/Didn't 의문문

Don't/Doesn't/Didn't + 주어 + 본동사(~가 하지 않는가/ 하지 않았는가)'는 주어와 본동사를 잘 듣는 것이 중요하다.

대표 질문 유형	대표 정답 유형		대표 오답 유형
	직접적인 응답	간접적인 응답	
Don't you plan to **contact** Ms. Nelson today? Nelson 씨에게 오늘 연락할 계획이시지 않나요? (= 연락할 계획이시죠?)	(Yes,) I'll call her after lunch. (O) (네,) 점심 식사 후에 전화할 겁니다.	Do you have Ms. Nelson's contact information? (O) Nelson 씨의 연락처를 가지고 계시나요?	Yes, we signed the contract. (✗) 네, 저희는 계약서에 서명했어요. → [오답type] contact와 소리가 비슷한 단어
Didn't you order more office supplies? 추가 사무용품을 주문하지 않았나요? (= ~ 주문했죠?)	(No,) Ms. Aubrey handles that. (O) (아뇨,) Aubrey 씨가 그 일을 처리합니다.	They haven't been shipped yet. (O) 그것들이 아직 배송되지 않았어요.	In the appropriate order. (✗) 적절한 순서로요. → [오답type] 같은 단어를 활용한 오답

◆ 출제 포인트 2 Isn't/Aren't/Wasn't/Weren't 의문문

Isn't/Aren't/Wasn't/Weren't+주어+보어(~가 ~아닌가/~아니었나)'는 주어와 보어를 잘 듣는 것이 중요하다.

대표 질문 유형	대표 정답 유형		대표 오답 유형
	직접적인 응답	간접적인 응답	
Isn't the **store closed** for the holiday? 휴일이라 상점이 문을 닫지 않았나요? (= ~ 문을 닫았죠?)	(No,) It is their busiest season. (O) (아뇨,) 요즘이 제일 바쁜 시즌이에요.	Oh, thank you for letting me know. (O) 아, 알려주셔서 감사합니다.	Yes, these items are on sale. (✗) 네, 이 제품들은 세일 중입니다. → [오답type] store에서 연상되는 단어
Wasn't the **budget report due** yesterday? 예산 보고서가 어제까지 아니었나요? (= ~ 어제까지였죠?)	Yes, but we are still working on it. (O) 네, 하지만 여전히 작업 중이에요.	It's taking longer than I expected. (O) 제가 예상한 것보다 더 오래 걸리고 있어요.	Yes, five thousand dollars. (✗) 네, 5천 달러요. → [오답type] budget에서 연상되는 단어

◆ 출제 포인트 3   Haven't/Hasn't 의문문

'Haven't/Hasn't + 주어 + p.p.(~가 하지 않았는가)'는 주어와 p.p.를 잘 듣는 것이 중요하다.

대표 질문 유형	대표 정답 유형		대표 오답 유형
	직접적인 응답	간접적인 응답	
Haven't you been **interviewed** yet? 이미 인터뷰를 하시지 않으셨나요? (= ~ 인터뷰를 하셨죠?)	(No,) I'm waiting for Ms. Kerns. (O) (아뇨,) Kerns 씨를 기다리고 있어요.	I just got here. (O) 저는 막 이곳에 왔어요.	For the marketing position. (✗) 마케팅 직책을 위해서요. → [오답type] interviewed 에서 연상되는 단어

🎵 빠른 700⁺점 달성 TIP

부정 의문문은 '부정어 not'이 질문에 포함되어 '~않나요?'로 해석되는 의문문 유형이지만, not을 무시하고 긍정 의문문처럼 듣는 것이 중요하다. 만약 질문의 not을 해석하며 듣게 되면, 오히려 응답으로 제시되는 Yes/No의 의미가 헷갈릴 수 있으므로 주의한다. 예를 들어 'Aren't you working tomorrow?'라고 물을 때 '내일 일하지 않아요?'라고 우리말로 해석하지 말고, you/working/tomorrow의 핵심어를 파악한 후 Yes는 일한다는 뜻으로, No는 일하지 않는 응답으로 이해하면 쉽다.

🎵 D08_01_T

PRACTICE | 기출 연습하기   문제를 푼 후, 질문과 정답을 2번씩 들으며 받아쓰기 해보세요.

1. (A) (B) (C)   1. Isn't there a _____ from Seoul to Los Angeles?
   [정답] I'll _____ the _____'s Web site.

2. (A) (B) (C)   2. Don't _____ some _____?
   [정답] Yes, _____ are they _____?

3. (A) (B) (C)   3. Isn't the _____ on _____?
   [정답] No, but he can _____ on _____.

4. (A) (B) (C)   4. Aren't _____ planning to take the _____ to the company retreat?
   [정답] I _____ the _____.

5. (A) (B) (C)   5. Didn't Helen give a _____ at the meeting?
   [정답] She's still _____.

6. (A) (B) (C)   6. Wasn't the _____ supposed to be _____ yesterday?
   [정답] The _____ has caused _____.

02 부가 의문문

🎵D08_02

부가 의문문은 '평서문 + 질문'의 구조로, 평서문 뒤에 평서문의 내용이 맞는지 확인하는 '그렇죠/그렇지 않나요?'를 의미하는 짧은 질문이 붙은 유형이다.

◆ 출제 포인트 1   Do/Be/Have 동사를 이용한 부가 의문문

평서문의 주어와 동사/보어/p.p.를 잘 듣는 것이 중요하다.

대표 질문 유형	대표 정답 유형		대표 오답 유형
	직접적인 응답	간접적인 응답	
This software comes with an instructional video, doesn't it? 이 소프트웨어에 사용 설명 동영상이 포함되어 있죠, 그렇지 않나요?	(Yes,) That's right. (O) (네,) 맞습니다.	Let's ask the salesperson. (O) 판매사원에게 물어 봅시다.	From 20 to 30 dollars. (✗) 20달러에서 30달러요. → [오답type] How much의 정답
You have an invitation for the awards ceremony, don't you? 시상식 초청장을 갖고 계시죠, 그렇지 않나요?	(Yes,) It is on my desk. (O) (네,) 제 책상 위에 있어요.	Didn't you get one? (O) 하나 받지 않으셨나요?	Ms. Sato has won it. (✗) Sato 씨가 그 상을 탔어요. → [오답type] awards ceremony에서 연상되는 단어
Water is leaking from the ceiling into the bathroom, isn't it? 물이 천장에서 화장실로 새고 있죠, 그렇지 않나요?	(Yes,) We need to call a plumber. (O) (네,) 배관공에게 전화해야 해요.	I didn't notice. (O) 그런 줄 몰랐어요.	The bathroom is down the hall to the right. (✗) 화장실은 복도를 따라 가다 오른쪽에 있습니다. → [오답type] 같은 단어를 활용한 오답
You haven't met Mr. Kimberly, have you? Kimberly 씨를 아직 만나지 못하신 것이 맞죠, 그렇죠?	(Yes,) I was introduced to him last year. (O) (네,) 작년에 그분을 소개 받았어요.	Was I supposed to? (O) 제가 만나기로 되어 있었나요?	It's in the metropolitan area. (✗) 대도시 권역에 있어요. → [오답type] Where의 정답

◆ 출제 포인트 2   Right을 이용한 부가 의문문

평서문의 주어와 동사/보어/p.p.를 잘 듣는 것이 중요하다.

대표 질문 유형	대표 정답 유형		대표 오답 유형
	직접적인 응답	간접적인 응답	
The package arrived this morning, right? 배송 물품이 오늘 아침에 도착한 것이 맞죠, 그렇죠?	(Yes,) I think it did. (O) (네,) 그런 것 같습니다.	Did you make an order? (O) 주문을 하셨나요?	I will do it today. (✗) 오늘 그것을 하겠습니다. → [오답type] this morning에서 연상되는 단어

🏃 빠른 700⁺점 달성 TIP

부가 의문문은 'You aren't working tomorrow, are you?(내일 일 안 하시죠, 그렇죠?)' 혹은 'You're working tomorrow, aren't you?(내일 일 하시죠, 그렇지 않나요?)' 혹은 'You're working tomorrow, right?(내일 일하시죠, 그렇죠?)'의 형태와 상관 없이 평서문 쪽의 you, working, tomorrow의 핵심어를 파악하는 것이 중요하다. 부정 의문문과 마찬가지로 대부분의 부가 의문문이 사실 확인을 하는 질문이므로 '그렇다'라는 뜻의 'That's right', 'That's correct'도 yes에 해당하는 정답이 된다는 것을 기억해두자.

🎵 D08_02_T

PRACTICE | 기출 연습하기   문제를 푼 후, 질문과 정답을 2번씩 들으며 받아쓰기 해보세요.

1. (A) (B) (C)   1. The dining _____ looks _____, doesn't it?
   [정답] Yes, the _____ really makes a _____.

2. (A) (B) (C)   2. We haven't _____ a _____ head _____ yet, have we?
   [정답] No, _____.

3. (A) (B) (C)   3. You _____ three _____ on the main stage, didn't you?
   [정답] I tried, but one _____.

4. (A) (B) (C)   4. The staff _____ was _____, wasn't it?
   [정답] _____, they _____ it.

5. (A) (B) (C)   5. Your _____ at Bryce Financial is _____, isn't it?
   [정답] I already _____ them.

6. (A) (B) (C)   6. We _____ a _____ on the sofa, right?
   [정답] What does the _____?

LC | DAY 08 실전문제

1. Mark your answer on your answer sheet. (A) (B) (C)

2. Mark your answer on your answer sheet. (A) (B) (C)

3. Mark your answer on your answer sheet. (A) (B) (C)

4. Mark your answer on your answer sheet. (A) (B) (C)

5. Mark your answer on your answer sheet. (A) (B) (C)

6. Mark your answer on your answer sheet. (A) (B) (C)

7. Mark your answer on your answer sheet. (A) (B) (C)

8. Mark your answer on your answer sheet. (A) (B) (C)

9. Mark your answer on your answer sheet. (A) (B) (C)

10. Mark your answer on your answer sheet. (A) (B) (C)

11. Mark your answer on your answer sheet. (A) (B) (C)

12. Mark your answer on your answer sheet. (A) (B) (C)

13. Mark your answer on your answer sheet. (A) (B) (C)

14. Mark your answer on your answer sheet. (A) (B) (C)

15. Mark your answer on your answer sheet. (A) (B) (C)

16. Mark your answer on your answer sheet. (A) (B) (C)

17. Mark your answer on your answer sheet. (A) (B) (C)

18. Mark your answer on your answer sheet. (A) (B) (C)

19. Mark your answer on your answer sheet. (A) (B) (C)

20. Mark your answer on your answer sheet. (A) (B) (C)

21. Mark your answer on your answer sheet. (A) (B) (C)

22. Mark your answer on your answer sheet. (A) (B) (C)

23. Mark your answer on your answer sheet. (A) (B) (C)

24. Mark your answer on your answer sheet. (A) (B) (C)

25. Mark your answer on your answer sheet. (A) (B) (C)

LC DAY 09 비 의문사 의문문(3)

선택 의문문은 매회 1~2문항, 평서문은 매회 3~4문항 정도 출제되며, 각각 Part 2 문제의 7%, 12.5%를 차지한다.

01 선택 의문문

선택 의문문은 or 앞 뒤로 선택 사항을 제시하는 의문문 유형으로, or가 연결하는 정보를 들어야 문제를 풀 수 있으며 거의 80% 이상이 '구 or 구'의 형태로 출제된다.

♪ D09_01

◆ 출제 포인트 1 '구 or 구' 구조의 선택 의문문

or로 연결되는 표현을 잘 듣는 것이 중요하다.

대표 질문 유형	대표 정답 유형		대표 오답 유형
	직접적인 응답	간접적인 응답	
Should I send this box by regular mail or by express mail? 이 상자를 일반 우편으로 보내야 하나요, 아니면 속달 우편으로 보내야 하나요?	Regular, please. (O) 일반으로 해주세요.	Either is fine. (O) 둘 중 어느 것이든 괜찮습니다.	Yes, you gave me the right address. (X) 네, 제게 정확한 주소를 알려 주셨어요. → [오답type] 선택 의문문은 Yes/No로 대답할 수 없다 / mail에서 연상되는 단어
Shall we order lunch or go out to a restaurant? 점심을 주문할까요, 아니면 나가서 식당으로 갈까요?	How about the bistro down the street? (O) 길 저쪽에 있는 식당 어때요?	Neither. I brought my own. (O) 둘 다 아니에요. 저는 제 것을 가져 왔어요.	A chicken sandwich, please. (X) 치킨 샌드위치로 주세요. → [오답type] lunch와 restaurant에서 연상되는 단어
Would you like the beef or the pork? 소고기로 하시겠어요, 아니면 돼지고기로 하시겠어요?	I am allergic to pork. (O) 저는 돼지고기 알레르기가 있어요.	Is the beef spicy? (O) 소고기 요리가 매운가요?	Yes, that would be fine. (X) 네, 그렇게 해 주시면 좋을 것 같아요. → [오답type] 선택의문문은 Yes/No로 대답할 수 없다

◆ 출제 포인트 2 '문장 or 문장' 구조의 선택 의문문

or로 연결되는 표현을 잘 듣는 것이 중요하다.

대표 질문 유형	대표 정답 유형		대표 오답 유형
	직접적인 응답	간접적인 응답	
Would you like to talk to Betty about the merger, or should I? Betty에게 합병에 대해서 이야기 하시겠어요, 아니면 제가 할까요?	(Yes,) I will do that. (O) (네,) 제가 할게요.	Ms. Kerry has the details. (O) Kerry 씨가 세부 정보를 알고 있어요.	It's a business merger. (X) 업체 합병입니다. → [오답type] 같은 단어를 활용한 오답

🚀 빠른 700⁺점 달성 TIP

선택 의문문에서는 둘 중 하나를 선택하는 답변 뿐만 아니라 둘 다 좋다거나 둘 다 아니라는 답변, 혹은 그 외의 다른 선택권을 제안하거나 둘 중 어느 하나를 선택하기 위한 조건을 묻는 질문도 정답이 될 수 있으므로 관련 표현을 알아두는 것이 중요하다.

🎵 D09_01_T

PRACTICE | 기출 연습하기 문제를 푼 후, 질문과 정답을 2번씩 들으며 받아쓰기 해보세요.

1. (A) (B) (C)   1. Should we use a recruitment _____ or look for applicants _____?
[정답] _____ will work fine.

2. (A) (B) (C)   2. Should we have _____ or _____ experts on the discussion panel?
[정답] I think _____ is _____.

3. (A) (B) (C)   3. Would you prefer a table in the dining _____ or on the _____?
[정답] I _____ to sit _____.

4. (A) (B) (C)   4. Would you like the suitcase in _____ or _____?
[정답] Which one _____?

5. (A) (B) (C)   5. Should we order _____ or _____ food?
[정답] I'm _____ from lunch.

6. (A) (B) (C)   6. Do _____ make the _____, or does the _____ _____ them?
[정답] _____ take care of everything.

02 평서문

🎵 D09_02

평서문은 물음표로 끝나는 의문문과는 달리 마침표로 끝나는 문장으로, 사실을 진술할 뿐만 아니라 정보를 묻거나 제안/제공/요청/의견제시 등의 다양한 의도를 나타낼 수 있다.

◆ 출제 포인트 1 정보 제공/의견 제시의 평서문

평서문의 주어와 동사를 잘 듣는 것이 중요하다.

대표 질문 유형	대표 정답 유형		대표 오답 유형
	직접적인 응답	간접적인 응답	
The parking lot behind the store will be closed for repairs tomorrow. 매장 뒤쪽에 있는 주차장이 내일 수리 작업으로 인해 문을 닫을 겁니다.	Okay, I'll let everyone know. (O) 알겠어요, 제가 모든 분들께 알릴게요.	There's more space at the lot down the street. (O) 길 저쪽에 있는 주차장에 공간이 더 많이 있어요.	I parked right on the street. (✗) 저는 길에 바로 주차했어요. → [오답type] parking과 소리가 비슷한 단어
Mr. Petrone's presentation was very impressive. Petrone 씨의 발표가 매우 인상적이었어요.	Yes, it was quite informative. (O) 네, 꽤 유익했어요.	What was it about? (O) 무엇에 관한 것이었나요?	I brought some presents for you. (✗) 당신에게 줄 선물을 좀 가져왔어요. → [오답type] presentation과 소리가 비슷한 단어

◆ 출제 포인트 2 문제점을 언급하는 평서문/Let's ~, Please ~의 평서문

평서문의 주어와 동사를 잘 듣는 것이 중요하다. Let's와 Please가 이끄는 구문은 바로 뒤에 연결되는 표현을 잘 듣는 것이 중요하다.

대표 질문 유형	대표 정답 유형		대표 오답 유형
	직접적인 응답	간접적인 응답	
The forklift in the warehouse doesn't work properly. 창고에 있는 지게차가 제대로 작동하지 않아요.	I can help you with that. (O) 제가 그 문제에 대해 도와 드릴 수 있어요.	There's another one in the parking lot. (O) 주차장에 한 대 더 있어요.	We lifted the boxes by ourselves. (✗) 저희가 직접 그 상자들을 들어 올렸어요. → [오답type] forklift와 소리가 비슷한 단어
Let's submit the proposal in a few minutes. 몇 분 후에 제안서를 제출합시다.	Okay, I'll turn it in to Mr. Suzuki. (O) 네, 제가 Suzuki 씨께 제출할게요.	I'm still reviewing the data. (O) 저는 여전히 데이터를 검토하는 중입니다.	No, a previous submission. (✗) 아뇨, 이전에 제출한 것이요. → [오답type] submit과 소리가 비슷한 단어
Please book a round-trip flight to Boston for me. 제 대신 보스턴으로 가는 왕복 항공편 좀 예약해 주세요.	I'll be sure to do that once lunch finishes. (O) 점심 식사가 끝나는 대로 꼭 그렇게 하겠습니다.	Mr. Marshall handles reservations now. (O) 지금은 Marshall 씨가 예약 업무를 처리하고 있어요.	No, it's an indirect flight. (✗) 아뇨, 경유 항공편입니다. → [오답type] 같은 단어를 활용한 오답

빠른 700⁺점 달성 TIP

의견을 제시하는 평서문은 동의하는 표현이, 제안/요청 유형에서는 'Sure(물론이죠)' 혹은 'We can do it(우리가 할 수 있어요)'과 같은 수락 표현이 자주 정답으로 출제되며, 문제점을 언급하는 유형은 문제점을 해결하는 방법에 대한 내용이 자주 정답으로 출제된다.

♪ D09_02_T

PRACTICE | 기출 연습하기
문제를 푼 후, 질문과 정답을 2번씩 들으며 받아쓰기 해보세요.

1. (A) (B) (C)   1. Be careful to _____ the laboratory _____ on your way out.
   [정답] Okay, _____ make sure I _____.

2. (A) (B) (C)   2. The maintenance team will _____ the floorboards _____.
   [정답] _____ for _____ me.

3. (A) (B) (C)   3. I'm _____ to _____ to my new apartment this weekend.
   [정답] You're welcome to _____ my _____.

4. (A) (B) (C)   4. Your _____ seems to be _____ the last page.
   [정답] Sorry, let me print _____.

5. (A) (B) (C)   5. _____ conduct the performance _____.
   [정답] We can _____ that to next week.

6. (A) (B) (C)   6. The _____ to your vehicle's engine have been _____.
   [정답] You're _____?

DAY 09 실전문제

1. Mark your answer on your answer sheet. (A) (B) (C)

2. Mark your answer on your answer sheet. (A) (B) (C)

3. Mark your answer on your answer sheet. (A) (B) (C)

4. Mark your answer on your answer sheet. (A) (B) (C)

5. Mark your answer on your answer sheet. (A) (B) (C)

6. Mark your answer on your answer sheet. (A) (B) (C)

7. Mark your answer on your answer sheet. (A) (B) (C)

8. Mark your answer on your answer sheet. (A) (B) (C)

9. Mark your answer on your answer sheet. (A) (B) (C)

10. Mark your answer on your answer sheet. (A) (B) (C)

11. Mark your answer on your answer sheet. (A) (B) (C)

12. Mark your answer on your answer sheet. (A) (B) (C)

13. Mark your answer on your answer sheet. (A) (B) (C)

14. Mark your answer on your answer sheet. (A) (B) (C)

15. Mark your answer on your answer sheet. (A) (B) (C)

16. Mark your answer on your answer sheet. (A) (B) (C)

17. Mark your answer on your answer sheet. (A) (B) (C)

18. Mark your answer on your answer sheet. (A) (B) (C)

19. Mark your answer on your answer sheet. (A) (B) (C)

20. Mark your answer on your answer sheet. (A) (B) (C)

21. Mark your answer on your answer sheet. (A) (B) (C)

22. Mark your answer on your answer sheet. (A) (B) (C)

23. Mark your answer on your answer sheet. (A) (B) (C)

24. Mark your answer on your answer sheet. (A) (B) (C)

25. Mark your answer on your answer sheet. (A) (B) (C)

LC | DAY 10 | 전반적인 내용을 묻는 유형

01 주제/목적/대화 장소를 묻는 문제 [매회 5문항 정도 출제]

BASIC 기본기 익히기

[주제/목적/대화 장소를 묻는 문제 유형]
매월 반복 출제되는 질문 유형이므로, 유형 파악을 통해 문제를 읽는 시간을 줄이고 대화를 듣는 데 더 집중할 수 있다.

◆ 주제
- What are the speakers (mainly) discussing?
  화자들은 (주로) 무엇을 논의하고 있는가?
- What is the conversation (mainly) about?
  대화는 (주로) 무엇에 관한 것인가?
- What is the (main) topic of the conversation?
  대화의 주제는 무엇인가?

◆ 목적
- Why is the man calling?
  남자가 전화한 이유는 무엇인가?
- What is the purpose of the woman's visit?
  여자의 방문 목적은 무엇인가?
- Why is the man at the store?
  남자는 왜 상점에 있는가?

◆ 대화 장소
- Where is the conversation (most likely) taking place?
  대화는 어디에서 이뤄지고 있는가?
- Where are the speakers?
  화자들은 어디에 있는가?

PATTERN 기출 유형 맛보기

🎵 D10_01

👀 눈으로 보기

Q. **What** is the conversation mainly **about**?
(A) Organizing an orientation session
(B) Preparing for a professional event
(C) Hiring a keynote speaker
(D) Writing an employee manual

↖ 대화를 듣기 전에 질문과 선택지를 빠르게 훑는다.
→ 질문의 핵심 어구를 통해 '주제' 문제임을 파악한다.

👂 귀로 듣기

W1: I'm pleased you could both attend this meeting. **It's time to figure out how we're going to handle the conference next month.** What should we focus on there?
W2: As you know, we've only rented a booth for the first three days of the event. We therefore need to make a powerful impression on attendees.
M: How about putting together a video of the media work we've done for our clients? If we expertly produce it, it will attract potential clients. Amy, do you think you can assist me with that?

↖ 대화를 듣는다.
→ 대화의 주제/목적/장소는 주로 초반부에 제시되므로 첫 대사가 시작될 때 특히 집중한다. 주제가 파악되는 순간 바로 선택지를 본다.

↖ 정답에 체크한다.
→ 파악된 주제(다음 달 컨퍼런스를 어떻게 처리할 것인지)와 의미가 일치하는 선택지에 표시한다.

🚀 빠른 700⁺점 달성 TIP

질문에 자주 보이는 mainly(주로), most likely(아마), probably(아마)는 군더더기 표현이므로 생략한 후 해석해도 질문의 요지를 파악할 수 있다.

PRACTICE | 기출 연습하기 문제를 푼 후, 대화를 다시 두 번 들으며 빈칸을 채워보세요.

1. What are the speakers mainly discussing?
   (A) A product launch
   (B) A company logo

2. What does the woman say she will do?
   (A) Send an e-mail
   (B) Call the design team

W: Hi, Tristan. _____ of the new _____ _____ that the design team presented in the meeting?
M: I liked the colors, but, unfortunately, I was sitting at the back of the room, so I couldn't see it very easily.
W: Oh, in that case, _____ of the file. Then you'll be able to see the image in detail.

3. Why is the man calling?
   (A) To inquire about a service
   (B) To order some equipment

4. What does the woman offer to do?
   (A) Provide a contract
   (B) Visit the man

M: Hello, I got a flyer for your business. It says that you provide _____. I'd like to know more about that.
W: We have several services available, and the costs depend on the size of your lawn. If you'd like, _____ _____ to discuss the work further. Then you can decide whether or not _____ us.
M: That would be great. How does Friday afternoon work for you?

5. Where is the conversation taking place?
   (A) At a computer repair shop
   (B) At an accounting firm

6. What does the woman plan to do next week?
   (A) Take a vacation
   (B) Start a new job

W: Hi, I'm here because I need to _____ _____. I was working on it last night, and the screen suddenly went black.
M1: OK, I'll have one of our technicians look at it. Matthew, do you have time to work on this laptop now?
M2: I can _____ this afternoon.
W: Do you know how long it will take? I'm _____ next week, and I'd really like to take my computer with me.
M2: I'll know more once I take a closer look.

02 직업/근무지를 묻는 문제 〔매회 4문항 정도 출제〕

BASIC 기본기 익히기

[직업/근무지를 묻는 문제 유형]
매월 반복 출제되는 질문 유형이므로, 유형 파악을 통해 문제를 읽는 시간을 줄이고 대화를 듣는 데 더 집중할 수 있다.

◆ 직업
- Who (most likely) are the speakers? 화자들은 누구인가?
- Who (most likely) is the woman? 여자는 누구인가?
- What (most likely) is the man's job[profession]? 남자의 직업은 무엇인가?

◆ 근무지
- Where do the speakers (most likely) work? 화자들은 어디에서 근무하는가?
- Where (most likely) does the woman work? 여자는 어디에서 근무하는가?
- What department does the man (probably) work in? 남자는 무슨 부서에서 근무하는가?

PATTERN 기출 유형 맛보기

🎵 D10_02

👀 눈으로 보기

Q. **Where** does the **woman work**?
(A) At a travel agency
(B) At a rental car agency
(C) At a health clinic
(D) At a hairdresser's

▸ 대화를 듣기 전에 질문과 선택지를 빠르게 훑는다.
→ 질문의 핵심 어구를 통해 '여자의 근무지'를 묻는 문제임을 파악한다.

👂 귀로 듣기

W: This is **Bethlem Royal Clinic**. How can I help you?
M: Hello. I'm Fred Thompson, and I'll be traveling abroad on vacation a month from now. I just realized that **I have to get some vaccinations before going**. Can I make an appointment with you?
W: Yes, Mr. Thompson, we have a few slots available later this week. How does this coming Friday sound? Is one thirty all right with you?
M: I'll be meeting with a client until two on that day.
W: Then how does three o'clock work? Can you be here then?
M: Yes, that's perfect. I'll see you on Friday.

▸ 대화를 듣는다.
→ 여자나 남자의 근무지는 상대방의 대사에서 단서가 나오는 경우도 자주 있으므로 이 부분을 항상 염두에 두고 상대방의 대사까지 집중해서 듣는다.

▸ 정답에 체크한다.
→ 파악된 여자의 근무지(업체명 Bethlem Royal Clinic과 예방 주사 접종)와 의미가 일치하는 선택지에 표시한다.

📌 빠른 700⁺점 달성 TIP
직업/근무지 유형은 대화에 언급된 어휘로 함정이 만들어지므로 한두 단어를 듣고 정답을 선택하지 않도록 주의하자. 예를 들어, 위 대화에서 traveling abroad를 듣고 travel agency를 선택하는 실수를 하지 않도록 주의해야 한다.

PRACTICE | 기출 연습하기 문제를 푼 후, 대화를 다시 두 번 들으며 빈칸을 채워보세요.

1. Where do the speakers most likely work?
   (A) At an electronics store
   (B) At a clothing store

2. What does the woman ask the man to do?
   (A) Put up a sign
   (B) Work additional hours

M: Erica, I was just helping a customer in _____ _____, and I noticed a problem with the cash register there. It wouldn't open when I was trying to process a customer's purchase.
W: Hmm… it might need to be replaced. _____ _____ an "Out of Order" sign on the machine? Then other employees will know that they're not supposed to use it.
M: Of course. I can _____ right now.

3. Who most likely is the woman?
   (A) A hotel receptionist
   (B) A store clerk

4. What does the man ask about?
   (A) Delivery fees
   (B) Furniture designs

W: _____ Harrison Furniture. Is there something I can help you find?
M: Hi, I'm interested in buying the black leather sofa over there. If _____ to my home, how much would that cost?
W: Since the price of the item is over three hundred dollars, _____. Will someone be home this afternoon to accept the item?
M: Yes, that's perfect. Let me give you my address.

5. Where most likely does the woman work?
   (A) At a real estate firm
   (B) At a travel agency

6. According to the woman, why should the man visit a Web site?
   (A) To make a payment
   (B) To view some photographs

M: Good morning. I'm calling _____ _____ to New York through your agency. I'd like to leave on July 6 and return on July 12.
W: All right, sir. _____ that include both the flight and the hotel. There are a few hotels to choose from.
M: That sounds good. What are my options?
W: If you visit our Web site, you can _____ _____ of the various hotels. I think that will help you to make your decision.

LC DAY 10

LC   DAY 10   실전문제   유형별로 학습한 내용들을 적용하면서 다음 실전문제를 풀어 보세요.

1. Who most likely is the woman?
   (A) An investor
   (B) An intern
   (C) A job applicant
   (D) A supervisor

2. What does the man suggest the woman do?
   (A) Download a program
   (B) Sign a form
   (C) Come back later
   (D) Share her opinions

3. According to the man, what is the woman eligible to receive?
   (A) A job promotion
   (B) A complimentary meal
   (C) An annual subscription
   (D) A computer training

4. What type of business is the man calling?
   (A) An office supply store
   (B) A book shop
   (C) An electronics store
   (D) A camping store

5. What does the man inquire about?
   (A) The details of a promotional sale
   (B) Driving directions to the business
   (C) The business's policy on returns
   (D) A job application process

6. What does the woman tell the man about?
   (A) A shipping fee
   (B) A closing time
   (C) A warranty period
   (D) A project deadline

7. What kind of business does the man work for?
   (A) An electronics store
   (B) A cleaning company
   (C) A legal firm
   (D) A job recruiter

8. What is the purpose of the call?
   (A) To make a complaint
   (B) To introduce a product
   (C) To update an address
   (D) To request a service

9. What does the man recommend the woman do?
   (A) Visit a Web site
   (B) Request a sample
   (C) Review a contract
   (D) Call another branch

10. Why is the woman calling?
    (A) To check some minimum qualifications
    (B) To inquire about a hiring process
    (C) To follow up on a purchase
    (D) To make a job offer

11. What does the man most likely mean when he says, "we received nearly two hundred applications"?
    (A) A task has been delayed.
    (B) A position has already been filled.
    (C) A deadline was moved up.
    (D) A goal was reached quickly.

12. What does the woman agree to do?
    (A) Meet the man's colleagues
    (B) Read some instructions
    (C) Attend a workshop
    (D) Call again next week

13. Where is the conversation taking place?
    (A) At an awards ceremony
    (B) At a planning meeting
    (C) At a product demonstration
    (D) At a training workshop

14. What were the women working on recently?
    (A) Securing an important client
    (B) Competing in a contest
    (C) Upgrading a Web site
    (D) Preparing for a job fair

15. What does the man say he is responsible for doing?
    (A) Teaching new employees
    (B) Organizing some résumés
    (C) Giving a presentation
    (D) Reviewing an interview schedule

16. What does the man ask about regarding a festival?
    (A) What the admission fee will be
    (B) Who has confirmed their performances
    (C) Why it will not be advertised online
    (D) When a site will be selected

17. In which department does Colleen most likely work?
    (A) Finance
    (B) Graphics
    (C) IT
    (D) Marketing

18. What does the man plan to review at the end of the month?
    (A) Employee achievements
    (B) Safety measures
    (C) News articles
    (D) Attendance data

Weather Forecast			
Wednesday	Thursday	Friday	Saturday
Rainy	Sunny	Sunny	Cloudy
66° F	80° F	75° F	68° F

19. What kind of event are the speakers discussing?
    (A) A community picnic
    (B) A sports competition
    (C) A volunteer project
    (D) An anniversary party

20. Look at the graphic. For which day is the event scheduled?
    (A) Wednesday
    (B) Thursday
    (C) Friday
    (D) Saturday

21. What will the man most likely do next?
    (A) Contact a musical group
    (B) Post an update online
    (C) Decorate an area
    (D) Visit a caterer

LC DAY 11 세부적인 내용을 묻는 유형 (1)

01 문제점을 묻는 문제 `매회 2-3문항 정도 출제`

BASIC 기본기 익히기

[문제점을 묻는 문제 유형]
매월 반복 출제되는 질문 유형이므로, 유형 파악을 통해 문제를 읽는 시간을 줄이고 대화를 듣는 데 더 집중할 수 있다.

◆ 문제점
- What problem does the woman mention[notice/have]? 여자는 무슨 문제점을 언급하는가[주목하는가/갖고 있는가]?
- What problem is being discussed? 무슨 문제점이 논의되고 있는가?
- Why is the man concerned? 남자는 왜 우려하는가?
- Why does the woman need assistance? 여자는 왜 도움을 필요로 하는가?

◆ 문제 원인
- What has caused a problem? 무엇이 문제점을 초래했는가?
- Why is the man unable to access the file? 남자는 왜 파일을 이용할 수 없는가?

PATTERN 기출 유형 맛보기 ♪ D11_01

👀 눈으로 보기

Q. **What problem** does the **woman mention**?
(A) Some employees quit their jobs.
(B) Bad weather is being predicted.
(C) Fewer customers have been coming.
(D) Complaints by customers have increased.

✎ 대화를 듣기 전에 질문과 선택지를 빠르게 훑는다.
→ 질문의 핵심 어구를 통해 '여자가 말하는 문제점'을 묻는 문제임을 파악한다.

👂 귀로 듣기

W: Greg, did you hear that **we might be getting a blizzard tomorrow?** The buses and trains probably won't be running, and I'm supposed to arrive early tomorrow.
M: I had no idea about that. If the forecast doesn't change, some of the other workers might not be able to make it here either. I'll have to decide whether to open the store late tomorrow morning.
W: If you need me to contact the other staff members scheduled to work, just ask.
M: Thanks a lot. I appreciate the offer.

✎ 대화를 듣는다.
→ 문제점 또는 그 원인을 묻는 문제는 대개 대화의 첫 번째 또는 두 번째 문제로 출제된다. 첫 번째 문제일 경우에는 대화 초반에, 두 번째 문제일 경우에는 중반에 단서가 제시되므로 문제 순서에 따라 초·중반부에 집중해 듣는다.

✎ 정답에 체크한다.
→ 파악된 문제점(내일 발생될 수 있는 눈보라)과 의미가 일치하는 선택지에 표시한다.

🏃 빠른 700⁺점 달성 TIP

문제점을 묻는 질문이 나오면, 부정적 상황과 관련된 내용이 대화에 나올 것임을 예상하고 들어야 한다. 또한 문제점 또는 그 원인을 묻는 문제의 선택지는 주로 문장으로 제시되기 때문에 대화를 듣기 전에 미리 읽어 의미를 파악해두는 것이 좋다. 이때 각 선택지의 핵심 어구를 표시해 두면 정답 선택이 용이하다.

PRACTICE | 기출 연습하기 문제를 푼 후, 대화를 다시 두 번 들으며 빈칸을 채워보세요.

1. What problem does the woman mention?
   (A) She has a scheduling conflict.
   (B) She ran out of supplies.

2. What does the man remind the woman about?
   (A) Keep a receipt
   (B) Use a coupon

M: Hi, Marilyn. I stopped by your office to find out if you have _____ for the annual banquet. I'd like to send them as soon as possible.
W: They're not ready yet. The problem is that _____ of the cream-colored paper, so I'm on my way to the stationery store now to buy more.
M: All right. Don't forget to _____ for the purchase. You'll need to give that to the finance team in order to get reimbursed.

3. What problem does the man mention?
   (A) Some equipment is not working.
   (B) A document is incorrect.

4. What will the woman most likely do next?
   (A) Place an order
   (B) Hold a meeting

W: Hi, Timothy. It's Jennifer. I just got back to my office, and I see that there is a message that I'm supposed to call you.
M: Thanks for _____. I'm trying to print some handouts for the staff meeting, but the _____.
W: You know, we've had this problem repeatedly, so _____ some new parts for it. I'll do that now, but you'll have to use the printer in another department in the meantime.

5. What has caused a problem?
   (A) A meeting was canceled.
   (B) Some items did not arrive.

6. What does the man suggest doing?
   (A) Delivering a product
   (B) Contacting another business

M: Hi, Pricilla. Hi, Robin. Is everything ready for tomorrow's sales pitch to our new client?
W1: Unfortunately, there's an issue with the conference room. _____ the projector and wireless speakers _____ from Ace Supplies.
W2: Right. We won't be able to do the presentation without them.
M: Hmm ... Robin, _____ Nordin Electronics to see if they have what you need in stock? Then we could pick it up today in person.
W1: OK. Then I can follow up with Ace Supplies later.

02 요청/제안 사항 문제 매회 6-7문항 정도 출제

BASIC 기본기 익히기

[요청/제안 사항을 묻는 문제 유형]
매월 반복 출제되는 질문 유형이므로, 유형 파악을 통해 문제를 읽는 시간을 줄이고 대화를 듣는 데 더 집중할 수 있다.

◆ 요청
- What does the woman ask the man to do? (행위 요청) 여자는 남자에게 무엇을 하도록 요청하는가?
- What information does the woman request? (정보 요청) 여자는 무슨 정보를 요청하는가?
- What does the man ask for(=request)? (정보 혹은 사물 요청) 남자는 무엇을 요청하는가?

◆ 제안
- What does the man suggest[recommend/propose]? 남자는 무엇을 제안하는가[권하는가/제안하는가]?
- What does the woman suggest[recommend/propose] doing? 여자는 무엇을 하도록 제안하는가[권하는가/제안하는가]?

What does the man offer to do? 문제 유형은 상대방에게 무언가를 하도록 제안하는 것이 아니라, 자신(the man)이 하겠다는 것이 무엇인지를 묻는 유형이다.

PATTERN 기출 유형 맛보기
♪ D11_02

👀 눈으로 보기
Q. **What** does the **woman ask** the man to do?
(A) Edit an article
(B) Renegotiate a price
(C) Ask for a refund
(D) Contact a manager

↖ 대화를 듣기 전에 질문과 선택지를 빠르게 훑는다.
→ 질문의 핵심 어구를 통해 '여자가 요청하는 내용을 묻는 문제'임을 파악한다.

👂 귀로 듣기
W: Good afternoon, Jeff. Could I get an update on the training manuals we're getting printed for the software?
M: The print shop sent me a sample this morning. However, I noticed several spelling mistakes. I informed the shop and received an apology. The manager said we'd get the corrected manuals on Thursday.
W: I'm afraid that's not good enough. The session is scheduled for Wednesday afternoon, so we need to hand out the manuals then. **Could you call the manager back** and request that we receive the manuals no later than Wednesday morning?

↖ 대화를 듣는다.
→ 요청/제안 내용은 주로 대화의 후반부에 제시되며, 질문의 주어가 하는 말에 단서가 있으므로 여자의 말에서 요청/제안 표현이 들릴 것이라 예상하고 듣는다.

↖ 정답에 체크한다.
→ 파악된 여자의 요청 사항(인쇄소에 연락해 특정 요일에 제품을 받는 일)과 의미가 일치하는 선택지에 표시한다.

🔖 빠른 700⁺점 달성 TIP
요청/제안 문제는 질문을 통해 여자의 요청/제안인지 남자의 요청/제안인지를 확인할 수 있으므로, 여자 또는 남자의 말에서 요청/제안 관련 표현이 나올 것임을 예상하고 들어야 한다. 또한 요청/제안 문제는 세 문제 중 세 번째 문제로 가장 많이 출제되지만 두 번째 문제로도 종종 출제되므로, 이 경우 대화의 마지막 부분까지 기다리지 말고 첫 문제의 단서 이후부터 집중해서 들어야 한다.

PRACTICE | 기출 연습하기 문제를 푼 후, 대화를 다시 두 번 들으며 빈칸을 채워보세요.

1. What does the man ask the woman to do?
   (A) Change a meeting date
   (B) Register for an event

2. What does the woman say she will do?
   (A) Approve an expense
   (B) Check a schedule

M: Susan, there's an industry conference on Thursday and Friday, so a lot of the salespeople on my team will not be able to attend the _____. Could you _____?
W: Sure. Thanks for bringing this to my attention. _____ to find out when the conference room is available.
M: Thanks. I know that you've got some new regulation changes to go over, so it's important for everyone to be there.

3. What does the man suggest doing?
   (A) Working extra hours
   (B) Hiring more workers

4. What does the man ask the woman to do?
   (A) Write a job description
   (B) Provide a Web site address

W: Mr. Song, the graphic design team is _____ with their tasks. The company has taken on a lot of new clients recently, so we're busier than ever.
M: Well, I think this trend is only going to continue. _____ part-time workers to help you?
W: Is there room in the budget to do that?
M: Definitely. Please write a _____ _____ and send it to me. Then I'll post it online.

5. What does the man offer to do?
   (A) Carry a bag
   (B) Cancel a reservation

6. What does the woman ask the man about?
   (A) A breakfast menu
   (B) A checkout time

M: All right, Ms. McIntyre. I have your reservation here, and you'll be in Room 406. If you'd like, I can _____ _____ your room for you.
W: Thanks, but I can manage it on my own. What time do I _____ of the hotel in the morning?
M: All guests must be checked out by 11 A.M. And don't forget that we offer a free breakfast in the morning. It's in the hotel lounge.
W: Thanks. I'll definitely _____ that.

DAY 11 실전문제

1. What goal does the woman mention?
   (A) Changing her career
   (B) Winning a prestigious award
   (C) Getting a book published
   (D) Displaying paintings publicly

2. What does the man offer to do?
   (A) Make arrangements for a meeting
   (B) Send the woman an application
   (C) Invest some money in a project
   (D) Accompany the woman to an event

3. What information does the woman ask for?
   (A) An e-mail address
   (B) A phone number
   (C) A business's name
   (D) A closing time

4. What is the main topic of the conversation?
   (A) A concert
   (B) A lecture
   (C) A health screening
   (D) A sporting event

5. According to the woman, what caused a problem?
   (A) A severe storm
   (B) A safety issue
   (C) A computer error
   (D) A broken microphone

6. What will the listeners hear next?
   (A) A new song
   (B) An interview
   (C) An advertisement
   (D) A traffic report

7. Where is the conversation most likely taking place?
   (A) At a hardware store
   (B) At a car dealership
   (C) At a moving company
   (D) At a bank

8. What are the speakers mainly discussing?
   (A) A competitor gaining market share
   (B) A shipment not arriving on time
   (C) Customers returning items frequently
   (D) Some employees who are not experienced

9. What do the speakers agree to do?
   (A) Hire more employees
   (B) Stop selling a brand
   (C) Lower some prices
   (D) Improve payment procedures

10. What are the speakers working on?
    (A) Looking for a laptop
    (B) Preparing for a sales meeting
    (C) Developing a new projector
    (D) Arranging some chairs

11. Who most likely is the man?
    (A) An IT technician
    (B) A sales director
    (C) A potential client
    (D) A building owner

12. What does the man suggest that the women do?
    (A) Postpone an event
    (B) Order new parts
    (C) Change locations
    (D) Restart a device

13. What does the woman ask the man for?
    (A) A contact number for a business
    (B) A recommendation for a lunch order
    (C) A copy of a contract
    (D) The name of a security guard

14. What does the man imply when he says, "Actually, I'm late for a meeting"?
    (A) He thinks the woman should give a presentation.
    (B) He wants to take a taxi to a site.
    (C) He cannot fulfill the woman's request.
    (D) He is upset about a schedule change.

15. What does the woman plan to do?
    (A) Postpone an event
    (B) Return to the building
    (C) Leave an office unlocked
    (D) Call another coworker

16. According to the woman, what caused some deliveries to be canceled?
    (A) A lack of supplies
    (B) Business closure
    (C) A late payment
    (D) A staff shortage

17. What does the woman want employees to do?
    (A) Repair items that customers bring in
    (B) Check the inventory more regularly
    (C) Use a new shipping system
    (D) Make alternative recommendations

18. What do the speakers plan to do this afternoon?
    (A) Announce a change
    (B) Contact a client
    (C) Create a schedule
    (D) Send a catalog

Set	Description
1	Clams in Garlic Cream Sauce
2	Roasted Chicken and Potatoes
3	Grilled Shrimp with Tomato Sauce
4	Pork Chops with Steamed Rice

19. What type of event is being discussed?
    (A) A product launch
    (B) An anniversary celebration
    (C) A welcome reception
    (D) An awards ceremony

20. Look at the graphic. Which menu set will be served to the woman?
    (A) Set 1
    (B) Set 2
    (C) Set 3
    (D) Set 4

21. What does the man request that the woman do?
    (A) Bring the invitation
    (B) Review a seating chart
    (C) Park on site
    (D) Dress formally

LC | DAY 12 — 세부적인 내용을 묻는 유형 (2)

01 앞으로 할 일을 묻는 문제 매회 3~4문항 정도 출제

BASIC 기본기 익히기

[앞으로 할 일을 묻는 문제 유형]
매월 반복 출제되는 질문 유형이므로, 유형 파악을 통해 문제를 읽는 시간을 줄이고 대화를 듣는 데 더 집중할 수 있다.

◆ **대화에 곧이어 할 일**
- What will the speakers (most likely) do next? 화자들은 곧이어 무엇을 할 것인가?
- What will the woman (most likely) do next? 여자는 곧이어 무엇을 할 것인가?
- What does the man say he will do next? 남자는 곧이어 무엇을 할 것이라고 말하는가?

◆ **미래에 할 일**
- What does the man say he will do? 남자는 무엇을 할 것이라고 말하는가?
- What will the man probably do? 남자는 무엇을 할 것 같은가?

PATTERN 기출 유형 맛보기 ♪ D12_01

👀 눈으로 보기

Q. **What** will the **man do next**?
(A) Advertise an apartment
(B) Do some repair work
(C) Contact the maintenance team
(D) **Look into some prices**

> 🔍 대화를 듣기 전에 질문과 선택지를 빠르게 훑는다.
> → 질문의 핵심 어구를 통해 '남자가 곧이어 할 일'을 묻는 문제임을 파악한다.

👂 귀로 듣기

W: Steve, you know how we paint the apartments before new tenants move in, right? Well, our maintenance team can't always do that immediately, so we're encountering some problems.
M: Then let's hire some professional painters.
W: That would be ideal, but we can't afford to pay their rates.
M: That was true in the past, but we run several apartments now.
W: Yeah, I suppose. And now that I think about it, the maintenance team is busier than ever doing work other than painting.
M: So let's contract the work to another company. **I'll** make a few calls to painters and **get some price estimates**.

> 🔍 대화를 듣는다.
> → do next(곧이어 할 일) 문제는 대화 이후에 질문상의 주어가 할 일을 묻는 문제이며, 주로 세 문제 중 마지막에 출제된다. 단서가 주로 대화 후반부에 제시되므로, 후반부의 내용에 집중해 듣는다.

> 🔍 정답에 체크한다.
> → 대화에서 파악된 다음에 할 일(전화를 걸어 가격 견적을 받는 일)과 의미가 일치하는 선택지에 표시한다.

📌 **빠른 700⁺점 달성 TIP**

앞으로 할 일(do next? / will do?)을 묻는 문제의 단서 표현은 I'll([aɪl])로 시작되는 경우가 많다. I'll은 I will(나는 ~ 할 것이다)을 줄여 쓴 형태로 발음이 생소할 수 있으니 여러 번 들어 숙지해 두자.

PRACTICE | 기출 연습하기 문제를 푼 후, 대화를 다시 두 번 들으며 빈칸을 채워보세요.

1. Who most likely is the woman?
   (A) A property manager
   (B) A sales representative

2. What will the woman most likely do next?
   (A) Send a brochure
   (B) Contact a landlord

W: Hello, you've reached the Harbor Apartments property management office. How may I help you?
M: Hi, this is Lucas Cassano calling from apartment 43B. I have a lease until December, but I actually need to move out early. I've _____ in Boston, so I'm relocating there.
W: OK, Mr. Cassano. You'll _____ _____ from the landlord, or there might be a fee. _____ about this situation.

3. What are the speakers mainly discussing?
   (A) A work assignment
   (B) A budget report

4. What will the speakers most likely do next?
   (A) Review a policy
   (B) Create a survey

M: The manager _____ a program of monthly professional development lectures. The sessions should be aimed at helping employees to improve their business skills. I'm really not sure what topic we should cover, though.
W: Why don't we _____ _____ for employees? That way, we could find out which topics they're most interested in.
M: Good idea. We can _____ questions now. The sooner we send it out, the better.

5. Where does the man work?
   (A) At a repair shop
   (B) At a factory

6. What does the man say he will do?
   (A) Call Phelps Supplies later
   (B) Give a product a try

W1: Hello. May I speak to the manager, please?
W2: Yes, just a moment. Mr. Adams, there's someone on the line for you.
M: Hi, this is Leo Adams, the _____.
W1: Hi, Mr. Adams. I'm calling from Phelps Supplies. Since you've placed several orders with us in the past, I wanted to introduce you to our new cleaner, which is specially designed for machine parts.
M: Hmm... _____ one bottle with our next order so I can see _____ _____?

02 특정 시점의 일 / 과거에 한 일을 묻는 문제 매회 3문항 정도 출제

BASIC 기본기 익히기

[특정 시점의 일 / 과거에 한 일을 묻는 문제 유형]
매월 반복 출제되는 질문 유형이므로, 유형 파악을 통해 문제를 읽는 시간을 줄이고 대화를 듣는 데 더 집중할 수 있다.

◆ 특정 시점에 일어났거나 일어날 일
- What does the woman say she will do next year? 여자는 내년에 무엇을 할 것이라고 말하는가?
- What is the man doing on Tuesday? 남자는 화요일에 무엇을 하는가?
- What will take place next month? 다음 달에 무슨 일이 있을 것인가?
- What did the woman do this afternoon? 여자는 오늘 오후에 무엇을 했는가?

◆ 과거에 일어난 일
- What has the man recently done? 남자는 최근에 무엇을 했는가?
- What did the woman recently do? 여자는 최근에 무엇을 했는가?
- What does the woman say she has already done? 여자는 이미 무엇을 했다고 말하는가?
- According to the conversation, what did Mindy do earlier? 대화에 따르면, Mindy는 앞서 무엇을 했는가?

PATTERN 기출 유형 맛보기   ♪ D12_02

👀 눈으로 보기
Q. **What** will the **woman do on Wednesday**?
(A) Interview for a job
(B) Purchase some clothes
(C) Work with some clients
(D) Go out of town on business

👂 귀로 듣기
W: Hello, Mr. Anderson. I've got a blouse I'd like you to dry clean for me. I just realized it's got a couple of stains on it, though.
M: Let me take a look. It won't be a problem to remove the stains. I can have this and the clothes you dropped off yesterday ready for you by Friday.
W: If you don't mind, I'd like to have both of them before **my job interview scheduled for Wednesday afternoon**. Can you do that?
M: Sure, I'll work on them personally, so you can pick them up by ten in the morning on that day.

🔍 **대화를 듣기 전에 질문과 선택지를 빠르게 훑는다.**
→ 질문의 핵심 어구를 통해 '여자가 특정 시점(수요일)에 할 일'을 묻는 문제임을 파악한다.

🔍 **대화를 듣는다.**
→ 특정 시점의 일을 묻는 문제는 대화의 1-2-3번 문제로 고루 출제된다. 따라서 1번 문제일 경우는 대화의 초반부, 2번은 중반부, 3번은 후반부에 집중해서 듣는다. 영문의 특성상('주어+동사+시점'의 어순) 질문의 시점 표현이 정답 단서 표현보다 뒤에 제시되므로, 질문의 주어인 여자의 말에 집중해서 듣다가 질문의 시점 표현(Wednesday)이 들리면 바로 앞에 함께 들었던 내용을 정답으로 선택해야 한다.

🔍 **정답에 체크한다.**
→ 대화에서 파악된 특정 시점(Wednesday)에 할 일(구직 면접)과 의미가 일치하는 선택지에 표시한다.

📌 빠른 700⁺점 달성 TIP
- 질문에 제시되는 특정 시점은 패러프레이징되지 않고 대화 속에서 그대로 언급되는 경우가 대부분이다.
- 질문에 recently(최근에), already(벌써), earlier(앞서) 등의 부사와 함께 '최근/과거에 있었던 일'이 무엇인지를 묻는 문제의 단서는 주로 대화에서 과거 시제 또는 현재 완료 시제 동사로 표현된다.

PRACTICE | 기출 연습하기 문제를 푼 후, 대화를 다시 두 번 들으며 빈칸을 채워보세요.

1. What kind of event will take place this weekend?
   (A) A food festival
   (B) A technology trade show

2. What will the man most likely do next?
   (A) Speak to a coworker
   (B) Call a client

M: Marta, _____ the technology trade show this weekend. Would you mind trading shifts with me on Friday so I can leave earlier in the day?
W: I'd like to help you out, but I have tickets to a concert that night, so I can't work the evening shift. _____ Garrett? He has worked the evening shift many times, and he usually has a flexible schedule.
M: OK, _____ now. Thanks.

3. Who most likely are the speakers?
   (A) Accountants
   (B) Journalists

4. What does the woman plan to do tomorrow?
   (A) Attend an interview
   (B) Move to a new office

M: Hi, Nicole. It's great to see you! I didn't know that you were coming to this year's _____.
W: I try to come every year because I feel like it helps me improve _____.
M: I feel the same way. Are you still working for the Trenway Times?
W: Yes, but I've actually applied for a new job at a magazine. In fact, _____ at their head office tomorrow.

5. What does the woman suggest doing?
   (A) Opening another branch
   (B) Changing to a new supplier

6. According to the woman, what has recently happened?
   (A) Some materials have become more expensive.
   (B) A competitor has gone out of business.

W: Mr. Shepherd, I'm wondering if it would be possible to _____ for our fabric needs. I think it would be better for our company.
M: Oh, really? Why is that?
W: Our current supplier _____ of their fabrics. I think we can _____ somewhere else.
M: OK. Why don't you do some research and get back to me with some figures?

LC DAY 12 실전문제

1. What are the speakers doing next week?
   (A) Welcoming some buyers
   (B) Taking a trip
   (C) Moving to a new home
   (D) Attending a festival

2. What does the woman suggest doing?
   (A) Exchanging some money
   (B) Purchasing insurance
   (C) Taking a lot of pictures
   (D) Doing some online research

3. What will the man send to the woman?
   (A) A map
   (B) An itinerary
   (C) A confirmation code
   (D) A hotel brochure

4. What problem does the man mention?
   (A) Some employees are absent.
   (B) Some equipment is noisy.
   (C) An air conditioner is not working properly.
   (D) A room is currently locked.

5. What does the woman plan to do after lunch?
   (A) Meet with a client
   (B) Leave for a business trip
   (C) Inspect a building
   (D) Interview a job candidate

6. What does the woman say she will do?
   (A) Print out some forms
   (B) Check a waiting list
   (C) Contact a repair person
   (D) Set up a device

7. What kind of event is being discussed?
   (A) An awards banquet
   (B) A retirement celebration
   (C) A product launch
   (D) An anniversary party

8. What does the woman ask about?
   (A) Decorations
   (B) Parking
   (C) Catering
   (D) Accommodations

9. What has the facility recently added?
   (A) A modern sound system
   (B) Outdoor dining space
   (C) A free Internet connection
   (D) Upgraded security measures

10. Where is the conversation taking place?
    (A) At a graphic design business
    (B) At a marketing firm
    (C) At a job recruitment agency
    (D) At a law office

11. What is the woman concerned about?
    (A) Missing a training session
    (B) Exceeding a project budget
    (C) Upsetting a client
    (D) Finding accommodations

12. What does the man say he will do?
    (A) Review a presentation
    (B) Reserve a meeting room
    (C) E-mail a schedule
    (D) Meet with a coworker

13. What did the woman do yesterday?
    (A) Helped a tenant move
    (B) Installed some equipment
    (C) Attended a meeting
    (D) Signed a new lease

14. Why is the man surprised?
    (A) He expected a water bill to be lower.
    (B) He expected the woman to take the day off.
    (C) He thought an event would be more popular.
    (D) He thought a problem had been resolved.

15. What does the man agree to do?
    (A) Send some figures
    (B) Review a document
    (C) Turn off some lights
    (D) Put up a notice

16. What is the man asking the woman to do?
    (A) Send some information
    (B) Place an order
    (C) Verify some figures
    (D) Set up some equipment

17. What does the man say he will do this afternoon?
    (A) Give a sales presentation
    (B) Conduct an interview
    (C) Print some documents
    (D) Visit a client

18. Why does the man say, "I just joined the team last year"?
    (A) To explain why he has not attended an event
    (B) To express appreciation for being a team member
    (C) To highlight how quickly he has been promoted
    (D) To show he is worried about explaining policies on his own

Flight Number	Departure Time	Arrival Time
PL-162	8:10 A.M.	9:36 A.M.
PL-249	9:20 A.M.	10:58 A.M.
PL-280	10:45 A.M.	12:11 A.M.
PL-346	11:30 A.M.	12:58 A.M.

19. What does the woman apologize for?
    (A) A lost bag
    (B) A canceled flight
    (C) An unavailable service
    (D) An incorrect fee

20. Look at the graphic. Which flight would be best for the man?
    (A) PL-162
    (B) PL-249
    (C) PL-280
    (D) PL-346

21. What does the man plan to do in Vancouver?
    (A) Meet an investor
    (B) Have a job interview
    (C) Negotiate a contract
    (D) Inspect a factory

LC | DAY 13 | 세부적인 내용을 묻는 유형 (3)

01 기타 세부 사항 문제 매회 9문항 정도 출제

BASIC 기본기 익히기

[기타 세부 사항을 묻는 문제 유형]
매월 반복 출제되는 질문 유형이므로, 유형 파악을 통해 문제를 읽는 시간을 줄이고 대화를 듣는 데 더 집중할 수 있다.

Why is the woman disappointed? 여자는 왜 실망하는가?
What is mentioned about the exhibit? 전시회에 관해 무엇이 언급되는가?
What does the man say about his company? 남자는 자신의 회사에 관해 무슨 말을 하는가?
What does the man say he wants to do? 남자는 무엇을 하고 싶다고 말하는가?
How did the man learn about the program? 남자는 어떻게 해당 프로그램에 대해 알게 되었는가?
What feature of the item is the woman excited about? 여자는 제품의 무슨 특징에 대해 흥미로워하는가?
What additional benefit does Frederick mention? Frederick 씨는 무슨 추가 혜택을 언급하는가?

PATTERN 기출 유형 맛보기

🎵 D13_01

👀 눈으로 보기

Q. **What** does the **man say Emily is good at**?
(A) Customer service
(B) Drink preparation
(C) Graphic design
(D) Renovation work

👂 귀로 듣기

W: Dave, ever since we started renovating the shop, we've gotten fewer customers. Do you have any idea how to get them to come back?
M: You know, it's possible people think our coffee shop is closed since there are many people working on the building. How about putting up a big sign pointing out we're still open for business?
W: Good thinking. If we make it big enough and hang it on the front of the building, everyone will know they can drop by anytime.
M: Exactly. **Let's ask Emily** for assistance since **she's good at making graphic designs**. I've seen her work, and it's really impressive.

> 🔍 **대화를 듣기 전에 질문과 선택지를 빠르게 훑는다.**
> → 매회 약 20% 정도가 정형화되지 않은 특정 세부 사항 문제로 다양하게 출제되지만, 의문사와 키워드를 중심으로 질문의 핵심을 빠르게 파악하는 것이 중요하다. 질문의 핵심 어구를 통해 '남자가 말하는 Emily가 잘 하는 일'을 묻는 문제임을 파악한다.

> 🔍 **대화를 듣는다.**
> → 다양한 세부 사항 문제는 대화의 1-2-3번 문제로 고르게 출제되므로 출제 순서와 키워드를 미리 충분히 파악하는 것이 좋다. 예를 들어, 왼쪽의 예시 문제가 세 번째 문제일 경우, 『후반부 단서 – 남자 대사 – Emily – good』과 같이 정보를 미리 파악하고 대화를 듣는 것이 좋다.

> 🔍 **정답에 체크한다.**
> → 대화에서 파악된 Emily가 잘 하는 일 (그래픽 디자인 작업)과 일치하는 선택지에 표시한다.

📌 **빠른 700⁺점 달성 TIP**
질문에 여자/남자(the woman/the man)가 아닌 제3자의 이름이 있는 경우가 있는데, 대부분의 대화에서 정답 단서보다 질문에 나온 이름이 더 먼저 제시되며 이름이 들린 후 얼마 지나지 않아 단서 내용이 제시되므로, 이름이 들린 이후의 내용에 집중해서 들으면 된다.

PRACTICE | 기출 연습하기 문제를 푼 후, 대화를 다시 두 번 들으며 빈칸을 채워보세요.

1. What does the man want to do?
   (A) Attend a dance performance
   (B) Organize a sporting event

2. What does the woman apologize for?
   (A) Some seats are not available.
   (B) The business does not accept credit cards.

M: Hello, _____ to the Montello Dance Troupe's performance on June 4. We'd like to sit on the main floor, as close to the stage as possible.
W: I'm sorry, sir, but _____ of the tickets for the main floor. We only have _____ _____ left.
M: That's too bad. I'll take whatever you have then. Can I pay for the tickets over the phone by credit card?

3. What does the woman want to do?
   (A) Sign up for a membership
   (B) Take a guided tour

4. What does the man say about the Egyptian Artifacts exhibit?
   (A) It requires an additional fee.
   (B) It will reopen soon.

W: Good afternoon. I _____ a one-year membership for the museum.
M: All right, ma'am. It costs eighty dollars, and it will allow you unlimited visits to the museum and all of its special exhibits.
W: That's perfect. Actually, I'm _____ Egyptian history, but I noticed that part of the museum is closed.
M: Yes, we're repairing some water damage in the Egyptian Artifacts exhibit now. However, it _____ _____ a couple of weeks.

5. How did the man hear about the product recall?
   (A) By reading the newspaper
   (B) By speaking to a coworker

6. What does the woman give to the man?
   (A) A replacement product
   (B) A set of instructions

M: Hi, I stopped in because _____ my coworkers that the Eastland-210 fan heater has been recalled. I just purchased one a few weeks ago.
W: Yes, the company has recalled that item due to a potential safety issue.
M: What do I need to do to get a replacement? Should I bring the heater here to the store?
W: It has to be sent directly to the manufacturer. _____ _____ about the recall. It explains step by step _____.

02 의도 파악 문제 매회 2문항 정도 출제

BASIC 기본기 익히기

[의도 파악 문제 유형]
"~"의 형태로 질문에 대화 속 문장이 제시되면 모두 의도 파악 문제이므로, 질문에서 "~" 외의 부분은 해석할 필요 없이 "~"에 해당하는 문장만 이해하면 된다.

What does the woman mean when she says, "It doesn't make any sense"?
여자가 "It doesn't make any sense"라고 말할 때 무엇을 의미하는가?
Why does the woman say, "I think that can happen"? 여자는 왜 "I think that can happen"이라고 말하는가?
What does the woman imply when she says, "Mr. Cooper is currently out of town"?
여자가 "Mr. Cooper is currently out of town"이라고 말할 때 무엇을 암시하는가?

PATTERN 기출 유형 맛보기 ♪D13_02

👁 눈으로 보기

Q. What does the man mean when he says, "**I've got a dinner appointment with Mr. Reynolds**"?
(A) He has to hurry to run some errands.
(B) He cannot speak to the woman any longer.
(C) He has to leave work early for the day.
(D) **He does not have time for an event.**

👂 귀로 듣기

W: Victor, did you know **Dr. Aaron North will be the final speaker at tomorrow's conference**?
M: Yes, I heard that. He's such an impressive architect. **Unfortunately, I've got a dinner appointment with Mr. Reynolds**.
W: In that case, I'll let you know how the talk goes.
M: That's all right. I've read all his books, so I'm familiar with his theories on urban architecture.
W: I still need to purchase his latest work.
M: Just borrow my copy when we return to the office.
W: Wow, thanks for the offer. I'd love to get my hands on it.

✎ 대화를 듣기 전에 질문과 선택지를 빠르게 훑는다.
→ 질문의 형태를 통해 '의도를 파악하는' 문제임을 알 수 있다. "~"로 제시된 문장을 먼저 읽고 의미를 파악한다.

✎ 대화를 듣는다.
→ "~"로 제시된 문장보다 단서가 먼저 나오는 경우가 대부분이므로 "~" 문장이 들릴 때까지 기다리지 말고 대화의 흐름을 파악하며 듣는다.

✎ 정답에 체크한다.
→ 대화에서 파악된 의도(Aaron North 박사의 연설에 참석할 수 없다)와 의미가 일치하는 선택지에 표시한다.

✏ 빠른 700⁺점 달성 TIP

의도 파악 문제는 질문에 제시된 화자의 대사보다 상대방의 대사가 단서인 경우가 많으므로 질문에 제시된 화자가 말하는 대사에만 집중해서는 안된다.

PRACTICE | 기출 연습하기 문제를 푼 후, 대화를 다시 두 번 들으며 빈칸을 채워보세요.

1. Where most likely is the conversation taking place?
   (A) In a library
   (B) In a restaurant

2. What does the woman imply when she says, "I was just leaving"?
   (A) She does not have time to discuss an issue.
   (B) She will give the man her table.

M: Oh, hello Susan! I never usually bump into anyone from work _____. I rarely see anyone from the office in this part of town.
W: Hi, Richard. Well, I read a review that said not only that the food is excellent, but also that the view from the patio is amazing. And, I must admit, it is impressive.
M: It's wonderful, isn't it? I always try to _____ out on the patio.
W: Actually, I was just leaving, if you _____.
M: Are you sure? I'd appreciate that, as I might have to wait a while for another one.

3. Where do the speakers work?
   (A) At an interior design studio
   (B) At a dental clinic

4. What does the man imply when he says, "but that was a few years ago"?
   (A) A task should be done again.
   (B) A business may have closed.

M: We need to find a way to improve the appearance of _____. The interior is the first thing that people notice when they visit us, and it's important for them to _____.
W: You know, we did _____ and decorated by professionals from Ramirez Inc.
M: Yes, but that was a few years ago. The paint is already starting to show some signs of wear.

5. What are the speakers mainly discussing?
   (A) A visit from investors
   (B) An overseas job opportunity

6. What does the woman imply when she says, "I'm interviewing job candidates all morning"?
   (A) She is surprised by the number of applications.
   (B) She is unable to attend a presentation.

W: I'm really looking forward to _____ from the financial firm in Japan.
M: Same here. I just _____, and they'll be arriving at 9 a.m. tomorrow. They'll be coming straight here for our CEO's presentation at 10.
W: Oh, the _____? I'm interviewing job candidates all morning.
M: Don't worry, they'll be with us all day. Can you join us for the factory tour in the afternoon?
W: Yeah, that shouldn't be a problem. I'll be free right after lunch.

DAY 13 실전문제

1. What does the man thank the woman for?
   (A) Creating a presentation for a manager
   (B) Completing an assigned task quickly
   (C) Accepting a job transfer
   (D) Recommending him for a promotion

2. What kind of business do the speakers work for?
   (A) A courier service
   (B) An advertising agency
   (C) A supermarket
   (D) An insurance company

3. What is scheduled for Friday?
   (A) An inspection
   (B) A training session
   (C) A celebration
   (D) A board meeting

4. What kind of event is being held?
   (A) A grand opening
   (B) A business seminar
   (C) An awards ceremony
   (D) A career fair

5. What does the man's company sell?
   (A) Billing software
   (B) Office furniture
   (C) Cleaning products
   (D) Security systems

6. How will the man contact the woman?
   (A) By mail
   (B) By fax
   (C) By e-mail
   (D) By telephone

7. What type of product is being discussed?
   (A) Laptop computers
   (B) Mobile phones
   (C) Hybrid vehicles
   (D) Printing equipment

8. What is the man disappointed about?
   (A) A software problem
   (B) A customer complaint
   (C) A budget issue
   (D) A performance rating

9. What does the woman agree to do?
   (A) Review a policy
   (B) Hire more employees
   (C) Conduct some tests
   (D) Increase advertising

10. Where do the speakers work?
    (A) At a post office
    (B) At a hair salon
    (C) At a bookstore
    (D) At an electronics shop

11. Why does the man want to hire another employee?
    (A) To answer the phone
    (B) To upgrade a Web site
    (C) To clean the facility
    (D) To process customer bills

12. What information about Career Finder does the woman provide?
    (A) Its free advice
    (B) Its friendly staff
    (C) Its low fees
    (D) Its fast responses

13. Why did the men take a trip to Rochester?
    (A) To sign a contract
    (B) To promote a product
    (C) To inspect a plant
    (D) To meet a colleague

14. What problem does Paul mention?
    (A) He had difficulty finding a venue.
    (B) He was unable to negotiate some terms.
    (C) Some samples did not arrive in time.
    (D) Attendance at an event was low.

15. According to the woman, what will be added to a flyer?
    (A) A new logo
    (B) Some photographs
    (C) A discount coupon
    (D) Contact information

16. What kind of product are the speakers discussing?
    (A) A portable computer
    (B) A recording device
    (C) A piece of luggage
    (D) An article of clothing

17. What feature of the product is the man impressed with?
    (A) The durable exterior
    (B) The variety of colors
    (C) The eco-friendly materials
    (D) The lightweight design

18. Why does the man say, "I have tickets to a symphony concert"?
    (A) To decline an invitation
    (B) To extend an invitation
    (C) To show appreciation
    (D) To ask for an extension

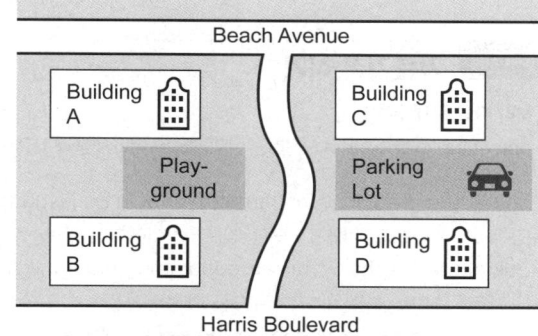

19. What are the speakers mainly discussing?
    (A) A building design
    (B) A job interview
    (C) A sales presentation
    (D) A safety inspection

20. Look at the graphic. Which building should the woman visit?
    (A) Building A
    (B) Building B
    (C) Building C
    (D) Building D

21. What does the man mention about visitors?
    (A) They can park near the main entrance.
    (B) They must sign a form upon arrival.
    (C) They should be accompanied by an employee.
    (D) They must wear a visitor badge.

LC DAY 14 시각 자료 연계 유형

01 2열 도표/3열 이상 도표 매회 2문항 정도 출제

BASIC 기본기 익히기

[시각 자료 문제 유형]
Look at the graphic으로 시작하는 문제는 모두 대화 내용과 시각 자료를 연계하여 풀어야 하는 문제이다.

Look at the graphic. What amount should be refunded from the order form?
시각 자료를 보시오. 주문서에서 어느 금액이 환불되어야 하는가?
Look at the graphic. Which product code does the man choose?
시각 자료를 보시오. 남자는 어느 제품 코드를 선택하는가?
Look at the graphic. When do the speakers want to start their tour?
시각 자료를 보시오. 화자들은 언제 투어를 시작하고 싶어 하는가?

PATTERN 기출 유형 맛보기   ♪ D14_01

👀 눈으로 보기

Dynasty Hotel

Floor 1	Lobby
Floor 2	Restaurant
Floor 3	**Business Center**
Floor 4	Meeting Rooms
Floor 5	Guest Rooms

Q. Look at the graphic. **Which floor** will the **man go to next**?
(A) Floor 2   **(B) Floor 3**   (C) Floor 4   (D) Floor 5

> ◀ 대화를 듣기 전에 질문/선택지/시각 자료를 빠르게 훑는다.
> → 질문의 형태를 통해 '시각 자료'를 이용하는 문제임을 알 수 있으며, 남자가 곧이어 갈 장소를 묻는 문제임을 확인한다.

👂 귀로 듣기

W: Hello, Mr. Murphy. I hope you're enjoying your stay here. Do you have any questions about the facilities at the Dynasty Hotel?
M: Actually, yes, I do. I'm attending the Weston Marketing Seminar here, and I wonder if you can tell me where the meeting rooms are.
W: You can take a look at this brochure to see where everything is located.
M: Thanks a lot. In addition, I wonder if you have some place where I can hire a translator. I need to meet with a client from Russia while I'm in town.
W: **You should visit the business center.** Someone there can help you out.
M: Great. **I'll go there right now.**

> ◀ 대화를 듣는다.
> → 단서는 호텔의 세부 장소가 될 것이므로 대화에서 '남자가 곧이어 갈 호텔의 세부 장소'에 관한 내용에 집중해서 듣는다.

> ◀ 정답에 체크한다.
> → 도표를 통해 대화에서 단서로 제시된 장소(비즈니스 센터)에 해당되는 선택지에 표시한다.

🔖 빠른 700⁺점 달성 TIP

시각 자료가 도표일 경우, 표에 나타난 항목 중에서 선택지로 제시된 것이 아닌 항목이 대화에 단서로 언급된다. 따라서 도표와 선택지를 미리 비교해 대화에서 들어야 할 단서 항목의 종류가 무엇인지 확인한다.

PRACTICE | 기출 연습하기 문제를 푼 후, 대화를 다시 두 번 들으며 빈칸을 채워보세요.

Project Schedule	
Stage 1	Remove grass
Stage 2	Dig drainage hole
Stage 3	Add sand
Stage 4	Arrange bricks

W: Harold, how are things coming along on the project at Ms. Wilson's property? Will all of _____ be completed by the end of the week?
M: Yes, _____ as planned. _____ _____ tomorrow after it is delivered in the morning.
W: Great! Please be sure to take photos of the final result so we can put them on our Web site.

1. What kind of business do the speakers work for?
   (A) A hardware store
   (B) A landscaping company

2. Look at the graphic. Which stage of the project will start tomorrow?
   (A) Stage 1
   (B) Stage 2
   (C) Stage 3
   (D) Stage 4

Product Code	Built-In Projector	Fingerprint Unlock	Storage Capacity
G-58		✓	Low
R-11	✓		Medium
K-90		✓	High
T-63	✓		High

M: Hello, I'm interested in buying a tablet computer. _____ _____ this morning about the various options available.
W: Great! We have several models to choose from. What did you have in mind?
M: I need a tablet with a _____ _____.
And, since I'll be using it for work from time to time, it should have a _____. Do you have anything in stock that has both of these features?

3. What did the man do in the morning?
   (A) Downloaded a coupon
   (B) Read some product reviews

4. Look at the graphic. Which product would be best for the man?
   (A) G-58
   (B) R-11
   (C) K-90
   (D) T-63

02 약도/그래프 및 기타 _{매회 1문항 정도 출제}

BASIC 기본기 익히기

[시각 자료 문제 유형]
Look at the graphic으로 시작하는 문제는 모두 대화 내용과 시각 자료를 연계하여 풀어야 하는 문제이다.

Look at the graphic. Which building is scheduled to be closed? 시각 자료를 보시오. 어느 건물이 폐쇄될 예정인가?
Look at the graphic. Which route will visitors take this weekend?
시각 자료를 보시오. 방문객들은 이번 주말에 어느 경로를 이용할 것인가?
Look at the graphic. Where is the event venue located? 시각 자료를 보시오. 행사 개최 장소는 어디에 위치해 있는가?

PATTERN 기출 유형 맛보기

🎵 D14_02

👀 눈으로 보기

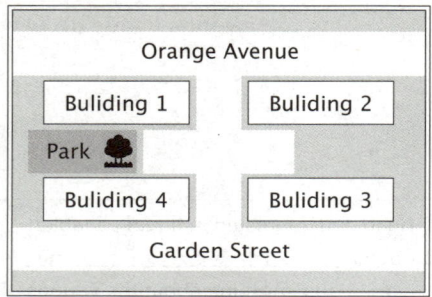

Q. Look at the graphic. **Which building** is **Hampton Manufacturing located** in?
(A) Building 1   (B) Building 2   (C) Building 3   **(D) Building 4**

> ✎ 대화를 듣기 전에 질문/선택지/시각 자료를 빠르게 훑는다.
> → 질문의 형태를 통해 '시각 자료'를 이용하는 문제임을 알 수 있으며, 회사 건물의 위치를 묻는 문제임을 확인한다.
> → 근처 사물이나 장소와의 위치 관계를 통해 단서가 제시되므로, 위치 파악의 기준이 될 수 있는 장소(park)나 거리 이름(Orange Avenue, Garden Street) 등을 빠르게 확인한다.

👂 귀로 듣기

W: Good morning, Mr. Carter. This is Susan Briggs from **Hampton Manufacturing**. We'd like you to come in for a job interview. How does this Friday at 3 P.M. sound?
M: That's perfect as I'm available then. Where should I go?
W: We recently moved to a new location in the city's business complex. **You can find us on Garden Street right next to the park.**
M: I'm sure I'll have no problem finding it. I'll be driving, so where should I park my car?
W: There's a lot in the center of the complex. Simply tell the parking attendant you're coming to visit us, and he'll give you a guest pass.

> ✎ 대화를 듣는다.
> → '회사의 위치'에 집중해 듣는다. 2개 이상의 단서가 제시될 수 있으므로 시각 자료를 보며 정답을 좁혀 나간다. 회사가 위치한 거리(Garden Street)를 통해 Building 3과 4로 좁혀지며, 근처 장소와의 관계(next to the park)를 통해 Building 4가 회사의 위치임을 알 수 있다.

> ✎ 정답에 체크한다.

🏃 빠른 700⁺점 달성 TIP

위치를 묻는 문제는 근처에 있는 사물이나 장소와의 위치 관계가 주요 단서가 된다. 따라서 ~ 옆(next to), ~ 뒤(behind), ~ 사이(between), 맞은 편(across from), ~ 근처(by), ~ 앞(in front of) 등의 위치 표현을 잘 알아두어야 한다. on+거리명(~ Road, ~ Avenue, ~ Lane) 표현을 함께 들어야 정답을 찾을 수 있는 문제도 출제되니 유의하자.

PRACTICE | 기출 연습하기 문제를 푼 후, 대화를 다시 두 번 들으며 빈칸을 채워보세요.

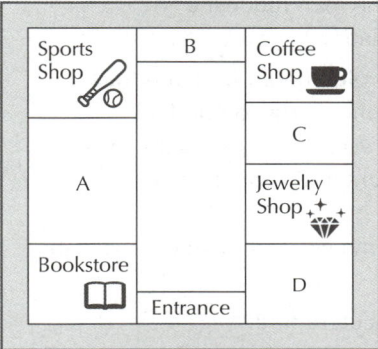

1. Why will the speakers relocate their business?
   (A) To have more space
   (B) To reduce expenses

2. Look at the graphic. Which unit does the woman suggest renting?
   (A) Unit A
   (B) Unit B
   (C) Unit C
   (D) Unit D

W: I'm glad we're relocating our health food store. We really _____ to accommodate the increase in demand. You got the details from the commercial realtor, right?
M: Yes, she suggested getting a unit in the Urban Shopping Center. You can _____ _____ on this floor plan. Unfortunately, the one right by the entrance is out of our budget.
W: Then _____ _____ the bookstore and the sports shop? Since a lot of athletes buy our products, it could be the perfect fit.

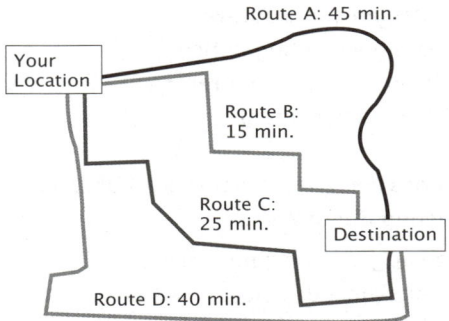

3. Why does the man thank the woman?
   (A) For giving him a ride
   (B) For inviting him to a conference

4. Look at the graphic. Which route does the man suggest taking?
   (A) Route A
   (B) Route B
   (C) Route C
   (D) Route D

M: _____ _____, Amanda. I was planning on driving to the conference on my own, but I've been having car trouble.
W: No problem. I'm happy to help. Actually, it wasn't very far out of my way. Now, I usually take the route which takes only 15 minutes to the conference center, but it's _____.
M: Well, we still have plenty of time. If we take this route suggested by my GPS app, we can _____ twenty-five minutes.
W: That's not so bad.

LC DAY 14 실전문제

1. What type of the business do the speakers work for?
   (A) A hardware store
   (B) An Internet service provider
   (C) A public library
   (D) A post office

2. What is the topic of the conversation?
   (A) An advertising campaign
   (B) A late delivery
   (C) A faulty device
   (D) A billing error

3. What does the man ask the woman to do?
   (A) Forward a message
   (B) Restart a computer
   (C) Calculate a fee
   (D) Complete a form

4. Where is the conversation taking place?
   (A) At a financial institution
   (B) At a moving company
   (C) At a department store
   (D) At a travel agency

5. What does the man make a complaint about?
   (A) Waiting in line
   (B) Changing a sign
   (C) Moving to a new room
   (D) Making daily calls

6. What does the woman agree to give the man after lunch?
   (A) A contract
   (B) A magazine article
   (C) A catalog
   (D) A user manual

7. Why does the man request a recommendation?
   (A) He has volunteered for a fundraiser.
   (B) He is trying to stay on budget.
   (C) He has recently moved to the area.
   (D) He will entertain some clients.

8. What does the woman mention about the restaurant?
   (A) It is difficult to find.
   (B) Its menu is limited.
   (C) It does not offer delivery.
   (D) Its prices are high.

9. What does the man plan to do now?
   (A) Make a guest list
   (B) Download a brochure
   (C) Send an invitation
   (D) Make a reservation

10. What does the woman need assistance with?
    (A) Installing some software
    (B) Posting a meeting notice
    (C) Moving some furniture
    (D) Saving a document

11. Why does Jerry say, "there's a lot of space in Meeting Room 2"?
    (A) To suggest changing a plan
    (B) To explain a decision
    (C) To show appreciation
    (D) To support his request

12. What will the woman most likely do next?
    (A) Order some equipment
    (B) Speak to a maintenance worker
    (C) Contact a customer
    (D) Print some promotional materials

Settings
- ☐ Contrast
- ☐ Tracking
- ☐ Display
- ☐ Sharpness

13. What is the woman having trouble with?
    (A) Setting up a television
    (B) Printing some handouts
    (C) Reading text on a screen
    (D) Contacting group members

14. Look at the graphic. Which category does the man suggest adjusting?
    (A) Contrast
    (B) Tracking
    (C) Display
    (D) Sharpness

15. Where will the woman meet the man soon?
    (A) At an orientation session
    (B) At a job interview
    (C) At an industry conference
    (D) At a committee meeting

History Museum Lectures

April 17	Pottery through the Ages
April 19	The Viking Era
April 24	Ancient Weapons
April 26	Copper Mining

16. How did the woman learn about the lectures?
    (A) By watching a TV commercial
    (B) By receiving a flyer in the mail
    (C) By hearing a radio ad
    (D) By reading a newsletter

17. Look at the graphic. Which date does the woman purchase a ticket for?
    (A) April 17
    (B) April 19
    (C) April 24
    (D) April 26

18. What does the man suggest doing?
    (A) Using public transportation
    (B) Parking on the street
    (C) Arriving early to get a seat
    (D) Purchasing a guidebook

LC DAY 15 전반적인 내용을 묻는 유형

01 주제/목적/담화 장소를 묻는 문제 매회 5-6문항 정도 출제

BASIC 기본기 익히기

[주제/목적/담화 장소를 묻는 문제 유형]
매월 반복 출제되는 질문 유형이므로, 유형 파악을 통해 문제를 읽는 시간을 줄이고 담화를 듣는 데 더 집중할 수 있다.

◆ 주제
- What is the (main) topic of the talk[meeting/announcement/workshop/broadcast]?
  담화[회의/공지/워크숍/방송]의 주제는 무엇인가?
- What is the talk[message/announcement/broadcast/report] (mainly/mostly) about?
  담화[메시지/공지/방송/보도]는 (주로) 무엇에 관한 것인가?
- What is the speaker calling[talking] about? 화자는 무엇에 관해 전화하는가[이야기하는가]?
- What (product/event) is being discussed? 무엇이[무슨 제품이/행사가] 이야기되고 있는가?

◆ 목적
- What is the purpose of the talk[message/call/event/meeting]? 담화[메시지/전화/행사/회의]의 목적은 무엇인가?
- Why is the event being held? 행사는 왜 개최되고 있는가?

◆ 담화의 장소
- Where most likely is the speaker? 화자는 어디에 있을 것 같은가?
- Where most likely are the listeners? 청자들은 어디에 있을 것 같은가?
- Where is the tour[announcement/talk/meeting] (most likely) taking place?
  투어[공지/담화/회의]가 어디에서 이뤄지고 있는가?

PATTERN 기출 유형 맛보기   ♪ D15_01

👀 눈으로 보기

Q. **Where** does the **talk take place**?
(A) At a government office
(B) At a factory
(C) At a car repair shop
(D) At an electronics store

▲ 담화를 듣기 전에 질문과 선택지를 빠르게 훑는다.
→ 질문의 핵심 어구를 통해 '담화 장소' 문제임을 파악한다.

👂 귀로 듣기

I'd like to start today's meeting by discussing an issue several people have brought up. **Here at the MTR Factory**, safety is our utmost concern. However, it appears as though some of you believe the equipment we're using is faulty and in need of replacing. Let me tell you that we'll be inspecting every piece of equipment in this facility. If we detect something wrong, we'll either repair it or replace it.

▲ 담화를 듣는다.
→ 담화의 주제/목적/장소는 주로 초반부에 제시되므로 첫 문장부터 집중해서 듣는다. 담화 장소가 파악되는 순간 바로 선택지를 본다.

▲ 정답에 체크한다.
→ 파악된 장소(공장)와 의미가 일치하는 선택지에 표시한다.

🏃 빠른 700⁺점 달성 TIP

'주제/목적/담화 장소/근무지/직업'을 묻는 문제가 담화의 1, 2번 문제로 나란히 출제되는 경우, 담화의 초반부에 단서가 겹쳐서 제시될 수도 있으므로 두 문제의 키워드를 모두 염두에 두고 담화를 듣자.

PRACTICE | 기출 연습하기 문제를 푼 후, 담화를 다시 두 번 들으며 빈칸을 채워보세요.

1. What event is the speaker discussing?
   (A) A race
   (B) A picnic

2. What does the speaker's company most likely sell?
   (A) Clothing
   (B) Beverages

W: I'll keep this meeting brief because I know you are all busy. I just want to _____ regarding the Annual Summer Marathon on May 25. As you know, we will have a booth to _____ to participants and spectators. We'll be preparing a variety of our company's _____ for sale. It'll be a great opportunity to introduce people to our products, especially the new flavors. We're also thinking about giving out some free samples for people to try.

3. Where is the announcement most likely taking place?
   (A) On an airplane
   (B) In a train station

4. What is causing a problem?
   (A) Inclement weather
   (B) An equipment failure

M: May I have your attention, please? _____ _____ that is passing through the area, delays are _____ from Warrenburg. We apologize for any inconvenience caused. Passenger safety is our top priority, so we must adjust our speeds _____. You can find up-to-the-minute departure and arrival times on the electronic display boards positioned throughout the station. We appreciate your understanding. Thank you for your patronage.

5. What is the purpose of the event?
   (A) To celebrate a manager's career
   (B) To introduce a new employee

6. What will most likely happen next?
   (A) An award will be presented.
   (B) A talk will be given.

W: Thank you all for coming to this farewell party for our sales manager, Henry Branum. We want to _____ _____ to our company, and we wish him all the best. As you all know, Mr. Branum successfully led our company as we joined the European market. This has _____ _____ as well as the creation of new jobs. Now, we'd like to have Mr. Branum come forward and _____ _____ about his time here at Lakewood Inc. and his future plans.

02 직업/근무지를 묻는 문제 _{매회 3문항 정도 출제}

BASIC 기본기 익히기

[직업/근무지를 묻는 문제 유형]
매월 반복 출제되는 질문 유형이므로, 유형 파악을 통해 문제를 읽는 시간을 줄이고 담화를 듣는 데 더 집중할 수 있다.

◆ **직업**
- Who is Anne Madison? Anne Madison은 누구인가?
- Who is the speaker? 화자는 누구인가?
- Who most likely are the listeners? 청자는 누구일 것 같은가?

◆ **근무지**
- Where does[do] the speaker[listeners] (most likely) work? 화자[청자들]는 어디에서 근무하는가?
- What industry does the speaker work in[for]? 화자는 무슨 업계에서 근무하는가?
- What business does the speaker work in[for]? 화자는 무슨 업체에서 근무하는가?
- Which department does the speaker work in[for]? 화자는 어느 부서에서 근무하는가?
- What kind[type] of business[store] is the speaker calling? 화자는 무슨 종류의 업체[매장]에 전화하는가?

PATTERN 기출 유형 맛보기

♪ D15_02

👀 눈으로 보기

Q. **Where** do the **listeners** most likely **work**?
(A) At a shoe store
(B) At a television station
(C) At an advertising agency
(D) At a newspaper

👂 귀로 듣기

Good morning, everyone. I'd like to talk about **the Hamilton Shoes account**. Five weeks ago, **we launched an ad campaign for** Hamilton Shoes which featured a couple of professional basketball players as spokesmen. It's my great pleasure to inform you that the company has seen sales of its latest line of sneakers increase by more than thirty percent since the ads came out. They're extremely pleased with the results, so they want us to produce more ads for them.

↖ 담화를 듣기 전에 질문과 선택지를 빠르게 훑는다.
→ 질문의 핵심 어구를 통해 '청자의 근무지'를 묻는 문제임을 파악한다.

↖ 담화를 듣는다.
→ 화자나 청자, 또는 제3자의 근무지나 직업 중에서 2개 이상이 담화에 제시되는 경우가 많으므로 질문이 누구의 직업/근무지를 묻는지를 반드시 구별해 들어야 한다.

↖ 정답에 체크한다.
→ 담화에서 파악된 근무지(우리가 광고 캠페인을 시작했다)와 의미가 일치하는 선택지에 표시한다.

🚀 빠른 700⁺점 달성 TIP

'Who is 사람 이름?' 질문 유형은 담화에 나오는 인물 간의 관계를 묻는 것이 아니라 특정인의 직업을 묻는 유형이 대부분이다. 이처럼 질문만으로 내용 파악이 어려울 때는 보기를 훑어보면 질문의 의도를 정확히 파악할 수 있다.

PRACTICE | 기출 연습하기 문제를 푼 후, 담화를 다시 두 번 들으며 빈칸을 채워보세요.

1. Who is Carrie Harris?
   (A) A business owner
   (B) A university professor

2. What will Carrie Harris be talking about?
   (A) Cleaning methods
   (B) Recycling tips

W: In our local calendar of events, residents are invited to a free lecture by _____
Carrie Harris of Hensley University. _____ at Clarence Hall at 3 P.M. on Saturday. Professor Harris will _____ you can clean your home without using harsh chemicals. A question-and-answer session will be held at the end of the lecture.

3. What kind of business does the speaker work for?
   (A) A magazine publisher
   (B) A software developer

4. What is the speaker announcing?
   (A) A new employee
   (B) An award nomination

M: It is my pleasure to announce that we have _____ _____ for the Magazine Innovation Award, and we will enter the finals next week. We have been considered for this award many times, but we have never made it this far. No matter what happens, I would like to thank you all for your contributions to _____ _____ it can be. In particular, Ms. Mercier on the editorial team has _____ _____ since she joined us one year ago.

5. Who most likely is the speaker?
   (A) An apartment manager
   (B) A laboratory technician

6. What is the speaker calling about?
   (A) Some broken lights
   (B) A safety alarm

M: Hi, Ms. Blakely. This is Tony _____ _____ of Hartland Apartments. I'm calling regarding your message saying that some of the lights in _____.
I agree with you that this is a safety issue for tenants. Therefore, I'll send one of our technicians to _____ _____. Thank you for bringing this matter to my attention. If you notice anything else, please don't hesitate to call.

LC DAY 15 실전문제

지문 유형별로 학습한 내용들을 적용하면서 다음 실전문제를 풀어 보세요.

1. Where most likely are the listeners?
   (A) At a bus station
   (B) At a restaurant
   (C) At a hardware store
   (D) At a medical facility

2. What is the speaker giving instructions about?
   (A) A software program
   (B) A vacation policy
   (C) Customer feedback forms
   (D) Payment procedures

3. What does the speaker suggest when he says, "Stephen is working a long shift today"?
   (A) The hours of operation have recently changed.
   (B) The business is expected to be busy.
   (C) Stephen has a lot of tasks to finish.
   (D) Stephen knows how to set up accounts.

4. Which department does the speaker most likely work in?
   (A) Research and development
   (B) Marketing
   (C) Human resources
   (D) Security

5. What does the speaker imply when she says, "your details were updated this morning"?
   (A) Some old documents should be discarded.
   (B) A system may be offline for a while.
   (C) Someone discovered Mr. Lopez's error quickly.
   (D) Mr. Lopez does not need to make a visit.

6. According to the speaker, what should the listener do this week?
   (A) Order business cards
   (B) Attend a staff meeting
   (C) Ask for authorization
   (D) Move to a new office

7. What is the talk mainly about?
   (A) An accounting program
   (B) A security alarm
   (C) A reservation system
   (D) A label printer

8. What benefit of the product does the speaker mention?
   (A) Its functions can be learned quickly.
   (B) Its warranty is valid for a long period of time.
   (C) It can share information between branches.
   (D) It sends updates to the manager's e-mail account.

9. According to the speaker, what has the company received?
   (A) A backup battery
   (B) A tablet computer
   (C) A partial refund
   (D) A user manual

10. What is the talk mainly about?
    (A) A job candidate
    (B) A team leader
    (C) A potential client
    (D) An award winner

11. According to the speaker, what did Rodney Claire recently do?
    (A) He started teaching some classes.
    (B) He created a software program.
    (C) He graduated from university.
    (D) He relocated to a different city.

12. What does the speaker plan to do later today?
    (A) Update a Web site
    (B) Place an order
    (C) Attend an industry conference
    (D) Send some paperwork

13. What is being advertised?
    (A) A fitness center
    (B) A language institute
    (C) An art school
    (D) A concert hall

14. According to the speaker, what can listeners do from October 1?
    (A) View some images
    (B) Meet staff members in person
    (C) Complete the registration online
    (D) Sign up for a contest

15. Why are listeners invited to visit a Web site?
    (A) To inquire about availability
    (B) To schedule a tour
    (C) To access a brochure
    (D) To get driving directions

---

16. Where does the speaker most likely work?
    (A) At a bank
    (B) At a hotel
    (C) At a flower shop
    (D) At a radio station

17. What does the speaker say is famous about the Cypress Hotel?
    (A) Its grand entrance
    (B) Its outdoor space
    (C) Its decorated rooms
    (D) Its customer service

18. Why most likely does the speaker say, "Yes, you heard that correctly... five thousand dollars"?
    (A) To apologize for an earlier error
    (B) To confirm the cost of a renovation
    (C) To show that a prize is impressive
    (D) To show support for an investment

Tower A Directory

Prudential Inc ············· Floors 2–6
Florence Co ················ Floors 7–10
Extron Industries ········ Floors 11–13
Almont Enterprises ····· Floors 14–16

19. What is the purpose of the telephone message?
    (A) To introduce a service
    (B) To confirm a meeting time
    (C) To renew a contract
    (D) To apply for a job

20. According to the speaker, why should the listener visit reception?
    (A) To pick up an ID badge
    (B) To sign a visitor form
    (C) To get a parking pass
    (D) To request a site map

21. Look at the graphic. On which floor will the speaker meet the listener?
    (A) Floor 2
    (B) Floor 7
    (C) Floor 10
    (D) Floor 14

LC DAY 16 세부적인 내용을 묻는 유형 (1)

01 요청/제안 사항 문제 [매회 4문항 정도 출제]

BASIC 기본기 익히기

[요청/제안 사항을 묻는 문제 유형]
매월 반복 출제되는 질문 유형이므로, 유형 파악을 통해 문제를 읽는 시간을 줄이고 담화를 듣는 데 더 집중할 수 있다.

◆ 요청
- What does the speaker ask[want/remind] the listener to do?
  화자는 청자에게 무엇을 하도록 요청하는가[원하는가/상기시키는가]?
- What are listeners asked[encouraged] to do? 청자들은 무엇을 하도록 요청[권고] 받는가?

◆ 제안
- What does the speaker suggest the listener do? 화자는 청자에게 무엇을 하도록 제안하는가?
- What does the speaker recommend (that the listener do)? 화자는 무엇을[청자에게 무엇을 하도록] 권하는가?
- What recommendation does the speaker make? 화자는 무슨 제안을 하는가?

PATTERN 기출 유형 맛보기 ♪D16_01

👀 눈으로 보기

Q. **What** does the **speaker suggest** that listeners do?
(A) Leave their homes early
(B) Avoid the downtown area
(C) Make a phone call
(D) Take public transportation

👂 귀로 듣기

Good morning, everyone. It's time for the WTRE Radio traffic report. If you're heading downtown, expect delays of up to one hour in some places. The reason is that the storm last night knocked down lots of trees and electric poles. Work crews are busy trying to clean up everything, but it's going to take a while. If you haven't left home yet, **I encourage you to take the subway or a commuter train** to avoid the city streets.

▸ 담화를 듣기 전에 질문과 선택지를 빠르게 훑는다.
→ 질문의 핵심 어구를 통해 '요청 내용'을 묻는 문제임을 파악한다.

▸ 담화를 듣는다.
→ 요청/제안 내용은 주로 3번째 문제로 출제되지만, 종종 2번째 문제로도 출제된다. 따라서 2번째 문제일 경우에는 담화 중반부에, 3번째 문제일 경우에는 후반부에 집중해서 듣는다.

▸ 정답에 체크한다.
→ 파악된 제안 사항(지하철이나 통근열차 이용)과 의미가 일치하는 선택지에 표시한다.

📌 **빠른 700⁺점 달성 TIP**

요청/제안을 나타내는 단서 표현은 Could you ~ / If you can ~ / Please ~ / I'd like us to ~ / I'll need you to ~ / Please make sure[be sure] to ~ / Can you please~ / Why don't you~ / Remember ~ / I encourage you to ~ / What you need to do ~ / I recommend[suggest] ~ / be advised to ~ 등이 있으며, 반복 출제되는 표현들이므로 반드시 알아두자.

PRACTICE | 기출 연습하기 문제를 푼 후, 담화를 다시 두 번 들으며 빈칸을 채워보세요.

1. What is the talk mainly about?
   (A) Planning a parade
   (B) Cleaning up a park

2. What are the listeners asked to do?
   (A) Find potential employees
   (B) Contact local businesses

> W: Thank you all for being here for this committee meeting. As you all know, we've been _____ _____ a parade to celebrate the town's founding day. However, we need to find a way to cover the expenses of this event, and we're currently short on funds. Therefore, we'll try to _____ _____. I've made a list of potential donors. I'd like each of you to _____ on your section of the list and find out whether they'd like to contribute to this event.

3. What have the company's managers decided to do?
   (A) Hire more staff
   (B) Relocate a business

4. What does the speaker ask the listeners to do?
   (A) Create a work schedule
   (B) Report their duties

> M: Next on today's meeting agenda, I'd like to _____ _____. We understand that you have all been under a lot of pressure due to the rapid growth of our business. It's wonderful that our brand is becoming more popular, but it also creates more work. The management team has _____ more full-time employees. To maximize our workforce, we'd like to assign them to the tasks that are the most understaffed. So, if you can _____ _____ of your duties today, please do so.

5. What product is being reviewed?
   (A) A fitness tracker
   (B) An exercise bike

6. What does the speaker recommend that the listeners do?
   (A) Get a warranty for a product
   (B) Make a purchase this month

> W: Hi, I'm Jenifer, and _____ the new fitness tracker recently released by Veasley Electronics. I've been using this product for three weeks, and I'm completely satisfied with it. At first, I was worried that it would overheat during my workouts, but it is heat- and sweat-resistant. Also, it was easy to _____ _____ and view my progress. If you're interested, I _____ _____ the end of the month. The company is having a sale right now, and you can get it for the lowest price of the season.

02 기타 세부 사항 문제 _{매회 12-13문항 정도 출제}

BASIC 기본기 익히기

[기타 세부 사항을 묻는 문제 유형]
매월 반복 출제되는 질문 유형이므로, 유형 파악을 통해 문제를 읽는 시간을 줄이고 담화를 듣는 데 더 집중할 수 있다.

◆ 문제점/언급/이유
- What problem does the speaker mention? 화자는 무슨 문제점을 언급하는가?
- What does the speaker say[emphasize] about the company? 화자는 회사에 관해 무엇을 말하는가[강조하는가]?
- What does the speaker thank the listeners for? 화자는 청자들에게 무엇에 대해 감사하는가?

◆ 다음에 할 일/특정 시점의 일(미래/과거)
- What most likely will the speaker[listeners] do next? 화자는[청자들은] 곧이어 무엇을 할 것 같은가?
- What does the speaker say she will do tomorrow? 화자는 내일 무엇을 할 것이라고 말하는가?
- What does the speaker say he has done? 화자는 무엇을 했다고 말하는가?
- According to the speaker, what will Emily Watson do? 화자의 말에 따르면, Emily Watson 씨는 무엇을 할 것인가?

◆ 기타
- What does the speaker like about the product? 화자는 제품에 관해 무엇을 마음에 들어 하는가?
- What does the speaker say is available on a Web site? 화자는 웹 사이트에서 무엇이 이용 가능하다고 말하는가?
- What should the listeners avoid doing? 청자들은 무엇을 하는 것을 피해야 하는가?

PATTERN 기출 유형 맛보기

♪ D16_02

눈으로 보기
Q. **Why** does the **speaker thank** the listeners?
(A) They created a new project.
(B) They landed a new client.
(C) They worked extra hours.
(D) They successfully moved to a new building.

귀로 듣기
Before we head to lunch, **I want to thank everyone for volunteering to come in on weekends** to make sure we finished the Anderson project on time. Because you all put in extra effort, we were able to send the blueprints for the building to Mr. Anderson yesterday. He called me this morning and stated that he's extremely pleased with our performance.

▸ 담화를 듣기 전에 질문과 선택지를 빠르게 훑는다.
→ 질문의 핵심 어구를 통해 '감사의 이유'를 묻는 문제임을 파악한다.

▸ 담화를 듣는다.
→ 감사의 이유를 묻는 질문이 있을 경우, 감사 표현이 제시되는 부분에서 그 이유가 함께 언급된다는 것을 의미한다. 따라서 감사 표현이 제시되는 부분을 놓치지 말고 들어야 한다.

▸ 정답에 체크한다.
→ 파악된 감사 이유(주말에 일하러 나온 것)와 의미가 일치하는 선택지에 표시한다.

빠른 700⁺점 달성 TIP

유형별 출제 빈도의 차이는 있으나 Part 3와 Part 4에 출제되는 질문 유형 및 단서의 위치는 큰 차이가 없다. 문제점 문제는 주로 담화의 초/중반에, 다음에 할 일 문제는 주로 후반부에 단서가 제시된다. 나머지 세부 사항 문제는 1-2-3번 문제로 고루 출제되므로 문제 순서에 따라 담화의 초/중/후반부에 집중해서 듣는다.

PRACTICE | 기출 연습하기 문제를 푼 후, 담화를 다시 두 번 들으며 빈칸을 채워보세요.

1. What will be changing at the business?
   (A) How customers will be billed
   (B) How deliveries will be monitored

2. What will Ms. Reynolds be doing?
   (A) Training staff members
   (B) Installing new equipment

M: To begin, I'd like to address your concerns about _____ for customers. In the past, customers were asked to pay their bills after their equipment was installed. However, to help us with our cash flow, we will now charge a fifteen percent deposit _____. You'll need to enter this charge into the system differently, so you must all learn how to do this. Vivian Reynolds, who will be here next week, will _____ for staff members.

3. What does the speaker thank the listeners for?
   (A) Sharing their opinions
   (B) Working additional hours

4. What will the listeners have to do in April?
   (A) Work from home
   (B) Attend an industry conference

W: Attention, all employees. First of all, I'd like to _____ your honest opinions about the working environment at the session last month. It was really helpful for us. One of the biggest complaints was _____. Therefore, we will have some major renovations done to our building. We've hired the industry's top designer! The only downside is that the building must be completely empty for the crew to work, so you must _____ in April. We'll have more details as the project gets closer.

5. How does the product differ from other products on the market?
   (A) It has a high safety rating.
   (B) It has a lot of different settings.

6. What can listeners do to get an accessory for free?
   (A) Complete a questionnaire
   (B) Sign up for a mailing list

M: Thanks for stopping by the Thurber Electronics trade show booth. My name is Cheolsu, and I'd like to tell you about my company's newest blender, the T-900. _____ is not the number of settings. We have about the same options as other products in this category. However, _____ is safety—it has the best rating in the industry. The T-900 also can be used with various accessories. If you _____, you can get one of these accessories for free.

LC DAY 16 실전문제

1. What kind of product is the speaker discussing?
   (A) A laser printer
   (B) A mobile phone
   (C) A digital recorder
   (D) A portable radio

2. What benefit of the product does the speaker mention?
   (A) It is small enough to carry around easily.
   (B) It operates with a long-lasting battery.
   (C) It helps users keep important information.
   (D) It comes in a variety of colors.

3. What will the speaker most likely do next?
   (A) Show a video
   (B) Respond to inquiries
   (C) Pass out samples
   (D) Give a demonstration

4. What is the broadcast mainly about?
   (A) Contract negotiation
   (B) Budget management
   (C) Employee motivation
   (D) Hiring practices

5. What does the speaker say that Harold Pearson has recently done?
   (A) Started teaching classes
   (B) Agreed to a merger
   (C) Published a new book
   (D) Received an award

6. What are the listeners asked to do?
   (A) Sign up for a newsletter
   (B) Provide their opinions
   (C) Suggest a guest speaker
   (D) Attend a grand opening

7. Why does the speaker apologize to the listeners?
   (A) He sent out an outdated file.
   (B) He had to postpone a company event.
   (C) He gave short notice for a meeting.
   (D) He had to move a meeting location.

8. What has the business received complaints about?
   (A) The inventory shortages
   (B) The inaccurate prices
   (C) The return policy
   (D) The business hours

9. What is scheduled to take place tomorrow?
   (A) A celebrity will visit the business.
   (B) A staff will undergo some training.
   (C) A promotional event will begin.
   (D) A software program will be installed.

10. What kind of business does the speaker most likely work for?
    (A) A software development firm
    (B) A job recruitment company
    (C) An architecture firm
    (D) A fashion company

11. What does the speaker suggest the listeners do?
    (A) Reassign tasks
    (B) Work overtime
    (C) Give clear instructions
    (D) Review policies

12. What will most likely happen next?
    (A) A new employee will be introduced.
    (B) A handout will be distributed.
    (C) The listeners will form discussion groups.
    (D) The speaker will share his experience.

13. Why is the speaker giving the talk?
    (A) To train some new employees
    (B) To announce a schedule change
    (C) To show appreciation for staff members
    (D) To welcome new investors

14. What does the speaker suggest doing?
    (A) Reserving a seat
    (B) Taking a short break
    (C) Retaining a document
    (D) Calling a business partner

15. What will the speaker most likely do next?
    (A) Pass out a sign-up sheet
    (B) Introduce some employees
    (C) Set up a meeting room
    (D) Take the listeners on a tour

16. Where most likely does the speaker work?
    (A) At a shipping company
    (B) At a hotel
    (C) At an airline
    (D) At a café

17. What does the speaker imply when he says, "we're focused on the customer experience"?
    (A) He would like the listener to complete a questionnaire.
    (B) He is busy training some new employees.
    (C) He is working hard to find a solution.
    (D) He is confident that a competitor will lose clients.

18. What is the listener asked to do?
    (A) Select a food option
    (B) Issue a payment
    (C) View a Web site
    (D) Send e-mail confirmation

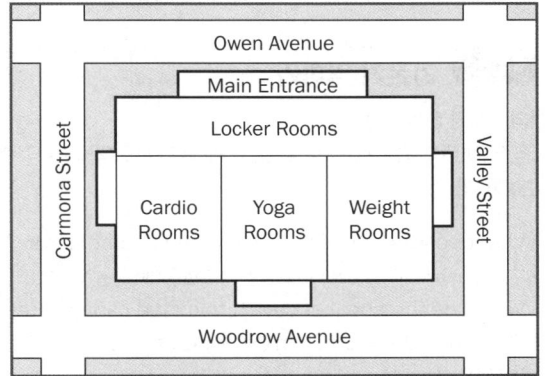

19. What is the purpose of the meeting?
    (A) To arrange some employee reviews
    (B) To make plans for a membership drive
    (C) To train new fitness instructors
    (D) To prepare for an athletic competition

20. Look at the graphic. Which entrance should the listeners use on June 12?
    (A) The main entrance
    (B) The Carmona Street entrance
    (C) The Woodrow Avenue entrance
    (D) The Valley Street entrance

21. What does the speaker say she wants employees to do at the end of the event?
    (A) Take down some decorations
    (B) Serve some refreshments
    (C) Assist with completing paperwork
    (D) Distribute some prizes

LC | DAY 17　세부적인 내용을 묻는 유형 (2)

01 의도 파악 문제　매회 3문항 정도 출제

BASIC 기본기 익히기

[의도 파악 문제 유형]
" ~ "의 형태로 질문에 담화 속의 문장이 제시되면 모두 의도 파악 문제이므로, 질문에서 " ~ " 외의 부분은 해석할 필요 없이 해당 문장의 내용만 이해하면 된다.

What does the speaker mean when she[he] says, "I'm not quite sure"?
화자가 'I'm not quite sure"라고 말할 때 무엇을 의미하는가?
Why does the speaker say, "I think we can go later"? 화자는 왜 "I think we can go later"라고 말하는가?
What does the woman imply when she says, "Mr. Henderson is out of town for an urgent issue"?
여자가 "Mr. Henderson is out of town for an urgent issue"라고 말할 때 무엇을 암시하는가?

PATTERN 기출 유형 맛보기　♪ D17_01

👀 눈으로 보기

Q. What does the speaker imply when he says, **"This will be a big show"**?
(A) Few tickets have been sold.
(B) A bigger venue must be found.
(C) A performance will be on television.
(D) A group is very popular.

👂 귀로 듣기

Hello, listeners, and thanks for tuning in. Before I begin, let me remind everybody that the city's summer festival is starting this weekend. On the first day, **there's going to be a concert by noted band Derrick and the Waves, so this will be a big show**. The event will be held at Duncan Park on Friday at six thirty, but you should probably get there early to guarantee a good seat. You're allowed to bring your own food and beverages with you.

▲ 담화를 듣기 전에 질문과 선택지를 빠르게 훑는다.
→ 질문의 형태를 통해 '의도 파악' 문제임을 알 수 있으며, " ~ " 부분의 문장을 미리 읽고 의미를 파악한다.

▲ 담화를 듣는다.
→ 의도 파악 문장에 앞서 단서가 제시되는 경우가 대부분이므로 의도 파악 문장이 들릴 때까지 기다려서는 안 된다. 또한 의도 파악 문장에 대명사가 자주 포함되기 때문에 대명사가 지칭하는 대상을 이해하기 위해서는 담화의 흐름을 파악하며 들어야 한다.

▲ 정답에 체크한다.
→ 파악된 의도(유명한 밴드)와 의미가 일치하는 선택지에 표시한다.

🚀 빠른 700⁺점 달성 TIP

고난도인 의도 파악 문제를 풀기 위해 고민하느라 바로 뒤에 나오는 쉬운 문제를 놓치기 십상이므로, 정답을 찾을 수 없다면 고민하지 말고 바로 다음 문제로 넘어가야 한다.

PRACTICE | 기출 연습하기 문제를 푼 후, 담화를 다시 두 번 들으며 빈칸을 채워보세요.

1. What does the speaker say about the utilities?
   (A) They are one month overdue.
   (B) They are not included in the rent.

2. Why does the speaker say, "this is a very popular apartment"?
   (A) To request a quick decision
   (B) To explain why the rent is expensive

W: Hi, Mr. Anderson. This is Sandra from Meadow Realty. Thanks for taking the time to tour the apartment in the Geneva Building that has just come up for rent. You had asked about the _____ and water. Well, I checked with the landlord, and these are _____, so you'd have to pay for them separately. You should be aware that this is a very popular apartment, so I need to know as soon as possible _____.

3. What does the speaker imply when he says, "we're approaching the peak season"?
   (A) A job opening should be filled soon.
   (B) He does not have time to help the listener.

4. What will the speaker do next?
   (A) Contract a recruiter
   (B) Send an interview schedule

M: Hi, Christine. It's Jason. We still need to _____ _____ for the shop's weekend shifts. As you know, we're approaching the peak season. The recruiter sent over plenty of résumés. I've _____ _____ six people on Friday, and I'd like you to _____ _____ these meetings so that I can get a second opinion. I'll e-mail you the schedule now. Please let me know if you have any conflicts.

5. What is the broadcast mainly about?
   (A) Parking regulations
   (B) City elections

6. What does the speaker most likely mean when he says, "the new rules were passed quickly this time"?
   (A) The council members need to work faster.
   (B) The support for a change is surprising.

M: You're listening to the lunchtime update on Radio 99. On today's program, we'll be talking about the _____ regarding where vehicles can park. The city council has decided to begin _____ to park on the streets in the downtown district and to raise the rates for all lots owned by the city. The council held a meeting to gather public opinions. _____ a lot of concerns. However, the new rules were passed quickly this time. Now, let's welcome city council member Roberta Torres to discuss this further.

02 시각 자료 문제 　매회 2문항 정도 출제

BASIC 기본기 익히기

[시각 자료 문제 유형]
Look at the graphic으로 시작하는 문제는 모두 담화 내용과 시각 자료를 연계하여 풀어야 하는 문제이다.

Look at the graphic. Which quantity on the invoice should be changed?
시각 자료를 보시오. 거래 내역서의 어느 수량이 변경되어야 하는가?
Look at the graphic. Which building is the speaker's company in? 시각 자료를 보시오. 어느 건물에 화자의 회사가 있는가?
Look at the graphic. Why is the speaker unable to get a refund for his item?
시각 자료를 보시오. 화자는 왜 자신의 제품에 대해 환불을 받을 수 없는가?

PATTERN 기출 유형 맛보기　♪ D17_02

👀 눈으로 보기

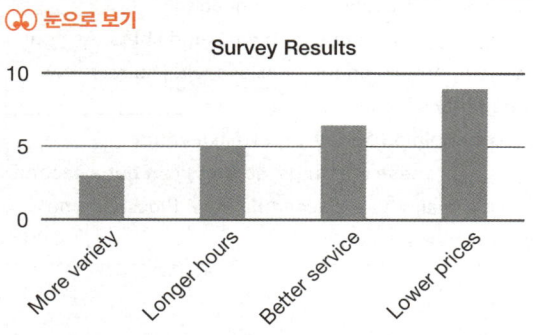

Q. **Look at the graphic. Which suggestion** will the company begin to **work on**?
(A) More variety
(B) Longer hours
(C) Better service
(D) Lower prices

🎧 귀로 듣기

The first thing we need to do now is go over the results of the customer satisfaction survey we conducted last month. It should come as no surprise that our customers want lower prices. That's to be expected due to the poor economy, but we can't do that. However, **we can work on the second most popular suggestion**, so we're going to make changes at the store immediately.

> ↖ 담화를 듣기 전에 질문/선택지/시각 자료를 빠르게 훑는다.
> → 질문의 형태를 통해 '시각 자료'를 이용해 푸는 문제임을 알 수 있으며, '회사가 조치를 시작하려는 항목'을 묻는 문제임을 파악한다.
> → 그래프 유형이며 가로축의 항목들이 선택지로 제시되어 있으므로 세로축을 구성하는 수치 관련 표현이나 순위를 나타내는 표현이 담화에 단서로 등장할 것임을 예상하고 들어야 한다.

> ↖ 담화를 듣는다.
> → '가장 많은/높은', '가장 낮은', 또는 '두 번째로 많은' 등의 표현을 통해 정답에 대한 단서를 알려주므로 최상급 또는 숫자 표현에 집중해서 듣는다. 해당 순위가 파악되는 순간 바로 그래프를 본다.

> ↖ 정답에 체크한다.
> → 파악된 순위(두 번째로 많은)의 그래프와 일치하는 선택지에 표시한다.

🚀 빠른 700⁺점 달성 TIP

2열/3열 도표는 선택지가 아닌 항목이 담화에서 단서로 제시되며, 막대 그래프 문제는 세로축의 수치나 순위를 나타내는 표현(the most ~, the second most ~, the lowest 등)이, 지도나 평면도는 위치를 나타내는 표현(next to, in front of, closest 등)이 단서로 제시된다.

PRACTICE | 기출 연습하기 문제를 푼 후, 담화를 다시 두 번 들으며 빈칸을 채워보세요.

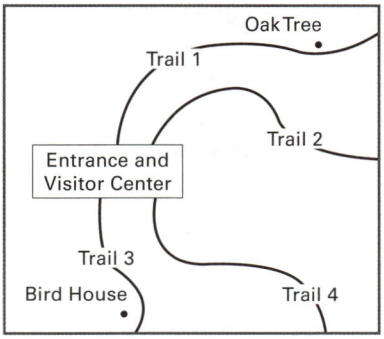

1. Who is the talk intended for?
   (A) New park employees
   (B) City officials

2. Look at the graphic. Which trail is closed?
   (A) Trail 1
   (B) Trail 2
   (C) Trail 3
   (D) Trail 4

W: We're pleased that _____ _____ the new employee orientation at Summit National Park. You can see the main trails on this map. We'll start on Trail 3 so I can show you the activity at our bird house. You'll hike parts of all the trails today except this one here, as _____ put up some fencing around the oak tree. It is over two hundred years old, so we want to protect it and _____ _____ it.

Employee Business Expenses: Walter Bennett		
DATE	AMOUNT	BUSINESS
August 1	$25	Mahlon Café
August 9	$40	Groton Inc.
August 24	$15	Jacobs Taxis
August 25	$130	Deleo Hotel

3. Why is the speaker calling?
   (A) A charge needs to be authorized.
   (B) A receipt has the wrong information.

4. Look at the graphic. Which business does the speaker inquire about?
   (A) Mahlon Café
   (B) Groton Inc.
   (C) Jacobs Taxis
   (D) Deleo Hotel

W: Good afternoon, Walter. This is Jacqueline, from the finance team. I'm ____ _____ for August, but there is one charge that _____. I've looked at your report, and it shows that you spent $40 on August 9, but there isn't any _____ _____. Could you call me back and let me know what is going on with this charge? You'll probably have to pick up the form from my office and complete it before returning it again. You can reach me at extension 34. Thanks.

DAY 17 실전문제

1. According to the speaker, what was recently decided?
   (A) A building design
   (B) A stadium's name
   (C) A construction location
   (D) A final budget

2. Why do some residents oppose the project?
   (A) It will be noisy.
   (B) It is too expensive.
   (C) It will create traffic problems.
   (D) It is bad for the environment.

3. What does the speaker plan to do next?
   (A) Gather some opinions
   (B) Visit the city center
   (C) Take a tour
   (D) Contact the mayor

4. Who most likely are the listeners?
   (A) Laboratory technicians
   (B) Financial advisors
   (C) Computer salespeople
   (D) Web site developers

5. What benefit of some equipment does the speaker mention?
   (A) A larger customer base
   (B) Shorter wait times
   (C) Improved safety features
   (D) More useful search results

6. What is scheduled to happen next week?
   (A) A training event will take place.
   (B) A new service will be launched.
   (C) Some visitors will take a tour.
   (D) Some consultants will have a meeting.

7. Why is the speaker giving the speech?
   (A) To recognize an employee's achievement
   (B) To introduce a new service
   (C) To celebrate a company's anniversary
   (D) To announce a business merger

8. What is Ms. Lee's field of expertise?
   (A) Finance
   (B) Transportation
   (C) Mining
   (D) Education

9. According to the speaker, what will Ms. Lee do next month?
   (A) Give a presentation
   (B) Select team members
   (C) Test some equipment
   (D) Take a business trip abroad

10. Why does the speaker want to postpone a meeting?
    (A) A client has made a complaint.
    (B) There are no available meeting rooms.
    (C) He has to take a business trip.
    (D) Some items have not arrived.

11. What did the listener write a report about?
    (A) Ideas for reducing energy usage
    (B) Companies that can supply fabric
    (C) An analysis of a feedback session
    (D) Ways to attract more customers

12. What does the speaker most likely mean when he says, "we need to discuss this further"?
    (A) He plans to consult an industry expert.
    (B) He is unsure that a suggestion will work.
    (C) He will lengthen the duration of a meeting.
    (D) He is concerned about a safety issue.

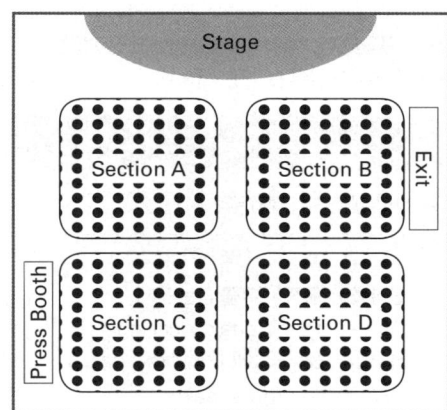

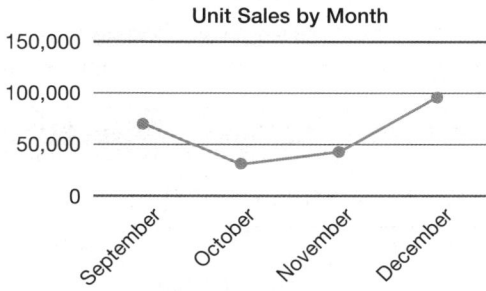

13. Who most likely is the intended audience of this talk?
    (A) Musicians
    (B) Athletes
    (C) Photographers
    (D) Journalists

14. Look at the graphic. Where can the listeners find empty seats?
    (A) Section A
    (B) Section B
    (C) Section C
    (D) Section D

15. What will the listeners do at the end of the event?
    (A) Have another performance
    (B) Respond to questions
    (C) Take a photo together
    (D) Participate in a tour

16. What kind of business does the speaker most likely work for?
    (A) A software development company
    (B) A financial consulting firm
    (C) A magazine publisher
    (D) A television studio

17. Look at the graphic. When did the company run some advertisements?
    (A) In September
    (B) In October
    (C) In November
    (D) In December

18. According to the speaker, what will the business do next month?
    (A) Merge with a partner
    (B) Decrease its prices
    (C) Introduce a new product
    (D) Hire more workers

LC DAY 18 담화 유형_전화 메시지/광고

01 전화 메시지(Telephone Message)

Part 4의 전화 메시지 담화 유형은 매회 2~3 지문 정도 출제되며 매회 전개 순서가 비슷한 편이다. 따라서 내용이 어떻게 전개되는지, 관련된 빈출 질문 유형은 무엇인지, 자주 나오는 단서 표현은 무엇인지 알아두면 예측 듣기가 가능하다.

♪ D18_01

◆ 출제 포인트 1 초반부에 단서가 제시되는 유형

화자나 청자의 근무지와 직업을 묻는 문제, 전화의 목적이나 이유를 묻는 문제는 주로 담화 초반부에 단서가 제시된다.

전개 내용		단서 표현	질문 유형
초반부	자기 소개 전화 목적	**전화를 건 목적/이유** 1. **I'm calling with some information about** the home you're interested in. 귀하께서 관심 있어 하시는 주택에 관한 정보를 드리려고 전화 드립니다. 2. **I'm calling regarding** the status of your recent order. 귀하의 최근 주문품에 대한 상황과 관련해 전화 드립니다. **화자[청자]의 근무지/직업** 1. **I'm calling from** the city's electric company. 시의 전기 회사에서 전화 드립니다. 2. Hello. **This is** Carmen Walker **from** the Milton County Library. 여보세요. 저는 Milton County Library의 Carmen Walker입니다. 3. **Thanks for sending me the information about** the repair work you intend to do. 귀하께서 계획하고 계신 수리 작업에 관한 정보를 제게 보내 주셔서 감사 드립니다.	**전화를 건 목적/이유를 묻는 문제** - What is the speaker calling about? 화자는 무엇에 관해 전화를 거는가? - Why does the speaker congratulate the listener? 화자는 왜 청자에게 축하 인사를 하는가? **화자[청자]의 근무지/직업을 묻는 문제** - Where does the speaker[listener] most likely work? 화자[청자]는 어디에서 근무하고 있을 것 같은가? - Who most likely is the speaker? 화자는 누구일 것 같은가?

◆ 출제 포인트 2 중반부에 단서가 제시되는 유형

세부 사항을 묻는 문제는 주로 담화 중반부에 단서가 제시된다.

전개 내용		단서 표현	질문 유형
중반부	세부 사항	**세부 사항** 1. **The problem is that** you failed to make your last two payments. 문제는 귀하께서 지난 두 번의 비용 납입을 하지 못하셨다는 점입니다. 2. **I'll e-mail you** the itinerary once everything is confirmed. 모든 것이 확인되는 대로 귀하께 일정표를 이메일로 보내 드리겠습니다. 3. **I was pleased with** how you handled the customer. 당신이 고객들을 대하는 방식이 만족스러웠습니다.	**세부 사항을 묻는 문제** - What problem does the speaker mention? 화자는 무슨 문제점을 언급하는가? - What will the speaker e-mail to the listener? 화자는 청자에게 무엇을 이메일로 보낼 것인가? - What is the speaker pleased with? 화자는 무엇에 대해 기뻐하는가?

◆ 출제 포인트 3   후반부에 단서가 제시되는 유형

요청 사항/제공 사항을 묻는 문제는 주로 담화 후반부에 단서가 제시된다.

전개 내용		단서 표현	질문 유형
후반부	요청 사항 제공 사항	**요청 사항** 1. **Could you please let me** know which shifts you prefer to work this week? 이번 주에 어느 교대 근무조로 일하시는 것을 선호하시는지 제게 알려 주시겠어요? 2. **I'll need you to** sign the contract if you agree to the terms. 조건에 동의하시면 계약서에 서명해 주셨으면 합니다. 3. You will **be required to** take a test before working on the assembly line. 조립 라인에서 근무하시기 전에 시험을 보셔야 할 것입니다. **제안/제공 사항** 1. If you finish your report by noon, **I'll let you** attend the speech at 3:00. 정오까지 보고서를 완료하시면, 3시에 열리는 연설 행사에 참석하시도록 해 드리겠습니다. 2. **I'd be happy to** provide you with the documents you requested. 요청하신 서류를 기꺼이 제공해 드리겠습니다.	요청 및 제안/제공 내용을 묻는 문제 - What does the speaker ask the listener to do? 화자는 청자에게 무엇을 하도록 요청하는가? - What does the speaker suggest the listener do? 화자는 청자에게 무엇을 하도록 제안하는가? - What does the speaker offer the listener? 화자는 청자에게 무엇을 제공하는가? - What does the speaker offer to do? 화자는 무엇을 하겠다고 제안하는가?

PRACTICE | 기출 연습하기 문제를 푼 후, 담화를 다시 두 번 들으며 빈칸을 채워보세요.

1. Where does the speaker work?
   (A) At a computer repair store
   (B) At a hardware store

2. What does the speaker offer?
   (A) A product warranty
   (B) A rush service

W: Hi, Mr. Koehn. This Andy Dengler calling from Spirit Computers. I've finished the updates you _____ _____. However, I'm afraid there's a problem with your cooling fan. _____ _____, it could cause overheating and damage your device. I know you weren't expecting this extra change, so I'm sorry about that. We can offer to _____ _____ as possible at no extra charge. Please call us at 555-4675 to confirm.

3. Who most likely is the speaker?
   (A) A real estate agent
   (B) A travel agent

4. What does the speaker ask the listener to do?
   (A) Send a deposit payment
   (B) Express interest in a visit

M: Hi, this is Shogo. There's a spacious three-bedroom apartment that just came _____, and I think it might be just what you're looking for. It's ___ _____ of the station. I know that was a feature you wanted. It's in the Gazella Building, which is very popular. I expect it to be rented quickly. So, I'll need you to let me know whether or not you want to _____. Please call me back as soon as you can. Thanks.

5. Where does the listener most likely work?
   (A) At an accounting firm
   (B) At a moving company

6. What problem does the speaker mention?
   (A) A suggested fee exceeds the planned budget.
   (B) A service is needed sooner than expected.

M: Good morning. This is Cory Juarez from Langley Accounting. Thanks for sending me the information about the fees for _____ and items to a new location. We're _____ _____, especially since you have such a great reputation. However, we're concerned that you won't be able to take on the job because our schedule has suddenly changed. We need to do the _____ _____, on March 3. Please let me know if that will work for you. Thanks.

02 광고(Advertisement)

Part 4의 광고 담화 유형은 매회 1지문 정도 출제되며 매회 전개 순서가 비슷한 편이다. 따라서 내용이 어떻게 전개되는지, 관련된 빈출 질문 유형은 무엇인지, 자주 나오는 단서 표현은 무엇인지 알아두면 예측 듣기가 가능하다.

♪ D18_02

◆ 출제 포인트 1   초반부에 단서가 제시되는 유형

관심을 유발하거나 광고되는 제품/서비스/업체를 소개하는 내용은 주로 담화 초반부에 단서가 제시된다.

전개 내용		단서 표현	질문 유형
초반부	관심 유발 제품/ 서비스 소개	**관심 유발** 1. **Are you tired of** the poor service from your cable operator? 이용 중이신 케이블 업체의 형편없는 서비스가 지겨우신가요? 2. **Would you like** a stylish home **but don't have time for** redecorating? 멋진 주택을 원하시지만 재단장하실 시간이 없으신가요? 3. **If** your firm is **looking for** a reliable cleaning service, ~ 귀사에서 신뢰하실 만한 청소 서비스를 찾고 계신다면, ~ 4. **Do you have** any unused luggage? 사용하지 않는 가방을 갖고 계신가요? **제품/서비스/업체 소개** 1. **Why not bring it to** the Belmont Community Center? Belmont Community Center로 가져 오시는 것은 어떠세요? 2. **Then switch to** Beta Cable. 그러시다면 저희 Beta Cable로 변경해 보십시오. 3. Samuelson Interior **is here to help**. 저희 Samuelson Interior 사가 도와 드리겠습니다. 4. **Then call** Matrix, Inc. 그러시면 Matrix, Inc.로 전화 주십시오.	**광고되는 서비스/상품/업체를 묻는 문제** - What service is being advertised? 무슨 서비스가 광고되고 있는가? - What products does the company sell? 회사는 무슨 제품을 판매하는가? - What type of business is being advertised? 무슨 종류의 업체가 광고되고 있는가? - What is the advertisement mainly about? 광고는 주로 무엇에 관한 것인가? - What is BestClick? BestClick은 무엇인가? **광고 대상을 묻는 문제** - Who is the advertisement intended for? 광고는 누구를 대상으로 하는가?

◆ 출제 포인트 2   중반부에 단서가 제시되는 유형

제품이나 서비스의 특장점을 묻는 문제는 주로 담화 중반부에 단서가 제시된다.

전개 내용		단서 표현	질문 유형
중반부	제품/서비스 특장점	**제품/서비스의 특장점** 1. **Our** Internet **service is available** in more than 100 countries. 저희 인터넷 서비스는 100곳이 넘는 국가에서 이용 가능합니다. 2. **With our wide variety of** women's clothes, you'll definitely find something you like. 아주 다양한 저희 여성 의류를 통해, 분명 원하시는 것을 찾게 되실 것입니다. 3. **The benefit** is you'll lose weight in no time. 이점은 여러분께서 즉시 체중을 감량하시게 된다는 것입니다.	**제품/서비스의 특징을 묻는 문제** - What does the speaker emphasize about the products[service]? 화자는 제품[서비스]에 관해 무엇을 강조하는가? - What benefit does the advertisement emphasize? 광고는 무슨 혜택을 강조하는가?

◆ 출제 포인트 3   후반부에 단서가 제시되는 유형

웹사이트에 방문할 것을 권고하거나, 추가 혜택에 관한 내용은 주로 담화 후반부에 단서가 제시된다.

전개 내용		단서 표현	질문 유형
후반부	웹 사이트 방문 권고 추가 혜택	**웹 사이트 방문 권고** 1. **For** a free consultation, **visit our Web site and** make a reservation. 무료 상담을 받으시려면, 저희 웹 사이트를 방문해 예약하시기 바랍니다. 2. **Visit our Web site to** learn all about the services we offer. 저희 웹 사이트를 방문해 저희가 제공해 드리는 모든 서비스를 알아 보십시오. 3. **Go to our Web site, where you can** chat with our customer representatives. 저희 웹 사이트를 방문하시면, 저희 고객 서비스 직원들과 채팅을 하실 수 있습니다. **추가 혜택** 1. **If you purchase** a membership **before** July 15, we'll give you a **free** 6-month magazine subscription. 7월 15일 이전에 회원권을 구입하시면, 무료 6개월 잡지 구독 서비스를 받게 되실 것입니다. 2. **We're offering discounts for** those who spend at least $100 on our Web site. 저희 웹 사이트에 최소 100달러를 소비하시는 분들께 할인을 제공해 드립니다.	**웹 사이트에서 할 수 있는 일을 묻는 문제** - What does the speaker say the listeners can do on a Web site? 화자는 청자들이 웹 사이트에서 무엇을 할 수 있다고 말하는가? - Why does the speaker invite the listeners to visit a Web site? 화자는 왜 청자들에게 웹 사이트를 방문하도록 요청하는가? - What does the speaker say can be found on the Web site? 화자는 웹 사이트에서 무엇을 찾아 볼 수 있다고 말하는가? **혜택을 묻는 문제** - What offer does the speaker mention? 화자는 무슨 제공 서비스를 언급하는가? - How can the listeners receive a discount[free gift]? 청자들은 어떻게 할인[사은품]을 받을 수 있는가?

PRACTICE | 기출 연습하기 문제를 푼 후, 담화를 다시 두 번 들으며 빈칸을 채워보세요.

1. What service is being advertised?
   (A) A delivery service
   (B) An Internet service

2. What does the speaker say can be found on the Web site?
   (A) A booking form
   (B) A product list

W: Are you a business owner _____ a fast and reliable _____? Then switch to Blane Communications. We have the fastest download speeds in the area and the lowest amount of outage time. For our easy _____ your set-up appointment, visit our Web site and click on the "Appointment" tab. We'll get you online in no time!

3. What business is being advertised?
   (A) A Web design company
   (B) A language school

4. What offer does the speaker mention?
   (A) A complimentary trial
   (B) A money-back guarantee

M: If you've ever wished that you could speak a _____ _____, then Lexsy Institute is here to help. We provide online lessons that you can download and listen to anytime, anywhere. Our system is easy to use, and you can _____. You'll be amazed at how quickly you start seeing results. Not sure if the Lexsy Institute is right for you? Visit our Web site, where we're offering a _____ so you can check us out.

5. What products does the company sell?
   (A) Printed signs
   (B) Display cases

6. What does the speaker emphasize about the products?
   (A) They come in various sizes.
   (B) They are made from recycled materials.

W: Do you own a retail business? Then you understand that the right sign can _____. Here at Colston Printing, we can _____ _____ that will get your customers interested in your business. All of our products are custom-made, so you can get exactly what you want. Whether you need large-scale banners, standard posters, or small cards, we've got you covered. Also, if you don't have an image ready yourself, we also have designers _____ _____.

LC   DAY 18 실전문제

1. What type of business is being advertised?
   (A) A real estate company
   (B) An interior design firm
   (C) A landscaping company
   (D) A hardware store

2. What can listeners do to receive a free gift?
   (A) Have a consultation in April
   (B) Recommend the business to a friend
   (C) Upgrade to a higher service package
   (D) Join the business's mailing list

3. Why are listeners encouraged to visit a Web site?
   (A) To get a cost estimate
   (B) To chat with employees
   (C) To download a brochure
   (D) To view some images

4. What service is being advertised?
   (A) A print shop
   (B) An electronics store
   (C) A courier service
   (D) A book publisher

5. What benefit does the advertisement emphasize?
   (A) Affordable prices
   (B) Effective protection
   (C) Friendly staff
   (D) Fast responses

6. What does the speaker say the listeners can do on a Web site?
   (A) Read customer reviews
   (B) Schedule a visit
   (C) Download a coupon
   (D) View a price list

7. Where does the speaker work?
   (A) At a marketing firm
   (B) At a construction company
   (C) At a dental office
   (D) At a hair salon

8. What is the purpose of the call?
   (A) To introduce a new service
   (B) To apologize for an error
   (C) To request a payment
   (D) To confirm an appointment

9. According to the speaker, what has recently changed?
   (A) A sign-up procedure
   (B) A parking situation
   (C) The business owner
   (D) The opening hours

10. What is mainly being advertised?
    (A) A final sale
    (B) A store relocation
    (C) A local contest
    (D) A job opportunity

11. What type of business most likely is Flannigan's?
    (A) A camping store
    (B) A car dealership
    (C) A clothing shop
    (D) A jewelry store

12. What does the speaker say can be done on the Web site?
    (A) Viewing some images
    (B) Downloading a coupon
    (C) Getting directions to a site
    (D) Reserving a ticket

13. What kind of items does the speaker's company sell?

    (A) Cleaning products
    (B) Athletic apparel
    (C) Vitamin supplements
    (D) Electronic devices

14. Why is the speaker calling?

    (A) To confirm a shipping address
    (B) To apologize for a delay
    (C) To report an incorrect order
    (D) To promote some new merchandise

15. What is the listener asked to do?

    (A) Cancel a service
    (B) Send an instruction manual
    (C) Refund a purchase
    (D) Deliver the items tomorrow

16. What does the speaker say is special about the coffee shop?

    (A) It offers discounts to local residents.
    (B) It donates a portion of its profits.
    (C) It has recently changed locations.
    (D) It grows some of its own ingredients.

17. Who is Reuben Webster?

    (A) The founder of a club
    (B) The director of a study
    (C) The mayor of a city
    (D) The owner of a business

18. Why does the speaker say, "I have one every day"?

    (A) She wants to recommend a beverage.
    (B) She thinks a price is reasonable.
    (C) She plans to change to part-time work.
    (D) She believes a task is easy to do.

19. In which department does the listener work?

    (A) Maintenance
    (B) Security
    (C) Sales
    (D) Accounting

20. Look at the graphic. What information should be changed?

    (A) 2A
    (B) 04689
    (C) 361
    (D) 43

21. What is the listener asked to do?

    (A) Return a document
    (B) Check a directory
    (C) Visit the speaker's office
    (D) Schedule an appointment

LC DAY 19 담화 유형_회의 발췌록/투어 정보

01 회의 발췌록(Excerpt from a Meeting)

Part 4의 회의 발췌록 담화 유형은 매회 3지문 정도 출제되며 매회 전개 순서가 비슷한 편이다. 따라서 내용이 어떻게 전개되는지, 관련된 빈출 질문 유형은 무엇인지, 자주 나오는 단서 표현은 무엇인지 알아두면 예측 듣기가 가능하다.

♪ D19_01

◆ 출제 포인트 1 초반부에 단서가 제시되는 유형

회의의 주제나 참석자의 신분/근무지를 묻는 문제는 주로 담화 초반부에 단서가 제시된다.

전개 내용		단서 표현	질문 유형
초반부	회의 주제	회의 주제/참석자 1. **I called this meeting to** describe how we plan to handle the merger. 우리가 어떻게 합병 문제를 처리할 계획인지 설명해 드리기 위해 이 회의를 소집했습니다. 2. **The first agenda item for** today's meeting is the budget for the upcoming year. 오늘 회의의 첫 번째 안건은 내년 예산 문제입니다. 3. **I'd like to go over** the results of last month's customer survey. 지난달에 있었던 고객 설문 조사의 결과를 검토해 보고자 합니다. 4. **As you know, our** media **firm started** a new ad campaign for our clients. 아시다시피, 우리 미디어 회사는 고객들을 대상으로 새로운 광고 캠페인을 시작했습니다.	회의 주제/청자의 신분/근무지를 묻는 문제 - What is the main topic of the meeting? 회의의 주제는 무엇인가? - Who mostly likely are the listeners? 청자들은 누구일 것 같은가? - What kind of business do the listeners most likely work for? 청자들은 무슨 종류의 회사에서 근무하고 있을 것 같은가?

◆ 출제 포인트 2 중반부에 단서가 제시되는 유형

세부 사항을 묻는 문제는 주로 담화 중반부에 단서가 제시된다.

전개 내용		단서 표현	질문 유형
중반부	세부 사항	세부 사항 1. **Terry Gonzalez, who is** organizing the spring festival, will use a few volunteers. 봄철 축제를 준비 중이신 Terry Gonzalez 씨께서 몇몇 자원 봉사자들을 활용하실 것입니다. 2. When **Derek Ring** started his business **last month**, he wasn't sure of his success. Derek Ring 씨께서 지난달에 개인 사업을 시작하셨을 때, 성공을 확신하지 못하셨습니다. 3. **It is our hope that** the meeting can be rescheduled for later in the week. 회의가 주 후반부로 조정될 수 있기를 바라고 있습니다. 4. **The most popular feature of** the fan is the timer that turns it off automatically. 그 선풍기의 가장 인기 있는 특징은 자동으로 꺼지게 해 주는 타이머입니다.	세부 사항을 묻는 문제 - Who is Terry Gonzales? Terry Gonzales 씨는 누구인가? - What does the speaker say Derek Ring recently did? 화자는 Derek Ring 씨가 최근에 무엇을 했다고 말하는가? - What is Paleo Publishing hoping to do? Paleo Publishing 사는 무엇을 하기를 바라고 있는가? - What feature of the product does the speaker mention? 화자는 제품의 어떤 특징을 언급하는가? - According to the speaker, what is scheduled for next year? 화자의 말에 따르면, 내년에 무엇이 예정되어 있는가?

| 중반부 | 세부 사항 | 5. We will have a display booth at the sales fair **coming up next year** in Dublin. 우리는 내년에 Dublin에서 열릴 예정인 판매 박람회에서 전시 부스를 운영할 것입니다. | |

◆ 출제 포인트 3 후반부에 단서가 제시되는 유형

요청 사항이나 앞으로 있을 일을 묻는 문제는 주로 담화 후반부에 단서가 제시된다.

전개 내용		단서 표현	질문 유형
후반부	요청 사항 앞으로 있을 일	**요청 사항** 1. **I'd like us[you all/each of you] to** come up with possible solutions. 저는 우리가[여러분 모두가/여러분 각자가] 가능성 있는 해결책을 내놓았으면 합니다. 2. **Be sure to** congratulate Kimberly on winning the award. 상을 받으신 Kimberly 씨를 꼭 축하해 주시기 바랍니다. 3. **Remember you can** return it for a full refund at anytime. 전액 환불을 받기 위해 언제든지 반품하실 수 있다는 점을 기억해 주시기 바랍니다. **앞으로 있을 일** 1. **I'm now going to have you** fill out some forms. 이제 여러분께 몇몇 양식을 작성하시도록 부탁드리겠습니다. 2. **I'm ready to** consider hiring additional staff members if necessary. 저는 필요하면 추가 직원들을 고용하는 것을 고려해 볼 준비가 되어 있습니다. 3. All tenants will **need to** sign new leases by **next month**. 모든 세입자들께서는 다음 달까지 새로운 임대 계약서에 서명하셔야 할 것입니다.	**요청 사항/앞으로의 일을 묻는 문제** - What are the listeners asked to do? 청자들은 무엇을 하도록 요청 받는가? - What will the speaker do next? 화자는 곧이어 무엇을 할 것인가? - What does the speaker say will happen on Monday? 화자는 월요일에 무슨 일이 있을 것이라고 말하는가? - What will the listeners have to do next month? 청자들은 다음 달에 무엇을 해야 하는가?

PRACTICE | 기출 연습하기 문제를 푼 후, 담화를 다시 두 번 들으며 빈칸을 채워보세요.

1. What is the speaker mainly talking about?
   (A) Nurse staffing
   (B) A branch opening

2. What does the speaker remind the listeners to do?
   (A) Forward a link
   (B) Submit an application

M: I called this meeting to _____ here at our clinic. We have a growing number of patients, so _____ to keep up with the demand. I have posted the job openings online, but we would also appreciate your help. I'll e-mail you the link to the job posting. If you know anyone who might be interested in one of these positions, _____ _____ right away, as the application deadline is March 31.

3. What kind of business do the listeners most likely work for?
   (A) An advertising agency
   (B) A financial institution

4. What does the speaker ask the listeners to do by Friday?
   (A) Create a budget proposal
   (B) Report their availability

M: As you know, we've recently _____ _____ with Yang International. This is a major achievement for us, as we'll be _____ _____ for television and Web sites for this well-known brand. To get off to a good start, we plan to hold a half-day brainstorming session sometime next week with all of you in the creative department. We're not sure which day would be more convenient. Therefore, I'd like you to e-mail me with information about _____ _____. Thanks.

5. Who most likely are the listeners?
   (A) Office receptionists
   (B) Retail cashiers

6. What is the topic of the meeting?
   (A) Using a different machine
   (B) Promoting new products

W: Good afternoon, everyone. I wanted to schedule this meeting with all of _____ to discuss the _____ the new products. As you know, our clothing store has recently started selling accessories. Displays of these goods are positioned in the checkout area so that they will be easily noticed by customers. However, we would also like _____ _____ for accessories to purchase based on what the customer is buying. I've prepared a list of suggestions to give you an idea of what I'm talking about.

02 투어 정보(Tour Information)

Part 4의 투어 담화 유형은 매회 1지문 정도 출제되며 매회 전개 순서가 비슷한 편이다. 따라서 내용이 어떻게 전개되는지, 관련된 빈출 질문 유형은 무엇인지, 자주 나오는 단서 표현은 무엇인지 알아두면 예측 듣기가 가능하다.

♪ D19_02

◆ 출제 포인트 1 초반부에 단서가 제시되는 유형

투어를 소개하거나 방문지의 특징에 대한 내용은 주로 담화 초반부에 단서가 제시된다.

전개 내용		단서 표현	질문 유형
초반부	투어 소개	투어 장소/종류/가이드 1. **Welcome to** Deacon Pottery. Deacon Pottery를 방문하신 것을 환영합니다. 2. **During this tour of** Washburn Culinary's manufacturing plant, please keep your safety equipment on at all times. 이번 Washburn Culinary의 제조 공장 견학 중에는, 항상 안전 장비를 착용한 상태로 계시기 바랍니다. 3. **I was** born and raised in this town. 저는 이 도시에서 태어나고 자랐습니다.	투어 장소/종류/화자(가이드)를 묻는 문제 - Where is the tour most likely taking place? 투어는 어디에서 진행되고 있을 것 같은가? - What product will listeners learn about during the tour? 청자들은 투어 중에 무슨 제품에 관해 알게 될 것인가? - What does the speaker mention about himself? 화자는 자신에 관해 무엇을 언급하는가?
	방문지 특징	방문지 특징 1. **You will be impressed with the museum's** modern art collection. 이 박물관의 현대 미술 소장품에 대해 깊은 인상을 받게 되실 것입니다. 2. **This factory is well-known for** its advanced machinery. 이 공장은 첨단 기계들로 잘 알려져 있습니다.	방문지 특징을 묻는 문제 - According to the speaker, what is impressive about the museum? 화자의 말에 따르면, 박물관과 관련해 무엇이 인상적인가? - What does the speaker emphasize about the factory? 화자는 공장에 관해 무엇을 강조하는가?

◆ 출제 포인트 2 중반부에 단서가 제시되는 유형

투어 일정에 대한 내용은 주로 담화 중반부에 단서가 제시된다.

전개 내용		단서 표현	질문 유형
중반부	투어 일정	투어 세부 일정 1. **Normally**, the tour lasts one hour, **but today** it will take ninety minutes to complete. 보통, 이 투어는 1시간 동안 지속되지만, 오늘은 종료되는 데 90분의 시간이 걸릴 것입니다. 2. **We'll take a rest** for a few minutes, **so** you can have time to take some photos. 우리는 몇 분간 휴식을 취할 것이므로, 여러분들께서는 사진 찍을 시간을 가지셔도 좋습니다.	투어 세부 사항을 묻는 문제 - What does the speaker say has changed about the tour? 화자는 투어와 관련해 무엇이 변경되었다고 말하는가? - According to the speaker, why will the group take a rest? 화자의 말에 따르면, 해당 그룹은 왜 휴식을 취할 것인가?

◆ 출제 포인트 3   후반부에 단서가 제시되는 유형

투어 후의 일정이나 금지·권고 사항에 대한 문제는 주로 담화 후반부에 단서가 제시된다.

전개 내용		단서 표현	질문 유형
후반부	투어 후 일정 금지 또는 권고 사항	**투어 후 일정** 1. **Once the tour is over, I encourage you to** check out our special programs. 투어가 종료되는 대로, 저희 특별 프로그램들을 확인해 보시기를 권해 드립니다. 2. **At the end of the tour, I'll pass out** some evaluation forms for you to fill out. 투어가 종료되는 시점에, 여러분께서 작성하실 평가 양식들을 나눠 드리겠습니다. **금지 또는 권고 사항** 1. **Remember that** cameras are not allowed here, **so please don't** take any pictures. 이곳에서는 카메라가 허용되지 않는다는 것을 기억하시고, 사진은 찍지 마십시오. 2. **I'd just like to ask you not to** speak loudly. 큰 소리로 말씀하시지 않도록 요청 드리고자 합니다.	**투어 후 일정을 묻는 문제** - What does the speaker recommend doing after the tour? 화자는 투어 후에 무엇을 하도록 권하는가? - What does the speaker say she will distribute? 화자는 무엇을 배부할 것이라고 말하는가? **금지 또는 권고 사항을 묻는 문제** - What does the speaker say is prohibited on the tour? 화자는 투어 중에 무엇이 금지되어 있다고 말하는가? - What should the listeners avoid doing? 청자들은 무엇을 하는 것을 피해야 하는가? - What does the speaker suggest the listeners do? 화자는 청자들에게 무엇을 하도록 권하는가?

PRACTICE | 기출 연습하기 문제를 푼 후, 담화를 다시 두 번 들으며 빈칸을 채워보세요.

1. Where is the tour most likely taking place?
   (A) At a fabric factory
   (B) At a career fair

2. What does the speaker suggest doing?
   (A) Picking up a brochure
   (B) Visiting a gift shop

M: Welcome to the tour of the Alhambra _____ _____. We are proud to be one of the largest producers of fabric in the country, and we stand behind the quality of our goods. Today, you'll get to see each step in the process. We'll first watch the thread being loaded into our weavers. Then, you'll see the weaving process at work, followed by the dyeing stage. At the end of the tour, _____ our on-site shop to _____, and ... of course ... plenty of fabric?

3. What does the speaker mention about Randolph National Park?
   (A) It has recently opened new hiking trails.
   (B) It is the most popular park in the area.

4. Why will the listeners stop in an hour?
   (A) To have a meal together
   (B) To hear a lecture on wildlife

M: Good morning, everyone. My name is Chris, and I'd like to welcome you to Randolph National Park. The park just _____ last week, so you are one of the first groups to take advantage of the change. We'll go along at quite a fast pace, but _____ _____ at the first lookout point so you can _____. If anyone has any questions about the plants or trees you see along the way, just let me know. If we're lucky, we'll also see some wildlife.

5. What does the speaker emphasize about the zoo?
   (A) Its age
   (B) Its size

6. According to the speaker, what is not allowed?
   (A) Using a camera
   (B) Bringing in food

W: Thank you all for signing up for this tour of the Brannon Zoo. We are proud to _____ _____ in the southwest. In fact, many of today's modern zoos used ours as a model when being built. We've timed this tour so that you will see some of the animals being fed. _____ the Reptile House first. We do _____ in there, so thanks in advance for not taking pictures.

DAY 19 실전문제

1. Who most likely is the speaker?
   (A) A building owner
   (B) A factory manager
   (C) A product reviewer
   (D) A security director

2. What is being replaced at the business in May?
   (A) Some lights
   (B) Some furniture
   (C) Some uniforms
   (D) Some equipment

3. What does the speaker ask the listeners to do?
   (A) Attend a workshop
   (B) Complete a survey
   (C) Read a training manual
   (D) Come to work early

4. What does the speaker tell the listeners about?
   (A) An office relocation
   (B) An annual meeting
   (C) A Web site relaunch
   (D) An industry conference

5. What does the speaker ask the listeners to do?
   (A) Print out some information
   (B) Tell some clients about a change
   (C) Update some software
   (D) Check their e-mail frequently

6. Who is Elaine Patterson?
   (A) A delivery person
   (B) A computer expert
   (C) An HR representative
   (D) A job applicant

7. What is the talk mainly about?
   (A) Methods for attracting clients
   (B) Preferred travel destinations
   (C) Company reimbursement policies
   (D) Ways to reduce wasteful spending

8. Why should the listeners speak to Erica?
   (A) To volunteer for a task
   (B) To request a form
   (C) To ask for a transfer
   (D) To sign up for an event

9. What does the speaker say the business will do at a later time?
   (A) Issue credit cards
   (B) Distribute some pamphlets
   (C) Finalize a contract
   (D) Upgrade some devices

10. Where is the tour taking place?
    (A) At a photography studio
    (B) At a research laboratory
    (C) At an art museum
    (D) At a cooking school

11. What does the speaker say is not allowed during the tour?
    (A) Speaking to employees
    (B) Touching the items
    (C) Making a lot of noise
    (D) Leaving the group

12. What does the speaker recommend doing?
    (A) Picking up a brochure
    (B) Purchasing some souvenirs
    (C) Registering for a workshop
    (D) Writing down some questions

13. According to the speaker, what is impressive about a building?

    (A) It has historically accurate furnishings.
    (B) It offers large meeting rooms.
    (C) It has several secret passageways.
    (D) It is located near a hill.

14. What does the speaker recommend doing after the tour?

    (A) Reading a history book
    (B) Watching a video
    (C) Joining a mailing list
    (D) Purchasing some dishes

15. What should the listeners avoid doing?

    (A) Using cell phones
    (B) Carrying food items
    (C) Losing a ticket
    (D) Taking photographs

---

16. Where most likely is the talk taking place?

    (A) At an art institute
    (B) At a manufacturing plant
    (C) At a fitness facility
    (D) At a department store

17. Why does the speaker say, "this is a popular time"?

    (A) To predict that the tour may be delayed
    (B) To praise the listeners for making a good decision
    (C) To explain why he is busier than usual
    (D) To warn listeners that an option may be unavailable

18. What are the listeners reminded to pick up?

    (A) A brochure
    (B) A visitor badge
    (C) A coupon
    (D) A parking pass

Arrangement A 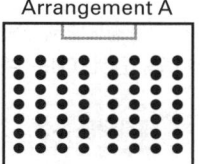　　Arrangement B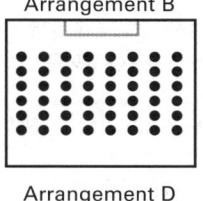

Arrangement C 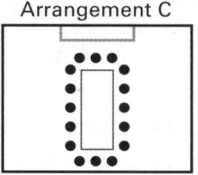　　Arrangement D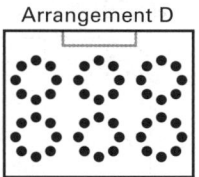

19. What kind of event is being discussed?

    (A) A painting class
    (B) A technology conference
    (C) A science workshop
    (D) A history lecture

20. According to the speaker, why did tickets sell out quickly?

    (A) A famous lecturer will attend.
    (B) The entrance fee was discounted.
    (C) A number of prizes will be given away.
    (D) The event was heavily advertised.

21. Look at the graphic. Which arrangement will be used in Room 17?

    (A) Arrangement A
    (B) Arrangement B
    (C) Arrangement C
    (D) Arrangement D

LC DAY 20 담화 유형_안내 방송/방송/뉴스

01 안내 방송(Announcement)

Part 4의 안내 방송 담화 유형은 매회 1~2지문 정도 출제되며 매회 전개 순서가 비슷한 편이다. 따라서 내용이 어떻게 전개되는지, 관련된 빈출 질문 유형은 무엇인지, 자주 나오는 단서 표현은 무엇인지 알아두면 예측 듣기가 가능하다.

♪ D20_01

◆ 출제 포인트 1 초반부에 단서가 제시되는 유형

안내 방송의 목적/주제/장소나 화자[청자]의 직업 관련 문제는 주로 담화 초반부에 단서가 제시된다.

전개 내용		단서 표현	질문 유형
초반부	인사말 및 목적	**인사말** 1. **Welcome to** our monthly seminar for financial analysts. 재정 분석 전문가들을 위한 저희 월간 세미나에 오신 것을 환영합니다. 2. **Thanks for coming to** the Jefferson Staffing Agency this afternoon. 오늘 오후에 저희 Jefferson Staffing Agency에 와 주셔서 감사 드립니다. **안내 방송의 이유/회사 소개** 1. The **flight** from Manchester to Copenhagen has been **delayed**. Manchester에서 Copenhagen으로 떠나는 항공편이 지연되었습니다. 2. **Here at** Delta Manufacturing, we provide our customers with quality products. 저희 Delta Manufacturing에서는, 고객 여러분께 고품질의 제품을 제공해 드립니다.	**안내 방송 장소를 묻는 문제** - Where is the announcement taking place? 안내 방송은 어디에서 이뤄지고 있는가? - Where is the announcement being made? 안내 방송은 어디에서 이뤄지고 있는가? **주제/직업을 묻는 문제** - What is the announcement about? 안내 방송은 무엇에 관한 것인가? - Who most likely is[are] the speaker[listeners]? 화자[청자]들은 누구일 것 같은가?

◆ 출제 포인트 2 중반부에 단서가 제시되는 유형

세부 사항을 묻는 문제는 주로 담화 중반부에 단서가 제시된다.

전개 내용		단서 표현	질문 유형
중반부	세부 사항	**세부 사항** 1. **Because of** the snowy conditions, several flights have been canceled today. 눈이 내리는 기상 상태로 인해, 여러 항공편이 오늘 취소되었습니다. 2. **Unfortunately**, Flight 372 is overbooked, so some passengers need to take a later flight. 안타깝게도, 372 항공편은 초과 예약이 되어 있어서, 일부 승객들께서는 나중에 떠나는 항공편을 이용하셔야 합니다. 3. **The gift shop** on the first floor sells all kinds of souvenirs. 1층에 있는 선물 매장에서는 모든 종류의 기념품을 팔고 있습니다.	**세부 사항을 묻는 문제** - What caused the problem? 무엇이 문제를 야기했는가? - What problem does the speaker mention? 화자는 무슨 문제를 언급하는가? - What does the speaker say about the gift shop? 화자는 선물 매장에 관해 무슨 말을 하는가?

✦ 출제 포인트 3   후반부에 단서가 제시되는 유형

미래의 일을 묻거나 제공되는 것을 묻는 문제는 주로 담화 후반부에 단서가 제시된다.

전개 내용		단서 표현	질문 유형
후반부	미래의 일	**앞으로 해야 할 일/일어날 일** 1. **If you'd like to** attend the conference **next month**, talk to Peggy Steele. 다음 달 컨퍼런스에 참석하기를 원하시면, Peggy Steele 씨에게 말씀하십시오. 2. **Why don't you** turn on your laptops and log in **now**? 노트북 컴퓨터를 켜시고 지금 로그인해 보시겠습니까? 3. **Don't forget to** submit your timesheet by **three o'clock** tomorrow. 내일 3시까지 근무 시간 기록지를 잊지 말고 제출하시기 바랍니다.	**앞으로 해야 할 일/일어날 일을 묻는 문제** - What will the listeners most likely do next month? 청자들은 다음 달에 무엇을 할 것 같은가? - What are the listeners instructed to do next? 청자들은 곧이어 무엇을 하도록 안내 받는가? - What is scheduled to take place at three o'clock? 3시에 무슨 일이 있을 예정인가?
	제공 정보	**제공되는 것** 1. **Derrick will come around and hand out** application forms soon. Derrick 씨께서 곧 돌아다니시면서 신청서를 배부할 것입니다. 2. **The employees will be rewarded with** bonuses for their outstanding performances. 직원들은 뛰어난 성과에 대해 보너스로 보상 받게 될 것입니다.	**제공되는 것을 묻는 문제** - According to the speaker, what will be distributed? 화자의 말에 따르면, 무엇이 배부될 것인가? - What does the speaker say the employees will receive? 화자는 직원들이 무엇을 받을 것이라고 말하는가?

PRACTICE | 기출 연습하기 문제를 푼 후, 담화를 다시 두 번 들으며 빈칸을 채워보세요.

1. Where is the announcement being made?
   (A) At an airport
   (B) At a bus terminal

2. What does the speaker say will be distributed?
   (A) Food vouchers
   (B) New tickets

M: Attention, _____ on Lia Airlines flight 451 to Shanghai. This flight had been _____ _____ three hours. We apologize for the inconvenience. We expect no further delays after this time, so there is no need to change your boarding passes. By way of apology, one of our staff members will come around and _____ ____ a set lunch menu at participating businesses on-site. There is plenty of time to use those. Sorry again for this delay. We will be making more announcements closer to the boarding time.

3. What kind of business does the speaker most likely work for?
   (A) An employment agency
   (B) A computer repair shop

4. What does the speaker ask the listeners to do?
   (A) Complete a form in advance
   (B) Hold their questions until the end

W: I'd like to welcome you all to the Appleton _____ _____. We hold this group interview session once a month to add more people to our computer database. Our goal is to _____ that will fit your skills and interests. As you can see, there are a lot of people here today, so we'd like to get through the process as quickly as possible. Could you help us speed things up by completing your _____ _____? You can get one from the desk over there.

5. Who most likely are the listeners?
   (A) Factory workers
   (B) Government officials

6. According to the speaker, what will Mr. Mindel do?
   (A) Prepare a report
   (B) Place an order

W: I'd like to make an announcement before _____ _____. We've just received the report from our recent safety inspection. We scored high on most categories, but there are still a lot of employees who are not wearing _____.
I understand that some of this gear is uncomfortable, but it is for your own protection, not to mention that it is required. If you need more items because yours are lost or damaged, please let us know. Mr. Mindel will be _____ _____ tomorrow morning.

02 방송/뉴스(Broadcast/News Report)

Part 4의 방송/뉴스 담화 유형은 매회 1~2지문 정도 출제되며 매회 전개 순서가 비슷한 편이다. 따라서 내용이 어떻게 전개되는지, 관련된 빈출 질문 유형은 무엇인지, 자주 나오는 단서 표현은 무엇인지 알아두면 예측 듣기가 가능하다.

♪ D20_02

◆ 출제 포인트 1 　 초반부에 단서가 제시되는 유형

인사말이나 방송의 주제, 초대 손님 등에 대한 내용은 주로 담화 초반부에 단서가 제시된다.

전개 내용		단서 표현	질문 유형
초반부	인사말 방송/뉴스 주제 초대 손님/ 회사 소개	**인사말** 1. **Thanks for listening to** [Welcome to/And now for/You're listening to] KTN Radio's Weekly News.　KTN Radio의 주간 뉴스를 청취해 주셔서 감사합니다[환영합니다/지금은 ~ 시간입니다/듣고 계십니다]. 2. **Thanks for tuning in to** our traffic update.　저희 교통 소식에 채널을 맞춰 주셔서 감사 드립니다. **방송/뉴스 주제** 1. The Bellevue Group will be **hosting a fundraiser** tomorrow night.　Bellevue Group은 내일 밤 모금 행사를 개최할 예정입니다. 2. Today, we'll be **talking about** the medical breakthrough announced by Dr. Melville.　오늘은, Melville 박사님께서 발표하신 중대한 의학적 발견에 관해 이야기해 보겠습니다. **초대 손님/회사 소개** 1. **With me in the studio is** Herb Sanchez, a bestselling novelist.　저와 함께 스튜디오에 베스트셀러 소설가 Herb Sanchez 씨께서 나와 계십니다. 2. **Today I'll be speaking to** the city's mayor, Abby West. 오늘 Abby West 시장님과 이야기 나눠 보겠습니다. 3. **Our story is about recent developments at** Jenkins, Inc., the largest manufacturer in the city.　전해 드릴 이야기는 시에서 가장 큰 제조사인 Jenkins Inc.의 최근 동향에 관한 것입니다.	**주제를 묻는 문제** - What is the broadcast[talk] mainly about?　방송[담화]는 주로 무엇에 관한 것인가? - What is the (main) topic of the workshop?　워크숍의 주제는 무엇인가? **화자/초대 손님/회사에 관해 묻는 문제** - Who is the speaker?　화자는 누구인가? - Who is Mark Putlack? Mark Putlack은 누구인가? - What is Ms. Kim's area of expertise?　Kim 씨의 전문 분야는 무엇인가? - What does JBC Studios make? JBC Studios는 무엇을 만드는가?

◆ 출제 포인트 2   중반부에 단서가 제시되는 유형

세부 사항을 묻는 문제는 주로 담화 중반부에 단서가 제시된다.

전개 내용		단서 표현	질문 유형
중반부	세부 사항	**세부 사항** 1. **We are expecting** snowy weather all weekend long. 주말 동안 내내 눈이 날리는 날씨가 예상됩니다. 2. Ms. Janet's third book was **just** published **last month**. Janet 씨의 세 번째 책이 지난 달에 막 출간되었습니다. 3. **We encourage you to** call in with your questions for Dr. Wellborn. Wellborn 박사님께 질문이 있으시면 전화 주시기를 권해 드립니다. 4. The zoo's panda exhibit **is set to** close **in July**. 동물원의 팬더 공개 행사가 7월에 종료될 예정입니다.	**세부 사항을 묻는 문제** - Why was the event canceled? 행사는 왜 취소되었는가? - According to the speaker, what did Janet Brunner recently do? 화자에 따르면, Janet Brunner 씨는 최근에 무엇을 했는가? - What does the speaker recommend? 화자는 무엇을 추천하는가? - According to the speaker, what will happen in July? 화자에 따르면, 7월에 무슨 일이 있을 것인가?

◆ 출제 포인트 3   후반부에 단서가 제시되는 유형

제안하는 내용이 무엇인지 묻거나 다음 방송 순서를 소개하는 내용은 주로 담화 후반부에 단서가 제시된다.

전개 내용		단서 표현	질문 유형
후반부	제안 다음 방송 순서 소개	**제안** 1. Due to the stormy weather, commuters **are advised to** avoid the Lexington Bridge. 폭풍우가 몰아치는 날씨로 인해, 통근자들은 Lexington Bridge를 피하도록 권고됩니다. 2. **I encourage you to** make a detour to avoid the affected area. 영향을 받은 구역을 피하실 수 있도록 우회로를 이용하시기를 권해 드립니다. **다음 방송 순서 소개** 1. **Now, I'll turn you over to** Harold Watson with today's local news. 이제, 오늘의 지역 뉴스를 전해 드릴 Harold Watson 씨에게 순서를 넘기겠습니다. 2. **Next**, let me describe the benefits of this new policy. 다음으로, 이 새로운 정책의 혜택을 설명해 드리겠습니다. 3. Mr. Tudor and I will discuss the company he just founded **in one moment**. Tudor 씨께서 막 설립하신 회사에 관한 이야기를 잠시 후에 함께 나눠 보겠습니다.	**제안 내용을 묻는 문제** - What does the speaker recommend[suggest] the listeners do? 화자는 청자들에게 무엇을 하도록 권하는가? **다음에 나올 내용을 묻는 문제** - What will the listeners hear next? 청자들은 곧이어 무엇을 들을 것인가? - What will the speaker most likely do next? 화자는 곧이어 무엇을 할 것 같은가?

PRACTICE | 기출 연습하기 문제를 푼 후, 담화를 다시 두 번 들으며 빈칸을 채워보세요.

1. Who is Elaine Richmond?
   (A) A health expert
   (B) A financial advisor

2. According to the speaker, what will happen next month?
   (A) A book will go on the market.
   (B) A business will have its grand opening.

M: You're listening to Everyday Tips on KRRM Radio. I'm your host, Martin Polk. With me in the studio is Elaine Richmond, a _____.
For the past decade, she has been teaching people how to change their daily habits to help them get in shape and feel great. Thanks for joining us today, Ms. Richmond. I've been told that _____ about your recommendations and that it will be _____ _____ next month. How about telling our listeners a little bit about it?

3. What is the broadcast mainly about?
   (A) Current weather
   (B) Traffic conditions

4. What does the speaker recommend?
   (A) Watching carefully for signs
   (B) Calling to report an accident

W: _____ this traffic update. Roadways are clear in the northern end of town. However, those traveling in the southern end should expect delays. Due to a burst water pipe on Topeka Road, a section of the road _____. Officials are rerouting drivers at this time. If you are driving in this area, be sure to pay close attention and _____ _____. This will help you to get where you're going easily and safely.

5. What is the news report about?
   (A) Expansion to the City Hall building
   (B) Construction of a new library

6. What advantage of a site does the speaker mention?
   (A) Access to public transportation
   (B) Proximity to residential properties

M: It's five o'clock, time for the local news report. At a press conference this morning, Avery Adams, the head of the city council, _____ _____ of a public library at 8th Street and Wilkens Drive. The new building will be the third library in the city, and it is _____ within about two and a half years. Several locations were considered for the project. However, planners selected the 8th Street site because it has the _____ a lot of residential apartment buildings.

LC DAY 20 실전문제

1. Who is Judy Liang?
   (A) A car mechanic
   (B) A legal expert
   (C) A radio show host
   (D) A university professor

2. Why should listeners call the number provided?
   (A) To volunteer for a study
   (B) To review a product
   (C) To enter a contest
   (D) To share an opinion

3. What will the listeners hear next?
   (A) The local news
   (B) The sports report
   (C) An interview
   (D) An advertisement

4. Who is the speaker?
   (A) A radio host
   (B) A bank employee
   (C) An inventor
   (D) A politician

5. What topic will be covered in the show?
   (A) Investment funds
   (B) Hiring practices
   (C) Marketing strategies
   (D) Business trips

6. What are the listeners asked to do?
   (A) Make a donation
   (B) Call in with questions
   (C) Vote on a proposal
   (D) Sign up for a convention

7. What is the broadcast mainly about?
   (A) A park cleanup project
   (B) An annual festival
   (C) A transportation program
   (D) A reelection campaign

8. What does the speaker mean when she says, "these things often have a lot of opposition"?
   (A) A project was surprisingly popular.
   (B) A decision upset the public.
   (C) A proposal will be debated further.
   (D) A start date may be delayed.

9. What will Samantha Graham tell the listeners about?
   (A) Where to meet for an event
   (B) Whom to contact with questions
   (C) When to expect a result
   (D) How to make an application

10. Where are the listeners?
    (A) On an airplane
    (B) At an airport
    (C) On a train
    (D) At a train station

11. What problem does the speaker mention?
    (A) Some tickets had the wrong information.
    (B) The luggage areas have too many items.
    (C) Some items are not properly labeled.
    (D) The team does not have enough workers.

12. Why does the speaker encourage listeners to read a card?
    (A) To learn about a return policy
    (B) To review safety procedures
    (C) To check a seating chart
    (D) To view meal choices

13. Why does the speaker thank the listeners?
    (A) They finished a task on time.
    (B) They had perfect attendance at a meeting.
    (C) They came to work on the weekend.
    (D) They made some useful suggestions.

14. In which department do the listeners probably work?
    (A) Shipping and receiving
    (B) Customer service
    (C) Product development
    (D) IT support

15. What will be announced later today?
    (A) Packaging designs
    (B) Sales figures
    (C) Material costs
    (D) Group leaders

16. Who most likely are the listeners?
    (A) Professors
    (B) Medical personnel
    (C) Journalists
    (D) Computer programmers

17. What is the main purpose of the talk?
    (A) To explain some company policies
    (B) To introduce a series of activities
    (C) To review a business's performance
    (D) To announce an interview opportunity

18. What does the speaker most likely mean when he says, "Ms. McGrath has prepared tea and coffee"?
    (A) The listeners will be able to take breaks.
    (B) The listeners should help pay for some items.
    (C) The listeners need to give a coworker a hand.
    (D) The listeners can try some product samples.

Section A	Section B	Section C	Section D
Rings	Bracelets	Necklaces	Earrings

19. What is being celebrated?
    (A) A business anniversary
    (B) A product launch
    (C) A store relocation
    (D) An award nomination

20. When will the event end?
    (A) This evening
    (B) Tomorrow evening
    (C) Next week
    (D) Next month

21. Look at the graphic. Which section has a fifty percent discount?
    (A) Section A
    (B) Section B
    (C) Section C
    (D) Section D

PART 5&6

DAY 01 빠른 700⁺점 달성을 위한 전략
DAY 02 주어 자리와 동사 자리
DAY 03 태/시제/가정법
DAY 04 명사
DAY 05 대명사
DAY 06 형용사/부사
DAY 07 부정사/동명사
DAY 08 분사
DAY 09 전치사
DAY 10 부사절 접속사/등위·상관 접속사
DAY 11 명사절 접속사/형용사절 접속사(=관계 대명사)
DAY 12 비교
DAY 13 어휘-동사/형용사/부사
DAY 14 어휘-명사/전치사
DAY 15 Part 6

정재현 토익
똑똑한 기본서
LC+RC

PART 7

DAY 16 주제, 목적 및 대상을 묻는 유형
DAY 17 세부 사항을 묻는 유형
DAY 18 진위 확인 유형
DAY 19 문장 넣기/의도 파악/동의어 찾기 유형
DAY 20 다중 지문 연계 유형

RC | DAY 01   빠른 700⁺점 달성을 위한 전략

RC Part 별 문제 풀이 방법
TOEIC RC 파트는 총 100문제이며 주어진 시간은 75분이다. 학습자에 따라 일부 편차가 있을 수 있지만, Part 5는 10분, Part 6는 8분, 마킹 시간(약 3분)을 제외한 나머지 시간인 54분을 Part 7에 배분하는 것이 적절하다. 빠른 시간에 700점을 달성하기 위해서는 질문 유형별 접근법과 시험장에서 적용해야 할 풀이 전략들을 파트별로 숙지하는 것이 바람직하다.

01 Part 5 문제 풀이 방법   30문항 (배분 시간 10분)

Part 5는 문장 속 빈칸을 채워 넣는 유형으로 총 30문제가 출제된다. RC 파트에는 문제 풀이 방법(directions)을 읽어주는 시간이 없으므로, LC 정답 마킹이 끝난 즉시 바로 RC의 101번 문제부터 순서대로 속도감 있게 풀기 시작한다.

문법 문제 풀이
POINT 1
문법 문제는 빈칸 주변의 단서를 중심으로 접근하면 대부분 정답을 찾을 수 있다. 이때 빈칸의 앞 혹은 뒤만 보고 풀이할 경우 함정에 빠지기 쉬우므로 조심해야 한다.

Mr. Kane was commended for ------- the safety of the museum's collection during last week's storm.
(A) to preserve
(B) preserving
(C) preserve
(D) preservation

[STEP 1] 보기 확인 후 문제 유형 파악하기
보기에 동일한 단어에서 파생된 형태가 나열되어 있으므로 품사 선택 문제임을 알 수 있다.

[STEP 2] 빈칸 앞과 뒤의 단서 파악 후 적합한 품사 선택하기
전치사(for) 뒤에 올 수 있으며 동시에 빈칸 뒤의 명사(the safety)를 목적어로 취할 수 있는 동명사 보기 (B) preserving이 정답이다.

빈칸 앞만 볼 경우: 전치사 뒤에 명사가 올 수 있으므로 오답인 (D) preservation을 고를 수 있다.
빈칸 뒤만 볼 경우: 명사 앞에 동사가 올 수 있으므로 오답인 (C) preserve를 고를 수 있다.

POINT 2
빈칸 주변만을 읽고 정답을 찾을 수 없는 경우에는 주어와 동사를 중심으로 전체 문장 구조를 파악해야 한다.

------- the city approves the permits, construction at the site on 97th Street will remain suspended.
(A) Soon
(B) Until
(C) Even
(D) With

[STEP 1] 보기 확인 후 문제 유형 파악하기
접속사, 전치사, 부사가 함께 보기에 있는 경우 문장 전체의 구조를 파악해야 하는 문제이다.

[STEP 2] 전체 문장 구조 확인 후 적합한 품사 선택하기
빈칸 뒤에 '주어 + 동사 ~'의 구조가 2개가 있으므로 접속사가 필요한 문장이다. 따라서 보기 중 유일한 접속사인 (B) Until이 정답이다.

어휘 문제 풀이
POINT 1
어휘 문제는 빈칸 주변의 단서를 중심으로 해석하여 정답을 찾을 수 있는 경우가 많다.

> Despite increased competition in the industry, the Nova S phone maintained ------- sales throughout the year.
> (A) renewable
> **(B) steady**
> (C) correct
> (D) final

[STEP 1] 보기 확인 후 문제 유형 파악하기
보기에 서로 다른 의미의 단어가 나열된 경우 어휘 문제임을 알 수 있다.

[STEP 2] 빈칸 주변을 중심으로 해석한 후 적합한 단어 선택하기
'일년 내내 ~한 매출을 유지하다'에 의미상 적합한 형용사인 (B) steady(꾸준한)를 정답으로 선택한다.

POINT 2
빈칸 주변만을 읽고 정답을 찾을 수 없는 경우에는 전체 문장을 해석하여 문제를 푼다.

> Due to the sensitive nature of the company's work, Bio Labs ------- controls entry to its facilities.
> (A) tensely
> **(B) strictly**
> (C) hardly
> (D) merely

→ '회사 업무의 민감한 성격으로 인해 시설 출입을 ~하게 통제한다'에 의미상 적합한 부사는 '엄격하게'를 뜻하는 (B) strictly이다.

🚀 PART 5 빠른 700⁺점 달성 TIP
1. Part 5에 등장하는 문법의 유형은 정해져 있다. 따라서 출제 유형과 유형별 문제풀이 방법을 정리해 두는 것이 문제를 빠르고 정확하게 풀기 위해 매우 중요하다.
2. 속도감 있게 문제를 푸는 것이 중요하다. 시간 안배가 매우 중요한 파트로서 막히는 문제가 있을 경우 오래 고민하지 말고 과감하게 정답을 선택해야 Part 6, 7을 위한 풀이 시간을 충분히 확보할 수 있다.

02 Part 6 문제 풀이 방법 [16문항 (배분 시간 8분)]

Part 6는 독해 지문 속의 빈칸을 완성하는 유형으로 총 4개의 지문이 등장하며 지문당 4문제가 출제된다.

POINT 1. 문법 문제 풀이

시제와 대명사 문제를 제외한 문법 문제는 대부분 문맥을 볼 필요 없이 빈칸이 속한 문장만 보면 되며 Part 5와 동일한 방법으로 풀이하면 된다.

> Interest in the film has grown among younger audience members through social media. Several popular online blogs ------ recommended the movie and its exploration of issues faced by the younger generation.
> (A) strong
> (B) strengthen
> (C) stronger
> **(D) strongly**

→ 문장의 주어와 동사 사이에 위치한 빈칸은 동사를 수식할 부사 자리이므로 (D) strongly가 정답이다.

POINT 2. 어휘 문제 풀이

빈칸 주변을 중심으로 해석하여 정답을 찾으며 해당 문장만으로 정답을 찾을 수 없는 경우에는 문맥 속에서 단서를 찾아야 한다. 이때, 첫 번째 문장은 문맥 파악을 위해 가장 중요하므로 반드시 읽어야 한다.

> Dear Ms. Jackson,
>
> We at the Irving Public Library thank you for your donation of $5,000 to the general fund. Your support will allow us to purchase more books for our patrons to read. We at the library constantly strive to improve our collection so that future generations can appreciate the gift of reading.
>
> Enclosed please find the plans for the new wing we intend to build next year. It is designed to hold thousands of books and will also contain an A/V room and several meeting rooms. Should you decide to ------ the construction of one of these rooms, we will name it after you.
>
> Regards,
>
> Janet Mason
> Irving Public Library
>
> (A) research
> (B) organize
> (C) apply
> **(D) fund**

[STEP 1] 첫 번째 문장 읽기
수신인(Ms. Jackson)이 도서관의 후원자라는 사실을 파악할 수 있다.

[STEP 2] 빈칸 문장 중심으로 해석한 후 적합한 단어 선택하기
해당 문장의 these rooms는 앞 문장에 있는 회의실(meeting rooms)을 지칭하는데, 수신인이 도서관의 후원자이므로, 회의실 공사와 관련하여 '자금을 대다'라는 의미인 (D) fund가 정답이다.

POINT 3. 빈칸에 알맞은 문장 넣기 풀이

빈칸 앞과 뒤 문장을 읽으며 가장 자연스럽게 어울리는 문장을 찾는다. 보기에 접속부사나 대명사가 있는 경우 이에 유의하여 논리를 파악한다.

> I know that your store's policy is that no books are permitted to be returned to the store if their plastic covering has been removed.
>
> ——. I bought a book for my class but then dropped it the following day. I therefore no longer require the textbook.
>
> (A) Please inform me of how much I owe for the purchase I made.
> (B) I am writing to let you know that I already received it.
> (C) This policy has been extremely helpful to me in the past.
> **(D) Nevertheless, I hope you will make an exception in my case.**

[STEP 1] 앞 뒤 문장 해석하기
앞 문장에서 반품이 허용되지 않는 정책을 알고 있다는 내용을, 뒤 문장에서 자신이 구입한 책이 필요 없게 되었다는 내용을 파악한다.

[STEP 2] 빈칸에 논리적으로 가장 적합한 문장 선택하기
Nevertheless(그럼에도 불구하고)와 함께 자신의 경우를 예외로 해 주기를 바란다는 의미의 (D)가 문맥상 가장 적합하다.

✈ PART 6 빠른 700⁺점 달성 TIP

1. 첫 번째 문장에 단서가 많이 등장하므로 첫 문장은 반드시 확인해야 한다.
2. 빈칸 문장만 읽어서는 정답이 보이지 않는 경우가 많다. 하지만 대부분 바로 앞/뒤 문장에서 단서를 찾을 수 있다는 점을 기억한다.

03 Part 7 문제 풀이 방법 `54문항 (배분 시간 54분)`

총 10개의 단일 지문이 출제되며 관련된 여러 지문의 관계를 파악해서 풀이하는 이중 및 삼중 지문이 각각 2개, 3개가 출제된다. **빠르게 필요한 정보를 찾아내는 것이 중요한 파트**로서, 주로 출제되는 지문의 종류로는 e-mail, letter, memo, notice, article, advertisement, online chat discussion, text message chain 등이 있다.

POINT 1. 단일 지문 문제 풀이

단일 지문은 지문당 2~4문제가 출제되며 주제 및 목적, 세부 사항, 진위 확인 유형 등이 주를 이룬다. 질문 혹은 보기의 키워드가 본문에서 주로 재표현(paraphrasing)된다는 점에 유의하여 문제를 푼다.

> **Sun Jet Airlines**
>
> Thank you for flying with Sun Jet Airlines. We greatly value the feedback of our passengers, as it helps us to continually improve our services. Please complete this short survey and give it to a flight attendant before disembarking from the airplane.
>
> **What did you think of your flight with Sun Jet Airlines?**

Please mark an 'X' for each category:

	Excellent	Satisfactory	Needs Improvement
Check-in Process			X
Airplane Amenities	X		
Airplane Cleanliness	X		
Crew Politeness	X		

Q. What are passengers asked to do?

  (A) Suggest new airline destinations
  (B) Ask a flight attendant about amenities
  (C) Hand over a completed survey
  (D) Enter a competition

[STEP 1] 질문에서 의문사 및 키워드 파악하기
의문사 What과 키워드 'asked to do'를 파악한다. 요청 사항을 묻는 문제임을 알 수 있다.

[STEP 2] 본문 중 관련 내용 찾기
요청 사항이 언급된 문장 'Please complete this short survey and give it to ~'에서 단서를 찾는다.

[STEP 3] 적절한 정답 선택하기
본문의 give it to를 hand over로 재표현(paraphrasing)한 (C)를 정답으로 선택한다.

POINT 2. 다중 지문 문제 풀이

이중 지문(두 개의 지문이 한 세트)에서는 두 지문을 연계한 문제가 1~2문제 정도 출제되며, 삼중 지문(세 개의 지문이 한 세트)에서는 보통 2개의 연계 문제가 출제된다. 표의 항목이나 지문의 여러 고유 명사가 보기에 등장할 경우 두 지문을 연계한 문제일 확률이 높다. 또한, 질문에 most likely, probably, implied/suggested 등의 표현이 있는 경우 연계 문제일 확률이 높다.

Admissions Department
Callahan Technology Institute
1819 Oakmound Road
Chicago, IL 60628

To Whom It May Concern:

I am interested in registering for a class on PhotoAce Software. I want to start my own photography blog, and I think this will be useful in making changes to my photos. I have read excellent reviews about the program, and I know that national magazines like Nature Monthly and Artist's Corner use it. I also think it will help me save a lot of time and get more things done. Additionally, I like the fact that I can just use my regular mouse with the program and I don't have to buy a digital drawing tablet or anything like that.

I'm wondering if you can recommend a class for me. I have never used any kind of photo editing software before. I'm available all day on Tuesdays, Wednesdays, and Thursdays for the entire duration of the term.

Please give me a call at 555-3909 at your earliest convenience so we can discuss this further. Thank you in advance for your help.

Sincerely,
Alice McKee

Fall Class Schedule: PhotoAce Software			
Class	Instructor	Day / Start Time	Level
PA121	Clarence Knudson	Monday / 10:00A.M.	Basic
PA341	Jason Bishop	Monday / 10:30 A.M.	Advanced
PA122	Ann Phelps	Tuesday / 9:00 A.M.	Basic
PA251	Shoshana Lira	Tuesday / 11:00 A.M.	Intermediate

→ 각 지문의 첫 부분을 읽으며 두 지문의 관계를 파악한다. 초반부를 읽어보면 첫 지문은 특정 소프트웨어 강좌 수강에 관심이 있는 학생이 쓴 글이고, 두 번째 지문은 해당 소프트웨어의 강좌 일정임을 알 수 있다.

1. What is indicated about PhotoAce? – 연계 문제 아닌 경우
(A) It does not require special equipment.
(B) It is available in more than one language.
(C) It is increasing in popularity among novices.
(D) It is used by professional writers.

[STEP 1] 해당 문제의 단서가 속한 지문 찾기
PhotoAce에 관한 설명은 첫 지문에 언급되어 있으므로 첫 지문에서 단서를 찾는다.
[STEP 2] 본문 중 관련 내용 찾기
첫 단락 마지막 부분에 일반 마우스만 필요하고 드로잉 태블릿 등은 살 필요 없다는 내용에서 (A)가 정답임을 알 수 있다.

2. Which class would be most suitable for Ms. McKee? – 연계 문제인 경우
(A) PA121
(B) PA341
(C) PA122
(D) PA251

[STEP 1] 보기를 통해 연계 문제임을 짐작하기
본문의 표의 항목이 보기에 등장했으므로 연계 문제일 것으로 짐작할 수 있다.
[STEP 2] 두 지문에서 관련 내용 찾기
첫 지문 두 번째 단락에서 사진 편집 소프트웨어 사용 경험이 없다는 사실과 시간이 가능한 요일을 확인하면 두 번째 지문에서 가장 알맞은 강좌는 PA122임을 알 수 있으므로 (C)를 정답으로 선택한다.

✎ PART 7 빠른 700⁺점 달성 TIP

1. Part 7도 문제 유형별 / 지문 유형별 반복되는 출제 유형이 있으므로, **출제 유형과 유형별 풀이 방법을 정리해 두면 문제 풀이 시간을 많이 단축할 수 있다.**
2. Part 7은 질문을 먼저 읽고 지문을 읽어야 한다.
3. 이중 지문과 삼중 지문은 문제를 풀기 전에 가장 먼저 두 지문 간의 관계, 세 지문 간의 관계를 파악하는 것이 중요하다. 지문 간 관계가 파악되면 각 문제의 단서가 몇 번째 지문에 있는지, 연계 문제의 단서는 어디에 있는지 쉽게 파악할 수 있다.

700⁺점 목표라면 과감히 버려도 되는 문제

TOEIC 700점을 목표로 한다면, 일반적으로 LC보다 RC 점수를 올리기가 어려우므로 RC 점수는 300-350점을 목표로 하는 것이 좋다. RC 300-350점을 위해서는 대략적으로 100문제 중 25~30개 정도 틀리면 되는데, 틀려도 목표 점수를 달성하는 데 지장이 없는 고난도 문제가 무엇인지 알아둔다면 풀어서 맞힐 수 있는 문제에 좀 더 집중할 수 있다.

01 Part 5 후반부에 등장하는 어휘 문제

Part 5 후반부(121-130번)에는 과거에 출제되지 않은 새로운 어휘가 보통 1문제 정도 등장하는데 고득점자도 풀기 어려운 높은 난도의 어휘인 경우가 많다. 따라서, 문장 전체를 해석했는데도 정답을 찾을 수 없는 경우라면 더 이상 고민하지 말고 다른 문제로 넘어가는 것이 좋다.

> Overall, sales have been increasing ------ despite rising competition from overseas.
> (A) arguably
> **(B) incrementally**
> (C) instinctively
> (D) mutually

보기가 다소 어려운 어휘들로 구성되어 고난이도 문제임을 짐작할 수 있다. 오랜 시간을 할애하지 않고 다음 문제로 넘어간다.

→ 동사 increase(증가하다)를 수식하기에 적합한 부사인 (B) incrementally(점진적으로)가 정답이다.

02 복합관계대명사, 명사절 접속사 문제

복합관계대명사(whoever, whatever, whichever 등)와 명사절 접속사(who, what, which 등)의 의미 및 용법 구별 문제는 900점 이상의 학습자에게도 결코 쉽지 않은 유형이다. 문장 구조가 잘 보이지 않거나 문장 구조를 파악한 후에도 정답을 찾을 수 없는 경우 다음 문제로 넘어가는 것이 바람직하다.

> The workers are allowed to store food shipments ------ there is empty space.
> (A) whoever
> **(B) wherever**
> (C) whatever
> (D) whichever

보기를 보면 복합관계대명사 문제임을 알 수 있다. 정답이 잘 보이지 않는다면 오랜 시간을 할애하지 않고 다음 문제로 넘어간다.

→ 빈칸 이하의 완전한 문장을 받을 수 있는 복합관계대명사 (B) wherever가 정답이다.

03 Part 7 기사문 (article)

Part 7의 기사문은 어려운 어휘와 표현들이 다수 등장하여 내용 이해가 어려운 경우가 많은데, 특히 172-175번에 등장하는 4문항으로 구성된 기사문은 지문의 길이 또한 만만치 않으므로 다른 지문을 먼저 풀이한 후 시간이 남을 경우 풀이하는 것이 바람직하다. 이중 지문이나 삼중 지문에 기사문이 포함된 경우도 마찬가지로 난도가 대부분 높은 경우에 해당하므로 상대적으로 쉬운 다른 지문을 먼저 풀이하는 것이 좋다.

> It takes great courage to start a business. It is perhaps an even greater challenge to change the direction of a successful business. That's exactly what chef Sue Rodding did when she converted her successful fine dining establishment *The Golden Oyster* into a casual diner serving Asian items with bold new flavor combination alongside assistant chef Trey Barnett. —[2]— Sue even went as far as to hire interior designer Peter Bairstow, who recently received the Albrighton prize for outstanding work in his field. Restaurant patrons have commented on how Peter's vibrant

접속사와 수식어 등으로 인해 문장의 길이가 길며 복잡한 문장 구조로 인해 해석이 쉽지 않다.

street food called *Street Eats*. "I was so inspired by my travels and my love for the region. I just knew it was something I had to do," Sue says. —[1]—

Industry expert Peter Landon feels making such a drastic change is inherently risky. "You are basically starting over. Your previous reputation doesn't count for much and you have to build a new brand up from the ground again," says Mr. Landon. "Loyal customers may dislike the changes and stop visiting your premises." Nevertheless, Ms. Rodding is fully committed to her vision, devising succulent menu

design features have created the feeling of being in a bustling Asian city. —[3]—

So two months after opening, is Ms. Rodding happy with the changes? "Absolutely," she says. "Business is thriving, and we've managed to attract a much younger crowd that may have been put off by the formal setting of *The Golden Oyster*." As for the future, Sue has no plans to stop now, and hopes to open new branches of *Street Eats* in Chicago and New York. —[4]— With the passion and drive Sue clearly possesses, there is no reason why her vision would not be a nationwide success.

> 사람, 회사명, 지역 등의 여러 고유 명사가 등장하여 내용 파악에 오랜 시간이 소요된다.

> PART 5에 등장하지 않는 어려운 어휘 및 표현들(노랑 바탕 표시)이 다수 등장하여 지문 해석을 더욱 어렵게 만든다.

04 Part 7 전체 진위 확인 유형

단일 지문인 경우

'전체 진위 확인 유형'에 해당하는 다음과 같은 질문은 보통 단서가 지문 전반에 흩어져 있는 경우이므로 풀이하는 데 상대적으로 오랜 시간이 소요된다. 따라서 마지막에 풀거나, 풀지 않고 다음 지문으로 넘어가는 것이 좋다.

– What is **suggested[indicated]** in the e-mail? 이메일에서 암시된[언급된] 것은 무엇인가?
– What is **NOT true** about the presentation? 발표에 관해 사실이 아닌 것은 무엇인가?

Press Release

Sampson Enterprises / Further information is available from Denise Irwin at irwind@sampsonent.net.

ARDBROOK (April 5)—Sampson Enterprises has completed all construction on the highly anticipated Everton Shopping Mall. This commercial building houses (D)123 retail units, the majority of which have already been reserved by local businesses and national chains. Colorful artwork adorns the interior walls, and the facility has been fitted with solar panels to reduce the site's carbon footprint.

(B)Each unit comes with its own secure storage area, and (A)lighting and other fixtures are included in the lease price. All units are zoned for retail activities, but potential renters with food service businesses should note that (C)they may be subject to additional licensing requirements.

The convenient location and the spacious parking areas make the Everton Shopping Mall an attractive option for businesses that rely heavily on foot traffic rather than advertising. Those interested in viewing the remaining available units, which come in a range of sizes, are encouraged

① 지문의 첫 문장에서 Everton Shopping Mall의 완공을 알림 (Everton Shopping Mall이 지문의 주제임을 알 수 있다.)

② 두 번째 단락 첫 부분 Each unit(각각의 상점)은 Everton Shopping Mall의 unit을 가리킴.

③ 세 번째 단락 첫 부분에서 The convenient location(편리한 위치)과 the spacious parking areas (넓은 주차 공간)와 같은 Everton Shopping Mall의 장점이 언급됨

to do so. They can be toured by appointment any weekday from 9 A.M. to 5 P.M. Our team is ready to answer any questions you may have. Contact us at 555-8622.

Q. What is mentioned about the Everton Shopping Mall?
(A) There is an extra fee for light fixtures.
(B) It is equipped with security cameras.
(C) Renters may need to obtain further permits.
(D) All the units have been rented out.

> Everton Shopping Mall은 지문의 주제이므로, 관련된 정보가 지문 전반에 흩어져 있다.

'전체 진위 확인 유형'은 다음과 같이 보기 하나 하나의 진위 여부를 지문과 대조해야 정답을 찾을 수 있다.

[STEP 1] 문제 유형 및 키워드 파악하기
Everton Shopping Mall이 지문의 주제임을 파악하고, 보기 내용과 본문을 하나씩 대조한다.

[STEP 2] 보기 (A)의 진위 여부 파악하기
본문의 'lighting and other fixtures are included in the lease price(조명 및 기타 설비는 임대료에 포함된다)' 부분을 통해 (A)가 오답임을 알 수 있다.

[STEP 3] 보기 (B)의 진위 여부 파악하기
본문의 'Each unit comes with its own secure storage area(각 소매 상가는 안전한 보관 창고를 갖추고 있다)'에서 (B)의 security camera가 아닌 secure storage area를 갖추고 있음을 알 수 있다.

[STEP 4] 보기 (C)의 진위 여부 파악하기
본문의 'they may be subject to additional licensing requirements(추가적인 면허 요건이 필요할 수 있다)'에서 (C)가 정답임을 알 수 있다.

[STEP 5] 보기 (D)의 진위 여부 파악하기
본문의 '~ the majority of which have already been reserved(123개의 상가 중 대부분은 이미 예약이 된 상태이다)'에서 (D) 역시 오답임을 알 수 있다.

다중 지문인 경우

이중 지문이나 삼중 지문에서 다음과 같이 지문의 발신자[작성자]/수신자에 관한 진위 확인 문제가 출제될 경우, 2개 이상의 지문 전반을 훑어야 정답의 단서를 찾을 수 있는 경우가 많으므로 다른 문제를 풀고 시간이 남으면 푸는 것이 좋다.

– **What** is **suggested[indicated]** about Mr. Albert? Albert 씨에 관해 암시된[언급된] 것은 무엇인가?

Article & Review

BLOOMINGTON (June 3)—Trystan Electronics, the manufacturer of a bladeless heating/cooling fan, has been successful in seeking damages for patent infringement by Heiser Appliances. A spokesperson for Trystan Electronics said that the developers of Heiser's AirSmart-360 copied the design of the Dual Breeze made by Trystan. The judge overseeing the case ruled that the differences in features between the two devices were not clear enough for consumers to tell them apart. Heiser Appliances was ordered to pay an undisclosed sum to Trystan Electronics as well as stop selling the AirSmart-360 immediately. Customers who purchased the AirSmart-360 thinking that it was the Dual Breeze may be able to return it to Heiser for a refund. See the company's Web site for details.

http://www.heiserappliances.com/catalog/heating_cooling/airsmart360

HOME	ORDER ONLINE	MERCHANDISE	**CUSTOMER REVIEWS**

Category: Heating/Cooling　　Product: AirSmart-360
Reviewer: Diana Bogan　　　　Posted: June 9

I have been using the AirSmart-360 for about six months, and it is a wonderful addition to my home. It does not consume a lot of electricity, so I often use it instead of turning on the central heating system. It doesn't have a lot of small parts, so it can be dusted in just a few seconds, and there's nowhere for the dust to build up. I knew that this device was not the Dual Breeze from Trystan Electronics when I purchased it. Even though they look very similar, the logo is prominently displayed on the box and the device, so I don't understand how people could be confused.

> Diana Bogan은 고객후기 작성자임을 알 수 있다.

Q. What is suggested about Ms. Bogan?
(A) She purchased the AirSmart-360 at a discount.
(B) She thinks the logo on the device is too large.
(C) She does not plan to return her AirSmart-360.
(D) She needs to make a warranty claim on the device.

> Ms. Bogan은 후기 작성자이므로 두 번째 지문 전반에 Ms. Bogan에 관해 정보가 흩어져 있으며, 나머지 한 지문에도 관련 정보가 있을 확률이 높다.

[STEP 1] 문제 유형 및 키워드 파악하기
Ms. Bogan이 후기 작성자임을 파악하고, 보기 내용과 본문을 하나씩 대조한다.

[STEP 2] 첫 번째 지문 내용 파악하기
첫 번째 지문에서 AirSmart-360의 디자인이 Dual Breeze를 모방하여 소비자가 두 제품의 차이점을 구별하기 어렵다는 점과 법원 판결 내용 및 AirSmart-360을 구매한 경우 환불이 가능하다는 내용을 확인한다.

[STEP 3] 두 번째 지문 내용 파악하기
두 번째 지문에서 Bogan 씨는 AirSmart-360의 구매 시점에 Dual Breeze가 아닌 것을 알고 있었으며 두 제품을 혼동하는 이유를 알 수 없다고 적고 있다.

[STEP 4] 두 본문의 내용과 일치하는 보기 선택하기
두 지문의 내용을 연계하면 Bogan 씨가 제품을 환불할 의사가 없음을 유추할 수 있다. 따라서, (C)를 정답으로 선택한다.

RC DAY 02 주어 자리와 동사 자리

BASIC 기본기 익히기

1. 문장의 기본 구조
모든 문장에는 주어와 동사가 필요하다.

The manager agreed. 매니저는 동의했다.
　주어　　　　동사

Mr. Morris accepted the offer. Morris 씨는 제안을 받아들였다.
　주어　　　　동사　　　목적어

2. 주어와 동사의 수 일치
단수 주어에는 단수 동사를, 복수 주어에는 복수 동사를 쓴다.

The list has been sent to Adam Locker. 리스트가 Adam Locker 씨에게 보내졌다.
　단수 주어 단수 동사

The lists have been sent to Adam Locker. 리스트들이 Adam Locker 씨에게 보내졌다.
　복수 주어 복수 동사

3. 동사의 종류
문장의 동사에 따라 동사 뒤에 오는 품사가 달라진다.

The mayor smiles warmly. 시장은 따뜻하게 미소 짓는다.
　주어　　자동사　부사

→ 목적어를 갖지 못하는 자동사(smile) 뒤에 올 수 있는 것은 부사이다.

Ms. Clayton cleaned the office. Clayton 씨는 사무실을 청소했다.
　주어　　　타동사　　목적어

→ 목적어를 가지는 타동사(clean) 뒤에는 목적어 역할을 하는 명사가 온다.

PATTERN 기출 유형 맛보기

Q. Air Pacific ------ its first-class passengers free internet access and a complimentary beverage upon boarding.
(A) to offer
(B) offering
(C) having offered
(D) offers → 빈칸은 주어 뒤 동사 자리이므로 유일한 동사 형태인 (D)가 정답이다.

Air Pacific은 탑승 시 1등석 승객들에게 인터넷 무료 이용과 무료 음료를 제공한다.

출제 경향 토익은 빈칸이 동사 자리인지 아닌지를 묻는 문제를 출제한다. 따라서 문장의 구조를 알아야 하고, 보기에서 동사와 동사가 아닌 것을 구별할 수 있어야 한다.

[이렇게도 출제된다]
- 보기에 동사를 2개 이상 주고 주어의 수(단수/복수)에 어울리는 동사를 고르도록 한다.
- 동사 뒤에 빈칸을 주고 동사와 어울리는 품사가 무엇인지 고르도록 한다.

◆ 출제 포인트 1 주어 자리

매년 7~8문제 출제

주어 자리에는 명사가 위치한다.
<u>The shipment</u> arrived at the dock. 화물이 부두에 도착했다.
　주어(명사)　　　동사

<u>That Mr. Casey declined the offer</u> is disappointing. Casey 씨가 그 제안을 거절한 것은 실망스럽다.
　　주어(명사절)　　　　　　　동사

토익에 출제되는 명사 형태

-tion [-sion]: reserva**tion** 예약	**-ment**: pay**ment** 지불
-ance [-ence]: attend**ance** 참석	**-er [-or]**: lead**er** 선두, 대표
-ist: journal**ist** 저널리스트, 기자	**-ity**: abil**ity** 능력

PRACTICE | 기출 연습하기

1. The (acquisition / acquire) was approved at the board meeting on March 23.
2. (Attendance / Attended) at the AdSense Conference was lower than in previous years.
3. Our (dividing / division) is primarily focused on creating effective marketing campaigns.

◆ 출제 포인트 2 동사의 위치

매년 3~4문제 출제

주어 뒤에는 동사가 위치하며 to부정사나 -ing 형태는 동사가 될 수 없다.
The ferry **operates** from Monday to Friday. 여객선은 월요일부터 금요일까지 운행한다.
　주어　　　동사
　　　　to operate (X)
　　　　operating (X)

[비교] 명령문은 주어 없이 '(Please) + 동사원형'으로 시작한다.
Please bring extra copies of your résumé. 이력서 추가 사본을 가져 오세요.

PRACTICE | 기출 연습하기

1. The senior manager (provided / to provide) a list of qualified candidates.
2. Please (forward / forwarding) my calls to Mr. Kensington while I am away from the office.
3. When making a reservation, first (select / selects) your preferred location from the list.

◆ 출제 포인트 3 동사의 형태

매년 약 3문제 출제

조동사 뒤에는 동사원형이 온다.
Mr. Sanchez **must leave** the office by 3 P.M. Sanchez 씨는 오후 3시까지 사무실을 떠나야 합니다.
　　　　　　조동사 + 동사원형

꼭 기억해야 할 조동사

will/be going to ~할 것이다	can ~할 수 있다	may/might ~일지도 모른다	must ~해야 한다	should ~해야 한다
would ~일 것이다	could ~할 수도 있다			

부정문을 만드는 do[does/did] not 뒤에는 동사원형이 온다.
Kemlane Systems **does not have** an online store. Kemlane Systems는 온라인 상점이 없다.
　　　　　　　　does not + 동사원형

have[has] 뒤에는 p.p.(과거분사)가 와서 현재완료 시제를 나타낸다.
Rose Electronics **has developed** a new mobile phone. Rose Electronics는 새로운 휴대 전화를 개발했다.
　　　　　　　현재완료 (have + p.p.)

PRACTICE | 기출 연습하기

1. All employees should (receive / receives) their new uniforms later today.
2. The budget does not (includes / include) transportation and other incidental expenses.
3. The company has (announce / announced) that Ms. Rider will be promoted to Head Accounting Manager.

◆ 출제 포인트 4 주어와 동사의 수 일치

매년 2~3문제 출제

be동사는 시제와 주어의 수에 따라 형태가 달라진다.
The promotional program **was** so successful. 홍보 프로그램은 매우 성공적이었다.
　　　　3인칭 단수 주어

인칭과 수, 시제에 따른 be동사의 변화

	1인칭 단수/복수	2인칭 단수/복수	3인칭 단수/복수
현재	am/are	are/are	is/are
과거	was/were	were/were	was/were

일반 동사는 주어가 3인칭 단수인 경우 현재 시제 동사에 -(e)s를 붙인다. 현재완료 시제는 'has+p.p.'로 나타낸다.
Mr. Nichols **oversees** the marketing department. Nichols 씨는 마케팅 부서를 감독한다.
3인칭 단수 주어

The managers of the hotel **meet** with the staff regularly. 그 호텔의 매니저들은 직원들과 정기적으로 만난다.
　복수 주어

The demand **has increased** considerably over the past year. 수요가 지난 1년간 상당히 증가했다.
3인칭 단수 주어

PRACTICE | 기출 연습하기

1. Until it went bankrupt, K-Textiles (offer / offered) fabrics from around the world.
2. The engineering plans for the project (expects / are expected) to be submitted by February.
3. (Tourism / Tourists) in Havana, Cuba, has decreased considerably since the hurricane.

◆ 출제 포인트 5   수 일치의 예외

매년 1~2문제 출제

주장/요구/제안 동사 혹은 의무/필수 형용사 뒤의 that절에는 '(should) + 동사원형'이 온다.

The director **asks** that Mr. Brehm **(should) meet** the deadline. 이사는 Brehm 씨에게 마감일을 지켜줄 것을 요청한다.
　　　　　'요구' 동사

It is **critical** that the product **(should) be** shipped tomorrow. 상품이 내일 발송되는 것이 중요하다.
　　'필수' 형용사

'(should) + 동사원형' 구문을 이끄는 동사와 형용사

| 동사 | ask 요청하다 | request 요구하다 | suggest 제안하다 | recommend 권고하다 | insist 주장하다 |
| 형용사 | vital 필수적인 | essential 필수적인 | critical 필수적인 | important 중요한 | imperative 반드시 해야 하는 |

PRACTICE | 기출 연습하기

1. We request that every participant (meets / meet) in the lobby at 8 A.M.
2. SemCo recommends that vacuum filters (were changed / be changed) once a year.
3. It is (actual / critical) that new employees be present at the upcoming training seminar.

◆ 출제 포인트 6   1형식 문장과 출제 유형

매년 4~5문제 출제

1형식 문장은 '주어 + 동사'의 구조이며 뒤에 동사를 수식하는 부사(구)가 오기도 한다.

Ms. Moore works diligently. Moore 씨는 부지런히 일한다.
주어　　동사　　부사

We will travel to Madrid next month. 우리는 다음 달에 마드리드로 여행을 갈 것이다.
주어　동사　　부사구　　　부사구

꼭 기억해야 할 1형식 동사

work 일하다	differ 다르다	arrive 도착하다	rise 상승하다
expire 만료되다	proceed 진행되다	travel 여행하다	function 작동되다
act 행동하다	behave 처신[행동]하다	shop 쇼핑하다	respond 반응하다

PRACTICE | 기출 연습하기

1. The HR team typically responds (prompt / promptly) to staff inquiries.
2. Local companies should act (responsibilities / responsibly) to protect the environment.
3. Actual color may (differ / calculate) slightly from the images presented online.

◆ 출제 포인트 7 2형식 문장과 출제 유형

매년 8~9문제 출제

2형식 문장은 '주어 + 동사 + 주격 보어(형용사 혹은 명사)'의 구조이다.

The design of the website is attractive. 웹사이트의 디자인이 매력적이다.
　　주어　　　　　　　　동사　주격 보어

The island has become a popular destination. 그 섬은 인기 있는 여행지가 되었다.
　주어　　　동사　　　　주격 보어

→ 주격 보어가 명사인 경우 주어와 동격을 이룬다. (The island = a popular destination)

꼭 기억해야 할 2형식 동사!

| be ~이다 | become ~이 되다 | remain 여전히 ~이다 | seem(=appear) ~인 것 같다 | prove ~로 증명되다 |

PRACTICE | 기출 연습하기

1. Unfortunately, it is (necessary / necessarily) to delay the speech until 2 P.M.
2. If shipping problems become more (frequent / frequency), customer complaints will likely increase.
3. Staffing Solutions guarantees that all personal information collected will remain (confidential / confidentially).

◆ 출제 포인트 8 3형식 문장과 출제 유형

매년 14~15문제 출제

3형식 문장은 '주어 + 동사 + 목적어'의 구조이다.

The company hired additional workers last week. 그 회사는 지난주에 추가 직원을 고용했다.
　주어　　　동사　　　목적어

The government will resume the construction of the library. 정부는 도서관 건설을 재개할 것이다.
　주어　　　　　동사　　　　　　목적어

cf.) Normal service will resume shortly. 정상 서비스가 곧 재개될 것이다.
　　　주어　　　동사　　부사

→ 하나의 동사(resume)가 자동사와 타동사 모두로 쓰일 수 있다.

PRACTICE | 기출 연습하기

1. Helping House provides (assisted / assistance) to families struggling to meet basic needs.
2. Please review your résumé (careful / carefully) before submitting it for consideration.
3. Cooper Marx cannot (attend / arrive) tomorrow's meeting due to a conflicting appointment.

◆ 출제 포인트 9 4형식 문장과 출제 유형

매년 약 1문제 출제

4형식 문장은 '주어 + 동사 + 간접목적어(~에게) + 직접목적어(~을[를])'의 구조이다.
<u>The store</u> <u>will offer</u> <u>its employees</u> <u>cash incentives</u>. 그 상점은 직원들에게 현금 인센티브를 제공할 것이다.
　주어　　　동사　　　　간접목적어　　　직접목적어

4형식 문장은 3형식 문장으로 전환 가능하다.
[4형식]　<u>The department</u> <u>will send</u> <u>you</u> <u>a security manual</u>. 그 부서가 당신에게 보안 매뉴얼을 보내 드릴 겁니다.
　　　　　　주어　　　　　동사　　간접목적어　　직접목적어

[3형식]　<u>The department</u> <u>will send</u> <u>a security manual</u> <u>(to you)</u>.
　　　　　　주어　　　　　동사　　　　목적어　　　　　부사구

→ 간접목적어를 전치사(주로 to)와 함께 뒤로 보내면 3형식 문장이 된다.

꼭 기억해야 할 4형식 동사

| give 주다 | offer 제공하다 | award 수여하다 | grant 허가하다 | send 보내다 | assign 할당하다 |

PRACTICE | 기출 연습하기

1. To request a refund, please send (we / us) the product and your original receipt.
2. Dr. Xander has offered us (assurance / assuredly) that results will be available soon.
3. The government (implemented / granted) the state the necessary additional agricultural funding.

◆ 출제 포인트 10 5형식 문장과 출제 유형

매년 약 2문제 출제

5형식 문장은 '주어 + 동사 + 목적어 + 목적격 보어(형용사 혹은 명사)'의 구조이다.
<u>Most students</u> <u>find</u> <u>Ms. Ryan's lectures</u> <u>informative</u>. 대부분의 학생들은 Ryan 씨의 강의가 유익하다고 생각한다.
　　주어　　　　동사　　　목적어　　　　목적격 보어

<u>The degree</u> <u>will make</u> <u>you</u> <u>an ideal candidate for the position</u>. 학위는 당신을 그 직책에 이상적인 지원자로 만들 것이다.
　주어　　　동사　　목적어　　　　　목적격 보어

→ 목적격 보어가 명사인 경우 목적어와 동격을 이룬다. (you = an ideal candidate for the position)

꼭 기억해야 할 5형식 동사

| make ~을 -하게 만들다 | find ~을 -라고 생각하다 | consider ~을 -라고 간주하다 | keep ~을 -한 상태로 유지시키다 |

PRACTICE | 기출 연습하기

1. PlayMore makes its toys (educational / educationally) and fun at the same time.
2. First Bank recommends not sharing your password to keep your account (secure / securely).
3. A survey shows that about 75% of subscribers (find / feel) the layout of *Travel Digest* appealing.

RC | DAY 02 실전문제

1. The spending report ------- a summary of all expenses paid with company credit cards.
   (A) contain
   (B) containing
   (C) to contain
   (D) contains

2. Given her skills in event planning, management ------- to put Peggy Lane in charge of organizing the benefit.
   (A) to decide
   (B) decision
   (C) deciding
   (D) decided

3. Winners of the New Taste Award have ------- Merle's Café in Burbank and Choptastic in Los Angeles.
   (A) including
   (B) include
   (C) includes
   (D) included

4. Marks, Inc., provides employees with soundproof rooms for making telephone calls so other employees can ------- on their work.
   (A) to focus
   (B) focuses
   (C) focus
   (D) focusing

5. ------- to the special event have been extended to all members of the Dallas Museum of Art.
   (A) Invitations
   (B) Invited
   (C) Invites
   (D) Invitation

6. To assemble the Wonderguard bookshelf, ------- the provided tools to attach the shelves to the frame.
   (A) to use
   (B) useful
   (C) use
   (D) using

7. The customer service department mostly deals with complaints, so representatives are excited when they receive -------.
   (A) compliments
   (B) complimentarily
   (C) complimented
   (D) complimentary

8. Unless customers choose automatic renewal, subscriptions to *World Business and Market Reporting* ------- after a year.
   (A) expire
   (B) expires
   (C) expiring
   (D) to expire

9. The mayor considers it ------- to launch the clean-energy initiative before this year's election.
   (A) necessity
   (B) necessary
   (C) necessitate
   (D) necessarily

10. The highway has been reduced to two lanes due to construction, so drivers should proceed -------.
    (A) cautioning
    (B) cautious
    (C) cautiously
    (D) cautioned

11. Studies show that consumer preferences are more ------- with the use of the data analysis software.
    (A) predict
    (B) prediction
    (C) predictable
    (D) predictably

12. The head of the firm appeared ------- to the terms of the merger but has not yet made a decision.
    (A) agreement
    (B) agreeable
    (C) agree
    (D) agrees

13. According to a recent survey, more than 20% of the company's employees do not ------- proper safety procedures.
    (A) following
    (B) followed
    (C) follow
    (D) followingly

14. Now that the computer system works -------, the company can operate more efficiently than ever.
    (A) perfect
    (B) perfection
    (C) perfected
    (D) perfectly

15. Mr. Ulysses believes offering lower interest rates will make our loans more ------- to business owners.
    (A) attracted
    (B) attractive
    (C) attractively
    (D) attraction

16. It is ------- that this form be filled out completely and accurately before seeing a doctor.
    (A) persuasive
    (B) imperative
    (C) authoritative
    (D) disruptive

Questions 17-20 refer to the following Web page.

---

www.yogibutter.com

Since its inception, Yogi Butter has been producing cosmetics free from ---17--- ingredients or chemicals. Our loyal customers are what have transformed us into one of the largest companies in the industry, which is why we want to say thank you. We hope to show our gratitude with a series of special giveaways, which will begin next month. Also, if you have not yet done so, ---18--- sure to sign up for our existing rewards program. Members can accrue 10 points for every $10 spent. These will ---19--- be added to your account and can be used for any future purchase. ---20---.

---

17. (A) illegible
    (B) artificial
    (C) fragile
    (D) finite

18. (A) have made
    (B) to make
    (C) making
    (D) make

19. (A) voluntarily
    (B) progressively
    (C) considerably
    (D) automatically

20. (A) Other cosmetics companies often use harsh chemicals.
    (B) Our spring line will be available for purchase next week.
    (C) Sign up now online or visit one of our stores to register for free.
    (D) Purchases of more than $100 are eligible for complimentary shipping.

RC DAY 03   태 / 시제 / 가정법

BASIC 기본기 익히기

1. 능동태와 수동태의 의미

능동태 문장은 주어가 행위의 주체가 되어 주어가 '~하다'의 의미를 갖는다.
The management **examined** the new plan. 경영진은 새로운 계획을 검토했다.
      주어   동사   목적어

수동태 문장은 주어가 행위의 대상이 되어 주어가 '~되다'의 의미를 갖는다.
The new plan **was examined** by the management. 새로운 계획이 경영진에 의해 검토되었다.
   주어   동사

2. 기본 3시제 (현재, 과거, 미래)

	형태 및 의미	예문
현재	동사원형 (~한다)	We often **travel** to India. 우리는 종종 인도로 여행을 간다.
과거	동사원형 + (e)d (~했다)	We **traveled** to India last year. 우리는 작년에 인도로 여행을 갔다.
미래	will + 동사원형 (~할 것이다)	We **will travel** to India next year. 우리는 내년에 인도로 여행을 갈 것이다.

* 현재 시제는 주어가 3인칭 단수인 경우 「동사원형 + (e)s」의 형태를 사용한다.

3. 주요 시제 별 수동태 형태

현재 수동	The equipment **is checked** regularly.	장비는 정기적으로 점검된다.
과거 수동	The equipment **was checked**.	장비는 점검되었다.
미래 수동	The equipment **will be checked**.	장비는 점검될 것이다.
현재완료 수동	The equipment **has been checked**.	장비는 점검이 완료되었다.
현재진행 수동	The equipment **is being checked**.	장비는 점검되는 중이다.

PATTERN 기출 유형 맛보기

Q. Dr. Jeremy Dougal ------ the latest medical advances in eyewear technology next Friday.
(A) had discussed
(B) will be discussing → next Friday(다음 주 금요일)는 미래를 나타내고, 의미상 주어와 동사의 관계가 능동이므로
(C) will be discussed   미래 시제 능동태인 (B)가 정답이다.
(D) was discussing
Jeremy Dougal 박사는 다음 주 금요일에 안경 기술의 최근 의학 발전에 대해 논의할 예정입니다.

출제 경향 동사 자리가 빈칸인 경우, 여러 개의 동사 보기 중 시제와 태가 적합한 동사를 선택하는 문제가 출제된다. 문장에 사용된 시간 부사를 적절히 활용할 줄 알아야 하며, 주어와 동사의 의미 관계에 따라 능동/수동을 구별할 수 있어야 한다.

[이렇게도 출제된다]
• 시간 부사절과 주절의 시간 관계를 파악하여 적절한 시제의 동사를 선택하는 문제가 출제된다.
• 문장에 동사를 제시한 후, 해당 동사의 시제와 어울리는 부사 어휘를 선택하는 문제가 출제된다.

◆ 출제 포인트 1   능동태와 수동태 구별

매년 약 14문제 출제

능동태는 주어가 '~하다'는 의미이며 목적어를 갖는다.
Mr. Taylor **will inspect** the building.   Taylor 씨가 건물을 점검할 것이다.
　　　　　 능동태　　　목적어

수동태는 주어가 '~되다/당하다'의 의미이며 목적어를 갖지 않는다.
The package **was delivered** to the office.   소포가 사무실로 배달되었다.
　　　　　　수동태(be + p.p.)　전치사구

자동사는 목적어를 가지지 않으므로 수동태로 쓸 수 없고 능동태만 가능하다.
The project **proceeded** quickly.   프로젝트는 빠르게 진행되었다.
　　　　　　능동태

PRACTICE | 기출 연습하기

1. Strong storms (were forced / forced) Valley Resort to close its swimming pools until the weather cleared.
2. Erin Carter's works have been (displaying / displayed) in museums and galleries around the world.
3. The first act of the play was (followed / proceeded) by a 15-minute intermission.

◆ 출제 포인트 2   감정 동사의 태 구별

매년 1~2문제 출제

감정 동사의 능동태는 주어가 '~한 감정을 느끼게 만들다'의 의미이다.
The topic will surely **interest** you.   그 주제는 분명 당신을 흥미롭게 할 것이다.
　　　　　　　　　　　능동태

감정 동사의 수동태는 주어가 '~한 감정을 느끼다'의 의미이다.
I **am interested** in joining the tour.   저는 관광 참여에 관심이 있습니다.
　　수동태

We **are pleased** to invite you to the dinner.   우리는 당신을 저녁 식사에 초대하게 되어 기쁩니다.
　　수동태　　　감정의 원인

→ 감정의 원인은 주로 to부정사, 전치사구 혹은 that절로 표현한다.

토익에 출제되는 감정 동사

| please 기쁘게 하다 | excite 흥분시키다 | delight 즐겁게 하다. | satisfy 만족시키다 |
| disappoint 실망시키다 | interest 흥미를 일으키다 | fascinate 매혹하다 | frustrate 좌절시키다 |

PRACTICE | 기출 연습하기

1. Ms. Chen reported that she is (satisfying / satisfied) with the tires we installed.
2. We are very (pleased / pleasing) that you have agreed to speak at this year's conference.
3. Henderson Corp. is (exciting / excited) to announce the opening of a new branch.

◆ 출제 포인트 3　현재 시제

매년 2~3문제 출제

현재 시제는 일반적·반복[습관]적인 사실을 나타낸다.
The center **regularly holds** seminars for residents.　그 센터는 주민들을 위해 정기적으로 세미나를 개최한다.

토익에 출제되는 현재 시제와 어울리는 부사

| frequently(=often) 자주, 종종 | occasionally 때때로 | regularly 정기적으로 | routinely 일상적으로 |
| typically 전형적으로 | normally 일반적으로 | usually 주로 | periodically 주기적으로 | every year[month] 매년[월] |

시간/조건의 부사절에서는 미래 시제 대신 현재 시제를 사용한다.
Jason Cain will take over as president **when Kelly Friel retires** next month.
　　　　　　　　　　　　　　　　　　　　　　　　　　시간 부사절
Kelly Friel 씨가 다음 달에 은퇴하면 Jason Cain 씨가 회장직을 이어받을 것이다.

If the weather is nice tomorrow, Ms. Mathis will attend the picnic.　내일 날씨가 좋다면, Mathis 씨는 소풍에 참석할 것이다.
　　　　조건 부사절

토익에 출제되는 시간/조건 부사절 접속사

| when ~할 때 | while ~하는 동안 | before ~하기 전에 | after ~한 후에 | until ~할 때까지 |
| by the time ~할 때 쯤에는 | once 일단 ~하면 | as soon as ~하자마자 | if ~라면 | unless ~하지 않는다면 |

PRACTICE | 기출 연습하기

1. The department (enormously / frequently) checks that all fire alarms are working properly.
2. Mr. Moodly will review the proposal when he (returns / returned) this afternoon.
3. The museum (previously / occasionally) offers private viewings of the collection to members.

◆ 출제 포인트 4　과거 시제 / 미래 시제

매년 4~5문제 출제

과거 시제는 과거의 행위나 상태를 나타내며 last(지난), yesterday(어제), ago(~전에) 등과 어울린다.
We **launched** the new software **last week**.　우리는 지난주에 새 소프트웨어를 출시했다.

미래 시제는 미래에 예정된 일 혹은 예측을 나타내며 next(다음), tomorrow(내일) 등과 어울린다.
The winner of the prize **will be announced next week**.　수상자는 다음 주에 발표될 것이다.

PRACTICE | 기출 연습하기

1. A new accountant (will be recruited / were recruited) through an employment agency next month.
2. Last week, Ms. Pitt (has decided / decided) we need to focus on the online campaign.
3. Mr. Oswald (had been studied / studied) American politics years ago while at New York University.

◆ 출제 포인트 5　완료 시제

매년 약 2문제 출제

현재완료 시제(have + p.p.)는 이미 완료되거나 과거의 한 시점부터 현재까지 지속되는 행위나 상태를 나타낸다.
A projector **has already been set up** in the meeting room.　회의실에 프로젝터가 이미 설치되어 있습니다.
Mr. Lanner **has been** a senior manager **for 10 years**.　Lanner 씨는 10년동안 선임 매니저로 있다.

🚀 빠른 700⁺점 달성 TIP

현재완료 진행 시제는 현재까지 지속되는 행위나 상태만을 의미한다.
Ms. Horvath **has been working** at the bank for two years. Horvath 씨는 2년 동안 그 은행에서 일해 왔다.
= has worked

토익에 출제되는 현재완료와 어울리는 표현

| over[for/in/during] the last[past] + 기간 지난 ~동안 | for + 기간 ~동안 | since + 과거 시점 ~이래로 | lately 최근에 |

과거완료 시제(had + p.p.)는 과거의 특정 사건보다 더 이전에 발생한 사건을 나타낸다.
The presentation **had begun** before Ms. Garcia **arrived**. 발표는 Garcia 씨가 도착하기 전에 시작되었다.
　　　　　　　　과거완료 (과거보다 이전)　　　　　　　　　　과거
= The presentation **began** before Ms. Garcia **arrived**.
→ before/after가 두 절을 연결하는 경우 시간의 전후 관계가 명백하므로 완료 시제를 사용하지 않아도 된다.

미래완료 시제(will have + p.p.)는 미래의 특정 사건보다 더 이전에 발생할 사건을 나타낸다.
By the time the manager **returns** next week, the project **will have been completed**.
　　　　　　　　　　　　　　　　　　미래　　　　　　　　　　　　　　　　미래완료 (미래보다 이전)
다음 주에 매니저가 돌아올 때쯤에는, 프로젝트가 종료되었을 것이다.

PRACTICE | 기출 연습하기

1. Apple Vineyard (is offering / has been offering) free wine tastings for the past 10 years.
2. Since the collapse of the bridge, Mayor Muller (has considered / will consider) road safety an important issue.
3. By the time the world-famous musician arrived, more than 100 fans (will gather / had gathered).

◆ 출제 포인트 6 가정법

매년 약 1문제 출제

가정법 미래는 가능성이 희박한 미래의 상황을 가정할 때 사용한다.
If you **should cancel** the reservation, you **will not get** a refund. 만약 예약을 취소하시면 환불을 받으실 수 없습니다.
　　　should + 동사원형　　　　　　　　　미래(will/can/may 등)
= Should you cancel the reservation, you will not get a refund. (If가 생략될 경우 주어와 조동사의 위치가 바뀐다.)

가정법 과거는 현재 사실과 반대의 상황을 가정할 때 사용한다.
If I **were** Mr. Brown, I **would accept** the job offer. 내가 만약 Brown 씨라면 그 일자리 제의를 받아들일 텐데.
　　　과거　　　　　　　would/could + 동사원형

가정법 과거완료는 과거 사실과 반대의 상황을 가정할 때 사용한다.
If we **had been given** more time, the project **could have been** successful.
　　　　과거완료　　　　　　　　　　　　　　　would/could + have + p.p.
만약 우리에게 더 많은 시간이 주어졌더라면, 그 프로젝트는 성공할 수 있었을 텐데.

PRACTICE | 기출 연습하기

1. If the city had approved the permit earlier, construction (has resumed / would have resumed) already.
2. (Should / When) the itinerary change, Trip Asia will contact you immediately.
3. If we had delayed the event, guests (had been choosing / could have chosen) not to attend.

RC DAY 03 실전문제

1. In preparation for President Manuel Rodriguez's appearance, metal detectors ------- at all of the building's entrances.
   (A) will install
   (B) are installing
   (C) will be installed
   (D) to install

2. Starting next month, we ------- classes on organic gardening on Tuesdays and Thursdays at noon.
   (A) were offered
   (B) offering
   (C) will offer
   (D) offered

3. The brochure ------- interest in the apartments available for rent on Charleston Avenue.
   (A) generate
   (B) generating
   (C) is generated
   (D) has generated

4. Due to numerous cases of food-related illnesses, Café 29 ------- by the health department.
   (A) inspection
   (B) is being inspected
   (C) were inspecting
   (D) inspector

5. The TM-860 ------- to consumers as a laptop that is both high-tech and affordable.
   (A) has promoted
   (B) has been promoted
   (C) was promoting
   (D) has been promoting

6. If the musical band is ------- with the offer, the contract dispute should be resolved soon.
   (A) pleased
   (B) pleasant
   (C) pleasing
   (D) pleasure

7. The plant ------- the revised safety protocols last year, but some employees are still not familiar with them.
   (A) implementation
   (B) implements
   (C) implemented
   (D) was implemented

8. The representatives at Darwin, Inc., are ------- to customer needs regardless of the time of day.
   (A) responsive
   (B) responsively
   (C) responder
   (D) responded

9. Before the machine ------- the analysis of the sample, it will make a series of short sounds.
   (A) began
   (B) begins
   (C) to begin
   (D) begin

10. Tourists ------- travel to the traditional markets to find cheap souvenirs and unique local foods.
    (A) shortly
    (B) rather
    (C) formerly
    (D) often

11. In the last few years, retailers ------- offering more merchandise available only for purchase online.
    (A) will begin
    (B) have begun
    (C) will have begun
    (D) to begin

12. If Keith Rider ------- two more cars by Saturday, he will have the highest sales of the month.
    (A) will sell
    (B) to sell
    (C) sells
    (D) sell

13. If Parkston Labs had not developed a drug with fewer side effects, another company ------- so eventually.
    (A) should do
    (B) will be doing
    (C) has done
    (D) would have done

14. Thanks to generous donors, the doctors at First Care Hospital ------- attend medical conferences across the country.
    (A) recently
    (B) regularly
    (C) quickly
    (D) brightly

15. By the time Ms. Walker arrives this afternoon, we ------- the necessary repairs on her device.
    (A) will have completed
    (B) is completing
    (C) completed
    (D) completes

16. Please note that only successful candidates ------- by Human Resources by next Wednesday.
    (A) would contact
    (B) will contact
    (C) will be contacted
    (D) have been contacted

Questions 17-20 refer to the following announcement.

Alice Seon's Communications Seminar

Alice Seon is a well-known -------(17)------- on crisis management and media strategies. She -------(18)------- as Director of Public Relations at Kilowatt Films for 15 years. In January, Ms. Seon will be holding a communications seminar designed to help others use the knowledge she has accumulated. During the event, she will help participants understand essential concepts by using innovative instructional techniques. -------(19)-------. As a result, seminar attendees will gain valuable practice that they can apply at the office. Due to high demand, spots for the sessions on January 2 and 3 have already filled up. -------(20)-------, some spaces are still available on January 4 and 5.

17. (A) authorizes
    (B) authorizing
    (C) authorize
    (D) authority

18. (A) had been serving
    (B) will serve
    (C) has served
    (D) serves

19. (A) Since leaving Kilowatt Films, she has been working as a consultant.
    (B) Ms. Seon was recently given an honorary degree from Boston University.
    (C) One will be to practice problem-solving by presenting real situations.
    (D) Each session will last for three hours with two 15-minute breaks.

20. (A) Unfortunately
    (B) Specifically
    (C) However
    (D) Consequently

RC | DAY 04   명사

BASIC 기본기 익히기

1. 명사의 정의 및 형태
명사는 사람, 사물 및 추상적인 것을 나타내는 단어로 주로 다음과 같은 형태를 갖는다.

사람	buy**er** 구매자 invest**or** 투자자 applic**ant** 지원자 cli**ent** 고객 employ**ee** 직원
사물	equipm**ent** 장비 facil**ity** 시설 resid**ence** 주택
추상적인 것	promot**ion** 홍보 decis**ion** 결정 happin**ess** 행복 leng**th** 길이 tour**ism** 관광 사업

2. 가산 명사와 불가산 명사
가산 명사는 단수는 a/an와 함께 쓸 수 있고, 복수는 -(e)s 형태로 쓴다.

단수	**a** customer 한 명의 고객
복수	several customer**s** 여러 명의 고객(들)

불가산 명사는 개수를 셀 수 없는 명사로 단수 형태로만 사용되며 a/an과 함께 쓰일 수 없다.

단수	information 정보 *cf.*) **an** information (✗) 하나의 정보
복수	존재하지 않음

PATTERN 기출 유형 맛보기

> Q. The Waterman Foundation provides financial ------ to young people pursuing a career in science or technology.
> (A) assisting
> **(B) assistance** → 빈칸은 동사(provides)의 목적어 자리이므로 명사 보기 (B) assistance가 정답이다.
> (C) assisted
> (D) assist
>
> Waterman Foundation은 과학이나 기술 분야의 직업을 꿈꾸는 젊은이들에게 재정적 지원을 제공한다.
>
> **출제 경향** 문장의 주어 혹은 목적어 자리에 명사를 선택하는 문제가 출제되는데 목적어 자리를 묻는 문제가 훨씬 많이 출제되는 추세이다. 문장의 주어와 목적어 자리를 파악할 수 있어야 하며 제시된 보기 중 무엇이 명사인지 고를 수 있어야 한다.

[이렇게도 출제된다]
- 가산 명사와 불가산 명사의 문법적 차이를 묻는 문제가 출제된다.
- 사람 명사와 사물 명사를 함께 보기에 제시하여 의미상 적합한 명사를 선택하는 문제가 출제된다.

◆ 출제 포인트 1   명사 자리

매년 33~34문제 출제

명사는 문장의 주어, 목적어, 보어 자리에 위치한다.

주어   The **renovation** will take approximately five months.   보수 공사는 약 5개월이 걸릴 것이다.

목적어   The new policy will promote economic **growth**.   새 정책은 경제 성장을 촉진할 것이다.
　　　　　　　　　　　　타동사　　　　　　　타동사의 목적어

　　　　You will be working under the **direction** of Mr. Sager.   당신은 Sager 씨의 지도 하에서 일하게 될 것입니다.
　　　　　　　　　　　　　　　　전치사　　　전치사의 목적어

보어   Ms. Sturt was **a former client** of the company.   Sturt 씨는 그 회사의 전 고객이었다.
　　　　　　　　2형식 동사

명사는 '관사/소유격 + 형용사 + 명사'의 순서로 쓰인다.

Some employees are unhappy with the new **regulations**.   일부 직원들은 새로운 규정에 불만이다.
　　　　　　　　　　　　　　　　　　　　관사 + 형용사 + 명사

PRACTICE | 기출 연습하기

1. The (acquisitional / acquisition) of additional trucks will allow Avira to expand its service area.
2. The sales department has made a slight (modification / modify) to its billing system.
3. In (anticipation / anticipating) of her interview with Ted Patel, Ms. Flores read his book.

◆ 출제 포인트 2   형용사나 동사로 착각하기 쉬운 형태의 명사

매년 5~6문제 출제

-al, -tive, -ing 의 형용사형 어미를 가진 명사에 주의해야 한다.

We will submit a **proposal** for a construction project.   우리는 건설 프로젝트를 위한 제안서를 제출할 것입니다.
The power must be disconnected before **cleaning**.   세척하기 전에 전원을 분리해야 합니다.

-al	propos**al** 제안(서) approv**al** 승인 rent**al** 임대 profession**al** 전문가 ⑱ 전문적인 potenti**al** 잠재력 ⑱ 잠재적인
-tive	initia**tive** 진취성, 주도 alterna**tive** 대안 ⑱ 대안의 representa**tive** 대표, 대리인 ⑱ 대표하는
-ing	clean**ing** 청소/세척 pric**ing** 가격책정 open**ing** 일자리/개최 account**ing** 회계 shipp**ing** 배송 handl**ing** 취급
기타	response 응답 emphasis 강조 ease 쉬움 assembly 조립 pleasure 즐거움 receipt 영수증 loss 손실

명사와 동사의 역할이 둘 다 가능한 단어에 주의해야 한다.

The city is encouraging the **use** of public transportation.   시는 대중 교통의 이용을 권장하고 있다.
　　　　　　　　　　　　　　명사 (사용)

Please **use** the attached form to register.   등록하시려면 첨부된 양식을 사용하세요.
　　　동사 (사용하다)

estimate 견적(을 내다)	access 접근(하다)	approach 접근(하다)	lack 부족(하다)	use 사용(하다)	caution 경고(하다)
change 변화(하다)	increase 증가(하다)	decrease 감소(하다)	detail 세부사항; 상세히 설명하다		purchase 구매(하다)
work 일(하다)	review 검토(하다)	plan 계획(하다)	visit 방문(하다)	supplement 보충(하다)	experience 경력, 경험(하다)

PRACTICE | 기출 연습하기

1. The engine requires more fuel but has enormous (potential / potent) to reduce pollution.
2. The band will perform at the (openness / opening) of Luggage Zone's Maplewood store.
3. The annual staff picnic generated an overwhelmingly positive (respond / response) from employees.

◆ 출제 포인트 3   가산 명사

매년 1~2문제 출제

가산 명사는 앞에 한정사(관사/소유격/each/every/any 등)가 없다면 복수형을 사용해야 한다.
The manager will contact **each applicant** tomorrow. 매니저는 내일 각 지원자들에게 연락할 것이다.
We are expecting over 100 attendees this year. 우리는 올해 100명 이상의 참석자를 기대하고 있다.
New employee should have two years of experience. (✗) 신입 사원은 2년의 경력을 가지고 있어야 한다.
→ New employees (O)

토익에 출제되는 가산 명사

| 사람/업체 | professional 전문가 | attendee 참가자 | applicant 지원자 | distributor 유통업자[업체] |
| 직업/부서/일자리 | job 직업 | profession (전문) 직업 | department(=division) 부서 | opening 일자리 |

셀 수 없어 보이지만 가산 명사인 경우에 유의해야 한다.
We provide special rates to students. 우리는 학생들에게 특별 요금을 제공한다.

| rate 요금 | fare 교통요금 | cost 원가, 비용 | discount 할인 | fund 자금 | refund 환불 | compliment 칭찬 |
| request 요청 | approach 접근법 | task 일, 과제 | plan 계획 | farm 농장 | market 시장 | limit 한계 |

PRACTICE | 기출 연습하기

1. OrgTech needs engineers who can create innovative (approach / **approaches**) to design issues.
2. Motor Electronics offers (discount / **discounts**) to customers who fill out an online survey.
3. The aim of this program is to recruit top-level designers for full-time (**employee** / employment).

◆ 출제 포인트 4   불가산 명사

매년 약 1문제 출제

불가산 명사는 부정관사 a/an과 함께 쓸 수 없으며 복수형이 불가능하다.
Ms. Allen wishes to receive information about special events. Allen 씨는 특별 행사에 대한 정보를 받고 싶어 한다.
   an information (X), informations (X)
The equipment needs regular maintenance. 그 장비는 정기적인 정비가 필요하다.
→ 정관사(the)는 불가산 명사와 사용 가능하다.

토익에 출제되는 불가산 명사

| equipment 장비 | luggage(= baggage) 짐 | merchandise 상품 | planning 기획 | farming 농업 | |
| marketing 마케팅 | funding 자금 지원 | access 접근 | information 정보 | work 일 | news 소식 |

PRACTICE | 기출 연습하기

1. Residents of Harwood Apartments get free (**access** / accesses) to the fitness center and pool.
2. Dr. Ivanov is asking for (fund / **funding**) for his research on heart disease.
3. Our team is looking for a contributor to write a short (**article** / news) about the finance industry.

◆ 출제 포인트 5 복합 명사

매년 약 7문제 출제

복합 명사는 두 개 이상의 명사가 결합된 것으로 앞의 명사는 단수 형태가 원칙이다.

We strive to maintain a high level of **client satisfaction**. 우리는 높은 수준의 고객 만족도를 유지하기 위해 노력하고 있다.
clients satisfaction (X)

토익에 출제되는 복합 명사

rental space 임대 공간	loan payment 대출 지불금	design competition 디자인 경연대회	office supplies 사무 용품
security reason 보안상의 이유	job opening 일자리	travel expense reimbursement 출장 경비 상환	

앞의 명사가 -s 형태인 예외적인 복합 명사에 주의한다.

Mr. Ortiz intends to apply for a **sales position**. Ortiz 씨는 영업 사원직에 지원할 생각이다.
sale position (X)

sales figures 매출액	savings plan 저축 플랜	awards ceremony 시상식	public relations program 홍보 프로그램

PRACTICE | 기출 연습하기

1. The office (supplied / supplies) can be found in the closet next to the exit.
2. A short presentation on workplace (safely / safety) will be held in the conference center.
3. Ms. Roth is currently seeking (rents / rental) space for her new cosmetics company.

◆ 출제 포인트 6 사람 명사 vs. 사물 명사

매년 11~12문제 출제

형태가 비슷한 사람 명사와 사물 명사를 구분해 알아두어야 한다.

The **application** has been received by the HR department. 지원서는 인사과에 의해 수령되었습니다.
Applicants for the position must have a university degree. 그 직책의 지원자는 대학 학위가 있어야 한다.

토익에 출제되는 사람 명사 ↔ 사물 명사

manufacturer 제조업체 ↔ manufacture 제조	attendant 안내원 ↔ attention 관심, 집중
applicant 지원자, 신청자 ↔ application 신청, 지원(서)	attendee 참석자 ↔ attendance 참석, 참석자 수
resident 거주자 ↔ residence 주택, 거주	donor 기부자 ↔ donation 기부
enthusiast 애호가 ↔ enthusiasm 열정	contributor 기고가 ↔ contribution 기여
supplier 공급업자 ↔ supply 공급	producer 생산자 ↔ product 제품, ~의 산물[결과물]
architect 건축가 ↔ architecture 건축	distributor 유통회사 ↔ distribution 유통, 배급
accountant 회계사 ↔ accounting 회계	correspondent 특파원 ↔ correspondence 서신 (교환)
analyst 분석가 ↔ analysis 분석	consultant 컨설턴트, 고문 ↔ consultation 자문, 협의
advisor 고문, 조언자 ↔ advice 조언	professional 전문가 ↔ profession 직업
	professionalism 전문성

PRACTICE | 기출 연습하기

1. Please contact the (manufacturer / manufacture) directly with any questions regarding your warranty.
2. All interoffice (correspondent / correspondence) should be formatted according to the established guidelines.
3. This four-week program will allow participants to gain knowledge in food (distributor / distribution) and health care.

RC DAY 04 실전문제

1. The foreman was over an hour late to the meeting as a result of ------- on Highway 101.
   (A) congested
   (B) congestion
   (C) congestive
   (D) congests

2. Ms. Mifflin would like to express her sincere ------- for the volunteers' hard work at Saturday's event.
   (A) appreciative
   (B) appreciated
   (C) appreciates
   (D) appreciation

3. To receive ------- for vacation requests, employees must have been with the company for more than six months.
   (A) approved
   (B) approval
   (C) approving
   (D) approves

4. The sales ------- at Burnstone Industries are required to handle all business correspondence via a work e-mail address.
   (A) represent
   (B) represents
   (C) representatives
   (D) representational

5. The educators at the Morrissey Institute teach a variety of subjects with an ------- on art, music, and theater.
   (A) emphasize
   (B) emphasis
   (C) emphasized
   (D) emphasizes

6. The marketing team believes a better slogan and redesigned packaging will increase the product's -------.
   (A) recognition
   (B) recognizing
   (C) recognize
   (D) recognized

7. Though she is new to management, Jinny Moon handled the labor shortage with great -------.
   (A) profession
   (B) professional
   (C) professionally
   (D) professionalism

8. Designed by a famous -------, the Quincy Tower has been a feature of the city skyline for decades.
   (A) architectural
   (B) architecture
   (C) architect
   (D) architects

9. The Rug Bazaar offers complimentary ------- for any rug or mat purchased in its store.
   (A) clean
   (B) cleanest
   (C) cleaned
   (D) cleaning

10. Guests who do not indicate any meal ------- will automatically be served steak with carrots and potatoes.
    (A) preferential
    (B) preferences
    (C) prefers
    (D) preferable

11. The latest issue of *Normandy Monthly* features an interview with Danielle Toole, a local wildlife -------.
    (A) enthused
    (B) enthusiastically
    (C) enthusiast
    (D) enthusiasm

12. Though the chemical may be obtained for industrial purposes, it has not yet been approved for consumer -------.
    (A) usable
    (B) use
    (C) useful
    (D) used

13. For ------- reasons, customers will never be asked for any personal information online.
    (A) security
    (B) secure
    (C) securely
    (D) secured

14. Most survey respondents said they did not have an opinion on the product due to ------- of information.
    (A) lacking
    (B) having lacked
    (C) lack
    (D) lacked

15. ------- at yesterday's game reached more than 30,000, proving once again how loyal fans of the Giants are.
    (A) Attended
    (B) Attendance
    (C) Attendant
    (D) Attendee

16. ------- for group tours must be submitted at least 24 hours in advance of the desired date.
    (A) Requested
    (B) Request
    (C) Requests
    (D) To request

Questions 17-20 refer to the following article.

RIVERDALE (September 4) — Once a town of no more than 300 people, Riverdale has become home to almost 2,000 residents. Over the past five years, the city of Riverdale has been offering large tax ------- to new property owners. This has been one of the main factors in the ------- increase in population. According to a survey of new residents, however, the city's proximity to Lake Itaska has ------- attracted buyers. City councilwoman Meredith Mars is hopeful that the overall increase in tax revenue will help the city develop its infrastructure. -------.

17. (A) to benefit
    (B) benefits
    (C) benefited
    (D) beneficial

18. (A) rapid
    (B) brief
    (C) narrow
    (D) anxious

19. (A) ahead
    (B) nearly
    (C) yet
    (D) also

20. (A) Moreover, she wonders whether the surrounding towns will provide similar benefits.
    (B) Therefore, she believes many people will move away from Riverdale.
    (C) In fact, she indicated that planning for a new public park has already begun.
    (D) She noted that residents of Riverdale tend to commute for at least an hour a day.

RC DAY 05 대명사

BASIC 기본기 익히기

1. 대명사의 정의
대명사는 보통 동일한 명사(구)의 반복을 피하기 위해 이를 대신하여 사용하는 말이다.

Ms. Jones was so busy yesterday that **she** forgot to send me the report.
　　　　　　　　　　　　　　　　　　　　Ms. Jones를 대신하는 대명사
Jones 씨는 어제 너무 바빠서 나에게 보고서를 보내는 것을 잊었다.

Mr. Goodman wants to exchange the broken **printer** for a new **one**.
　　　　　　　　　　　　　　　　　　　　　　　　　　　　printer를 대신하는 대명사
Goodman 씨는 고장난 프린터를 새 프린터로 교환하고 싶어 합니다.

2. 인칭대명사의 격 변화
인칭대명사는 사람 혹은 사물을 가리키는 대명사로서 인칭과 격 등에 따라 다른 형태를 갖는다.

인칭 \ 격	주격 (~은/는/이/가)	소유격 (~의)	목적격 (~을/를, ~에게)	소유대명사 (~의 것)	재귀대명사 (~자신, 스스로)
1인칭	I	my	me	mine	myself
	we	our	us	ours	ourselves
2인칭	you	your	you	yours	yourself
3인칭	she/he/it	her/his/its	her/him/it	hers/his/-	herself/himself/itself
	they	their	them	theirs	themselves

3. 부정대명사의 정의
부정대명사는 정해지지 않은 사람 혹은 사물을 가리키는 대명사이다.

I will ask **someone** to pick up the package. 누군가에게 소포를 가져오라고 부탁할게요.
Many of the attendees came from nearby cities. 참석자들 중 많은 이들은 인근 도시에서 왔다.

PATTERN 기출 유형 맛보기

Q. Ronald Chou was able to condense ------- years of research on fertilizer into a 60-minute presentation.
(A) he
(B) his → 명사 앞에는 대명사의 소유격이 와야 하므로 정답은 (B) his이다.
(C) him
(D) himself

Ronald Chou 씨는 비료에 대한 그의 오랜 연구를 60분짜리 발표에 요약할 수 있었다.

출제 경향 빈칸에 적합한 대명사의 격을 묻는 문제를 출제하는데, 소유격을 묻는 문제가 가장 많이 출제되고 있으며 그 다음은 주격과 목적격 순서로 출제 빈도가 높다.

[이렇게도 출제된다]
- 부사 자리 혹은 목적어 자리에 재귀대명사를 선택하는 문제를 출제한다.
- 수량을 나타내는 one, few, much 등의 대명사의 용법을 묻는 문제를 출제한다.

◆ 출제 포인트 1   주격 / 목적격 / 재귀대명사

매년 9~10문제 출제

인칭대명사의 주격은 주어 자리에, 목적격은 목적어 자리에 쓴다.

주격   **We** will hold a job fair on March 10.   우리는 3월 10일에 취업 박람회를 개최할 것이다.

목적격   Please complete the documents and send **them** by June 30.   서류들을 작성해서 6월 30일까지 보내 주세요.
동사의 목적어

Ms. Hall has been working **with us** for the past five years.   Hall 씨는 지난 5년간 저희와 함께 일해 왔습니다.
전치사의 목적어

재귀대명사는 주어와 목적어가 같을 때 목적어 자리에 쓰며, '직접'의 의미일 때 부사 자리에 쓴다.

목적어 자리   Ms. Guerra has dedicated **herself** to charity.   Guerra 씨는 자선 사업에 자기 자신을 바쳐 왔다.
'(자기) 자신'이란 의미

부사 자리   You need to install the software **yourself**.   당신은 직접 소프트웨어를 설치해야 합니다.
'직접'이란 의미

'by + 재귀대명사'는 '혼자, 스스로'라는 의미의 숙어이다.
I was unable to do the job **by myself**.   나는 그 일을 혼자 할 수 없었다.
= alone, on my own

PRACTICE | 기출 연습하기

1. Mr. Ewing informed me that (he / him) will not be able to attend the meeting.
2. We will notify (yourself / you) immediately when there is any problem with your order.
3 During the presentation, Ms. Lee will demonstrate how to operate the machinery (her / herself).

◆ 출제 포인트 2   소유격 / 소유대명사

매년 약 10문제 출제

소유격은 명사 앞에 위치하며 own(~자신의)과 함께 쓰일 수 있다.
We will allow employees to change **their** work schedule.   우리는 직원들이 자신의 근무 시간을 변경하는 것을 허용할 것이다.
Ms. Lang started **her own** business ten years ago.   Lang 씨는 10년 전에 자신의 사업을 시작했다.

소유대명사는 주어/목적어/보어 자리에 올 수 있으며 '~의 것'이라는 의미이다.
The envelope on the desk is **yours**.   책상 위의 봉투는 당신의 것입니다.
= your envelope

All computers are working fine except **mine**.   나의 것을 제외하고는 모든 컴퓨터가 잘 작동하고 있다.
= my computer

PRACTICE | 기출 연습하기

1. Fashion designer Luna Everton will present (her / hers) fall collection this week.
2. All employees will be expected to pay for (their own / them) meals at the conference.
3. Mr. Nelson is using the fax machine at the library because (he / his) is broken.

◆ 출제 포인트 3   this / that / these / those

매년 1~2문제 출제

this / that / these / those는 대명사 뿐만 아니라 형용사로도 사용된다.
You are invited to participate in the event. **This** will last about 90 minutes.
귀하를 행사 참가에 초대합니다. 이것은 약 90분 동안 지속될 것입니다.
Thank you for your purchase of the printers and monitors, but **these** items are currently out of stock.   프린터와 모니터를 구매해 주셔서 감사드립니다. 하지만 이 품목들은 현재 품절입니다.
→ this / that은 단수 명사와 these / those는 복수 명사와 어울린다.

those는 '~하는 사람들'이라는 의미로도 쓰이며 who나 전치사구/~ing / p.p. 등의 수식을 받는다.
Discounts are available to **those who** register early.   일찍 등록하는 사람들에게는 할인이 가능하다.
Only **those with** a permit are allowed to park in the green zone.   허가증이 있는 사람들만 녹색 구역에 주차할 수 있다.

PRACTICE | 기출 연습하기

1. Outstanding workers are (that / those) who arrive on time and maintain a positive attitude.
2. Preference will be given to (those / them) with extensive experience in advertising.
3. (This / These) documents are highly sensitive and must be kept secure at all times.

◆ 출제 포인트 4   전체 중 일부를 나타내는 대명사

매년 3~4문제 출제

'------ + of the[소유격] + 복수 명사' 구조와 어울리는 대명사는 정해져 있다.

| one / each / (a) few / several / some / many / most / all / both / neither / none + of the[소유격] + 복수 명사 |

Some of the industry leaders will give presentations at the conference.
업계의 리더들 중 몇몇이 컨퍼런스에서 발표를 할 것이다.
TIP   someone, everyone, every, the one, something, nothing 등이 해당 구조에 오답으로 자주 출제되므로 주의한다.

'one / each + of the[소유격] + 복수 명사'는 단수 취급한다.
One of our interns was assigned to Team A.   우리 인턴들 중 한 명이 A팀에 배정되었다.

'------ + of the[소유격] + 불가산 명사' 구조와 어울리는 대명사는 정해져 있다.

| (a) little / some / much / most / all + of the[소유격] + 불가산 명사 |

Much of the information seems useful.   정보 중 많은 것이 유용한 것 같다.
Mr. Swanson plans to finish **all of his work** by next Thursday.
Swanson 씨는 다음 주 목요일까지 그의 모든 일을 끝낼 계획이다.

전체 중 일부를 나타내는 대명사는 of 이하 없이 단독으로 부정대명사의 역할이 가능하다.
We interviewed a total of 56 applicants, and **most** were qualified.
                                              = most of the applicants
우리는 총 56명의 지원자들을 인터뷰했는데, 대부분 자질이 있었다.

PRACTICE | 기출 연습하기

1. (Each / Every) of our photocopiers comes with complimentary service and repairs for a year.
2. (Some / Something) of the companies at the job fair are hiring recent graduates.
3. Two designers were hired recently, but (both / any) left the company after only a few weeks.

◆ 출제 포인트 5 부정대명사 -one / -body / -thing

매년 약 2문제 출제

-one / -body는 불특정 사람을 나타내며 -thing은 불특정 사물을 나타낸다.

| everyone 모든 사람 | someone 누군가 | no one / nobody 아무도 ~아닌 | everything 모든 것 | nothing 아무 것도 ~않은 |

No one was present in the office when the furniture arrived. 가구가 도착했을 때 사무실에는 아무도 없었다.
Everything has been set up for the presentation. 발표를 위해 모든 것이 준비되었다.

someone은 긍정문에, anyone은 보통 부정문/의문문/조건문에 사용된다.
I will arrange for **someone** to meet Mr. Idler at the airport. 나는 누군가가 Idler 씨를 공항에서 마중하도록 준비할 것이다.
This information should not be shared with **anyone** outside the company.
이 정보는 회사 외부의 누구와도 공유해서는 안 됩니다.

cf.) 긍정문에 anyone이 사용될 경우 '누구든, 모든 사람'의 의미이다.
    I would recommend this book to **anyone** interested in Thai history. 태국 역사에 관심 있는 누구에게든 이 책을 추천하겠다.

PRACTICE | 기출 연습하기

1. The technician did (everything / anybody) he could to repair the computer network.
2. (Someone / Any) needs to supervise the volunteers working at the campaign office.
3. (Anyone / Another) available to plan this year's Ride for Children should contact Marcus Simpson.

◆ 출제 포인트 6 another / other / others / each other

매년 1~2문제 출제

another는 가산 단수 명사와 어울리며 other는 복수 명사 혹은 불가산 명사와 어울린다.
Mount Co. will soon merge with **another** company. Mount 사는 곧 다른 회사와 합병할 것이다.
This coupon cannot be used with **other** discounts. 이 쿠폰은 다른 할인들과 함께 사용할 수 없습니다.

동일한 명사가 앞에 언급된 경우 'another + 단수 명사'는 another, 'other + 복수 명사'는 others로 표현할 수 있다.
A book borrowed at one branch may be returned to **another**. 한 지점에서 대여한 책은 다른 지점에 반납할 수 있다.
    = another branch
Some projects will take much longer than **others**. 몇몇 프로젝트들은 다른 것들보다 시간이 오래 걸린다.
    = other projects

'서로서로'란 의미의 each other / one another는 목적어 자리에만 쓰인다.
Participants will be able to share ideas with **each other**. 참가자들은 서로서로 생각을 공유할 수 있을 것이다.
    = one another

PRACTICE | 기출 연습하기

1. If you already took a long vacation, management is unlikely to approve (another / other one).
2. (Other / Others) appliance stores are unable to beat the prices at Hometastic in Louisville.
3. The conference gives managers from different cities a chance to meet (one another / other).

RC DAY 05 실전문제

1. Ms. Porter regularly evaluates the members of ------- department so that everyone is aware of the company's expectations.
   (A) herself
   (B) she
   (C) her
   (D) hers

2. To avoid confusion, Mr. Roth has asked that employees communicate only with ------- regarding the guest list.
   (A) his
   (B) him
   (C) he
   (D) his own

3. Hans Richter founded the Merlin Corporation by ------- more than thirty years ago and has become an industry leader.
   (A) he
   (B) his
   (C) him
   (D) himself

4. Ms. Corbet was notified that ------- was selected to fill the position immediately after the interview.
   (A) her
   (B) hers
   (C) she
   (D) herself

5. Thanks to the ten new branches, the Wellman Company will expand ------- customer base throughout Asia.
   (A) itself
   (B) its
   (C) them
   (D) themselves

6. Ms. Mayfield had to borrow Mr. Becker's printer card today because she left ------- at home.
   (A) her
   (B) hers
   (C) herself
   (B) she

7. JP Motors offers a free vehicle inspection to ------- who purchased a car at one of the retailer's branches.
   (A) them
   (B) which
   (C) those
   (D) these

8. Taking a patient's blood pressure is just one of the ------- of the nurses at Memorial Lake Hospital.
   (A) responsible
   (B) responsibly
   (C) responsibility
   (D) responsibilities

9. ------- of the films nominated for Best Picture was a commercial success, particularly the one entitled *Bridge to Nowhere*.
   (A) Each
   (B) Most
   (C) Every
   (D) All

10. With her outstanding sense of humor and charming personality, ------- entertains clients better than Linda Kincaid.
    (A) nothing
    (B) nobody
    (C) whoever
    (D) either

11. The customers sitting by the window ordered two plates of sushi, but ------- has been prepared yet.
    (A) nobody
    (B) neither
    (C) either
    (D) whichever

12. Volton, Inc., is constructing a new manufacturing plant in Houston and ------- in San Jose.
    (A) other
    (B) each other
    (C) another
    (D) neither

13. ------- of Ms. Nunez's top choices for the account manager position attended Dappline University in Australia.
    (A) Those
    (B) Both
    (C) Each other
    (D) Anyone

14. Virtually ------- at the book-signing purchased a copy of the author's latest novel in advance.
    (A) everyone
    (B) anything
    (C) which
    (D) each other

15. Several agencies will need to collaborate with ------- in order to solve the country's pollution crisis.
    (A) whomever
    (B) each other
    (C) other
    (D) its own

16. Eating at the hotel buffet is the most convenient option for guests, but ------- are available.
    (A) other
    (B) any other
    (C) others
    (D) another

Questions 17-20 refer to the following article.

DETROIT (November 14) — Two of the world's largest automobile manufacturers, Hanata Motors (HM) and Waters-Mark Group (WMG), ------- into one company. The deal will be effective as of December 7. -------. The newly ------- firm will be based out of Detroit, where WMG's headquarters are located. HM currently employs around 330,000 workers, while WMG's employees total around 60,000. HM CEO Garrett Easton and WMG CEO Ingrid Stanton released a joint statement saying there would not be any employee layoffs. ------- also said there were no plans to move production facilities overseas.

17. (A) is merged
    (B) merged
    (C) will be merging
    (D) have been merging

18. (A) Government approval for the agreement was received last week.
    (B) Parts must be imported before vehicles can be assembled.
    (C) Both firms specialize in the high-end clothing market.
    (D) Both companies are strong competitors in their respective industries.

19. (A) informed
    (B) created
    (C) reviewed
    (D) renovated

20. (A) He
    (B) They
    (C) It
    (D) We

RC DAY 06 — 형용사 / 부사

BASIC 기본기 익히기

1. 형용사의 역할
형용사는 명사를 수식하거나 보충 설명한다.

명사 수식	You should wear **protective** glasses. 보호 안경을 써야 합니다.
주격 보어	The event was **successful**. 행사는 성공적이었다.

2. 부사의 역할
부사는 동사, 형용사, 부사, 동명사, 전치사구 등 명사 이외의 품사를 수식한다.

동사 수식	You should speak **quietly** during the visit. 방문 중에는 조용히 말해야 합니다.
	We **proudly** announce the opening of a new branch. 새로운 지사의 개장을 자랑스럽게 발표합니다.
형용사 수식	The registration process was **extremely** difficult. 등록 절차는 극도로 어려웠다.
부사 수식	You can locate the shop **fairly** easily. 그 상점을 꽤 쉽게 찾으실 수 있습니다.
동명사 수식	Please register by **completely** filling out the form. 양식을 완전히 작성해서 등록해 주세요.
전치사구 수식	The project was delayed **largely** due to funding problems. 그 프로젝트는 주로 자금 문제로 인해 연기되었다.

3. 형용사와 부사의 주요 형태

형용사			부사	
-able	reason**able** 합리적인	형용사 + -ly	reasonab**ly** 합리적으로
-ful	use**ful** 유용한		usefu**lly** 유용하게
-ive	effect**ive** 효과적인		effective**ly** 효과적으로
-al	addition**al** 추가적인		additiona**lly** 추가적으로
-ous	cauti**ous** 신중한		cautious**ly** 신중하게
-y	eas**y** 쉬운		easi**ly** 쉽게
-ent[ant]	excell**ent** 뛰어난		excellent**ly** 뛰어나게

PATTERN 기출 유형 맛보기

Q. Before operating your new steam cleaner, make sure that you ------ close the lid to the water tank.
(A) tighter
(B) tightness
(C) tight
(D) tightly → 빈칸은 동사(close)를 수식하는 위치이므로 부사 보기 (D) tightly가 정답이다.

새 스팀 청소기를 작동하기 전에 반드시 물통 뚜껑을 꽉 닫도록 하십시오.

출제 경향 형용사와 부사의 위치를 구별하는 문제를 출제한다. 동사를 수식하는 부사의 출제 빈도가 가장 높으며 명사 앞에서 수식하는 형용사의 용법을 묻는 유형 또한 자주 출제되고 있다.

[이렇게도 출제된다]
- 가산 명사와 불가산 명사에 각각 어울리는 수량 형용사의 용법을 묻는 문제가 출제된다.
- 문법적 쓰임새를 구별해야 하는 부사 yet, ever, enough 등의 용법을 묻는 문제가 출제된다.

◆ 출제 포인트 1 형용사 자리

매년 약 24문제 출제

형용사는 명사 앞이나 뒤에 위치하여 명사를 수식하거나 보어 자리에 위치한다.

The museum is undergoing **extensive** renovation. 그 박물관은 광범위한 개조를 하고 있다.
　　　　　　　　　　　　　　　　　　명사 수식

The seminar about investments was very **informative**. 투자에 관한 세미나는 매우 유익했다.
　주어　　　　　　　　　　　　　　2형식 동사　　주격 보어

I found the jazz classes particularly **beneficial**. 나는 재즈 수업이 특히 유용하다고 생각했다.
5형식 동사　　목적어　　　　　　　　　목적격 보어

토익에 출제되는 보어를 이끄는 동사

주격 보어를 이끄는 2형식 동사				
be ~이다	become ~이 되다	remain 여전히 ~이다	seem(=appear) ~인 것 같다	prove ~로 판명되다
목적격 보어를 이끄는 5형식 동사				
make ~한 상태로 만들다	find ~라고 생각하다	consider ~라고 간주하다	keep ~한 상태로 유지시키다	

PRACTICE | 기출 연습하기

1. A major celebrity endorsement can generate (substantial / substantially) interest in a product.
2. Representative Matthew Kerns has been (active / actively) in local politics since graduating from university.
3. Appropriate office furniture will make your workspace more (professional / professionally) to visiting clients.

◆ 출제 포인트 2 형태에 주의해야 하는 형용사

매년 약 7문제 출제

일반적 형태가 아닌 형용사들은 별도로 암기해야 한다.

명사 + -ly	timely 시기 적절한	orderly 질서 정연한	friendly 친근한	costly 값비싼	leisurely 여유로운
분사 형태	limited 한정된	detailed 상세한	extended 연장된	experienced 노련한	qualified 자질을 갖춘
	promising 유망한	rising 상승하는	surrounding 주변의	leading 주도적인	challenging 어려운
기타	complete 끝난, 완전한	secure 안전한	diverse 다양한	lengthy 너무 긴	distinct 뚜렷이 구별되는

Your order will arrive in a **timely** manner. 귀하의 주문은 제때에 도착할 것입니다.
A **complete** itinerary of your trip will be sent soon. 귀하의 전체 여행 일정이 곧 발송될 것입니다.

PRACTICE | 기출 연습하기

1. Questions submitted online will be answered by our manager in a (timely / timed) manner.
2. When staying at Longhorn Hotel, keep your valuables (secure / securely) in the room's safe.
3. Our Mango Delight flavor will be available for a (limited / limitation) time only.

◆ 출제 포인트 3　수량 형용사 (1)

매년 3~4문제 출제

가산 명사의 단수/복수를 구별하여 적절한 수량 형용사를 선택한다.

one / each / every + 가산 단수 명사
(a) few / several / many / numerous / both + 가산 복수 명사

Ms. Krahn greets **every** customer with a smile.　Krahn 씨는 모든 고객을 미소로 맞이합니다.
Mr. Alley has served as a consultant for **several** large companies.　Alley 씨는 몇몇 대기업의 컨설턴트로 일해 왔다.

불가산 명사와 어울리는 수량 형용사를 선택한다.

(a) little / much + 불가산 명사

The brochure provides **little** information about the program.　그 책자는 프로그램에 대한 정보를 거의 제공하지 않는다.

PRACTICE | 기출 연습하기

1. The musical fountain is one of the (many / much) attractive features of Dunphy Park.
2. (Each / Several) applicant for the position must submit at least two references.
3. In truth, early bookings may have (little / few) influence on the price of airfare.

◆ 출제 포인트 4　수량 형용사 (2)

매년 약 2문제 출제

가산/불가산 명사 모두와 함께 쓸 수 있는 수량 형용사는 별도로 기억해 둔다.

no / any / some / most / a lot of(=plenty of) / all + 가산 명사/불가산 명사

TIP　no, any는 가산 명사의 단수와 복수 형태 모두와 사용 가능하다.

All employees working in a laboratory must wear protective gear.
　　　　가산 명사
실험실에서 근무하는 모든 직원은 보호 장비를 착용해야 한다.

We would be happy to provide **any** additional information about the event.
　　　　　　　　　　　　　　　　　　　　　　　　　　불가산 명사
행사에 대한 어떤 추가 정보라도 기꺼이 제공해 드리겠습니다.

PRACTICE | 기출 연습하기

1. (Any / All) employee unable to attend Tuesday's training session must still complete the online program.
2. (All / Every) expenses incurred during the trip will be reimbursed upon submission of receipts.
3. You are responsible for (any / many) recording equipment lost or damaged during the rental period.

◆ 출제 포인트 5   부사 자리 (1) 동사 수식

매년 약 23문제 출제

부사는 동사의 앞 혹은 뒤에서 동사를 수식한다.

타동사 수식   The editorial team **thoroughly** reviewed the article.   편집팀은 그 기사를 철저히 검토했다.

= The editorial team reviewed the article **thoroughly**.

자동사 수식   Blaxton Company's earnings rose **sharply**.   Blaxton 사의 수익이 급격히 증가했다.

부사는 동사구 사이에 위치하여 동사를 수식한다.

be동사와 p.p. 사이   The situation was **promptly** resolved.   사태는 즉시 해결되었다.
= The situation was resolved **promptly**.

조동사와 동사원형 사이   The committee must **regularly** meet with the board of directors.
위원회는 정기적으로 이사회와 만나야 한다.

have와 p.p. 사이   Ms. Pierce has **successfully** completed the training program.
Pierce 씨는 훈련 과정을 성공적으로 마쳤다.

PRACTICE | 기출 연습하기

1. It's crucial that each department works (**cooperatively** / cooperative) to meet the updated deadline.
2. Few people read terms of service agreements (careful / **carefully**) before using an application.
3. Some cereal manufacturers (strategic / **strategically**) advertise to children by using cartoon characters.

◆ 출제 포인트 6   부사 자리 (2) 동사 이외 수식

매년 약 10문제 출제

부사는 형용사, 분사, 부사, 동명사, 전치사구 등의 앞에서 이를 수식한다.

The park has become an **increasingly** popular destination for tourists.
형용사 수식

그 공원은 관광객들에게 점점 더 인기 있는 목적지가 되었다.

Car rental is available at a **greatly** discounted rate.   차량 렌트는 대폭 할인된 요금으로 이용할 수 있다.
분사 수식

'be + ------ + 관사 + 명사'의 자리에 부사가 위치한다.

The hotel was **originally** a cafeteria.   그 호텔은 원래 카페테리아였다.

PRACTICE | 기출 연습하기

1. Critical reception of the latest novel from Nick Brooks has been (consistent / **consistently**) positive.
2. Horizon Travels can plan an (affordable / **affordably**) priced vacation for both families and individuals.
3. Premiere Insurance has engaged in a (deciding / **decidedly**) fresh approach to social media advertising.

◆ 출제 포인트 7   주의해야 할 부사의 용법 (1)

매년 약 2문제 출제

ever, yet은 부정문과 의문문에 주로 사용된다.
Mr. Norman has not signed the contract yet. Norman 씨는 아직 계약서에 서명하지 않았다.
The rent hardly ever goes down in this city. 이 도시에서는 집세가 좀처럼 내려가지 않는다.
cf.) ever, yet은 다음의 경우 긍정문에서 사용 가능하다.
   have yet to + 동사원형 '아직 ~않다'   최상급 + ever/yet '여태껏 중 가장'   than + ever '어느 때보다도'
   I **have yet to** receive a confirmation e-mail. 저는 아직 확인 메일을 받지 못했습니다.

so/very(매우), quite(꽤), relatively(상대적으로), extremely(극도로)는 원급 형용사/부사만 수식한다.
Your skill as a designer is quite admirable. 디자이너로서 당신의 솜씨는 정말 감탄스러워요.
Some of our products are performing extremely well. 일부 제품은 실적이 극도로 좋다.
cf.) Some of our products are performing extremely. (✗)
→ extremely의 동사 수식은 불가능하므로 틀린 문장이다.

PRACTICE | 기출 연습하기

1. Staff who have not (yet / only) requested holiday leave should contact Mr. Collins in HR.
2. You can be confident that your financial data is secure than (ever / never).
3. The Toronto Twisters have been (very / yet) successful this season despite numerous injuries.

◆ 출제 포인트 8   주의해야 할 부사의 용법 (2)

매년 약 4문제 출제

숫자 표현 앞에 자주 사용되는 부사를 기억한다.

| approximately / nearly / almost / about 대략, 거의 | over / more than ~이상 |
| up to (최대) ~까지 | exactly 정확하게 | only / just 단지 | at least 적어도 |

Cancellations must be made at least two weeks in advance. 취소는 최소 2주 전에 해야 합니다.
Approximately half of the residents are not satisfied with the policy. 주민의 약 절반이 그 정책에 만족하지 않는다.

enough는 형용사/부사를 뒤에서 수식한다.
The waiting room is large enough for 20 people. 대기실은 20명이 들어갈 만큼 충분히 크다

cf.) enough가 형용사인 경우 명사 앞에서 수식이 가능하다.
   The city does not have enough funds for the project. 그 도시는 그 프로젝트를 위한 충분한 자금을 가지고 있지 않다.

soon, shortly는 주로 미래 시제와 함께 쓰인다.
The restaurant will soon move to a new building. 그 식당은 곧 새 건물로 옮겨갈 것이다.
cf.) The demand for the product is expected to rise shortly. 그 제품에 대한 수요는 곧 증가할 것으로 예상된다.
→ 'be expected to V(~할 것으로 예상되다)'와 같이 미래 의미를 나타내는 표현과도 사용 가능하다.

PRACTICE | 기출 연습하기

1. The flight to Vancouver will depart at 11:00 A.M. and take (approximated / approximately) four hours.
2. Since everyone also ordered dessert, the company dinner became (enough / quite) expensive.
3. (About / Ever) 70% of staff admitted they had used office property for personal use.

✦ 출제 포인트 9   의미에 주의해야 하는 유사 형태 형용사

매년 약 1문제 출제

형태가 비슷하여 의미가 혼동될 수 있는 형용사에 주의한다.

□ confident 자신 있는, 확신하는 □ confidential 비밀의, 기밀의	□ dependent(=reliant) 의존적인 □ dependable(=reliable) 믿을 만한	□ considerable 상당한 □ considerate 사려 깊은
□ favorable 호의적인 □ favorite 가장 좋아하는	□ weekly 매주의 □ weeklong 일주일에 걸친	□ responsible (for) (~에) 책임이 있는 □ responsive (to) (~에) 민감하게 반응하는
□ respectful 존중하는, 정중한 □ respectable 존경할 만한 □ respective 각각의	□ extensive 포괄적인 □ extended 연장된	□ various 다양한 □ variable 변동이 심한
□ understanding 이해심 많은 □ understandable 이해될 수 있는	□ advisable 권할 만한 □ advisory 조언의, 자문의	□ seasonal 제철의, 계절적인 □ seasoned 노련한, 경험 많은

The starting salary is **dependent** on the candidate's experience. 초봉은 지원자의 경력에 달려 있다.
Praddock was ranked one of the most **dependable** brands.
Praddock은 가장 신뢰할 수 있는 브랜드 중 하나로 선정되었다.

PRACTICE | 기출 연습하기

1. The product launch was successful due to the efforts of the (various / variable) departments involved.
2. Zenith Studios is so (confident / confidential) in the film's success that it's already planning a sequel.
3. Wilcore Industries would have agreed to the merger under more (favorable / favorite) circumstances.

✦ 출제 포인트 10   의미에 주의해야 하는 유사 형태 부사

매년 약 2문제 출제

형태가 비슷하여 의미가 혼동될 수 있는 부사에 주의한다.

□ high ⑱ 높은 ⑲ 높게 □ highly ⑲ 매우	□ close ⑱ 가까운 ⑲ 가깝게 □ closely ⑲ 밀접하게, 면밀히	□ late ⑱ 늦은 ⑲ 늦게 □ lately ⑲ 최근에
□ hard ⑱ 어려운 ⑲ 열심히 □ hardly ⑲ 거의 ~않다	□ short ⑱ 짧은 □ shortly ⑲ 곧	□ near ⑲ ~가까이 □ nearly ⑲ 거의 □ nearby ⑱ 가까운 ⑲ 가까이에

The building is **hardly** visible from the road. 그 건물은 도로에서 거의 보이지 않는다.
We work **hard** to ensure your safety and security. 우리는 당신의 안전과 보안을 위해 열심히 노력하고 있습니다.

PRACTICE | 기출 연습하기

1. Dr. Pedanski is (high / highly) regarded among both patients and medical professionals.
2. The news report about the election results should be airing (short / shortly).
3. Throughout the film's production, the screenwriter will work very (close / closely) with the director.

RC DAY 06 실전문제

1. Bali Designs reacted ------- to the production issues caused by several delayed deliveries of fabric.
   (A) prompt
   (B) promptly
   (C) prompting
   (D) promptness

2. The floor manager is in charge of conducting a ------- inventory of the merchandise every Sunday.
   (A) completing
   (B) completely
   (C) complete
   (D) completion

3. If items must be shipped -------, Trader Wear does not require customers to pay additional delivery fees.
   (A) separately
   (B) separation
   (C) separating
   (D) separate

4. Given the great round of applause at the end, it seems the audience found the show quite -------.
   (A) impressive
   (B) impression
   (C) impressively
   (D) impresses

5. The CEO reminded employees that any information regarding company affairs must remain -------.
   (A) confidence
   (B) confidentially
   (C) confidentiality
   (D) confidential

6. Owing to low subscription rates, the *Galiston Times* will not hire ------- writers in the near future.
   (A) addition
   (B) additional
   (C) additions
   (D) additionally

7. The flight attendants on Irish Air are ------- asked for extra pillows and blankets.
   (A) frequent
   (B) frequency
   (C) frequently
   (D) more frequent

8. Before the course starts, it would be ------- to familiarize yourself with the content of the leaflet.
   (A) beneficial
   (B) benefited
   (C) benefits
   (D) beneficially

9. We are proud to provide the finest quality products from local manufacturers at ------- prices.
   (A) affords
   (B) affording
   (C) affordable
   (D) afforded

10. Though not available in every unit, ------- apartments at 556 Stonehenge Avenue have large built-in closets.
    (A) every
    (B) each
    (C) many
    (D) plenty

11. Although there are some crucial deadlines approaching, working overtime is strictly -------.
    (A) volunteering
    (B) voluntarily
    (C) voluntary
    (D) volunteers

12. Although it is located far away from towns, the Nelson Hotel is an ------- popular destination.
    (A) astonished
    (B) astonishment
    (C) astonishingly
    (D) astonish

13. The printing fee is ------- on whether the flyers will be in color or black and white.
    (A) dependent
    (B) dependence
    (C) dependable
    (D) depend

14. We apologize for ------- inconvenience caused by our inability to complete the order.
    (A) both
    (B) these
    (C) any
    (D) few

15. Making a reservation at Chateau Blanc is ------- impossible, but spots are occasionally open for weekday lunches.
    (A) nearly
    (B) nearing
    (C) nearby
    (D) nears

16. "Tonight" is the most popular song of the summer, even though critics complain that its chorus is too -------.
    (A) repetition
    (B) repetitive
    (C) repeating
    (D) repeat

Questions 17-20 refer to the following article.

After 12 years of headlining at the Oasis Hotel & Casino, jazz musician Charlotte Kline will ------- **17.** perform for the last time on the Oasis stage. -------. "It's been a pleasure to be here for all **18.** these years," the artist said, "but I'm excited to get back into the studio." In addition to her talent as a vocalist, Ms. Kline is gifted on both the piano and guitar. Following Ms. Kline's final performance, an auction of several ------- used during her show will be held. The event will be **19.** for ticket holders only, but the general public is invited to join an online auction of ------- items **20.** donated by Ms. Kline.

17. (A) regret
    (B) regrets
    (C) regretful
    (D) regretfully

18. (A) Her predecessor at the Oasis was vocalist Martin Reardon.
    (B) Ms. Kline plans to focus on recording music for a new album.
    (C) Ms. Kline dropped out of college to pursue her passion for music.
    (D) Her shows typically start at 7 P.M., though there is a Sunday matinee.

19. (A) intentions
    (B) sculptures
    (C) instruments
    (D) appliances

20. (A) another
    (B) each other
    (C) other
    (D) further

RC DAY 07 to부정사 / 동명사

BASIC 기본기 익히기

1. to부정사와 동명사의 형태
to부정사는 'to + 동사원형', 동명사는 '동사원형 + ing'의 형태이다.

to부정사	Mr. Britt wishes **to purchase** a house. Britt 씨는 집을 구매하길 원한다.
동명사	Ms. Ferda is considering **selling** her car. Ferda 씨는 차를 파는 것을 고려 중이다.

2. to부정사의 역할
to부정사는 명사, 형용사, 부사의 역할을 한다.

명사	The goal of the company is **to provide** the highest level of customer service. 회사의 목표는 최고 수준의 고객 서비스를 제공하는 것이다.
형용사	Thank you for the opportunity **to speak** with you. 귀하와 이야기할 기회를 주셔서 감사합니다.
부사	P&J Ltd. is working hard **to protect** the environment. P&J 사는 환경을 보호하기 위해 열심히 노력하고 있다.

3. 동명사의 역할
동명사는 명사의 역할을 하며 '~하는 것'이란 의미를 갖는다.

주어	**Entering** a new market can be exciting. 새로운 시장에 진입하는 것은 흥미로울 수 있다.
목적어	We recommend **changing** your passwords often. 암호를 자주 변경할 것을 권고 드립니다.
	Service quality can be improved without **increasing** the cost. 비용을 늘리지 않고도 서비스 품질을 개선할 수 있습니다.
보어	The goal of this event is **introducing** you to each other. 이번 행사의 목표는 여러분을 서로에게 소개하는 것입니다.

PATTERN 기출 유형 맛보기

Q. The delicious flavors offered by Broward's are sure ------ all of your ice cream needs.
(A) will satisty
(B) to satisfy → 문장에 동사(are)가 있으므로 유일하게 동사가 아닌 보기 (B) to satisfy가 정답이다.
(C) satisfies
(D) is satisfying

Broward가 제공하는 훌륭한 맛은 여러분의 모든 아이스크림 요구를 만족시킬 것입니다.

출제 경향 문장에 동사가 이미 있는 경우, to부정사나 동명사 등 준동사를 정답으로 선택하는 문제의 출제 비중이 가장 높다. 목적어를 취할 수 있는 준동사의 동사적 특징을 묻는 문제 또한 자주 출제되고 있다.

[이렇게도 출제된다]
- 명사와 동명사를 함께 보기에 출제하여 둘의 용법 차이를 묻는 문제가 출제된다.
- to부정사와 어울리는 어휘를 고르는 문제가 출제된다.

◆ 출제 포인트 1   to부정사와 동명사의 특징

매년 6~7문제 출제

to부정사와 동명사는 동사의 자리에 위치할 수 없다.
We **have installed** a new security system.   우리는 새로운 보안 시스템을 설치했다.
    to install (X), installing (X)

→ to부정사와 동명사는 동사 이외의 역할을 수행하므로 동사 자리에는 올 수 없다.

부정사와 동명사는 동사처럼 뒤에 부사, 목적어, 보어 등을 가질 수 있다.
Employees are required **to travel** **regularly**.   직원들은 정기적으로 출장을 가야 한다.
                         to + 자동사   부사

We encourage you **to submit** **suggestions** for new products.   신제품에 대한 제안을 제출할 것을 권고합니다.
                        to + 타동사   목적어

You must be a resident **to be** **eligible** for the prize.   이 상을 받을 자격이 있으려면 거주자여야 합니다.
                      to + 2형식 동사   보어

부정사와 동명사는 동사와 마찬가지로 주어와의 의미 관계에 따라 능동과 수동을 구별하여 표현한다.

능동   The chef made every effort **to develop** creative recipes.
         주방장은 창의적인 요리법을 개발하기 위해 모든 노력을 다했다.

수동   The project is scheduled **to be completed** in two weeks.   그 프로젝트는 2주 후에 완료될 예정이다.

PRACTICE | 기출 연습하기

1. Mr. Craft asked an intern (to record / will record) the sales presentation.
2. E-Auction is obligated to collect (paid / payment) once the bidding ends.
3. Business consultants assert that the key to maximizing (profitable / profitability) is low overhead costs.

◆ 출제 포인트 2   동사 + to부정사

매년 1~2문제 출제

to부정사를 목적어로 가지는 동사가 있다.

토익에 출제되는 to부정사와 어울리는 동사

intend 계획하다	wish 바라다	plan 계획하다	hope 희망하다	offer 제의하다
arrange 일정을 잡다	decide/choose 결정하다	strive 노력하다	aim 목표로 하다	hesitate 주저하다
expect 기대하다	ask 부탁하다	manage 성공하다	fail 실패하다	would like 바라다

Ms. Nielsen hopes **to renew** her membership.   Nielsen 씨는 멤버십을 갱신하기를 희망하고 있다.
                 hopes의 목적어 (갱신하는 것을)

PRACTICE | 기출 연습하기

1. Mayor Thompson plans (to submit / submitted) a proposal for a riverside bike path.
2. Junior staff who wish (to pursue / pursuing) executive positions should be competitive and efficient.
3. The Columbus Dispatch always (assumes / strives) to publish informative and factual articles.

◆ 출제 포인트 3 명사 + to부정사

매년 1~2문제 출제

to부정사의 수식을 받는 명사가 있다.

토익에 출제되는 to부정사의 수식을 받는 명사

right 권리	effort 노력	ability 능력	intention(=intent) 의도
opportunity 기회	decision 결정	proposal 제안	way 방법

The firm announced its <u>intention</u> **to expand** into Mexico. 그 회사는 멕시코로 확장하겠다는 의사를 발표했다.
　　　　　　　　　　　↑_____|
　　　　　　　　　　　intention 수식 (확장할)

You will have <u>the opportunity</u> **to ask** questions after the class.
　　　　　　　　　　↑_____|
　　　　　　　　　　opportunity 수식 (질문을 할)
여러분은 수업이 끝난 후에 질문을 할 기회를 갖게 될 것입니다.

PRACTICE | 기출 연습하기

1. In an effort (to ensure / ensuring) quality, coffee beans are roasted for twenty minutes.
2. All festival vendors reserve the (selection / right) to refuse cash payments.
3. Product testers are given the (situation / opportunity) to try new technology before it is released.

◆ 출제 포인트 4 형용사 + to부정사

매년 약 3문제 출제

to부정사와 자주 함께 쓰이는 형용사가 있다.

토익에 출제되는 to부정사와 어울리는 형용사

likely ~할 것 같은	[un]able ~할 수 있는[없는]	willing ~할 의향이 있는	reluctant(=unwilling) ~을 꺼려하는
eager ~을 갈망하는	scheduled ~할 일정이 잡힌	hesitant ~을 주저하는	eligible ~할 자격이 있는
available 이용 가능한	set 예정된	prepared(=ready) ~할 준비가 된	bound 틀림없이 ~할 것 같은

[감정 형용사]
pleased / delighted / excited / happy 기쁜　　proud 자랑스러운　　fortunate 다행스러운, 운이 좋은　　surprised 놀란

The chairman is <u>likely</u> **to approve** the new budget. 의장이 새 예산을 승인할 것 같다.
　　　　　　　　　　↑_____|
　　　　　　　　　　미래 (승인할)

I am very <u>excited</u> **to hear** about your new book. 당신의 신간에 대해 듣게 되어 매우 기쁩니다.
　　　　　　↑_____|
　　　　　　감정의 원인 (듣게 되어)

PRACTICE | 기출 연습하기

1. Our legal department was able (to define / defines) the terms of the business acquisition.
2. Pruitt Limousine Services is always (skillful / ready) to transport you in style.
3. The Wilshire Hotel is pleased (to welcome / welcoming) the executive staff from Lowell Co.

◆ 출제 포인트 5   동사 + 목적어 + to부정사

매년 2~3문제 출제

to부정사를 목적격 보어로 가지는 동사가 있다.

토익에 출제되는 to부정사를 목적격 보어로 취하는 동사

ask 요구하다	require 요구하다	request 요청하다	invite 요청하다
instruct 지시하다	encourage 격려하다	remind 상기시키다	enable 가능하게 하다
advise 조언하다	expect 기대하다, 요청하다	permit / allow 허락하다	persuade 설득하다

Online banking enables you to view your account history at any time.
　　　　　　　　　　　　목적어　목적격 보어
온라인 뱅킹은 언제라도 계좌 기록을 보는 것을 가능하게 한다.

The company is expected to win the building contract. 그 회사는 건축 계약을 따낼 것으로 예상된다.
→ to부정사를 목적격 보어로 취하는 동사의 수동태에 유의한다.

PRACTICE | 기출 연습하기

1. The PetSmart camera allows owners to (monitor / monitoring) their pets while at work.
2. Passengers are advised (to return / returning) to their seats while in-flight meals are being distributed.
3. All participants are (applied / required) to pay their registration fee by Sunday evening.

◆ 출제 포인트 6   (in order) to부정사

매년 3~4문제 출제

'~하기 위해'의 의미인 경우 '(in order) to V' 형태를 사용한다.

Mr. Ryan called the hotel to make a reservation. Ryan 씨는 예약하기 위해 호텔에 전화했다.
Please submit expense reports in order to receive reimbursement. 환급을 받기 위해 지출 보고서를 제출하세요.
cf.) to부정사의 to와 명사나 동명사가 뒤따르는 전치사 to를 구별해야 한다.
　　We are committed to keeping customer information secure.
　　저희는 고객 정보를 안전하게 유지하기 위해 최선을 다하고 있습니다.

토익에 출제되는 (동)명사를 동반하는 전치사 to 표현

look forward to + -ing ~을 고대하다	be committed[dedicated/devoted] to + -ing ~에 헌신하다
lead to + -ing ~을 초래하다	be subject to + -ing ~여하에 달려있다
in addition to + -ing ~외에도	be opposed to(=object to) + -ing ~에 반대하다

PRACTICE | 기출 연습하기

1. Interns will organize the storage room to (make / making) space for old office appliances.
2. Attendees must wear VIP wristbands (in order to / when) enter the backstage area.
3. Contest winners should visit a participating store (to / so) redeem their prize.

◆ 출제 포인트 7   동사 + 동명사

매년 1문제 출제

동사를 목적어로 가지는 동사가 있다.

토익에 출제되는 동명사를 목적어로 취하는 동사

| consider 고려하다 | recommend 추천하다 | suggest 제안하다 | mind 꺼리다 |
| include 포함하다 | involve 수반하다, 포함하다 | avoid 피하다 | discontinue 중단하다 |

Drivers should <u>avoid parking</u> on the street while the snow is cleared.
　　　　　　　　　avoid의 목적어 (주차하는 것을)
눈을 치우는 동안 운전자들은 거리에 주차하는 것을 피해야 합니다.

We <u>recommend registering</u> for the tour in advance. 투어에 미리 등록하는 것을 권장합니다.
　　　recommend의 목적어 (등록하는 것을)

PRACTICE | 기출 연습하기

1. The owner of Raccoon Coffee is considering (to open / opening) a second location.
2. To attract a wider audience, the film's producer has suggested (casting / to cast) a famous actress.
3. The receptionist's responsibilities include (reserving / reservation) a room for weekly department meetings.

◆ 출제 포인트 8   전치사 + 동명사

매년 약 8문제 출제

전치사 뒤에 부정사는 올 수 없으며 명사 혹은 동명사만 올 수 있다.
The firm is in the process <u>of relocating</u> its headquarters. 그 회사는 본사를 이전하는 중이다.
　　　　　　　　　　　　　　　　to relocate (X)

토익에 출제되는 동명사를 목적어로 취하는 전치사

before + -ing(= prior to + -ing) ~하기 전에	after + -ing ~하고 나서	by + -ing ~함으로써
instead of + -ing ~하는 것 대신에	despite + -ing ~에도 불구하고	without + -ing ~하지 않고
in addition to + -ing(= besides + -ing) ~하는 것 외에도	on / upon + -ing ~하자마자	

You are required to show your ticket <u>prior to boarding</u> the train. 기차에 타시기 전에 표를 보여주셔야 합니다.

PRACTICE | 기출 연습하기

1. Policy makers are still debating about (limiting / to limit) toxic emissions from factories.
2. In addition to (improve / improving) alertness, Trinity energy drinks prevent afternoon drowsiness.
3. (Instead of / In case) renovating the restaurant, the owner wants to move to a new location.

◆ 출제 포인트 9 　동명사 vs. 명사 (1)

매년 12~13문제 출제

동명사와 명사는 둘 다 명사 자리에 위치하지만 동명사만이 목적어를 가진다.
Mr. Lawlor is responsible for **promoting** the upcoming exhibit. 　Lawlor 씨는 다가오는 전시회 홍보를 담당하고 있다.
　　　　　　　　　　　　　　　　　promotion (X) 　　　목적어

cf.) You need to receive **approval** from the board. 　당신은 이사회의 승인을 받아야 합니다.
　　　　　　　　　　　　approving (X)

→ 명사는 뒤에 목적어를 동반하지 않는다.

PRACTICE | 기출 연습하기

1. Redwood Diner closed in April without (notifying / notification) customers as to the reason.
2. (Recovery / Recovering) deleted files may cost you a lot of money.
3. Commuters should take exit 32 to avoid (congestion / congesting) on the highway.

◆ 출제 포인트 10 　동명사 vs. 명사 (2)

매년 약 2문제 출제

동명사는 부사의 수식을 받고, 명사는 형용사의 수식을 받는다.
Jet Co. was able to make **significant** profits by **dramatically** improving productivity.
　　　　　　　　　　　　　 형용사로 수식　　　　　 부사로 수식

Jet 사는 생산성을 크게 향상시킴으로써 상당한 수익을 올릴 수 있었다.

관사(a(n)/the)는 동명사 앞에는 쓰일 수 없고, 명사 앞에는 쓰일 수 있다.
Ms. Morton will finalize the **proposal** by the end of the week. 　Morton 씨는 이번 주말까지 그 제안을 확정할 것이다.
　　　　　　　　　　　　　　 → proposing (X)

PRACTICE | 기출 연습하기

1. By (slow / slowly) releasing plot details, the studio increased interest in the movie.
2. Mr. Mason announced his retirement after the (completing / completion) of the project.
3. Zenva Technologies is known for (prompt / promptly) responding to customer inquiries.

RC DAY 07 실전문제

1. The Flower Market would like ------- all customers to complete an evaluation of the service they received.
   (A) invitingly
   (B) invitation
   (C) to invite
   (D) inviting

2. Our new mobile app ------- users to take virtual tours of popular destinations throughout Europe.
   (A) provides
   (B) gives
   (C) allows
   (D) promotes

3. Instructions are provided on the back of the bottle ------- proper application of the cream.
   (A) will ensure
   (B) to ensure
   (C) is ensuring
   (D) ensures

4. The warranty will cease to be ------- if the item is repaired or modified by any unauthorized person.
   (A) validate
   (B) validity
   (C) validates
   (D) valid

5. By ------- the infected e-mail, Ms. Nielsen unknowingly allowed a virus to enter her computer.
   (A) opens
   (B) opening
   (C) opened
   (D) open

6. Shoppers are invited ------- the customer-service desk to pick up a mall guide and book of coupons.
   (A) having visited
   (B) visits
   (C) to visit
   (D) visiting

7. The board is prepared -------- another bid on the old factory in Marquette, which is ideally located.
   (A) offering
   (B) has offered
   (C) to offer
   (D) offers

8. Customers may view their personal details at any time by ------- their account through our website.
   (A) accessed
   (B) accessing
   (C) access
   (D) accesses

9. In an ------- to better organize the office filing system, Mr. Larson labeled all documents according to date.
   (A) advice
   (B) idealism
   (C) effort
   (D) impression

10. ------- supervising the construction of Howard Bridge, Orlando Consultants is collaborating on the renovation of Diamond Street Park.
    (A) Such as
    (B) Moreover
    (C) In addition to
    (D) As soon as

11. Jackson Corp. does not make new contracts with suppliers ------- visiting their manufacturing facilities first.
    (A) without
    (B) instead
    (C) over
    (D) only

12. Anyone who has resided in Sandersville for more than 30 days is ------- to apply for a library card.
    (A) possible
    (B) eligible
    (C) considerable
    (D) flexible

13. At Star Hotels, we look forward to ------- our guests with the comforts of home at reasonable prices.
    (A) provided
    (B) provide
    (C) providing
    (D) provides

14. I am writing to let you know that the new deadline for ------- office supplies is November 30.
    (A) ordered
    (B) ordering
    (C) order
    (D) orders

15. In order to ------- larger groups, Fredo's Italian Restaurant has a private room that seats up to 20 people.
    (A) accommodates
    (B) accommodate
    (C) accommodation
    (D) accommodating

16. The manager is ------- to consider candidates without experience as long as they have a marketing degree.
    (A) useful
    (B) willing
    (C) necessary
    (D) possible

Questions 17-20 refer to the following e-mail.

From: peter.black@goodliving.com
To: russell@handcrafted.com
Subject: Cherry wood bookcase

Dear. Mr. Russell,

I am writing to you on behalf of Good Living, a home furnishings store in Seattle. We are interested in ---**17.**--- our stock of artisan furniture with pieces such as the ones you create. We are particularly interested in the bookcase you make from cherry wood. One of our managers saw this ---**18.**--- at last spring's Design Expo and insisted we contact you immediately. According to your Web site, the piece is for sale, but the value is not listed. If it is ---**19.**--- possible to buy the bookcase, we would like to know the price. For now, we are only interested in acquiring just a few pieces. ---**20.**---.
I look forward to hearing from you.

Sincerely,
Peter Black
Good Living

---

17. (A) expand
    (B) expands
    (C) expanded
    (D) expanding

18. (A) invoice
    (B) method
    (C) portion
    (D) item

19. (A) indeed
    (B) quite
    (C) alone
    (D) likewise

20. (A) Our shop also offers expert advice on interior design.
    (B) However, we may purchase more if customers respond well.
    (C) Unfortunately, it is similar to something else we have available.
    (D) If you do, just send us an e-mail with your name and address.

RC DAY 08 분사

BASIC 기본기 익히기

1. 분사의 정의와 종류
분사는 동사에서 나온 형용사로 현재분사(동사원형 + -ing)와 과거분사(p.p.)로 나뉜다.

동사 indicate (보여주다, 명시하다)
— 현재분사 indicating (~을 보여주는, 명시하는)
— 과거분사 indicated (보여지는, 명시된)

ex) a calendar **indicating** special events 특별 행사를 보여주는 달력
　　　명사(calendar) 수식

　　the amount **indicated** on the receipt 영수증에 명시된 금액
　　　명사(amount) 수식

2. 현재분사와 과거분사의 차이
현재분사는 능동의 의미(~하는)를 가지며 과거분사는 수동의 의미(~된, ~되는)를 갖는다.

현재분사　G&I Food is a **growing** company, with more than 200 employees.
　　　　　　　　　　　　　　능동 (성장하는)
　　　　　G&I Food는 200명 이상의 직원을 둔 성장하는 회사이다.

과거분사　I have enclosed the **revised** guidelines. 개정된 지침을 동봉했습니다.
　　　　　　　　　　　　　　　수동 (개정된)

PATTERN 기출 유형 맛보기

Q. Please mail the ------ registration form along with payment in full to the address below.
(A) attach
(B) attached　→ 빈칸은 명사(registration form)를 수식하는 형용사 자리이다. 형용사 역할이 가능한 보기는 (B) attached와
(C) attaching　　　(C) attaching 두 개가 있는데 '첨부된'이란 수동의 의미가 적합하므로 과거분사인 (B)가 정답이다.
(D) attachment
첨부된 등록 양식을 대금 전액과 함께 아래 주소로 우송해 주세요.

출제 경향　형용사 자리에 현재분사(-ing)와 과거분사(-ed)를 제시한 후, 의미상 무엇이 적절한지를 묻는 문제가 가장 많이 출제되며 형용사 자리에 분사 보기가 하나만 출제되는 유형 또한 출제 빈도가 높다.

[이렇게도 출제된다]
- 감정동사의 -ing와 p.p.의 의미상의 차이를 묻는 문제가 출제된다.
- 분사구문에서 -ing와 p.p.를 제시하여 무엇이 적절한지를 묻는 문제가 출제된다.

◆ 출제 포인트 1   분사의 역할

매년 3~4문제 출제

분사는 형용사 역할을 하거나 보어 역할을 한다.

명사 수식   Many people are worried about the **rising** cost of fuel.
　　　　　많은 사람들이 상승하는 연료비에 대해 걱정하고 있다.

　　　　　Some items **listed** in the catalog may not be available.
　　　　　카탈로그에 나열된 일부 품목들은 재고가 없을 수도 있습니다.

주격 보어   Mr. Vinson is well **qualified** for the position.　Vinson 씨는 그 직책을 위한 자격을 잘 갖추고 있다.

목적격 보어 The dance performance made the audience **delighted**.　댄스 공연은 관객을 즐겁게 했다.

PRACTICE | 기출 연습하기

1. Book your tickets in advance because flights to the Maldives are (limitation / limited).
2. All members should update their (preferred / preference) method of contact on their user profile.
3. Recipes (originate / originating) from the southern regions of China feature spicy ingredients.

◆ 출제 포인트 2   현재분사(-ing) vs. 과거분사(p.p.)

매년 약 7문제 출제

수식받는 명사와 분사의 관계가 능동이면 현재분사(-ing)를, 수동이면 과거분사(p.p.)를 쓴다.
Due to the **approaching** storm, we will be closed this weekend.
다가오는 폭풍으로 인해, 저희는 이번 주말에 문을 닫을 것입니다.
→ storm(폭풍)과 approach(다가오다)는 능동 관계이다.

The event will be open only to **invited** guests.　그 행사는 초대받은 손님들에게만 공개될 것이다.
→ guests(손님들)와 invite(초대하다)는 수동 관계이다.

PRACTICE | 기출 연습하기

1. David James is one of the (leading / led) experts on the history of fashion.
2. All campers must be in their (assigning / assigned) room by 10 A.M. every night.
3. Mr. Jenkins will review the purchase orders (submitting / submitted) by each department.

◆ 출제 포인트 3   -ing와 p.p.의 구별이 모호한 분사

매년 약 5문제 출제

능동과 수동의 의미 구별이 분명하지 않은 분사 형태의 형용사는 별도로 기억한다.

-ing 형태의 형용사				
surrounding 주변의	promising 유망한	encouraging 고무적인	demanding 힘든	following 다음의
challenging 도전적인	winning 우승한	inviting 매력적인	convincing 설득력 있는	entertaining 흥미로운

p.p. 형태의 형용사				
dedicated 헌신적인	talented 재능 있는	motivated 진취적인	qualified 자질 있는	experienced 노련한
skilled 숙련된	limited 제한된	detailed 상세한	accomplished 조예가 깊은	damaged 손상된
complicated 복잡한	extended 연장된	distinguished 유명한	finished 완성된	established 기반이 확고한

Ms. Haley was offered a **promising** position at Cardiff Labs.
Haley 씨는 Cardiff 연구소에서 전도 유망한 자리를 제의 받았다.

The mountain is accessible only to **experienced** hikers. 그 산은 노련한 등산객들만 접근할 수 있다.

PRACTICE | 기출 연습하기

1. Each employee will write a (detailing / detailed) development plan that outlines their career goals.
2. Mr. Patel excels in her (challenging / challenger) position as art director of Cliffton Advertising.
3. Langston Dynamics, an (establishing / established) Boston-based company, provides incentives to employees who exercise regularly.

◆ 출제 포인트 4 감정 동사의 -ing / p.p.

매년 약 3문제 출제

감정 동사의 -ing 형태는 '~을 느끼게 만드는'이라는 의미이고, -ed 형태는 '~을 느끼는'이란 의미이다.

Gardening can be a **satisfying** hobby for you. 정원을 가꾸는 것은 여러분에게 만족을 느끼게 만드는 취미일 수 있습니다.
　　　　　　　　　　만족을 느끼게 만드는

We are always proud of our long list of **satisfied** customers. 저희는 만족하신 고객들의 긴 리스트가 늘 자랑스럽습니다.
　　　　　　　　　　　　　　　　　　　　만족을 느끼는

토익에 출제되는 감정 동사

excite 신나게 하다	interest 흥미를 갖게 하다	please 기쁘게 하다	amuse 즐겁게 하다
delight 즐겁게 하다	fascinate 매혹시키다	satisfy 만족시키다	disappoint 실망시키다
confuse 혼동시키다	bore 지루하게 하다	tire 지치게 하다	surprise 놀라게 하다

PRACTICE | 기출 연습하기

1. Haruki Ishiguro read a (fascinating / fascinated) excerpt from his upcoming autobiography.
2. The Marietta Fire Department will offer a class for anyone (interesting / interested) in learning first aid.
3. Bob Forte has decided to pursue an (exciting / excited) career as a professional photographer.

◆ 출제 포인트 5 자동사의 분사 : -ing형 형용사

매년 약 2문제 출제

자동사의 분사는 현재분사 형태를 사용한다.

We would like to enhance our company's **existing** logo. 우리는 우리 회사의 기존 로고를 개선하길 원한다.
　　　　　　　　　　　　　　　　　　→ 자동사 exist (존재하다)

In the **coming** year, we plan to develop a fast food chain. 내년에 우리는 패스트푸드 체인점을 개발할 계획이다.
　　→ 자동사 come (오다)

토익에 출제되는 자동사의 -ing형 형용사

| rising 상승하는 | existing 현재의, 기존의 | lasting 지속적인 | coming 다가오는 | upcoming 곧 있을 |
| remaining 남아있는 | participating 참가하는 | working 일하는 | growing 증가하는 | emerging 신흥의 |

PRACTICE | 기출 연습하기

1. Due to (rising / risen) fuel costs, Fox Shipping will be increasing its current rates.
2. Westport's (growing / grown) population led to the development of several satellite cities.
3. Whether customers will remember to use their membership points is the only (remaining / remained) problem.

◆ 출제 포인트 6 분사구문

매년 1~2문제 출제

부사절과 주절의 주어가 같은 경우 '부사절 접속사 + 주어 + 동사'를 -ing/p.p.가 이끄는 분사구문으로 바꿀 수 있다.

Because it provides excellent service, Tomson Bistro attracts a lot of customers.
= **Providing excellent service**, Tomson Bistro attracts a lot of customers.
훌륭한 서비스를 제공하기 때문에, Tomson Bistro는 많은 고객을 끌어들인다.

→ 부사절의 동사가 능동태인 경우 현재분사를 사용한다.

Although it was established only one year ago, Morning Herald has more than 10,000 subscribers.
= **Established only one year ago**, Morning Herald has more than 10,000 subscribers.
불과 1년 전에 설립되었지만, <Morning Herald>는 1만명이 넘는 구독자를 가지고 있다.

→ 부사절의 동사가 수동태인 경우 과거분사를 사용한다.

관계대명사 which가 앞 문장 전체를 받는 경우, 'which + 동사'를 분사로 바꿀 수 있다.
We have moved to a larger office, **which allows us to provide much better service**.
= We have moved to a larger office, **allowing us to provide much better service**.
우리는 더 큰 사무실로 이전했는데, 이것은 더 나은 서비스를 제공하는 것을 가능하게 했다.

TIP thereby/thus/therefore는 -ing를 수식하여 '그러므로 ~하다'라는 의미로 사용된다.
The new system will enable us to operate more efficiently, **thus reducing the total costs**.
이 새로운 시스템을 통해 우리는 더 효율적으로 운영할 수 있고, 그러므로 총 비용을 절감할 수 있을 것이다.

PRACTICE | 기출 연습하기

1. (Being / Has been) a main investor, Ms. Alkire was concerned about the restaurant's poor reviews.
2. Dylarama announced a new tablet yesterday, (confirming / confirmed) its intent to enter an already-competitive market.
3. We have moved to a larger location, (such as / thereby) allowing us to stock a wider selection of merchandise.

RC DAY 08 실전문제

1. The ------- candidate will have at least ten years of experience working with billing systems.
   (A) qualify
   (B) qualifier
   (C) qualified
   (D) qualification

2. The kitchen starter set comes with two pots, a large knife, and five bowls of ------- sizes.
   (A) vary
   (B) varies
   (C) varying
   (D) variation

3. The bathroom and kitchen sinks are made with high quality materials ------- from Spain.
   (A) import
   (B) importing
   (C) importer
   (D) imported

4. The ------- flyer lists the sales at our Fredericktown branch, which is closing at the end of March.
   (A) enclosure
   (B) enclosed
   (C) enclosing
   (D) enclose

5. The city council will meet this week to discuss the ------- construction of a tunnel under the Lucca River.
   (A) propose
   (B) proposed
   (C) proposes
   (D) proposal

6. Employees ------- in joining the company's softball team should send an e-mail to Valerie Dixon in Human Resources.
   (A) interest
   (B) interested
   (C) interesting
   (D) interests

7. According to city regulations, all ------- structures must maintain a certain appearance to preserve local cultural history.
   (A) exist
   (B) existence
   (C) existing
   (D) existed

8. Meeting attendees were each provided with a printed copy of the ------- agreement as well as a digital one.
   (A) revision
   (B) revised
   (C) revising
   (D) revise

9. Due to the summer parade, parking in downtown Wayzata and the ------- area is likely to be difficult this Saturday.
   (A) surrounds
   (B) surround
   (C) surrounded
   (D) surrounding

10. Despite the heavy rain, Ms. Martinez's flight was able to leave at the ------- departure time.
    (A) scheduling
    (B) schedule
    (C) scheduled
    (D) schedules

11. Unlike many other products, Orange Power not only cleans surfaces but has a ------- scent.
    (A) pleases
    (B) pleasing
    (C) please
    (D) pleased

12. A fresh coat of paint has changed the old building into an ------- property that is full of charm.
    (A) invites
    (B) invited
    (C) invitation
    (D) inviting

13. Mr. Ackerman keeps a record of everything he eats, ------- that his calorie intake remains at a reasonable level.
    (A) ensures
    (B) will ensure
    (C) ensuring
    (D) be ensured

14. A generous donation of $10,000 was received at the last minute, ------- allowing the museum to continue operations.
    (A) thereby
    (B) such as
    (C) throughout
    (D) which

15. Staff members are invited to a banquet ------- Justin Shaffer, who will be retiring after 30 years of service.
    (A) honor
    (B) honors
    (C) honoring
    (D) honored

16. The newly ------- test will assist doctors in better assessing the discomfort level of their patients.
    (A) creates
    (B) creation
    (C) creator
    (D) created

Questions 17-20 refer to the following e-mail.

To: All staff
From: Minjune Park
Date: July 4
Subject: Electric Safety program

During the period of July 20 – 25, Metro Power ------- its Electric Safety program. To bring
                                                 17.
attention to the initiative, a variety of events have been planned for the week. -------.
                                                                                18.
A number of ------- have also been prepared as part of the publicity campaign. These will list the
              19.
week's events as well as provide simple tips for safely using electricity.

This information will be affixed to notice boards in ------- public facilities. It will also be posted
                                                    20.
to our Web site and available for download. We ask for your assistance in spreading the word about this important outreach effort.

17. (A) were being launched
    (B) were launching
    (C) will have launched
    (D) will be launching

18. (A) These include prize drawings and presentations on safety measures.
    (B) Metro Power has been providing homes with electricity for three decades.
    (C) Such events are subject to cancellation if weather conditions are poor.
    (D) Accidents involving electric appliances and outlets are often preventable.

19. (A) opinions
    (B) payments
    (C) books
    (D) posters

20. (A) participates
    (B) participating
    (C) participated
    (D) participant

RC | DAY 09 전치사

BASIC 기본기 익히기

1. 전치사와 전치사구
전치사는 (대)명사나 동명사의 '앞'에 위치하므로 '전치사'로 부르며, 이때 전치사와 뒤에 오는 (대)명사 혹은 동명사를 묶어서 '전치사구'라고 한다.

Due to the bad weather, the event was canceled. 악천후로 행사가 취소되었다
　　전치사구 (전치사 + 명사)　　　　완전한 문장 구조

Users may cancel the contract **without** paying a fee. 이용자들은 수수료를 지불하지 않고 계약을 취소할 수 있다.
　　　완전한 문장 구조　　　　　전치사구 (전치사 + 동명사)

2. 전치사구의 역할
전치사구는 문장에서 형용사 혹은 부사의 역할을 한다.

The details **of the order** will be sent soon. 주문의 세부 내역은 곧 발송될 것입니다.
　　　　　형용사 역할 (명사 수식)

You can return this item **within two weeks**. 이 상품은 2주 이내에 반품하실 수 있습니다.
　　　　　　부사 역할 (동사 수식)

PATTERN 기출 유형 맛보기

Q. Mr. Kincaid was unable to answer any e-mails ------ the month-long vacation.

(A) whether
(B) while
(C) during → 빈칸은 명사를 연결하는 전치사 자리이다. 전치사 보기인 (C) during과 (D) between 중 의미상 '휴가 동안'이
(D) between　　적합하므로 '~동안'의 의미를 갖는 (C) during이 정답이다.

Kincaid 씨는 한 달의 휴가 동안 어떤 이메일에도 답을 하지 못했다.

출제 경향　'시간'의 의미를 갖는 전치사의 의미 및 용법을 구별하는 유형의 출제 빈도가 가장 높으며 '장소'의 의미를 갖는 전치사의 의미 구별을 묻는 문제 또한 출제 비중이 높은 편이다.

[이렇게도 출제된다]
- 전치사, 접속사, 접속부사가 함께 보기에 출제되어 용법의 차이를 구별하는 문제가 출제된다.
- 방향, 이유, 양보, 목적 등의 의미를 갖는 전치사의 용법을 묻는 문제가 출제된다.

◆ 출제 포인트 1   시간 전치사 (1)

매년 약 3문제 출제

시간을 나타내는 전치사

at + 시점/시각	at 3 o'clock 3시에 at noon 정오에 at midnight 자정에
on + 요일/날짜	on Friday 금요일에 on July 10 7월 10일에
in + 월/연도	in March 3월에 in 2020 2020년에
before(=prior to)/after + 시점, 날짜, 요일, 월/연도	before/after Tuesday 화요일 전에/후에 before/after noon 정오 전에/후에 before/after September 17 9월 17일 전에/후에

The cooking class will be held **at** noon. 요리 수업은 정오에 열릴 것이다.
Ms. Hallick will be out of office **on** Wednesday. Hallick 씨는 수요일에 사무실에 없을 것이다.
Participants should arrive **before** 2 o'clock. 참가자들은 2시 전에 도착해야 합니다.

PRACTICE | 기출 연습하기

1. The lecture series will start (on / at) February 15 and continue until the following Friday.
2. This year's fire inspection will begin this afternoon (at / for) 1:00 P.M. as planned.
3. Evening appointments are available for patients who can only come (between / after) 6:00 P.M.

◆ 출제 포인트 2   시간 전치사 (2) : 시점 vs. 기간

매년 약 11문제 출제

시점과 어울리는 전치사

at ~에	by/until ~까지	since + 과거시점 ~이래로	toward ~ 무렵에	before ~전에	after ~후에

Mr. Brown will finalize the proposal **by** Tuesday. Brown 씨는 화요일까지 그 제안을 마무리 지을 것이다.
The discount will be applied **at** the time of purchase. 할인은 구매 시점에 적용될 것이다.
→ 시점을 나타내는 명사는 특정 시각, 날짜/요일 뿐만 아니라 the beginning(시작), the end(끝), the time of(~의 시점), the deadline(마감 시한) 등이 있다.

기간과 어울리는 전치사

within ~이내에	for/during ~동안	throughout ~내내	over ~동안에 걸쳐	in ~ 후에, ~ 동안	after ~ 후에

Mr. Nellans is retiring **after** 20 years of service. Nellans 씨는 20년간 근무한 후에 은퇴한다.
The shop will extend its operating hours **during** the summer. 그 가게는 여름 동안 영업시간을 연장할 것이다.
→ 기간을 나타내는 명사는 30 days(30일)와 같은 숫자로 표현된 것뿐만 아니라 vacation(휴가), meeting(회의), summer(여름), duration(지속 기간), business hours(영업 시간)와 같이 기간을 함축하는 명사도 포함한다.

PRACTICE | 기출 연습하기

1. Expense reports must be submitted to Accounting (by / with) Friday afternoon.
2. Notify City Hall of a change of address (among / within) 14 days of moving.
3. (During / Into) the meeting, Mr. Han explained the purpose of the new research department.

◆ 출제 포인트 3 장소 전치사

매년 약 5문제 출제

장소를 나타내는 전치사

at + 지점, 장소	at the intersection 교차로 (지점)에서	at the library 도서관에서
on + (2차원) 평면, 표면	on the second floor 2층에서	on the outside of the packaging 포장 외부에
in + (3차원) 공간, 넓은 장소	in the room 방에서	in the lobby 로비에서	in the envelop 봉투 안에

near the bank 은행 근처에   **throughout**(=across) the region 전 지역에 걸쳐
along the coast 해안을 따라서   **across** the bridge 다리 건너에   **beside**(=**next to**) the entrance 출입구 옆에
hang **above**(=**over**) the table 테이블 위에 걸려 있다   **under** the desk 책상 아래에   **behind** the stage 무대 뒤에서

The mayor will appear **on** the cover of the magazine. 시장이 잡지 표지에 등장할 것이다.
We plan to open about 100 branches **across** the country. 우리는 전국에 걸쳐 약 100개의 지점을 개설할 계획이다.

PRACTICE | 기출 연습하기

1. Gifts may be left on the counter (until / near) the information desk.
2. Several restaurants are conveniently located (on / in) the hotel's first-floor lobby.
3. Free Wi-Fi connections are readily available (into / throughout) the hospital's numerous buildings.

◆ 출제 포인트 4 방향/이유/양보/목적/범위/관련 전치사

매년 13~14문제 출제

방향/이유/양보/목적/범위/관련을 나타내는 전치사

방향/출처	**to** ~로, ~에게 **from** ~로부터, ~에서	relocate **to** another city 다른 도시로 이전하다 purchase a book **from** the store 상점에서 책을 구매하다
이유	**due to, owing to, because of** ~때문에	**due to** the rising cost 증가하는 비용 때문에
양보	**despite, in spite of** ~에도 불구하고	**despite** the risks 위험에도 불구하고
목적/이유	**for** ~을 위해, ~때문에	**for** your safety 귀하의 안전을 위해 win an award **for** one's excellent performance 뛰어난 실적으로 상을 받다
범위	**within** ~이내에 **among** ~에 포함된, ~중 하나인	**within** walking distance 걸을 수 있는 거리에 be **among** the world's best workplaces 전세계에서 가장 좋은 일터 중 하나이다
관련	**about, as to, regarding, concerning** ~에 관한	information **about** the event 행사에 관한 정보

Ms. Batty lives **within** one mile of the office. Batty 씨는 사무실에서 1마일 이내에 산다.

PRACTICE | 기출 연습하기

1. Designs must be submitted (out / to) Mr. Boice by lunchtime to be considered.
2. The game was relocated (instead of / due to) problems with the stadium's plumbing.
3. The construction will continue (despite / behind) concern from business owners regarding customer parking.

◆ 출제 포인트 5 기타 빈출 전치사

매년 약 7문제 출제

기타 빈출 전치사

except ~을 제외하고	no one except the director 이사 이외에는 누구도 아닌	at (가격) ~로	at reasonable prices 합리적인 가격으로
with ~와 함께	a meeting with a client 고객과의 미팅	according to ~에 따르면	according to a recent report 최근 보도에 따르면
without ~없이	without permission 허가 없이	such as ~와 같은	a talented musician such as you 당신과 같은 재능 있는 음악가
unlike ~와 달리	unlike other companies 다른 회사들과 달리	regardless of ~와 상관없이	regardless of age 나이와 상관없이
through ~을 통해	through the main entrance 정문을 통해	between ~사이에	between the 1st and 2nd Avenues 1번가와 2번가 사이에

You are not allowed to enter **without** a visitor's pass. 방문객 출입증 없이는 입장할 수 없습니다.

PRACTICE | 기출 연습하기

1. Apartment tenants (over / with) pets are required to arrange professional cleaning when moving out.
2. All employees (along / except) those in Marketing will participate in the survey.
3. (Such as / According to) the agreement, Matterhorn Studios has exclusive distribution rights for the film.

◆ 출제 포인트 6 용법에 주의해야 하는 유사 의미 전치사

매년 1~2문제 출제

의미는 유사하지만 용법이 다른 전치사에 주의한다.

by (늦어도) ~까지 until ~까지	완료의 개념 지속의 개념	arrive by 2 P.M. (늦어도) 2시까지 도착하다 stay open until 10 P.M. 밤 10시까지 문을 열다
in ~안에 into ~안으로	상태의 개념 동작의 개념	stay in the hotel 호텔에 머무르다 expand into Europe 유럽으로 확장하다
for ~ 동안 during ~ 동안	+ 숫자로 표현된 명사 + 기간을 함축하는 명사	for 10 years 10년 동안 during the conference 회의 동안
between ~사이에 among ~ 사이에	+ 두 개의 특정 대상 + 셋 이상의 불특정 다수	between airport and hotel 공항과 호텔 간에 among coworkers 동료들 사이에

All supplies will be delivered **by** Friday. 모든 물품은 금요일까지 배달될 것이다.
The seminar will last **until** October 15. 세미나는 10월 15일까지 계속됩니다.

PRACTICE | 기출 연습하기

1. The express train to Halifax runs most frequently (between / among) 5 and 7 P.M.
2. The bridge renovation should be completed (by / until) next Wednesday.
3. Under company policy, the use of personal phones is prohibited (for / during) business hours.

1. Cancellations will be accepted for full refunds up to 24 hours ------- the performance.
   (A) previous
   (B) advanced
   (C) prior to
   (D) in fact

2. Please be advised that the restaurant will be closed ------- renovations starting on March 10.
   (A) on
   (B) for
   (C) at
   (D) of

3. A favorite of local residents, Mickey's Diner stays open ------- 2 A.M. and offers free refills on coffee.
   (A) by
   (B) within
   (C) during
   (D) until

4. For the contract to go into effect, it must be signed and received by our office ------- May 31.
   (A) before
   (B) since
   (C) upon
   (D) over

5. Walker Institute was able to reach its fundraising goal ------- 30 days of launching the campaign.
   (A) during
   (B) within
   (C) into
   (D) on

6. To protect against harmful emissions, safety goggles must be worn ------- the duration of the test.
   (A) about
   (B) throughout
   (C) upon
   (D) behind

7. The seminar led by Felicia Jones was moved to another room ------- technical issues in the Emerald Room.
   (A) instead of
   (B) as a result
   (C) because of
   (D) in order to

8. The Vineyard announced its plan to open 10 new branch offices ------- the nation over the next three years.
   (A) beside
   (B) regarding
   (C) after
   (D) across

9. Mr. Ranker was nominated as Best Teacher of the Year ------- his commitment to the field of education.
   (A) since
   (B) about
   (C) for
   (D) by

10. Several five-star restaurants are located ------- walking distance of the conference center.
    (A) into
    (B) within
    (C) nearby
    (D) across

11. Treetop Greenhouse offers a wide range of flowers to choose from, ------- Spanish pink roses and Herston lilies.
    (A) in addition
    (B) such as
    (C) while
    (D) even if

12. The tax benefit for education expenses is available to all citizens of New Hope, Virginia, ------- income level.
    (A) prior to
    (B) along with
    (C) regardless of
    (D) instead of

13. ------- his numerous achievements, Oswald Trent is best known for inventing a revolutionary vacuum cleaner.
(A) At
(B) About
(C) Regarding
(D) Among

14. Sinter Corp. maintains a professional atmosphere, but ------- most other companies, it has a casual office dress code.
(A) contrary
(B) unlike
(C) aside
(D) except

15. All visitors are required to put on one of the lab coats hanging ------- the hook next to the entrance.
(A) on
(B) of
(C) in
(D) to

16. Stores have been contacting us ------- a new line of mixers as their customers are requesting newer models.
(A) onto
(B) through
(C) regarding
(D) around

Questions 17-20 refer to the following article.

Tasty Plate to Enter the Frozen Dessert Market

CHICAGO (June 15) — Tasty Plate, the Chicago-based -------**17.** of frozen meals, will be launching a new line of dessert products. The company was started more than 30 years ago by chef Diana Wong, who wanted to bring delicious Chinese food to the frozen section. Since then, its offerings have grown to include a wide range of cuisines, including Indian and Mexican.

-------**18.**.

Tasty Plate plans to release its first desserts -------**19.** the end of this year, but they have yet to develop final recipes. Blaine Morris, the head chef at Tasty Plate, remains sure that the company will be able to find ingredients and flavors that freeze and reheat well. "This will present numerous -------**20.** as desserts are new to us," he said, "but making frozen food taste good is what Tasty Plate specializes in."

---

17. (A) produce
(B) producer
(C) producing
(D) produced

18. (A) All frozen meals must be stamped with an expiration date.
(B) It has manufacturing facilities in Zimbabwe and Argentina as well.
(C) The restaurant has locations in most major countries worldwide.
(D) Multiple other cuisines are also being developed by the company.

19. (A) over
(B) as
(C) of
(D) by

20. (A) occasions
(B) projects
(C) challenges
(D) programs

RC DAY 10 부사절 접속사 / 등위·상관 접속사

BASIC 기본기 익히기

1. 부사절 접속사

부사절 접속사는 주절과 종속절(부사절)을 연결하는 접속사이다. 부사절은 문장 속에서 부사의 역할을 하는 종속절로서 완전한 문장으로 이루어진 주절의 앞 혹은 뒤에 위치한다.

After we launched a new marketing campaign, our sales increased quickly.
　　　　　종속절(부사절)　　　　　　　　　　　　　주절
우리가 새로운 마케팅 캠페인을 시작한 후, 우리의 매출은 빠르게 증가했다.

The road will be closed **while** pipes are being replaced. 파이프가 교체되는 동안 도로가 폐쇄될 것이다.
　　주절　　　　　　　　　　　종속절(부사절)

2. 등위 접속사

등위 접속사는 명사와 명사, 동사와 동사, 절과 절 등 같은 단위를 연결하는 접속사이다.

You may pay with cash **or** a credit card. 현금이나 신용카드로 지불하실 수 있습니다.
　　　　　　　　　명사　　　명사

The office has been renovated **and** is scheduled to reopen in June. 사무실은 개조되었으며 6월에 다시 문을 열 예정이다.
　　　　　　동사　　　　　　　　동사

The event is free, **but** advance registration is required. 이벤트는 무료이지만 사전 등록이 필요합니다.
　　　　절　　　　　　　　절

PATTERN 기출 유형 맛보기

Q. ------- the Luxury Suite has been booked for next week, the Royal Hotel has many other rooms available.
(A) Instead
(B) Despite
(C) Although → 빈칸은 완전한 두 절을 연결하는 접속사의 자리이므로 보기 중 유일한 부사절 접속사인 (C) Although가 정답이다.
(D) Regarding

Luxury Suite 룸은 다음 주에 예약이 되어있지만, Royal Hotel에는 예약 가능한 다른 많은 방이 있다.

출제 경향 부사절 접속사의 위치에 빈칸을 출제하고 보기에는 부사절 접속사가 하나만 등장하는 유형의 출제 빈도가 가장 높다. 이때 보기에 등장하는 전치사와 부사를 오답으로 소거할 수 있는 능력이 필요하다.

[이렇게도 출제된다]
- 부사절 접속사 보기를 여러 개 제시하여 이 중 문맥상 적절한 것이 무엇인지 묻는 문제가 출제된다.
- both A and B, either A or B와 같은 상관 접속사에서 적절한 짝을 선택하는 문제가 출제된다.

◆ 출제 포인트 1　부사절 접속사 자리

매년 약 11문제 출제

완전한 두 절을 연결하는 부사절 접속사는 문장의 맨 앞 또는 절과 절의 사이에 위치한다.

When Mr. Luzi loaded the software, he received an error message.
　　　　완전한 절　　　　　　　　　　　　　　　완전한 절
Luzi 씨가 소프트웨어를 로딩했을 때 오류 메시지를 받았다.

We have to purchase the tickets **before** they sell out.　우리는 다 팔리기 전에 표를 구매해야 합니다.
　　　　완전한 절　　　　　　　　　　　　　완전한 절

부사절 접속사 자리에 전치사나 접속부사는 올 수 없다.
Although she is a new employee, Ms. Neal is very professional.　비록 신입 직원이지만 Neal 씨는 매우 전문적이다.
Despite (X), Nevertheless (X)

부사절 접속사 자리에 오답으로 출제되는 접속부사

however 하지만	therefore(=thus) 그러므로	otherwise 그렇지 않으면	moreover(=in addition) 게다가
even so 그렇긴 하지만	likewise 마찬가지로	instead 대신에	nevertheless(=nonetheless) 그럼에도 불구하고
meanwhile 그동안	afterwards 그 후에	then 그 다음에	in fact 사실은　　indeed 실제로

PRACTICE | 기출 연습하기

1. (Despite / Unless) it stops raining soon, the game will be rescheduled for a later time.
2. The restaurant's grand opening was delayed (because / moreover) several staff members left unexpectedly.
3. (Then / Once) the item becomes available, we will send you an e-mail notification.

◆ 출제 포인트 2　부사절 접속사 (1) 이유/양보

매년 8~9문제 출제

'이유/양보'의 의미를 갖는 부사절 접속사

| 이유 | because ~때문에 | since ~이므로 | now (that) ~이니까 | as ~때문에 |
| 양보 | although/though/even though 비록 ~이지만 | | while 비록 ~이지만, ~인 반면 | whereas ~인 반면 |

I arrived on time for the meeting **since** there wasn't much traffic.
교통량이 많지 않았기 때문에 나는 회의 시간에 맞게 도착했다.

Even though it may be costly, it will be helpful to seek professional advice.
비용이 많이 들 수도 있지만 전문가의 조언을 구하는 것이 도움이 될 것이다.

PRACTICE | 기출 연습하기

1. The Whiteflower offers low rates (as if / even though) it is a luxurious hotel.
2. (Unless / Since) she is new to the company, Ms. Farewell is not familiar with company policies.
3. (So that / Although) company cars are available for business trips, most employees use personal vehicles.

◆ 출제 포인트 3   부사절 접속사 (2) 시간/조건

매년 약 12문제 출제

'시간/조건'의 의미를 갖는 부사절 접속사

시간	once/as soon as ~하자마자	when ~할 때	while ~하는 동안
	before ~전에	after ~후에	until ~까지 since ~이래로
조건	if ~라면	unless ~아니라면	assuming (that) ~라면 as long as ~하는 한
	even if 만약 ~이라 할지라도	only if 오직 ~인 경우에만	provided (that) ~라는 조건 하에
	whether ~ or (not) ~이든 아니든 관계 없이		in the event (that)/in case ~인 경우에 대비하여, ~이라면

TIP before, after, until, since는 접속사와 전치사로 모두 쓰일 수 있다.

No one was present in the office **when** our workers arrived.
저희 직원들이 도착했을 때 사무실에는 아무도 없었습니다.

If your friend joins the gym, you will receive a prize.
친구가 체육관에 가입한다면, 당신은 상을 받을 것이다.

PRACTICE | 기출 연습하기

1. (So that / Before) the negotiations began, the CEO guaranteed no jobs would be lost.
2. The music concert will be moved indoors (if / until) there is inclement weather.
3. Staff photos will be uploaded online (as soon as / whether) Ms. Rodriguez finishes editing them.

◆ 출제 포인트 4   부사절 접속사 (3) 목적/결과

매년 약 2문제 출제

'목적/결과'의 의미를 갖는 부사절 접속사

목적	so (that) ~ can[may/will] / in order that ~할 수 있도록
결과	so[such] ~ that ... 너무 ~해서 …하다

Please contact us **so that** we **can** schedule the interview.
면접 일정을 잡을 수 있도록 저희에게 연락 주세요.

Mr. James worked **so** hard **that** he received a pay raise.
James 씨는 너무 열심히 일해서 급여 인상을 받았다.

PRACTICE | 기출 연습하기

1. Please let me know whether you can participate by November 1 (while / so that) we may arrange the seating.
2. The reduced speed limit was so effective (that / which) annual accidents dropped by 50%.
3. Please pay your overdue bill immediately (yet / so) your service can continue uninterrupted.

◆ 출제 포인트 5   부사절의 축약

매년 약 5문제 출제

두 절의 주어가 같은 경우 부사절을 '부사절 접속사 + -ing/p.p.' 형태로 바꿀 수 있다.
When making a reservation, you must provide a credit card number.
　　= When you make a reservation
예약하실 때 신용카드 번호를 주셔야 합니다.
→ 부사절이 능동태인 경우 '부사절 접속사 + -ing' 형태로 쓸 수 있다.

The contract will be only valid **if signed** by both parties. 그 계약은 양측이 서명한 경우에만 유효하다.
　　　　　　　　　　　　　= if it is signed by both parties
→ 부사절이 수동태인 경우 '부사절 접속사 + p.p.' 형태로 쓸 수 있다.

토익에 출제되는 '부사절 접속사 + -ing/p.p. 구조'

| when/while/before/after/since + **-ing** |
| when/while/as/unless/if/though + **p.p.** |

PRACTICE | 기출 연습하기

1. When (speaking / spoken) to the reporter, Sara Baker emphasized the importance of the merger.
2. All cruise passengers are encouraged to check their luggage (so / before) boarding the ship.
3. (As / When) indicated in the report, consumer interest in audiobooks has increased significantly.

◆ 출제 포인트 6   등위 접속사 / 상관 접속사

매년 약 7문제 출제

등위 접속사는 같은 단위를 대등하게 연결하는 접속사이다.

| and 그리고　　but(=yet) 그러나　　or 또는　　so 그래서 |

I went to the bookstore yesterday, **but** it was closed. 어제 서점에 갔지만, 문이 닫혀 있었다.
　　　　　　절　　　　　　　　　　　　절
Renewing your subscription is <u>simple</u> **and** <u>easy</u>. 구독을 갱신하는 것은 간단하고 쉽습니다.
　　　　　　　　　　　　　　형용사　　　형용사

상관 접속사는 짝을 맞추어 사용한다.

| both A and B A와 B 모두 | either A or B A 혹은 B |
| neither A nor B A도 B도 아닌 | not only A but (also) B A뿐만 아니라 B도 |

The restaurant is open for **both** lunch **and** dinner. 그 레스토랑은 점심과 저녁 모두 문을 연다.
The product was **neither** damaged **nor** defective. 그 제품은 손상되지도 결함이 있지도 않았다.

PRACTICE | 기출 연습하기

1. The article was removed from our site, (and / or) we apologize for its inaccuracies.
2. This weekend, movie ticket purchases include either a free popcorn (and / or) soda.
3. Driving in Tokyo may be confusing, (whereas / so) it's helpful to use a navigation system.

RC DAY 10 실전문제

1. ------- the city approves the permits, construction at the site on 97th Street will remain suspended.
   (A) Soon
   (B) Until
   (C) Even
   (D) With

2. Boxes should be loaded after ------- the tracking number and package weight have been entered into the computer.
   (A) nor
   (B) either
   (C) both
   (D) so

3. The human resources manager will make a hiring decision ------- she completes all of the interviews.
   (A) then
   (B) with
   (C) after
   (D) from

4. Yolanda Gates announced her campaign for mayor this morning, ------- she has yet to start fundraising.
   (A) likewise
   (B) but
   (C) whether
   (D) next

5. -------- employees are allowed to make color copies, management requests that they use black ink whenever possible.
   (A) Whether
   (B) However
   (C) Despite
   (D) Although

6. Ms. Bradford will be visiting our office tomorrow ------- that we can finalize the contract details.
   (A) if
   (B) so
   (C) then
   (D) such

7. Dr. Kenny's lectures are always well received, ------- he has the ability to explain important information clearly.
   (A) if so
   (B) not only
   (C) because
   (D) unless

8. ------- sorting through some old files, we discovered a picture of the founder with a former president.
   (A) In addition
   (B) While
   (C) Because of
   (D) As though

9. An insurance agent will assess the home's value again ------- the renovations have been completed.
   (A) still
   (B) once
   (C) later
   (D) while

10. ------- exploring the Madison Aquarium, we ask that you refrain from tapping on the glass or feeding the animals.
    (A) During
    (B) So that
    (C) When
    (D) In order to

11. ------- Jeff Thomas will be unable to attend the meeting in person, he will participate via video conferencing.
    (A) While
    (B) As if
    (C) Immediately
    (D) Whether

12. ------- peak season has begun, hotels and restaurants in the Virginia Beach area are busier than normal.
    (A) In that
    (B) In particular
    (C) Now that
    (D) Because of

13. ------- Ms. Draper meets with a new client, she always makes sure to leave one of her business cards.
    (A) As if
    (B) Though
    (C) Whereas
    (D) When

14. Machine operators must remain next to their equipment at all times ------- otherwise instructed by a manager.
    (A) unless
    (B) because
    (C) not only
    (D) either

15. The caterer at Heaven's Café can accommodate special requests ------- they are made at least 48 hours in advance.
    (A) prior to
    (B) unless
    (C) according to
    (D) as long as

16. Applications will be accepted ------- they are received by the end of the business day on Friday.
    (A) regardless of
    (B) provided that
    (C) as a result of
    (D) rather than

Questions 17-20 refer to the following notice.

Attention All Employees:

We would like to invite all of you to a special showcase of art, entitled *Risen from Waste*, by local artist Cathy Krum. This event will be held in the main atrium during August 17-29 as part of our Art in the Square series. ------- this exhibition has traveled to more than 300 cities, this will be its first time in Greensboro.
                                                              17.

Risen from Waste features pieces made entirely of ------- materials, such as old tires and
                                                      18.
discarded furniture. Ms. Krum believes that using these will help spread a message about the importance of environmental conservation.

Visiting the exhibition is, of course, -------, but we encourage all employees to take a few
                                        19.
moments to stop by. Ms. Krum's work is one-of-a-kind and will only be here for a short time.

-------.
20.

---

17. (A) But
    (B) Besides
    (C) Therefore
    (D) Although

18. (A) recycling
    (B) recycled
    (C) recycles
    (D) recycle

19. (A) available
    (B) optional
    (C) accessible
    (D) irrelevant

20. (A) We believe viewing it will bring some relaxation to your day.
    (B) All of the pieces were available for purchase at the end of the event.
    (C) Plastic bottles, broken glass, and newspaper were also used.
    (D) This is why it is necessary to protect the planet we live on.

RC DAY 11   명사절 접속사 / 형용사절 접속사(=관계대명사)

BASIC 기본기 익히기

1. 명사절의 역할

명사절은 '명사절 접속사 + (주어) + 동사 ~'의 형태이며 명사(구)와 마찬가지로 문장의 주어, 목적어, 보어의 역할을 한다.

Whether Mr. Lee will be hired depends on his qualifications.   Lee 씨가 채용될지의 여부는 그의 자질에 달려 있다.
       주어 역할

The manager wondered **who suggested the idea**.   매니저는 누가 그 아이디어를 제안했는지 궁금해 했다.
              목적어 역할

The problem is **that I received a wrong item**.   문제는 내가 잘못된 물품을 받았다는 것이다.
             보어 역할

2. 형용사절의 역할

형용사절은 '관계대명사(형용사절 접속사)' + 불완전한 절'의 형태이며 앞에 있는 명사를 수식하는 형용사 역할을 한다. 이 때 수식받는 명사를 선행사라고 부른다.

We will develop a Web site **that is easy to use**.   우리는 사용하기 쉬운 웹사이트를 개발할 것이다.
         선행사   형용사절

Anyone **who did not attend the meeting** should contact Mr. Beckner.
  선행사   형용사절

회의에 참석하지 않은 사람은 Beckner 씨에게 연락해야 합니다.

PATTERN 기출 유형 맛보기

Q. Sherwin Theater posted a list of the actors ------- will be appearing in its production of *Wall Street Days*.
(A) since
(B) who → 두 절을 연결하는 접속사가 필요한 자리이다. 선행사가 사람(actors)이고 빈칸 이하의 절에 주어가 없으므로 사람 주격 관계 대명사 (B) who가 정답이다.
(C) where
(D) they

Sherwin Theater는 <Wall Street Days> 작품에 출연할 배우들의 명단을 게시했다.

출제 경향 선행사의 사람, 사물 여부와 격에 따라 적절한 관계대명사를 선택하는 문제가 출제된다. 또한 관계대명사, 대명사, 부사 등을 함께 보기에 출제하여 용법을 구별하는 문제 또한 자주 출제되고 있다.

[이렇게도 출제된다]
- 명사절 접속사와 부사절 접속사를 함께 보기에 포함시켜 문장 구조에 적절한 것이 무엇인지 묻는다.
- 보기에 명사절 접속사를 여러 개 포함시켜 용법을 구별하는 문제가 출제된다.

◆ 출제 포인트 1   명사절의 위치

매년 약 2문제 출제

명사절은 명사절 접속사(that / whether / 의문사)가 이끌며 문장에서 주어, 목적어, 보어 자리에 위치한다.

주어   **That the product arrived damaged** is disappointing.
　　　　　　　　　　　　　　　　　　　　동사
　　　= It is disappointing **that the product arrived damaged**.
　　　제품이 파손된 상태로 도착한 것은 실망스럽다.
　　　→ 명사절이 주어 자리에 오는 경우 가주어/진주어 구문으로 표현하는 것이 더욱 일반적이다.

목적어   The supervisor will decide **who will be promoted**.   상사가 누가 승진될지 결정할 것이다.
　　　　　　　　　　　　타동사
　　　　Ms. Ching is not sure about **how much discount she will get**.
　　　　　　　　　　　　　　　전치사
　　　　Ching 씨는 얼마나 많은 할인을 받을지 확신하지 못하고 있다.

보어   Our concern is **whether we can obtain enough funds**.   우리의 걱정은 충분한 자금을 획득할 수 있을지이다.
　　　　　　　동사

PRACTICE | 기출 연습하기

1. (So / **That**) Ms. Mitchell's proposal was not approved by the committee was surprising.
2. Many customers called the company this morning to ask (**whether** / although) service will be restored soon.
3. Regardless of (even / **whether**) it rains, group photographs will be taken in Chester Park.

◆ 출제 포인트 2   명사절 접속사 (1) that / whether / how

매년 약 3문제 출제

명사절을 이끄는 that(~라는 점[것])과 whether(~인지 아닌지) 뒤에는 완전한 절이 온다.
The president announced **that** the company will build a new factory.
회장은 회사가 새로운 공장을 지을 것이라는 것을 발표했다.

The customer wants to know **whether** he is eligible for free shipping (or not).
그 고객은 자신이 무료 배송을 받을 수 있는지 없는지를 알고 싶어 합니다.

명사절을 이끄는 how는 단독으로 쓰이면 '어떻게'의 의미이고, 'how+형용사/부사'의 형태로 쓰이면 '얼마나'의 의미이다. 두 경우 모두 뒤에는 완전한 절이 온다.
We need to find **how** customer service can be improved.
고객 서비스를 어떻게 개선할 수 있는지 알아낼 필요가 있다.

Many are surprised by **how** rapidly the company is growing.
많은 사람들은 그 회사가 얼마나 빠르게 성장하고 있는지에 놀란다.

PRACTICE | 기출 연습하기

1. The coordinator of the charity event estimates (**that** / which) it will raise over $10,000.
2. Bonuses will differ depending on (**how** / so) many vacation days an employee has used.
3. The incident report will determine (**whether** / so that) Gyatt's latest sedan needs to be recalled.

◆ 출제 포인트 3   명사절 접속사 (2) who / what / which

매년 약 1문제 출제

명사절을 이끄는 who(누가, 누구를)와 what(무엇이, 무엇을)은 명사절 내에서 주어나 목적어 역할을 한다.
Ms. Riedel will explain **what** the workshop covers.   Riedel 씨는 워크숍이 무엇을 다루는지 설명할 것이다.
　　　　　　　　　　　　목적어(무엇을)　목적어 없는 불완전한 절

Please let me know **who** will make a presentation.   누가 발표를 할지 알려주세요.
　　　　　　　　　　주어(누가)　　주어 없는 불완전한 절

명사절을 이끄는 which(어떤)는 명사를 수식하여 '선택'의 뉘앙스로 사용된다.
I would like to see **which** room is currently available.   현재 어떤 방이 이용 가능한지 알고 싶습니다.

It is not clear **which** train I should take.   내가 어떤 기차를 타야 할지 확실하지 않다.

PRACTICE | 기출 연습하기

1. During this promotion, the customers will decide (whom / which) ice cream flavor is best.
2. Analysts will likely determine exactly (what / that) caused the surprising election results.
3. We should decide (who / which) will be attending the conference before we book accommodations.

◆ 출제 포인트 4   명사절 접속사 + to부정사

매년 약 1문제 출제

what/how/whether가 이끄는 명사절에는 절 대신 to부정사를 사용할 수 있다.
You will learn **how** you can install the program.   그 프로그램을 어떻게 설치하는지 배울 것이다.
= You will learn **how** to install the program.

Mr. Weaver must decide **whether** he should accept the proposal or not.
= Mr. Weaver must decide **whether** to accept the proposal or not.
Weaver 씨는 제안을 수락할지 말지 결정해야 한다.

'which + 명사 + 절'은 'which + 명사 + to부정사'로 표현할 수 있다.
Ms. Chapman has not decided **which plan** she should choose.
= Ms. Chapman has not decided **which plan** to choose.
Chapman 씨는 어떤 계획을 선택해야 할지 결정하지 못했다.

PRACTICE | 기출 연습하기

1. Our various vacation packages let you choose (which / whether) to pursue adventure or relaxation.
2. Nolan Communications is hiring a technician who knows (how / that) to use various programming languages.
3. Our stylist will help you determine (how / which) shoes to select for your outfit.

◆ 출제 포인트 5 형용사절 접속사(관계대명사)의 종류 (1)

매년 6~7문제 출제

선행사가 사람/사물인지에 따라, 형용사절에서의 역할에 따라 사용하는 관계대명사가 달라진다.

선행사 \ 격	주격	목적격 (생략 가능)	소유격
사람	who[that]	whom[that]	whose
사물	which[that]	which[that]	whose

TIP that은 콤마와 전치사 뒤에는 사용하지 않는다.

관계대명사(주격) Anna Rode is a journalist **who** writes articles on investment.
Anna Rode는 투자에 관한 기사를 쓰는 기자이다.
→ 사람(a journalist)을 지칭하며 동사(writes)의 주어 역할을 하는 사람 주격이 필요한 자리이다.

관계대명사(목적격) Below are some of the topics **that** we are going to discuss.
아래 있는 것은 우리가 논의할 몇 가지 주제입니다.
→ 선행사(topics)는 사물이며 to부정사(to discuss)의 목적격이 필요한 자리이다.

We have interviewed seven candidates, **each of whom** has a university degree. 우리는 일곱 명의 후보자를 인터뷰했는데, 그들 각각은 대학 학위를 가지고 있다.
→ 전체 중 일부를 나타내는 대명사(one/each/several/some/most/all/none 등)와 of which/whom은 함께 자주 사용된다.

PRACTICE | 기출 연습하기

1. Any customer (they / who) mentions the radio advertisement gets a free order of breadsticks.
2. Trent Elliot hopes to start a business (when / that) facilitates the distribution of wind energy.
3. Nashville Chicken has five locations, one of (who / which) is currently closed for renovations.

◆ 출제 포인트 6 형용사절 접속사(관계대명사)의 종류 (2)

매년 약 1문제 출제

관계대명사 소유격은 선행사가 사람과 사물인 경우 모두 whose를 사용한다.

대명사(소유격) We will hire Ms. Lafont. **Her** résumé is particularly impressive.
우리는 Lafont 씨를 채용할 것이다. 그녀의 이력서는 특히 인상적이다.

관계대명사(소유격) We will hire Ms. Lafont, **whose** résumé is particularly impressive.
우리는 Lafont 씨를 채용할 것인데, 그녀의 이력서가 특히 인상적이다.
→ 사람(Ms. Lafont)을 지칭하며 명사(résumé) 앞이므로 사람 소유격이 필요한 자리이다.

PRACTICE | 기출 연습하기

1. We have decided on another candidate (who / whose) expertise better suits our needs.
2. The teams (that / whose) members work different shifts must arrange their own meeting times.
3. A 30 percent discount will be available to customers (who / whose) purchase a one-year subscription.

RC DAY 11 실전문제

1. The company will not discuss the contract terms ------- were negotiated with Eclectic Motors until the deal is final.
   (A) they
   (B) that
   (C) where
   (D) whose

2. Subscribers -------- have signed up for the *Toronto Daily* digital package have unlimited access to online articles.
   (A) when
   (B) all
   (C) who
   (D) also

3. The firm still needs to release last year's budget report, -------- describes its overseas investment.
   (A) what
   (B) where
   (C) this
   (D) which

4. Scientists want to find out ------- water pollution is responsible for high rates of skin diseases in the community.
   (A) whether
   (B) although
   (C) so that
   (D) either

5. Kirking Hotels CEO Bella Johnson announced ------- the company will be opening a new chain of luxury accommodations.
   (A) once
   (B) that
   (C) while
   (D) what

6. Baritone Corp. purchased the accounting firm ------- offices are on the third floor of the Waters Building.
   (A) which
   (B) whose
   (C) what
   (D) how

7. The chef must decide ------- to serve the chicken with potatoes or the baked fish and vegetables.
   (A) so
   (B) which
   (C) both
   (D) whether

8. Most residents of Morris City work in the steel industry, ------- accounts for about 30% of the local economy.
   (A) whatever
   (B) which
   (C) who
   (D) this

9. According to the agenda, we will discuss ------- well the current office features suit the needs of the company.
   (A) so
   (B) only
   (C) therefore
   (D) how

10. The actors are in final rehearsals for the play, ------- set to debut at 7 P.M. this evening.
    (A) that having
    (B) what is
    (C) the one that
    (D) which is

11. Right Start is an educational program that helps high school students choose ------- career path to pursue.
    (A) how
    (B) where
    (C) who
    (D) which

12. Our investors will be visiting the New Haven facility to see -------- work on the prototype is progressing.
    (A) whom
    (B) how
    (C) upon
    (D) during

13. It remains to be seen ------- Mr. Moreno's request to be transferred to Perth will be approved.
    (A) such that
    (B) whether
    (C) as if
    (D) whereas

14. ------- passengers are able to cancel their reservations for free depends on the type of ticket they purchased.
    (A) Thus
    (B) Whether
    (C) Additionally
    (D) Even if

15. Malcolm Engineering has hired thirty new employees, ------- are recent graduates.
    (A) as far as
    (B) because of them
    (C) in order that
    (D) most of whom

16. To gain insight on staff productivity, the new manager has asked employees to describe ------- their jobs involve.
    (A) about
    (B) when
    (C) how
    (D) what

Questions 17-20 refer to the following article.

Phoenix Star — Business Briefs

PHOENIX (February 3) — Otto G. Clancy has been promoted to chief financial officer (CFO) of Nile River Manufacturing. The promotion was ------- through a press release on Tuesday. -------.
                                                                                    17.   **18.**
As CFO, he will oversee company investments and financial reporting. -------, he will be charged
                                                                      19.
with determining which areas of the company are likely to be most profitable in the future. Mr. Clancy was also the employee ------- Nile River Manufacturing's charitable contributions last
                                                          20.
year.

17. (A) denied
    (B) confirmed
    (C) earned
    (D) requested

18. (A) The firm is also seeking a new entry-level accountant.
    (B) Nile River Manufacturing will work with a number of appliance companies.
    (C) The board of directors will be meeting Mr. Clancy for the first time.
    (D) Mr. Clancy has been senior accounting director for five years.

19. (A) Consequently
    (B) Instead
    (C) On the contrary
    (D) Additionally

20. (A) whose coordination
    (B) coordinated that
    (C) who coordinated
    (D) that coordinates

RC DAY 12 비교

BASIC 기본기 익히기

1. 원급/비교급/최상급의 형태 및 의미
형용사와 부사는 원급(기본 형태)의 어형을 변화시켜 비교급(-er)과 최상급(-est)의 형태를 만들 수 있다. 3음절 이상인 경우 보통 비교급은 앞에 more를, 최상급에는 most를 붙인다.

	원급	비교급 (더 ~한[하게])	최상급 (가장 ~한[하게])
2음절 이하	low ⑱ 낮은 fast ⑱ 빠른 ⑲ 빠르게	low**er** ⑱ 더 낮은 fast**er** ⑱ 더 빠른 ⑲ 더 빠르게	low**est** ⑱ 가장 낮은 fast**est** ⑱ 가장 빠른 ⑲ 가장 빠르게
3음절 이상	important ⑱ 중요한 rapidly ⑲ 빠르게	**more** important ⑱ 더 중요한 **more** rapidly ⑲ 더 빠르게	**most** important ⑱ 가장 중요한 **most** rapidly ⑲ 가장 빠르게

- **원급** Lerma Printing is known for its **fast** services. Lerma Printing은 빠른 서비스로 알려져 있다.
- **비교급** This printer is **faster** than the previous model. 이 프린터는 이전 모델보다 빠르다.
- **최상급** Paulto Co. is one of the **fastest** growing companies. Paulto 사는 가장 빠르게 성장하는 회사 중 하나이다.

2. 비교급/최상급의 불규칙 변화
-er/-est 혹은 more/most 형태가 아닌 비교급/최상급 어휘들은 별도로 기억해 두어야 한다.

원급	비교급 (더 ~한[하게])	최상급 (가장 ~한[하게])
good 좋은, well 잘	better 더 좋은/더 잘	best 가장 좋은/가장 잘
many/much 많은	more 더 많은	most 가장 많은
little 적은	less 더 적은	least 가장 적은

PATTERN 기출 유형 맛보기

Q. Jewelry Expo organizers were disappointed to discover that attendance was ------- than last year despite active marketing.

(A) lowest
(B) lowering
(C) lower → 빈칸 뒤에 than이 있으므로 이와 어울리는 비교급 (C) lower가 정답이다.
(D) low

보석 박람회 주최측은 활발한 마케팅에도 불구하고 참석률이 작년보다 낮다는 것을 발견하고 실망했다.

출제 경향 than을 단서로 제시한 후 비교급을 정답으로 선택하거나 반대로 비교급을 제시한 후 than을 선택하는 유형의 출제 비중이 가장 높다.

[이렇게도 출제된다]
- 정관사 혹은 소유격을 빈칸 앞에 제시한 후 최상급을 선택하는 문제가 출제된다.
- 비교급이나 최상급과 어울리는 부사 표현이 무엇인지 묻는 문제가 출제된다.

◆ 출제 포인트 1　원급

매년 약 1문제 출제

원급 비교는 두 대상의 상태나 특징이 동등할 경우에 쓰며, 'as + 원급 형용사/부사 + as(…만큼 ~한)'로 표현한다.

Adam Vinson's new novel is **as popular as** his first book.
　　　　　　　　　　　　　　more popular (X) / most popular (X)

Adam Vinson의 새 소설은 그의 첫 번째 책만큼 인기가 있다.

Please finalize the paperwork **as quickly as** possible. 서류를 가능한 빨리 완성해 주세요.
　　　　　　　　　　　　　　more quickly (X) / most quickly (X)

원급 비교의 as~as에 형용사를 쓸지 부사를 쓸지는 문장 구조를 살펴 판단한다.

The bedroom <u>is</u> as **spacious** as the living room area. 침실이 거실만큼 넓다.
　　　　　　　　　　spaciously (X)

→ 2형식 동사(is)의 보어가 필요하므로 형용사가 와야 한다.

Please complete this form as **accurately** as possible. 이 양식을 최대한 정확하게 작성해 주세요.
　　　　　　　　　　　　　accurate (X)

→ 앞에 완전한 문장이 있으므로 부사가 와야 한다.

PRACTICE | 기출 연습하기

1. Vendors should be as (flexible / flexibility) as possible when requesting preferred booth locations.
2. Novak Chemicals disposes of its waste products as (safer / safely) as possible.
3. Few nurses are as (responsive / responsively) to patients' needs as those at Camden Hospital.

◆ 출제 포인트 2　비교급 (1)

매년 2~3문제 출제

비교급은 두 대상의 상태나 특징에 우열이 있을 때 쓰며, '비교급 형용사/부사 + than(…보다 ~한)'으로 표현한다.

Blind Comet offers **lower** prices **than** its competitors. Blind Comet은 경쟁자들보다 낮은 가격을 제공한다.
　　　　　　　　　low (X) / lowest (X)

cf.) This program will help you perform tasks **more efficiently**.
　　이 프로그램은 작업을 (기존보다) 더욱 효율적으로 수행하도록 도울 것입니다.

→ 문맥상 비교 대상을 알 수 있을 경우 'than ~'을 생략하는 것이 가능하다.

형용사의 비교급인지 부사의 비교급인지는 문장 구조를 살펴 판단한다.

The company needs to <u>be</u> more **competitive** to attract investment.
　　　　　　　　　　　　　　competitively (X)

그 회사는 투자를 유치하기 위해 경쟁력을 높일 필요가 있다.

→ be동사 뒤에 보어가 필요하므로 형용사가 와야 한다.

The electrical system will be inspected more **frequently**. 전기 시스템은 더 자주 점검될 것이다.
　　　　　　　　　　　　　　　　　　　frequent (X)

→ 앞에 동사가 있으므로 이를 수식하는 부사가 와야 한다.

PRACTICE | 기출 연습하기

1. The latest e-reader from Bonfire Designs is (slim / slimmer) than the previous models.
2. Preparing monthly business reports is more time-consuming (than / from) preparing weekly ones.
3. This farewell gathering has been planned (more careful / more carefully) than other events.

◆ 출제 포인트 3   비교급 (2)

매년 1문제 출제

much, still, even, far은 비교급을 강조하여 '훨씬'이란 의미를 갖는다.
The museum will relocate to a **much** larger building. 그 박물관은 훨씬 더 큰 건물로 이전할 것이다.
We are looking for ways to work **even** more productively. 우리는 훨씬 더 생산적으로 일할 수 있는 방법을 찾고 있다.

라틴계 비교급은 -or로 끝나며 than이 아닌 to를 사용한다.
This camera is far **superior to** the one we had before. 이 카메라는 우리가 전에 가지고 있던 것보다 훨씬 낫다.

토익에 출제되는 라틴계 비교급

superior to ~보다 뛰어난	inferior to ~보다 열등한	prior to ~보다 이전에

PRACTICE | 기출 연습하기

1. Ms. Murillo is now required to perform (more / even) wider tasks than before.
2. The newly built highway makes it much (easy / easier) to drive across the city.
3. The atmosphere of Blue Moon is (superior / better) to that of more expensive restaurants.

◆ 출제 포인트 4   최상급 (1)

매년 약 2문제 출제

최상급은 셋 이상 대상의 상태나 특징을 비교할 경우에 쓰며, 'the[소유격] + 최상급 형용사/부사'로 표현한다.
Thor Magnison is one of **the most popular** authors in Iceland.
Thor Magnison은 아이슬란드에서 가장 인기 있는 작가 중 한 사람이다.
We visited **Europe's most densely** populated area. 우리는 유럽에서 가장 인구 밀도가 높은 지역을 방문했다.

형용사의 최상급인지 부사의 최상급인지는 문장 구조를 살펴 판단한다.
Mr. Ohlsen is going to take the most **convenient** route. Ohlsen 씨는 가장 편리한 길을 택할 것이다.
                                              conveniently (X)
→ 명사(route)를 수식해야 하므로 형용사가 들어가야 한다.
The city will repave **the most heavily** travelled part of the highway.
                           heaviest (X)
그 도시는 고속도로에서 차량의 이동이 가장 많았던 구간을 다시 포장할 것이다.
→ 분사(travelled)를 수식해야 하므로 부사가 들어가야 한다.

PRACTICE | 기출 연습하기

1. Watch the film in a movie theater to enjoy it to the (fuller / fullest) extent possible.
2. Last year, employment growth was the (greatness / greatest) in tourism and health services sector.
3. We offer one of the (most comprehensive / most comprehensively) training programs in the country.

◆ 출제 포인트 5   최상급 (2)

매년 1~2문제 출제

최상급의 비교 대상·범위는 of(~중에서), among(~사이에서), in(~에서)과 함께 표현한다.
Of the ten applicants, Mr. Hornsby is the most qualified. 10명의 지원자 중에서 Hornsby 씨가 가장 적임자다.
This lake is the most popular location **in the park**. 이 호수는 공원에서 가장 인기 있는 장소이다.

ever/yet/so far(여태껏, 역대), only(오직, ~만), available/possible(이용 가능한/가능한)은 최상급을 강조하는 표현으로 자주 사용된다.
The committee will make this year's event **the best ever**. 위원회는 올해 행사를 역대 최고로 만들 것이다.
We use **only the freshest** ingredients. 우리는 가장 신선한 재료만을 사용한다.
This app will help you find **the cheapest** flights **available**.
이 앱은 구할 수 있는 가장 저렴한 항공편을 찾는 데 도움을 줄 것이다.

PRACTICE | 기출 연습하기

1. Sunbrella canvas is among the (stronger / strongest) fabrics available for boat covers.
2. (By / Of) all the courses Professor Dutton teaches, Medieval Literature is the most challenging.
3. *Precinct's* latest episode is its most exciting (just / yet) and showcases excellent character development.

◆ 출제 포인트 6   관용 표현

매년 약 1문제 출제

원급/비교급/최상급 관용 표현

just as + 원급 + as 딱 …만큼 ~한	This material is **just as durable as** metal. 이 재료는 금속만큼 내구성이 있다.
twice[three times] as + 원급 + as 두 배[세 배] 만큼 더 ~한	Merley Hall is **twice as large as** Allen Hall. Merley 홀은 Allen 홀보다 두 배 만큼 더 크다.
no later than (늦어도) ~까지	Please reply to this letter **no later than** March 1. 늦어도 3월 1일까지 이 편지에 답장해 주세요.
비교급 + than ever 그 어느 때보다 더	Creating a Web site has become **easier than ever**. 웹사이트를 만드는 것이 그 어느 때보다도 더 쉬워졌다.
비교급 + than predicted[anticipated] 예측했던[계획했던] 것보다 더	The project took much **longer than predicted**. 그 프로젝트는 예상했던 것보다 더 오래 걸렸다.
one[some] of the + 최상급 가장 ~한 것 중의 하나[일부]	The article featured **some of the most beautiful** beaches in the world. 그 기사는 세계에서 가장 아름다운 해변들 중 일부를 특집으로 다루었다.
the second[third] + 최상급 두 번째로[세 번째로] 가장 ~한	**The second longest** bridge in the country is located in Covia. 그 나라에서 두 번째로 긴 다리는 Covia에 위치해 있다.

PRACTICE | 기출 연습하기

1. Participants should vote for their favorite story (no later / as quickly) than September 29.
2. Tiramisu is the fourth (more frequently / most frequently) ordered item on our dessert menu.
3. Maintaining a perfect lawn is easier than (once / ever) thanks to Sadler Landscaping.

RC DAY 12 실전문제

1. According to the test results, the hybrid engine was ------- than the electric one in terms of gas mileage.
   (A) as efficiently
   (B) most efficiently
   (C) more efficient
   (D) very efficient

2. Garrison Dean's new photography exhibit is good, but it isn't as impressive ------- some of his earlier work.
   (A) like
   (B) either
   (C) of
   (D) as

3. We ask that you board the bus no -------- than 3:15 P.M. so that the tour can stay on schedule.
   (A) late
   (B) later
   (C) latest
   (D) lately

4. The panelists will be discussing playwright Rachel Nunez and the impact of her ------- plays on modern society.
   (A) most popular
   (B) popularity
   (C) more popularly
   (D) popularizes

5. With the revised instruction manual, our customers should be able to assemble the bookcase much --------.
   (A) most easily
   (B) easy
   (C) easily
   (D) more easily

6. Located in the center of downtown Dallas, Fashion Bin sells designer clothing at a discount of more -------- 50%.
   (A) over
   (B) even
   (C) as
   (D) than

7. Power lines were severely damaged by the storm, but Nikita Electric promises to restore power as ------- as possible.
   (A) quickest
   (B) more quickly
   (C) quickly
   (D) quicker

8. To the board's surprise, the merger with Onestar, Inc., has been -------- more beneficial than originally predicted.
   (A) even
   (B) about
   (C) alone
   (D) soon

9. Despite its faults, analysts agree that the governor's tax proposal is by far the -------- so far.
   (A) most innovatively
   (B) innovation
   (C) most innovative
   (D) innovate

10. The clients care more about purchasing a house that is the right size -------- finding one in their preferred location.
    (A) than
    (B) which
    (C) that
    (D) what

11. Desert Technologies claims the ProtonX5 is both lightweight and the -------- computer on the market today.
    (A) most speed
    (B) speedily
    (C) speediest
    (D) more speed

12. During the meeting, Ms. Kerry stressed that working together as a team is the ------- on the new project.
    (A) important
    (B) importantly
    (C) most important
    (D) importance

13. With only 10 minutes left in his presentation, Ms. Weber will give the -------- possible explanation of the manufacturing process.
    (A) briefly
    (B) more briefly
    (C) briefest
    (D) brief

14. The project budget needs to be adjusted as the cost of the venue is higher than -------.
    (A) anticipating
    (B) anticipates
    (C) anticipate
    (D) anticipated

15. Of all the speakers at the symposium, the consensus was that Carl Bowman was the -------.
    (A) more eloquently
    (B) eloquently
    (C) most eloquent
    (D) eloquent

16. No one campaigned ------- for better health care than Ms. Ventura, but she couldn't receive enough support.
    (A) more energetically
    (B) energetically
    (C) more energetic
    (D) energetic

Questions 17-20 refer to the following Web page.

> The Fairstone Institute will soon begin its ------- study on carbohydrate consumption to date.
> **17.**
> -------. The other half will be able to choose from a ------- list of carbohydrates. Participants
> **18.** **19.**
> will also be asked to keep a record of all the food they eat. -------, they will need to complete
> **20.**
> a survey assessing their energy levels after each meal. The experiment will take place over a period of 30 days. Lead researchers are still looking for volunteers, so please contact us at carbstudy@fairstone.com if interested.

17. (A) most comprehensively
    (B) comprehensive
    (C) most comprehensive
    (D) compression

18. (A) Some participants consumed an excessive amount of carbohydrates.
    (B) Eaten in the proper amounts, carbohydrates are part of a balanced diet.
    (C) Participants will be men and women between the ages of 18 and 49.
    (D) Half of participants will be allowed to eat unlimited carbohydrates.

19. (A) selection
    (B) selected
    (C) selects
    (D) selecting

20. (A) For example
    (B) In addition
    (C) In contrast
    (D) Instead

RC DAY 13 — 어휘 - 동사 / 형용사 / 부사

◆ 출제 포인트 1 동사 어휘 (1)

매년 약 26문제 출제

동사 어휘 문제는 목적어와 의미상 가장 잘 어울리는 동사를 선택한다.
The supervisor has (**expressed** / ~~congratulated~~) concern about the changes in the work schedules. 상사는 작업 일정 변경에 대해 우려를 표했다.

빈칸 뒤에 전치사가 있는 경우 이와 어울리는 동사를 선택한다.
All employees must (**participate** / ~~attend~~) in the special training session this Friday.
모든 직원은 이번 금요일 특별 교육 세션에 참석해야 합니다.

토익에 출제되는 '동사 + 전치사'

invest in ~에 투자하다	specialize in ~을 전문으로 하다	cooperate with ~와 협력하다	communicate with ~와 연락을 주고받다
enroll in ~에 등록하다	rely[depend] on ~에 의존하다	register for ~에 등록하다	compete with[against] ~와 경쟁하다
deal with ~을 다루다	participate in ~에 참석하다	consist of ~로 구성되다	coincide with ~와 일치하다
result in[from] ~을 야기하다[~로부터 초래되다]		collaborate on[with] ~에 대해[~와] 협력하다	
comply with = conform to = adhere to ~을 준수하다			

PRACTICE | 기출 연습하기

1. We recommend that you (enroll / apply) in the introductory marketing course offered at the community center.
2. Construction was halted because the architect's plans did not (assign / comply) with local regulations.
3. The manuals available online should (address / install) issues you may encounter with our software.

◆ 출제 포인트 2 동사 어휘 (2)

매년 3~4문제 출제

빈칸 뒤에 'A to[from] B' 혹은 that절 등의 구문이 있는 경우 이와 어울리는 동사를 선택한다.
You may (~~store~~ / **ship**) the computer to one of our authorized service centers.
컴퓨터를 공인 서비스 센터 중 하나로 보내실 수 있습니다.

토익에 출제되는 '동사 구문'

동사 + A to B A를 B에게 ~하다	ship/send 보내다 forward 전달하다 submit 제출하다 delegate 위임하다 donate 기부하다
동사 + A from -ing A가 ~하지 못하게 하다	prevent/prohibit/keep/discourage/stop 막다[방해하다]
동사 + that절 that절을 ~하다	ensure 확실히 하다 agree 동의하다 argue 주장하다 indicate 나타내다 announce 발표하다

사람만을 목적어로 취하는 동사에 주의한다.
The Hudson Center will hold a job fair in Detroit to (**recruit** / ~~complete~~) new researchers.
Hudson Center는 새로운 연구자들을 모집하기 위해 디트로이트에서 취업 박람회를 열 것이다.

Ms. Ence called this morning to (~~remind~~ / **confirm**) the details of the reservation.
Ence 씨가 예약 내용을 확인하기 위해 오늘 아침에 전화했다.

토익에 출제되는 '사람만을 목적어로 취하는 동사'

inform[notify] 통보하다   convince[assure] 납득[확신]시키다   remind 상기시키다   appoint 임명하다   elect 선출하다   recruit 채용하다

TIP inform[notify], convince[assure], remind는 '회사[단체]', '부서' 등을 목적어로 취할 수도 있다.

PRACTICE | 기출 연습하기

1. Quarterly inspections will (ensure / reserve) that the factory's machinery remains in excellent condition.
2. Jennifer revised the article and (exchanged / forwarded) the final draft to her head editor.
3. The Department of Transportation has (informed / announced) the extension of the Astoria subway line.

✦ 최빈출 ✦ 확인 문제

1. New advertising firms need to ------- strong relationships with clients to gain a clear understanding of their needs.
   (A) treat
   (B) build
   (C) raise
   (D) locate

2. Parkland Heights residents ------- that improvements must be made to the rooftop swimming pool.
   (A) contain
   (B) agree
   (C) revise
   (D) defer

3. The staff at Shriner's Hospital ------- in the care and treatment of children and young people.
   (A) identifies
   (B) processes
   (C) specializes
   (D) finalizes

4. Writer Emma Kay and Mountaintop Publishing have ------- an agreement to increase the royalty payments by 10%.
   (A) reached
   (B) notified
   (C) resulted
   (D) invited

5. The IT department's report suggests that updating the company's firewall program would ------- computer network failures.
   (A) enhance
   (B) prevent
   (C) organize
   (D) upgrade

6. Executives at Streetlight Studios ------- additional changes to the film's script before they would proceed with production.
   (A) advised
   (B) requested
   (C) informed
   (D) complied

7. Graduates of Oberlin's School of Law will continue to ------- against each other as they pursue careers in top law firms.
   (A) associate
   (B) compete
   (C) decide
   (D) finance

8. Mr. Hasan needs to ------- the first draft of his novel to his publisher by 4:30 P.M. this afternoon.
   (A) comply
   (B) urge
   (C) submit
   (D) advise

9. For every annual edition, the head editor of *Best American Poetry* ------- a guest editor who decides which poems to include.
   (A) predicts
   (B) operates
   (C) develops
   (D) appoints

10. Mellinger's acquisition of Southcoast Foods will ------- in a 15% increase in the grocer's market share.
    (A) expect
    (B) spend
    (C) finish
    (D) result

11. Any mail containing voter registration information must be ------- to Larry Watson on the fourth floor.
    (A) delivered
    (B) stored
    (C) handled
    (D) responded

12. The state government ------- new environmental policies to reduce the amount of industrial pollutants.
    (A) convinced
    (B) achieved
    (C) implemented
    (D) preserved

◆ 출제 포인트 3　형용사 어휘 (1)

매년 약 26문제 출제

형용사 어휘 문제는 수식받는 명사와 의미상 가장 잘 어울리는 형용사를 선택한다.
We offer 20 (~~considerable~~ / spacious) rooms with patios and amazing views.
저희는 테라스와 멋진 전망이 있는 넓은 객실을 제공합니다.

보어 자리인 경우 주어 혹은 목적어와 어울리는 형용사를 선택한다.
All our tour guides are experienced and (knowledgeable / ~~enjoyable~~) about the local history.
우리의 모든 여행 가이드들은 경험이 많고 지역 역사에 대해 박식합니다.

The company wishes to make its Web site design more (~~conclusive~~ / attractive).
회사는 웹 사이트 디자인을 보다 매력적으로 만들기를 원한다.

PRACTICE | 기출 연습하기

1. Air Tropico experienced (completed / significant) growth after opening several direct routes to Hawaii.
2. Even with the rise of mobile technologies, demand for desktop computers has remained (casual / stable).
3. Donations will be used to keep the program fees (affordable / useful) for the residents of the community.

◆ 출제 포인트 4　형용사 어휘 (2)

매년 8~9문제 출제

복수 명사를 수식하는 형용사 numerous(수많은), multiple(다수의), various(다양한)에 주의한다.
An e-mail with your (~~numerous~~ / updated) itinerary will be sent to you by tomorrow.
업데이트된 여행 일정이 포함된 이메일이 내일까지 보내질 것입니다.

사람에게만 사용하는 형용사에 주의한다.
We offer (competitive / ~~experienced~~) compensation and an excellent benefits package.
우리는 경쟁력 있는 보상과 훌륭한 복리후생 제도를 제공합니다.

토익에 출제되는 '사람에게만 사용하는 형용사'

[in]experienced 경험이 있는[없는]　　skilled 숙련된　　talented 재능 있는　　motivated 진취적인　　convinced 확신하는
[un]willing 의향이 있는[내키지 않는]　　reluctant 꺼리는　　[un]aware 알고 있는[깨닫지 못하는]　　loyal 충성스러운
pleased/delighted/satisfied/excited 기쁜, 만족을 느낀　　fascinated 매료된　　[un]interested 관심이 있는[없는]

PRACTICE | 기출 연습하기

1. The lead designer has found the feedback very (interested / useful) and will modify the prototype.
2. Due to (numerous / supportive) problems encountered during production, the film premiere was delayed.
3. Include a letter of recommendation from your (various / previous) employer in your application packet.

✦ 최빈출 ✦ 확인 문제

1. Collin Publication's *Intro to Geometry* had to be re-published due to numerous ------- errors.
   (A) reliable
   (B) rapid
   (C) detailed
   (D) minor

2. Bangkok is home to many gourmet restaurants that serve incredible dishes at ------- prices.
   (A) operational
   (B) willing
   (C) reasonable
   (D) valuable

3. During a loan deferment period, -------- payments will be acceptable, but interest will continue to grow.
   (A) considerate
   (B) sensible
   (C) desirable
   (D) partial

4. The corporate restructuring caused six sales representatives to apply for transfers, leaving those positions -------.
   (A) potential
   (B) bright
   (C) hollow
   (D) vacant

5. The project directors found it ------- to delegate daily operational tasks so that they could focus on more creative issues.
   (A) financial
   (B) abundant
   (C) beneficial
   (D) legible

6. Due to ------- call volumes during the holidays, customers may prefer to use our online chat service.
   (A) steep
   (B) loud
   (C) heavy
   (D) wide

7. Our parking attendants are ------- to assist with any emergency situations that may arise.
   (A) available
   (B) obvious
   (C) voluntary
   (D) probable

8. Universal Architecture uses ------- 3D printing technology to provide inexpensive and sustainable housing.
   (A) surprised
   (B) pleased
   (C) delayed
   (D) advanced

9. The session entitled "Leadership for the 21st Century" was brief but very -------.
   (A) informative
   (B) eventual
   (C) advisory
   (D) helping

10. Kate Schmidt was nominated in the Best Actress category for her ------- performance in *The Simple Life*.
    (A) responsive
    (B) exceptional
    (C) multiple
    (D) whole

11. Despite increased competition in the industry, the Nova S phone maintained -------- sales throughout the year.
    (A) renewable
    (B) steady
    (C) correct
    (D) final

12. Hospital management placed three twin beds in the break room to make it more ------- for staff working 24-hour shifts.
    (A) capable
    (B) probable
    (C) favorable
    (D) comfortable

◆ 출제 포인트 5　부사 어휘 (1)

매년 24~25문제 출제

부사 어휘 문제는 수식받는 단어와 의미상 가장 잘 어울리는 부사를 선택한다.
The beach has become (**increasingly** / ~~differently~~) popular among tourists.
그 해변은 관광객들 사이에서 점점 더 인기를 얻고 있다.

The restaurant offers (~~sparsely~~ / **reasonably**) priced menus that change every day.
그 식당은 매일 바뀌는 합리적인 가격의 메뉴를 제공한다.

시제와 어울리는 부사를 정답으로 선택한다.
Sattler employees (**often** / ~~nearly~~) eat lunch in the company's cafeteria.
Sattler 직원들은 종종 회사의 구내 식당에서 점심을 먹는다.

PRACTICE | 기출 연습하기

1. Hammer Studios will (soon / once) release *Dungeon Crawl* 3 on every game console.
2. The newest branches of Anytime Health are (conveniently / fluently) located in Waterford and Vienna.
3. Due to faulty equipment, the Cleveland factory has not met its weekly quotas (briefly / recently).

◆ 출제 포인트 6　부사 어휘 (2)

매년 8~9문제 출제

정도를 나타내는 부사가 자주 출제된다.

slightly/marginally 근소하게	moderately 적당히	somewhat 다소	relatively 상대적으로	partially 부분적으로
very 매우	highly 매우, 많이	fully 완전히	quite/rather 꽤	extremely 극도로	markedly 현저히
dramatically 극적으로	substantially/significantly/considerably 상당히			

Prices are (**considerably** / ~~voluntarily~~) higher during the peak months.
성수기 동안에는 가격이 상당히 더 높다.

시간의 전후 및 신속함을 나타내는 부사가 자주 출제된다.

once 한때	formerly/previously 이전에	originally 애초에, 본래	later 나중에	finally 마침내	now 지금
still 여전히	immediately 즉시	soon/shortly 곧	promptly 지체 없이	abruptly 갑작스럽게	

The updated copy of the contract will be sent to you (~~recently~~ / **immediately**).
업데이트된 계약서 사본이 즉시 발송될 것입니다.

The video game will be released across the country (**later** / ~~next~~) this month.
그 비디오 게임은 이달 말에 전국에 출시될 것이다.

PRACTICE | 기출 연습하기

1. Roman Academy's three-month intensive Italian course is regarded as (highly / correctly) effective.
2. After living in Tokyo for a decade, Mr. Kellison (once / still) struggles to understand Japanese.
3. Compared with other major cities, the cost of living in Dallas is (efficiently / relatively) low.

◆ 최빈출 ◆ 확인 문제

1. The opinion column was ------- removed from the Web site after some readers complained about its content.
   (A) equally
   (B) randomly
   (C) promptly
   (D) comparatively

2. Popular tax preparation software such as E-Crunch helps users to calculate their income tax returns -------.
   (A) relatively
   (B) widely
   (C) indefinitely
   (D) precisely

3. Dr. Tanaka retired from the newspaper after 30 years and ------- works part-time in a quiet café.
   (A) very
   (B) last
   (C) now
   (D) once

4. Extended leave requests should be submitted ------- to Barbara Weiss in HR and not to department managers.
   (A) directly
   (B) busily
   (C) nearly
   (D) basically

5. While an oil change ------- costs $30 at Motor-Pro, they're 50% off from now until the end of March.
   (A) familiarly
   (B) personally
   (C) typically
   (D) previously

6. Construction work on Dunphy Tower will be able to begin ------- after City Hall approves the building permit.
   (A) unevenly
   (B) immediately
   (C) habitually
   (D) currently

7. The opening of the new subway line has ------- reduced the commute for the majority of our employees.
   (A) drastically
   (B) necessarily
   (C) strictly
   (D) formerly

8. Jim Harrison, the youngest member of the team, ------- worked in Singapore office for five years.
   (A) still
   (B) previously
   (C) highly
   (D) always

9. Employees are ------- encouraged to attend the presentation on using social media for small companies.
   (A) strongly
   (B) extremely
   (C) mutually
   (D) closely

10. Office workers who ------- complained about the online scheduling system now prefer it over the old method.
    (A) favorably
    (B) quite
    (C) initially
    (D) annually

11. With the hiring of Toby Capparelle as assistant chef, Acorn Bistro is expected to begin serving Italian dishes -------.
    (A) nearly
    (B) recently
    (C) shortly
    (D) initially

12. Jonathan Davis became a member of the Folk Music Hall of Fame for his ------- outstanding albums and live performances.
    (A) jointly
    (B) consistently
    (C) exactly
    (D) reluctantly

RC DAY 13 실전문제

1. Delta Corp. CEO Ariel Blackstone announced her retirement at yesterday's gala and ------- Sofia Lee as her successor.
   (A) operated
   (B) founded
   (C) granted
   (D) named

2. More and more tourists have begun traveling to other countries as international flights have become more --------.
   (A) comparable
   (B) expressive
   (C) affordable
   (D) capable

3. The new welding machine will allow the factory to ------- production, helping the company meet rising demand.
   (A) subscribe
   (B) accelerate
   (C) inform
   (D) resist

4. Due to the sensitive nature of the company's work, Bio Labs ------- controls entry to its facilities.
   (A) tensely
   (B) strictly
   (C) hardly
   (D) merely

5. Allow the glue on the back of the hook to dry fully so that it properly ------- to the wall.
   (A) adheres
   (B) complies
   (C) performs
   (D) utilizes

6. During the interview, Mr. Suzuki elaborated on his ------- experience working with heavy machinery.
   (A) prospective
   (B) imperative
   (C) extensive
   (D) punctual

7. The cast and crew of Deep Space are ------- awaiting the list of nominees for the Critics' Awards.
   (A) greatly
   (B) accurately
   (C) eagerly
   (D) commonly

8. All students enrolled in the business program must ------- a basic writing course before they can qualify for graduation.
   (A) retire
   (B) complete
   (C) deserve
   (D) present

9. Speedy Shipping's ------- GPS-tracking system allows customers to go online and find the exact location of their delivery.
   (A) innovative
   (B) alert
   (C) uncertain
   (D) assorted

10. Ms. Donaldson instructed us to review the proposed contract ------- before the negotiations with Elstar Industries.
    (A) previously
    (B) relatively
    (C) highly
    (D) thoroughly

11. Stone Tires had to hire ------- new operators to handle the influx of calls related to the recall.
    (A) periodical
    (B) fierce
    (C) multiple
    (D) interested

12. Protecting sensitive data files with encryption software will ------- hackers from being able to access them.
    (A) present
    (B) ignore
    (C) prevent
    (D) reduce

13. In order to ------- a driver's license, applicants must prove they are residents of the area.
    (A) achieve
    (B) review
    (C) obtain
    (D) define

14. The meeting room on the fifth floor will be ------- until the installation of the air conditioner is complete.
    (A) irresponsible
    (B) inaccessible
    (C) undeniable
    (D) improbable

15. Governor Carson's high approval ratings have been attributed ------- to his effectiveness at reducing pollution in the region.
    (A) extremely
    (B) diligently
    (C) primarily
    (D) importantly

16. The anti-smoking campaign has been ------- successful, reducing smoking among adults by over 15%.
    (A) markedly
    (B) loosely
    (C) intimately
    (D) affordably

Questions 17-20 refer to the following advertisement.

It's time once again for the annual fall sale at Maury's Used Vehicles. If you're in the market for a used car, stop by and take a completely risk-free test drive. -------. Our sales associates will only discuss prices if you ask! In the event you purchase a car, Maury's will guarantee the vehicle for ------- 180 days. If you experience any mechanical issues during this time, ------- bring your vehicle to one of our expert mechanics and receive free repairs. Visit us today, and be sure to ------- a valid driver's license!
17.
18.
19.
20.

17. (A) Preview our new line of vehicles at maurysvehicles.com.
    (B) A 10% down payment is required on all purchases.
    (C) Smaller cars are not always more fuel efficient.
    (D) You won't be asked to pay or sign anything.

18. (A) as much
    (B) over
    (C) no more
    (D) not even

19. (A) simply
    (B) evenly
    (C) generally
    (D) justly

20. (A) achieve
    (B) bring
    (C) renew
    (D) initiate

RC DAY 14 — 어휘 – 명사 / 전치사

◆ 출제 포인트 1   명사 어휘 (1)

매년 37~38문제 출제

명사 어휘 문제는 특정 단어에만 집중할 경우 함정에 빠질 수 있으므로 문장 전체의 꼼꼼한 해석이 필요하다.

We will conduct a full (~~option~~ / **evaluation**) of the training program.
　　　　　단서　　　　　함정단어
우리는 그 훈련 프로그램에 대한 완전한 평가를 실시할 것이다.

Mr. McBride received positive (**feedback** / ~~impact~~) on his presentation.
　　　　　　　　　　단서　　　　함정단어
McBride 씨는 그의 발표에 대해 긍정적인 피드백을 받았다.

빈칸 뒤에 전치사 혹은 부정사가 있는 경우 이와 어울리는 명사를 선택한다.
The company has achieved a 10% (**increase** / ~~production~~) in sales.
그 회사는 매출의 10% 증가를 달성했다.

토익에 출제되는 '명사 + 전치사'

increase/decrease in ~의 증가/감소	proximity to ~와의 근접성	access to ~에의 접근(권)	admission to ~에의 입장
comment[opinion/view/stance] on ~에 대한 의견[견해]			

PRACTICE | 기출 연습하기

1. The logistics team provides timely (estimates / delivery) of the transportation cost for all international orders.
2. The (addition / content) of unlimited video calls to NetCast's mobile plan will make it more appealing.
3. Solar panels have proven to be a cleaner and cheaper (option / alternative) to coal and natural gas.

◆ 출제 포인트 2   명사 어휘 (2)

매년 1~2문제 출제

빈칸 뒤에 that절이 있는 경우 이와 어울리는 명사를 선택한다.
These documents provide (~~foundation~~ / **evidence**) that Ms. Clark is qualified for the job.
이 서류들은 Clark 씨가 그 일에 적격이라는 증거를 제공한다.

토익에 출제되는 'that절과 어울리는 명사'

fact 사실	indication(=sign) 조짐, 징후	indicator 지표	confirmation 확인	speculation 추측

'목적'을 의미하는 명사와 'low/high'와 어울리는 명사는 자주 출제된다.

목적을 의미하는 명사
goal	aim	purpose	objective	mission	intention

low/high와 어울리는 명사
standard 기준	volume 양	morale 사기	demand 수요	priority 우선순위	productivity 생산성

The Eastern Co. has managed to maintain high (~~behavior~~ / **morale**) among the staff.
Eastern 사는 직원들의 높은 사기를 유지할 수 있었다.

PRACTICE | 기출 연습하기

1. The financial director has made balancing the budget a high (adjustment / priority) for this fiscal year.
2. The (fact / gossip) that most rural residents lack adequate healthcare was highlighted in the article.
3. The (purpose / indication) of this research is to identify common causes of delayed orders.

◆ 최빈출 ◆ 확인 문제

1. Hopeworks Charity will provide the tools, paints, materials, and other ------- required during construction.
   (A) capabilities
   (B) supplies
   (C) attributes
   (D) facilities

2. Nationwide Home Insurance, unlike other agencies, provides full ------- of damages caused by flooding.
   (A) guarantees
   (B) potential
   (C) coverage
   (D) discounts

3. Leanders Co. has stopped production of its line of digital music players to reduce -------.
   (A) credits
   (B) customs
   (C) expenses
   (D) values

4. Employees who cannot attend the company trip will need to obtain ------- from their department managers.
   (A) registration
   (B) commission
   (C) suggestion
   (D) permission

5. The ------- of this committee is to prepare our workforce for upcoming advancements in information technology.
   (A) solution
   (B) aim
   (C) experience
   (D) guide

6. Businesses interested in supporting the Chicago Marathon can find an ------- for sponsorship on our Web site.
   (A) addition
   (B) impression
   (C) application
   (D) entirety

7. The design team will finish all ------- to the prototype before the start of the convention next week.
   (A) provisions
   (B) revisions
   (C) techniques
   (D) nominations

8. Greenhaven Heights is an ideal apartment complex for families because of its ------- to prestigious schools.
   (A) diligence
   (B) competence
   (C) proximity
   (D) achievement

9. While the ------- for installing marble countertops appears to be easy, even one mistake could be costly.
   (A) capacity
   (B) category
   (C) procedure
   (D) likelihood

10. Mayor Harris appeared on several popular podcasts in his most recent ------- to connect with younger voters.
    (A) attempt
    (B) omission
    (C) evaluation
    (D) conclusion

11. Stockholders requested CEO Mark Rafferty's official ------- on the company's disappointing performance.
    (A) increase
    (B) attraction
    (C) comment
    (D) preparation

12. The strong real estate market is a good ------- that the economy has recovered from the recession.
    (A) procedure
    (B) indicator
    (C) reference
    (D) objective

◆ 출제 포인트 3   전치사 어휘 (1)

매년 2~3문제 출제

빈출 전치사 어휘

upon ~하자마자	**upon** completion 완성하자마자
as ~로서	**as** a consultant 컨설턴트로서
beyond ~을 넘어, ~이후에	**beyond** regular business hours 정규 근무 시간 이후에
including ~을 포함하여	amenities **including** the fitness center 피트니스 센터를 포함한 편의 시설
by ~만큼	rise **by** 15% 15% (만큼) 상승하다
given(=considering) ~을 감안하면	**given** the high cost 높은 비용을 감안하면
aboard (비행기, 배 등에) 탑승하여	**aboard** the plane 기내에서
worth ~의 가치가 있는	a coupon **worth** $10 10달러 짜리 쿠폰
amid ~의 와중에, ~ 속에	**amid** widespread concerns 만연한 우려 속에

PRACTICE | 기출 연습하기

1. Jason worked (as / to) a columnist for Metro Daily before joining Prism Magazine.
2. (Apart / Upon) retiring from Mercy Hospital, Dr. Smith will produce online seminars for medical students.
3. (Like / Given) the recent surge in local tourism, residents should prepare for increased traffic.

◆ 출제 포인트 4   전치사 어휘 (2)

매년 약 2문제 출제

두 단어 이상으로 이루어진 빈출 전치사

instead of ~ 대신에	**instead of** a package tour 패키지 여행 대신에
ahead of ~보다 앞서, ~ 앞에	**ahead of** the deadline 마감 시한 전에
along with ~와 더불어, ~와 함께	**along with** the receipts 영수증과 함께
contrary to ~와 대조적으로, ~와 반대로	**contrary to** what we knew 우리가 알고 있던 것과는 반대로
in addition to(=besides) ~외에도	**in addition to** an annual bonus 연간 상여금 외에도
in response to ~에 응하여	**in response to** customer complaints 고객의 불평에 대응하여
as a result of ~의 결과로서	**as a result of** the merger 합병의 결과로
in advance of ~보다 앞서	**in advance of** the event 행사에 앞서
in accordance with ~에 따라	**in accordance with** the government policy 정부 정책에 따라

PRACTICE | 기출 연습하기

1. Mr. Freeland will attend the trade negotiations (as a result of / on behalf of) Canadian Steel.
2. Due to poor weather, the music festival will take place next weekend (instead of / aside from) this Saturday.
3. The Omega laptop offers a touch bar interface (along / in addition to) a fully customizable keyboard.

최빈출 확인 문제

1. Due to maintenance costs, membership fees at Oxbow Golf Club will increase ------- 15% next year.
   (A) by
   (B) onto
   (C) for
   (D) across

2. To enter the convention for free, show your VIP pass ------- your company identification badge at the front entrance.
   (A) additionally
   (B) on behalf of
   (C) along with
   (D) out of

3. Turner Studios has acquired film rights to Midnight Monster in a deal ------- up to 8 million dollars.
   (A) in spite of
   (B) together with
   (C) worth
   (D) except

4. Praxis Inc. was able to expand into a new market ------- its acquisition of Delcor Appliances.
   (A) moreover
   (B) away from
   (C) as a result of
   (D) since

5. The university's literature festival will feature readings from its own faculty members, ------- Anita Davis and Jay Moss.
   (A) including
   (B) pertaining
   (C) about
   (D) above

6. Critics attending the Vancouver Film Festival can watch Tom Brautigan's Silver Suns two weeks ------- its theatrical release.
   (A) except
   (B) ahead of
   (C) during
   (D) between

7. ------- concerns about a defective steering system, Takoma Motors recalled their latest sedan.
   (A) Apart
   (B) Amid
   (C) Atop
   (D) Abroad

8. Always willing to take on responsibilities ------- his required role, Mr. Sager is often overwhelmed in the office.
   (A) along
   (B) towards
   (C) beyond
   (D) among

9. All vehicles must undergo yearly inspections ------- state regulations.
   (A) in accordance with
   (B) as opposed to
   (C) on account of
   (D) in advance of

10. Free WiFi is available to all passengers ------- the ferry, though the connection may be weak.
    (A) aboard
    (B) beyond
    (C) past
    (D) into

11. ------- demand from fans, the band created a social media page to communicate directly with them.
    (A) Alongside of
    (B) In place of
    (C) As a result
    (D) In response to

12. ------- the official release of the product, we will be conducting several last-minute tests in the lab.
    (A) In advance of
    (B) Whether
    (C) As opposed to
    (D) As long as

◆ 출제 포인트 5　전치사를 포함한 숙어 (1)

매년 약 4문제 출제

형용사 + 전치사

be eligible for ~의 자격이 있다	be adequate for ~에 적합하다	be exempt from ~에서 면제되다	be appreciative of ~을 고맙게 여기다
be indicative of ~을 보여주다	be (un)aware of ~을 알다[모르다]	be equivalent to ~와 맞먹다	be subject to ~에 달려있다
be known[noted/notable/renowned] for ~때문에 유명하다		be concerned about ~에 대해 걱정하다	be scheduled for ~로 예정되다

The system inspection is scheduled (**for** / ~~in~~) October 5. 시스템 검사는 10월 5일로 예정되어 있다.

명사 + 전치사

influence[effect / impact] on ~에 미치는 영향	solution to ~의 해결(책)	shift in ~의 변화	restriction on ~에 대한 제약
in honor of ~을 축하[기념]하여	in recognition of ~을 인정하여	experience in ~의 경력	advances in ~의 발전
demand for ~의 수요	reputation for ~에 대한 명성	preparation for ~을 위한 준비	preference for ~의 선호

The award was given to Ms. Park in (**recognition** / ~~admission~~) **of** her contribution.
그 상은 기여한 공로를 인정하여 Park 씨에게 수여되었다.

실전 PRACTICE

1. The new Tracer app is (reflective / compatible) with most smart phone operating systems.
2. The International Development Department is responsible (in / for) managing our business interests abroad.
3. A person must be 18 or older to be (considerate / eligible) for the club membership.

◆ 출제 포인트 6　전치사를 포함한 숙어 (2)

매년 4~5문제 출제

동사 + 목적어 + 전치사

select A from B B에서 A를 선별[선택]하다	obtain/purchase/order A from B B에서 A를 얻다/구매하다/주문하다
remove[eliminate] A from B B에서 A를 제거하다	exchange A for B A를 B와 교환하다
provide/present/supply A with B A에게 B를 제공하다/증정하다/공급하다 (= provide/present/supply B to A)	
commend/honor/recognize A for ~에 대해 A를 칭찬하다/명예를 부여하다/인정하다	

We would like to (~~realize~~ / **commend**) Ms. Collins **for** her professional attitude.
Collins 씨의 직업적인 태도에 대해 칭찬하고 싶습니다.

기타 전치사 숙어

under the supervision/direction/management of ~의 감독/지시/관리 하에	until further notice 추후 공지가 있을 때까지
ahead of schedule 일정보다 빨리　on schedule 일정에 맞게	behind schedule 일정보다 늦게
for your convenience 귀하의 편의를 위해　a series of 일련의	a(n) array[variety/range] of 다양한
a total of 총 ~의　a wealth of 풍부한　a selection of 엄선된	a shortage of ~의 부족　a summary of ~의 요약

You will be working (**under** / ~~around~~) **the direction** of Mr. Lewis.
Lewis 씨의 지시에 따라 일을 하시게 될 겁니다.

PRACTICE | 기출 연습하기

1. The development team provides its director (with / for) progress reports on a weekly basis.
2. The Children's Hospital charity event earned a (result / total) of $557,000 from corporate donors.
3. The Harbrook University campus provides an (array / entity) of transportation options for students.

◆ 최빈출 ◆ 확인 문제

1. Mack's Supermarket will not be stocking chili peppers from Carolina Farms until further -------.
   (A) status
   (B) notice
   (C) concern
   (D) knowledge

2. Most drivers are still ------- of the reduced speed limit along Riverview Drive.
   (A) competent
   (B) unaware
   (C) sensitive
   (D) willing

3. Since several people are currently on vacation, the marketing team is not finished ------- the quarterly reports.
   (A) at
   (B) from
   (C) out
   (D) with

4. Cali Electronics allows its customers to exchange two old games ------- a newly released title.
   (A) on
   (B) into
   (C) as
   (D) for

5. Bluth Real Estate initiated the Westchester development project in response to the high ------- for affordable suburban housing.
   (A) population
   (B) demand
   (C) percentage
   (D) occurrence

6. Surprisingly, the participants in Burgerland's focus group did not have a strong ------- for either of the new sauce flavors.
   (A) courtesy
   (B) decision
   (C) preference
   (D) choice

7. At the Cosgrove Center's annual banquet, renowned painter Amelia Kurst was ------- for her contributions to the arts.
   (A) completed
   (B) resumed
   (C) afforded
   (D) recognized

8. All helmets produced by Nolan Athletics are put through a ------- of tests to guarantee their durability.
   (A) series
   (B) shortage
   (C) length
   (D) presence

9. It is recommended to bring your own gear since rentals are ------- to the availability of the equipment.
   (A) accountable
   (B) subject
   (C) popular
   (D) public

10. Murray Construction spent about 10 million dollars on the project, which is ------- to over 70% of the budget.
    (A) significant
    (B) equivalent
    (C) appropriate
    (D) reasonable

11. With each entrée purchase, Malcom Steakhouse guests can select two side dishes ------- the list.
    (A) about
    (B) from
    (C) among
    (D) following

12. Having traveled through South America by motorbike, Mr. Caron has a ------- of knowledge about the region.
    (A) fame
    (B) labor
    (C) height
    (D) wealth

RC DAY 14 실전문제

1. Carver City will turn the former ------- of an old food processing plant into a public park.
   (A) placement
   (B) arena
   (C) site
   (D) travel

2. The experts at Natural Homes will assemble all furniture ------- delivery for a low fee of $50.
   (A) onto
   (B) next
   (C) upon
   (D) afterward

3. Under the ------- of manager Leroy Varga, the sales team increased profits by 18% last quarter.
   (A) provision
   (B) expansion
   (C) supervision
   (D) attendance

4. Despite some negative publicity regarding safety standards, investors continue to express ------- in the company.
   (A) exception
   (B) gratitude
   (C) sympathy
   (D) confidence

5. The Ashley Center is equipped with ------- such as a fitness center and a movie theater.
   (A) conventions
   (B) procedures
   (C) facilities
   (D) guidelines

6. Only employees who attended the training seminar in April are ------- from the one being held on Monday.
   (A) exempt
   (B) observed
   (C) ready
   (D) distinct

7. The keynote speech will be delivered by this year's ------- of the Xavier Award, Valerie Gruber.
   (A) ceremony
   (B) recipient
   (C) member
   (D) client

8. There is an information booth at the east entrance ------- the one at the front door.
   (A) as if
   (B) in addition to
   (C) still
   (D) regardless of

9. Mr. Braun has a limited amount of time, so only the questions that are ------- to his presentation will be accepted.
   (A) definite
   (B) relevant
   (C) finished
   (D) potential

10. Due to safety concerns, only medical staff performing the procedure may gain ------- to the patient's room.
    (A) access
    (B) solution
    (C) placement
    (D) direction

11. Yolanda's Café gives a 5% discount to any customers who use reusable cups ------- paper or plastic ones.
    (A) as to
    (B) instead of
    (C) through
    (D) except

12. The seminar is running ------- schedule, so there will be an extra ten minutes for the Q&A session.
    (A) aboard
    (B) outside
    (C) ahead of
    (D) next to

13. Mr. Willem's ------- included organizing multiple international conferences, the largest of which was attended by over 5,000 people.
    (A) authorities
    (B) accomplishments
    (C) capabilities
    (D) proficiencies

14. In the event a receipt cannot be provided ------- proof of purchase, store credit may be offered.
    (A) through
    (B) as
    (C) except
    (D) along

15. Farrah Hansen's ------- for all athletics is what makes her such a successful sports reporter.
    (A) elevation
    (B) likeness
    (C) assortment
    (D) enthusiasm

16. Lindberg & Nowak is the area's leading provider of accounting services because of its ------- for attention to detail.
    (A) preparation
    (B) destination
    (C) confirmation
    (D) reputation

Questions 17-20 refer to the following article.

Rainier Tourism Board Increases Budget

The Rainier Board of Tourism will be spending more than 5 million dollars over the next three years to promote local tourism. This figure is higher than that of the board's ------- investments, **17.** which helped to attract more than 850,000 tourists last year and 600,000 the year before. These gains are primarily due to intensified marketing campaigns, ------- the one about weekend **18.** trips to the area's beautiful beaches. In contrast to the rise in visitors to Rainier, travel to other domestic locations has shown little ------- in recent years. -------.
19. **20.**

---

17. (A) prospective
    (B) previous
    (C) current
    (D) following

18. (A) including
    (B) included
    (C) includes
    (D) include

19. (A) effect
    (B) value
    (C) competition
    (D) growth

20. (A) Board members will vote on this issue soon.
    (B) The area is most easily accessible by train or bus.
    (C) Another campaign promoted local art festivals.
    (D) Experts attribute this partly to the weak economy.

RC DAY 15 PART 6

◆ 출제 포인트 1   대명사/지시어

매년 19~20문제 출제

실전 적용 전략
- 어휘나 시제 문제 등에서 빈칸이 있는 문장에 지시어(this, that, such 등), 대명사(he, she, they, each, both, one 등) 혹은 정관사(the)가 있는 경우 앞 문장에서 단서를 찾는다.
- 보기에 대명사(he, she, they, each, both, one 등)가 있는 경우 앞 문장에서 단서를 찾는다.

PATTERN   기출 유형 맛보기

Attention: All employees

To kick off our February Health Drive, we would like to remind everyone of some basic ways to increase energy.

Eating right and staying active are two of the best ways to maintain high energy. ② Instead of grabbing a bag of chips as a snack, try having some fresh fruit or a handful of almonds. Or the next time you're waiting for the elevator, consider taking the stairs.

① **These** simple ------- will improve your overall health and give you more energy throughout the day.

(A) elements
(B) features
(C) measures
(D) statements

② 감자칩 대신 과일과 아몬드를 섭취하고 엘리베이터 대신 계단을 이용하라는 권고가 있는데, 이는 일종의 '조치' 혹은 '방책'으로 볼 수 있으므로 (C) measures가 정답이다.

① '당신의 전반적인 건강을 개선할 것이다'의 주어로 적합한 명사를 찾아야 하는데, 빈칸 앞에 지시어(these)가 있으므로 앞 문장에 단서가 있을 것임을 알 수 있다.

PRACTICE | 기출 연습하기 다음을 읽고 빈칸에 알맞은 것을 고르세요.

1.

From this coming Monday, associates from a corporate accounting firm will be visiting our offices. As discussed at last week's meeting, our company has been dealing with some accounting problems since the acquisition of the commercial properties in Birmingham and Stafford.

In dealing with those -------, the accountants may require a variety of documents. We ask that you remain cooperative and provide them with any necessary information.

(A) challenges   (B) suggestions   (C) inquiries   (D) clients

2.

Ms. Offerman will be out of town through May 19. While she is away, Mr. Randolph will be in charge of purchasing. Thus, all requests or inquiries regarding purchasing should be sent directly to -------. Any correspondence sent to Ms. Offerman will not be dealt with until after she returns.

(A) them   (B) it   (C) these   (D) him

3.

It's my pleasure to provide this letter of recommendation for Carol Kudrow. Ms. Kudrow ------- in our sales department as head of international sales. Her primary responsibility here is to maintain relationships with overseas clients in order to sell our products abroad. Based on the work she has done for our company, I am sure she would be a valuable asset to your team.

(A) was employed   (B) is employed   (C) will employ   (D) employs

4.

To accompany the interior renovations, the management of Burger Jack's has decided to make some changes in the staff uniform. ------- will be shared at a restaurant-wide meeting to be held at 10 A.M. on Saturday, January 29. New menu items will also be presented at this meeting, so attendance for all employees is required.

(A) Theirs   (B) We   (C) These   (D) Either

5.

CHICAGO, April 27—Local singer Lena Perkins appeared last night at an event for Save the Trees, a campaign to protect local forests. The evening kicked off with a cocktail hour and five-course dinner, which was followed by a performance by Ms. Perkins. The event was held at the Delaware Hotel. It ------- a crowd of over 250 guests.

(A) will draw   (B) was drawn   (C) drew   (D) draws

◆ 출제 포인트 2　시제

매년 17~18문제 출제

실전 적용 전략
- 첫 문장에 시제 문제의 단서가 있는 경우가 많으므로 첫 문장을 반드시 확인한다.
- 특히 메일 발송 날짜, 기사의 날짜가 제시된 경우 이에 주목한다.
- 빈칸이 있는 문장과 앞뒤 문장을 빠르게 읽으며 단서를 찾는다.
- 이때 지시어(this, that, such 등), 정관사(the), 대명사 등이 제시된 경우 이를 단서로 활용한다.

PATTERN　기출 유형 맛보기

To: r.tanner@fashionfactory.co.uk
From: customerservice@ironfabrics.co.uk
Subject: Your order
① Date: 15 April

Dear Mr. Tanner,

In the previous e-mail, we have informed you of the closure of our warehouse on 1 May. ② Regrettably, this means any deliveries scheduled to be shipped **on that date** -------. As a result, the shipment of fabric due to be sent to Fashion Factory will not be sent until 2 May.

We apologize for any inconvenience this may cause. As compensation, we would like to offer you a 5% discount on your next order with us.

Please contact us immediately if you have any questions.

(A) delayed
(B) will be delayed
(C) was delayed
(D) delaying

① 이메일 발송 날짜가 4월 15일임을 확인한다.

② 문장에 제시된 시간 단서 'on that date'는 앞 문장의 5월 1일을 가리키는데, 발송 날짜와 비교하면 미래 시점인 것을 알 수 있다. 따라서 정답은 미래 시제 (B) will be delayed이다.

PRACTICE | 기출 연습하기 다음을 읽고 빈칸에 알맞은 것을 고르세요.

1.

BANGKOK, November 11—Starting next month, WeTalk users will be able to send payments through the WeTalk application on their mobile devices. The application is mainly used for chatting and sharing media. With the new changes, it ------- users to transfer money to individuals or businesses as well. The move is part of WeTalk's efforts to create a more streamlined mobile experience.

(A) is allowed   (B) has been allowing   (C) will allow   (D) may have allowed

2.

Notes for yesterday's meeting were taken by Mr. Patterson and will be sent out later today. Important topics covered included the development status of our new line of sneakers and a reminder to follow building parking regulations.

Also, the sales figures for this month ------- at the meeting. These will be summarized and distributed along with the meeting notes.

(A) will be revealed   (B) will have revealed   (C) were revealed   (D) are being revealed

3.

New Station to Open on Sunset Boulevard

August 6—San Francisco Transit (SFT) has announced that it ------- a new subway station to extend the South Line. Work on the station is expected to begin next month. Currently, the South Line ends at Montgomery Avenue, but the new last stop will be at the bus terminal on Sunset Boulevard. Over 500,000 people ride on SFT trains each day, with the South Line being the busiest.

(A) has been constructing   (B) is constructed   (C) will be constructing   (D) has constructed

4.

As discussed during our conference call, we have been looking for ways to increase sales. Per Ms. Davenport's suggestion, we have decided to redo our window displays and place a full-page ad in the newspaper. We believe these measures ------- more customers. Furthermore, it is essential that we implement these decisions before the release of our fall line.

(A) attracted   (B) are attracting   (C) have attracted   (D) will attract

5.

Thank you for taking the time yesterday to sit down for an interview. Your willingness to answer questions -------. I especially benefited from the tour you gave me of your factory, which allowed me to get a closer look at how your products are assembled. The interview will appear in the September issue of our magazine, which I will send you a copy of soon.

(A) might appreciate   (B) was appreciated   (C) appreciates   (D) will be appreciated

◆ 출제 포인트 3   접속부사

매년 15~16문제 출제

실전 적용 전략
- 보기에 접속부사가 있는 경우 빈칸 앞 뒤 문장의 논리 관계를 파악하여 정답을 선택한다.

토익에 출제되는 접속부사

의미	접속부사
역접, 대조	however 하지만 on the contrary 그와 반대로 in contrast 그에 반해서
양보	nevertheless/nonetheless 그럼에도 불구하고 even so 비록 그렇지만
결과	therefore/thus 그러므로 accordingly 그에 따라서 consequently/as a result 그 결과
조건	if so 만약 그렇다면 otherwise 그렇지 않으면 in this case 이러한 경우에
시간	then 그리고 나서 afterwards 그 후에 at the same time 그와 동시에
추가, 부연설명	in addition/additionally/besides/plus/furthermore/moreover 게다가 also 또한
예시	for example/for instance 예를 들면
기타	alternatively 대안으로 instead (부정문 뒤에서) 그 대신 likewise/similarly 마찬가지로 in particular 특히 to that end 그 목적을 위해 as a matter of fact/in fact 사실은, 실은 in summary 요약하면 unfortunately 불행히도

PATTERN 기출 유형 맛보기

Dear Editor,

In last month's issue of your magazine, you included a review of director Stacey Moore's film Planets. The review described the movie as unoriginal and boring. ① It also suggested that the movie was **disappointing** because Ms. Moore is **inexperienced**. -------, ② I enjoyed the film and thought it had many **positive** qualities. The acting was outstanding, and the plot was quite creative. Also, the director has been working in the industry for a decade, so she knows what she is doing. I highly recommend this film to all moviegoers.

Sincerely
James Thatcher

(A) In addition
(B) As a result
(C) However
(D) Therefore

① 앞 문장에는 감독의 경험이 부족하여 영화가 실망스러웠다는 부정적인 내용이 언급되고 있다.

② 뒤 문장에는 영화에 많은 긍정적인 특징들이 있다고 언급하고 있는데, 이는 앞 문장과 서로 상반되는 내용이므로 (C) However가 정답이다.

PRACTICE | 기출 연습하기 다음을 읽고 빈칸에 알맞은 것을 고르세요.

1.

Dear Mr. Grant,

We regret to inform you that we are unable to process your booking for our 3-day tour of Madrid. Due to a large soccer tournament, the city will experience a huge influx of visitors during the days you requested. -------, the majority of the city's hotels will be completely full. If your dates are flexible, we would be happy to assist you in booking a later tour.

(A) As a result   (B) In the first place   (C) Despite this   (D) On the other hand

2.

Atlantic Airways tries to accommodate the dietary needs of all of its passengers. Special meals, however, are not available on board unless specifically asked for. -------, any passenger with dietary restrictions must contact a representative at least 48 hours in advance of departure to request a special meal.

(A) Nevertheless   (B) For example   (C) Meanwhile   (D) Therefore

3.

To make an appointment at Sunlake Dental, visit www.sunlakedental.com/book. -------, you can call our office at 952-555-6134 and make an appointment over the phone. If it is your first time visiting us, we ask that you arrive at least 15 minutes before your scheduled appointment. Please also make sure to bring proof of insurance.

(A) Alternatively   (B) Accordingly   (C) For instance   (D) Favorably

4.

With its simple cabins and beautiful lakeside views, Coopersville may look like a quiet village, but it is so much more. Not only does it have some of the best hiking trails in Montana, but it boasts outstanding cuisine and is home to an award-winning spa. Over the past few years, it has gained popularity as a relaxing honeymoon destination for newlyweds. -------, it was recently named "Honeymoon Spot of the Year" by *Wedding* magazine.

(A) By comparison   (B) However   (C) If so   (D) In fact

5.

DETROIT, September 22—ChemZ Industries has been ordered to temporarily suspend operations until its facilities are deemed safe. This comes after a chemical being produced at the factory leaked last month after the failure of a safety mechanism. Large quantities of the chemical were accidentally released into a nearby river. -------, analysis showed that traces of the chemical had been absorbed by plants and animals downstream.

(A) Instead   (B) Regardless   (C) On the contrary   (D) In addition

◆ 출제 포인트 4   어휘

매년 약 59문제 출제

실전 적용 전략

- 첫 문장에 어휘 문제의 단서가 제시되는 경우가 많으므로 첫 문장을 반드시 확인한다.
- 빈칸이 포함된 문장에 단서가 없는 경우, 주변 문장도 함께 읽으며 단서를 찾는다.
- 이때 지시어(this, that, such 등), 접속부사(however, therefore 등), 대명사가 제시된 경우 이를 단서로 활용한다.
- 앞서 언급된 표현을 다르게 바꾸어 표현하는 패러프레이징에 유의한다.

ex) a seminar(세미나) → this event(이 행사)

a time-consuming system(시간 소모가 많은 시스템) → the inefficient process(비효율적인 절차)

PATTERN 기출 유형 맛보기

To: All Kose Media Staff
From: Linda Fernandez, Human Resources Specialist
Date: June 30
RE: Opportunity

① The gym at Rose Industries offers experienced personal trainers and the latest equipment. By providing such a facility, we hope to improve employee welfare.

Many of you have been asking whether the gym can be accessed by the public. ② Currently, the facility is for ------ use only. ③ **However**, in response to these inquiries, we are considering **opening** the gym to employee friends and family.

Your opinion on this matter is appreciated, so please fill out the survey found at www.roseintranet.com/gymsurvey.

(A) flexible
(B) internal
(C) early
(D) regular

① 첫 문장을 읽고 사내 헬스클럽에 관한 내용임을 파악한다.

② 해당 문장을 읽고 정답을 찾을 수 없는데, 접속부사(However)가 포함된 다음 문장에 단서가 있을 것임을 알 수 있다.

③ However(하지만)로 연결되는 뒤 문장은 헬스 클럽을 직원 친구나 가족에게 개방하는 것을 고려 중이라는 내용이므로, 앞 문장에는 현재는 내부 직원들만 이용할 수 있다는 내용이 적합하다. 따라서 (B) internal이 정답이다.

PRACTICE | 기출 연습하기 다음을 읽고 빈칸에 알맞은 것을 고르세요.

1.

Your e-mail has been received by our service department. According to the e-mail, there is a crack across the screen of your cell phone. Given that the device is still under warranty and you purchased additional insurance with us, the cost of a new screen should be free. Please ship the ------- item to our center or drop it off at the nearest NexCom location.

(A) harmful   (B) final   (C) damaged   (D) incorrect

2.

Dear Ms. Nelson,

Thank you for your invitation to the 12th annual Heroes of Perth Gala on August 23. While I am honored to have been asked to attend, I will be on a business trip to Moscow on the date of the event. Therefore, I will be ------- to join you. I would, however, like to donate $1,000 to the fundraising effort for the new community center. Please let me know the best way to send you the money.

(A) doubtful   (B) expected   (C) unable   (D) prepared

3.

Located in the heart of Cape Town, Safran Center is the place to go when buying or selling -------. We have gently used guitars, drums, pianos, violins and much more for sale. And if you're looking to sell something for a little extra cash, we buy anything from flutes to accordions. Stop by today and check out what we have in stock.

(A) instruments   (B) supplies   (C) cleaners   (D) appliances

4.

Attention: All Staff

Routine maintenance on the building's fire alarms will begin today at 11:30 A.M. We hope to have this ------- finished within an hour so as not to disturb the work environment. Nevertheless, if unforeseen issues arise, it may take a bit longer. We ask for your understanding and patience if the technicians are still working on this after lunch.

(A) location   (B) process   (C) document   (D) training

5.

Dear Mr. Yamamoto,

I am pleased to report that your lost luggage has been recovered. The missing bags are currently in Munich, where they were supposed to have been loaded onto your transfer flight. They are scheduled to reach Berlin tomorrow morning. After they arrive, we will return your ------- to you as quickly as possible at the address indicated on your claim form.

(A) tickets   (B) possessions   (C) products   (D) payments

◆ 출제 포인트 5   빈칸에 알맞은 문장 넣기

매년 48문제 출제

실전 적용 전략
- 첫 문장을 읽고 지문의 전반적인 주제를 파악한다.
- 빈칸의 앞과 뒤 문장에 집중하여 흐름에 가장 적합한 문장을 찾는다.
- 앞뒤 문장과의 연결이 매끄럽지 않은 보기는 오답으로 소거한다.
- 보기 혹은 뒤 문장에 지시어, 대명사, 접속부사 등이 제시된 경우 이를 단서로 적극 활용한다.

PATTERN   기출 유형 맛보기

Date: December 2
To: Customer Service Team <csteam@taloncorp.com>
From: Peter North <peter.north@taloncorp.com>
Subject: LV600 power cord

To all customer service representatives:

① We have recently been receiving multiple complaints about the LV600 microwave. Many customers have reported that the device suddenly shuts off while in use. ② After examining some of the returned microwaves, it has been determined that the electrical cord is **faulty**. -------. ③ Since the problem does not pose a safety risk, there will not be a product recall. Instead, customers who experience this issue will be sent a new power cord free of charge. In addition, all shipments of the LV600 have been halted until enough cords can be produced to replace the faulty ones.

Thank you,

Peter North
Head of Customer Service, Talon Corporation

(A) Older models do not include the same advanced features.
④ **(B) This defect is responsible for the sudden loss of power.**
(C) It is explained in the FAQ section of our Web site.
(D) An extended warranty is available at an additional cost.

① 글의 첫 부분을 읽고 제품의 전원이 갑자기 꺼지는 문제가 있었음을 알 수 있다.

② 빈칸 앞 문장에서 검사 결과 전기 코드에 결함을 발견했다는 내용을 파악한다.

③ 뒤 문장에서 제품의 리콜은 없을 것이라고 한 내용을 읽는다.

④ 앞 문장의 faulty(불량의)를 This defect(이러한 결함)로 표현하여 코드의 결함이 불량의 원인이라는 내용인 (B)가 빈칸에 오는 것이 흐름상 가장 적합하다.

PRACTICE | 기출 연습하기 다음을 읽고 빈칸에 알맞은 것을 고르세요.

1.
> Created more than 50 years ago by landscape architect Nels Lindberg, Holmes Park is a place for people of all ages. The park boasts five gardens, three fountains, and many walking trails. There is also a large lake located in the center of the park, attracting wild birds of all colors and sizes. Given the size of the park, visitors may find a map useful. -------.

(A) They plan to see some birds the park is known for.
(B) The most visited garden is the Rose Garden.
(C) One can be picked up at any park information center.
(D) Children under 5 years old are not allowed in the park.

2.
> To Whom It May Concern:
>
> Last spring, I purchased a jacket at Washington Coat Factory's end-of-season sale. I put it in storage but recently took it out as the weather is cooler. Upon trying it on, I noticed that there is some damage to one of the zippers. I know that allowing me to return or exchange the item at this point is against your return policy. -------. If the item is no longer in stock, I would be happy to accept store credit. Please let me know how to proceed.

(A) I am still waiting for the item to be delivered.
(B) Nevertheless, I am hoping to receive an exception.
(C) A new shipping policy is explained in this document.
(D) The payment was made in cash, but I have the receipt.

3.
> Dear Hiring Manager,
>
> I would like to submit my résumé for consideration for the position of Associate Editor at the *Los Angeles Daily*.
>
> -------. For the last five years, I have been the content director and editor of the arts section at the *Dallas Times*. Prior to that, I was employed at Chronicle News, where I contributed to a number of newspapers and magazines. I believe my background would assist me in helping your paper grow both in print and online.

(A) I would also like to apply for an internship at your organization.
(B) I have extensive experience working in the field of publishing.
(C) Thank you for taking the time to sit down for an interview.
(D) Most newspapers are working to gain readers through the Internet.

4.
> Bandoo Industries built its newest fridge, the Quatro, with features designed to make your grocery shopping easier. A built-in camera allows you to take a picture of the contents of your fridge without opening the door. -------. That way, you can easily see if there is anything you forgot to add to your shopping list.

(A) The product was debuted at this year's Kitchen Expo.
(B) You can even connect to the camera from your mobile phone.
(C) There are also temperature-controlled drawers for fresh fruit.
(D) A service technician will come to your home to install the fridge.

RC DAY 15 실전문제

Questions 1-4 refer to the following press release.

On March 28, Tristone Construction was awarded the contract for the redesign of the National History Museum of Sydney(NHMS). The museum, originally built in 1975, will receive upgrades that will modernize and better utilize the museum's facilities. -------(1)-------. Additionally, certain improvements, -------(2)------- advanced air filtration and a climate control system, will make the building's infrastructure more efficient. Tristone successfully completed other similar projects in the past, including its -------(3)------- of Melbourne's Modern Art Museum. Marissa Nguyen, NHMS's Facilities Manager, -------(4)------- the project in cooperation with Tristone representatives.

1. (A) Tristone submitted a budget proposal for the renovation project last spring.
   (B) Ms. Nguyen is responsible for the museum's building and grounds.
   (C) The updates include the construction of a new gallery on the first floor.
   (D) Adding sensor-controlled lighting is a common method for saving on energy bills.

2. (A) such as
   (B) in order
   (C) likewise
   (D) in spite of

3. (A) purchases
   (B) renovations
   (C) promotions
   (D) revisions

4. (A) were overseeing
   (B) overseeing
   (C) to oversee
   (D) will oversee

Questions 5-8 refer to the following article.

Walker Studios plans to make a sequel to *Friday Night*, which is currently in theaters across the country. The head of the studio, Henry Chen, made the decision based on a sudden surge in ticket ------- for the movie. The move for a sequel has come as quite a surprise to industry
5.
experts as the film has received ------- reviews from professional critics. -------. Interest in the
6. 7.
film, however, has grown among younger audience members through social media. Several popular online blogs ------- recommended the movie and its exploration of issues faced by the
8.
younger generation.

5. (A) to sell
   (B) sell
   (C) salable
   (D) sales

6. (A) warm
   (B) harsh
   (C) steep
   (D) brilliant

7. (A) Many theaters offer tickets for purchase on their Web sites.
   (B) The director attended the opening night of the film.
   (C) The movie was also performing poorly at the box office.
   (D) Moreover, it featured some award-winning actors.

8. (A) strongly
   (B) strengthen
   (C) stronger
   (D) strong

Questions 9-12 refer to the following e-mail.

To: staff@elementarypublishing.com
From: s.lewis@elementarypublishing.com
Date: November 16
Subject: Policy Change

Dear Employees,

Elementary Publishing ------- a new procedure for tracking employee hours. As of January, all staff members will be required to record their arrival and departure. This may be an ------- for all of you. However, management would like to ensure that all employees are accounted for. Beginning on January 1, do not go straight to your desk when arriving at the office. -------, please start by scanning your employee ID card at the reception desk. Scan it again before you leave for the day. In addition, please sign and return the attached form to me by Wednesday, November 30. -------.

Thank you for your cooperation.

Stan Lewis
Human Resources Manager

9. (A) is implementing
   (B) may be implementing
   (C) was implementing
   (D) would have implemented

10. (A) alleviation
    (B) inconvenience
    (C) exaggeration
    (D) alternative

11. (A) Likewise
    (B) Depending on that
    (C) Instead
    (D) If so

12. (A) There are some technical problems with the new system.
    (B) The employee ID cards contain small electronic chips.
    (C) Our company hires both full-time and part-time workers.
    (D) This is to show that you have been informed of the policy.

Questions 13-16 refer to the following article.

Ashford-Foley Industries to Close Plant

DALLAS—At its annual investors meeting, Ashford-Foley Industries (AFI) announced that ------- would be closing the company's manufacturing plant in Houston, Texas. This will likely save the company over $100 million dollars.

After the plant closes, all orders will be handled by AFI's existing production facilities. -------.
"Ashford-Foley is the country's leading tire company," says industry analyst Virgil Graves, "but their ------- are quickly gaining market share. Consolidating production will help the company stay profitable."

AFI will gradually reduce operations at the Houston facility over the next five years. -------, the site will be sold or put up for auction.

13. (A) anyone
    (B) those
    (C) he
    (D) it

14. (A) An offer for the property has been declined.
    (B) All four are also located in North America.
    (C) The company's corporate office is in Texas too.
    (D) The decision is largely the result of its success.

15. (A) competitors
    (B) participants
    (C) suppliers
    (D) advocates

16. (A) In summary
    (B) Despite this
    (C) After that time
    (D) As a matter of fact

RC | DAY 16   주제, 목적 및 대상을 묻는 유형

매년 약 84문제 출제 13%

BASIC 기본기 익히기

빈출 질문 유형

주제를 묻는 문제
What is the main **topic** of the article? 이 기사의 주요 주제는 무엇인가?
What does the memo mainly **discuss**? 회람은 주로 무슨 내용을 다루고 있는가?

목적을 묻는 문제
What is the **purpose** of the e-mail? 이메일의 목적은 무엇인가?
Why was the e-mail **sent[written]**? 이메일은 왜 발송되었는가[쓰였는가]?

대상을 묻는 문제
For whom is the advertisement **intended**? 광고는 누구를 대상으로 한 것인가?
To whom is the letter **written**? 편지는 누구에게 쓰여졌는가?

실전 적용 전략
글의 주제 및 목적을 묻는 문제의 약 70% 정도는 단서가 앞 부분에 등장하므로 제목과 첫 단락을 읽고 내용을 요약하는 것이 중요하다. 첫 단락에 주제 및 목적이 명확하게 드러나지 않는 경우, 나머지 단락의 첫 1~2문장에 집중하면 정답을 찾을 수 있다.

PATTERN 기출 유형 맛보기

To: All Oakridge Insurance Employees
From: David Lester, HR Manager
Date: July 15
Re: Vacation requests

② Beginning August 1, all employees must have their vacation time approved at least two weeks in advance. There is a form in the HR office that you should pick up and complete. Your supervisor should then sign it. Please note that we can still give time off for an emergency on short notice, if necessary.

Thank you for your cooperation.

① Q. Why was the memo written?
(A) To respond to an inquiry
③ **(B) To explain a new policy**
(C) To announce a staff retreat
(D) To introduce a supervisor

② 지문의 첫 부분을 먼저 읽는다. 8월 1일부터 직원들은 2주 전에 미리 휴가 승인을 받아야 한다는 내용을 확인한다.

① 질문의 'Why ~ written?'을 통해 목적을 묻는 문제임을 알 수 있다.

③ 이와 같은 내용이 담긴 보기인 (B) To explain a new policy(새로운 정책을 설명하기 위해)를 정답으로 선택한다.

PRACTICE | 기출 연습하기

Please refer to the following invitation.

~ You're Invited ~
Quarterly Professional Development Seminar
Thursday, March 3, 7 P.M. Utica Hall

Speaker: Dr. Theresa Synder, Psychologist at Snyder Counseling
Topic: "Boosting Motivation in Students"

This event is limited to Guerrero University personnel who are directly involved in teaching students. Those who attend the seminar are advised to prepare for the event by going over the topic points on the Web site in advance at www.guerrerouni.edu.

Event planner: Yvonne Stark

1. Who most likely are the intended recipients of this invitation?
   (A) University students
   (B) HR employees
   (C) Professors
   (D) Psychologists

Please refer to the following announcement.

RESTORATION PROJECT

The Clarkston Historical Society will sponsor building projects in the Clarkston area. The goal is to help to restore old buildings in town. The group will issue a grant of $100,000 to five different sites. Owners of residential or commercial buildings that are more than fifty years old can apply. The money must be used to make building improvements. Contact Rita Becker at 555-7003 for more information.

2. Why was the announcement written?
   (A) To discuss a city tour
   (B) To announce a grand opening
   (C) To explain a funding opportunity
   (D) To introduce award winners

Please refer to the following e-mail.

Dear Marketing Staff,

At the last management meeting, Mr. Wong put forward a proposal regarding our new ad campaign. He thought it would be a good idea to use ads on social media. I have researched the costs of advertising on various social media sites. The information is attached here for you to review before the next meeting.

Sincerely,

Sabrina Perez
Marketing Director

3. Why did Ms. Perez send the e-mail?
   (A) To report on the success of an advertising campaign
   (B) To request help for a special visitor
   (C) To follow up on a proposal made at a meeting
   (D) To ask for a payment for a completed project

PARAPHRASING 패러프레이징 연습

A. 비슷한 의미를 가진 표현끼리 연결하세요.

1. take 20 percent off the price
2. damaged chairs
3. expand substantially
4. a copy of a contract
5. available every summer

(A) grow significantly
(B) a legal document
(C) receive a discount
(D) offered on a seasonal basis
(E) ruined furniture

B. 패러프레이징에 유의하여 정답을 고르세요.

6. We would appreciate if you would send us the completed survey by March 15.
   Q. Why did Mr. Rager write to Ms. Britt?
   (A) To explain the results of a test
   (B) To ask for her feedback

   📌 패러프레이징 확인하기
   survey → _____

7. Please follow these simple steps if you would like to sign up for our rewards program.
   Q. Why was the e-mail sent?
   (A) To explain how to register
   (B) To schedule an appointment

   📌 패러프레이징 확인하기
   _____ → register

8. We would like to see you again, so let us know when you are available.
   Q. Why does Mr. Hofuku send the e-mail to Ms. Edwards?
   (A) To inquire about a reservation
   (B) To request a meeting

   📌 패러프레이징 확인하기
   see → _____

9. This is a reminder that the spring sale at Maxi Dress will soon start.
   Q. What does the e-mail mainly discuss?
   (A) an upcoming event
   (B) an annual sales goal

   📌 패러프레이징 확인하기
   soon start → _____
   spring sale → _____

10. Today the workers will repaint and replace old flooring instead of installing new doors.
    Q. Why was the memo written?
    (A) To report a change in schedule for renovations
    (B) To address complaints about the lack of space

    📌 패러프레이징 확인하기
    repaint and replace old flooring → _____

| 정답 | 1. (C)   2. (E)   3. (A)   4. (B)   5. (D)
6. (B), feedback   7. (A), sign up   8. (B), meeting   9. (A), upcoming, event   10. (A), renovations

Questions 1-2 refer to the following memo.

To: All King Burger employees
From: Melanie Gibb, Restaurant Owner
Date: December 14
Subject: Staff Announcement

In light of the rising number of cases where individuals are coming in late for their shifts, we feel it is necessary to remind all workers to be punctual. At our restaurant, it is critical that we stick closely to the daily shift schedule. If a worker does not show up when they are supposed to, then their coworkers will need to work late to cover for them. This is not acceptable. In addition, please remember our policy regarding lateness. If you think you will be delayed, you must call the shift manager at least one hour before your scheduled start time. Those who fail to do so will pay a ten dollar fee, and if this happens three times within a three month period, the employee will face disciplinary action. Please keep this in mind. If there is anything you are unsure about, simply ask your shift manager.

1. What is the purpose of the memo?
   (A) To announce a change to a work schedule
   (B) To discuss a problem with restaurant equipment
   (C) To remind staff about arriving at work on time
   (D) To request volunteers to work during an event

2. What should employees do if they have a query?
   (A) Check a notice board
   (B) Arrange a meeting with Ms. Gibb
   (C) Review an employee handbook
   (D) Contact their supervisor

Questions 3-5 refer to the following letter.

Not Another Cheap Imitation
345 South Audley, 25b
London WC 9309X10

Lynn Wellyn
Crafty Kid's Clothes Closet
27 Cawley Road, Brooklyn, Victoria 0384

August 12

Dear Ms. Wellyn,

Thank you for your interest in our one-of-a-kind clothing line in your letter of August 1. The following information should address all your questions:

1. We do design and manufacture our own line of kids-outdoor wear, indoor wear and pajamas. These clothes are colorful, durable, and washable. The outdoor wear is made using brand-name synthetic materials and is breathable and warm. We think that these products are the highest quality available.

2. With prior notice we can embroider any choice of names, designs or logos on our clothing, at a minimal additional cost.

3. Most orders are guaranteed to ship within two weeks. Additional shipping time is needed for orders of more than 200 units. These are usually shipped within three weeks.

If you have further questions, please contact me. I have enclosed our current catalog with the updated price list. We will send you the holiday catalog as soon as it is available. Thanks again for your interest!

Sincerely,
Joey Singh
Joey Singh

3. What is the purpose of this letter?
   (A) To thank a customer for a recent purchase
   (B) To ask for information about a clothing line
   (C) To respond to a request for information
   (D) To apologize for a late shipment

4. What does the letter guarantee?
   (A) Shipping within a certain time
   (B) A discount for large orders
   (C) Refunds for missing or damaged deliveries
   (D) Prompt customer service

5. What did the writer send with the letter?
   (A) Order forms
   (B) A previous order
   (C) A holiday catalog
   (D) A price listing

Questions 6-9 refer to the following article.

Delight for Electronics Manufacturer Digiprompt

CAIRO (October 7) — Robert Ennels, managing director of Digiprompt, today announced the opening of a new distribution plant in Egypt. Construction is expected to take approximately six months, with the plant due to open by April 2. Mr. Ennels told reporters at a press conference that he believes this move is key in helping Digiprompt's range of affordable laptop computers reach consumers throughout the African continent. He claims that he was inspired by a holiday to the region the month before, where he realized many businesses and schools were using outdated equipment. Mr. Ennels believes that he has identified what it takes to be successful in the African marketplace. "It's not enough to just have a great product", he said. "Nor is advertising particularly important. For me, the key factor is in reducing the money spent on distribution. That's what we are hoping to achieve with this new venture." Mr. Ennels is perhaps best known for his role as joint director of globally renowned firm Assistatec. However, he voluntarily left this post in order to found Digiprompt. "There was no argument or anything with my co-manager", he reports. "In fact, we still get on well to this day. I just felt a strong urge to work entirely for myself." Another feature of this new project is that it allows Mr. Ennels the opportunity to continue exploring the continent in his free time. "That's certainly a nice bonus, but it's not the main reason for coming here," he laughed.

6. What is the article mainly about?
   (A) The tourist attractions of the African continent
   (B) The construction of some new premises
   (C) The launch of a new product
   (D) The business relationship of two colleagues

7. According to the article, what has Mr. Ennels recently done?
   (A) He spoke to a colleague.
   (B) He purchased some new IT equipment.
   (C) He founded a construction company.
   (D) He took a vacation.

8. What does Mr. Ennels say is the most important consideration for success in Africa?
   (A) Tailoring products to the local marketplace
   (B) Having a strong marketing campaign
   (C) Keeping distribution costs low
   (D) Having a range of high-quality products

9. Why did Mr. Ennels found Digiprompt?
   (A) He had a desire to work independently.
   (B) He was fired from his previous job.
   (C) He discovered a love for the African landscape.
   (D) He wanted to do some charitable work.

RC DAY 17 세부 사항을 묻는 유형

매년 약 275문제 출제 39%

BASIC 기본기 익히기

빈출 질문 유형

Who is Mitchell Adams? Michell Adams 씨는 누구인가?
What will happen on July 10? 7월 10일에 무슨 일이 일어나는가?
What are employees asked to do? 직원들에게 무엇을 하라고 요청하는가?
How many uniforms were ordered? 얼마나 많은 유니폼들이 주문되었는가?
Where is the travel agency located? 여행사는 어디에 위치해 있는가?
By when must Mr. Bruce pay the bill? Bruce 씨는 언제까지 대금을 지불해야 하는가?

실전 적용 전략

질문을 읽고 질문의 핵심 키워드를 파악한 후, 본문에서 관련 내용이 언급된 부분을 빠르게 찾는 것이 핵심이다. 이때 질문의 키워드가 고유 명사(인명/지명/업체명) 혹은 날짜/요일인 경우, 본문에서 동일한 표현을 찾아 연결된 문장을 읽으면 정답을 찾을 수 있다. 질문의 키워드가 고유 명사나 날짜/요일이 아닌 경우, 지문의 첫 문장부터 주어-동사 중심으로 빠르게 읽으며 키워드가 다른 표현으로 paraphrasing된 부분을 찾으면 된다.

PATTERN 기출 유형 맛보기

To: Diane Clark <diane.clark@westforddesigns.com>
From: Alan Scofield <scofield.a@floreston.gov>
Subject: Summer Fun Run
Date: June 4

Dear Ms. Clark,

As a member of the city council, I am in charge of planning this year's Summer Fun Run. Last week, I ordered 500 flyers from your business to advertise the race. I need to add 500 more flyers to my order. If possible, ② I would like to have all of the flyers by June 11. That's because volunteers will help to pass them out the next day. I will call you later today to make the payment for the new flyers.

Thank you,

Alan Scofield

① Q. When will the flyers be distributed?
(A) On June 5
(B) On June 11
③ **(C) On June 12**
(D) On June 21

② 같은 의미의 표현 'pass out'이 언급된 부분을 읽어보면 전단지를 6월 11일 다음 날(the next day)에 배포한다는 내용을 확인할 수 있다.

① 의문사 When을 통해 세부사항을 묻는 문제임을 알 수 있으며, 질문의 키워드 'be distributed(배포되다)'을 파악한다.

③ 따라서 (C) On June 12를 정답으로 선택한다.

PRACTICE | 기출 연습하기

Please refer to the following information.

> Printing in a Hurry
> www.lux-printing.com
>
> With Lux Printing, last-minute printing jobs don't have to be a hassle. Simply upload your photograph/logo/text, provide notes on sizing and layout preferences, and hit the Preview button. Our team of professionals will create a made-to-order image for you in less than thirty minutes. Printed materials can be shipped within as little as 2 hours. If you are not satisfied with the design, you can request changes at no extra charge. Your image will be saved on our secure Web site for six months, and you can access it at any time by using the 5-digit code provided by our staff.

1. What can the 5-digit code be used for?
   (A) Paying for a service
   (B) Tracking a delivery
   (C) Viewing an image online
   (D) Requesting a discount

Please refer to the following advertisement.

> Modern Apartment with Great View!
>
> A two-bedroom apartment in the new Cicero Tower building is available from March 1. The outdoor balcony overlooks the beautiful Cheshire River. The apartment comes with an oven, refrigerator, and microwave. Assigned parking can be obtained for a small fee. The rental fee of $1,150 per month includes water and trash removal at no extra cost. Call 555-0497 for more information.

2. What is included in the monthly rent?
   (A) An electricity bill
   (B) A parking spot
   (C) A garbage service
   (D) A washing machine

Please refer to the following e-mail.

To: All Culver Appliances Employees <stafflist@culver-appliances.com>
From: Leo Derosa <l_derosa@culver-furniture.com>
Date: October 16
Subject: For Your Attention

On October 1, our store began providing free delivery on all orders exceeding $200. Please note that while delivery is free, there is still a $50 charge for installations. This has caused some confusion among both customers and employees. It is important that you fully understand the rules regarding free and paid services, and that you outline the applicable fees to customers at the time of purchase. If anyone needs to have items delivered outside of our standard delivery zone, please refer them to Dale Schaff.

Thank you for your cooperation,

Leo Derosa
General Manager, Culver Appliances

3. According to the e-mail, what will Mr. Schaff do?
   (A) Assist with bulk purchases
   (B) Handle special requests
   (C) Reimburse installation fees
   (D) Send employees product details

PARAPHRASING 패러프레이징 연습

A. 비슷한 의미를 가진 표현끼리 연결하세요.

1. top-rated eateries
2. All sales are final.
3. explore its possibility
4. located just minutes from the station
5. refrigerators and dishwashers

(A) determine whether it is feasible
(B) very popular restaurants
(C) conveniently located
(D) no returns or exchanges
(E) some household appliances

B. 패러프레이징에 유의하여 정답을 고르세요.

6. Please find attached a summary of this quarter's earnings and revenue.
   Q. What did Mr. Bridges include with the e-mail?
   (A) Financial information
   (B) A list of potential purchases

   ★ 패러프레이징 확인하기
   _____ → include with the e-mail
   _____ → Financial information

7. Donations for the Children's Fund can be placed in the box at the reception desk.
   Q. What are visitors asked to do?
   (A) Donate more time to the program
   (B) Leave money in a container

   ★ 패러프레이징 확인하기
   place → _____
   box → _____

8. Only personnel with a staff badge will be allowed into the testing facility.
   Q. What can the badge be used for?
   (A) Receiving a discount on parking
   (B) Accessing a restricted area

   ★ 패러프레이징 확인하기
   be allowed into → _____
   facility → _____

9. Guides at Downtown Tours must be familiar with tourist spots around the city.
   Q. What is a required qualification for the position?
   (A) Knowledge of sightseeing in the area
   (B) Expertise in the local history

   ★ 패러프레이징 확인하기
   _____ with tourist spots
   → _____ of sightseeing

10. Changes to your billing or contact information can be securely made at www.pricehouse.co.uk/myaccount.
    Q. How can someone update an e-mail address?
    (A) By making a phone call
    (B) By visiting a Web site

    ★ 패러프레이징 확인하기
    changes → _____
    contact information → _____
    www.pricehouse.co.uk ~
    → _____

| 정답 | 1. (B) 2. (D) 3. (A) 4. (C) 5. (E)
6. (A), attached, earnings and revenue   7. (B), leave, container
8. (B), access, area   9. (A) be familiar, knowledge   10. (B), update, an e-mail address, a Web site

Questions 1-3 refer to the following instructions.

Thank you for your purchase of a Shinn Electronics blender. Please follow the steps below to keep your appliance in good condition.

- All parts, except for the electric base, are dishwasher-safe. Use care when handling the set of blades.
- Store the blender with the pitcher removed to prevent trapped water.
- Never put soups or other heated liquids into the blender straight from the stovetop, as this may cause the plastic pitcher to crack.
- Make sure the rubber seal and lid are in the right position so that the blender does not leak.
- All parts have passed government safety tests. However, long-term use of the electric cord could result in a safety issue, so it should be inspected once every few months.
- Do not throw away the packaging that the blender was delivered in. Shinn Electronics requires it to be sent to the manufacturer, along with the blender and parts, for return requests.

1. What is mentioned as something that may damage the blender?
   (A) A loose lid while in operation
   (B) Exposure to hot substances
   (C) A long operation time
   (D) Use of a dishwasher

2. What are customers encouraged to do with the blender regularly?
   (A) Check its power cord
   (B) Replace its rubber seal
   (C) Sharpen its set of blades
   (D) Review its safety features

3. According to the instructions, why are customers advised to retain the packaging?
   (A) It includes information about cleaning the item.
   (B) It must be included if the item is returned.
   (C) It prevents damage to the item during storage.
   (D) It provides the address of the manufacturer.

Questions 4-6 refer to the following Web page.

Faronia Theater

Celebrating Music from Around the World
Upcoming Event: Celtic Music Concert

Engage with the richness of another culture with Faronia Theater's first-ever Celtic Music Concert on Saturday, February 19, at 7 P.M. The opening act will be a local group that plays music as a hobby, but the rest of the show will include four professional performance groups. Audience members will hear music spanning two centuries, with instruments such as the fiddle and the tin whistle providing accompaniment.

The concert program was planned by Amelia Palen, who meticulously researched the Celtic music scene. Prior to joining the theater's planning team, Ms. Palen traveled throughout Europe, studying the heritage of a variety of groups, so she was the perfect fit for this job.

Tickets for the event are available now at the box office, and they include the concert itself and a question-and-answer session with the musicians following the show. Those interested in learning some basic Celtic dance moves may sign up for a three-hour workshop taking place on the same day as the concert. There is an extra charge of $8 per person to take part in this unique activity.

4. What is true about the Celtic Music Concert?
   (A) It is held annually at the Faronia Theater.
   (B) It will be available for two shows only.
   (C) It exclusively includes contemporary music.
   (D) It features professional and amateur musicians.

5. Who is Ms. Palen?
   (A) A historian
   (B) A theater employee
   (C) A singer
   (D) A travel agent

6. According to the Web page, what is available for an additional fee?
   (A) An orientation program
   (B) A recording of the concert
   (C) A dance lesson
   (D) A question-and-answer session

Questions 7-9 refer to the following letter.

241 Grey Road, Victoria, BC P4T 9E4

September 6

Greg Dubois
Connect to All, Customer Service
65 Winston Center
Victoria, BC P3L 8A5

RE: Member Account: 207-83-69

Dear Mr. Greg,

I currently belong to Connect to All's basic membership package. This subscription package entitles me to local phone calls, caller ID and call waiting. Since the regular monthly rate for this package is $27, I am wondering why I have been charged $40 as indicated on my August bill. I believe that the higher rate applies only to subscribers of the premium membership package.

I joined Connect to All two years ago as a basic member and have not made any changes to my services. You can verify this by looking through my records carefully.

Up until now, I have found all your telephone services satisfactory and I intend to keep my current subscription. I would be very grateful if you could correct this error and send me a new bill for August. If you require any more information regarding this, my number is (716) 633-8021.

Thank you very much for your time and effort.

Sincerely,
Ellen Gibbs

7. Why was this letter written?
   (A) To request a monthly payment
   (B) To report an error on a bill
   (C) To provide a new phone number
   (D) To inquire about membership rates

8. What does Ms. Gibbs ask the phone company to do?
   (A) Repair her phone line
   (B) Upgrade her membership plan
   (C) Mail a corrected bill to her
   (D) Cancel her caller ID service

9. What does Ms. Gibbs say about her subscription?
   (A) It costs $40 per month.
   (B) She is a premium member.
   (C) She will not renew it.
   (D) It is two years old.

RC | DAY 18 | 진위 확인 유형

매년 약 120문제 출제 21.9%

BASIC 기본기 익히기

빈출 질문 유형
What is **indicated/mentioned/stated** about the company? 회사에 관해 언급된 것은?
What is **suggested/implied** about the position? 직책에 관해 암시된 것은?
What is **true** about the invoice? 송장에 대해 사실인 것은?
What NOT indicated/mentioned/stated about Mr. Lee? Lee 씨에 대해 언급되지 않은 것은?

실전 적용 전략
진위 확인 유형은 크게 단서가 지문의 한 부분에 있는 '세부 진위 확인 유형'과 단서가 지문 전반에 고르게 흩어져 있는 '전체 진위 확인 유형'으로 나눌 수 있다. 질문의 about 뒤에 제시되거나 보기에 등장하는 키워드를 확인 후 본문의 관련 부분과 비교하여 정답을 찾는다. 이때 질문과 보기에 등장하는 표현들은 본문 속에서 대부분 다른 말로 패러프레이징되어 등장한다는 점에 유의해야 한다. 단서가 지문 전반에 고르게 흩어져 있는 경우도 많으므로 정답을 찾기 어려운 경우 다른 문제를 먼저 풀며 지문의 구조 및 정보들의 위치를 파악한 후 나중에 풀이하는 것이 좋다.

PATTERN 기출 유형 맛보기

Demko Dry Cleaning has been serving the Oakway community proudly for the past decade, and we are celebrating this milestone. ② Anytime in the week of February 7, hand in this coupon to receive 10% off. Please note this applies to cleaning only and cannot be used toward delivery or our mending service.

Thank you for being a Demko Dry Cleaning customer!

① Q. What is indicated about the offer?
(A) It cannot be used with other discounts.
(B) Multiple items must be cleaned.
③ **(C) It is valid for one week only.**
(D) Customers can use it more than once.

② 본문 속에서 offer와 관련된 내용을 읽으며 2월 7일의 주에 쿠폰을 제시하면 10% 할인을 받을 수 있다는 내용 등을 파악한다.

① 질문을 읽고 진위 확인 유형 문제임을 알 수 있다. 키워드 offer(할인, 가격 인하)를 확인한다.

③ 보기의 내용을 하나씩 본문과 대조하며 정답을 찾는다. 보기 중 할인이 일주일간 유효하다는 내용의 (C)가 본문의 정보와 일치하므로 정답으로 선택한다.

PRACTICE | 기출 연습하기

Please refer to the following form.

Thank you for purchasing a Smilebright-360 electric toothbrush from Shelby Oral Care. You can extend the lifespan of your device by adhering to a schedule of regular maintenance. After each use, or at least once a day, rinse the head of the toothbrush to remove any excess toothpaste or trapped food particles. Give your toothbrush a more thorough cleaning weekly by removing the brush head, running warm water over the handle, and wiping down the metal shaft.

The brush head should be replaced every three months for optimal bristle performance. Once fully charged, the brush has enough power for approximately two weeks of use, depending on the frequency of brushing. The charging station can be left plugged in because it automatically turns off when there is no toothbrush on it.

Smilebright-360: We help you to keep smiling!

---

1. What is mentioned about the charging station?
   (A) It should be wiped down to keep it clean.
   (B) It can fully charge the device very quickly.
   (C) It does not need to be unplugged when not in use.
   (D) It can be powered by a backup battery.

Please refer to the following memo.

To: All Aragon Consulting Staff
From: Kristin Lockhart
Re: Barbara Wilk
Date: November 9

On behalf of Aragon Consulting, I would like to express my excitement that Ms. Barbara Wilk will be in charge of the marketing department from next week. Ms. Wilk has received several awards throughout her career, including the prestigious Desalvo Prize. Her long career history will be an invaluable asset to us. Currently, the marketing department is mostly made up of staff members who are new to the field, so they need someone accomplished to guide and mentor them.

We will officially welcome Ms. Wilk to the team with a dinner on Monday, November 14, at 6:30 P.M. Just head down to the first floor, where several tables will be waiting for us at the Safari Grill.

---

2. What is mentioned about Ms. Wilk?
   (A) She has written several books.
   (B) She teaches at a university.
   (C) She has won multiple awards.
   (D) She has worked with Ms. Lockhart before.

Please refer to the following form.

Cleo Catering Company: Exquisite Food for Every Special Occasion

We look forward to serving you at Cleo Catering Company. Please take a moment to fill out the information below. We can then call you with recommendations to suit your personal desires.

Customer: _____   Phone Number: _____   Event Date(s): _____

Desired Meal Type: [ ] Buffet-Style   [ ] Sit-Down Dinner   [ ] Refreshments Only

Type of Event: [ ] Casual   [ ] Semi-Formal   [ ] Formal
Number of Guests: [ ] Up to 20   [ ] 21–50   [ ] 51–100   [ ] 101+
Event City: [ ] Delmar   [ ] Glenview   [ ] Kendale   [ ] Overton
Decorations Required: [ ] Yes   [ ] No
Receipt of Food: [ ] Pick-Up   [ ] Delivery

---

3. What is indicated about Cleo Catering Company?
   (A) It specializes in supplying food for formal events.
   (B) It makes suggestions based on the supplied answers.
   (C) It is unable to provide food on short notice.
   (D) It can serve events with up to one hundred people.

PARAPHRASING 패러프레이징 연습

A. 비슷한 의미를 가진 표현끼리 연결하세요.

1. doctors and nurses
2. in business for ten years
3. refine the operations
4. both hikers and motorists
5. a new kind of footwear

(A) improve the procedures
(B) shoes that you haven't seen elsewhere
(C) be established a decade ago
(D) medical workers
(E) pedestrians and drivers

B. 패러프레이징에 유의하여 정답을 고르세요.

6. Customers can shop for athletic wear at more than 100 locations across the country.
   Q. What is indicated about the company?
   (A) It operates multiple stores.
   (B) It opens on the weekend.

   ★ 패러프레이징 확인하기
   100 locations → _____

7. The head of construction for the Ford Bridge says workers need more time than anticipated.
   Q. What is mentioned about the project?
   (A) It will take longer than expected.
   (B) It is currently under inspection.

   ★ 패러프레이징 확인하기
   _____ → take longer than expected

8. The potato soup at Glanmire Café was voted Favorite New Dish by *Atlanta News* readers.
   Q. What is suggested about Glanmire Café?
   (A) It serves a popular menu item.
   (B) It is a new restaurant in the area.

   ★ 패러프레이징 확인하기
   favorite → _____

9. Appointments for our free tasting usually fill up fast, so don't wait to book yours!
   Q. What is mentioned about the free tasting event?
   (A) It is offered throughout the year.
   (B) It will likely be in high demand.

   ★ 패러프레이징 확인하기
   Appointments fill up fast
   → _____

10. Landscape architect Rodrigo Diego designed the building's gardens to harmonize with the surrounding environment.
    Q. What is suggested about the gardens?
    (A) It took a long time to complete them.
    (B) They blend well with the natural setting.

    ★ 패러프레이징 확인하기
    _____ → blend well with
    surrounding environment
    → _____

| 정답 | 1. (D) 2. (C) 3. (A) 4. (E) 5. (B)
6. (A), multiple stores   7. (A), need more time than anticipated
8. (A), popular   9. (B), in high demand   10. (B), harmonize with, natural setting

RC DAY 18 실전문제

Question 1-2 refer to the following invoice.

Invoice   Evergreen Movers

Customer: Jessie Bartz
Meeting at pickup point: 658 Ashcroft Way
Moving items to: 1392 Rutherford Court
Start Time and Date: 8 A.M. on May 10

Description	Quantity	Price Per Unit	Subtotal
Medium Boxes (24" x 18" x 16")	12	$2.75	$33.00
Small Boxes (18" x 12" x 12")	12	$1.95	$23.40
Bubble Wrap (80-foot roll)	1	$8.99	$8.99
Sticker Labels (25-count roll)	1	$0.00	$0.00
Packing and Transport Crew (2 people)	7.5 hours (excluding lunch break)	$55.00 per 2-person crew	$412.50

Please remit the total payment no later than May 12 to Cynthia Glenn in our accounting office. She can be reached by phone at 555-4113.

---

1. What kind of business is Evergreen Mobility?
   (A) A supplier of packing materials
   (B) A moving company
   (C) A landscaping firm
   (D) A furniture store

2. What is NOT indicated in the invoice?
   (A) To whom to submit a payment
   (B) Where the crew should go first
   (C) What sizes of containers are used
   (D) How long a lunch break will last

Questions 3-6 refer to the following Web site.

Educomp
Online Perfection

The Educomp Foundation has been educating learners on critical issues facing the law industry for over ten years now. Our seminars, which are exclusively available to view online, have proved extremely popular with students and young professionals alike. To date, 1.5 million subscribers have watched the videos, with many leaving positive feedback. Learners often state the duration of our seminars to be one of the most pleasing aspects. As each is a maximum length of 45 minutes, it makes them ideal for those with busy schedules and lifestyles.

To find out about our upcoming range of lectures and seminars, simply enter your name and address on the "Tell me more" section of this Web site. Our staff will then send you our annual catalog. On occasion, we allow some individuals and companies to obtain a DVD copy of our lectures to keep. If you are interested in this, you will need to fill out a money order form for $25. You can download this from our Web site. Please print this and then fill out your details. Once complete, you can take this to your bank to complete the order. When we receive this sum, our courier will then deliver the DVD within 10 working days.

3. The word "critical" in paragraph 1, line 1, is closest in meaning to
   (A) dangerous
   (B) negative
   (C) important
   (D) uncertain

4. What is NOT mentioned about Educomp's seminars?
   (A) They have been viewed by over a million people.
   (B) They may only be attended by students.
   (C) They are only available to watch on the Internet.
   (D) They last for under an hour.

5. What is indicated about Educomp?
   (A) It has been in business for over 15 years.
   (B) It is currently relocating to another city.
   (C) It produces catalogs once a year.
   (D) It recorded large profits in the previous year.

6. How can readers obtain a DVD copy of lecture material?
   (A) By submitting information to a Web site
   (B) By paying a fee
   (C) By downloading video files
   (D) By contacting a courier

Questions 7-9 refer to the following advertisement.

Lamont Landscaping: Increase your property's value and keep your yard looking its best!

Lamont Landscaping was founded about thirty years ago by Jason Lamont, who relocated to Meadowcreek to attend the local university but later decided to start his own business here.

Lamont Landscaping is a family-owned-and-operated business that strives to create the perfect blend of style and functionality for its customers. When starting out, the team only worked on small residential projects. However, over time, the business has established itself as an industry leader, taking on larger projects and working at commercial properties as well. Lamont Landscaping now even has its own greenhouse to provide flowers, trees, and shrubs for its projects. The business has also added an emergency response service, in which crews will respond to emergency calls around the clock in cases of broken irrigation pipes or fallen trees.

Two years ago, Rachel Zager assumed control of the business, and she is continuing the tradition of excellent customer service. To learn more about Lamont Landscaping, visit www.lamontlandscaping.com.

7. Where would this advertisement most likely appear?
   (A) In a travel guide
   (B) In a local newspaper
   (C) At a university
   (D) At a career fair

8. What is most likely true about Ms. Zager?
   (A) She opened a customer service call center.
   (B) She has moved out of Meadowcreek.
   (C) She wants to change the direction of the business.
   (D) She is a relative of Jason Lamont.

9. What is NOT indicated as a way that the business has changed?
   (A) It has made some services available 24 hours a day.
   (B) It has secured projects for government properties.
   (C) It has expanded the types of properties it serves.
   (D) It has begun supplying some of its own materials.

RC DAY 19 문장 넣기 / 의도 파악 / 동의어 찾기 유형

01 문장 넣기 유형

매년 2~4문제 출제 3.7%

BASIC 기본기 익히기

빈출 질문 유형

In which of the positions marked [1], [2], [3], and [4] does the following sentence best belong?
[1], [2], [3] 그리고 [4]로 표시된 위치들 중에서 다음 문장이 들어가기에 가장 적절한 곳은 어디인가?

실전 적용 전략

주어진 문장이 들어갈 가장 적합한 위치를 고르는 문제이다. 보통 제시된 문장에 지시어(this, that, such 등), 대명사(he, she, they, each, both, one 등), 접속부사(therefore, however, also, for example 등) 혹은 시간 및 장소 관련 표현(then, before/after, here, there)이 단서로 제시되는 경우가 많으므로 빈칸 앞 문장과의 논리를 파악하는 것이 중요하다. 단서가 빈칸 뒤 문장에 제시되는 경우는 4~5% 정도로 비중이 크지 않다.

PATTERN 기출 유형 맛보기

[지시어가 단서인 경우]

② The restaurant manager needed a creative way to handle more customers, so he cleaned up the building's rooftop and set up tables and chairs. —[1]—. Now the business gets nearly double the number of reservations in the spring and summer, boosting sales and creating a memorable experience. —[2]—.

Q. In which of the positions marked [1] and [2] does the following sentence best belong?

① "That area soon became popular with diners."
③ **(A) [1]**
(B) [2]

② 건물의 옥상에 테이블과 의자를 세팅 하였다는 내용을 읽으며, 주어진 문장의 'That area'가 the building's roof top을 지칭하고 있음을 알 수 있다.

① 주어진 문장을 읽으며 지시어가 포함된 단서 'That area(그 공간)'를 파악한다. 앞 문장에는 이와 관련된 장소 명사가 언급될 것임을 짐작할 수 있다.

③ 따라서 (A) [1]을 정답으로 선택한다.

[접속부사가 단서인 경우]

At yesterday's city council meeting, members approved a plan to offer over $25,000 in city funds to local community groups. These will be issued in amounts ranging from $500 to $1000. —[1]—. Groups must be registered with the city and have at least ten active members. ② To apply for the funds, visit www.cottonwoodcity.gov/funding and complete the required fields. —[2]—.

Q. In which of the positions marked [1] and [2] does the following sentence best belong?

① "Alternatively, pick up a paper application at City Hall."
(A) [1]
③ **(B) [2]**

② 홈페이지를 방문하는 것은 자금 신청을 위한 또 하나의 방법이므로 Alternatively로 시작하는 문장과 자연스럽게 연결된다.

① 주어진 문장을 읽으며 접속부사 단서인 Alternatively(또는, 아니면)를 파악한다. 앞 문장에는 신청서를 직접 가져가는 것 이외의 다른 방안이 제시될 것임을 짐작할 수 있다.

③ 따라서 (B) [2]를 정답으로 선택한다.

PRACTICE | 기출 연습하기

Please refer to the following e-mail.

> Dear Ms. Molina,
>
> —[1]—. Our records show that your subscription to *Home Decorating Monthly* will expire on August 31. —[2]—. If you would like to continue receiving monthly issues of our magazine, please send back the enclosed application for renewal. —[3]—. To ensure that you don't miss a single issue, please do not delay in taking care of this matter. —[4]—.

1. In which of the positions marked [1], [2], [3], and [4] does the following sentence best belong?
   "The accounts team will then send you a bill for the service."
   (A) [1]   (B) [2]   (C) [3]   (D) [4]

Please refer to the following letter.

> Dear Mr. Nazario,
>
> Every year, we send out a reader survey to all subscribers of *Insider Monthly* magazine to find out what sections of our publication they enjoy and what kinds of articles they would like to see. You have yet to return your survey form. —[1]—. Through feedback from readers like you, we can ensure that we remain a respected authority on extraction equipment, drilling safety, and mine-related regulations. —[2]—. I have enclosed another copy of the survey for your convenience. —[3]—. You should complete it and return it to the address printed on the back. —[4]—. If you do so, you will be automatically entered into a drawing for a $1,000 gift certificate from Walton Industries.
>
> Warmest regards,
>
> Darwin Alvez

2. In which of positions marked [1], [2], [3], and [4] does the following sentence best belong?
   "If this is simply an oversight, rest assured that there is still time to participate."
   (A) [1]   (B) [2]   (C) [3]   (D) [4]

Please refer to the following announcement.

Applications Being Accepted

The Kenwood Nature Trust (KNT) is seeking a nonprofit organization to develop a community garden project. —[1]—. Four acres of land at the northern end of town has been donated to the city. KNT will finance a project to convert the land to small plots for individual use. —[2]—. It will make the enjoyable hobby of gardening available to residents of Kenwood, the majority of whom live in apartment buildings with nowhere to plant their own flowers or vegetables except in plant pots.

Interested parties should visit the trust's Web site at www.kenwoodnature.org. —[3]—. They should upload a design for the proposed garden along with a certificate showing the group's nonprofit status. —[4]—.

---

3. In which of the marked [1], [2], [3], and [4] does the following sentence best belong?
   "Additional paperwork, such as an estimated timeline, would also be appreciated."
   (A) [1]   (B) [2]   (C) [3]   (D) [4]

02 의도 파악 유형

매년 24문제 출제 3.7%

BASIC 기본기 익히기

빈출 질문 유형
At 9:15 A.M., what does Ms. Morton most likely mean when she writes, "Certainly"?
오전 9시 15분에, Morton 씨가 "Certainly"라고 썼을 때 의미한 것은 무엇인가?

실전 적용 전략
의도를 파악해야 하는 표현의 위치를 지문에 표시한 후, 메시지의 맥락 속에서 의도를 파악한다. 'Sorry', 'Why wait?'과 같은 짧막하고 쉬운 구어체 표현들이 주로 출제되며 앞뒤 맥락만으로 의도를 찾을 수 없다면 이전까지의 메시지의 흐름을 파악하여 문제를 풀이한다.

＊ 의도 파악 유형의 빈출 상황

① 요청을 수락하는 경우
[맥락] 새로운 디자인에 관한 의견을 주실 수 있을까요?
[표현] Of course. / Certainly. / Sure thing. / No problem. 물론이죠.
[정답] She is willing to help. 그녀는 기꺼이 도우려고 한다.

② 상대의 의견 및 제안에 동의하는 경우
[맥락] Haley 씨의 강연은 언제나 흥미로워요.
[표현] No doubt. / That's true. / Certainly. / That's what I thought. 맞아요.
[정답] He agrees with her opinion about Ms. Haley. 남자는 Haley 씨에 대한 그녀의 의견에 동의한다.

③ 도움을 제시하는 경우
[맥락] 새로 생긴 컨퍼런스 센터가 우리 직원을 모두 수용할 수 있을지 모르겠어요.
[표현] I'll find out. / Let me check (on that). / I'll go ahead and ask. 제가 알아볼게요.
[정답] He will research the center's capacity. 남자는 센터의 수용 인원을 조사할 것이다.

PATTERN 기출 유형 맛보기

Charles Jensen [9:26 A.M.] Great news! The agreement with Stockton Inc. has been settled. As our new partner, they will handle the northwest region from next month.

Ki-woo Choi [9:27 A.M.] Fantastic! ② That will cut down on the time it takes to ship items to customers.

Beth Saldivar [9:28 A.M.] ① My thoughts exactly.

① Q. At 9:28 A.M., what does Ms. Saldivar most likely mean when she writes, "My thoughts exactly"?
(A) The company should move its office to another region.
③ **(B) The company's deliveries will be made more quickly.**

② 해당 표현의 앞선 맥락을 읽고 새로운 계약이 체결되어 제품 배송 시간이 단축될 것이라는 내용을 파악한다.

① 질문에 언급된 표현 'My thoughts exactly(제 생각도 그래요)' 및 해당 시각을 확인한다.

③ 배송 시간이 단축될 것이라는 상대의 말에 'My thoughts exactly'라며 맞장구를 치는 상황이므로 마찬가지의 내용을 담은 (B)를 정답으로 선택한다.

PRACTICE | 기출 연습하기

Please refer to the following online chat discussion.

Vineet Dhebar, 8:32 A.M.
Jieun, are you almost here? The presentations start in about ninety minutes.

Jieun Choi, 8:33 A.M.
I'm on my way. There was an accident on Custer Bridge, so traffic is backed up. Could you start getting things ready?

Vineet Dhebar, 8:34 A.M.
All right. I can hook up the microphones and projector.

Jieun Choi, 8:35 A.M.
Thanks. The venue may have extra power cords if you need them.

Vineet Dhebar, 8:36 A.M.
Okay. Wow, people are already lining up at the registration table, which doesn't even open until nine thirty.

Jieun Choi, 8:37 A.M.
No way! I guess they want to get good seats near the front.

---

1. At 8:37 A.M., what does Ms. Choi mean when she writes, "No way"?
    (A) She is disappointed that no seats near the front are available.
    (B) She is surprised that some people have arrived early.
    (C) She strongly disagrees with Mr. Dhebar's proposal.
    (D) She does not think that she can get to the venue by nine thirty.

Please refer to the following text message chain.

Marco Malakian [1:12 P.M.]
Wendy... A representative from Viscotti Fine Foods called to say they won't be able to cater our product launch event on April 8 due to a staffing issue.

Wendy Partridge [1:15 P.M.]
Hmm... Do you want me to ask the marketing manager what we should do?

Marco Malakian [1:18 P.M.]
Well, we could try Primo Catering on Ramsay Road. It's a popular place for business events, but they might already have a full schedule.

Wendy Partridge [1:20 P.M.]
I'll check it out.

Marco Malakian [1:24 P.M.]
Perfect. And if they are too busy, I'll get together with the marketing manager and make alternative plans.

Wendy Partridge [1:27 P.M.]
Great. Let's talk again soon.

---

2. At 1:20 P.M., what does Ms. Partridge mean when she writes, "I'll check it out"?
   (A) She will find out whether a product launch event can be postponed.
   (B) She will review the details of a service provided by Viscotti Fine Foods.
   (C) She will inquire about Primo Catering's availability.
   (D) She will attempt to reserve a venue on Ramsay Road.

03 동의어 찾기 유형

매년 약 25문제 출제 3.7%

BASIC 기본기 익히기

빈출 질문 유형
The word "term" in paragraph 1, line 2, is closest in meaning to
첫 번째 단락, 두 번째 줄의 단어 'term'과 의미가 가장 가까운 것은?

실전 적용 전략
제시된 단어의 문맥 속 의미를 묻는 문제로 대부분 다의어가 출제된다. 따라서, 제시된 단어만 보고 정답을 선택해서는 안 되며 반드시 문맥상의 의미를 파악해서 정답을 선택해야 한다.

Part 7 동의어에 출제되는 빈출 다의어

cover	1. 보도하다 (report on) 2. (비용) 충당하다, 치르다 (pay) 3. 다루다 (discuss, deal with)
reflect	1. 보여 주다 (show) 2. 나타내다 (indicate) 3. 반영하다, 맞추다 (match)
condition	1. 상태 (state) 2. 조건 (terms) 3. 상황 (circumstances)
draw	1. 끌다 (attract) 2. (칭찬/비판 등) 받다 (receive) 3. 그리다 (produce a picture, illustrate)
recognize	1. (사실) 인정하다 (acknowledge) 2. (공로) 인정하다 (honor)
secure	1. 얻다, 확보하다 (obtain) 2. 고정하다 (fasten) 3. 안정된, 자신감 있는 (confident)
as	1. ~ 때문에 (because) 2. ~할 때 (when)
assume	1. 맡다 (take on, take over) 2. 추정하다 (presume)
term	1. 기간 (duration) 2. 조건 (conditions)
mark	1. 기념하다 (celebrate) 2. 표시하다 (write on something)

PATTERN 기출 유형 맛보기

② The office supply store will **cover** the shipping costs for any orders of supplies that total at least two hundred dollars.

① Q. The word "cover" in paragraph 1, line 1, is closest in meaning to
(A) explain ③ **(B) pay** (C) guard (D) hide

② 해당 문장 속에서 cover the costs는 '비용을 충당하다[치르다]'는 의미로 쓰이고 있음을 파악한다.

① 질문을 읽고 해당 단어의 위치를 파악한다.

③ 이와 가장 가까운 의미를 갖고 있는 (B) pay를 정답으로 선택한다.

PRACTICE | 기출 연습하기 음영으로 표시된 단어와 동의어를 고르세요.

1. The list of journalists invited to cover the event on March 3 can be found on our Web site.
   (A) report on
   (B) protect
   (C) create
   (D) pay

2. The results from a single focus group do not necessarily reflect public opinion, so further market research is advisable.
   (A) attend
   (B) think about
   (C) remember
   (D) show

3. The city is expected to see economic growth as tourists and business people are drawn to the area.
   (A) provoked
   (B) attracted
   (C) illustrated
   (D) moved

4. We will hold a ceremony in order to recognize those who make a significant contribution to the firm.
   (A) realize
   (B) accept
   (C) honor
   (D) approve of

5. While we do our best to deliver every package in perfect condition, fragile items may break sometimes.
   (A) state
   (B) provision
   (C) practice
   (D) rule

6. Mr. Brooks will look through the first half of the applications, and Ms. Cooper will handle the rest.
   (A) basis
   (B) remainder
   (C) reminder
   (D) pause

7. The XL300 laptop is lightweight and compact, making it a great value for the money.
   (A) payment
   (B) estimate
   (C) principle
   (D) bargain

8. Your entry *Children in the Rain* was chosen as the winner of the 7th annual Amateur Art Challenge.
   (A) effort
   (B) subscription to a magazine
   (C) doorway
   (D) submission to a contest

9. The professor chose a textbook featuring interviews with leading figures in the field of chemical engineering.
   (A) ideas
   (B) shapes
   (C) people
   (D) numbers

10. Animal House promises to treat your pets with the utmost care while you are away on vacation.
    (A) delight
    (B) consider
    (C) handle
    (D) repair

11. To maintain your vehicle in top condition, be sure to regularly change the oil and rotate the tires.
    (A) keep
    (B) deliver
    (C) declare
    (D) test

12. The schedule is tentative, but for now Mr. Fox is set to give his presentation at 2 P.M.
    (A) full
    (B) experimental
    (C) hesitant
    (D) indefinite

RC DAY 19 실전문제

Questions 1-3 refer to the following online chat session.

Roseanne Trantham [9:13 A.M.]: To make the most of our March 17 planning meeting, I'd like you all to do make some preparations. Fierce competition has adversely affected our revenues. I think it's time to branch out.

Todd Connelly [9:15 A.M.]: What did you have in mind?

Roseanne Trantham [9:16 A.M.]: More and more stores are stocking art supplies, so to set ourselves apart, we need to add a greater variety of items to our inventory.

Phil Kang [9:17 A.M.]: It would be useful to our customers to stock reference books related to different techniques.

Santosh Munshif [9:18 A.M.]: Good idea! This might make our business more appealing to beginners.

Todd Connelly [9:19 A.M.]: Right! And we could also consider selling coffee mugs with famous paintings printed on them. They would make great gifts.

Roseanne Trantham [9:20 A.M.]: I knew you'd come up with some helpful ideas. Look into the best place to buy these kinds of products wholesale and report back to me at the meeting.

Phil Kang [9:21 A.M.]: No problem.

1. What kind of goods is the writers' company currently selling?
   (A) Athletic apparel
   (B) Coffee mugs
   (C) Art supplies
   (D) Reference books

2. At 9:13 A.M., what does Ms. Trantham mean when she writes, "I think it's time to branch out"?
   (A) The company should open more retail stores.
   (B) The business should offer a wider selection of goods.
   (C) The meeting agenda should have more discussion points.
   (D) The group should add more members.

3. What does Mr. Kang agree to do?
   (A) Set up a meeting room
   (B) E-mail a recommendation
   (C) Proofread a final report
   (D) Conduct some research

Questions 4-7 refer to the following article.

HENTHORN VALLEY—Caprea Gallery owner Desmond Alarcon has a creative side that shines through, but his background is not what you may expect. —[1]— Mr. Alarcon started working in the field of art after giving up his original job as a tax accountant. He has had a passion for art since he was a young adult, but it was not until decades later that he turned this hobby into a full-time job.

The Caprea Gallery opened three years ago, and it has slowly been gaining in popularity. —[2]— Mr. Alarcon faced major obstacles in the early days, as the level of interest in art-related activities and events in Henthorn Valley was very low. "At the time, people didn't have any opportunities to see paintings and sculptures in person. I've been working hard to change that."

It seems that Mr. Alarcon's hard work is paying off. —[3]— The number of visitors to his gallery has been growing steadily, and several art-based community groups have sprung up. Mr. Alarcon hosts numerous lectures and other special events on site. He is also looking for ways to reach more people. —[4]—

Starting from next month, some of the paintings in the Caprea Gallery's collection will be on loan to city hall, the Henthorn Valley library, and other city-owned buildings for display in their lobbies and corridors.

4. The word "turned" in paragraph 1, line 5, is closest in meaning to
   (A) reversed
   (B) brought
   (C) transformed
   (D) revolved

5. What does Mr. Alarcon think has contributed to the community's lack of interest in art?
   (A) The high cost of producing art
   (B) The reduction in art classes
   (C) The closure of an art museum
   (D) The lack of exposure to art

6. What is suggested about the Caprea Gallery?
   (A) It will provide artwork to public buildings.
   (B) It will host an art competition.
   (C) It only displays work from local artists.
   (D) It plans to hire some new guides.

7. In which of the marked [1], [2], [3], and [4] does the following sentence best belong?
   "In fact, he's come up with a unique solution to do so."
   (A) [1]
   (B) [2]
   (C) [3]
   (D) [4]

RC DAY 20   다중 지문 연계 유형

매년 약 96문제 출제 15%

BASIC 기본기 익히기

빈출 질문 유형
What position did Ms. Nichols apply for? Nichols 씨는 어떤 직책에 지원했는가?
Which item is currently out of stock? 어떤 품목이 현재 품절되었나?
What is **most likely[probably]** true about the event? 행사에 대해 사실인 것은 무엇인가?
What is **suggested** about Mr. Leeves? Leeves 씨에 대해 암시된 것은 무엇인가?

실전 적용 전략
한 지문에 단서가 충분하지 않은 경우 다른 지문에서 관련된 내용을 종합하여 정답을 찾는다. 표 및 리스트에 있는 각 항목, 숫자(날짜, 시각, 금액) 혹은 지문에 있는 고유 명사(지명, 인명 등)가 보기에 등장하는 경우 대부분 두 지문 이상을 연계하여 정답을 찾아야 한다. 또한, 본문에 여러 선택권이 언급되거나, 일정이 변경된 경우 혹은 할인의 조건 등이 언급된 경우 연계 문제일 확률이 높다는 점을 알아두자.

PATTERN 기출 유형 맛보기

1. 이중 지문

Kirkland Aquarium: Admission Information
Kirkland Aquarium is open daily from 10 A.M. to 8 P.M. Our ticket options are listed below.

Ticket Category	Price	Provides
Basic	$8.00	Access to all tank exhibits
Bronze	$12.00	Basic access + guided tour
Silver	$15.00	Bronze access + admission to the penguin enclosure
② Gold	$25.00	Silver access + admission to Shark Dive live show

② 첫 지문의 표에서 Ticket Category는 가격이나 티켓이 제공하는 내용에 따라 달라지는 것을 알 수 있으므로 두번째 지문에서 해당 내용을 찾는다.

To: info@kirklandaqua.com
From: b.davis@rightwayins.com
Date: April 5
Subject: Visit to Kirkland Aquarium

To Whom It May Concern:

I am the HR director of Rightway Insurance. Our staff takes a group trip every spring, and this year we have decided to visit your aquarium. We will have a group of twenty-five people in total. Therefore, we would like to make sure that we can stay together during our visit. Is it possible to book a specific time to visit the penguin enclosure? ③ We're also looking forward to seeing the Shark Dive event. Please call me at 555-0479.

Sincerely,

Barney Davis

③ Davis 씨가 원하는 것은 Shark Dive Event이므로, (D) Gold가 정답임을 알 수 있다.

① Q. What kind of tickets will Mr. Davis most likely purchase?
(A) Basic   (B) Bronze   (C) Silver   **(D) Gold**

① 질문과 보기의 키워드를 확인 후 본문에서 관련 단서를 찾는다. 보기가 표의 항목으로 구성되어 있으므로 연계 문제일 것으로 추측할 수 있다. 질문이 '티켓의 종류'를 묻고 있으므로 티켓 종류가 나와있는 첫 지문의 표를 먼저 살펴본다.

2. 삼중 지문

http://www.lexingtoncommunityconnect.org/housing

Looking for Apartment to Rent

Date: September 12

I am a financial advisor who is relocating to Lexington for work. I would like to find a two-bedroom apartment near the city center for around $1,600 per month. My first day of work at the new location is December 1.

---

http://www.lexingtoncommunityconnect.org/housing

Stunning Two-Bedroom Apartment for Rent

Date: September 12

Located in the Purcell Building downtown, this beautiful apartment overlooks Roland Park. The interior has been recently renovated, and ③ the new tenant can move in on November 15 or later. The monthly rent is $1,500, which includes water and gas.

③ 11월 15일부터 입주가 가능하므로 (C)가 정답임을 알 수 있다.

To: Andres Watkins <andres@watkinsproperties.com>
From: Virginia Spencer <v_spencer@yorkshire-inc.com>
Date: September 13
Subject: Two-bedroom Apartment

Dear Mr. Watkins,

I saw your posting on Lexington Community Connect about the apartment in the Purcell Building. ② I'd like to move in on the first day that it is available. If possible, I'd like to tour the apartment on September 17, as I'll be in town on business. Thanks!

Virginia Spencer
(638) 555-9926

② Spencer 씨가 입주 가능한 첫 날 이사를 원한다는 내용만으로는 정답을 찾을 수 없다. 따라서, 입주 가능 날짜가 언급된 두 번째 지문을 살펴본다.

① Q. On what date does Ms. Spencer want to begin living in the Purcell Building?
(A) September 11
(B) September 17
(C) November 15
(D) December 1

① 보기가 날짜로 구성되어 있으므로 연계 문제일 것으로 추측할 수 있다. 질문이 'Spencer 씨의 입주 희망 날짜'를 묻고 있으므로 Spencer 씨가 작성한 세 번째 지문을 먼저 살펴본다.

PRACTICE | 기출 연습하기

Please refer to the following e-mails.

To: Dennis Seiler <seilerd@reinltd.com>
From: Mina Nayar <nayarm@reinltd.com>
Date: January 6
Subject: Employee banquet

Dear Mr. Seiler,

The planning committee has selected March 3 as the date of our employee banquet. Vice President Timothy Almaraz has agreed to fly here to Houston to attend the event. The Sapphire Plaza, which is our preferred location, is too expensive for our budget. However, I will try to negotiate with the venue to get a lower price because it is low season. If that does not work, we will have to book space at Lanham Hall instead. I'll keep you updated.

Sincerely,

Mina Nayar

To: Timothy Almaraz <almarazt@reinltd.com>
From: Mina Nayar <nayarm@reinltd.com>
Date: February 27
Subject: Houston branch employee banquet

Dear Mr. Almaraz,

I have received your flight details from your assistant. We are so pleased that you will be able to attend our employee banquet in Houston. My colleague, John Herbert, will pick you up at the airport and take you to the hotel. After you have a chance to get checked in and drop off your bags, he will then take you to the Sapphire Plaza for the banquet. If there is anything I can do to make your visit more enjoyable, please let me know.

Warmest regards,

Mina Nayar

1. What is probably true about Ms. Nayar?
   (A) She plans to meet Mr. Almaraz at the airport.
   (B) She successfully negotiated a price decrease.
   (C) Her preferred caterer was not available.
   (D) Her event had to be postponed.

Please refer to the following memo and e-mail.

Date: September 16
From: Tony Stevens, Security Manager
To: All Valley Laboratories Staff
Re: Security Changes

Technicians will visit the Valley Laboratories building to install electronic locks on all doors. This is a way for us to protect both the employees and the company's property. Employees will be given ID badges by their managers. These badges will give you access to the rooms you need. We will start to use the new system on September 25. If you have any questions or comments, please contact me at tstevens@valley-lab.com.

To: tstevens@valley-lab.com
From: jmaguire@valley-lab.com
Date: September 29
Subject: Problem with ID badge

Dear Mr. Stevens,

I would like to inform you about an issue with my employee ID badge. Whenever I swipe the badge, the door does not open. I only get an "Error" message. My badge stopped working the day after we started using the system. Fortunately, my coworkers have been letting me into the labs. However, I need to come in early on October 3, so I'd like to fix the problem before then. Please let me know how I can get my ID badge replaced.

Thank you,

Jill Maguire

---

2. When did Ms. Maguire first notice a problem with her ID badge?
   (A) On September 16
   (B) On September 26
   (C) On September 29
   (D) On October 3

Please refer to the following product description, customer review, and online response.

Newport Home: Hand Blender, Model R85

No kitchen is complete without this versatile kitchen tool! The R85 is perfect for blending soups, making smoothies, and much more. The compact size is ideal for kitchens with little storage. But don't let the size fool you—the powerful motor can handle a wide variety of foods. The device features three speed settings and a lightweight design.

Retail Price: $65.00 / Newport Rewards Members Special Price: $55.00.

---

www.newporthome.com/customerreviews/R85/0124

HOME	CATALOG	REVIEWS	CONTACT

R85 Hand Blender Reviews: Rated 4.5/5 by Christina Neville on June 4

Overall, I am very impressed by how powerful this hand blender is, especially considering its small size. I am a Newport Rewards Member, so I got it at a discount. However, seeing its performance, I would be happy to pay full price. The only downside of this device is that the blades have to be washed by hand. I was expecting to be able to put all components in the dishwasher.

---

www.newporthome.com/customerreviews/R85/cs476

HOME	CATALOG	REVIEWS	CONTACT

Derrick Mason [Newport Customer Service] replying to review by Christina Neville

Thank you for sharing your review of the R85 hand blender. We are pleased that you are finding many uses for it in your cooking. Regarding your comments, you may consider purchasing our R83 model. It is not as light as the R85, but it does address your complaint. You can find this and similar models by clicking on the Catalog button above. Thank you for being a Newport Home customer!

---

3. What is implied about Ms. Neville?
   (A) She received free shipping on her order.
   (B) She used a coupon to make a purchase.
   (C) She bought the hand blender for $55.00.
   (D) She was given the hand blender as a gift.

4. Why does Mr. Mason recommend the R83 model to Ms. Neville?
   (A) Its parts can be cleaned in the dishwasher.
   (B) It is able to fit into a small space.
   (C) It has a lightweight design.
   (D) Its battery lasts for a long time.

Please refer to the following online form, e-mail, and Web site.

---

www.commerciallinens.com/contact

Commercial Linens Contact Form

Full Name: Elizabeth Ralston   E-mail Address: ralston_e@seasidegrillrestaurant.com

Comments: I am the manager of Seaside Grill in Cape Charles, and our restaurant has been purchasing the Patino line of tablecloths for many years. Unfortunately, our most recent order was a disappointment. The tablecloths seemed to be much thinner, and they had an unpleasant waxy texture.

To: ralston_e@seasidegrillrestaurant.com
From: caleb@commerciallinens.com
Date: February 18
Subject: Reply to customer comments

Dear Ms. Ralston,

We apologize that you had a disappointing experience with your purchase. Our manufacturer for some of our products went out of business, and it seems that the replacement is not offering the same level of quality. We are working to remedy this situation. In the meantime, we are happy to accept returns of any items that do not meet your standards. We would also like to give you a free sample of our newest product, E422, for you to try. Thank you for your understanding.

Caleb Escobar

---

www.commerciallinens.com/catalog/restaurant_supplies

Newest additions to the Commercial Linens catalog! We are pleased to bring you the new Cotton-Rich line, which provides napkins made from heavy premium cotton for durability and a luxurious feel.

Item Number	Size	Price per Unit
G348	16" x 16"	$0.75
E422	18" x 18"	$0.90
L197	20" x 20"	$1.05
A506	21" x 21"	$1.20

---

5. What is implied about the Patino tablecloths?
(A) Their price has recently increased.
(B) Their manufacturer has changed.
(C) They are the most popular line.
(D) They have been discontinued.

6. What napkin size will be sent to Ms. Ralston?
(A) 16" x 16"   (B) 18" x 18"   (C) 20" x 20"   (D) 21" x 21"

Questions 1-5 refer to the following advertisement and e-mail.

Astro Educational Institute
Workshop Series

We at Astro Education Inc. consider ourselves one of the leading facilities in the country for helping learners upgrade their skills and enabling them to advance in their career. Our courses are delivered by experts all with a Master's Degree or above in their respective field, and are very competitively priced. Furthermore, we have offices in ten states, including New York and California, meaning you are sure to be able to learn at a convenient location.

The following courses are available to enroll in for October:

Course Name	Description	Price per Person
Online Advertising	Learn the secrets of Web Advertising from industry expert Mark Pilate	$450.00
Employee Management	Find out how to get the very best performance from your staff	$550.00
The Secrets of Sales	Do you want to hone your marketing skills? Then this intensive, week-long course is for you!	$400.00
Successful Presentation	Learn how to wow colleagues and customers through confidently and expertly delivered presentations	$425.00

As a special promotion, we will offer a 10% discount if more than one person attends from the same company. To take advantage of this fabulous offer, simply quote reference SAVE10 when booking over the phone.

TO : customerservice@astroed.com
FROM : t.hurney@jjenterprises.net
DATE : September 25
SUBJECT : Inquiry

To whom it may concern,

I booked a place on one of your courses for myself and 5 other colleagues here at JJ Enterprises. Although I thought we would greatly benefit from the Online Advertising course, due to budget constraints we have had to go for your cheapest available option instead. We are very much looking forward to attending next week what I'm sure will be a memorable learning experience.

I would just like to clarify a couple of points before I can finalize my travel arrangements. I was wondering how often your complimentary shuttle service runs from the airport. That will help me decide where to book our hotel. Also, I was told by your employee to print some handouts before the course, but I can't seem to find them on your website. Could you tell me where these are?

Thanks in advance for your help.

Thelma Hurney

1. What is NOT announced in the advertisement?
   (A) Course leaders have professional qualifications.
   (B) A number of courses will be delivered online.
   (C) The company has facilities in multiple locations.
   (D) Course places can be reserved by telephone.

2. Which course will Ms. Hurney most likely attend?
   (A) The Secrets of Sales
   (B) Successful Presentation
   (C) Online Advertising
   (D) Employee Management

3. Which of the following does the Astro Educational Institute offer?
   (A) Reduced hotel rates
   (B) Discounted airline tickets
   (C) An online booking system
   (D) A free transportation service

4. What is suggested about Ms. Hurney?
   (A) She has previously worked as a lecturer.
   (B) She will receive a discount on her booking.
   (C) She has attended a course at Astro Educational Institute before.
   (D) She is an expert in online sales techniques.

5. According to the e-mail, what information is Ms. Hurney looking for?
   (A) The final total of an invoice
   (B) The location of some files
   (C) Directions to an office
   (D) The name of a course leader

Questions 6-10 refer to the following excerpt from an article, instructions, and e-mail.

Health First Magazine: January

Reach Your Fitness Goals with These Helpful Smartphone Apps!

#1: Pro-Health
Pro-Health is a fitness app that will help you make the most of your workouts. At the touch of a button, you can measure your achievements over time, set goals, and get exercise tips.

With the Pro-Health app, you no longer need to measure your walking or jogging routes. Simply turn on the app and take any route you want. The app will calculate the distance you traveled using your phone's GPS function. It will also keep track of your average speed and calories burned, keeping them in an easy-to-use database so you can see how you have improved. Exercising at home? The Pro-Health video library allows you to stream a variety of workout videos that require little to no equipment. Some Pro-Health packages also allow you to create custom workouts based on your specific body type, fitness level, and goals. The Novice package includes all of the features for tracking your fitness data as well as access to a mini-library of 30 videos for just $6 per month. Those more devoted to their fitness routine may opt for larger packages with more videos and features.

Thank you for your interest in the Pro-Health smartphone app. Complete the information below to get started. We are also offering a discount for friends or family members of Pro-Health users. If you were referred by a friend, be sure to input the referral code below.

User Information
Name: Ada Borelli
E-mail: borellia@monteagleco.com
Phone Number: 897-555-68820

How did you hear about Pro-Health? Magazine article
How would you describe your fitness level? Intermediate

Pro-Health Package
Novice: $6/month [ ]   Maintain: $10/month [ ]
Challenge: $12/month [X]   Master: $15/month [ ]

Referral Code: N/A

To: borellia@monteagleco.com
From: info@prohealthapp.com
Date: May 9
Subject: Important Update

Dear Pro-Health user:

In line with our terms and conditions, Pro-Health reserves the right to make changes to the application's packages once per year. We have decided to increase some package prices to add a new function that will keep track of users' sleep patterns and provide a section teaching you how to make dishes packed with nutrition. Additionally, all tools will be made available not only in English as they are now, but also in Spanish and Mandarin. Please see our updated rates below, effective July 1.

Package	Video Library Access	Monthly Charge
Novice	20	$6
Maintain	50	$12
Challenge	80	$15
Master	120	$20

As our way of thanking current users for their patronage, those with the Challenge or Master package will be sent a free resistance band.

6. According to the article excerpt, what can users do with the Pro-Health smartphone app?
   (A) Get jogging route recommendations
   (B) Find nearby workout facilities
   (C) Track fitness progress
   (D) Order workout equipment

7. What is implied about the Pro-Health smartphone app?
   (A) It was released in January.
   (B) It makes use of a phone's location function.
   (C) It must always be connected to the Internet.
   (D) It has been a best-selling app for three years.

8. Why will Ms. Borelli be sent a free resistance band?
   (A) She has purchased the Challenge package.
   (B) She recommended the service to a friend.
   (C) She completed a customer feedback survey.
   (D) She participated in a fitness competition.

9. What is NOT indicated in the e-mail as a planned improvement for the app?
   (A) Offering some healthy recipes
   (B) Downloading trail maps from other countries
   (C) Adding a sleep-tracking feature
   (D) Providing content in different languages

10. How will the Novice package be changed from July 1?
    (A) Features on the sign-in page will be simplified.
    (B) The numbers of videos will be decreased.
    (C) A new payment method will be available.
    (D) The monthly fee will be raised.

ACTUAL TEST

정재현 토익
똑똑한 기본서
LC+RC

LISTENING TEST

In the Listening test, you will be asked to demonstrate how well you understand spoken English. The entire Listening test will last approximately 45 minutes. There are four parts, and directions are given for each part. You must mark your answers on the separate answer sheet. Do not write your answers in your test book.

PART 1

Directions : For each question in this part, you will hear four statements about a picture in your test book. When you hear the statements, you must select the one statement that best describes what you see in the picture. Then find the number of the question on your answer sheet and mark your answer. The statements will not be printed in your test book and will be spoken only one time.

Statement (C), "They are sitting at a table." is the best description of the picture so you should select answer (C) and mark it on your answer sheet.

1.

2.

3.

4.

5.

6.

PART 2

Directions: You will hear a question or statement and three responses spoken in English. They will not be printed in your test book and will be spoken only one time. Select the best response to the question or statement and mark the letter (A), (B) or (C) on your answer sheet.

7. Mark your answer on your answer sheet.
8. Mark your answer on your answer sheet.
9. Mark your answer on your answer sheet.
10. Mark your answer on your answer sheet.
11. Mark your answer on your answer sheet.
12. Mark your answer on your answer sheet.
13. Mark your answer on your answer sheet.
14. Mark your answer on your answer sheet.
15. Mark your answer on your answer sheet.
16. Mark your answer on your answer sheet.
17. Mark your answer on your answer sheet.
18. Mark your answer on your answer sheet.
19. Mark your answer on your answer sheet.
20. Mark your answer on your answer sheet.
21. Mark your answer on your answer sheet.
22. Mark your answer on your answer sheet.
23. Mark your answer on your answer sheet.
24. Mark your answer on your answer sheet.
25. Mark your answer on your answer sheet.
26. Mark your answer on your answer sheet.
27. Mark your answer on your answer sheet.
28. Mark your answer on your answer sheet.
29. Mark your answer on your answer sheet.
30. Mark your answer on your answer sheet.
31. Mark your answer on your answer sheet.

PART 3

Directions: You will hear some conversations between two or more people. You will be asked to answer three questions about what the speakers say in each conversation. Select the best response to each question and mark the letter (A), (B), (C) or (D) on your answer sheet. The conversations will not be printed in your test book and will be spoken only one time.

32. How did the woman learn about the business?
    (A) By speaking to a friend
    (B) By reading a magazine
    (C) By listening to the radio
    (D) By receiving a flyer

33. According to the man, what makes the business unique?
    (A) Its reasonable prices
    (B) Its convenient location
    (C) Its knowledgeable staff
    (D) Its environmentally friendly goods

34. What does the woman plan to do next week?
    (A) Go on vacation
    (B) Meet a customer
    (C) Give a speech
    (D) Relocate her office

35. What does the woman inquire about?
    (A) The subway fare
    (B) A business's closing time
    (C) Directions to a site
    (D) A traffic delay

36. What does the woman plan to do this afternoon?
    (A) Attend an interview
    (B) Go to a concert
    (C) Take a historical tour
    (D) Visit an exhibit

37. What does the man suggest doing?
    (A) Taking a taxi
    (B) Checking a Web site
    (C) Calling an office
    (D) Downloading a map

38. Where most likely does the man work?
    (A) At a pharmacy
    (B) At a clothing shop
    (C) At a café
    (D) At a dental clinic

39. What problem does the man mention?
    (A) A team is short-staffed.
    (B) A policy has recently changed.
    (C) A computer is not working.
    (D) An order form was not signed.

40. What does the man offer to the woman?
    (A) A business catalog
    (B) A free delivery service
    (C) A product sample
    (D) A discount coupon

41. What does the man suggest about his business?
    (A) It will get new equipment.
    (B) It will hire more employees.
    (C) It will purchase a competitor.
    (D) It will add a new service.

42. What is one feature that is essential for the man?
    (A) Tight security
    (B) A break room
    (C) Underground parking
    (D) A loading area

43. According to the man, why is he unable to change a moving date?
    (A) An opening event has been promoted.
    (B) A building will be torn down.
    (C) A moving service has been booked.
    (D) A lease agreement will expire.

GO ON TO THE NEXT PAGE

44. What is the main topic of the conversation?
    (A) A business agreement
    (B) An equipment repair
    (C) A product delivery
    (D) A new employee

45. What does the woman remind the man about?
    (A) She has plans to meet the man later.
    (B) She will leave the office early today.
    (C) She will attend an out-of-town conference.
    (D) She is awaiting budget approval.

46. Why will the man speak to Mr. Reeves?
    (A) To request changing a reservation
    (B) To give him a new work assignment
    (C) To invite him to a special event
    (D) To ask for feedback on a document

47. What happened last month?
    (A) A building lease expired.
    (B) A return policy was updated.
    (C) An additional branch opened.
    (D) A new product was launched.

48. According to the man, what feature impressed customers?
    (A) The affordable delivery
    (B) The wide selection
    (C) The knowledgeable staff
    (D) The fast checkout times

49. What does the man say he will do?
    (A) Copy some documents
    (B) Speak to a caterer
    (C) Promote an employee
    (D) Select a design

50. Where do the speakers most likely work?
    (A) At a marketing firm
    (B) At a real estate agency
    (C) At an insurance company
    (D) At a financial institution

51. What did Geraldo Sanz recommend?
    (A) Browsing competitors' Web sites
    (B) Reading a newly published book
    (C) Taking a photography course
    (D) Holding more staff meetings

52. What does the man plan to do?
    (A) Schedule shorter breaks
    (B) Download some software
    (C) Get a price estimate
    (D) Post a sign-up sheet

53. Where most likely do the women work?
    (A) At an airline
    (B) At a taxi service
    (C) At a hotel
    (D) At a hospital

54. What is the man surprised about?
    (A) A booking fee
    (B) A late departure
    (C) A refund policy
    (D) A service upgrade

55. What do the women require?
    (A) A credit card number
    (B) A membership confirmation
    (C) A reservation date
    (D) A voucher code

56. What does Mr. Palmer want to change about the cabinet doors?
    (A) The wood type
    (B) The door thickness
    (C) The exterior color
    (D) The handle sizes

57. Why does the woman say, "we can't get a refund for those items"?
    (A) She is concerned about unnecessary spending.
    (B) She thinks they should use a different business.
    (C) She does not know how to make a request.
    (D) She wants an error to be changed.

58. What does the man plan to do?
    (A) Adjust a contract
    (B) Take some measurements
    (C) Hire a crew
    (D) Make a payment

59. What does the woman imply when she says, "I'm headed to a meeting with Mr. Calhoun"?
    (A) She is only available for a brief talk.
    (B) She expects an issue to be resolved.
    (C) She received the man's message.
    (D) She is unable to attend an event.

60. What does the man say he is concerned about?
    (A) The dependability of a print shop
    (B) The accuracy of a product description
    (C) The deadline for a contract negotiation
    (D) The cost of importing some goods

61. Why does the woman thank the man?
    (A) He offered to work additional hours.
    (B) He completed an assignment quickly.
    (C) He recommended a qualified consultant.
    (D) He prevented an unnecessary cost.

Departures to Hillside

Departure Time	Platform
7:55 A.M.	7
8:35 A.M.	CANCELED
9:10 A.M.	3
9:40 A.M.	DELAYED
10:05 A.M.	6
10:30 A.M.	2

62. Look at the graphic. From which platform will the woman depart?
    (A) Platform 7
    (B) Platform 3
    (C) Platform 6
    (D) Platform 2

63. What does the man ask the woman about?
    (A) Some reimbursement requests
    (B) Some staff reviews
    (C) Her presentation to a client
    (D) Her approval of a proposal

64. What does the man offer to do?
    (A) Postpone an event
    (B) Set up some equipment
    (C) Record a meeting
    (D) Reserve a meeting room

GO ON TO THE NEXT PAGE

Bayside Boat Tours

Boat Type	Max Passengers
Gudgeon	20
Davit	35
Ballaster	40
Scuttle	55

Invoice: Ace Printing	
12" × 18"	$30
18" × 24"	$35
24" × 36"	$50
36" × 48"	$75
TOTAL	$190

65. According to the man, what was finalized for the staff outing this morning?

(A) The group size
(B) The budget
(C) The duration
(D) The date

66. Look at the graphic. Which boat model do the speakers select?

(A) Gudgeon
(B) Davit
(C) Ballaster
(D) Scuttle

67. What does the woman say she will do?

(A) Contact a tour company
(B) Print out a map
(C) Arrange a meal
(D) Post a sign-up sheet

68. What does the man plan to do with the banners?

(A) Direct potential employees
(B) Advertise a property
(C) Promote a new device
(D) Welcome company investors

69. Look at the graphic. Which amount should be deleted from the invoice?

(A) $30
(B) $35
(C) $50
(D) $75

70. What will the woman's colleague do next?

(A) Label some containers
(B) Print a new bill
(C) Speak to a manager
(D) Give a demonstration

PART 4

Directions: You will hear some talks given by a single speaker. You will be asked to answer three questions about what the speaker says in each talk. Select the best response to each question and mark the letter (A), (B), (C) or (D) on your answer sheet. The talks will not be printed in your test book and will be spoken only one time.

71. What kind of service does the speaker's company provide?
    (A) Web design
    (B) Product testing
    (C) Building renovations
    (D) Financial consulting

72. What is the speaker mainly discussing?
    (A) A budget report
    (B) Team assignments
    (C) A new employee
    (D) Delivery delays

73. What are the listeners asked to do today?
    (A) E-mail some suggestions
    (B) Meet a client
    (C) Review some information
    (D) Give a sales pitch

74. By which city department was the message made?
    (A) Labor
    (B) Health
    (C) Transportation
    (D) Energy

75. According to the message, why has a project been delayed?
    (A) There was severe weather in the area.
    (B) There was not enough room in the budget.
    (C) Some residents made some complaints.
    (D) Some materials were not delivered.

76. What are the listeners reminded to do?
    (A) Call back later
    (B) Update a schedule
    (C) Sign a form
    (D) Join a mailing list

77. Where most likely do the listeners work?
    (A) At a post office
    (B) At a fashion studio
    (C) At a tour company
    (D) At a business institute

78. What does the speaker imply when he says, "Now, we've purchased several company phones"?
    (A) An issue has been resolved.
    (B) A directory will be updated.
    (C) A product was highly recommended.
    (D) Some funds are no longer available.

79. What does the speaker plan to do on Mondays?
    (A) Provide financial details
    (B) Analyze some feedback
    (C) Announce schedule changes
    (D) Check some devices

80. Where is the talk taking place?
    (A) At a supermarket
    (B) At an orchard
    (C) At a garden store
    (D) At a restaurant

81. Why is the speaker giving the talk?
    (A) To correct an error
    (B) To explain job responsibilities
    (C) To give an activity overview
    (D) To provide safety advice

82. What does the speaker encourage the listeners to do?
    (A) Write down questions
    (B) Pick up a catalog
    (C) Turn off cell phones
    (D) Try some products

GO ON TO THE NEXT PAGE

83. What is the speaker mainly discussing?
(A) A stock trend
(B) A business expansion
(C) A corporate merger
(D) An industry award

84. Who is Greg McEvoy?
(A) A university professor
(B) A company CEO
(C) A financial expert
(D) A graphic designer

85. What is the Mankato Corporation planning to do next month?
(A) Make a donation
(B) Hold job interviews
(C) Start a building project
(D) Host a convention

86. What type of equipment will be delivered tomorrow?
(A) Copy machines
(B) Security cameras
(C) Projectors
(D) Shredders

87. What feature of the equipment is the speaker pleased about?
(A) It has a low price.
(B) It connects wirelessly.
(C) It operates quietly.
(D) It is lightweight.

88. Why does the speaker say, "but they are short-staffed"?
(A) To explain the reason for a delay
(B) To ask for volunteers for a project
(C) To show support for hiring more workers
(D) To recommend doing a task without help

89. Why does the speaker apologize to the listeners?
(A) A presenter is not available.
(B) A registration process was complicated.
(C) There are not enough seats.
(D) The start time has changed.

90. Who is Alicia Marshall?
(A) A news broadcaster
(B) A business owner
(C) A best-selling author
(D) A city official

91. What will be the topic of Alicia Marshall's workshop?
(A) Marketing techniques
(B) Time management
(C) Effective teamwork
(D) Overseas investments

92. Who most likely are the listeners?
(A) Construction workers
(B) Bank tellers
(C) Real estate agents
(D) Laboratory technicians

93. What does the speaker imply when he says, "Most people have a lot of questions during the visit"?
(A) Some instructions are not clear enough.
(B) More information should be posted online.
(C) An activity may take longer than expected.
(D) An information file should be read carefully.

94. According to the speaker, what is a top priority?
(A) Working together as a team
(B) Responding to messages quickly
(C) Having a secure e-mail password
(D) Complying with regulations

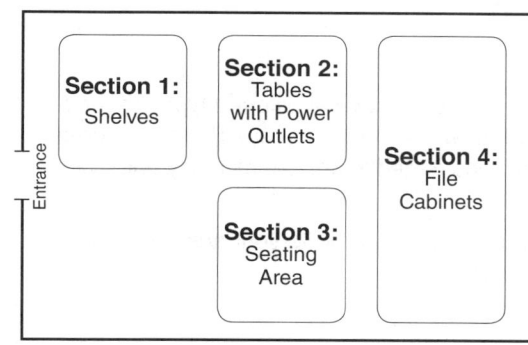
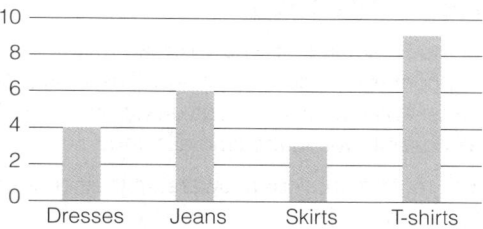

95. Who most likely is the speaker?
    (A) A computer programmer
    (B) A department store manager
    (C) A building owner
    (D) A trade show organizer

96. What does the speaker mention about some tablet computers?
    (A) They are offered at a reasonable price.
    (B) They will be shipped soon.
    (C) They have been popular with customers.
    (D) They can be positioned near the entrance.

97. Look at the graphic. Which section has been added?
    (A) Section 1
    (B) Section 2
    (C) Section 3
    (D) Section 4

98. What kind of business do the listeners work for?
    (A) A clothing manufacturer
    (B) An accounting firm
    (C) A retail chain
    (D) A fashion magazine

99. Look at the graphic. According to the speaker, what product will be moved near the entrances?
    (A) Dresses
    (B) Jeans
    (C) Skirts
    (D) T-shirts

100. What does the speaker plan to do?
    (A) Contact some supervisors
    (B) Tour some stores
    (C) Distribute a survey
    (D) Announce a staff promotion

This is the end of the Listening test. Turn to Part 5 in your test book.

GO ON TO THE NEXT PAGE

READING TEST

In the Reading test, you will read a variety of texts and answer several different types of reading comprehension questions. The entire Reading test will last 75 minutes. There are three parts, and directions are given for each part. You are encouraged to answer as many questions as possible within the time allowed.

You must mark your answers on the separate answer sheet. Do not write your answers in your test book.

PART 5

Directions: A word or phrase is missing in each of the sentences below. Four answer choices are given below each sentence. Select the best answer to complete the sentence. Then mark the letter (A), (B), (C), or (D) on your answer sheet.

101. Because the author was so late, only a small ------- of his fans remained at the book signing event.
    (A) crowded
    (B) crowd
    (C) crowding
    (D) crowds

102. Workers in all departments are requested to submit ------- official timesheets by Friday afternoon.
    (A) their
    (B) them
    (C) theirs
    (D) they

103. The contract ------- the rental of the entire fourth floor of the building for use as office space.
    (A) applies
    (B) wraps
    (C) spends
    (D) covers

104. Mr. Reynolds is taking some time off ------- he is suffering from minor health issues.
    (A) because
    (B) concerning
    (C) whether
    (D) despite

105. The boxes in the warehouse must be moved carefully in order to ------- damage to their contents.
    (A) ignore
    (B) postpone
    (C) prevent
    (D) interrupt

106. Ms. Jones has been placed in charge of the ceremony being held for the ------- of the new store.
    (A) opens
    (B) openly
    (C) openness
    (D) opening

107. ------- members of the theatrical organization are permitted backstage prior to the beginning of a show.
    (A) Easily
    (B) Provided
    (C) Until
    (D) Only

108. Davidson Motors plans to introduce additional vehicles to be more ------- with buyers in their twenties.
    (A) competitively
    (B) competitive
    (C) competition
    (D) competing

109. All concertgoers are required to present a ------- ticket to gain admission to the theater.
(A) direct
(B) varied
(C) prompt
(D) valid

110. Dr. Norris, a local resident, was recognized for innovative ------- in the field of dentistry.
(A) achievable
(B) achievement
(C) achieving
(D) achieves

111. Prices at Harold's Pharmaceuticals have remained constant ------- its entire line of healthcare products.
(A) onto
(B) beside
(C) across
(D) between

112. The qualifications of the five applicants for the supervisor position differ ------- by education and experience.
(A) greatest
(B) greatly
(C) greater
(D) great

113. ------- Mr. Tanaka arrives at the facility, please be sure to take him to the conference room.
(A) As well as
(B) Not only
(C) As soon as
(D) So that

114. A reporter for a local news station reported on the ------- construction of a suspension bridge across Blueline Bay.
(A) propose
(B) proposal
(C) proposing
(D) proposed

115. While it has ------- lasted for three days, the Emerson County Fair will be held for one week this summer.
(A) exceptionally
(B) financially
(C) positively
(D) traditionally

116. Because of a major shipping problem, no items from MacGregor are due to arrive for ------- weeks.
(A) another
(B) variable
(C) plentiful
(D) several

117. Once the contract is signed by both parties, no further ------- to the conditions can be made.
(A) commitments
(B) adjustments
(C) conversions
(D) selections

118. Every business card for employees at Harper Media has been ------- to reflect each individual's personality.
(A) customizes
(B) customizing
(C) customize
(D) customized

119. Ms. Watts will not return to work until 11 A.M., but she is available to meet anytime ------- that.
(A) behind
(B) along
(C) during
(D) after

120. The store sells jewelry at ------- reduced prices despite its location in an exclusive neighborhood.
(A) slightly
(B) slighting
(C) slighted
(D) slightest

121. The receptionist at the front desk can transfer all calls made by outside parties to the ------- department.
(A) intentional
(B) subsequent
(C) appropriate
(D) significant

122. Mr. Prentice in HR ------- the firm's new guidelines for dealing with clients at a meeting tomorrow afternoon.
(A) should be presented
(B) will be presented
(C) is presenting
(D) had been presenting

123. Although the errors in the report were ------- noticeable, the manager asked it to be completely rewritten.
(A) preferably
(B) correctly
(C) carefully
(D) barely

124. It is imperative that any price ------- not affect the company's targeted revenue numbers for the quarter.
(A) reductions
(B) sensations
(C) institutions
(D) reservations

125. Mr. Benson increased the speed at which he completed his assignments without compromising -------.
(A) clearly
(B) clarity
(C) clear
(D) clearing

126. Because the Weston Hotel has no vacancies this month, Mr. Jenkins must book a room -------.
(A) elsewhere
(B) somewhat
(C) already
(D) furthermore

127. A ceremony is being held for the Tyler Institute's annual ------- of outstanding performance.
(A) omission
(B) recognition
(C) standard
(D) exception

128. Because he does not like speaking in public, Mr. Turner is ------- to present his work at the conference.
(A) reluctant
(B) reluctance
(C) more reluctantly
(D) reluctance

129. ------- purchasing her flight ticket, Ms. Vernon confirmed that it was the cheapest one available.
(A) Owing to
(B) Provided that
(C) Prior to
(D) Instead

130. ------- the repairs on the bridge were finished, vehicular traffic had already crossed over it on numerous occasions.
(A) Due to
(B) Unless
(C) Whenever
(D) By the time

PART 6

Directions: Read the texts that follow. A word, phrase, or sentence is missing in parts of each text. Four answer choices for each question are given below the text. Select the best answer to complete the text. Then mark the letter (A), (B), (C), or (D) on your answer sheet.

Questions 131-134 refer to the following e-mail.

To: Sylvia Bannister
From: Carl Jepson
Date: March 12
Subject: Interior Work

Dear Ms. Bannister,

We have been busy with the interior work you requested on your new home. First, we ------- some tiles from a manufacturer in Bolivia renowned for the quality of its designs. As a
131.
precaution, we ordered a ------- small number of tiles. However, upon receiving them and testing
132.
them, I confirmed their quality and ordered enough for the kitchen and bathrooms. We have also decided to use wallpaper rather than paint the walls, thereby allowing my workers to do their jobs faster. -------.
133.

We are delighted ------- the appearance of the house and invite you to visit anytime to check on
134.
our progress.

Sincerely,

Carl Jepson
Jepson Home Interior

131. (A) purchased
(B) purchase
(C) are purchasing
(D) will purchase

132. (A) rather
(B) soon
(C) much
(D) well

133. (A) The kitchen is one of the largest rooms in the house.
(B) This is the work we are doing on the outside of your home.
(C) This will allow us to finish everything within two weeks.
(D) We hope to convince the owner to give us a larger budget.

134. (A) in
(B) beyond
(C) with
(D) over

Questions 135-138 refer to the following article.

A lawyer associated with Donald Kern ------- (135.) that the businessman made a large donation to the city. The funds will be used to complete the construction of the community center being built near Hamburg Park. "We appreciate Mr. Kern's generosity," said Mayor Elliot Stevens, "especially during this time of financial trouble for the city."

------- (136.). Now, thanks to Mr. Kern, a second building can be constructed beside the ------- (137.) one. The center will have more room for classes, athletic events, and seminars. In addition, a new swimming pool will be located ------- (138.) the center's parking lot.

135. (A) will announce
 (B) has announced
 (C) announcement
 (D) announce

136. (A) Mr. Kern owns several successful businesses in the city.
 (B) Construction of the center had been halted due to a lack of funds.
 (C) The community center is a popular place with local families.
 (D) Mayor Stevens is running for reelection this coming fall.

137. (A) noticed
 (B) conserved
 (C) existing
 (D) tangible

138. (A) such as
 (B) except for
 (C) even though
 (D) adjacent to

Questions 139-142 refer to the following advertisement.

Are you interested in having your home redecorated?

Would you like to make your house look modern, but are you worried about the cost? Then you should contact Morrison Home Decorating. -------. These include works of art, furniture, and appliances. You'll love our selection.
                                                            139.

At Morrison Home Decorating, we care ------- our clients. That's ------- we listen carefully to what
                                        140.   141.
they want and then help them make the right decisions regarding how their homes should look.

To see our ------- collection of items, visit us online at www.morrisonhd.com.
            142.

139. (A) Our office is located at 985 West Haven Street.
     (B) Be sure to ask about the special discount we're offering this month.
     (C) We have all sorts of decorations that will not exceed your budget.
     (D) Our experts are standing by to answer all of your questions.

140. (A) around
     (B) with
     (C) about
     (D) onto

141. (A) which
     (B) why
     (C) where
     (D) when

142. (A) completes
     (B) completion
     (C) completely
     (D) complete

Questions 143-146 refer to the following article.

Nashville Job Fair, April 11 — The annual Nashville Job Fair was held in the city on Saturday, April 9. -------. Like every year, technology and manufacturing firms were ------- represented.
143.   144.
-------, much more engineering companies than normal were present this year. Observers
145.
speculated that they chose to attend this ------- due to the number of highly educated students
146.
in the Nashville area.

143. (A) The keynote speaker will also highlight this year's theme.
(B) The fair attracts businesses from around the entire Southeast.
(C) Several employees recognized the hard work of the volunteers.
(D) Attendance was not as high as it had been in previous years.

144. (A) heavily
(B) heaviness
(C) heavier
(D) heavy

145. (A) Therefore
(B) Instead
(C) For example
(D) Moreover

146. (A) happening
(B) event
(C) display
(D) class

PART 7

Directions: In this part you will read a selection of texts, such as magazine and newspaper articles, e-mails, and instant messages. Each text or set of texts is followed by several questions. Select the best answer for each question and mark the letter (A), (B), (C), or (D) on your answer sheet.

Questions 147-148 refer to the following notice.

Get our lowest prices of the year at Halifax Jewelry!

We've expanded our selection at our city center location, and you can pick up these deals:

All necklaces: 30% off · All rings: 40% off · All bracelets: 50% off

You won't find prices like these online or anywhere else!
We also offer a 5-year warranty on top of the 2-year warranty provided by the manufacturer.
Financing is available on select items with only 10% down!

The sale runs from August 5 to August 8.

147. By whom was this notice most likely issued?

(A) A marketing executive
(B) A financial advisor
(C) A store manager
(D) A manufacturing engineer

148. What is implied about Halifax Jewelry?

(A) It only holds a sale once a year.
(B) It has a location in the downtown area.
(C) It has been in operation for two years.
(D) It has recently expanded its building.

Questions 149-150 refer to the following Web page.

149. What is suggested about Aurora Tech's staff members?

(A) They receive competitive compensation.
(B) They have worked in other industries.
(C) They developed efficient trading practices.
(D) They are able to think creatively.

150. Why did Aurora Tech create the Blue Skies Program?

(A) To connect employees at different branches
(B) To receive feedback from current customers
(C) To teach people how to use technological devices
(D) To open stores in Australian cities

Questions 151-152 refer to the following online chat discussion.

Ryan Maranto [1:38 P.M.]: Thank you for contacting Colson Communications. How may I help you?

Wanda Hester [1:39 P.M.]: I've just received my bill for September, and it seems that I've been overcharged. My business only signed up for the basic corporate package.

Ryan Maranto [1:40 P.M.]: Could you please give me the customer ID code that appears at the top of your bill?

Wanda Hester [1:42 P.M.]: Sure. It's TL-93849.

Ryan Maranto [1:43 P.M.]: Thank you. According to our records, Sungate changed its address three weeks ago. The new building did not have a broadband Internet line, so you were charged a one-time installation fee.

Wanda Hester [1:44 P.M.]: That makes sense. I remember we had to have a technician visit. Thanks for answering my question.

151. What is suggested about Sungate?
(A) It is an Internet service provider.
(B) It is Mr. Maranto's employer.
(C) It recently underwent a relocation.
(D) It upgraded its monthly service package.

152. At 1:44 P.M., what does Ms. Hester most likely mean when she writes, "That makes sense"?
(A) She understands why a bill was higher than expected.
(B) She remembered that the company increased its monthly fees.
(C) She was able to locate the customer ID code.
(D) She found an earlier e-mail explaining the problem.

Questions 153-154 refer to the following e-mail.

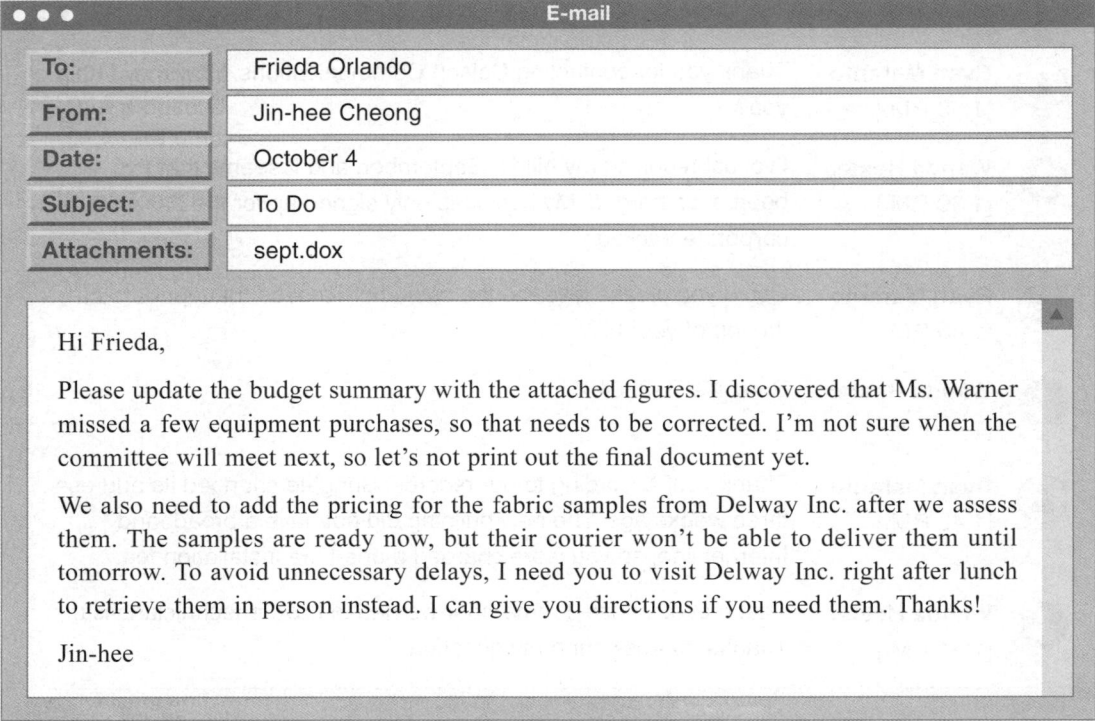

To:	Frieda Orlando
From:	Jin-hee Cheong
Date:	October 4
Subject:	To Do
Attachments:	sept.dox

Hi Frieda,

Please update the budget summary with the attached figures. I discovered that Ms. Warner missed a few equipment purchases, so that needs to be corrected. I'm not sure when the committee will meet next, so let's not print out the final document yet.

We also need to add the pricing for the fabric samples from Delway Inc. after we assess them. The samples are ready now, but their courier won't be able to deliver them until tomorrow. To avoid unnecessary delays, I need you to visit Delway Inc. right after lunch to retrieve them in person instead. I can give you directions if you need them. Thanks!

Jin-hee

153. What is the purpose of the e-mail?
(A) To approve a budget
(B) To postpone a committee meeting
(C) To order some equipment
(D) To update a report

154. What does Ms. Cheong ask Ms. Orlando to do?
(A) Pick up some items
(B) Call Delway Inc.
(C) Print some documents
(D) Prepare a price list

Questions 155-157 refer to the following e-mail.

To: Aberdeen Realty Sales Team <saleslist@aberdeenrty.com>
From: Gwen Reyes <reyesg@aberdeenrty.com>
Date: July 16

Hello, Everyone.

Recent budget cuts at Aberdeen Realty have resulted in having to lay off two of our three full-time graphic designers. As a result, salespeople will be expected to take on some additional tasks, such as creating brochures for open houses. Therefore, we are offering graphic design classes to help you improve these skills so that you may carry them out more easily.

The classes will be held in our conference room, and the instructor will be Edward Stokes of the prestigious Kappa Institute. There will be five sessions in total for each level, running once a week for five weeks. The classes will take place over the noon break so that you don't have to stay late. The planned schedule is as follows: Tuesdays—Beginner Level, Wednesdays—Intermediate Level, and Fridays—Advanced Level. Please select the level that best suits you.

We thank you for your flexibility with your job duties, and we will continue to do our best to provide you with the tools you need to make your sales efforts a success.

Sincerely,

Gwen Reyes

155. Why is Aberdeen Realty offering classes?
(A) Employees requested ongoing professional development.
(B) A team at the business has been downsized.
(C) The business will launch a Web site soon.
(D) An institute is providing a free trial.

156. What is implied about some Aberdeen Realty sales team members?
(A) They will visit the Kappa Institute together.
(B) They usually work later than other employees.
(C) They have been asked to take on additional customers.
(D) They already have some graphic design experience.

157. What is NOT indicated about the classes?
(A) They will be held at lunchtime.
(B) They will be taught by an outside instructor.
(C) They will require a test for entry.
(D) They will be held for five weeks.

Questions 158-160 refer to the following company newsletter.

Singapore Summary

We are pleased to announce the return of the design team, whose six members have just spent four days in Singapore. —[1]— The team, which is led by Carrie Eagan, worked on a project for the Interactive Media category of the International Design Competition.

This is the first time our company has submitted an entry in this highly-competitive industry event. —[2]— Although the team did not advance to the final round, team members enjoyed networking with other creative professionals. Carrie already has some ideas to help the team develop a distinctive identity and make their entry for next year stand out. —[3]— We look forward to seeing the work! —[4]—

158. Why was the article written?

(A) To explain a company's return policy
(B) To highlight a team's event participation
(C) To generate ideas for a project
(D) To announce the restructuring of teams

159. What is mentioned about Ms. Eagan?

(A) She has won an industry award.
(B) She is known for her unique style.
(C) She plans to enter a contest again.
(D) She recently joined the team.

160. In which of the positions marked [1], [2], [3], and [4] does the following sentence best belong?

"This year, it included representatives from the top companies in the world."

(A) [1]
(B) [2]
(C) [3]
(D) [4]

Questions 161-163 refer to the following e-mail.

From: cdiaz@diazuniforms.com
To: dmartinez@evebistro.com
Subject: Aug 19 Order
Date: August 21

Dear Mr. Martinez,

We are happy to inform you that the following items that you ordered on August 19 are ready for shipping:

3x White Chef Coats, Medium x1, Large x2
10x Trenton Wait Staff Vests, Small x3, Medium x4, Large x3, Grey
10x Rushmore Ties, Grey

Due to low stock levels, the items listed below are on back order and will be available in approximately 10 days:
10x Trenton Wait Staff Shirts, Small x3, Medium x4, Large x3, Black
10 x Marico Waist Apron, 28-centimeter length, Black

The Marico waist aprons are available only in the 25-centimeter variety, which cost for $5.50 each, and we have Rushmore shirts, in the sizes you wanted, for $28.00 each. Please accept our apologies for the delay and inform me whether you would like to wait and receive these items together in ten days, receive a partial order now and another in ten days, or substitute some items and receive the order immediately.

Until I hear back from you, I'll place your order on hold and not charge anything to your customer account.

We appreciate your patronage!

Craig Diaz
Diaz Uniforms

---

161. What is the purpose of the e-mail?

(A) To confirm that a payment was received
(B) To suggest using expedited shipping
(C) To update a customer on an order
(D) To apologize for sending faulty goods

162. What is indicated about the Marico waist aprons?

(A) They are available in multiple colors.
(B) They cost 28 dollars each.
(C) They come in different lengths.
(D) They will be returned to Diaz Uniforms.

163. What is Mr. Martinez asked to do?

(A) Tell Mr. Diaz how he wishes to proceed
(B) Check some items in a product catalog
(C) Make a payment using his customer account
(D) State his preferred shipping company

Questions 164-167 refer to the following online chat discussion.

Patricia Way [3:26 P.M.]
Ian, has the schedule for the company retreat been sent around yet?

Ian Cheng [3:30 P.M.]
Not yet. Susan was supposed to send it out on Monday morning, but she's been off sick this week.

Patricia Way [3:31 P.M.]
Will the retreat still go ahead as planned on Thursday?

Alistair Bruce [3:35 P.M.]
I really hope so. The deposit on the venue has already been paid, and we have had to move an important business meeting to Friday in order to accommodate staff going.

Ian Cheng [3:41 P.M.]
Don't worry about it. I'll speak to Susan's assistant and get it sent out by tomorrow morning. Everything will be taken care of.

Patricia Way [3:45 P.M.]
Superb. I shall look forward to receiving the itinerary. Have the venue staff confirmed our booking for the team-building activity in the evening?

Ian Cheng [3:49 P.M.]
I haven't heard back from them. I'll phone them and make sure the reservation is confirmed.

Alistair Bruce [3:52 P.M.]
Thanks a lot for your support, Ian. I know all employees are really looking forward to this year's retreat.

164. What is the purpose of the discussion?
 (A) To request a refund for an event
 (B) To schedule a business meeting
 (C) To discuss the details of an activity
 (D) To review a company's sick leave policy

165. According to the discussion, when should the itinerary have been sent out?
 (A) On Monday
 (B) On Tuesday
 (C) On Wednesday
 (D) On Friday

166. At 3:41 P.M., what does Mr. Cheng most likely mean when he writes, "Don't worry about it"?
 (A) He can circulate a schedule.
 (B) He can find directions to a venue.
 (C) He can book some entertainment.
 (D) He can attend a business meeting.

167. What will Mr. Cheng most likely do next?
 (A) Prepare some presentation slides
 (B) Take a sick day
 (C) Make a call
 (D) Transfer some funds

Questions 168-171 refer to the following article.

Meetings–More Harm Than Good?
by Ellen Perna

The average office worker attends over thirty meetings per month, and that figure is even higher for those working at the management level. —[1]— Many companies are experimenting with implementing a meeting-free day once a week, which involves banning all group meetings on the selected day. —[2]— Employers who have used this system have experienced an increase in work output. This is because staff members can focus on their assigned projects more easily. Employees also report having a more favorable view of the company.

Employers who implement such a policy should be strict about enforcing the policy. —[3]— Without doing so, old habits are likely to creep back into the company culture, and employees will soon be overloaded with unnecessary meetings again. Depending on the nature of the company, some exceptions may need to be made. —[4]—

To ensure that a meeting-free day is the right move for the company, employers should evaluate the needs of the staff at least every other month to determine what adjustments to the policy should be made, if any.

168. Who most likely is the intended audience of this article?
(A) Event planners
(B) Staff trainers
(C) Business owners
(D) Market analysts

169. What is NOT indicated in the article as a benefit of a meeting-free day?
(A) It makes staff members feel more positive about the company.
(B) It can improve the efficiency of employees.
(C) It helps staff members get to know each other better.
(D) It allows employees to concentrate on their tasks.

170. What does the article recommend doing regularly?
(A) Updating some software
(B) Reassessing employees' needs
(C) Planning staff outings
(D) Adjusting a travel schedule

171. In which of the positions marked [1], [2], [3], and [4] does the following sentence best belong?

"For instance, client meetings may still be available on all weekdays."

(A) [1]
(B) [2]
(C) [3]
(D) [4]

GO ON TO THE NEXT PAGE

Questions 172-175 refer to the following schedule of events.

The Winnipeg Creative Writing Festival (WCWF)
January 14-16 Vanderbilt Plaza Winnipeg, Canada

January 14 Order of Events

Writer's Block: The Path Out — 12:30 A.M.-1:15 P.M.
Bison Hall

Through years of writing workshops and feedback sessions, novelist Alan Cruz has gathered information about the most common obstacles to creativity. In this informative presentation, he gives tips on how writers can keep their ideas flowing.

Making an Impact — 1:30 P.M.-2:30 P.M.
Marten Room

Writing professor Arjuna Parikh from Rasmussen University will share the common pitfalls that inexperienced writers make. Then audience members will be invited to show excerpts from their own work to receive responses from Mr. Parikh and his experienced colleagues.

Literary Review — 2:45 P.M.-3:15 P.M.
Gannett Hall

Watch a panel of experts give their opinions on a short story from established writer Melinda Sanchez.

From Pen to Purchase: Getting Your Work Published — 3:30 P.M.-5:30 P.M.
Eider Room

Navigating the publication process can be challenging and confusing for first-time authors. Commissioning Editor for Maxwell Publishing, Glenda Cordero, walks you through the steps from preparing your first manuscript to seeing your book on shelves in bookstores.

Seating for all sessions is available on a first-come, first-served basis.
- Rather than distributing supplementary materials as handouts in advance this year, they will be available for download on our Web site at www.wcwf.org. A free Wi-fi connection is available throughout the venue, and printing can be done at the business center.
- Owing to the WCWF's low operational budget, we rely on you to spread the word to get others involved, so please do so.

172. What is true about the Winnipeg Creative Writing Festival?
 (A) Activities are held in the morning and afternoon.
 (B) It is always hosted by Vanderbilt Plaza.
 (C) The duration of each session is different.
 (D) Some sessions partially overlap each other.

173. Where can attendees get feedback about their writing?
 (A) In Bison Hall
 (B) In the Eider Room
 (C) In Gannett Hall
 (D) In the Marten Room

174. What is indicated about supplemental materials?
 (A) They will be distributed during the first session.
 (B) They should be downloaded by participants.
 (C) They will be mailed to attendees in advance.
 (D) They should be purchased at the business center.

175. What are people asked to do?
 (A) Select their seats online
 (B) Make a donation to a budget
 (C) Tell others about the event
 (D) Save questions for the end

Questions 176-180 refer to the following Web page and e-mail.

http://www.petstock.com

| HOME | ONLINE CATALOG | CUSTOMER REVIEWS | INFORMATION | CONTACT |

Pet Stock

The supplies you need for a happy and healthy pet!

We can take orders over the phone or online. We do our best to deliver your order promptly and safely. Should you receive broken, torn, or bent merchandise, you can send it back for a full refund. In these cases, we will also reimburse you for any shipping costs you incur.

Delivery Fees

Destination	Overnight with Tracking	Standard with Tracking	Standard without Tracking
Domestic (within the U.S.)	$12.95	$9.95	$8.45
Canada/Mexico	$29.95	$19.95	$17.95
Outside North America	Unavailable	$49.95	$47.95

To: Pet Stock <customerservice@petstock.com>
From: Lillian Castleberry <lcastleberry@kearneymail.com>
Date: March 13
Subject: Pet Stock order

To Whom It May Concern:

I purchased some Kiko brand dog food from your store online to be sent domestically, and it arrived yesterday by overnight shipping. I was extremely disappointed to discover that the food was unusable. It seems that Kiko has changed its recipe, and my dog won't eat it now. At first, I thought there was a problem with the specific bag I received, so I went to a local shop this morning to check whether or not the recipe had indeed been adjusted. There was no mention of a new recipe on your Web site, which I believe is a significant oversight. Please make the appropriate updates so that other customers do not have the same issue.

Sincerely,

Lillian Castleberry

176. In the Web page, the word "take" in paragraph 1, line 1, is closest in meaning to
(A) select
(B) hold
(C) accept
(D) remove

177. What is indicated about Pet Stock?
(A) It does not offer overnight delivery to Canada.
(B) It charges less for shipping on large purchases.
(C) It has recently started offering its goods online.
(D) It pays the expenses of returning damaged items.

178. Why did Ms. Castleberry send the e-mail?
(A) To request a refund
(B) To check a delivery's status
(C) To make a complaint
(D) To cancel an order

179. How much was Ms. Castleberry most likely charged for shipping?
(A) $9.95
(B) $12.95
(C) $19.95
(D) $29.95

180. According to the e-mail, why did Ms. Castleberry visit a local business on March 13?
(A) She planned to compare product prices.
(B) She needed to purchase a replacement item.
(C) She wanted to exchange some items.
(D) She decided to confirm a change.

Questions 181-185 refer to the following schedule and e-mail.

International Conference on Sustainability (ICS)
Atwater Conference Center, Stockholm, Sweden, August 7-9
Tentative Schedule for DAY 2/ Updated March 27

8:30 A.M.-9:30 A.M.	Breakfast Reception and Daily Sign-In
9:30 A.M.-10:00 A.M.	"Responsible Business Expansion" Craig Kerr, General Manager, Vantaa Industries, Helsinki, Finland
10:00 A.M.-11:00 A.M.	"New Technologies in Wind Power" Amrit Chopade, Lead Project Engineer, WHB Wind, Kolkata, India
11:00 A.M.-12:30 P.M.	"Driving Change: Government vs. Private Sector" Gebre Adonay, Dahlia Research Institute, Vancouver, Canada
12:30 P.M.-1:30 P.M.	Buffett Lunch in the Clover Room
1:30 P.M.-2:30 P.M.	"Managing Shareholder Expectations" Celine Blanc, Malquin Industries, Melbourne, Australia
2:30 P.M.-4:00 P.M.	The presenter for this time slot has not been confirmed yet. Contact event planners Raquel Lagesse and Ignazio Cetta with suggestions.
4:00 P.M.-5:00 P.M.	"Developing Effective Partnerships with Private Companies" Halima Palomino, Cheron Co., Florence, Italy

To: Raquel Lagesse <raquellegesse@icsustainability.org>
From: Ignazio Cetta <cetta_ignozio@westchesteruni.edu>
Date: April 20
Subject: Schedule updates

Dear Raquel,

As you requested, I have extended an invitation to speak at the conference to a number of prominent figures in the field. Fortunately, Manuela Gomes of Bahia Co. in Sao Paulo, Brazil, volunteered to take the empty time slot after Ms. Blanc's presentation. At Brazil's energy summit last year, Ms. Gomes gave a talk on the cost-effectiveness of residential solar panels. She will prepare a modified version of this presentation for our conference.

Additionally, I've been contacted by Amrit Chopade, who must withdraw from the event due to a medical ailment. His colleague, Kumari Dheer, has agreed to take his spot. Her area of expertise differs from that of Mr. Chopade, so later this week she will let me know what subject she plans to cover. I'll e-mail you as soon as I find out more.

Cheers,

Ignazio

181. What is true about Ms. Blanc?
    (A) She requested to speak in the morning.
    (B) She currently resides in Stockholm, Sweden.
    (C) She is scheduled to give a presentation on August 8.
    (D) She will cover the topic of government assistance.

182. When will the conference attendees learn about forming business relationships?
    (A) At 9:30 A.M.
    (B) At 11:00 A.M.
    (C) At 1:30 P.M.
    (D) At 4:00 P.M.

183. In the e-mail, the word "extended" in paragraph 1, line 1, is closest in meaning to
    (A) developed
    (B) prolonged
    (C) enlarged
    (D) offered

184. Which talk has been canceled?
    (A) Responsible Business Expansion
    (B) New Technologies in Wind Power
    (C) Driving Change: Government vs. Private Sector
    (D) Managing Shareholder Expectations

185. What does Mr. Cetta expect Ms. Dheer to do?
    (A) Cover her own travel expenses for the event
    (B) Inform him of a topic selection soon
    (C) Make adjustments to an existing presentation
    (D) Recruit a replacement speaker this week

Questions 186-190 refer to the following e-mails and press release.

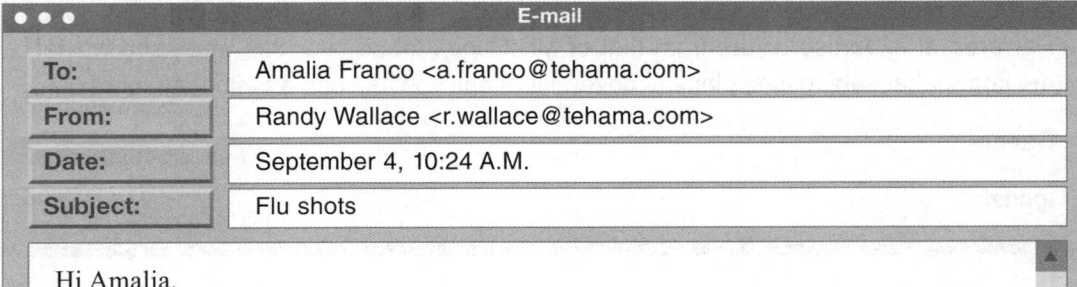

To:	Amalia Franco <a.franco@tehama.com>
From:	Randy Wallace <r.wallace@tehama.com>
Date:	September 4, 10:24 A.M.
Subject:	Flu shots

Hi Amalia,

Lena Boesen, the project manager at the Birmingham office, just called me here at the headquarters. She has the draft of the press release regarding the One Stop Shot Program sponsored by Tehama, and she recommended adding the number for our customer service line so that people may contact us with any questions they have. She said that it is vital to get free clinics to participate in the program, as they often have vaccine shortages and have a tendency to limit their use to young children and pregnant women. According to Ms. Boesen, this leaves the elderly particularly vulnerable to the flu virus. I hope you have time to deal with this today. Let me know if you run into any problems.

Cheers,

Randy

To: Randy Wallace <r.wallace@tehamapharm.com>
From: Amalia Franco <a.franco@tehamapharm.com>
Date: September 4, 3:19 P.M.
Subject: RE: Flu shots
Attachment: press_release.doc

Hi Randy,

I have updated the press release based on the guidance from Ms. Boesen, and it is now ready for publication. Because you stressed the importance of this program, I would appreciate it if you checked the attached file one more time to ensure that it is exactly the right approach. Ms. Boesen may also want to have a second look before contacting press outlets to distribute the message.

Thanks,

Amalia

For Immediate Release

Tehama Seeks to Improve Flu Vaccination Rates

Tehama is announcing its One Stop Shot Program. Through the program, the organization will make 1.8 million doses of the flu vaccine available for free to low-income individuals through free clinics in major cities. The program will also make available free one-day workshops for doctors and nurses to help them better manage the resources at clinics that are overburdened. These workshops will take place at the organization's head office in St. Louis, as well as in its branch offices in Detroit, Cleveland, and Birmingham. Inquiries about the program should be directed to 1-800-555-7733.

About Tehama: Tehama is a nonprofit organization dedicated to improving the nation's health. It is financially supported by donations from corporations and individuals.

186. What is implied about Ms. Boesen?
    (A) She wants to set up a phone meeting with Ms. Franco.
    (B) She will transfer to a new branch soon.
    (C) She is acquainted with medical clinic operations.
    (D) She oversaw the One Stop Shot Program last year.

187. What has Ms. Franco recently done?
    (A) Conducted customer service training
    (B) Uploaded some information to a Web site
    (C) Led a press conference for the company
    (D) Added contact details to a document

188. What is one purpose of the One Stop Shot Program?
    (A) To give health checkups to people with a low income
    (B) To provide training to medical personnel
    (C) To distribute vaccines to schools
    (D) To build free health clinics in major cities

189. What information is provided in the press release?
    (A) The benefits of taking the flu vaccine
    (B) The requirements that clinics must meet
    (C) The deadline for applying for vaccines
    (D) The source of Tehama's funding

190. Where does Mr. Wallace work?
    (A) Birmingham
    (B) Cleveland
    (C) Detroit
    (D) St. Louis

Questions 191-195 refer to the following Web page, e-mail, and notice.

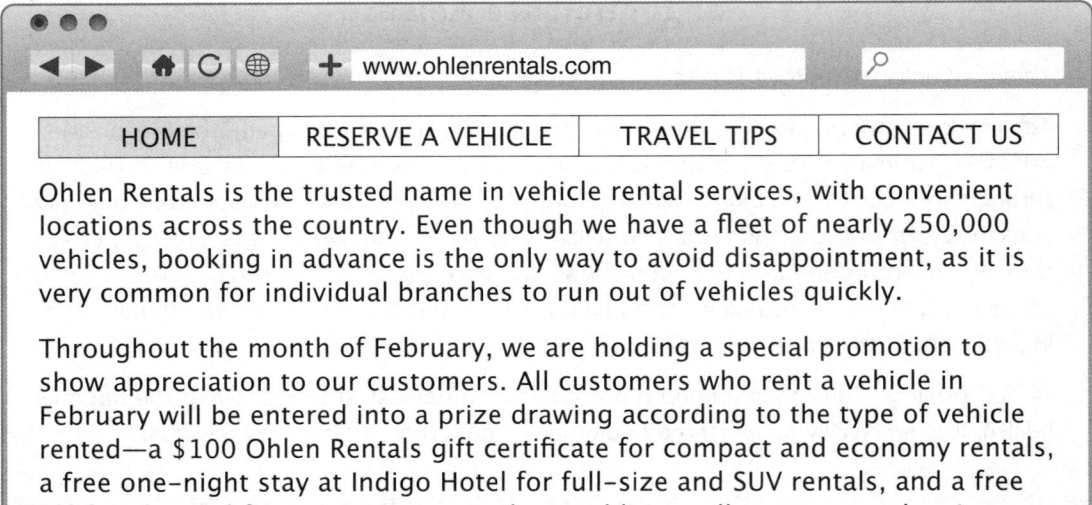

www.ohlenrentals.com

| HOME | RESERVE A VEHICLE | TRAVEL TIPS | CONTACT US |

Ohlen Rentals is the trusted name in vehicle rental services, with convenient locations across the country. Even though we have a fleet of nearly 250,000 vehicles, booking in advance is the only way to avoid disappointment, as it is very common for individual branches to run out of vehicles quickly.

Throughout the month of February, we are holding a special promotion to show appreciation to our customers. All customers who rent a vehicle in February will be entered into a prize drawing according to the type of vehicle rented—a $100 Ohlen Rentals gift certificate for compact and economy rentals, a free one-night stay at Indigo Hotel for full-size and SUV rentals, and a free weekend rental for moving van rentals. In addition, all customers who sign up for our monthly newsletter will be given a travel mug.

Click here to start the reservation process.

To: Brianna Archambault <archambault_b@gladstone.net>
From: Ohlen Rentals <bookings@ohlenrentals.com>
Date: February 4
Subject: Reservation Confirmation

Dear Ms. Archambault,

Thank you for reserving a rental vehicle from Ohlen Rentals. The details of your reservation are as follows:

Pick-up date/Location	February 16/Chicago O'Hare International Airport
Drop-off date/Location	February 21/Chicago O'Hare International Airport
Package type	Standard
Vehicle type	Full-size SUV
Daily rate	$79.99
Requested add-ons	None
Newsletter Sign-up	Yes
Reservation Confirmation	TL49502R7

A deposit of $100 has been charged to your credit card ending in 8861. When you pick up the vehicle, you must show the same credit card you used to make the reservation. However, you will not pay the remaining balance until you return the car. Should you need special accessories such as a GPS device, baby seat, etc., please inform us at least 48 hours in advance.

Notice to Ohlen Rentals Customers:

The following information applies to all Ohlen Rentals branches:

1. All vehicle rentals come with basic insurance that covers injuries and damage to third-party vehicles and drivers/passengers, but supplemental liability protection is available for an additional fee. At the service counter where you pick up your keys, please inquire about the method for purchasing other options that may better suit your needs.

2. Our Ohlen Rewards Program ends on February 22. Points can still be used after this time, but new points cannot be earned.

3. We no longer allow customers to add a second driver with our standard package. You must upgrade to a premium package if you wish to do so.

---

191. What is suggested on the Web page about Ohlen Rentals?
 (A) It has domestic and international branches.
 (B) It will purchase more vehicles.
 (C) It gives discounts for online reservations.
 (D) Its services are in high demand.

192. What will Ms. Archambault be expected to do on February 16?
 (A) Present a credit card
 (B) Request special accessories
 (C) Make a payment
 (D) Show an airline ticket

193. What prize might Ms. Archambault win in a drawing?
 (A) A gift certificate
 (B) A free stay at a hotel
 (C) A free weekend rental
 (D) A travel mug

194. According to the notice, what should customers inquire about at the pick-up counter?
 (A) When to return the vehicle
 (B) Where to get updated driving directions
 (C) What to do for vehicle maintenance
 (D) How to buy insurance policies

195. What is true about Ms. Archambault?
 (A) She is the only one allowed to operate the vehicle.
 (B) She requested an upgrade to her reservation.
 (C) She plans to return the vehicle to a different location.
 (D) She will not be able to earn points for her rental.

Questions 196-200 refer to the following memo, advertisement, and e-mail.

To: All Lawrence Aquarium Employees
From: Evelyn Gibbons, Site Manager
Re: Changes ahead
Date: February 25

Hello Everyone,

The Lawrence Aquarium will undergo a number of changes to attract more visitors to the facility and to better serve our visitors. Spring is a common time for schools to hold field trips, so we will run a special promotion for school groups in order to encourage them to take a tour here. The management team has come up with the following plan: throughout the month of April, elementary school students will be able to take a tour of the aquarium for three dollars, which is a 75% reduction in the usual admission fee. Up to five adults accompanying school groups will also be admitted for free.

Darlene Keller has completed the assessment of the flow of visitors through our site, including which exhibits get the most visits and the average amount of time people spend at each point. Having reviewed the results of this assessment, we have decided to close down the Marine Plants exhibit, starting from March 1. This will free up some much-needed space in the west wing, and we will move either the gift shop or the café to that area. We would appreciate your feedback before making this decision, so please e-mail me sometime this week. If we expand the café, we will order tables and chairs for a seating area instead of only offering to-go options like we currently do.

Field Trip Deals at Lawrence Aquarium!

From April 1 to May 15, Lawrence Aquarium will offer discounted admission for elementary school groups. Students will be charged just $3 each, and the group's chaperones (up to five) will be admitted at no cost. We will also provide two high-quality 24' X 36' posters of marine animals to each class that visits. Additional posters and other souvenirs are on sale at our gift shop, which has moved to the west end of the building and has an extended selection of marine-themed gift options for you to choose from. Call 555-9931 to book your tickets.

To: Evelyn Gibbons <gibobnse@lawrenceaqua.com>
From: Cecelia Chavez <chavezc@lawrenceaqua.com>
Date: May 31
Subject: School tours

Dear Ms. Gibbons,

I have reviewed the figures for the past two months, and I'm pleased to say that our decision to reach out to elementary schools was a success. We had thirty classes visit our site during the promotion, and I think the children had a great time. In addition to the classroom posters, we also sent a flyer home with each child. It had facts about marine animals on one side and annual membership information for parents on the other side. We hope this will encourage some parents to become aquarium members.

The agreement to partner with Ambry Amusement Park has been finalized. Next month, they will install a small on-premises fish tank sponsored by our aquarium, the aim of which is to generate interest in our site. I will explain this in greater detail at the next planning meeting.

Sincerely,

Cecelia

196. What is suggested about the Marine Plants exhibit?
   (A) It is the largest room in the building.
   (B) Its equipment is too expensive to repair.
   (C) It did not get many visitors.
   (D) It used to be the starting point for tours.

197. What did Ms. Gibbons ask the memo recipients to do?
   (A) Provide suggestions for group activities
   (B) Volunteer to lead additional tours
   (C) Review information about a special offer
   (D) Share their opinions about two options

198. How did the original plan for elementary schools change?
   (A) The hours of operation were extended.
   (B) The children's tickets were further reduced.
   (C) The discount period was extended.
   (D) The admission fee was waived for adults.

199. What is implied about the Lawrence Aquarium?
   (A) It purchased furniture for its café seating area.
   (B) It distributed sixty marine animal posters.
   (C) It held a poster design contest for children.
   (D) It sold some new memberships to parents.

200. Why does Ms. Chavez mention Ambry Amusement Park?
   (A) It has formed a business relationship with the aquarium.
   (B) It is offering a similar tour discount to elementary schools.
   (C) It is currently one of the aquarium's largest competitors.
   (D) It has plans to sponsor a charity fundraising event.

Stop! This is the end of the test. If you finish before time is called, you may go back to Parts 5, 6, and 7 and check your work.

더 얇게, 더 쉽게 20일 만에 700+ 달성하는

정재현 토익 똑똑한 기본서

LC + RC

SMART

정재현

해설집

더 얇게, 더 쉽게 20일 만에 700+ 달성하는

정재현 토익 똑똑한 기본서

SMART

정재현

해설집

LC + RC

DAY 02 시제·태 / 오답 유형

01 문장의 시제와 태

PRACTICE | 기출 연습하기 본책 p.17

정답 1 (B) 2 (D) 3 (C) 4 (B)

1.
(A) A man is putting an item into a bag.
(B) A man is looking at some merchandise.
(C) A man is pushing a shopping cart.
(D) A man is trying on his shirt.

(A) 한 남자가 제품을 가방에 넣고 있다.
(B) 한 남자가 일부 상품을 보고 있다.
(C) 한 남자가 쇼핑 카트를 밀고 있다.
(D) 한 남자가 셔츠를 착용해 보고 있다.

| 해설 |
한 손에 상품을 들고 쳐다보고 있는 남자의 자세에 초점을 맞춰 묘사한 (B)가 정답이다. 사진에서 가방이 보이지 않고, 카트를 미는 동작과 셔츠를 착용하는 동작도 아니다.

| 어휘 | put A into B A를 B에 넣다 merchandise 상품 try on ~을 착용해 보다

2.
(A) The woman is reaching for a glass.
(B) The woman is using some silverware.
(C) The man is wiping a table.
(D) The man is holding a serving tray.

(A) 여자가 유리잔을 향해 팔을 뻗고 있다.
(B) 여자가 일부 은식기를 사용하고 있다.
(C) 남자가 탁자를 닦고 있다.
(D) 남자가 서빙용 쟁반을 들고 있다.

| 해설 |
쟁반을 들고 있는 남자의 동작에 초점을 맞춰 묘사한 (D)가 정답이다. 여자가 팔을 뻗는 동작과 식기를 사용하는 동작, 그리고 남자가 탁자를 닦는 동작은 모두 사진에서 보이지 않는다.

| 어휘 | reach for ~을 향해 팔을 뻗다, ~을 붙잡기 위해 팔을 뻗다 silverware 은식기(류) wipe (행주 등으로) ~을 닦다 hold ~을 들다, 붙잡다, 쥐다 tray 쟁반

3.
(A) There's some luggage on the platform.
(B) Passengers are stepping down from a train.
(C) The train is stopped at the station.
(D) Some tracks are being repaired.

(A) 승강장에 일부 수하물이 있다.
(B) 승객들이 기차에서 내리고 있다.
(C) 기차가 역에 정차해 있다.
(D) 일부 선로가 수리되는 중이다.

| 해설 |
기차가 역에 정차된 상태에 초점을 맞춰 묘사한 (C)가 정답이다. 수하물과 승객들, 수리하는 동작은 모두 사진에서 볼 수 없다.

| 어휘 | luggage 수하물, 짐 platform 승강장 passenger 승객 step down from ~에서 내리다 repair ~을 수리하다

4.
(A) Some chairs have been stacked by the table.
(B) Some potted plants have been placed in a corner.
(C) A rug is being replaced.
(D) A light fixture is being installed.

(A) 몇몇 의자가 탁자 옆에 차곡차곡 쌓여 있다.
(B) 몇몇 화분에 심겨진 식물이 한쪽 구석에 놓여 있다.
(C) 양탄자가 교체되는 중이다.
(D) 조명 기기가 설치되는 중이다.

| 해설 |
방 한쪽 구석에 식물을 심은 화분이 놓여 있는 모습에 초점을 맞춰 묘사한 (B)가 정답이다. 의자가 쌓여 있는 모습과 양탄자를 교체하는 동작, 조명을 설치하는 동작은 모두 사진에서 확인할 수 없다.

| 어휘 | stack ~을 차곡차곡 쌓다 by ~ 옆에 potted plant 화분에 심은 식물 be placed in ~에 놓여 있다 rug 양탄자, 깔개 replace ~을 교체하다 light fixture 조명 기기 install ~을 설치하다

02 오답 유형

PRACTICE | 기출 연습하기 본책 p.19

정답 1 (B) 2 (C) 3 (D) 4 (A)

1.
(A) He is removing his sweater.
(B) He is walking down a staircase.
(C) The stairs are being fixed.
(D) Some artwork is propped against the railing.

(A) 남자가 스웨터를 벗고 있다.
(B) 남자가 계단을 내려오고 있다.
(C) 계단이 수리되는 중이다.
(D) 일부 미술품이 난간에 기대어 놓여 있다.

| 해설 |
남자가 계단을 내려오는 동작에 초점을 맞춰 묘사한 (B)가 정답이다. 스웨터를 벗는 동작과 계단을 수리하는 동작, 난간에 기대 놓인 미술품은 모두 사진에 없다.

| 어휘 | remove ~을 벗다, 제거하다, 없애다 staircase 계단 fix ~을 수리하다, 고치다 be propped against ~에 기대어 놓여 있다 railing (계단 등의) 난간, 손잡이

2.
(A) Some people are getting into a truck.
(B) One of the men is putting on a hat.
(C) Some people are loading boxes onto a vehicle.
(D) A truck is being parked in a garage.

(A) 몇몇 사람들이 트럭에 올라타고 있다.
(B) 남자들 중 한 명이 모자를 착용하는 중이다.
(C) 몇몇 사람들이 상자를 차량에 싣고 있다.
(D) 트럭 한 대가 차고에 주차되는 중이다.

| 해설 |
상자를 차에 싣는 사람들의 동작에 초점을 맞춰 묘사한 (C)가 정답이다. 트럭에 올라타는 동작과 모자를 착용하는 동작은 나타나 있지 않으며, 차고도 보이지 않는다.

| 어휘 | get into ~ 안으로 들어 가다 put on (동작) ~을 착용하다, 입다, 걸치다 load A onto B A를 B에 싣다 vehicle 차량 park ~을 주차하다 garage 차고, 주차장

3.
(A) A man is turning on a laptop.
(B) A man is taking off his shirt.
(C) The table is unoccupied.
(D) Some documents are spread out on a desk.

(A) 한 남자가 노트북 컴퓨터를 켜고 있다.
(B) 한 남자가 셔츠를 벗고 있다.
(C) 탁자에 사람이 아무도 없다.
(D) 일부 문서가 책상 위에 펼쳐져 있다.

| 해설 |
문서가 책상 위에 펼쳐져 있는 모습에 초점을 맞춰 묘사한 (D)가 정답이다. 노트북 컴퓨터를 켜는 동작과 셔츠를 벗는 동작은 사진에서 볼 수 없다.

| 어휘 | turn on ~을 켜다, 틀다   take off ~을 벗다   unoccupied 사람이 없는, 사용되지 않고 있는   be spread out on ~ 위에 펼쳐져 있다

4.
(A) Some artwork has been mounted on the wall.
(B) Some furniture is being assembled.
(C) There is a desk under the paintings.
(D) A drawer has been left open.

(A) 일부 미술품이 벽에 걸려 있다.
(B) 일부 가구가 조립되는 중이다.
(C) 그림 밑에 책상이 하나 있다.
(D) 서랍 하나가 열린 채로 있다.

| 해설 |
벽에 미술품이 걸려 있는 모습에 초점을 맞춰 묘사한 (A)가 정답이다. 사진에서 가구를 조립하는 동작은 찾아볼 수 없고, 책상 위에 그림이 보이지 않으며, 열려 있는 서랍도 없다.

| 어휘 | be mounted on ~에 걸려 있다   assemble ~을 조립하다   painting 그림   drawer 서랍   be left + 형용사 ~된 채로 있다

DAY 02 | 실전문제   본책 p.21

정답 1 (A)   2 (C)   3 (B)   4 (B)   5 (C)   6 (D)

1.
(A) A woman is examining some clothing.
(B) A woman is putting on her jacket.
(C) A woman is paying for some merchandise.
(D) A woman is being assisted.

(A) 한 여자가 일부 의류를 살펴보고 있다.
(B) 한 여자가 재킷을 착용하고 있다.
(C) 한 여자가 일부 상품에 대한 값을 지불하고 있다.
(D) 한 여자가 도움을 받고 있다.

| 해설 |
여자가 옷을 살펴보는 모습에 초점을 맞춰 묘사한 (A)가 정답이다. 재킷을 착용하는 동작과 돈을 지불하는 동작, 도움을 받는 모습은 모두 사진에서 볼 수 없다.

| 어휘 | examine ~을 살펴보다, 점검하다   clothing 의류, 옷   put on (동작) ~을 착용하다   pay for ~에 대한 값을 지불하다   merchandise 상품   assist ~을 돕다

2.
(A) Some people are sitting by the airplane.
(B) Some luggage is being taken out of the aircraft.
(C) Some passengers are boarding an airplane.
(D) An aircraft is descending toward a runway.

(A) 몇몇 사람들이 비행기 옆에 앉아 있다.
(B) 일부 수하물이 비행기에서 꺼내지는 중이다.
(C) 몇몇 승객들이 비행기에 탑승하고 있다.
(D) 비행기 한 대가 활주로 쪽으로 하강하고 있다.

| 해설 |
승객들이 비행기에 탑승하는 동작에 초점을 맞춰 묘사한 (C)가 정답이다. 앉아 있는 사람과 수하물을 꺼내는 동작, 비행기가 하강하는 모습은 모두 사진에서 확인할 수 없다.

| 어휘 | by ~ 옆에   luggage 수하물, 짐   take A out of B B에서 A를 꺼내다   aircraft 비행기   passenger 승객   board ~에 탑승하다   descend 하강하다, 내려오다   toward ~ 쪽으로, ~을 향해   runway 활주로

3.
(A) She's putting away a microscope.
(B) She's wearing gloves.
(C) She's picking up some equipment.
(D) She's leaving the laboratory.

(A) 여자가 현미경을 치우고 있다.
(B) 여자가 장갑을 착용한 상태이다.
(C) 여자가 일부 장비를 집어 들고 있다.
(D) 여자가 실험실에서 나가고 있다.

| 해설 |
여자가 장갑을 착용한 상태에 초점을 맞춰 묘사한 (B)가 정답이다. 현미경을 치우는 동작과 장비를 집어 드는 동작, 실험실에서 나가는 동작은 모두 사진에서 보이지 않는다.

| 어휘 | put away ~을 치우다   microscope 현미경   wear (상태) ~을 착용하다   pick up ~을 집어 들다   equipment 장비   leave ~에서 나가다, 떠나다   laboratory 실험실, 연구실

4.
(A) Some people are standing at the front of the room.
(B) Some people are watching a presentation.
(C) A woman is distributing notepads.
(D) A man is drawing on the board.

(A) 몇몇 사람들이 방 앞쪽에 서 있다.
(B) 몇몇 사람들이 발표를 보고 있다.
(C) 한 여자가 메모지를 나눠 주고 있다.
(D) 한 남자가 보드에 그림을 그리고 있다.

| 해설 |
발표 중인 한 사람을 여러 사람이 앉아서 지켜보고 있는 모습에 초점을 맞춰 묘사한 (B)가 정답이다. 여러 사람들이 서 있는 모습과 메모지를 나눠 주는 동작, 그림을 그리는 동작은 사진에서 보이지 않는다.

| 어휘 | at the front of ~의 앞쪽에, 앞부분에   presentation 발표(회)   distribute ~을 나눠주다, 배부하다   notepad 메모지   draw 그림을 그리다

5.
(A) The man is adjusting his headphones.
(B) The man is putting items in a backpack.
(C) There's a fountain in front of a building.
(D) There's a shirt on the ground.

(A) 남자가 헤드폰을 바로잡고 있다.
(B) 남자가 배낭에 물품을 넣고 있다.
(C) 건물 앞에 분수대가 있다.
(D) 바닥에 셔츠가 놓여 있다.

| 해설 |
건물 앞에 분수대가 위치해 있는 모습에 초점을 맞춰 묘사한 (C)가 정답이다. 헤드폰을 바로잡는 동작과 물품을 배낭에 넣는 동작, 셔츠가 바닥에 놓여 있는 모습은 사진에서 보이지 않는다.

| 어휘 | adjust (모양, 위치 등) ~을 바로잡다   put A in B A를 B에 넣다, 놓다, 두다   fountain 분수(대)   in front of ~ 앞에

6.
(A) Carpeting is being unrolled in a room.

(B) A briefcase has been left on a table.
(C) There's a lamp in the center of the room.
(D) Some pillows are lined up in a row.

(A) 카펫이 방 안에서 펼쳐지는 중이다.
(B) 서류 가방이 탁자 위에 놓여 있다.
(C) 방 가운데에 전등이 하나 있다.
(D) 몇몇 쿠션이 일렬로 정렬되어 있다.

| 해설 |
소파 위에 일렬로 정렬되어 있는 쿠션의 모습에 초점을 맞춰 묘사한 (D)가 정답이다. 카펫을 펼치는 동작과 서류 가방이 놓여 있는 모습은 사진에서 볼 수 없고, 전등은 가운데가 아닌 한쪽 구석에 놓여 있다.

| 어휘 | carpeting 카펫 unroll (말려 있는 것) ~을 펼치다 briefcase 서류 가방 be left on ~ 위에 놓여 있다 pillow 쿠션, 베개 be lined up in a row 일렬로 정렬되어 있다

DAY 03 1인·2인 사진 / 다인·사물·풍경 사진

01 1인·2인 사진

PRACTICE | 기출 연습하기   본책 p.23
정답 1 (D)   2 (C)   3 (D)   4 (D)

1.
(A) The man is drinking from a mug.
(B) The man is using a pen.
(C) The man is writing on a notepad.
(D) The man is working at a laptop computer.

(A) 남자가 머그잔에 든 것을 마시고 있다.
(B) 남자가 펜을 사용하고 있다.
(C) 남자가 메모지에 필기를 하고 있다.
(D) 남자가 노트북 컴퓨터로 일하고 있다.

| 해설 |
남자가 노트북 컴퓨터로 일하고 있는 모습에 초점을 맞춰 묘사한 (D)가 정답이다. 머그잔에 든 것을 마시는 동작과 펜을 사용하는 동작, 필기하는 동작은 모두 사진에서 확인할 수 없다.

| 어휘 | drink from ~에 든 것을 마시다 notepad 메모지

2.
(A) A man is copying a document.
(B) A man is opening a window.
(C) A copy machine is being examined.
(D) Some equipment is being moved into the room.

(A) 한 남자가 서류를 복사하고 있다.
(B) 한 남자가 창문을 열고 있다.
(C) 복사기가 점검되는 중이다.
(D) 일부 장비가 방 안으로 옮겨지는 중이다.

| 해설 |
복사기를 점검하는 동작에 초점을 맞춰 묘사한 (C)가 정답이다. 복사를 하는 동작과 창문을 여는 동작, 장비를 옮기는 동작은 모두 사진에서 확인할 수 없다.

| 어휘 | examine ~을 점검하다, 살펴보다 equipment 장비 be moved into ~ 안으로 옮겨지다

3.
(A) The man is holding onto the handrail.
(B) The man is waving to the woman.
(C) The woman is resting on the steps.
(D) The woman is carrying some food.

(A) 남자가 난간을 붙잡고 있다.
(B) 남자가 여자에게 손을 흔들고 있다.
(C) 여자가 계단에서 쉬고 있다.
(D) 여자가 일부 음식을 나르고 있다.

| 해설 |
여자가 계단에 앉아 쉬고 있는 모습에 초점을 맞춰 묘사한 (C)가 정답이다. 남자가 난간을 잡고 있는 모습과 손을 흔드는 동작, 여자가 음식을 나르는 동작은 모두 사진에서 보이지 않는다.

| 어휘 | hold onto ~을 붙잡다 handrail (계단 등의) 난간, 손잡이 wave to ~에게 손을 흔들다 rest 쉬다, 휴식하다 carry ~을 나르다, 옮기다, 휴대하다

4.
(A) They are shaking hands.
(B) They are seated behind the counter.
(C) The man is setting his glasses on the desk.
(D) The counter has been cleared of items.

(A) 사람들이 악수하고 있다.
(B) 사람들이 카운터 뒤쪽에 앉아 있다.
(C) 남자가 책상 위에 안경을 놓고 있다.
(D) 카운터에 물품이 깨끗이 치워져 있다.

| 해설 |
물건이 하나도 없이 깨끗한 상태인 카운터에 초점을 맞춰 묘사한 (D)가 정답이다. 두 사람이 악수를 하는 것은 아니며, 카운터 뒤쪽에 사람이 앉은 모습과 안경을 내려놓는 동작은 사진에서 볼 수 없다.

| 어휘 | shake hands 악수하다 be seated 앉아 있다 behind ~ 뒤쪽에 set A on B A를 B 위에 놓다 be cleared of A A가 깨끗이 치워져 있다

02 다인/사물·풍경 사진

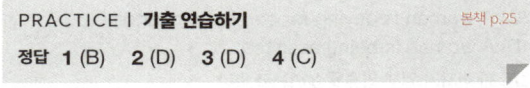

PRACTICE | 기출 연습하기   본책 p.25
정답 1 (B)   2 (D)   3 (D)   4 (C)

1.
(A) Some people are standing in line.
(B) Some people are seated in a waiting area.
(C) One of the people is pulling a suitcase.
(D) One of the people is talking on the phone.

(A) 몇몇 사람들이 줄지어 서 있다.
(B) 몇몇 사람들이 대기 공간에 앉아 있다.
(C) 사람들 중 한 명이 여행 가방을 끌고 있다.
(D) 사람들 중 한 명이 전화 통화를 하고 있다.

| 해설 |
사람들이 대기 공간에 함께 앉아 있는 모습에 초점을 맞춰 묘사한 (B)가 정답이다. 사람들이 줄지어 서 있는 모습과 여행 가방을 끄는 동작, 전화 통화를 하는 모습은 모두 사진에서 볼 수 없다.

| 어휘 | stand in line 줄지어 서 있다 be seated 앉아 있다 pull ~을 끌다, 잡아당기다 suitcase 여행 가방 talk on the phone 전화 통화하다

2.
(A) A streetlamp is being repaired.
(B) Some pedestrians are walking down the sidewalk.
(C) A car is pulled up to the curb.

(D) Some people are crossing the street.

(A) 가로등이 수리되고 있다.
(B) 몇몇 보행자들이 보도를 따라 걷고 있다.
(C) 자동차 한 대가 도로 경계석에 정차해 있다.
(D) 몇몇 사람들이 길을 건너고 있다.

| 해설 |
사람들이 함께 길을 건너는 동작에 초점을 맞춰 묘사한 (D)가 정답이다. 가로등을 수리하는 동작과 보도를 따라 걷는 동작, 자동차가 정차해 있는 모습은 모두 사진에서 볼 수 없다.

| 어휘 | repair ~을 수리하다 pedestrian 보행자 down (길 등) ~을 따라 sidewalk 보도 pull up (자동차) ~을 정차하다, 세우다 curb 도로 경계석 cross ~을 건너다

3.
(A) The beach is crowded with bathers.
(B) A boat is approaching the shore.
(C) Some umbrellas are arranged in a circle.
(D) Some chairs are facing the water.

(A) 해변이 해수욕하는 사람들로 붐빈다.
(B) 보트 한 대가 해안으로 다가가고 있다.
(C) 몇몇 파라솔이 원형으로 정렬되어 있다.
(D) 몇몇 의자가 물가를 향해 있다.

| 해설 |
물가를 바라보는 방향으로 배치되어 있는 의자들에 초점을 맞춰 묘사한 (D)가 정답이다. 사람들로 붐비는 모습과 이동 중인 보트는 보이지 않으며 파라솔은 나란히 줄지어 놓여 있다.

| 어휘 | be crowded with ~로 붐비다 bather 해수욕하는 사람 approach ~로 다가가다, 다가오다 shore 물가, 해안 arrange ~을 정렬하다, 정리하다 in a circle 원형으로 umbrella 파라솔, 우산 face ~을 향해있다

4.
(A) Some doors have been opened.
(B) The pavement is being swept.
(C) Some tables have been set up outdoors.
(D) The chairs are occupied.

(A) 몇몇 문이 열려 있다.
(B) 포장도로가 빗자루로 청소되는 중이다.
(C) 몇몇 탁자가 옥외에 설치되어 있다.
(D) 여러 의자에 사람들이 앉아 있다.

| 해설 |
탁자들이 건물 앞에 놓여 있는 모습에 초점을 맞춰 묘사한 (C)가 정답이다. 문이 열려 있는 상태가 아니며, 청소하는 동작과 사람들이 앉아 있는 모습은 사진에서 볼 수 없다.

| 어휘 | pavement 포장도로 sweep (빗자루로) ~을 청소하다, 쓸다 set up ~을 설치하다 outdoors 옥외에, 야외에 occupied 사람이 있는, 사용 중인

DAY 03 | 실전문제   본책 p.27

정답 1 (B) 2 (D) 3 (C) 4 (D) 5 (A) 6 (B)

1.
(A) Some trees are being planted.
(B) She's standing on a bridge.
(C) She's leaning against the railing.
(D) Water is flowing over the bridge.

(A) 몇몇 나무가 심어지는 중이다.
(B) 여자가 다리 위에 서 있다.
(C) 여자가 난간에 (등을) 기대고 있다.
(D) 물이 다리 위로 넘쳐 흐르고 있다.

| 해설 |
다리 위에 서 있는 여자의 모습에 초점을 맞춰 묘사한 (B)가 정답이다. 나무를 심는 동작과 난간에 기대어 있는 모습, 물이 다리 위로 넘치는 모습은 모두 사진에서 볼 수 없다.

| 어휘 | plant (식물) ~을 심다 lean against ~에 (등을) 기대다 railing (계단 등의) 난간, 손잡이 flow over ~ 위로 넘쳐 흐르다

2.
(A) The girl is paying at a cash register.
(B) The boy is baking some cakes.
(C) The baked goods have been cleared from the shelves.
(D) Some bread is being displayed in a glass case.

(A) 소녀가 계산대에서 돈을 지불하고 있다.
(B) 소년이 몇몇 케이크를 굽고 있다.
(C) 제과제품이 선반에서 치워져 있다.
(D) 몇몇 빵이 유리 진열장 안에 진열되어 있다.

| 해설 |
진열장 안에 진열되어 있는 빵의 모습에 초점을 맞춰 묘사한 (D)가 정답이다. 돈을 지불하는 동작과 케이크를 굽는 동작은 확인할 수 없으며, 진열장이 채워져 있는 것으로 보아 제품이 치워져 있는 상태도 아니다.

| 어휘 | cash register 계산대, 금전 등록기 bake (빵 등) ~을 굽다 baked goods 제과제품 be cleared from ~에서 치워지다 shelf 선반 display ~을 진열하다, 전시하다 glass case 유리 진열장

3.
(A) A woman is wrapping up a necklace.
(B) A woman is cleaning a display case.
(C) Some jewelry is on display.
(D) Merchandise is being rearranged.

(A) 한 여자가 목걸이를 포장하고 있다.
(B) 한 여자가 진열장을 청소하고 있다.
(C) 몇몇 장신구가 진열되어 있다.
(D) 상품이 재배치되고 있다.

| 해설 |
장신구가 진열되어 있는 모습에 초점을 맞춰 묘사한 (C)가 정답이다. 물품을 포장하는 동작과 청소하는 동작, 상품을 재배치하는 동작은 모두 사진에서 볼 수 없다.

| 어휘 | wrap up ~을 포장하다, 싸다 display case 진열장 jewelry 장신구, 보석 제품 on display 진열 중인, 전시 중인 merchandise 상품 rearrange ~을 재배치하다, 다시 정리하다

4.
(A) A field of grass is being cut.
(B) A bicycle is leaning against a fence.
(C) They are strolling in a park.
(D) They are sitting on a bench.

(A) 잔디밭이 깎이는 중이다.
(B) 자전거 한 대가 담장에 기대어져 있다.
(C) 사람들이 공원에서 산책하고 있다.
(D) 사람들이 벤치에 앉아 있다.

| 해설 |
사람들이 벤치에 앉아 있는 모습에 초점을 맞춰 묘사한 (D)가 정답이다. 잔디를 깎는 동작과 자전거가 담장에 기대어 있는 모습, 사람들이 산책하는 동작은 모두 사진에서 볼 수 없다.

| 어휘 | field of grass 잔디밭 lean against ~에 기대고 있다 stroll 산책하다, 거닐다

5.
(A) A man is preparing some food.
(B) A man is washing some vegetables.
(C) A man is covering a bowl.
(D) A man is stacking a pile of dishes.

(A) 한 남자가 일부 음식을 준비하고 있다.
(B) 한 남자가 일부 채소를 씻고 있다.
(C) 한 남자가 그릇을 덮고 있다.
(D) 한 남자가 그릇을 차곡차곡 쌓고 있다.

| 해설 |
음식 준비를 하는 남자의 모습에 초점을 맞춰 묘사한 (A)가 정답이다. 채소를 씻는 동작과 그릇을 덮는 동작, 그릇을 쌓는 동작은 모두 사진에서 볼 수 없다.

| 어휘 | prepare ~을 준비하다 cover ~을 덮다 bowl (움푹한) 그릇 stack a pile of ~을 차곡차곡 쌓다, 겹겹이 쌓다

6.
(A) Some curtains have been closed.
(B) Chairs are arranged on either side of the table.
(C) Some furniture is being carried outside.
(D) The window is being cleaned.

(A) 몇몇 커튼이 닫혀 있다.
(B) 의자가 탁자 양옆에 정렬되어 있다.
(C) 일부 가구가 밖에서 옮겨지고 있다.
(D) 창문이 청소되고 있다.

| 해설 |
의자가 탁자 양옆에 놓여 있는 모습에 초점을 맞춰 묘사한 (B)가 정답이다. 커튼은 젖혀진 상태이며, 가구를 옮기는 동작과 창문을 닦는 동작은 사진에서 볼 수 없다.

| 어휘 | arrange ~을 정렬하다, 정리하다 on either side of ~의 양옆에, 양측에 carry ~을 옮기다, 나르다, 휴대하다

DAY 04 의문사 의문문(1) – Who/What/Which

01 Who 의문문

PRACTICE | 기출 연습하기 본책 p.29

정답 1 (A) 2 (C) 3 (C) 4 (B) 5 (C) 6 (A)

1. Who's handling the reservation for the retirement party?
(A) Lucy is in charge.
(B) For shipping and handling.
(C) He's retiring after twenty-five years.

은퇴 기념 파티에 필요한 예약을 누가 처리하고 있나요?
(A) Lucy 씨가 맡고 있습니다.
(B) 운송 및 처리 작업을 위해서요.
(C) 그분은 25년간의 재직 끝에 은퇴하는 겁니다.

| 해설 |
은퇴 기념 파티에 필요한 예약을 처리하는 사람을 묻는 Who 의문문에 대해 책임자의 이름을 직접 언급하는 (A)가 정답이다.
(B) 목적을 나타내는 For 전치사구로 답변하고 있으므로 Why 의문문에 어울리는 오답이다.
(C) 가리키는 대상을 알 수 없는 He를 언급한 오답이다.

| 어휘 | handle ~을 처리하다, 다루다 reservation 예약 retirement 은퇴 in charge 맡고 있는, 책임지는 shipping and handling 운송 및 처리 retire 은퇴하다

2. Who should I speak with to return this oven?
(A) No, I haven't spoken to him.
(B) I can cook it in your oven.
(C) I'll get the manager for you.

이 오븐을 반품하려면 누구와 얘기해야 하나요?
(A) 아뇨, 저는 그분과 얘기한 적이 없어요.
(B) 제가 당신 오븐으로 그걸 요리할 수 있어요.
(C) 제가 책임자를 불러오겠습니다.

| 해설 |
오븐 반품과 관련해 얘기해야 하는 사람을 묻는 Who 의문문에 대해 책임자를 불러오겠다는 말로 책임자와 얘기하면 된다는 것을 알려주는 (C)가 정답.
(A) 의문사 의문문에 맞지 않는 No로 대답한 오답.
(B) 요리 가능 여부를 말하는 답변이므로 제품 반품과 관련해 묻는 질문의 핵심에서 벗어난 오답.

| 어휘 | return ~을 반품하다, 반납하다 get ~을 불러오다, 데려오다

3. Who typed up the summary of the new tax regulations?
(A) Certainly, I've got time now.
(B) Within the past few weeks.
(C) Someone on the accounting team.

새로운 세금 규제 요약본을 누가 타이핑했나요?
(A) 물론이죠, 제가 지금 시간이 있습니다.
(B) 지난 몇 주 내에요.
(C) 회계팀에 있는 사람이요.

| 해설 |
세금 규제 요약본을 타이핑한 사람이 누구인지 묻는 Who 의문문에 대해 해당 인물의 소속 부서를 언급하는 것으로 답변하는 (C)가 정답.
(A) 요청에 대한 수락을 나타내는 답변이므로 Who 의문문에 맞지 않는 오답.
(B) 과거의 기간 내에 있었던 일을 말하는 답변이므로 When 또는 How long ago 의문문에 어울리는 오답.

| 어휘 | type up ~을 타이핑하다 summary 요약(본) tax 세금 regulation 규제, 규정 Certainly. (강한 긍정이나 동의) 물론이죠, 당연하죠. within ~ 이내에 accounting 회계

4. Who are you currently working for?
(A) Starting next Monday.
(B) A company in the robotics industry.
(C) Sorry, not yet.

현재 어디서 근무하고 계신가요?
(A) 다음 주 월요일부터요.
(B) 로봇 공학 업계의 회사에서요.
(C) 죄송하지만, 아직이요.

| 해설 |
work for와 함께 쓰이는 Who 의문문은 근무지를 묻는 질문이므로 특정 업계의 회사를 언급한 (B)가 정답.
(A) 미래 시점을 나타내는 말이므로 When 의문문에 어울리는 오답.
(C) 완료 여부와 관련된 대답이므로 Who 의문문에 맞지 않는 오답.

| 어휘 | currently 현재 work for ~에서 근무하다 robotics 로봇 공학 industry 업계

5. Who was selected to represent our firm at the conference?

(A) The speech was well received.
(B) Sometime later this afternoon.
(C) Nobody has said anything yet.
누가 콘퍼런스에서 우리 회사를 대표하도록 선정되었나요?
(A) 그 연설은 좋은 반응을 얻었습니다.
(B) 이따가 오늘 오후 중으로요.
(C) 아직 뭐라고 말한 사람이 없었습니다.

| 해설 |
콘퍼런스에서 회사를 대표하도록 선정된 사람이 누구인지를 묻는 Who 의문문에 대해 아직 아무도 말한 사람이 없었다는 말로 아직 결정되지 않은 상태임을 나타내는 (C)가 정답.
(A) 연설에 대한 반응을 나타내는 답변이므로 회사 대표자를 묻는 질문의 핵심에서 벗어난 오답.
(B) 대략적인 미래 시점을 나타내므로 When 의문문에 어울리는 오답.

| 어휘 | select ~을 선정하다, 선택하다   represent ~을 대표하다   firm 회사   speech 연설   well received 좋은 반응을 얻은, 호평을 받은

6. Who's responsible for correcting errors in the document?
(A) Did you find some?
(B) More than 250 pages.
(C) I found several errors.
누가 문서의 오류를 바로잡는 일을 책임지고 있나요?
(A) 좀 찾으셨나요?
(B) 250페이지가 넘습니다.
(C) 제가 여러 오류를 발견했습니다.

| 해설 |
오류를 바로잡는 일을 책임지고 있는 사람이 누구인지 묻는 Who 의문문에 대해 뭔가 찾았는지를 반문하는 것으로 오류가 있는지를 먼저 확인하려는 의도를 나타낸 (A)가 정답.
(B) 분량을 나타내는 말이므로 How many 의문문에 어울리는 오답.
(C) 답변자 자신이 과거 시점에 오류를 찾은 사실을 말하고 있으므로 질문의 핵심에서 벗어난 오답.

| 어휘 | be responsible for ~을 책임지다   correct ~을 바로잡다, 고치다   more than ~가 넘는   several 여럿의, 몇몇의

02 What/Which 의문문

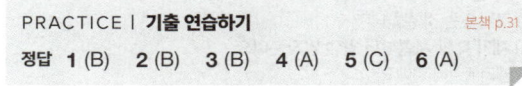

1. Which magazine should we subscribe to this year?
(A) About five pages long.
(B) I'm interested in *Sports Weekly*.
(C) He works as a journalist.
우리가 올해 어떤 잡지를 구독해야 하나요?
(A) 약 5페이지 정도의 분량입니다.
(B) 저는 <Sports Weekly>에 관심이 있습니다.
(C) 그는 기자로 일하고 있습니다.

| 해설 |
구독해야 하는 잡지가 어느 것인지 묻는 Which 의문문에 대해 특정 잡지 이름과 함께 그것에 관심 있다는 말로 답변하는 (B)가 정답.
(A) 분량과 관련된 말이므로 How long 의문문에 어울리는 오답.
(C) 가리키는 대상을 알 수 없는 He를 언급한 오답.

| 어휘 | subscribe to ~을 구독하다   about 약, 대략   be interested in ~에 관심이 있다   as (신분, 자격 등) ~로서   journalist 기자, 저널리스트

2. Which designer is creating the posters for the upcoming performance?
(A) A dramatic performer.
(B) The same one we hired in spring.
(C) I requested that they arrive this Wednesday.
어느 디자이너가 곧 있을 공연에 필요한 포스터를 만들고 있나요?
(A) 인상적인 연주자요.
(B) 우리가 봄에 고용했던 바로 그분이요.
(C) 그것들이(그 포스터들이) 이번 주 수요일에 도착하도록 요청했습니다.

| 해설 |
공연에 필요한 포스터를 만드는 디자이너가 누구인지 묻는 Which 의문문에 대해 designer를 대신하는 대명사 one과 함께 과거에 고용했던 디자이너와 같은 사람임을 밝히는 (B)가 정답.
(A) 디자이너가 아닌 연주자의 특성과 관련된 답변이므로 질문의 핵심에서 벗어난 오답.
(C) 포스터의 도착 시점을 언급하는 말이므로 질문의 핵심에서 벗어난 오답.

| 어휘 | create ~을 만들어 내다   upcoming 곧 있을, 다가오는   performance 공연, 연주(회)   dramatic 인상적인, 극적인   performer 연주자, 공연자   hire ~을 고용하다   request that ~하도록 요청하다   arrive 도착하다

3. Which flight are you planning to book a seat on?
(A) I think this Thursday is fine.
(B) It depends on the price.
(C) She's flying tomorrow.
어느 항공편에 자리를 예약할 계획이신가요?
(A) 저는 목요일이 좋을 것 같아요.
(B) 가격에 따라 다릅니다.
(C) 그녀는 내일 비행기를 타고 가요.

| 해설 |
자리를 예약할 항공편이 어느 것인지 묻는 Which 의문문에 대해 가격에 따라 다르다는 조건을 언급하는 말로 아직 알 수 없음을 나타내는 (B)가 정답.
(A) 시점과 관련된 의견을 밝히는 말이므로 When 의문문에 어울리는 오답.
(C) 답변자 자신이 아니라 가리키는 대상을 알 수 없는 She의 일정을 말하고 있으므로 오답. / flight과 발음이 비슷한 flying을 사용한 오답.

| 어휘 | plan to do ~할 계획이다   book ~을 예약하다   depend on ~에 따라 다르다, ~에 달려 있다   fly 비행기를 타고 가다

4. What time does the train for Milan leave?
(A) In thirty minutes.
(B) Twenty percent off.
(C) I have my ticket.
Milan 행 기차가 몇 시에 출발하나요?
(A) 30분 후에요.
(B) 20퍼센트 할인됩니다.
(C) 저는 티켓을 갖고 있습니다.

| 해설 |
Milan 행 기차가 출발하는 시간을 묻는 What time 의문문에 대해 미래 시점 표현으로 답변하는 (A)가 정답.
(B) 할인 비율을 말하는 답변이므로 기차 출발 시간을 묻는 질문의 핵심에서 벗어난 오답.
(C) 티켓 소지 여부를 밝히는 답변이므로 질문의 핵심에서 벗어난 오답.

| 어휘 | leave 출발하다, 떠나다   in + 시간 ~ 후에

5. What's the delivery fee for this carpet?
(A) It's easy to clean.
(B) To match the wall.
(C) It might be included.

이 카펫에 대한 배송 요금이 얼마인가요?
(A) 세척하기 쉽습니다.
(B) 벽과 어울리게 하기 위해서요.
(C) 그것(요금)이 포함되어 있을 수도 있습니다.

| 해설 |
카펫 배송 요금을 묻는 What's ~ fee 의문문에 대해 해당 요금을 It으로 지칭해 제품 가격에 포함되어 있을 수도 있다는 말로 배송 요금을 낼 필요가 없음을 나타내는 (C)가 정답.
(A) 제품 세척과 관련된 말이므로 질문의 핵심에서 벗어난 오답.
(B) 목적을 나타내는 to부정사로 답변하고 있으므로 Why 의문문에 어울리는 오답.

| 어휘 | delivery fee 배송 요금   match (색, 스타일 등이) ~와 어울리다, 맞다, 일치시키다   include ~을 포함하다

6. What did you think of the marketing workshop?
(A) I attended a different event.
(B) She's not around.
(C) I'll get to work on it.

마케팅 워크숍에 대해 어떻게 생각하셨어요?
(A) 저는 다른 행사에 참석했어요.
(B) 그녀는 근처에 있지 않습니다.
(C) 제가 그 작업에 착수할게요.

| 해설 |
마케팅 워크숍에 대한 상대방의 의견을 묻는 What did you think of 의문문에 대해 다른 행사에 참석했다는 말로 의견을 제시할 수 없음을 나타내는 (A)가 정답.
(B) 가리키는 대상을 알 수 없는 She를 언급한 오답.
(C) 마케팅 워크숍에 대한 의견을 묻는 질문의 핵심에서 벗어난 오답.

| 어휘 | attend ~에 참석하다   around 근처에 있는, 주변에 있는   get to do ~하는 것에 착수하다, ~하게 되다   work on ~에 대해 작업하다

DAY 04 | 실전문제 본책 p.32

정답 1 (B)   2 (A)   3 (A)   4 (B)   5 (B)   6 (A)
      7 (B)   8 (A)   9 (A)   10 (B) 11 (B) 12 (A)
      13 (C) 14 (A) 15 (A) 16 (C) 17 (B) 18 (A)
      19 (B) 20 (B) 21 (A) 22 (A) 23 (C) 24 (C)
      25 (C)

1. What kinds of vehicles does the company manufacture?
(A) At the new factory.
(B) Trucks and vans.
(C) For low prices.

그 회사는 어떤 종류의 차량을 생산하나요?
(A) 새로운 공장에서요.
(B) 트럭과 승합차요.
(C) 저렴한 가격으로요.

| 해설 |
생산하는 차량의 종류를 묻는 What kinds 의문문에 대해 차량의 종류를 제시하는 것으로 답변하는 (B)가 정답.
(A) 장소 표현이므로 Where 의문문에 어울리는 오답.
(C) 가격 수준을 말하는 답변이므로 오답.

| 어휘 | vehicle 차량   manufacture ~을 제조하다   van 승합차

2. Who sent you the questions for the political debate?
(A) The event planner, Ramón Lopez.
(B) Sure, I'd be happy to answer it.
(C) To my work e-mail address, please.

누가 그 정치적 토론을 위한 질문들을 당신에게 보냈나요?
(A) 행사 기획자인 Ramón Lopez 씨요.
(B) 물론이죠, 기꺼이 답변해 드리겠습니다.
(C) 제 회사 이메일 주소로 부탁 드립니다.

| 해설 |
상대방에게 질문을 보낸 사람이 누구인지 묻는 Who 의문문에 대해 특정 업무를 맡고 있는 담당자의 이름으로 답변하는 (A)가 정답.
(B) Yes와 동일한 역할을 하는 Sure는 의문사 의문문에 어울리지 않는 반응이므로 오답.
(C) 수신할 이메일 주소를 알려주는 답변이므로 Where 또는 How 의문문에 어울리는 오답.

| 어휘 | political 정치적인, 정치와 관련된   debate 토론, 논쟁   event planner 행사 기획자   be happy to do 기꺼이 ~하다

3. Which of these colors would you prefer to paint the living room?
(A) The blue looks the nicest.
(B) Yes, we have plenty of room.
(C) I think she prefers the top floor.

거실에 페인트 칠을 하는 데 이 색상들 중 어느 것을 선호하시나요?
(A) 파란색이 가장 좋아 보여요.
(B) 네, 저희에게 공간이 많이 있습니다.
(C) 그녀는 맨 위층을 선호하는 것 같아요.

| 해설 |
선호하는 색상이 어느 것인지 묻는 Which 의문문에 대해 특정 색상을 언급하는 것으로 답변하는 (A)가 정답.
(B) 의문사 의문문에 적합하지 않은 Yes로 답변하는 오답.
(C) 가리키는 대상을 알 수 없는 she를 언급한 오답.

| 어휘 | prefer ~을 선호하다   look + 형용사 ~인 것 같다, ~하는 것처럼 보이다   plenty of 많은   room 공간

4. Who's the new director of the Sales Division?
(A) I believe that's correct.
(B) A man I know from university.
(C) Next to the elevator.

누가 영업부의 신임 책임자인가요?
(A) 그게 맞는 것 같습니다.
(B) 제가 대학 시절부터 알던 남자분이요.
(C) 엘리베이터 옆에요.

| 해설 |
영업부의 신임 책임자가 누구인지를 묻는 Who 의문문에 대해 한 사람의 신원과 관련된 정보로 답변하는 (B)가 정답.
(A) 동의하는 표현이므로 Who 의문문에 적합하지 않은 오답.
(C) 위치 표현이므로 Where 의문문에 어울리는 오답.

| 어휘 | director 책임자, 관리자, 임원, 이사   Sales Division 영업부   correct 맞는, 옳은, 정확한   next to ~ 옆에

5. Which restaurant did you reserve a table at?
(A) By calling the place.
(B) The Greek restaurant down the street.
(C) We're eating there at six thirty.

어느 레스토랑에 테이블을 예약하셨나요?
(A) 그곳에 전화를 거는 방법으로요.
(B) 길 저쪽에 있는 그리스 레스토랑이요.
(C) 우리는 그곳에서 6시 30분에 식사합니다.

| 해설 |
테이블을 예약한 레스토랑이 어느 곳인지 묻는 Which 의문문에 대해 위치 표현과 함께 특정 레스토랑을 직접 제시하는 (B)가 정답.
(A) 방법을 나타내는 By 전치사구로 답변하고 있으므로 How 의문문에 어울리는 오답.
(C) there가 지칭하는 장소가 어디인지 알 수 없으며, 시간 표현이 함께 포함되어 있으므로 Which 의문문에 맞지 않는 오답.

| 어휘 | reserve ~을 예약하다 by (방법) ~하는 방법으로, ~함으로써 down the street 길 저쪽에

6. Who organized last year's company banquet?
(A) One of my former coworkers.
(B) The bank's building expansion, I think.
(C) That's what Jacob told me.

누가 작년에 열린 회사 연회를 준비했나요?
(A) 제 이전 동료 직원들 중의 한 명이요.
(B) 은행의 건물 확장 공사인 것 같습니다.
(C) Jacob 씨가 제게 그렇게 말했습니다.

| 해설 |
작년에 열린 연회를 준비한 사람이 누구인지 묻는 Who 의문문에 대해 그 사람의 신원과 관련된 정보로 답변하는 (A)가 정답.
(B) 공사의 특징과 관련된 답변이므로 Who 의문문에 맞지 않는 오답.
(C) 사람의 이름이 언급되기는 하지만 행사를 준비한 담당자를 알려주는 답변이 아니므로 오답.

| 어휘 | organize ~을 조직하다, 준비하다 banquet 연회 former 이전의, 과거의 expansion 확장 (공사), 확대

7. What accounting software do you recommend?
(A) We should do it this way.
(B) I don't remember the name.
(C) She's the best accountant.

무슨 회계 소프트웨어를 추천하시나요?
(A) 우리는 그것을 이런 방식으로 해야 합니다.
(B) 이름이 기억나지 않네요.
(C) 그녀는 최고의 회계사입니다.

| 해설 |
선호하는 회계 소프트웨어를 묻는 What 의문문에 대해 해당 소프트웨어의 이름이 생각나지 않는다는 말로 지금 얘기해 줄 수 없음을 나타내는 (B)가 정답.
(A) 특정 방식에 해당되는 this way가 무엇인지 알 수 없으므로 오답.
(C) 가리키는 대상을 알 수 없는 She를 언급한 오답.

| 어휘 | accounting 회계 recommend ~을 추천하다 this way 이런 방식으로, 이렇게 accountant 회계사

8. Who left this phone charger in the conference room?
(A) Looks like it's mine.
(B) To discuss negotiation strategies.
(C) Please reserve it in advance.

누가 이 휴대 전화 충전기를 대회의실에 놓아두었나요?
(A) 제 것 같아 보이네요.
(B) 협상 전략을 논의하기 위해서요.
(C) 미리 그것을 예약해 두세요.

| 해설 |
휴대 전화 충전기를 대회의실에 놓아둔 사람이 누구인지 묻는 Who 의문문에 대해 phone charger를 it과 mine으로 표현해 자신이 놓아 둔 사람임을 밝히는 (A)가 정답.
(B) 목적을 나타내는 to부정사로 답변하고 있으므로 Why 의문문에 어울리는 오답.
(C) 과거의 일을 묻는 질문과 달리 미래의 일에 대한 요청을 나타내는 오답.

| 어휘 | leave A in B A를 B에 놓다, 두다 charger 충전기 Looks like ~인 것 같아요 discuss ~을 논의하다 negotiation 협상, 협의 strategy 전략 reserve ~을 예약하다 in advance 미리, 사전에

9. Which healthcare plan would you like to sign up for?
(A) All of them offer similar benefits.
(B) She wrote her name on the card.
(C) I'm healthier than ever before.

어느 의료 서비스 계획을 신청하고 싶으신가요?
(A) 전부 비슷한 혜택을 제공하고 있네요.
(B) 그녀는 카드에 자신의 이름을 썼습니다.
(C) 저는 그 어느 때보다 더 건강합니다.

| 해설 |
신청하기를 원하는 의료 서비스 계획이 어느 것인지 묻는 Which 의문문에 대해 대상 범위에 해당되는 것을 them으로 지칭해 전부 비슷하다는 말로 답하는 (A)가 정답.
(B) 대상을 알 수 없는 She를 언급한 오답.
(C) 자신의 건강 상태와 관련된 말이므로 질문의 핵심에서 벗어난 오답.

| 어휘 | healthcare plan 의료 서비스 계획 would like to do ~하고 싶다 sign up for ~을 신청하다, ~에 등록하다 similar 비슷한, 유사한 benefit 혜택, 이점 than ever before 그 어느 때보다

10. Who's going to demonstrate how to use the new copier?
(A) Yes, I'll print you another.
(B) Angela Mathis is.
(C) Thanks for your hard work.

누가 새 복사기 사용법을 시연할 예정인가요?
(A) 네, 제가 한 장 더 출력해 드릴게요.
(B) Angela Mathis 씨요.
(C) 당신의 노고에 감사 드립니다.

| 해설 |
새 복사기 사용법을 시연할 사람이 누구인지 묻는 Who 의문문에 대해 질문에 사용된 동사와 동일한 is와 함께 직접 그 사람의 이름을 밝히는 (B)가 정답.
(A) 의문사 의문문에 맞지 않는 Yes로 답변하는 오답.
(C) 감사의 뜻을 나타내는 표현이므로 질문의 핵심에서 벗어난 오답.

| 어휘 | demonstrate ~을 시연하다, 시범을 보이다 how to do ~하는 법

11. Who can I ask about fixing this vending machine?
(A) He fixed my car's engine.
(B) There should be a phone number on the side.
(C) No, I don't think I can.

이 자판기를 수리하는 일과 관련해 누구에게 물어볼 수 있나요?
(A) 그가 제 차의 엔진을 수리했어요.
(B) 옆면에 전화번호가 있을 겁니다.
(C) 아뇨, 제가 할 수 있을 것 같지 않아요.

| 해설 |
자판기를 수리하는 일을 물어볼 수 있는 사람을 묻는 Who 의문문에 대해 기계 옆면에 전화번호가 있다는 말로 연락 방법을 알리는 (B)가 정답.
(A) 대상을 알 수 없는 He를 언급한 오답. / fixing과 발음이 비슷한 fixed를 사용한 오답.
(C) 의문사 의문문에 맞지 않는 No로 대답한 오답.

| 어휘 | ask A about B A에게 B에 관해 묻다 fix ~을 수리하다, 고치다 vending machine 자판기

12. Which book should we put at the front of the display?
(A) The most popular one.

DAY 04   009

(B) That's what I think, too.
(C) For a few more days.

진열 공간 앞부분에 어느 책을 놓아야 하나요?
(A) 가장 인기 있는 것이요.
(B) 저도 그렇게 생각해요.
(C) 며칠 더요.

| 해설 |
진열 공간 앞부분에 놓아야 할 책을 묻는 Which 의문문에 대해 book을 대신하는 대명사 one과 함께 필요한 책의 특징을 언급하는 (A)가 정답.
(B) 동의를 나타내는 말이므로 정보를 구하는 의문사 의문문엔 어울리지 않는 오답.
(C) 기간 표현이므로 How long 의문문에 어울리는 오답.

| 어휘 | put ~을 놓다, 두다 at the front of ~의 앞부분에 display 진열 (공간) popular 인기 있는

13. Who determines each employee's work assignments?
(A) Either in July or August.
(B) Five days a week.
(C) The section head does.

누가 각 직원의 배정 업무를 결정하나요?
(A) 7월 또는 8월 둘 중의 하나입니다.
(B) 일주일에 5일이요.
(C) 부장님께서 하십니다.

| 해설 |
직원의 배정 업무를 결정하는 사람이 누구인지 묻는 Who 의문문에 대해 determines를 대신하는 does와 함께 구체적인 직책을 직접 밝히는 것으로 답변하는 (C)가 정답.
(A) 시점 표현이므로 When 의문문에 어울리는 오답.
(B) 빈도 표현이므로 How often 의문문에 어울리는 오답.

| 어휘 | determine ~을 결정하다 work assignment 배정된 업무 either A or B A 또는 B 둘 중의 하나 section head 부장

14. What car model do you drive?
(A) Are you planning to buy one?
(B) A highly-skilled mechanic.
(C) I also take the bus.

무슨 자동차 모델을 운전하시나요?
(A) 한 대 구입할 계획이신가요?
(B) 고도로 숙련된 정비사입니다.
(C) 저는 버스도 탑니다.

| 해설 |
소유한 차량의 모델을 묻는 What 의문문에 대해 car를 대신하는 대명사 one과 함께 한 대 구입할 계획인지 반문하는 것으로 질문의 의도를 먼저 확인하고자 하는 (A)가 정답.
(B) 정비사의 능력과 관련된 답변이므로 질문의 핵심에서 벗어난 오답.
(C) 자신이 일반적으로 이용하는 교통 수단을 말하고 있으므로 질문의 핵심에서 벗어난 오답.

| 어휘 | plan to do ~할 계획이다 highly-skilled 고도로 숙련된 mechanic 정비사

15. Who can I talk to about my missing laptop?
(A) The lost and found office.
(B) That's not my computer.
(C) Before six in the evening.

분실한 제 노트북 컴퓨터와 관련해 누구에게 얘기할 수 있나요?
(A) 분실물 보관소요.
(B) 그건 제 컴퓨터가 아닙니다.
(C) 저녁 6시 이전이에요.

| 해설 |
분실한 노트북 컴퓨터와 관련해 얘기할 수 있는 사람을 묻는 Who 의문문에 대해 분실물 담당자를 찾을 수 있는 장소로서 분실물 보관소를 언급한 (A)가 정답.
(B) 질문자의 분실물이 아닌 자신의 상황을 말하는 오답. / laptop에서 연상되는 computer를 사용한 오답.
(C) 시점을 나타내는 표현이므로 When 의문문에 어울리는 오답.

| 어휘 | missing 분실된, 빠진, 없는 lost and found office 분실물 보관소

16. Which venue should we arrange to host the seminar in?
(A) I'll organize the files later today.
(B) I don't have time for a meeting with you.
(C) Mark is familiar with the places nearby.

우리가 어느 행사장에서 세미나를 주최하도록 준비해야 하나요?
(A) 제가 오늘 이따가 파일들을 정리하겠습니다.
(B) 당신과 회의를 할 시간이 없습니다.
(C) Mark 씨가 근처에 있는 장소들을 잘 알고 있습니다.

| 해설 |
어느 행사장에서 세미나를 주최해야 하는지 묻는 Which 의문문에 대해 그와 관련된 정보를 알만한 사람을 알려 주는 것으로 답변하는 (C)가 정답.
(A) 파일 정리 작업을 할 시점을 언급하는 답변이므로 질문의 핵심에서 벗어난 오답.
(B) 자신의 일정과 관련된 말이므로 질문의 핵심에서 벗어난 오답.

| 어휘 | venue 행사장 arrange ~을 준비하다, 마련하다 host ~을 주최하다 organize ~을 정리하다, 마련하다 be familiar with ~을 잘 알고 있다, ~에 익숙하다 nearby 근처에

17. What are these skirts made of?
(A) The black, white, and gray ones.
(B) They're one hundred percent silk.
(C) I'm glad you like it.

이 치마들은 무엇으로 만들어진 건가요?
(A) 검정색, 흰색, 그리고 회색이 있습니다.
(B) 100퍼센트 실크입니다.
(C) 마음에 드신다니 기쁩니다.

| 해설 |
치마를 만든 재료가 무엇인지 묻는 What 의문문에 대해 '실크'라는 직물을 언급한 (B)가 정답.
(A) 색상의 종류를 나열하는 답변이므로 질문의 핵심에서 벗어난 오답.
(C) 상대방의 긍정적인 반응에 대한 기쁨을 나타내는 답변이므로 질문의 핵심에서 벗어난 오답.

| 어휘 | be made of ~로 만들어져 있다 be glad (that) ~해서 기쁘다

18. Who's planning the fundraiser?
(A) I thought it was canceled.
(B) At the Copper Hotel.
(C) A large amount of money.

누가 기금 마련 행사를 계획하고 있나요?
(A) 저는 그것이 취소되었다고 생각했어요.
(B) Copper 호텔에서요.
(C) 많은 액수의 돈이요.

| 해설 |
기금 마련 행사를 계획하고 있는 사람이 누구인지 묻는 Who 의문문에 대해 그 행사가 취소된 것으로 생각했다는 말로 우회적으로 모른다고 답변하는 (A)가 정답.
(B) 장소 표현이므로 Where 의문문에 어울리는 오답.

(C) 금액과 관련된 말이므로 How much 의문문에 어울리는 오답.

| 어휘 | plan ~을 계획하다   fundraiser 기금 마련 행사, 모금 행사   cancel ~을 취소하다   a large amount of 많은 액수의, 많은 양의

19. Which time slot should I choose for my presentation?
(A) She's discussing marketing.
(B) Any one you prefer.
(C) No, it wasn't selected.

제 발표를 위해 어느 시간대를 선택해야 하나요?
(A) 그녀가 마케팅에 관해 논의합니다.
(B) 선호하시는 어느 때이든지요.
(C) 아뇨, 그것은 선정되지 않았어요.

| 해설 |
자신의 발표를 위해 선택해야 하는 시간대를 묻는 Which 의문문에 대해 time slot을 대신하는 대명사 one을 사용해 어느 시간대든 상관없다고 말하는 (B)가 정답.
(A) 가리키는 대상을 알 수 없는 She를 언급한 오답.
(C) 의문사 의문문에 맞지 않는 No로 답변한 오답.

| 어휘 | time slot 시간대   choose ~을 선택하다   presentation 발표(회)   discuss ~을 논의하다   prefer ~을 선호하다   select ~을 선정하다, 선택하다

20. Who's expected to be promoted to fill Byron's position?
(A) He's in his office on the third floor.
(B) They're still considering several applicants.
(C) Fill out this form, please.

Byron 씨의 자리를 충원하기 위해 누가 승진될 것으로 예상하시나요?
(A) 그분은 3층에 있는 사무실에 계십니다.
(B) 여전히 여러 지원자들을 고려하는 중입니다.
(C) 이 양식을 작성해 주시기 바랍니다.

| 해설 |
승진 대상자가 누구인지를 묻는 Who 의문문에 대해 여전히 고려하는 중이라는 말로 아직 결정되지 않았음을 나타낸 (B)가 정답.
(A) 위치를 알려주는 답변이므로 승진 대상자를 묻는 질문의 핵심에서 벗어난 오답.
(C) 양식 작성을 요청하는 말이므로 마찬가지로 승진 대상자를 묻는 질문의 핵심에서 벗어난 오답.

| 어휘 | be expected to do ~할 것으로 예상되다   be promoted 승진되다   fill ~을 충원하다   position 직책, 자리   consider ~을 고려하다   several 여럿의, 몇몇의   applicant 지원자   fill out ~을 작성하다   form 양식, 서식

21. What are we offering customers who attend our grand opening sale?
(A) I'll make a decision soon.
(B) No, we're closed for the day.
(C) It's being offered to customers.

우리 개장식 세일 행사에 참석하는 고객들에게 무엇을 제공하나요?
(A) 제가 곧 결정을 내리겠습니다.
(B) 아뇨, 저희는 오늘 하루 문을 닫았습니다.
(C) 그것이 고객들에게 제공되고 있습니다.

| 해설 |
개장식 세일 행사에 참석하는 고객들에게 제공하는 것이 무엇인지 묻는 What 의문문에 대해 오늘 결정을 내리겠다는 말로 아직 정해지지 않았음을 나타내는 (A)가 정답.
(B) 의문사 의문문에 맞지 않는 No로 답변하는 오답.
(C) 제공되는 것으로 언급된 It이 무엇을 지칭하는지 알 수 없으므로 오답.

| 어휘 | offer A B A에게 B를 제공하다   attend ~에 참석하다   make a decision 결정을 내리다

22. Who did you call at the store about your recent order?
(A) His name was David.
(B) I'm going shopping later today.
(C) No, my clothes haven't arrived yet.

귀하의 최근 주문 사항에 관해 매장에 있는 누구에게 전화하셨나요?
(A) 그분 이름이 David 씨였어요.
(B) 저는 오늘 늦게 쇼핑하러 갈 겁니다.
(C) 아뇨, 제 옷이 아직 도착하지 않았어요.

| 해설 |
주문 사항에 관해 전화한 대상자를 묻는 Who 의문문에 대해 did와 시제가 동일한 과거 동사 was와 함께 그 사람의 이름을 직접 언급한 (A)가 정답.
(B) 질문의 did와 시제 관계가 맞지 않는 미래 부사구 later today로 답변한 오답.
(C) 의문사 의문문에 맞지 않는 No로 대답한 오답.

| 어휘 | recent 최근의   order 주문(품)   clothes 의류   arrive 도착하다

23. Which graphic design was awarded the top prize?
(A) Yes, everyone demonstrated their creativity.
(B) You could probably find a better price.
(C) The winner will be announced next week.

어느 그래픽 디자인이 대상을 수상했나요?
(A) 네, 모든 사람이 각자의 창의성을 보여 주었습니다.
(B) 아마 더 저렴한 가격을 찾으실 수 있을 겁니다.
(C) 수상자가 다음 주에 발표될 겁니다.

| 해설 |
대상을 수상한 그래픽 디자인이 어느 것인지 묻는 Which 의문문에 대해 수상자가 다음 주에 발표된다는 말로 아직 알 수 없다고 하는 (C)가 정답.
(A) 의문사 의문문에 맞지 않는 Yes로 답변하는 오답.
(B) 가격 수준과 관련된 내용이므로 질문의 핵심에서 벗어난 오답.

| 어휘 | award A B A에게 B를 수여하다, 주다   top prize 대상   winner 수상자   announce ~을 발표하다

24. What if we worked late tonight to meet the deadline?
(A) In the conference room.
(B) Maybe after eight.
(C) I'd say that's a good idea.

마감시한을 맞추기 위해 오늘 밤 늦게까지 일하는 게 어떨까요?
(A) 회의실에서요.
(B) 아마 8시 이후에요.
(C) 좋은 생각인 것 같습니다.

| 해설 |
늦게까지 일하자고 제안하는 What if 의문문에 대해 좋은 생각이라는 말로 동의를 나타내는 (C)가 정답.
(A) 장소 표현이므로 Where 의문문에 어울리는 오답.
(B) 시점 표현이므로 When 의문문에 어울리는 오답.

| 어휘 | meet ~을 충족하다   deadline 마감시한   I'd say ~인 것 같아요

25. Who's checked this inventory list for the warehouse?
(A) A late shipment of merchandise.
(B) By October 1.
(C) Look for the signature at the bottom.

누가 창고에 필요한 이 재고 목록을 확인했나요?
(A) 늦은 상품 배송이요.

(B) 10월 1일까지입니다.
(C) 하단에서 서명을 찾아보세요.

| 해설 |
재고 목록을 확인한 사람을 묻는 Who 의문문에 대해 하단의 서명을 찾아 보라는 말로 그 사람을 알아낼 수 있으므로 방법을 언급한 (C)가 정답.
(A) 배송 지연 문제를 언급하고 있어 Who 의문문에 맞지 않는 오답.
(B) 완료 기한을 나타내는 대답이므로 When 의문문에 어울리는 오답.

| 어휘 | inventory 재고(품) warehouse 창고 shipment 배송(품) merchandise 상품 by (기한) ~까지 look for ~을 찾다 signature 서명 bottom 하단, 아랫부분

DAY 05 의문사 의문문(2) –When/Where

01 When 의문문

PRACTICE | 기출 연습하기   본책 p.35
정답 1 (B) 2 (C) 3 (B) 4 (A) 5 (C) 6 (A)

1. When was the deadline for application for the position?
(A) He hasn't applied.
(B) A couple of days ago.
(C) Thanks a lot.

그 직책에 대한 지원 마감 시한이 언제였나요?
(A) 그는 지원하지 않았어요.
(B) 이틀 전이요.
(C) 정말 감사합니다.

| 해설 |
지원 마감 시한을 묻는 When 의문문에 대해 과거 시점 표현으로 답변하는 (B)가 정답.
(A) 가리키는 대상을 알 수 없는 He를 언급한 오답.
(C) 감사의 표현이므로 질문의 핵심에서 벗어난 오답.

| 어휘 | deadline 마감 시한 application 지원(서), 신청(서) position 직책, 일자리 apply 지원하다, 신청하다

2. When will Mr. Weber assign next week's work shifts?
(A) At least eight hours a day.
(B) It's a brand-new assignment.
(C) No later than Friday.

Weber 씨가 언제 다음 주 교대 근무를 배정하나요?
(A) 하루에 최소한 8시간이요.
(B) 완전히 새로 배정된 업무입니다.
(C) 늦어도 금요일까지는 하실 거예요.

| 해설 |
Weber 씨가 교대 근무를 배정하는 시점을 묻는 When 의문문에 대해 특정 시점 표현으로 답변하는 (C)가 정답.
(A) 지속 시간으로 답변하고 있으므로 How long 의문문에 어울리는 오답.
(B) 배정 업무의 특성과 관련된 말이므로 질문의 핵심에서 벗어난 오답.

| 어휘 | assign ~을 배정하다, 할당하다 work shift 교대 근무(조) at least 최소한, 적어도 brand-new 완전히 새로운 assignment 배정된 업무, 할당된 일 no later than 늦어도 ~까지는

3. When should I return this library book?
(A) For all patrons.
(B) By June 3 at the latest.
(C) The end was surprising.

이 도서관 책을 언제 반납해야 하나요?
(A) 모든 고객들을 위해서요.
(B) 늦어도 6월 3일까지요.
(C) 결말 부분이 놀라웠어요.

| 해설 |
책을 반납해야 하는 시점을 묻는 When 의문문에 대해 기한을 나타내는 By 전치사구로 답변하는 (B)가 정답.
(A) 특정 대상을 나타내는 For 전치사구로 답변하고 있으므로 질문의 핵심에서 벗어난 오답.
(C) 이야기의 결말이 지니는 특징과 관련된 내용이므로 질문의 핵심에서 벗어난 오답.

| 어휘 | return ~을 반납하다, 반품하다 patron 고객 by (기한) ~까지 at the latest 늦어도 surprising 놀라게 하는

4. When do you have time to review the budget?
(A) How about after lunch?
(B) Yes, I looked at it.
(C) On my computer.

언제 예산을 검토하실 시간이 있으신가요?
(A) 점심 시간 이후는 어떤가요?
(B) 네, 제가 그것을 확인해 봤습니다.
(C) 제 컴퓨터에요.

| 해설 |
예산을 검토할 시점을 묻는 When 의문문에 대해 대략적인 미래 시점을 제안하는 (A)가 정답.
(B) 의문사 의문문에 맞지 않는 Yes로 답변하는 오답.
(C) 정보 저장 위치와 관련된 말이므로 Where 의문문에 어울리는 오답.

| 어휘 | review ~을 검토하다, 살펴보다 budget 예산 How about ~? ~는 어떤가요? look at ~을 보다

5. When will the new office furniture be delivered?
(A) It's a new desk.
(B) By ferry.
(C) In two days.

언제 새 사무용 가구가 배송되나요?
(A) 새 책상입니다.
(B) 선박으로요.
(C) 이틀 후에요.

| 해설 |
새 사무용 가구가 배송되는 시점을 묻는 When 의문문에 대해 미래 시점을 나타내는 In 전치사구로 답변하는 (C)가 정답.
(A) 제품의 종류를 나타내는 말이므로 배송 시점을 묻는 질문의 핵심에서 벗어난 오답. / furniture에서 연상되는 desk를 사용한 오답.
(B) 운송 수단을 나타내는 말이므로 방법을 묻는 How 의문문에 어울리는 오답.

| 어휘 | deliver ~을 배송하다, 배달하다 ferry (운송용) 여객선, 연락선

6. When is the first day of the biotechnology conference?
(A) I marked it on your calendar.
(B) The conference call is set for three.
(C) At a large hospital in Birmingham.

생명 공학 콘퍼런스의 첫째 날이 언제인가요?
(A) 제가 그것을 당신 달력에 표시해 두었습니다.
(B) 전화 회의가 3시로 예정되어 있습니다.
(C) Birmingham에 있는 대형 병원에서요.

| 해설 |
생명 공학 콘퍼런스의 첫째 날이 언제인지 묻는 When 의문문에 대해 달력에 표시해 두었다는 말로 해당 정보를 확인할 수 있는 방법을 알려 주는 (A)가 정답.
(B) When에 어울리는 시간 표현이 제시되기는 하지만 질문의 핵심에서 벗어난 오답. / 질문의 conference를 반복 사용한 오답.
(C) 장소 표현이므로 Where 의문문에 어울리는 오답.

| 어휘 | biotechnology 생명 공학   mark ~을 표시하다   conference call 전화 회의   be set for + 시점 ~로 예정되어 있다

02 Where 의문문

PRACTICE | 기출 연습하기 본책 p.37
정답 1 (B) 2 (B) 3 (B) 4 (C) 5 (C) 6 (C)

1. Where is a good place to get my car fixed?
(A) For insurance purposes.
(B) Try the shop across the street.
(C) No, it's in the garage.

제 차를 수리 받기에 좋은 곳이 어디에 있나요?
(A) 보험용으로요.
(B) 길 건너편에 있는 정비소에 한번 가 보세요.
(C) 아뇨, 그것은 차고에 있습니다.

| 해설 |
차 수리를 맡기기에 좋은 곳을 묻는 Where 의문문에 대해 위치를 나타내는 across 전치사구와 함께 특정 장소에 가 보도록 권하는 (B)가 정답.
(A) 목적을 나타내는 For 전치사구로 답변하고 있으므로 Why 의문문에 어울리는 오답.
(C) 의문사 의문문에 맞지 않는 No로 답변하는 오답.

| 어휘 | get A p.p. A가 ~되게 하다   fix ~을 고치다, 바로잡다   insurance 보험   purpose 목적   try ~에 한번 가 보다, ~을 한번 해 보다   across the street 길 건너편에   garage 차고, 주차장

2. Where did the delivery man leave the package?
(A) To Seoul.
(B) On your desk.
(C) Yes, I live in the city.

배송 기사가 어디에 배송 물품을 놓아 두었나요?
(A) 서울로요.
(B) 당신 책상에요.
(C) 네, 저는 도시에 살고 있습니다.

| 해설 |
배송 기사가 물품을 놓아 둔 곳을 묻는 Where 의문문에 대해 전치사 on을 이용해 위치 표현으로 답변하는 (B)가 정답.
(A) Where와 어울리는 전치사 to가 쓰이기는 했지만 목적지 또는 이동 방향을 나타내므로 오답.
(C) 의문사 의문문에 맞지 않는 Yes로 답변하는 오답.

| 어휘 | leave ~을 놓다 두다   package 배송 물품, 소포

3. Where can I find out about employee benefits?
(A) Another vacation day.
(B) On the company's Web site.
(C) A full retirement package.

직원 복지 혜택에 관해 어디에서 알아볼 수 있나요?
(A) 하루 휴가가 추가됩니다.
(B) 회사의 웹 사이트에서요.
(C) 퇴직금 전액이요.

| 해설 |
직원 복지 혜택에 관해 알아볼 수 있는 곳을 묻는 Where 의문문에 대해 관련 정보를 확인할 수 있는 방법으로 회사의 웹 사이트를 언급한 (B)가 정답.
(B) 추가되는 휴가일과 관련된 정보를 제시하는 답변이므로 질문의 핵심에서 벗어난 오답.
(C) 퇴직 시의 혜택을 알리는 답변이므로 질문의 핵심에서 벗어난 오답.

| 어휘 | find out about ~에 관해 확인해 보다, 알아 보다   employee benefits 직원 복지 혜택, 복리 후생   retirement package 퇴직금 (제도)

4. Where's the duty-free store?
(A) You're free to use it.
(B) Until the end of August.
(C) On the fifth floor.

면세점이 어디에 있나요?
(A) 그것을 마음껏 쓰셔도 됩니다.
(B) 8월 말까지요.
(C) 5층에요.

| 해설 |
면세점이 있는 곳을 묻는 Where 의문문에 대해 5층이라는 위치 정보로 답변하는 (C)가 정답.
(A) 허용을 나타내는 말이므로 질문의 핵심에서 벗어난 오답.
(B) 지속 상태가 완료되는 시점을 나타내는 말이므로 When 의문문에 어울리는 오답.

| 어휘 | duty-free store 면세점   be free to do 마음껏 ~해도 좋다   until (지속) ~까지

5. Where is the journalism conference scheduled to take place?
(A) She's the keynote speaker.
(B) In late October.
(C) At a hotel in New York.

저널리즘 콘퍼런스가 어디에서 개최될 예정인가요?
(A) 그녀가 기조 연설자입니다.
(B) 10월 말에요.
(C) New York에 있는 호텔에서요.

| 해설 |
저널리즘 콘퍼런스가 개최되는 곳을 묻는 Where 의문문에 대해 장소 전치사 At과 in을 활용해 특정 장소를 언급하는 (C)가 정답.
(A) 가리키는 대상을 알 수 없는 She를 언급한 오답.
(B) 시점 표현이므로 When 의문문에 어울리는 오답.

| 어휘 | be scheduled to do ~할 예정이다   take place (행사, 일 등이) 개최되다, 발생되다   keynote speaker 기조 연설자

6. Where should we put these potted plants?
(A) Water them once a week.
(B) A gift from the manager.
(C) This room is already crowded.

이 화분에 심은 식물을 어디에 두어야 하나요?
(A) 일주일에 한번 물을 주세요.
(B) 부장님께서 주신 선물이에요.
(C) 이 방은 이미 꽉 차 있어요.

| 해설 |
화분에 심은 식물을 두어야 하는 곳을 묻는 Where 의문문에 대해 현재 두 사람이 있는 방이 꽉 차 있다는 말로 다른 곳에 두어야 한다고 우회적으로 나타내는 (C)가 정답.
(A) 물을 주는 빈도를 나타내는 말이므로 How often 의문문에 어울리는 오답.
(B) 제공자를 나타내는 답변이므로 질문의 핵심에서 벗어난 오답.

| 어휘 | put ~을 놓다, 두다   potted plant 화분에 심은 식물   water ~에 물을 주다   crowded (물건으로) 꽉 찬, 가득한

DAY 05 | 실전문제
본책 p.39

정답
1 (B)   2 (B)   3 (B)   4 (C)   5 (C)   6 (C)
7 (C)   8 (B)   9 (B)   10 (B)   11 (C)   12 (C)
13 (C)   14 (B)   15 (A)   16 (B)   17 (B)   18 (B)
19 (C)   20 (A)   21 (A)   22 (B)   23 (C)   24 (A)
25 (C)

1. Where should we go for lunch today?
(A) Around noon.
(B) To the café on Pine Street.
(C) A ham and cheese sandwich.

오늘 점심 식사 하러 어디로 가야 하나요?
(A) 정오쯤에요.
(B) Pine Street에 있는 카페로요.
(C) 햄 치즈 샌드위치요.

| 해설 |
점심 식사를 하러 갈 곳을 묻는 Where 의문문에 대해 목적지나 이동 방향을 나타내는 To 전치사와 함께 특정 식당을 언급하는 (B)가 정답.
(A) 시점 표현이므로 When 의문문에 어울리는 오답.
(C) 음식의 종류를 말하는 답변이므로 What kind 의문문에 어울리는 오답.

| 어휘 | around ~쯤에, ~경에   noon 정오

2. When did Ms. Potter approve the proposal?
(A) Two hours long.
(B) Just last week.
(C) For a new project.

Potter 씨가 언제 그 제안을 승인했나요?
(A) 2시간 길이입니다.
(B) 불과 지난주에요.
(C) 새로운 프로젝트를 위해서요.

| 해설 |
Potter 씨가 제안을 승인한 시점을 묻는 When 의문문에 대해 과거 시점 표현으로 답변하는 (B)가 정답.
(A) 기간을 나타내는 말이므로 How long 의문문에 어울리는 오답.
(C) 목적을 나타내는 For 전치사구로 답변하고 있으므로 Why 의문문에 어울리는 오답.

| 어휘 | approve ~을 승인하다   proposal 제안(서)

3. When will the next express train depart?
(A) About twenty-five dollars.
(B) Not until 5 P.M.
(C) Line up on Platform 2.

다음 급행 열차는 언제 출발하나요?
(A) 약 25달러입니다.
(B) 오후 5시나 되어야 합니다.
(C) 2번 승강장에서 줄 서세요.

| 해설 |
다음 급행 열차가 출발하는 시점을 묻는 When 의문문에 대해 특정 미래 시점 표현으로 답변하는 (B)가 정답.
(A) 금액을 나타내는 말이므로 How much 의문문에 어울리는 오답.
(C) 줄을 서는 위치를 나타내는 말이므로 Where 의문문에 어울리는 오답.

| 어휘 | express 급행의, 신속한, 속달의   depart 출발하다, 떠나다   about 약, 대략   not until + 시점 ~나 되어야 한다   line up 줄을 서다

4. Where do you want to set up our booth at the fair?
(A) Registration for the seminar.
(B) Another booth at a trade show.
(C) In the auditorium by the front entrance.

박람회에서 어디에 우리 부스를 설치하기를 원하세요?
(A) 세미나 등록이요.
(B) 무역 박람회장에 있는 또 다른 부스요.
(C) 정문 출입구 옆에 있는 강당에요.

| 해설 |
박람회에서 설치할 부스의 위치를 묻는 Where 의문문에 대해 특정 위치와 장소를 나타내는 표현으로 답변하는 (C)가 정답.
(A) 행사 참석 방법과 관련된 말이므로 How 의문문에 어울리는 오답.
(B) Where와 어울리기는 하지만 부스 설치 위치가 아니므로 질문의 핵심에서 벗어난 오답.

| 어휘 | set up ~을 설치하다, 마련하다   booth 부스, 칸막이 공간   fair 박람회   registration 등록   trade show 무역 박람회   auditorium 강당

5. When do I need to respond to the invitation?
(A) Yes, that's what happened.
(B) Everyone in the office.
(C) By the end of the week.

제가 언제 초청에 답변해야 하나요?
(A) 네, 그래서 그런 겁니다.
(B) 사무실에 있는 모든 사람들이요.
(C) 이번 주말까지요.

| 해설 |
초청에 대해 답변해야 하는 시점을 묻는 When 의문문에 대해 기한을 나타내는 By 전치사구로 답변하는 (C)가 정답.
(A) 의문사 의문문에 맞지 않는 Yes로 답변하는 오답.
(B) Who 의문문이나 How many 의문문에 어울리는 오답.

| 어휘 | respond to ~에 답변하다, 반응하다   invitation 초대(장)   happen 일어나다, 발생되다   by (기한) ~까지

6. Where can I buy the latest issue of the magazine?
(A) No, I might have to stay late.
(B) Did the subscription fee increase?
(C) At the newsstand on the corner.

그 잡지의 최신 호를 어디에서 구입할 수 있나요?
(A) 아뇨, 저는 늦게까지 있어야 할지도 몰라요.
(B) 구독 요금이 인상되었나요?
(C) 모퉁이에 있는 잡지 가판대에서요.

| 해설 |
잡지의 최신 호를 구입할 수 있는 곳을 묻는 Where 의문문에 대해 위치를 나타내는 At 전치사구로 답변하는 (C)가 정답.
(A) 의문사 의문문에 맞지 않는 No로 답변하는 오답.
(B) 구독 요금 인상 여부를 되묻는 말이므로 질문의 핵심에서 벗어난 오답.

| 어휘 | latest 최신의   issue (잡지 등의) 호   might have to do ~해야 할 지도 모른다   subscription 구독, 서비스 가입   fee 요금, 수수료   increase 인상되다, 증가되다   newsstand 잡지 가판대   on the corner 모퉁이에

7. Where is the nearest post office?
(A) No, not much.
(B) Every weekday.
(C) On the next block.

가장 가까운 우체국이 어디에 있나요?
(A) 아뇨, 그렇게 많지 않아요.
(B) 주중에 매일이요.
(C) 다음 블록에요.

| 해설 |
가장 가까운 우체국이 있는 곳을 묻는 Where 의문문에 대해 위치를 나타내는 On 전치사구로 답변하는 (C)가 정답.
(A) 의문사 의문문에 맞지 않는 No로 답변하는 오답.
(B) 빈도를 나타내는 답변이므로 How often 의문문에 어울리는 오답.

| 어휘 | nearest 가장 가까운

8. When can couriers drop off packages?
(A) The side entrance, please.
(B) Anytime during business hours.
(C) A box of product samples.

언제 택배 업체에서 배송 물품을 갖다 줄 수 있나요?
(A) 옆쪽의 출입문을 이용해 주세요.
(B) 업무 시간 중에 언제든지요.
(C) 제품 샘플들이 담긴 상자입니다.

| 해설 |
택배 업체에서 배송 물품을 갖다 주는 시점을 묻는 When 의문문에 대해 during 전치사구를 포함한 시간 범위로 답변하는 (B)가 정답.
(A) 출입 방식을 말하는 답변이므로 오답.
(C) 배송 물품의 특징과 관련된 말이므로 질문의 핵심에서 벗어난 오답.

| 어휘 | courier 택배 업체, 배송 업체   drop off ~을 갖다 놓다, 내려놓다   package 배송 물품, 소포   entrance 출입문   anytime 언제든지

9. Where is the baseball stadium?
(A) A glove and a bat, please.
(B) Go straight three blocks and turn right.
(C) The game starts at seven.

야구 경기장이 어디에 있나요?
(A) 글러브와 배트 하나씩 주세요.
(B) 세 블록 직진하신 다음에 우회전하세요.
(C) 경기가 7시에 시작합니다.

| 해설 |
야구 경기장이 있는 곳을 묻는 Where 의문문에 대해 해당 장소로 가는 방법으로 답변하는 (B)가 정답.
(A) 야구용품을 구입할 때 할 수 있는 말이므로 질문의 핵심에서 벗어난 오답. / baseball에서 연상되는 glove, bat를 사용한 오답.
(C) 경기 시작 시간을 말하는 답변이므로 When 의문문에 어울리는 오답.

| 어휘 | go straight 직진하다   turn right 우회전하다

10. When will the cafeteria reopen?
(A) Because renovations are done.
(B) This Thursday, actually.
(C) For an affordable meal.

구내 식당이 언제 다시 문을 여나요?
(A) 개조 공사가 완료된 상태이기 때문입니다.
(B) 실은, 이번 주 목요일입니다.
(C) 가격이 적당한 식사를 위해서요.

| 해설 |
구내 식당이 다시 문을 여는 시점을 묻는 When 의문문에 대해 특정 요일로 답변하는 (B)가 정답.
(A) 이유를 나타내는 Because로 답변하고 있으므로 Why 의문문에 어울리는 오답.
(C) 목적을 나타내는 For 전치사구로 답변하고 있으므로 Why 의문문에 어울리는 오답.

| 어휘 | cafeteria 구내 식당   reopen 다시 문을 열다, 재개장하다   renovation 개조, 보수   actually 실은, 사실은   affordable 가격이 알맞은

11. Where would I go to see Mr. Jenkins this morning?
(A) To set up an appointment.
(B) Yes, right before lunch.
(C) You can find him in the laboratory.

오늘 아침에 Jenkins 씨를 뵈려면 어디로 가야 할까요?
(A) 예약 일정을 잡기 위해서요.
(B) 네, 점심 시간 직전에요.
(C) 실험실에서 찾으실 수 있습니다.

| 해설 |
Jenkins 씨를 만날 수 있는 곳을 묻는 Where 의문문에 대해 Mr. Jenkins를 him으로 지칭해 그 사람을 찾을 수 있는 장소를 언급한 (C)가 정답.
(A) 목적을 나타내는 to부정사구로 답변하고 있으므로 Why 의문문에 어울리는 오답.
(B) 의문사 의문문에 맞지 않는 Yes로 답변하는 오답.

| 어휘 | set up an appointment 예약 일정을 잡다, 약속 일정을 잡다   right before ~ 직전에   laboratory 실험실, 연구실

12. When will the new line of sneakers be released?
(A) There's a sporting goods store nearby.
(B) We intend to lease everything.
(C) I'll have to ask someone in Sales.

새로운 운동화 제품 라인은 언제 출시되나요?
(A) 근처에 스포츠용품 매장이 하나 있습니다.
(B) 우리는 모든 것을 임대할 계획입니다.
(C) 영업부에 있는 사람에게 물어봐야 합니다.

| 해설 |
새 운동화 제품이 출시되는 시점을 묻는 When 의문문에 대해 담당 부서에 확인해 봐야 알 수 있다는 말로 답변하는 (C)가 정답.
(A) 스포츠용품 매장 위치와 관련된 답변이므로 Where 의문문에 어울리는 오답.
(B) released와 발음이 유사한 lease를 활용한 오답으로 질문의 핵심에서 벗어난 답변

| 어휘 | line 제품 라인, 제품군   release ~을 출시하다, 공개하다   sporting goods 스포츠용품   nearby 근처에   intend to do ~할 계획이다, 작정이다   lease ~을 임대하다, 대여하다   Sales 영업부

13. When will the construction project be complete?
(A) I don't know him.
(B) A five-story building.
(C) Within a year.

공사 프로젝트가 언제 완료되나요?
(A) 저는 그를 모릅니다.
(B) 5층짜리 건물입니다.
(C) 1년 안으로요.

| 해설 |
공사 프로젝트가 완료되는 시점을 묻는 When 의문문에 대해 대략적인 미래 시점을 나타내는 표현으로 답변하는 (C)가 정답.
(A) 가리키는 대상을 알 수 없는 him을 언급한 오답.
(B) 건물의 특징과 관련된 말이므로 질문의 핵심에서 벗어난 오답.

| 어휘 | construction 공사, 건설   complete 완료된, 완전한   five-story 5층 높이의   within ~이내에

14. When does the performance begin?
(A) An excellent actor.
(B) About an hour from now.
(C) It's in the theater on Main Street.

공연이 언제 시작하나요?
(A) 훌륭한 배우입니다.
(B) 지금으로부터 약 1시간 후에요.
(C) Main Street에 위치한 극장에서요.

| 해설 |
공연이 시작되는 시점을 묻는 When 의문문에 대해 대략적인 미래 시점을 나타내는 표현으로 답변하는 (B)가 정답.
(A) 배우의 특징과 관련된 말이므로 질문의 핵심에서 벗어난 오답.
(C) 장소 표현이므로 Where 의문문에 어울리는 오답.

| 어휘 | performance 공연, 연주(회) excellent 훌륭한, 우수한 about 약, 대략

15. When does the last payment need to be sent?
(A) I lost that information when my computer crashed.
(B) To any branch of Desmond Bank.
(C) I will talk to her this afternoon.

최종 지불 금액이 언제 송금되어야 하나요?
(A) 제 컴퓨터가 고장 났을 때 그 정보를 잃어버렸어요.
(B) Desmond 은행의 어느 지점으로든지요.
(C) 제가 오늘 오후에 그녀와 얘기해 보겠습니다.

| 해설 |
최종 지불 금액이 송금되어야 하는 시점을 묻는 When 의문문에 대해 컴퓨터 문제로 그 정보를 잃어버려 알 수 없는 상태임을 나타내는 (A)가 정답.
(B) 목적지나 이동 방향을 나타내는 To 전치사로 답변하고 있으므로 Where 의문문에 어울리는 오답.
(C) 시점 표현이 포함되어 있기는 하지만 질문의 핵심에서 벗어난 오답.

| 어휘 | payment 지불(금) crash (컴퓨터 등) 갑자기 고장 나다, 멈추다 branch 지점, 지사

16. Where will this year's awards ceremony be?
(A) At the end of the year.
(B) Ms. Chapman hasn't decided yet.
(C) No, I didn't win anything.

올해의 시상식이 어디에서 있나요?
(A) 연말에요.
(B) Chapman 씨가 아직 결정하지 않았습니다.
(C) 아뇨, 저는 아무 상도 받지 못했어요.

| 해설 |
시상식이 열리는 곳을 묻는 Where 의문문에 대해 Chapman 씨가 아직 결정하지 않았다는 말로 여전히 알 수 없는 상태임을 나타내는 (B)가 정답.
(A) 시점 표현이므로 When 의문문에 어울리는 오답.
(C) 의문사 의문문에 맞지 않는 No로 답변하는 오답.

| 어휘 | awards ceremony 시상식 decide ~을 결정하다 win (상 등) ~을 받다, 타다

17. Where can I find the Accounting Department?
(A) Sorry, I didn't count them.
(B) Check out the building directory.
(C) For help with the budget.

어디에서 회계부를 찾을 수 있나요?
(A) 죄송하지만, 저는 그것들을 세지 않았습니다.
(B) 건물 안내도를 확인해 보세요.
(C) 예산에 대해 도움을 받기 위해서요.

| 해설 |
회계부가 있는 곳을 묻는 Where 의문문에 대해 건물 안내도를 확인해 보라는 말로 해당 부서를 찾는 방법을 알려 주는 (B)가 정답.
(A) Accounting과 발음이 유사한 count를 활용한 답변으로 질문과 전혀 관련 없는 오답.
(C) 목적을 나타내는 For 전치사로 답변하고 있으므로 Why 의문문에 어울리는 오답.

| 어휘 | accounting 회계 count ~을 세다 check out ~을 확인해 보다 directory (건물 입구 등에 있는) 안내 목록 help with ~에 대한 도움 budget 예산

18. When did you get a gym membership?
(A) I work out about three times a week.
(B) In March, when I tried the free class.
(C) The one on Mason Avenue.

언제 체육관 회원권을 구입하셨어요?
(A) 저는 일주일에 약 세 번 운동합니다.
(B) 3월에 무료 강좌를 한번 들어 봤을 때요.
(C) Mason Avenue에 위치한 곳이요.

| 해설 |
체육관 회원권을 구입한 시점을 묻는 When 의문문에 대해 특정 과거 시점으로 답변하는 (B)가 정답.
(A) 반복 주기와 관련된 답변이므로 How often 의문문에 어울리는 오답.
(C) 장소 표현이므로 Where 의문문에 어울리는 오답.

| 어휘 | gym 체육관 work out 운동하다 about 약, 대략 try ~을 한번 해 보다 free 무료의

19. Where's the break room?
(A) For the entire staff.
(B) Fifteen minutes or more.
(C) At the end of the hallway.

휴게실이 어디에 있나요?
(A) 전체 직원들을 위해서요.
(B) 15분 이상이요.
(C) 복도 끝에요.

| 해설 |
휴게실 위치를 묻는 Where 의문문에 대해 위치를 나타내는 At 전치사구로 답변하는 (C)가 정답.
(A) 대상을 나타내는 For 전치사구로 답변하고 있으므로 질문의 핵심에서 벗어난 오답.
(B) 지속 시간을 나타내는 말이므로 How long 의문문에 어울리는 오답.

| 어휘 | break room 휴게실 entire 전체의, 모든 hallway 복도

20. When did my client call to speak with me?
(A) After you went to lunch.
(B) Yes, I spoke with her.
(C) I called some new customers.

제 고객께서 저와 얘기하기 위해 언제 전화하셨나요?
(A) 당신이 점심 식사 하러 간 후에요.
(B) 네, 제가 그녀와 얘기했습니다.
(C) 제가 몇몇 신규 고객들께 전화했습니다.

| 해설 |
고객이 전화한 시점을 묻는 When 의문문에 대해 특정 과거 시점을 언급하는 (A)가 정답.
(B) 의문사 의문문에 맞지 않는 Yes로 답변하는 오답.
(C) 답변자 자신이 과거 시점에 한 일을 말하고 있으므로 질문의 핵심에서 벗어난 오답.

| 어휘 | client 고객, 의뢰인 speak with ~와 얘기하다

21. Where are the final results of the test?
(A) Didn't Rachel file them in the cabinet?
(B) Overall, we were satisfied.
(C) That's the wrong one.

테스트 최종 결과물이 어디에 있나요?
(A) Rachel 씨가 그것들을 캐비닛에 파일로 정리해 두지 않았나요?
(B) 전반적으로, 우리는 만족했습니다.
(C) 그것이 아닙니다.

| 해설 |
테스트 결과물이 있는 곳을 묻는 Where 의문문에 대해 results를 them으

로 지칭하면서 보관 장소에 관해 반문하는 (A)가 정답.
(B) 테스트 결과의 만족도와 관련된 답변이므로 질문의 핵심에서 벗어난 오답.
(C) 질문의 복수명사 results를 단수대명사 That과 one으로 지칭하여 답변할 수 없으므로 오답.

| 어휘 | result 결과(물) file ~을 파일로 정리하다 overall 전반적으로 satisfied 만족한 wrong 잘못된, 엉뚱한

22. Where's the speech taking place?
(A) Next Friday at seven.
(B) By Professor Warren Anderson.
(C) I heard you couldn't make it.

연설이 어디에서 진행되나요?
(A) 다음 주 금요일 7시입니다.
(B) Warren Anderson 교수님께서 진행하십니다.
(C) 당신은 오지 못한다고 들었는데요.

| 해설 |
연설이 진행되는 곳을 묻는 Where 의문문에 대해 상대방이 참석할 수 없는 것으로 알고 있었다는 말로 우회적인 답변을 하는 (C)가 정답.
(A) 미래 시점 표현이므로 When 의문문에 어울리는 오답.
(B) 연설자를 나타내는 말이므로 Who 의문문에 어울리는 오답.

| 어휘 | take place (행사, 일 등이) 개최되다, 발생되다 by (행위 주체) ~에 의해 professor 교수 make it (제때) 가다, 도착하다

23. Where did Mr. Kennedy first work when he transferred here?
(A) Sometime around a decade ago.
(B) Usually by public transportation.
(C) In the R&D Department.

Kennedy 씨가 이곳으로 전근 왔을 때 어디에서 처음 근무하셨나요?
(A) 대략 10년 전쯤에요.
(B) 보통 대중교통으로요.
(C) 연구개발부에서요.

| 해설 |
Kennedy 씨가 전근한 후에 처음 근무한 곳을 묻는 Where 의문문에 대해 특정 부서 명칭으로 답변하는 (C)가 정답.
(A) 과거의 특정 시점을 나타내는 말이므로 When 의문문에 어울리는 오답.
(B) 교통 수단을 의미하는 말이므로 방법을 묻는 How 의문문에 어울리는 오답.

| 어휘 | transfer 전근가다 around 대략, 약 usually 보통, 일반적으로 public transportation 대중교통 R&D 연구개발

24. When do we get reimbursed for the airplane tickets?
(A) Once they're approved.
(B) On Hamilton Airlines.
(C) About one thousand dollars.

우리가 언제 항공권에 대한 비용을 환급 받나요?
(A) 승인되는 대로요.
(B) Hamilton 항공편으로요.
(C) 약 1천 달러입니다.

| 해설 |
항공권 비용 환급을 받을 수 있는 시점을 묻는 When 의문문에 대해 조건이나 때를 나타내는 접속사 Once와 함께 승인을 먼저 받아야 함을 알리는 (A)가 정답.
(B) 특정 항공사를 제시하는 답변이므로 질문의 핵심에서 벗어난 오답.
(C) 금액을 제시하는 답변이므로 How much 의문문에 어울리는 오답.

| 어휘 | get reimbursed for ~에 대해 비용을 환급 받다 once (일단) ~하는 대로, ~하자마자 approve ~을 승인하다 about 약, 대략

25. Where can I donate these children's books?
(A) Anytime before 6 P.M.
(B) It's overbooked.
(C) There's a collection box at the library.

어디에 이 아동 도서를 기부할 수 있나요?
(A) 오후 6시 이전에 아무때나요.
(B) 초과 예약되어 있습니다.
(C) 도서관에 수거함이 있어요.

| 해설 |
기부를 할 수 있는 곳을 묻는 Where 의문문에 대해 장소 전치사 at과 함께 수거함이 비치된 곳을 알려주는 (C)가 정답.
(A) 시점 표현이므로 When 의문문에 어울리는 오답.
(B) 예약 상태를 나타내는 말이므로 질문의 의도에 맞지 않는 오답.

| 어휘 | donate ~을 기부하다 overbooked 초과 예약된 collection 수거, 모음

DAY 06 의문사 의문문(3) - How/Why

01 How 의문문

PRACTICE | 기출 연습하기   본책 p.41

정답 1 (B) 2 (C) 3 (B) 4 (C) 5 (A) 6 (B)

1. How long will you be gone this time?
(A) In Dubai on business.
(B) I'm not sure.
(C) For the first time.

이번에는 얼마나 오래 가 계시나요?
(A) Dubai에 출장 때문에요.
(B) 확실치 않습니다.
(C) 처음으로요.

| 해설 |
다른 곳에 가 있는 기간을 묻는 How long 의문문에 대해 확실하지 않다는 말로 정확히 알 수 없다고 답변하는 (B)가 정답.
(A) 장소를 나타내는 말이므로 Where 의문문에 어울리는 오답.
(C) 경험 또는 횟수와 관련된 답변이므로 질문의 핵심에서 벗어난 오답.

| 어휘 | on business 출장 때문에 for the first time 처음으로

2. How much would it be to repair this cracked window?
(A) It overlooks a large public park.
(B) No longer than twenty minutes.
(C) Approximately two hundred fifty dollars.

이 깨진 창문을 수리하는 데 비용이 얼마나 들까요?
(A) 큰 공원이 내려다보입니다.
(B) 20분 이내입니다.
(C) 약 250달러입니다.

| 해설 |
창문 수리 비용을 묻는 How much 의문문에 대해 대략적인 비용을 직접 알려 주는 (C)가 정답.
(A) 건물의 특징과 관련된 답변이므로 질문의 핵심에서 벗어난 오답.
(B) 소요 시간을 나타내는 말이므로 How long 의문문에 어울리는 오답.

| 어휘 | repair ~을 수리하다 cracked 부서진, 깨진, 망가진 overlook (건물

등이) ~을 내려다보다   no longer than ~ 이하의   approximately 약, 대략

3. How often does the company hire new employees?
(A) Around fifty of them.
(B) At least twice a year.
(C) The company's ranking is getting higher.

회사에서 얼마나 자주 신입 직원들을 고용하나요?
(A) 약 50명의 사람들이요.
(B) 최소한 1년에 두 번이요.
(C) 회사의 순위가 점점 더 높아지고 있어요.

| 해설 |
얼마자 자주 신입 직원들을 고용하는지 묻는 How often 의문문에 대해 대략적인 빈도를 알려주는 (B)가 정답.
(A) 사람 수를 제시하는 답변이므로 How many 의문문에 어울리는 오답.
(C) 회사의 순위 변화를 나타내는 말이므로 질문의 핵심에서 벗어난 오답.

| 어휘 | hire ~을 고용하다   around 약, 대략   at least 최소한, 적어도   ranking 순위   get + 형용사 ~한 상태가 되다

4. How will you get around while visiting Berlin?
(A) Yes, I should get there on time.
(B) I could visit you on Thursday.
(C) Mostly by public transportation.

Berlin을 방문하시는 중에 어떻게 다니실 건가요?
(A) 네, 저는 그곳에 제때 가야 합니다.
(B) 목요일에 당신을 방문할 수 있을 거예요.
(C) 대체로 대중교통을 이용해서요.

| 해설 |
Berlin 방문 중의 이동 방법을 묻는 How 의문문에 대해 교통 수단으로 답변하는 (C)가 정답.
(A) 의문사 의문문에 맞지 않는 Yes로 답변하는 오답.
(B) 방문 시점을 알리는 답변이므로 When 의문문에 어울리는 오답.

| 어휘 | get around 돌아다니다   while ~하는 동안   on time 제때   mostly 대체로, 대부분   by (수단) ~로, ~을 이용해   public transportation 대중교통

5. How was the International Science Symposium?
(A) I learned a lot.
(B) Yes, I suppose so.
(C) Three days in total.

국제 과학 심포지엄은 어땠나요?
(A) 저는 많은 것을 배웠습니다.
(B) 네, 그런 것 같아요.
(C) 전부 합쳐서 3일이요.

| 해설 |
국제 과학 심포지엄에 대한 의견을 묻는 How 의문문에 대해 많이 배웠다는 말로 유용했음을 밝히는 (A)가 정답.
(B) 의문사 의문문에 맞지 않는 Yes로 답변하는 오답.
(C) 기간 표현이므로 How long 의문문에 어울리는 오답.

| 어휘 | in total 모두 합쳐, 총

6. How can I operate this machinery?
(A) They are made of metal.
(B) Didn't you attend the training session?
(C) Yes, it's a brand-new item.

이 기계를 어떻게 작동할 수 있나요?
(A) 그것들은 금속으로 만들어져 있어요.
(B) 교육 시간에 참석하지 않으셨나요?
(C) 네, 완전히 새 상품입니다.

| 해설 |
기계 작동 방법을 묻는 How 의문문에 대해 교육 시간에 참석하지 않았는지를 반문하는 말로 그 방법을 배우지 않았는지를 확인하는 (B)가 정답.
(A) 재료를 언급하고 있으므로 What 의문문에 어울리는 오답.
(C) 의문사 의문문에 맞지 않는 Yes로 답변하는 오답.

| 어휘 | operate ~을 작동하다, 가동하다   machinery 기계   be made of ~로 만들어져 있다   training session 교육 시간   brand-new 완전히 새로운

02 Why 의문문

PRACTICE | 기출 연습하기   본책 p.43

정답 1 (A)   2 (C)   3 (B)   4 (A)   5 (A)   6 (C)

1. Why don't we request extra funding this quarter?
(A) What a good idea!
(B) He's on vacation now.
(C) They haven't spent much lately.

이번 분기에 추가 자금을 요청하는 게 어떨까요?
(A) 좋은 생각입니다!
(B) 그는 지금 휴가 중입니다.
(C) 그들은 최근에 많이 소비하지 않았어요.

| 해설 |
추가 자금을 요청하도록 제안하는 Why don't we 의문문에 대해 좋은 아이디어라는 말로 동의를 나타내는 (A)가 정답.
(B) 가리키는 대상을 알 수 없는 He를 언급한 오답.
(C) They가 지칭하는 복수 대명사가 질문에 나타나 있지 않으므로 오답. / funding에서 연상되는 spent를 사용한 오답.

| 어휘 | request ~을 요청하다   extra 추가의, 여분의   funding 자금   quarter 분기   on vacation 휴가 중인   lately 최근에

2. Why don't you agree to give a speech at the convention?
(A) Didn't you already go there?
(B) This Saturday afternoon.
(C) I don't have time to attend.

컨벤션에서 연설을 하기로 동의하시는 게 어때요?
(A) 이미 그곳에 가지 않았나요?
(B) 이번 주 토요일 오후에요.
(C) 참석할 시간이 없습니다.

| 해설 |
연설을 하는 데 동의하도록 제안하는 Why don't you 의문문에 대해 참석할 시간이 없다는 말로 거절 의사를 밝히는 (C)가 정답.
(A) 미래의 일과 관련된 제안을 하는 상황에 맞지 않게 과거의 일을 확인하는 질문이므로 오답.
(B) 미래 시점 표현이므로 When 의문문에 어울리는 오답.

| 어휘 | agree to do ~하는 데 동의하다   give a speech 연설하다   attend 참석하다

3. Why did you submit the budget report so late?
(A) Yes, this is next year's budget.
(B) Because of my heavy workload.
(C) No thanks, I don't need any help.

예산 보고서를 왜 그렇게 늦게 제출하신 거죠?
(A) 네, 이것이 내년 예산입니다.
(B) 과중한 제 업무량 때문에요.
(C) 괜찮습니다, 저는 어떤 도움도 필요하지 않습니다.

| 해설 |
예산 보고서를 늦게 제출한 이유를 묻는 Why 의문문에 대해 Why와 호응하는 Because of 구문을 써서 많은 업무량 때문이라고 한 (B)가 정답.
(A) 이유를 묻는 Why 의문문에 맞지 않는 Yes로 답변하는 오답.
(C) 거절 의사를 나타내는 말이므로 제안 의문문에 어울리는 오답.

| 어휘 | submit ~을 제출하다 budget 예산 because of ~ 때문에 heavy (양, 정도 등이) 많은, 심한 workload 업무량

4. Why haven't the invitations been sent yet?
(A) We're still collecting addresses.
(B) A few celebrations.
(C) At least two hundred more.

왜 초대장이 아직 발송되지 않았나요?
(A) 우리는 아직 주소를 모으는 중입니다.
(B) 몇몇 축하 행사요.
(C) 최소한 200개 더요.

| 해설 |
초대장이 아직 발송되지 않은 이유를 묻는 Why 의문문에 대해 아직 주소를 모으는 중이라는 말로 답변하는 (A)가 정답.
(B) invitations에서 연상되는 celebrations를 사용한 오답.
(C) 수량 표현이므로 How many 의문문에 어울리는 오답.

| 어휘 | invitation 초대(장) collect ~을 모으다, 수집하다 celebration 축하 행사, 기념 행사 at least 최소한, 적어도

5. Why are you going to Toronto?
(A) For an interview.
(B) From 10 A.M. to 6 P.M.
(C) Go up to the third floor.

왜 Toronto에 가시는 건가요?
(A) 면접 때문에요.
(B) 오전 10시부터 오후 6시까지요.
(C) 3층으로 올라가세요.

| 해설 |
Toronto에 가는 이유를 묻는 Why 의문문에 대해 목적을 나타내는 For 전치사구로 답변하는 (A)가 정답.
(B) 기간 표현이므로 How long 의문문에 어울리는 오답.
(C) 이동 방향을 알려 주는 말이므로 Where 의문문에 어울리는 오답.

| 어휘 | interview 면접 go up to ~로 올라가다

6. Why can't I log in to my company account?
(A) In the computer lab.
(B) Yes, we're having company soon.
(C) Did you type the correct password?

왜 제 회사 계정에 로그인할 수 없는 건가요?
(A) 컴퓨터실에요.
(B) 네, 곧 손님이 올 겁니다.
(C) 정확한 비밀번호를 입력하셨나요?

| 해설 |
회사 계정에 로그인할 수 없는 이유를 묻는 Why 의문문에 대해 로그인 시 발생 가능한 문제점과 관련해 확인하려는 의도로 반문하는 (C)가 정답.
(A) 장소 표현이므로 Where 의문문에 어울리는 오답.
(B) 이유를 묻는 의문사 Why에 맞지 않는 Yes로 답변하는 오답.

| 어휘 | log in to ~에 로그인하다 account 계정, 계좌 computer lab 컴퓨터실 company (관사 없이) 손님, 방문객 correct 정확한, 맞는, 옳은

DAY 06 | 실전문제 본책 p.44

정답 1 (C) 2 (A) 3 (C) 4 (A) 5 (C) 6 (A)
      7 (C) 8 (A) 9 (B) 10 (A) 11 (B) 12 (C)
      13 (B) 14 (C) 15 (C) 16 (C) 17 (C) 18 (C)
      19 (B) 20 (C) 21 (B) 22 (C) 23 (C) 24 (B)
      25 (B)

1. How many people will be attending the client dinner?
(A) On a monthly basis.
(B) The food was really good.
(C) About forty.

고객과의 저녁 식사에 얼마나 많은 사람들이 참석하나요?
(A) 한 달 단위로요.
(B) 음식이 정말 맛있었어요.
(C) 약 40명이요.

| 해설 |
고객과의 저녁 식사에 참석하는 사람 수를 묻는 How many 의문문에 대해 대략적인 인원수를 밝히는 (C)가 정답.
(A) 반복 주기와 관련된 답변이므로 How often 의문문에 어울리는 오답.
(B) 음식의 만족도와 관련된 말이므로 정도나 의견을 묻는 How 의문문에 어울리는 오답.

| 어휘 | attend ~에 참석하다 on a monthly basis 한 달 단위로 about 약, 대략

2. Why is the store closed early today?
(A) Because we are expecting a snowstorm.
(B) No, it's open until ten.
(C) I hope to finish later in the day.

매장이 오늘 왜 일찍 문을 닫는 건가요?
(A) 눈보라가 예상되기 때문입니다.
(B) 아뇨, 10시까지 문을 엽니다.
(C) 이따가 끝낼 수 있기를 바라고 있어요.

| 해설 |
매장이 오늘 일찍 문을 닫는 이유를 묻는 Why 의문문에 대해 날씨 문제를 언급하는 (A)가 정답.
(B) 이유를 묻는 의문사 Why에 맞지 않는 No로 답변하는 오답.
(C) 미래의 완료 시점을 말하는 답변이므로 When 의문문에 어울리는 오답.

| 어휘 | expect ~을 예상하다, 기대하다 until (지속) ~까지 hope to do ~하기를 바라다

3. How far away is the convention center?
(A) I already registered.
(B) Did you go there this morning?
(C) A bit more than five miles.

컨벤션 센터가 얼마나 멀리 떨어져 있나요?
(A) 저는 이미 등록했어요.
(B) 오늘 아침에 그곳에 가셨나요?
(C) 5마일 조금 넘습니다.

| 해설 |
컨벤션 센터와의 거리를 묻는 How far 의문문에 대해 직접적으로 대략적인 거리를 밝히는 (C)가 정답.
(A) 과거 시점에 등록한 사실을 밝히는 답변이므로 질문의 핵심에서 벗어난 오답.
(B) 특정 장소에 갔었는지를 확인하기 위해 반문하는 말이므로 질문의 핵심에서 벗어난 오답.

| 어휘 | far away 멀리 떨어진 register 등록하다 a bit 조금, 약간 more than ~가 넘는

4. Why did you fail to complete the report on time?
(A) Is it due already?
(B) The past four times.
(C) He reports to Mr. Anderson.

왜 보고서를 제때 완료하지 못하셨나요?
(A) 벌써 기한이 되었나요?
(B) 지난 네 번이요.
(C) 그는 Anderson 씨 직속으로 근무합니다.

| 해설 |
보고서를 제때 완료하지 못한 이유를 묻는 Why 의문문에 대해 벌써 기한이 되었는지 반문하는 것으로 제출 기한에 대해 확인하는 (A)가 정답.
(B) 횟수를 나타내는 말이므로 How many 의문문에 어울리는 오답. / time과 발음이 비슷한 times를 사용한 오답.
(C) 가리키는 대상을 알 수 없는 He를 언급한 오답.

| 어휘 | fail to do ~하지 못하다 complete ~을 완료하다 on time 제때 due 기한이 된 past 지난, 이전의 report to ~ 직속이다, ~에게 업무 보고를 하다

5. How long has the flight to Athens been delayed?
(A) A very pleasant flight.
(B) I'll be arriving soon.
(C) By about an hour.

Athens행 항공편이 얼마나 오래 지연되었나요?
(A) 아주 즐거운 비행이었습니다.
(B) 저는 곧 도착합니다.
(C) 약 1시간 정도요.

| 해설 |
항공편이 지연된 시간의 길이를 묻는 How long 의문문에 대해 대략적인 경과 시간으로 답변하는 (C)가 정답.
(A) 항공기 여행의 만족도를 나타내는 답변이므로 질문의 핵심에서 벗어난 오답.
(B) 현재 완료 시제로 과거에 발생한 일의 상태를 묻는 질문과 맞지 않는 미래 시제로 답변하는 오답.

| 어휘 | flight 항공편, 비행 delayed 지연된, 지체된 pleasant 즐거운, 기쁜 arrive 도착하다 by (차이) ~만큼, ~ 정도 about 약, 대략

6. How can we set up everything before the store opens?
(A) Janet said she'll help.
(B) At nine in the morning.
(C) It's a large supermarket.

매장이 문을 열기 전에 어떻게 모든 것을 준비할 수 있나요?
(A) Janet이 도와줄 수 있다고 말했어요.
(B) 오전 9시에요.
(C) 대형 슈퍼마켓입니다.

| 해설 |
매장이 문을 열기 전에 모든 것을 준비하는 것이 가능한지 묻는 How 의문문에 대해 Janet이 도와주기로 한 사실을 말하는 것으로 가능하다고 답변하는 (A)가 정답.
(B) 시간 표현이므로 When 의문문에 어울리는 오답.
(C) 슈퍼마켓의 규모를 말하는 답변이므로 질문의 핵심에서 벗어난 오답.

| 어휘 | set up ~을 준비하다, 설치하다

7. Why did Amy park on the street?
(A) Usually on weekdays.
(B) Yes, that's right.
(C) The parking lot was full.

Amy 씨가 왜 거리에 주차한 건가요?
(A) 보통 주중에요.
(B) 네, 맞습니다.
(C) 주차장이 꽉 차 있었어요.

| 해설 |
Amy 씨가 거리에 주차한 이유를 묻는 Why 의문문에 대해 주차장의 상태를 알려 주는 (C)가 정답.
(A) 시점 표현이므로 When 의문문에 어울리는 오답.
(B) 이유를 묻는 의문사 Why에 맞지 않는 Yes로 답변하는 오답.

| 어휘 | park 주차하다 usually 보통, 일반적으로 parking lot 주차장

8. How did you learn about the open position?
(A) I went to a job fair.
(B) That's why I'm interested.
(C) What did you have in mind?

그 공석에 대해 어떻게 알게 되셨나요?
(A) 취업 박람회에 갔었어요.
(B) 그게 바로 제가 관심이 있는 이유입니다.
(C) 생각해 두신 것이 있으신가요?

| 해설 |
공석에 대해 알게 된 방법을 묻는 How 의문문에 대해 취업 박람회에 참석했다는 말로 관련 정보를 얻게 된 계기를 밝히는 (A)가 정답.
(B) 관심을 갖게 된 이유를 제시하는 답변이므로 질문의 핵심에서 벗어난 오답.
(C) 무언가를 선택하는 상황에서 상대방의 의견을 묻기 위해 반문하는 말이므로 질문의 핵심에서 벗어난 오답.

| 어휘 | learn about ~에 대해 알게 되다 open position 공석 job fair 취업 박람회 interested 관심이 있는 have A in mind A를 생각해 두다, 염두에 두다

9. How old is the town's art museum?
(A) Five hundred different paintings.
(B) It was built sixty years ago.
(C) He's having a birthday party next week.

시의 미술관이 얼마나 오래 되었나요?
(A) 500가지 다른 그림들이요.
(B) 60년 전에 지어졌어요.
(C) 그가 다음 주에 생일 파티를 엽니다.

| 해설 |
미술관이 운영되어 온 기간을 묻는 How old 의문문에 대해 해당 건물이 지어진 과거 시점을 밝히는 (B)가 정답.
(A) 그림의 숫자를 나타내는 말이므로 How many 의문문에 어울리는 오답.
(C) 가리키는 대상을 알 수 없는 He를 언급한 오답.

| 어휘 | painting 그림

10. How did the caterer respond to our special requests?
(A) You'd better ask Shawn.
(B) Some vegetarian dishes.
(C) Thanks for your quick response.

출장 요리업체에서 우리의 특별 요청에 어떻게 반응했나요?
(A) Shawn에게 물어보시는 게 좋을 거예요.
(B) 몇몇 채식 요리들이요.
(C) 빠른 답변에 감사드립니다.

| 해설 |
특별 요청에 대한 반응이 어땠는지 묻는 How 의문문에 대해 Shawn에게 물어보라는 말로 관련 정보를 확인할 수 있는 방법을 알려 주는 (A)가 정답.
(B) 음식의 종류를 제시하는 답변이므로 What kind 의문문에 어울리는 오

답.
(C) 감사의 인사를 나타내는 말이므로 질문의 핵심에서 벗어난 오답.

| 어휘 | caterer 출장 요리업체 respond to ~에 반응하다, 답변하다 request 요청 had better + 동사 원형 ~하는 게 좋다 vegetarian dish 채식 요리 response 답변, 반응

11. Why don't we schedule a meeting with Mr. Leonard?
(A) Yes, we do.
(B) Okay, I'll give him a call.
(C) That's not on my calendar.

Leonard 씨와 회의 일정을 잡는 게 어떨까요?
(A) 네, 그렇습니다.
(B) 좋아요, 제가 그에게 전화할게요.
(C) 그건 제 달력에 쓰여 있지 않아요.

| 해설 |
Leonard 씨와 회의 일정을 잡도록 제안하는 Why don't we 의문문에 대해 수락을 뜻하는 Okay와 함께 일정을 잡을 방법을 말하는 (B)가 정답.
(A) Why don't we ~?는 제안 의문문이므로 수락/거절의 의미를 포함한 말로 답변해야 하지만 Yes, we do는 특정 사실을 확인하기 위한 Do 일반 의문문에 대한 긍정만을 나타내므로 오답.
(C) That이 상대방의 제안을 가리키는 것으로 볼 수 있지만 뒤에 이어지는 말이 수락이나 거절의 표현이 아니라서 오답.

| 어휘 | schedule ~의 일정을 잡다 give A a call A에게 전화하다

12. How do you intend to promote your firm?
(A) She was promoted last week.
(B) No, it's not a good offer.
(C) Mainly with online ads.

어떻게 당신 회사를 홍보할 계획이신가요?
(A) 그녀는 지난주에 승진했어요.
(B) 아뇨, 그건 좋은 제안이 아닙니다.
(C) 주로 온라인 광고를 통해서요.

| 해설 |
상대방 회사를 홍보할 방법을 묻는 How 의문문에 대해 온라인 광고라는 구체적 방법을 직접 밝히는 (C)가 정답.
(A) 가리키는 대상을 알 수 없는 She를 언급한 오답.
(B) 의문사 의문문에 맞지 않는 No로 답변하는 오답.

| 어휘 | intend to do ~할 계획이다, 작정이다 promote ~을 홍보하다, 승진시키다 firm 회사 offer 제안, 제공 mainly 주로 ad 광고

13. Why is the user's manual for the software missing?
(A) Thanks for all of your assistance.
(B) I asked Marie to review it.
(C) Yes, I'll do it by hand.

왜 그 소프트웨어의 사용자 설명서가 빠져 있는 건가요?
(A) 당신의 모든 도움에 대해 감사드립니다.
(B) 제가 Marie에게 검토하도록 요청했습니다.
(C) 네, 제가 손으로 하겠습니다.

| 해설 |
소프트웨어의 사용자 설명서가 빠져 있는 이유를 묻는 Why 의문문에 대해 user's manual을 it으로 지칭해 제3자에게 검토 요청을 한 사실을 말하는 (B)가 정답.
(A) 감사의 인사이므로 질문의 핵심에서 벗어난 오답.
(C) 이유를 묻는 의문사 Why에 맞지 않는 Yes로 답변하는 오답.

| 어휘 | user's manual 사용자 설명서 missing 빠진, 없는, 분실된 assistance 도움 ask A to do A에게 ~하도록 요청하다 review ~을 검토하다 by hand 손으로, 수기로

14. Why do you want Mr. Harper's contract?
(A) Yes, that's his signature.
(B) I actually need Mr. Hooper's contract.
(C) In the file cabinet in his office.

왜 Harper 씨의 계약서를 원하시는 건가요?
(A) 네, 그게 그분의 서명입니다.
(B) 실은 Hooper 씨의 계약서가 필요합니다.
(C) 그분 사무실에 있는 파일 캐비닛에요.

| 해설 |
상대방이 Harper 씨의 계약서를 원하는 이유를 묻는 Why 의문문에 대해 그것이 아닌 다른 계약서가 필요하다는 말로 잘못된 정보를 정정해 주는 (B)가 정답.
(A) 이유를 묻는 의문사 Why에 맞지 않는 Yes로 답변하는 오답.
(C) 위치 표현이므로 Where 의문문에 어울리는 오답.

| 어휘 | contract 계약(서) signature 서명 actually 실은, 사실은

15. How much do you charge for international shipping?
(A) Yes, I live in Germany.
(B) For a fast delivery.
(C) Let me check our price list.

해외 배송에 대해 얼마나 많은 요금을 부과하시나요?
(A) 네, 저는 독일에 살고 있습니다.
(B) 빠른 배송에 대해서요.
(C) 저희 가격 목록을 확인해 보겠습니다.

| 해설 |
해외 배송에 대해 부과하는 요금의 액수를 묻는 How much 의문문에 대해 가격 목록을 확인해 보겠다는 말로 관련 정보를 알아볼 수 있는 방법을 언급하는 (C)가 정답.
(A) 의문사 의문문에 맞지 않는 Yes로 답변하는 오답.
(B) 배송 방법과 관련된 내용이므로 질문의 핵심에서 벗어난 오답. / shipping에서 연상되는 delivery를 사용한 오답.

| 어휘 | charge ~을 부과하다, 청구하다 shipping 배송, 선적 delivery 배송(품), 배달

16. How soon will the city council make a decision?
(A) Local traffic policies.
(B) She joined last year, I think.
(C) In about two weeks.

시의회가 얼마나 빨리 결정을 내릴까요?
(A) 지역 내 교통 정책이요.
(B) 그녀는 작년에 합류한 것 같아요.
(C) 약 2주 후에요.

| 해설 |
결정을 내리는 미래 시점을 묻는 How soon will 의문문에 대해 In 전치사 구와 함께 대략적인 미래 시점으로 답변하는 (C)가 정답.
(A) 논의 주제 등에 해당되는 답변이므로 What 의문문에 어울리는 오답.
(B) 가리키는 대상을 알 수 없는 She를 언급한 오답.

| 어휘 | council 의회 make a decision 결정을 내리다 local 지역의, 현지의 traffic 교통, 차량들 policy 정책 join 합류하다, 가입하다, 입사하다 in + 기간 ~ 후에 about 약, 대략

17. Why did Erica leave during the meeting?
(A) Make sure you bring your lunch.
(B) Because she was late for an appointment.
(C) We hope to see you there.

Erica 씨가 왜 회의 중에 나간 건가요?
(A) 반드시 점심 식사를 챙겨 오도록 하세요.

(B) 약속 시간에 늦었기 때문입니다.
(C) 저희는 당신을 그곳에서 뵐 수 있기를 바랍니다.

| 해설 |
Erica 씨가 회의 중에 나간 이유를 묻는 Why 의문문에 대해 Why와 호응하는 Because와 함께 약속 시간에 늦었다는 말로 이유를 제시한 (B)가 정답.
(A) 점심 식사를 챙겨 오도록 요청하는 말이므로 질문의 핵심에서 벗어난 오답.
(C) 과거의 일을 묻는 질문과 달리 미래의 희망 사항을 말하고 있어 질문의 핵심에서 벗어난 오답.

| 어휘 | leave 나가다, 떠나다 make sure (that) 반드시 ~하도록 하다 appointment 약속, 예약

18. How can we save money on commuting costs?
(A) The communications department.
(B) Hundreds of dollars per month.
(C) Jack suggested sharing rides.

통근 비용에 드는 돈을 어떻게 절약할 수 있나요?
(A) 정보통신부입니다.
(B) 한 달에 수백 달러요.
(C) Jack이 차를 함께 탈 것을 제안했어요.

| 해설 |
통근 비용 절약 방법을 묻는 How 의문문에 대해 Jack이 제안한 이동 방법을 알려 주는 (C)가 정답.
(A) 부서 명칭에 해당되는 말이므로 who 의문문에 어울리는 오답.
(B) 금액을 말하는 답변이므로 How much 의문문에 어울리는 오답.

| 어휘 | commuting 통근 communications department 정보통신부 suggest -ing ~하도록 제안하다 share rides 차를 함께 타다

19. Why don't you hire more workers?
(A) No, the other one.
(B) I'll think about it.
(C) Just a little lower.

추가 직원을 고용해 보시는 게 어떨까요?
(A) 아뇨, 나머지 한 사람이요.
(B) 생각해 볼게요.
(C) 조금만 더 낮게요.

| 해설 |
추가 직원을 고용하도록 제안하는 Why don't you 의문문에 대해 생각해 보겠다는 말로 제안에 대한 수락 여부를 보류하는 (B)가 정답.
(A) 제안에 대한 거절을 뜻하는 No 뒤에 이어지는 말이 질문의 핵심과 어울리지 않는 오답.
(C) 높낮이와 관련된 말이므로 질문의 핵심에서 벗어난 오답.

| 어휘 | hire ~을 고용하다 the other one (둘 중 하나를 제외한) 나머지 하나 a little 조금, 약간

20. Why hasn't the training session started yet?
(A) Check the train schedule.
(B) It was very useful.
(C) Let me go and find out.

교육 시간이 왜 아직 시작되지 않은 거죠?
(A) 열차 시간표를 확인해 보세요.
(B) 매우 유용했습니다.
(C) 제가 가서 알아보겠습니다.

| 해설 |
교육이 아직 시작되지 않은 이유를 묻는 Why 의문문에 대해 자신이 직접 확인해 보겠다는 말로 이유를 파악하기 위한 조치를 언급하는 (C)가 정답.
(A) 열차 시간표를 확인하도록 제안하는 말이므로 질문의 핵심에서 벗어난 오답. / training과 발음이 비슷한 train을 사용한 오답.

(B) 정보의 특성과 관련된 답변이므로 질문의 핵심에서 벗어난 오답.

| 어휘 | training session 교육 시간 useful 유용한 find out 알아보다, 확인해 보다

21. Why did you place the catering order today?
(A) Enough for sixty people.
(B) It's the last day to get a discount.
(C) Mostly sandwiches and desserts.

왜 오늘 출장 요리를 주문하신 건가요?
(A) 60명의 사람들에게 충분합니다.
(B) 할인을 받을 수 있는 마지막 날입니다.
(C) 대부분 샌드위치와 디저트입니다.

| 해설 |
오늘 출장 요리 주문을 한 이유를 묻는 Why 의문문에 대해 할인을 받는 마지막 날이라는 사실을 밝히는 (B)가 정답.
(A) 인원수와 관련된 답변이므로 질문의 핵심에서 벗어난 오답.
(C) 음식 종류를 말하는 답변이므로 What kind 의문문에 어울리는 오답.

| 어휘 | place an order 주문하다 catering 출장 요리(업) mostly 대부분, 대체로

22. How often does Ms. Caine visit the main facility?
(A) It's the newest facility.
(B) In Richmond, I believe.
(C) She hasn't been needed there recently.

Caine 씨께서 얼마나 자주 본사 시설을 방문하시나요?
(A) 최신 시설입니다.
(B) Richmond에 있는 것 같아요.
(C) 그분은 최근에 그곳에서 필요하지 않으셨어요.

| 해설 |
Caine 씨가 본사 시설을 방문하는 빈도를 묻는 How often 의문문에 대해 최근에 그 사람이 필요치 않았다는 말로 자주 방문하지 않았음을 나타내는 (C)가 정답.
(A) 시설의 특징과 관련된 말이므로 질문의 핵심에서 벗어난 오답.
(B) 장소 표현이므로 Where 의문문에 어울리는 오답.

| 어휘 | facility 시설(물) newest 최신의 recently 최근에

23. How did everyone enjoy the restaurant?
(A) Downtown near the theater district.
(B) They loved it since it wasn't crowded.
(C) Yes, that's the one we visited.

모든 사람이 레스토랑에서 즐거워했나요?
(A) 극장가 근처의 시내 구역에서요.
(B) 붐비지 않아서 아주 마음에 들어 했어요.
(C) 네, 그곳이 우리가 방문했던 곳입니다.

| 해설 |
레스토랑에서 보낸 시간과 관련된 의견을 묻는 How 의문문에 대해 아주 마음에 들어 했다는 말로 사람들이 매우 긍정적인 반응을 보였음을 의미하는 (B)가 정답.
(A) 위치 표현이므로 Where 의문문에 어울리는 오답.
(C) 의문사 의문문에 맞지 않는 Yes로 답변하는 오답.

| 어휘 | near ~ 근처의 theater district 극장가 since ~ 때문에 crowded (사람들로) 붐비는

24. Why was the tour of the apartment canceled?
(A) A week before the opening.
(B) Someone already rented it.
(C) I completely agree.

그 아파트 방문이 왜 취소되었나요?
(A) 개장 일주일 전에요.

(B) 누군가가 이미 임대했습니다.
(C) 전적으로 동의합니다.

| 해설 |
아파트 방문이 취소된 이유를 묻는 Why 의문문에 대해 이미 임대되었다는 말로 견학을 할 수 없었음을 알리는 (B)가 정답.
(A) 시점 표현이므로 When 의문문에 어울리는 오답.
(C) 상대방의 말에 대한 동의를 나타내는 표현이므로 질문의 핵심에서 벗어난 오답.

| 어휘 | tour 견학, 시찰   cancel ~을 취소하다   rent ~을 임대하다, 대여하다   completely 전적으로, 완전히   agree 동의하다

25. Why don't I edit this article?
(A) In the newspaper.
(B) That would be great.
(C) Sure, I'm an editor.

제가 이 기사를 편집해 드릴까요?
(A) 신문에서요.
(B) 그렇게 해 주시면 좋겠네요.
(C) 물론이죠, 제가 편집자입니다.

| 해설 |
자신이 기사를 편집해 주겠다고 제안하는 Why don't I 의문문에 대해 그 일을 That으로 지칭해 그렇게 하는 것이 좋겠다는 말로 수락을 나타낸 (B)가 정답.
(A) 출처와 관련된 답변이므로 질문의 핵심에서 벗어난 오답.
(C) 수락을 뜻하는 Sure 뒤에 이어지는 말이 앞뒤가 맞지 않는 오답.

| 어휘 | edit ~을 편집하다   article (신문 등의) 기사   editor 편집자

DAY 07   비 의문사 의문문 (1)

01 Do/Be/Have 동사로 시작하는 의문문

PRACTICE | 기출 연습하기   본책 p.47
정답 1 (C)   2 (C)   3 (C)   4 (C)   5 (B)   6 (C)

1. Did you remember to write that memo we talked about?
(A) A membership card.
(B) It was Wednesday.
(C) No, but I'll write it soon.

우리가 얘기했던 그 메모를 쓰는 것을 기억하고 계셨나요?
(A) 회원 카드요.
(B) 그건 수요일이었어요.
(C) 아뇨, 하지만 곧 쓸 겁니다.

| 해설 |
메모를 쓰는 일을 기억하고 있었는지 묻는 Did 일반 의문문에 대해 부정을 뜻하는 No와 함께 곧 할 예정임을 알리는 (C)가 정답.
(A) 회원 카드를 언급하는 말이므로 메모 작성 여부와 관련 없는 오답.
(B) 특정 요일을 언급하는 답변으로 When 의문문에 어울리는 오답.

| 어휘 | remember to do ~하는 것을 기억하다   soon 곧, 머지않아

2. Have you passed out copies of the pamphlet?
(A) Black and white photos.
(B) Do you want some coffee?
(C) Yes, at yesterday's staff meeting.

팸플릿 사본을 나눠 주셨나요?

(A) 흑백 사진들이요.
(B) 커피 좀 드시겠어요?
(C) 네, 어제 열린 직원 회의에서요.

| 해설 |
팸플릿 사본을 나눠 줬는지 묻는 Have 일반 의문문에 대해 긍정을 나타내는 Yes와 함께 나눠준 시기와 장소를 덧붙인 (C)가 정답.
(A) 사진의 특성을 나타내는 말이므로 질문의 핵심에서 벗어난 오답. / pamphlet에서 연상되는 photos를 사용한 오답.
(B) 커피를 마실 것인지 묻는 말이므로 질문의 핵심에서 벗어난 오답. / 질문의 copies와 발음이 비슷한 coffee를 사용한 오답.

| 어휘 | pass out ~을 나눠 주다   pamphlet 팸플릿, 안내 책자   black and white photo 흑백 사진

3. Excuse me. Are you waiting for a table?
(A) No, I just bought a sofa.
(B) Check under the paperwork.
(C) Yes, we'll need seating for four.

실례합니다. 테이블이 나기를 기다리고 계신가요?
(A) 아뇨, 저는 소파를 구입했어요.
(B) 서류 밑을 확인해 보세요.
(C) 네, 저희는 4인용 자리가 필요합니다.

| 해설 |
테이블이 나기를 기다리고 있는지 묻는 Are 일반 의문문에 대해 긍정을 뜻하는 Yes와 함께 인원수를 추가로 알리는 (C)가 정답.
(A) 부정을 나타내는 No로 답변하고 있지만, 그 뒤에 이어지는 말이 대기 여부와 관련 없는 오답.
(B) 물건을 찾을 수 있는 위치를 알리는 말이므로 질문의 핵심에서 벗어난 오답.

| 어휘 | wait for ~을 기다리다   paperwork 서류 (작업)   seating 앉는 자리, 좌석

4. Do you want to review these performance evaluations today?
(A) One of the company's top performers.
(B) A better view from the roof.
(C) I have several important appointments.

이 업무 능력 평가서들을 오늘 검토하고 싶으신가요?
(A) 회사에서 최고의 실적을 낸 사람들 중 한 명입니다.
(B) 옥상에서 보이는 더 좋은 전망이요.
(C) 제가 중요한 약속들이 여러 개 있습니다.

| 해설 |
업무 능력 평가서들을 오늘 검토하기를 원하는지 묻는 Do 일반 의문문에 대해 여러 중요한 약속이 있다는 말로 부정의 뜻을 나타내는 (C)가 정답.
(A) 특정 범위에 속한 사람들을 가리키는 말이므로 서류 검토 여부와 관련 없는 오답. / performance와 발음이 비슷한 performer를 사용한 오답.
(B) 옥상에서의 전망을 언급하는 답변이므로 질문의 핵심에서 벗어난 오답. / review와 발음이 비슷한 view를 사용한 오답.

| 어휘 | review ~을 검토하다   performance 수행 능력, 실적, 성과   evaluation 평가(서)   top performer 최고의 실적을 낸 사람   view 전망, 경관   roof 옥상   several 여럿의, 몇몇의   appointment 약속, 예약

5. Do you know where I can get more staples?
(A) Hasn't the deadline passed?
(B) Probably in the storage closet.
(C) The economy is very stable.

어디에서 스테이플러 침을 더 구할 수 있는지 아시나요?
(A) 마감 시한이 지나지 않았나요?
(B) 아마 수납장에 있을 겁니다.
(C) 경제가 매우 안정적입니다.

DAY 07   023

| 해설 |
스테이플러 침을 더 구할 수 있는 곳을 묻는 Do you know where 간접 의문문에 대해 in 전치사구와 함께 보관 장소로 답변하는 (B)가 정답.
(A) Do you know where와 맞지 않는 마감 시한을 언급하고 있으므로 질문의 핵심에서 벗어난 오답.
(C) 경제의 상태와 관련된 말이므로 질문의 핵심에서 벗어난 오답. / staple과 발음이 비슷한 stable을 사용한 오답.

| 어휘 | staple 스테이플러 침 deadline 마감 시한 pass 지나가다 probably 아마 storage closet 수납장 economy 경제 stable 안정적인

6. Is the monthly utility payment due today?
(A) A personal check.
(B) Electricity for the whole building.
(C) It's already been paid.

월간 공과금 납부 기한이 오늘인가요?
(A) 개인 수표요.
(B) 건물 전체에 대한 전기 서비스요.
(C) 이미 납부되었습니다.

| 해설 |
월간 공과금 납부 기한이 오늘인지 묻는 Is 일반 의문문에 대해 이미 납부되었다고 답변하는 (C)가 정답.
(A) 비용 지불 방식에 해당되는 말이므로 질문의 핵심에서 벗어난 오답.
(B) 전기가 제공되는 범위를 나타내는 말이므로 질문의 핵심에서 벗어난 오답. / utility에서 연상되는 electricity를 사용한 오답.

| 어휘 | monthly 월간의, 달마다의 utility payment 공과금 due + 시점 ~가 기한인 check 수표 electricity 전기 whole 전체의

02 Can/Could/Would/Should로 시작하는 의문문

PRACTICE | 기출 연습하기   본책 p.49

정답 1 (B) 2 (B) 3 (B) 4 (A) 5 (B) 6 (C)

1. Can you pass me that folder, please?
(A) Yes, I need one.
(B) Sure. Here it is.
(C) We passed the test.

그 폴더를 제게 좀 건네주시겠어요?
(A) 네, 하나 필요합니다.
(B) 그럼요. 여기 있습니다.
(C) 우리는 테스트를 통과했습니다.

| 해설 |
폴더를 건네 달라고 요청하는 Can you 일반 의문문에 대해 수락을 뜻하는 Sure와 함께 물건을 건넬 때 사용하는 말을 덧붙인 (B)가 정답.
(A) 긍정을 나타내는 Yes로 답변하고 있지만, 그 뒤에 이어지는 말이 요청 질문과 관련 없는 오답.
(C) 과거에 테스트를 통과한 사실을 알리는 답변이므로 질문의 핵심에서 벗어난 오답. / 질문의 pass를 반복 사용한 오답.

| 어휘 | pass ~을 건네 주다, (시험 등) ~을 통과하다

2. Would you like to take a trip to Europe?
(A) Yes, I just fell down.
(B) Yes, when is it?
(C) In several countries.

유럽으로 여행을 가시겠어요?
(A) 네, 제가 막 넘어졌어요.
(B) 네, 언제인가요?
(C) 여러 나라에요.

| 해설 |
유럽으로 여행을 가자고 제안하는 Would you like 일반 의문문에 대해 수락을 뜻하는 Yes와 함께 trip을 대신하는 it을 사용하여 여행 시기를 되묻는 (B)가 정답.
(A) 긍정을 뜻하는 Yes로 답변하고 있지만 그 뒤에 이어지는 말이 질문의 핵심에서 벗어난 오답.
(C) 장소 표현이므로 Where 의문문에 어울리는 오답.

| 어휘 | take a trip to ~로 여행 가다 fall down 넘어지다, 쓰러지다 several 여럿의, 몇몇의

3. Could you double-check these sales figures for me?
(A) The results of the product launch.
(B) I'll look them over this afternoon.
(C) He's an experienced accountant.

이 매출 수치를 제 대신 다시 한번 확인해 주시겠어요?
(A) 제품 출시에 대한 결과물이요.
(B) 오늘 오후에 살펴보겠습니다.
(C) 그는 경험 많은 회계사입니다.

| 해설 |
매출 수치를 다시 한번 확인해 달라고 요청하는 Could you 일반 의문문에 대해 sales figures를 them으로 지칭해 확인할 수 있는 시점을 알리는 말로 요청을 수락하는 (B)가 정답.
(A) 제품 출시에 따른 결과를 언급하고 있으므로 요청 질문에 대한 반응으로 맞지 않는 오답.
(C) 가리키는 대상을 알 수 없는 He를 언급한 오답.

| 어휘 | double-check ~을 다시 한번 확인하다 sales 매출, 판매(량), 영업 figure 수치, 숫자 result 결과(물) launch 출시, 공개 look A over A를 살펴보다, 검토하다 experienced 경험 많은 accountant 회계사

4. Would you mind training the new interns?
(A) OK, I'll take care of that.
(B) A summer internship.
(C) The next train to New York.

신입 인턴 직원들을 교육해 주시겠어요?
(A) 좋아요, 제가 처리할게요.
(B) 여름 인턴 과정이요.
(C) New York으로 가는 다음 기차요.

| 해설 |
신입 인턴 직원들을 교육해 달라고 요청하는 Would you mind 일반 의문문에 대해 수락을 나타내는 OK와 함께 그 일을 that으로 지칭해 자신이 하겠다는 의사를 나타낸 (A)가 정답.
(B) 특정 기간에 열리는 인턴 프로그램을 언급하는 말로서, 요청 질문과 관련 없는 오답. / interns와 발음이 비슷한 internship을 사용한 오답.
(C) New York으로 가는 기차를 언급하는 답변이므로 요청 질문과 관련 없는 오답. / training과 발음이 비슷한 train을 사용한 오답.

| 어휘 | Would you mind -ing? ~해 주시겠어요? train ~을 교육하다 take care of ~을 처리하다, 다루다

5. Can I get an update on the merger?
(A) No, our competitor.
(B) I'm on my way out.
(C) Michael has some extras.

합병에 관한 정보 좀 알려 주시겠어요?
(A) 아뇨, 우리의 경쟁사요.
(B) 제가 밖에 나가는 중입니다.
(C) Michael에게 여분이 좀 있습니다.

| 해설 |
합병에 관한 정보를 알려 달라고 요청하는 Can 일반 의문문에 대해 외출하는 중이라는 말로 지금 얘기해 줄 수 없다고 밝히는 (B)가 정답.

(A) 거절을 뜻하는 No로 답변하고 있지만, 그 뒤에 이어지는 말이 요청에 대한 반응으로 맞지 않는 오답.
(C) 합병 관련 정보가 아닌 Michael의 물품 소유 여부를 알리는 말이므로 질문의 핵심에서 벗어난 오답.

| 어휘 | get an update on ~에 관한 정보를 얻다, 소식을 듣다 merger 합병 competitor 경쟁사, 경쟁자 on one's way out 밖으로 나가는 중인 extra 여분, 추가분

6. Should I leave my laptop in the conference room?
(A) Promptly at three o'clock.
(B) To discuss the investments.
(C) We won't be coming back here.

제 노트북 컴퓨터를 회의실에 놓아둬야 하나요?
(A) 3시 정각에요.
(B) 투자 문제를 논의하기 위해서요.
(C) 우리는 이곳으로 돌아오지 않습니다.

| 해설 |
자신의 노트북 컴퓨터를 놓아둬야 하는지 묻는 Should I 일반 의문문에 대해 다시 돌아오지 않는다는 말로 놓아두지 말라고 하는 (C)가 정답.
(A) 시점 표현이므로 When 의문문에 어울리는 오답.
(B) 목적을 나타내는 to부정사로 답변하고 있으므로 Why 의문문에 어울리는 오답.

| 어휘 | leave A in B A를 B에 놓다, 두다 promptly ~ 정각에, 제시간에, 지체 없이 discuss ~을 논의하다 investment 투자(금)

DAY 07 | 실전문제   본책 p.50

정답 1 (C)   2 (A)   3 (B)   4 (A)   5 (C)   6 (B)
      7 (B)   8 (A)   9 (C) 10 (A) 11 (B) 12 (C)
     13 (C) 14 (B) 15 (C) 16 (A) 17 (C) 18 (A)
     19 (C) 20 (B) 21 (A) 22 (C) 23 (B) 24 (B)
     25 (A)

1. Do you know Ms. Stewart?
(A) In her office.
(B) No, that can't be right.
(C) We've met twice in the past.

Stewart 씨를 아시나요?
(A) 그녀의 사무실에요.
(B) 아뇨, 그게 맞을 리가 없습니다.
(C) 우리는 전에 두 번 만난 적이 있어요.

| 해설 |
Stewart 씨를 아는지 묻는 Do 일반 의문문에 대해 두 번 만난 적이 있다는 말로 간접적으로 긍정의 답변을 하는 (C)가 정답.
(A) 장소 표현이므로 Where 의문문에 어울리는 오답.
(B) 부정을 뜻하는 No로 답변하고 있지만, 그 뒤에 이어지는 말이 질문의 핵심과 관련 없는 오답.

| 어휘 | in the past 전에, 과거에

2. Did you set the store's security alarm?
(A) Yes, right before I left.
(B) A new security guard.
(C) To prevent unauthorized access.

매장의 보안 알람을 설정하셨나요?
(A) 네, 제가 퇴근하기 직전에요.
(B) 신입 보안 근무자요.
(C) 무단 출입을 예방하기 위해서요.

| 해설 |
매장의 보안 알람을 설정했는지 묻는 Did 일반 의문문에 대해 긍정을 뜻하는 Yes와 함께 그렇게 한 시점을 덧붙인 (A)가 정답.
(B) 보안 알람 설정 여부가 아닌 보안 근무자를 언급하고 있어 질문의 핵심에서 벗어난 오답. / 질문의 security를 반복 사용한 오답.
(C) 목적을 나타내는 to부정사로 답변하고 있으므로 Why 의문문에 어울리는 오답.

| 어휘 | set ~을 설정하다 security 보안, 경비 right before ~하기 직전에 leave 퇴근하다, 나가다, 떠나다 prevent ~을 예방하다 unauthorized 승인되지 않은, 인가되지 않은 access 출입, 접근, 이용

3. Would you like me to arrange a cab for you?
(A) In room 463.
(B) I had planned to take the bus.
(C) Please arrange them in rows.

제가 택시를 준비시켜 드릴까요?
(A) 463호실에요.
(B) 저는 버스를 탈 계획이었습니다.
(C) 그것들을 줄 맞춰 정리해 주세요.

| 해설 |
자신이 택시를 준비시켜 주겠다고 제안하는 Would you 일반 의문문에 대해 버스를 탈 계획이었다는 말로 거절의 뜻을 나타내는 (B)가 정답.
(A) 장소 표현이므로 Where 의문문에 어울리는 오답.
(C) 대상을 알 수 없는 복수 명사를 지칭하는 them이 언급된 오답. / 질문의 arrange를 반복 사용한 오답.

| 어휘 | arrange ~을 준비하다, 마련하다, 정렬하다 cab 택시 plan to do ~할 계획이다 take (교통편) ~을 이용하다, 타다 in rows 줄 맞춰, 줄 세워

4. Do you like working as a museum volunteer?
(A) I definitely enjoy teaching others about history.
(B) Every Saturday afternoon.
(C) No, I live near the theater.

박물관 자원 봉사자로 근무하는 게 좋으세요?
(A) 역사에 관해 다른 사람들을 가르치는 일이 확실히 즐겁습니다.
(B) 매주 토요일 오후에요.
(C) 아뇨, 저는 극장 근처에 살아요.

| 해설 |
자원 봉사자로 일하는 것이 좋은지 묻는 Do 일반 의문문에 대해 그 일을 즐기는 이유를 언급하는 말로 긍정의 답변을 하는 (A)가 정답.
(B) 반복 주기와 관련된 답변이므로 How often 의문문에 어울리는 오답.
(C) No 뒤에 이어지는 말이 자신의 거주 위치를 알리고 있으므로 질문의 핵심과 관련 없는 오답.

| 어휘 | volunteer 자원 봉사자 definitely 확실히, 분명히 others 다른 사람들 near ~ 근처에, 가까이에

5. Should I remove the old notices from the bulletin board?
(A) Flyers from local businesses.
(B) I read about it yesterday.
(C) Thanks. That would be helpful.

게시판에서 오래된 공지들을 제거할까요?
(A) 지역 내 기업들이 만든 전단이요.
(B) 어제 그것에 관해 읽어 봤어요.
(C) 감사합니다. 그렇게 해 주시면 도움이 될 거예요.

| 해설 |
게시판에서 오래된 공지들을 자신이 제거해도 되는지 묻는 Should I 일반 의문문에 대해 감사의 말과 함께 그 일을 that으로 지칭해 도움이 될 것이라

DAY 07 025

고 알리는 (C)가 정답.
(A) 게시물 제거 여부가 아닌 전단의 특징을 말하고 있으므로 질문의 핵심에서 벗어난 오답.
(B) 질문의 핵심인 복수명사 notices를 대신할 수 없는 단수대명사 it으로 답변하는 오답.

| 어휘 | remove ~을 제거하다, 없애다 notice 공지, 공고 bulletin board 게시판 flyer 전단 local 지역의, 현지의 business 회사, 업체, 매장 helpful 도움이 되는, 유익한

6. Can you notify me when the package arrives?
(A) Fabric samples from the supplier.
(B) Sure, I'll send you a text message.
(C) The office building's reception desk.

배송 물품이 도착하면 제게 통지해 주시겠어요?
(A) 공급업체에서 보내는 직물 샘플이요.
(B) 그럼요, 문자 메시지를 보내 드리겠습니다.
(C) 그 사무용 건물의 안내 데스크요.

| 해설 |
배송 물품이 도착하면 통지해 달라고 요청하는 Can you 일반 의문문에 대해 수락을 뜻하는 Sure와 함께 통지 방법을 덧붙이는 (B)가 정답.
(A) 물품의 종류를 나타내는 말이므로 질문의 핵심에서 벗어난 오답.
(C) 주체를 나타내는 말이므로 Who 의문문에 어울리는 오답.

| 어휘 | notify ~에게 통지하다, 알리다 package 배송 물품, 소포 arrive 도착하다 fabric 직물, 천 supplier 공급업체 text message 문자 메시지 reception desk 안내 데스크

7. Could you tell me where the security office is?
(A) To pick up an ID badge.
(B) It's next to the elevators.
(C) There are a few pages left.

보안 관리실이 어디에 있는지 알려 주시겠어요?
(A) 사원증을 가져가기 위해서요.
(B) 엘리베이터 옆에 있습니다.
(C) 몇 페이지 남았습니다.

| 해설 |
보안 관리실이 있는 곳을 알려 달라는 요청을 나타내는 Could you 일반 의문문에 대해 위치 표현으로 답변하는 (B)가 정답.
(A) 목적을 나타내는 to부정사로 답변하고 있으므로 Why 의문문에 어울리는 오답.
(C) 남은 페이지 분량을 알리는 말이므로 질문의 핵심에서 벗어난 오답.

| 어휘 | security 보안 pick up ~을 가져가다, 가져오다 ID badge 신분증, 사원증 next to ~ 옆에

8. Is there a service for gift-wrapping my purchases?
(A) That's only during the holidays.
(B) When is the birthday party?
(C) This department store is popular.

제 구매 제품에 대한 선물 포장 서비스가 있나요?
(A) 그건 오직 휴일 중에만 가능합니다.
(B) 생일 파티가 언제인가요?
(C) 이 백화점은 인기 있는 곳입니다.

| 해설 |
구매 제품에 대한 선물 포장 서비스가 있는지 묻는 Is 일반 의문문에 대해 해당 서비스를 That으로 지칭해 이용 가능한 특정 기간을 알려 주는 말로 답변한 (A)가 정답.
(B) 생일 파티 개최 시점을 되묻고 있으므로 질문의 핵심에서 벗어난 오답. / gift-wrapping에서 연상되는 birthday를 사용한 오답.
(C) 특정 백화점의 인기 정도를 말하는 답변이므로 마찬가지로 질문의 핵심에서 벗어난 오답.

| 어휘 | gift-wrap ~을 선물 포장하다 purchase 구매(품) popular 인기 있는

9. Have all the promotional brochures been printed?
(A) Thank you for your support.
(B) A few hours at most.
(C) Check with the advertising department.

홍보 안내 책자가 모두 인쇄되었나요?
(A) 도움에 감사드립니다.
(B) 많아야 몇 시간입니다.
(C) 광고부에 확인해 보세요.

| 해설 |
홍보 안내 책자가 모두 인쇄되었는지 묻는 Have 일반 의문문에 대해 광고부에 확인해 보라는 말로 인쇄 여부를 파악할 방법을 알리는 (C)가 정답.
(A) 감사 인사에 해당되는 답변이므로 질문의 핵심에서 벗어난 오답.
(B) 소요 시간을 알리는 말이므로 How long 의문문에 어울리는 오답.

| 어휘 | promotional 홍보의, 판촉의 brochure 안내 책자, 소책자 support 도움, 지지, 후원 at most 많아야, 기껏해야 check with ~에게 확인해 보다 advertising 광고 department 부서

10. Does this restaurant only serve vegetarian dishes?
(A) You must be thinking of a different one.
(B) No, I also eat meat regularly.
(C) Leave it at the table.

이 식당은 오직 채식주의자용 음식만 제공하나요?
(A) 다른 곳(식당)을 생각하고 계시군요.
(B) 아뇨, 저도 고기를 주기적으로 먹어요.
(C) 탁자 옆에 놓아두세요.

| 해설 |
한 레스토랑이 채식 음식만 제공하는지 묻는 Did 일반 의문문에 대해 restaurant을 one으로 지칭해 다른 곳을 생각하고 있다는 말로 상대방의 정보가 잘못 되었음을 알려 주는 (A)가 정답.
(B) 부정을 나타내는 No로 답변하고 있지만, 그 뒤에 개인의 식습관에 관해 말하므로 질문의 핵심에서 벗어난 오답.
(C) 물건을 놓아둘 장소를 알리는 답변이므로 질문의 핵심에서 벗어난 오답.

| 어휘 | serve (음식 등) ~을 제공하다, 내오다 vegetarian 채식주의자 dish 음식, 요리 must ~하는 것이 틀림없다 regularly 주기적으로 leave ~을 놓다, 두다

11. Will the kitchen renovations be finished by next month?
(A) The deadline's August 5.
(B) I really enjoy cooking.
(C) No, the work crew.

주방 개조 공사가 다음 달까지 완료될까요?
(A) 마감 시한이 8월 5일입니다.
(B) 저는 요리하는 것을 정말로 즐깁니다.
(C) 아뇨, 작업팀이요.

| 해설 |
주방 개조 공사가 다음 달까지 완료되는지 묻는 Will 일반 의문문에 대해 정확한 마감 시한 날짜를 알려 주는 (A)가 정답.
(B) 자신이 요리하는 것을 좋아한다는 것을 밝히고 있으므로 질문의 핵심에서 벗어난 오답. / kitchen에서 연상되는 cooking을 사용한 오답.
(C) 부정을 뜻하는 No로 답변하고 있지만, 그 뒤에 이어지는 말이 공사 완료 시점과 관련 없는 오답.

| 어휘 | renovation 개조, 보수 by (기한) ~까지 deadline 마감시한 crew (함께 일하는) 팀, 조

12. Would you mind checking this document for me?

(A) No, that's not correct.
(B) It's in Mr. Klein's office.
(C) Actually, I'm meeting a client.

제 대신 이 서류 좀 확인해 주시겠어요?
(A) 아뇨, 그건 맞지 않습니다.
(B) 그건 Klein 씨 사무실에 있습니다.
(C) 실은, 제가 고객을 만날 예정입니다.

| 해설 |
서류를 확인해 달라고 요청하는 Would you mind 일반 의문문에 대해 Actually와 함께 고객을 만난다는 말로 우회적으로 거절 의사를 밝히는 (C)가 정답.
(A) 거절을 뜻하는 No로 답변하고 있지만, 그 뒤에 이어지는 말이 질문의 핵심에서 벗어난 오답.
(B) 장소를 알려 주는 말이므로 Where 의문문에 어울리는 오답.

| 어휘 | correct 맞는, 옳은, 정확한 actually 실은, 사실은

13. Are you familiar with the client management program?
(A) We need more clients.
(B) I've met him a few times.
(C) Yes, I'll show you what to do.

고객 관리 프로그램에 익숙하신가요?
(A) 우리는 고객들이 더 필요합니다.
(B) 저는 그를 몇 번 만나 봤어요.
(C) 네, 제가 무엇을 해야 하는지 알려 드릴게요.

| 해설 |
고객 관리 프로그램에 익숙한지를 묻는 Are 일반 의문문에 대해 긍정을 뜻하는 Yes와 함께 해야 하는 것을 가르쳐 주겠다는 말로 잘 알고 있다고 답변하는 (C)가 정답.
(A) 고객들이 더 필요하다는 사실을 말하는 답변이므로 질문의 핵심에서 벗어난 오답. / 질문의 client를 반복 사용한 오답.
(B) 가리키는 대상을 알 수 없는 him을 언급한 오답.

| 어휘 | be familiar with ~에 익숙하다, ~을 잘 알다 management 관리 a few times 몇 번 show A B A에게 B를 알려 주다

14. Has the courier dropped off the paint samples yet?
(A) I prefer painting landscape scenes.
(B) Not that I know of.
(C) The temperature has dropped.

배송 기사가 페인트 샘플을 갖다 주었나요?
(A) 저는 풍경화를 그리는 것을 선호합니다.
(B) 제가 알기로는 아니에요.
(C) 기온이 떨어졌어요.

| 해설 |
배송 기사가 페인트 샘플을 갖다 주었는지 묻는 Has 일반 의문문에 대해 자신이 알기로는 그렇지 않다는 말로 부정의 답변을 하는 (B)가 정답.
(A) 선호하는 그림의 종류를 언급하는 답변이므로 질문의 핵심에서 벗어난 오답. / paint와 발음이 비슷한 painting을 사용한 오답.
(C) 기온이 하락한 사실을 알리는 말이므로 페인트 샘플 배송 여부와 관련 없는 오답. / 질문의 dropped를 반복 사용한 오답.

| 어휘 | courier 배송 기사, 배송 업체 drop off (물건) ~을 갖다 놓다, (사람) ~을 내려 주다 Not that I know of 내가 알기로는 아니다 temperature 기온, 온도 drop 떨어지다, 하락하다

15. Could you please call the head accountant to set up a meeting?
(A) Employee salaries and overtime payments.
(B) The equipment is all set up.
(C) Sure. What's the extension?

수석 회계사에게 전화하셔서 회의 일정을 잡아 주시겠어요?
(A) 직원 연봉과 초과 근무 수당이요.
(B) 장비가 모두 설치되어 있습니다.
(C) 물론이죠. 내선 번호가 뭐죠?

| 해설 |
수석 회계사에게 전화 해서 회의 일정을 잡아 달라고 요청하는 Could you 일반 의문문에 대해 수락을 뜻하는 Sure와 함께 내선 번호를 묻는 것으로 연락 방법을 확인하는 (C)가 정답.
(A) 직원 혜택의 종류를 언급하는 말이므로 요청 질문에 맞지 않는 오답.
(B) 장비 설치 완료 상태를 알리는 말이므로 질문의 핵심에서 벗어난 오답.

| 어휘 | accountant 회계사 set up ~의 일정을 잡다, 설정하다, 설치하다 overtime payment 초과 근무 수당 equipment 장비 extension 내선 전화 (번호)

16. Can you give me a ride to work on Friday?
(A) I have that day off.
(B) The machine is working again.
(C) They're giving us more.

금요일에 저를 회사까지 차로 태워 주시겠어요?
(A) 저는 그날 휴무입니다.
(B) 기계가 다시 작동 중입니다.
(C) 그들이 우리에게 더 제공해 줄 겁니다.

| 해설 |
금요일에 회사까지 차로 태워 달라고 요청하는 Can you 일반 의문문에 대해 해당 요일을 that day로 지칭해 그때 휴무라는 말로 우회적으로 요청을 거절하는 (A)가 정답.
(B) 기계의 작동 상태를 알리는 말이므로 질문의 핵심에서 벗어난 오답. / work와 발음이 비슷한 working을 사용한 오답.
(C) 가리키는 대상을 알 수 없는 They를 언급한 오답.

| 어휘 | give A a ride A를 차로 태워 주다 to work 회사까지, 직장까지 have A off A에 일을 쉬다 work (기계 등이) 작동되다

17. Have they replaced the wallpaper?
(A) There are several colors available.
(B) In my latest e-mail.
(C) It does look more modern now.

그 사람들이 벽지를 교체했나요?
(A) 이용 가능한 여러 색상이 있습니다.
(B) 제 최근 이메일에요.
(C) 지금 확실히 더 현대적으로 보여요.

| 해설 |
they로 지칭한 사람들이 벽지를 교체했는지 묻는 Have 일반 의문문에 대해 현재의 외관이 보여주는 특성을 언급하는 것으로 벽지를 교체했음을 나타내는 (C)가 정답.
(A) 이용 가능한 색상의 다양성을 말하는 답변이므로 질문의 핵심에서 벗어난 오답.
(B) 자료 등의 위치를 말하는 답변이므로 Where 의문문에 어울리는 오답.

| 어휘 | replace ~을 교체하다 wallpaper 벽지 several 여럿의, 몇몇의 available 이용 가능한 latest 최근의, 최신의 look + 형용사 ~하게 보이다

18. Do you have some extra printer paper?
(A) What size do you want?
(B) My printer has been set up.
(C) Place the extras on my desk.

여분의 인쇄용지가 좀 있으신가요?
(A) 어느 사이즈를 원하세요?
(B) 제 프린터가 설치되어 있습니다.
(C) 여분의 것을 제 책상에 놓아주세요.

| 해설 |
여분의 인쇄용지가 있는지 묻는 Do 일반 의문문에 대해 원하는 사이즈를 반문하는 것으로 용지가 있음을 나타내는 (A)가 정답.
(B) 용지 보유 여부가 아닌 자신의 프린터 설치 여부를 말하고 있어 질문의 핵심에서 벗어난 오답. / 질문의 printer를 반복 사용한 오답.
(C) 물품을 놓을 위치를 말하는 답변이므로 Where 의문문에 어울리는 오답. / 질문의 extra를 반복 사용한 오답.

| 어휘 | extra a. 여분의, 추가의 n. 여분의 것, 추가되는 것   set up ~을 설치하다, 설정하다   place A on B A를 B에 놓다, 두다

19. Is your software giving you an error message too?
(A) A few more minutes.
(B) It's the button on the left.
(C) I've just asked IT to check it out.

당신 소프트웨어에도 오류 메시지가 뜨나요?
(A) 몇 분만 더요.
(B) 왼쪽에 있는 버튼입니다.
(C) 저는 막 정보 기술팀에 확인해 달라고 요청했어요.

| 해설 |
상대방의 소프트웨어에도 오류 메시지가 나타나는지 묻는 Is 일반 의문문에 대해 담당 부서에 확인 요청을 했다는 말로 자신에게도 오류 메시지가 나타나고 있음을 알리는 (C)가 정답.
(A) 추가로 필요한 시간을 말하는 답변이므로 질문의 핵심에서 벗어난 오답.
(B) 특정 버튼의 위치를 알리는 말이므로 질문의 핵심에서 벗어난 오답.

| 어휘 | on the left 왼쪽에   ask A to do A에게 ~하도록 요청하다   IT 정보 기술(부)   check A out A를 확인하다

20. Does anyone need to add requests to this equipment order form?
(A) In my desk drawer.
(B) Alicia said she needs a keyboard.
(C) At least an hour.

이 장비 주문서에 요청 사항을 추가하셔야 하는 분이 계신가요?
(A) 제 책상 서랍에요.
(B) Alicia 씨가 키보드가 필요하다고 얘기했어요.
(C) 최소한 1시간이요.

| 해설 |
주문서에 요청 사항을 추가할 사람이 있는지 묻는 Does 일반 의문문에 대해 특정인이 필요로 하는 물품을 언급하는 (B)가 정답.
(A) 위치 표현이므로 Where 의문문에 어울리는 오답.
(C) 소요 시간을 말하는 답변이므로 How long 의문문에 어울리는 오답.

| 어휘 | add ~을 추가하다   request 요청, 신청   equipment 장비   order form 주문서   drawer 서랍   at least 최소한, 적어도

21. Have you tried the new lunch specials at the cafeteria yet?
(A) I've been away all week.
(B) A health food store.
(C) Sure, I'm free after lunch.

구내식당에서 새로운 점심 특선 메뉴를 드셔 보셨나요?
(A) 저는 일주일 내내 부재중이었습니다.
(B) 건강 식품 매장이요.
(C) 그럼요, 저는 점심 식사 후에 시간이 됩니다.

| 해설 |
구내 식당에서 새로운 점심 특선 메뉴를 먹어 봤는지 묻는 Have 일반 의문문에 대해 부재중이었다는 말로 먹어 볼 기회가 없었음을 알리는 (A)가 정답.
(B) 한 매장의 종류를 언급하는 말이므로 점심 특선 메뉴 식사 여부와 관련 없는 오답.
(C) 긍정을 나타내는 Sure로 답변하고 있지만, 그 뒤에 이어지는 말이 질문의 핵심과 관련 없는 오답.

| 어휘 | try ~을 한번 먹어 보다, 해 보다   cafeteria 구내 식당   away 부재중인, 자리를 비운   free 시간이 나는

22. Could you drop off these shirts at the dry cleaner's?
(A) A stain on the front.
(B) Turn left at the corner.
(C) I think it closed at six.

이 셔츠들을 세탁소에 맡겨 주시겠어요?
(A) 앞면에 있는 얼룩이요.
(B) 모퉁이에서 좌회전하세요.
(C) 그곳은 6시에 문을 닫는 것 같은데요.

| 해설 |
셔츠들을 세탁소에 맡겨 달라고 요청하는 Could you 일반 의문문에 대해 6시에 문을 닫는다는 말로 맡길 수 없음을 알리는 (C)가 정답.
(A) 얼룩의 위치를 알리는 말이므로 요청 질문의 반응으로 부적합한 오답. / dry cleaner에서 연상되는 stain을 사용한 오답.
(B) 이동 방향을 알리는 답변이므로 질문의 핵심에서 벗어난 오답.

| 어휘 | drop off (물건) ~을 갖다 주다, (사람) ~을 내려 주다   dry cleaner's 세탁소   stain 얼룩   front 앞면, 앞쪽   turn left 좌회전하다   corner 모퉁이, 구석

23. Should we replace the furniture in the waiting room?
(A) You can place it on the wall.
(B) I think it's still in good condition.
(C) Thanks for waiting for me.

우리가 대기실에 있는 가구를 교체해야 할까요?
(A) 벽에 붙여 놓으시면 됩니다.
(B) 아직 상태가 좋은 것 같아요.
(C) 저를 기다려 주셔서 감사합니다.

| 해설 |
대기실에 있는 가구를 교체해야 하는지 묻는 Should we 일반 의문문에 대해 상태가 좋다는 말로 교체할 필요가 없음을 나타내는 (B)가 정답.
(A) 부착 위치를 알리는 말이므로 Where 의문문에 어울리는 오답.
(C) 기다려 준 것에 대한 감사 인사이므로 질문의 핵심에서 벗어난 오답. / 질문의 waiting을 반복 사용한 오답.

| 어휘 | replace ~을 교체하다   waiting room 대기실   place ~을 놓다, 두다   in good condition 상태가 좋은

24. Are the hotel rooms in Fiji always this expensive?
(A) I'd be happy to give you a tour.
(B) You should see the peak-season prices.
(C) I'd like to stay for two nights.

Fiji에 있는 호텔 객실들이 항상 이렇게 비싼가요?
(A) 제가 기꺼이 투어를 제공해 드리겠습니다.
(B) 성수기 가격을 보시고 말씀하세요.
(C) 2박을 하려고 합니다.

| 해설 |
Fiji에 있는 호텔 객실 가격이 항상 비싼지 묻는 Are 일반 의문문에 대해 성수기 가격을 봐야 한다는 말로 성수기에 비하면 그렇게 비싼 편이 아니라는 의미로 상대방의 말을 부정하는 (B)가 정답.
(A) 투어 제공 의사를 나타내는 말이므로 객실 가격 수준과 관련 없는 오답.
(C) 객실 예약 시 할 수 있는 말이므로 질문의 핵심에서 벗어난 오답. / hotel room에서 연상되는 stay를 사용한 오답.

| 어휘 | this 이렇게, 이 정도로   expensive 비싼   be happy to do 기꺼이 ~하다

peak-season 성수기의   stay for two nights 2박을 하다

25. May I speak to the pharmacist on duty?
(A) She'll be right back.
(B) It may be locked.
(C) You have a point.

근무 중이신 약사와 통화할 수 있을까요?
(A) 금방 자리로 돌아오실 겁니다.
(B) 잠겨 있을지도 모릅니다.
(C) 일리 있는 말씀입니다.

| 해설 |
근무 중인 약사와 통화할 수 있는지 묻는 May I 일반 의문문에 대해 그 사람을 She로 지칭해 곧 돌아온다는 말로 곧 통화가 가능함을 알리는 (A)가 정답.
(B) 가리키는 대상을 알 수 없는 단수 명사를 대신하는 It이 언급된 오답.
(C) 상대방의 의견에 대한 동의를 나타낼 때 사용하는 말이므로 질문의 핵심에서 벗어난 오답.

| 어휘 | pharmacist 약사   on duty 근무 중인   be right back 금방 돌아오다   lock ~을 잠그다

DAY 08   비 의문사 의문문 (2)

01 부정 의문문

PRACTICE | 기출 연습하기   본책 p.53
정답 1 (A)   2 (B)   3 (C)   4 (B)   5 (B)   6 (B)

1. Isn't there a direct flight from Seoul to Los Angeles?
(A) I'll check the airline's Web site.
(B) No, I'm taking the train.
(C) I think he probably will.

서울에서 Los Angeles로 가는 직항편이 있지 않나요? (= ~있죠?)
(A) 제가 항공사 웹 사이트를 확인해 보겠습니다.
(B) 아뇨, 저는 기차를 탈 겁니다.
(C) 아마 그가 그럴 것 같아요.

| 해설 |
서울에서 Los Angeles로 가는 직항편이 있는지 확인하는 Isn't 부정 의문문에 대해 항공사 웹 사이트를 확인하겠다는 말로 관련 정보를 파악할 방법을 언급하는 (A)가 정답.
(B) 부정을 나타내는 No 뒤에 답변자 자신의 계획을 말하고 있으므로 질문의 핵심에서 벗어난 오답.
(C) 가리키는 대상을 알 수 없는 he를 언급한 오답.

| 어휘 | direct flight 직항편   take (교통편) ~을 타다, 이용하다   probably 아마

2. Don't you need some folders?
(A) I'll hold it for you.
(B) Yes, where are they stored?
(C) The printed résumés.

폴더들이 좀 필요하지 않으신가요? (= ~ 필요하시죠?)
(A) 제가 대신 그걸 들어 드릴게요.
(B) 네, 어디에 보관되어 있나요?
(C) 인쇄된 이력서들이요.

| 해설 |
폴더들이 필요하지 않은지 확인하는 Don't 부정 의문문에 대해 긍정을 뜻하는 Yes와 함께 folders를 they로 지칭해 보관 장소를 되묻는 (B)가 정답.

(A) it에 해당되는 단수 명사로 언급된 것이 없으므로 오답.
(C) 폴더가 아닌 이력서의 상태를 언급하고 있어 질문의 핵심에서 벗어난 오답.

| 어휘 | hold ~을 들다, 붙잡다   store ~을 보관하다, 저장하다   résumé 이력서

3. Isn't the doctor available on Sundays?
(A) There's a new medical clinic.
(B) From the hospital.
(C) No, but he can see you on Saturdays.

의사 선생님께서 매주 일요일에 시간이 되시지 않나요? (= ~ 되시죠?)
(A) 새로 문을 연 진료소가 있습니다.
(B) 병원으로부터요.
(C) 아뇨, 하지만 매주 토요일에 진료하실 수 있습니다.

| 해설 |
의사가 매주 일요일에 시간이 되는지 여부를 확인하는 Isn't 부정 의문문에 대해 부정을 나타내는 No와 함께 진료 가능한 다른 요일을 언급하는 (C)가 정답.
(A) 의사의 진료 가능 여부가 아닌 새 진료소의 존재를 말하고 있으므로 질문의 핵심에서 벗어난 오답. / doctor에서 연상되는 medical clinic을 사용한 오답.
(B) 출발점이나 출처 등을 나타내는 말이므로 질문의 핵심에서 벗어난 오답. / doctor에서 연상되는 hospital을 사용한 오답.

| 어휘 | available (사람이) 시간이 나는   medical clinic 진료소

4. Aren't you planning to take the train to the company retreat?
(A) Over the next few days.
(B) I prefer the bus.
(C) Please take a brochure.

회사 야유회에 기차를 타고 가실 계획이지 않나요? (= ~ 계획이시죠?)
(A) 앞으로 며칠 동안에 걸쳐서요.
(B) 저는 버스를 선호합니다.
(C) 안내 책자를 하나 가져가세요.

| 해설 |
회사 야유회에 기차를 타고 갈 것인지 확인하기 위한 Aren't 부정 의문문에 대해 버스를 선호한다는 말로 기차를 타지 않을 것임을 알리는 (B)가 정답.
(A) 이동 수단이 아닌 시간을 나타내는 말이므로 질문의 핵심에서 벗어난 오답.
(C) 안내 책자를 가져가도록 권하는 말이므로 질문의 핵심과 관련 없는 오답. / 질문의 take를 반복 사용한 오답.

| 어휘 | plan to do ~할 계획이다   take (교통편) ~을 타다, 이용하다   retreat 야유회   over ~ 동안에 걸쳐   prefer ~을 선호하다   brochure 안내 책자

5. Didn't Helen give a presentation at the meeting?
(A) Keep it under thirty minutes.
(B) She's still out of town.
(C) I have an interview at five.

Helen 씨가 회의에서 발표하지 않았나요? (= ~ 발표하셨죠?)
(A) 30분 미만으로 유지해 주세요.
(B) 그녀는 아직 다른 지역에 있습니다.
(C) 저는 5시에 면접이 있습니다.

| 해설 |
Helen 씨가 회의에서 발표했는지 여부를 확인하기 위한 Didn't 부정 의문문에 대해 Helen을 She로 지칭해 다른 곳에 가 있다는 말로 그 사람이 발표하지 않았다고 답변하는 (B)가 정답.
(A) 시간 길이를 제한할 때 하는 말이므로 질문의 핵심에서 벗어난 오답. / presentation에서 연상되는 thirty minutes를 사용한 오답.
(C) Helen 씨의 발표 여부가 아닌 자신의 일정을 말하는 답변이므로 오답.

| 어휘 | keep A under B A를 B 미만으로 유지하다   out of town 다른 지역에 가 있는

6. Wasn't the furniture supposed to be delivered yesterday?
(A) No, you can sit wherever you like.
(B) The snowstorm has caused delays.
(C) We now use a tracking code.

가구가 어제 배송되기로 되어 있지 않았나요? (= ~ 배송되어야 했죠?)
(A) 아뇨, 원하시는 곳에 어디든지 앉으시면 됩니다.
(B) 눈보라가 배송 지연을 초래했어요.
(C) 저희는 현재 추적 코드를 활용하고 있습니다.

| 해설 |
가구가 예정대로 어제 배송되었는지 여부를 확인하는 Wasn't 부정 의문문에 대해 배송 지연 원인을 알리는 것으로 배송되지 않았음을 말하는 (B)가 정답.
(A) Wasn't와 호응하는 No가 쓰였지만, 이어지는 말이 상대방에게 앉으라고 권하는 내용이므로 질문의 핵심에서 벗어난 오답.
(C) 과거 시점의 배송 완료 여부를 묻는 질문과 달리 배송 추적 방법을 알리는 말이므로 질문의 핵심에서 벗어난 오답.

| 어휘 | wherever ~하는 곳은 어디든지   cause ~을 초래하다   delay 지연, 지체   tracking code 추적 코드

02 부가 의문문

PRACTICE | 기출 연습하기   본책 p.55

정답 1 (A)   2 (A)   3 (A)   4 (B)   5 (C)   6 (A)

1. The dining room looks elegant, doesn't it?
(A) Yes, the tablecloth really makes a difference.
(B) Get a reservation at Antonio's Steakhouse.
(C) A dinner party for twelve guests.

식당이 고급스러워 보이네요, 그렇지 않나요?
(A) 네, 테이블보가 정말로 큰 차이를 만들어 주네요.
(B) Antonio's Steakhouse에 예약해 두세요.
(C) 12명의 손님들을 위한 저녁 식사 파티요.

| 해설 |
식당이 고급스러워 보이지 않는지 확인하는 부가 의문문에 대해 긍정을 나타내는 Yes와 함께 그렇게 보이는 이유를 언급하는 (A)가 정답.
(B) 특정 장소에 예약하도록 제안하는 말이므로 질문의 핵심에서 벗어난 오답.
(C) 예약할 때 밝히는 정보에 해당되는 말이므로 질문의 핵심에서 벗어난 오답.

| 어휘 | elegant 고급스러운, 우아한   tablecloth 테이블보

2. We haven't found a new head accountant yet, have we?
(A) No, not yet.
(B) A savings account.
(C) Of course I'll help you.

우리가 아직 새로운 수석 회계사를 찾지 못한 것이 맞죠, 그렇죠?
(A) 네, 아직이요.
(B) 보통 예금 계좌요.
(C) 물론 당신을 도와 드릴 겁니다.

| 해설 |
아직 신임 수석 회계사를 찾지 못한 것이 맞는지 확인하는 부가 의문문에 대해 부정을 나타내는 No와 함께 아직 찾지 못했음을 알리는 (A)가 정답.
(B) 계좌의 특징과 관련된 답변이므로 질문의 핵심에서 벗어난 오답.

(C) 요청에 대한 수락을 나타내는 말이므로 질문의 핵심과 관련 없는 오답.

| 어휘 | head accountant 수석 회계사   not yet 아직 아니다   savings account 보통 예금 계좌

3. You set up three microphones on the main stage, didn't you?
(A) I tried, but one wasn't working.
(B) No, he didn't win the award.
(C) The view from the front row is best.

중앙 무대에 세 개의 마이크를 설치하셨죠, 그렇지 않나요?
(A) 그러려고 했지만, 하나가 작동되지 않았어요.
(B) 아뇨, 그는 상을 받지 못했어요.
(C) 앞줄의 시야가 가장 좋습니다.

| 해설 |
중앙 무대에 세 개의 마이크를 설치했는지 여부를 확인하는 부가 의문문에 대해 microphone을 대신하는 대명사 one과 함께 작동되지 않았다는 말로 세 개를 전부 설치하지는 못했음을 나타내는 (A)가 정답.
(B) 부정을 뜻하는 No로 답변하고 있지만, 그 뒤에 이어지는 말이 대상을 알 수 없는 he에 관한 것이므로 질문의 핵심에서 벗어난 오답.
(C) 공연을 관람하기 좋은 위치를 언급하는 말이므로 질문의 핵심에서 벗어난 오답. / stage에서 연상되는 front row를 사용한 오답.

| 어휘 | set up ~을 설치하다, 마련하다   work (기계 등이) 작동되다   win an award 상을 받다   view 시야   front row 앞줄

4. The staff meeting was postponed, wasn't it?
(A) The billing department.
(B) Actually, they canceled it.
(C) A busy agenda.

직원 회의가 연기되었죠, 그렇지 않나요?
(A) 청구서 담당 부서요.
(B) 실은, 취소됐습니다.
(C) 바쁜 의사 일정입니다.

| 해설 |
직원 회의가 연기되었는지 여부를 확인하는 부가 의문문에 대해 주최측의 사람들을 they로, meeting을 it으로 지칭해 연기된 것이 아니라 취소되었음을 밝히는 (B)가 정답.
(A) 부서 명칭에 해당되는 말이므로 who 의문문에 어울리는 오답.
(C) 바쁜 일정임을 알리는 말이므로 회의 연기 여부와 관련 없는 오답. / meeting에서 연상되는 agenda를 사용한 오답.

| 어휘 | postpone ~을 연기하다   billing 청구서 발송   actually 실은, 사실은   cancel ~을 취소하다   agenda 의사 일정, 안건

5. Your interview at Bryce Financial is tomorrow, isn't it?
(A) It's an amazing view.
(B) He interviewed for the position.
(C) I already spoke with them.

Bryce Financial 사의 면접이 내일이죠, 그렇지 않나요?
(A) 아주 멋진 전망이네요.
(B) 그는 그 직책을 위해 면접을 봤습니다.
(C) 이미 그쪽 분들과 얘기 나눴습니다.

| 해설 |
Bryce Financial 사에 있을 면접이 내일인지 확인하려는 부가 의문문에 대해 그 회사의 사람들을 them으로 지칭해 이미 면접 본 상황임을 밝히는 (C)가 정답.
(A) 면접이 아닌 전망과 관련된 말이므로 질문의 핵심에서 벗어난 오답. / interview와 발음이 비슷한 view를 사용한 오답.
(B) 가리키는 대상을 알 수 없는 He의 면접과 관련된 말이므로 질문의 핵심에서 벗어난 오답.

| 어휘 | amazing 아주 멋진, 놀라운   view 전망, 경관   interview 면접을 보다   position 직책, 자리

6. We got a discount on the sofa, right?
(A) What does the invoice say?
(B) It is very comfortable.
(C) Feel free to turn on the light.

우리가 그 소파에 대해 할인을 받았죠, 그렇죠?
(A) 거래 내역서에 뭐라고 쓰여 있나요?
(B) 매우 편안합니다.
(C) 편하게 전등을 켜도 됩니다.

| 해설 |
소파에 대해 할인 받은 것이 맞는지 확인하는 부가 의문문에 대해 거래 내역서의 내용을 되물음으로써 자신도 잘 알지 못함을 나타내는 (A)가 정답.
(B) 제품의 특성과 관련된 말이므로 질문의 핵심에서 벗어난 오답. / sofa에서 연상되는 comfortable을 사용한 오답.
(C) 전등을 켜도 좋다고 허락하는 말이므로 질문의 핵심과 관련 없는 오답. / right과 발음이 비슷한 light을 사용한 오답.

| 어휘 | invoice 거래 내역서, 송장   comfortable 편안한   Feel free to do 편히 ~하세요, 마음껏 ~하세요   turn on ~을 켜다

DAY 08 | 실전문제   본책 p.56

정답 1 (A)   2 (C)   3 (A)   4 (C)   5 (A)   6 (B)
      7 (C)   8 (B)   9 (C)   10 (A) 11 (B) 12 (C)
      13 (A) 14 (A) 15 (B) 16 (A) 17 (C) 18 (A)
      19 (B) 20 (A) 21 (C) 22 (A) 23 (B) 24 (C)
      25 (A)

---

1. Shouldn't we hire more technicians?
(A) We have four already.
(B) No, a broken copier.
(C) You can join us.

우리가 추가 기술자를 고용해야 하지 않나요? (= ~ 고용해야죠?)
(A) 우리에게 이미 네 명이 있어요.
(B) 아뇨, 고장 난 복사기요.
(C) 저희와 함께 하실 수 있어요.

| 해설 |
추가 기술자를 고용해야 하지 않냐는 Shouldn't 부정 의문문에 대해 이미 네 명이 있다는 말로 고용할 필요가 없음을 알리는 (A)가 정답.
(B) 복사기의 상태를 나타내는 말이므로 질문의 핵심에서 벗어난 오답. / technician에서 고장 난 복사기를 수리하는 상황을 연상하게 하는 오답.
(C) 자신들과 함께 하도록 권하는 말이므로 마찬가지로 질문의 핵심에서 벗어난 오답.

| 어휘 | hire ~을 고용하다   technician 기술자, 기사   broken 고장 난   join ~와 함께하다, ~에 합류하다

2. Steven designed the new advertisement for the product line, didn't he?
(A) I'll test it for you.
(B) Just sign at the bottom.
(C) No, that was Rachel's work.

Steven 씨가 그 제품 라인에 대한 새로운 광고를 디자인했죠, 아닌가요?
(A) 제가 대신 테스트해보겠습니다.
(B) 하단에 서명하시면 됩니다.
(C) 아뇨, 그건 Rachel 씨의 작품입니다.

| 해설 |
Steven 씨가 제품 라인에 대한 새로운 광고를 디자인했는지 여부를 확인하는 부가 의문문에 대해 부정을 뜻하는 No와 함께 실제 작업자의 이름을 밝히는 (C)가 정답.
(A) 자신의 의지를 나타내는 말이므로 Steven 씨의 광고 디자인 여부와 관련 없는 오답.
(B) 서명 위치를 알려 줄 때 하는 말이므로 질문의 핵심에서 벗어난 오답. / design과 발음이 비슷한 sign을 사용한 오답.

| 어휘 | advertisement 광고   product line 제품 라인, 제품군   at the bottom 하단에   work 작품, 작업(물)

3. Hasn't that perfume been discontinued?
(A) No, it's a popular product.
(B) She likes the floral scent.
(C) It continues on the next page.

저 향수는 단종되지 않았나요? (= ~ 단종되었죠?)
(A) 아뇨, 인기 있는 제품입니다.
(B) 그녀는 꽃 향기를 좋아합니다.
(C) 다음 페이지로 이어집니다.

| 해설 |
특정 향수의 단종 여부를 확인하기 위한 Hasn't 부정 의문문에 대해 단종되지 않았음을 뜻하는 No와 뒤에 그 이유를 덧붙이는 (A)가 정답.
(B) 가리키는 대상을 알 수 없는 She를 언급한 오답.
(C) 책이나 잡지 등의 내용이 다음 페이지에 이어진다는 말이므로 질문의 핵심에서 벗어난 오답. / discontinued와 발음이 비슷한 continues를 사용한 오답.

| 어휘 | perfume 향수   discontinue ~을 단종시키다   floral 꽃의, 꽃으로 된   scent 향, 향기   continue 이어지다, 계속되다

4. The lighting in this restaurant isn't bright enough, is it?
(A) I've tried a few different dishes.
(B) They had trouble getting here.
(C) You're right. I can hardly see my menu.

이 레스토랑의 조명이 충분히 밝지 않네요, 그렇죠?
(A) 저는 몇 가지 다른 음식들을 먹어 본 적이 있어요.
(B) 그들이 이곳으로 오는 데 문제가 있었습니다.
(C) 맞아요. 메뉴가 거의 보이지 않네요.

| 해설 |
레스토랑의 조명이 충분히 밝지 않다는 것에 대해 확인하려는 부가 의문문에 대해 동의를 나타내는 말과 함께 그 근거를 함께 언급하는 (C)가 정답.
(A) 식사와 관련된 자신의 경험을 말하는 답변이므로 질문의 핵심에서 벗어난 오답.
(B) 조명의 밝기가 아닌, 대상을 알 수 없는 They와 관련된 말이므로 질문의 핵심에서 벗어난 오답.

| 어휘 | lighting 조명   bright 밝은   enough (형용사 뒤에서) 충분히   try ~을 한번 먹어 보다   dish 요리   get here 이곳으로 오다   hardly 거의 ~ 않다

5. A meal will be served on this flight, right?
(A) Let's try the Raintree Café.
(B) I'll have the pasta.
(C) Unfortunately, it won't.

이 비행기에서 식사가 제공되죠, 맞죠?
(A) Raintree Café에 한번 가 봅시다.
(B) 저는 파스타로 하겠습니다.
(C) 안타깝게도, 그렇지 않습니다.

| 해설 |
비행기에서 식사가 제공되는 것이 맞는지 확인하는 부가 의문문에 대해 유감을 나타낼 때 사용하는 Unfortunately와 함께 부정문 won't으로 답변

한 (C)가 정답.
(A) 특정 카페로 가 보자고 제안하는 말이므로 질문의 핵심에서 벗어난 오답. / meal에서 연상되는 특정 식당명을 사용한 오답.
(B) 음식을 주문할 때 할 수 있는 말이므로 기내 식사 제공 여부를 확인하는 질문의 핵심과 관련 없는 오답. / meal에서 연상되는 pasta를 사용한 오답.

| 어휘 | serve (음식 등) ~을 제공하다, 내오다   try ~에 한번 가 보다, ~을 한번 해 보다   unfortunately 안타깝게도, 아쉽게도

6. You've submitted your job application, haven't you?
(A) He found it online.
(B) I'm still writing it.
(C) Several applicants.

구직 지원서를 제출하셨죠, 그렇지 않나요?
(A) 그가 그것을 온라인에서 찾아 냈어요.
(B) 아직 작성하는 중입니다.
(C) 여러 지원자들이요.

| 해설 |
상대방이 구직 지원서를 제출했는지 여부를 확인하는 부가 의문문에 대해 job application을 it으로 지칭해 여전히 작성하고 있다는 말로 아직 제출하지 않았음을 나타내는 (B)가 정답.
(A) 가리키는 대상을 알 수 없는 He를 언급한 오답.
(C) 지원자 수와 관련된 말이므로 질문의 핵심에서 벗어난 오답. / application과 발음이 비슷한 applicants를 사용한 오답.

| 어휘 | submit ~을 제출하다   application 지원(서), 신청(서)   online 온라인에서   several 여럿의, 몇몇의   applicant 지원자

7. You were able to get into the laboratory, weren't you?
(A) Some scientific research.
(B) The equipment is very modern.
(C) No, the access code was changed.

실험실에 들어갈 수 있으셨죠, 그렇지 않나요?
(A) 일부 과학 연구요.
(B) 장비가 매우 현대적입니다.
(C) 아뇨, 출입 코드가 변경되었어요.

| 해설 |
실험실에 들어갈 수 있었는지 여부를 확인하는 부가 의문문에 대해 부정을 뜻하는 No와 함께 그곳에 들어 갈 수 없었던 이유를 덧붙인 (C)가 정답.
(A) 연구의 특징과 관련된 말이므로 질문의 핵심에서 벗어난 오답. / laboratory에서 연상되는 research를 사용한 오답.
(B) 장비의 특징과 관련된 답변이므로 질문의 핵심과 관련 없는 오답. / laboratory에서 연상되는 equipment를 사용한 오답.

| 어휘 | get into ~ 안으로 들어가다   laboratory 실험실, 연구실   research 연구, 조사   equipment 장비   access 출입, 접근, 이용

8. Doesn't Thomas usually drive to work?
(A) He works full time.
(B) Yes, but his car is being repaired.
(C) Actually, I like taking the subway.

Thomas 씨는 보통 차를 운전해 출근하지 않나요? (= ~ 출근하죠?)
(A) 그는 정규직으로 근무하고 있습니다.
(B) 네, 하지만 그분의 차량은 수리 중입니다.
(C) 실은, 저는 지하철을 타는 게 좋습니다.

| 해설 |
Thomas 씨가 보통 차를 운전해 출근하는지 여부를 확인하는 Doesn't 부정 의문문에 대해 긍정을 뜻하는 Yes와 함께 Thomas 씨를 he로 지칭해 일시적으로 차를 이용할 수 없는 이유를 말하는 (B)가 정답.
(A) Thomas 씨의 차량 이용 여부가 아닌 근무 형태와 관련된 말이므로 질문의 핵심에서 벗어난 오답.
(C) Thomas 씨가 아닌 답변자 자신이 선호하는 교통편을 말하고 있으므로 질문의 핵심에서 벗어난 오답.

| 어휘 | usually 보통, 일반적으로   drive to work 차를 운전해 출근하다   work full time 정규직으로 근무하다   repair ~을 수리하다   actually 실은, 사실은   take (교통편) ~을 타다, 이용하다

9. We can park in the underground lot after hours, can't we?
(A) It will take thirty minutes.
(B) There is a nice picnic area.
(C) I'm sure we can.

우리가 영업 시간 이후에 지하 주차장에 주차할 수 있죠, 그렇지 않나요?
(A) 30분이 걸릴 겁니다.
(B) 멋진 피크닉 구역이 있습니다.
(C) 분명 그렇게 할 수 있습니다.

| 해설 |
영업 시간 이후에 지하 주차장에 주차할 수 있는지 여부를 확인하는 부가 의문문에 대해 동일 조동사 can을 반복 사용해 가능성에 대한 확신을 나타내는 (C)가 정답.
(A) 소요 시간을 의미하는 답변이므로 질문의 핵심에서 벗어난 오답.
(B) 피크닉 구역이 존재함을 알리는 말이므로 주차와 관련 없는 오답.

| 어휘 | park 주차하다   underground lot 지하 주차장   after hours 영업 시간 이후에   take + 시간 ~의 시간이 걸리다

10. You're attending the symphony concert this Saturday, right?
(A) A professional musician.
(B) Check the group's Web site.
(C) No, the show was sold out.

이번 주 토요일에 교향악 연주회에 참석하시는 것이 맞죠?
(A) 전문 음악가입니다.
(B) 그 그룹의 웹 사이트를 확인해 보세요.
(C) 아뇨, 그 공연은 매진되었어요.

| 해설 |
토요일에 교향악 연주회에 참석하는 것이 맞는지 확인하는 부가 의문문에 대해 부정을 나타내는 No와 함께 참석할 수 없는 이유로 매진 상태를 언급한 (C)가 정답.
(A) 한 음악가의 특징과 관련된 말이므로 질문의 핵심에서 벗어난 오답.
(B) 답변자의 행사 참석 여부는 웹 사이트에서 확인할 수 없는 것이므로 오답.

| 어휘 | attend ~에 참석하다   symphony 교향악   sold out 매진된, 품절된

11. The side entrance should be left locked, shouldn't it?
(A) No, the clock is broken.
(B) Yes, it has to be secured.
(C) Yes, a little bit to the right.

옆쪽 출입문이 잠긴 상태로 있어야 하죠, 그렇지 않나요?
(A) 아뇨, 시계가 고장 난 상태입니다.
(B) 네, 안전한 상태가 되어야 합니다.
(C) 네, 조금만 더 오른쪽으로요.

| 해설 |
옆쪽 출입문이 잠긴 상태여야 하지 않는지 확인하는 부가 의문문에 대해 안전한 상태여야 한다는 말로 잠가야 한다는 뜻을 나타낸 (B)가 정답.
(A) 시계의 상태를 알리는 말이므로 질문의 핵심에서 벗어난 오답. / 질문의 locked와 발음이 비슷한 clock을 사용한 오답.
(C) 위치 이동과 관련된 답변이므로 질문의 핵심에서 벗어난 오답. / left에서 연상되는 right를 사용한 오답.

| 어휘 | be left + 형용사 ~한 상태로 있다, 남겨지다　locked 잠긴　broken 고장 난, 망가진　secure ~을 안전하게 하다　a little bit 조금, 약간　to the right 오른쪽으로

12. Isn't Sylvia Atkinson going to meet the interns?
(A) It was a competitive program.
(B) A workshop for the entire staff.
(C) No, she has to visit a client.

Sylvia Atkinson 씨가 인턴 직원들과 만날 예정이지 않나요? (= ~ 예정이죠?)
(A) 경쟁력 있는 프로그램이었습니다.
(B) 전체 직원들을 위한 워크숍입니다.
(C) 아뇨, 그분은 고객을 방문해야 합니다.

| 해설 |
Sylvia Atkinson 씨가 인턴 직원들과 만나는지 여부를 확인하는 Isn't 부정 의문문에 대해 부정을 뜻하는 No와 함께 Sylvia 씨를 she로 지칭해 그 이유를 언급하는 (C)가 정답.
(A) Sylvia 씨의 일정이 아닌 프로그램의 특성을 말하고 있어 질문의 핵심에서 벗어난 오답.
(B) 마찬가지로, Sylvia 씨의 일정이 아닌 워크숍의 목적을 말하고 있어 질문의 핵심에서 벗어난 오답.

| 어휘 | competitive 경쟁력 있는, 경쟁하는　entire 전체의, 전부의

13. Don't you want to check out the new art exhibition?
(A) Who is the featured artist?
(B) A dark paint color.
(C) Sarah will check for you.

새 미술 전시회를 확인해 보고 싶지 않으신가요? (= ~ 확인해 보고 싶으시죠?)
(A) 누가 그 전시회의 주요 미술가인가요?
(B) 어두운 색채입니다.
(C) Sarah 씨가 당신을 위해 확인해 드릴 겁니다.

| 해설 |
새 미술 전시회를 확인해 보고 싶지 않은지 묻는 Don't 부정 의문문에 대해 누가 주요 미술가인지 반문하는 것으로 해당 전시회에 대한 세부 정보를 요청하는 (A)가 정답.
(B) 색상의 특징을 말하는 답변이므로 질문의 핵심에서 벗어난 오답.
(C) 답변자 자신의 의견이 아닌 제3자인 Sarah 씨가 하려는 일을 말하고 있어 질문의 핵심에서 벗어난 오답.

| 어휘 | check out ~을 확인해보다　exhibition 전시(회)　featured 주요한, 주연으로 출연한, 특집으로 실린

14. We don't need to decorate the ballroom, do we?
(A) No, the venue staff will handle that.
(B) I like the colors you chose.
(C) I think live music would be good.

우리가 연회장을 장식할 필요가 없죠, 그렇죠?
(A) 없어요, 행사장 직원들이 그 일을 처리할 겁니다.
(B) 당신이 선택한 색상이 마음에 듭니다.
(C) 라이브 음악이 좋을 것 같아요.

| 해설 |
연회장을 장식할 필요가 없는 것이 맞는지 확인하는 부가 의문문에 대해 하지 않아도 된다는 내용을 나타내는 No와 함께 해당 작업을 처리하는 주체가 따로 있음을 언급하는 (A)가 정답.
(B) 색상에 대한 의견을 말하는 답변이므로 연회장 장식 작업의 필요성과 관련 없는 오답. / decorate에서 연상되는 colors를 사용한 오답.
(C) 라이브 음악이 좋을 것이라는 말로 의견을 제시하는 답변이므로 질문의 핵심에서 벗어난 오답.

| 어휘 | decorate ~을 장식하다　ballroom 연회장　venue 행사장　handle ~을 처리하다, 다루다　choose ~을 선택하다

15. Didn't you mention that you're looking for a new car?
(A) How about the repair shop?
(B) Yes, I've saved up for one.
(C) No, it was cheaper.

새 차를 찾고 있다고 말씀하시지 않았나요? (= ~ 말씀하셨죠?)
(A) 수리점은 어떠신가요?
(B) 네, 한 대 구입하려고 저축했어요.
(C) 아뇨, 가격이 더 저렴했어요.

| 해설 |
새 차를 찾고 있는지 여부를 확인하는 Didn't 부정 의문문에 대해 찾고 있다는 의미를 나타내는 Yes와 함께 신차 구입을 위해 자신이 한 일을 알리는 (B)가 정답.
(A) 제안을 나타내는 말이므로 상대방 질문의 핵심에서 벗어난 오답.
(C) Didn't과 호응하는 No가 쓰이기는 했지만, 가격 수준과 관련된 말이므로 질문의 핵심에서 벗어난 오답.

| 어휘 | mention that ~라고 말하다, 언급하다　look for ~을 찾다　repair shop 수리점, 정비 공장　save up for ~을 위해 저축하다　cheap 저렴한, 싼

16. Wasn't Benjamin interested in the performance?
(A) A few times a year.
(B) Yes, I'll give him a flyer.
(C) The show was impressive.

Benjamin 씨가 그 공연에 관심 있지 않으셨나요? (= ~ 있으셨죠?)
(A) 일 년에 몇 차례요.
(B) 네, 제가 그분께 전단을 드릴 거예요.
(C) 공연이 인상적이었어요.

| 해설 |
Benjamin 씨가 특정 공연에 관심 있지 않았는지 확인하는 Wasn't 부정 의문문에 대해 긍정을 나타내는 Yes와 함께 관심을 보인 것에 따른 조치로 전단을 줄 것임을 알리는 (B)가 정답.
(A) 횟수를 나타내는 답변이므로 How often 또는 How many times 의문문에 어울리는 오답.
(C) Benjamin 씨의 관심 여부가 아닌 공연의 특성을 말하는 답변이므로 질문의 핵심에서 벗어난 오답. / performance에서 연상되는 show, impressive를 사용한 오답.

| 어휘 | be interested in ~에 관심 있다　performance 공연, 연주(회)　flyer 전단　impressive 인상적인

17. You'll attend Tuesday's trade show, won't you?
(A) I thought it was helpful.
(B) Ten will be enough.
(C) Yes, but just for a few hours.

화요일에 열리는 무역 박람회에 참석하시죠, 그렇지 않나요?
(A) 도움이 되었다고 생각했습니다.
(B) 10명이면 충분할 겁니다.
(C) 네, 하지만 단지 몇 시간 동안만요.

| 해설 |
화요일에 열리는 무역 박람회에 상대방이 참석하는지 여부를 확인하는 부가 의문문에 대해 긍정을 뜻하는 Yes와 함께 참석 가능한 시간을 알리는 (C)가 정답.
(A) 아직 열리지 않은 행사에 이미 참여해 경험한 것처럼 답변하므로 오답.
(B) 사람이나 물품의 숫자와 관련된 말이므로 질문의 핵심에서 벗어난 오답.

| 어휘 | attend ~에 참석하다　trade show 무역 박람회　helpful 도움이 되는, 유익한　enough 충분한

18. There are no rooms available here for December 31st, are there?
(A) No, but there's another hotel nearby.
(B) A double room would be better.
(C) I'll be sure to send it by then.

이곳에 12월 31일에 이용 가능한 방이 없죠, 그렇죠?
(A) 없어요, 하지만 근처에 다른 호텔이 있습니다.
(B) 2인실이 더 좋을 겁니다.
(C) 그때까지 꼭 보내 드리도록 하겠습니다.

| 해설 |
12월 31일에 이용 가능한 방이 없는 것이 맞는지 확인하는 부가 의문에 대해 부정을 뜻하는 No와 함께 객실을 구할 수 있는 다른 방법을 제안하는 (A)가 정답.
(B) 객실의 종류에 대해 의견을 제시하는 말이므로 예약 가능 여부와 관련 없는 오답. / 질문의 room을 반복 사용한 오답.
(C) 가리키는 대상을 알 수 없는 it과 함께 발송 기한을 나타내는 말이므로 질문의 핵심에서 벗어난 오답.

| 어휘 | available 이용 가능한 nearby 근처에 be sure to do 꼭 ~하다 by then 그때까지

19. Won't Ms. Collins be promoted to assistant manager?
(A) Yes, I could use your help.
(B) It hasn't been decided yet.
(C) A new sales promotion.

Collins 씨께서 차장으로 승진되시지 않을까요? (= ~ 승진되시겠죠?)
(A) 네, 당신의 도움이 필요합니다.
(B) 아직 결정되지 않았습니다.
(C) 새로운 판매 촉진 행사입니다.

| 해설 |
Collins 씨가 차장으로 승진되는지 여부를 확인하는 Won't 부정 의문에 대해 그 일을 It으로 지칭해 아직 결정되지 않은 상태임을 나타내는 (B)가 정답.
(A) 긍정을 나타내는 Yes 뒤에 이어지는 말이 Collins 씨의 승진 여부와 관련 없는 오답.
(C) 행사의 특징에 해당되는 말이므로 질문의 핵심에서 벗어난 오답. / promoted와 발음이 비슷한 promotion을 사용한 오답.

| 어휘 | be promoted to ~로 승진되다 assistant manager 차장 could use ~가 필요하다 decide ~을 결정하다 sales 판매, 영업, 매출 promotion 판촉, 홍보

20. Rachel was planning to donate to our charity, wasn't she?
(A) Haven't you received her check?
(B) A shelter for homeless animals.
(C) I'll be there.

Rachel 씨가 우리 자선 단체에 기부할 계획이셨죠, 그렇지 않으셨나요?
(A) 그분의 수표를 받지 못하셨나요?
(B) 집 없는 동물들을 위한 보호소요.
(C) 저는 참석할 거예요..

| 해설 |
Rachel 씨가 자선 단체에 기부할 계획이지 않았는지 확인하는 부가 의문에 대해 Rachel을 her로 지칭해 기부를 위한 수표를 받지 않았는지 되묻는 (A)가 정답.
(B) 보호소의 용도와 관련된 답변이므로 질문의 핵심에서 벗어난 오답.
(C) Rachel의 기부 계획과 관련 없이, 답변자 자신의 참석 여부를 말하고 있으므로 오답.

| 어휘 | plan to do ~할 계획이다 donate to ~에 기부하다 charity 자선 단체, 자선 활동 receive ~을 받다 check 수표 shelter 보호소, 쉼터

21. Breakfast was included in the hotel's room fee, wasn't it?
(A) Usually two double beds.
(B) For a business trip.
(C) Yes, at the on-site restaurant.

아침 식사가 호텔 객실 요금에 포함되어 있었죠, 그렇지 않았나요?
(A) 보통 2개의 더블 침대요.
(B) 출장 때문에요.
(C) 네, 구내 레스토랑에서요.

| 해설 |
아침 식사가 호텔 객실 요금에 포함되어 있지 않은지 확인하는 부가 의문에 대해 긍정을 나타내는 Yes와 함께, 식사가 가능한 장소를 덧붙여 말하는 (C)가 정답.
(A) 객실의 종류와 관련된 말이므로 질문의 핵심에서 벗어난 오답. / hotel's room에서 연상되는 double beds를 사용한 오답.
(B) For 전치사구를 통해 목적을 알리는 말이므로 Why 의문문에 어울리는 오답.

| 어휘 | include ~을 포함하다 fee 요금 usually 보통, 일반적으로 business trip 출장 on-site 구내의, 현장의

22. Haven't the award winners been announced yet?
(A) The entry deadline was only yesterday.
(B) You have a good chance.
(C) An annual photography contest.

수상자들이 아직 발표되지 않았나요? (= ~ 이미 발표되었죠?)
(A) 출품 마감 시한이 불과 어제였어요.
(B) 가능성이 충분히 있습니다.
(C) 연례 사진 촬영 경연대회입니다.

| 해설 |
수상자들이 아직 발표되지 않았는지 확인하기 위한 Haven't 부정 의문문에 대해 출품 마감시한이 어제였다는 말로 수상자를 결정하는 데 시간이 필요함을 암시한 (A)가 정답.
(B) 수상자 선정 여부가 아닌 상대방과 관련된 말이므로 질문의 핵심에서 벗어난 오답.
(C) 대회의 특성을 알리는 말이므로 질문의 핵심과 관련 없는 오답. / winner에서 연상되는 contest를 사용한 오답.

| 어휘 | award winner 수상자 announce ~을 발표하다 entry 출품(작), 참가 deadline 마감시한 have a chance 가능성이 있다 annual 연례의, 해마다의 photography 사진 촬영

23. Aren't we supposed to turn left at this intersection?
(A) They haven't arrived yet.
(B) There's bad traffic that way.
(C) We divided it into sections.

이 교차로에서 좌회전해야 하는 것 아닌가요? (= ~ 좌회전해야 하죠?)
(A) 그들은 아직 도착하지 않았어요.
(B) 그 길은 교통 상황이 좋지 않아요.
(C) 우리는 그것을 여러 부분으로 나눴어요.

| 해설 |
교차로에서 좌회전해야 하는 것이 아닌지 확인하기 위한 Aren't 부정 의문문에 대해 그 방향을 that way로 지칭해 교통 상황이 좋지 않다는 말로 좌회전할 필요가 없음을 나타내는 (B)가 정답.
(A) 교차로에서 좌회전하는 일과 관련 없는 도착 여부를 언급하는 오답.
(C) 뭔가를 분리 또는 구분할 때 할 수 있는 말이므로 질문의 핵심과 관련 없는 오답. / intersection과 발음이 비슷한 section을 사용한 오답.

| 어휘 | intersection 교차로 arrive 도착하다 traffic 교통, 차량들 that way 그쪽에, 그 길에 divide A into B A를 B로 나누다 section 부분, 영역, 부문

24. Didn't you renew the magazine subscription?
(A) On the second page.
(B) I think it's a used one.
(C) They nearly doubled the price.

잡지 구독 서비스를 갱신하지 않으셨나요? (= ~ 갱신하셨죠?)
(A) 두 번째 페이지예요.
(B) 제 생각에 그건 중고인 것 같아요.
(C) 그곳이 가격을 거의 두 배로 올렸습니다.

| 해설 |
잡지 구독 서비스를 갱신했는지 여부를 묻는 Didn't 부정 의문문에 대해 가격을 두 배로 올렸다는 말로 갱신하지 않았음을 나타내는 (C)가 정답.
(A) 특정 페이지를 말하는 답변이므로 Where 의문문에 어울리는 오답.
(B) 잡지 구독 갱신 여부가 아닌 제품의 사용 상태를 말하고 있어 질문의 핵심에서 벗어난 오답.

| 어휘 | renew ~을 갱신하다 subscription 구독, 서비스 가입 used 중고의 nearly 거의 double ~을 두 배로 만들다

25. You're a fan of poetry, aren't you?
(A) Yes, I read it quite often.
(B) A new best-seller.
(C) From the public library.

당신은 시를 좋아하는 팬이죠, 그렇지 않나요?
(A) 네, 꽤 자주 읽습니다.
(B) 신작 베스트셀러요.
(C) 공공 도서관에서요.

| 해설 |
상대방이 시를 좋아하는 사람인지 묻는 부가 의문문에 대해 긍정을 뜻하는 Yes와 함께, 시를 좋아한다는 사실에 대한 근거를 언급하는 (A)가 정답.
(B) 책의 특징을 말하는 답변이므로 질문의 핵심에서 벗어난 오답.
(C) 출처를 언급하고 있으므로 Where 의문문에 어울리는 오답.

| 어휘 | poetry 시 quite 꽤, 상당히

DAY 09 비 의문사 의문문 (3)

01 선택 의문문

PRACTICE | 기출 연습하기 본책 p.59
정답 1 (A) 2 (B) 3 (A) 4 (C) 5 (C) 6 (B)

1. Should we use a recruitment agency or look for applicants ourselves?
(A) Either will work fine.
(B) Yes, you have a point.
(C) The deadline has changed.

채용 대행사를 이용해야 하나요, 아니면 우리가 직접 지원자들을 찾아야 하나요?
(A) 둘 중 어느 것이든 잘 될 거예요.
(B) 네, 일리 있는 말씀이요.
(C) 마감 시한이 변경되었어요.

| 해설 |
지원자를 찾는 일과 관련해 두 가지 방법을 놓고 묻는 선택 의문문에 대해 둘 중 어느 것이든 좋다고 답변하는 (A)가 정답.
(B) 선택 의문문에 맞지 않는 Yes로 답변하는 오답.
(C) 마감 시한을 언급하는 말이므로 질문의 핵심에서 벗어난 오답.

| 어휘 | recruitment agency 채용 대행사 look for ~을 찾다 applicant 지원자, 신청자 either 둘 중 어느 것이든 work fine 잘 되다 you have a point 일리 있는 말씀입니다 deadline 마감 시한

2. Should we have four or five experts on the discussion panel?
(A) To discuss economic issues.
(B) I think four is plenty.
(C) Next Friday at five.

토론 위원단에 전문가들이 4명 있어야 하나요, 5명 있어야 하나요?
(A) 경제 문제를 논의하기 위해서요.
(B) 4명이면 충분한 것 같아요.
(C) 다음 금요일 5시에요.

| 해설 |
토론 위원단에 필요한 전문가의 인원수와 관련해 묻는 선택 의문문에 대해 4명을 언급하는 (B)가 정답.
(A) 목적을 나타내는 to부정사구로 답변하고 있으므로 Why 의문문에 어울리는 오답.
(C) 미래 시점 표현이므로 When 의문문에 어울리는 오답.

| 어휘 | expert 전문가 discussion 토론, 논의 panel (토론 등을 하는) 위원단, 패널 discuss ~을 논의하다 economic 경제의, 경제에 관한 issue 문제, 사안 plenty 충분한, 많은

3. Would you prefer a table in the dining room or on the patio?
(A) I prefer to sit inside.
(B) It received excellent reviews.
(C) I'd like an appetizer.

식당 내에 있는 테이블과 테라스에 있는 테이블 중에 어떤 쪽을 선호하시나요?
(A) 저는 실내에 앉는 것을 선호합니다.
(B) 그것은 대단한 호평을 받았습니다.
(C) 애피타이저를 먹고 싶습니다.

| 해설 |
식당에서 앉을 자리와 관련해 묻는 선택 의문문에 대해 실내에 앉는 것을 선호한다는 말로 식당 내의 테이블에 앉겠다는 의사를 밝히는 (A)가 정답.
(B) it이 가리키는 구체적 대상이 무엇인지 알 수 없으므로 오답.
(C) 음식의 종류를 언급하는 말이므로 질문의 핵심에서 벗어난 오답.

| 어휘 | patio 테라스 prefer to do ~하는 것을 선호하다 receive ~을 받다 appetizer (주 요리 전에 나오는) 애피타이저

4. Would you like the suitcase in canvas or leather?
(A) In the display case.
(B) I can carry it.
(C) Which one lasts longer?

캔버스 천으로 된 것과 가죽으로 된 것 중에서 어느 여행 가방이 좋으신가요?
(A) 진열장 안에요.
(B) 제가 옮길 수 있습니다.
(C) 어느 것이 더 오래 가나요?

| 해설 |
여행 가방의 재질과 관련해 두 가지 종류를 제시하는 선택 의문문에 대해 어느 한쪽을 선택하기 위한 조건을 먼저 확인하는 (C)가 정답.
(A) 위치 표현이므로 Where 의문문에 어울리는 오답.
(B) it이 가리키는 특정 대상이 무엇인지 알 수 없으므로 오답.

| 어휘 | suitcase 여행 가방 canvas 캔버스 천 leather 가죽 display case 진열장 carry ~을 옮기다, 나르다 last 지속되다 longer 더 오래

5. Should we order Chinese or Italian food?
(A) They can deliver it.
(B) She speaks a few languages.
(C) I'm still full from lunch.

중식 요리와 이탈리안 요리 중에 어느 것을 주문해야 하나요?
(A) 그쪽에서 그것을 배달해 줄 수 있습니다.
(B) 그녀는 몇 가지 다른 언어를 할 줄 압니다.
(C) 저는 여전히 점심 먹은 게 배가 불러요.

| 해설 |
주문할 음식과 관련해 두 가지 음식 종류를 놓고 묻는 선택 의문문에 대해 여전히 배가 부르다는 말로 어느 것도 선택하지 않겠다는 뜻을 나타낸 (C)가 정답.
(A) 배달 가능 여부와 관련된 답변이므로 질문의 핵심에서 벗어난 오답.
(B) 가리키는 대상을 알 수 없는 She를 언급한 오답.

| 어휘 | order ~을 주문하다   deliver ~을 배달하다, 배송하다   a few 몇몇의, 몇 가지의   full 배가 부른

6. Do I make the reservations, or does the secretary handle them?
(A) I'm booked on a flight to Cairo.
(B) Let him take care of everything.
(C) At the Rosemont Hotel.

제가 예약을 하는 건가요, 아니면 비서가 처리해 주나요?
(A) 저는 Cairo행 항공편이 예약되어 있어요.
(B) 그에게 모든 것을 처리하게 하세요.
(C) Rosemont 호텔이에요.

| 해설 |
예약 업무의 주체와 관련해 묻는 선택 의문문에 대해 secretary를 him으로 지칭해 그 사람에게 맡기라고 답변하는 (B)가 정답.
(A) 자신이 예약한 항공편을 언급하는 말이므로 질문의 핵심에서 벗어난 오답. / reservations에서 연상되는 booked를 사용한 오답.
(C) 특정 호텔을 언급하고 있으므로 예약의 주체와 관련 없는 오답.

| 어휘 | secretary 비서   handle(= take care of) ~을 처리하다, 다루다   book A on B A를 B에 예약해 주다   let A do A에게 ~하게 하다

02 평서문

PRACTICE | 기출 연습하기   본책 p.61

정답 1 (C)   2 (C)   3 (A)   4 (A)   5 (C)   6 (B)

1. Be careful to lock the laboratory door on your way out.
(A) No, not very often.
(B) A cutting-edge experiment.
(C) Okay, I'll make sure I do.

나가시는 길에 실험실 문을 잠그는 것을 명심하세요.
(A) 아뇨, 그렇게 자주는 아니에요.
(B) 최첨단 실험입니다.
(C) 알겠습니다, 반드시 그렇게 하겠습니다.

| 해설 |
나갈 때 실험실 문을 잠그도록 당부하는 평서문에 대해 수락을 나타내는 Okay와 함께 그렇게 하겠다고 약속하는 (C)가 정답.
(A) 거절을 뜻하는 No로 답변하고 있지만, 뒤에 이어지는 말이 핵심에서 벗어난 오답.
(B) 실험의 종류를 언급하는 말이므로 당부에 대한 답변으로 맞지 않는 오답. / laboratory에서 연상되는 experiment를 사용한 오답.

| 어휘 | lock ~을 잠그다   laboratory 실험실, 연구실   on one's way out 나가는 길에   cutting-edge 최첨단의   experiment 실험   make sure 반드시 ~하다

2. The maintenance team will repair the floorboards tomorrow.
(A) She's on the third floor.
(B) I got a new pair.
(C) Thanks for informing me.

시설 관리팀이 내일 마룻바닥을 수리할 거예요.
(A) 그녀는 3층에 있습니다.
(B) 저는 새로 한 짝을 구했습니다.
(C) 알려 주셔서 감사합니다.

| 해설 |
시설 관리팀이 내일 수리 작업을 한다는 사실을 알리는 평서문에 대해 그 사실을 알려 준 것에 대해 감사 인사를 하는 (C)가 정답.
(A) 대상을 알 수 없는 She를 언급한 오답. / floorboards와 발음이 비슷한 floor를 사용한 오답.
(B) 자신이 과거 시점에 한 일을 말하는 답변이므로 핵심에서 벗어난 오답. / repair와 발음이 비슷한 pair를 사용한 오답.

| 어휘 | maintenance 시설 관리, 유지 관리   repair ~을 수리하다   floorboards 마루 바닥   inform ~에게 알리다

3. I'm planning to move to my new apartment this weekend.
(A) You're welcome to borrow my truck.
(B) No, I decided to renew my lease.
(C) Isn't the department doing well?

저는 이번 주말에 새 아파트로 이사할 계획입니다.
(A) 언제든지 제 트럭을 빌려가셔도 좋습니다.
(B) 아뇨, 저는 임대 계약을 갱신하기로 결정했어요.
(C) 그 부서는 잘 하고 있지 않나요?

| 해설 |
이번 주말에 새 아파트로 이사할 계획임을 알리는 평서문에 대해 자신의 트럭을 빌려가도 좋다는 말로 이사하는 데 필요한 도움을 제공하겠다는 뜻을 나타낸 (A)가 정답.
(B) 답변자 자신의 임대 계약 갱신 결정 여부를 밝히는 답변이므로 핵심에서 벗어난 오답. / move ~ apartment에서 연상되는 lease를 사용한 오답.
(C) 이사와 관련 없는, 부서의 업무 진행 상태를 묻고 있어 핵심에서 벗어난 오답. / apartment와 발음이 비슷한 department를 사용한 오답.

| 어휘 | plan to do ~할 계획이다   move to ~로 이사하다   be welcome to do 언제든지 ~해도 좋다   borrow ~을 빌리다   decide to do ~하기로 결정하다   renew ~을 갱신하다   lease 임대 계약(서)   department 부서

4. Your report seems to be missing the last page.
(A) Sorry, let me print another copy.
(B) The reporter works for a local paper.
(C) Unfortunately, I missed my flight.

당신 보고서는 마지막 페이지가 빠진 것 같아요.
(A) 죄송합니다, 한 장 다시 출력하겠습니다.
(B) 그 기자는 지역 신문사에서 근무합니다.
(C) 안타깝게도, 저는 비행기를 놓쳤어요.

| 해설 |
보고서에 마지막 페이지가 빠져 있다는 문제점을 알리는 평서문에 대해 사과의 말과 함께 다시 출력하겠다는 말로 해결책을 제시하는 (A)가 정답.
(B) 가리키는 대상을 알 수 없는 The reporter를 언급한 오답. / report와 발음이 비슷한 reporter를 사용한 오답.
(C) 과거 시점에 항공편을 놓친 사실을 밝히고 있으므로 핵심에서 벗어난 오답. / missing과 발음이 비슷한 missed를 사용한 오답.

| 어휘 | copy 한 장, 한 부, 한 권   work for ~에서 근무하다   local 지역의, 현지의   unfortunately 안타깝게도, 아쉽게도

5. Let's conduct the performance reviews today.
(A) Did you enjoy the musical performance?
(B) Yes, a construction company.
(C) We can postpone that to next week.

오늘 업무 능력 평가를 실시합시다.
(A) 음악 공연이 즐거우셨나요?
(B) 네, 건설회사입니다.
(C) 그 일은 다음 주로 연기해도 됩니다.

| 해설 |
오늘 평가를 실시하자고 권하는 평서문에 대해 그 일을 that으로 지칭해 다음 주로 연기해도 된다는 말로 오늘 할 필요가 없음을 밝히는 (C)가 정답.
(A) 과거 시점에 있었던 공연에 대한 의견을 묻고 있으므로 핵심에서 벗어난 오답. / 질문의 performance를 반복 사용한 오답.
(B) 동의를 뜻하는 Yes로 답변하고 있지만 뒤에 이어지는 말이 핵심과 관련 없는 오답.

| 어휘 | conduct ~을 실시하다, 수행하다 performance 업무 능력, 성과, 실적, 공연, 연주 review 평가, 검토, 의견, 후기 construction 공사, 건설 postpone A to B A를 B로 연기하다, 미루다

6. The repairs to your vehicle's engine have been completed.
(A) A few old components.
(B) You're finished already?
(C) I usually drive to work.

고객님의 차량 엔진에 대한 수리 작업이 완료되었습니다.
(A) 몇몇 낡은 부품들이요.
(B) 벌써 끝내셨나요?
(C) 저는 보통 차를 운전해 출근합니다.

| 해설 |
차량 엔진에 대한 수리 작업이 완료되었음을 알리는 평서문에 대해 빨리 끝난 것에 대한 놀라움을 나타내는 (B)가 정답.
(A) 부품의 특성을 말하는 답변이므로 핵심에서 벗어난 오답. / engine에서 연상되는 components를 사용한 오답.
(C) 자신의 평소 출근 방식을 말하고 있으므로 핵심에서 벗어난 오답. / vehicle에서 연상되는 drive를 사용한 오답.

| 어휘 | repair 수리 vehicle 차량 complete ~을 완료하다, 완수하다 component 부품 usually 보통, 일반적으로

DAY 09 | 실전문제
본책 p.62

정답
1 (A) 2 (A) 3 (A) 4 (A) 5 (C) 6 (A)
7 (A) 8 (B) 9 (B) 10 (B) 11 (A) 12 (B)
13 (B) 14 (C) 15 (B) 16 (B) 17 (B) 18 (B)
19 (B) 20 (C) 21 (C) 22 (B) 23 (B) 24 (A)
25 (C)

1. Are you interested in the metal or wooden file cabinets?
(A) The metal ones, please.
(B) I thought the talk was interesting.
(C) They have three drawers.

금속 파일 캐비닛과 목재 파일 캐비닛 중에 어느 것에 관심이 있으세요?
(A) 금속으로 된 것으로 주세요.
(B) 연설이 흥미롭다고 생각했어요.
(C) 그것들은 서랍이 3개입니다.

| 해설 |
파일 캐비닛의 두 가지 재질을 언급하는 선택 의문문에 대해 금속 제품을 선택하여 답하는 (A)가 정답.
(B) 담화에 대한 자신의 의견을 밝히는 말이므로 질문의 핵심에서 벗어난 오답. / interested와 발음이 비슷한 interesting을 사용한 오답.
(C) 서랍의 개수를 말하고 있으므로 질문에서 묻는 재질과 관련 없는 오답. / cabinet에서 연상되는 drawer를 사용한 오답.

| 어휘 | be interested in ~에 관심이 있다 wooden 목재로 된 drawer 서랍

2. Should we book a direct flight or have a layover somewhere?
(A) Direct flights are expensive.
(B) The annual medical conference.
(C) I don't see why not.

직항편을 예매해야 하나요, 아니면 어디선가 경유해야 하나요?
(A) 직항편은 비쌉니다.
(B) 연례 의료 콘퍼런스요.
(C) 안 될 이유가 없죠.

| 해설 |
예매할 항공편과 관련해 두 가지 종류를 놓고 묻는 선택 의문문에 대해 직항편이 비싸다는 말로 간접적으로 경유하는 항공편을 선택하고 있는 (A)가 정답.
(B) 행사의 종류를 말하고 있으므로 질문의 핵심에서 벗어난 오답.
(C) 동의나 허락을 나타낼 때 사용하는 말이므로 질문의 핵심과 관련 없는 오답.

| 어휘 | direct flight 직항편 layover 경유(지), 기착지 annual 연례적인, 해마다의 I don't see why not 안 될 이유가 없죠, 되고 말고요

3. Pardon me, Mr. Bradley needs to sign for this parcel.
(A) Try office 417.
(B) You can get more at the post office.
(C) He couldn't agree more.

실례합니다만, Bradley 씨가 이 소포에 서명하셔야 합니다.
(A) 417호 사무실로 가 보세요.
(B) 우체국에서 더 구하실 수 있어요.
(C) 그는 전적으로 동의했어요.

| 해설 |
Bradley 씨가 소포에 서명해야 한다는 사실을 밝히는 평서문에 대해 그 사람을 만날 수 있는 장소를 알려 주는 (A)가 정답.
(B) 물품 구입 방법에 해당되는 말이므로 핵심에서 벗어난 오답. / parcel에서 연상되는 post office를 사용한 오답.
(C) He가 Mr. Bradley를 지칭하는 것으로 생각할 수 있지만 뒤에 이어지는 말이 맞지 않는 오답.

| 어휘 | sign ~에 서명하다 parcel 소포 try ~에 한번 가 보다, ~을 한번 해 보다

4. The author's second book was not as good.
(A) Right. I preferred the first one too.
(B) No, this is my second visit.
(C) The bookstore opens at eight o'clock.

그 작가의 두 번째 책은 그렇게 좋지 않았어요.
(A) 맞아요. 저도 첫 번째 것이 더 좋았어요.
(B) 아뇨, 이번이 제 두 번째 방문입니다.
(C) 그 서점은 8시에 문을 엽니다.

| 해설 |
한 작가의 두 번째 책이 그렇게 좋지 않았다는 의견을 말하는 평서문에 대해 동의를 나타내는 Right과 함께 그 이유를 덧붙인 (A)가 정답.
(B) 부정을 나타내는 No 뒤에 이어지는 말이 특정 책에 대한 의견과 관련 없는 오답.

(C) 서점이 문을 여는 시간을 말하고 있으므로 When 의문문에 어울리는 오답.

| 어휘 | author 작가, 저자   not as good 그렇게 좋지 않은   prefer ~을 더 좋아하다, 선호하다

5. I'm having trouble logging on to the database.
(A) Today's date is July 28.
(B) A recent research project.
(C) Let me give you a hand.

제가 데이터베이스에 로그인하는 데 문제를 겪고 있어요.
(A) 오늘 날짜는 7월 28일입니다.
(B) 최근의 연구 프로젝트요.
(C) 제가 도와 드릴게요.

| 해설 |

데이터베이스에 로그인하는 데 문제를 겪고 있다고 알리는 평서문에 대해 자신이 도와 주겠다고 제안하는 (C)가 정답.
(A) 오늘 날짜를 알리는 말이므로 핵심에서 벗어난 오답. / database와 발음이 비슷한 date를 사용한 오답.
(B) 가까운 과거에 있었던 연구 프로젝트를 언급하고 있으므로 핵심에서 벗어난 오답. / database에서 연상되는 research를 사용한 오답.

| 어휘 | have trouble -ing ~하는 데 문제를 겪다, 어려움이 있다   log on to ~에 로그인하다   recent 최근의   research 연구, 조사   Let me do 제가 ~해 드릴게요   give A a hand A를 도와 주다

6. Sorry, but the sales team has the conference room reserved.
(A) OK, we'll be finished in a minute.
(B) In the restaurant's private room.
(C) Where are the discounted items?

죄송하지만, 영업팀이 대회의실을 예약해 두었습니다.
(A) 알겠어요, 저희는 금방 끝납니다.
(B) 그 레스토랑의 개별 식사 공간에서요.
(C) 할인 제품들은 어디에 있나요?

| 해설 |

영업팀이 대회의실을 예약해 둔 상태임을 알리는 평서문에 대해 곧 끝난다는 말로 영업팀을 위해 자리를 비워주겠다고 알리는 (A)가 정답.
(B) 회의실이 아닌 특정 레스토랑 이용 상황과 관련된 말이므로 핵심에서 벗어난 오답.
(C) 회의실이 아닌 할인 제품 이용과 관련해 되묻는 말이므로 핵심에서 벗어난 오답.

| 어휘 | sales 영업, 판매, 매출   have A p.p. A가 ~되게 하다, A를 ~해 두다   reserve ~을 예약하다   in a minute 금방, 잠시 후에   private 사적인, 개별적인, 전용의   discounted 할인된

7. I could move you to a quieter workstation if that's better.
(A) Thanks, but it's not necessary.
(B) I live near Freemont Station.
(C) Please e-mail me the latest copy.

더 조용한 업무 공간이 더 나을 것 같으시면 제가 옮겨 드릴 수 있어요.
(A) 감사합니다만, 그러실 필요는 없습니다.
(B) 저는 Freemont역 근처에 살고 있어요.
(C) 최신본을 제게 이메일로 보내 주세요.

| 해설 |

더 조용한 업무 공간으로 옮겨 줄 수 있다고 제안하는 평서문에 대해 그럴 필요 없다는 말로 거절 의사를 밝힌 (A)가 정답.
(B) 거주 지역을 알리는 말이므로 핵심에서 벗어난 오답.
(C) 이메일로 자료를 보내도록 요청하는 말이므로 핵심에서 벗어난 오답.

| 어휘 | move A to B A를 B로 옮기다   workstation 업무 공간, 근무 자리   necessary 필요한, 필수의   near ~ 근처에   latest 최신의   copy 한 부, 한 장, 한 권

8. Would you like to rent an SUV or a hybrid car?
(A) I rent a two-bedroom apartment.
(B) Does the hybrid have trunk space?
(C) Yes, that sounds perfect.

SUV와 하이브리드 차량 중 어느 것을 대여하고 싶으신가요?
(A) 저는 방 2개짜리 아파트를 임대해요.
(B) 하이브리드 차량에 트렁크 공간이 있나요?
(C) 네, 아주 좋습니다.

| 해설 |

대여할 차량의 종류 두 가지를 놓고 묻는 선택 의문문에 대해 하이브리드 차량을 선택하기 위한 조건으로 트렁크 공간의 존재 여부를 먼저 확인하는 (B)가 정답.
(A) 아파트 임대에 관한 답변이므로 질문의 핵심에서 벗어난 오답. / 질문의 rent를 반복 사용한 오답.
(C) 선택 의문문에 맞지 않는 Yes로 답변하는 오답.

| 어휘 | rent ~을 대여하다, 임대하다   that sounds perfect 아주 좋습니다, 완벽한 것 같아요

9. Should we wait for the elevator or take the stairs?
(A) The staff is taking a break.
(B) These boxes are difficult to carry.
(C) His office was recently moved.

엘리베이터를 기다려야 하나요, 아니면 계단을 이용해야 하나요?
(A) 직원들이 휴식 중입니다.
(B) 이 상자들은 옮기기 힘들어요.
(C) 그의 사무실은 최근에 이전되었어요.

| 해설 |

두 가지 이동 수단을 언급하는 선택 의문문에 대해 상자들이 옮기기엔 힘들다는 말로 엘리베이터를 타는 쪽을 선택한 (B)가 정답.
(A) 직원들이 현재 하고 있는 일을 말하고 있으므로 질문의 핵심에서 벗어난 오답.
(C) 가리키는 대상을 알 수 없는 His를 언급한 오답.

| 어휘 | take the stairs 계단을 이용하다   take a break 휴식하다   carry 옮기다, 나르다   recently 최근에

10. The investors from Singapore will visit the office tomorrow.
(A) A major source of funding.
(B) Our department is ready for them.
(C) I've been there a few times.

싱가포르에서 오시는 투자자들께서 내일 사무실을 방문하실 겁니다.
(A) 주요 자금 공급처요.
(B) 저희 부서는 그분들을 맞이할 준비가 되어 있습니다.
(C) 저는 그곳에 몇 번 가 봤어요.

| 해설 |

싱가포르에서 오는 투자자들이 내일 사무실을 방문할 예정임을 알리는 평서문에 대해 investors를 them으로 지칭해 그 사람들을 맞이할 준비가 되어 있음을 알리는 (B)가 정답.
(A) 투자자 방문 행사가 아닌 자금 공급 방법과 관련된 답변이므로 핵심에서 벗어난 오답. / investors에서 연상되는 funding을 사용한 오답.
(C) 과거에 특정 장소를 방문한 경험에 관해 말하고 있으므로 핵심에서 벗어난 오답.

| 어휘 | investor 투자자   major 주요한   source 공급원, 원천, 출처   funding 자금 (제공)   department 부서   be ready for ~에 대한 준비가 되다   a few times 몇 번, 몇 차례

11. We should talk about the decorations for the retirement party.
(A) I'm not busy tomorrow.
(B) At least fifty guests.
(C) A speech from the CEO.

우리는 은퇴 기념 파티에 필요한 장식품들에 관해 논의해야 합니다.
(A) 저는 내일 바쁘지 않습니다.
(B) 최소한 50명의 손님들이요.
(C) 대표이사님의 연설이요.

| 해설 | 은퇴 기념 파티에 필요한 장식품들에 관해 얘기하자고 제안하는 평서문에 대해 내일 바쁘지 않다는 말로 수락/동의의 의사를 밝히는 (A)가 정답.
(B) 초대 손님의 숫자를 언급하고 있으므로 How many 의문문에 어울리는 오답. / party에서 연상되는 guests를 사용한 오답.
(C) 연설자의 신분을 알리는 말이므로 핵심에서 벗어난 오답.

| 어휘 | decoration 장식(물)   retirement 은퇴, 퇴직   at least 최소한, 적어도   speech 연설

12. Should we rent a car or rely on public transportation?
(A) A variety of vehicles.
(B) I don't mind driving.
(C) It was a business trip.

차를 대여해야 하나요, 아니면 대중교통에 의존해야 하나요?
(A) 다양한 차량들이요.
(B) 저는 운전해도 상관없어요.
(C) 출장이었습니다.

| 해설 | 이용할 교통 수단과 관련해 두 가지 종류를 언급하는 선택 의문문에 대해 운전해도 상관없다는 말로 차량을 대여하는 쪽을 선택하는 (B)가 정답.
(A) 차량의 종류와 관련된 답변이므로 질문의 핵심에서 벗어난 오답. / car에서 연상되는 vehicles를 사용한 오답.
(C) 여행의 목적과 관련된 말이므로 질문의 핵심에서 벗어난 오답.

| 어휘 | rent ~을 대여하다, 임대하다   rely on ~에 의존하다   public transportation 대중교통   a variety of 다양한   vehicle 차량   don't mind -ing ~해도 상관없다   business trip 출장

13. Do you want to prepare the guest list for the party, or should I?
(A) I think Friday night would be best.
(B) Well, I'm not sure who should come.
(C) Yes, they're planning to attend.

파티에 필요한 초대 손님 명단을 준비하고 싶으신가요, 아니면 제가 할까요?
(A) 금요일 밤이 가장 좋을 것 같아요.
(B) 글쎄요, 저는 누가 와야 하는지 잘 모르겠어요.
(C) 네, 그들은 참석할 계획을 세우고 있어요.

| 해설 | 초대 손님 명단 준비를 할 사람을 정하는 선택 의문문에 대해 자신은 누가 와야 하는지 모르겠다는 말로 상대방에게 처리를 맡기는 (B)가 정답.
(A) 시점을 말하는 답변이므로 When 의문문에 어울리는 오답.
(C) 의문문 두 개가 or로 연결된 선택 의문문에는 Yes/No로 응답할 수 있으나 가리키는 대상을 알 수 없는 they로 답변하고 있으므로 오답.

| 어휘 | prepare ~을 준비하다   plan to do ~할 계획이다   attend 참석하다

14. The building renovations will begin next week.
(A) I'd be happy to.
(B) He approved the guest list?
(C) Who told you that?

건물 개조 공사가 다음 주에 시작될 겁니다.
(A) 기꺼이 그렇게 하겠습니다.
(B) 그분이 초대 손님 명단을 승인했나요?
(C) 누가 그걸 말해주었나요?

| 해설 | 건물 개조 공사가 다음 주에 시작된다고 알리는 평서문에 대해 해당 정보를 that으로 지칭해 누가 그 말을 했는지 되묻는 것으로 놀라움을 나타내는 (C)가 정답.
(A) 요청 등에 대해 수락을 나타낼 때 할 수 있는 말이므로 핵심에서 벗어난 오답.
(B) 가리키는 대상을 알 수 없는 He를 언급한 오답.

| 어휘 | renovation 개조, 보수   be happy to do 기꺼이 ~하다   approve ~을 승인하다   tell A B A에게 B를 말하다

15. I'd like to discuss my business loan with Ms. Marshall.
(A) Mainly for startup companies.
(B) She's transferred to another branch.
(C) No, the discussion was quite friendly.

Marshall 씨와 제 사업 대출 문제를 논의하고 싶습니다.
(A) 주로 신생 기업들을 위해서요.
(B) 그분은 다른 지점으로 전근했습니다.
(C) 아뇨, 논의가 꽤 우호적이었어요.

| 해설 | Marshall 씨와 사업 대출 문제를 논의하고 싶다는 뜻을 나타내는 평서문에 대해 Ms. Marshall을 She로 지칭해 다른 곳으로 전근한 상태라 논의가 불가능하다고 말하는 (B)가 정답.
(A) 대출금의 용도와 관련된 말이므로 핵심에서 벗어난 오답. / business loan에서 연상되는 startup companies를 사용한 오답.
(C) 과거 시점(was)에 있었던 일을 말하고 있으므로 앞으로 하려는 일을 언급하는 상황에 맞지 않는 오답.

| 어휘 | discuss ~을 논의하다   loan 대출   mainly 주로   startup company 신생 기업   transfer to ~로 전근하다   branch 지점, 지사   discussion 논의, 토론   quite 꽤, 상당히   friendly 우호적인

16. The dentist can see you tomorrow or Friday.
(A) The store closes early on Saturdays.
(B) Later in the week would be better.
(C) An annual checkup.

치과 의사 선생님께서 내일 또는 금요일에 당신을 진료해 드릴 수 있습니다.
(A) 그 매장은 토요일에 일찍 문을 닫습니다.
(B) 이번 주 후반이 더 좋겠어요.
(C) 연례 검진입니다.

| 해설 | 진료 가능한 두 시점을 제시하는 평서문에 대해 이번 주 후반이 더 좋겠다는 말로 금요일을 선택하는 (B)가 정답.
(A) 한 매장이 매주 일반적으로 문을 닫는 요일을 언급하고 있으므로 질문의 핵심에서 벗어난 오답.
(C) 검진의 종류를 말하는 답변이므로 질문의 핵심과 관련 없는 오답. / dentist에서 연상되는 annual checkup을 사용한 오답.

| 어휘 | dentist 치과 의사   later in the week 이번 주 후반   annual 연례적인, 해마다의   checkup (정기) 검진, 점검

17. I'm not sure how to get the copy machine to print double-sided.
(A) I would appreciate that.
(B) The presentation slides.
(C) I don't have the manual.

저는 복사기로 양면 인쇄하는 방법을 잘 모르겠습니다.
(A) 그렇게 해 주시면 감사하겠습니다.
(B) 발표용 슬라이드요.
(C) 저는 설명서가 없습니다.

| 해설 |
복사기로 양면 인쇄하는 방법을 잘 모른다는 평서문에 대해 설명서를 갖고 있지 않아 답변자 자신도 알지 못한다고 밝히는 (C)가 정답.
(A) 감사 인사에 해당되는 말이므로 문제점을 알리는 상황에 어울리지 않는 오답.
(B) 자료의 용도와 관련된 말이므로 핵심에서 벗어난 오답.

| 어휘 | how to do ~하는 법   get A to do A가 ~하게 하다   print double-sided 양면 인쇄하다   appreciate ~에 대해 감사하다   presentation 발표(회)   manual 설명서, 안내서

18. I can't find the list of workshop participants.
(A) That's where I buy my clothing.
(B) Ask Molly to e-mail it again.
(C) It will cover leadership skills.

워크숍 참가자 명단을 찾을 수가 없어요.
(A) 그곳이 제가 옷을 사는 곳입니다.
(B) Molly 씨에게 다시 이메일로 보내 달라고 요청하세요.
(C) 리더십 능력에 대해서 다룰 겁니다.

| 해설 |
워크숍 참가자 명단을 찾을 수 없다고 알리는 평서문에 대해 list를 it으로 지칭해 그것을 다시 구할 수 있는 방법을 알려 주는 (B)가 정답.
(A) 답변자 자신의 의류 구매 장소에 관한 내용이므로 대화 상황과 무관한 오답.
(C) 워크숍 주제에 관한 내용이므로 대화 상황과 무관한 오답. / workshop에서 연상되는 leadership skills를 사용한 오답.

| 어휘 | participant 참가자   clothing 옷, 의류   ask A to do A에게 ~하도록 요청하다   cover (주제 등) ~을 다루다   skill 능력, 기술

19. Should we post the information on the company Web site or the bulletin board?
(A) A list of potential clients.
(B) Some employees don't have online access.
(C) Thanks for discovering the errors.

그 정보를 회사 웹사이트에 게시해야 하나요, 아니면 공고판에 게시해야 하나요?
(A) 잠재 고객 명단이요.
(B) 일부 직원들은 온라인으로 접속하지 못합니다.
(C) 오류를 발견해 주셔서 감사합니다.

| 해설 |
정보 공유와 관련해 두 가지 방법을 놓고 묻는 선택 의문문에 대해 일부 직원들이 온라인으로 접속하지 못한다는 말로 공고판에 게시하는 쪽을 선택하는 (B)가 정답.
(A) 명단의 내용을 나타내는 말이므로 질문의 핵심에서 벗어난 오답.
(C) 감사 인사에 해당되는 답변이므로 선택 의문문에 대한 반응으로 맞지 않는 오답.

| 어휘 | post ~을 게시하다   bulletin board 공고판, 게시판   potential 잠재적인   access 접속, 접근, 이용   discover ~을 발견하다

20. A leather briefcase was left in the conference room.
(A) The contract negotiations.
(B) I'll keep my comments brief.
(C) Steve was just in there.

가죽 서류 가방 하나가 회의실에 놓여 있었어요.
(A) 계약 협상이요.

(B) 제 의견을 간단히 말씀드릴게요.
(C) Steve 씨가 조금 전에 그곳에 있었어요.

| 해설 |
가죽 서류 가방이 회의실에 놓여 있었다고 알리는 평서문에 대해 그 장소를 there로 지칭해 Steve 씨가 그곳에 있었다는 말로 Steve 씨의 물건임을 나타낸 (C)가 정답.
(A) 회의의 내용에 해당되는 말이므로 핵심에서 벗어난 오답.
(B) 회의 등에서 의견을 제시하기 전에 할 수 있는 말이므로 상황에 맞지 않는 오답. / briefcase와 발음이 비슷한 brief를 사용한 오답.

| 어휘 | leather 가죽   briefcase 서류 가방   be left in ~에 놓여 있다, 남겨져 있다   contract 계약(서)   negotiation 협상, 협의   keep A brief A를 간단하게 하다   comment 의견

21. This museum has the best collection of sculptures.
(A) The guide is waiting for us.
(B) Discounted tickets for senior citizens.
(C) You haven't been to the Harmony Gallery, have you?

이 박물관은 최고의 조각품들을 소장하고 있습니다.
(A) 가이드가 우리를 기다리고 있어요.
(B) 노인들을 위한 할인 입장권이요.
(C) Harmony Gallery에 가본 적 없으시죠, 그렇죠?

| 해설 |
박물관이 최고의 조각품들을 소장하고 있다고 말하는 평서문에 대해 특정 미술관을 언급해 그곳에 가보지 않았으니 그런 이야기를 하는 거라는 뜻으로 상대방의 의견에 동의하지 않음을 나타내는 (C)가 정답.
(A) 조각품들에 관한 의견이 아닌 가이드의 대기 상태와 관련된 말이므로 핵심에서 벗어난 오답.
(B) 마찬가지로, 조각품이 아닌 입장권 종류와 관련된 말이므로 핵심에서 벗어난 오답. / museum에서 연상되는 discounted tickets를 사용한 오답.

| 어휘 | collection 소장(품), 수집(품)   sculpture 조각품   wait for ~을 기다리다   discounted 할인된   senior citizen 노인   have been to ~에 가 본 적이 있다

22. Would you prefer the chicken salad or the tomato soup?
(A) This café is very popular.
(B) Actually, a sandwich is enough.
(C) I have my own vegetable garden.

치킨 샐러드가 더 좋으세요, 아니면 토마토 수프가 더 좋으세요?
(A) 이 카페는 매우 인기가 좋습니다.
(B) 사실, 샌드위치면 충분합니다.
(C) 제 소유의 채소밭이 있습니다.

| 해설 |
치킨 샐러드와 토마토 수프 중에 어느 것이 더 좋은지 묻는 선택 의문문에 대해 샌드위치면 충분하다는 말로 둘 모두 선택하지 않는 (B)가 정답.
(A) 음식 종류가 아닌 카페의 인기 정도를 말하고 있어 질문의 핵심에서 벗어난 오답.
(C) 자신이 소유하고 있는 채소밭이 있음을 알리는 말이므로 마찬가지로 질문의 핵심에서 벗어난 오답.

| 어휘 | prefer ~을 더 좋아하다, 선호하다   popular 인기 있는   actually 실은, 사실은   enough 충분한   one's own 자신 소유의, 자신만의   vegetable garden 채소밭, 텃밭

23. I'm surprised that Mr. Robinson never called me back.
(A) He works in the Shipping Department.
(B) Didn't you receive an e-mail from him?
(C) Use the back entrance, then.

Robinson 씨께서 저에게 다시 전화하지 않으셔서 놀라워요.
(A) 그분은 발송부에서 근무합니다.
(B) 그분에게서 이메일을 받지 않으셨나요?
(C) 그럼 뒷문을 이용하세요.

| 해설 |
Robinson 씨가 답신 전화를 하지 않은 것이 놀랍다는 평서문에 대해 Mr. Robinson을 him으로 지칭해 전화 대신 다른 방법으로 연락한 것이 아닌지 되묻는 (B)가 정답.
(A) 근무 부서를 말하는 답변이므로 핵심에서 벗어난 오답.
(C) 뒷문을 이용하도록 부탁하는 말이므로 핵심에서 벗어난 오답. / 질문의 back을 반복 사용한 오답.

| 어휘 | call back 답신 전화하다   receive ~을 받다   back entrance 뒷문   then 그럼, 그렇다면

24. The plane will arrive about ninety minutes late.
(A) We'd better let our driver know.
(B) Gate 30 in Terminal 2.
(C) I prefer the plain style.

비행기가 약 90분 늦게 도착할 겁니다.
(A) 우리 기사님께 알려 드리는 게 좋겠어요.
(B) 2번 터미널의 30번 탑승구입니다.
(C) 저는 평범한 스타일을 선호합니다.

| 해설 |
비행기가 약 90분 늦게 도착한다고 알리는 평서문에 대해 자신들의 기사에게 그 사실을 알리는 게 좋다는 말로 후속 조치를 언급하는 (A)가 정답.
(B) 탑승 위치를 알리는 말이므로 대화 주제를 벗어난 오답.
(C) 답변자 자신이 선호하는 스타일과 관련된 의견을 말하는 답변이므로 대화 주제를 벗어난 오답. / plane과 발음이 동일한 plain을 사용한 오답.

| 어휘 | plane 비행기   arrive 도착하다   about 약, 대략   had better + 동사원형 ~하는 게 좋다   let A know A에게 알리다   prefer ~을 선호하다, 더 좋아하다   plain 평범한, 보통의, 단조로운

25. Should I throw away these bottles, or did you want to use them again?
(A) We saved about twenty dollars.
(B) Some beverages for the welcome party.
(C) Just put them in the recycling bin, thanks.

이 병들을 버려야 하나요, 아니면 다시 사용하고 싶으셨나요?
(A) 우리는 약 20달러를 절약했어요.
(B) 환영 파티에 필요한 일부 음료들이요.
(C) 그냥 재활용 쓰레기통에 넣어주세요, 고맙습니다.

| 해설 |
병을 처리하는 일과 관련해 두 가지 방법을 언급하는 선택 의문문에 대해 재활용 쓰레기통에 넣어 달라고요 청하는 (C)가 정답.
(A) 과거 시점의 일(saved)을 말하고 있으므로 미래의 일과 관련된 질문 내용에 맞지 않는 오답.
(B) 음료의 용도를 말하는 답변이므로 질문의 핵심에서 벗어난 오답. / bottle에서 연상되는 beverages를 사용한 오답.

| 어휘 | throw away ~을 버리다   save ~을 절약하다, 저축하다   about 약, 대략   beverage 음료   recycling bin 재활용 쓰레기통

DAY 10 전반적인 내용을 묻는 유형

01 주제/목적/대화 장소를 묻는 문제

기출 유형 맛보기   본책 p.64

Q. 대화는 주로 무엇에 관한 것인가?
(A) 오리엔테이션 시간 마련하기
(B) 전문적인 행사 준비하기
(C) 기조 연설자 고용하기
(D) 직원용 안내서 내용 작성하기

여1: 두 분 모두 이 회의에 참석하실 수 있어서 기쁩니다. 다음 달에 있을 콘퍼런스를 어떻게 처리할 것인지를 알아봐야 할 때입니다. 그곳에서 무엇에 중점을 두어야 할까요?
여2: 아시다시피, 행사의 첫 3일 동안만 부스를 대여했어요. 따라서 참석자들에게 강력한 인상을 남겨야 합니다.
남: 우리가 고객들을 대상으로 했었던 미디어 작업물 동영상을 준비하는 건 어떨까요? 우리가 전문적으로 만들어 낸다면, 잠재 고객들을 끌어들이게 될 거예요. Amy, 이 일에 대해서 저 좀 도와주실 수 있으세요?

PRACTICE | 기출 연습하기   본책 p.65

정답 1 (B)   2 (A)   3 (A)   4 (B)   5 (A)   6 (A)

Questions 1-2 refer to the following conversation.

W: Hi, Tristan. **1** What did you think of the new logo for our company that the design team presented in the meeting?
M: I liked the colors, but, unfortunately, I was sitting at the back of the room, so I couldn't see it very easily.
W: Oh, in that case, **2** I'll e-mail you a copy of the file. Then you'll be able to see the image in detail.

1-2번 문제는 다음 대화를 참조하시오.
여: 안녕하세요, Tristan 씨. 디자인팀이 회의에서 발표한 우리 회사의 새 로고에 대해 어떻게 생각하셨어요?
남: 색상이 마음에 들기는 했지만, 아쉽게도, 제가 회의실 뒤쪽에 앉아 있었기 때문에 잘 안보였어요.
여: 아, 그러시면, 제가 파일 복사본을 이메일로 보내 드릴게요. 그렇게 하면 그 이미지를 자세히 보실 수 있을 거예요.

1. 화자들은 주로 무엇에 관해 이야기하고 있는가?
(A) 제품 출시
(B) 회사 로고

| 해설 |
대화를 시작하면서 여자가 회사의 새 로고에 대해 어떻게 생각했는지를 (What did you think of the new logo for our company ~) 물은 뒤로 그 로고와 관련된 내용으로 대화가 진행되고 있으므로 (B)가 정답이다.

2. 여자는 무엇을 할 것이라고 말하는가?
(A) 이메일 보내기
(B) 디자인팀에 전화하기

| 해설 |
여자가 할 일이 언급되는 대화 마지막에, 여자가 파일 복사본을 이메일로 보내겠다고(I'll e-mail you a copy of the file) 알리는 부분이 있으므로 (A)가 정답이다.

| 어휘 | present ~을 발표하다 unfortunately 아쉽게도, 안타깝게도 easily 쉽게, 수월하게 in that case 그런 경우라면 then 그렇게 하면, 그때, 그런 다음 in detail 자세히 launch 출시, 공개

Questions 3-4 refer to the following conversation.

> M: Hello, I got a flyer for your business. It says that you provide ③ **weekly lawn maintenance. I'd like to know more about that.**
> W: We have several services available, and the costs depend on the size of your lawn. ④ **If you'd like, I can visit your property** to discuss the work further. Then you can decide whether or not you'd like to hire us.
> M: That would be great. How does Friday afternoon work for you?

3-4번 문제는 다음 대화를 참조하시오.
남: 안녕하세요, 귀사에 관련된 전단을 봤는데요. 매주 잔디 관리 서비스를 제공하신다고 쓰여 있던데요. 그 서비스에 관해 좀 더 알고 싶습니다.
여: 이용 가능한 여러 서비스가 있는데, 비용은 잔디 면적에 따라 다릅니다. 괜찮으시면, 고객님의 건물에 방문해서 서비스 작업에 관해 더 논의해 볼 수 있습니다. 그런 다음에 저희를 고용하실지 말지 결정하시면 됩니다.
남: 그렇게 하면 아주 좋을 것 같습니다. 금요일 오후가 어떠세요?

3. 남자는 왜 전화를 거는가?
(A) 서비스에 관해 문의하기 위해
(B) 일부 장비를 주문하기 위해

| 해설 |
대화 초반부에 남자가 잔디 관리 서비스를 언급하면서 더 알아보고 싶다고 (~ weekly lawn maintenance. I'd like to know more about that) 말하고 있으므로 서비스 문의가 목적이라고 한 (A)가 정답이다.

4. 여자는 무엇을 하겠다고 제안하는가?
(A) 계약서 제공하기
(B) 남자를 방문하기

| 해설 |
대화 중반부에 여자가 추가 논의를 위해 남자의 건물을 방문할 의사가 있다고(If you'd like, I can visit your property ~) 밝히고 있으므로 (B)가 정답이다.

| 어휘 | flyer 전단 business 업체, 회사 provide ~을 제공하다 lawn 잔디 maintenance 유지 관리 several 여러 가지의 depend on ~에 따라 다르다, ~에 달려 있다 property 건물, 부동산 discuss ~을 논의하다 further 추가로, 한층 더 then 그런 다음, 그때, 그렇게 하면 decide ~을 결정하다 whether or not ~인지 아닌지 hire ~을 고용하다 inquire about ~에 관해 문의하다 equipment 장비 contract 계약(서)

Questions 5-6 refer to the following conversation with three speakers.

> W: Hi, ⑤ **I'm here because I need to have my laptop fixed.** I was working on it last night, and the screen suddenly went black.
> M1: OK, I'll have one of our technicians look at it. Matthew, do you have time to work on this laptop now?
> M2: I can get started on it this afternoon.
> W: Do you know how long it will take? ⑥ **I'm going on vacation next week**, and I'd really like to take my computer with me.
> M2: I'll know more once I take a closer look.

5-6번 문제는 다음 세 사람의 대화를 참조하시오.
여: 안녕하세요, 제 노트북 컴퓨터를 수리 받아야 해서 왔습니다. 제가 어젯밤에 노트북 컴퓨터로 일을 하고 있었는데, 화면이 갑자기 보이지 않았어요.
남1: 알겠습니다, 저희 기술자들 중 한 명에게 살펴봐 달라고 할게요. Matthew 씨, 지금 이 노트북 컴퓨터 좀 봐 주실 시간이 되세요?
남2: 오늘 오후에 시작할 수 있습니다.
여: 시간이 얼마나 걸릴지 아시나요? 제가 다음 주에 휴가를 가는데, 제 컴퓨터를 꼭 갖고 가고 싶어서요.
남2: 자세히 살펴보고 나면 더 잘 알 수 있을 겁니다.

5. 대화가 어디에서 이뤄지고 있는가?
(A) 컴퓨터 수리 업체에서
(B) 회계 법인 회사에서

| 해설 |
대화를 시작하면서 여자가 노트북 컴퓨터를 수리 받으러 왔다고(I'm here because I need to have my laptop fixed) 방문 목적을 밝히는 것으로 보아 컴퓨터 수리 업체에서 이뤄지는 대화임을 알 수 있으므로 (A)가 정답이다.

6. 여자는 다음 주에 무엇을 할 계획인가?
(A) 휴가 가기
(B) 새 직장에 출근하기

| 해설 |
여자의 말에서 next week이라는 시점 키워드가 언급되는 후반부에, 다음 주에 휴가를 간다고(I'm going on vacation next week) 알리고 있으므로 (A)가 정답이다.

| 어휘 | fix ~을 고치다, 바로잡다 work on ~에 대한 일을 하다 suddenly 갑자기 go + 형용사 ~한 상태가 되다 get started 시작하다 how long it will take 시간이 얼마나 걸릴지 go on vacation 휴가를 가다 take ~을 가져가다 once (일단) ~하고 나면, ~하는 대로 take a close look 면밀히 살펴보다 take place (일, 행사 등이) 발생되다, 일어나다 repair 수리 accounting firm 회계 법인

02 직업/근무지를 묻는 문제

기출 유형 맛보기
본책 p.66

Q. 여자는 어디에서 근무하는가?
(A) 여행사에서
(B) 렌터카 대리점에서
(C) 진료소에서
(D) 미용실에서

> 여: Bethlem Royal Clinic입니다. 무엇을 도와 드릴까요?
> 남: 안녕하세요. 저는 Fred Thompson이며, 지금부터 한 달 후에 휴가로 해외 여행을 가려고 합니다. 가기 전에 예방 접종을 받아야 한다는 사실을 막 알았어요. 그곳에 예약할 수 있나요?
> 여: 네, Thompson 씨, 이번 주 후반에 이용 가능하신 시간대가 좀 있습니다. 이번 금요일은 어떠신가요? 1시 30분에 괜찮으세요?
> 남: 제가 그날 2시까지 고객과 만날 예정입니다.
> 여: 그러시면 3시는 어떠세요? 그때 이쪽으로 오실 수 있으세요?
> 남: 네, 아주 좋습니다. 그럼 금요일에 뵙겠습니다.

PRACTICE | 기출 연습하기

정답 1 (B) 2 (A) 3 (B) 4 (A) 5 (B) 6 (B)

Questions 1-2 refer to the following conversation.

M: Erica, I was just helping a customer in **1 our women's sweaters section**, and I noticed a problem with the cash register there. It wouldn't open when I was trying to process a customer's purchase.
W: Hmm… it might need to be replaced. **2 Could you put an "Out of Order" sign on the machine?** Then other employees will know that they're not supposed to use it.
M: Of course. I can take care of that right now.

1-2번 문제는 다음 대화를 참조하시오.
남: Erica, 제가 우리 여성 스웨터 코너에서 한 손님들 도와 드리고 있었는데, 그곳 금전 등록기에 문제가 있다는 것을 알았어요. 제가 고객의 구매를 처리해 드리려고 했을 때 그게 열리지 않았어요.
여: 흠… 교체되어야 할지도 모르겠네요. 그 기계에 "고장"이라는 안내 표지를 붙여 주시겠어요? 그렇게 하면 다른 직원들이 그걸 사용하면 안 된다는 것을 알 수 있을 거예요.
남: 물론입니다. 지금 바로 처리할 수 있어요.

1. 화자들은 어디에서 근무하겠는가?
(A) 전자 제품 매장에서
(B) 의류 매장에서

| 해설 |
대화 시작 부분에 화자들이 근무하는 장소와 관련해 남자가 '우리 여성 스웨터 코너(our women's sweaters section)'라고 지칭하고 있으므로 (B)가 정답이다.

2. 여자는 남자에게 무엇을 하도록 요청하는가?
(A) 안내 표지 붙이기
(B) 추가 근무하기

| 해설 |
여자의 요청 사항이 언급되는 중반부에, "고장" 안내 표지를 붙여 달라고(Could you put an "Out of Order" sign ~?) 부탁하고 있으므로 (A)가 정답이다.

| 어휘 | cash register 금전 등록기 try to do ~하려 하다 process ~을 처리하다 purchase 구매(품) replace ~을 교체하다 put ~을 붙이다, 놓다, 두다 out of order 고장 난 then 그렇게 하면, 그때, 그런 다음 be supposed to do ~해야 하다, ~할 예정이다 take care of ~을 처리하다 electronics 전자 제품 put up ~을 붙이다, 내걸다 additional 추가의

Questions 3-4 refer to the following conversation.

W: **3 Welcome to Harrison Furniture.** Is there something I can help you find?
M: Hi, I'm interested in buying the black leather sofa over there. **4 If I get it delivered to my home, how much would that cost?**
W: Since the price of the item is over three hundred dollars, there would be no charge. Will someone be home this afternoon to accept the item?
M: Yes, that's perfect. Let me give you my address.

3-4번 문제는 다음 대화를 참조하시오.
여: Harrison 가구점에 오신 것을 환영합니다. 제가 찾으시는 것을 도와 드릴까요?
남: 안녕하세요, 저는 저쪽에 있는 검정 가죽 소파를 구입하는 데 관심이 있습니다. 제 집으로 배송시키려면 비용이 얼마나 들까요?
여: 그 제품의 가격이 300달러가 넘기 때문에 무료입니다. 오늘 오후에 제품을 받으실 분이 댁에 계신가요?
남: 네, 아주 좋습니다. 제 주소를 알려 드리겠습니다.

3. 여자는 누구일 것 같은가?
(A) 호텔 안내 담당 직원
(B) 매장 점원

| 해설 |
대화 초반부에 여자가 Harrison Furniture에 온 것을 환영한다고(Welcome to Harrison Furniture) 인사하는 것으로 보아 가구점 직원임을 알 수 있으므로 (B)가 정답이다.

4. 남자는 무엇에 관해 묻는가?
(A) 배송 요금
(B) 가구 디자인

| 해설 |
대화 중반부에 나오는 남자의 질문 사항을 확인하면, 배송시키는 데 비용이 얼마나 드는지(If I get it delivered to my home, how much would that cost?) 묻고 있으므로 (A)가 정답이다.

| 어휘 | leather 가죽 cost ~의 비용이 들다 over ~가 넘는 charge 청구 요금, 부과 요금 accept ~을 받다, 수용하다 receptionist 안내 담당 직원 clerk 점원 fee 요금, 수수료

Questions 5-6 refer to the following conversation.

M: Good morning. **5 I'm calling about booking a trip to New York through your agency.** I'd like to leave on July 6 and return on July 12.
W: All right, sir. We have affordable packages that include both the flight and the hotel. There are a few hotels to choose from.
M: That sounds good. What are my options?
W: **6 If you visit our Web site, you can check out our photo gallery of the various hotels.** I think that will help you to make your decision.

5-6번 문제는 다음 대화를 참조하시오.
남: 안녕하세요. 그쪽 대행사를 통해 New York으로 가는 여행을 예약하는 것에 관해 전화 드렸습니다. 저는 7월 6일에 떠나서 7월 12일에 돌아오려고 합니다.
여: 알겠습니다, 고객님. 항공편과 호텔 모두가 포함된, 가격이 저렴한 패키지들이 있습니다. 선택하실 수 있는 호텔들도 몇 군데 있습니다.
남: 좋은 것 같습니다. 저한테 어떤 선택권이 있나요?
여: 저희 웹 사이트를 방문하시면, 다양한 호텔을 담은 사진 갤러리를 확인해 보실 수 있습니다. 그것이 고객님께서 결정을 내리시는 데 도움이 될 것 같습니다.

5. 여자는 어디에서 근무하고 있을 것 같은가?
(A) 부동산 중개업체에서
(B) 여행사에서

| 해설 |
대화를 시작하면서 남자가 여자의 대행사를 통해 New York 행 여행을 예약하기 위해 전화했다고(I'm calling about booking a trip to New York through your agency) 알리는 부분을 통해 여자가 여행사 직원임을 알 수 있으므로 (B)가 정답이다.

6. 여자의 말에 따르면, 남자는 왜 웹 사이트를 방문해야 하는가?
(A) 비용을 지불하기 위해
(B) 일부 사진들을 보기 위해

| 해설 |
여자의 말에서 웹 사이트가 언급되는 후반부에, 웹 사이트에서 다양한 호텔을 담은 사진 갤러리를 볼 수 있다고(If you visit our Web site, you can check out our photo gallery ~) 알리고 있으므로 (B)가 정답이다.

| 어휘 | book ~을 예약하다   agency 대행사, 업체   leave 떠나다, 출발하다   affordable 가격이 저렴한, 알맞은   include ~을 포함하다   choose from ~에서 선택하다   option 옵션, 선택권   check out ~을 확인해 보다   various 다양한   make one's decision 결정을 내리다   real estate 부동산   firm 업체, 회사   make a payment 비용을 지불하다   view ~을 보다

DAY 10 | 실전문제   본책 p.68

정답 1 (B)   2 (D)   3 (C)   4 (D)   5 (A)   6 (B)
      7 (B)   8 (D)   9 (A)   10 (B) 11 (A) 12 (D)
      13 (D) 14 (D) 15 (B) 16 (C) 17 (B) 18 (D)
      19 (D) 20 (C) 21 (A)

Questions 1-3 refer to the following conversation.

M: Hi, Teri. You've done a great job in the first week of **1** your internship here. As the office manager, **2** I'd like to know what you think of the program so far. If I can get some feedback, it would be a great help.
W: I've learned so much in a short period of time, and the entire staff has been open to teaching me about the publishing business.
M: I'm glad to hear that. You know, **3** everyone in our internship program is eligible to receive an annual subscription to the magazine. If you're interested in this free gift, just talk to the HR department.
W: Thanks. I'll do that.

1-3번 문제는 다음 대화를 참조하시오.
남: 안녕하세요, Teri 씨. 이곳에서의 인턴 근무 첫 주에 일을 아주 잘해 주셨어요. 사무실 책임자로서, 지금까지 프로그램에 대해 어떻게 생각하고 계신지 알고 싶습니다. 제가 피드백을 받을 수 있다면, 많은 도움이 될 것 같아요.
여: 짧은 기간 내에 아주 많은 것을 배웠고, 전체 직원들께서 출판업에 관해 제게 열린 마음으로 가르쳐 주셨습니다.
남: 그 말씀을 들으니 기쁘네요. 아시겠지만, 우리 인턴 프로그램에 참가하신 모든 분들은 잡지 연간 구독 서비스를 받을 자격이 있습니다. 이 무료 선물에 관심이 있으시면 인사부에 얘기하기만 하면 됩니다.
여: 감사합니다. 그렇게 하겠습니다.

| 어휘 | so far 지금까지   in a short period of time 짧은 기간 내에   entire 전체의   publishing 출판(업)   be eligible to do ~할 자격이 있다   receive ~을 받다   annual 연간의, 해마다의   subscription 구독   be interested in ~에 관심이 있다   free 무료의   HR department 인사부

1. 여자는 누구일 것 같은가?
(A) 투자자
(B) 인턴
(C) 구직 지원자
(D) 관리자

| 해설 |
대화 초반부에 남자가 여자의 신원과 관련해 'your internship'이라고 지칭하는 것으로 보아 인턴 직원임을 알 수 있으므로 (B)가 정답이다.

| 어휘 | applicant 지원자   supervisor 관리자, 책임자, 상사

2. 남자는 여자에게 무엇을 하도록 제안하는가?
(A) 프로그램 다운로드하기
(B) 양식에 서명하기
(C) 나중에 다시 오기
(D) 의견 공유하기

| 해설 |
남자의 요청 사항이 언급되는 초반부에, 프로그램에 대해 어떻게 생각하고 있는지 알고 싶으며, 피드백이 도움이 될 것이라는 (I'd like to know what you think of the program ~ a great help) 말로 의견을 제공하도록 요청하고 있으므로 (D)가 정답이다.

| 어휘 | form 양식, 서식   share ~을 공유하다   opinion 의견

3. 남자의 말에 따르면, 여자는 무엇을 받을 자격이 있는가?
(A) 승진
(B) 무료 식사
(C) 연간 구독 서비스
(D) 컴퓨터 훈련

| 해설 |
대화 후반부에, 인턴 프로그램 참가자는 잡지 연간 구독 서비스를 받을 자격이 있다고 (~ is eligible to receive an annual subscription to the magazine) 알리고 있으므로 (C)가 정답이다.

| 어휘 | promotion 승진   complimentary 무료의

Questions 4-6 refer to the following conversation.

W: **4** Thanks for calling Westway Camping Supplies. How may I help you?
M: Hello. I heard on the radio that **5** your store is having a major sale on tents. Does that sale apply to all tents or just certain brands?
W: It's for all of the tents that we have in stock. You can save up to sixty percent off the suggested retail price.
M: That's fantastic. Thanks for the information. I'll head over there now to take a look.
W: All right, but **6** please note that we close at seven o'clock, so you'll have to hurry if you want to come today.

4-6번 문제는 다음 대화를 참조하시오.
여: Westway 캠핑용품에 전화 주셔서 감사합니다. 무엇을 도와 드릴까요?
남: 안녕하세요. 그쪽 매장에서 텐트 제품에 대해 대규모 세일 행사를 한다고 라디오에서 들었어요. 그 세일이 모든 텐트에 적용되나요, 아니면 특정 브랜드에만 적용되나요?
여: 저희가 재고로 보유하고 있는 모든 텐트에 해당됩니다. 제시된 소매가에서 최대 60퍼센트까지 비용을 절약하실 수 있습니다.
남: 정말 좋네요. 정보를 알려 주셔서 감사합니다. 지금 그쪽으로 가서 한번 살펴 볼게요.
여: 좋습니다, 하지만 저희가 7시에 문을 닫기 때문에 오늘 오시고 싶으시면 서두르셔야 한다는 점에 유의하시기 바랍니다.

| 어휘 | have a major sale on ~에 대해 대규모 세일을 하다   apply to ~에 적용되다   certain 특정한, 일정한   have A in stock A를 재고로 갖고 있다   up to 최대 ~까지   suggested 제시된, 제안된   retail price 소매가   head over there 그쪽으로 가다, 향하다   take a look 한번 보다   note that ~라는 점에 유의하다

4. 남자는 무슨 종류의 업체에 전화를 거는가?
(A) 사무용품 매장
(B) 서점
(C) 전자제품 매장
(D) 캠핑용품 매장

| 해설 |
대화를 시작하면서 전화를 받는 여자가 Westway Camping Supplies에 전화한 것에 대해 감사하다고(Thanks for calling Westway Camping Supplies) 인사하고 있으므로 (D)가 정답이다.

5. 남자는 무엇에 관해 묻는가?
(A) 판촉 세일 행사의 상세 정보
(B) 업체에 차를 운전해 가는 길
(C) 반품에 대한 업체의 정책
(D) 입사 지원 과정

| 해설 |
남자의 문의 사항이 언급되는 대화 초반부에, 텐트 세일이 모든 텐트 제품에 적용되는지 아닌지를(~ your store is having a major sale on tents. Does that sale apply to all tents or just certain brands?) 묻고 있는데, 이는 세일과 관련된 상세 정보를 확인하려는 것이므로 (A)가 정답이다.

| 어휘 | inquire about ~에 관해 문의하다   details 상세 정보   promotional 판촉의, 홍보의   directions to ~로 찾아가는 길, 방법   business 업체, 회사   policy 정책   return 반품   application 지원(서)

6. 여자는 남자에게 무엇에 관해 말하는가?
(A) 배송 요금
(B) 문을 닫는 시간
(C) 품질 보증 기간
(D) 프로젝트 마감시한

| 해설 |
여자가 대화 마지막에 7시에 문을 닫는다는 사실에 유의하라고(please note that we close at seven o'clock ~) 알리고 있으므로 (B)가 정답이다.

| 어휘 | fee 요금   warranty 품질 보증(서)   deadline 마감시한

Questions 7-9 refer to the following conversation.

M: Good morning, **7 Annie's Cleaning.** How may I help you?
W: Hello. I'm the manager of a small company that has just moved to the Amato Building. **8 I'm calling to see if you have a crew that can visit our site after the office closes to do some light tasks,** **7 such as vacuuming and dusting.**
M: I'm sure we can handle that. **9 There's a schedule of our open time slots on our Web site. It may be a good idea to look that over for yourself first.**
W: All right. I'll do that now and get back to you. Thanks.

7-9번 문제는 다음 대화를 참조하시오.

남: 안녕하세요, Annie's Cleaning입니다. 무엇을 도와 드릴까요?
여: 안녕하세요. 저는 Amato Building으로 막 이전한 한 소기업의 책임자입니다. 저희 사무실이 문을 닫은 이후에 방문해서 진공 청소기로 청소하거나 먼지를 제거하는 것과 같은 가벼운 일을 해주실 수 있는 작업팀이 있는지 알아보기 위해 전화 드립니다.
남: 저희는 물론 그 일을 처리해 드릴 수 있습니다. 저희 웹 사이트에 가시면 비어 있는 저희 작업 시간대를 보실 수 있는 일정표가 있습니다. 먼저 직접 그것을 살펴보시는 것이 좋을 듯합니다.

여: 알겠습니다. 지금 그렇게 한 다음에 다시 연락 드리겠습니다. 감사합니다.

| 어휘 | move to ~로 이사하다   crew (함께 일하는) 팀, 조   site 장소, 현장, 부지   light 가벼운, 쉬운   task 일, 업무   vacuuming 진공 청소   dusting 먼지 제거   handle ~을 처리하다, 다루다   open time slot 비어 있는 시간대   look over ~을 살펴보다, 검토하다   for oneself 직접, 스스로   get back to ~에게 다시 연락하다

7. 남자는 무슨 종류의 업체에서 근무하고 있는가?
(A) 전자 제품 매장
(B) 청소 전문 회사
(C) 법률 회사
(D) 채용 대행 업체

| 해설 |
대화를 시작하면서 전화를 받는 남자가 'Annie's Cleaning'이라는 말로 업체 이름을 알리고 있고, 뒤이어 진공 청소와 먼지 제거(such as vacuuming and dusting) 서비스가 언급되고 있으므로 (B)가 정답이다.

| 어휘 | work for ~에서 근무하다

8. 전화의 목적은 무엇인가?
(A) 불만 제기하기
(B) 제품 소개하기
(C) 주소 업데이트하기
(D) 서비스 요청하기

| 해설 |
여자가 전화의 목적을 언급하는 중반부에 진공 청소와 먼지 제거 같은 작업을 하러 올 작업팀이 있는지 알아보기 위해 전화한다는 내용(I'm calling to see if you have a crew ~ such as vacuuming and dusting)이 있으므로 (D)가 정답이다.

| 어휘 | make a complaint 불만을 제기하다   introduce ~을 소개하다   request ~을 요청하다

9. 남자는 여자에게 무엇을 하도록 권하는가?
(A) 웹 사이트 방문하기
(B) 샘플 요청하기
(C) 계약서 검토하기
(D) 다른 지점에 전화하기

| 해설 |
대화 후반부에, 웹 사이트의 일정표를 언급하면서 그것을 확인해 보는 것이 좋겠다고(There's a schedule of our open time slots on our Web site. It may be a good idea to look that over ~) 권하고 있으므로 (A)가 정답이다.

| 어휘 | review ~을 검토하다   contract 계약(서)   branch 지점, 지사

Questions 10-12 refer to the following conversation.

W: Hello. My name is Marissa Gerard. **10 I applied online for your open senior lab technician position. I'm wondering what the next step will be.**
M: **11 We had hoped to start contacting those who passed the screening process yesterday, but** we received nearly two hundred applications.
W: I see. Well, I hope to be considered, since I have seven years of experience in a similar position.
M: Where were you working?
W: Andrex Pharmaceuticals. I was a group leader on the main research team.
M: It sounds like you have the qualifications we are looking for. **12 Could you call back after the**

weekend to make sure your application is put forward to the next stage?
W: 12 **Certainly. I'll be sure to do that.**

10-12번 문제는 다음 대화를 참조하시오.
여: 안녕하세요. 제 이름은 Marissa Gerard입니다. 제가 공석인 귀사의 수석 실험실 기사 직책에 온라인으로 지원했습니다. 다음 단계가 무엇이 될지 궁금해서요.
남: 저희는 지원서 선별 과정을 통과한 분들께 연락 드리는 일을 어제 시작할 수 있기를 바랐지만, 거의 200개에 달하는 지원서를 받았습니다.
여: 알겠습니다. 음, 저는 제가 고려되기를 바라고 있는데, 유사한 직책에서 7년간 일한 경력이 있기 때문입니다.
남: 어느 회사였나요?
여: Andrex 제약 회사입니다. 저는 핵심 연구팀의 팀장이었습니다.
남: 저희가 찾고 있는 자격 요건을 갖추신 분인 것 같네요. 귀하의 지원서가 다음 단계로 넘어가 있는지 확인하기 위해 주말 이후에 다시 전화해 주시겠어요?
여: 물론입니다. 꼭 그렇게 하겠습니다.

| 어휘 | apply 지원하다 open 공석인, 비어 있는 lab 실험실 step 단계 contact ~에게 연락하다 application 지원(서) pass ~을 통과하다 screening 선별 process 과정 receive ~을 받다 nearly 거의 consider ~을 고려하다 similar 유사한 It sounds like ~인 것 같다 qualification 자격 요건

10. 여자는 남자에게 왜 전화를 거는가?
(A) 일부 최소한의 자격 요건을 확인하기 위해
(B) 채용 과정에 관해 문의하기 위해
(C) 구매 제품에 대한 후속 조치를 취하기 위해
(D) 일자리 제의를 하기 위해

| 해설 |
대화를 시작하면서 여자가 수석 실험실 기사 직책에 지원한 사실과 함께 다음 단계가 궁금하다고(I applied online ~ I'm wondering what the next step will be) 말하고 있는데, 이는 채용 과정에 문의하는 것이므로 (B)가 정답이다.

| 어휘 | qualification 자격, 자질, 능력 minimum 최소한의 inquire about ~에 관해 문의하다 hiring 채용, 고용 follow up on ~에 대해 후속 조치를 취하다 purchase 구매(품) job offer 고용 제안

11. 남자가 "we received nearly two hundred applications"라고 말할 때 무엇을 의미할 것 같은가?
(A) 업무가 지연되었다.
(B) 한 직책이 이미 충원되었다.
(C) 마감시한이 앞당겨졌다.
(D) 목표에 빠르게 도달했다.

| 해설 |
초반부에 남자가 지원서 선별 과정을 통과한 사람들에게 어제부터 연락할 수 있기를 바랐다는(We had hoped to start contacting those who passed applications passed ~) 말에 이어 '거의 200개를 받았다'고 말하는 상황이다. 즉, 지원자가 많아 선별 과정이 지연되었다는 말이므로 (A)가 정답이다.

| 어휘 | task 일, 업무 delayed 지연된 fill ~을 충원하다 deadline 마감시한 move up ~을 앞당기다 reach ~에 도달하다

12. 여자는 무엇을 하는 데 동의하는가?
(A) 남자의 동료 직원 만나기
(B) 일부 설명서 읽어 보기
(C) 워크숍에 참석하기
(D) 다음 주에 다시 전화하기

| 해설 |
대화 후반부에, 남자가 주말이 지난 뒤에 다시 전화하라고(Could you call back after the weekend ~) 요청하자 여자가 긍정의 답변과 함께 그러겠다고(Certainly. I'll be sure to do that) 수락하고 있으므로 (D)가 정답이다.

| 어휘 | colleague 동료 직원 instructions 설명, 안내, 지시 attend ~에 참석하다

Questions 13-15 refer to the following conversation with three speakers.

M: Hi, Kamala. Hi, Ruhi. I'm surprised to see you 13 **here at the training workshop.** Didn't you attend a similar session last month?
W1: We were supposed to, but an urgent project came up.
M: Oh, that's right. 14 **You two were assigned to attend the regional career fair.**
W2: Well, we were more than just attending it. 14 **We had to make all of the preparations** to operate a booth there.
M: You must have done a great job because I saw that you gathered a lot of 15 **résumés. I'm in charge of sorting them** and deciding which people to invite for interviews.

13-15번 문제는 다음 세 명의 대화를 참조하시오.
남: 안녕하세요, Kamala 씨. 안녕하세요, Ruhi 씨. 두 분을 이곳 교육 워크숍에서 만나니 놀랍네요. 지난달에 비슷한 워크숍에 참석하지 않으셨나요?
여1: 그럴 예정이었지만, 급한 프로젝트가 생겼어요.
남: 아, 그렇군요. 두 분께서는 지역 취업 박람회에 참석하도록 배정 받으셨죠.
여2: 음, 저희는 단순히 참석만 한 것이 아니었어요. 그곳에서 부스를 운영하는 데 필요한 모든 준비 작업을 해야 했어요.
남: 아주 잘 해내신 것이 분명해요, 두 분께서 많은 이력서를 받으셨다는 것을 보면요. 제가 그것들을 분류하고 어떤 사람들을 면접에 부를 것인지를 결정하는 일을 맡고 있습니다.

| 어휘 | be surprised to do ~해서 놀라다 training 교육 attend ~에 참석하다 similar 유사한 session (특정 활동을 위한) 시간 be supposed to do ~할 예정이다, ~하기로 되어 있다 urgent 긴급한 come up 발생되다, 생기다 be assigned to do ~하도록 배정받다 regional 지역의 career fair 취업 박람회 more than ~ 이상인 make a preparation 준비하다 operate ~을 운영하다 booth 부스, 칸막이 공간 must have p.p. ~한 것이 분명하다 gather ~을 모으다 résumé 이력서 in charge of ~을 맡고 있는 sort ~을 분류하다 decide ~을 결정하다 invite ~을 초대하다

13. 대화가 어디에서 이뤄지고 있는가?
(A) 시상식장에서
(B) 기획 회의에서
(C) 제품 시연회에서
(D) 교육 워크숍에서

| 해설 |
대화 초반부에 남자가 현재 화자들이 있는 장소를 'here at the training workshop'이라고 지칭하고 있으므로 (D)가 정답이다.

| 어휘 | take place (일, 행사 등이) 발생되다, 일어나다 demonstration 시연(회)

14. 여자들은 최근에 무엇에 대한 일을 해 오고 있었는가?
(A) 중요한 고객 확보하기
(B) 경연대회에서 경쟁하기
(C) 웹 사이트 업그레이드하기
(D) 취업 박람회 준비하기

| 해설 |

대화 중반부에 남자가 여자들을 You two로 지칭해 지역 취업 박람회에 참석하도록 배정받은 일을(You two were assigned to attend the regional career fair) 언급하자, 여자 한 명이 자신들이 모든 준비 작업을 해야 한다(We had to make all of the preparations ~) 알리고 있다. 따라서 (D)가 정답이다.

| 어휘 | work on ~에 대한 일을 하다 recently 최근에 secure ~을 확보하다 compete 경쟁하다 prepare for ~을 준비하다, ~에 대비하다

15. 남자는 무슨 일을 하는 것을 책임지고 있다고 말하는가?
(A) 신입 사원들 가르치기
(B) 일부 이력서 정리하기
(C) 발표하기
(D) 면접 일정 검토하기

| 해설 |

남자가 자신이 맡은 일을 설명하는 후반부에, 이력서를 분류하는 일을 맡고 있다고(~ résumés. I'm in charge of sorting them ~) 하는 것으로 보아 이력서 정리를 담당하고 있음을 알 수 있으므로 (B)가 정답이다.

| 어휘 | be responsible for ~을 책임지다 organize ~을 정리하다, 체계화하다

Questions 16-18 refer to the following conversation.

> M: Jane, I was looking over your proposed promotional campaign for the Classic Music Festival, and **16** I noticed that you don't plan to put any ads on Web sites. We usually use a variety of media outlets. **16** Why did you decide to do something different?
> W: I thought newspaper advertisements would be the best use of our limited funds. The types of people who would enjoy this event are likely to get their information from the local press. And **17** Colleen has designed an advertisement that will look great printed in black and white.
> M: Okay. I'm interested to see how this strategy works. **18** I'll review how many people attended the festival at the end of the month, after the event is over.

16-18번 문제는 다음 대화를 참조하시오.

남: Jane, 클래식 음악 축제에 대해 당신이 제안한 홍보 캠페인 자료를 검토하고 있었는데, 웹 사이트에 광고를 낼 계획이 없다는 점을 알게 되었습니다. 우리는 보통 다양한 언론 매체들을 활용하잖아요. 왜 다른 것을 하기로 결정하신 거죠?
여: 저는 신문 광고가 제한적인 우리 자금에 대한 최적의 활용 방법이라고 생각했습니다. 이 행사를 즐기려는 유형의 사람들은 아마도 지역 신문을 통해 정보를 얻을 것 같습니다. 그리고 Colleen 씨가 흑백으로 인쇄되면 아주 멋지게 보일 광고를 디자인해 주셨어요.
남: 알겠습니다. 이 전략이 얼마나 효과가 있을지 확인하고 싶습니다. 행사가 종료되고 나서 이달 말에 얼마나 많은 사람들이 축제에 참여했는지 검토해 보겠습니다.

| 어휘 | look over ~을 검토하다 proposed 제안된 promotional 홍보의, 판촉의 notice that ~임을 알게 되다 plan to do ~할 계획이다 put an ad 광고를 내다 a variety of 다양한 media outlet 언론 매체 decide to do ~하기로 결정하다 limited 제한적인 fund 자금 be likely to do ~할 가능성이 있다 local press 지역 신문 look + 형용사 ~하게 보이다 printed in black and white 흑백으로 인쇄된 strategy 전략 work 효과가 있다 review ~을 검토하다 over 종료된

16. 남자는 축제와 관련해 무엇에 관해 묻는가?
(A) 입장료가 얼마일 것인지
(B) 누가 공연을 확정해 주었는지
(C) 왜 온라인으로 광고되지 않을 것인지
(D) 언제 장소가 선정될 것인지

| 해설 |

대화 초반부에, 남자는 웹 사이트에 광고를 내지 않기로 한 계획을(I noticed that you don't plan to put any ads on Web sites) 언급하면서, 그렇게 결정한 이유를 묻고 있으므로(Why did you decide to do something different?) (C)가 정답이다.

| 어휘 | regarding ~와 관련해 admission fee 입장료 confirm ~을 확정하다 advertise ~을 광고하다 site 장소, 부지 select ~을 선정하다

17. Colleen 씨는 어느 부서에서 근무할 것 같은가?
(A) 재무
(B) 그래픽
(C) IT
(D) 마케팅

| 해설 |

이름 키워드 Colleen이 언급되는 중반부에, 여자는 Colleen 씨가 광고를 디자인한(Colleen has designed an advertisement) 사실을 밝히고 있으므로 (B)가 정답이다.

18. 남자는 월말에 무엇을 검토할 계획인가?
(A) 직원들의 성과
(B) 안전 조치
(C) 뉴스 기사
(D) 참석자 데이터

| 해설 |

월말이라는 시점 키워드가 언급되는 후반부에 남자는 이달 말에 축제 참가자 수에 대해 검토하겠다고(I'll review how many people attended the festival at the end of the month ~) 밝히고 있으므로 (D)가 정답이다.

| 어휘 | achievement 업적, 성취 measures 조치 attendance 참석(자의 수)

Questions 19-21 refer to the following conversation and weather forecast.

> W: I was worried when we decided to hold **19** our company's 25th-anniversary party outdoors, but it seems like the weather is going to be good.
> M: Yes, I was just looking at the weather forecast for our event day.
> W: Oh, so you see what I mean. It will be **20** seventy-five degrees, and there won't be any clouds or rain.
> M: I guess **21** I should call the band and let them know what time to arrive.
> W: Yes, please do that. The food will be delivered at noon, so they should start setting up before then.

Weather Forecast			
Wednesday	Thursday	**20** Friday	Saturday
Rainy	Sunny	Sunny	Cloudy
66°F	80°F	75°F	68°F

19-21번 문제는 다음 대화와 일기 예보에 관한 문제입니다.

여: 저는 우리 회사의 25주년 기념일 파티를 야외에서 개최하기로 결정했을 때 걱정했었지만, 날씨가 좋을 것 같아요.

남: 네, 제가 막 우리 행사 당일의 일기 예보를 보고 있었어요.
여: 아, 그럼 제 말이 무슨 뜻인지 아시겠네요. 기온이 75도인데요, 구름이나 비가 전혀 없을 거예요.
남: 밴드에게 전화를 걸어서 몇 시에 도착해야 하는지를 알려 줘야 할 것 같아요.
여: 네, 그렇게 해 주세요. 음식이 정오에 배달될 것이기 때문에, 그 전에 그들이 준비를 시작해야 합니다.

일기 예보			
수요일	목요일	금요일	토요일
비	맑음	맑음	흐림
화씨 66°	화씨 80°	화씨 75°	화씨 68°

| 어휘 | decide to do ~하기로 결정하다 hold ~을 개최하다 anniversary (해마다 돌아오는) 기념일 it seems like ~인 것 같다 degree (온도의) 도 let A know A에게 알리다 what time to do 몇 시에 ~하는지 arrive 도착하다 noon 정오 set up 준비하다, 마련하다 then 그때

19. 화자들은 무슨 종류의 행사에 관해 이야기하고 있는가?
(A) 지역 주민 야유회
(B) 스포츠 경기 대회
(C) 자원 봉사 프로젝트
(D) 기념일 파티

| 해설 |
대화를 시작하면서 여자가 회사의 25주년 기념일 파티를(our company's 25th-anniversary party) 언급하며 그 행사의 진행과 관련된 내용으로 대화가 전개되고 있으므로 (D)가 정답이다.

| 어휘 | community 지역 사회 competition 경기, 대회 volunteer 자원 봉사

20. 시각 자료를 보시오. 행사는 어느 요일로 예정되어 있는가?
(A) 수요일
(B) 목요일
(C) 금요일
(D) 토요일

| 해설 |
행사 당일 날씨가 언급되는 중반부에, 여자가 기온이 75도이고 구름이나 비가 전혀 없을 것이라고(~ seventy-five degrees, and there won't be any clouds or rain) 알리고 있는데, 시각 자료에서 이에 해당되는 요일이 Friday이므로 (C)가 정답이다.

21. 남자는 다음에 무엇을 할 것 같은가?
(A) 음악 그룹에게 연락하기
(B) 새 정보를 온라인으로 게시하기
(C) 한 구역을 장식하기
(D) 출장 요리 업체를 방문하기

| 해설 |
남자가 자신이 할 일을 밝히는 후반부에, 밴드에게 전화해야 한다고(I should call the band ~) 알리고 있으므로 (A)가 정답이다.

| 어휘 | contact ~에게 연락하다 post ~을 게시하다 decorate ~을 장식하다 caterer 출장 요리 업체

DAY 11 세부적인 내용을 묻는 유형 (1)

01 문제점을 묻는 문제

기출 유형 맛보기 본책 p.70

Q. 여자는 무슨 문제점을 언급하는가?

(A) 일부 직원들이 직장을 그만두었다.
(B) 악천후가 예상되고 있다.
(C) 더 적은 수의 고객들이 찾아오고 있다.
(D) 고객들의 불만 사항이 증가되었다.

여: Greg, 내일 눈보라가 발생할지도 모른다는 얘기 들었어요? 버스와 기차가 아마 운행되지 않을 수도 있는데, 제가 내일 일찍 도착할 예정이거든요.
남: 그 얘기는 처음 듣는데요. 일기 예보가 바뀌지 않는다면, 일부 다른 직원들도 이곳에 제때 올 수 없을지도 몰라요. 내일 아침에 매장 문을 늦게 열어야 할지를 제가 결정해야 할 것 같네요.
여: 출근 예정인 다른 직원들에게 제가 연락하기를 원하시면, 말씀만 하세요.
남: 정말 고마워요. 제안 감사해요.

PRACTICE | 기출 연습하기 본책 p.71

정답 1 (B) 2 (A) 3 (A) 4 (A) 5 (B) 6 (B)

Questions 1-2 refer to the following conversation.

M: Hi, Marilyn. I stopped by your office to find out if you have finished preparing the invitations for the annual banquet. I'd like to send them as soon as possible.
W: They're not ready yet. **1** The problem is that I used up all of the cream-colored paper, so I'm on my way to the stationery store now to buy more.
M: All right. **2** Don't forget to keep the receipt for the purchase. You'll need to give that to the finance team in order to get reimbursed.

1-2번 문제는 다음 대화를 참조하시오.
남: 안녕하세요, Marilyn. 연례 연회 행사에 필요한 초대장을 준비하시는 일을 완료하셨는지 알아보려고 당신 사무실에 들렀어요. 가능한 한 빨리 발송했으면 합니다.
여: 아직 준비되지 않았어요. 문제는 크림 색상의 용지를 모두 사용했다는 것입니다, 그래서 추가로 구입하기 위해 지금 문구점에 가는 길입니다.
남: 알겠습니다. 구매 제품에 대한 영수증을 잊지 말고 보관하세요. 비용을 환급 받으시려면 재무팀에 그것을 제출하셔야 합니다.

1. 여자는 무슨 문제점을 언급하는가?
(A) 일정이 겹치는 문제가 있다.
(B) 용품을 다 사용했다.

| 해설 |
여자의 문제점이 언급되는 중반부에, 크림 색상의 용지를 모두 사용했다고(I used up all of the cream-colored paper) 알리고 있으므로 (B)가 정답이다.

2. 남자는 여자에게 무엇을 하도록 상기시키는가?
(A) 영수증 보관하기
(B) 쿠폰 사용하기

| 해설 |
대화 후반부에, 남자가 여자에게 영수증을 잊지 말고 보관해 놓으라고 (Don't forget to keep the receipt ~) 당부하고 있으므로 (A)가 정답이다.

| 어휘 | stop by ~에 들르다 invitation 초대(장) banquet 연회 use up ~을 다 쓰다 on one's way to ~로 가는 길에, 오는 길에 stationery store 문구점

forget to do ~하는 것을 잊다   receipt 영수증   get reimbursed 비용 환급을 받다   run out of ~을 다 쓰다   supplies 용품, 물품   remind A to do A에게 ~하도록 상기시키다

Questions 3-4 refer to the following conversation.

W: Hi, Timothy. It's Jennifer. I just got back to my office, and I see that there is a message that I'm supposed to call you.
M: Thanks for getting back to me. I'm trying to print some handouts for the staff meeting, but **3** the printer is down again.
W: You know, we've had this problem repeatedly, so **4** I'll need to order some new parts for it. I'll do that now, but you'll have to use the printer in another department in the meantime.

3-4번 문제는 다음 대화를 참조하시오.
여: 안녕하세요, Timothy 씨. Jennifer입니다. 제가 막 사무실로 돌아왔는데, 당신께 전화 드려야 한다는 내용의 메시지가 보이네요.
남: 제게 다시 연락 주셔서 감사합니다. 제가 직원 회의에 필요한 일부 유인물을 출력하려고 하는데, 프린터가 또 고장 났어요.
여: 있잖아요, 이 문제가 반복해서 일어나고 있어서, 제가 몇몇 새 부품들을 주문해야 할 것 같아요. 지금 바로 하기는 하겠지만, 그 사이에 다른 부서에 있는 프린터를 사용하셔야 할 겁니다.

3. 남자는 무슨 문제점을 언급하는가?
(A) 일부 장비가 작동되지 않고 있다.
(B) 문서에 오류가 있다.

| 해설 |
대화 중반부에, 프린터가 또 고장 났다는(the printer is down again) 문제점을 알리는 남자의 말로 보아 장비가 작동되지 않고 있음을 알 수 있으므로 (A)가 정답이다.

4. 여자는 곧이어 무엇을 할 것 같은가?
(A) 주문하기
(B) 회의 개최하기

| 해설 |
대화 후반부에, 여자가 새 부품을 주문하는 일을 언급하면서 지금 하겠다고 (I'll need to order some new parts for it. I'll do that now ~) 알리고 있으므로 (A)가 정답이다.

| 어휘 | get back to ~로 돌아오다, ~에게 다시 연락하다   be supposed to do ~해야 하다, ~할 예정이다   try to do ~하려 하다   handout 유인물   down (기계 등이) 고장 난, 꺼진   repeatedly 반복해서, 되풀이되어   part 부품   department 부서   in the meantime 그 사이에, 그러는 동안   equipment 장비   work (기계 등이) 작동되다   hold ~을 개최하다

Questions 5-6 refer to the following conversation with three speakers.

M: Hi, Pricilla. Hi, Robin. Is everything ready for tomorrow's sales pitch to our new client?
W1: Unfortunately, there's an issue with the conference room. **5** We never received the projector and wireless speakers we ordered from Ace Supplies.
W2: Right. We won't be able to do the presentation without them.
M: Hmm... Robin, **6** why don't you call Nordin Electronics to see if they have what you need in stock? Then we could pick it up today in person.
W1: OK. Then I can follow up with Ace Supplies later.

5-6번 문제는 다음 세 사람의 대화를 참조하시오.
남: 안녕하세요, Pricilla 씨. 안녕하세요, Robin 씨. 우리 신규 고객을 대상으로 내일 있을 영업 발표에 대한 준비가 모두 끝났나요?
여1: 안타깝게도, 대회의실에 문제가 있습니다. 우리가 Ace Supplies에서 주문한 프로젝터와 무선 스피커를 전혀 받지 못했습니다.
여2: 맞아요. 그것들 없이는 발표를 할 수 없을 거예요.
남: 흠… Robin 씨, Nordin Electronics에 전화하셔서 필요로 하시는 것이 재고에 있는지 확인해 보시는 건 어떨까요? 그런 다음에 우리가 오늘 직접 가서 가져올 수 있을 겁니다.
여1: 알겠습니다. 그럼 Ace Supplies에 대해서는 나중에 후속 조치를 취할 수 있을 거예요.

5. 무엇이 문제점을 초래했는가?
(A) 회의가 취소되었다.
(B) 일부 물품들이 도착하지 않았다.

| 해설 |
대화 초반부에, 주문한 프로젝터와 무선 스피커를 받지 못했다는(We never received the projector and wireless speakers we ordered ~) 문제점을 언급하고 있으므로 (B)가 정답이다.

6. 남자는 무엇을 하도록 제안하는가?
(A) 상품 배달하기
(B) 다른 업체에 연락하기

| 해설 |
대화 후반부에, 남자가 Nordin Electronics에 전화해 볼 것을(why don't you call Nordin Electronics ~) 제안하는 부분이 있는데, 이는 앞서 언급된 Ace Supplies가 아닌 다른 업체에 알아보라는 것이므로 (B)가 정답이다.

| 어휘 | sales pitch 영업 발표, 제품 구입 권유   unfortunately 안타깝게도, 아쉽게도   receive ~을 받다   be able to do ~할 수 있다   presentation 발표(회)   see if ~인지 확인해 보다   have A in stock A를 재고로 갖고 있다   pick up ~을 가져오다   in person 직접 (가서)   follow up with ~에 대해 후속 조치를 하다

02 요청/제안 사항 문제

기출 유형 맛보기
본책 p.72

Q. 여자는 남자에게 무엇을 하도록 요청하는가?
(A) 기사 편집하기
(B) 가격 재협상하기
(C) 환불 요청하기
(D) 책임자에게 연락하기

여: 안녕하세요, Jeff. 우리가 소프트웨어를 위해 인쇄하고 있는 교육용 설명서에 관한 진행 상황 좀 알려 주시겠어요?
남: 인쇄소에서 오늘 아침에 제게 샘플을 보내 주었습니다. 그런데, 몇 가지 오타를 발견했어요. 인쇄소에 알렸고 사과를 받았습니다. 우리가 목요일에 수정된 설명서를 받을 거라고 그 책임자가 말해 주었습니다.
여: 그걸로 충분하지 않은 것 같아요. 행사 시간이 수요일 오후로 예정되어 있기 때문에 그때 유인물을 나눠 줘야 합니다. 그 책임자에게 다시 전화해서 늦어도 수요일 오전까지는 우리가 설명서를 받아야 한다고 요청해주시겠어요?

PRACTICE | 기출 연습하기

본책 p.73

정답 1 (A)　2 (B)　3 (B)　4 (A)　5 (A)　6 (B)

Questions 1-2 refer to the following conversation.

> M: Susan, there's an industry conference on Thursday and Friday, so a lot of the salespeople on my team will not be able to attend **1 the monthly meeting. Could you reschedule it for next week?**
> W: Sure. Thanks for bringing this to my attention. **2 I'll check the reservation schedule** to find out when the conference room is available.
> M: Thanks. I know that you've got some new regulation changes to go over, so it's important for everyone to be there.

1-2번 문제는 다음 대화를 참조하시오.
남: Susan, 목요일과 금요일에 업계 콘퍼런스 행사가 있기 때문에, 우리 팀에 있는 많은 영업 사원들이 월간 회의 시간에 참석할 수 없을 거예요. 그 회의를 다음 주로 일정을 변경해 주시겠어요?
여: 그럼요. 이 부분에 제가 주의를 기울일 수 있게 해 주셔서 감사합니다. 예약 일정표를 확인해서 언제 대회의실이 이용 가능한지 알아보겠습니다.
남: 감사합니다. 짚고 넘어 가야 할 몇몇 새로운 규정 변경 사항이 있는 것으로 알고 있기 때문에, 모든 사람이 그곳에 가는 게 중요합니다.

1. 남자는 여자에게 무엇을 하도록 요청하는가?
(A) 회의 날짜 변경하기
(B) 행사에 등록하기

| 해설 |
남자가 요청 사항을 밝히는 초반부에, 월간 회의를 언급하면서 그 일정을 재조정해 달라고(~ the monthly meeting. Could you reschedule it for next week?) 요청하고 있는데, 이는 날짜 변경을 뜻하므로 (A)가 정답이다.

2. 여자는 무엇을 할 것이라고 말하는가?
(A) 지출 비용 승인하기
(B) 일정표 확인하기

| 해설 |
여자가 앞으로 할 일이 언급되는 대화 중반부에, 예약 일정표를 확인해 보겠다고(I'll check the reservation schedule ~) 알리고 있으므로 (B)가 정답이다.

| 어휘 | industry 업계　salespeople 영업 사원들　attend ~에 참석하다　reschedule ~의 일정을 재조정하다　bring A to one's attention A에 ~가 주의[관심]을 기울이게 하다　reservation 예약　regulation 규정, 규제　go over ~을 짚어 주다, 검토하다

Questions 3-4 refer to the following conversation.

> W: Mr. Song, the graphic design team is having trouble keeping up with their tasks. The company has taken on a lot of new clients recently, so we're busier than ever.
> M: Well, I think this trend is only going to continue. **3 How about hiring a few part-time workers** to help you?
> W: Is there room in the budget to do that?
> M: Definitely. **4 Please write a description of the job's duties and send it to me.** Then I'll post it online.

3-4번 문제는 다음 대화를 참조하시오.
여: Song 씨, 그래픽 디자인팀이 업무를 따라잡는 데 어려움을 겪고 있어요. 회사에서 최근에 많은 신규 고객들을 맡게 되었기 때문에 우리가 그 어느 때보다 더 바쁩니다.
남: 저, 제 생각에는 이러한 추세가 계속될 것 같아요. 당신을 도울 수 있는 몇몇 시간제 근무자를 고용해 보는 건 어떠세요?
여: 예산에 그렇게 할 수 있는 여유가 있나요?
남: 물론입니다. 그 자리의 직무에 관한 설명을 작성하셔서 제게 보내 주세요. 그럼 제가 온라인에 게시하겠습니다.

3. 남자는 무엇을 하도록 제안하는가?
(A) 추가 근무하기
(B) 더 많은 직원 고용하기

| 해설 |
대화 중반부에, 남자가 시간제 근무자를 고용하는 것을(How about hiring a few part-time workers ~) 제안하는 부분이 있으므로 (B)가 정답이다.

4. 남자는 여자에게 무엇을 요청하고 있는가?
(A) 직무 설명 내용 작성하기
(B) 웹 사이트 주소 제공하기

| 해설 |
남자가 여자에게 요청하는 일이 언급되는 후반부에, 직무 설명 내용을 작성해 보내 달라고(Please write a description of the job's duties and send it to me) 알리고 있으므로 (A)가 정답이다.

| 어휘 | keep up with (진행 속도 등) ~을 따라잡다　task 업무, 일　take on ~을 맡다　recently 최근에　than ever 그 어느 때보다도　trend 경향, 추세　continue 계속되다　room 여유, 여지　budget 예산　Definitely (강한 긍정) 물론이죠, 당연하죠　description 설명　duty 업무, 직무　then 그러면, 그때, 그런 다음　post ~을 게시하다　extra 추가의, 별도의

Questions 5-6 refer to the following conversation.

> M: All right, Ms. McIntyre. I have your reservation here, and you'll be in Room 406. **5 If you'd like, I can take your suitcase up to your room** for you.
> W: Thanks, but I can manage it on my own. **6 What time do I need to check out** of the hotel in the morning?
> M: All guests must be checked out by 11 A.M. And don't forget that we offer a free breakfast in the morning. It's in the hotel lounge.
> W: Thanks. I'll definitely take advantage of that.

5-6번 문제는 다음 대화를 참조하시오.
남: 좋습니다, McIntyre 씨. 여기 귀하의 예약 사항이 보이는데, 406호실에 머무르시게 됩니다. 원하신다면, 제가 대신 객실까지 여행 가방을 올려다 드리겠습니다.
여: 감사합니다만, 제가 할 수 있습니다. 아침에 이 호텔에서 몇 시에 퇴실해야 하나요?
남: 모든 고객들께서는 반드시 오전 11시까지 퇴실하셔야 합니다. 그리고 저희가 오전에 무료 아침 식사를 제공해 드린다는 점을 잊지 마세요. 이곳 로비로 오시면 됩니다.
여: 감사합니다. 꼭 그 서비스를 이용할 겁니다.

5. 남자는 무엇을 해 주겠다고 제안하는가?
(A) 가방 옮기기
(B) 예약 취소하기

| 해설 |
남자의 제안 사항이 언급되는 초반부에, 가방을 대신 들어다 주겠다고(If you'd like, I can take your suitcase up to your room ~) 제안하는 말이 있으므로 (A)가 정답이다.

6. 여자는 남자에게 무엇에 관해 묻는가?
(A) 아침 식사 메뉴
(B) 퇴실 시간

| 해설 |
여자의 질문 사항이 제시되는 중반부에, 몇 시에 퇴실해야 하는지를(What time do I need to check out ~?) 묻고 있으므로 (B)가 정답이다.

| 어휘 | reservation 예약　manage ~을 처리하다, 해내다　on one's own 혼자, 스스로　by (기한) ~까지　forget that ~라는 점을 잊다　free 무료의　definitely 분명히, 꼭　take advantage of ~을 이용하다

DAY 11 | 실전문제　　　　　　　　　　본책 p.74

정답　1 (D)　2 (A)　3 (B)　4 (A)　5 (C)　6 (D)
　　　7 (A)　8 (C)　9 (B)　10 (B)　11 (A)　12 (D)
　　　13 (A)　14 (C)　15 (D)　16 (A)　17 (D)　18 (C)
　　　19 (C)　20 (B)　21 (D)

Questions 1-3 refer to the following conversation.

M: Thanks for showing me around your studio, Tammy. Everything is so beautiful.
W: Thanks! I spend all of my free time working on **1 my paintings. My goal is to have them exhibited in an art gallery someday.**
M: Well, you certainly have the talent for it. You know, **2 my cousin works at the Falbo Gallery. I could set up an appointment for you two to get together.**
W: I'd really appreciate that! Actually, it might be better if I call and introduce myself. **3 Do you have the number of the gallery?**
M: Of course. Let me find it.

1-3번 문제는 다음 대화를 참조하시오.
남: 당신의 스튜디오를 둘러볼 수 있게 해 주셔서 감사합니다, Tammy 씨. 모든 것이 너무 아름다워요.
여: 감사합니다! 저는 제 모든 여유 시간을 제 그림 작업을 하는 데 써요. 제 목표는 언젠가 미술관에서 그것들이 전시되도록 하는 거예요.
남: 저, 당신은 분명 그럴 만한 능력이 있어요. 있잖아요, 제 사촌이 Falbo Gallery에서 일하고 있어요. 두 사람이 만남을 가질 수 있도록 제가 약속을 주선해 드릴 수 있어요.
여: 그렇게 해 주시면 정말로 감사할 거예요! 사실, 제가 전화를 드리고 직접 소개를 하면 더 나을지도 몰라요. 그 미술관 전화번호를 갖고 계세요?
남: 물론이죠. 찾아볼게요.

| 어휘 | show A around B A에게 B를 둘러보게 해 주다　work on ~에 대한 작업을 하다　painting 그림　exhibit ~을 전시하다　set up an appointment 약속 일정을 잡다　get together 만나다, 모이다　appreciate ~에 대해 감사하다　it might be better if ~한다면 더 좋을지도 모른다　introduce ~을 소개하다

1. 여자는 무슨 목표를 언급하는가?
(A) 자신의 진로 변경하기
(B) 권위 있는 상 받기
(C) 책 출판하기
(D) 공개적으로 그림 전시하기

| 해설 |
대화 초반부에, 여자는 자신의 그림 작품을 언급하면서 미술관에서 그것들이 전시되도록 하는 것이 목표라고 하는(~ my paintings. My goal is to have them exhibited in an art gallery someday) 알리고 있으므로 (D)가 정답이다.

| 어휘 | career 진로, 근무 경력　win (상 등) ~을 받다, 타다　prestigious 권위 있는　display ~을 전시하다, 진열하다　publicly 공개적으로

2. 남자는 무엇을 해주겠다고 하는가?
(A) 만남 일정 잡기
(B) 여자에게 지원서 보내기
(C) 한 프로젝트에 일부 자금 투자하기
(D) 한 행사장으로 여자와 동행하기

| 해설 |
대화 중반부에, 남자는 사촌이 Falbo Gallery에서 일한다는 사실과 함께 만남을 가질 수 있도록 약속을 잡아줄 수 있다고(~ my cousin works at the Falbo Gallery. I could set up an appointment for you two to get together) 말하고 있으므로 (A)가 정답이다.

| 어휘 | application 지원(서)　invest A in B A를 B에 투자하다　accompany ~와 동행하다, ~을 동반하다

3. 여자는 무슨 정보를 요청하는가?
(A) 이메일 주소
(B) 전화번호
(C) 업체 이름
(D) 폐장 시간

| 해설 |
대화 후반부에, 여자가 남자에게 미술관 전화번호를 갖고 있는지(Do you have the number of the gallery?) 묻고 있으므로 (B)가 정답이다.

Questions 4-6 refer to the following conversation.

M: In local news, the **4 Summer Music Festival wrapped up last night with a final performance from singer Sarina Ramos, who is in the studio today.** Welcome, Sarina.
W: Thanks. It's a pleasure to be here. We had a fantastic crowd last night with lots of energy. Unfortunately, **5 due to a computer malfunction, there was some trouble** with the ticket readers at the entrances, so the start time of the concert was delayed.
M: Well, from what I hear, everyone had a great time after that got sorted out. **6 Now, it's time for a brief update on the traffic situation,** and then we'll have more from Sarina.

4-6번 문제는 다음 대화를 참조하시오.
남: 지역 뉴스입니다, 어젯밤 여름 음악 축제가 오늘 스튜디오에 자리하신 가수 Sarina Ramos 씨의 최종 공연을 끝으로 마무리되었습니다. 어서 오세요, Sarina 씨.
여: 감사합니다. 이 자리에 나올 수 있게 되어 기쁩니다. 저희는 어젯밤에 어마어마한 에너지를 지닌 환상적인 관중들과 함께 했습니다. 안타깝게도, 컴퓨터 오작동으로 인해, 출입구의 티켓 판독기에 일부 문제가 생기는 바람에, 콘서트 시작 시간이 지연되었습니다.
남: 음, 제가 들은 바로는, 모든 사람들이 그 문제가 해결된 후로는 아주 멋진 시간을 보냈다고 합니다. 이제, 교통 상황에 관해 간단히 새로운 소식을 전해 드릴 순서이며, 그 다음에 Sarina 씨와 더 얘기를 나눠 보겠습니다.

| 어휘 | local 지역의, 현지의　wrap up 마무리되다, 끝나다　crowd 관중, 군중　unfortunately 안타깝게도　due to ~로 인해　malfunction 오작동　reader 판독기　delayed 지연된　sort out (문제 등) ~을 해결하다　brief 간단한, 잠시의　traffic 교통, 차량들　situation 상황

4. 대화의 주제는 무엇인가?
(A) 콘서트
(B) 강연
(C) 건강 검진
(D) 스포츠 행사

| 해설 |
대화를 시작하면서 남자가 어제 끝난 Summer Music Festival을 언급한 후에 마지막 공연을 한 가수 Sarina Ramos를(singer Sarina Ramos) 스튜디오에 초대한 상황임을 밝히고 있으므로 (A)가 정답이다.

5. 여자의 말에 따르면, 무엇이 문제를 야기했는가?
(A) 심각한 폭풍우
(B) 안전 문제
(C) 컴퓨터 오류
(D) 고장 난 마이크

| 해설 |
문제점이 언급되는 중반부에, 여자가 컴퓨터 오작동으로 인해 일부 문제가 발생했음을(~ due to a computer malfunction, there was some trouble ~) 알리고 있으므로 (C)가 정답이다.

| 어휘 | cause ~을 야기하다   severe 심각한, 극심한   broken 고장 난, 망가진

6. 청자들은 곧이어 무엇을 들을 것인가?
(A) 새로운 노래
(B) 인터뷰
(C) 광고
(D) 교통 소식

| 해설 |
다음 방송 순서를 밝히는 후반부에, 남자가 교통 상황에 관해 간단히 새로운 소식을 전할 차례라고(Now, it's time for a brief update on the traffic situation ~) 알리고 있으므로 (D)가 정답이다.

| 어휘 | advertisement 광고

Questions 7-9 refer to the following conversation.

> W1: Jean, I've reviewed the data on the transactions **7** here at our store over the past few months. **8** Customers are returning **7** the power tools and ladders made by Quimby Co. at the highest rate we've ever seen.
> W2: Yeah, it seems like a lot of the complaints we get at the store are about that brand. When people try to use their products, they don't meet their expectations.
> W1: Exactly. How can we resolve this problem?
> W2: Hmm… I don't think the price is the problem—it's the product themselves. **9** Let's remove that brand from our shelves and look for a different manufacturer instead.
> W1: **9** Yes, that's the best way forward.

7-9번 문제는 다음 대화를 참조하시오.
여1: Jean, 제가 지난 몇 달에 걸쳐 이곳 우리 매장의 거래에 대한 데이터를 검토해 왔습니다. 우리가 그동안 봐 온 것 중에서 가장 높은 비율로 Quimby Co.에서 제조한 전동 공구와 사다리를 고객들이 반품하고 있어요.
여2: 네, 우리가 매장에서 접수하는 많은 불만 사항들이 그 브랜드와 관련된 것 같아요. 사람들이 그 제품을 사용하려 할 때, 기대치를 충족시키지 못하고 있습니다.
여1: 바로 그거예요. 우리가 이 문제를 어떻게 해결할 수 있을까요?
여2: 흠… 가격이 아니라 제품 자체가 문제인 것 같아요. 그 브랜드를 우리 진열 선반에서 없애고, 대신 다른 제조사를 찾아봅시다.
여1: 네, 그게 나중을 위한 최선의 방법입니다.

| 어휘 | review ~을 검토하다   transaction 거래   over ~ 동안에 걸쳐   return ~을 반품하다   power tool 전동 공구   ladder 사다리   rate 비율   complaint 불만   expectation 기대(치)   Exactly (강한 동조) 바로 그거예요, 맞아요   resolve ~을 해결하다   oneself (명사 뒤에서 강조하여) 그 자체   remove ~을 없애다, 제거하다   look for ~을 찾다   manufacturer 제조사   instead 대신에   the best way forward 앞날을 위한 최선의 방법

7. 대화가 어디에서 이뤄지고 있을 것 같은가?
(A) 철물점에서
(B) 자동차 판매 대리점에서
(C) 이사 전문 회사에서
(D) 은행에서

| 해설 |
여자 한 명이 대화를 시작하면서 '우리 매장(here at our store)'이라고 지칭한 후에 제품의 종류와 관련해 전동 공구와 사다리(the power tools and ladders)를 언급하고 있으므로 (A)가 정답이다.

| 어휘 | take place (일, 행사 등이) 발생되다, 일어나다   dealership 판매 대리점

8. 화자들은 주로 무엇에 관해 이야기하고 있는가?
(A) 시장 점유율을 얻고 있는 경쟁사
(B) 제때 도착하지 않는 배송 물품
(C) 자주 반품을 하는 고객들
(D) 경험이 많지 않은 일부 직원들

| 해설 |
문제점이 언급되는 초반부에, 여자 한 명이 특정 전동 공구와 사다리가 반품되고 있는 상황임을(Customers are returning the power tools and ladders ~) 알리고 있으므로 (C)가 정답이다.

| 어휘 | competitor 경쟁사   gain ~을 얻다   market share 시장 점유(율)   arrive 도착하다   on time 제때   frequently 자주   experienced 경험이 많은

9. 화자들은 무엇을 하는 데 동의하는가?
(A) 추가 직원 고용하기
(B) 한 브랜드의 판매 중단하기
(C) 일부 가격 낮추기
(D) 비용 지불 절차 개선하기

| 해설 |
대화 후반부에, 한 여자가 특정 브랜드를 진열 선반에서 없애자고(Let's remove that brand from our shelves ~) 제안하자, 다른 여자가 'Yes'라고 동의하고 있다. 이는 해당 제품의 판매 중단을 뜻하는 것이므로 (B)가 정답이다.

| 어휘 | lower ~을 낮추다, 내리다   improve ~을 개선하다   payment 비용 지불(액)   procedure 절차

Questions 10-12 refer to the following conversation with three speakers.

> W1: Hi, Susan. I've saved the slideshow **10** presentation for our sales meeting on this portable drive.
> W2: Thanks. I've connected the projector to the laptop, but I'm just getting a blue screen. **11** Could you call someone from the IT department to help us with this issue? The clients will be here soon.
> W1: Sure. **11** Let me call right away … Oh, hi, Brady. It's Susan. I'm in the third-floor meeting room, and the projector isn't displaying the image

from the laptop.
M: It does that sometimes. **12 You should try turning it off and turning it on again.**
W1: We can try that, but I don't think it will work.
M: All right. I'll be there in a few minutes.

10-12번 문제는 다음 세 명의 대화를 참조하시오.
여1: 안녕하세요, Susan 씨. 제가 이 휴대용 드라이브에 우리 매출 회의에 관한 슬라이드쇼 발표 자료를 저장해 뒀어요.
여2: 감사합니다. 제가 프로젝터를 노트북 컴퓨터에 연결시켰는데, 파란색 화면만 보이고 있어요. IT 부서의 직원에게 전화하셔서 이 문제에 대해 우리를 도와 달라고 해 주시겠어요? 고객들이 곧 여기로 올 거예요.
여1: 물론이죠. 당장 전화할게요… 아, 안녕하세요, Brady 씨. 저는 Susan입니다. 제가 3층 회의실에 와 있는데, 프로젝터가 노트북 컴퓨터의 이미지를 보여주지 못하고 있어요.
남: 가끔씩 그럽니다. 껐다가 그 후에 다시 한번 켜 보세요.
여1: 그렇게 해 볼 수는 있지만, 효과가 있을 것 같지 않아요.
남: 알겠습니다. 몇 분 후에 그리로 갈게요.

| 어휘 | presentation 발표 sales 매출, 영업, 판매(량) portable 휴대용의 connect A to B A를 B에 연결하다 display (화면 등에서) ~을 보여 주다, 나타내다 turn off[on] ~을 끄다[켜다] work 효과가 있다, 작동되다 in + 시간 ~ 후에

10. 화자들은 무엇에 대한 일을 하고 있는가?
(A) 노트북 컴퓨터 찾기
(B) 매출 회의 준비하기
(C) 새 프로젝터 개발하기
(D) 일부 의자들 배치하기

| 해설 |
대화 초반부에, 여자 한 명이 휴대용 드라이브에 저장한 매출 회의에 관한 발표 자료를 건네 주는(~ presentation for our sales meeting on this portable drive) 상황이 나오므로 (B)가 정답이다.

| 어휘 | look for ~을 찾다 prepare for ~을 준비하다 develop ~을 개발하다 arrange ~을 배치하다, 마련하다

11. 남자는 누구일 것 같은가?
(A) IT 기술자
(B) 영업부장
(C) 잠재 고객
(D) 건물 주인

| 해설 |
대화 중반부에, 여자 한 명이 IT 부서의 직원에게 전화하도록(Could you call someone from the IT department ~) 요청하자, 다른 여자가 남자와 통화를 시작하는(Let me call right away. Hmm … Oh, hi, Brady) 부분에서 남자의 신원을 확인할 수 있다. 따라서 남자는 IT 부서 직원임을 알 수 있으므로 (A)가 정답이다.

| 어휘 | potential 잠재적인

12. 남자는 여자들에게 무엇을 하도록 권하는가?
(A) 행사 연기하기
(B) 새로운 부품 주문하기
(C) 위치 변경하기
(D) 기기를 다시 시작하기

| 해설 |
남자가 권하는 일이 언급되는 후반부에, 프로젝터를 껐다가 다시 한번 켜 보도록(Try turning it off and then back on again) 권하고 있으므로 (D)가 정답이다.

| 어휘 | postpone ~을 연기하다 part 부품 location 위치, 지점 device 기기, 장치

Questions 13-15 refer to the following conversation.

M: Hi, you've reached Andrew Saunders.
W: Hi, Andrew. I'm glad I caught you before you left for lunch. There's a business card on my desk for Corbin Industries. **13 14 I'm wondering if you could tell me the phone number on it. Could you help me with that?**
M: Actually, I'm late for a meeting. My committee is discussing the quarterly budget over lunch.
W: Oh, I see. Then I don't want to keep you.
M: **15 I think Angela was planning to stay here during lunch, so you could call her.** I'm sure she wouldn't mind going up to your office and looking for the card.
W: Thanks. **15 That's what I'll do.** I'm downtown now, so I really want to avoid going all the way back to our building.

13-15번 문제는 다음 대화를 참조하시오.
남: 안녕하세요, 저는 Andrew Saunders입니다.
여: 안녕하세요, Andrew 씨. 점심 식사하러 나가시기 전에 연락이 되어 다행입니다. 제 책상에 보시면 Corbin Industries 사로 된 명함이 하나 있어요. 거기에 적힌 전화번호를 제게 알려 주실 수 있는지 궁금해서요. 저를 도와주실 수 있을까요?
남: 사실, 제가 회의에 늦은 상태라서요. 제가 속한 위원회에서 점심 식사를 하면서 분기 예산 문제를 논의할 예정이에요.
여: 아, 알겠습니다. 그럼 제가 당신을 붙잡고 있으면 안 되겠네요.
남: Angela 씨가 점심 시간 중에 계속 여기 있을 계획이셨던 것 같으니, 그분께 전화해 보세요. 분명 당신 사무실로 올라가서 그 명함을 찾아봐 줄 겁니다.
여: 감사합니다. 그렇게 해야겠네요. 제가 지금 시내에 있기 때문에, 우리 건물로 다시 되돌아 가는 일을 정말로 피하고 싶어서요.

| 어휘 | reach ~에게 연락하다 catch (때마침) 연락이 닿다, 만나다 leave for ~하러 나가다 wonder if ~인지 궁금하다 actually 실은, 사실은 committee 위원회 quarterly 분기의 budget 예산 over (식사 등) ~하면서 downtown 시내에 있는 avoid -ing ~하는 것을 피하다 all the way to ~까지 계속, 쭉

13. 여자는 남자에게 무엇을 요청하는가?
(A) 한 업체의 연락처
(B) 점심 식사 주문에 대한 추천
(C) 계약서 사본
(D) 한 보안 직원의 이름

| 해설 |
여자가 요청 사항을 언급하는 초반부에, 특정 회사를 밝히면서 그곳의 전화번호를 알려줄 수 있는지(I'm wondering if you could tell me the phone number on it) 요청하고 있으므로 (A)가 정답이다.

| 어휘 | contract 계약(서)

14. 남자가 "Actually, I'm late for a meeting"이라고 말할 때 무엇을 암시하는가?
(A) 여자가 발표를 해야 한다고 생각한다.
(B) 한 장소로 택시를 타고 가고 싶어 한다.
(C) 여자의 요청 사항을 이행할 수 없다.
(D) 일정 변경에 대해 언짢아 하고 있다.

| 해설 |
대화 초반부에, 여자가 특정 회사를 밝히면서 그곳의 전화번호를 알려 줄 수 있는지(I'm wondering if you could tell me the phone number on it) 요청하자 남자가 '사실, 회의 시간에 늦은 상태이다'라고 말하는 상황이다. 따라서 여자의 요청을 들어줄 수 없음을 밝히는 말임을 알 수 있으므로

(C)가 정답이다.

| 어휘 | site 장소, 현장　fulfill ~을 이행하다　request 요청　be upset about ~에 대해 언짢아 하다

15. 여자는 무엇을 할 계획인가?
(A) 행사 연기하기
(B) 건물로 돌아 가기
(C) 사무실을 잠그지 않은 채로 두기
(D) 다른 동료 직원에게 전화하기

| 해설 |
대화 후반부에, 남자가 Angela 씨에게 전화해 보도록 권하자(I think Angela was planning to stay here ~ so you could call her) 여자가 그래야겠다고(That's what I'll do) 동의하고 있으므로 (D)가 정답이다.

| 어휘 | postpone ~을 연기하다　return to ~로 돌아가다　leave A p.p. A를 ~된 상태로 두다　coworker 동료 직원

Questions 16-18 refer to the following conversation.

> M: Leah, I've had several calls from customers about their **16** **orders being canceled** without notice. Did you have a computer glitch in the shipping department?
> W: No, it's a problem with our supply chain. **16** **We completely ran out of the Martex brand of kitchen appliances**, so there was nothing we could do.
> M: I see. Is there any way to prevent this in the future?
> W: We can't always predict what customers will order. However, **17** **we should teach our staff to suggest other items from our catalog when this happens.** What do you think about the plan?
> M: Great idea! **18** **Let's meet this afternoon to draw up a schedule** for training employees.
> W: All right. It would be best to have the details worked out before we announce it.

16-18번 문제는 다음 대화를 참조하시오.

남: Leah 씨, 제가 고객들로부터 사전 공지 없이 주문이 취소되는 것과 관련해 여러 전화를 받았어요. 배송부에 컴퓨터와 관련된 문제가 있었나요?
여: 아뇨, 그건 우리 공급망과 관련된 문제입니다. Martex 브랜드의 주방 기기가 완전히 다 떨어졌기 때문에, 우리가 할 수 있는 건 전혀 없었어요.
남: 알겠습니다. 앞으로 이 문제를 방지할 수 있는 방법이 있을까요?
여: 고객들이 무엇을 주문할 것인지를 항상 예측할 수는 없어요. 하지만, 이런 일이 생길 때 우리 직원들에게 카탈로그에 들어 있는 다른 제품을 권하도록 가르쳐야 해요. 이 방안에 대해 어떻게 생각하세요?
남: 좋은 생각입니다! 직원 교육에 대한 일정표를 작성할 수 있도록 오늘 오후에 만납시다.
여: 좋습니다. 우리가 공지하기 전에 세부 방안을 생각해 내는 것이 가장 좋을 거예요.

| 어휘 | several 여럿의　cancel ~을 취소하다　without notice 사전 공지 없이　glitch 작은 문제, 결함　shipping 배송, 선적　supply chain 공급망　completely 완전히, 전적으로　run out of A A가 다 떨어지다, 다 쓰다　appliance (가전) 기기　prevent ~을 방지하다　predict ~을 예측하다　draw up ~을 작성하다　work out ~을 생각해 내다　announce ~을 공지하다, 발표하다

16. 여자의 말에 따르면, 무엇 때문에 일부 배송이 취소되는 일이 초래되었는가?
(A) 물품 부족
(B) 폐업

(C) 지불 연체
(D) 직원 부족

| 해설 |
대화 초반부에, 남자가 고객들의 주문 취소 문제(orders being canceled)를 언급한 뒤로, 여자가 특정 브랜드의 제품이 다 떨어졌다는(We completely ran out of the Martex brand of kitchen appliances ~) 말로 그 이유를 말하고 있다. 따라서 물품 부족 문제가 원인임을 알 수 있으므로 (A)가 정답이다.

| 어휘 | lack of ~의 부족　supplies 물품, 용품　shortage 부족

17. 여자는 직원들에게 무엇을 하기를 원하는가?
(A) 고객들이 가져오는 제품 수리하기
(B) 더 주기적으로 재고 물품 확인하기
(C) 새로운 배송 시스템 활용하기
(D) 대안이 되는 추천 사항을 말해 주기

| 해설 |
여자의 말에서 교육 관련 정보가 제시되는 후반부에 다른 제품을 권하도록 직원들을 가르쳐야 한다고(we should teach our staff to suggest other items ~) 밝히고 있는데, 이는 대체 제품을 권하는 것이므로 (D)가 정답이다.

| 어휘 | repair ~을 수리하다　bring in ~을 가져오다, 들여오다　inventory 재고(품), 재고 목록　regularly 주기적으로　alternative 대안이 되는, 대체하는

18. 화자들은 오늘 오후에 무엇을 할 계획인가?
(A) 변동 사항 공지하기
(B) 고객에게 연락하기
(C) 일정표 만들기
(D) 카탈로그 보내기

| 해설 |
'오늘 오후'라는 시점 키워드가 제시되는 후반부에, 일정표를 만들기 위해 오늘 오후에 만나자고(Let's meet this afternoon to draw up a schedule ~) 제안하고 있으므로 (C)가 정답이다.

| 어휘 | contact ~에게 연락하다　create ~을 만들어 내다

Questions 19-21 refer to the following conversation and menu.

> W: Good afternoon. This is Maxine Griffin. I'm calling in response to **19** **your invitation to the welcome party** for new investors. I plan on attending the event.
> M: That's wonderful, Ms. Griffin. And did you have a chance to look at the menu options?
> W: Hmm ... well, **20** **I'm allergic to seafood**, so I need to take that into consideration.
> M: We have two sets without seafood— **20** **the roasted chicken and potatoes and the pork chops with steamed rice.**
> W: Oh, **20** **I don't eat pork either.**
> M: All right. **21** **And please note that this is a formal event, so you should wear appropriate clothing.**

Set	Description
1	Clams in Garlic Cream Sauce
20 2	Roasted Chicken and Potatoes
3	Grilled Shrimp with Tomato Sauce
4	Pork Chops with Steamed Rice

19-21번 문제는 다음 대화와 메뉴를 참조하시오.
여: 안녕하세요. 저는 Maxine Griffin이라고 합니다. 신규 투자자들을 위해 열리는 환영 파티 초대에 대한 답변으로 전화 드렸습니다. 저는 그 행사에 참석할 계획입니다.
남: 아주 좋습니다. Griffin 씨. 그리고 메뉴 선택을 확인할 기회가 있었나요?
여: 흠… 저, 제가 해산물에 알레르기가 있기 때문에, 그 점을 고려해야 합니다.
남: 해산물이 들어 있지 않은 세트는 두 가지가 있는데, 구운 닭고기와 감자 요리가 있고, 밥이 곁들여진 폭 찹이 있습니다.
여: 아, 저는 돼지고기도 먹지 않아요.
남: 알겠습니다. 그리고 격식을 갖춘 행사이기 때문에, 적절한 복장을 차려 입으셔야 한다는 점에 유의하시기 바랍니다.

세트	설명
1	마늘 크림 소스로 된 조개 요리
2	구운 닭고기와 감자 요리
3	토마토 소스로 그릴에 구운 새우 요리
4	밥이 곁들여진 폭 찹

| 어휘 | in response to ~에 대한 답변으로, ~에 대응해 investor 투자자 be allergic to ~에 알레르기가 있다 take A into consideration A를 고려하다 roasted 구운 steamed 찐 either (부정문에서) ~도 formal 격식을 갖춘 appropriate 적절한 clothing 옷, 의류 description 설명 clam 조개

19. 어떤 종류의 행사에 관해 얘기하고 있는가?
(A) 제품 출시
(B) 기념일 행사
(C) 환영 축하 행사
(D) 시상식

| 해설 |
대화 초반부에, 여자가 환영 파티 초대에(your invitation to the welcome party) 대한 답변으로 전화한다고 알리고 있으므로 (C)가 정답이다.

| 어휘 | launch 출시, 공개 anniversary (해마다 돌아오는) 기념일 reception 축하 행사, 기념 행사

20. 시각 자료를 보시오. 여자에게 어느 메뉴 세트가 제공될 것인가?
(A) 세트 1
(B) 세트 2
(C) 세트 3
(D) 세트 4

| 해설 |
대화 중반부에, 여자가 해산물 알레르기가 있다고 언급했고(I'm allergic to seafood), 후반부에 남자가 'roasted chicken and potatoes'와 'pork chops with steamed rice'라는 두 가지 선택 사항을 제시하자, 여자가 돼지고기도 먹지 않는다고(I don't eat pork either) 말하고 있다. 따라서 'roasted chicken and potatoes'를 선택할 것임을 알 수 있으므로 이 세트 번호에 해당되는 (B)가 정답이다.

21. 남자는 여자에게 무엇을 하도록 요청하는가?
(A) 초대장 가지고 오기
(B) 좌석 배치도 확인하기
(C) 구내에 주차하기
(D) 격식을 갖춰 차려 입기

| 해설 |
남자의 권고 사항이 언급되는 후반부에, 격식을 갖춘 행사에 맞게 차려 입도록(And please note that this is a formal event, so you should wear appropriate clothing) 권고하고 있으므로 (D)가 정답이다.

| 어휘 | review ~을 확인하다, 검토하다 seating chart 좌석 배치도 formally 격식을 갖춰

DAY 12 세부적인 내용을 묻는 유형 (2)

01 앞으로 할 일을 묻는 문제

기출 유형 맛보기 본책 p.76

Q. 남자는 곧이어 무엇을 할 것인가?
(A) 한 아파트 광고하기
(B) 일부 수리 작업 하기
(C) 시설 관리팀에 연락하기
(D) 일부 가격 조사하기

여: Steve, 새 세입자들이 이사 오기 전에 우리가 어떻게 아파트에 페인트칠을 하는지 알고 계시죠? 저, 우리 시설 관리팀이 이 일을 항상 즉시 해 줄 수 있는 것이 아니라서, 몇몇 문제점과 맞닥뜨리고 있어요.
남: 그럼 전문 페인트칠 업체를 고용합시다.
여: 그러면 이상적이겠지만, 우리는 그 비용을 지불할 여유가 없어요.
남: 전에는 그랬지만, 지금은 우리가 여러 아파트를 운영하고 있잖아요.
여: 네, 그렇죠. 그리고 지금 생각해 보니까, 시설 관리팀이 페인트 작업 외에 다른 일을 하느라 그 어느 때보다 더 바빠요.
남: 그럼 그 일을 다른 업체와 계약해서 맡깁시다. 제가 몇몇 페인트칠 전문 업체에 전화해서 가격 견적서를 받아 볼게요.

PRACTICE | 기출 연습하기 본책 p.77
정답 1 (A) 2 (B) 3 (A) 4 (B) 5 (B) 6 (B)

Questions 1-2 refer to the following conversation.

W: Hello, **1** you've reached the Harbor Apartments property management office. How may I help you?
M: Hi, this is Lucas Cassano calling from apartment 43B. I have a lease until December, but I actually need to move out early. I've accepted a new position in Boston, so I'm relocating there.
W: OK, Mr. Cassano. You'll have to **2** get approval from the landlord, or there might be a fee. **2** I'll e-mail him now about this situation.

1-2번 문제는 다음 대화를 참조하시오.
여: 여보세요, 여기는 Harbor 아파트 건물 관리 사무소입니다. 무엇을 도와 드릴까요?
남: 안녕하세요, 저는 아파트 43B에서 전화 드리는 Lucas Cassano라고 합니다. 제가 12월까지 임대 계약이 되어 있기는 하지만, 사실은 일찍 이사를 가야 합니다. 제가 Boston에 있는 새 일자리를 수락했기 때문에, 그곳으로 이주할 예정입니다.
여: 알겠습니다, Cassano 씨. 건물주의 승인을 받으셔야 하는데, 그렇지 않으면 수수료가 있을 수도 있습니다. 제가 지금 이 상황에 관해 그분께 이메일을 보내겠습니다.

1. 여자는 누구일 것 같은가?
(A) 부동산 관리자
(B) 판매 직원

| 해설 |
여자의 말에서 여자가 근무하는 장소가 건물 관리 사무소(you've reached the Harbor Apartments property management office)임을 알 수 있으므로 정답은 (A)이다.

2. 여자는 곧이어 무엇을 할 것 같은가?
(A) 안내 책자 보내기
(B) 건물주에게 연락하기

| 해설 |
여자가 앞으로 할 일을 언급하는 후반부에, 건물주의 승인을 받아야 한다면서(get approval from the landlord) 그 사람에게 이메일을 보내겠다고 (I'll e-mail him now ~) 알리고 있으므로 (B)가 정답이다.

| 어휘 | property 건물, 부동산 lease 임대 계약(서) move out 이사 가다 position 직책, 일자리 relocate 이전하다, 이사하다 get approval from ~로부터 허락[승인]을 받다 landlord 건물주, 집주인 fee 수수료, 요금 representative 대리인, 대표자 brochure 안내 책자

Questions 3-4 refer to the following conversation.

> M: 3 **The manager wants us to develop a program of monthly professional development lectures.** The sessions should be aimed at helping employees to improve their business skills. I'm really not sure what topic we should cover, though.
> W: 4 **Why don't we make a questionnaire** for employees? That way, we could find out which topics they're most interested in.
> M: Good idea. 4 **We can brainstorm the survey questions now.** The sooner we send it out, the better.

3-4번 문제는 다음 대화를 참조하시오.
남: 부장님께서 우리가 월간 직업 능력 개발 강좌 프로그램을 개발하기를 원하세요. 이 시간들은 직원들이 각자의 비즈니스 능력을 향상시키는 데 도움을 주는 것을 목표로 해야 합니다. 하지만 우리가 무슨 주제를 다뤄야 하는지 통 모르겠어요.
여: 직원들을 대상으로 하는 설문지를 만들어 보는 건 어때요? 그렇게 하면, 그들이 무슨 주제에 가장 관심이 있는지 알아볼 수 있을 거예요.
남: 좋은 생각이에요. 지금 설문지 질문들에 관한 아이디어를 떠올려 볼 수 있을 겁니다. 더 빨리 보낼수록, 더 좋을 거예요.

3. 화자들은 주로 무엇에 관해 이야기하고 있는가?
(A) 배정된 업무
(B) 예산 보고서

| 해설 |
대화 초반부에, 남자가 부서장이 원하는 일을(The manager wants us to develop a program ~) 언급한 뒤로 그 방법에 관해 대화가 진행되고 있는데, 이는 자신들에게 배정된 업무를 의미하는 것이므로 (A)가 정답이다.

4. 화자들은 곧이어 무엇을 할 것 같은가?
(A) 정책 검토하기
(B) 설문지 만들기

| 해설 |
대화 중반부에, 여자가 설문지를 만들자고 제안하자(Why don't we make a questionnaire ~), 남자가 설문지 질문들에 관한 아이디어 회의를 지금 할 수 있다고(We can brainstorm the survey questions now) 밝히고 있다. 이는 설문지를 만드는 것에 동의하는 말이므로 (B)가 정답이다.

| 어휘 | professional development 직업 능력 개발 session (특정 활동을 위한) 시간 be aimed at ~을 목표로 하다 improve ~을 향상시키다, 개선하다

though (문장 끝이나 중간에서) 하지만 questionnaire 설문(지)(= survey) That way 그렇게 하면, 그런 방법으로 find out ~을 알아내다 brainstorm ~에 관한 아이디어 회의를 하다

Questions 5-6 refer to the following conversation with three speakers.

> W1: Hello. May I speak to the manager, please?
> W2: Yes, just a moment. Mr. Adams, there's someone on the line for you.
> M: Hi, 5 **this is Leo Adams, the factory manager.**
> W1: Hi, Mr. Adams. I'm calling from Phelps Supplies. Since you've placed several orders with us in the past, 6 **I wanted to introduce you to our new cleaner,** which is specially designed for machine parts.
> M: Hmm ... 6 **why don't you send one bottle with our next order so I can see how well it works?**

5-6번 문제는 다음 세 명의 대화를 참조하시오.
여1: 안녕하세요. 책임자와 얘기 좀 할 수 있을까요?
여2: 네, 잠시만요. Adams 씨, 누군가가 당신을 찾는 전화가 왔습니다.
남: 안녕하세요, 공장 책임자 Leo Adams입니다.
여1: 안녕하세요, Adams 씨. 저는 Phelps Supplies에서 전화 드리고 있습니다. 전에 저희 쪽에 여러 차례 주문을 하신 적이 있으시기 때문에, 기계 부품을 위해 특별히 고안된 저희 새 세척제를 소개해 드리고자 합니다.
남: 흠… 얼마나 효과가 좋은지 확인해 볼 수 있도록 다음 번 저희 주문에 한 통 함께 보내 주시는 건 어떠세요?

5. 남자는 어디에서 근무하는가?
(A) 수리 업체에서
(B) 공장에서

| 해설 |
남자가 자신의 신원을 밝히는 중반부에, 공장 책임자라고(this is Leo Adams, the factory manager) 소개하고 있으므로 (B)가 정답이다.

6. 남자는 무엇을 할 것이라고 말하는가?
(A) 나중에 Phelps Supplies에 전화하기
(B) 제품을 시험 사용해 보기

| 해설 |
새로운 세제를 소개하려 한다는(~ introduce you to our new cleaner) 여자의 말 뒤에, 남자가 그 효과를 확인해 볼 수 있도록 나중에 한 통 보내 달라고(why don't you send one bottle ~ see how well it works?) 요청하고 있다. 이는 시험 사용을 통해 제품의 성능을 알아보려는 것이므로 (B)가 정답이다.

| 어휘 | on the line 전화상에 place an order 주문하다 several 여럿의 be designed for ~을 위해 고안되다, ~을 목적으로 만들어지다 part 부품 work 효과가 있다, 작용하다 repair 수리 give A a try A를 시험 사용해 보다, A를 한번 해 보다

02 특정 시점의 일 / 과거에 한 일을 묻는 문제

기출 유형 맛보기
본책 p.78

Q. 여자는 수요일에 무엇을 할 것인가?
(A) 구직 면접 보기
(B) 몇몇 의류 구입하기
(C) 고객들과 협업하기
(D) 외부 지역으로 출장 가기

여: 안녕하세요, Anderson 씨. 드라이클리닝을 해 주셨으면 하는 블라우스가 있습니다. 그런데 두어 군데 얼룩이 있다는 것을 막 알았어요.
남: 한번 볼게요. 얼룩을 지우는 것은 문제가 되지 않을 겁니다. 이것과 어제 놓고 가신 옷들을 금요일까지 준비해 드릴 수 있습니다.
여: 괜찮으시면, 수요일 오후로 예정되어 있는 제 구직 면접 전에 두 가지 모두 받았으면 합니다. 그렇게 해 주실 수 있으세요?
남: 네, 그날 오전 10시까지 가져가실 수 있도록 직접 작업해 드릴게요.

PRACTICE | 기출 연습하기
본책 p.79

정답 1 (B) 2 (A) 3 (B) 4 (A) 5 (B) 6 (A)

Questions 1-2 refer to the following conversation.

M: Marta, [1] **I'm participating in the technology trade show this weekend.** Would you mind trading shifts with me on Friday so I can leave earlier in the day?
W: I'd like to help you out, but I have tickets to a concert that night, so I can't work the evening shift. [2] **Why don't you try asking Garrett? He has worked the evening shift many times, and he usually has a flexible schedule.**
M: OK, [2] **I'll go look for him now.** Thanks.

1-2번 문제는 다음 대화를 참조하시오.
남: Marta, 제가 이번 주말에 기술 무역 박람회에 참가할 예정입니다. 제가 금요일에 더 일찍 떠날 수 있도록 그날 저와 교대 근무를 바꿔 주실 수 있으세요?
여: 도와 드리고는 싶지만, 제가 그날 밤에 콘서트를 보려고 티켓을 구입해 놔서, 저녁 교대 근무를 할 수 없어요. Garrett 씨께 한번 여쭤 보는 건 어때요? 그분은 저녁 교대 근무를 여러 차례 하셨었는데, 보통 일정이 유연하시거든요.
남: 알겠습니다, 지금 그분을 찾으러 가 볼게요. 감사합니다.

1. 이번 주말에 무슨 종류의 행사가 열리는가?
(A) 음식 축제
(B) 기술 박람회

| 해설 |
'이번 주말'이라는 시점 키워드가 언급되는 초반부에, 남자가 이번 주말에 기술 무역 박람회에 참가한다고(I'm participating in the technology trade show this weekend) 알리고 있으므로 (B)가 정답이다.

2. 남자는 곧이어 무엇을 할 것 같은가?
(A) 동료 직원과 이야기하기
(B) 고객에게 전화하기

| 해설 |
대화 후반부에 여자가 Garrett 씨에게 물어보도록 권하면서(Why don't you try asking Garrett? ~) 그 이유를 언급하자, 남자가 그를 지금 찾아보겠다고(I'll go look for him now) 답변하고 있다. 따라서 대화 후 동료 직원과 이야기할 것임을 알 수 있으므로 (A)가 정답이다.

| 어휘 | participate in ~에 참가하다 trade ~을 바꾸다, 교환하다 shift 교대 근무(조) leave 떠나다, 출발하다 help A out A를 돕다 usually 보통, 일반적으로 flexible 유연한, 탄력적인 go do ~하러 가다, 어서 ~하다 look for ~을 찾다 take place (일, 행사 등) 발생되다, 열리다

Questions 3-4 refer to the following conversation.

M: Hi, Nicole. It's great to see you! I didn't know that [3] **you were coming to this year's journalism convention.**
W: I try to come every year because I feel like it [3] **helps me improve my reporting skills.**
M: I feel the same way. Are you still working for the *Trenway Times*?
W: Yes, but I've actually applied for a new job at a magazine. In fact, [4] **I'll go to an interview at their head office tomorrow.**

3-4번 문제는 다음 대화를 참조하시오.
남: 안녕하세요, Nicole 씨. 만나서 반갑습니다! 당신이 올해 열리는 저널리즘 컨벤션에 올 줄은 몰랐어요.
여: 저는 매년 오려고 하는데, 제 보도 능력을 향상시키는 데 도움이 되는 것처럼 느껴지기 때문이에요.
남: 저도 똑같이 느껴요. 여전히 <Trenway Times>에서 일하고 계신가요?
여: 네, 하지만, 실은 한 잡지사의 새 직책에 지원했어요. 사실, 내일 그곳 본사로 면접을 보러 갑니다.

3. 화자들은 누구일 것 같은가?
(A) 회계사
(B) 기자

| 해설 |
신문 관련 단서가 제시되는 초반부에, 저널리즘 컨벤션에 온 상황임을 나타내는 말과(~ this year's journalism convention) 보도 능력 향상(~ improve my reporting skills) 같은 언급으로 보아 두 사람이 기자임을 알 수 있으므로 (B)가 정답이다.

4. 여자는 내일 무엇을 할 계획인가?
(A) 면접에 참석하기
(B) 새 사무실로 이전하기

| 해설 |
여자의 말에서 '내일'이라는 시점 키워드가 제시되는 후반부에, 내일 한 잡지사의 본사로 면접을 보러 간다고(I'll go to an interview at their head office tomorrow) 알리고 있으므로 (A)가 정답이다.

| 어휘 | improve ~을 향상시키다, 개선하다 reporting 보도 skill 능력, 기술 work for ~에서 근무하다 actually 실은, 사실은 apply for ~에 지원하다 in fact 실제로, 사실은 head office 본사 plan to do ~할 계획이다 attend ~에 참석하다

Questions 5-6 refer to the following conversation.

W: Mr. Shepherd, [5] **I'm wondering if it would be possible to change to a different supplier** for our fabric needs. I think it would be better for our company.
M: Oh, really? Why is that?
W: [6] **Our current supplier just increased the price of their fabrics.** I think we can find a better deal somewhere else.
M: OK. Why don't you do some research and get back to me with some figures?

5-6번 문제는 다음 대화를 참조하시오.
여: Shepherd 씨, 우리가 필요로 하는 직물에 대해 다른 공급업체로 바꾸는 것이 가능한지 궁금합니다. 제 생각에는 그게 우리 회사에 더 좋을 것 같아요.

남: 아, 정말요? 왜 그렇죠?
여: 저희가 현재 거래하는 공급업체가 자사의 직물 제품에 대한 가격을 막 인상했어요. 어딘가 다른 곳에서 더 나은 거래 조건을 찾을 수 있을 것 같아요.
남: 좋아요. 조사를 좀 해 보시고 수치 자료와 함께 제게 다시 연락 주시겠어요?

5. 여자는 무엇을 하라고 제안하는가?
(A) 또 다른 지사 개설하기
(B) 새 공급업체로 변경하기

| 해설 |
대화 초반부에서 여자가 다른 공급업체로 바꿀 것을(change to a different supplier) 제안하고 있으므로 (B)가 정답이다.

6. 여자의 말에 따르면, 최근에 무슨 일이 있었는가?
(A) 일부 재료가 더 비싸졌다.
(B) 경쟁사가 폐업했다.

| 해설 |
여자가 최근의 일에 관해 언급되는 후반부에, 공급업체가 자사의 직물 가격을 막 인상한(Our current supplier just increased the price of their fabrics) 사실을 밝히고 있는데, 이는 재료 값의 증가를 뜻하므로 (A)가 정답이다.

| 어휘 | wonder if ~인지 궁금하다 supplier 공급업체 fabric 직물, 천 needs 필요(로 하는 것) current 현재의 increase ~을 인상하다, 증가시키다 deal 거래 조건, 거래 상품 somewhere else 어딘가 다른 곳에서 Why don't you ~? 하는 게 어떠세요? do research 조사하다 get back to ~에게 다시 연락하다 figure 수치, 숫자 branch 지사, 지점 material 재료, 자재, 물품 competitor 경쟁사 go out of business 폐업하다

DAY 12 | 실전문제   본책 p.80

정답 1 (B)   2 (A)   3 (C)   4 (C)   5 (A)   6 (B)
      7 (B)   8 (B)   9 (D)   10 (B) 11 (A) 12 (D)
      13 (C) 14 (D) 15 (D) 16 (C) 17 (C) 18 (D)
      19 (C) 20 (D) 21 (D)

Questions 1-3 refer to the following conversation.

W: I'm so excited that **1 we're traveling to Barcelona next week.** We're going to have a great time!
M: Yes, I'm really looking forward to it. Is there anything else we need to prepare?
W: Hmm... **2 how about exchanging some currency in advance?** It would be convenient to have some euros in cash as soon as we arrive.
M: Good point. I can take care of that as soon as the bank opens tomorrow. Oh, and I've received **3 the confirmation code for our hotel reservation. I'll e-mail it to you.**
W: Thanks.

1-3번 문제는 다음 대화를 참조하시오.
여: 우리가 다음 주에 Barcelona로 여행을 가게 되어서 너무 흥분돼요. 아주 멋진 시간을 보내게 될 거예요!
남: 네, 저도 정말로 고대하고 있어요. 우리가 준비해야 하는 다른 게 있을까요?
여: 흠… 미리 환전을 좀 하는 건 어떨까요? 우리가 도착하자마자 유로화를 갖고 있으면 편할 거예요.

남: 좋은 지적입니다. 내일 은행이 문을 여는 대로 제가 그 부분을 처리할게요. 아, 그리고 우리 호텔 예약에 대한 확인 코드를 받았어요. 제가 이메일로 보내 드릴게요.
여: 감사합니다.

| 어휘 | look forward to ~을 고대하다 prepare ~을 준비하다 how about -ing? ~하는 건 어때요? exchange currency 환전하다 in advance 미리, 사전에 as soon as ~하자마자, ~하는 대로 arrive 도착하다 take care of ~을 처리하다 receive ~을 받다 confirmation 확인 reservation 예약

1. 화자들은 다음 주에 무엇을 하는가?
(A) 일부 구매자 환영하기
(B) 여행 떠나기
(C) 새 집으로 이사하기
(D) 축제에 참석하기

| 해설 |
'다음 주'라는 시점 키워드가 제시되는 초반부에, 여자가 다음 주에 Barcelona로 여행을 간다고(we're traveling to Barcelona next week) 말하고 있으므로 (B)가 정답이다.

| 어휘 | attend ~에 참석하다

2. 여자는 무엇을 하도록 권하는가?
(A) 환전하기
(B) 보험 구입하기
(C) 사진을 많이 찍기
(D) 온라인으로 조사하기

| 해설 |
여자가 권하는 일이 제시되는 중반부에, 미리 환전을 하는 건 어떤지(how about exchanging some currency in advance?) 제안하고 있으므로 (A)가 정답이다.

| 어휘 | purchase ~을 구입하다 insurance 보험 take a picture 사진을 찍다 do research 조사하다

3. 남자는 여자에게 무엇을 보낼 것인가?
(A) 지도
(B) 일정표
(C) 확인 코드
(D) 호텔 안내 책자

| 해설 |
대화 후반부에, 남자가 자신이 받은 호텔 예약 확인 코드를 이메일로 보내겠다고(~ the confirmation code for our hotel reservation. I'll e-mail it to you) 알리고 있으므로 (C)가 정답이다.

| 어휘 | itinerary 일정(표) brochure 안내 책자, 소책자

Questions 4-6 refer to the following conversation.

M: Cheryl, would it be all right **4 if I worked in your office today? The air conditioner in mine is broken, and it's too hot for me to concentrate.**
W: Well, normally that would be fine, but **5 a client is coming here for a meeting after lunch.** I'll need to use the space myself.
M: I understand. I put in a maintenance request, but they said it could take more than a week to get to it.
W: That's unacceptable. **6 I'll call a repair technician right now.** You shouldn't have to wait so long to get this problem resolved.

4-6번 문제는 다음 대화를 참조하시오.
남: Cheryl, 제가 오늘 당신의 사무실에서 일해도 괜찮을까요? 제 사무실에

있는 에어컨이 고장 났는데, 집중하기에는 너무 더워서요.
여: 저, 보통은 그렇게 하셔도 괜찮지만, 점심 시간 이후에 고객 한 분이 회의를 하러 이곳에 오실 예정이라서요. 제가 직접 사무실 공간을 사용해야 합니다.
남: 알겠습니다. 제가 시설 관리를 요청해 봤지만, 이 일을 시작하는 데 일주일이 넘게 걸릴 수 있다고 하더라고요.
여: 받아들일 수 없는 부분이네요. 제가 당장 수리 기사에게 전화할게요. 이 문제가 해결되는 데 그렇게 오래 기다리셔야 하면 안 되죠.

| 어휘 | broken 고장 난, 망가진   concentrate 집중하다   normally 보통, 일반적으로   oneself (부사적으로) 직접, 스스로   put in a request 요청하다, 신청하다   maintenance 시설 관리, 유지 관리   more than ~가 넘는   get to ~을 시작하다, ~에 착수하다   unacceptable 받아들일 수 없는   repair 수리   resolve ~을 해결하다

4. 남자는 무슨 문제점을 언급하는가?
(A) 일부 직원들이 결근한 상태이다.
(B) 일부 장비에서 소음이 난다.
(C) 에어컨이 제대로 작동하지 않는다.
(D) 한 방이 현재 잠겨 있다.

| 해설 |
남자가 문제점을 언급하는 초반부에, 상대방 사무실에서 일할 수 있는지 물으면서 자신의 사무실이 너무 덥다는(~ if I worked in your office today? ~ it's too hot for me to concentrate) 문제점을 알리고 있으므로 (C)가 정답이다.

| 어휘 | absent 결근한, 부재중인   equipment 장비   noisy 소음이 나는   currently 현재

5. 여자는 점심 시간 이후에 무엇을 할 계획인가?
(A) 고객과 만나기
(B) 출장 가기
(C) 건물 점검하기
(D) 구직 지원자 면접하기

| 해설 |
'점심 시간 이후'라는 시점 키워드가 제시되는 중반부에, 여자가 점심 시간 이후에 고객이 회의를 하러 온다고(a client is coming here for a meeting after lunch) 알리고 있으므로 (A)가 정답이다.

| 어휘 | meet with (약속하여) ~와 만나다   leave for ~하러 떠나다, 출발하다   inspect ~을 점검하다   job candidate 구직 지원자

6. 여자는 무엇을 할 것이라고 말하는가?
(A) 일부 양식 출력하기
(B) 대기 명단 확인하기
(C) 수리 담당자에게 연락하기
(D) 기기 설치하기

| 해설 |
여자가 곧이어 할 일을 말하는 후반부에, 당장 수리 기사에게 전화하겠다고(I'll call a repair technician right now) 밝히고 있으므로 (C)가 정답이다.

| 어휘 | form 양식, 서식   contact ~에게 연락하다   set up ~을 설치하다, 마련하다   device 기기, 장치

Questions 7-9 refer to the following conversation with three speakers.

M1: Welcome, Ms. Hampton, to Arlana Plaza. I'm Oliver. We spoke on the phone earlier. And this is Floyd. So, you said you're considering **7 holding an event** at our site.
W: That's right. I'm planning a dinner for Tyndall Supplies. **7 Our president will retire at the end of next month, so we're holding a celebration in his honor.**
M2: That's wonderful. There are several banquet halls to choose from, accommodating up to five hundred guests.
W: We're expecting around two hundred people. Most of them will be driving here. **8 Are there enough spots for their vehicles?**
M1: Yes, we've got plenty of space.
M2: And **9 we've recently added free high-speed Wi-fi** throughout the building, which is a top priority for many people.

7-9번 문제는 다음 세 명의 대화를 참조하시오.
남1: Arlana Plaza에 오신 것을 환영합니다, Hampton 씨. 저는 Oliver입니다. 우리 일전에 전화 통화를 한 적이 있었죠. 그리고 이쪽은 Floyd 씨입니다. 자, 저희 장소에서 행사를 개최하는 것을 고려하고 계신다고 말씀하셨죠.
여: 맞습니다. Tyndall Supplies 사를 위해 저녁 만찬 행사를 계획하고 있습니다. 저희 대표님께서 다음 달 말에 은퇴하시기 때문에, 기념해 드리기 위해 축하 행사를 개최할 예정입니다.
남2: 아주 멋진 일입니다. 선택하실 수 있는 연회 홀들이 여러 개 있는데, 최대 500명까지 손님들을 수용할 수 있습니다.
여: 저희는 약 200명의 인원을 예상하고 있어요. 대부분 차를 운전해 이곳으로 오실 거예요. 차량을 주차할 수 있는 자리가 충분히 있나요?
남1: 네, 저희는 공간을 많이 보유하고 있습니다.
남2: 그리고 저희가 최근에 건물 전역에 걸쳐 무료 초고속 와이파이를 추가했는데, 이는 많은 분들에게 있어 최우선 사항인 부분입니다.

| 어휘 | site 장소, 현장, 부지   plan ~을 계획하다   retire 은퇴하다   celebration 축하 행사, 기념 행사   in one's honor ~을 기념하기 위해, 기리기 위해   several 여럿의   banquet 연회   accommodate ~을 수용하다   up to 최대 ~까지   expect ~을 예상하다   around 약, 대략   enough 충분한   spot 자리, 공간, 지점   vehicle 차량   plenty of 많은   recently 최근에   free 무료의   throughout ~ 전역에 걸쳐   top priority 최우선 사항

7. 무슨 종류의 행사가 이야기되고 있는가?
(A) 시상식 연회
(B) 은퇴 기념 행사
(C) 제품 출시
(D) 기념일 파티

| 해설 |
대화 초반부에, 남자 한 명이 행사 개최(holding an event)를 언급한 뒤로, 여자가 소속 회사의 대표가 다음 달에 은퇴하기 때문에 행사를 연다고(Our president will retire ~ so we're holding a celebration in his honor) 알리고 있으므로 (B)가 정답이다.

| 어휘 | retirement 은퇴   launch 출시, 공개   anniversary (해마다 돌아오는) 기념일

8. 여자는 무엇에 관해 문의하는가?
(A) 장식품
(B) 주차
(C) 출장 요리 제공
(D) 숙박 시설

| 해설 |
대화 후반부에, 여자가 차량 주차 공간이 충분한지(Are there enough spots for their vehicles?) 문의하고 있으므로 (B)가 정답이다.

| 어휘 | decoration 장식품   catering 출장 요리 제공(업)   accommodation 숙박 시설

9. 해당 시설물은 최근에 무엇을 추가했는가?
(A) 현대적인 음향 시스템
(B) 옥외 식사 공간
(C) 무료 인터넷 연결 서비스
(D) 업그레이드된 보안 조치

| 해설 |
'최근'이라는 시점 키워드가 제시되는 마지막 부분에, 남자 한 명이 최근에 무료 초고속 와이파이를 추가한(we've recently added free high-speed Wi-fi ~) 사실을 말하고 있으므로 (C)가 정답이다.

| 어휘 | connection 연결   measure 조치

Questions 10-12 refer to the following conversation.

W: Carlos, I heard that the company will arrange on-site workshops **10** here at our marketing firm. I think it's a great idea. Do you know when the first one will be held?
M: Yes, the HR team just finalized the schedule yesterday. The first workshop is scheduled for March 18.
W: Oh, that could be a problem for my team. Several of us will be out of town on a business trip. **11** I really don't want to miss the workshop. Is there anything that can be done?
M: Hmm… **12** Let me go talk to Ms. Brown, since she's in charge of this project. Maybe she would consider postponing the workshop.

10-12번 문제는 다음 대화를 참조하시오.
여: Carlos, 이곳 우리 마케팅 회사에서 열리는 현장 워크숍 행사를 회사 측에서 마련할 것이라는 얘기를 들었어요. 아주 좋은 생각 같아요. 첫 번째 행사가 언제 열리는지 아세요?
남: 네, 인사팀이 어제 막 그 일정을 최종 확정했어요. 첫 번째 워크숍은 3월 18일로 예정되어 있습니다.
여: 아, 그럼 저희 팀에게는 문제가 될 수 있겠어요. 저희들 중 몇몇이 출장 때문에 다른 지역에 갈 예정이거든요. 저는 그 워크숍을 정말 놓치고 싶지 않아요. 뭔가 할 수 있는 일이 없을까요?
남: 흠… Brown 씨께서 이 프로젝트를 맡고 계시니 제가 가서 그분과 얘기해 볼게요. 아마 워크숍을 연기하는 것을 고려해 보실 수 있을 거예요.

| 어휘 | arrange ~을 마련하다, 조치하다   on-site 현장의   firm 회사, 업체   hold ~을 개최하다   HR team 인사팀   finalize ~을 최종 확정하다   be scheduled for + 날짜 ~로 예정되다   several 몇몇, 여러 명   out of town 다른 지역에 가 있는   on a business trip 출장   miss ~을 놓치다, 지나치다   go talk to 가서 ~와 얘기하다   since ~이기 때문에   in charge of ~을 맡고 있는   consider -ing ~하는 것을 고려하다   postpone ~을 연기하다

10. 대화가 어디에서 이뤄지고 있는가?
(A) 그래픽 디자인 업체에서
(B) 마케팅 회사에서
(C) 취업 알선 대행사에서
(D) 법률 사무소에서

| 해설 |
대화를 시작하면서 여자가 소속 회사를 'here at our marketing firm'이라고 지칭하고 있으므로 (B)가 정답이다.

| 어휘 | take place (일, 행사 등이) 발생되다, 일어나다   job recruitment 취업 알선   agency 대행사

11. 여자는 무엇에 대해 우려하고 있는가?
(A) 교육 시간을 놓치는 것
(B) 프로젝트 예산을 초과하는 것
(C) 고객을 언짢게 만드는 것
(D) 숙소를 찾는 것

| 해설 |
여자의 우려 사항이 언급되는 중반부에, 워크숍을 정말 놓치고 싶지 않다는 (I really don't want to miss the workshop) 말로 그 행사를 놓치는 것에 대한 우려를 나타내고 있으므로 (A)가 정답이다.

| 어휘 | be concerned about ~에 대해 우려하다   exceed ~을 초과하다   budget 예산   upset ~을 언짢게 만들다

12. 남자는 무엇을 할 것이라고 말하는가?
(A) 발표 내용 검토하기
(B) 회의실 예약하기
(C) 일정표를 이메일로 보내기
(D) 동료 직원과 만나기

| 해설 |
대화 마지막에, 남자가 Brown 씨에게 가서 얘기해 보겠다고(Let me go talk to Ms. Brown) 알리고 있으므로 Brown 씨를 동료 직원으로 지칭한 (D)가 정답이다.

| 어휘 | review ~을 검토하다   reserve ~을 예약하다   meet with (약속하여) ~와 만나다

Questions 13-15 refer to the following conversation.

M: **13** You went to the monthly tenants' meeting last night, right? How did it go?
W: As always, I gathered a lot of useful feedback. There is one issue that we got a lot of complaints about, though. **14** Tenants say that the hot water system is malfunctioning.
M: **14** Again? I can't believe that! Didn't we already have it fixed?
W: Yes, but it seems that it didn't fully get rid of the problem. I've scheduled more work to be done on Thursday. **15** Could you put up a notice to let tenants know that the water will be shut off on that day?
M: **15** Of course.

13-15번 문제는 다음 대화를 참조하시오.
남: 어젯밤에 열린 월례 입주자 회의에 가셨었죠, 그렇죠? 어떻게 되었나요?
여: 늘 그렇듯이, 많은 유용한 의견을 얻었어요. 하지만 우리가 많은 불만을 받은 문제가 하나 있어요. 입주자들은 온수 시스템이 오작동되고 있다고 합니다.
남: 또 그런다고요? 믿을 수가 없네요! 우리가 이미 그 문제를 바로잡지 않았나요?
여: 네, 하지만 우리가 문제를 완전히 처리하지 못했던 것 같아요. 목요일에 추가 작업이 완료되도록 일정을 잡아 두었어요. 그날 수도가 단수될 것이라고 입주자들에게 알릴 수 있도록 공고를 게시해 주시겠어요?
남: 물론입니다.

| 어휘 | tenant 입주자, 세입자   as always 늘 그렇듯이   gather ~을 모으다   useful 유용한   feedback 의견   complaint about ~에 관한 불만   though (문장 끝이나 중간에서) 하지만   malfunction 오작동되다   fix ~을 바로잡다, 고치다   fully 완전히, 전적으로   get rid of ~을 없애다, 처리하다   put up ~을 게시하다, 내걸다   notice 공고, 공지   shut off ~을 중단하다, 차단하다

13. 여자는 어제 무엇을 했는가?
(A) 한 입주자가 이사하는 것을 돕기
(B) 일부 장비 설치하기
(C) 회의에 참석하기
(D) 새로운 임대 계약서에 서명하기

| 해설 |
어제에 해당되는 시점 키워드가 제시된 초반부에, 남자가 여자에게 월례 입주자 회의에 간 것이 맞는지(You went to the monthly tenants meeting last night ~) 확인하고 있으므로 (C)가 정답이다.

| 어휘 | install ~을 설치하다   equipment 장비   attend ~에 참석하다   lease 임대 계약(서)

14. 남자는 왜 놀라워하는가?
(A) 수도 요금이 더 적게 나올 것으로 예상했다.
(B) 여자가 하루 휴가를 가질 것으로 예상했다.
(C) 한 행사가 더 인기가 많을 것으로 생각했다.
(D) 한 문제점이 해결되었다고 생각했다.

| 해설 |
대화 중반부에, 여자가 온수 시스템 오작동 문제를(~ hot water system is malfunctioning) 언급하자, 남자가 믿을 수 없다고 놀라면서 그 문제를 바로잡지 않았는지(~ I can't believe that! Didn't we already have it fixed?) 되묻고 있다. 이는 처리한 문제가 다시 발생한 것에 따른 놀라움에 해당하므로 (D)가 정답이다.

| 어휘 | take A off A 기간 동안 쉬다   resolve ~을 해결하다

15. 남자는 무엇을 하는 데 동의하는가?
(A) 일부 수치 자료 보내기
(B) 문서 검토하기
(C) 일부 조명 끄기
(D) 공고 게시하기

| 해설 |
대화 후반부에, 여자가 공고를 게시하도록 요청하자(Could you put up a notice ~?) 남자가 'Of course'라는 말로 수락하고 있으므로 (D)가 정답이다.

| 어휘 | agree to do ~하는 데 동의하다   figure 수치, 숫자   review ~을 검토하다   turn off ~을 끄다

Questions 16-18 refer to the following conversation.

M: Bernadette, **16 could you please confirm that these sales figures are correct?**
W: Let's see ... yes, those are accurate figures from last month's sales.
M: Thanks. That's the last report we'll need for the orientation session with new hires on Thursday. **17 I'm going to print some copies of the agenda this afternoon.**
W: Okay. And, just to let you know, I might have to interview some job candidates on Thursday. If so, **18 you'd have to explain the company's policies to the new hires on your own.**
M: **18 The group is likely to have a lot of questions,** and I just joined the team last year.
W: I'm sure you would do fine.

16-18번 문제는 다음 대화를 참조하시오.

남: Bernadette, 이 매출 수치가 맞는지 확인 좀 해 주시겠어요?
여: 어디 봅시다… 네, 지난달 매출에 대한 정확한 수치네요.
남: 감사합니다. 그게 목요일에 있을 신입 사원 대상 오리엔테이션 시간에 필요한 마지막 보고서입니다. 오늘 오후에 제가 안건에 대한 몇몇 사본을 출력할 예정입니다.
여: 좋습니다. 그리고 한 가지 알려 드리자면, 제가 목요일에 몇몇 구직 지원자들을 면접해야 할지도 몰라요. 그럴 경우에, 신입 사원들에게 당신 혼자서 회사의 정책을 설명해 주셔야 할 겁니다.
남: 그 그룹이 질문을 많이 할 것 같은데, 저는 불과 작년에 팀에 합류했는걸요.
여: 분명 잘하실 거예요.

| 어휘 | confirm ~을 확인해 주다   sales 매출, 판매(량)   figure 수치, 숫자   correct 맞는, 정확한   accurate 정확한   session (특정 활동을 위한) 시간   new hire 신입 사원   agenda 안건, 의제   job candidate 구직 지원자   explain ~을 설명하다   policy 정책   on one's own 혼자서   be likely to do ~할 가능성이 있다   join ~에 입사하다, 합류하다

16. 남자는 여자에게 무엇을 하라고 요청하는가?
(A) 일부 정보 보내기
(B) 주문하기
(C) 일부 수치 확인해 주기
(D) 일부 장비 설치하기

| 해설 |
남자가 여자에게 요청하는 사양이 제시되는 초반부에, 매출 수치가 맞는지 확인 좀 해 달라고(could you please confirm that these sales figures ~) 요청하고 있으므로 (C)가 정답이다.

| 어휘 | verify ~을 확인하다, 입증하다   set up ~을 설치하다, 준비하다   equipment 장비

17. 남자는 오늘 오후에 무엇을 할 것이라고 말하는가?
(A) 매출 관련 발표하기
(B) 면접 실시하기
(C) 일부 문서 출력하기
(D) 고객 방문하기

| 해설 |
'오늘 오후'라는 시점 키워드가 제시되는 중반부에, 남자가 오늘 오후에 안건에 대한 사본을 출력할 것이라고(I'm going to print some copies of the agenda this afternoon) 알리고 있으므로 (C)가 정답이다.

| 어휘 | give a presentation 발표하다   conduct ~을 실시하다, 수행하다

18. 남자는 왜 "I just joined the team last year"라고 말하는가?
(A) 왜 한 행사에 참석하지 않았는지 설명하기 위해
(B) 팀원인 것에 대한 감사의 뜻을 표현하기 위해
(C) 얼마나 빠르게 승진되었는지를 강조하기 위해
(D) 혼자 정책을 설명하는 일을 걱정하고 있음을 나타내기 위해

| 해설 |
대화 후반부에, 여자가 남자 혼자서 신입 사원들에게 회사의 정책을 설명해야 한다고(you'd have to explain the company's policies to the new hires on your own) 알리자, 남자가 신입 사원들이 질문을 많이 할 것 같다고(The group is likely to have a lot of questions) 말하면서 '자신은 작년에 합류했다'고 알리는 상황이다. 이는 혼자 정책을 설명을 하는 일에 대한 걱정에서 나온 반응에 해당하므로 (D)가 정답이다.

| 어휘 | attend ~에 참석하다   express ~을 표현하다   appreciation 감사(의 뜻)   highlight ~을 강조하다   promote ~을 승진시키다

Questions 19-21 refer to the following conversation and schedule.

W: Thanks for calling Plymouth Airlines. How may I help you?
M: Hello. I tried to use your smartphone app to book a flight, but it doesn't seem to be working. I need to travel to Vancouver on August 10.

W: **19** I'm very sorry about that, sir. We've been having problems with the app, so it's currently down for maintenance. I can assist you with the booking over the phone, though.
M: Great! **20** I'd like to depart no earlier than 11 A.M because I don't want to be rushed in the morning. **21** I have to perform a factory inspection in Vancouver, but it's not until very late in the day.

Flight Number	**20** Departure Time	Arrival Time
PL-162	8:10 A.M.	9:36 A.M.
PL-249	9:20 A.M.	10:58 A.M.
PL-280	10:45 A.M.	12:11 A.M.
20 PL-346	11:30 A.M.	12:58 A.M.

19-21번 문제는 다음 대화와 일정표를 참조하시오.
여: Plymouth Airlines에 전화 주셔서 감사합니다. 무엇을 도와 드릴까요?
남: 안녕하세요. 제가 항공편을 예약하기 위해 귀사의 스마트폰 앱을 이용하려고 했는데, 작동되지 않는 것 같습니다. 저는 8월 10일에 Vancouver로 출장을 가야 합니다.
여: 그 부분에 대해 대단히 죄송합니다, 고객님. 저희 앱에 문제가 생기고 있기 때문에, 현재 유지 관리를 위해 차단된 상태입니다. 하지만 제가 전화상으로 예약을 도와드릴 수 있습니다.
남: 잘됐네요! 저는 아침에 서둘러 가는 것을 원치 않기 때문에, 빨라도 오전 11시 이후에 출발하고 싶습니다. 제가 Vancouver에서 공장 점검을 실시해야 하기는 하지만, 그날 아주 늦게나 이뤄질 겁니다.

편명	출발 시간	도착 시간
PL-162	오전 8:10	오전 9:36
PL-249	오전 9:20	오전 10:58
PL-280	오전 10:45	오전 12:11
PL-346	오전 11:30	오전 12:58

| 어휘 | try to do ~하려 하다 book ~을 예약하다 currently 현재 down (시스템 등이) 차단된, 작동이 되지 않는 maintenance 유지 관리 assist A with B B에 대해 A를 돕다 booking 예약 over the phone 전화상으로 though (문장 끝이나 중간에서) 하지만 be rushed 서두르다 depart 출발하다 no earlier than 빨라도 ~ 후에 perform ~을 실시하다, 수행하다 inspection 점검 not until A A나 되어야 하다 departure 출발 arrival 도착

19. 여자는 무엇에 대해 사과하는가?
(A) 분실된 가방
(B) 취소된 항공편
(C) 이용할 수 없는 서비스
(D) 부정확한 요금

| 해설 |
여자가 중반부에 사과의 말을 하며 앱에 문제가 생겨서 유지 관리를 위해 앱이 차단되어 있다고 알리는 것으로 보아(~ We've been having problems with the app, so it's currently down for maintenance) 현재 특정 서비스를 이용할 수 없음을 알 수 있으므로 (C)가 정답이다.

| 어휘 | apologize for ~에 대해 사과하다 lost 분실된, 잃어버린 canceled 취소된 unavailable 이용할 수 없는 incorrect 부정확한 fee 요금

20. 시각 자료를 보시오. 남자에게 어느 항공편이 가장 좋을 것인가?
(A) PL-162
(B) PL-249
(C) PL-280
(D) PL-346

| 해설 |
남자가 말하는 항공편 조건이 제시되는 후반부에, 빨라도 오전 11시 이후에 출발하고 싶다고(I'd like to depart no earlier than 11 A.M.) 밝히고 있다. 시각 자료에서 출발 시간이 11시 이후인 것은 11시 30분으로 표기된 PL-346뿐이므로 (D)가 정답이다.

21. 남자는 Vancouver에서 무엇을 할 계획인가?
(A) 투자자와 만나기
(B) 구직 면접 보기
(C) 계약 협상하기
(D) 공장 점검하기

| 해설 |
Vancouver라는 장소 키워드가 제시된 후반부에, Vancouver에서 공장 점검을 실시해야 한다고(I have to perform a factory inspection in Vancouver ~) 알리고 있으므로 (D)가 정답이다.

| 어휘 | plan to do ~할 계획이다 investor 투자자 negotiate ~을 협상하다 contract 계약(서) inspect ~을 점검하다

DAY 13 세부적인 내용을 묻는 유형 (3)

01 기타 세부 사항 문제

기출 유형 맛보기 본책 p.82

Q. 남자는 Emily 씨가 무엇을 잘 한다고 말하는가?
(A) 고객 서비스
(B) 음료 준비
(C) 그래픽 디자인
(D) 개조 작업

여: Dave, 매장 개조 공사를 시작한 이후로 줄곧, 손님들이 더 적게 오고 있어요. 그들이 다시 찾아오게 만들 방법에 대한 아이디어가 있으세요?
남: 저, 많은 사람들이 건물에서 작업하고 있기 때문에 우리 커피 매장이 문을 닫았다고 사람들이 생각할 가능성이 있죠. 우리가 여전히 영업 중이라고 가리키는 큰 표지판을 세워 두는 건 어떨까요?
여: 좋은 생각이에요. 충분히 크게 만들어서 건물 앞에 걸어 두면, 모든 사람이 언제든지 들를 수 있다는 것을 알게 될 거예요.
남: 맞습니다. Emily 씨가 그래픽 디자인 작업을 잘하니까 그분에게 도움을 요청해 봅시다. 그분의 작업물을 본 적이 있는데, 정말로 인상적이에요.

PRACTICE | 기출 연습하기 본책 p.83

정답 1 (A) 2 (A) 3 (A) 4 (B) 5 (B) 6 (B)

Questions 1-2 refer to the following conversation.

M: Hello, **1** I'd like to buy three tickets to the Montello Dance Troupe's performance on June 4. We'd like to sit on the main floor, as close to the stage as possible.
W: **2** I'm sorry, sir, but we've sold out of the tickets for the main floor. We only have seats in

the balcony left.
M: That's too bad. I'll take whatever you have then. Can I pay for the tickets over the phone by credit card?

1-2번 문제는 다음 대화를 참조하시오.
남: 안녕하세요, 7월 4일 무용단의 공연을 관람할 수 있는 입장권 3장을 구입하고 싶습니다. 저희는 중앙 관람 구역에 앉았으면 하는데, 가능한 한 무대와 가까운 곳으로요.
여: 죄송하지만 손님, 중앙 관람 구역의 입장권은 매진된 상태입니다. 발코니 좌석만 남아 있습니다.
남: 아쉽네요. 그럼 무엇이든 남아 있는 것으로 살게요. 전화상에서 신용카드로 입장권 가격을 지불할 수 있나요?

1. 남자는 무엇을 하고 싶어 하는가?
(A) 무용 공연에 참석하기
(B) 스포츠 행사 조직하기

| 해설 |
대화 초반부에, 남자가 Montello Dance Troupe 공연 입장권을(~ tickets to the Montello Dance Troupe's performance) 구입하고 싶다고 알리고 있으므로 (A)가 정답이다.

2. 여자는 무엇에 대해 사과하는가?
(A) 일부 좌석이 이용 불가능하다.
(B) 업체가 신용카드를 받지 않는다.

| 해설 |
중반부에, 여자가 사과 표현과 함께 중앙 관람 구역 입장권이 매진된 상태임을(I'm sorry, sir, but we've sold out of the tickets for the main floor) 알리고 있는데, 이는 해당 좌석을 이용할 수 없음을 뜻하는 것이므로 (A)가 정답이다.

| 어휘 | troupe 공연단, 극단   as A as possible 가능한 한 A   close to ~와 가까운   sell out of ~가 매진되다   have A left A가 남아 있다   whatever 무엇이든 ~하는 것, ~하는 무엇이든   then 그럼, 그렇다면   over the phone 전화상에서   attend ~에 참석하다   available 이용 가능한   accept ~을 받다

Questions 3-4 refer to the following conversation.

W: Good afternoon. 3 I would like to get a one-year membership for the museum.
M: All right, ma'am. It costs eighty dollars, and it will allow you unlimited visits to the museum and all of its special exhibits.
W: That's perfect. Actually, I'm highly interested in Egyptian history, but I noticed that part of the museum is closed.
M: Yes, we're repairing some water damage in 4 the Egyptian Artifacts exhibit now. However, it will reopen in just a couple of weeks.

3-4번 문제는 다음 대화를 참조하시오.
여: 안녕하세요. 박물관 1년 회원권을 구입하려고 합니다.
남: 알겠습니다, 고객님. 비용은 80달러이며, 회원권을 통해 박물관과 모든 특별 전시회에 무제한으로 입장하실 수 있습니다.
여: 아주 좋네요. 실은, 제가 이집트 역사에 관심이 아주 많은데, 박물관 일부가 문을 닫았다는 걸 알았어요.
남: 네, 저희가 현재 이집트 공예품 전시회 행사장에 일부 누수 피해 구역을 수리하고 있습니다. 하지만, 2주만 있으면 재개장할 것입니다.

3. 여자는 무엇을 하고 싶어 하는가?
(A) 회원 자격 신청하기
(B) 가이드 동반 투어 하기

| 해설 |
여자가 원하는 일을 언급하는 초반부에, 박물관 1년 회원권을 구입하고 싶다고(I would like to get a one-year membership ~) 알리고 있으므로 (A)가 정답이다.

4. 남자는 이집트 공예품 전시회에 관해 무슨 말을 하는가?
(A) 추가 요금을 필요로 한다.
(B) 곧 재개장할 것이다.

| 해설 |
'이집트 공예품 전시회'라는 키워드가 제시되는 후반부에, 수리 작업 때문에 2주 후에 재개장한다고(~ the Egyptian Artifacts exhibit now. However, it will reopen in just a couple of weeks) 알리고 있으므로 (B)가 정답이다.

| 어휘 | unlimited 무제한의   exhibit 전시회   highly 아주, 대단히   notice that ~임을 알게 되다   repair ~을 수리하다   damage 피해, 손상   however 하지만, 그러나   in + 기간 ~ 후에   sign up for ~을 신청하다   guided 가이드를 동반한   require ~을 필요로 하다   addition 추가의   fee 요금

Questions 5-6 refer to the following conversation.

M: Hi, I stopped in because 5 I heard from one of my coworkers that the Eastland-210 fan heater has been recalled. I just purchased one a few weeks ago.
W: Yes, the company has recalled that item due to a potential safety issue.
M: What do I need to do to get a replacement? Should I bring the heater here to the store?
W: It has to be sent directly to the manufacturer. 6 Here's an information sheet about the recall. It explains step by step how to return the item.

5-6번 문제는 다음 대화를 참조하시오.
남: 안녕하세요, 제 동료들 중 한 명에게서 Eastland-210 온풍기 제품이 리콜되었다는 얘기를 듣고 들렀습니다. 저는 불과 일주일 전에 그 제품을 한 대 구입했어요.
여: 네, 회사에서 잠재적인 안전 문제로 인해 그 제품을 리콜했습니다.
남: 교체 받으려면 어떻게 해야 하나요? 이곳 매장으로 온풍기를 가져오면 되나요?
여: 제조사로 곧장 보내져야 합니다. 여기 이 리콜과 관련된 안내지가 있습니다. 제품을 반품하는 방법을 단계별로 설명해 드립니다.

5. 남자는 제품 리콜에 관해 어떻게 듣게 되었는가?
(A) 신문 기사를 읽음으로써
(B) 동료 직원과 얘기함으로써

| 해설 |
남자의 말에서 리콜이 언급되는 초반부에, 동료들 중 한 명에게서 제품 리콜에 관해 들었다고(I heard from one of my coworkers that ~ has been recalled) 밝히고 있으므로 (B)가 정답이다.

6. 여자는 남자에게 무엇을 주는가?
(A) 교체 제품
(B) 일련의 설명

| 해설 |
후반부에서 여자가 리콜 관련 안내지를 주면서 반품 방법이 설명되어 있다고(Here's an information sheet ~ how to return the item) 알리고 있으므로 (B)가 정답이다.

| 어휘 | stop in 들르다   coworker 동료 직원   recall (결함 제품에 대해) ~을 리콜하다, 회수하다   purchase ~을 구입하다   due to ~로 인해   potential

잠재적인   issue 문제, 사안   replacement 교체(품)   directly to ~로 곧장   manufacturer 제조사   sheet 종이 (한 장)   explain ~을 설명하다   step by step 단계적으로   how to do ~하는 법   return ~을 반품하다   instructions 설명, 안내, 지시

02 의도 파악 문제

기출 유형 맛보기
본책 p.84

Q. 남자가 "I've got a dinner appointment with Mr. Reynolds"라고 말할 때 무엇을 의미하는가?
(A) 서둘러 볼 일을 보러 가야 한다.
(B) 더 이상 여자와 얘기를 할 수 없다.
(C) 오늘 일과를 일찍 마치고 퇴근해야 한다.
(D) 행사에 갈 시간이 나지 않는다.

> 여: Victor, Aaron North 박사님이 내일 콘퍼런스에서 최종 연설자가 되신다는 사실을 알고 계셨나요?
> 남: 네, 들었어요. 그분은 정말 인상적인 건축가입니다. 안타깝게도, 저는 Reynolds 씨와 저녁 약속이 있어요.
> 여: 그러시면, 연설이 어떻게 진행되는지 알려 드릴게요.
> 남: 괜찮아요. 제가 그분의 책을 전부 읽어 봤기 때문에, 도시 건축과 관련된 그분의 이론에 익숙합니다.
> 여: 저는 여전히 그분의 최신 작품을 구입해야 해요.
> 남: 우리가 사무실로 돌아가면 그냥 제 것을 빌려 가세요.
> 여: 와, 그렇게 제안해 주셔서 고마워요. 꼭 받아서 보고 싶네요.

PRACTICE | 기출 연습하기
본책 p.85

정답   1 (B)   2 (B)   3 (B)   4 (A)   5 (A)   6 (B)

Questions 1-2 refer to the following conversation.

> M: Oh, hello, Susan! I never usually bump into anyone from work 1 here at this restaurant. I rarely see anyone from the office in this part of town.
> W: Hi, Richard. Well, I read a review that said not only that the food is excellent, but also that the view from the patio is amazing. And, I must admit, it is impressive.
> M: It's wonderful, isn't it? 2 I always try to get a table out on the patio.
> W: Actually, I was just leaving, 2 if you want this one.
> M: Are you sure? I'd appreciate that, as I might have to wait a while for another one.

1-2번 문제는 다음 대화를 참조하시오.
남: 아, 안녕하세요, Susan 씨! 보통 이 레스토랑에서 회사 사람을 우연히 마주칠 일이 없었어요. 도시의 이쪽 지역에서 사무실 사람을 좀처럼 보지 못하거든요.
여: 안녕하세요, Richard 씨. 저, 음식이 훌륭한 것뿐만 아니라 테라스에서 바라보는 경관까지 놀랍다고 쓴 후기를 읽었어요. 그리고, 정말이지, 인상적입니다.
남: 아주 멋지지 않나요? 저는 항상 밖에 있는 테라스에 테이블을 잡으려고 해요.
여: 사실, 저는 막 나가려던 참이었어요, 이 자리를 원하신다면요.
남: 정말입니까? 그렇다면 감사합니다, 다른 자리를 잡기 위해 잠시 대기해야 할지도 모르거든요.

1. 대화가 어디에서 이뤄지고 있는 것 같은가?
(A) 도서관에서
(B) 레스토랑에서

| 해설 |
대화 시작 부분에, 남자가 here at this restaurant라는 표현으로 대화의 장소를 언급하고 있으므로 (B)가 정답이다.

2. 여자가 "I was just leaving"이라고 말할 때 암시하는 것은 무엇인가?
(A) 문제를 논의할 시간이 없다.
(B) 남자에게 자신의 테이블을 내어 줄 것이다.

| 해설 |
대화 후반부에 남자가 항상 테라스에 있는 테이블을 잡으려 한다고 말하자(I always try to get a table out on the patio), 여자가 막 나가려던 참이었다고 알리면서 '이 자리를 원한다면(if you want this one)'이라는 조건을 덧붙이고 있다. 이는 테라스에서 자신이 이용하던 테이블을 남자가 이용하도록 하려는 것이므로 (B)가 정답이다.

| 어휘 | usually 보통, 일반적으로   bump into ~와 우연히 마주치다   rarely 좀처럼 ~않다   review 후기, 의견, 평가   not only A but also B A뿐만 아니라 B도   view 경관, 조망   patio 테라스   amazing 놀라운   I must admit 사실, 정말이지   leave 나가다, 떠나다   appreciate ~에 대해 감사하다   might have to do ~해야 할지도 모르다   a while 잠시, 잠깐   discuss ~을 논의하다, 이야기하다   issue 문제, 사안

Questions 3-4 refer to the following conversation.

> M: We need to find a way to improve the appearance of 3 our dental clinic. The interior is the first thing that people notice when they visit us, and it's important for them to get a good impression.
> W: You know, 4 we did have the entire lobby repainted and decorated by professionals from Ramirez Inc.
> M: Yes, but that was a few years ago. 4 The paint is already starting to show some signs of wear.

3-4번 문제는 다음 대화를 참조하시오.
남: 우리 치과를 단장할 수 있는 방법을 찾아봐야 합니다. 사람들이 우리를 방문할 때 가장 먼저 알아보는 것이 실내이고, 그들이 좋은 인상을 받는 것이 중요합니다.
여: 아시다시피, Ramirez Inc.의 전문가들에게서 로비 전체를 다시 페인트 칠 받고 장식 서비스도 받았잖아요.
남: 네, 하지만 그건 몇 년 전의 일이었습니다. 그 페인트는 이미 닳은 표시가 나기 시작하고 있어요.

3. 화자들은 어디에서 근무하는가?
(A) 실내 디자인 스튜디오에서
(B) 치과에서

| 해설 |
대화 초반부에, 남자가 자신의 근무지를 '우리 치과(our dental clinic)'라고 지칭하고 있으므로 (B)가 정답이다.

4. 남자가 "but that was a few years ago"라고 말할 때 암시하는 것은 무엇인가?
(A) 작업이 다시 이루어져야 한다.
(B) 업체가 문을 닫았을 수도 있다.

| 해설 |
여자가 전문가에게서 서비스를 받았다고 알린(we did have the entire lobby repainted ~) 것에 대한 반응으로 남자가 '몇 년 전의 일이었다'라고 답변하고 있다. 곧이어 남자가 페인트가 닳은 표시가 나고 있다고(The

paint is already starting to show some signs of wear) 말하는 것을 통해 다시 작업이 필요한 상황임을 알 수 있으므로 (A)가 정답이다.

| 어휘 | way to do ~하는 방법   improve ~을 개선하다, 향상시키다   appearance 모습, 외관   dental clinic 치과   notice ~을 알아차리다   entire 전체의   repaint ~을 다시 페인트 칠하다   decorate ~을 장식하다   professional 전문가   task 업무, 일

Questions 5-6 refer to the following conversation.

W: 5 I'm really looking forward to meeting our new investors from the financial firm in Japan.
M: Same here. I just checked their itinerary, and they'll be arriving at 9 a.m. tomorrow. They'll be coming straight here for our CEO's presentation at 10.
W: Oh, 6 the presentation is at 10? I'm interviewing job candidates all morning.
M: Don't worry, they'll be with us all day. Can you join us for the factory tour in the afternoon?
W: Yeah, that shouldn't be a problem. I'll be free right after lunch.

5-6번 문제는 다음 대화를 참조하시오.
여: 일본에 있는 금융 회사에서 오는 우리의 새 투자자들을 만나는 것이 정말로 고대됩니다.
남: 저도요. 제가 막 그분들 일정표를 확인했는데, 내일 오전 9시에 도착하실 예정입니다. 10시에 진행되는 우리 대표이사님의 발표를 위해 이곳으로 곧장 오실 거예요.
여: 아, 그 발표가 10시인가요? 저는 오전 내내 취업 지원자들을 면접할 예정입니다.
남: 걱정 마세요, 투자자들은 우리와 하루 종일 있을 겁니다. 오후에는 함께 공장 견학을 하실 수 있으세요?
여: 네, 그건 문제가 되지 않을 겁니다. 점심 식사 직후에는 시간이 있을 거예요.

5. 화자들은 주로 무엇을 이야기하고 있는가?
(A) 투자자들의 방문
(B) 해외 취업 기회

| 해설 |
대화 시작 부분에, 여자가 일본에 있는 금융 회사에서 오는 새 투자자들을 만나는 것이 고대된다고(~ looking forward to meeting our new investors ~) 알린 뒤로, 이들의 방문 일정에 관해 이야기하고 있으므로 (A)가 정답이다.

6. 여자가 "I'm interviewing job candidates all morning"이라고 말할 때 암시하는 것은 무엇인가?
(A) 지원서 숫자에 놀라워하고 있다.
(B) 발표에 참석할 수 없다.

| 해설 |
대화 중반부에 여자는, 발표가 10시인지 물으면서(~ the presentation is at 10?) 오전 내내 취업 지원자들을 면접할 것이라 알린다. 이는 면접 일정으로 인해 그 발표에 참석할 수 없다는 말이므로 (B)가 정답이다.

| 어휘 | look forward to -ing ~하기를 고대하다   investor 투자자   financial firm 금융 회사   itinerary 일정(표)   arrive 도착하다   come straight 곧장 오다   presentation 발표(회)   job candidate 취업 지원자   join ~와 함께 하다, ~에 합류하다   free 시간이 있는   right after ~ 직후에   overseas 해외의   job opportunity 취업 기회   be surprised by ~에 놀라다   application 지원(서)   be unable to do ~할 수 없다   attend ~에 참석하다

DAY 13 | 실전문제 본책 p.86

정답 1 (D)   2 (C)   3 (B)   4 (B)   5 (C)   6 (D)
      7 (C)   8 (D)   9 (C) 10 (B) 11 (A) 12 (C)
     13 (B) 14 (D) 15 (D) 16 (C) 17 (D) 18 (A)
     19 (C) 20 (B) 21 (D)

Questions 1-3 refer to the following conversation.

M: Rebecca, 1 I wanted to thank you for recommending me for the promotion to assistant manager. I got the job! I'll be working at 2 our grocery store branch in Eastlake.
W: Congratulations! I know you'll do a great job making that store a success. Since you'll be transferring branches, will there be a farewell party for you?
M: I don't think there will be time. 3 I have to attend a training seminar with the manager of the Eastlake branch. 3 That's this Friday.
W: Well, maybe we could find time to have lunch together before that.

1-3번 문제는 다음 대화를 참조하시오.
남: Rebecca 씨, 저를 부점장 직책으로의 승진 대상자로 추천해 주신 것에 대해 감사드리고자 합니다. 제가 그 직책에 선정되었습니다! Eastlake에 있는 우리 식료품 매장 지점에서 일하게 되었어요.
여: 축하드립니다! 그 매장을 성공적으로 이끄는 일을 아주 잘해 주실 거라고 생각해요. 지점을 옮기실 예정이시니까, 송별 파티가 열리는 건가요?
남: 그럴 시간이 있을 것 같지 않습니다. Eastlake 지점장님과 함께 교육 세미나에 참석해야 합니다. 이번 금요일에 있어요.
여: 그럼, 아마 그전에 함께 점심 식사라도 할 시간은 만들 수 있을 거예요.

| 어휘 | promotion 승진   assistant manager 부점장, 차장   grocery store 식료품 매장   branch 지점, 지사   success 성공   since ~이기 때문에   transfer ~을 옮기다   farewell party 송별 파티   attend ~에 참석하다   training 교육

1. 남자는 무엇에 대해 여자에게 감사하는가?
(A) 책임자를 위해 발표 자료를 만든 것
(B) 빠르게 배정받은 일을 완료한 것
(C) 전근을 수용한 것
(D) 승진 대상자로 남자를 추천한 것

| 해설 |
남자가 감사의 인사와 그 이유를 말하는 초반부에, 자신을 승진 대상자로 추천해 준 것에 대해 감사하다고(I wanted to thank you for recommending me for the promotion) 알리고 있으므로 (D)가 정답이다.

2. 화자들은 무슨 종류의 업체에서 근무하는가?
(A) 택배 서비스 회사
(B) 광고 대행사
(C) 슈퍼마켓
(D) 보험 회사

| 해설 |
대화 초반부에, 남자가 소속 업체를 'our grocery store'라고 지칭하고 있으므로 grocery store와 같은 종류에 해당되는 (C)가 정답이다.

3. 금요일에 무엇이 예정되어 있는가?
(A) 점검
(B) 교육 시간

DAY 13 065

(C) 축하 행사
(D) 이사회 회의

| 해설 |
'금요일'이라는 시점 키워드가 제시된 후반부에, 남자가 교육 세미나에 참석해야 한다고(I have to attend a training seminar) 알리면서 금요일에 열린다고(That's this Friday) 말하고 있으므로 (B)가 정답이다.

| 어휘 | create ~을 만들어 내다   presentation 발표   complete ~을 완료하다   assigned 배정된   task 업무, 일   accept ~을 수용하다, 받아들이다   job transfer 전근   courier service 택배 서비스   agency 대행사   insurance 보험   session (특정 활동을 위한) 시간   celebration 축하 행사, 기념 행사   board 이사회

Questions 4-6 refer to the following conversation.

> W: Is this seat free? I'd like to sit close to the stage, if possible.
> M: Go right ahead. I've heard that ❹ this lecture on small business ventures is very informative. Some of my colleagues attended it last week.
> W: That's great. What's your company's name?
> M: I work for Empire Limited. ❺ We are a producer of environmentally friendly kitchen cleansers and other items used for household cleaning.
> W: You know, I work for the Venus Inn, and we are thinking about changing our supplier for the housekeeping staff.
> M: I could send you some free samples to try. If you give me your business card, ❻ I'll call you next week to discuss this further.

4-6번 문제는 다음 대화를 참조하시오.

여: 이 자리는 비어 있는 건가요? 가능하면 제가 무대와 가까이 앉고 싶어서요.
남: 앉으셔도 됩니다. 저는 소규모 벤처 기업에 관한 이 강연이 매우 유익하다고 들었습니다. 일부 제 동료 직원들이 지난주에 참석했었거든요.
여: 잘됐네요. 다니시는 회사 이름이 뭐가요?
남: 저는 Empire Limited에서 근무합니다. 저희는 친환경 주방 세제를 비롯해서 가정에서 청소용으로 사용되는 기타 제품들을 만드는 생산업체입니다.
여: 있잖아요, 제가 Venus Inn에서 근무하는데, 저희는 객실 관리 담당 직원들을 위해 물품 공급업체를 변경하는 것에 대해 생각해 보는 중이에요.
남: 시험 사용해 보실 수 있도록 무료 샘플을 좀 보내 드릴 수 있습니다. 제게 명함을 주시면, 이 부분에 대해 더 논의해 볼 수 있도록 다음 주에 전화 드리겠습니다.

| 어휘 | free 비어 있는, 무료의   close to ~에 가까이   if possible 가능하면, 가급적   Go right ahead (앞서 언급된 일에 대해) 어서 하세요   informative 유익한   colleague 동료 직원   attend ~에 참석하다   work for ~에서 근무하다   environmentally friendly 친환경적인   household 가정   supplier 공급업체   housekeeping 객실 관리   try ~을 시험해 보다   discuss ~을 논의하다   further 더욱, 추가로

4. 무슨 종류의 행사가 개최되고 있는가?
(A) 개장식
(B) 비즈니스 세미나
(C) 시상식
(D) 취업 박람회

| 해설 |
대화 초반부에, 남자가 '소규모 벤처 기업에 관한 이 강연(this lecture on small business ventures)'이라는 말로 참가 중인 행사를 언급하고 있으므로 (B)가 정답이다.

5. 남자의 회사는 무엇을 판매하는가?
(A) 비용 청구 소프트웨어
(B) 사무용 가구
(C) 청소용품
(D) 보안 시스템

| 해설 |
남자가 소속 회사의 특징을 말하는 중반부에, 청소용으로 사용되는 친환경적인 주방 세제를 만드는 회사라고(We are a producer of environmentally friendly kitchen cleansers ~) 알리고 있으므로 (C)가 정답이다.

| 어휘 | billing 비용 청구

6. 남자는 여자에게 어떻게 연락할 것인가?
(A) 우편으로
(B) 팩스로
(C) 이메일로
(D) 전화로

| 해설 |
대화 후반부에, 남자가 여자에게 명함을 요청하면서 전화를 하겠다는(I'll call you ~) 말로 연락 방법을 언급하고 있으므로 (D)가 정답이다.

| 어휘 | contact ~에게 연락하다

Questions 7-9 refer to the following conversation.

> M: Hi, Kimberly. It's Alex. I wanted to give you a call about ❽ the performance rating for our ❼ hybrid automobiles.
> W: I haven't had a chance to read the report yet. How did we do?
> M: I'm afraid it's not good news. ❽ I'm disappointed that our cars got an average score in most of the categories.
> W: That's a shame. Well, maybe our engineers need to make adjustments.
> M: You know, they are already working on some prototypes. ❾ Would you mind running some tests on them to get some preliminary data?
> W: ❾ I can take care of that. I'll let you know what I find out.

7-9번 문제는 다음 대화를 참조하시오.

남: 안녕하세요, Kimberly 씨. 저는 Alex입니다. 우리 하이브리드 차량에 대한 성능 평가 등급에 관해 전화 드리고 싶었습니다.
여: 아직 보고서를 읽을 기회가 없었어요. 어땠는데요?
남: 좋은 소식이 아니라 안타깝습니다. 대부분의 항목에서 우리 자동차들이 평균 점수를 받은 것이 실망스럽습니다.
여: 안타깝네요. 저, 아마 우리 엔지니어들이 조정 작업을 해야 할 것 같아요.
남: 저기, 이미 일부 시제품에 대해 작업을 하는 중입니다. 예비 데이터를 좀 얻을 수 있도록 그 시제품들에 대해 일부 테스트를 좀 해 주시겠어요?
여: 제가 그것을 처리해 드릴 수 있습니다. 제가 알아낸 것을 알려 드릴게요.

| 어휘 | performance rating 성능 평가 등급   automobile 자동차   average 평균의   category 항목, 부문   make an adjustment 조정하다, 조절하다   work on ~에 대한 일을 하다   prototype 시제품   preliminary 예비의, 초기의   take care of ~을 처리하다   find out ~을 알아내다, 확인하다

7. 무슨 종류의 제품이 이야기되고 있는가?
(A) 노트북 컴퓨터
(B) 휴대 전화

(C) 하이브리드 차량
(D) 인쇄 장비

| 해설 |
대화 초반부에서 남자가 hybrid automobiles라고 언급하고 있으므로 (C)가 정답이다.

| 어휘 | equipment 장비

8. 남자는 무엇에 대해 실망하고 있는가?
(A) 소프트웨어 문제
(B) 고객 불만 사항
(C) 예산 문제
(D) 성능 평가 등급

| 해설 |
대화 중반부에, 남자가 대부분의 항목에서 자동차들이 평균 점수를 받은 것이 실망스럽다고(I'm disappointed that our cars got an average score in most of the categories) 하는데, 이는 초반부에 제시된 성능 평가 등급(the performance rating)과 관련된 것이므로 (D)가 정답이다.

| 어휘 | complaint 불만   budget 예산

9. 여자는 무엇을 하는 데 동의하는가?
(A) 정책 검토하기
(B) 추가 직원 고용하기
(C) 일부 테스트 수행하기
(D) 광고 늘리기

| 해설 |
대화 후반부에, 남자가 데이터를 얻을 수 있도록 테스트를 해 달라고(Would you mind running some tests on them to get some preliminary data?) 요청하자 여자가 자신이 처리하겠다고(I can take care of that) 동의하고 있으므로 (C)가 정답이다.

| 어휘 | agree to do ~하는 데 동의하다   review ~을 검토하다   policy 정책   conduct ~을 수행하다   increase ~을 늘리다, 증가시키다   advertising 광고(활동)

Questions 10-12 refer to the following conversation.

M: Now that **10 our hair salon** has expanded, it's getting difficult to keep up with all of the duties.
W: I know what you mean. When I'm cutting someone's hair, I don't want to be interrupted to take a booking.
M: Exactly. So, **11 I'd like to hire another employee to handle incoming calls.** We have enough room in the budget for that.
W: All right. I can post the job opening on the **12 Career Finder Web site. It's great because they only charge three dollars to add a listing.** Let's get together later this week to figure out the details, such as the preferred skills and the hourly wage.

10-12번 문제는 다음 대화를 참조하시오.

남: 이제 우리 미용실이 확장되었기 때문에, 모든 업무를 신속히 처리하기가 어려워질 겁니다.
여: 무슨 말씀이신지 알고 있습니다. 제가 누군가의 머리를 자르고 있을 때, 예약을 받느라 방해받고 싶지 않습니다.
남: 맞습니다. 따라서, 걸려 오는 전화를 처리할 다른 직원을 고용하려고 합니다. 이 부분에 대해 예산에 여유가 충분히 있어요.
여: 좋습니다. 제가 Career Finder 웹 사이트에 구인 공고를 게시할 수 있어요. 목록을 하나 추가하는 데 겨우 3달러밖에 청구하지 않기 때문에 아주 좋습니다. 우대하는 기술이나 시급과 같이 세부 사항들을 확인해 볼 수 있도록 이번 주 후반에 자리를 갖도록 해요.

| 어휘 | now that 이제 ~이므로   expand 확장되다, 확대되다   keep up with (진행 상황 등) ~을 따라잡다   duty 업무, 직무   interrupt ~을 방해하다   take a booking 예약을 받다   Exactly (동조를 나타내어) 맞습니다, 바로 그겁니다   hire ~을 고용하다   handle ~을 처리하다   incoming call 수신 전화   room 여지, 여유   budget 예산   post ~을 게시하다   charge ~을 청구하다, 부과하다   get together 만나다, 모이다   figure out ~을 확인하다, 알아내다

10. 화자들은 어디에서 근무하는가?
(A) 우체국에서
(B) 미용실에서
(C) 서점에서
(D) 전자 제품 매장에서

| 해설 |
대화 초반부에, 남자가 자신의 근무 장소를 'our hair salon'이라고 지칭하고 있으므로 (B)가 정답이다.

| 어휘 | electronics 전자 제품

11. 남자는 왜 또 다른 직원을 고용하고 싶어 하는가?
(A) 전화를 받기 위해
(B) 웹 사이트를 업그레이드하기 위해
(C) 시설물을 청소하기 위해
(D) 고객용 청구서를 처리하기 위해

| 해설 |
남자가 직원 고용 문제를 언급하는 중반부에, 걸려 오는 전화를 처리하기 위해 다른 직원을 고용하고 싶다고(I'd like to hire another employee to handle incoming calls) 밝히고 있으므로 (A)가 정답이다.

| 어휘 | facility 시설(물)   process ~을 처리하다   bill 청구서, 고지서

12. 여자는 Career Finder에 관해 무슨 정보를 제공하는가?
(A) 무료 조언
(B) 친절한 직원
(C) 저렴한 요금
(D) 빠른 대응

| 해설 |
Career Finder라는 업체명이 언급되는 후반부에, 여자는 그 웹 사이트가 목록을 추가하는 데 3달러 밖에 청구하지 않는다는(~ Career Finder Web site. It's great because they only charge three dollars ~) 점을 알리고 있으므로 (C)가 정답이다.

| 어휘 | free 무료의   friendly 친절한   fee 요금, 수수료   response 대응, 반응

Questions 13-15 refer to the following conversation with three speakers.

W: Welcome back to the office, Walter and Paul. How did everything go with **13 your trip to Rochester?**
M1: We worked hard at the trade expo **13 to introduce our new wireless headphones.** But Paul and I agreed that it could have been better.
W: Oh, really? **14 Paul,** were there any issues?
M2: **14 There was less than half the number of visitors at the expo compared to last year.** We were able to distribute most of our flyers, though. And we wrote our e-mail addresses on the back so suppliers could contact us directly with questions.
W: That's a good idea. **15 I'm actually planning to have the design team add the salespeople's office phone number and e-mail address to the**

flyer.
M2: Great! That would look more professional.

13-15번 문제는 다음 세 명의 대화를 참조하시오.

여: 사무실로 돌아오신 것을 환영합니다, Walter 씨와 Paul 씨. Rochester 로의 출장에서 모든 일이 잘 되었나요?
남1: 우리는 무역 박람회에서 우리 회사의 새 무선 헤드폰을 소개하기 위해 열심히 노력했습니다. 하지만 Paul과 저는 더 잘 될 수도 있었을 것이라는 점에 동의했습니다.
여: 아, 그래요? Paul 씨, 무슨 문제가 있었나요?
남2: 박람회장에 작년에 비해 절반도 되지 않는 방문객들이 왔습니다. 하지만 우리는 대부분의 전단을 배부할 수 있었습니다. 그리고 질문이 있는 공급 업체들이 곧장 우리에게 연락할 수 있도록 뒷면에 우리 이메일 주소를 적어 놓았습니다.
여: 좋은 생각이네요. 사실 제가 전단에 우리 영업 사원들의 사무실 전화번호와 이메일 주소를 추가하도록 디자인팀에 부탁할 계획입니다.
남2: 좋습니다! 그렇게 하면 더 전문적으로 보일 겁니다.

| 어휘 | trade expo 무역 박람회   introduce ~을 소개하다   agree that ~라는 점에 동의하다   less than ~가 채 되지 않는, ~ 미만의   half 절반   compared to ~와 비교해   distribute ~을 배부하다   most of 대부분의   flyer 전단   though (문장 끝이나 중간에서) 하지만   supplier 공급업체   contact ~에게 연락하다   directly 곧장   actually 실은, 사실   salespeople 영업 사원들   look + 형용사 ~하게 보이다

13. 남자들은 왜 Rochester로 출장을 갔는가?
(A) 계약서에 서명하기 위해
(B) 제품을 홍보하기 위해
(C) 공장을 점검하기 위해
(D) 동료 직원을 만나기 위해

| 해설 |
'Rochester'라는 장소 키워드가 언급되는 초반부에(~ your trip to Rochester?), 그곳으로 출장 간 이유와 관련해 남자 한 명이 새 무선 헤드폰을 소개하는 일을(~ to introduce our new wireless headphones) 했다고 한 것으로 보아 제품 홍보 목적의 출장이었음을 알 수 있으므로 (B) 가 정답이다.

| 어휘 | contract 계약(서)   promote ~을 홍보하다   inspect ~을 점검하다   plant 공장   colleague 동료 직원

14. Paul 씨는 무슨 문제점을 언급하는가?
(A) 행사장을 찾는 데 어려움이 있었다.
(B) 일부 조항들을 협의할 수 없었다.
(C) 일부 샘플이 제때 도착하지 않았다.
(D) 행사 참가자 수가 저조했다.

| 해설 |
대화 중반부에, Paul이라는 이름이 언급된 바로 다음에 답변하는 남자가 작년에 비해 절반도 채 되지 않는 방문객들이 왔다는(There was less than half the number of visitors ~ compared to last year.) 문제점을 알리고 있으므로 (D)가 정답이다.

| 어휘 | venue 행사장   negotiate ~을 협의하다   terms (계약서 등의) 조항   arrive 도착하다   in time 제때   attendance 참가(자의 수)

15. 여자의 말에 따르면, 전단에 무엇이 추가될 것인가?
(A) 새로운 로고
(B) 몇몇 사진들
(C) 할인 쿠폰
(D) 연락처

| 해설 |
'전단(flyer)'이라는 키워드가 언급되는 후반부에, 여자가 전단에 영업 사원들의 사무실 전화번호와 이메일 주소를 추가하게 할 계획을(~ have the

design team add the salespeople's office phone number and e-mail address to the flyer) 언급하고 있으므로 (D)가 정답이다.

Questions 16-18 refer to the following conversation.

M: Ms. Rosario, I'd like to congratulate you and your team on the fine work you did for the Maestro-4X. It has the potential to become our company's top-selling 16 suitcase.
W: Thank you, Mr. Burkett. We wanted the 16 suitcase to be both practical and stylish. So the product is up to your standards?
M: Definitely. In fact, 17 there was one feature that particularly impressed me.
W: Oh, I'd love to hear what it is.
M: 17 The bag is designed to be lightweight. A lot of travelers are looking for that feature.
W: Great. You know, 18 the R&D team is going for dinner tonight. Would you like to join us?
M: Thanks, but I have tickets to a symphony concert.

16-18번 문제는 다음 대화를 참조하시오.

남: Rosario 씨, Maestro-4X에 대해 훌륭하게 일을 해 주셔서 당신과 당신의 팀에 축하 인사를 전해 드리고 싶습니다. 우리 회사의 베스트셀러 여행 가방이 될 수 있는 잠재력이 있어요.
여: 감사합니다, Burkett 씨. 저희는 그 여행 가방이 실용적이면서도 세련되기를 원했습니다. 그럼 그 제품이 당신의 기준을 충족하는 건가요?
남: 물론입니다. 실제로, 특히 제게 깊은 인상을 남긴 특징이 하나 있었어요.
여: 아, 그게 뭔지 꼭 들어 보고 싶네요.
남: 그 가방이 경량으로 디자인되어 있다는 것입니다. 많은 여행객들이 그 특징을 찾고 있거든요.
여: 아주 좋습니다. 저기, 연구개발팀이 오늘 저녁에 회식을 하러 갈 예정입니다. 저희와 함께 가시겠어요?
남: 감사합니다만, 교향악 연주회에 가려고 티켓을 구입해 놔서요.

| 어휘 | fine 훌륭한, 뛰어난   practical 실용적인   stylish 세련된, 멋진   up to ~을 충족하는   standard 기준   Definitely (강한 긍정) 물론입니다, 당연합니다   in fact 실제로, 사실은   feature 특징   particularly 특히   impress ~에게 깊은 인상을 남기다   be designed to do ~하도록 고안되다   lightweight 경량의   look for ~을 찾다   R&D 연구개발   join ~에 입사하다, 합류하다   symphony 교향악

16. 화자들은 무슨 종류의 제품에 관해 이야기하고 있는가?
(A) 휴대용 컴퓨터
(B) 녹음기
(C) 여행용 가방
(D) 의류 한 점

| 해설 |
대화 초반부에, Maestro-4X라는 제품명을 말하면서 그것이 여행 가방(suitcase)이라고 화자들이 모두 언급하고 있으므로 (C)가 정답이다.

| 어휘 | portable 휴대용의   device 기기, 장치   luggage 여행용 가방   an article of clothing 의류 한 점

17. 남자는 제품의 무슨 특징에 깊은 인상을 받았는가?
(A) 내구성이 좋은 외관
(B) 다양한 색상
(C) 친환경적인 소재
(D) 경량 디자인

| 해설 |
중반부에서, 남자가 제품에 대해 깊은 인상을 받았음을(there was

one feature that particularly impressed me) 언급한 뒤로, 그 가방이 경량으로 디자인되어 있다는 특징을(The bag is designed to be lightweight) 알리고 있으므로 (D)가 정답이다.

| 어휘 | durable 내구성이 좋은   exterior 외관   the variety of 다양한   eco-friendly 친환경적인   material 소재, 재료

18. 남자는 왜 "I have tickets to a symphony concert"라고 말하는가?
(A) 초대를 거절하기 위해
(B) 초대장을 발송하기 위해
(C) 감사의 뜻을 전하기 위해
(D) 연장을 요청하기 위해

| 해설 |
대화 후반부에서, 여자가 오늘 저녁 회식 자리에 함께 가자고 (~ the R&D team is going for dinner tonight. Would you like to join us?) 제안하자 남자가 '교향악 연주회 티켓을 구해 놨다'고 반응하는 상황이다. 이는 거절의 의사를 나타내는 것이므로 (A)가 정답이다.

| 어휘 | decline (정중히) 거절하다   extend (초대장을) 보내다   appreciation 감사(의 마음)   ask for ~을 요청하다   extension 연장, 확장

Questions 19-21 refer to the following conversation and map.

M: Good afternoon, Ms. Pinkerton. This is Claude Salazar, the purchasing manager at Niles Inc. I'm pleased that you'll be visiting me Thursday to give 19 **the sales presentation for your newest line of facial creams.**
W: I'm sure you'll be satisfied with what we can offer. Is your building difficult to find?
M: There are several buildings in our complex. 20 **Ours is on Harris Boulevard, next to the playground.**
W: Okay. And do I need to show an ID when I arrive?
M: No, but due to our security procedures, 21 **all visitors have to wear a special badge** while in the building. You can get one near the main entrance.

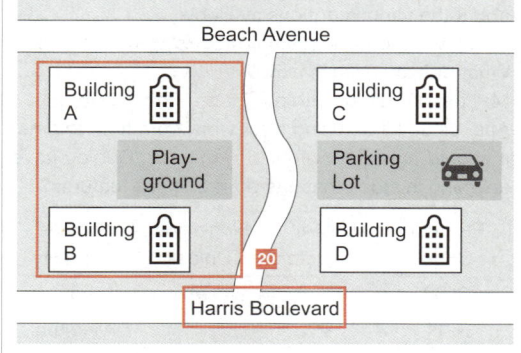

19-21번 문제는 다음 대화와 지도를 참조하시오.
남: 안녕하세요, Pinkerton 씨. 저는 Niles Inc.의 구매부장인 Claude Salazar입니다. 목요일에 귀사의 최신 얼굴 크림 제품 라인에 대한 판매 홍보용 발표를 위해 저를 방문하실 예정이라니 기쁩니다.
여: 저희가 제공해 드릴 수 있는 것에 대해 분명 만족하실 것입니다. 건물이 찾기 어려운가요?
남: 저희 단지 내에 여러 건물들이 있습니다. 저희 건물은 운동장 옆에 있는 Harris Boulevard에 있고, 운동장 옆에 위치해 있습니다.
여: 알겠습니다. 그리고 제가 도착하면 신분증을 제시해야 하나요?
남: 아뇨, 하지만 저희 보안 절차로 인해, 모든 방문객들은 건물 내에 있는 동안 특별 출입증을 착용해야 합니다. 중앙 출입구 근처에서 하나 받으실 수 있습니다.

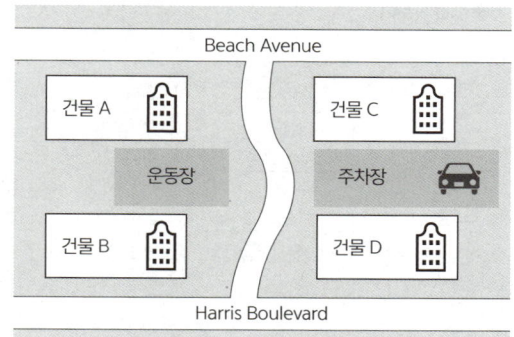

| 어휘 | purchasing manager 구매부장   sales 판매(량), 영업, 매출   presentation 발표(회)   line 제품 라인   offer ~을 제공하다   several 여럿의   complex (복합) 단지   next to ~ 옆에   arrive 도착하다   due to ~로 인해   procedure 절차   while ~하는 동안   near ~ 근처에   parking lot 주차장

19. 화자들은 주로 무엇에 관해 이야기하고 있는가?
(A) 건물 설계
(B) 구직 면접
(C) 판매 홍보용 발표
(D) 안전 점검

| 해설 |
대화 초반부에, 남자가 상대방이 최신 제품에 관해 하려는 판매 홍보 발표 (~ the sales presentation for your newest line ~)에 관해 언급한 뒤로, 그와 관련된 방문에 관해 대화가 이어지고 있으므로 (C)가 정답이다.

| 어휘 | inspection 점검

20. 시각 자료를 보시오. 여자는 어느 건물을 방문해야 하는가?
(A) 건물 A
(B) 건물 B
(C) 건물 C
(D) 건물 D

| 해설 |
남자가 건물 위치를 언급하는 중반부에, Harris Boulevard에 있고 운동장 옆에 위치해 있다고(Ours is on Harris Boulevard, next to the playground) 알려 주고 있다. 시각 자료에서 운동장 옆에 있는 건물 A와 B 중에서 Harris Boulevard 쪽에 있는 것이 건물 B이므로 (B)가 정답이다.

21. 남자는 방문객과 관련해 무엇을 언급하는가?
(A) 중앙 출입구 근처에 주차할 수 있다.
(B) 반드시 도착하자마자 양식에 서명해야 한다.
(C) 직원 한 명과 동행해야 한다.
(D) 반드시 방문객 출입증을 착용해야 한다.

| 해설 |
방문객 관련 정보가 제시되는 후반부에, 남자가 모든 방문객들은 특별 출입증을 착용해야 한다고(~ all visitors have to wear a special badge ~) 알리고 있으므로 (D)가 정답이다.

| 어휘 | park 주차하다   form 양식, 서식   upon ~하자마자   arrival 도착   be accompanied by ~와 동행하다, ~을 동반하다

DAY 14 시각 자료 연계 유형

01 2열 도표/3열 이상 도표

기출 유형 맛보기 본책 p.88

Dynasty 호텔

1층	로비
2층	식당
3층	비즈니스 센터
4층	회의실
5층	객실

Q. 시각 자료를 보시오. 남자는 곧이어 어느 층으로 갈 것인가?
(A) 2층
(B) 3층
(C) 4층
(D) 5층

여: 안녕하세요, Murphy 씨. 이곳에서 즐겁게 머물고 계시기를 바랍니다. 저희 Dynasty 호텔의 시설에 관해 질문이 있으신가요?
남: 실은, 네, 있습니다. 제가 이곳에서 열리는 Weston 마케팅 세미나에 참석하는데, 회의실들이 있는 곳을 알려 주실 수 있는지 궁금합니다.
여: 모든 시설의 위치를 확인하실 수 있도록 이 안내 책자를 한번 보시기 바랍니다.
남: 정말 감사합니다. 추가로, 제가 통역사를 고용할 수 있는 곳이 있는지도 궁금합니다. 제가 이 도시에 있는 동안 러시아에서 오신 고객을 만나야 해서요.
여: 비즈니스 센터를 방문하셔야 합니다. 그곳에 있는 분들이 도와 드릴 수 있습니다.
남: 잘됐네요. 지금 바로 그곳에 가 볼게요.

PRACTICE | 기출 연습하기 본책 p.89

정답 1 (B) 2 (C) 3 (B) 4 (D)

Questions 1-2 refer to the following conversation and schedule.

W: Harold, how are things coming along on the project at Ms. Wilson's property? Will all of **1** the landscaping work be completed by the end of the week?
M: Yes, everything is going smoothly as planned. **2** We'll add the sand tomorrow after it is delivered in the morning.
W: Great! Please be sure to take photos of the final result so we can put them on our Web site.

Project Schedule	
Stage 1	Remove grass
Stage 2	Dig drainage hole
2 Stage 3	Add sand
Stage 4	Arrange bricks

1-2번 문제는 다음 대화와 일정표를 참조하시오.
여: Harold 씨, Wilson 씨의 건물에서 진행되는 프로젝트는 어떻게 되어 가고 있나요? 모든 조경 작업이 이번 주말까지 완료되나요?
남: 네, 모든 것이 계획대로 순조롭게 진행되고 있습니다. 오전에 모래가 배달되면 내일 추가할 겁니다.
여: 잘됐네요! 우리 웹 사이트에 올릴 수 있도록 최종 결과물을 반드시 사진으로 찍어 주세요.

프로젝트 일정	
1단계	잔디 제거하기
2단계	배수구 파기
3단계	모래 추가하기
4단계	벽돌 배치하기

1. 화자들은 무슨 종류의 업체에서 근무하는가?
(A) 철물점
(B) 조경 회사

| 해설 |
화자들의 업체에서 하는 일이 언급되는 초반부에, 여자가 조경 작업(the landscaping work)의 완료 여부를 묻고 있으므로 (B)가 정답이다.

2. 시각 자료를 보시오. 내일 시작될 프로젝트는 어느 단계인가?
(A) 단계 1
(B) 단계 2
(C) 단계 3
(D) 단계 4

| 해설 |
'내일'이라는 시점 키워드가 제시되는 중반부에, 남자가 내일 모래를 추가한다고(We'll add the sand tomorrow) 알리고 있는데, 시각 자료에서 모래를 추가 작업은 Stage 3에 해당되므로 (C)가 정답이다.

| 어휘 | property 건물, 부동산 landscaping 조경 complete ~을 완료하다 by (기한) ~까지 so (that) (목적) ~할 수 있도록 remove ~을 제거하다 grass 잔디 dig 땅을 파다 drainage hole 배수구 arrange ~을 배치하다, 정렬하다

Questions 3-4 refer to the following conversation and chart.

M: Hello, I'm interested in buying a tablet computer. **3** I was reading some reviews this morning about the various options available.
W: Great! We have several models to choose from. What did you have in mind?
M: I need a tablet with a **4** high storage capacity. And, since I'll be using it for work from time to time, it should have **4** a built-in projector. Do you have anything in stock that has both of these features?

Product Code	Built-In Projector	Fingerprint Unlock	Storage Capacity
G-58		✔	Low
R-11	✔		Medium
K-90		✔	High
4 T-63	✔		High

3-4번 문제는 다음 대화와 표를 참조하시오.
남: 안녕하세요, 제가 태블릿 컴퓨터를 구입하는 데 관심이 있습니다. 오늘 아침에 이용 가능한 다양한 옵션에 관한 일부 후기를 읽어 봤습니다.
여: 좋습니다! 저희는 선택하실 수 있는 모델들이 여러 개 있습니다. 무엇을

염두에 두고 계신가요?
남: 저는 저장 용량이 큰 태블릿이 필요합니다. 그리고, 때때로 일하는 데 사용할 것이기 때문에, 내장 프로젝터가 있어야 합니다. 이 두 가지 특징을 모두 갖춘 것이 재고로 있나요?

제품 코드	내장 프로젝터	지문 잠금 해제	저장 용량
G-58		✓	작음
R-11	✓		중간
K-90		✓	큼
T-63	✓		큼

3. 남자는 아침에 무엇을 했는가?
(A) 쿠폰 다운로드하기
(B) 일부 제품 후기 읽어 보기

| 해설 |
'아침'이라는 시점 키워드가 제시되는 초반부에, 남자가 오늘 아침에 후기를 읽은(I was reading some reviews this morning ~) 사실을 밝히고 있으므로 (B)가 정답이다.

4. 시각 자료를 보시오. 어느 제품이 남자에게 최적이겠는가?
(A) G-58
(B) R-11
(C) K-90
(D) T-63

| 해설 |
대화 후반부에, 남자는 자신이 원하는 조건으로 큰 저장 용량(high storage capacity)과 내장 프로젝터(a built-in projector)를 언급하고 있다. 시각 자료에서 이 두 가지 조건에 해당되는 것이 T-63이므로 (D)가 정답이다.

| 어휘 | review 후기, 의견, 평가   various 다양한   available 이용 가능한   several 여럿의   choose from ~에서 선택하다   storage capacity 저장 용량   since ~이기 때문에   from time to time 때때로   built-in 내장된   feature 특징, 기능   fingerprint 지문

02 약도/그래프 및 기타

기출 유형 맛보기

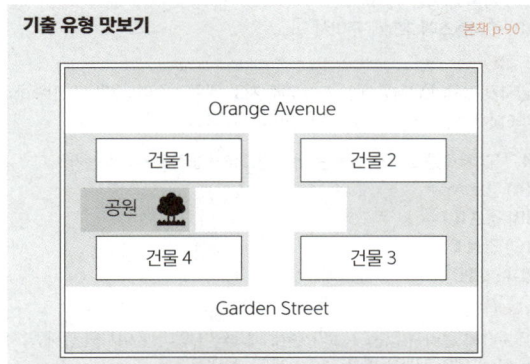

Q. 시각 자료를 보시오. Hampton Manufacturing은 어느 건물에 위치해 있는가?
(A) 건물 1
(B) 건물 2
(C) 건물 3
(D) 건물 4

여: 안녕하세요, Carter 씨. 저는 Hampton Manufacturing의 Susan Briggs입니다. 당신이 면접을 보러 오셨으면 하는데요. 이번 주 금요일 오후 3시 어떠세요?

남: 제가 그때 시간이 나기 때문에 아주 좋습니다. 어디로 가야 하죠?
여: 저희가 최근에 시의 상업 단지에 있는 새 위치로 이전했습니다. Garden Street 쪽의 공원 바로 옆에 위치한 건물에서 찾으실 수 있습니다.
남: 그곳을 찾는 데 분명 아무 문제가 없을 겁니다. 제가 운전을 해서 갈 예정이라서요, 어디에 주차해야 하나요?
여: 단지 내 중앙 구역에 주차장이 있습니다. 저희 회사를 방문하신다고 주차 안내원에게 얘기하기만 하시면, 방문객 주차증을 줄 겁니다.

PRACTICE | 기출 연습하기

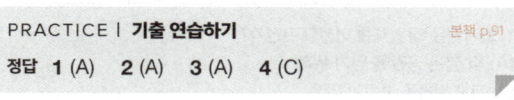

Questions 1-2 refer to the following conversation and floor plan.

W: I'm glad we're relocating our health food store. **1 We really need a larger space** to accommodate the increase in demand. You got the details from the commercial realtor, right?
M: Yes, she suggested getting a unit in the Urban Shopping Center. You can see the available spots on this floor plan. Unfortunately, the one right by the entrance is out of our budget.
W: Then **2 how about the unit between the bookstore and the sports shop?** Since a lot of athletes buy our products, it could be the perfect fit.

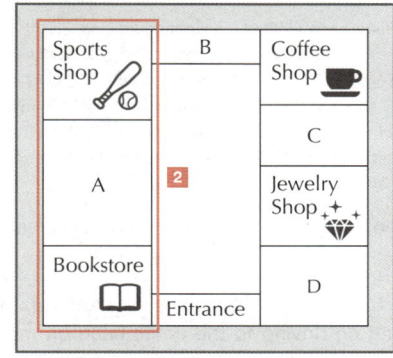

1-2번 문제는 다음 대화와 평면도를 참조하시오.
여: 우리 건강 식품 매장을 이전하게 되어서 기뻐요. 우리가 수요 증가를 감당하려면 더 큰 공간이 꼭 필요해요. 상업용 부동산 중개업자에게서 상세 정보를 받으신 것이 맞죠?
남: 네, 그분이 Urban Shopping Center 내의 점포를 얻도록 제안해 주셨어요. 이 평면도에서 이용 가능한 자리들을 보실 수 있습니다. 안타깝게도, 입구 바로 옆에 있는 곳은 우리의 예산을 초과해요.
여: 그럼 서점과 스포츠용품 매장 사이에 있는 점포는 어때요? 많은 운동 선수들이 우리 제품을 구입하기 때문에, 아주 적합한 자리가 될 수 있어요.

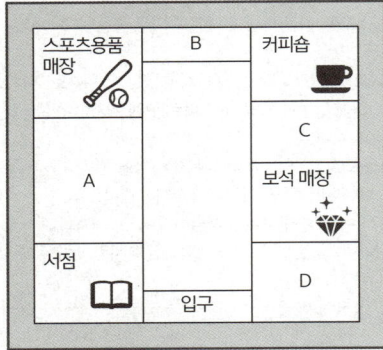

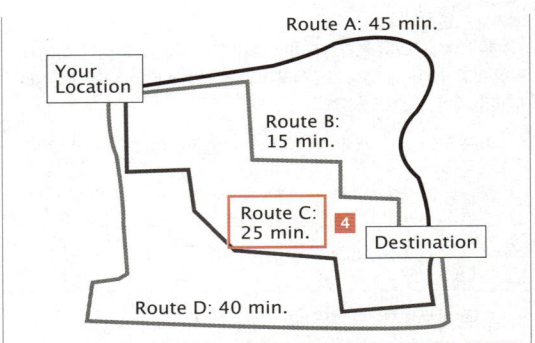

1. 화자들은 왜 업체를 이전할 것인가?
(A) 더 넓은 공간을 얻기 위해
(B) 지출 비용을 줄이기 위해

| 해설 |
위치 이전 및 그 이유가 언급되는 초반부에, 여자가 더 넓은 공간이 꼭 필요하다고(We really need a larger space ~) 밝히고 있으므로 (A)가 정답이다.

2. 시각 자료를 보시오. 여자는 어느 점포를 임대하도록 권하는가?
(A) 점포 A
(B) 점포 B
(C) 점포 C
(D) 점포 D

| 해설 |
대화 후반부에, 여자는 서점과 스포츠용품 매장 사이에 있는 점포를(how about the unit between the bookstore and the sports shop?) 권하고 있는데, 시각 자료에서 해당 위치에 있는 것이 점포 A이므로 (A)가 정답이다.

| 어휘 | relocate ~을 이전하다   accommodate ~을 감당하다, 수용하다   increase in ~의 증가   demand 수요   details 상세 정보   commercial 상업의   realtor 부동산 중개업자   unit (상가 등의) 점포, (아파트 등의) 한 세대   available 이용 가능한   spot 자리, 지점, 위치   unfortunately 안타깝게도   right by ~ 바로 옆에   out of ~을 벗어나는   budget 예산   since ~이기 때문에   athlete 운동 선수   perfect fit 완벽히 어울리는 것   reduce ~을 줄이다   expense 지출 (비용)   rent ~을 임대하다

Questions 3-4 refer to the following conversation and map.

> M: **3 Thanks for picking me up, Amanda.** I was planning on driving to the conference on my own, but I've been having car trouble.
> W: No problem. I'm happy to help. Actually, it wasn't very far out of my way. Now, I usually take the route which takes only 15 minutes to the conference center, but it's closed for repairs.
> M: Well, we still have plenty of time. **4 If we take this route suggested by my GPS app, we can get there in just twenty-five minutes.**
> W: That's not so bad.

3-4번 문제는 다음 대화와 지도를 참조하시오.
남: 태워다 주셔서 감사합니다, Amanda. 제가 직접 운전해서 콘퍼런스 행사장에 갈 계획이었지만, 계속 차량에 문제가 있었어요.
여: 별 말씀을요. 도와드릴 수 있어서 기뻐요. 실은, 제가 가는 길에서 그렇게 멀리 떨어져 있지 않았어요. 저는 보통 콘퍼런스 센터까지 15분밖에 걸리지 않는 경로로 다니지만, 그곳은 지금 수리 작업 때문에 폐쇄되어 있어요.
남: 저, 우리는 아직 시간이 많이 있어요. 제 GPS 앱에서 권해 주는 이 경로를 따라 가면, 불과 25분 만에 그곳에 갈 수 있습니다.
여: 그렇게 나쁘지 않네요.

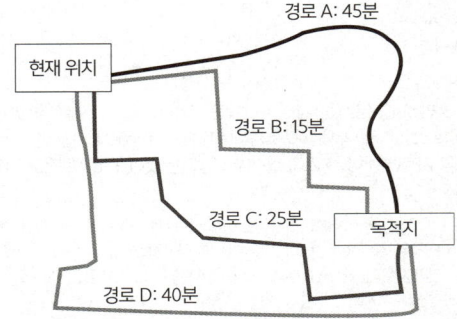

3. 남자는 왜 여자에게 감사하는가?
(A) 차를 태워 주어서
(B) 콘퍼런스에 초청해 주어서

| 해설 |
남자가 감사의 인사를 하는 초반부에, 차로 태워다 주어 고맙다고(Thanks for picking me up, Amanda) 말하고 있으므로 (A)가 정답이다.

4. 시각 자료를 보시오. 남자는 어느 경로를 이용하도록 권하는가?
(A) 경로 A
(B) 경로 B
(C) 경로 C
(D) 경로 D

| 해설 |
15분밖에 걸리지 않는 경로가 현재 폐쇄되어 있다는 여자의 말에 남자는 GPS 앱의 정보에 따라 25분만에 갈 수 있음을(If we take this route suggested by my GPS app, we can get there in just twenty-five minutes) 밝히고 있다. 시각 자료에서 25분으로 표기된 경로가 C이므로 (C)가 정답이다.

| 어휘 | pick up ~를 차로 데려 가다   on one's own 혼자, 스스로   actually 실은, 사실은   far out of ~에서 멀리 떨어진   usually 보통, 일반적으로   get to ~로 가다   repair 수리   plenty of 많은   suggest ~을 권하다, 제안하다   in + 시간 ~ 만에, ~ 후에   location 위치, 지점   destination 목적지

DAY 14 | 실전문제

본책 p.92

정답 1 (B)   2 (D)   3 (A)   4 (A)   5 (B)   6 (C)
     7 (D)   8 (B)   9 (D) 10 (C) 11 (A) 12 (B)
    13 (C) 14 (B) 15 (D) 16 (A) 17 (C) 18 (A)

Questions 1-3 refer to the following conversation.

W: Mr. Dorsett, I got an e-mail from Melanie Babcock, who recently signed up for **1 our Internet service.** She said **2 she got her first bill** and that there's a charge for installing the line.
M: Let's see ... there was already a line at that address. We just needed to switch over the service.
W: Right. So, **2 there should only be a sign-up fee, not an installation fee.** How can I issue a new bill?
M: **3 Could you forward me Ms. Babcock's e-mail?** I'll take care of it.

1-3번 문제는 다음 대화를 참조하시오.
여: Dorsett 씨, 최근에 우리 인터넷 서비스를 신청한 Melanie Babcock 씨로부터 이메일을 받았습니다. 그분께서 첫 고지서를 받으셨는데, 연결선 설치 작업에 대한 청구 요금이 있다고 하시더라고요.
남: 어디 보자… 그 주소지에는 이미 선이 있었는데요. 우리는 그저 서비스를 전환하기만 하면 되었어요.
여: 그렇군요. 그럼, 설치 요금이 아니라 가입비만 있어야겠네요. 제가 어떻게 새 고지서를 발급할 수 있죠?
남: Babcock 씨의 이메일을 제게 전송해 주시겠어요? 제가 처리할게요.

| 어휘 | recently 최근에   sign up for ~을 신청하다   bill 고지서, 청구서   charge 청구 요금   install ~을 설치하다   switch over ~을 전환하다   sign-up fee 가입비   installation 설치   issue ~을 발급하다   forward A B A에게 B를 전송하다, 회송하다   take care of ~을 처리하다

1. 화자들은 무슨 종류의 업체에서 근무하는가?
(A) 철물점
(B) 인터넷 서비스 제공업체
(C) 공공 도서관
(D) 우체국

| 해설 |
대화 초반부에, 여자가 소속 회사를 'our Internet service'라고 지칭하고 있으므로 (B)가 정답이다.

| 어휘 | provider 공급업체

2. 대화의 주제는 무엇인가?
(A) 광고 캠페인
(B) 늦은 배송
(C) 결함이 있는 기기
(D) 비용 청구상의 오류

| 해설 |
대화 초반부에 여자가 한 고객이 받은 고지서를(she got her first bill) 언급한 데 이어, 중반부에서는 그 고지서에 설치비 없이 가입비만 있어야 한다고(there should only be a sign-up fee, not an installation fee) 알리고 있다. 즉, 고지서에 오류가 있음을 지적하는 내용이므로 (D)가 정답이다.

| 어휘 | advertising 광고 (활동)   faulty 결함이 있는   device 기기, 장치   billing 비용 청구

3. 남자는 여자에게 무엇을 하도록 요청하는가?
(A) 메시지 전송하기
(B) 컴퓨터 다시 시작하기
(C) 요금 계산하기
(D) 양식 작성 완료하기

| 해설 |
남자의 요청 사항이 언급되는 후반부에, Babcock 씨의 이메일을 전송해 달라고 요청하고(Could you forward me Ms. Babcock's e-mail?) 있으므로 (A)가 정답이다.

| 어휘 | calculate ~을 계산하다   complete ~을 작성 완료하다   form 양식, 서식

Questions 4-6 refer to the following conversation.

W: Eddie, customers seem to be responding positively to your idea to post the daily exchange rates **4 here at our bank.** I've had several people tell me how helpful it is.
M: I'm glad to hear that. **5 But I don't like having to put up a new sign every morning.** It seems like a waste of paper.
W: I know what you mean. Actually, I think we have room in the budget to purchase a digital display screen. **6 I've got a catalog** with that kind of equipment in my office.
M: Oh, I'd really like to take a look at the catalogue. The sooner we place an order, the better.
W: **6 I'll drop it off after lunch.**

4-6번 문제는 다음 대화를 참조하시오.
여: Eddie 씨, 여기 우리 은행에서 일일 환율을 게시하는 당신의 아이디어에 고객들이 긍정적으로 반응하고 있는 것 같아요. 제게 그것이 얼마나 도움이 되는지를 말씀하신 분이 여럿 있었어요.
남: 그 얘기를 들으니 기쁘네요. 하지만 매일 아침에 새로운 표지판을 내걸어야 하는 게 마음이 들진 않아요. 종이 낭비 같거든요.
여: 무슨 말씀이신지 알아요. 실은, 우리 예산에 디지털 표시 화면을 구입할 만한 여유가 있는 것 같아요. 제 사무실에 그와 같은 종류의 장비를 볼 수 있는 카탈로그가 있어요.
남: 아, 그 카탈로그를 한번 꼭 보고 싶어요. 우리가 더 빨리 주문하면 할수록 더 좋을 거예요.
여: 제가 점심 식사 후에 갖다 드릴게요.

| 어휘 | respond 반응하다   positively 긍정적으로   post ~을 게시하다   exchange rate 환율   several 여럿의   helpful 도움이 되는   put up ~을 게시하다, 내걸다   actually 실은, 사실   room 여지, 여유   budget 예산   purchase ~을 구입하다   equipment 장비   drop off ~을 갖다 놓다, 내려 놓다

4. 대화가 어디에서 이뤄지고 있는가?
(A) 금융 기관에서
(B) 이사 전문 회사에서
(C) 백화점에서
(D) 여행사에서

| 해설 |
대화 초반부에, 여자가 대화 장소와 관련해 'here at our bank'라고 지칭하고 있으므로 (A)가 정답이다.

| 어휘 | take place (일, 행사 등이) 발생되다, 일어나다

5. 남자는 무엇에 대해 불만을 제기하고 있는가?
(A) 줄을 서서 대기하기
(B) 표지판 변경하기
(C) 새로운 방으로 옮기기
(D) 날마다 전화 걸기

DAY 14 073

| 해설 |
남자가 불만을 말하는 중반부에, 매일 아침에 새로운 표지판을 내걸어야 하는 게 마음에 들진 않는다고(~ I don't like having to put up a new sign every morning) 밝히고 있으므로 (B)가 정답이다.

| 어휘 | make a complaint about ~에 대해 불만을 제기하다   move to ~로 옮기다, 이전하다   make a call 전화하다

6. 여자는 점심 시간 이후에 남자에게 무엇을 주기로 동의하는가?
(A) 계약서
(B) 잡지 기사
(C) 카탈로그
(D) 사용자 설명서

| 해설 |
'점심 시간 이후'라는 시점 키워드가 언급되는 후반부에, 여자가 점심 시간 이후에 뭔가를 갖다 주겠다고(I'll drop it off after lunch) 하는데, 여기서 말하는 it은 앞서 자신이 갖고 있다고 말한 카탈로그(I've got a catalog ~)를 가리키므로 (C)가 정답이다.

| 어휘 | agree to do ~하는 데 동의하다

Questions 7-9 refer to the following conversation.

> M: Audrey, you dine out fairly often, right?
> W: Yes, I love trying new restaurants.
> M: **7 Our company has some clients visiting from Singapore, and I'm supposed to show them around town.** I'm looking for a nice place to take them to dinner. Any recommendations?
> W: Well, Tawani Grill is very popular because the chefs prepare the food for you right at the table. **8 The only problem is that there aren't many menu items to choose from.**
> M: That should be okay. No one in the group has any special dietary needs.
> W: If you're planning on going there on a Friday or Saturday, **9 you'd better reserve a table in advance.**
> M: Good point. **9 I'll do that now.**

7-9번 문제는 다음 대화를 참조하시오.
남: Audrey 씨, 꽤 자주 외식하시죠?
여: 네, 새로운 레스토랑에 가 보는 것을 정말 좋아하거든요.
남: 우리 회사에 싱가포르에서 방문하시는 몇몇 고객들이 계시는데, 제가 그 분들을 모시고 시내 구경시켜 드리려고 해요. 저녁 식사를 대접해 드릴 만한 좋은 곳을 찾고 있어요. 추천해 주실 만한 곳이 있나요?
여: 음, Tawani Grill이 아주 인기가 많은 곳인데, 요리사들이 테이블에서 바로 음식을 준비해 주기 때문이에요. 유일한 문제는 선택할 수 있는 메뉴가 많지 않다는 것입니다.
남: 그건 괜찮을 거예요. 그 방문단에서 어느 분도 음식과 관련해 특별히 요구하는 것이 없거든요.
여: 금요일이나 토요일에 그곳에 가실 계획이시라면, 미리 테이블을 예약하시는 게 좋아요.
남: 좋은 지적입니다. 지금 그렇게 할게요.

| 어휘 | dine out 외식하다   fairly 꽤, 상당히   try ~에 한번 가 보다   recommendation 추천(하는 것)   prepare ~을 준비하다   dietary 음식과 관련된   reserve ~을 예약하다   in advance 미리, 사전에   Good point (동의를 나타내어) 좋은 지적입니다

7. 남자는 왜 추천을 부탁하는가?
(A) 모금 행사에 자원했다.
(B) 예산 범위를 지키려 하고 있다.

(C) 최근에 그 지역으로 이사했다.
(D) 일부 고객들을 즐겁게 해 줄 것이다.

| 해설 |
남자가 추천 사항을 요청하는 초반부에, 싱가포르에서 오는 고객들에게 시내 구경을 시켜줘야 한다고(~ clients visiting from Singapore, and I'm supposed to show them around town) 말한 후에 식사 장소를 추천해 달라고 요청하고 있다. 따라서 (D)가 정답이다.

| 어휘 | volunteer for ~에 자원하다   fundraiser 모금 행사   stay on budget 예산 범위를 지키다   recently 최근에   entertain ~을 즐겁게 해 주다

8. 여자는 한 레스토랑에 관해 무엇을 언급하는가?
(A) 찾기 어렵다.
(B) 메뉴가 제한적이다.
(C) 배달 서비스를 제공하지 않는다.
(D) 가격이 높다.

| 해설 |
여자가 특정 레스토랑의 특징을 언급하는 중반부에, 선택할 수 있는 음식이 많지 않다는(The only problem is that there aren't many menu items to choose from) 사실을 알리고 있으므로 (B)가 정답이다.

| 어휘 | offer ~을 제공하다

9. 남자는 지금 무엇을 할 계획인가?
(A) 고객 명단 만들기
(B) 안내 책자 다운로드하기
(C) 초대장 보내기
(D) 예약하기

| 해설 |
대화 후반부에, 여자가 미리 예약을 하는 게 좋다고(you'd better reserve a table in advance) 조언을 하자 남자가 지금 그렇게 하겠다고(I'll do that now) 답변하고 있으므로 (D)가 정답이다.

| 어휘 | brochure 안내 책자

Questions 10-12 refer to the following conversation with three speakers.

> W: Hi, Jerry. Hi, Sean. **10 Could you help me move some chairs** into **11 Meeting Room 3?**
> M1: Sorry, but we're just leaving to meet a client, and we're already running late. But there's a lot of space in Meeting Room 2.
> W: **11 Yes, Jerry, but that's already booked by another team.** It'll take me a long time to move these chairs, and my training workshop starts in fifteen minutes.
> M2: You know, I thought there was a cart in this building.
> M1: Right. That would make the job faster.
> W: Who would know more about that?
> M2: **12 Just ask someone from the maintenance team.** I'm sure they'd let you borrow it or give you a hand.
> W: **12 I'll try that.** Thanks.

10-12번 문제는 다음 세 명의 대화를 참조하시오.
여: 안녕하세요, Jerry 씨. 안녕하세요, Sean 씨. 의자 몇 개를 3번 회의실로 옮기는 일 좀 도와주시겠어요?
남1: 죄송하지만, 저희는 고객을 만나러 막 나가려는 참인데, 이미 좀 늦었습니다. 하지만 2번 회의실에 공간이 많이 있습니다.
여: 네, Jerry 씨, 하지만 그곳은 이미 다른 팀에 의해 예약되어 있어요. 이

의자들을 제가 옮기는 데 오랜 시간이 걸릴 텐데, 제 교육 워크숍이 15분 후에 시작됩니다.
남2: 저기, 이 건물에 카트가 있었던 것 같아요.
남1: 맞아요. 그걸 이용하면 더 빨리 하실 수 있을 겁니다.
여: 그것에 관해 누가 더 잘 알고 있을까요?
남2: 시설 관리팀에 있는 사람에게 물어보시면 될 겁니다. 분명 그쪽 사람들이 그것을 빌려 가도록 해 드리거나 도와 드릴 겁니다.
여: 그렇게 해 볼게요. 감사합니다.

| 어휘 | leave 나가다, 떠나다   run late 늦다   book ~을 예약하다   training 교육   in + 시간 ~ 후에   maintenance 시설 관리, 유지 관리   let A do A가 ~하게 하다   borrow ~을 빌리다   give A a hand A를 돕다   try ~을 한번 해 보다

10. 여자는 무엇에 대해 도움을 필요로 하는가?
(A) 일부 소프트웨어 설치하기
(B) 회의 공고 게시하기
(C) 일부 가구 옮기기
(D) 문서 저장하기

| 해설 |
여자가 도움을 요청하는 말이 제시되는 초반부에, 의자를 옮기는 것을 도와 줄 수 있냐고(Could you help me move some chairs ~) 묻고 있으므로 (C)가 정답이다.

| 어휘 | assistance with ~에 대한 도움   install ~을 설치하다   post ~을 게시하다   notice 공고

11. Jerry 씨는 왜 "there's a lot of space in Meeting Room 2"라고 말하는가?
(A) 계획을 변경하도록 권하기 위해
(B) 결정 사항을 설명하기 위해
(C) 감사의 뜻을 전하기 위해
(D) 자신의 요청 사항을 뒷받침하기 위해

| 해설 |
초반부에, 여자가 3번 회의실로(Meeting Room 3) 의자를 옮기는 걸 도와달라고 하자, Jerry 씨가 도울 수 없는 이유와 함께 '2번 회의실에 공간이 많다'고 말하는 상황이다. 이는 3번 회의실 대신 2번 회의실을 이용하라고 권하는 말에 해당되므로 이를 '계획 변경'으로 표현한 (A)가 정답이다.

| 어휘 | suggest -ing ~하도록 권하다   explain ~을 설명하다   decision 결정   appreciation 감사(의 마음)   support ~을 뒷받침하다, 지지하다   request 요청

12. 여자는 곧이어 무엇을 할 것 같은가?
(A) 일부 장비 주문하기
(B) 시설 관리 직원과 얘기하기
(C) 고객에게 연락하기
(D) 일부 홍보용 자료 출력하기

| 해설 |
대화 후반부에, 남자 한 명이 시설 관리팀에 있는 사람에게 도움을 청하라고 권하자(Just ask someone from the maintenance team) 여자가 그렇게 해 보겠다고(I'll try that) 답변하고 있으므로 (B)가 정답이다.

| 어휘 | equipment 장비   contact ~에게 연락하다   promotional 홍보의, 판촉의   material 자료, 재료, 물품

Questions 13-15 refer to the following conversation and display.

M: Hi, Elaine. Do you have everything ready for your presentation at the advisory committee meeting?
W: I have my slides ready, but the projector doesn't seem to be working. **13 If you look on the screen, you'll see that the words are blurry. I can hardly read anything.**
M: Hmm… there should be some settings options on the projector's display screen.
W: Let's see… here they are. I'm not sure which one is the problem, though.
M: Last time this happened to me, I tried the third option, but it didn't work. **14 Adjusting the second option might resolve your problem.**
W: Okay, I'll give that a try. **15 I'll see you at the advisory committee meeting in a few minutes.**

```
Settings
☐ Contrast
14 ☐ Tracking
☐ Display
☐ Sharpness
```

13-15번 문제는 다음 대화와 디스플레이를 참조하시오.

남: 안녕하세요, Elaine 씨. 자문 위원회 회의에서 있을 발표 준비가 다 되셨나요?
여: 슬라이드를 준비해 놓기는 했는데, 프로젝터가 작동하지 않는 것 같아요. 화면을 보시면, 단어들이 흐릿하다는 게 보이실 거예요. 거의 아무 것도 읽을 수가 없어요.
남: 흠… 프로젝터의 표시 화면에 설정 옵션이 있을 텐데요.
여: 한번 볼게요… 여기 있네요. 하지만 어느 것이 문제인지 잘 모르겠어요.
남: 지난번에 제게 이런 문제가 발생했을 때, 세 번째 옵션을 선택해 봤지만, 소용 없었어요. 두 번째 옵션을 조절하는 것이 문제를 해결해 줄 수도 있습니다.
여: 알겠어요, 그렇게 해 볼게요. 몇 분 후에 자문 위원회 회의에서 뵙겠습니다.

```
설정
☐ 명암
☐ 트래킹
☐ 디스플레이
☐ 선명도
```

| 어휘 | presentation 발표   advisory committee 자문 위원회   work 작동되다, 효과가 있다   blurry 흐릿한, 뿌연   hardly 거의 ~ 않다   setting 설정   though (문장 끝이나 중간에서) 하지만   adjust ~을 조절하다   resolve ~을 해결하다   contrast (화면의) 명암   tracking (화면의 노이즈를 조절하는) 트래킹   sharpness 선명(도)

13. 여자는 무엇에 대해 어려움을 겪고 있는가?
(A) 텔레비전 설치하기
(B) 일부 유인물 출력하기
(C) 화면의 글자 읽기
(D) 그룹 구성원들에게 연락하기

| 해설 |
여자가 겪는 문제점이 상세히 설명되는 초반부에, 화면상의 단어들이 흐릿해서 거의 읽을 수 없다고(~ you'll see that the words are blurry. I can hardly read anything) 알리고 있으므로 (C)가 정답이다.

| 어휘 | handout 유인물   text 글자, 문자   contact ~에게 연락하다

14. 시각 자료를 보시오. 남자는 어느 항목을 조절하도록 권하는가?
(A) 명암
(B) 트래킹

(C) 디스플레이
(D) 선명도

| 해설 |
남자의 조언이 제시되는 후반부에, 두 번째 옵션을 조절하면 문제가 해결될 수도 있을 것이라는(Adjusting the second option might resolve your problem) 내용이 나온다. 시각 자료에서 두 번째 항목에 해당되는 것이 Tracking이므로 (B)가 정답이다.

| 어휘 | category 항목, 부문   suggest -ing ~하도록 권하다

15. 여자는 곧 어디에서 남자를 만날 것인가?
(A) 오리엔테이션 시간에
(B) 구직 면접 자리에서
(C) 업계 콘퍼런스 행사에서
(D) 위원회 회의에서

| 해설 |
대화의 맨 마지막에서, 잠시 후에 자문 위원회 회의에서 보자는(I'll see you at the advisory committee meeting in a few minutes) 여자의 말로 보아 (D)가 정답이다.

| 어휘 | soon 곧, 머지않아   session (특정 활동을 위한) 시간   industry 업계

Questions 16-18 refer to the following conversation and schedule.

W: Hi. I'm signed up for **16** the museum's monthly newsletter, and I read about your lecture series in the last issue. I'd like to get a ticket for the "Pottery through the Ages" lecture on April 17.
M: Unfortunately, we don't have any tickets left for that event. **17** The next lecture that still has tickets left is the one on ancient weapons.
W: Oh, all right. **17** I'll get a ticket for that one then.
M: OK. It's twelve dollars total. And, just so you know, we'll be resurfacing our parking lot at that time, so it'll be off limits. **18** You should take the bus or subway here if you can.

History Museum Lectures	
April 17	Pottery through the Ages
April 19	The Viking Era
17 April 24	**Ancient Weapons**
April 26	Copper Mining

16-18번 문제는 다음 대화와 일정표를 참조하시오.
여: 안녕하세요. 제가 박물관의 월간 소식지를 신청한 상태인데, 지난 호에서 그곳의 강연 시리즈에 대해 읽었습니다. 저는 4월 17일에 있을 "대대로 전해지는 도자기" 강연 입장권을 구하고자 합니다.
남: 안타깝게도, 그 행사는 남아 있는 입장권이 전혀 없습니다. 여전히 입장권이 남아 있는 다음 강연은 고대의 무기에 관한 것입니다.
여: 아, 알겠습니다. 그럼 그 행사의 입장권을 구입하겠습니다.
남: 좋습니다. 전부 12달러입니다. 그리고, 참고로 말씀드리자면, 저희가 그때 주차장 바닥 재포장 공사를 할 예정이라서 출입이 제한될 것입니다. 가능하시다면 버스나 지하철을 타고 이곳으로 오셔야 합니다.

역사 박물관 강연	
4월 17일	대대로 전해지는 도자기
4월 19일	바이킹 시대
4월 24일	고대의 무기
4월 26일	구리 채광

| 어휘 | be signed up for ~에 신청되어 있다, 가입되어 있다   issue (잡지 등의) 호   pottery 도자기   unfortunately 안타깝게도   ancient 고대의   weapon 무기   then 그럼, 그렇다면   resurface (바닥, 도로 등) ~을 재포장하다   parking lot 주차장   be off limits 출입이 제한되다   era 시대   copper 구리   mining 채광

16. 여자는 어떻게 강연에 관해 알게 되었는가?
(A) TV 광고를 시청함으로써
(B) 우편으로 전단을 받음으로써
(C) 라디오 광고를 청취함으로써
(D) 소식지를 읽음으로써

| 해설 |
여자가 강연 관련 정보를 언급하는 초반부에, 자신이 신청한 월간 소식지에서 그 정보를 읽었다고(~ the museum's monthly newsletter, and I read about your lecture series in the last issue) 밝히고 있으므로 (D)가 정답이다.

17. 시각 자료를 보시오. 여자는 어느 날의 입장권을 구매하는가?
(A) 4월 17일
(B) 4월 19일
(C) 4월 24일
(D) 4월 26일

| 해설 |
대화 중반부에, 남자가 아직 남아 있는 입장권은 고대 무기에 관한 것이라고(~ still has tickets left is the one on ancient weapons) 알려 주자 여자가 그 입장권을 구입하겠다고(I'll get a ticket for that one then) 답변하고 있다. 시각 자료에서 해당 강연의 날짜가 April 24로 되어 있으므로 (C)가 정답이다.

18. 남자는 무엇을 하도록 권하는가?
(A) 대중교통 이용하기
(B) 거리에 주차하기
(C) 좌석을 확보하도록 일찍 도착하기
(D) 가이드북 구입하기

| 해설 |
대화 후반부에, 남자가 버스나 지하철을 타고 오도록(You should take the bus or subway here ~) 권하고 있으므로 (A)가 정답이다.

| 어휘 | learn about ~에 관해 알다   commercial 광고 방송   receive ~을 받다   flyer 전단   ad 광고   public transportation 대중교통   park 주차하다   arrive 도착하다

DAY 15 전반적인 내용을 묻는 유형

01 주제/목적/담화 장소를 묻는 문제

기출 유형 맛보기   본책 p.94

Q. 담화가 어디에서 이뤄지고 있는가?
(A) 정부 관청에서
(B) 공장에서
(C) 자동차 정비소에서
(D) 전자제품 매장에서

저는 여러 사람들이 제기한 한 가지 사안을 논의하는 것으로 오늘 회의를 시작하고자 합니다. 우리 MTR Factory에서는 안전이 최대 관심사입니다. 하지만, 여러분 중 일부는 우리가 사용하고 있는 장비가 결함이 있고 교체를 필요로 한다고 생각하는 것처럼 보입니다. 저는 우리가 이 시설 내의 모든 장비를 하나하나 점검할 예정이라는 점을 말씀드리고자 합니다. 우리가 뭔가 잘못된 부분을 발견할 경우, 그것을 수리하거나 교체할 것입니다.

PRACTICE | 기출 연습하기

본책 p.95

정답 1 (A) 2 (B) 3 (B) 4 (A) 5 (A) 6 (B)

Questions 1-2 refer to the following excerpt from a meeting.

W: I'll keep this meeting brief because I know you are all busy. **1** I just want to go over some details regarding the Annual Summer Marathon on May 25. As you know, we will have a booth to sell our goods to participants and spectators. **2** We'll be preparing a variety of our company's sports drinks and bottled water for sale. It'll be a great opportunity to introduce people to our products, especially the new flavors. We're also thinking about giving out some free samples for people to try.

1-2번 문제는 다음 회의 발췌록을 참조하시오.
여: 여러분 모두 바쁘시다는 것을 알고 있기 때문에 이 회의를 간략하게 하도록 하겠습니다. 저는 5월 25일에 열릴 연례 여름 마라톤 행사와 관련된 일부 세부 사항들을 짚고 넘어 가고자 합니다. 아시다시피, 우리는 참가자과 관중들에게 우리 상품을 판매하기 위해 부스를 설치할 것입니다. 우리는 판매용으로 우리 회사의 다양한 스포츠 음료와 생수를 준비할 예정입니다. 이는 사람들에게 우리 제품들, 특히 새로운 맛으로 된 제품들을 소개할 수 있는 아주 좋은 기회가 될 것입니다. 우리는 또한 사람들이 시음해 볼 수 있도록 무료 샘플 제품들을 나눠 주는 것도 생각하고 있습니다.

1. 화자는 무슨 행사를 이야기하고 있는가?
(A) 경주 대회
(B) 야유회

| 해설 |
담화 초반부에, Annual Summer Marathon 행사와 관련된(~ regarding the Annual Summer Marathon ~) 일부 세부 사항들을 짚고 넘어 가겠다고 알리고 있으므로 '마라톤'을 '경주 대회'로 표현한 (A)가 정답이다.

2. 화자의 회사는 무엇을 판매할 것 같은가?
(A) 의류
(B) 음료

| 해설 |
중반부에, 판매용으로 다양한 스포츠 음료와 생수를 준비할 것이라고(~ preparing a variety of our company's sports drinks and bottled water ~) 언급하고 있으므로 (B)가 정답이다.

| 어휘 | brief 간략한 go over ~을 짚고 넘어 가다, 검토하다 details 세부 사항 regarding ~와 관련해 booth 부스, 칸막이 공간 goods 상품 participant 참가자 spectator 관중 a variety of 다양한 for sale 판매 중인 opportunity 기회 introduce A to B B를 A에게 소개하다 especially 특히 flavor 맛 give out ~을 나눠 주다 try ~을 한번 먹어 보다

Questions 3-4 refer to the following announcement.

M: May I have your attention, please? **3 4** Due to the severe weather that is passing through the area, delays are expected on most trains departing from Warrenburg. We apologize for any inconvenience caused. Passenger safety is our top priority, so we must adjust our speeds according to the conditions. You can find up-to-the-minute departure and arrival times on the electronic display boards positioned throughout the station. We appreciate your understanding. Thank you for your patronage.

3-4번 문제는 다음 안내를 참조하시오.
남: 잠시 주목해 주시겠습니까? 우리 지역을 거쳐 지나가는 험한 날씨로 인해, Warrenburg에서 출발하는 대부분의 열차에 지연이 예상됩니다. 저희는 이로 인해 초래된 모든 불편함에 대해 사과 드립니다. 탑승객 안전이 저희의 최우선 사항이므로, 저희는 반드시 기상 상태에 따라 속도를 조절할 것입니다. 여러분께서는 역 전체에 걸쳐 설치된 전광판을 통해 최신 출발 및 도착 시간을 확인해 보실 수 있습니다. 여러분의 양해에 감사 드립니다. 항상 이용해 주셔서 감사합니다.

| 어휘 | due to ~로 인해 severe weather 험한 날씨, 극심한 날씨 pass through ~을 통과해 지나다 delay 지연, 지체 expect ~을 예상하다 depart from ~에서 출발하다, 떠나다 cause ~을 초래하다, 야기하다 top priority 최우선 사항 adjust ~을 조절하다, 조정하다 according to ~에 따라 condition 상태, 조건 up-to-the-minute 최신의, 첨단의 departure 출발 arrival 도착 electronic display board 전광판 position ~을 놓다 throughout ~ 전체에 걸쳐 appreciate ~에 대해 감사하다 patronage 애용, 성원

3. 공지가 어디에서 이뤄지고 있는 것 같은가?
(A) 항공기 내에서
(B) 기차역에서

| 해설 |
담화 초반부에, 기차 운행이 지연되는 상황을(~ delays are expected on most trains ~) 언급하고 있으므로 (B)가 정답이다.

4. 무엇이 문제점을 초래하고 있는가?
(A) 악천후
(B) 장비 고장

| 해설 |
담화 초반부에, 험한 날씨로 인해(Due to the severe weather ~) 열차 운행이 지장이 있음을 알리고 있으므로 (A)가 정답이다.

Questions 5-6 refer to the following introduction.

W: **5** Thank you all for coming to this farewell party for our sales manager, Henry Branum. **5** We want to honor his many years of service to our company, and we wish him all the best. As you all know, Mr. Branum successfully led our company as we joined the European market. This has contributed to enormous growth as well as the creation of new jobs. **6** Now, we'd like to have Mr. Branum come forward and give some brief comments about his time here at Lakewood Inc. and his future plans.

5-6번 문제는 다음 소개를 참조하시오.
여: 우리의 영업부장님인 Henry Branum을 위한 이 송별 파티에 와 주신

여러분 모두에게 감사 드립니다. 우리는 우리 회사에서 오랜 기간 재직하신 Branum 부장님을 기리고자 하며, 부장님께 행운을 빌어 드립니다. 모두 아시다시피, Branum 부장님께서는 우리가 유럽 시장에 진출했을 때 우리 회사를 성공적으로 이끌어 주셨습니다. 이는 새로운 일자리 창출뿐만 아니라 엄청난 성장에도 기여했습니다. 이제, Branum 부장님께서 이곳 Lakewood Inc. 사에 보내신 시간과 앞으로의 계획에 관한 간단한 말씀을 전하실 수 있도록 앞으로 모시겠습니다.

5. 행사의 목적은 무엇인가?
(A) 부장의 근무 경력을 축하하는 것
(B) 새로운 직원을 소개하는 것

| 해설 |
담화 초반부에, 송별 파티에 와 주셔서 감사하며(Thank you all for coming to this farewell party), 오랜 기간 재직한 Branum 부장을 기리기를 원한다고(We want to honor his many years of service to our company ~) 언급하고 있으므로 (A)가 정답이다.

6. 곧이어 무슨 일이 있을 것 같은가?
(A) 상이 수여될 것이다.
(B) 연설이 있을 것이다.

| 해설 |
담화 후반부에, Branum 부장이 앞으로 나와 간단한 말을 전할 것이라는(we'd like to have Mr. Branum come forward and give some brief comments ~) 언급으로 보아 (B)가 정답이다.

| 어휘 | farewell party 송별 파티 honor ~을 기리다, ~에게 영예를 주다 wish A all the best A에게 행운을 빌어 주다 successfully 성공적으로 lead ~을 이끌다 join ~에 입사하다, 합류하다 contribute to ~에 기여하다, 공헌하다 enormous 엄청난 growth 성장 B as well as A A뿐만 아니라 B도 creation 만듦, 창작(물) brief 간단한 celebrate ~을 축하하다, 기념하다 present ~을 주다, 제시하다

02 직업/근무지를 묻는 문제

기출 유형 맛보기
본책 p.96

Q. 청자들은 어디에서 근무하는가?
(A) 신발 매장에서
(B) 텔레비전 방송국에서
(C) 광고 대행사에서
(D) 신문사에서

여러분, 안녕하세요. 저는 Hamilton Shoes 고객사에 관해 이야기하고자 합니다. 5주 전에, 우리는 두 명의 프로 농구 선수를 대표로 내세운 Hamilton Shoes를 위한 광고 캠페인을 시작했습니다. 광고가 나온 이후로 이 회사의 최신 운동화 제품 라인의 매출이 30퍼센트 이상 증가했다는 점을 알려 드리게 되어 대단히 기쁩니다. 이 회사는 그 결과에 대해 매우 만족하고 있기에 우리가 추가 광고를 만들어 주기를 원하고 있습니다.

PRACTICE | 기출 연습하기
본책 p.97

정답 1 (B) 2 (A) 3 (A) 4 (B) 5 (A) 6 (A)

Questions 1-2 refer to the following broadcast.

W: In our local calendar of events, residents are invited to a free lecture by **1** environmental science professor Carrie Harris of Hensley University. This event will be held at Clarence Hall at 3 P.M. on Saturday. **2** Professor Harris will give a lecture about ways you can clean your home without using harsh chemicals. A question-and-answer session will be held at the end of the lecture.

1-2번 문제는 다음 방송을 참조하시오.
여: 우리 지역 행사 안내 달력을 보면, 주민들은 Hensley 대학의 Carrie Harris 환경 과학 교수님께서 진행하시는 무료 강연에 초대받았습니다. 이 행사는 토요일 오후 3시에 Clarence Hall에서 개최될 예정입니다. Harris 교수님께서 유독 화학 제품을 사용하지 않고도 여러분의 집을 청소할 수 있는 방법들에 관해 강연을 해 주실 것입니다. 강연 끝에는 질의 응답 시간도 열립니다.

1. Carrie Harris 씨는 누구인가?
(A) 사업체 소유주
(B) 대학 교수

| 해설 |
담화 초반부에, Carrie Harris 씨가 환경 과학 교수라고(environmental science professor Carrie Harris) 밝히는 부분이 있으므로 (B)가 정답이다.

2. Carrie Harris 씨는 무엇에 관해 이야기할 것인가?
(A) 청소 방법
(B) 재활용 관련 팁

| 해설 |
담화 후반부에, 유독 화학 제품을 사용하지 않고 집을 청소하는 방법을 알려 준다고(~ will give a lecture about ways you can clean your home ~) 언급하고 있으므로 (A)가 정답이다.

| 어휘 | local 지역의, 현지의 resident 주민 invite ~을 초대하다 free 무료의 hold ~을 개최하다, 열다 give a lecture 강연하다 way 방법 without -ing ~하지 않고 harsh chemicals 유독 화학 제품 question-and-answer session 질의 응답 시간 method 방법

Questions 3-4 refer to the following excerpt from a meeting.

M: It is my pleasure to announce that **3 4** we have received a nomination for the Magazine Innovation Award, and we will enter the finals next week. We have been considered for this award many times, but we have never made it this far. No matter what happens, I would like to thank you all for your contributions to making our business the best it can be. In particular, Ms. Mercier on the editorial team has shown great leadership since she joined us one year ago.

3-4번 문제는 다음 회의 발췌록을 참조하시오.
남: 우리가 Magazine Innovation 상의 후보로 지명받았고 다음 주에 있을 최종 결선에 포함될 것임을 알려 드리게 되어 기쁩니다. 우리가 이 상에 대해 여러 차례 고려된 바가 있었지만, 이만큼까지 온 적은 한번도 없었습니다. 결과가 어떻게 되든 상관 없이, 저는 우리 회사를 가능한 한 최고로 만드는 데 있어 여러분 모두의 공헌에 대해 감사 드리고자 합니다. 특히, 편집팀의 Mercier 씨께서 1년 전에 우리 회사에 입사하신 이후로 뛰어난 리더십을 보여 주셨습니다.

3. 화자는 무슨 종류의 회사에서 근무하는가?
(A) 잡지 출판사
(B) 소프트웨어 개발업체

| 해설 |

담화 초반부에, Magazine Innovation Award에 후보 지명된 사실을(~ a nomination for the Magazine Innovation Award) 알리고 있으며, 이 상의 명칭으로 보아 화자는 잡지 출판사에서 근무하고 있음을 알 수 있다. 따라서 (A)가 정답이다.

| 어휘 | announce that ~임을 알리다, 발표하다 receive a nomination for ~에 대한 후보 지명을 받다 final 최종 결선, 결승전 consider ~을 고려하다 make it this far 이만큼까지 이루다, 이만큼까지 도달하다 no matter what ~하든 상관 없이 contribution to ~에 대한 공헌, 기여 in particular 특히 editorial 편집의 developer 개발업체, 개발자

4. 화자는 무엇을 알리는가?
(A) 신입 사원
(B) 수상 후보 지명

| 해설 |

담화 초반부에, Magazine Innovation Award에 후보 지명된 사실을(~ a nomination for the Magazine Innovation Award) 알리는 내용이 있으므로 (B)가 정답이다.

Questions 5-6 refer to the following telephone message.

M: Hi, Ms. Blakely. **5** This is Tony from the management office of Hartland Apartments. I'm calling regarding your message saying that **6** some of the lights in the parking lot aren't working. I agree with you that this is a safety issue for tenants. Therefore, I'll send one of our technicians to investigate the problem right away. Thank you for bringing this matter to my attention. If you notice anything else, please don't hesitate to call.

5-6번 문제는 다음 전화 메시지를 참조하시오.

남: 안녕하세요, Blakely 씨. 저는 Hartland 아파트의 관리 사무소의 Tony 입니다. 주차장의 일부 전등이 작동되지 않고 있다고 말씀하신 메시지에 관해 전화드립니다. 이것이 입주자들의 안전 문제에 해당된다는 점에서 당신의 말에 동의합니다. 따라서, 즉시 이 문제점을 점검해 볼 수 있도록 저희 기술자들 중 한 명을 보내겠습니다. 제가 이 문제에 주의를 기울일 수 있도록 해 주신 데 대해 감사 드립니다. 그 외의 다른 문제를 알아차리게 되실 경우, 주저하지 마시고 전화 주시기 바랍니다.

5. 화자는 누구일 것 같은가?
(A) 아파트 관리 책임자
(B) 실험실 기술자

| 해설 |

담화 초반부에, 화자가 Hartland Apartments의 관리 사무소에서 전화하는 사람이라고(~ Tony calling from the management office of Hartland Apartments) 알리고 있으므로 (A)가 정답이다.

| 어휘 | parking lot 주차장 work (기계 등이) 작동되다 agree with A that ~라는 점에 대해 A의 말에 동의하다 tenant 입주자, 세입자 investigate ~을 점검하다, 조사하다 right away 즉시, 당장 bring A to one's attention A에 ~가 주의를 기울이게 하다 notice ~을 알아차리다 hesitate to do ~하는 것을 주저하다 laboratory 실험실

6. 화자는 무엇에 관해 전화하는가?
(A) 일부 고장 난 전등
(B) 안전 경보 장치

| 해설 |

담화 초반부에, 주차장의 일부 전등이 작동되지 않는 문제를(~ some of the lights in the parking lot aren't working) 언급한 뒤로 그 조치 방법을 알리고 있으므로 (A)가 정답이다.

DAY 15 | 실전문제 본책 p.98

정답
1 (B) 2 (A) 3 (D) 4 (C) 5 (D) 6 (A)
7 (C) 8 (C) 9 (B) 10 (A) 11 (B) 12 (D)
13 (C) 14 (A) 15 (C) 16 (D) 17 (B) 18 (C)
19 (B) 20 (C) 21 (B)

Questions 1-3 refer to the following instructions.

M: Before we begin today's shift, I wanted to let you know that many of **1** our restaurant's servers have been working longer hours than their assigned shifts. To resolve this issue, **2** we've purchased some new employee time-tracking software, which I'll show you how to use today. When you start your shift, simply sign in on the computer in the break room, then sign out again when you leave. The first time you use it, **3** you'll need to set up an account. It's easy to do, but if you have any issues, Stephen is working a long shift today.

1-3번 문제는 다음 설명을 참조하시오.

남: 우리가 오늘 교대 근무를 시작하기 전에, 우리 레스토랑의 많은 종업원들이 각자에게 할당된 교대 근무보다 더 많은 시간을 근무해 왔다는 사실을 알려 드리고자 합니다. 이 문제를 해결하기 위해, 우리는 새로운 직원 근무 시간 추적 소프트웨어를 구입했으며, 오늘 여러분께 그 사용법을 알려 드리겠습니다. 여러분께서 교대 근무를 시작하실 때, 휴게실에 마련된 컴퓨터에 로그인하셨다가 퇴근하실 때 로그아웃하시기만 하면 됩니다. 처음 이것을 이용하실 때, 계정을 설정하셔야 할 것입니다. 쉽게 하실 수 있기는 하지만, 어떠한 문제라도 있으실 경우에는 Stephen 씨께서 오늘 오랜 시간 동안 교대 근무를 하실 예정입니다.

| 어휘 | shift 교대 근무(조) assigned 할당된, 배정된 resolve ~을 해결하다 issue 문제, 사안 purchase ~을 구입하다 time-tracking 시간을 추적하는 sign in 로그인하다 break room 휴게실 sign out 로그아웃하다 set up ~을 설정하다 account 계정

1. 청자들은 어디에 있을 것 같은가?
(A) 버스 정류장에
(B) 레스토랑에
(C) 철물점에
(D) 의료 시설에

| 해설 |

담화 초반부에, 화자가 소속 업체를 'our restaurant'라고 지칭하고 있으므로 (B)가 정답이다.

| 어휘 | facility 시설(물)

2. 화자는 무엇에 관해 설명하고 있는가?
(A) 소프트웨어 프로그램
(B) 휴가 정책
(C) 고객 의견 양식
(D) 비용 지불 절차

| 해설 |

담화 초반부에, 화자는 새로운 직원 근무 시간 추적 소프트웨어를 구입한 사실을(we've purchased some new employee time-tracking software ~) 언급하면서 그 사용법을 알려 주겠다고 밝히고 있으므로 (A)가 정답이다.

| 어휘 | instructions 설명, 안내, 지시 policy 정책 form 양식, 서식 procedure 절차

3. 화자가 "Stephen is working a long shift today"라고 말할 때 암시하는 것은 무엇인가?
(A) 운영 시간이 최근에 변경되었다.
(B) 해당 업체가 바쁠 것으로 예상된다.
(C) Stephen 씨에게 끝내야 할 일이 많다.
(D) Stephen 씨가 계정 설정 방법을 알고 있다.

| 해설 |
담화 후반부에, 계정을 설정해야 한다고 알리면서 문제가 있을 경우를 언급한 뒤에(~ you'll need to set up an account. It's easy to do, but if you have any issues ~) 'Stephen 씨가 오늘 오랜 시간 동안 교대 근무를 할 것이다'라고 말하는 상황이다. 이는 Stephen 씨가 계정 설정 방법을 알고 있으니 그에게 물어보라는 의미이므로 (D)가 정답이다.

| 어휘 | hours of operation 운영 시간   recently 최근에   be expected to do ~할 것으로 예상되다   task 업무, 일

Questions 4-6 refer to the following telephone message.

> W: Hi, Mr. Lopez. **4** Thanks for reaching out to the human resources department. I got your message saying that **5** you wanted to visit my office to change your job title because of your recent promotion. I'm calling to inform you that your details were updated this morning. This change will be reflected in all parts of the system, including our employee directory, which can be found on the company Web site. You will, however, **6** need to get business cards with your new title, so you should order those sometime this week.

4-6번 문제는 다음 전화 메시지를 참조하시오.
여: 안녕하세요, Lopez 씨. 인사부에 연락해 주셔서 감사합니다. 최근 승진하셔서 직함을 변경할 수 있도록 제 사무실을 방문하고 싶으시다고 말씀하신 메시지를 받았습니다. 저는 해당 세부 정보가 오늘 아침에 업데이트되었음을 알려 드리기 위해 전화 드렸습니다. 이 변경 사항은 회사 시스템의 모든 부분에 반영될 것이며, 여기에는 회사 웹 사이트에서 찾아보실 수 있는 직원 안내 목록도 포함됩니다. 하지만, 새로운 직함이 포함된 명함을 받으셔야 하므로, 이번 주 중으로 주문하셔야 합니다.

| 어휘 | reach out to ~에 연락하다   human resources department 인사부   job title 직함   recent 최근의   promotion 승진, 진급   inform A that A에게 ~라고 알리다   details 세부 정보   reflect ~을 반영하다   including ~을 포함해   employee directory 직원 안내 목록

4. 화자는 무슨 부서에서 근무하고 있을 것 같은가?
(A) 연구개발부
(B) 마케팅부
(C) 인사부
(D) 보안 관리부

| 해설 |
담화를 시작하면서 화자가 인사부에 연락한 것에 대해 감사 인사를 하고 (Thanks for reaching out to the human resources department) 있으므로 (C)가 정답이다.

5. 화자가 "your details were updated this morning"이라고 말할 때 암시하는 것은 무엇인가?
(A) 일부 오래된 문서들이 폐기되어야 한다.
(B) 시스템이 한동안 오프라인 상태일 수 있다.
(C) 누군가가 Lopez 씨의 오류를 빠르게 발견했다.
(D) Lopez 씨가 방문할 필요가 없다.

| 해설 |
담화 초반부에, 상대방이 직함을 변경할 수 있도록 사무실을 방문하고 싶다고(~ you wanted to visit my office to change your job title ~) 말한 사실을 언급하면서 "당신의 세부 정보가 오늘 아침에 업데이트되었다"고 알리는 상황이다. 따라서 상대방의 요구사항이 이미 해결되었으니 화자의 사무실을 방문할 필요가 없음을 알리기 위한 말이라는 것을 알 수 있으므로 (D)가 정답이다.

| 어휘 | discard ~을 폐기하다   for a while 한동안   discover ~을 발견하다   make a visit 방문하다

6. 화자의 말에 따르면, 청자는 이번 주에 무엇을 해야 하는가?
(A) 명함 주문하기
(B) 직원 회의에 참석하기
(C) 승인 요청하기
(D) 새 사무실로 옮기기

| 해설 |
'이번 주'라는 시점 키워드가 제시되는 후반부에, 명함을 받아야 한다는 사실과 함께 그것을 이번 주에 주문해야 한다고(~ need to get business cards with your new title, so you should order those sometime this week) 알리고 있으므로 (A)가 정답이다.

| 어휘 | ask for ~을 요청하다   authorization 승인

Questions 7-9 refer to the following talk.

> W: Good afternoon, and thank you all for attending this training session. Today, I'll be teaching you about the features of the **7** new system that our hotel has purchased to manage reservations, the XK24. The feature I like best about this product is that **8** it allows you to share incoming data from each Pembroke Hotel location. That means you'll be able to check the availability of rooms at any branch in real time. In addition, **9** the product's developers gave us a tablet computer for logging into the system anywhere. This will be very useful for us.

7-9번 문제는 다음 담화를 참조하시오.
여: 안녕하세요, 그리고 이번 교육 시간에 참석해 주신 여러분 모두에게 감사 드립니다. 오늘, 저는 우리 호텔이 예약을 관리하기 위해 구입한 새로운 시스템인 XK24의 특징들을 여러분께 가르쳐 드릴 것입니다. 제가 이 제품에 대해 가장 마음에 들어 하는 기능은 이것을 통해 여러분께서 각 Pembroke 호텔 지점으로부터 유입되는 데이터를 공유하실 수 있다는 점입니다. 이는 여러분께서 실시간으로 어느 지점에 있는 객실이든 그 이용 가능 여부를 확인할 수 있게 된다는 것을 의미합니다. 추가로, 이 제품의 개발자들이 우리에게 어디에서도 로그인하게 해 주는 태블릿 컴퓨터 한 대를 제공해 주었습니다. 이는 우리에게 매우 유용할 것입니다.

| 어휘 | feature 특징, 기능   purchase ~을 구입하다   reservation 예약   allow A to do A가 ~할 수 있게 하다   incoming 유입되는, 들어 오는   location 지점, 위치   availability 이용 가능성   branch 지점, 지사   in real time 실시간으로   in addition 추가로   developer 개발자, 개발업체

7. 담화는 주로 무엇에 관한 것인가?
(A) 회계 프로그램
(B) 보안 경보기
(C) 예약 시스템
(D) 라벨 프린터

| 해설 |
담화 초반부에, 호텔에서 예약을 관리하기 위해 구입한 새로운 시스

템을(new system that our hotel has purchased to manage reservations) 언급한 뒤로 그 특징을 간략히 설명하고 있으므로 (C)가 정답이다.

| 어휘 | accounting 회계

8. 화자는 제품의 무슨 이점을 언급하는가?
(A) 제품의 기능을 빠르게 익힐 수 있다.
(B) 품질 보증이 오랜 기간 유효하다.
(C) 지점들 간의 정보를 공유할 수 있다.
(D) 책임자의 이메일 계정으로 새 정보를 보낸다.

| 해설 |
담화 중반부에, 각 Pembroke 호텔 지점으로부터 유입되는 데이터를 공유할 수 있다는(~ it allows you to share incoming data from each Pembroke Hotel location) 제품의 기능이 언급되고 있으므로 (C)가 정답이다.

| 어휘 | benefit 이점, 혜택   function 기능   warranty 품질 보증(서)   valid 유효한   account 계정

9. 화자의 말에 따르면, 회사는 무엇을 받았는가?
(A) 여분의 배터리
(B) 태블릿 컴퓨터
(C) 부분 환불
(D) 사용자 설명서

| 해설 |
담화 후반부에, 제품 개발자들이 태블릿 컴퓨터 한 대를 제공해 준(~ the product's developers gave us a tablet computer ~) 사실을 알리고 있으므로 (B)가 정답이다.

| 어휘 | partial 부분적인, 일부   refund 환불

Questions 10-12 refer to the following excerpt from a meeting.

M: Good morning, everyone. I've just been informed that 10 **the person we selected for the IT technician position has turned down our job offer.** Therefore, we need to find someone else. I propose that we go with Rodney Claire, who was the second choice for many of us on the hiring committee. 11 **Mr. Claire has just developed his own time management software program**, so he definitely has the skills that we need. 12 **I'll e-mail you a sample contract of the terms that we would offer to Mr. Claire. I can do so this afternoon** so you can look it over before I contact him.

10-12번 문제는 다음 회의 발췌록을 참조하시오.
남: 안녕하세요, 여러분. 우리가 IT 기술 담당자 직책에 선정된 분께서 우리의 채용 제안을 거절하셨다는 사실을 막 통보받았습니다. 따라서, 우리는 다른 분을 찾아야 합니다. 저는 우리 채용 위원회의 많은 구성원들에게 있어 두 번째 선택 대상이셨던 Rodney Claire로 결정하도록 제안합니다. Claire 씨께서는 본인만의 시간 관리 소프트웨어 프로그램을 막 개발해 내셨기 때문에, 분명 우리가 필요로 하는 능력을 갖추고 계신 분입니다. 우리가 Claire 씨께 제안해 드릴 수 있는 조건들을 담은 샘플 계약서를 여러분께 이메일로 보내 드리겠습니다. 오늘 오후에 그렇게 해 드릴 텐데, 그래야 제가 그분께 연락하기 전에 검토하실 수 있으실 겁니다.

| 어휘 | be informed that ~라고 통보받다   select ~을 선정하다   turn down ~을 거절하다   propose 제안하다   go with ~로 정하다   hiring committee 채용 위원회   develop ~을 개발하다   one's own 자신만의   definitely 분명히, 확실히

contract 계약(서)   terms 조건, 조항   look A over A를 검토하다   contact ~에게 연락하다

10. 담화는 주로 무엇에 관한 것인가?
(A) 구직 지원자
(B) 팀장
(C) 잠재 고객
(D) 수상자

| 해설 |
담화 초반부에, IT 기술 담당자 직책에 선정되었던 사람이 채용 제안을 거절한(~ the person we selected for the IT technician position has turned down our job offer) 사실을 언급한 후에 대체 후보에 관해 이야기하고 있으므로 구직 지원자를 뜻하는 (A)가 정답이다.

| 어휘 | candidate 후보자   potential 잠재적인

11. 화자의 말에 따르면, Rodney Claire 씨는 최근에 무엇을 했는가?
(A) 몇몇 강의를 가르치기 시작했다.
(B) 소프트웨어 프로그램을 만들어 냈다.
(C) 대학교를 졸업했다.
(D) 다른 도시로 이사했다.

| 해설 |
Claire 씨가 최근에 한 일이 언급되는 중반부에, 시간 관리 소프트웨어 프로그램을 개발한 사실을(Mr. Claire has just developed his own time management software program ~) 알리고 있으므로 (B)가 정답이다.

| 어휘 | graduate from ~을 졸업하다   relocate to ~로 이전하다

12. 화자는 오늘 이따가 무엇을 할 계획인가?
(A) 웹 사이트 업데이트하기
(B) 주문하기
(C) 업계 콘퍼런스에 참석하기
(D) 일부 문서 보내기

| 해설 |
'later today'라는 시점 키워드에 해당되는 표현이 제시되는 후반부에, 샘플 계약서를 이메일로 보내겠다면서 오늘 오후에 그렇게 하겠다고(I'll e-mail you a sample contract of the terms that we would offer to Mr. Claire. I can do so this afternoon ~) 알리고 있으므로 (D)가 정답이다.

| 어휘 | paperwork 문서 (작업)

Questions 13-15 refer to the following advertisement.

M: 13 **Do you love art? The Verano Academy of the Arts can teach you how to create stunning paintings.** No matter your ability level, our highly-experienced instructors can help you improve your skills as well as your confidence. And 14 **beginning October 1, you can visit our Web site to browse photographs of artwork** that our students have made. We hope you'll be inspired by these beautiful pieces! 15 **Visit our Web site to download an informational brochure.** We hope to hear from you soon.

13-15번 문제는 다음 광고를 참조하시오.
남: 미술을 아주 좋아하시나요? 저희 Verano Academy of the Arts에서 여러분께 굉장히 멋진 그림들을 그리는 방법을 가르쳐 드릴 수 있습니다. 여러분의 능력 수준에 상관없이, 뛰어난 경험을 지닌 저희 강사들이 여러분의 능력뿐만 아니라 자신감까지도 향상시켜 드리도록 도와 드릴 수 있습니다. 그리고 10월 1일부터, 저희 웹 사이트를 방문하셔서 저희 학생들이 만든 미

술 작품 사진들을 둘러보실 수 있습니다. 이 아름다운 작품들을 통해 여러분께서 영감을 받으시기를 바랍니다! 저희 웹 사이트를 방문하셔서 정보 안내 책자를 다운로드하시기 바랍니다. 곧 여러분으로부터 연락받을 수 있기를 바랍니다.

| 어휘 | create ~을 만들어 내다 stunning 굉장히 멋진, 아주 훌륭한 No matter + 명사 ~에 상관없이 highly-experienced 뛰어난 경험을 지닌 instructor 강사 improve ~을 향상시키다 as well as ~뿐만 아니라 (…도) confidence 자신감 browse ~을 둘러보다 artwork 미술품 be inspired by ~에서 영감을 받다 piece (글, 그림, 음악 등의) 작품 brochure 안내 책자

13. 무엇이 광고되고 있는가?
(A) 피트니스 센터
(B) 어학원
(C) 미술학원
(D) 콘서트 홀

| 해설 |
담화 시작 부분에, 미술을 아주 좋아하는지 물으면서 멋진 그림을 그리는 법을 가르쳐 줄 수 있다는(Do you love art? The Verano Academy of the Arts can teach you how to create stunning paintings) 말로 보아 미술을 가르치는 기관에 대한 광고임을 알 수 있으므로 (C)가 정답이다.

14. 화자의 말에 따르면, 청자들은 10월 1일부터 무엇을 할 수 있는가?
(A) 일부 이미지 확인하기
(B) 직접 직원들과 만나기
(C) 온라인으로 등록 완료하기
(D) 경연대회에 참가 등록하기

| 해설 |
'10월 1일'이라는 시점 키워드가 제시되는 중반부에, 10월 1일부터 웹 사이트를 방문해 학생들이 만든 미술 작품 사진들을 둘러볼 수 있다고(~ beginning October 1, you can visit our Web site to browse photographs of artwork ~) 알리고 있으므로 (A)가 정답이다.

| 어휘 | in person 직접 (가서) complete ~을 작성 완료하다 registration 등록 sign up for ~에 등록하다, ~을 신청하다

15. 청자들은 왜 웹 사이트를 방문하도록 요청받는가?
(A) 이용 가능 여부를 문의하기 위해
(B) 견학 일정을 잡기 위해
(C) 안내 책자를 이용하기 위해
(D) 차로 운전해 가는 길을 알기 위해

| 해설 |
웹 사이트와 관련된 요청 사항이 제시되는 후반부에, 웹 사이트를 방문해 정보 안내 책자를 다운로드하라고(Visit our Web site to download an informational brochure) 하고 있으므로 (C)가 정답이다.

| 어휘 | inquire about ~에 관해 문의하다 availability 이용 가능성 access ~을 이용하다, ~에 접근하다 directions 찾아가는 길

Questions 16-18 refer to the following broadcast.

M: **16** That was the *Hour of Music* program here on KRT Radio. Up next is the local news. The Cypress Hotel has been granted the status of a historical building thanks to a recent campaign of support. **17** The hotel, which is well-known for its beautiful flower gardens and perfectly landscaped lawn, has been in operation for one hundred fifty years. To celebrate its anniversary, it is holding events for the public throughout the week, including a prize drawing. **18** Anyone can register to win the grand prize, which is five thousand dollars. Yes, you heard that correctly… five thousand dollars! Visit the hotel's Web site for more information.

16-18번 문제는 다음 방송을 참조하시오.

남: 방금 들으신 것은 저희 KRT 라디오의 <Hour of Music> 프로그램이었습니다. 다음 순서는 지역 뉴스입니다. Cypress 호텔이 최근의 지지 캠페인 덕분에 역사적인 건물 등급을 승인받았습니다. 이 호텔은 아름다운 화원과 완벽하게 조경 작업이 된 잔디로 잘 알려져 있으며, 150년 동안 운영되어 왔습니다. 이 기념일을 축하하기 위해, 이 호텔에서는 경품 추첨 행사를 포함해 이번 주 내내 일반 대중을 위한 행사들을 개최할 예정입니다. 누구든지 등록하셔서 1등 상품을 타실 수 있는데, 이 금액이 5,000달러입니다. 네, 제대로 들으신 것이 맞습니다… 5,000달러입니다! 이 호텔의 웹 사이트를 방문하셔서 더 많은 정보를 알아보시기 바랍니다.

| 어휘 | Up next is A (방송 등에서) 다음 순서는 A입니다 be granted A A를 승인받다, 부여받다 status 지위, 신분 historical 역사적인 thanks to ~로 인해, ~ 덕분에 recent 최근의 be well-known for ~로 잘 알려져 있다 landscaped 조경 작업이 된 be in operation 운영되다, 가동되다 celebrate ~을 축하하다, 기념하다 anniversary (해마다 돌아오는) 기념일 hold ~을 개최하다 the public 일반 대중 throughout ~ 동안 내내 including ~을 포함해 prize drawing 경품 추첨 register 등록하다 win (상 등) ~을 타다, 받다 correctly 제대로, 정확히

16. 화자는 어디에서 일하고 있을 것 같은가?
(A) 은행에서
(B) 호텔에서
(C) 꽃 가게에서
(D) 라디오 방송국에서

| 해설 |
담화를 시작 부분에서, 방금 들은 것은 KRT 라디오 방송국의 <Hour of Music> 프로그램이라고(That was the *Hour of Music* program here on KRT Radio) 알리고 있으므로 (D)가 정답이다.

17. 화자는 Cypress 호텔에 관해 무엇이 유명하다고 말하는가?
(A) 웅장한 입구
(B) 야외 공간
(C) 장식된 객실
(D) 고객 서비스

| 해설 |
중반부에, 호텔이 유명한 이유로 아름다운 화원과 완벽하게 조경 작업이 된 잔디를(The hotel, which is well-known for its beautiful flower gardens and perfectly landscaped lawn ~) 언급하고 있으므로 이를 야외 공간으로 표현한 (B)가 정답이다.

| 어휘 | decorated 장식된

18. 화자가 왜 "Yes, you heard that correctly … five thousand dollars"라고 말하는 것 같은가?
(A) 앞서 발생된 실수에 대해 사과하기 위해
(B) 개조 공사 비용을 확인해 주기 위해
(C) 상금 액수가 인상적임을 나타내기 위해
(D) 투자에 대한 지지를 나타내기 위해

| 해설 |
담화 후반부에, 누구든지 등록해 1등 상금을 탈 수 있고 금액이 5,000달러라고(Anyone can register to win the grand prize, which is five thousand dollars) 알린 후에 "5,000달러라는 금액을 제대로 들은 것이 맞다"고 알리는 상황이다. 즉, 상금의 액수가 매우 크다는 것을 강조하는 말이므로 (C)가 정답이다.

| 어휘 | apologize for ~에 대해 사과하다 confirm ~을 확인해 주다 renovation 개조, 보수 impressive 인상적인 support 지지, 후원 investment 투자(금)

Questions 19-21 refer to the following telephone message and directory.

W: Hello, Mr. Rios. It's Emma Fitch. I'm glad that we'll finally get a chance to meet tomorrow. **19 You suggested a 10 A.M. meeting, and I wanted to let you know that's fine for me.** As you know, we're talking to several companies to find the one with the best insurance coverage for a reasonable price. Since you said you'd be driving here, don't forget to **20 stop by reception. They will give you a voucher for parking** that is valid for two hours. You just need to present it to the ticket agent on your way out. **21 Our company, Florence Co., takes up four floors in Tower A. My office is on the lowest floor of our section**, so just meet me there.

```
          Tower A Directory
  Prudential Inc ················· Floors 2–6
21 Florence Co ··················· Floors 7–10
  Extron Industries ············· Floors 11–13
  Almont Enterprises ··········· Floors 14–16
```

19-21번 문제는 다음 전화 메시지와 안내 목록을 참조하시오.

여: 안녕하세요, Rios 씨. 저는 Emma Fitch입니다. 드디어 내일 저희가 만날 기회가 생겨 기쁘게 생각합니다. 귀하께서 오전 10시 회의를 제안해 주셨는데, 제게도 그 일정이 좋다는 사실을 알려 드리고 싶었습니다. 아시다시피, 저희는 합리적인 가격으로 최고의 보험 혜택을 제공하는 곳을 찾기 위해 여러 회사와 이야기하는 중입니다. 귀하께서 이곳으로 차를 운전해 오시겠다고 말씀하셨으므로, 잊지 말고 안내 데스크에 들르시기 바랍니다. 그곳의 직원이 2시간 동안 유효한 주차 쿠폰을 제공해 줄 것입니다. 나가실 때 이것을 티켓 안내원에게 제시해 주셔야 합니다. 저희 Florence Co. 사는 A동의 4개 층을 차지하고 있습니다. 제 사무실은 저희 회사 구역에서 가장 아래층에 있으므로, 그곳에서 저를 만나시면 됩니다.

```
          A동 층별 안내
  Prudential Inc. ················ 2–6층
  Florence Co. ···················· 7–10층
  Extron Industries ············· 11–13층
  Almont Enterprises ··········· 14–16층
```

| 어휘 | get a chance to do ~할 기회가 생기다 suggest ~을 제안하다, 권하다 let A know A에게 알리다 insurance 보험 coverage (보험 등이 보장하는) 혜택, 보장 범위 reasonable 합리적인 since ~이므로 forget to do ~하는 것을 잊다 stop by ~에 들르다 reception 안내 데스크 voucher 쿠폰, 상품권 valid 유효한 present ~을 제시하다 on one's way out 나가는 길에 take up ~을 차지하다 directory (건물 입구 등에 있는) 안내 목록

19. 전화 메시지의 목적은 무엇인가?
(A) 서비스를 소개하는 것
(B) 회의 시간을 확인해 주는 것
(C) 계약을 갱신하는 것
(D) 일자리에 지원하는 것

| 해설 |
담화 초반부에, 상대방이 회의 시간을 오전 10시로 제안한 것에 대해 자신도 좋다고(You suggested a 10 A.M. meeting, and I wanted to let you know that's fine for me) 알리고 있으므로 (B)가 정답이다.

| 어휘 | introduce ~을 소개하다 confirm ~을 확인해 주다 renew ~을 갱신하다 contract 계약(서) apply for ~에 지원하다

20. 화자의 말에 따르면, 청자는 왜 안내 데스크를 방문해야 하는가?
(A) 출입증을 가져가기 위해
(B) 방문객 출입 양식에 서명하기 위해
(C) 주차권을 받기 위해
(D) 구내 안내도를 요청하기 위해

| 해설 |
'안내 데스크'라는 키워드가 제시되는 중반부에, 그곳에 들르면 주차권이 제공될 것이라고(~ stop by reception. They will give you a voucher for parking ~) 알리고 있으므로 (C)가 정답이다.

| 어휘 | pick up ~을 가져가다 parking pass 주차권 request ~을 요청하다 site map 안내도

21. 시각 자료를 보시오. 화자는 어느 층에서 청자를 만날 것인가?
(A) 2층
(B) 7층
(C) 10층
(D) 14층

| 해설 |
담화 후반부에, Florence Co.라는 회사명과 함께 이 회사가 사용하는 네 개의 층에서 가장 낮은 층에 화자의 사무실이 있다고(~ Florence Co., takes up four floors in Tower A. My office is on the lowest floor of our section ~) 알리고 있다. 시각 자료에 이 회사가 7층~10층까지 입주해 있는 것으로 표기되어 있으므로 이 중 가장 낮은 층인 (B)가 정답이다.

DAY 16 세부적인 내용을 묻는 유형 (1)

01 요청/제안 사항 문제

기출 유형 맛보기

본책 p.100

Q. 화자는 청자들에게 무엇을 하도록 제안하는가?
(A) 집에서 일찍 출발하기
(B) 시내 지역 피하기
(C) 전화하기
(D) 대중교통 이용하기

안녕하세요, 여러분. WTRE 라디오 교통 소식입니다. 시내로 가고 계신다면, 일부 구역에서 최대 1시간까지 지연 상황을 예상하시기 바랍니다. 그 이유는 어젯밤에 발생한 폭풍우가 많은 나무와 전신주를 쓰러뜨렸기 때문입니다. 작업 인부들이 바쁘게 모든 것을 치우기 위해 노력하고 있지만, 한동안 시간이 걸릴 것입니다. 아직 댁에서 나오지 않으셨다면, 시내 거리를 피하실 수 있도록 지하철이나 통근 열차를 이용하시기를 권해 드립니다.

PRACTICE | 기출 연습하기

본책 p.101

정답 1 (A) 2 (B) 3 (A) 4 (B) 5 (A) 6 (B)

Questions 1-2 refer to the following excerpt from a meeting.

W: Thank you all for being here for this committee meeting. **1 As you all know, we've been working to organize a parade to celebrate the town's founding day.** However, we need to find a way to cover the expenses of this event, and we're currently short on funds. Therefore, **2 we'll try to solicit donations from local businesses**. I've made a list of potential donors. **2 I'd like each of you to call the business owners** on your section of the list and find out whether they'd like to contribute to this event.

1-2번 문제는 다음 회의 발췌록을 참조하시오.
여: 이번 위원회 회의를 위해 이 자리에 와 주신 여러분 모두에게 감사 드립니다. 모두 아시다시피, 우리는 시의 창립일을 기념하는 퍼레이드 행사를 마련하기 위해 힘써 왔습니다. 하지만, 우리는 이 행사의 지출 비용을 충당할 방법을 찾아야 하며, 현재 자금이 부족한 상태입니다. 따라서, 지역 내 기업들에게 기부를 요청하려 노력할 것입니다. 제가 잠재 기부자들의 명단을 만들었습니다. 저는 명단에서 여러분 각자에게 해당되는 섹션에 있는 사업체 소유주들에게 전화를 걸어 그분들이 이번 행사에 기부하고자 하는지를 알아봐 주셨으면 합니다.

1. 담화는 주로 무엇에 관한 것인가?
(A) 퍼레이드 행사 기획하기
(B) 공원 정화 작업하기

| 해설 |
담화 초반부에, 시의 창립일을 기념하는 퍼레이드 행사를 준비하는 일을(~ we've been working to organize a parade ~) 언급한 후로 그 일에 필요한 자금 상황을 이야기하고 있으므로 (A)가 정답이다.

2. 청자들은 무엇을 하도록 요청 받는가?
(A) 잠재 직원들 찾기
(B) 지역 기업에 연락하기

| 해설 |
담화 중반부에, 지역 기업으로부터 기부를 받는 방법을(~ we'll try to solicit donations from local businesses) 언급하면서, 이를 위해 기업 소유주들에게 전화해 보도록(I'd like each of you to call the business owners ~) 청자들에게 요청하고 있으므로 (B)가 정답이다.

| 어휘 | committee 위원회 organize ~을 마련하다, 조직하다 celebrate ~을 기념하다, 축하하다 founding day 창립일 way to do ~하는 방법 cover (비용 등) ~을 충당하다 expense 지출 (비용) currently 현재 be short on A A가 부족하다 solicit ~을 요구하다, 간청하다 donation 기부(금) potential 잠재적인 donor 기부자 would like A to do A에게 ~하기를 원하다 find out ~을 알아 보다, 확인하다 whether ~인지 (아닌지) contribute to ~에 기부하다 contact ~에게 연락하다

Questions 3-4 refer to the following excerpt from a meeting.

M: Next on today's meeting agenda, I'd like to discuss the current workload. We understand that you have all been under a lot of pressure due to the rapid growth of our business. It's wonderful that our brand is becoming more popular, but it also creates more work. **3 The management team has made the decision to hire more full-time employees.** To maximize our workforce, we'd like to assign them to the tasks that are the most understaffed. So, **4 if you can write up a description of your duties today, please do so.**

3-4번 문제는 다음 회의 발췌록을 참조하시오.
남: 오늘 회의의 다음 안건으로, 현재의 업무량을 논의하고자 합니다. 우리는 여러분 모두가 회사의 빠른 성장으로 인해 많은 압박감을 받아 왔음을 알고 있습니다. 우리 브랜드가 더 많은 인기를 얻고 있어 아주 좋기는 하지만, 이는 또한 더 많은 일을 만들어 냅니다. 경영진에서는 추가 정규직 직원들을 고용하기로 결정을 내렸습니다. 회사의 인력을 최대로 활용하기 위해, 우리는 가장 인원이 부족한 상태인 업무에 그 직원들을 배정하고자 합니다. 따라서, 오늘 여러분의 업무에 관한 설명을 작성하실 수 있다면, 그렇게 해주시기 바랍니다.

3. 회사의 책임자들은 무엇을 하기로 결정했는가?
(A) 추가 직원 고용하기
(B) 업체 이전하기

| 해설 |
결정 사항이 언급되는 중반부에, 추가 정규직 직원들을 고용하기로 결정을 내렸다고(The management team has made the decision to hire more full-time employees) 알리고 있으므로 (A)가 정답이다.

4. 화자는 청자들에게 무엇을 하도록 요청하는가?
(A) 업무 일정표 만들기
(B) 각자의 업무 보고하기

| 해설 |
담화 후반부에, 각자의 업무에 관한 설명을 작성할 수 있다면 그렇게 해 달라고(if you can write up a description of your duties today, please do so) 요청하고 있으므로 (B)가 정답이다.

| 어휘 | agenda 안건, 의제 current 현재의 workload 업무량 under (영향 등) ~하게 있는 pressure 압박(감) due to ~로 인해 growth 성장 create ~을 만들어 내다 make a decision 결정을 내리다 maximize ~을 최대한 활용하다 workforce 인력, 직원들 assign A to B A를 B에 배정하다, 할당하다 task 업무, 일 understaffed 인원이 부족한 write up ~을 완전히 작성하다 description 설명 duty 업무, 직무 relocate (위치) ~을 이전하다

Questions 5-6 refer to the following talk.

W: Hi, I'm Jenifer, and **5 I'll be reviewing the new fitness tracker** recently released by Veasley Electronics. I've been using this product for three weeks, and I'm completely satisfied with it. At first, I was worried that it would overheat during my workouts, but it is heat- and sweat-resistant. Also, it was easy to choose different settings and view my progress. If you're interested, **6 I suggest you buy one before the end of the month.** The company is having a sale right now, and you can get it for the lowest price of the season.

5-6번 문제는 다음 담화를 참조하시오.
여: 안녕하세요, 저는 Jenifer이며, Veasley Electronics 사에서 최근에 출시한 새 피트니스 측정기 제품에 대한 사용 후기를 말씀 드리고자 합니다. 저는 이 제품을 3주 동안 사용해 왔으며, 전적으로 만족합니다. 처음엔 운동 중에 과열되지 않을까 걱정했지만, 이 제품은 열과 땀에 강합니다. 또한, 다른 설정을 선택하고 향상 과정을 확인하기가 쉬웠습니다. 관심이 있으시면, 이달 말 전에 한 대 구입하시도록 권해 드립니다. 이 회사에서 현재 세일 행사를 진행하고 있으므로, 시즌 중 가장 저렴한 가격으로 구입하실 수 있습니다.

5. 무슨 제품이 평가되고 있는가?
(A) 피트니스 측정기
(B) 운동용 자전거

| 해설 |
제품의 종류가 언급되는 초반부에, 피트니스 측정기 제품에 대한 사용 후기를 말하겠다고(I'll be reviewing the new fitness tracker ~) 알리는 부

분이 있으므로 (A)가 정답이다.

6. 화자는 청자들에게 무엇을 하도록 권하는가?
(A) 제품에 대한 품질 보증 서비스 구입하기
(B) 이번 달에 제품 구입하기

| 해설 |
담화 후반부에, 화자는 이달 말이 되기 전에 하나 구입하도록 권하고 있으므로(I suggest you buy one before the end of the month) (B)가 정답이다.

| 어휘 | review ~에 대한 사용 후기를 말하다, ~을 평가하다 recently 최근에 release ~을 출시하다 completely 전적으로, 완전히 be satisfied with ~에 만족하다 be worried that ~라는 점을 걱정하다 overheat 과열되다 workout 운동 resistant ~에 강한, 잘 견디는 setting (기기 등의) 설정 view ~을 보다 progress 진전; 진척 suggest (that) ~하도록 권하다, 제안하다 warranty 품질 보증(서)

02 기타 세부 사항 문제

기출 유형 맛보기   본책 p.102

Q. 화자는 왜 청자들에게 감사하는가?
(A) 새로운 프로젝트를 기획했다.
(B) 신규 고객을 확보했다.
(C) 추가 근무를 했다.
(D) 새 건물로 성공적으로 이사를 했다.

점심 식사를 하러 가기 전에, 우리가 반드시 Anderson 프로젝트를 제때 완료할 수 있도록 주말에도 자원해서 나와 주신 여러분께 감사 드리고자 합니다. 여러분이 별도의 노력을 기울여 주었기 때문에, 어제 Anderson 씨께 건물 설계도를 보내 드릴 수 있었습니다. 그분께서 오늘 아침에 제게 전화하셔서 우리의 작업 능력에 대단히 만족한다고 말씀해 주셨습니다.

PRACTICE | 기출 연습하기   본책 p.103

정답 1 (A) 2 (A) 3 (A) 4 (A) 5 (A) 6 (B)

Questions 1-2 refer to the following excerpt from a meeting.

M: To begin, I'd like to address your concerns about **1** our new billing system for customers. In the past, customers were asked to pay their bills after their equipment was installed. However, to help us with our cash flow, we will now charge a fifteen percent deposit before the work begins. You'll need to enter this charge into the system differently, so you must all learn how to do this. **2** Vivian Reynolds, who will be here next week, will conduct the training for staff members.

1-2번 문제는 다음 회의 발췌록을 참조하시오.
남: 가장 먼저, 고객들을 대상으로 하는 우리의 새 비용 청구 시스템에 관한 여러분의 우려를 해결해 드리고자 합니다. 과거에는, 고객들은 장비가 설치된 후에 청구 대금을 지불하도록 요청 받았습니다. 하지만, 우리의 현금 흐름에 도움이 되기 위해, 우리는 이제 작업이 시작되기 전에 15퍼센트의 선금을 청구할 것입니다. 여러분은 이 청구 금액을 시스템에 다르게 입력해야 할 것이므로, 이렇게 하는 방법을 반드시 모두가 익히셔야 합니다. Vivian Reynolds 씨께서 다음 주에 이곳으로 오셔서 직원들을 대상으로 하는 교육을 실시하실 것입니다.

1. 업체에서 무엇이 변경될 것인가?
(A) 고객들에게 어떻게 비용이 청구될 것인지
(B) 배송 물품이 어떻게 추적 관찰될 것인지

| 해설 |
담화 초반부에, 고객들을 대상으로 하는 새 비용 청구 시스템(our new billing system for customers)을 언급한 뒤로 새로운 청구 방식을 설명하고 있으므로 (A)가 정답이다.

2. Reynolds 씨는 무엇을 할 예정인가?
(A) 직원들 교육하기
(B) 새로운 장비 설치하기

| 해설 |
'Reynolds'라는 이름 키워드가 제시되는 후반부에, Vivian Reynolds 씨가 다음 주에 와서 직원들을 대상으로 교육을 할 것이라고(Vivian Reynolds ~ will conduct the training for staff members) 알리고 있으므로 (A)가 정답이다.

| 어휘 | address ~을 해결하다, 처리하다 concern 우려, 걱정 billing 비용 청구, 고지서 발송 equipment 장비 install ~을 설치하다 cash flow 현금 흐름 charge ~을 청구하다; 청구(액) deposit 선금, 예치금 enter ~을 입력하다 conduct ~을 실시하다, 수행하다 training 교육 bill ~에게 비용을 청구하다 monitor ~을 관찰하다, 감시하다

Questions 3-4 refer to the following announcement.

W: Attention, all employees. First of all, **3** I'd like to thank you for sharing your honest opinions about the working environment at the session last month. It was really helpful for us. One of the biggest complaints was the outdated facilities. Therefore, we will have some major renovations done to our building. We've hired the industry's top designer! The only downside is that the building must be completely empty for the crew to work, so **4** you must work remotely from home in April. We'll have more details as the project gets closer.

3-4번 문제는 다음 안내를 참조하시오.
여: 모든 직원들께 알립니다. 우선, 지난달에 있었던 모임에서 업무 환경에 관해 솔직한 의견을 공유해 주셔서 감사 드리고자 합니다. 이는 우리에게 정말로 도움이 되었습니다. 가장 큰 불만 사항들 중의 하나는 낡은 시설이었습니다. 따라서, 우리는 우리 건물에 대해 대대적인 개조 공사를 완료할 것입니다. 우리는 업계 최고의 디자이너를 고용했습니다! 유일한 단점이라면 공사팀이 작업할 수 있도록 건물이 완전히 비워져야 한다는 것이므로, 여러분은 4월에 재택 근무를 해야 합니다. 이 프로젝트가 더 임박해지면 더 많은 세부 정보를 알게 될 것입니다.

3. 화자는 무엇에 대해 청자들에게 감사하는가?
(A) 각자의 의견을 공유한 것
(B) 추가 근무를 한 것

| 해설 |
감사 인사가 제시되는 초반부에, 솔직한 의견을 공유해주어 고맙다고(I'd like to thank you for sharing your honest opinions ~) 전하고 있으므로 (A)가 정답이다.

4. 청자들은 4월에 무엇을 해야 할 것인가?
(A) 재택 근무하기
(B) 업계 콘퍼런스에 참석하기

| 해설 |
'4월'이라는 시점 키워드가 제시되는 후반부에, 공사로 인해 4월에 재택 근무를 해야 한다고(~ you must work remotely from home in April) 알리고 있으므로 (A)가 정답이다.

| 어휘 | share ~을 공유하다 opinion 의견 working environment 업무 환경 session (특정 활동을 위한) 시간; 모임 complaint 불만 outdated 낡은, 구식의 facility 시설(물) have A p.p. A가 ~되게 하다 major 대대적인, 대규모의 renovation 개조, 보수 industry 업계 downside 단점, 부정적인 면 work remotely from home 재택 근무를 하다 details 세부 정보 get closer 더 가까워지다 additional 추가의

Questions 5-6 refer to the following talk.

> M: Thanks for stopping by the Thurber Electronics trade show booth. My name is Cheolsu, and I'd like to tell you about my company's newest blender, the T-900. What makes this blender unique is not the number of settings. We have about the same options as other products in this category. However, 5 what sets ours apart is safety—it has the best rating in the industry. The T-900 also can be used with various accessories. 6 If you join our mailing list, you can get one of these accessories for free.

5-6번 문제는 다음 담화를 참조하시오.

남: Thurber Electronics의 무역 박람회 부스에 들러 주셔서 감사 드립니다. 제 이름은 철수이며, 저희 회사의 최신 믹서기인 T-900에 관해 여러분께 말씀 드리고자 합니다. 이 믹서기를 특별하게 하는 것은 설정 기능의 개수가 아닙니다. 저희에게는 이 범주에 속한 기타 제품들만큼 대략적으로 동일한 옵션들이 있습니다. 하지만, 저희 제품을 차별화시키는 것은 안전성이며, 업계 내에서 최고의 등급을 받았습니다. T-900 제품은 또한 다양한 부대용품들과 함께 사용될 수 있습니다. 저희 우편물 발송 대상자 명단에 등록하시면 이 부대용품들 중 하나를 무료로 받아 보실 수 있습니다.

5. 해당 제품은 시중에 나와 있는 기타 제품들과 어떻게 다른가?
(A) 높은 안전성 등급을 받았다.
(B) 많은 다른 설정 기능들이 있다.

| 해설 |
제품의 특성이 언급되는 중반부에, 안전성에 대해 업계에서 최고 등급을 받았다고(what sets ours apart is safety — it has the best rating in the industry) 알리고 있으므로 (A)가 정답이다.

6. 청자들은 무료로 부대용품을 받기 위해 무엇을 할 수 있는가?
(A) 설문지 작성하기
(B) 우편물 발송 대상자로 신청하기

| 해설 |
무료 부대용품을 받는 방법이 설명되는 후반부에, 우편물 발송 대상자 명단에 등록하기만 하면 부대용품들 중 하나를 무료로 받는다고(If you join our mailing list, you can get one of these accessories for free) 알리고 있으므로 (B)가 정답이다.

| 어휘 | stop by ~에 들르다 trade show 무역 박람회 booth 부스, 칸막이 공간 What makes A B A가 B한 이유 unique 특별한, 독특한 setting (기기 등의) 설정 about 대략, 약 category 범주, 항목 however 하지만 what sets A apart A를 차별화시키는 것 rating 등급, 평가 점수 industry 업계 accessories 부대용품 at no cost 무료로(= for free) by (방법) mailing list 우편물 발송 대상자 명단 on the market 시중에 나온 complete ~을 작성 완료하다 questionnaire 설문지 sign up for ~을 신청하다, ~에 등록하다

DAY 16 | 실전문제 본책 p.104

정답 1 (C) 2 (C) 3 (B) 4 (C) 5 (C) 6 (B)
       7 (C) 8 (A) 9 (D) 10 (C) 11 (A) 12 (D)
       13 (D) 14 (C) 15 (B) 16 (B) 17 (C) 18 (D)
       19 (B) 20 (D) 21 (C)

Questions 1-3 refer to the following talk.

> M: Good morning, everyone. I'm pleased to represent Vista Solutions here at this trade expo. Do you have trouble keeping up with fast-paced meetings? Then, 1 you'll love our latest digital recorder. We understand how difficult it is to take notes during meetings or other events. With our device, 2 you won't have to worry about failing to catch the important points. You can play the recording back as many times as you need. 3 Now, I'd like to address any questions you may have about the device. Please just raise your hand if you have something to share.

1-3번 문제는 다음 담화를 참조하시오.

남: 안녕하세요, 여러분. 저는 이곳 무역 박람회장에서 Vista Solutions를 대표하게 되어 기쁘게 생각합니다. 빠르게 진행되는 회의를 쫓아가는 데 어려움을 겪고 계신가요? 그러시다면, 저희 최신 디지털 녹음 기기가 아주 마음에 드실 것입니다. 저희는 회의나 기타 행사 중에 메모를 하는 것이 얼마나 어려운 일인지 알고 있습니다. 저희 기기를 이용하시면, 중요한 사항들을 놓칠까 봐 걱정하실 필요가 없습니다. 필요한 만큼 여러 차례 녹음된 내용을 재생하실 수 있습니다. 이제, 여러분께서 이 기기에 대해 갖고 계신 어떤 질문이든 제가 해결해 드리겠습니다. 함께 공유하고 싶으신 것이 있으신 분은 손만 들어 주십시오.

| 어휘 | be pleased to do ~해서 기쁘다 represent ~을 대표하다 trade expo 무역 박람회 have trouble -ing ~하는 데 어려움을 겪다 keep up with ~을 따라잡다 fast-paced 빠른 속도의 latest 최신의 take notes 메모하다 device 기기 fail to do ~하지 못하다 catch ~을 (놓치지 않고) 이해하다, 알아듣다 address (문제 등) ~을 해결하다, 처리하다 raise ~을 들다

1. 화자는 무슨 종류의 제품에 관해 이야기하고 있는가?
(A) 레이저 프린터
(B) 휴대 전화기
(C) 디지털 녹음 기기
(D) 휴대용 라디오

| 해설 |
담화 초반부에, 자사의 제품으로 최신 디지털 녹음 기기를(~ you'll love our latest digital recorder) 언급하고 있으므로 (C)가 정답이다.

| 어휘 | portable 휴대용의

2. 화자는 제품의 무슨 이점을 언급하는가?
(A) 편리하게 휴대하고 다닐 만큼 충분히 작다.
(B) 장시간 지속되는 배터리로 작동된다.
(C) 사용자들이 중요 정보를 유지하는 데 도움이 된다.
(D) 다양한 색상으로 나온다.

| 해설 |
제품의 특징이 언급되는 중반부에, 회의나 행사 중에 메모를 하는 일의 어려움을 말하면서 중요 사항들을 놓칠까 봐 걱정할 필요가 없다고(~ you won't have to worry about failing to catch the important points) 알리고 있다. 이는 중요 정보 유지에 도움이 된다는 말과 같으므로 (C)가 정답이다.

| 어휘 | benefit 이점, 혜택   carry around ~을 휴대하고 다니다   operate 작동되다   long-lasting 장시간 지속되는   come in ~의 상태로 나오다   a variety of 다양한

3. 화자는 곧이어 무엇을 할 것 같은가?
(A) 동영상 보여주기
(B) 문의 사항에 답변하기
(C) 샘플 나눠 주기
(D) 시연하기

| 해설 |
담화 후반부에, 화자는 청자들의 질문을 해결해 주겠다고(Now, I'd like to address any questions you may have ~) 알리고 있으므로 (B)가 정답이다.

| 어휘 | respond to ~에 답변하다   pass out ~을 나눠 주다   demonstration 시연(회)

Questions 4-6 refer to the following broadcast.

> W: We're back with *Business Boost*, the show that brings you useful tips for running your business. **4** **Our topic today is about how business owners can increase their staff's enthusiasm and keep them working hard** toward a goal. In the studio today is an expert in this field, Harold Pearson. He has written several books on the subject over the years. In addition, **5** **just last month, Mr. Pearson's fourth book hit the market.** He's going to share some of his best advice with you today. **6** **Then, we'd love to hear from you. Call the station** to tell us what you think about these strategies.

4-6번 문제는 다음 방송을 참조하시오.

여: 여러분의 사업체를 운영하는 데 유용한 팁을 전해 드리는 프로그램인 <Business Boost>가 계속 이어지겠습니다. 오늘 주제는 사업체 소유주들이 소속 직원들의 열정을 어떻게 끌어올릴 수 있는지, 그리고 어떻게 계속하여 목표를 향해 열심히 일하게 할 수 있는지에 관한 것입니다. 오늘 이곳 스튜디오에는 이 분야의 전문가이신 Harold Pearson 씨께서 나와 계십니다. 이분께서는 수년간에 걸쳐 해당 주제에 관해 여러 권의 책을 저술하신 바 있습니다. 추가로, 바로 지난달에, Pearson 씨의 네 번째 도서가 출시되었습니다. Pearson 씨께서 오늘 여러분께 최고의 조언 몇 가지를 공유해 드릴 예정입니다. 그런 다음, 여러분의 얘기를 들어 보고자 합니다. 저희 방송국으로 전화 주셔서 이 전략들에 관해 어떻게 생각하시는지 말씀해 주시기 바랍니다.

| 어휘 | bring 전달하다, 알려 주다   run ~을 운영하다   increase ~을 끌어올리다, 증대하다   enthusiasm 열정, 열의   keep A -ing A가 계속 ~하도록 유지하다   toward (목표 등) ~을 위해, 향해   expert 전문가   field 분야   subject 주제   in addition 추가로   station 방송국   strategy 전략

4. 방송은 주로 무엇에 관한 것인가?
(A) 계약 협상
(B) 예산 관리
(C) 직원 동기 부여
(D) 고용 관행

| 해설 |
방송의 주제가 제시되는 초반부에, 직원들의 열정을 끌어올리고 계속해서 목표를 향해 열심히 일하도록 만드는 방법에 관해(Our topic today is about how business owners can increase their staff's enthusiasm and keep them working hard ~) 이야기하겠다고 말하고 있다. 이는 동기 부여와 관련된 것이므로 (C)가 정답이다.

| 어휘 | negotiation 협의, 협상   budget 예산   practice 관행, 관례

5. 화자는 Harold Pearson 씨가 최근에 무엇을 했다고 말하는가?
(A) 수업을 가르치는 일을 시작했다.
(B) 합병에 동의했다.
(C) 새로운 책을 출간했다.
(D) 상을 받았다.

| 해설 |
'Harold Pearson'라는 이름 키워드와 'recently'라는 시점 키워드에 해당되는 표현이 제시되는 중반부에, 바로 지난달에 Pearson 씨의 네 번째 책이 나왔다고(~ just last month, Mr. Pearson's fourth book hit the market) 알리고 있으므로 (C)가 정답이다.

| 어휘 | merger 합병

6. 청자들은 무엇을 하도록 요청받는가?
(A) 소식지 신청하기
(B) 각자의 의견 제공하기
(C) 초청 연사 제안하기
(D) 개장식에 참석하기

| 해설 |
담화 후반부에, 청자들의 얘기를 들어 보고 싶다는 말과 함께 방송국으로 전화해 달라고(Then, we'd love to hear from you. Call the station ~) 요청하고 있으므로 의견 제공을 의미하는 (B)가 정답이다.

| 어휘 | sign up for ~을 신청하다, ~에 등록하다   suggest ~을 제안하다

Questions 7-9 refer to the following excerpt from a meeting.

> M: Good afternoon, staff. Before we get things underway, I'd like to say that **7** **I'm sorry that I called this meeting without much warning.** The management team made a decision that will affect the business, so we wanted to let you know about it right away. Lately, **8** **our store has been getting a lot of complaints from customers because we often run out of merchandise.** No one wants to go shopping and see empty shelves. It is essential that we maintain consistent levels of stock. **9** **Tomorrow, in the morning, we will install some software** that will help us to track our items better. We hope this will remedy the situation.

7-9번 문제는 다음 회의 발췌록을 참조하시오.

남: 안녕하세요, 직원 여러분. 시작하기에 앞서, 충분한 통지 없이 이번 회의를 소집해 죄송하다는 말씀을 드리고자 합니다. 경영진에서 회사에 영향을 미치게 될 결정을 내렸기 때문에, 즉시 이에 관해 여러분께 알려 드리고 싶었습니다. 최근, 우리 매장은 고객들로부터 많은 불만 사항을 접수해 왔는데, 우리 매장에 종종 상품이 다 떨어지는 일이 생기기 때문입니다. 그 누구도 쇼핑을 하러 가서 비어 있는 선반을 보고 싶어 하지 않습니다. 우리가 일정한 수준의 재고를 유지하는 것이 필수적입니다. 내일 아침에, 우리는 제품을 더 잘 파악하는 데 도움을 줄 일부 소프트웨어를 설치할 것입니다. 우리는 이것이 상황을 해결해 주기를 바라고 있습니다.

| 어휘 | get A underway A를 시작하다, 진행하다   call a meeting 회의를 소집하다   without much warning 충분한 통지 없이   make a decision 결정을 내리다   affect ~에 영향을 미치다   business 회사, 업체   right away 즉시   complaint 불만   run out of A A가 다 떨어지다, 다 쓰다   merchandise 상품   It is essential that ~하는 것이 필수적이다   maintain ~을 유지하다   consistent 한결같은   stock 재고(품)   install ~을 설치하다   track ~을 파악하다, 추적하다   remedy ~을 해결하다

7. 화자는 청자들에게 왜 사과하는가?
(A) 오래된 파일을 발송했다.
(B) 회사의 행사를 연기해야 했다.
(C) 회의에 대해 급히 공지했다.
(D) 회의 장소를 옮겨야 했다.

| 해설 |
담화 초반부에, 충분한 통지 없이 회의를 소집한 것에 대해 사과하고(~ I'm sorry that I called this meeting without much warning) 있으므로 (C)가 정답이다.

| 어휘 | outdated 오래된, 낡은   postpone ~을 연기하다   give short notice 급히 공지하다

8. 회사는 무엇에 대해 불만을 접수했는가?
(A) 재고 부족
(B) 부정확한 가격
(C) 반품 정책
(D) 영업 시간

| 해설 |
불만 사항과 그 이유가 제시되는 중반부에, 종종 상품이 다 떨어져서 고객들의 불만이 접수되고 있다고(our store has been getting a lot of complaints ~ we often run out of merchandise) 알리고 있다. 이는 재고 부족 문제를 뜻하므로 (A)가 정답이다.

| 어휘 | inventory 재고(품), 재고 목록   shortage 부족   inaccurate 부정확한   return policy 반품 정책

9. 내일 무슨 일이 있을 예정인가?
(A) 유명 인사가 회사를 방문할 것이다.
(B) 직원들이 일부 교육을 받을 것이다.
(C) 홍보 행사가 시작될 것이다.
(D) 소프트웨어 프로그램이 설치될 것이다.

| 해설 |
'내일'이라는 시점 키워드가 제시되는 후반부에, 내일 아침에 소프트웨어를 설치할 것이라고(Tomorrow, in the morning, we will install some software ~) 알리고 있으므로 (D)가 정답이다.

| 어휘 | celebrity 유명 인사   undergo ~을 겪다, 거치다   promotional 홍보의

Questions 10-12 refer to the following talk.

M: Good morning, everyone. I've called this management meeting to address some complaints about **10 the workloads for the architects on our various building design projects.** As managers, you are ultimately responsible for the quality of the finished design. Because of that, you may feel like you have to do everything yourself. This just won't work in the long run. **11 You need to reassign your less important tasks to your team members** to free up more time. I started doing this a few months ago, and **12 I'd now like to tell you how that worked in my case.** I think you'll agree that it's an effective strategy.

10-12번 문제는 다음 담화를 참조하시오.
남: 안녕하세요, 여러분. 우리의 다양한 건물 설계 프로젝트에 대한 건축가들의 업무량 관련 일부 불만을 해결하기 위해 이 경영진 회의를 소집했습니다. 책임자로서, 여러분께서는 완료된 설계의 질에 대해 최종적으로 책임을 지게 됩니다. 이로 인해, 여러분께서는 모든 것을 직접 해야 하는 것처럼 느끼실 수도 있습니다. 이는 장기적으로 볼 때 좋은 효과를 내지 못할 뿐입니다. 여러분께서는 더 많은 시간을 확보하실 수 있도록 덜 중요한 업무들을 팀원들에게 다시 배정해 주셔야 합니다. 저는 몇 달 전에 이렇게 하기 시작했는데, 이것이 제 경우에 어떻게 효과가 있었는지를 지금 여러분께 말씀드리고자 합니다. 저는 여러분께서 이것이 효과적인 전략이라는 데 동의하시리라 생각합니다.

| 어휘 | workload 업무량   architect 건축가   various 다양한   ultimately 최종적으로   be responsible for ~을 책임지다   quality 품질   feel like ~한 것처럼 느끼다   work 효과가 있다, 작용하다   in the long run 장기적으로   reassign A to B A를 B에게 다시 배정하다   task 업무, 일   free up more time 더 많은 시간을 확보하다   case 경우, 사례   effective 효과적인   strategy 전략

10. 화자는 무슨 종류의 업체에서 근무하고 있을 것 같은가?
(A) 소프트웨어 개발 업체
(B) 채용 대행 업체
(C) 건축 회사
(D) 패션 회사

| 해설 |
화자의 업무에 관한 정보가 언급되는 초반부에, 건물 설계 프로젝트에 대한 건축가들의 업무량이(~ the workloads for the architects on our various building design projects) 언급되고 있으므로 (C)가 정답이다.

| 어휘 | firm 회사   recruitment 채용

11. 화자는 청자들에게 무엇을 하도록 제안하는가?
(A) 업무 다시 배정하기
(B) 추가 근무하기
(C) 명확한 지시 내리기
(D) 정책 검토하기

| 해설 |
화자의 제안 사항이 제시되는 중반부에, 덜 중요한 업무를 팀원들에게 다시 배정해야 한다고(You need to reassign your less important tasks to your team members ~) 말하므로 (A)가 정답이다.

| 어휘 | instructions 지시, 안내, 설명   review ~을 검토하다   policy 정책

12. 곧이어 무슨 일이 있을 것 같은가?
(A) 신입 사원이 소개될 것이다.
(B) 유인물이 배부될 것이다.
(C) 청자들이 토론 그룹을 구성할 것이다.
(D) 화자가 자신의 경험을 공유해 줄 것이다.

| 해설 |
담화 후반부에, 화자는 자신이 몇 달 전부터 덜 중요한 일을 팀원들에게 배정하기 시작했다면서 그것이 어떻게 효과적이었는지를 지금 말해 주겠다고(~ I'd now like to tell you how that worked in my case) 알리고 있다. 이는 자신의 경험담을 들려 주겠다는 뜻이므로 (D)가 정답이다.

| 어휘 | introduce ~을 소개하다   handout 유인물   distribute ~을 배부하다   form ~을 구성하다, 형성하다

Questions 13-15 refer to the following talk.

W: Good morning. My name is Anna Everett, and I'll be telling you about Shinn Enterprises today. This is a great turnout. **13 It's wonderful to see that so many people have decided to put money into our company.** By investing in this opportunity, you are likely to get amazing results. Now, **14 I've given each of you a document that summarizes our business model and monthly revenue. I suggest keeping that** for your records. We'll take a tour of the entire facility later today. But first, **15 I'd like to introduce you to our executive team.** I'll tell you a little about each member now.

13-15번 문제는 다음 담화를 참조하시오.

여: 안녕하세요. 제 이름은 Anna Everett이며, 오늘 Shinn Enterprises에 관해 여러분께 말씀드릴 것입니다. 이 자리에 많은 분들께서 참석해 주셨네요. 이렇게 많은 분들께서 저희 회사에 자금을 투자하시기로 결정해 주셨다는 것을 알게 되어 놀랍습니다. 이번 기회에 투자를 함으로써, 놀라운 결과를 얻으시게 될 가능성이 있습니다. 자, 제가 저희 사업 모델과 월간 수익을 요약한 문서를 여러분 각자에게 나눠 드렸습니다. 그것을 보관용으로 갖고 계시도록 권해 드립니다. 우리는 오늘 이따가 전체 시설에 대한 견학을 실시할 것입니다. 하지만 우선, 저희 임원진을 소개해 드리겠습니다. 이제 각 임원에 관해 간단히 말씀드리겠습니다.

| 어휘 | turnout 참가자의 수   decide to do ~하기로 결정하다   put money into ~에 자금을 투자하다   invest in ~에 투자하다   opportunity 기회   be likely to do ~할 가능성이 있다   amazing 놀라운   result 결과(물)   summarize ~을 요약하다   revenue 수익   for one's records 보관용으로   entire 전체의   executive team 임원진

13. 화자는 왜 담화를 진행하고 있는가?
(A) 일부 신입 사원들을 교육하기 위해
(B) 일정 변경을 공지하기 위해
(C) 직원들에게 감사의 뜻을 전하기 위해
(D) 새로운 투자자들을 환영하기 위해

| 해설 | 담화 초반부에, 참석자가 많다는 말과 함께 많은 사람들이 자신의 회사에 자금 투자를 결정한 것이 놀랍다고(It ~ to see that so many people have decided to put money ~) 알리고 있으므로 투자자들을 대상으로 하는 담화임을 알 수 있다. 따라서 (D)가 정답이다.

| 어휘 | announce ~을 공지하다, 발표하다   appreciation 감사(의 마음)   investor 투자자

14. 화자는 무엇을 하도록 권하는가?
(A) 좌석 예약하기
(B) 잠시 휴식 취하기
(C) 문서 보관하기
(D) 사업 파트너에게 전화하기

| 해설 | 화자의 권고 사항이 언급되는 중반부에, 사업 모델과 월간 수익을 요약한 문서를 나눠 주었다는 말과 함께 그것을 잘 보관하도록 권하고 있으므로(I've given each of you a document ~ I suggest keeping that ~) (C)가 정답이다.

| 어휘 | reserve ~을 예약하다   take a break 잠시 휴식하다   retain ~을 보관하다, 유지하다

15. 화자는 곧이어 무엇을 할 것 같은가?
(A) 신청 용지 나눠 주기
(B) 일부 직원들 소개하기
(C) 회의실 마련하기
(D) 청자들을 견학시켜 주기

| 해설 | 담화 후반부에, 회사의 임원진을 소개해 주겠다고(~ I'd like to introduce you to our executive team) 알리고 있으므로 (B)가 정답이다.

| 어휘 | handout 유인물   pass out ~을 나눠 주다   sign-up 신청, 등록   set up ~을 마련하다, 설치하다

Questions 16-18 refer to the following telephone message.

M: Good afternoon, this is Jeremiah from Wallace Court. **16** We received your booking request for a room with a seaside view for your upcoming trip. Unfortunately, due to a computer problem, the room was not saved for you, and now we have no more available. I propose putting you in one of our suites. It doesn't have a view, but **17** you would only be charged the standard rate. We don't usually do this, but we're focused on the customer experience. **18** I've sent you a temporary booking form to your e-mail address. Please reply to that message to confirm that you agree with the change. Thank you.

16-18번 문제는 다음 전화 메시지를 참조하시오.

남: 안녕하세요, 저는 Wallace Court의 Jeremiah입니다. 곧 있을 귀하의 출장을 위해 해변 경관이 보이는 객실에 대한 예약 요청서를 받았습니다. 안타깝게도, 컴퓨터 문제로 인해, 해당 객실이 귀하에게 배정되지 않았으며, 현재 이용 가능한 것이 없습니다. 저는 귀하께 저희 스위트 객실 중의 하나에 배정해 드리는 것을 제안합니다. 경관이 보이지는 않지만, 스탠다드 객실 요금만 귀하께 청구될 것입니다. 일반적으로 이렇게 해 드리지 않지만, 저희는 고객 경험에 중점을 둡니다. 제가 귀하의 이메일 주소로 임시 예약 양식을 발송해 드렸습니다. 이와 같은 변동 사항에 동의하시는지를 확인해 주실 수 있도록 해당 메시지에 답장해 주시기 바랍니다. 감사합니다.

| 어휘 | booking 예약   request 요청(서)   view 경관, 조망   upcoming 곧 있을, 다가오는   unfortunately 안타깝게도   due to ~로 인해   save ~을 남겨 놓다   propose -ing ~하도록 제안하다   charge A B A에게 B를 청구하다, 부과하다   rate 요금   be focused on ~에 초점을 맞추다   temporary 임시의, 일시적인   reply to ~에 답장하다   confirm that ~임을 확인해 주다

16. 화자는 어디에서 근무하고 있을 것 같은가?
(A) 배송 회사에서
(B) 호텔에서
(C) 항공사에서
(D) 카페에서

| 해설 | 업체의 특성이 제시되는 초반부에, 해변 경관이 보이는 객실에 대한 예약 요청을 받은 사실이(We received your booking request for a room ~) 언급되고 있으므로 (B)가 정답이다.

17. 화자가 "we're focused on the customer experience"라고 말할 때 암시하는 것은 무엇인가?
(A) 청자가 설문지를 작성하기를 원한다.
(B) 일부 신입 직원들을 교육하느라 바쁘다.
(C) 해결책을 찾기 위해 열심히 노력하고 있다.
(D) 경쟁사가 고객을 잃을 것으로 확신하고 있다.

| 해설 | 담화 중반부에, 스탠다드 객실 요금만 청구하겠다는 말과 함께 일반적으로 이렇게 하지 않는다고(~ you would only be charged the standard rate. We don't usually do this) 알린 후에 "고객 경험에 초점을 맞추고 있다"고 덧붙이는 상황이다. 이는 객실 예약이 제대로 되지 않은 문제를 해결하기 위한 최선의 조치임을 강조하는 말이므로 (C)가 정답이다.

| 어휘 | would like A to do A에게 ~하기를 원하다   complete ~을 작성 완료하다   questionnaire 설문지   be busy -ing ~하느라 바쁘다   solution 해결책   be confident that ~임을 확신하다   competitor 경쟁사

18. 청자는 무엇을 하도록 요청받는가?
(A) 음식 옵션 선택하기
(B) 비용 지불하기
(C) 웹 사이트 방문하기
(D) 확인 이메일 보내기

| 해설 | 담화 후반부에, 이메일로 예약 양식을 보낸 사실과 함께 동의 여부를 확인

하는 답장을 해 달라고(I've sent you a temporary booking form to your e-mail address. Please reply to that message to confirm ~) 요청하고 있으므로 (D)가 정답이다.

| 어휘 | select ~을 선택하다 issue a payment 비용을 지불하다 confirmation 확인(서)

Questions 19-21 refer to the following excerpt from a meeting and floor plan.

W: Good afternoon. I've organized this meeting 19 **because we need to make arrangements for our upcoming membership drive**, which will help us to get more people to join our gym. 20 **I need you all to come in early on June 12** to help prepare for the event. I know that most of you use the Woodrow Avenue entrance because it's near the yoga studio. However, 20 **on that day, you'll need to enter through the weight room, as it will be the only unlocked door.** The event will feature tours and free classes. 21 **When the event ends, please help participants to fill out their membership forms.** We want to make this process as easy as possible.

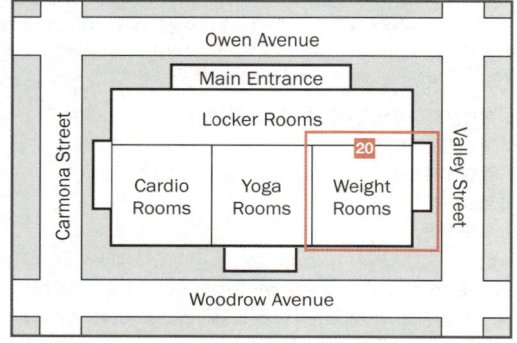

19-21번 문제는 다음 회의 발췌록과 평면도를 참조하시오.

여: 안녕하세요. 우리 체육관에 더 많은 사람들을 가입하게 하는 데 도움이 되는 것으로서 곧 진행될 우리의 회원 모집 활동을 준비해야 하기 때문에 제가 이번 회의 자리를 마련했습니다. 저는 여러분 모두가 6월 12일에 일찍 오셔서 이 행사 준비를 도와주셨으면 합니다. 여러분 대부분이 요가 스튜디오와 가깝다는 이유로 Woodrow Avenue 입구를 이용하고 계신다는 점을 알고 있습니다. 하지만, 그날, 여러분은 웨이트 트레이닝 룸을 통해 들어오셔야 하는데, 이 출입구가 유일하게 잠겨 있지 않은 문이 될 것이기 때문입니다. 이 행사는 견학과 무료 강습을 특징으로 할 것입니다. 행사가 종료될 때, 참가자들이 회원 가입 양식을 작성하도록 도와 주시기 바랍니다. 우리는 이 과정이 가능한 한 수월하게 진행되기를 원합니다.

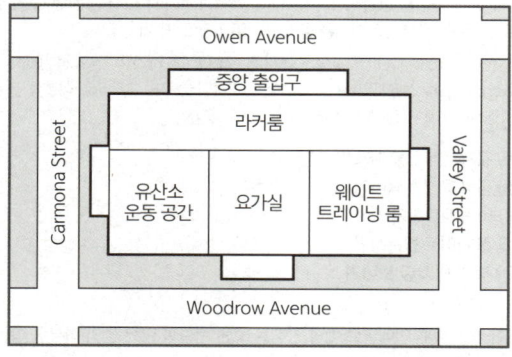

| 어휘 | organize ~을 마련하다, 조직하다 make arrangements for ~에 대한 준비를 하다 upcoming 곧 있을, 다가오는 drive (조직적인) 활동, 운동 join ~에 가입하다, 합류하다 prepare for ~을 준비하다 near ~ 가까이에 feature ~을 특징으로 하다 participant 참가자 fill out ~을 작성하다 form 양식, 서식 process 과정 as A as possible 가능한 한 A하게 cardio 심폐 강화 운동; 유산소 운동

19. 회의의 목적은 무엇인가?
(A) 직원 평가 시간을 마련하는 것
(B) 회원 모집 활동에 대한 계획을 세우는 것
(C) 신입 피트니스 강사들을 교육하는 것
(D) 운동 경기 대회를 준비하는 것

| 해설 |
회의를 여는 목적이 언급되는 초반부에, 회원 모집 활동을 준비해야 하기 때문에(~ because we need to make arrangements for our upcoming membership drive ~) 회의를 소집했다고 알리고 있으므로 (B)가 정답이다.

| 어휘 | arrange ~을 마련하다, 조정하다 review 평가, 의견, 후기 make plans for ~에 대한 계획을 세우다 athletic competition 운동 경기 대회

20. 시각 자료를 보시오. 청자들은 6월 12일에 어느 출입구를 이용해야 하는가?
(A) 중앙 출입구
(B) Carmona Street 출입구
(C) Woodrow Avenue 출입구
(D) Valley Street 출입구

| 해설 |
'6월 12일'은 직원들에게 행사 준비를 하러 오도록 요청하는 날짜로(I need you all to come in early on June 12 ~), 그날 웨이트 트레이닝 룸을 통해 들어오도록(~ on that day, you'll need to enter through the weight room) 요청하고 있다. 시각 자료에서 'weight rooms'가 Valley Street과 접해 있으므로 (D)가 정답이다.

21. 화자는 직원들이 행사 종료 시에 무엇을 하기를 원한다고 말하는가?
(A) 일부 장식물 떼어 내기
(B) 다과 제공하기
(C) 서류 작성 도와주기
(D) 상품 나눠 주기

| 해설 |
담화 후반부에, 행사가 종료될 때 참가자들의 회원 가입 양식을 작성하도록 도와 주라고(When the event ends, please help participants to fill out their membership forms) 알리고 있으므로 (C)가 정답이다.

| 어휘 | take down (해체 작업 등을 통해) ~을 떼어 내다, 걷어 내다 refreshments 다과 assist with ~을 돕다 complete ~을 작성 완료하다 distribute ~을 나눠 주다

DAY 17   세부적인 내용을 묻는 유형 (2)

01 의도 파악 문제

기출 유형 맛보기   본책 p.106

Q. 화자가 "This will be a big show"라고 말할 때 암시하는 것은 무엇인가?
(A) 입장권이 거의 판매되지 않았다.
(B) 더 큰 행사장을 반드시 찾아야 한다.
(C) 공연이 텔레비전에서 방송될 것이다.

(D) 한 그룹이 매우 인기가 높다.

안녕하세요, 청취자 여러분, 그리고 청취해 주셔서 감사 드립니다. 시작하기에 앞서, 모든 분들께 우리 시의 여름 축제가 이번 주말에 시작된다는 사실을 상기시켜 드립니다. 첫날에는, 유명한 밴드인 Derrick and the Waves의 콘서트가 있을 예정이므로, 이는 대단한 공연이 될 것입니다. 이 행사는 금요일 6시 30분에 Duncan Park에서 열리지만, 좋은 자리를 확보하시려면 아마 일찍 가셔야 할 것입니다. 각자 음식과 음료를 가지고 오셔도 됩니다.

PRACTICE | 기출 연습하기

본책 p.107

정답 1 (B) 2 (A) 3 (A) 4 (B) 5 (A) 6 (B)

Questions 1-2 refer to the following telephone message.

W: Hi, Mr. Anderson. This is Sandra from Meadow Realty. Thanks for taking the time to tour the apartment in the Geneva Building that has just come up for rent. You had asked about **1** the utilities such as electricity and water. Well, I checked with the landlord, and **1** these are not part of the monthly rent, so you'd have to pay for them separately. You should be aware that this is a very popular apartment, **2** so I need to know as soon as possible whether you'd like to take it.

1-2번 문제는 다음 전화 메시지를 참조하시오.
여: 안녕하세요, Anderson 씨. 저는 Meadow Realty의 Sandra입니다. 막 임대용으로 나온 Geneva Building의 아파트를 둘러보실 시간을 내 주셔서 감사합니다. 귀하께서는 전기나 수도 같은 공공 서비스에 관해 물어 보셨습니다. 제가 건물주에게 확인해 보았는데, 이는 월 임대료의 일부에 해당되지 않으므로, 별도로 그 비용을 지불하셔야 할 것입니다. 이 아파트는 매우 인기 있습니다. 따라서 이곳으로 정하실 것인지를 가능한 한 빨리 제가 알아야 한다는 점을 알아 두시기 바랍니다.

1. 화자는 공공 서비스에 관해 무슨 말을 하는가?
(A) 한 달 연체되었다.
(B) 임대료에 포함되어 있지 않다.

| 해설 |
담화 중반부에, 전기나 수도 같은 공공 서비스를 언급한 후에(the utilities such as electricity and water), 이것들은 월 임대료에 포함되지 않는다고(~ these are not part of the monthly rent ~) 알리고 있으므로 (B)가 정답이다.

2. 화자는 왜 "this is a very popular apartment"라고 말하는가?
(A) 신속한 결정을 요청하기 위해
(B) 임대료가 왜 비싼지 설명하기 위해

| 해설 |
담화 후반부에, 그곳으로 정할 것인지를 가능한 한 빨리 알아야 한다고(so I need to know as soon as possible whether you'd like to take it) 말하는 상황이다. 이는 청자가 빨리 결정하도록 촉구하는 것이므로 (A)가 정답이다.

| 어휘 | take the time to do ~할 시간을 내다 tour ~을 둘러보다, 견학하다 come up 나타나다 rent 임대(료), 대여(료) utilities (전기, 수도 등의) 공공 서비스 landlord 건물주 separately 별도로, 분리하여 be aware that ~라는 점을 알다, 인식하다 popular 인기 있는 as soon as possible 가능한 한 빨리

whether ~인지 (아닌지) overdue 연체된 include ~을 포함하다 request ~을 요청하다 decision 결정

Questions 3-4 refer to the following telephone message.

M: Hi, Christine. It's Jason. **3** We still need to find a manager for the shop's weekend shifts. As you know, we're approaching the peak season. The recruiter sent over plenty of résumés. **4** I've set up interviews with six people on Friday, and I'd like you to sit in on these meetings so that I can get a second opinion. **4** I'll e-mail you the schedule now. Please let me know if you have any conflicts.

3-4번 문제는 다음 전화 메시지를 참조하시오.
남: 안녕하세요, Christine. Jason입니다. 우리는 여전히 매장의 주말 교대 근무를 위한 책임자를 찾아야 합니다. 아시다시피, 우리에게 성수기가 다가오고 있습니다. 채용 대행 업체에서 많은 이력서들을 보내 왔습니다. 제가 금요일로 여섯 명의 사람들과 면접 일정을 잡아 두었으며, 제가 다른 사람의 의견을 얻을 수 있도록 당신이 이 면접 자리에 함께 해 주셨으면 합니다. 지금 이메일로 이 일정을 보내 드리겠습니다. 일정이 겹치지 않는지 제게 알려주시기 바랍니다.

3. 화자가 "we're approaching the peak season"라고 말할 때 암시하는 것은 무엇인가?
(A) 공석이 곧 충원되어야 한다.
(B) 청자를 도와줄 시간이 없다.

| 해설 |
담화 초반부에, 여전히 매장의 주말 교대 근무를 위한 책임자를 찾아야 한다고(We still need to find a manager for the shop's weekend shifts) 알린 후에 "성수기가 다가오고 있다"고 말하는 상황이다. 이는 빨리 해당 책임자를 찾아 채용해야 한다는 것을 강조하는 말이므로 (A)가 정답이다.

4. 화자는 곧이어 무엇을 할 것인가?
(A) 채용 대행 업체와 계약하기
(B) 면접 일정표 보내기

| 해설 |
중반부에, 여섯 명의 사람들과 면접 일정을 잡아 둔 사실을(I've set up interviews with six people on Friday ~) 언급한 뒤에, 후반부에 가서 이메일로 그 일정을 보내 주겠다고(I'll e-mail you the schedule now) 알리고 있으므로 (B)가 정답이다.

| 어휘 | shift 교대 근무(조) approach ~에 다가가다 recruiter 채용 대행 업체 send over ~을 전송하다, 보내다 plenty of 많은 résumé 이력서 set up ~의 일정을 잡다, ~을 마련하다 so that (목적) ~할 수 있도록 second opinion 다른 사람의 의견 conflict (일정상의) 겹침, 충돌 job opening 공석 fill ~을 충원하다, 채우다 contract ~와 계약하다

Questions 5-6 refer to the following broadcast.

M: You're listening to the lunchtime update on Radio 99. On today's program, **5** we'll be talking about the city's new rules regarding where vehicles can park. The city council has decided to begin charging a fee to park on the streets in the downtown district and to raise the rates for all lots owned by the city. The council held a meeting to gather public opinions. **6** Typically, residents share a lot of concerns. However, the new rules were passed quickly this time. Now, let's welcome city council member Roberta Torres to discuss this further.

DAY 17 091

5-6번 문제는 다음 방송을 참조하시오.

남: 여러분께서는 지금 라디오 99의 점심 뉴스를 청취하고 계십니다. 오늘 프로그램에서는, 차량들이 주차할 수 있는 장소와 관련된 우리 시의 새로운 규정에 관해 이야기해 볼 예정입니다. 시 의회는 시내 구역의 거리에 주차하는 데 요금을 부과하기 시작하고 시 소유의 모든 주차장에 대한 이용 요금을 인상하기로 결정을 내렸습니다. 의회는 일반 대중의 의견을 듣기 위한 회의를 개최했습니다. 늘 그렇듯이, 주민들이 함께 많은 우려를 합니다. 하지만, 새로운 규정이 이번에는 빠르게 통과되었습니다. 자, 이 문제를 더 깊이 이야기해 보기 위해 시 의회의 Roberta Torres 의원님을 모셔 보겠습니다.

5. 방송은 주로 무엇에 관한 것인가?
(A) 주차 규제
(B) 시의 선거

| 해설 |
담화 초반부에, 주차 장소와 관련된 새로운 규정에 관해 이야기하겠다고 (~ we'll be talking about the city's new rules regarding where vehicles can park) 알리고 있으므로 (A)가 정답이다.

6. 화자가 "the new rules were passed quickly this time"라고 말할 때 무엇을 의미할 것 같은가?
(A) 시의회 의원들은 더 빨리 일할 필요가 있다.
(B) 변화에 대한 지지가 놀라운 일이다.

| 해설 |
담화 중반부에, "주민들이 많은 우려 사항들을 공유한다"고 말한 뒤로 대조나 반대를 나타내는 However와 함께 새 규정이 빠르게 통과되었음을 (However, the new rules were passed quickly this time) 알리는 상황이다. 이는 일반적인 경우와 다른 상황에 대한 놀라움을 나타내는 말에 해당되므로 (B)가 정답이다.

| 어휘 | regarding ~에 관한 vehicle 차량 park 주차하다 council 의회 charge ~을 부과하다, 청구하다 fee 요금, 수수료 district 구역, 지구 raise ~을 인상하다 rate 요금 lot 주차장 own ~을 소유하다 gather ~을 모으다 public opinion 일반 대중의 의견 typically 일반적으로; 늘 그렇듯이 resident 주민 share concern 함께 염려하다 pass ~을 통과시키다 further 더욱 깊이, 한층 더 regulation 규제, 규정 election 선거 support 지지, 후원

02 시각 자료 문제

기출 유형 맛보기 본책 p.108

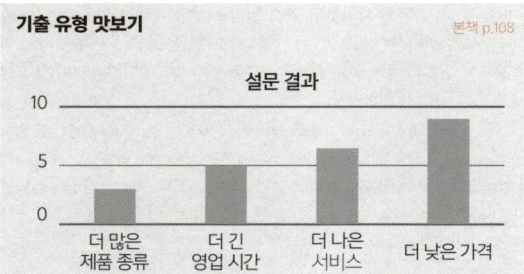

Q. 시각 자료를 보시오. 회사는 어느 의견에 대한 조치를 시작할 것인가?
(A) 더 많은 제품 종류
(B) 더 긴 영업 시간
(C) 더 나은 서비스
(D) 더 낮은 가격

지금 우리가 가장 먼저 해야 하는 것은 지난달에 실시한 고객 만족도 설문지의 결과를 살펴보는 것입니다. 우리 고객들이 더 낮은 가격을 원한다는 사실은 놀랍지 않습니다. 이는 침체된 경제로 인해 예상될 수 있는 부분이지만, 우리는 그렇게 할 수 없습니다. 하지만, 두 번째로 많은 의견에 대해서는 조치할 수 있으므로, 매장에서 즉시 변경 사항을 적용할 예정입니다.

PRACTICE | 기출 연습하기 본책 p.109

정답 1 (A) 2 (A) 3 (A) 4 (B)

Questions 1-2 refer to the following talk and map.

W: We're pleased that **1 you're here for the new employee orientation at Summit National Park**. You can see the main trails on this map. We'll start on Trail 3 so I can show you the activity at our bird house. You'll hike parts of all the trails today **2 except this one here, as it's closed to put up some fencing around the oak tree.** It is over two hundred years old, so we want to protect it and keep visitors from climbing it.

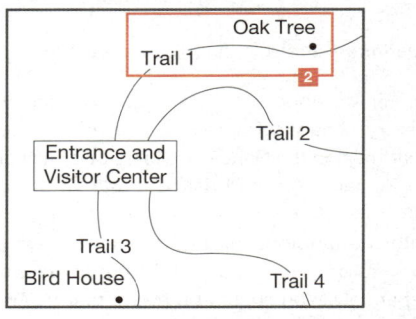

1-2번 문제는 다음 담화와 지도를 참조하시오.
여: Summit 국립공원의 신입 직원 오리엔테이션 시간을 위해 이곳에 와 주셔서 기쁘게 생각합니다. 여러분께서는 이 지도에서 주요 등산로를 보실 수 있을 겁니다. 3번 등산로에서 오리엔테이션을 시작해 새들이 살고 있는 곳에서 열리는 활동을 보여 드리겠습니다. 오늘 이곳을 제외하고 모든 등산로의 일부를 걷게 되실 텐데, 이곳은 오크 나무 주변에 일부 울타리를 설치하기 위해 폐쇄되어 있기 때문입니다. 이 나무는 200년도 더 된 것이기 때문에, 그것을 보호하고 방문객들이 오르지 못하게 하고자 하는 것입니다.

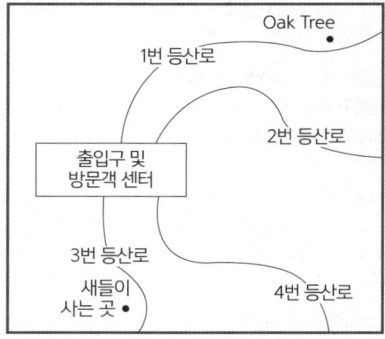

1. 담화는 누구를 대상으로 하는 것인가?
(A) 공원의 신입 직원들
(B) 시 관계자들

| 해설 |
담화 초반부에, 청자들을 가리켜 'Summit National Park의 신입 직원 오리엔테이션 시간에 온 사람들'이라고 (~ you're here for the new employee orientation at Summit National Park) 지칭하고 있으므로 (A)가 정답이다.

2. 시각 자료를 보시오. 어느 등산로가 폐쇄되어 있는가?
(A) 1번 등산로

(B) 2번 등산로
(C) 3번 등산로
(D) 4번 등산로

| 해설 |
탐방이 제외되는 등산로가 언급되는 후반부에, 그 이유로 오크 나무 주변에 울타리를 설치하기 위해 폐쇄되어 있다고(~ except this one here, as it's closed to put up some fencing around the oak tree) 알리고 있다. 시각 자료에서 'Oak Tree'로 표기가 되어 있는 등산로는 'Trail 1'이므로 (A)가 정답이다.

| 어휘 | main 주요한 trail 등산로, 산책로 except ~을 제외하고 put up ~을 설치하다, 놓다 fencing 울타리 over ~가 넘는 protect ~을 보호하다 keep A from -ing A가 ~하는 것을 방지하다, 막다 be intended for ~을 대상으로 하다 officials 관계자들, 당국자들

Questions 3-4 refer to the following talk and expense report.

W: Good afternoon, Walter. This is Jacqueline, from the finance team. **3** **I'm processing your business expenses for August, but there is one charge that needs to be authorized.** I've looked at your report, and it shows that **4** **you spent $40 on August 9, but there isn't any approval from your manager.** Could you call me back and let me know what is going on with this charge? You'll probably have to pick up the form from my office and complete it before returning it again. You can reach me at extension 34. Thanks.

Employee Business Expenses: Walter Bennett		
DATE	AMOUNT	BUSINESS
August 1	$25	Mahlon Café
4 August 9	**$40**	**Groton Inc.**
August 24	$15	Jacobs Taxis
August 25	$130	Deleo Hotel

3-4번 문제는 다음 담화와 경비 보고서를 참조하시오.

여: 안녕하세요, Walter 씨. 저는 재무팀의 Jacqueline입니다. 제가 당신의 8월분 업무 관련 경비를 처리하고 있는데, 승인되어야 하는 청구 비용이 하나 있습니다. 당신의 보고서를 보면 8월 9일에 40달러를 지출한 것으로 나와 있지만, 소속 부서장님의 승인이 어디에도 없습니다. 제게 다시 전화 주셔서 이 청구 비용이 어떻게 된 것인지 알려 주시겠습니까? 제 사무실에서 양식을 가져가셔서 작성하신 후에 다시 제출해 주셔야 할 것입니다. 내선 번호 34번으로 제게 연락하실 수 있습니다. 감사합니다.

직원 업무용 경비: Walter Bennett		
날짜	금액	업체
8월 1일	25달러	Mahlon 카페
8월 9일	40달러	Groton 사
8월 24일	15달러	Jacobs 택시
8월 25일	130달러	Deleo 호텔

3. 화자는 왜 전화를 거는가?
(A) 한 가지 청구 비용이 승인되어야 한다.
(B) 한 가지 영수증에 잘못된 정보가 들어 있다.

| 해설 |
담화 초반부에, 화자는 처리 중인 경비와 관련해 승인되어야 하는 청구 비용이 있다고(~ your business expenses for August, but there is one charge that needs to be authorized) 알리고 있으므로 (A)가 정답이다.

4. 시각 자료를 보시오. 화자는 어느 업체에 관해 문의하는가?
(A) Mahlon 카페
(B) Groton 사
(C) Jacobs 택시
(D) Deleo 호텔

| 해설 |
담화 중반부에, 8월 9일에 40달러를 지출한 것으로 나와 있지만 부서장의 승인이 없다고(~ you spent $40 on August 9, but there isn't any approval from your manager) 알리고 있다. 시각 자료에서 화자가 말한 날짜와 비용에 해당하는 업체가 'Groton Inc.'이므로 (B)가 정답이다.

| 어휘 | finance 재무, 재정 process ~을 처리하다 expense 경비, 지출 비용 charge 청구 비용 authorize ~을 승인하다 approval 승인 what is going on with A A가 어떻게 된 것인지 pick up ~을 가져가다 return 다시 제출하다, 되돌려 주다 reach ~에게 연락하다 extension 내선 전화 (번호) amount 액수 receipt 영수증

DAY 17 | 실전문제   본책 p.110

정답	1 (C)	2 (C)	3 (A)	4 (B)	5 (D)	6 (B)
	7 (A)	8 (B)	9 (C)	10 (D)	11 (A)	12 (C)
	13 (A)	14 (C)	15 (B)	16 (A)	17 (A)	18 (B)

Questions 1-3 refer to the following broadcast.

M: This is Robert Thorpe reporting live for *Channel 8 News*. I'm here at City Hall, where Mayor Anderson has just announced that **1** **the location of the city's new baseball stadium was decided this morning.** The facility will be built in the Highland neighborhood, on some land that is the current location of an old manufacturing plant. **2** **Many residents are against the project, as the high number of visitors to the stadium is expected to cause extensive traffic delays** throughout Highland. **3** **I've got a panel of local residents here, and I'm going to get their feedback on this matter.**

1-3번 문제는 다음 방송을 참조하시오.

남: 생방송으로 보도해 드리는 <채널 8 뉴스>의 Robert Thorpe입니다. 저는 지금 시청에 나와 있으며, 이곳에서 Anderson 시장이 오늘 아침에 우리 시의 새 야구 경기장 위치가 결정되었다고 막 발표했습니다. 이 시설은 Highland 지역의, 현재 낡은 제조 공장이 자리잡고 있는 부지에 지어질 예정입니다. 많은 주민들이 이 프로젝트에 반대하고 있는데, 경기장을 찾는 방문객들의 많은 숫자가 Highland 전역에 걸쳐 광범위한 교통 지연을 초래할 것으로 예상되기 때문입니다. 지금 이곳에 지역 주민들로 구성된 패널을 모셨으며, 이 문제에 관한 의견을 들어 보도록 하겠습니다.

| 어휘 | report live 생방송으로 보도하다 announce that ~라고 발표하다 neighborhood 지역, 인근 current 현재의 location 위치, 지점 manufacturing plant 제조 공장 resident 주민 against ~에 반대하여 be expected to do ~할 것으로 예상되다 cause ~을 초래하다 extensive 광범위한, 폭넓은 traffic 차량들, 교통 delay 지연, 지체 throughout ~ 전역에 걸쳐 feedback 의견 matter 일, 문제, 사안

1. 화자에 따르면, 최근에 무엇이 결정되었는가?
(A) 건물 디자인
(B) 경기장 명칭

(C) 건설 위치
(D) 최종 예산

| 해설 |
가까운 과거 시점에 결정된 일이 언급되는 초반부에, 오늘 아침에 시의 새 야구 경기장 위치가 결정되었다고(~ the location of the city's new baseball stadium was decided this morning) 알리고 있으므로 (C)가 정답이다.

| 어휘 | budget 예산

2. 일부 주민들은 왜 해당 프로젝트에 반대하는가?
(A) 소음을 일으킬 것이다.
(B) 너무 비용이 많이 든다.
(C) 교통 문제를 유발할 것이다.
(D) 환경에 좋지 않다.

| 해설 |
주민들이 반대하는 이유가 제시되는 후반부에, 경기장을 찾는 방문객들이 많아지면 광범위한 교통 지연을 초래할 것이라고(Many residents are against the project, as the high number of visitors to the stadium is expected to cause extensive traffic delays ~) 언급하고 있으므로 (C)가 정답이다.

| 어휘 | oppose ~에 반대하다   create ~을 만들어 내다

3. 화자는 곧이어 무엇을 할 것인가?
(A) 일부 의견 모으기
(B) 도심 구역 방문하기
(C) 견학하기
(D) 시장에게 연락하기

| 해설 |
담화 후반부에, 화자는 패널로 나온 주민들의 의견을 들어 보겠다고(I've got a panel of local residents here, and I'm going to get their feedback ~) 알리고 있으므로 (A)가 정답이다.

| 어휘 | gather ~을 모으다   contact ~에게 연락하다

Questions 4-6 refer to the following excerpt from a meeting.

W: First on the meeting agenda, later today, the IT team will install new software on your computers. The program will offer **4 our financial consultants, each of you**, an easy way to search market trends. You can also check the history of company stocks. I'm particularly excited about this program because its database is updated a few times a minute. **5 That means your search results will be much more useful than before.** I'll go over some of the features so that you're ready to use it for **6 the start of our new service for customers next week.**

4-6번 문제는 다음 회의 발췌록을 참조하시오.
여: 첫 번째 회의 안건으로, 오늘 이따가, IT팀에서 여러분의 컴퓨터에 새로운 소프트웨어를 설치할 것입니다. 이 프로그램은 우리 재무 컨설턴트인 여러분 각자에게 시장 동향을 찾아보는 편리한 방법을 제공해 줄 것입니다. 여러분은 또한 회사 주식에 대한 기록도 확인하실 수 있습니다. 저는 이 프로그램의 데이터베이스가 1분마다 몇 번씩 업데이트되기 때문에 특히 흥미롭다고 생각합니다. 이는 여러분의 검색 결과가 예전보다 훨씬 더 유용해질 것임을 의미합니다. 다음 주에 고객들을 대상으로 하는 신규 서비스의 시작을 위해 여러분이 이것을 사용할 준비가 될 수 있도록 일부 특징들을 살펴 보겠습니다.

| 어휘 | agenda 안건, 의제   install ~을 설치하다   offer ~를 제공하다   financial 재무의, 재정의   consultant 컨설턴트, 상담 전문가, 자문   search ~을 찾아보다, 검색하다   stock 주식   particularly 특히   a few times a minute 1분마다 몇 번씩   go over ~을 살펴보다, 검토하다   feature 특징   so that (목적) ~할 수 있도록

4. 청자들은 누구일 것 같은가?
(A) 실험실 기술자들
(B) 재무 상담 전문가들
(C) 컴퓨터 판매 사원들
(D) 웹 사이트 개발자들

| 해설 |
담화 초반부에, 청자들을 통해 'our financial consultants, each of you'라고 지칭하고 있으므로 (B)가 정답이다.

| 어휘 | laboratory 실험실   salespeople 판매 사원들   developer 개발자

5. 화자는 일부 장비의 무슨 이점을 언급하는가?
(A) 더 규모가 큰 고객층
(B) 더 짧은 대기 시간
(C) 개선된 안전 관련 기능
(D) 더욱 유용한 검색 결과

| 해설 |
담화 중반부에, 화자는 한 프로그램의 기능을 설명하면서 그 기능으로 인해 검색 결과가 예전보다 훨씬 더 유용해질 것이라는(That means your search results will be much more useful than before) 긍정적인 결과를 예상하고 있으므로 (D)가 정답이다.

| 어휘 | equipment 장비   customer base 고객층   wait times 대기 시간   improve ~을 향상시키다

6. 다음 주에 무슨 일이 있을 예정인가?
(A) 교육 행사가 열릴 것이다.
(B) 신규 서비스가 시작될 것이다.
(C) 일부 방문객들이 견학을 할 것이다.
(D) 일부 컨설턴트들이 회의를 할 것이다.

| 해설 |
'다음 주'라는 시점 키워드가 제시되는 후반부에, 고객들을 대상으로 하는 신규 서비스가 시작되는 시점이 다음 주라고(~ the start of our new service for customers next week) 말하고 있으므로 (B)가 정답이다.

| 어휘 | take place (일, 행사 등이) 일어나다, 발생되다   launch ~을 시작하다, 출시하다

Questions 7-9 refer to the following speech.

M: Good evening, ladies and gentlemen. **7 Thank you all for being here to acknowledge the hard work of one of our staff members, Ms. Hyunjung Lee.** Ms. Lee was recently awarded the prestigious Baron Prize for Innovation, so we have gathered together to celebrate this accomplishment with her. Ms. Lee impressed the judging committee **8 by designing a railway system that is partially powered by solar energy.** This is definitely the kind of thinking we need in our field. A prototype of the train is nearly completed, and **9 Ms. Lee will begin testing the train's power supply system next month.** We look forward to getting updates on this amazing project.

7-9번 문제는 다음 연설을 참조하시오.
남: 안녕하십니까, 신사 숙녀 여러분. 우리 직원들 중 한 분이신 Hyunjung

Lee 씨의 노고를 치하하기 위한 자리에 와 주신 여러분 모두에게 감사 드립니다. Lee 씨는 최근 권위 있는 Baron Prize for Innovation을 수상하셨으므로, 이 업적을 함께 기념하기 위해 이렇게 한 자리에 모였습니다. Lee 씨는 태양열 에너지로 부분적인 동력을 얻는 철도 시스템을 고안한 것으로 심사위원단에게 깊은 인상을 남기셨습니다. 이는 분명 우리 분야에서 우리가 필요로 하는 종류의 생각입니다. 그 열차의 시제품이 거의 완료되었으며, Lee 씨께서 다음 달에 이 열차의 전력 공급 시스템을 테스트하기 시작하실 것입니다. 우리는 이 놀라운 프로젝트에 관한 새로운 소식을 들을 수 있기를 고대하고 있습니다.

| 어휘 | acknowledge ~을 치하하다, 인정하다   recently 최근에   be awarded A A를 수상하다, A가 수여되다   prestigious 권위 있는   gather 모이다   celebrate ~을 기념하다, 축하하다   accomplishment 업적, 성취   impress ~에게 깊은 인상을 남기다   judging committee 심사 위원단   partially 일부분, 부분적으로   be powered by ~로 동력을 얻다   definitely 분명히, 확실히   field 분야   prototype 시제품   nearly 거의   complete ~을 완료하다   power supply 전력 공급   look forward to -ing ~하기를 고대하다

7. 화자는 왜 연설을 하는가?
(A) 한 직원의 업적을 인정하기 위해
(B) 신규 서비스를 소개하기 위해
(C) 회사의 창립 기념일을 축하하기 위해
(D) 회사 합병을 공지하기 위해

| 해설 |
담화의 목적이 언급되는 초반부에, Hyunjung Lee라는 직원의 노고를 치하하기 위한 자리에 온 것에 대해 감사 인사를(Thank you all for being here to acknowledge the hard work of one of our staff members, Ms. Hyunjung Lee) 하고 있으므로 (A)가 정답이다.

| 어휘 | recognize ~을 인정하다, 표창하다   achievement 업적, 성과   introduce ~을 소개하다   anniversary (해마다 돌아오는) 기념일   merger 합병

8. Lee 씨의 전문 분야는 무엇인가?
(A) 재무
(B) 교통
(C) 광업
(D) 교육

| 해설 |
Lee 씨가 상을 받은 이유가 설명되는 중반부에, 태양열 에너지로 일부분 동력을 얻는 철도 시스템을 고안한 일이(~ by designing a railway system that is partially powered by solar energy) 언급되고 있으므로 (B)가 정답이다.

| 어휘 | field of expertise 전문 분야

9. 화자의 말에 따르면, Lee 씨는 다음 달에 무엇을 할 것인가?
(A) 발표하기
(B) 팀원 선정하기
(C) 일부 장비 테스트하기
(D) 해외로 출장 가기

| 해설 |
'다음 달'이라는 시점 키워드가 제시되는 후반부에, Lee 씨가 다음 달에 열차의 전력 공급 시스템 테스트를 시작할 것이라고(~ Ms. Lee will begin testing the train's power supply system next month) 알리고 있으므로 (C)가 정답이다.

| 어휘 | select ~을 선정하다   equipment 장비   abroad 해외로, 해외에

Questions 10-12 refer to the following telephone message.

M: Hi, Rita. This is Victor. I know we were supposed to meet today, but I think **10** we should postpone it. The delivery of fabric samples from Batavia Supplies is late, so there would be nothing for us to look at. The shipping company has guaranteed that they'll be here on Wednesday, so let's plan for Thursday morning. Also, **11** I've reviewed your report on possible changes we can make to cut our electricity consumption. **12** Your main recommendation was to install smart meters on all of the machines. The cost would be substantial, so… um… we need to discuss this further.

10-12번 문제는 다음 전화 메시지를 참조하시오.
남: 안녕하세요, Rita 씨. 저는 Victor입니다. 우리가 오늘 만나기로 되어 있었다는 것을 알기는 하지만, 연기해야 할 것 같습니다. Batavia Supplies에서 보내 오는 직물 샘플의 배송이 늦어지고 있어서, 우리가 살펴봐야 할 것이 없습니다. 배송 업체에서 수요일에 이곳 도착한다고 보장했기 때문에, 목요일 오전으로 계획을 잡읍시다. 또한, 전력 소비를 줄이기 위해 우리가 해 볼 수 있는 변경 사항에 관한 당신의 보고서를 검토해 봤습니다. 당신의 중점적인 권고 사항은 모든 기계에 스마트 계량기를 설치하는 것이었습니다. 비용이 상당할 것이므로… 음… 이 문제를 더 깊이 있게 논의해 봐야 합니다.

| 어휘 | be supposed to do ~할 예정이다, ~하기로 되어 있다   postpone ~을 연기하다   delivery 배송(품)   fabric 직물   guarantee that ~라고 보장하다   make a change 변경하다   electricity consumption 전력 소비   recommendation 추천   install ~을 설치하다   meter 계량기   substantial 상당한, 많은   further 더 깊이, 한층 더

10. 화자는 왜 회의를 연기하고 싶어 하는가?
(A) 고객이 불만을 제기했다.
(B) 이용 가능한 회의실이 없다.
(C) 출장을 떠나야 한다.
(D) 일부 제품이 도착하지 않았다.

| 해설 |
회의 연기와 그 이유가 제시되는 초반부에, Batavia Supplies에서 보내오는 직물 샘플의 배송이 늦어지고 있다는(~ we should postpone it. The delivery of fabric samples from Batavia Supplies is late ~) 사실을 말하고 있으므로 (D)가 정답이다.

| 어휘 | make a complaint 불만을 제기하다   available 이용 가능한   arrive 도착하다

11. 청자는 무엇에 관해 보고서를 작성했는가?
(A) 에너지 사용량을 줄이기 위한 아이디어
(B) 직물을 공급해 줄 수 있는 회사들
(C) 의견 제공 시간에 대한 분석
(D) 더 많은 고객을 끌어들이는 방법

| 해설 |
상대방이 작성한 보고서를 언급하는 중반부에, '전력 소비를 줄이기 위해 시도해 볼 수 있는 변경 사항에 관한 보고서'라는(~ your report on possible changes we can make to cut our electricity consumption) 내용으로 보아 (A)가 정답이다.

| 어휘 | reduce ~을 줄이다   supply ~을 공급하다   analysis 분석   session (특정 활동을 위한) 시간; 모임   attract ~을 끌어들이다

12. 화자가 "we need to discuss this further"라고 말할 때 무엇을 의미하는 것 같은가?
(A) 업계 전문가와 상의할 계획이다.
(B) 제안 사항이 효과가 있을지 확실하지 않다.
(C) 회의 지속 시간을 늘릴 것이다.
(D) 안전 문제를 우려하고 있다.

| 해설 |
담화 후반부에, 상대방이 제안한 스마트 계량기 설치 작업에 비용이 많이 든다고(Your main recommendation was to install smart meters ~ The cost would be substantial ~) 알린 후에 "더 논의해야 한다"고 말하는 상황이다. 이는 상대방의 제안에 대한 의구심을 나타내는 말이므로 (B)가 정답이다.

| 어휘 | consult ~와 상의하다 industry 업계 expert 전문가 be unsure that ~인지 확실하지 않다 suggestion 제안, 의견 lengthen ~을 늘리다, 길게 하다 duration 지속 시간 be concerned about ~을 우려하다

Questions 13-15 refer to the following instructions and seating chart.

W: I'd like to take this opportunity to thank 13 **all of you orchestra members** for playing in our concert this evening. We are very pleased with the community's response to this event. Now, there are several groups performing today. After you've finished, you are welcome to join the audience. 14 **We have purposely not sold tickets for the section closest to the press booth, so there should be plenty of empty seats there.** 15 **Following the event, please meet in the lobby, as there will be reporters there who may have questions** about the show itself or your rehearsal techniques.

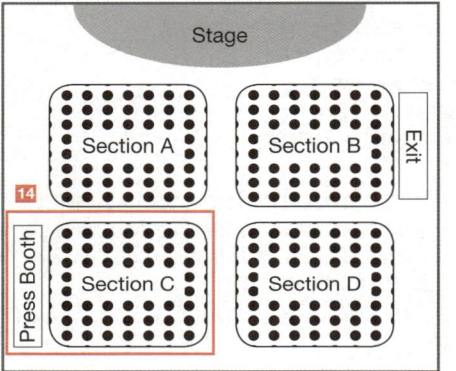

13-15번 문제는 다음 설명과 좌석 배치도를 참조하시오.
여: 저는 이 자리를 빌어 오늘 저녁 우리 콘서트에서 연주하시게 될 오케스트라 단원 여러분 모두에게 감사 드리고자 합니다. 우리는 이번 행사에 대한 지역 사회의 반응에 대해 매우 기쁘게 생각하고 있습니다. 자, 오늘 여러 그룹들이 공연을 합니다. 여러분께서 연주를 마치신 후에는, 객석에서 얼마든지 함께 하셔도 좋습니다. 우리가 기자석에서 가장 가까운 구역에 대해서는 의도적으로 티켓을 판매하지 않았으므로, 그곳에는 빈 좌석들이 많이 있을 것입니다. 행사 후에는, 공연 자체나 여러분의 리허설 기술에 관해 질문이 있을 수도 있는 기자들이 그곳에 있을 것이기 때문에 로비로 모여 주시기 바랍니다.

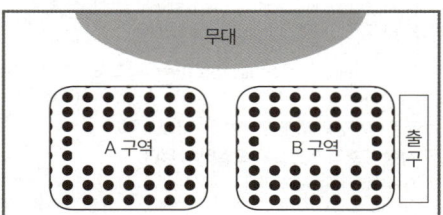

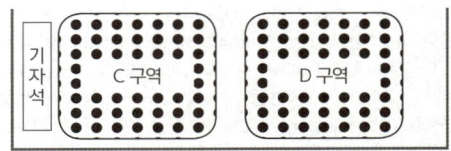

| 어휘 | I'd like to take this opportunity to do 이 자리를 빌어 ~하고자 합니다 community 지역 사회 response to ~에 대한 반응 perform 공연하다, 연주하다 be welcome to do 얼마든지 ~해도 좋다 audience 관객, 청중 purposely 의도적으로 close to ~와 가까운 press booth 기자석 plenty of 많은 following ~ 후에 itself (사물 명사 뒤에서) ~ 자체 rehearsal 리허설, 예행연습

13. 이 담화의 대상이 되는 청자들은 누구일 것 같은가?
(A) 음악가들
(B) 운동 선수들
(C) 사진 기자들
(D) 기자들

| 해설 |
담화 초반부에, 감사 인사를 하면서 청자들을 'all of you orchestra members'라고 지칭하고 있으므로 (A)가 정답이다.

| 어휘 | intended 대상이 되는

14. 시각 자료를 보시오. 청자들은 어디에서 빈 좌석을 찾을 수 있는가?
(A) A 구역
(B) B 구역
(C) C 구역
(D) D 구역

| 해설 |
담화 중반부에, 기자석에서 가장 가까운 구역은 의도적으로 티켓을 판매하지 않아 빈 좌석들이 많이 있을 것이라고(We have purposely not sold tickets for the section closest to the press booth, so there should be plenty of empty seats there) 알리고 있다. 시각 자료에서 기자석에서 가장 가까운 구역이 'Section C'이므로 (C)가 정답이다.

15. 청자들은 행사가 끝날 때 무엇을 할 것인가?
(A) 공연 한번 더 하기
(B) 질문에 답변하기
(C) 함께 사진 촬영하기
(D) 투어에 참여하기

| 해설 |
담화 후반부에, 행사가 끝나고 나면 기자들이 질문을 할 것이니 로비로 모이라고 요청하고(Following the event, please meet in the lobby, as there will be reporters there who may have questions ~) 있으므로 (B)가 정답이다.

| 어휘 | participate in ~에 참여하다

Questions 16-18 refer to the following talk and graph.

M: To begin, I'd like to review the sales trends for 16 **our products here at Stegman Software Co.** You can see from this chart that the programs we've developed have been selling well. We usually see our highest sales in December, and that was also true about this year. But 17 **you'll notice the second-highest sales here. That's when we ran our TV advertising campaign.** To help generate further interest in our products, 18 **we're going to lower our prices next month.** This may be permanent or temporary, depending on the market response that we get. I'll keep you posted on that.

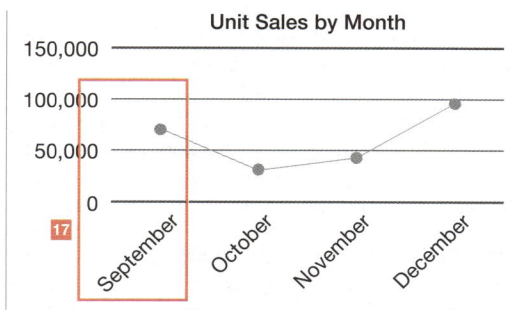

16-18번 문제는 다음 담화와 그래프를 참조하시오.
남: 먼저, 이곳 우리 Stegman Software 사의 제품들에 대한 판매 추세를 살펴보고자 합니다. 여러분께서는 이 차트를 통해 우리가 개발한 프로그램들이 잘 팔리고 있다는 것을 보실 수 있습니다. 우리는 보통 12월에 가장 높은 판매량을 보이는데, 이는 올해에도 역시 적용되었습니다. 하지만, 두 번째로 높은 판매량을 기록한 이 부분이 보이실 겁니다. 이 부분은 바로 우리가 TV 광고 캠페인을 진행했던 때였습니다. 우리 제품에 대한 더 많은 관심을 유발하는 데 도움이 될 수 있도록, 우리는 다음 달에 가격을 내릴 예정입니다. 이는 우리가 얻게 될 시장 반응에 따라 영구적일 수도, 또는 일시적일 수도 있습니다. 이 점에 대해서는 계속 여러분께 공지해 드리겠습니다.

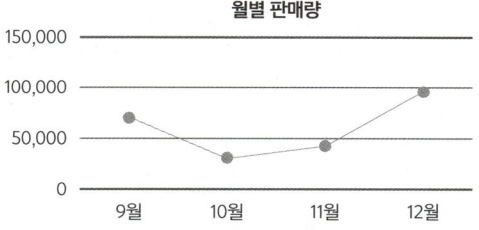

| 어휘 | sales 판매(량), 매출 trend 경향 develop ~을 개발하다 usually 보통, 일반적으로 notice ~을 알아차리다 second-highest 두 번째로 높은 run ~을 진행하다, 운영하다 advertising 광고 generate ~을 발생시키다, 만들어 내다 lower ~을 내리다, 낮추다 permanent 영구적인 temporary 일시적인 depending on ~에 따라 다른, ~에 달려 있는 keep A posted A에게 계속 공지하다, 알리다 unit (제품 등의) 1개, 구성 단위

16. 화자는 무슨 종류의 업체에서 근무하고 있을 것 같은가?
(A) 소프트웨어 개발 회사
(B) 금융 컨설팅 회사
(C) 잡지 출판사
(D) 텔레비전 스튜디오

| 해설 |
담화를 시작하면서 화자가 소속 업체를 'our products here at Stegman Software Co.'라고 지칭하고 있으므로 (A)가 정답이다.

| 어휘 | financial 금융의, 재무의 firm 회사

17. 시각 자료를 보시오. 회사는 언제 몇몇 광고를 냈는가?
(A) 9월에
(B) 10월에
(C) 11월에
(D) 12월에

| 해설 |
담화 중반부에, 두 번째로 높은 판매량을 기록한 시기를 언급하면서 그 때 TV 광고 캠페인을 진행했다고(~ you'll notice the second-highest sales here. That's when we ran our TV advertising campaign) 알리고 있다. 시각 자료에서 두 번째로 판매량 수치가 높은 달이 'September'이므로 (A)가 정답이다.

| 어휘 | advertisement 광고

18. 화자의 말에 따르면, 업체는 다음 달에 무엇을 할 것인가?
(A) 제휴 업체와 합병하기
(B) 가격 인하하기
(C) 신제품 소개하기
(D) 추가 직원 고용하기

| 해설 |
'다음 달'이라는 시점 키워드가 제시되는 후반부에, 다음 달에 가격을 내릴 예정이라고(we're going to lower our prices next month) 언급하고 있으므로 (B)가 정답이다.

| 어휘 | merge with ~와 합병하다 decrease ~을 인하하다, 내리다

DAY 18 담화 유형_전화 메시지/광고

01 전화 메시지(Telephone Message)

PRACTICE | 기출 연습하기

정답 1 (A) 2 (B) 3 (A) 4 (B) 5 (B) 6 (B)

Questions 1-2 refer to the following telephone message.

W: Hi, Mr. Koehn. This is Andy Dengler **1** calling from Spirit Computers. I've finished the updates you requested for your laptop. However, I'm afraid there's a problem with your cooling fan. **1** If it does not get replaced, it could cause overheating and damage your device. I know you weren't expecting this extra change, so I'm sorry about that. **2** We can offer to get it done as quickly as possible at no extra charge. Please call us at 555-4675 to confirm.

1-2번 문제는 다음 전화 메시지를 참조하시오.
여: 안녕하세요, Koehn 씨. 저는 Spirit 컴퓨터에서 전화 드리는 Andy Dengler입니다. 귀하께서 요청하신 노트북 컴퓨터의 업데이트 작업을 완료했습니다. 하지만, 냉각 팬에 문제가 있는 것 같습니다. 이 부품이 교체되지 않는다면, 과열을 초래해 기기에 손상을 입힐 수도 있습니다. 귀하께서는 이 추가 변동 사항을 예상하지 못하셨다는 점을 알고 있기 때문에, 이 부분에 대해 유감스럽게 생각합니다. 저희가 추가 비용 없이 이 작업을 가능한 빨리 처리해 드릴 수 있습니다. 저희에게 555-4657번으로 전화하셔서 확인해 주시기 바랍니다.

1. 화자는 어디에서 근무하는가?
(A) 컴퓨터 수리점에서
(B) 철물점에서

| 해설 |
담화 초반부에 나오는 사업장 명칭(Spirit Computers)과 노트북 컴퓨터 업데이트 작업(updates you requested for your laptop)이나 부품 교체 작업(If it does not get replaced) 같은 언급을 통해 컴퓨터를 수리하는 곳임을 알 수 있으므로 (A)가 정답이다.

2. 화자는 무엇을 제공하는가?
(A) 제품 품질 보증
(B) 빠른 서비스

| 해설 |
담화 후반부에, 가능한 한 빨리 작업을 처리해 줄 수 있다고(We can offer to get it done as quickly as possible ~) 알리고 있으므로 (B)가 정답

이다.

| 어휘 | request ~을 요청하다   I'm afraid (that) (부정적인 일에 대해) ~인 것 같다   replace ~을 교체하다   cause ~을 초래하다   overheating 과열   damage ~을 손상시키다, ~에 피해를 주다   device 기기, 장치   expect ~을 예상하다   extra 추가의, 별도의   offer to do ~해주겠다고 말하다   as ~ as possible 가능한 한 ~하게   at no extra charge 추가 비용 없이   confirm 확인해 주다   warranty 품질 보증(서)   rush 빠른, 급한

Questions 3-4 refer to the following telephone message.

M: Hi, this is Shogo. **3** There's a spacious three-bedroom apartment that just came available for rent, and I think it might be just what you're looking for. It's within walking distance of the station. I know that was a feature you wanted. It's in the Gazella Building, which is very popular. I expect it to be rented quickly. So, **4** I'll need you to let me know whether or not you want to go to the property. Please call me back as soon as you can. Thanks.

3-4번 문제는 다음 전화 메시지를 참조하시오.
남: 안녕하세요, 저는 Shogo입니다. 공간이 넓은 침실 3개짜리 아파트가 막 임대용으로 이용 가능하게 되었는데, 이 아파트가 바로 귀하께서 찾고 계신 곳일 수 있다는 생각이 들었습니다. 이 아파트는 역에서 걸어서 갈 수 있는 거리에 있습니다. 이것이 귀하께서 원하셨던 특징이었다는 것을 알고 있습니다. 이 아파트는 매우 인기가 높은 Gazella Building에 있습니다. 저는 이곳이 빠르게 임대될 것으로 예상하고 있습니다. 따라서, 이 건물에 가 보고 싶으신지를 제게 알려 주셔야 할 것입니다. 가능한 한 빨리 제게 다시 전화 주시기 바랍니다. 감사합니다.

3. 화자는 누구일 것 같은가?
(A) 부동산 중개업체 직원
(B) 여행사 직원

| 해설 |
담화 초반부에, 공간이 넓은 침실 3개짜리 아파트를 언급하면서 상대방이 원하는 곳일 수 있다는 점을(There's a spacious three-bedroom apartment ~ I think it might be just what you're looking for) 언급하는 것으로 볼 때 부동산을 중개하는 사람임을 알 수 있으므로 (A)가 정답이다.

4. 화자는 청자에게 무엇을 하도록 요청하는가?
(A) 선금 송금하기
(B) 방문에 대한 관심 나타내기

| 해설 |
담화 후반부에, 해당 건물에 가 보고 싶은지를 자신에게 알려 달라고(~ let me know whether or not you want to go to the property) 요청하고 있으므로 (B)가 정답이다.

| 어휘 | spacious (공간이) 널찍한   come ~한 상태가 되다   available 이용 가능한   rent 임대, 대여; ~을 임대하다   look for ~을 찾다   within walking distance of ~에서 걸어서 갈 수 있는 거리에 있는   feature 특징   expect A to do A가 ~할 것으로 예상하다   need A to do A에게 ~하기를 원하다   let A know A에게 알리다   whether or not ~인지 아닌지   property 건물, 부동산   as soon as you can 가능한 빨리   deposit payment 선금, 예치금   express (감정 등) ~을 나타내다, 표현하다   interest in ~에 대한 관심

Questions 5-6 refer to the following telephone message.

M: Good morning. This is Cory Juarez from Langley Accounting. **5** Thanks for sending me the information about the fees for moving our office furniture and items to a new location. We're satisfied with the quote, especially since you have such a great reputation. However, we're concerned that you won't be able to take on the job because our schedule has suddenly changed. **6** We need to do the relocation one week early, on March 3. Please let me know if that will work for you. Thanks.

5-6번 문제는 다음 전화 메시지를 참조하시오.
남: 안녕하세요. 저는 Langley 회계의 Cory Juarez입니다. 새로운 곳으로 저희 사무 가구와 물품들을 옮기는 요금과 관련된 정보를 보내주셔서 감사합니다. 저희는 가격 견적서에 만족하는데, 특히 귀사에 대한 평판이 매우 좋기 때문입니다. 하지만, 저희 일정이 갑자기 변경되었기 때문에 귀사에서 이 일을 맡아 주실 수 있을지 우려됩니다. 저희는 이번 이전 작업을 일주일 더 이른 3월 3일에 해야 합니다. 이 일정이 괜찮으신지 제게 알려 주시기 바랍니다. 감사합니다.

5. 청자는 어디에서 근무하고 있을 것 같은가?
(A) 회계 법인에서
(B) 이사 전문 업체에서

| 해설 |
담화 초반부에, 새로운 곳으로 사무 가구와 물품들을 옮기는 것에 대한 요금 정보를 받았다고(We've received the information about the fees for moving ~) 알리고 있으므로 청자가 이사 서비스를 제공하는 업체에 소속되어 있음을 알 수 있으므로 (B)가 정답이다.

6. 화자는 무슨 문제점을 언급하는가?
(A) 제안된 요금이 계획된 예산을 초과한다.
(B) 서비스가 예상보다 더 빨리 필요하다.

| 해설 |
담화 후반부에, 일정 변경을 언급하면서 일주일 더 빨리 작업을 해야 한다고(We need to do the relocation one week early ~) 알리고 있으므로 (B)가 정답이다.

| 어휘 | fee 요금, 수수료   location 지점, 위치   be satisfied with ~에 만족하다   quote 가격 견적(서)   especially 특히   since ~이기 때문에   reputation 명성, 평판   be concerned that ~라는 점을 우려하다   take on ~을 맡다   suddenly 갑자기   relocation (위치) 이전   let A know if A에게 ~인지 알리다   work for (날짜, 일정 등이) ~에게 맞다, 적합하다   suggested 제안된   exceed ~을 초과하다   budget 예산   than expected 예상보다

02 광고(Advertisement)

PRACTICE | 기출 연습하기   본책 p.117

정답   1 (B)   2 (A)   3 (B)   4 (A)   5 (A)   6 (A)

Questions 1-2 refer to the following advertisement.

W: Are you a business owner who depends on **1** a fast and reliable Internet connection? Then switch to Blane Communications. We have the fastest download speeds in the area and the lowest amount of outage time. **2** For our easy online form to book your set-up appointment, visit our Web site and click on the "Appointment" tab. We'll get you online in no time!

1-2번 문제는 다음 광고를 참조하시오.
여: 빠르고 신뢰할 수 있는 인터넷 연결 서비스에 의존하는 사업체 소유주

이신가요? 그러시다면 Blane 통신으로 바꿔 보시기 바랍니다. 저희는 지역 내에서 가장 빠른 다운로드 속도를 보유하고 있으며, 서비스 중단 시간이 가장 짧습니다. 설치 예약을 하시는 데 필요한 간편한 저희 온라인 양식을 보시려면, 저희 웹 사이트를 방문하셔서 "예약" 탭을 클릭하시기 바랍니다. 순식간에 온라인에 접속하실 수 있게 해 드립니다!

1. 무슨 서비스가 광고되고 있는가?
(A) 배송 서비스
(B) 인터넷 서비스

| 해설 |
담화 초반부에, 빠르고 신뢰할 수 있는 인터넷 연결 서비스를 언급하면서 특정 업체로 바꿔 보라고(~ a fast and reliable Internet connection? Then switch to Blane Communications) 권하고 있으므로 (B)가 정답이다.

2. 화자는 웹 사이트에서 무엇을 찾아볼 수 있다고 말하는가?
(A) 예약 양식
(B) 제품 목록

| 해설 |
'웹 사이트'라는 키워드가 언급되는 후반부에, 간편한 설치 예약 온라인 양식을 보려면 웹 사이트를 방문하라고(For our easy online form to book your set-up appointment, visit our Web site ~) 알리고 있으므로 (A)가 정답이다.

| 어휘 | depend on ~에 의존하다   reliable 신뢰할 수 있는   connection 연결   switch to ~로 바꾸다, 변경하다   amount (시간의) 양   outage (서비스 등의) 중단, 정지   book an appointment 예약하다   set-up 설치   get A online A를 온라인에 접속시키다   in no time 순식간에, 즉시

Questions 3-4 refer to the following advertisement.

M: 3 If you've ever wished that you could speak a second language fluently, then Lexsy Institute is here to help. We provide online lessons that you can download and listen to anytime, anywhere. Our system is easy to use, and you can work at your own pace. You'll be amazed at how quickly you start seeing results. Not sure if the Lexsy Institute is right for you? 4 Visit our Web site, where we're offering a thirty-day free trial so you can check us out.

3-4번 문제는 다음 광고를 참조하시오.
남: 제2의 언어를 유창하게 말할 수 있기를 한번이라도 원하셨던 분이시라면, Lexsy Institute가 도와드리기 위해 있습니다. 저희는 언제 어디서든 다운로드 받아 들으실 수 있는 온라인 강의를 제공해 드립니다. 저희 시스템은 간편하게 이용하실 수 있으며, 여러분만의 속도로 학습하실 수 있습니다. 여러분께서는 얼마나 빠르게 성과가 나타나기 시작하는지 보시면 놀라실 것입니다. 저희 Lexsy Institute가 여러분께 맞는 곳인지 확신이 서지 않으시나요? 30일 무료 체험 서비스를 제공해 드리는 저희 웹 사이트를 방문하셔서 확인해 보세요.

3. 무슨 업체가 광고되고 있는가?
(A) 웹 디자인 업체
(B) 어학원

| 해설 |
담화를 시작하면서 제2의 언어를 유창하게 말하기를 원하는 사람들을 도와 준다고(If you've ever wished that you could speak a second language fluently, then Lexsy Institute is here to help) 알리고 있으므로 (B)가 정답이다.

4. 화자는 어떤 서비스가 제공된다고 말하는가?
(A) 무료 체험
(B) 환불 보장

| 해설 |
담화 후반부에, 웹 사이트에서 제공되는 30일 무료 체험 서비스가(Visit our Web site, where we're offering a thirty-day free trial ~) 언급되고 있으므로 (A)가 정답이다.

| 어휘 | second language 제2의 언어   fluently 유창하게   provide ~을 제공하다   anytime, anywhere 언제 어디서든   at one's own pace 자신만의 속도로   be amazed at ~에 놀라다   quickly 빠르게   result 결과(물), 성과   offer ~을 제공하다; 제공(되는 것)   free trial 무료 체험   complimentary 무료의   money-back 환불   guarantee 보장

Questions 5-6 refer to the following advertisement.

W: Do you own a retail business? Then you understand that the right sign can attract more customers. 5 Here at Colston Printing, we can create eye-catching signs that will get your customers interested in your business. All of our products are custom-made, so you can get exactly what you want. 6 Whether you need large-scale banners, standard posters, or small cards, we've got you covered. Also, if you don't have an image ready yourself, we also have designers on-site to share their expertise.

5-6번 문제는 다음 광고를 참조하시오.
여: 소매 업체를 소유하고 계신가요? 그러시다면 제대로 된 간판이 더 많은 고객들을 끌어들일 수 있다는 점을 알고 계실 것입니다. 저희 Colston 인쇄에서는, 고객들이 여러분의 업체에 관심을 갖게 할 눈길을 끄는 간판을 만들어 드릴 수 있습니다. 저희의 모든 제품은 맞춤 제작되고 있으므로, 정확히 원하시는 것을 받아 보실 수 있습니다. 대형 현수막이나 일반 포스터를 필요로 하시든, 또는 작은 카드가 필요하시든 상관없이, 저희가 충족시켜 드리겠습니다. 또한, 직접 이미지를 준비하지 못하실 경우에, 전문 지식을 공유해 드릴 디자이너들도 대기하고 있습니다.

5. 해당 업체는 무슨 제품을 판매하는가?
(A) 인쇄된 간판
(B) 진열장

| 해설 |
담화 초반부에, Colston Printing이라는 업체 이름과 함께 눈에 띄는 간판을 만들어 준다고(Here at Colston Printing, we can create eye-catching signs ~) 알리고 있으므로 (A)가 정답이다.

6. 화자는 제품과 관련해 무엇을 강조하는가?
(A) 사이즈가 다양하다.
(B) 재활용된 재료로 만든다.

| 해설 |
제품 관련 특징이 언급되는 후반부에, 대형 현수막이나 일반 포스터, 또는 작은 카드가 필요하든 상관없이 원하는 것을 충족시켜 준다고(Whether you need large-scale banners, standard posters, or small cards, ~) 알리고 있다. 이는 다양한 사이즈로 제품이 제공되는 것을 의미하므로 (A)가 정답이다.

| 어휘 | retail business 소매 업체   sign 간판, 표지(판)   attract ~을 끌어들이다   create ~을 만들어 내다   eye-catching 눈길을 끄는   custom-made 맞춤 제작의   exactly 정확히   whether A, B, or C A나 B, 또는 C이든 상관 없이   large-scale 대형의, 대규모의   banner 현수막   cover ~을 충족하다   have A on-site A를 대기시키다   share ~을 공유하다   expertise 전문 지식   display 진열, 전시   emphasize ~을 강조하다   come in various sizes 다양한 사이즈로 나오다   be made from ~로 만들어지다   recycled 재활용된   material 재료, 자재

DAY 18 | 실전문제

본책 p.118

정답
1 (B) 2 (A) 3 (D) 4 (C) 5 (B) 6 (A)
7 (C) 8 (D) 9 (B) 10 (A) 11 (B) 12 (C)
13 (A) 14 (C) 15 (D) 16 (B) 17 (D) 18 (A)
19 (B) 20 (D) 21 (D)

Questions 1-3 refer to the following advertisement.

M: **1 Do you want a fresh look for your home but can't decide which colors and decorations to choose?** Regal Inc. is here to help. We can design any room to match your ideal style, and we'll help you select everything from the paint color to the furniture and accessories. And **2 if you book a consultation for anytime in April, we'll give you a free vase** for your home. It's yours to keep whether you continue with our service or not. Ready for the next step? **3 Visit www.regalinc.net to look at photos of our latest projects.**

1-3번 문제는 다음 광고를 참조하시오.
남: 여러분의 집을 새로운 모습으로 단장하길 원하시지만 어떤 색상과 장식물을 선택하셔야 할지 결정하실 수 없으신가요? 저희 Regal Inc.가 도와 드리겠습니다. 저희는 여러분의 이상적인 스타일에 맞춰 어느 공간이든 디자인할 수 있으며, 페인트 색상에서부터 가구와 부대용품에 이르기까지 모든 것을 선택하시는 데 도움을 드릴 것입니다. 그리고 4월 중에 언제든지 상담 서비스를 예약하실 경우, 여러분의 집에서 사용하실 수 있는 무료 꽃병을 제공해 드립니다. 저희 서비스를 계속 이용하실 것인지의 여부는 여러분께 달려 있습니다. 다음 단계로 나아가실 준비가 되셨나요? www.regalinc.net을 방문하셔서 저희의 최근 프로젝트 사진들을 확인해 보시기 바랍니다.

| 어휘 | look 모습, 외관 decoration 장식(물) match ~에 맞추다, 어울리게 하다 ideal 이상적인 accessories 부대용품 book ~을 예약하다 consultation 상담 free 무료의 vase 꽃병 whether ~ or not ~인지 아닌지 continue with ~을 계속하다

1. 무슨 종류의 업체가 광고되고 있는가?
(A) 부동산 중개 회사
(B) 인테리어 디자인 회사
(C) 조경 전문 회사
(D) 철물점

| 해설 |
담화 시작 부분에, 주택을 새롭게 단장하고 싶을 때 색상과 장식물을 선택하는 일과 관련된(Do you want a fresh look for your home but can't decide which colors and decorations to choose?)라고 설명하고 있으므로 (B)가 정답이다.

| 어휘 | real estate 부동산 (중개업) landscaping 조경

2. 청자들은 무료 선물을 받기 위해 무엇을 할 수 있는가?
(A) 4월 중에 상담 받기
(B) 해당 업체를 친구에게 추천하기
(C) 더 높은 서비스 패키지로 업그레이드하기
(D) 해당 업체의 우편물 발송 대상자 명단에 가입하기

| 해설 |
무료 선물이 언급되는 중반부에, 4월 중에 언제든지 상담 서비스를 예약하면 무료 꽃병을 준다고(if you book a consultation for anytime in April, we'll give you a free vase ~) 말하고 있으므로 (A)가 정답이다.

| 어휘 | mailing list 우편물 발송 대상자 명단

3. 청자들은 왜 웹 사이트를 방문하도록 권장되는가?
(A) 비용 견적서를 받기 위해
(B) 직원들과 채팅하기 위해
(C) 안내 책자를 다운로드하기 위해
(D) 일부 이미지를 보기 위해

| 해설 |
웹 사이트 관련 정보가 제시되는 후반부에 웹 사이트에서 최신 프로젝트 사진을 볼 수 있다고(Visit www.regalinc.net to look at photos of our latest projects) 알리고 있으므로 (D)가 정답이다.

| 어휘 | cost estimate 가격 견적(서) brochure 안내 책자 view ~을 보다

Questions 4-6 refer to the following advertisement.

W: **4 If you have sensitive or important documents that you need to send, then call Concord Couriers.** We can deliver your items to anywhere in the country. We use a state-of-the-art tracking system to make sure we know where your items are at all times. That means **5 you can be confident that you're getting the top level of security available.** We have experience handling irreplaceable items such as handwritten manuscripts and signed contracts. **6 Visit our Web site to read what our customers have to say about us.** Choose Concord for your peace of mind!

4-6번 문제는 다음 광고를 참조하시오.
여: 발송하셔야 하는 민감하거나 중요한 문서가 있으시다면 저희 Concord 택배에 전화 주십시오. 저희는 여러분의 물품을 전국 어느 곳이든 배송해 드릴 수 있습니다. 저희는 항상 여러분의 물품이 어디에 있는지 확실히 알기 위해 최신 추적 시스템을 이용하고 있습니다. 이는 여러분께서 이용 가능한 최고 수준의 보안 서비스를 받고 있음을 확신하실 수 있다는 것을 의미합니다. 저희는 손으로 작성한 원고나 서명된 계약서와 같은 대체 불가능한 물품들을 처리한 경험이 있습니다. 저희 웹 사이트를 방문하셔서 고객들께서 저희에 관해 어떻게 말씀하고 계신지 읽어 보시기 바랍니다. 마음의 평안을 위해 저희 Concord를 선택하십시오!

| 어휘 | sensitive 민감한 courier 택배 (회사) anywhere 어디든지 state-of-the-art 최신의 tracking system 추적 시스템 make sure (that) 반드시 ~하도록 하다 at all times 항상 be confident that ~임을 확신하다 security 보안 handle ~을 처리하다 irreplaceable 대체 불가능한 handwritten 손으로 쓴 manuscript 원고 signed 서명된 contract 계약(서)

4. 무슨 서비스 업체가 광고되고 있는가?
(A) 인쇄소
(B) 전자 제품 매장
(C) 택배 서비스 업체
(D) 도서 출판 업체

| 해설 |
제공 서비스의 특징이 언급되는 초반부에, 민감하거나 중요한 문서를 발송하는 일과(If you have sensitive or important documents that you need to send, then call Concord Couriers) 관련된 업체라고 말하고 있으므로 택배 서비스 업체를 뜻하는 (C)가 정답이다.

| 어휘 | electronics 전자 제품

5. 광고는 무슨 혜택을 강조하고 있는가?
(A) 알맞은 가격
(B) 효과적인 보호
(C) 친절한 직원
(D) 빠른 대응

| 해설 |
장점이 언급되는 중반부에, 이용 가능한 최고 수준의 보안 서비스를 받는다고(~ you can be confident that you're getting the top level of security available) 알리고 있으므로 (B)가 정답이다.

| 어휘 | emphasize ~을 강조하다   affordable (가격이) 알맞은   effective 효과적인   response 대응, 반응

6. 화자는 청자들이 웹 사이트에서 무엇을 할 수 있다고 말하는가?
(A) 고객들의 후기 읽어 보기
(B) 일정 잡기
(C) 쿠폰 다운로드하기
(D) 가격 목록 확인해 보기

| 해설 |
웹 사이트가 언급되는 후반부에, 웹 사이트에서 고객들이 말하는 내용을 읽어 볼 수 있다고(Visit our Web site to read what our customers have to say about us) 알리고 있는데, 이는 이용 후기를 읽어 볼 수 있다는 말이므로 (A)가 정답이다.

| 어휘 | review 후기, 의견, 평가

Questions 7-9 refer to the following telephone message.

> W: Hi, Ms. Dalavi. This is Simone **7 from Victoria Dental Clinic.** You called last week to schedule an appointment for tomorrow at 2 P.M., but you said that you might have to change it. **8 I'm just calling to check that you plan to be here at that time.** If you could call me back to let me know either way, I would really appreciate it. Also, please note that **9 we no longer have a parking lot nearby, as that lot is under construction.** That might affect how you plan to get here.

7-9번 문제는 다음 전화 메시지를 참조하시오.
여: 안녕하세요, Dalavi 씨. 저는 Victoria 치과의 Simone입니다. 귀하께서는 지난주에 전화하셔서 내일 오후 2시로 예약 일정을 잡으셨지만, 변경하셔야 할 수도 있다고 말씀하셨습니다. 저는 귀하께서 해당 시간에 이곳으로 오실 계획이신지 확인해 보기 위해 전화 드렸습니다. 어느 쪽이든지 제게 알려 주시기 위해 다시 전화 주실 수 있으시면, 대단히 감사하겠습니다. 또한, 근처에 있는 주차장이 공사 중이기 때문에, 더 이상 그 주차장을 이용하실 수 없다는 점에 유의하시기 바랍니다. 이는 귀하께서 이곳으로 어떻게 오실지를 계획하시는 데 영향을 미칠 수도 있습니다.

| 어휘 | appointment 예약, 약속   might have to do ~해야 할 수도 있다   either way (둘 중) 어느 쪽이든   appreciate ~에 대해 감사하다   note that ~라는 점에 유의하다   no longer 더 이상 ~않다   parking lot 주차장   nearby 근처에   under construction 공사 중인   affect ~에 영향을 미치다   get here 이곳으로 오다

7. 화자는 어디에서 근무하는가?
(A) 마케팅 회사에
(B) 건설 회사에서
(C) 치과에서
(D) 미용실에서

| 해설 |
담화 초반부에, 화자가 자신을 소개하면서 'from Victoria Dental Clinic'이라고 소속 업체를 알리고 있으므로 (C)가 정답이다.

8. 전화의 목적은 무엇인가?
(A) 새로운 서비스를 소개하는 것
(B) 오류에 대해 사과하는 것
(C) 비용 지불을 요청하는 것
(D) 예약 사항을 확인하는 것

| 해설 |
초반부에 화자는 내일 오후 2시를 언급하면서 상대방이 그때 올 수 있는지를 확인하기 위해 전화했다고(I'm just calling to check that you plan to be here at that time) 알리고 있다. 이는 예약 시간을 확인하려는 것이므로 (D)가 정답이다.

| 어휘 | apologize for ~에 대해 사과하다   request ~을 요청하다   payment 비용 지불   confirm ~을 확인하다

9. 화자의 말에 따르면, 최근에 무엇이 변경되었는가?
(A) 등록 절차
(B) 주차 상황
(C) 업체 소유주
(D) 운영 시간

| 해설 |
변경 사항과 관련된 정보가 제시되는 후반부에, 근처에 있는 주차장을 더 이상 이용할 수 없다고(we no longer have a parking lot nearby ~) 알리고 있으므로 (B)가 정답이다.

| 어휘 | sign-up 등록, 신청   procedure 절차   situation 상황

Questions 10-12 refer to the following advertisement.

> M: After thirty years in business, Flannigan's is closing its doors. **10 We are holding one last sale** to get rid of our merchandise, and the deals are the best you'll ever see. The sale starts on Friday, April 20, and runs for one week. **11 You can pick up a great vehicle for a fantastic price** and be happy with your purchase. Don't miss this opportunity. Visit Flannigan's, located just outside the city. **12 For driving directions to our business, visit our Web site at www.myflannigans.com.** We hope to see you soon!

10-12번 문제는 다음 광고를 참조하시오.
남: 30년간의 운영 끝에, Flannigan's가 문을 닫습니다. 저희는 상품을 처리하기 위해 마지막으로 한번 더 세일 행사를 개최할 예정이며, 이번 할인은 앞으로 다시는 찾아보실 수 없을 최고의 할인 조건입니다. 이 세일 행사는 4월 20일 금요일에 시작되며, 일주일 동안 진행됩니다. 환상적인 가격에 훌륭한 차량을 구입하실 수 있으며, 구입 제품에 만족하실 수 있습니다. 이번 기회를 놓치지 마십시오. 도시 바로 외곽에 위치한 저희 Flannigan's를 방문해 보시기 바랍니다. 저희 업체로 차를 운전해 찾아오시는 방법을 확인해 보시려면, 저희 웹 사이트 www.myflannigans.com을 방문하시기 바랍니다. 여러분을 곧 뵐 수 있기를 바랍니다!

| 어휘 | hold ~을 개최하다   get rid of ~을 없애다, 제거하다   merchandise 상품   deal 거래 제품, 거래 조건   run 진행되다, 지속되다   pick up ~을 구입하다   vehicle 차량   purchase 구입(품)   miss ~을 놓치다, 지나치다   opportunity 기회   located just outside ~ 바로 외곽에 위치한   directions to ~로 찾아 가는 방법

10. 무엇이 주로 광고되고 있는가?
(A) 최종 세일 행사
(B) 매장 이전
(C) 지역 경연 대회
(D) 구직 기회

| 해설 |
담화 초반부에, 마지막으로 개최하는 세일이라고(We are holding one last sale ~) 알린 후에 그 세일 행사와 관련된 정보를 제공하고 있으므로 (A)가 정답이다.

| 어휘 | relocation (위치) 이전

11. Flannigan's는 무슨 종류의 업체일 것 같은가?
(A) 캠핑용품 매장
(B) 자동차 판매 대리점
(C) 의류 매장
(D) 보석 제품 매장

| 해설 |
제품의 종류가 언급되는 중반부에, 환상적인 가격에 훌륭한 차량을 구입할 수 있다고(You can pick up a great vehicle for a fantastic price ~) 말하고 있으므로 (B)가 정답이다.

| 어휘 | dealership 판매 대리점

12. 화자는 웹 사이트에서 무엇을 할 수 있다고 말하는가?
(A) 일부 이미지 보기
(B) 쿠폰 다운로드하기
(C) 한 장소로 가는 방법 확인하기
(D) 티켓 예매하기

| 해설 |
웹 사이트 관련 정보가 제시되는 후반부에, 차를 운전해 찾아오는 방법을 확인해 보려면 웹 사이트를 방문하라고(For driving directions to our business, visit our Web site at www.myflannigans.com.) 알리고 있으므로 (C)가 정답이다.

| 어휘 | view ~을 보다 site 장소, 위치 reserve ~을 예약하다

Questions 13-15 refer to the following telephone message.

> W: Hi, this message is for Donald Keegan. This is Linda from Alberta Co. Your company sent us some boxes that we plan to use to transport **13** our floor cleaners and countertop cleansing spray. They arrived earlier this week, but we didn't notice an issue until today, when we started trying to pack up the items. **14** Unfortunately, the storage space in these boxes is too small. They're not the size we ordered. We have some shipments going out soon, so **15** would it be possible to get the replacements tomorrow? We would really appreciate it. Thanks.

13-15번 문제는 다음 전화 메시지를 참조하시오.
여: 안녕하세요, 이 메시지는 Donald Keegan 씨께 전해 드리는 것입니다. 저는 Alberta Co.에서 근무하는 Linda입니다. 저희가 바닥 세척제와 조리대 세척 스프레이를 운송하는 데 사용할 계획인 몇몇 상자들을 귀하의 회사에서 보내 주셨습니다. 이번 주 초에 도착하기는 했지만, 물품을 포장하려고 시작한 오늘에서야 문제를 알아차렸습니다. 안타깝게도, 이 상자의 보관 공간이 너무 좁습니다. 이 상자들은 저희가 주문한 사이즈가 아닙니다. 저희에게는 곧 발송해야 하는 배송 물품들이 있어서, 내일 대체 물품을 받아 보는 것이 가능할까요? 그럴 수 있다면 대단히 감사드리겠습니다. 고맙습니다.

| 어휘 | transport ~을 운송하다 countertop 조리대 notice ~을 알아차리다 not A until B B가 되어서야 A하다 pack up ~을 포장하다, 싸다 unfortunately 안타깝게도 storage 보관, 저장 shipment 배송(품) replacement 대체(품) appreciate ~에 대해 감사하다

13. 화자의 회사는 무슨 종류의 제품을 판매하는가?
(A) 세척용품
(B) 운동복
(C) 비타민 보충제
(D) 전자 기기

| 해설 |
담화 초반부에, 화자가 'our floor cleaners and countertop cleansing spray' 같은 제품을 언급하는 것으로 보아 세척용품을 판매하는 업체임을 알 수 있으므로 (A)가 정답이다.

| 어휘 | athletic 운동의 supplement 보충(제) device 기기, 장치

14. 화자는 왜 전화를 거는가?
(A) 배송 주소를 확인해 주기 위해
(B) 지연 문제에 대해 사과하기 위해
(C) 잘못된 주문을 알리기 위해
(D) 일부 새 상품을 홍보하기 위해

| 해설 |
담화 중반부에, 화자가 상자의 보관 공간이 너무 좁다는 말과 함께 주문한 사이즈가 아니라고(Unfortunately, the storage space in these boxes is too small. They're not the size we ordered) 말하고 있으므로 (C)가 정답이다.

| 어휘 | confirm ~을 확인해 주다 apologize for ~에 대해 사과하다 delay 지연, 지체 incorrect 잘못된, 부정확한 promote ~을 홍보하다 merchandise 상품

15. 청자는 무엇을 하도록 요청받는가?
(A) 서비스 취소하기
(B) 안내 설명서 보내기
(C) 구매에 대해 환불해 주기
(D) 내일 물품을 배송하기

| 해설 |
담화 후반부에, 내일 대체 물품을 받아 보는 것이 가능할지(would it be possible to get the replacements tomorrow?) 묻는 것으로 보아 내일 물품을 배송해 주길 요청하고 있음을 알 수 있으므로 (D)가 정답이다.

| 어휘 | cancel ~을 취소하다 instruction manual 안내 설명서 refund ~에 대해 환불하다 purchase 구입(품)

Questions 16-18 refer to the following talk.

> W: Hello, and welcome to Fairside Café. Since you said this is your first time visiting here, I'd like to tell you a bit about our coffee shop. We are a locally owned business that **16** gives five percent of all profits to charities in the community. **17** Reuben Webster, the coffee shop's owner, is dedicated to making this city a better place to live. Now, this month we've added a new drink to our menu, **18** the Hot Mint Mocha. It has a coffee base with mint syrup and whipped cream on top. I have one every day. If you have any questions before you order, just let me know.

16-18번 문제는 다음 담화를 참조하시오.
여: 안녕하세요, 그리고 Fairside 카페에 오신 것을 환영합니다. 이번이 이곳을 처음 방문하시는 것이라고 말씀해 주셨기 때문에, 저희 커피 매장에 관해 조금 말씀드리고자 합니다. 저희는 지역 사회의 자선 단체에 모든 수익금의 5퍼센트를 기부하는 지역 고유의 업체입니다. 이 커피 매장의 소유주이신 Reuben Webster 씨께서는 이 도시를 더 살기 좋은 곳으로 만드는 데 전념하고 계십니다. 자, 이번 달에 저희는 메뉴에 새로운 음료인 핫 민트 모카를 추가했습니다. 이 제품은 커피를 바탕으로 하는 음료로서 민트 시럽이 들어 있고 휘핑 크림을 올려 드립니다. 저는 매일 한 잔씩 마시고 있습니다. 주문하시기에 앞서 질문이 있으실 경우, 제게 말씀해 주시기 바랍니다.

| 어휘 | since ~이기 때문에 a bit 조금, 약간 locally owned 지역 고유의, 지역 자체의 profit 수익 charity 자선 단체 community 지역 사회 be dedicated to -ing ~하는 데 전념하다, 헌신하다 add ~을 추가하다 base 바탕, 기반

16. 화자는 해당 커피 매장과 관련해 무엇이 특별하다고 말하는가?
(A) 지역 주민들에게 할인을 제공한다.

(B) 수익의 일부를 기부한다.
(C) 최근 매장 위치를 변경했다.
(D) 일부 자체 재료를 재배하고 있다.

| 해설 |
담화 초반부에, 지역 사회의 자선 단체에 모든 수익금의 5퍼센트를 기부한다는 사실을(~ gives five percent of all profits to charities in the community) 언급하고 있으므로 (B)가 정답이다.

| 어휘 | offer ~을 제공하다 local 지역의, 현지의 resident 주민 donate ~을 기부하다 portion 일부, 부분 recently 최근에 grow ~을 기르다 ingredient (음식) 재료, 성분

17. Reuben Webster 씨는 누구인가?
(A) 한 동호회의 설립자
(B) 한 연구의 책임자
(C) 한 도시의 시장
(D) 한 업체의 소유주

| 해설 |
'Reuben Webster'라는 이름 키워드가 등장하는 중반부에, 'Reuben Webster, the coffee shop's owner'라는 말로 보아 커피 매장의 소유주임을 알 수 있으므로 (D)가 정답이다.

| 어휘 | founder 설립자 mayor 시장

18. 화자는 왜 "I have one every day"라고 말하는가?
(A) 한 음료를 추천하고 싶어 한다.
(B) 가격이 합리적이라고 생각한다.
(C) 시간제 근무로 변경할 계획이다.
(D) 한 가지 일이 하기 쉽다고 생각한다.

| 해설 |
담화 후반부에, Hot Mint Mocha라는 제품의 특징을 말하면서(~ the Hot Mint Mocha. It has a coffee base with mint syrup and whipped cream on top) "매일 한 잔씩 마신다"고 알리고 있다. 이는 그만큼 맛이 좋다는 것을 강조해 해당 제품을 추천하는 것이므로 (A)가 정답이다.

| 어휘 | beverage 음료 reasonable 합리적인 plan to do ~할 계획이다 task 업무, 일

Questions 19-21 refer to the following telephone message and employee badge.

W: Hello. This is Marie Fleming **19 calling for the security director, Bailey Evans.** I just joined the company yesterday. My employee badge was delivered by your security team to my office, which is number three sixty-one, just a few minutes ago. Unfortunately, I noticed that **20 there is an error on the badge. My phone extension should be listed as fifty-five.** I don't think the matter is very urgent, but **21 could you please set up a time when I can stop by your office** and get this matter resolved? Thank you very much.

Marie Fleming
Security Level: 2A
Staff ID: 04689
Office Number: 361
20 Phone Extension: 43

19-21번 문제는 다음 전화 메시지와 사원증을 참조하시오.
여: 안녕하세요. 저는 보안 책임자이신 Bailey Evans 씨께 전화 드리는 Marie Fleming입니다. 저는 어제 막 입사했습니다. 제 사원증이 불과 몇 분 전에 귀하의 보안팀으로부터 제 사무실로 전달되었으며, 번호는 361입니다. 안타깝게도, 이 사원증에 오류가 있는 것을 알게 되었습니다. 제 내선 전화번호가 55번으로 기재되어야 합니다. 이 문제가 그렇게 긴급한 것 같지는 않지만, 제가 귀하의 사무실에 들러 이 문제를 해결할 수 있는 시간을 정해 주시겠습니까? 대단히 감사합니다.

Marie Fleming
보안 등급: 2A
사원 번호: 04689
사무실 번호: 361
내선 번호: 43

| 어휘 | join ~에 입사하다, 합류하다 notice that ~임을 알아 차리다 extension 내선 전화 (번호) matter 문제, 사안, 일 urgent 긴급한 set up ~을 정하다, 설정하다 stop by ~에 들르다 resolve ~을 해결하다

19. 청자는 어느 부서에 근무하고 있는가?
(A) 시설 관리
(B) 보안
(C) 영업
(D) 회계

| 해설 |
화자가 전화 메시지 수신자를 언급하는 초반부에, 보안 책임자인 Bailey Evans 씨에게 전화한다고(~ calling for the security director, Bailey Evans) 알리고 있으므로 (B)가 정답이다.

20. 시각 자료를 보시오. 무슨 정보가 변경되어야 하는가?
(A) 2A
(B) 04689
(C) 361
(D) 43

| 해설 |
담화 중반부에 사원증에 오류가 있다면서 내선 전화번호가 55번이 되어야 한다고(~ there is an error on the badge. My phone extension should be listed as fifty-five) 알리고 있다. 시각 자료에서 내선 번호 (phone extension)가 '43'으로 표기되어 있으므로 (D)가 정답이다.

21. 청자는 무엇을 하도록 요청 받는가?
(A) 서류 되돌려 주기
(B) 직원 안내 목록 확인하기
(C) 화자의 사무실 방문하기
(D) 약속 시간 정하기

| 해설 |
담화 후반부에, 자신이 상대방의 사무실에 들를 수 있는 시간을 정해 달라고 (could you please set up a time when I can stop by your office ~) 요청하고 있으므로 (D)가 정답이다.

| 어휘 | return ~을 되돌려 주다 directory 직원 안내 목록, 건물 안내 목록 appointment 약속, 예약

DAY 19　담화 유형_회의 발췌록/투어 정보

01 회의 발췌록(Excerpt from a Meeting)

PRACTICE I | 기출 연습하기　본책 p.122

정답　1 (A)　2 (A)　3 (A)　4 (B)　5 (B)　6 (B)

Questions 1-2 refer to the following excerpt from a meeting.

M: **1 I called this meeting to talk about staffing** here at our clinic. We have a growing number of patients, so **1 we need more nurses** to keep up with the demand. I have posted the job openings online, but we would also appreciate your help. I'll e-mail you the link to the job posting. If you know anyone who might be interested in one of these positions, **2 be sure to forward the link right away**, as the application deadline is March 31.

1-2번 문제는 다음 회의 발췌록을 참조하시오.

남: 이곳 우리 진료소의 인력과 관련해 이야기하고자 회의를 소집했습니다. 우리에게 점점 더 많은 환자들이 찾아오고 있기 때문에, 이 수요에 발맞추기 위해 더 많은 간호사들이 필요합니다. 제가 온라인으로 공석들을 게시하기는 했지만, 우리는 여러분께서 도와주실 수 있다면 감사할 것입니다. 제가 이 구인 공고의 링크를 여러분께 이메일로 보내 드리겠습니다. 지원 마감시한이 3월 31일이므로 누구든 이 직책들 중의 하나에 관심이 있을 수 있는 사람을 알고 계실 경우에, 즉시 이 링크를 꼭 보내 주시기 바랍니다.

1. 화자는 주로 무엇에 관해 이야기하고 있는가?
(A) 간호사 직원 채용
(B) 지점 개설

| 해설 |
담화의 초반부에, 인력과 관련해 이야기하고자 회의를 소집했다(I called this meeting to talk about staffing)고 했으며 더 많은 간호사들이 필요하다고(~ we need more nurses ~) 알리고 있으므로 (A)가 정답이다.

2. 화자는 청자들에게 무엇을 하도록 상기시키는가?
(A) 링크 전송하기
(B) 지원서 제출하기

| 해설 |
담화 후반부에 관심이 있을 만한 사람을 알고 있으면 즉시 링크를 보내 주라고(~ be sure to forward the link right away ~) 알리고 있으므로 (A)가 정답이다.

| 어휘 | staffing 인력 구성, 직원 채용　a growing number of 점점 더 많은 수의　keep up with (진행, 속도 등) ~에 발맞추다, ~을 따라잡다　demand 수요　post ~을 게시하다　job opening 공석　appreciate ~에 대해 감사하다　job posting 구인 공고　be sure to do 꼭 ~하다　forward ~을 전송하다　right away 즉시　application 지원(서)　deadline 마감시한　branch 지점, 지사　submit ~을 제출하다

Questions 3-4 refer to the following excerpt from a meeting.

M: As you know, we've recently **finalized the contract** with Yang International. This is a major achievement for us, as **3 we'll be developing numerous advertisements for television and Web sites** for this well-known brand. To get off to a good start, we plan to hold a half-day brainstorming session sometime next week with all of you in the creative department. We're not sure which day would be more convenient. Therefore, **4 I'd like you to e-mail me with information about when you're free by Friday.** Thanks.

3-4번 문제는 다음 회의 발췌록을 참조하시오.

남: 아시다시피, 우리는 최근에 Yang International과의 계약을 최종 확정했습니다. 이는 우리에게 있어 매우 큰 성과인데, 잘 알려진 이 브랜드를 위해 텔레비전과 여러 웹 사이트에 사용할 다수의 광고를 개발하게 될 것이기 때문입니다. 순조롭게 시작할 수 있도록, 우리는 크리에이티브 부서에 속한 여러분 모두와 함께 다음 주 중으로 반나절 동안 아이디어 회의 시간을 열 계획입니다. 우리는 어느 요일이 더 편리할지 알지 못합니다. 따라서, 금요일까지 여러분이 언제 시간이 있는지와 관련된 정보를 제게 이메일로 보내 주셨으면 합니다. 감사합니다.

3. 청자들은 무슨 종류의 업체에서 근무하고 있을 것 같은가?
(A) 광고 대행사
(B) 금융 기관

| 해설 |
담화 초반부에, 화자가 자신과 청자들을 we로 지칭하면서 텔레비전과 여러 웹 사이트에 사용할 다수의 광고를 개발할 것이라고(~ we'll be developing numerous advertisements for television and Web sites ~) 알리고 있으므로 (A)가 정답이다.

4. 화자는 청자들에게 금요일까지 무엇을 하도록 요청하는가?
(A) 예산 제안서 만들기
(B) 시간이 나는지의 여부 알리기

| 해설 |
'금요일'이라는 시점 키워드가 제시되는 후반부에, 금요일까지 청자들이 언제 시간이 있는 지와 관련된 정보를 이메일로 보내 달라고(I'd like you to e-mail me with information about when you're free by Friday) 알리고 있으므로 (B)가 정답이다.

| 어휘 | recently 최근에　finalize ~을 최종 확정하다　contract 계약(서)　achievement 성과, 업적　develop ~을 개발하다　numerous 다수의　advertisement 광고　well-known 잘 알려진　get off to a good start 순조롭게 시작하다, 좋은 출발을 보이다　hold ~을 개최하다, 열다　brainstorming 아이디어 회의　session (특정 활동을 위한) 시간; 모임　creative 창의적인　department 부서　convenient 편리한

Questions 5-6 refer to the following excerpt from a meeting.

W: Good afternoon, everyone. I wanted to schedule **5 this meeting with all of our store's cashiers to discuss 6 the best way to promote the new products.** As you know, our clothing store has recently started selling accessories. Displays of these goods are positioned in the checkout area so that they will be easily noticed by customers. However, we would also like **you to make recommendations** for accessories to purchase based on what the customer is buying. I've prepared a list of suggestions to give you an idea of what I'm talking about.

5-6번 문제는 다음 회의 발췌록을 참조하시오.
여: 안녕하세요, 여러분. 저는 신제품들을 홍보할 수 있는 가장 좋은 방법을 논의하기 위해 우리 매장의 모든 계산 담당 직원들과 함께 하는 이번 회의 일정을 잡고 싶었습니다. 아시다시피, 우리 의류 매장은 최근에 액세서리들을 판매하기 시작했습니다. 고객들이 쉽게 알아차릴 수 있도록 이 상품의 진열대가 계산대 구역에 놓여 있습니다. 하지만, 우리는 또한 고객이 구입하는 것을 바탕으로 함께 구입할 액세서리에 대해서도 여러분께서 추천을 해 주셨으면 합니다. 제가 이야기하고자 하는 것에 대한 아이디어를 드리기 위해 제안 사항들이 담긴 목록을 준비했습니다.

5. 청자들은 누구일 것 같은가?
(A) 사무실 접수 담당자들
(B) 소매 업체 계산대 직원들

| 해설 |
담화 초반부에, 화자가 모든 계산 담당 직원들과 하는 회의라고(~ this meeting with all of our store's cashiers ~) 언급하고 있으므로 (B)가 정답이다.

6. 회의의 주제는 무엇인가?
(A) 다른 기계 이용하기
(B) 신제품 홍보하기

| 해설 |
회의의 목적이 제시되는 초반부에, 신제품들을 홍보할 수 있는 가장 좋은 방법과 관련된(~ the best way to promote the new products) 회의라고 알리고 있으므로 (B)가 정답이다.

| 어휘 | cashier 계산 담당 직원 promote ~을 홍보하다 display 진열(품), 전시(품) goods 상품 be positioned in ~에 놓이다 checkout 계산대 so that (목적) ~할 수 있도록 notice ~을 알아차리다 make a recommendation for ~에 대해 추천해 주다 purchase ~을 구입하다 based on ~을 바탕으로 prepare ~을 준비하다 suggestion 제안, 의견 receptionist 접수 담당자 retail 소매(업)

02 투어 정보(Tour Information)

PRACTICE | 기출 연습하기   본책 p.125

정답 1 (A)   2 (B)   3 (A)   4 (A)   5 (A)   6 (B)

Questions 1-2 refer to the following tour information.

M: **1 Welcome to the tour of the Alhambra Textiles factory.** We are proud to be one of the largest producers of fabric in the country, and we stand behind the quality of our goods. Today, you'll get to see each step in the process. We'll first watch the thread being loaded into our weavers. Then, you'll see the weaving process at work, followed by the dyeing stage. At the end of the tour, **2 how about stopping by our on-site shop to get gifts, souvenirs,** and … of course… plenty of fabric?

1-2번 문제는 다음 투어 정보를 참조하시오.
남: Alhambra 섬유 공장 견학에 오신 것을 환영합니다. 저희는 전국에서 가장 규모가 큰 직물 생산 업체 중의 하나인 것을 자랑스럽게 여기고 있으며, 저희 제품의 품질에 대해 책임을 집니다. 오늘, 여러분께서는 생산 과정의 각 단계를 보시게 됩니다. 가장 먼저 실이 방직 기계에 얹어지는 모습을 보시게 됩니다. 그런 다음, 방직 과정이 이뤄지는 것을 보실 예정이며, 염색 단계가 뒤를 이을 것입니다. 견학의 마지막에는, 건물 구내에 있는 매장에 들르셔서 선물과 기념품, 그리고… 당연히… 다량의 직물을 구입해 보시는 것은 어떠십니까?

1. 견학이 어디에서 이뤄지고 있을 것 같은가?
(A) 직물 공장에서
(B) 직업 박람회장에서

| 해설 |
견학 장소가 언급되는 초반부에, 'Welcome to the tour of the Alhambra Textiles factory'라고 알리고 있으므로 'Textiles factory'와 같은 의미에 해당되는 (A)가 정답이다.

2. 화자는 무엇을 하도록 권하는가?
(A) 안내 책자 가져가기
(B) 선물 매장 방문하기

| 해설 |
담화 후반부에, 선물과 기념품을 구입할 수 있는 매장에 들러 보도록(how about stopping by our on-site shop to get gifts, souvenirs ~) 권하고 있으므로 (B)가 정답이다.

| 어휘 | be proud to do ~해서 자랑스럽다 fabric 직물, 섬유 stand behind ~을 책임지다, 지지하다 quality 품질 get to do ~하게 되다 process 과정 thread 실 be loaded into ~에 실리다 weaver 방직 기계 at work (일, 과정 등이) 이뤄지는, 되고 있는 followed by A A가 뒤따르는 dyeing 염색 stop by ~에 들르다 on-site 구내의, 현장의 souvenir 기념품 plenty of 다량의, 많은 career fair 직업 박람회 pick up ~을 가져가다

Questions 3-4 refer to the following tour information.

M: Good morning, everyone. My name is Chris, and I'd like to welcome you to Randolph National Park. **3 The park just opened three more trails last week**, so you are one of the first groups to take advantage of the change. We'll go along at quite a fast pace, but **4 we'll stop in about an hour at the first lookout point so you can enjoy your packed lunches.** If anyone has any questions about the plants or trees you see along the way, just let me know. If we're lucky, we'll also see some wildlife.

3-4번 문제는 다음 투어 정보를 참조하시오.
남: 안녕하세요, 여러분. 제 이름은 Chris이며, Randolph 국립공원에 오신 것을 환영합니다. 우리 공원은 지난주에 세 곳의 추가 등산로를 막 개방했기 때문에, 여러분께서는 이 변동 사항을 처음 이용하시는 그룹 중의 하나이십니다. 우리는 꽤 빠른 속도로 이동하겠지만, 여러분께서 싸 오신 점심 식사를 즐기실 수 있도록 약 1시간 후에 첫 번째 전망대에서 멈출 것입니다. 그 과정에서 마주치는 식물이나 나무들에 관해 질문이 있으신 분은, 제게 말씀만 해 주십시오. 운이 좋을 경우, 몇몇 야생 동물을 보실 수도 있습니다.

3. 화자는 Randolph 국립공원에 관해 무엇을 언급하는가?
(A) 최근에 새로운 등산로를 열었다.
(B) 지역 내에서 가장 인기 있는 공원이다.

| 해설 |
담화 초반부에, 지난주에 막 세 곳의 추가 등산로를 개방했다고(The park just opened three more trails last week ~) 알리고 있으므로 (A)가 정답이다.

4. 청자들은 왜 1시간 후에 멈출 것인가?
(A) 함께 식사하기 위해
(B) 야생 동물에 관한 강연을 듣기 위해

| 해설 |
담화 중반부에, 점심 식사를 즐길 수 있도록 1시간 후에 첫 번째 전망대 지점에 멈춘다고(~ we'll stop in about an hour ~ so you can enjoy your packed lunches) 알리고 있으므로 (A)가 정답이다.

| 어휘 | trail 등산로, 산책로 take advantage of ~을 이용하다 go along 계속

이동하다, 계속 진행하다   quite 꽤, 상당히   pace 속도   lookout point 전망대 지점   packed 싸 놓은, 포장된   along the way 그 과정에서

Questions 5-6 refer to the following tour information.

W: Thank you all for signing up for this tour of the Brannon Zoo. 5 We are proud to operate the oldest zoo in the southwest. In fact, many of today's modern zoos used ours as a model when being built. We've timed this tour so that you will see some of the animals being fed. We'll head into the Reptile House first. 6 We do not permit any photography in there, so thanks in advance for not taking pictures.

5-6번 문제는 다음 투어 정보를 참조하시오.
여: 이번 Brannon 동물원 견학에 등록해 주신 여러분 모두에게 감사 드립니다. 저희는 남서부 지역에서 가장 오래된 동물원을 운영하는 것을 자랑스럽게 여기고 있습니다. 실제로, 오늘날의 많은 현대적인 동물원들이 지어질 때 저희를 모델로 이용했습니다. 저희는 여러분께서 일부 동물들에게 먹이를 주는 모습을 보실 수 있도록 이번 투어의 시간을 맞췄습니다. 가장 먼저 파충류관으로 향하겠습니다. 그곳에서는 어떠한 사진 촬영도 허용하지 않고 있기 때문에, 사진을 촬영하지 않으시는 것에 대해 미리 감사의 말씀 드립니다.

5. 화자는 동물원에 관해 무엇을 강조하는가?
(A) 운영 기간
(B) 규모

| 해설 |
담화 초반부에, 남서부 지역에서 가장 오래된 동물원을 운영하는 것이 자랑스럽다고(We are proud to operate the oldest zoo ~) 말하고 있는데, 이는 운영 기간을 강조하는 말이므로 (A)가 정답이다.

6. 화자의 말에 따르면, 무엇이 허용되지 않는가?
(A) 카메라 사용하기
(B) 음식 반입하기

| 해설 |
담화 후반부에, 어떠한 사진 촬영도 허용하지 않는다는(We do not permit any photography in there ~) 정책을 말하고 있으므로 (A)가 정답이다.

| 어휘 | sign up for ~에 등록하다, ~을 신청하다   be proud to do ~해서 자랑스러워하다   operate ~을 운영하다   in fact 사실, 실제로   time ~의 시간을 맞추다   so that (목적) ~할 수 있도록   feed ~에게 먹이를 주다   head into ~로 향해 가다   reptile 파충류   permit ~을 허용하다(= allow)   photography 사진 촬영   in advance 미리, 사전에   emphasize ~을 강조하다   bring in ~을 들여 오다

DAY 19 | 실전문제   본책 p.126

정답 1 (B)   2 (D)   3 (C)   4 (C)   5 (A)   6 (B)
      7 (C)   8 (B)   9 (A)   10 (A) 11 (D) 12 (C)
      13 (A) 14 (D) 15 (A) 16 (C) 17 (D) 18 (C)
      19 (C) 20 (D) 21 (D)

Questions 1-3 refer to the following excerpt from a meeting.

M: Next on the agenda, I have some news that I think you'll all be happy to hear. As you know, we conducted an employee survey here at 1 our manufacturing facility. Many of you reported to the management team that you were frustrated with the outdated machinery. We understand that improving the tools you have will make the working environment better. Therefore, 2 at the beginning of May, we plan to replace several of our machines on the production floor. To help you learn how to use the new machines in advance, 3 I'd like all of you to read the user manual, which I'm passing out now.

1-3번 문제는 다음 회의 발췌록을 참조하시오.
남: 다음 안건으로, 여러분께서 들으시면 모두 기뻐하시리라 생각하는 뉴스가 있습니다. 아시다시피, 이곳 우리 제조 시설에서 직원 설문 조사를 실시했습니다. 많은 분들이 낡은 기기가 불만이라고 경영진에 알려 주셨습니다. 우리는 여러분이 사용하는 작업 도구들을 개선하면 업무 환경이 더 나아질 것임을 알고 있습니다. 따라서, 5월초에, 우리는 생산 작업장에 있는 여러 기계들을 교체할 계획입니다. 미리 새 기계를 사용하는 방법을 여러분께서 배우는 데 도움을 드리기 위해, 여러분 모두 제가 지금 나눠 드릴 사용자 설명서를 읽어 봐 주셨으면 합니다.

| 어휘 | agenda 안건, 의제   conduct ~을 실시하다, 수행하다   survey 설문 조사(지)   manufacturing 제조   facility 시설   report to ~에게 알리다   be frustrated with ~을 불만스러워하다   outdated 낡은, 오래된   machinery 기계들   improve ~을 개선하다   tool 수단, 공구   working environment 업무 환경   replace ~을 교체하다   several 여러 가지   production floor 생산 작업장   in advance 미리, 사전에   pass out ~을 나눠 주다

1. 화자는 누구일 것 같은가?
(A) 건물 소유주
(B) 공장 책임자
(C) 제품 평가자
(D) 보안 책임자

| 해설 |
담화 초반부에, 화자는 자신이 근무하는 곳을 'our manufacturing facility'라고 지칭한 후에 소속 직원들의 불만을 개선하기 위해 생산 작업장의 기계를 교체할 것이라는 조치를 설명하고 있으므로 (B)가 정답이다.

| 어휘 | reviewer 평가자

2. 5월에 해당 업체에서 무엇이 교체되는가?
(A) 일부 조명
(B) 일부 가구
(C) 일부 유니폼
(D) 일부 장비

| 해설 |
'5월'이라는 시점 키워드가 제시되는 중반부에, 5월 초에 여러 기계들을 교체할 계획이라고(~ at the beginning of May, we plan to replace several of our machines ~) 알리고 있으므로 (D)가 정답이다.

| 어휘 | equipment 장비

3. 화자는 청자들에게 무엇을 하도록 요청하는가?
(A) 워크숍에 참석하기
(B) 설문지 작성하기
(C) 교육 자료 읽어 보기
(D) 일찍 출근하기

| 해설 |
담화 후반부에, 자신이 나눠 주는 사용자 설명서를 읽어 보라고(I'd like all of you to read the user manual, which I'm passing out now) 요청하고 있으므로 (C)가 정답이다.

| 어휘 | training manual 교육 자료

Questions 4-6 refer to the following excerpt from a meeting.

> W: To wrap up today's meeting, I'd like to announce that **4 the company's Web site will be unavailable** for several hours tomorrow. This is due to taking the site offline **4 while we relaunch it with the new design.** During this time, you will not be able to access information like the company directory and the client list. If you plan to use this information, **5 please print out the details you need today**, as we don't know exactly when full service will be restored. If you have any problems with the new site after it goes live, please call **6 Elaine Patterson, the computer specialist** who is handling the change. She can be reached at extension 10.

4-6번 문제는 다음 회의 발췌록을 참조하시오.

여: 오늘 회의를 마무리하면서, 저는 회사의 웹 사이트가 내일 몇 시간 동안 이용 불가능할 것이라는 점을 알려 드리고자 합니다. 이는 우리가 새로운 디자인과 함께 웹 사이트를 새롭게 선보이는 동안 오프라인 상태로 전환하는 작업으로 인한 것입니다. 이 시간 동안, 여러분께서는 회사 안내 목록과 고객 명단 같은 정보를 이용하실 수 없을 것입니다. 이 정보를 이용할 계획이시면 언제 모든 서비스가 복구될지 정확히 알지 못하기 때문에, 오늘 필요한 상세 정보를 출력하시기 바랍니다. 새로운 사이트가 가동된 후에 어떠한 문제든지 겪게 되실 경우에는, 이 변경 사항을 처리하고 계신 컴퓨터 전문가 Elaine Patterson 씨에게 전화하시기 바랍니다. 내선 번호 10번으로 연락하시면 됩니다.

| 어휘 | wrap up ~을 마무리하다   announce that ~임을 알리다, 공지하다   unavailable 이용할 수 없는   due to ~로 인한   take A offline A를 오프라인 상태로 전환하다   relaunch ~를 새롭게 선보이다   access ~을 이용하다, ~에 접근하다   directory 안내 목록   details 상세 정보, 세부 사항   exactly 정확히   restore ~을 복구하다   go live 가동되다   specialist 전문가   handle ~을 처리하다   reach ~에게 연락하다   extension 내선 전화 (번호)

4. 화자는 청자들에게 무엇에 관해 이야기하는가?
(A) 사무실 이전
(B) 연례 회의
(C) 웹 사이트 재공개
(D) 업계 콘퍼런스

| 해설 |
담화 초반부에, 내일 회사의 웹 사이트를 이용할 수 없다고(~ the company's Web site will be unavailable ~) 알리면서 그 이유가 새로운 디자인으로 다시 선보이기 위한 것이라고(~ while we relaunch it with the new design) 밝히고 있다. 따라서 (C)가 정답이다.

| 어휘 | relocation (위치) 이전   annual 연례적인, 해마다의   industry 업계

5. 화자는 청자들에게 무엇을 하도록 요청하는가?
(A) 정보 출력하기
(B) 고객들에게 변화에 관해 말하기
(C) 소프트웨어 업데이트하기
(D) 이메일을 자주 확인하기

| 해설 |
담화 중반부에, 필요한 상세 정보를 오늘 출력해 놓으라고(~ please print out the details you need today ~) 요청하고 있으므로 (A)가 정답이다.

| 어휘 | frequently 자주

6. Elaine Patterson 씨는 누구인가?
(A) 배송 담당자
(B) 컴퓨터 전문가
(C) 인사부 직원
(D) 구직 지원자

| 해설 |
이름 키워드 'Elaine Patterson'이 언급되는 후반부에, 'Elaine Patterson, the computer specialist'라고 컴퓨터 전문가라고 알리고 있으므로 (B)가 정답이다.

| 어휘 | HR 인사부   representative 직원   applicant 지원자

Questions 7-9 refer to the following talk.

> M: If I could have your attention for a moment, **7 I'd like to clear up some confusion regarding our guidelines for reimbursement.** Whenever you are traveling for business or entertaining clients, you are eligible to have your expenses paid by the company. Simply provide a copy of your credit card statement showing the charge along with **8 form C-12. You can talk to Erica in the administration office to get the form.** We know that it may be inconvenient for you to pay these charges yourselves. **9 That's why we plan to issue company credit cards to most employees later this year.**

7-9번 문제는 다음 담화를 참조하시오.

남: 잠시 제게 주목해 주실 수 있다면, 비용 환급에 필요한 우리의 가이드라인과 관련된 일부 혼란을 말끔히 정리해 드리고자 합니다. 업무를 위해, 또는 고객 접대를 위해 출장을 가실 때마다, 여러분은 경비를 회사에서 지불하도록 하실 수 있는 자격이 있습니다. 제출 양식 C-12와 함께 청구 비용을 보여주는 신용카드 내역서 사본을 제공해 주시기만 하면 됩니다. 행정팀의 Erica 씨에게 말씀하셔서 해당 양식을 받으실 수 있습니다. 우리는 이 청구 비용들을 여러분이 직접 지불하는 것이 불편할 수도 있다는 점을 알고 있습니다. 이것이 바로 우리가 올해 후반에 대부분의 직원들에게 회사 법인 카드를 발급할 계획을 세우는 이유입니다.

| 어휘 | attention 주목, 주의, 관심   clear up ~을 말끔히 정리하다   confusion 혼동, 혼란   regarding ~와 관련해   reimbursement 비용 환급   whenever ~할 때마다   entertain ~을 즐겁게 해 주다   be eligible to do ~할 자격이 있다   expense 지출 (비용)   statement 내역서   charge 청구 비용   along with ~와 함께   administration 행정   inconvenient 불편한   issue ~을 발급하다

7. 담화는 주로 무엇에 관한 것인가?
(A) 고객들을 끌어들이는 방법
(B) 선호하는 여행지
(C) 회사의 비용 환급 정책
(D) 낭비를 줄이는 방법

| 해설 |
담화 초반부에, 화자는 비용 환급에 필요한 가이드라인과 관련된 혼란을 정리해 주겠다고(I'd like to clear up some confusion regarding our guidelines for reimbursement) 알리고 있으므로 (C)가 정답이다.

| 어휘 | method 방법   attract ~을 끌어 들이다   preferred 선호하는   destination 목적지, 도착지   policy 정책   reduce ~을 줄이다   spending 소비

8. 청자들은 왜 Erica 씨에게 얘기해야 하는가?
(A) 한 가지 일에 자원하기 위해
(B) 양식을 요청하기 위해
(C) 전근을 요청하기 위해
(D) 한 행사에 등록하기 위해

| 해설 |
이름 키워드 'Erica'가 제시되는 중반부에, 화자는 C-12라는 양식을 언급하면서 Erica 씨를 통해 그 양식을 받을 수 있다는(~ form C-12. You can talk to Erica in the administration office to get the form) 알리고 있으므로 (B)가 정답이다.

| 어휘 | volunteer for ~에 자원하다   request ~을 요청하다(= ask for)   transfer 전근   sign up for ~에 등록하다, ~을 신청하다

9. 화자는 회사가 나중에 무엇을 할 것이라고 말하는가?
(A) 신용카드 발급하기
(B) 일부 팸플릿 배부하기
(C) 계약 최종 확정하기
(D) 일부 기기 업그레이드하기

| 해설 |
회사가 하려는 일이 언급되는 후반부에, 회사에서 올해 후반에 대부분의 직원들에게 회사 법인 카드를 발급할 것이라는(~ we plan to issue company credit cards to most employees later this year) 사실을 밝히고 있으므로 (A)가 정답이다.

| 어휘 | distribute ~을 배부하다   finalize ~을 최종 확정하다   device 기기, 장치

Questions 10-12 refer to the following tour information.

> M: Good afternoon. My name is Armando, and I'd like to welcome you to **10** Milani Photos. Throughout our tour today, **10** you'll see a few different photography studios. Some have unique sets, so I think you'll find them interesting. If one of our employees is free, you might even get to ask a few questions. I just want to remind you that **11** you must not separate from the group at any time. At the end of the tour, **12** I'll tell you about some of the on-site workshops we have available. I highly encourage you to sign up for one.

10-12번 문제는 다음 투어 정보를 참조하시오.
남: 안녕하세요. 제 이름은 Armando이며, Milani Photos에 오신 여러분을 환영합니다. 오늘 견학 시간 내내, 여러분께서는 몇몇 다른 사진 촬영 스튜디오를 보시게 될 것입니다. 일부 스튜디오에는 독특한 세트들이 있으므로, 흥미롭게 생각하실 것으로 보입니다. 저희 직원들 중의 한 명이 시간이 나면, 심지어 몇몇 질문들을 하게 되실 수도 있습니다. 여러분께서는 반드시 항상 견학 그룹에서 떨어져 계시지 말아야 한다는 점을 꼭 상기시켜 드리고자 합니다. 견학이 종료될 때, 이용 가능하신 몇몇 현장 워크숍에 관해 말씀 드릴 것입니다. 한 가지에 등록해 보시도록 적극 권해 드립니다.

| 어휘 | throughout ~ 동안 내내   photography 사진 촬영   unique 독특한, 특별한   find A + 형용사 A를 ~하다고 생각하다   free 시간이 나는   even 심지어 (~도)   get to do ~하게 되다   remind A that A에게 ~라고 상기시키다   separate from ~에서 떨어져 있다, 분리되다   at any time 항상, 언제든지   on-site 현장의, 구내의   available 이용 가능한   highly encourage A to do A에게 ~하도록 적극 권하다   sign up for ~에 등록하다

10. 견학이 어디에서 진행되고 있는가?
(A) 사진 촬영 스튜디오에서
(B) 연구 실험실에서
(C) 미술관에서
(D) 요리 학교에서

| 해설 |
담화 초반부에, 'Milani Photos'라는 업체 이름과 사진 촬영 스튜디오를 볼 수 있다는(you'll see a few different photography studios) 사실이 언급되고 있으므로 (A)가 정답이다.

| 어휘 | research 연구, 조사   laboratory 실험실

11. 화자는 견학 중에 무엇이 허용되지 않는다고 말하는가?
(A) 직원들에게 말 걸기
(B) 물품에 손 대기
(C) 크게 소음 내기
(D) 그룹에서 벗어나 있기

| 해설 |
담화 후반부에, 항상 견학 그룹에서 떨어져 있지 말아야 한다고(~ you must not separate from the group at any time) 알리고 있으므로 (D)가 정답이다.

| 어휘 | make noise 소음을 내다   leave ~에서 벗어나 있다, 떠나 있다

12. 화자는 무엇을 하도록 권하는가?
(A) 안내 책자 가져가기
(B) 일부 기념품 구입하기
(C) 워크숍에 등록하기
(D) 몇몇 질문 적어 놓기

| 해설 |
담화 후반부에 화자는 이용 가능한 몇몇 현장 워크숍에 관해 알려 주겠다는 말과 함께 그 중 하나에 등록해 보도록 적극 권한다고(I'll tell you about some of the on-site workshops ~ I highly encourage you to sign up for one) 말하고 있으므로 (C)가 정답이다.

| 어휘 | pick up ~을 가져가다   brochure 안내 책자   souvenir 기념품   register for ~에 등록하다   write down ~을 적어 놓다

Questions 13-15 refer to the following tour information.

> W: It's great to see so many people here for this tour of Coulter Manor. Once we enter the building, I think **13** you'll be impressed that all of the furniture and decorations accurately show the historical time period during which this majestic home was built. We'll visit the gift shop as our last stop. **14** There we sell plates and bowls with traditional colors. I highly recommend getting some of those. And, just a reminder, **15** please turn off your cell phones and store them in your pocket or bag for the duration of the tour.

13-15번 문제는 다음 투어 정보를 참조하시오.
여: 이 Coulter Manor 견학에 이렇게 많은 분들께서 오신 것을 보니 대단히 기쁩니다. 일단 건물에 들어가고 나면, 저는 모든 가구와 장식물들이 이 웅장한 저택이 지어졌을 당시의 역사적인 시대를 정확히 보여준다는 점에서 여러분이 깊은 인상을 받으실 것으로 생각합니다. 우리는 마지막 순서로 선물 매장을 방문할 것입니다. 그곳에서 저희는 전통적인 색상으로 된 접시와 그릇들을 판매하고 있습니다. 이들 중의 몇몇을 구입하시기를 적극 권해 드립니다. 그리고, 한 가지 상기시켜 드리고 싶은 것은, 견학이 지속되는 동안에 여러분의 휴대 전화기를 끄신 후에 주머니나 가방에 넣어 주시기 바랍니다.

| 어휘 | once 일단 ~하면, ~하자마자   be impressed that ~에 깊은 인상을 받다   decoration 장식(물)   historical 역사적인   majestic 웅장한, 장엄한   plate 접시   bowl (움푹한) 그릇   traditional 전통적인   highly recommend -ing ~하도록 적극 권하다   reminder (메시지, 말 등의) 상기시키는 것   turn off ~을 끄다   store ~을 보관하다   for the duration of ~가 지속되는 동안

13. 화자의 말에 따르면, 건물에 대해 무엇이 인상적인가?
(A) 역사적 시간을 정확히 보여주는 가구들이 있다.
(B) 커다란 회의실을 제공한다.
(C) 여러 비밀 통로들이 있다.

(D) 언덕 근처에 자리잡고 있다.

| 해설 | 담화 초반부에, 모든 가구와 장식물들이 과거의 역사적인 시대를 정확히 보여준다는 점에 깊은 인상을 받을 것이라고(~ you'll be impressed that all of the furniture and decorations accurately show the historical time period ~) 말하고 있으므로 역사적인 정확성을 언급한 (A)가 정답이다.

| 어휘 | impressive 인상적인   historically 역사적으로   accurate 정확한   furnishings 비품(가구, 카펫, 커튼 등), 집기   passageway (연결) 통로

14. 화자는 견학 후에 무엇을 하도록 권하는가?
(A) 역사책 읽어 보기
(B) 동영상 시청하기
(C) 우편물 발송 대상자 명단에 가입하기
(D) 몇몇 그릇 구입하기

| 해설 | 담화 중반부에, 전통적인 색상으로 된 접시와 그릇들을 판매한다는 사실과 함께 몇 개 구입하도록 권하고(There we sell plates and bowls with traditional colors. I highly recommend getting some of those) 있으므로 (D)가 정답이다.

| 어휘 | mailing list 우편물 발송 대상자 명단   purchase ~을 구입하다

15. 청자들은 무엇을 하는 것을 피해야 하는가?
(A) 휴대 전화 사용
(B) 음식물 휴대
(C) 티켓 분실
(D) 사진 촬영

| 해설 | 담화 후반부에, 휴대 전화기를 끈 후에 주머니나 가방에 넣어 두라고(~ please turn off your cell phones and store them in your pocket or bag ~) 알리고 있는데, 이는 휴대 전화 사용이 금지된다는 뜻이므로 (A)가 정답이다.

| 어휘 | avoid -ing ~하는 것을 피하다   carry ~을 휴대하다

Questions 16-18 refer to the following introduction.

> M: Thank you for participating in this tour of Riley's. My name is Jeff, and **16 I'll be showing you our workout equipment and rooms for group classes** during this tour. **17 We like to let visitors try some of the machines for themselves, whenever possible.** But … um … this is a popular time. I'm happy to answer any questions you may have throughout the tour. When we're finished, **18 don't forget to stop by the front desk to get your coupon** for ten percent off membership fees.

16-18번 문제는 다음 소개를 참조하시오.

남: 오늘 열리는 저희 Riley's 견학에 참가해 주셔서 감사 드립니다. 제 이름은 Jeff이며, 이번 견학 동안 저희 운동 장비와 단체 강습 공간들을 여러분께 보여 드릴 예정입니다. 저희는 가급적이면 방문객들께 직접 일부 기구들을 시험 사용해 보시도록 해 드립니다. 하지만 … 음 … 지금은 사람들이 많은 시간대입니다. 견학 시간 내내 여러분께서 갖고 계실 수 있는 모든 질문에 기꺼이 답변해 드리겠습니다. 견학이 끝날 때, 잊지 말고 프런트 데스크에 들르셔서 회비를 10퍼센트 할인해 드리는 쿠폰을 받아 가시기 바랍니다.

| 어휘 | participate in ~에 참가하다   workout 운동   equipment 장비   let A do A에게 ~하게 하다   try ~을 시험 사용해 보다   for oneself 스스로, 혼자   whenever possible 가급적이면   popular 사람이 많은   throughout ~ 동안 내내   forget to do ~하는 것을 잊다   stop by ~에 들르다

16. 담화가 어디에서 진행되고 있을 것 같은가?
(A) 미술학원에서
(B) 제조 공장에서
(C) 피트니스 시설에서
(D) 백화점에서

| 해설 | 시설 관련 특징이 제시되는 초반부에, 운동 장비와 단체 강습 공간들을 보여 주겠다고(~ I'll be showing you our workout equipment and rooms for group classes ~) 알리고 있으므로 (C)가 정답이다.

| 어휘 | take place (일, 행사 등) 일어나다, 발생되다   institute 학원, 기관, 협회   manufacturing 제조   plant 공장   facility 시설(물)

17. 화자는 왜 "this is a popular time"라고 말하는가?
(A) 견학이 지연될 수 있음을 예측하기 위해
(B) 좋은 결정을 내린 것에 대해 청자들을 칭찬하기 위해
(C) 자신이 왜 평소보다 더 바쁜지 설명하기 위해
(D) 한 가지 옵션이 이용 불가능할 수 있다고 주의를 주기 위해

| 해설 | 담화 중반부에, 화자가 가급적이면 방문객들에게 직접 일부 기구들을 시험 사용해 보도록 한다고(We like to let visitors try some of the machines for themselves, whenever possible) 알린 후에 "지금은 사람들이 많은 시간대"라고 말하는 상황이다. 따라서 기구들을 시험 사용해 보는 일이 불가능할 수 있음을 미리 알리려는 의도라는 것을 알 수 있으므로 (D)가 정답이다.

| 어휘 | predict that ~라고 예측하다   delayed 지연된   praise A for B B에 대해 A를 칭찬하다   make a decision 결정하다   explain ~을 설명하다   than usual 평소보다   warn A that A에게 ~라고 주의를 주다   unavailable 이용 불가능한

18. 청자들에게 무엇을 가져가라고 상기시키는가?
(A) 안내 책자
(B) 방문객 출입증
(C) 쿠폰
(D) 주차권

| 해설 | 담화 후반부에, 프런트 데스크에 들러서 회비를 10퍼센트 할인해 주는 쿠폰을 받아 가라고(~ don't forget to stop by the front desk to get your coupon ~) 알리고 있으므로 (C)가 정답이다.

| 어휘 | be reminded to do ~하도록 상기되다   pick up ~을 가져가다

Questions 19-21 refer to the following excerpt from a meeting and diagrams.

> M: To begin, I'd like to thank you for joining the planning committee for **19 this year's biology workshop**. There will be a lot of interesting topics covered in the field of biology, and we have finalized the schedule of presenters. Thanks to an increase in our budget, **20 we were able to run an extensive ad campaign for the event. Because of this, tickets sold out in record time.** Now, some of the tickets include **21 a special group discussion led by Dr. Beverly Ellis in room 17.** We don't need the chairs lined up in long rows like in the other rooms. Instead, **21 we'll have small circles of chairs to help facilitate discussions.** I'd like one of you to be in charge of making the necessary arrangements.

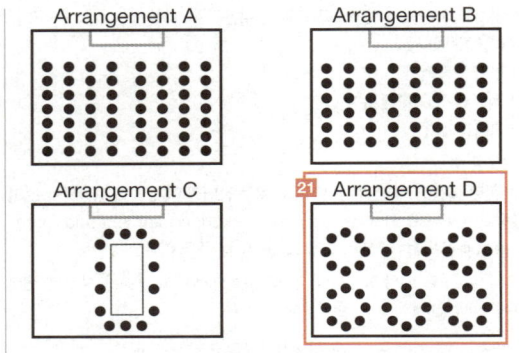

(C) 많은 상품이 증정될 것이다.
(D) 행사가 대대적으로 광고되었다.

| 해설 |
담화 중반부에, 화자는 대대적인 광고 캠페인을 진행했다는 말과 함께 그 때문에 입장권이 기록적인 시간 내에 매진되었음을(~ we were able to run an extensive ad campaign ~ Because of this, tickets sold out in record time) 알리고 있으므로 (D)가 정답이다.

| 어휘 | entrance fee 입장료   a number of 많은   prize 상, 상품   give away ~을 나눠 주다, 증정하다   heavily (양, 정도 등이) 엄청나게, 많이   advertise ~을 광고하다

21. 시각 자료를 보시오. 17번 방에서 어느 배치 방식이 이용될 것인가?
(A) 배치 방식 A
(B) 배치 방식 B
(C) 배치 방식 C
(D) 배치 방식 D

| 해설 |
담화 후반부에, 17번 방에서 Beverly Ellis 박사가 진행하는 그룹 토론회를 언급하면서 그 시간을 위해 의자를 여러 작은 원 형태로 만들어 둘 것이라고(~ we'll have small circles of chairs to help facilitate discussions) 말하고 있으므로 (D)가 정답이다.

DAY 20 담화 유형_안내 방송/방송/뉴스

01 안내 방송(Announcement)

PRACTICE I 기출 연습하기   본책 p.130

정답   1 (A)   2 (A)   3 (A)   4 (A)   5 (A)   6 (B)

Questions 1-2 refer to the following announcement.

M: **1 Attention, all passengers traveling on Lia Airlines flight 451 to Shanghai.** This flight had been delayed by approximately three hours. We apologize for the inconvenience. We expect no further delays after this time, so there is no need to change your boarding passes. By way of apology, one of our staff members will **2 come around and provide gift certificates for** a set lunch menu at participating businesses on-site. There is plenty of time to use those. Sorry again for this delay. We will be making more announcements closer to the boarding time.

1-2번 문제는 다음 안내를 참조하시오.
여: Shanghai로 향하는 Lia Airlines 451 항공편을 이용하시는 탑승객 여러분께 알립니다. 이 항공편은 약 3시간 정도 지연되었습니다. 불편에 대해 사과 드립니다. 이 시간 이후에는 더 이상 지연되지 않을 것으로 예상하고 있으므로 탑승권을 변경하실 필요가 없습니다. 사과의 의미로, 저희 직원들 중 한 명이 돌아 다니면서 공항 구내에 있는 참여 업체에서 점심 세트 메뉴를 이용하실 수 있는 상품권을 제공해 드릴 것입니다. 이 상품권을 이용하실 수 있는 시간은 많이 있습니다. 이 지연 문제에 대해 다시 한번 사과 드립니다. 탑승 시간이 가까워질 때 추가 공지를 해 드릴 예정입니다.

1. 안내 방송이 어디에서 이뤄지고 있는가?
(A) 공항에서

19-21번 문제는 다음 회의 발췌록과 도해를 참조하시오.
남: 먼저, 올해의 생물학 워크숍 행사를 위한 기획 위원회에 함께 해주셔서 감사합니다. 생물학 분야에서 다뤄질 수 있는 흥미로운 주제들이 많이 있을 것이며, 우리는 발표자들의 일정을 최종 확정했습니다. 예산 증액 덕분에, 우리는 이 행사에 대해 대대적인 광고 캠페인을 진행할 수 있었습니다. 이로 인해, 행사 입장권이 기록적인 시간 내에 매진되었습니다. 현재, 일부 입장권에는 17번 방에서 Beverly Ellis 박사님께서 진행하시는 특별 그룹 토론회가 포함되어 있습니다. 우리는 다른 방들처럼 의자를 긴 줄로 정렬해 둘 필요가 없습니다. 대신, 토론을 용이하게 하는 데 도움이 될 수 있도록 의자를 여러 작은 원 형태로 만들어 둘 것입니다. 저는 여러분 중의 한 명이 필요한 준비 작업을 맡아 주셨으면 합니다.

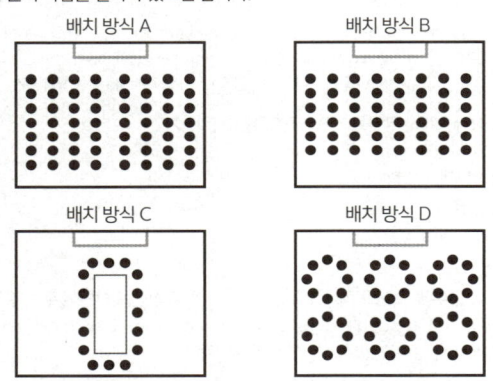

| 어휘 | join ~에 함께 하다   planning committee 기획 위원회   biology 생물학   cover (주제 등)을 다루다   field 분야   finalize ~을 최종 확정하다   presenter 발표자   thanks to ~로 인해, ~ 덕분에   increase in ~의 증가   budget 예산   extensive 폭넓은, 광범위한   ad 광고   sell out 매진되다   in record time 기록적인 시간에   include ~을 포함하다   discussion 토론(회)   led by ~가 진행하는, 이끄는   line up ~을 일렬로 정리하다   row 줄, 열   instead 대신   facilitate ~을 용이하게 하다   in charge of ~을 맡은   make an arrangement 준비하다, 조정하다   necessary 필요한   arrangement 배치, 배열

19. 무슨 종류의 행사가 이야기되고 있는가?
(A) 그림 수업
(B) 기술 콘퍼런스
(C) 과학 워크숍
(D) 역사 강좌

| 해설 |
담화 초반부에, 화자가 'this year's biology workshop'이라는 말로 생물학 워크숍 행사를 언급한 뒤로 해당 행사와 관련된 정보를 제시하고 있으므로 (C)가 정답이다.

20. 화자의 말에 따르면, 입장권이 왜 빠르게 매진되었는가?
(A) 유명 강연자가 참석할 것이다.
(B) 입장료가 할인되었다.

(B) 버스 터미널에서

| 해설 |
담화 시작 부분에, Shanghai로 향하는 Lia Airlines 451 항공편을 이용하는 탑승객에게 알리는(Attention, all passengers traveling on Lia Airlines flight 451 to Shanghai) 공지임을 알리고 있으므로 (A)가 정답이다.

2. 화자는 무엇이 배부될 것이라고 말하는가?
(A) 음식 쿠폰
(B) 새로운 티켓

| 해설 |
담화 후반부에, 점심 세트 메뉴를 이용할 수 있는 상품권을 제공하겠다고(~ provide gift certificates for a set lunch menu ~) 알리고 있으므로 (A)가 정답이다.

| 어휘 | passenger 탑승객 delayed 지연된, 지체된 by (차이) ~ 정도, ~만큼 approximately 약, 대략 apologize for ~에 대해 사과하다 inconvenience 불편함 expect ~을 예상하다 further 추가의 boarding pass 탑승권 by way of apology 사과의 의미로 gift certificate 상품권 participating 참여하는 on-site 구내에, 현장에 plenty of 많은 make an announcement 공지하다 closer to ~와 더 가까이 distribute ~을 배부하다 voucher 쿠폰, 상품권

Questions 3-4 refer to the following announcement.

W: I'd like to ③ welcome you all to the Appleton Staffing Agency. We hold this group interview session once a month to add more people to our computer database. Our goal is to help you find the right job that will fit your skills and interests. As you can see, there are a lot of people here today, so we'd like to get through the process as quickly as possible. ④ Could you help us speed things up by completing your application form ahead of time? You can get one from the desk over there.

3-4번 문제는 다음 안내를 참조하시오.
여: Appleton Staffing Agency에 오신 여러분 모두를 환영합니다. 저희는 회사의 컴퓨터 데이터베이스에 더 많은 분들을 추가하기 위해 한 달에 한번 단체 면접 시간을 개최합니다. 저희 목표는 여러분의 능력과 관심 분야에 맞는 적합한 일자리를 찾는 데 도움을 드리는 것입니다. 보시다시피, 오늘 이 자리에 많은 분들께서 와 계시므로, 가능한 한 신속히 과정을 진행하고자 합니다. 미리 여러분의 지원서를 작성하셔서 저희가 진행 속도를 낼 수 있도록 도와 주시겠습니까? 저쪽에 있는 데스크에서 한 부 받으실 수 있습니다.

3. 화자는 무슨 종류의 회사에서 근무하는 것 같은가?
(A) 채용 대행사
(B) 컴퓨터 수리점

| 해설 |
담화 초반부에, Appleton Staffing Agency에 온 것을 환영하는 인사와 함께 소속 업체를 We로 지칭하고(~ Appleton Staffing Agency. We hold ~) 있으므로 화자는 일자리를 알선해 주는 업종에 종사하고 있음을 알 수 있으므로 (A)가 정답이다.

4. 화자는 청자들에게 무엇을 하도록 요청하는가?
(A) 미리 양식 작성하기
(B) 종료 시까지 질문 보류하기

| 해설 |
담화 후반부에, 미리 지원서를 작성해(~ by completing your application form ahead of time?) 빨리 진행되도록 도와 달라고 요청하고 있으므로 (A)가 정답이다.

| 어휘 | group interview session 단체 면접 시간 add A to B A를 B에 추가하다 fit ~에 적합하다, 알맞다 interest 관심(사) get through ~을 거치다 process 과정 as ~ as possible 가능한 ~하게 speed things up 일의 속도를 높이다 complete ~을 작성 완료하다 application form 지원서, 신청서 ahead of time 미리, 앞서 repair 수리 in advance 미리, 사전에 hold ~을 중단하다, 보류하다

Questions 5-6 refer to the following announcement.

W: I'd like to make an announcement before ⑤ the next factory shift begins. We've just received the report from our recent safety inspection. We scored high on most categories, but there are still a lot of employees who are not wearing the proper safety gear. I understand that some of this gear is uncomfortable, but it is for your own protection, not to mention that it is required. If you need more items because yours are lost or damaged, please let us know. ⑥ Mr. Mindel will be putting in a supply order tomorrow morning.

5-6번 문제는 다음 안내를 참조하시오.
여: 공장의 다음 교대 근무가 시작되기 전에 공지를 해 드리고자 합니다. 우리는 최근의 안전 점검을 통해 나온 보고서를 막 받았습니다. 우리는 대부분의 항목에서 높은 점수를 받았지만, 여전히 적절한 안전 장비를 착용하지 않는 직원들이 많이 있습니다. 일부 이 장비가 불편하다는 것을 알지만, 이것이 필수라는 점은 언급할 필요도 없을 뿐만 아니라 여러분 자신을 보호하기 위한 것입니다. 분실하셨거나 손상되어 추가 물품이 필요하실 경우, 저희에게 알려 주시기 바랍니다. Mindel 씨께서 내일 아침에 물품 공급 주문을 하실 예정입니다.

5. 청자들은 누구일 것 같은가?
(A) 공장 직원들
(B) 정부 관계자들

| 해설 |
업무와 관련된 정보가 제시되는 초반부에, 공장의 교대 근무가(~ the next factory shift begins) 언급되고 있으므로 (A)가 정답이다.

6. 화자의 말에 따르면, Mindel 씨는 무엇을 할 것인가?
(A) 보고서 준비하기
(B) 주문하기

| 해설 |
'Mr. Mindel'이라는 이름 키워드가 제시되는 후반부에, Mindel 씨가 내일 아침에 물품 공급 주문을 할 것이라고(Mr. Mindel will be putting in a supply order tomorrow morning) 말하고 있으므로 (B)가 정답이다.

| 어휘 | make an announcement 공지하다, 발표하다 shift 교대 근무(조) recent 최근의 safety inspection 안전 점검 score 점수를 기록하다 category 항목, 범주 proper 적절한, 제대로 된 safety gear 안전 장비 uncomfortable 불편한 one's own 자기 자신의 protection 보호 not to mention that ~라는 점은 언급할 필요도 없고 required 필수인 damaged 손상된 let A know A에게 알리다 put in an order 주문하다(= place an order) supply 공급 officials 관계자들, 당국자들

02 방송/뉴스(Broadcast/News Report)

PRACTICE | 기출 연습하기 본책 p.133

정답 **1** (A) **2** (A) **3** (B) **4** (A) **5** (A) **6** (B)

Questions 1-2 refer to the following broadcast.

M: You're listening to *Everyday Tips* on KRRM Radio. I'm your host, Martin Polk. With me in the studio is **1** **Elaine Richmond, a specialist in the field of health**. For the past decade, she has been teaching people how to change their daily habits to help them get in shape and feel great. Thanks for joining us today, Ms. Richmond. I've been told that **2** **you will publish a book about your recommendations and that it will be on shelves starting from next month.** How about telling our listeners a little bit about it?

1-2번 문제는 다음 방송을 참조하시오.
남: 여러분은 지금 KRRM 라디오의 <Everyday Tips>를 청취하고 계십니다. 저는 진행자 Martin Polk입니다. 오늘 저와 함께 스튜디오에 계신 분은 Elaine Richmond 씨로 건강 분야의 전문가입니다. 지난 10년 동안, Richmond 씨는 건강한 몸매를 가꾸고 좋은 기분을 유지하도록 사람들에게 도움을 주기 위해 일일 습관을 바꾸는 방법을 가르쳐 왔습니다. 오늘 자리해 주셔서 감사 드립니다, Richmond 씨. 사람들에게 권장하는 것들에 관한 책을 출간하신다는 사실과 그것이 다음 달부터 서점에 진열될 것이라는 얘기를 들었습니다. 이에 관해 저희 청취자들께 조금 말씀해 주시면 어떨까요?

1. Elaine Richmond 씨는 누구인가?
(A) 건강 전문가
(B) 재정 자문

| 해설 |
이름 키워드 'Elaine Richmond'가 언급되는 초반부에, 'Elaine Richmond, a specialist in the field of health'라며 건강 분야의 전문가라고 알리고 있으므로 (A)가 정답이다.

2. 화자의 말에 따르면, 다음 달에 무슨 일이 있을 것인가?
(A) 책 한 권이 시중에 나올 것이다.
(B) 한 업체가 개업식을 할 것이다.

| 해설 |
담화 후반부에, 책이 출간된다는 사실과 함께 그것이 다음 달에 서점에 진열된다고(~ you will publish a book ~ it will be on shelves starting from next month) 언급하고 있으므로 (A)가 정답이다.

| 어휘 | host (방송 프로그램 등의) 진행자 specialist 전문가(= expert) field 분야 decade 10년 get in shape 건강한 몸매를 가꾸다 be told that ~라는 얘기를 듣다 publish ~을 출간하다 recommendation 추천, 권고 a little bit 조금, 약간 financial 재정의, 재무의 advisor 자문, 고문 on the market 시중에 나와 있는

Questions 3-4 refer to the following broadcast.

W: **3** **Thanks for tuning in to this traffic update.** Roadways are clear in the northern end of town. However, those traveling in the southern end should expect delays. Due to a burst water pipe on Topeka Road, a section of the road has been temporarily closed. Officials are rerouting drivers at this time. If you are driving in this area, **4** **be sure to pay close attention and look for the detour signs.** This will help you to get where you're going easily and safely.

3-4번 문제는 다음 방송을 참조하시오.
여: 저희 교통 정보 채널을 청취해 주셔서 감사합니다. 우리 도시의 북부 끝자락에 위치한 도로들이 한산한 상태입니다. 하지만, 남쪽 끝 방면으로 이동하시는 분들께서는 지체를 예상하셔야 합니다. Topeka Road에 발생된 수도관 파열로 인해, 해당 도로의 한 구간이 일시적으로 폐쇄되어 있습니다. 당국자들은 현재 운전자들에게 경로 변경을 요청하고 있습니다. 이 구역에서 운전하고 계신다면, 반드시 세심한 주의를 기울이시고 '우회 도로' 표지판을 찾아보시기 바랍니다. 이렇게 하면 편리하고 안전하게 원하시는 곳으로 도달하시는 데 도움이 될 것입니다.

3. 방송은 주로 무엇에 관한 것인가?
(A) 현재 날씨
(B) 교통 상황

| 해설 |
담화를 시작하면서 교통 정보 채널을 청취해 주어 감사하다는 인사를 (Thanks for tuning in to this traffic update) 전하고 있으므로 (B)가 정답이다.

4. 화자는 무엇을 권하는가?
(A) 세심하게 표지판 찾아보기
(B) 전화로 사고 상황 알리기

| 해설 |
담화 후반부에, 반드시 세심한 주의를 기울이고 우회 도로 표지판을 찾아보도록 권하고(~ be sure to pay close attention and look for the detour signs) 있으므로 (A)가 정답이다.

| 어휘 | tune in to ~을 청취하다, ~에 채널을 맞추다 traffic 교통, 차량들 travel 이동하다 expect ~을 예상하다 burst 파열된 section 구간, 구역 temporarily 일시적으로 officials 당국자들, 관계자들 reroute (경로 등) ~을 변경하다 be sure to do 반드시 ~하다 pay close attention 세심한 주의를 기울이다 look for ~을 찾다 detour 우회 도로 current 현재의 condition 상태, 조건 carefully 세심하게, 조심하여 accident 사고

Questions 5-6 refer to the following news report.

M: It's five o'clock, time for the local news report. At a press conference this morning, Avery Adams, the head of the city council, **5** **announced plans for the construction of a public library** at 8th Street and Wilkens Drive. The new building will be the third library in the city, and it is expected to be completed within about two and a half years. Several locations were considered for the project. However, planners selected the 8th Street site because **6** **it has the advantage of being near a lot of residential apartment buildings.**

5-6번 문제는 다음 뉴스 보도를 참조하시오.
남: 현재 시각은 5시이며, 지역 뉴스 보도 시간입니다. 오늘 아침에 열린 기자 회견에서, 시 의회 의장이신 Avery Adams 씨께서 8th Street과 Wilkens Drive가 만나는 지점에 공공 도서관을 짓는 계획을 발표하셨습니다. 이 새로운 건물은 우리 도시의 세 번째 도서관이 될 것이며, 약 2년 반 내에 완공될 것으로 예상됩니다. 이 프로젝트에 대해 여러 장소가 고려되었습니다. 하지만, 공사 기획자들은 8th Street에 있는 장소를 선정했는데, 많은 주거용 아파트 건물들과 가깝게 위치해 있다는 장점이 있기 때문입니다.

5. 뉴스 보도는 무엇에 관한 것인가?
(A) 시청 건물에 대한 확장
(B) 새로운 도서관 건설 공사

| 해설 |
담화 초반부에, 공공 도서관을 짓는 계획이 발표되었음을 (~ announced plans for the construction of a public library ~) 알린 후에 그와 관련된 소식을 전하고 있으므로 (B)가 정답이다.

6. 화자는 한 장소의 무슨 장점을 언급하는가?
(A) 대중교통에 대한 접근성
(B) 주거용 건물들과의 근접성

| 해설 |
담화 후반부에, 많은 주거용 아파트 건물들과 가깝게 위치해 있다는 장점을(~ it has the advantage of being near a lot of residential apartment buildings) 언급하고 있으므로 (B)가 정답이다.

| 어휘 | local 지역의, 현지의   press conference 기자 회견   council 의회   announce ~을 발표하다   be expected to do ~할 것으로 예상되다   complete ~을 완료하다   within ~ 이내에   consider ~을 고려하다   planner 기획자   select ~을 선정하다   advantage 장점   near ~ 근처에 있는   residential 주거의   expansion 확장, 확대   access to ~에 대한 접근, 이용   proximity to ~와의 근접(성)   property 건물, 부동산

DAY 20 | 실전문제   본책 p.134

정답	1 (D)	2 (A)	3 (D)	4 (A)	5 (C)	6 (B)
	7 (C)	8 (A)	9 (D)	10 (C)	11 (B)	12 (D)
	13 (A)	14 (C)	15 (D)	16 (C)	17 (B)	18 (A)
	19 (C)	20 (B)	21 (B)			

Questions 1-3 refer to the following broadcast.

M: This is Clark Snyder here on 1200 AM Radio. There's possible good news for people who have trouble sleeping. **1** **Dr. Judy Liang, a professor at San Diego University**, has developed a smartphone app that tracks sleep patterns. She and her team now plan to use the app in some research on sleep habits. **2** **If you'd like to participate in this study as a volunteer, call 555-6199.** We've got Dr. Liang in the studio today, so I'll be asking her more about this project **3** **right after this commercial break**.

1-3번 문제는 다음 방송을 참조하시오.
남: 저는 1200 AM 라디오의 Clark Snyder입니다. 잠 드는 데 어려움을 겪고 계신 분들에게 좋은 소식이 있습니다. San Diego 대학의 교수이신 Judy Liang 박사님께서 수면 패턴을 파악하는 스마트폰 앱을 개발하셨습니다. Liang 박사님께서는 자신의 팀과 함께 현재 수면 습관에 대한 연구를 하시는 데 이 앱을 사용하실 계획입니다. 자원 봉사자로서 이 연구에 참여하기를 원하실 경우, 555-6199번으로 전화하시기 바랍니다. 저희가 오늘 스튜디오에 Liang 박사님을 모셨으므로, 광고 방송 직후에 이 프로젝트에 관해 박사님께 더 많은 것을 여쭤보겠습니다.

| 어휘 | possible 가능한, 있을 수 있는   have trouble -ing ~하는 데 어려움을 겪다   develop ~을 개발하다   track ~을 파악하다, 추적하다   participate in ~에 참여하다   volunteer 자원 봉사자   right after ~ 직후에   commercial break 광고 방송

1. Judy Liang 씨는 누구인가?
(A) 자동차 정비공
(B) 법률 전문가
(C) 라디오 프로그램 진행자
(D) 대학 교수

| 해설 |
이름 키워드 'Judy Liang'이 언급되는 초반부에, 'Dr. Judy Liang, a professor at San Diego University'라고 대학 교수임을 알리고 있으므로 (D)가 정답이다.

| 어휘 | mechanic 정비공   expert 전문가   host (방송 프로그램 등의) 진행자

2. 청자들은 왜 제공된 번호로 전화해야 하는가?
(A) 연구에 자원하기 위해
(B) 제품을 평가하기 위해
(C) 경연대회에 참가하기 위해
(D) 의견을 공유하기 위해

| 해설 |
전화번호가 제시되는 중반부에, 자원 봉사자로서 연구에 참여하기를 원할 경우에 전화하라고(If you'd like to participate in this study as a volunteer, call 555-6499) 권하고 있으므로 (A)가 정답이다.

| 어휘 | volunteer for ~에 자원하다   review ~을 평가하다, 검토하다   share ~을 공유하다

3. 청자들은 곧이어 무엇을 들을 것인가?
(A) 지역 뉴스
(B) 스포츠 소식
(C) 인터뷰
(D) 광고

| 해설 |
담화 맨 마지막에, 광고 방송 직후에(~ right after this commercial break) 더 많은 얘기를 할 것이라고 알리고 있으므로 (D)가 정답이다. 방송 담화에서는 방송 순서와 관련된 정보에 특히 주의해야 한다.

| 어휘 | local 지역의

Questions 4-6 refer to the following broadcast.

W: **4** **Thanks for joining us today on *Business Beat*,** the show that helps you navigate the complex business world. Today, I'm pleased to welcome Lawrence Navarro, a successful entrepreneur and career coach, to the show. **5** **We'll be discussing the best strategies for marketing a small business.** If you're a small business owner, you may be seeking advice related to your particular circumstances. We'd love to hear from you. **6** **Call us at 555-3221 to share any questions you may have.** We'll try to get through as many as possible.

4-6번 문제는 다음 광고를 참조하시오.
여: 여러분께서 복잡한 기업 세계를 탐구하시는 데 도움을 드리는 프로그램인 <Business Beat>에 오늘 함께 해 주셔서 감사드립니다. 오늘, 저는 성공을 거둔 기업가이자 직업 경력 조언자이신 Lawrence Navarro 씨를 프로그램에 모시게 되어 기쁘게 생각합니다. 저희는 소기업을 마케팅하는 데 있어 가장 좋은 전략에 대해 논의할 예정입니다. 소기업 소유주이신 분들께서는, 여러분의 특정한 상황과 관련된 조언을 구하실 수도 있습니다. 저희는 여러분들의 이야기를 꼭 들어 보고자 합니다. 555-3221번으로 전화 주셔서 여러분께서 갖고 계실 수 있는 어떠한 질문이든 공유해 주시기 바랍니다. 가능한 한 많은 질문을 받아 보도록 하겠습니다.

| 어휘 | join ~와 함께 하다   navigate ~을 탐구하다, 여기저기 살펴보다   complex 복잡한   successful 성공적인   entrepreneur 기업가   discuss ~을 이야기하다   strategy 전략   small business 소기업   seek ~을 구하다, 찾다   related to ~와 관련된   particular 특정한   circumstance 상황, 환경   try to do ~하려 하다   get through ~을 거치다

4. 화자는 누구인가?
(A) 라디오 프로그램 진행자
(B) 은행 직원
(C) 발명가
(D) 정치인

| 해설 |
담화를 시작하면서 화자가 'Thanks for joining us today on *Business Beat*, ~'라는 말로 특정 방송 프로그램을 들어 주어 감사 하다고 인사하고 있으므로 (A)가 정답이다.

5. 프로그램에서 무슨 주제가 다뤄질 것인가?
(A) 투자 자금
(B) 고용 관행
(C) 마케팅 전략
(D) 출장

| 해설 |
방송의 주제가 제시되는 중반부에 소기업을 마케팅하는 데 있어 가장 좋은 전략을 이야기할 것이라고(We'll be discussing the best strategies for marketing a small business) 알리고 있으므로 (C)가 정답이다.

| 어휘 | investment 투자(금)   hiring 고용   practice 관행, 관례

6. 청자들은 무엇을 하도록 요청을 받는가?
(A) 기부하기
(B) 질문과 함께 전화하기
(C) 제안에 대해 투표하기
(D) 컨벤션에 등록하기

| 해설 |
담화 후반부에, 전화를 걸어 질문을 공유해 달라고(Call us at 555-3221 to share any questions you may have) 요청하고 있으므로 (B)가 정답이다.

| 어휘 | donation 기부(금)   vote on ~에 대해 투표하다   proposal 제안(서)   sign up for ~에 등록하다, ~을 신청하다

Questions 7-9 refer to the following broadcast.

W: This is the *Channel 3 Daily News Update*. Our main story tonight is **7** the new citywide program that will provide free bus passes for the elderly. From January first, all senior citizens who are Spring Valley residents will be eligible to join the program. **8** The proposal was passed last month by city council members. That caught my attention because … well … these things often have a lot of opposition. On the show tonight is **9** Samantha Graham, who is helping to organize the program. She'll explain the steps for applying for a pass.

7-9번 문제는 다음 방송을 참조하시오.
여: <Channel 3의 Daily News> Update입니다. 오늘 밤 주요 소식은 시 전역에서 시행되는 것으로서 노인들에게 무료 버스 승차권을 제공하는 새로운 프로그램입니다. 1월 1일부터, Spring Valley 지역의 주민인 모든 노인들은 이 프로그램에 가입하실 수 있는 자격을 얻게 될 것입니다. 이 제안은 지난달에 시 의회 의원들에 의해 통과되었습니다. 그 점이 제 주의를 끌게 되었는데… 음… 이러한 일들은 흔히 많은 반대에 부딪히기 때문입니다. 오늘 밤 저희 프로그램에는 이 프로그램을 마련하는 데 도움을 주고 계시는 Samantha Graham 씨께서 자리하실 것입니다. Graham 씨께서 승차권을 신청하는 단계를 설명해 주실 것입니다.

| 어휘 | citywide 시 전역의   free 무료의   the elderly 노인들   resident 주민   be eligible to do ~할 자격이 있다   join ~에 함께 하다, ~에 가입하다   proposal 제안(서)   pass ~을 통과시키다   council 의회   catch one's attention ~의 주의를 끌다   opposition 반대   organize ~을 마련하다, 편성하다   apply for ~을 신청하다, ~에 지원하다

7. 방송은 주로 무엇에 관한 것인가?
(A) 공원 정화 프로젝트

(B) 연례 축제 행사
(C) 교통편 이용 프로그램
(D) 재선거 유세 활동

| 해설 |
담화 초반부에, 화자는 시 전역에서 노인들에게 무료 버스 승차권을 제공하는 새로운 프로그램이 시행될 예정이라고(~ the new citywide program that will provide free bus passes for the elderly) 알리고 있으므로 (C)가 정답이다.

| 어휘 | cleanup 정화, 청소   annual 연례의, 해마다의   transportation 교통(편)   reelection 재선거   campaign 유세, 선거 운동

8. 화자가 "these things often have a lot of opposition"이라고 말할 때 무엇을 의미하는가?
(A) 한 프로젝트가 놀랍게도 인기가 있었다.
(B) 한 가지 결정이 일반 대중을 화나게 했다.
(C) 한 가지 제안이 더욱 깊이 있게 논의될 것이다.
(D) 시작 날짜가 지연될 수 있다.

| 해설 |
담화 중반부에, 화자가 지난달에 이 제안이 시 의회 의원들에 의해 통과되었다는 사실과 함께 그 점이 자신의 주의를 끌었다고(The proposal was passed last month by city council members. That caught my attention ~) 말한 후에 "이런 일이 흔히 많은 반대에 부딪힌다"고 그 이유를 말하는 상황이다. 즉, 큰 반대 없이 통과되었다는 것은 많은 사람들의 지지를 받는다는 의미라는 것을 강조하고 있으므로 (A)가 정답이다.

| 어휘 | surprisingly 놀랍게도   decision 결정   upset ~을 화나게 하다   the public 일반 대중   debate ~을 논의하다   further 더 깊이, 한층 더   delayed 지연된

9. Samantha Graham 씨는 청자들에게 무엇에 관해 이야기할 것인가?
(A) 행사를 위해 모이는 장소
(B) 질문과 함께 연락할 사람
(C) 결과가 예상되는 시점
(D) 신청하는 방법

| 해설 |
담화 후반부에 'Samantha Graham'이라는 이름 키워드가 제시된 뒤로 'She'라는 대명사와 함께 이 사람이 승차권 신청 단계를 설명해 줄 것이라고(Samantha Graham ~ She'll explain the steps for applying for a pass) 알리고 있다. 따라서 (D)가 정답이다.

| 어휘 | expect ~을 예상하다   result 결과(물)

Questions 10-12 refer to the following announcement.

W: Hello, and **10** welcome aboard this express train to Manchester. Our journey will be approximately three hours. Unfortunately, **11** our luggage areas at the ends of the cars are very full. To help with this, please move your small bags to the racks above your heads to make more space for the larger bags. If you need assistance, I'll be coming through shortly. Also, our on-board café is open for business. **12** If you're interested in buying lunch today, you can see the set menu options on the card in your seat pocket.

10-12번 문제는 다음 안내를 참조하시오.
여: 안녕하세요, 이 Manchester행 급행 열차에 탑승하신 것을 환영합니다. 오늘 여정은 약 3시간 정도가 될 것입니다. 안타깝게도, 열차 칸마다 끝 쪽에 위치한 저희 수하물 공간이 아주 가득 찬 상태입니다. 이 문제에 도움이 될 수 있도록, 작은 가방들을 머리 위의 선반으로 옮기셔서 더 큰 가방들을

위한 추가 공간이 생길 수 있게 해 주십시오. 도움이 필요하시면, 제가 곧 가도록 하겠습니다. 또한, 저희 열차 내 카페가 영업을 위해 문을 열었습니다. 오늘 점심 식사를 구입하는 데 관심이 있으실 경우, 여러분의 좌석 주머니에 들어 있는 카드에서 세트 메뉴 옵션을 확인해 보실 수 있습니다.

| 어휘 | aboard 탑승한   express 급행의   approximately 약, 대략   unfortunately 안타깝게도, 아쉽게도   luggage 수하물, 짐   car 열차 칸   help with ~에 도움이 되다   rack 선반   make space 공간을 만들다   assistance 도움   come through 도착하다, 가다   shortly 곧, 머지않아   on-board 열차 내의, 기내의   be interested in ~에 관심이 있다

10. 청자들은 어디에 있는가?
(A) 비행기에
(B) 공항에
(C) 열차에
(D) 기차역에

| 해설 |
담화를 시작하면서 화자가 'welcome aboard this express train'이라며 열차에 탑승한 승객들을 환영하는 인사를 하고 있으므로 (C)가 정답이다.

11. 화자는 무슨 문제점을 언급하는가?
(A) 일부 티켓에 잘못된 정보가 들어 있다.
(B) 수하물 공간에 물건이 너무 많다.
(C) 일부 물품에 제대로 라벨 표기가 되어 있지 않다.
(D) 팀에 직원들이 충분하지 않다.

| 해설 |
담화 초반부에, 열차 칸마다 끝 쪽에 위치한 수하물 공간이 가득 찼다는(~ our luggage areas at the ends of the cars are very full) 사실을 언급하고 있으므로 (B)가 정답이다.

| 어휘 | properly 제대로, 적절히   label ~을 라벨로 표기하다

12. 화자는 왜 청자들에게 카드를 읽도록 권하는가?
(A) 반품 정책에 관해 알기 위해
(B) 안전 절차를 살펴보기 위해
(C) 좌석 배치도를 확인하기 위해
(D) 식사 선택권을 확인해 보기 위해

| 해설 |
카드가 언급되는 후반부에, 점심 식사를 구입하는 데 관심이 있으면 좌석 주머니에 들어 있는 카드에서 세트 메뉴 옵션을 볼 수 있다고(If you're interested in buying lunch today, you can see the set menu options on the card ~) 알리고 있으므로 (D)가 정답이다.

| 어휘 | learn about ~에 관해 알다   return 반품, 반납   review ~을 살펴보다, 검토하다   procedure 절차   seating chart 좌석 배치도

Questions 13-15 refer to the following announcement.

W: May I have your attention, please? **13** I want to thank everyone for completing the most recent assignment by the deadline. I know it was tight, but you managed to do it. **14** The next project for our department will be creating some new body wash products that will appeal to teens. We'll analyze the properties and ingredients of some products already on the market and then use that as inspiration for making our own version. You'll be working in teams of four. **15** Later this afternoon, I'm going to tell you who will be the head of each team.

13-15번 문제는 다음 안내를 참조하시오.
여: 잠시 주목해 주시겠습니까? 가장 최근 배정된 업무를 마감시한까지 완료해 주신 것에 대해 모든 분들에게 감사하고자 합니다. 빡빡한 일정이었다는 것을 알고 있지만, 여러분은 그 일을 해 냈습니다. 우리 부서의 다음 프로젝트는 십대들의 마음을 끌 수 있는 새로운 바디 워시 제품을 만드는 일이 될 것입니다. 우리는 시중에 이미 나와 있는 일부 제품들의 특성과 성분을 분석한 다음, 그 내용을 우리 고유의 제품을 만드는 데 아이디어로 활용할 것입니다. 여러분은 네 명이 팀을 이뤄 일할 것입니다. 오늘 오후 늦게, 누가 각 팀의 팀장이 될 것인지를 여러분에게 말씀드리겠습니다.

| 어휘 | complete ~을 완료하다   recent 최근의   assignment 배정(된 일)   by (기한) ~까지   deadline 마감시한   tight 빡빡한   manage to do ~해 내다   department 부서   create ~을 만들어 내다   appeal to ~의 마음을 끌다   analyze ~을 분석하다   property 특성   ingredient 성분   on the market 시중에 나와 있는   inspiration 영감(을 주는 것), (기발한) 생각

13. 화자는 왜 청자들에게 감사하는가?
(A) 청자들이 제때 일을 완료했다.
(B) 청자들이 회의에 모두 참석했다.
(C) 주말에 근무하러 나왔다.
(D) 몇몇 유용한 제안을 했다.

| 해설 |
화자가 감사 인사를 하는 초반부에, 배정 업무를 마감시한까지 완료해 준 것에 대해 감사하다고(I want to thank everyone for completing the most recent assignment by the deadline) 말하고 있으므로 (A)가 정답이다.

| 어휘 | task 일, 업무   on time 제때   attendance 참석(자의 수)   make a suggestion 제안하다

14. 청자들은 어느 부서에서 근무할 것 같은가?
(A) 발송 접수부
(B) 고객 서비스부
(C) 제품 개발부
(D) IT 지원부

| 해설 |
부서의 업무적 특성이 제시되는 중반부에, 다음 프로젝트가 새로운 바디 워시 제품을 만드는 일이라고(The next project for our department will be creating some new body wash products ~) 말하고 있으므로 (C)가 정답이다.

15. 오늘 늦게 무엇이 공지될 것인가?
(A) 포장 디자인
(B) 매출 수치
(C) 자재 비용
(D) 팀장들

| 해설 |
'later today'라는 시점 키워드와 관련된 표현이 제시되는 후반부에, 오늘 오후 늦게 누가 각 팀의 팀장이 될 것인지를 알려 주겠다고(Later this afternoon, I'm going to tell you who will be the head of each team) 말하고 있으므로 (D)가 정답이다.

| 어휘 | packaging 포장재   figure 수치, 숫자   material 자재, 재료, 물품

Questions 16-18 refer to the following talk.

M: Thank you for attending this workshop on research methods, which we hope will help you as **16** you write various articles for our monthly publication. Now that everyone has arrived, **17** we will begin our planned procedures shortly. **17** First, you'll watch a video on making sure that

DAY 20 115

you have the correct facts in your writing. **17 Next**, there will be a discussion on interpreting results of scientific research. **17 After that**, I'll give a presentation on research methods. **18 There's quite a lot to learn today, but you won't have to do it nonstop.** Ms. McGrath has prepared tea and coffee.

16-18번 문제는 다음 담화를 참조하시오.
남: 여러분이 우리의 월간 출판물을 위해 다양한 기사를 작성할 때 도움이 되기를 바라는 이 조사 방법 워크숍에 참석해 주셔서 감사 드립니다. 이제 모두가 도착하였으므로 계획된 순서를 곧 시작해 보겠습니다. 우선, 여러분의 글에 정확한 사실이 포함되어 있는지를 확실히 해 두는 일에 관한 동영상을 시청할 것입니다. 다음으로, 과학 연구의 결과를 해석하는 것에 관한 토론이 있겠습니다. 그 후에는, 조사 방법에 관해 제가 발표를 할 것입니다. 오늘 배우실 내용이 꽤 많이 있지만, 한번도 쉬지 않고 진행할 필요는 없을 것입니다. McGrath 씨께서 차와 커피를 준비해 주셨습니다.

| **어휘** | method 방법 as ~할 때, ~하면서 various 다양한 article (잡지 등의) 기사 publication 출판(물) now that (이제) ~이므로 planned 계획된 procedure (진행) 순서, 절차 shortly 곧, 머지않아 make sure that ~임을 확실히 해 두다, 반드시 ~하도록 하다 correct 정확한, 옳은 discussion 토론, 논의 interpret ~을 이해하다, 해석하다 give a presentation 발표하다 quite 꽤, 상당히 nonstop 한번도 쉬지 않고 계속

16. 청자들은 누구일 것 같은가?
(A) 교수들
(B) 의료인들
(C) 기자들
(D) 컴퓨터 프로그래머들

| **해설** |
담화 초반부에, 화자가 청자들을 'you'로 지칭해 월간 출판물을 위해 다양한 기사를 작성하는 일을 한다고(~ you write various articles for our monthly publication) 언급하였으므로 (C)가 정답이다.

| **어휘** | personnel 직원들, 인원

17. 담화의 주 목적은 무엇인가?
(A) 회사의 몇몇 정책을 설명하는 것
(B) 일련의 활동들을 소개하는 것
(C) 회사의 성과를 살펴보는 것
(D) 인터뷰 기회를 알리는 것

| **해설** |
담화 초반부에, 계획된 순서를 곧 시작하겠다고(~ we will begin our planned procedures shortly) 말한 후에, First와 Next, 그리고 After that 같은 표현을 차례로 이용해 진행 순서를 설명하고 있으므로 (B)가 정답이다.

| **어휘** | explain ~을 설명하다 policy 정책, 방침 introduce ~을 소개하다 a series of 일련의 review ~을 살펴보다, 검토하다 performance 성과, 실적 opportunity 기회

18. 화자가 "Ms. McGrath has prepared tea and coffee"라고 말할 때 무엇을 의미하는 것 같은가?
(A) 청자들이 휴식 시간을 가질 수 있을 것이다.
(B) 청자들이 일부 물품에 대한 비용을 지불하는 것을 도와야 한다.
(C) 청자들이 동료 직원을 도와줘야 한다.
(D) 청자들이 몇몇 제품 샘플들을 시험 사용해 볼 수 있다.

| **해설** |
담화 후반부에, 알아 두어야 할 것이 꽤 많이 있지만 한번도 쉬지 않고 진행하는 것은 아니라고(There's quite a lot to learn today, but you won't have to do it nonstop) 말한 후에 "McGrath 씨가 차와 커피를 준비해 주었다"고 알리는 상황이다. 이는 다과를 먹으면서 휴식할 수 있는 시간이

있음을 나타내는 것이므로 (A)가 정답이다.

| **어휘** | take a break 휴식을 취하다 give A a hand A를 돕다 coworker 동료 직원 try ~을 한번 사용해 보다

Questions 19-21 refer to the following announcement and display case.

M: Good morning, Mayfair Jewelry customers. **19 We are pleased to offer significant discounts in celebration of moving our store to the Everett Mall.** Sale items are marked with a red tag, and we're offering some of the lowest prices of the season. **20 This event started yesterday and will continue until we close tomorrow at 8 P.M.** You won't want to miss our display case near the front of the store, **21 where the bracelets are half off**. If you'd like to try anything on, our friendly shop clerks are ready to give you assistance or respond to any inquiries you may have.

Section A	**21 Section B**	Section C	Section D
Rings	**Bracelets**	Necklaces	Earrings

19-21번 문제는 다음 안내와 진열대를 참조하시오.
남: 안녕하십니까, Mayfair 보석 고객 여러분. 저희는 Everett Mall로의 매장 이전을 기념하기 위해 상당한 할인을 제공해 드리게 되어 기쁘게 생각합니다. 세일 제품들은 빨간색 가격표로 표기되어 있으며, 시즌 중 가장 저렴한 가격으로 제공해 드리고 있습니다. 이번 행사는 어제 시작되었으며, 저희가 내일 오후 8시에 영업을 종료할 때까지 지속될 것입니다. 저희 매장의 앞쪽 근처에 놓인 진열대를 지나치지 않으시길 바라는데, 이곳에서 팔찌가 절반 가격으로 할인되어 판매됩니다. 어느 제품이든 착용해 보시기를 원하실 경우, 친절한 저희 매장 점원들이 도움을 드리거나 궁금하실 수 있는 어떠한 문의 사항에 대해서도 답변해 드릴 준비가 되어 있습니다.

A 구역	B 구역	C 구역	D 구역
반지	팔찌	목걸이	귀걸이

| **어휘** | offer ~을 제공하다 significant 상당한, 많은 in celebration of ~을 기념해 be marked with ~로 표기되어 있다 tag 가격표, 꼬리표 continue 지속되다 miss ~을 지나치다, 놓치다 display case 진열대 bracelet 팔찌 half off 절반 가격으로 할인된 try A on A를 한번 착용해 보다 clerk 점원 assistance 도움 respond to ~에 답변하다 inquiry 문의 necklace 목걸이

19. 무엇이 기념되고 있는가?
(A) 업체 기념일
(B) 제품 출시
(C) 매장 이전
(D) 수상 후보 지명

| **해설** |
담화 초반부에, Everett Mall로 매장을 이전한 것을 기념하기 위해 할인을 제공한다고(~ offer significant discounts in celebration of moving our store to the Everett Mall) 알리고 있으므로 (C)가 정답이다.

| **어휘** | celebrate ~을 기념하다, 축하하다 anniversary (해마다 돌아오는) 기념일 launch 출시, 공개 relocation (위치) 이전 nomination 후보 지명

20. 행사가 언제 끝날 것인가?
(A) 오늘 저녁
(B) 내일 저녁
(C) 다음 주

(D) 다음 달

| 해설 |
행사 기간 정보가 제시되는 중반부에, 행사가 어제 시작되었다는 말과 함께 내일 오후 8시까지 지속된다고(This event started yesterday and will continue until we close tomorrow at 8 P.M.) 알리고 있으므로 (B)가 정답이다.

21. 시각 자료를 보시오. 어느 구역에서 가격이 절반으로 할인되는가?
(A) A 구역
(B) B 구역
(C) C 구역
(D) D 구역

| 해설 |
담화 후반부에, 팔찌가 절반 가격으로 할인된다고(~ where the bracelets are half off) 알리고 있는데, 시각 자료에서 팔찌가 표기되어 있는 구역이 'Section B'이므로 (B)가 정답이다.

DAY 02 주어 자리와 동사 자리

◆ 출제 포인트 1 주어 자리   본책 p.149

1. acquisition
| 해석 |
그 기업 인수는 3월 23일에 열린 이사회 회의에서 승인되었다.
| 해설 |
문장 맨 앞에 위치한 정관사 The와 동사 was approved 사이에 쓰일 수 있는 단어는 주어 역할을 할 명사이므로 명사인 acquisition이 정답이다.
| 어휘 | acquisition (기업) 인수, 매입, 취득   acquire ~을 인수하다, 매입하다   approve ~을 승인하다   board 이사회

2. Attendance
| 해석 |
AdSense 콘퍼런스의 참석자 수가 지난 수년간보다 더 낮았다.
| 해설 |
동사 was 앞에 있는 at 전치사구의 수식을 받으면서 주어 역할을 할 명사가 그 앞에 위치해야 한다. 따라서 명사인 Attendance가 정답이다.
| 어휘 | attendance 참석, 참석자 수   attend ~에 참석하다   previous 이전의

3. division
| 해석 |
저희 부서는 효과적인 마케팅 캠페인을 만드는 데 주력하고 있습니다.
| 해설 |
문장 맨 앞에 위치한 소유격 대명사 Our와 동사 is 사이에 쓰일 수 있는 단어는 주어 역할을 할 명사이므로 명사인 division이 정답이다.
| 어휘 | divide ~을 나누다   division (단체 내의) 부, 과, 국   primarily 주로   be focused on ~에 주력하다, 초점을 맞추다   create ~을 만들어 내다   effective 효과적인

◆ 출제 포인트 2 동사의 위치   본책 p.149

1. provided
| 해석 |
선임 매니저는 적격인 후보자들의 명단을 제공했다.
| 해설 |
주어 역할을 하는 The senior manager 뒤에는 동사가 위치해야 하므로 동사의 형태인 provided가 정답이다.
| 어휘 | senior 고위의, 수석의, 상급의   provide ~을 제공하다   qualified 적격인, 자격을 갖춘   candidate 후보자

2. forward
| 해석 |
제가 사무실에 없는 동안 제게 오는 전화를 Kensington 씨께 돌려 주시기 바랍니다.
| 해설 |
Please로 시작하는 명령문이므로 동사원형인 forward가 정답이다.
| 어휘 | forward A to B A를 B에게 보내다, 회송하다   while ~하는 동안   be away from ~에서 떠나 있다, 떨어져 있다

3. select
| 해석 |
예약을 하실 때, 목록에서 선호하시는 지점을 먼저 선택해 주십시오.
| 해설 |
부사 first의 수식을 받는 동사로 시작되는 명령문이 되어야 하므로 동사원형인 select가 정답이다.
| 어휘 | make a reservation 예약하다   select ~을 선택하다, 고르다   preferred 선호되는   location 지점, 위치

◆ 출제 포인트 3 동사의 형태   본책 p.150

1. receive
| 해석 |
모든 직원들은 오늘 늦게 새 근무복을 받을 것이다.
| 해설 |
조동사 should 뒤에는 동사원형이 나와야 하므로 receive가 정답이다.
| 어휘 | receive ~을 받다

2. include
| 해석 |
예산은 교통비와 기타 부수적인 경비를 포함하고 있지 않다.
| 해설 |
부정문을 만드는 does not 뒤에는 동사원형이 위치해야 하므로 include가 정답이다.
| 어휘 | budget 예산   include ~을 포함하다   transportation 교통편   incidental 부수적인   expense 경비, 비용

3. announced
| 해석 |
회사는 Rider 씨가 회계부장으로 승진할 것이라고 발표했다.
| 해설 |
has 뒤에는 현재 완료 시제를 만드는 과거 분사가 쓰여야 하므로 announced가 정답이다.
| 어휘 | announce 발표하다, 공지하다   be promoted to ~로 승진하다   Accounting 회계(부)

◆ 출제 포인트 4 주어와 동사의 수 일치   본책 p.150

1. offered
| 해석 |
파산하기 전까지, K-Textiles 사는 전 세계에서 만들어지는 섬유 제품을 제공했다.
| 해설 |
K-Textiles는 하나의 회사 이름으로서 단수 취급하므로 수 일치의 영향을 받지 않는 과거 시제인 offered가 정답이다.
| 어휘 | until (지속) ~할 때까지   go bankrupt 파산하다   offer ~을 제공하다   fabric 섬유   from around the world 전 세계에서 만들어지는, 전 세계에서 나오는

2. are expected
| 해석 |
그 프로젝트에 대한 엔지니어링 작업 계획서가 2월까지 제출될 것으로 예상된다.
| 해설 |
문장의 주어 The engineering plans가 복수 명사이므로 수 일치가 되는 복수 동사의 형태인 are expected가 정답이다.
| 어휘 | plan 계획(서)   be expected to do ~할 것으로 예상되다   submit ~을 제출하다   by (기한) ~까지

3. Tourism
| 해석 |
쿠바의 Havana 지역의 관광 산업은 허리케인이 발생된 이후로 상당히 감소되어 왔다.
| 해설 |
문장의 동사 has decreased가 단수 동사이므로 단수 주어인 Tourism이 정답이다.
| 어휘 | tourism 관광 산업   decrease 감소되다, 줄어들다   considerably 상당히   since ~ 이후로

✦ 출제 포인트 5 수 일치의 예외

1. meet

| 해석 |
모든 참가자들은 오전 8시에 로비에서 모여주실 것을 요청 드립니다.

| 해설 |
주장/요구/제안/의무 동사들 중의 하나인 request 뒤에 위치한 that절의 동사는 동사 원형이어야 하므로 meet이 정답이다.

| 어휘 | request that ~하도록 요청하다   participant 참가자

2. be changed

| 해석 |
SemCo는 진공 필터가 일년에 한번 교체되도록 권장한다.

| 해설 |
주장/요구/제안/의무 동사들 중의 하나인 recommend 뒤에 위치한 that절의 동사는 동사 원형이어야 하므로 be changed가 정답이다.

| 어휘 | recommend that ~하도록 권장하다, 추천하다   vacuum filter 진공 필터   once a year 일 년에 한번

3. critical

| 해석 |
신입 사원들이 다가오는 교육 세미나에 참석하는 것이 매우 중요하다.

| 해설 |
that절의 동사가 원형인 be로 되어 있으므로 의무/필수 형용사 중 하나인 critical이 정답이다.

| 어휘 | It is critical that ~하는 것이 매우 중요하다, 반드시 ~해야 한다   present 참석한, 있는, 존재하는   upcoming 다가오는, 곧 있을   training 교육

✦ 출제 포인트 6 1형식 문장과 출제 유형

1. promptly

| 해석 |
인사팀은 일반적으로 직원들의 문의에 즉각적으로 대응한다.

| 해설 |
1형식 동사 responds와 전치사 to 사이에는 동사를 수식하는 부사가 쓰여야 하므로 promptly가 정답이다.

| 어휘 | HR 인사(부)   respond to ~에 대응하다, 응답하다   prompt 즉각적인, 지체 없는   promptly 즉각적으로   inquiry 문의

2. responsibly

| 해석 |
지역 회사들은 환경을 보호하기 위해 책임감 있게 행동해야 한다.

| 해설 |
목적어를 취하지 않는 1형식 동사 act 뒤에는 동사를 수식할 부사가 위치해야 하므로 responsibly가 정답이다.

| 어휘 | local 지역의, 현지의   responsibility 책임, 책무   responsibly 책임감 있게   protect 보호하다

3. differ

| 해석 |
실제 색상은 온라인에서 제시되는 이미지와 약간 다를 수 있습니다.

| 해설 |
목적어를 취하지 않고, 바로 뒤에 위치한 부사 slightly의 수식을 받아야 하므로 1형식 동사인 differ가 정답이다.

| 어휘 | actual 실제의   differ 다르다   calculate ~을 계산하다   slightly 약간, 조금   presented 제시된, 보여진, 나타난

✦ 출제 포인트 7 2형식 문장과 출제 유형

1. necessary

| 해석 |
안타깝게도, 연설을 오후 2시로 연기해야 할 필요가 있다.

| 해설 |
2형식 동사 is 뒤에는 주격 보어가 쓰여야 하므로 형용사인 necessary가 정답이다.

| 어휘 | unfortunately 안타깝게도, 아쉽게도   it is necessary to do ~해야 할 필요가 있다   necessarily 반드시, 꼭, 필수적으로   delay ~을 연기하다, 미루다   speech 연설

2. frequent

| 해석 |
배송 문제가 더 자주 발생될 경우, 고객 불만이 증가할 것이다.

| 해설 |
become은 주격 보어와 함께 쓰이는 2형식 동사이므로 형용사인 frequent가 정답이다.

| 어휘 | shipping 배송, 선적   frequent 잦은, 빈번한   frequency 빈도, 잦음   complaint 불만   likely ~할 것 같은   increase 증가하다, 오르다

3. confidential

| 해석 |
Staffing Solutions는 수집되는 모든 개인 정보가 기밀로 유지될 것임을 보장한다.

| 해설 |
remain은 주격 보어와 함께 쓰이는 2형식 동사이므로 형용사인 confidential이 정답이다.

| 어휘 | guarantee 보장하다, 보증하다   collected 수집된, 모은   remain + 형용사 ~한 상태로 유지되다, 남아 있다   confidential 기밀의, 비밀의   confidentially 은밀히, 비밀리에

✦ 출제 포인트 8 3형식 문장과 출제 유형

1. assistance

| 해석 |
Helping House는 기본적으로 필요한 것을 충족하는 데 어려움이 있는 가정에 도움을 제공한다.

| 해설 |
provide는 목적어를 필요로 하는 3형식 동사이므로 목적어 역할을 하는 명사 assistance가 정답이다.

| 어휘 | provide ~을 제공하다   assist ~을 돕다   assistance 도움   struggle to do ~하는 데 큰 어려움을 겪다, ~하기 위해 아등바등하다   meet ~을 충족하다   needs 필요로 하는 것

2. carefully

| 해석 |
고려 대상이 될 수 있도록 제출하시기 전에 이력서를 신중하게 검토해 보시기 바랍니다.

| 해설 |
3형식 동사 review와 목적어 your résumé 뒤에는 동사를 수식해 검토하는 방법을 나타낼 부사가 위치해야 알맞으므로 부사인 carefully가 정답이다.

| 어휘 | review ~을 검토하다   résumé 이력서   careful 신중한, 조심스러운   carefully 신중히, 조심스럽게   submit ~을 제출하다   consideration 고려

3. attend

| 해석 |
Cooper Marx는 일정이 겹치는 약속으로 인해 내일 있을 회의에 참석할 수 없다.

| 해설 |
빈칸 뒤에 목적어 역할을 하는 명사구 tomorrow's meeting이 있으므로 목적어를 취할 수 있는 3형식 동사 attend가 정답이다.
| 어휘 | attend ~에 참석하다 arrive 도착하다 due to ~로 인해 conflicting 일정이 겹치는, 충돌하는 appointment 약속, 예약

◆ 출제 포인트 9 | 4형식 문장과 출제 유형 (본책 p.153)

1. us
| 해석 |
환불을 요청하시려면, 해당 제품과 원본 영수증을 저희에게 보내 주시기 바랍니다.
| 해설 |
2개의 목적어를 취하는 4형식 동사 send 바로 뒤에는 받는 사람을 나타낼 간접목적어가 필요하므로 목적격 대명사인 us가 정답이다.
| 어휘 | request ~을 요청하다, 신청하다 refund 환불(금) original 원본의 receipt 영수증

2. assurance
| 해석 |
Xander 박사는 결과를 곧 알 수 있을 것이라고 우리에게 장담했다.
| 해설 |
2개의 목적어를 취하는 4형식 동사 offer 뒤로 받는 사람을 나타내는 간접목적어 us가 있으므로 그 뒤에 쓰일 단어로 직접목적어에 해당되는 명사인 assurance가 정답이다.
| 어휘 | assurance 확언, 장담, 확약 assuredly 틀림 없이, 분명히 result 결과(물) available 이용 가능한

3. granted
| 해석 |
정부는 필요한 추가 농업 자금을 그 주에 제공했다.
| 해설 |
뒤에 간접목적어(the state)와 직접목적어(the necessary additional agricultural funding)가 이어져 있으므로 두 개의 목적어를 취할 수 있는 4형식 동사 granted가 정답이다.
| 어휘 | government 정부 implement ~을 시행하다 state (행정 구역) 주 agricultural 농업의 funding 자금, 기금

◆ 출제 포인트 10 | 5형식 문장과 출제 유형 (본책 p.153)

1. educational
| 해석 |
PlayMore는 자사의 장난감을 교육적인 동시에 재미 있는 것으로 만든다.
| 해설 |
5형식 동사 make와 목적어 its toys 뒤에는 목적격 보어가 쓰여야 하므로 형용사인 educational이 정답이다.
| 어휘 | make A + 형용사 A를 ~한 상태로 만들다, ~하게 만들다 educational 교육적인 educationally 교육적으로 at the same time 동시에

2. secure
| 해석 |
First 은행은 여러분의 계좌를 안전하게 유지하기 위해 비밀 번호를 공유하지 않을 것을 권장합니다.
| 해설 |
5형식 동사 keep과 목적어 your account 뒤에는 목적격 보어가 쓰여야 하므로 형용사인 secure가 정답이다
| 어휘 | recommend (not) -ing ~하도록[하지 않도록] 권하다 share ~을 공유하다 keep A + 형용사 A를 ~한 상태로 유지하다, ~하게 유지하다 account 계좌, 계정 secure 안전한 securely 안전하게

3. find
| 해석 |
한 설문 조사에 따르면 약 75퍼센트의 구독자들이 <Travel Digest>의 지면 배치 방식을 매력적이라고 생각하는 것으로 나타나 있다.
| 해설 |
목적어 the layout of Travel Digest와 목적격 보어로 쓰인 형용사 appealing이 이어져 있어 5형식 문장 구조가 되어야 하므로 5형식 동사인 find가 정답이다
| 어휘 | survey 설문 조사(지) about 약, 대략 subscriber 구독자, 서비스 가입자 find A + 형용사 A를 ~하다고 생각하다 layout 배치, 구획 appealing 매력적인

DAY 02 | 실전문제 (본책 p.154)

정답						
	1 (D)	2 (D)	3 (D)	4 (C)	5 (A)	6 (C)
	7 (A)	8 (A)	9 (B)	10 (C)	11 (C)	12 (B)
	13 (C)	14 (D)	15 (B)	16 (B)	17 (B)	18 (D)
	19 (D)	20 (C)				

1. (D)
| 해석 |
지출 보고서는 회사의 법인 카드로 지불된 모든 지출 비용에 대한 요약 정보를 포함하고 있다.
| 해설 |
빈칸 앞뒤로 명사구와 전치사구만 있으므로(paid 이하는 수식어로 쓰인 분사구) 빈칸이 문장의 동사 자리인데, 단수 주어 The spending report와 수 일치가 되어야 하므로 (D) contains가 정답이다.
| 어휘 | spending 지출, 소비 summary 요약(본) expense (비용) 지출 contain ~을 포함하다

2. (D)
| 해석 |
그녀의 행사 기획 능력을 감안해, 경영진은 Peggy Lane에게 자선 모금 행사 조직에 대한 책임을 맡기기로 결정했다.
| 해설 |
빈칸 앞뒤로 명사와 to부정사구, 전치사구만 있으므로 빈칸이 문장의 동사 자리이다. 따라서 유일하게 동사의 형태인 (D) decided가 정답이다.
| 어휘 | given ~을 감안해, 고려해 skill 능력, 기술 event planning 행사 기획 decide to do ~하기로 결정하다 put A in charge of B A에게 B에 대한 책임을 맡기다 organize ~을 조직하다, 준비하다 benefit 자선 모금 행사 decision 결정

3. (D)
| 해석 |
New Taste 상의 수상 업체에는 Burbank 지역의 Merle's 카페와 Los Angeles 지역의 Choptastic이 포함되어 있었다.
| 해설 |
빈칸 앞에 위치한 have와 어울려야 하므로 have와 함께 현재 완료 시제를 만들 때 사용하는 과거 분사의 형태인 (D) included가 정답이다.
| 어휘 | winner 수상 업체, 수상자 include ~을 포함하다

4. (C)
| 해석 |
Marks 사는 다른 직원들이 각자의 업무에 집중할 수 있도록 직원들에게 전화를 하기 위한 방음 공간을 제공하고 있다.
| 해설 |
조동사 can 뒤에는 동사 원형이 이어져야 하므로 (C) focus가 정답이다.
| 어휘 | provide A with B A에게 B를 제공하다 soundproof 방음의 make a telephone call 전화를 걸다 focus on ~에 집중하다, 초점을 맞추다

5. (A)

| 해석 |
특별 행사 초대장이 Dallas 미술관의 모든 회원들에게 발송되었다.
| 해설 |
빈칸은 주어 역할을 할 명사 자리인데, 동사 have been extended는 복수 주어와 수 일치가 되는 형태이므로 복수 명사인 (A) Invitations가 정답이다.
| 어휘 | extend (초대장 등) ~을 발송하다, 보내다   invitation 초대(장)   invite ~을 초대하다, ~에게 요청하다

6. (C)

| 해석 |
Wonderguard 책장을 조립하시려면, 선반을 프레임에 부착할 수 있도록 제공된 도구를 사용하십시오.
| 해설 |
문장 전체에 동사가 없다. 따라서 빈칸에 문장의 동사가 들어가 명령문 구조가 되어야 하므로 (C) use가 정답이다.
| 어휘 | assemble ~을 조립하다   provide ~을 제공하다   tool 도구, 공구   attach ~을 부착하다, 붙이다   shelf 선반   frame (가구 등의) 프레임, 뼈대   useful 유용한

7. (A)

| 해석 |
고객 서비스부는 주로 불만 사항을 처리하는 곳이기 때문에, 직원들은 칭찬을 받을 때 무척 기뻐한다.
| 해설 |
빈칸 앞에 위치한 동사 receive는 목적어를 필요로 하는 3형식 동사이므로 목적어 역할을 할 명사인 (A) compliments가 정답이다.
| 어휘 | mostly 주로, 대체로   deal with ~을 처리하다, 다루다   complaint 불만   representative 직원   excited 신이 난, 들뜬   compliment n. 칭찬, 찬사 v. ~을 칭찬하다   complimentarily 칭찬하여   complimentary 칭찬하는, 무료의

8. (A)

| 해석 |
고객들께서 자동 갱신을 선택하지 않으실 경우, <World Business and Market Reporting> 지에 대한 구독 서비스는 1년 후에 만료됩니다.
| 해설 |
빈칸 앞뒤로 명사와 전치사구만 있으므로 빈칸은 문장의 동사 자리인데, 문장의 주어 subscriptions가 복수이므로 복수 주어와 수 일치가 되는 형태인 (A) expire가 정답이다.
| 어휘 | unless ~하지 않으면, ~가 아니라면   choose ~을 선택하다   renewal 갱신   subscription to ~에 대한 구독, 서비스 가입   expire 만료되다

9. (B)

| 해석 |
시장은 올해 있을 선거 이전에 청정 에너지 계획을 시작하는 것을 필수로 여기고 있다.
| 해설 |
5형식 동사 consider와 목적어 it 뒤에는 목적격 보어로 쓰일 형용사가 이어져야 하므로 형용사인 (B) necessary가 정답이다.
| 어휘 | mayor 시장   consider it A to do ~하는 것이 A하다고 여기다   launch ~을 시작하다, ~에 착수하다   clean-energy 청정 에너지   initiative (조직적인) 계획, 운동   election 선거   necessity 필수(품), 필요   necessary 필수의, 필요한   necessitate ~을 필요하게 만들다   necessarily 반드시, 꼭, 필수적으로

10. (C)

| 해석 |
공사로 인해 고속도로가 2차로로 줄어들었기 때문에, 차량 운전자들은 조심해서 이동해야 한다.
| 해설 |
빈칸 앞에 위치한 proceed는 1형식 동사이므로 빈칸은 이 동사를 수식할 부사 자리이다. 따라서 부사인 (C) cautiously가 정답이다.
| 어휘 | highway 고속도로   reduce ~을 줄이다, 감소시키다   lane 차선   due to ~로 인해   construction 공사, 건설   proceed 나아가다, 계속 진행하다   caution ~에게 주의를 주다, 경고하다   cautious 조심스러운, 신중한   cautiously 조심스럽게, 신중히

11. (C)

| 해석 |
연구들은 데이터 분석 소프트웨어를 사용하면 소비자 선호도가 더욱 예측 가능하다는 것을 보여준다.
| 해설 |
빈칸 앞에 2형식 동사(are)가 있으므로 빈칸에는 주격 보어로 쓰일 형용사가 필요하다. 따라서 형용사인 (C) predictable이 정답이다.
| 어휘 | study 연구   consumer 소비자   preference 선호   analysis 분석   predict 예측하다   prediction 예측   predictable 예측 가능한

12. (B)

| 해석 |
그 업체의 대표는 합병 조항에 동의하는 것처럼 보였지만, 아직 결정을 내리지는 않았다.
| 해설 |
빈칸 앞에 위치한 동사 appear는 주격 보어와 함께 사용하는 2형식 동사인데, 주어로 쓰인 사람(head of the firm)의 상태나 감정 등을 나타낼 형용사가 쓰여야 알맞으므로 (B) agreeable이 정답이다.
| 어휘 | firm 업체, 회사   appear + 형용사 ~한 것 같다, ~한 것처럼 보이다   terms 조항, 약관   merger 합병   make a decision 결정을 내리다   agreement 동의, 합의(서)   agreeable 동의하는, 찬성하는   agree 동의하다, 찬성하다

13. (C)

| 해석 |
최근 조사에 따르면, 회사 직원의 20% 이상이 적절한 안전 절차를 따르지 않는다고 한다.
| 해설 |
빈칸 앞에 부정문을 만드는 조동사 표현인 do not이 있으므로 빈칸에는 동사 원형이 와야 한다. 따라서 동사 원형 형태인 (C) follow가 정답이다.
| 어휘 | recent 최근의   survey 조사   employee 직원   proper 적절한   safety procedures 안전 절차   follow 따르다

14. (D)

| 해석 |
이제 컴퓨터 시스템이 완벽하게 작동하기 때문에 회사는 그 어느 때보다 더 효율적으로 운영될 수 있다.
| 해설 |
빈칸 앞의 work는 1형식 동사이므로 뒤에는 이를 수식하는 부사가 와야 한다. 따라서 부사 (D) perfectly가 정답이다.
| 어휘 | now that ~이므로   operate 운영되다   efficiently 효율적으로   than ever 어느 때보다   perfect a. 완벽한 v. 완벽하게 하다   perfection 완벽   perfectly 완벽하게

15. (B)

| 해석 |
Ulysses 씨는 더 낮은 이자율을 제공하면 사업자들에게 우리의 대출 상품을 더욱 매력적으로 느끼게 만들 것이라고 생각한다.
| 해설 |
5형식 동사 make와 목적어 our loans 뒤에는 목적격 보어로 쓰일 형용사가 이어져야 하므로 형용사인 (B) attractive가 정답이다. more는 이 목적격 보어를 수식하는 역할을 한다.
| 어휘 | believe (that) ~라고 생각하다   offer ~을 제공하다   interest rates 이자율   make A + 형용사 A를 ~하게 만들다, ~한 상태로 만들다   attractive to ~에게 매력적인   business owner 사업자, 업체 소유주   attract ~을 끌어들이다   attractively 매력적으로   attraction 명소, 인기 장소

16. (B)

| 해석 |
이 양식은 반드시 의사 선생님의 진찰을 받으시기 전에 빠짐없이 정확하게 작성되어야 합니다.

| 해설 |
빈칸 뒤에 이어지는 that절의 동사가 원형인 be filled out으로 되어 있어 빈칸에 의무/필수 형용사가 필요하다는 것을 알 수 있으므로 (B) imperative가 정답이다.

| 어휘 | It is imperative that 반드시 ~해야 하다, ~하는 것이 필수이다   form 양식, 서식   fill out ~을 작성하다   completely 완벽하게, 모두   accurately 정확하게   see a doctor 의사의 진찰을 받다   persuasive 설득력 있는   authoritative 권위적인, 권위 있는   disruptive 지장을 주는, 방해하는

17-20번 문제는 다음 웹페이지를 참조하시오.

www.yogibutter.com

창업 이후로, Yogi Butter는 **17** 인공 성분이나 화학 물질이 들어 있지 않은 화장품을 생산해 왔습니다. 저희 단골 고객들께서는 저희를 업계 최대 규모의 회사들 중 한 곳으로 탈바꿈시켜 주신 분들이며, 이것이 바로 저희가 여러분께 감사드리는 이유입니다. 저희는 일련의 특별 증정품을 통해 감사의 뜻을 전하고자 하며, 이는 다음 달에 시작될 것입니다. 또한, 아직 가입하지 않으신 분들은, 기존의 저희 보상 프로그램에 **18** 반드시 가입 신청하시기 바랍니다. 회원들께서는 10달러를 소비하실 때마다 10포인트를 쌓을 수 있습니다. 이는 **19** 자동으로 여러분의 계정에 추가될 것이며, 향후 어떤 구매 제품에 대해서도 사용될 수 있습니다. **20** 무료 등록을 위해 지금 온라인에서 신청하시거나, 저희 매장 중 한 곳을 방문하십시오.

| 어휘 | inception 창업, 시작   free from ~이 없는   ingredient 성분, 재료   chemical 화학품   transform A into B A를 B로 탈바꿈시키다   industry 업계   gratitude 감사(의 마음)   a series of 일련의   giveaway 증정품   sign up for ~을 신청하다   existing 기존의   reward 보상   accrue ~을 누적시키다   account 계정, 계좌

17. (B)

| 해설 |
chemicals와 함께 전치사 from의 또 다른 목적어로서 화장품에 들어 있지 않은 성분의 특성을 나타낼 형용사가 필요하므로 '인공의'라는 의미인 (B) artificial이 정답이다.

| 어휘 | illegible 판독할 수 없는   fragile 깨지기 쉬운   finite 한정된

18. (D)

| 해설 |
if절에 이어 콤마 뒤에 주절이 위치해야 하는데, 주어 없이 동사만으로 하나의 절을 구성하려면 명령문 구조가 되어야 하므로 명령문을 이끄는 동사원형 (D) make가 정답이다.

19. (D)

| 해설 |
동사 be added를 수식해 These가 지칭하는 일, 즉 앞서 언급된 포인트가 계정에 추가되는 방식을 나타내기에 적절한 부사가 빈칸에 필요하므로 '자동으로'를 의미하는 (D) automatically가 정답이다.

| 어휘 | voluntarily 자발적으로   progressively 계속해서   considerably 상당히, 많이

20. (C)

(A) 다른 화장품 회사들은 흔히 강한 화학품을 사용합니다.
(B) 저희 봄철 제품 라인은 다음 주부터 구매 가능할 것입니다.
(D) 100달러 이상 구매 시 무료 배송의 자격을 갖추게 됩니다.

| 해설 |
빈칸에 앞서 보상 프로그램 및 보상 방식을 설명하는 문장들이 쓰여 있으

므로 해당 프로그램을 이용할 수 있는 방법을 알리는 내용을 담은 (C)가 정답이다.

| 어휘 | harsh 강한, 센   available for purchase 구매 가능한   register 등록하다   for free 무료로   be eligible for ~에 대한 자격이 있다   complimentary 무료의

DAY 03   태/시제/가정법

◆ 출제 포인트 1   능동태와 수동태 구별   본책 p.157

1. forced

| 해석 |
강력한 폭풍우로 인해 밸리 리조트는 어쩔 수 없이 날씨가 맑아질 때까지 수영장 문을 닫아야 했다.

| 해설 |
바로 뒤에 위치한 명사 Valley Resort를 목적어로 취해야 하므로 능동태인 forced가 정답이다.

| 어휘 | force A to do 어쩔 수 없이 A가 ~하게 만들다, A에게 ~하도록 강요하다   clear (날씨가) 맑아지다, 개다

2. displayed

| 해석 |
Erin Carter의 작품들은 전 세계의 박물관과 미술관에 전시되었다.

| 해설 |
주어와 동사가 의미상 '전시되다'라는 수동의 관계이므로 수동태를 구성하는 과거 분사 displayed가 정답이다.

| 어휘 | work (음악, 미술 등) 작품   display 전시하다   museum 박물관

3. followed

| 해석 |
그 연극의 1막에 이어 15분간의 중간 휴식 시간이 있었다.

| 해설 |
be 동사 was와 함께 수동태를 구성하는 타동사의 과거 분사인 followed 가 정답이다. proceed는 자동사이므로 was와 함께 수동태를 구성할 수 없다.

| 어휘 | act (연극의) 막   be followed by A A가 뒤따르다, A가 이어지다   intermission 중간 휴식 시간   proceed 진행되다, 계속되다

◆ 출제 포인트 2   감정 동사의 태 구별   본책 p.157

1. satisfied

| 해석 |
Chen 씨는 우리가 설치한 타이어에 만족하고 있다고 알렸다.

| 해설 |
의미상 that절의 주어 she가 만족을 느끼는 주체가 되어야 하므로 수동태를 구성하는 satisfied가 정답이다.

| 어휘 | report that ~라고 알리다   be satisfied with ~에 만족하다   install ~을 설치하다   satisfy ~을 만족시키다

2. pleased

| 해석 |
저희는 귀하께서 올해의 콘퍼런스에서 연설하는 데 동의해 주셔서 매우 기쁘게 생각합니다.

| 해설 |
의미상 문장의 주어 We가 기쁨을 느끼는 주체가 되어야 하므로 수동태를 구성하는 pleased가 정답이다.

| 어휘 | be pleased that ~해서 기쁘다   agree to do ~하는 데 동의하다,

합의하다   speak 연설하다

3. excited
| 해석 |
저희 Henderson 사는 새로운 지점의 개점을 알려 드리게 되어 흥분됩니다.
| 해설 |
문장의 주어 Henderson Corp.가 흥분을 느끼는 주체가 되어야 하므로 수동태를 구성하는 excited가 정답이다.
| 어휘 | be excited to do ~해서 흥분되다, 들뜨다   announce ~을 알리다, 공지하다   opening 개점, 개장, 개업   branch 지점, 지사

◆ 출제 포인트 3   현재 시제   본책 p.158

1. frequently
| 해석 |
그 부서는 모든 화재 경보기가 제대로 작동되고 있는지 자주 확인한다.
| 해설 |
현재 시제로 쓰인 동사 checks와 의미가 어울려야 하므로 현재 시제 동사와 함께 빈도를 나타낼 때 사용하는 부사 frequently가 정답이다.
| 어휘 | department 부서   frequently 자주, 흔히   check that ~인지 확인하다   fire alarm 화재 경보(기)   work (기계 등이) 작동되다   properly 제대로, 적절히   enormously 엄청나게, 대단히

2. returns
| 해석 |
Moodly 씨가 오늘 오후에 돌아오면 그 제안서를 검토할 것이다.
| 해설 |
주절에 미래 시제 동사(will review)가 쓰일 경우, 시간/조건을 나타내는 when절에는 현재 시제 동사를 사용하므로 returns가 정답이다.
| 어휘 | review ~을 검토하다   proposal 제안(서)   return 돌아 오다, 돌아 가다

3. occasionally
| 해석 |
그 박물관은 종종 회원들을 대상으로 소장품에 대한 개별 관람 시간을 제공한다.
| 해설 |
현재 시제로 쓰인 동사 offers와 의미가 어울려야 하므로 현재 시제 동사와 함께 빈도를 나타낼 때 사용하는 부사 occasionally가 정답이다.
| 어휘 | occasionally 종종, 때때로   offer ~을 제공하다   private 개별의, 개인의, 사적인   viewing 관람, 시청, 둘러보기   collection 소장(품), 수집(품)   previously 이전에, 과거에

◆ 출제 포인트 4   과거 시제/미래 시제   본책 p.158

1. will be recruited
| 해석 |
신입 회계사 한 명이 다음 달에 고용 대행 업체를 통해 채용될 것이다.
| 해설 |
문장 끝에 쓰인 미래 시점 표현 next month와 의미가 어울려야 하므로 미래 시제인 will be recruited가 정답이다.
| 어휘 | accountant 회계사   recruit ~을 채용하다, 모집하다   through ~을 통해   employment agency 고용 대행 업체

2. decided
| 해석 |
지난주에, Pitt 씨는 우리가 온라인 캠페인에 중점을 두어야 한다고 결정을 내렸다.
| 해설 |
Last week이라는 과거 시점 표현과 의미가 어울려야 하므로 과거 시제인 decided가 정답이다.
| 어휘 | decide (that) ~라고 결정을 내리다   focus on ~에 중점을 두다

3. studied
| 해석 |
Oswald 씨는 몇 년 전에 뉴욕 대학교에 다니면서 미국 정치학을 공부했다.
| 해설 |
years ago라는 과거 시점 표현과 의미가 어울려야 하므로 과거 시제인 studied가 정답이다.
| 어휘 | politics 정치학   while ~하면서, ~하는 동안

◆ 출제 포인트 5   완료 시제   본책 p.158

1. has been offering
| 해석 |
Apple Vineyard는 지난 10년 동안 무료 와인 시음 행사를 제공해 왔다.
| 해설 |
과거에서 현재까지의 기간을 나타내는 for the past 10 years와 의미가 어울려야 하므로 현재 완료 진행 시제인 has been offering이 정답이다.
| 어휘 | offer ~을 제공하다   free 무료의   tasting 시음(회)

2. has considered
| 해석 |
그 다리의 붕괴 사건 이후로, Muller 시장은 도로 안전을 중요한 문제로 여겨 왔다.
| 해설 |
과거의 시작점을 의미하는 Since와 어울려 그 이후로 현재까지 지속되어 온 일을 나타내야 알맞으므로 이와 같은 의미로 쓰인 현재 완료 시제 has considered가 정답이다.
| 어휘 | since ~ 이후로   collapse 붕괴, 무너짐   mayor 시장   consider A B A를 B로 여기다   issue 문제, 사안

3. had gathered
| 해석 |
세계적으로 유명한 그 음악가가 도착했을 때쯤, 100명이 넘는 팬들이 이미 모여 있었다.
| 해설 |
By the time이 이끄는 절에 과거 시제(arrived)가 쓰이면 주절에는 이보다 이전을 나타내는 과거 완료 시제가 함께 쓰이므로 had gathered가 정답이다.
| 어휘 | by the time ~할 때쯤, ~할 무렵에   world-famous 세계적으로 유명한   arrive 도착하다   more than ~가 넘는   gather 모이다

◆ 출제 포인트 6   가정법   본책 p.159

1. would have resumed
| 해석 |
시에서 허가증을 더 일찍 승인해 주었다면, 공사가 이미 재개되었을 것이다.
| 해설 |
If절에 과거 완료 시제(had approved)가 쓰이면 주절에는 'would/could have p.p.'의 형태로 된 동사가 짝을 이뤄야 하므로 would have resumed가 정답이다.
| 어휘 | approve ~을 승인하다   permit 허가증   resume 재개되다

2. Should
| 해석 |
일정표가 변경될 경우에, Trip Asia가 귀하께 즉시 연락 드릴 것입니다.

| 해설 |
조건절의 주어와 동사가 수 일치를 이루지 않으므로 If가 생략되면서 Should가 원래 위치에서 앞으로 도치된 구조로 볼 수 있다. 따라서 Should가 정답이다.
| 어휘 | itinerary 일정(표) contact ~에게 연락하다 immediately 즉시

3. could have chosen
| 해석 |
우리가 그 행사를 연기했었다면, 손님들이 참석하지 않기로 결정했을 수도 있다.
| 해설 |
If절에 과거 완료 시제(had delayed)가 쓰이면 주절에는 'would/could have p.p.'의 형태로 된 동사가 짝을 이뤄야 하므로 could have chosen이 정답이다.
| 어휘 | delay ~을 연기하다, 미루다 choose (not) to do ~하기로[하지 않기로] 결정하다 attend 참석하다

DAY 03 | 실전문제
본책 p.160

정답 1 (C) 2 (C) 3 (D) 4 (B) 5 (B) 6 (A)
      7 (C) 8 (A) 9 (B) 10 (D) 11 (B) 12 (C)
      13 (D) 14 (B) 15 (A) 16 (C) 17 (B) 18 (C)
      19 (C) 20 (C)

1. (C)
| 해석 |
Manuel Rodriguez 회장의 등장에 대비해, 금속 탐지기가 건물의 모든 출입구에 설치될 것이다.
| 해설 |
주어인 metal detectors는 설치되어지는 수동의 의미가 적합하므로 install의 수동태인 (C) will be installed가 정답이다.
| 어휘 | in preparation for ~에 대비해 appearance 등장, 나타남, 출현 detector 탐지기, 감지기 install ~을 설치하다

2. (C)
| 해석 |
다음 달부터, 저희는 매주 화요일과 목요일 정오에 유기농 원예에 관한 강좌를 제공할 것입니다.
| 해설 |
Starting next month라는 미래 시점 표현과 의미가 어울려야 하므로 미래 시제인 (C) will offer가 정답이다.
| 어휘 | organic 유기농의 gardening 원예 noon 정오 offer ~을 제공하다

3. (D)
| 해석 |
안내 책자는 Charleston 가에 임대용으로 이용 가능한 아파트들에 대한 관심을 불러일으켰다.
| 해설 |
빈칸은 문장의 동사 자리인데, 빈칸 뒤에 목적어(interest)가 있으므로 능동태가 되어야 하며, 단수 주어(The brochure)와 수 일치가 되어야 하므로 (D) has generated가 정답이다.
| 어휘 | brochure 안내 책자, 소책자 interest in ~에 대한 관심 available 이용 가능한 for rent 임대용의 generate ~을 발생시키다

4. (B)
| 해석 |
음식과 관련된 다수의 질병 발생 사례로 인해, 카페 29는 보건부에 의해 점검을 받는 중이다.
| 해설 |
주어인 Café 29와 타동사 inspect는 '점검을 받다'라는 수동의 관계를 이루므로 수동태인 (B) is being inspected가 정답이다.
| 어휘 | numerous 다수의, 수많은 case 사례, 경우 food-related 음식과 관련된 illness 질병 health department 보건부 inspection 점검, 조사 inspect ~을 점검하다, 조사하다 inspector 점검관, 조사관

5. (B)
| 해석 |
TM-860은 소비자들을 대상으로 첨단 제품이면서 가격도 합리적이라는 두 가지 특성을 모두 지닌 노트북 컴퓨터로 홍보되어 왔다.
| 해설 |
주어 TM-860이 '홍보된다'는 수동의 의미가 적합하므로 promote의 수동태인 (B) has been promoted가 정답이다.
| 어휘 | consumer 소비자 both A and B A와 B 둘 모두 high-tech 첨단의 affordable 가격이 합리적인 promote ~을 홍보하다

6. (A)
| 해석 |
악단이 그 제안에 만족할 경우에, 계약 분쟁은 곧 해결될 것이다.
| 해설 |
'~에 대해 만족하다, 기뻐하다'라는 감정 동사의 수동적인 의미가 적합하므로 수동태를 구성할 수 있는 (A) pleased가 정답이다.
| 어휘 | musical band 악단 be pleased with ~에 만족하다, 기뻐하다 offer 제안 contract 계약(서) dispute 분쟁, 논쟁 resolve ~을 해결하다 pleasant 기분 좋은, 즐거운 please ~을 기쁘게 하다 pleasure 기쁨, 즐거움

7. (C)
| 해석 |
그 공장은 개정된 안전 규약을 작년에 시행했지만, 일부 직원들은 여전히 그것에 익숙하지 않다.
| 해설 |
빈칸 뒤의 목적어를 취할 수 있는 능동태이며, 과거 시점 표현 last year와 어울리는 과거 시제인 (C) implemented가 정답이다.
| 어휘 | revised 개정된, 수정된 protocol 규약, 협약 be familiar with ~에 익숙하다, 친숙하다 implementation 시행, 실행 implement ~을 시행하다, 실행하다

8. (A)
| 해석 |
Darwin 주식회사의 직원들은 하루 중 시간대에 상관 없이 고객이 필요로 하는 것에 즉각 대응한다.
| 해설 |
빈칸 앞뒤에 각각 위치한 be 동사 are, 전치사 to와 함께 어울려 '~에 즉각 대응하다'라는 의미를 구성할 수 있는 형용사 (A) responsive가 정답이다. 자동사 respond는 수동태를 구성할 수 없으므로 과거 분사 (D) responded는 오답이다.
| 어휘 | representative 직원 responsive to ~에 즉각 반응을 보이는 needs 필요로 하는 것 regardless of ~에 상관 없이 responsively 반응하여 responder 반응하는 사람, 응답기 respond 반응하다, 응답하다

9. (B)
| 해석 |
그 기기가 샘플 분석을 시작하기 전에, 일련의 짧은 소리를 낼 것입니다.
| 해설 |
주절에 미래 시제(will make)가 쓰일 경우, Before가 이끄는 시간 부사절에는 현재 시제가 필요한데, 단수 주어 the machine과 수 일치가 되어야 하므로 (B) begins가 정답이다.
| 어휘 | analysis 분석 make a sound 소리를 내다 a series of 일련의

10. (D)
| 해석 |
관광객들은 흔히 값싼 기념품과 독특한 지역 음식을 찾기 위해 전통 시장으로 간다.

| 해설 |
주어 Tourists와 동사 travel 사이에 위치한 빈칸은 동사를 수식할 부사 자리인데, travel이 현재 시제이므로 현재 시제와 함께 빈도를 나타낼 때 사용하는 부사 (D) often이 정답이다.
| 어휘 | travel to ~로 이동하다 traditional 전통적인 find ~을 찾다 souvenir 기념품 unique 독특한, 특별한 local 지역의, 현지의 shortly 곧 rather 좀, 약간, 다소, 오히려 formerly 이전에

11. (B)
| 해석 |
지난 몇 년 동안, 소매업자들은 오직 온라인 구매용으로만 이용 가능한 상품을 더 많이 제공하기 시작했다.
| 해설 |
과거에서 현재까지의 기간을 나타내는 In the last few years와 의미가 어울려야 하므로 현재 완료 시제 (B) have begun이 정답이다.
| 어휘 | retailer 소매업자 offer ~을 제공하다 merchandise 상품 available 이용 가능한 for purchase 구매용의 online 온라인에서

12. (C)
| 해석 |
Keith Rider 씨가 토요일까지 자동차 두 대를 더 판매한다면, 이번 달에 가장 높은 판매량을 기록하게 된다.
| 해설 |
주절에 미래 시제(will have)가 쓰일 경우에 If절에는 현재 시제가 쓰여야 하는데, 단수 주어 Keith Rider와 수 일치가 되어야 하므로 (C) sells가 정답이다.
| 어휘 | by (기한) ~까지 sales 판매(량), 매출, 영업

13. (D)
| 해석 |
Parkston Labs가 부작용이 더 적은 약품을 개발하지 않았다면, 다른 회사가 결국 그랬을 것이다.
| 해설 |
If절에 과거 완료 시제(had not developed)가 쓰이면 주절에는 'would/could have p.p.'의 형태로 된 동사가 짝을 이뤄야 하므로 (D) would have done이 정답이다.
| 어휘 | develop ~을 개발하다 fewer 더 적은 side effect 부작용 another 또 다른 하나의 eventually 결국, 마침내

14. (B)
| 해석 |
너그러운 기부자들로 인해, First Care 병원의 의사들은 전국에서 개최되는 의료 콘퍼런스에 주기적으로 참석하고 있다.
| 해설 |
빈칸 뒤에 위치한 현재 시제 동사 attend와 의미가 어울리는 부사가 필요하므로 현재 시제 동사와 함께 빈도를 나타낼 때 사용하는 (B) regularly가 정답이다.
| 어휘 | generous 너그러운, 후한, 아낌 없는 donor 기부자 attend ~에 참석하다 across ~ 전역에서 recently 최근에 regularly 주기적으로, 정기적으로 quickly 신속히 brightly 밝게, 환하게

15. (A)
| 해석 |
Walker 씨가 오늘 오후에 도착할 무렵이면, 우리는 그녀의 기기에 대해 필요한 수리 작업을 완료할 것이다.
| 해설 |
By the time이 이끄는 절에 현재 시제(arrives)가 쓰이면 주절에는 미래 완료 시제가 짝을 이뤄 사용되므로 (A) will have completed가 정답이다.
| 어휘 | by the time ~할 때쯤에, ~할 무렵에 arrive 도착하다 necessary 필요한, 필수의 repair 수리 device 기기, 장치 complete ~을 완료하다

16. (C)
| 해석 |
합격자만 다음 주 수요일까지 인사부의 연락을 받는다는 점에 유의하십시오.
| 해설 |
next Wednesday라는 미래 시점 표현과 어울리며 주어인 candidates가 '연락을 받다'라는 수동의 의미가 되게 하는 미래 시제 수동태인 (C) will be contacted가 정답이다.
| 어휘 | note that ~라는 점에 유의하다 successful candidate 합격자 Human Resources 인사부

17-20번 문제는 다음 발표를 참조하시오.

Alice Seon의 의사소통 세미나

Alice Seon 씨는 위기 관리 및 미디어 전략에 관해 잘 알려져 있는 **17** 권위자이십니다. Seon 씨는 15년째 Kilowatt Films 사의 대외 홍보 이사로 **18** 재직해 오고 계신 분입니다. 1월에, Seon 씨는 본인이 축적해 온 지식을 다른 이들이 활용하는 데 도움을 주기 위해 고안된 의사소통 세미나를 개최할 예정입니다. 이 행사 중에, Seon 씨는 혁신적인 교육 기술을 활용함으로써 참가자들이 필수 개념들을 이해하는 것을 도울 것입니다. **19** 그중 하나는 실제 상황을 제시함으로써 문제 해결을 연습해 보는 일이 될 것입니다. 결과적으로, 세미나 참석자들은 사무실에서 적용해 볼 수 있는 소중한 실전 경험을 얻게 됩니다. 높은 수요로 인해, 1월 2일과 3일에 열리는 행사 시간에 대한 자리가 이미 만석이 되었습니다. **20** 하지만, 1월 4일과 5일 행사에 대한 일부 자리는 아직 이용 가능합니다.

| 어휘 | well-known 잘 알려진 crisis management 위기 관리 strategy 전략 hold ~을 개최하다 designed to do ~하도록 고안된 help A do A가 ~하는 것을 돕다 accumulate ~을 축적하다 participant 참가자 essential 필수적인 by (방법) ~함으로써 innovative 혁신적인 instructional 교육용의 as a result 결과적으로 attendee 참석자 gain ~을 얻다 valuable 소중한 practice 실전 경험 apply 적용되다 due to ~로 인해 demand 수요, 요구 session (특정 활동을 위한) 시간 fill up 가득 차다 available 이용 가능한

17. (D)
| 해설 |
빈칸은 형용사 well-known의 수식을 받음과 동시에 be 동사 뒤에서 보어 역할을 할 명사 자리이다. 따라서 명사인 (D) authority가 정답이다.
| 어휘 | authorize ~을 인가하다 authority 권위, 권위자

18. (C)
| 해설 |
문장 맨 마지막에 위치한 for 15 years는 과거에서 현재까지의 근무 기간을 나타내며, 현재 완료 시제 동사와 함께 사용하는 전치사구이므로 (C) has served가 정답이다.
| 어휘 | serve as ~로서 근무하다

19. (C)
(A) Kilowatt Films에서 퇴사한 이후로, 그분은 컨설턴트로 일해 오고 있습니다.
(B) Seon 씨는 최근에 Boston 대학으로부터 명예 학위를 수여 받았습니다.
(D) 각 시간은 두 번의 15분 휴식 시간을 포함해 3시간 동안 진행됩니다.
| 해설 |
앞서 언급된 instructional techniques 중의 하나를 One으로 지칭해 그 교육 기술의 특징을 설명하는 내용을 담은 (C)가 정답이다.
| 어휘 | recently 최근에 honorary degree 명예 학위 practice ~을 연습하다 problem-solving 문제 해결 present ~을 제시하다 situation 상황 last 지속되다 break 휴식 시간

20. (C)

| 해설 |
빈칸 앞뒤에 각각 자리가 꽉 찬 날짜와 아직 이용 가능한 날짜들이 언급되어 있는데, 이는 서로 대조적인 상황에 해당된다. 따라서 '하지만'이라는 의미로 대조를 나타내는 (C) However가 정답이다.
| 어휘 | unfortunately 안타깝게도   specifically 특히   consequently 결과적으로

DAY 04   명사

◆ 출제 포인트 1   명사 자리   본책 p.163

1. acquisition
| 해석 |
추가 트럭의 구입으로 인해 Avira 사가 자사의 서비스 구역을 확대할 수 있을 것이다.
| 해설 |
정관사 The와 전치사 of 사이는 명사 자리이므로 acquisition이 정답이다.
| 어휘 | acquisitional 구입과 관련된   acquisition 구입(한 것), 인수, 매입   additional 추가의   allow A to do A가 ~할 수 있게 해 주다   expand ~을 확대하다, 확장하다

2. modification
| 해석 |
영업부는 비용 청구 시스템을 약간 변경했다.
| 해설 |
형용사 slight과 전치사 to 사이는 형용사의 수식을 받은 명사 자리이므로 modification이 정답이다.
| 어휘 | sales department 영업부   make a modification 변경하다, 수정하다   slight 약간의, 조금의   modify ~을 변경하다, 수정하다   billing system 비용 청구 시스템

3. anticipation
| 해석 |
Ted Patel 씨와 가질 인터뷰를 예상해, Flores 씨는 그가 쓴 책을 읽었다.
| 해설 |
전치사 In과 전치사 of 사이는 명사 자리이므로 anticipation이 정답이다.
| 어휘 | in anticipation of ~을 예상해   anticipate ~을 예상하다, 기대하다

◆ 출제 포인트 2   형용사나 동사로 착각하기 쉬운 형태의 명사
                                              본책 p.163

1. potential
| 해석 |
그 엔진은 더 많은 연료를 필요로 하지만, 오염 물질을 감소시킬 수 있는 엄청난 잠재성을 지니고 있다.
| 해설 |
형용사 enormous의 수식을 받음과 동시에 동사 has의 목적어 역할을 할 명사가 필요하므로 '가능성, 잠재성'을 의미하는 명사 potential이 정답이다. potent는 형용사이다.
| 어휘 | require ~을 필요로 하다   enormous 엄청난, 막대한   potential 가능성, 잠재성   potent 강한, 강력한   reduce ~을 감소시키다   pollution 오염 (물질)

2. opening
| 해석 |
그 밴드가 Luggage Zone의 Maplewood 매장 개장식에서 공연할 것이다.

| 해설 |
정관사 the 와 전치사 of 사이는 명사 자리인데, 두 보기 중 의미상 적절한 명사인 opening이 정답이다. openness는 '솔직함'이라는 뜻이다.
| 어휘 | perform 공연하다, 연주하다   opening 개장식, 개관식

3. response
| 해석 |
연례 직원 야유회는 직원들로부터 압도적으로 긍정적인 반응을 이끌어 냈다.
| 해설 |
형용사 positive의 수식을 받을 명사가 필요하므로 명사인 response가 정답이다.
| 어휘 | annual 연례적인, 해마다의   generate ~을 만들어 내다   overwhelmingly 압도적으로   positive 긍정적인   respond 반응하다, 응답하다   response 반응, 응답

◆ 출제 포인트 3   가산 명사   본책 p.164

1. approaches
| 해석 |
OrgTech는 디자인 문제에 대해 혁신적인 접근 방식을 만들어 낼 수 있는 엔지니어들을 필요로 한다.
| 해설 |
명사 approach는 가산 명사인데, 앞에 한정사가 없으므로 복수형인 approaches가 정답이다.
| 어휘 | create ~을 만들어 내다   innovative 혁신적인   approach 접근 방식   issue 문제, 사안

2. discounts
| 해석 |
Motor Electronics는 온라인 설문지를 작성하는 고객들에게 할인을 제공한다.
| 해설 |
명사 discount는 가산 명사이며, 앞에 한정사가 없으므로 복수형인 discounts가 정답이다.
| 어휘 | offer ~을 제공하다   fill out ~을 작성하다   survey 설문 조사(지)

3. employment
| 해석 |
이 프로그램의 목적은 정규직으로 최고의 디자이너를 채용하는 것이다.
| 해설 |
가산 단수 명사 employee는 한정사가 없이 단독으로 쓰이지 않으므로, employment를 정답으로 선택한다.
| 어휘 | aim 목적   recruit 채용하다   full-time 정규직의, 상근직의   employee 직원   employment 채용

◆ 출제 포인트 4   불가산 명사   본책 p.164

1. access
| 해석 |
Harwood 아파트의 주민들은 피트니스 센터와 수영장을 무료로 이용할 수 있다.
| 해설 |
불가산 명사에 해당되는 access는 복수 형태로 사용할 수 없으므로 access가 정답이다.
| 어휘 | resident 주민   get access to ~을 이용하다, ~에 접근하다   free 무료의

2. funding

| 해석 |
Ivanov 박사는 심장병에 관한 자신의 연구에 필요한 자금을 요청하고 있다.

| 해설 |
앞에 한정사가 없으므로 가산 명사의 복수 명사 또는 불가산 명사가 필요한데, fund는 가산 명사에 해당되므로 불가산 명사인 funding이 정답이다.

| 어휘 | ask for ~을 요청하다   funding 자금 (제공)   research 연구, 조사   heart disease 심장병

3. article

| 해석 |
우리 팀은 금융 산업에 관한 짧은 기사를 쓸 기고자를 찾고 있다.

| 해설 |
의미상으로는 둘 다 가능할 것 같지만, 앞에 부정 관사가 있으므로 불가산 명사인 news는 오답이 된다. 따라서 정답은 article이다.

| 어휘 | contributor 기고자, 기고 작가   article 기사   finance 금융

◆ 출제 포인트 5   복합 명사   본책 p.165

1. supplies

| 해석 |
사무용품은 출구 옆에 있는 벽장에서 찾아볼 수 있다.

| 해설 |
벽장에서 찾아볼 수 있는 것은 의미상 '사무용품'이 적합하므로 '용품, 물품' 등을 뜻하는 명사 supplies가 정답이다.

| 어휘 | office supplies 사무용품   closet 벽장   next to ~ 옆에   exit 출구

2. safety

| 해석 |
직장 내 안전에 관한 짧은 발표가 콘퍼런스 센터에서 개최될 것이다.

| 해설 |
의미상 workplace와 함께 복합 명사를 구성할 수 있는 또 다른 명사가 필요하므로 '안전'을 뜻하는 명사 safety가 정답이다.

| 어휘 | presentation 발표(회)   workplace safety 직장 내 안전   safely 안전하게   hold ~을 개최하다, 열다

3. rental

| 해석 |
Roth 씨는 현재 자신의 새 화장품 회사에 필요한 임대 공간을 찾고 있다.

| 해설 |
space와 함께 동사 is seeking의 목적어로 쓰일 복합 명사를 구성할 수 있는 또 다른 명사가 필요한데, space와 함께 '임대 공간'이라는 의미가 되어야 적절하므로 rental이 정답이다.

| 어휘 | currently 현재   seek ~을 찾다, 구하다   rent 집세, 방세   rental 임대, 대여   cosmetics 화장품

◆ 출제 포인트 6   사람 명사 vs. 사물 명사   본책 p.165

1. manufacturer

| 해석 |
품질 보증 서비스와 관련해 어떤 질문이든 있으실 경우에 제조사에 직접 연락하십시오.

| 해설 |
동사 contact의 목적어로서 연락을 받는 대상이 될 수 있는 명사가 필요하므로 '제조사'를 의미하는 manufacturer가 정답이다. manufacture는 '제조'를 의미하므로 contact의 목적어로 맞지 않는다.

| 어휘 | contact ~에 연락하다   manufacturer 제조사   manufacture n. 제조, 생산 v. ~을 제조하다   directly 직접, 곧장   regarding ~와 관련해, ~에 관한

warranty 품질 보증(서)

2. correspondence

| 해석 |
사내에서 주고 받는 모든 서신은 정해진 가이드라인에 따라 형식이 갖춰져야 합니다.

| 해설 |
동사 be formatted의 주어로서 형식이 갖춰질 수 있는 것을 나타낼 사물 명사가 필요하므로 '서신'을 의미하는 correspondence가 정답이다. correspondent는 사람 명사이므로 be formatted의 주어로 적합하지 않다.

| 어휘 | interoffice 사내의, 사무실 간의   correspondent 특파원, 통신원   correspondence 서신   format ~의 형식을 갖추다, 구성하다   according to ~에 따라   established 확정된, 확립된

3. distribution

| 해석 |
이 4주간의 프로그램은 참가자들이 음식 유통과 보건에 대한 지식을 얻을 수 있도록 해줄 것이다.

| 해설 |
knowledge in(~에 대한 지식) 뒤에 연결될 명사는 의미상 '유통'을 의미하는 distribution이 적합하다. distributor(유통회사)는 의미상 부적합할 뿐 아니라 가산 명사이므로 한정사를 붙이거나 복수 형태로 사용해야만 한다.

| 어휘 | allow A to do A로 하여금 ~하는 것을 가능케 하다   participant 참가자   gain 얻다   health care 보건, 의료

DAY 04 | 실전문제   본책 p.166

정답 1 (B) 2 (D) 3 (B) 4 (C) 5 (B) 6 (A)
     7 (D) 8 (C) 9 (D) 10 (B) 11 (C) 12 (B)
    13 (A) 14 (C) 15 (B) 16 (C) 17 (B) 18 (A)
    19 (D) 20 (C)

1. (B)

| 해석 |
현장 감독관이 101번 고속도로의 교통 혼잡에 따른 결과로 회의에 1시간 넘게 늦었다.

| 해설 |
전치사 of와 on 사이에 위치한 빈칸은 of의 목적어 역할을 할 명사 자리이므로 명사인 (B) congestion이 정답이다.

| 어휘 | foreman (공사장 등의) 현장 감독관   over ~가 넘는   as a result of ~의 결과로   congest ~을 혼잡하게 만들다, 정체시키다   congestion (교통) 혼잡   congestive 충혈성의

2. (D)

| 해석 |
Mifflin 씨는 토요일 행사에서 자원 봉사자들의 노고에 대해 진심으로 감사의 마음을 전하고 싶어 한다.

| 해설 |
빈칸은 앞의 소유격 대명사 her와 형용사 sincere의 수식을 받음과 동시에 to부정사로 쓰인 동사 express의 목적어 역할을 할 명사 자리이므로 명사인 (D) appreciation이 정답이다.

| 어휘 | would like to do ~하고자 하다, ~하고 싶다   express ~을 표현하다, 나타내다   sincere 진심의, 진정한   volunteer 자원 봉사자   hard work 노고   appreciative 감사하는   appreciate ~에 대해 감사하다   appreciation 감사(의 마음)

3. (B)
| 해석 |
휴가 신청에 대한 승인을 받으려면, 직원들은 반드시 6개월 넘게 회사에 소속되어 있어야 한다.
| 해설 |
to부정사로 쓰인 동사 receive와 전치사 for 사이에 위치한 빈칸은 receive의 목적어 역할을 할 명사 자리이므로 명사인 (B) approval이 정답이다.
| 어휘 | receive ~을 받다   request 신청(서), 요청(서)   more than ~가 넘는   approve ~을 승인하다   approval 승인

4. (C)
| 해석 |
Burnstone Industries의 영업 사원들은 회사 이메일 주소를 통해 모든 비즈니스 관련 서신을 처리해야 한다.
| 해설 |
의미상 sales와 함께 문장의 주어로 쓰일 복합 명사를 구성할 수 있는 또 다른 명사가 필요하므로 '직원'을 의미하는 명사 (C) representatives가 정답이다.
| 어휘 | sales 영업, 판매(량)   be required to do ~해야 하다   handle ~을 처리하다, 다루다   correspondence 서신   via ~을 통해   represent ~을 대표하다, 대신하다   representative 직원, 대표자, 대리인   representational 대표의, 대의의

5. (B)
| 해석 |
Morrissey 전문학교의 교육 전문가들은 미술과 음악, 그리고 극작품에 중점을 둔 다양한 과목을 가르친다.
| 해설 |
전치사 with의 목적어 자리인 빈칸은 부정 관사 an과 어울리는 단수 명사가 필요하므로 단수 명사인 (B) emphasis가 정답이다.
| 어휘 | educator 교육 전문가   a variety of 다양한   subject 과목   with an emphasis on ~에 중점을 두고, ~에 초점을 맞추고   theater 극작품, 연극   emphasize ~을 강조하다

6. (A)
| 해석 |
마케팅팀은 더 나은 슬로건과 다시 디자인한 포장지가 제품에 대한 인식을 높여 줄 것이라고 생각한다.
| 해설 |
소유격 product's의 수식을 받을 명사가 필요한 자리이므로 명사인 (A) recognition이 정답이다.
| 어휘 | slogan 슬로건, 구호   redesigned 다시 디자인된   packaging 포장(지)   increase ~을 높이다, 증가시키다   recognition 인식, 인정   recognize ~을 인식하다, 인정하다

7. (D)
| 해석 |
비록 경영진에 새로 합류한 사람이기는 하지만, Jinny Moon 씨는 뛰어난 전문성을 통해 인력 부족 문제를 처리했다.
| 해설 |
빈칸은 형용사 great의 수식을 받음과 동시에 전치사 with의 목적어 역할을 할 명사 자리이며, 빈칸 앞에 한정사가 없으므로 불가산 명사인 (D) professionalism이 정답이다. (A) profession과 (B) professional은 가산 명사이다.
| 어휘 | though 비록 ~이기는 하지만   management 경영(진)   handle ~을 처리하다, 다루다   labor 인력, 노동력   shortage 부족   profession 직업   professional a. 직업의, 전문적인 n. 전문가   professionalism 전문성, 직업 의식

8. (C)
| 해석 |
유명 건축가에 의해 디자인된 Quincy Tower는 수십 년 동안 도시 스카이라인의 특징이었다.
| 해설 |
부정 관사 a와 형용사 famous의 수식을 동시에 받는 단수 가산 명사가 필요한 자리이며, 의미상으로도 적절한 (C) architect가 정답이다.
| 어휘 | famous 유명한   feature 특징(적인 것)   skyline 스카이라인, 하늘과 맞닿은 윤곽선   decade 10년   architectural 건축학의, 건축상의   architecture 건축학, 건축 양식   architect 건축가

9. (D)
| 해석 |
Rug Bazaar는 자사의 매장에서 구입한 어느 양탄자나 매트 제품에 대해서든 무료 세척 서비스를 제공한다.
| 해설 |
빈칸은 형용사 complimentary의 수식을 받음과 동시에 동사 offers의 목적어 역할을 할 명사 자리이므로 명사인 (D) cleaning이 정답이다.
| 어휘 | offer ~을 제공하다   complimentary 무료의   rug 양탄자   purchase ~을 구입하다   clean a. 깨끗한 v. ~을 청소하다   cleaning 세척, 세탁

10. (B)
| 해석 |
선호 음식을 표기하지 않는 고객분께는 자동으로 당근과 감자를 곁들인 스테이크가 제공될 것입니다.
| 해설 |
명사 meal이 단독으로 동사 indicate의 목적어가 되기에는 의미상 부적합하므로, meal과 함께 indicate의 목적어로 쓰일 복합 명사를 구성할 수 있는 또 다른 명사가 필요하다. 따라서 명사인 (B) preferences가 정답이다.
| 어휘 | indicate ~을 표기하다, 가리키다   automatically 자동으로   serve (음식 등) ~을 제공하다, 내오다   carrot 당근   preferential 우선권을 주는, 특혜를 주는   preference 선호(하는 것)   prefer ~을 선호하다   preferable 선호되는

11. (C)
| 해석 |
<Normandy Monthly>의 최신 호는 지역 야생 동물 애호가인 Danielle Toole 씨와의 인터뷰 기사를 특집으로 실었다.
| 해설 |
빈칸은 부정 관사 a와 형용사 local의 수식을 동시에 받을 수 있는 단수 명사 자리이며, 콤마 앞의 사람 명사인 Danielle Toole과 동격을 이루는 자리이므로 이에 해당되는 사람 명사 (C) enthusiast가 정답이다.
| 어휘 | latest 최신의   issue (잡지 등의) 호   feature ~을 특집으로 싣다, 특징으로 하다   local 지역의, 현지의   wildlife 야생 동물   enthuse ~을 열광하게 만들다, ~을 열광해서 말하다   enthusiastically 열광적으로   enthusiast 애호가, 열성 팬   enthusiasm 열광, 열정

12. (B)
| 해석 |
비록 그 화학 제품이 공업용으로 구입될 수는 있지만, 아직 소비자용으로 승인을 받지는 못했다.
| 해설 |
가산 명사인 consumer가 한정사 없이 빈칸 앞에 위치해 있으므로 consumer와 함께 전치사 for의 목적어로 쓰일 복합 명사를 구성할 수 있는 또 다른 명사가 빈칸에 필요하다는 것을 알 수 있다. 따라서 명사인 (B) use가 정답이다.
| 어휘 | though 비록 ~이기는 하지만   chemical 화학 제품, 화학 물질   obtain ~을 구하다, 얻다   for industrial purposes 공업용으로, 산업용으로   approve ~을 승인하다   consumer 소비자   usable 사용 가능한   useful 유용한

13. (A)

| 해석 |
보안상의 이유로, 고객들은 온라인상에서 어떠한 개인 정보도 요구 받지 않을 것이다.

| 해설 |
빈칸은 명사 reasons를 수식하는 형용사 혹은 reasons와 함께 복합명사를 구성할 수 있는 또 다른 명사가 올 수 있는 자리인데, 의미상 '보안상의 이유'가 적합하므로 복합명사를 만드는 명사 (A) security가 정답이다.

| 어휘 | reason 이유 customer 고객 personal 개인적인 security 보안 secure a. 안전한 v. 얻다, 확보하다

14. (C)

| 해석 |
대부분의 설문 조사 응답자들은 정보의 부족으로 인해 그 제품에 대해 의견을 갖고 있지 않다고 말했다.

| 해설 |
전치사 due to와 of 사이에 위치한 빈칸은 due to의 목적어로서 of 전치사구의 수식을 받을 명사 자리이므로 명사인 (C) lack이 정답이다.

| 어휘 | survey 설문 조사(지) respondent 응답자 opinion 의견 due to ~로 인해 lack n. 부족 v. ~이 부족하다

15. (B)

| 해석 |
어제 열린 경기의 관중 수는 3만 명이 넘는 수준에 이르렀으며, 이는 Giants의 팬들이 얼마나 충성스러운지를 다시 한번 입증하는 것이었다.

| 해설 |
빈칸은 주어 자리이므로 명사가 필요한데 앞에 한정사가 없으므로 가산 명사의 단수 형태인 (C) Attendant와 (D) Attendee는 모두 오답이 된다. 따라서, 나머지 보기인 불가산 명사 (B) Attendance가 정답이다.

| 어휘 | reach ~에 이르다, 도달하다 more than ~가 넘는 prove ~을 입증하다, 증명하다 loyal 충성스러운 attend ~에 참석하다, 다니다 attendance 참석(자의 수) attendant 종업원, 안내원 attendee 참석자

16. (C)

| 해석 |
단체 여행에 대한 신청서는 반드시 원하시는 날짜보다 적어도 24시간 전에 미리 제출되어야 합니다.

| 해설 |
동사 must be submitted의 주어 역할을 할 명사가 빈칸에 필요한데, 그 앞에 부정 관사가 없으므로 복수 명사인 (C) Requests가 정답이다. request가 가산 명사이므로 단수로 쓰일 경우에는 부정 관사 a가 필요하다.

| 어휘 | submit ~을 제출하다 at least 적어도 in advance 미리, 사전에 desired 원하는, 바라는 request v. ~을 요청하다 n. 요청(서)

17-20번 문제는 다음 기사를 참조하시오.

RIVERDALE (9월 4일) — 한때 300명에 불과한 사람들이 살던 마을인 Riverdale은 거의 2,000명의 주민이 모여 사는 거주지가 되었습니다. 지난 5년 동안, Riverdale 시는 신규 부동산 소유자들을 대상으로 대대적인 세금 17 혜택을 제공해 왔습니다. 이는 18 빠른 거주자 증가의 주요 요소들 중 하나였습니다. 하지만, 새로운 주민들을 대상으로 한 설문 조사에 따르면, Lake Itaska와의 인접성 19 또한 주택 구매자들을 끌어들였습니다. Meredith Mars 시의원은 세입의 전반적인 증가가 도시의 사회 기반 시설을 개발하는 데 도움이 되기를 바라고 있습니다. 20 실제로, 그녀는 새 공원을 짓기 위한 계획이 이미 시작되었다고 밝혔습니다.

| 어휘 | no more than ~에 불과한 resident 주민 offer ~을 제공하다 property 건물, 부동산 factor 요소 increase in ~의 증가 population 인구 (수) according to ~에 따르면 survey 설문 조사(지) proximity to ~와의 인접(성) attract ~을 끌어들이다 councilwoman 시의원 overall 전반적인 revenue 수입, 수익 help A do A가 ~하는 것을 돕다 develop ~을 개발하다 infrastructure 사회 기반 시설

17. (B)

| 해설 |
빈칸 앞에 위치한 large tax만으로는 has been offering의 목적어로서 신규 부동산 소유자들에게 제공하는 대상을 나타내기에 의미가 부족하다. 따라서 '세금 혜택'이라는 복합 명사를 구성할 수 있는 또 다른 명사 (B) benefits가 정답이다.

| 어휘 | benefit v. ~에게 혜택이 되다 n. 혜택, 이득 beneficial 유익한

18. (A)

| 해설 |
'증가'를 의미하는 명사 increase를 수식하기에 적합하며, 문맥상 가정 적절한 것은 '빠른'을 의미하는 (A) rapid이다.

| 어휘 | brief 간단한, 잠시 동안의 narrow 좁은 anxious 불안해하는, 염려하는

19. (D)

| 해설 |
앞서 언급된 세금 혜택 외에 Lake Itaska와의 인접성도 거주자 증가의 또 다른 원인으로 언급되는 문장이 되어야 알맞다. 따라서 '또한'이라는 의미로 추가 정보를 나타낼 때 사용하는 (D) also가 정답이다.

| 어휘 | ahead (공간, 시간상으로) 앞선, 앞에 nearly 거의

20. (C)

(A) 더욱이, 그녀는 인근 마을들이 유사한 혜택을 제공할 것인지를 궁금해 하고 있습니다.
(B) 따라서, 그녀는 많은 사람들이 Riverdale을 떠나 이사할 것으로 생각하고 있습니다.
(D) 그녀는 Riverdale 주민들이 날마다 최소 1시간씩 통근하는 경향이 있다는 점에 주목했습니다.

| 해설 |
앞서 세입 증가가 사회 기반 시설을 개발하는 데 도움이 되기를 바라는 시의원의 희망이 언급되어 있으므로 In fact와 함께 그와 같은 개발 작업의 한 가지 예시를 들고 있는 (C)가 정답이다.

| 어휘 | moreover 더욱이 wonder whether ~인지 (아닌지) 궁금해하다 surrounding 인근의 similar 유사한 therefore 따라서 in fact 실제로, 사실 indicate that ~임을 나타내다 note that ~임에 주목하다 tend to do ~하는 경향이 있다 commute 통근하다 at least 최소한

DAY 05 — 대명사

출제 포인트 1 주격/목적격/재귀대명사 본책 p.169

1. he

| 해석 |
Ewing 씨는 자신이 회의에 참석할 수 없을 것이라고 내게 알려 주었다.

| 해설 |
that절의 동사 will be 앞에 위치한 빈칸은 that절의 주어 자리이므로 주격 대명사인 he가 정답이다.

| 어휘 | inform A that A에게 ~라고 알리다 be able to do ~할 수 있다 attend ~에 참석하다

2. you

| 해석 |
귀하의 주문에 어떤 문제라도 있을 경우에 즉시 귀하께 알려 드릴 것입니다.

| 해설 |
동사 notify의 목적어가 필요하므로 목적격 대명사인 you가 정답이다. 재귀 대명사인 yourself도 목적어 역할은 가능하지만 주어와 목적어가 같을 때 사용한다.
| 어휘 | notify ~에게 알리다   immediately 즉시   order 주문(품)

3. herself
| 해설 |
발표 중에, Lee 씨가 직접 기계를 작동하는 방법을 시연해 줄 것이다.
| 해설 |
빈칸은 부사 자리이므로 이와 같은 역할이 가능한 '직접'이란 의미의 재귀대명사 herself가 정답이다.
| 어휘 | during ~ 중에, ~ 동안   presentation 발표(회)   demonstrate ~을 시연하다   how to do ~하는 법   operate ~을 작동하다, 가동하다   machinery 기계

◆ 출제 포인트 2 소유격/소유대명사   본책 p.169

1. her
| 해설 |
패션 디자이너 Luna Everton 씨가 이번 주에 자신의 가을 컬렉션을 선보일 것이다.
| 해설 |
동사 present의 목적어인 복합 명사 fall collection을 앞에서 수식해야 하므로 명사 앞에 위치하는 소유격 대명사 her가 정답이다.
| 어휘 | present ~을 발표하다, 제시하다   collection (의류 등의) 컬렉션, 신상품들

2. their own
| 해설 |
전 직원은 콘퍼런스에서 자기 자신의 식사 비용을 지불해야 한다.
| 해설 |
전치사 for의 목적어인 명사 meals를 앞에서 수식해야 하므로 명사 앞에 위치할 수 있는 their own이 정답이다.
| 어휘 | be expected to do ~할 것으로 기대되다   pay for ~에 대한 비용을 지불하다   meal 식사

3. his
| 해설 |
Nelson 씨는 자신의 것이 고장 난 상태이기 때문에 도서관에 있는 팩스 기계를 사용하고 있다.
| 해설 |
접속사 because와 동사 is 사이는 because절의 주어 자리인데, 의미상 앞서 언급된 fax machine과 관련해 '그의 팩스 기계=그의 것'을 나타내야 알맞으므로 소유대명사 his가 정답이다.
| 어휘 | broken 고장난, 망가진

◆ 출제 포인트 3 this/that/these/those   본책 p.170

1. those
| 해설 |
뛰어난 직원들은 제때 도착하고 긍정적인 태도를 유지하는 사람들이다.
| 해설 |
뒤에 위치한 who절의 수식을 받아야 하므로 who절과 함께 '~하는 사람들'이라는 의미로 쓰이는 those가 정답이다.
| 어휘 | outstanding 뛰어난, 두드러진   on time 제때   maintain ~을 유지하다   positive 긍정적인   attitude 태도

2. those
| 해설 |
광고 분야에 경험이 많은 사람들이 선호될 것입니다.
| 해설 |
빈칸 뒤 전치사구(with extensive experience)의 수식을 받을 수 있는 대명사는 '사람들'이란 의미의 those이다. 인칭 대명사 them은 형용사구(전치사구, 관계사절 등)의 수식을 받을 수 없다.
| 어휘 | preference 선호   extensive 광범위한, 포괄적인   experience 경험

3. These
| 해설 |
이 문서들은 매우 민감해서 항상 안전하게 보관되어야 한다.
| 해설 |
빈칸 뒤의 복수 명사(documents)와 함께 사용할 수 있는 지시 형용사는 These이다.
| 어휘 | document 서류   highly 매우   sensitive 민감한   secure 안전한   at all times 늘, 항상

◆ 출제 포인트 4 전체 중 일부를 나타내는 대명사   본책 p.170

1. Each
| 해설 |
우리가 보유한 각각의 복사기에는 1년 동안의 무료 서비스와 수리 혜택이 딸려 있다.
| 해설 |
뒤에 위치한 'of + 소유격 + 복수 명사' 구조와 어울릴 수 있는 대명사 Each가 정답이다.
| 어휘 | photocopier 복사기   come with ~가 딸려 있다, ~을 포함하다   complimentary 무료의   repair 수리

2. Some
| 해설 |
취업 박람회에 참가한 일부 회사들이 최근 졸업자들을 고용하고 있다.
| 해설 |
뒤에 위치한 'of + the + 복수 명사' 구조와 어울릴 수 있는 대명사 Some이 정답이다.
| 어휘 | job fair 취업 박람회   hire ~을 고용하다   recent 최근의   graduate 졸업생

3. both
| 해설 |
두 명의 디자이너가 최근에 고용되었지만, 두 사람 모두 불과 몇 주 만에 회사를 그만두었다.
| 해설 |
앞서 언급된 두 명의 디자이너(Two designers)를 가리켜야 하므로 '둘 모두'를 의미하는 both가 정답이다.
| 어휘 | recently 최근에   leave ~을 그만두다, ~에서 떠나다

◆ 출제 포인트 5 부정대명사 -one/-body/-thing   본책 p.171

1. everything
| 해설 |
그 기술자는 컴퓨터 네트워크를 수리하기 위해 자신이 할 수 있는 모든 것을 했다.
| 해설 |
동사 did의 목적어로 쓰여 '~을 했다'라는 의미가 되어야 하므로 '모든 것'을 뜻하는 대명사 everything이 정답이다. anybody는 사람을 가리키므로 did의 목적어로 맞지 않는다.
| 어휘 | technician 기술자, 기사   repair ~을 수리하다

2. Someone

| 해석 |
누군가가 선거 사무소에서 근무하고 있는 자원 봉사자들을 관리해야 한다.
| 해설 |
문장의 주어로서 자원 봉사자들을 관리하는 주체에 해당되는 사람을 나타내야 하므로 Someone이 정답이다.
| 어휘 | supervise ~을 관리하다, 감독하다   volunteer 자원 봉사자

3. Anyone

| 해석 |
올해의 Ride for Children 행사를 계획할 시간이 있는 사람은 누구든지 Marcus Simpson 씨에게 연락해야 한다.
| 해설 |
빈칸 뒤에 위치한 형용사 available의 수식을 받아 '시간이 있는 사람은 누구든'이란 의미를 만드는 Anyone이 정답이다. Another는 대명사로 쓰일 경우 형용사의 수식을 받지 않으므로 오답이다.
| 어휘 | available (사람이) 시간이 나는   contact ~에게 연락하다

◆ 출제 포인트 6   another/other/others/each other

본책 p.171

1. another

| 해석 |
이미 장기 휴가를 다녀왔다면, 경영진에서 또 휴가를 승인할 것 같지 않다.
| 해설 |
to부정사로 쓰인 동사 approve의 목적어가 필요하므로 '또 다른 하나'를 의미하는 대명사 another(= another vacation)가 정답이다. other one은 another one 또는 other ones와 같은 형태가 되어야 알맞다.
| 어휘 | take a vacation 휴가를 떠나다   management 경영(진)   be unlikely to do ~할 것 같지 않다   approve ~을 승인하다

2. Other

| 해석 |
다른 가전 기기 매장들은 Louisville에 있는 Hometastic의 가격과는 경쟁이 되지 않는다.
| 해설 |
뒤에 위치한 복수 명사 appliance stores를 수식해야 하므로 Other가 정답이다. Others는 대명사이므로 명사 앞에 쓸 수 없다.
| 어휘 | appliance store 가전 기기 매장   be unable to do ~할 수 없다   beat the price 더 낮은 가격을 제시하다

3. one another

| 해석 |
그 콘퍼런스는 여러 다른 도시에서 온 관리자들에게 서로 만날 수 있는 기회를 제공한다.
| 해설 |
to부정사로 쓰인 동사 meet의 목적어가 필요하므로 '서로'라는 의미의 대명사 one another가 정답이다. other은 형용사이므로 meet의 목적어가 될 수 없다.
| 어휘 | give A a chance A ~에게 ~할 기회를 제공하다

DAY 05 | 실전문제

본책 p.172

정답 1 (C)   2 (B)   3 (D)   4 (C)   5 (B)   6 (B)
7 (C)   8 (D)   9 (A)   10 (B)   11 (B)   12 (C)
13 (B)   14 (A)   15 (B)   16 (C)   17 (C)   18 (A)
19 (B)   20 (B)

1. (C)

| 해석 |
Porter 씨는 모든 이들이 회사의 기대치를 알고 있도록 하기 위해 자신의 부서에 속한 구성원들을 정기적으로 평가한다.
| 해설 |
빈칸에는 전치사 of의 목적어 역할을 하는 명사 department를 앞에서 수식할 수 있는 말이 필요하므로 소유격 대명사 (C) her가 정답이다.
| 어휘 | regularly 정기적으로   evaluate ~을 평가하다   department 부서   so that (목적) ~할 수 있도록   be aware of ~을 알고 있다, 인식하다   expectation 기대(치)

2. (B)

| 해석 |
혼란을 피하기 위해, Roth 씨는 직원들에게 손님 명단과 관련해서는 오직 자신하고만 의사소통하도록 요청했다.
| 해설 |
빈칸이 전치사 with의 목적어 자리이므로 목적격 대명사인 (B) him이 정답이다.
| 어휘 | avoid ~을 피하다   confusion 혼란   ask that ~하도록 요청하다   communicate 의사소통하다   regarding ~와 관련해

3. (D)

| 해석 |
Hans Richter 씨는 30년도 더 이전에 혼자 Merlin 사를 설립했으며, 업계의 선두 주자가 되었다.
| 해설 |
빈칸은 전치사 by의 목적어 자리인데, 목적어로 쓰일 대명사가 주어 Hans Richter를 가리키므로 행위의 주체와 대상이 동일할 때 사용하는 재귀대명사 (D) himself가 정답이다.
| 어휘 | found ~을 설립하다   corporation 기업, 회사   industry 업계

4. (C)

| 해석 |
Corbet 씨는 면접 직후 그 직책을 충원하도록 선발되었다는 통보를 받았다.
| 해설 |
빈칸은 that절의 동사 was의 주어 자리이므로 주격 대명사인 (C) she가 정답이다.
| 어휘 | notify 통보하다   select 선별하다, 선발하다   fill the position 직책을 충원하다   immediately after ~ 직후에

5. (B)

| 해석 |
새로운 10개의 지점 덕분에 Wellman 사는 고객 기반을 아시아 전역으로 확대할 것이다.
| 해설 |
빈칸은 동사 expand의 목적어 역할을 하는 명사인 customer base를 앞에서 수식할 수 있는 소유격이 필요한 자리이다. 따라서 (B) its가 정답이다.
| 어휘 | thanks to ~ 덕택에   branch 지점   expand 확대하다   throughout ~ 전역에 걸쳐

6. (B)

| 해석 |
Mayfield 씨는 자신의 것을 집에 두고 왔기 때문에 오늘 Becker 씨의 프린터 카드를 빌려야만 했다.
| 해설 |
'left ~ at home(집에 두고 오다)'에서 left의 목적어로 적합한 것은 의미상 'her printer card'이므로 이를 줄여서 표현한 소유 대명사 (B) hers가 정답이다.
| 어휘 | borrow 빌리다   leave 두다, 남겨놓다

7. (C)
| 해석 |
JP Motors는 자사 소매 지점들 중 한 곳에서 차량을 구입한 사람들에게 무료 차량 점검 서비스를 제공한다.
| 해설 |
빈칸 뒤에 이어지는 who절의 수식을 받아야 하므로 who절과 함께 '~하는 사람들'이라는 의미를 나타낼 때 사용하는 (C) those가 정답이다.
| 어휘 | vehicle 차량 inspection 점검, 조사 purchase ~을 구입하다 retailer 소매 판매점 branch 지점, 지사

8. (D)
| 해석 |
환자들의 혈압을 측정하는 일은 Memorial Lake 병원 간호사들의 책무들 중 하나에 불과하다.
| 해설 |
빈칸 앞에 위치한 one of the는 복수 명사와 함께 사용하므로 (D) responsibilities가 정답이다.
| 어휘 | take one's blood pressure ~의 혈압을 측정하다 responsible 책임이 있는 responsibly 책임감 있게 responsibility 책무, 책임

9. (A)
| 해석 |
Best Picture 상 후보로 지명된 각각의 영화들은 상업적인 성공을 거뒀는데, 특히 <Bridge to Nowhere>라는 제목의 작품이 그러했다.
| 해설 |
빈칸 뒤에 위치한 'of the + 복수 명사'의 수식을 받을 수 있는 대명사가 필요한데, 동사 was와 수 일치가 되어야 하므로 'of the + 복수 명사' 구조와 함께 쓰이는 단수 대명사인 (A) Each가 정답이다. (C) Every는 형용사 역할만 가능하다.
| 어휘 | nominated for ~에 대해 후보로 지명된 commercial 상업적인 success 성공 particularly 특히 entitled A A라는 제목의

10. (B)
| 해석 |
뛰어난 유머 감각과 매력적인 성격으로 인해, Linda Kincaid보다 더 잘 고객들을 즐겁게 하는 사람은 아무도 없다.
| 해설 |
빈칸에는 비교급 표현 better than과 어울리는 대명사 주어가 쓰여야 하는데, 비교 대상이 사람이므로(Linda Kincaid) 비교급 표현과 함께 '더 잘 ~하는 사람은 아무도 없다'라는 의미를 나타낼 수 있는 (B) nobody가 정답이다.
| 어휘 | outstanding 뛰어난, 두드러진 sense of humor 유머 감각 charming 매력적인 personality 성격, 개성 entertain ~을 즐겁게 하다

11. (B)
| 해석 |
창가에 앉아 있는 고객들이 초밥 두 접시를 주문했지만, 아직 둘 중 어느 것도 준비되지 않았다.
| 해설 |
접속사 but과 동사 has been prepared 사이에 위치한 빈칸은 but절의 주어 자리이다. 앞서 언급된 두 접시(two plates)를 가리킬 수 있으면서 yet과 어울려 부정의 의미를 나타내야 알맞으므로 '둘 중 어느 것도 ~아니다'를 뜻하는 (B) neither가 정답이다.
| 어휘 | by ~ 옆에, ~가에 plate 접시 prepare ~을 준비하다 yet (부정문에서) 아직

12. (C)
| 해석 |
Volton 주식회사는 Houston에 새로운 제조 공장 하나를, 그리고 San Jose에 또 다른 하나를 짓고 있다.

| 해설 |
앞서 언급된 제조 공장과 같은 종류의 것을 나타낼 대명사가 쓰여야 알맞으므로 '또 다른 하나'라는 의미의 (C) another(= another manufacturing plant)가 정답이다. (A) other 뒤에는 명사가 이어져야 하며 (B) each other는 '서로'를 의미하므로 맞지 않는다. (D) neither는 앞서 언급된 두 가지 모두를 부정할 때 사용한다.
| 어휘 | construct ~을 짓다, 건설하다 manufacturing 제조 plant 공장

13. (B)
| 해석 |
Nunez 씨가 경리 책임자 직책에 선택한 최상위 두 사람 모두 호주에 있는 Dappline 대학교를 다녔다.
| 해설 |
빈칸 뒤에 위치한 'of + 소유격' 구조와 어울리는 대명사가 필요하므로 '~ 둘 모두'라는 의미를 나타낼 때 사용하는 (B) Both가 정답이다.
| 어휘 | top choice 최상의 선택, 최고의 선택 account (회계) 장부, 계정, 계좌 position 직책, 일자리 attend (학교 등) ~에 다니다, ~에 참석하다

14. (A)
| 해석 |
도서 사인회 행사에 참석한 거의 모든 사람들이 그 작가의 최신 소설 한 부씩을 미리 구입했다.
| 해설 |
virtually의 수식을 받아 '거의 모든 사람'이라는 의미를 갖는 대명사가 동사 purchased의 주어로서 적합하므로 (A) everyone이 정답이다.
| 어휘 | virtually 거의, 사실상 book-signing 도서 사인회 copy 한 부 author 작가, 저자 latest 최신의 in advance 미리, 사전에

15. (B)
| 해석 |
여러 정부 기관들이 국가의 공해 위기를 해결하기 위해 서로 협력해야 할 것이다.
| 해설 |
빈칸이 전치사 with의 목적어 자리이므로 동사나 전치사의 목적어로 쓰여 '서로'라는 의미를 갖는 (B) each other가 정답이다. (A) whomever는 주어와 동사가 포함된 절을 이끌어야 하며, (C) other는 명사를 수식할 때 사용한다.
| 어휘 | several 여럿의, 몇몇의 agency 정부 기관 collaborate with ~와 협업하다, 공동 작업하다 in order to do ~하기 위해 solve ~을 해결하다 pollution 공해, 오염 crisis 위기 one's own 자기 자신의

16. (C)
| 해석 |
호텔 뷔페 식당에서 식사를 하는 것이 고객들에게 가장 편리한 선택권이지만, 다른 것들도 이용 가능하다.
| 해설 |
접속사 but과 동사 are 사이에 위치한 빈칸은 but절의 주어 자리이며, 동사 are와 수 일치가 되어야 하므로 복수 대명사인 (C) others(= other options)가 정답이다. (A) other 뒤에는 명사가 이어져야 하며, (D) another는 단수 대명사이다.
| 어휘 | convenient 편리한 option 선택권, 옵션 available 이용 가능한

17-20번 문제는 다음 기사를 참조하시오.

DETROIT (11월 14일) — 세계에서 가장 큰 두 곳의 자동차 제조사인 Hanata Motors(HM)와 Waters-Mark Group(WMG)이 하나의 회사로 17 합병될 예정입니다. 이 합병 계약은 12월 7일부터 효력이 발생됩니다. 18 지난주에 이 계약에 대한 정부의 승인을 받았습니다. 새롭게 19 태어나는 회사는 Detroit를 기반으로 할 것이며, 이곳은 WMG의 본사가 위치해 있는 곳입니다. HM 사는 현재 약 33만 명의 직원을 고용하고 있는 반면, WMG 사의 총 직원은 약 6만 명에 달합니다. HM 사의 Garrett Easton 대표이사와 WMG 사의 Ingrid

Stanton 대표이사는 어떠한 직원 해고도 없을 것이라는 내용으로 공동 성명을 발표했습니다. 20 그들은 또한 해외로 제조 시설을 이전할 계획도 없다고 밝혔습니다.

| 어휘 | manufacturer 제조사 deal 거래 계약, 거래 조건 effective 효력이 있는 as of 시점 ~부터 firm 회사 be based out of ~을 기반으로 하다, 근거지로 하다 headquarters 본사 currently 현재 employ ~을 고용하다 around 약, 대략 while ~인 반면 total 총합이 ~이다 release ~을 발표하다 joint statement 공동 성명 layoff 해고 facility 시설(물) overseas 해외로

17. (C)
| 해설 |
다음 문장에 미래 시제 동사와 함께 합병이 효력을 발휘하는 날짜로 12월 7일이 쓰여 있는데, 이는 이 기사의 작성 날짜인 11월 4일보다 미래 시점이다. 따라서 미래 시제인 (C) will be merging이 정답이다.

| 어휘 | merge into ~로 합병하다[되다]

18. (A)
(B) 차량이 조립되기 전에 반드시 부품들이 수입되어야 합니다.
(C) 두 회사 모두 고급 의류 시장을 전문으로 합니다.
(D) 두 회사는 각각의 업계에서 강력한 경쟁사들입니다.
| 해설 |
앞선 문장에 언급된 합병 계약(The deal)을 the agreement로 바꿔 해당 계약이 정부로부터 승인 받은 시점을 알리는 (A)가 정답이다. 두 회사 모두 자동차 제조사이므로 (C)와 (D)는 오답이다

| 어휘 | approval 승인 agreement 계약(서), 합의(서) receive ~을 받다 import ~을 수입하다 vehicle 차량 assemble ~을 조립하다 specialize in ~을 전문으로 하다 high-end 고급 competitor 경쟁사 respective 각각의 industry 업계

19. (B)
| 해설 |
빈칸 앞에 위치한 The newly와 함께 앞서 언급된 합병에 따라 새롭게 시작되는 회사를 설명할 과거 분사가 필요하다. 따라서 '만들어진'을 뜻하는 (B) created가 정답이다.

| 어휘 | inform ~에게 알리다 review ~을 검토하다 renovate ~을 개조하다

20. (B)
| 해설 |
동사 said의 주체는 앞에 제시된 두 회사의 대표이사들이어야 알맞으므로 이 두 사람을 대신할 수 있는 대명사인 (B) They가 정답이다.

DAY 06 형용사/ 부사

◆ 출제 포인트 1 형용사 자리   본책 p.175

1. substantial
| 해설 |
주요 유명인이 나오는 광고는 상품에 대한 상당한 관심을 발생시킬 수 있다.
| 해설 |
동사 generate의 목적어로 쓰인 명사 interest를 수식해야 하므로 형용사 substantial이 정답이다.

| 어휘 | major 주요한 celebrity 유명인 endorsement (유명인이 나오는) 상품 광고 generate ~을 발생시키다, 만들어 내다 substantial 상당한, 많은 substantially 상당히, 많이 interest in ~에 대한 관심

2. active
| 해석 |
Matthew Kerns 의원은 대학교를 졸업한 이후로 지역 정계에서 활동해 왔다.
| 해설 |
be 동사 뒤에 위치할 보어가 필요하므로 보어 역할이 가능한 형용사 active가 정답이다.

| 어휘 | Representative 하원 의원 active 활동 중인, 활동적인, 적극적인 actively 활동적으로, 활발히, 적극적으로 local 지역의, 현지의 politics 정치

3. professional
| 해석 |
적절한 사무 가구는 방문 고객들에게 여러분의 업무 공간을 더욱 전문적으로 보이게 만들 것이다.
| 해설 |
'make + 목적어 + 목적격 보어'의 구조를 만들어 목적어를 보충 설명하는 목적격 보어로 쓰일 형용사가 필요하므로 professional이 정답이다.

| 어휘 | appropriate 적절한 workspace 업무 공간, 근무 자리 professional 전문적인 professionally 전문적으로

◆ 출제 포인트 2 형태에 주의해야 하는 형용사   본책 p.175

1. timely
| 해석 |
온라인으로 제출된 질문들은 저희 책임자에 의해 제때에 답변될 것입니다.
| 해설 |
부정 관사 a와 명사 manner 사이는 명사를 수식할 형용사 자리이므로 timely가 정답이다.

| 어휘 | submit ~을 제출하다 in a timely manner 때맞춰, 시기 적절하게

2. secure
| 해석 |
Longhorn 호텔에 머무르실 때, 귀중품은 객실 내 금고에 안전하게 보관하시기 바랍니다.
| 해설 |
'keep + 목적어 + 목적격 보어'의 구조를 만들어 목적어를 설명하는 목적격 보어로 쓰일 형용사가 필요하므로 secure가 정답이다.

| 어휘 | valuables 귀중품 secure 안전한 securely 안전하게 safe 금고

3. limited
| 해석 |
저희 Mango Delight 맛은 오직 한정된 기간에만 이용 가능할 것입니다.
| 해설 |
부정 관사 a와 명사 time 사이는 명사를 수식할 형용사 자리이므로 limited가 정답이다. time 앞에 또 다른 명사가 쓰여 복합 명사를 구성하는 것도 가능하지만 limitation은 time과 복합 명사를 구성하기에 의미가 적절치 않다.

| 어휘 | flavor 맛, 풍미 available 이용 가능한 limited 한정된, 제한된 limitation 한정, 제한

◆ 출제 포인트 3 수량 형용사 (1)   본책 p.176

1. many
| 해석 |
음악 분수대는 Dunphy 공원이 지닌 많은 매력적인 특징 중의 하나이다.
| 해설 |
가산 명사의 복수형인 features를 수식해야 하므로 가산 명사와 함께 사용하는 many가 정답이다.

| 어휘 | musical fountain 음악 분수대 attractive 매력적인 feature 특징

2. Each

| 해석 |
그 직책에 대한 각 지원자는 최소 2장의 추천서를 제출해야 한다.

| 해설 |
가산 명사의 단수형인 applicant를 수식해야 하므로 단수 명사와 함께 사용하는 Each가 정답이다.

| 어휘 | applicant 지원자   position 직책, 일자리   submit ~을 제출하다   at least 최소한, 적어도   reference 추천서, 추천인

3. little

| 해석 |
사실, 조기 예약은 항공료에 거의 영향을 미치지 않을지도 모른다.

| 해설 |
불가산 명사 influence를 수식해야 하므로 불가산 명사와 함께 사용하는 little이 정답이다.

| 어휘 | in truth 사실은, 실은   booking 예약   have little influence on ~에 거의 영향을 미치지 않다   airfare 항공료

✦ 출제 포인트 4 수량 형용사 (2)   본책 p.176

1. Any

| 해석 |
화요일 교육 시간에 참석할 수 없는 모든 직원은 여전히 온라인 프로그램을 완수해야만 한다.

| 해설 |
가산 명사의 단수형인 employee를 수식할 수 있는 Any가 정답이다. All은 가산 명사의 복수형과 어울린다.

| 어휘 | unable to do ~할 수 없는   training session 교육 (과정)   complete ~을 완수하다, 완료하다

2. All

| 해석 |
출장 중에 발생되는 모든 지출 비용은 영수증을 제출하자마자 환급될 것이다.

| 해설 |
가산 명사의 복수형인 expenses를 수식할 수 있는 All이 정답이다. Every 뒤에는 가산 명사의 단수형이 와야 한다.

| 어휘 | expense 지출 비용   incur (비용) ~을 발생시키다   reimburse ~을 환급해 주다   submission 제출(되는 것)   receipt 영수증

3. any

| 해석 |
대여 기간 중에 분실되거나 손상되는 어떠한 녹음 장비에 대해서든 귀하께 책임이 있습니다.

| 해설 |
불가산 명사 equipment를 수식해야 하므로 불가산 명사를 수식할 수 있는 any가 정답이다.

| 어휘 | be responsible for ~에 대한 책임이 있다   equipment 장비   lost 분실된   damaged 손상된   rental 대여, 임대

✦ 출제 포인트 5 부사 자리 (1) 동사 수식   본책 p.177

1. cooperatively

| 해석 |
업데이트된 마감 시한을 맞출 수 있도록 각 부서가 협력해 일하는 것이 중요하다.

| 해설 |
자동사 work는 뒤에 부사가 필요하므로 cooperatively가 정답이다.

| 어휘 | It's crucial that ~하는 것이 중요하다   department 부서   cooperatively 협력하여, 협조하여   cooperative 협력하는, 협조적인   meet ~을 충족하다   deadline 마감시한

2. carefully

| 해석 |
애플리케이션을 사용하기 전에 서비스 계약의 약관을 주의 깊게 읽어 보는 사람은 거의 없다.

| 해설 |
괄호 앞이 완전한 문장이므로 동사 read를 수식하는 부사 carefully가 정답이다.

| 어휘 | few 거의 없는   terms (계약서 등의) 약관, 조항   agreement 계약(서), 합의(서)

3. strategically

| 해석 |
몇몇 시리얼 제조사들은 만화 주인공들을 활용해 아이들을 대상으로 전략적으로 광고한다.

| 해설 |
뒤에 위치한 동사 advertise를 수식하는 부사가 필요하므로 strategically가 정답이다.

| 어휘 | manufacturer 제조사   strategic 전략적인   strategically 전략적으로   advertise to ~를 대상으로 광고하다   cartoon 만화

✦ 출제 포인트 6 부사 자리 (2) 동사 이외 수식   본책 p.177

1. consistently

| 해석 |
Nick Brooks의 최신 소설에 대한 평단의 반응은 지속적으로 긍정적이었다.

| 해설 |
뒤에 위치한 형용사 positive를 수식할 부사가 필요하므로 consistently가 정답이다.

| 어휘 | critical 평단의, 비평가들의   reception 반응   latest 최신의   consistent 지속적인   consistently 지속적으로   positive 긍정적인

2. affordably

| 해석 |
Horizon Travels는 가족과 개인 모두를 위해 알맞게 가격이 책정된 휴가 계획을 세울 수 있다.

| 해설 |
뒤에 위치한 분사 priced를 수식해 가격이 매겨진 방식을 나타내야 알맞으므로 부사 affordably가 정답이다.

| 어휘 | plan ~을 계획하다   affordable (가격이) 알맞은, 적절한   affordably 알맞게, 적절하게   priced 가격이 책정된   individual 개인, 사람

3. decidedly

| 해석 |
Premiere Insurance는 소셜 미디어 광고에 대해 확실히 신선한 접근 방식을 활용해 왔다.

| 해설 |
바로 뒤에 위치한 형용사 fresh를 수식해 그 의미를 강조할 부사가 와야 알맞으므로 decidedly가 정답이다

| 어휘 | engage in ~에 관여하다   deciding 결정적인   decidedly 확실히   approach 접근법   advertising 광고

✦ 출제 포인트 7 주의해야 할 부사의 용법 (1)   본책 p.178

1. yet

| 해석 |
아직 휴가를 신청하지 않은 직원들께서는 인사부의 Collins 씨께 연락하셔야 합니다.

| 해설 |
not이 포함된 부정문에 어울리는 부사가 필요하므로 yet이 정답이다.
| 어휘 | request ~을 요청하다   holiday leave 휴가   contact ~에게 연락하다   HR 인사(부)

2. ever
| 해설 |
여러분의 재무 데이터가 그 어느 때보다 안전하다는 것을 확신하셔도 좋습니다.
| 해설 |
than과 함께 '그 어느 때보다 더'라는 의미를 구성하는 ever가 정답이다.
| 어휘 | confident 자신하는, 확신하는   financial 재무의   secure 안전한

3. very
| 해설 |
Toronto Twisters는 다수의 부상 사례에도 불구하고 이번 시즌에 매우 성공적이었다.
| 해설 |
보어로 쓰인 원급 형용사 successful을 수식할 부사가 필요하므로 very가 정답이다.
| 어휘 | despite ~에도 불구하고   numerous 다수의, 수많은   injury 부상

✦ 출제 포인트 8 주의해야 할 부사의 용법 (2)
본책 p.178

1. approximately
| 해설 |
Vancouver로 향하는 항공편은 오전 11시에 출발할 것이며, 약 4시간이 소요될 것입니다.
| 해설 |
시간을 나타내는 숫자 표현 four를 앞에서 수식할 수 있는 부사가 필요하므로 approximately가 정답이다.
| 어휘 | depart 출발하다, 떠나다   approximate (수량 등이) ~에 가깝다, 거의 ~이다   approximately 약, 대략

2. quite
| 해설 |
모든 사람들이 디저트도 주문했기 때문에 회사의 회식에 상당히 돈이 많이 들게 되었다.
| 해설 |
원급 형용사 expensive를 앞에서 수식할 수 있는 부사가 필요하므로 quite이 정답이다. enough는 형용사를 뒤에서 수식한다.
| 어휘 | since ~하기 때문에   quite 상당히, 꽤

3. About
| 해설 |
약 70퍼센트의 직원들이 개인적인 용도로 사무실 자산을 사용한 적이 있었다고 인정했다.
| 해설 |
비율을 나타내는 숫자 표현 70%를 앞에서 수식할 수 있는 부사가 필요하므로 About이 정답이다.
| 어휘 | admit (that) ~임을 인정하다   property 자산   for personal use 개인적인 용도로

✦ 출제 포인트 9 의미에 주의해야 하는 유사 형태 형용사
본책 p.179

1. various
| 해설 |
다양한 관련 부서들의 노력으로 인해 제품 출시 행사가 성공적이었다.
| 해설 |
복수 명사 departments를 수식해 '다양한 부서들'이라는 의미가 되어야 알맞으므로 '다양한'을 뜻하는 various가 정답이다.
| 어휘 | launch 출시(회), 공개   due to ~로 인해   effort 노력   variable 가변적인, 변동이 심한   department 부서   involved 관련된

2. confident
| 해설 |
Zenith 스튜디오는 그 영화의 성공을 매우 확신하고 있어서 이미 속편을 계획하고 있다.
| 해설 |
전치사 in과 어울리면서 속편을 계획하는 이유와 관련되어야 하므로 '~을 확신하는, 자신하는'이라는 의미의 confident가 정답이다.
| 어휘 | so A that B 너무 A해서 B하다   confidential 기밀의, 비밀의   sequel 속편

3. favorable
| 해설 |
Wilcore Industries는 더 유리한 상황 하에서는 합병에 동의했었을 것이다.
| 해설 |
'상황, 사정' 등을 의미하는 circumstances와 의미가 어울리는 형용사가 필요하므로 '유리한, 호의적인'을 뜻하는 favorable이 정답이다.
| 어휘 | would have p.p. ~했을 것이다   merger 합병   favorite 매우 좋아하는   circumstance 상황, 사정

✦ 출제 포인트 10 의미에 주의해야 하는 유사 형태 부사
본책 p.179

1. highly
| 해설 |
Pedanski 의사 선생님은 환자와 의료 전문가들 사이에서 모두 매우 높이 평가되고 있다.
| 해설 |
regarded를 수식해 그 의미를 강조할 부사가 필요하므로 '매우, 대단히' 등을 뜻하는 highly가 정답이다.
| 어휘 | highly regarded 매우 높이 평가 받는   medical professional 의료 전문가

2. shortly
| 해설 |
선거 결과에 관한 뉴스 보도가 곧 방송될 것이다.
| 해설 |
동사 air를 뒤에서 수식할 부사가 필요하므로 대략적인 미래 시점을 나타낼 때 사용하는 shortly가 정답이다.
| 어휘 | election 선거   result 결과(물)   air 방송되다

3. closely
| 해설 |
그 영화의 제작 과정 전반에 걸쳐, 시나리오 작가는 감독과 매우 긴밀하게 작업할 것이다.
| 해설 |
자동사 work를 수식해 일하는 방식을 나타낼 부사가 쓰여야 알맞으므로 closely가 정답이다.
| 어휘 | throughout ~ 동안 내내   production 제작   screenwriter 시나리오 작가   closely 긴밀히, 면밀히

DAY 06 | 실전문제

본책 p.180

정답
1. (B) 2. (C) 3. (A) 4. (A) 5. (D) 6. (B)
7. (C) 8. (A) 9. (C) 10. (C) 11. (C) 12. (C)
13. (A) 14. (C) 15. (A) 16. (B) 17. (D) 18. (B)
19. (C) 20. (C)

1. (B)
| 해석 |
Bali Designs는 몇몇 지연된 직물 배송으로 인해 야기된 제품 생산 문제에 즉각적으로 대응했다.
| 해설 |
자동사 react와 전치사 to 사이에 위치한 빈칸은 동사를 수식할 부사 자리이므로 (B) promptly가 정답이다.
| 어휘 | react to ~에 대응하다   production 생산   issue 문제   caused by ~에 의해 야기된   delayed 지연된   delivery 배송   fabric 직물, 천   prompt a. 즉각적인 v. ~을 촉발시키다   promptly 즉각적으로   promptness 신속(함)

2. (C)
| 해석 |
매장 책임자는 매주 일요일에 상품에 대한 모든 재고 조사를 수행하는 일을 책임지고 있다.
| 해설 |
부정 관사 a와 명사 inventory 사이에 위치한 빈칸은 명사를 수식할 형용사 자리이므로 (C) complete이 정답이다. 또 다른 명사가 쓰여 복합 명사를 구성하는 것도 가능하기는 하지만 (D) completion은 inventory와 복합 명사를 이루기에 의미가 적절치 않으므로 오답이다.
| 어휘 | floor manager 매장 책임자   in charge of ~을 책임지는   conduct ~을 실시하다   inventory 재고 조사, 재고(품)   merchandise 상품   complete a. 모든, 완전한 v. ~을 완료하다   completely 완전히   completion 완료

3. (A)
| 해석 |
제품들이 별도로 배송되어야만 하는 경우에도, Trader Wear는 고객에게 추가 배송비를 지불하도록 요구하지 않습니다.
| 해설 |
수동태 동사 be shipped 뒤에 위치한 빈칸은 동사를 수식할 부사 자리이므로 (A) separately가 정답이다.
| 어휘 | ship ~을 배송하다   require A to do A에게 ~하도록 요구하다   additional 추가의   fee 요금, 수수료   separately 별도로   separation 분리   separate a. 분리된 v. ~을 분리하다

4. (A)
| 해석 |
마지막 순간에 나온 엄청난 박수 갈채를 감안하면, 관객들이 그 공연을 상당히 인상 깊게 생각한 것으로 보인다.
| 해설 |
'find + 목적어 + 목적격 보어'의 구조를 만들어 목적격 보어로 쓰일 형용사가 필요하므로 (A) impressive가 정답이다.
| 어휘 | given ~을 감안하면   round of applause 박수 갈채   audience 관객, 청중   impressive 인상 깊은   impression 인상, 감명   impressively 인상 깊게   impress ~에게 깊은 인상을 남기다

5. (D)
| 해석 |
대표 이사는 직원들에게 회사의 일과 관련된 어떠한 정보도 기밀로 유지되어야 한다고 상기시켰다.
| 해설 |
remain은 보어와 함께 사용하는 동사인데, 이 문장에서는 that절의 주어인 any information의 상태를 보충 설명할 형용사가 필요하므로 (D) confidential이 정답이다.
| 어휘 | remind A that A에게 ~라고 상기시키다   regarding ~와 관련된   affair 일, 문제, 사건   confidence 확신, 자신(감)   confidentially 기밀로   confidentiality 기밀   confidential 기밀의

6. (B)
| 해석 |
저조한 구독률 때문에 <Galiston Times>는 가까운 시일 내에는 작가를 추가로 채용하지 않을 것이다.
| 해설 |
타동사 hire와 목적어 writers 사이에 위치한 빈칸은 목적어를 수식하는 형용사 자리이므로 (B) additional이 정답이다.
| 어휘 | owing to ~ 때문에   subscription rate 구독률   in the near future 가까운 미래에   addition 추가   additional 추가적인   additionally 추가적으로

7. (C)
| 해석 |
Irish Air의 승무원들은 자주 여분의 베개와 담요를 요청 받고 있다.
| 해설 |
수동태 동사를 구성하는 are와 과거 분사 asked 사이에 위치한 빈칸은 부사 자리이므로 (C) frequently가 정답이다.
| 어휘 | flight attendant 승무원   ask A for B A에게 B를 요청하다   extra 여분의   pillow 베개   blanket 담요   frequent 잦은   frequency 잦음, 빈도   frequently 자주

8. (A)
| 해석 |
강좌가 시작되기 전에 전단의 내용을 숙지하는 것이 유익할 것이다.
| 해설 |
빈칸은 2형식 동사 be의 형용사 보어가 필요한 자리이므로 형용사인 (A) beneficial이 정답이다. be 동사와 함께 수동태 구조를 만들 수 있는 (B) benefited는 의미상 적절치 않으므로 오답이다.
| 어휘 | familiarize oneself with ~을 숙지하다   leaflet 전단   beneficial 유익한, 이로운   benefit v. ~을 이롭게 하다 n. 이점   beneficially 유익하게, 이롭게

9. (C)
| 해석 |
저희는 현지 제조업체들로부터 최고 품질의 제품을 저렴한 가격에 제공하게 되어 자랑스럽습니다.
| 해설 |
빈칸은 전치사의 목적어인 명사 prices를 수식하는 형용사의 자리이므로 형용사 (C) affordable이 정답이다.
| 어휘 | be proud to do ~하게 되어 자랑스럽다   local 지역의, 현지의   manufacturer 제조업체   affordable 저렴한

10. (C)
| 해석 |
모든 세대에서 이용 가능한 것은 아니지만, Stonehenge Avenue 556번지에 있는 많은 아파트에는 큰 붙박이장이 있다.
| 해설 |
가산 명사의 복수형인 apartments를 수식할 수 있는 형용사가 필요하므로 (C) many가 정답이다. (A) every와 (B) each는 단수 명사를 수식하며, (D) plenty는 plenty of의 형태로 명사를 수식하므로 오답이다.
| 어휘 | though (비록) ~이기는 하지만   available 이용 가능한   unit (아파트나 상가의) 세대, 점포   built-in 붙박이의

11. (C)
| 해석 |
비록 중요한 마감일이 다가오고 있지만, 야근을 하는 것은 전적으로 자발적이다.

| 해설 |
빈칸은 2형식 동사 is의 형용사 보어가 필요한 자리이므로 (C) voluntary가 정답이다. 빈칸 앞의 부사 strictly는 빈칸에 올 형용사를 수식하고 있다.
| 어휘 | crucial 중요한   approaching 다가오는   work overtime 야근하다, 초과 근무하다   strictly 엄격하게   voluntarily 자발적으로   voluntary 자발적인   volunteer n. 자원봉사자 v. 자원하다

12. (C)
| 해석 |
도시들로부터 멀리 떨어진 곳에 위치해 있기는 하지만, Nelson 호텔은 놀라울 정도로 인기가 많은 목적지이다.
| 해설 |
명사 destination을 수식하는 형용사 popular를 앞에서 수식할 부사가 필요하므로 (C) astonishingly가 정답이다.
| 어휘 | although (비록) ~이기는 하지만   be located far away from ~에서 멀리 떨어진 곳에 위치하다   destination 목적지, 도착지   astonished 크게 놀란   astonishment 크게 놀람   astonishingly 놀라울 정도로   astonish ~을 크게 놀라게 하다

13. (A)
| 해석 |
인쇄 비용은 전단이 컬러가 될 것인지 아니면 흑백이 될 것인지의 여부에 달려 있다.
| 해설 |
be 동사 is 뒤에 위치할 보어로서 전치사 on과 어울려 '~에 달려 있는, ~에 따라 다른'이라는 의미로 쓰이는 (A) dependent가 정답이다. 명사 (B) dependence는 주어와 동격이 아니므로 보어로 쓰일 수 없으며, 또 다른 형용사 (C) dependable은 '믿을 수 있는'이라는 의미이므로 문맥상 어울리지 않는다.
| 어휘 | be dependent on ~에 달려 있다, ~에 따라 다르다   whether A or B A인지 B인지(의 여부)   in color 컬러로   black and white 흑백   dependence 의존, 의지   depend 의존하다, 의지하다

14. (C)
| 해석 |
저희가 주문을 완수하지 못하여 야기된 어떠한 불편함에 대해서도 사과드립니다.
| 해설 |
불가산 명사 inconvenience를 수식할 형용사가 필요하므로 (C) any가 정답이다. (A) both와 (B) these, (D) few는 모두 가산 명사의 복수형을 수식하므로 정답이 될 수 없다.
| 어휘 | apologize for ~에 대해 사과하다   inconvenience 불편함   inability to do ~할 수 없음   order 주문(품)

15. (A)
| 해석 |
Chateau Blanc에 예약을 하는 일은 거의 불가능하지만, 주중에 점심 식사를 할 수 있는 자리가 때때로 생긴다.
| 해설 |
형용사 impossible을 앞에서 수식해 불가능한 정도를 나타낼 부사가 필요하므로 '거의'라는 의미의 부사 (A) nearly가 정답이다. (C) nearby도 부사로 쓰이는데, 거리의 근접함을 나타내므로 의미상 부적합하다.
| 어휘 | make a reservation 예약하다   impossible 불가능한   spot 자리   occasionally 때때로   open 이용 가능한   near a. 가까운 ad. 가까이   nearby ad. 근처에 a. 근처의

16. (B)
| 해석 |
비평가들이 후렴구가 너무 반복적이라고 불만을 표하고 있음에도 불구하고, <Tonight>은 여름의 가장 인기 있는 곡이다.

| 해설 |
빈칸은 2형식 동사 is의 주격 보어가 필요하므로 형용사인 (B) repetitive가 정답이다.
| 어휘 | popular 인기있는   critic 비평가   complain 불평하다, 항의하다   chorus (노래의) 후렴   repetition 반복   repetitive 반복적인   repeat 반복하다

17-20번 문제는 다음 기사를 참조하시오.

Oasis Hotel & Casino에서 주 공연자로 12년간 활동한 끝에, 재즈 음악가 Charlotte Kline 씨가 Oasis의 무대에서 17 아쉬운 마음으로 마지막 공연을 펼칠 것입니다. 18 Kline 씨는 신규 앨범에 필요한 음악을 녹음하는 데 집중할 계획입니다. "그 오랜 시간 동안 이곳에 있을 수 있어 기뻤습니다. 하지만 저는 스튜디오로 돌아갈 수 있게 되어 흥분됩니다."라고 이 음악가는 말했습니다. 보컬리스트로서의 재능뿐만 아니라, Kline 씨는 피아노와 기타 연주에도 재능이 있습니다. Kline 씨의 마지막 공연 후에, 공연 중에 사용된 여러 19 악기들에 대한 경매 행사가 개최될 것입니다. 이 행사는 티켓을 소지하신 분들만 입장 가능하지만, 일반 대중도 Kline 씨께서 기부한 20 다른 물품들에 대한 온라인 경매에 함께 하시기 바랍니다.

| 어휘 | headline 주 공연자로 출연하다   perform 공연하다   get back to ~로 돌아가다   in addition to ~뿐만 아니라   be gifted on ~에 재능이 있다, 타고나다   both A and B A와 B 둘 모두   following ~ 후에   auction 경매   several 여럿의   hold ~을 개최하다   general public 일반 대중   be invited to do ~하도록 요청 받다   join ~에 함께 하다   donate ~을 기부하다

17. (D)
| 해설 |
조동사 will과 동사 사이에 위치한 빈칸은 동사를 수식할 부사 자리이므로 (D) regretfully가 정답이다.
| 어휘 | regret 유감스럽게 생각하다, 후회하다   regretful 유감스러운   regretfully 유감스럽게

18. (B)
(A) Oasis에서 그녀의 전임자는 보컬리스트인 Martin Reardon이었습니다.
(C) Kline 씨는 음악을 향한 열정을 추구하기 위해 대학을 중퇴했습니다.
(D) 그녀의 공연은 일반적으로 오후 7시에 시작되지만, 일요일에는 낮 공연이 있습니다.
| 해설 |
다음 문장에 앞으로의 계획으로 스튜디오로 돌아 가는 일이 언급되어 있는데, 이는 녹음 작업을 위한 것으로 판단할 수 있다. 따라서 Kline 씨의 녹음 계획이 언급된 (B)가 정답이다.
| 어휘 | predecessor 전임자   plan to do ~할 계획이다   focus on ~에 초점을 맞추다   drop out of ~에서 중퇴하다   pursue ~을 추구하다   passion 열정   typically 일반적으로   though ~이기는 하지만   matinee 낮 공연

19. (C)
| 해설 |
공연 중에 사용된 물품으로서 경매에 내놓을 수 있는 것을 나타낼 명사가 필요하므로 문맥상 '악기'를 뜻하는 (C) instruments가 정답이다.
| 어휘 | intention 의도   sculpture 조각품   appliance (가전) 기기

20. (C)
| 해설 |
복수 명사 items를 수식할 형용사가 필요하므로 복수 명사 앞에 사용 가능하며, 의미상으로도 적합한 (C) other가 정답이다.
| 어휘 | another 또 다른 하나의   each other 서로   further 추가의, 한층 더한

DAY 07 to부정사/동명사

◆ 출제 포인트 1 to부정사와 동명사의 특징 본책 p.183

1. to record
| 해석 |
Craft 씨는 인턴 직원에게 판매 프레젠테이션을 녹화할 것을 요청했다.
| 해설 |
문장에 동사 asked가 있으므로 준동사가 와야 한다. 따라서 to record가 정답이다.
| 어휘 | sales 매출, 영업, 판매(량) presentation 발표(회)

2. payment
| 해석 |
E-Auction은 일단 입찰이 종료되는 대로 지불 금액을 받을 의무가 있다.
| 해설 |
to부정사로 쓰인 타동사 collect의 목적어가 필요하므로 명사인 payment가 정답이다.
| 어휘 | be obligated to do ~할 의무가 있다 collect (돈 등) ~을 받다 payment 지불(액) once 일단 ~하는 대로 bidding 입찰

3. profitability
| 해석 |
비즈니스 상담 전문가들은 수익성을 극대화하는 열쇠는 낮은 간접비라고 주장한다.
| 해설 |
동명사 maximizing의 목적어가 필요하므로 명사인 profitability가 정답이다.
| 어휘 | assert that ~라고 주장하다 maximize ~을 최대화하다 profitable 수익성 있는 profitability 수익성 overhead costs 간접비

◆ 출제 포인트 2 동사+to부정사 본책 p.183

1. to submit
| 해석 |
Thompson 시장은 강변 자전거 도로에 대한 제안서를 제출할 계획이다.
| 해설 |
동사 plan은 to부정사를 목적어로 취하는 동사이므로 to submit이 정답이다.
| 어휘 | submit ~을 제출하다 proposal 제안(서) bike path 자전거 도로

2. to pursue
| 해석 |
임원 직책으로 올라가기를 바라는 사원급 직원들은 경쟁력을 갖추고 유능해야 한다.
| 해설 |
동사 wish는 to부정사를 목적어로 취하는 동사이므로 to pursue가 정답이다.
| 어휘 | junior staff 사원급 직원들 pursue ~을 추구하다 executive 임원의 position 직책 competitive 경쟁력 있는 efficient (사람이) 유능한, (일 등이) 효율적인

3. strives
| 해석 |
The Columbus Dispatch는 항상 유익하고 사실에 기반한 기사를 싣기 위해 애쓴다.
| 해설 |
뒤에 이어지는 to부정사 to publish와 결합될 수 있는 동사가 필요하므로 to부정사와 함께 '~하기 위해 애쓰다'라는 의미로 쓰이는 동사 strives가 정답이다.
| 어휘 | assume ~라고 생각하다 strive to do ~하기 위해 애쓰다 publish (기사 등) ~을 싣다, 출간하다 informative 유익한 factual 사실에 기반한 article (잡지 등의) 기사

◆ 출제 포인트 3 명사+ to부정사 본책 p.184

1. to ensure
| 해석 |
품질을 보장하기 위한 노력의 일환으로, 커피 콩을 20분 동안 볶습니다.
| 해설 |
명사 effort는 to부정사의 수식을 받는 명사이므로 to ensure가 정답이다.
| 어휘 | in an effort to do ~하기 위한 노력의 일환으로 ensure ~을 보장하다 quality 질, 품질 roast ~을 볶다

2. right
| 해석 |
축제의 모든 판매업체들은 현금 지불을 거부할 권리를 갖고 있습니다.
| 해설 |
뒤에 이어지는 to부정사 to refuse의 수식을 받을 명사가 필요하므로 right이 정답이다.
| 어휘 | vendor 판매상 reserve the right to do ~할 권리를 갖다 selection 선정 refuse ~을 거부하다 payment 지불(액)

3. opportunity
| 해석 |
제품 테스트 담당자들에게는 새로운 기술이 공개되기에 앞서 그것을 시도해 볼 기회가 주어진다.
| 해설 |
뒤에 이어지는 to부정사 to try의 수식을 받으며 의미상으로 적합한 opportunity가 정답이다.
| 어휘 | situation 상황 opportunity to do ~할 기회 try ~을 시도해 보다, 한번 해 보다 release ~을 공개하다, 출시하다

◆ 출제 포인트 4 형용사 + to부정사 본책 p.184

1. to define
| 해석 |
우리 법무팀은 그 사업체 인수에 대한 조건을 명확히 규정할 수 있었다.
| 해설 |
형용사 able은 to부정사와 결합하여 '~할 수 있다'라는 의미로 쓰이므로 to define이 정답이다.
| 어휘 | legal department 법무팀 define 명확히 규정하다 terms 조건 acquisition 인수

2. ready
| 해석 |
Pruitt Limousine Services 사는 항상 근사하게 여러분을 모셔다드릴 준비가 되어 있습니다.
| 해설 |
뒤에 이어지는 to부정사 to transport와 잘 어울리며 의미상으로도 적합한 ready가 정답이다.
| 어휘 | skillful 숙련된 be ready to do ~할 준비가 되다 transport ~을 수송하다 in style 근사하게

3. to welcome
| 해석 |
The Wilshire 호텔은 Lowell 주식회사의 임원 여러분을 환영하게 되어 기쁘게 생각합니다.

| 해설 |
형용사 pleased는 to부정사와 결합하여 '~하게 되어 기쁘다'라는 의미로 쓰이므로 to welcome이 정답이다.
| 어휘 | executive 임원의, 간부의

◆ 출제 포인트 5   동사+목적어+to부정사   본책 p.185

1. monitor
| 해석 |
PetSmart 카메라는 주인들이 근무 중에 반려 동물을 관찰할 수 있게 해 준다.
| 해설 |
동사 allow는 목적어 뒤에 to부정사를 목적격 보어로 취하는 동사이므로 to부정사를 구성하는 동사원형인 monitor가 정답이다.
| 어휘 | owner 주인, 소유자 monitor ~을 관찰하다 at work 근무 중인

2. to return
| 해석 |
탑승객께서는 기내식이 전달되는 동안 각자의 좌석으로 돌아가 주시기 바랍니다.
| 해설 |
be advised는 to부정사와 결합되어 사용되므로 to return이 정답이다.
| 어휘 | passenger 탑승객 be advised to do ~하시기를 권합니다 return to ~로 돌아가다 in-flight 기내의 distribute ~을 나눠 주다

3. required
| 해석 |
모든 참가자들은 일요일 저녁까지 등록비를 지불해야 한다.
| 해설 |
뒤에 이어지는 to부정사 to pay와 결합될 수 있어야 하므로 to부정사와 함께 '~해야 하다'라는 의미로 사용하는 required가 정답이다.
| 어휘 | participant 참가자 be required to do ~해야 하다 apply 신청하다 registration fee 등록비

◆ 출제 포인트 6   (in order) to부정사   본책 p.185

1. make
| 해석 |
인턴들이 오래된 사무 기기들을 놓을 공간을 확보하기 위해 창고를 정리할 것이다.
| 해설 |
'공간을 확보하기 위해'라는 의미가 적합하므로 to부정사를 구성하는 동사 원형 make가 정답이다.
| 어휘 | organize ~을 정리하다 storage room 창고, 저장실 make space for ~을 놓을 공간을 확보하다 appliance 기기

2. in order to
| 해석 |
무대 뒤 구역에 출입하려면 참석자들은 반드시 VIP 손목 밴드를 착용해야 한다.
| 해설 |
동사 원형인 enter와 결합해 VIP 손목 밴드를 착용하는 목적을 나타내야 알맞으므로 in order to가 정답이다.
| 어휘 | attendee 참석자 wristband 손목 밴드 backstage area 무대 뒤 구역

3. to
| 해석 |
콘테스트 입상자들은 상품을 교환하기 위해 참여 매장을 방문해야 한다.

| 해설 |
동사 원형 redeem과 결합해 매장을 방문하는 '목적'을 나타내는 것이 의미상 적합하므로 to부정사를 만드는 to가 정답이다.
| 어휘 | winner 수상자, 우승자 participating 참여하는 redeem (쿠폰·상품권 등을) 상품으로 바꾸다

◆ 출제 포인트 7   동사+동명사   본책 p.186

1. opening
| 해석 |
Raccoon Coffee의 소유주는 두 번째 지점을 개장하는 것을 고려 중이다.
| 해설 |
consider는 동명사를 목적어로 취하는 동사이므로 opening이 정답이다.
| 어휘 | location 지점, 위치

2. casting
| 해석 |
더 폭넓은 관객을 끌어들이기 위해, 그 영화의 제작자는 유명 여배우를 캐스팅하도록 제안했다.
| 해설 |
suggest는 동명사를 목적어로 취하는 동사이므로 casting이 정답이다.
| 어휘 | attract ~을 끌어들이다 audience 관객, 청중 cast (배우 등) ~을 캐스팅하다

3. reserving
| 해석 |
안내 담당자의 직무에는 주간 부서 회의에 필요한 방을 예약하는 일이 포함되어 있다.
| 해설 |
동명사를 목적어로 취하는 동사 include와 어울리면서 동시에 빈칸 뒤의 명사 a room을 목적어로 취할 수 있는 동명사 reserving이 정답이다.
| 어휘 | receptionist 접수 담당자 responsibility 직무, 책무 reserve ~을 예약하다 reservation 예약 department 부서

◆ 출제 포인트 8   전치사+동명사   본책 p.186

1. limiting
| 해석 |
정책 입안자들은 공장에서 나오는 독성 배출 물질을 제한하는 것에 관해 여전히 논쟁을 벌이고 있다.
| 해설 |
전치사 about 뒤에 위치해 목적어 역할을 할 수 있는 것은 동명사이므로 limiting이 정답이다.
| 어휘 | policy maker 정책 입안자 debate 논쟁하다 limit ~을 제한하다 toxic 독성의 emission 배출 물질

2. improving
| 해석 |
각성 수준을 향상시켜 주는 것 외에도, Trinity 에너지 드링크는 오후의 나른함을 방지해 준다.
| 해설 |
전치사 in addition to 뒤에 위치해 목적어 역할을 할 수 있는 것은 동명사이므로 improving이 정답이다.
| 어휘 | improve ~을 향상시키다 alertness 각성 (수준) prevent ~을 방지하다, 막다 drowsiness 나른함, 졸림

3. Instead of
| 해석 |
레스토랑을 개조하는 대신에, 소유주는 새로운 곳으로 이전하고 싶어 한다.

| 해설 |
동명사 renovating을 목적어로 취할 수 있는 전치사가 쓰여야 알맞으므로 Instead of가 정답이다. In case(~의 경우에 대비하여)는 접속사로서 뒤에 절이 와야 한다.
| 어휘 | renovate ~을 개조하다, 보수하다

◆ 출제 포인트 9   동명사 vs. 명사 (1)   본책 p.187

1. notifying
| 해석 |
Redwood Diner는 고객들에게 이유에 관해 알리지 않고 4월에 문을 닫았다.
| 해설 |
뒤에 위치한 명사 customers를 목적어로 취함과 동시에 전치사 without의 목적어 역할을 할 수 있는 것은 동명사이므로 notifying이 정답이다.
| 어휘 | notify ~에게 알리다   notification 통보   as to ~와 관련해

2. Recovering
| 해석 |
삭제된 파일을 복구하는 것은 많은 돈이 들 수도 있다.
| 해설 |
뒤에 위치한 명사 deleted files를 목적어로 취하여 주어 자리에 올 수 있는 것은 동명사이므로 Recovering이 정답이다.
| 어휘 | recover 복구하다   deleted 삭제된   cost a lot of money 많은 비용이 들다

3. congestion
| 해석 |
통근자들은 고속도로상의 교통 혼잡을 피하기 위해 32번 출구를 이용해야 한다.
| 해설 |
동사 avoid는 명사와 동명사를 모두 목적어로 취할 수 있는데, 뒤에 on 전치사구가 있으므로 명사 congestion이 정답이다.
| 어휘 | commuter 통근자   exit 출구   avoid ~을 피하다   congestion (교통) 혼잡, 정체   congest ~을 혼잡하게 하다, 정체시키다   highway 고속도로

◆ 출제 포인트 10   동명사 vs. 명사 (2)   본책 p.187

1. slowly
| 해석 |
서서히 상세 줄거리를 공개함으로써, 그 스튜디오는 영화에 관한 관심을 높였다.
| 해설 |
전치사 By와 목적어인 동명사 releasing 사이에 위치할 수 있는 것은 동명사를 수식할 부사이므로 slowly가 정답이다.
| 어휘 | release ~을 공개하다, 출시하다   plot 줄거리   details 상세 내용, 세부 사항   increase ~을 높이다, 증가시키다   interest in ~에 대한 관심

2. completion
| 해석 |
Mason 씨는 프로젝트의 완료 후 은퇴를 선언했다.
| 해설 |
빈칸 앞의 관사(the)와 어울릴 수 있는 것은 명사이므로 completion이 정답이다.
| 어휘 | announce 발표하다   retirement 은퇴   completion 완료

3. promptly
| 해석 |
Zenva Technologies는 고객의 문의에 신속하게 대응하는 것으로 알려져 있다.

| 해설 |
동명사 responding을 수식하는 것은 부사이므로 promptly가 정답이다.
| 어휘 | be known for ~로 유명하다   promptly 빠르게   respond to ~에 대응하다   inquiry 문의

DAY 07 | 실전문제   본책 p.188

정답					
1 (C)	2 (C)	3 (B)	4 (D)	5 (B)	6 (C)
7 (C)	8 (B)	9 (C)	10 (C)	11 (A)	12 (B)
13 (C)	14 (B)	15 (B)	16 (B)	17 (D)	18 (D)
19 (A)	20 (B)				

1. (C)
| 해석 |
The Flower Market은 모든 고객들께 각자 받으셨던 서비스에 대한 평가서를 작성하도록 요청 드리고자 합니다.
| 해설 |
빈칸 앞에 위치한 would like는 to부정사와 결합하므로 (C) to invite이 정답이다. would like 뒤에 명사를 쓸 수도 있지만, 빈칸 뒤에 명사구(all customers)가 있으므로 준동사가 와야 한다.
| 어휘 | invite A to do A에게 ~하도록 요청하다   complete ~을 작성하다, 완료하다   evaluation 평가(서)   receive ~을 받다   invitingly 매력적으로   invitation 초대(장)

2. (C)
| 해석 |
우리의 새로운 모바일 앱은 사용자들이 유럽 전역에 있는 인기 여행지의 가상 투어를 할 수 있게 해준다.
| 해설 |
빈칸 뒤 '목적어 + to부정사'의 구조와 어울리며 의미상으로도 '~을 가능케 하다'가 적합하므로 이에 해당하는 보기인 (C) allows가 정답이다.
| 어휘 | take a tour of ~을 여행하다   virtual 가상의   destination (여행) 목적지, 행선지

3. (B)
| 해석 |
크림을 적절하게 바를 수 있게 하기 위해 병 뒷면에 설명이 제공되어 있습니다.
| 해설 |
빈칸 앞에 이미 문장의 동사 are provided가 있으므로 또 다른 동사 ensure는 준동사의 형태가 되어야 한다. 따라서 (B) to ensure가 정답이다. 나머지는 모두 동사의 형태이므로 오답이다.
| 어휘 | instructions 설명, 안내   provide ~을 제공하다   on the back of ~의 뒷면에   proper 적절한, 제대로 된   application 적용, (약제 등의) 바름   ensure ~을 보장하다

4. (D)
| 해석 |
누구든 인증 받지 않은 사람에 의해 제품이 수리되거나 개조될 경우에는 품질 보증이 더 이상 유효하지 않습니다.
| 해설 |
to부정사로 쓰인 be 뒤에는 보어가 위치해야 하는데, 이 문장에서는 주어 warranty의 상태와 관련되어야 하므로 형용사 (D) valid가 정답이다. 명사 (B) validity는 주어와 동격 관계가 아니므로 보어의 역할을 할 수 없다.
| 어휘 | cease to do ~하는 것을 중단하다   repair ~을 수리하다   modify ~을 개조하다   unauthorized 인증되지 않은   validate ~을 인증하다   validity 유효함   valid 유효한

5. (B)
| 해석 |
감염된 이메일을 열어 봄으로써, Nielsen 씨는 자신도 모르게 바이러스가 컴퓨터에 침입하게 만들었다.
| 해설 |
전치사 By의 목적어 역할을 함과 동시에 the infected e-mail을 목적어로 취할 수 있는 것은 동명사이므로 (B) opening이 정답이다.
| 어휘 | infected 감염된 unknowingly 자신도 모르게 allow A to do A가 ~할 수 있게 해 주다

6. (C)
| 해석 |
쇼핑객들께서는 쇼핑몰 가이드와 쿠폰북을 가져가실 수 있도록 고객 서비스 데스크를 방문해 주시기 바랍니다.
| 해설 |
동사 are invited는 to부정사와 결합해 '~하시기 바랍니다, ~하도록 요청됩니다' 등의 의미를 나타내므로 (C) to visit이 정답이다.
| 어휘 | be invited to do ~하도록 요청 받다 pick up ~을 가져가다, 가져오다 mall guide 쇼핑몰 가이드 책자

7. (C)
| 해석 |
이사진은 이상적인 곳에 위치한 Marquette 지역의 낮은 공장에 대한 또 다른 입찰 금액을 제안할 준비가 되어 있다.
| 해설 |
동사 is prepared는 to부정사와 결합해 '~할 준비가 되다'라는 의미를 나타내므로 (C) to offer가 정답이다.
| 어휘 | board 이사진 bid 입찰(액) ideally 이상적으로 located 위치한

8. (B)
| 해석 |
고객은 언제든지 당사 웹 사이트를 통해 자신의 계정에 접근하여 개인 정보를 볼 수 있습니다.
| 해설 |
전치사 by의 목적어 역할을 함과 동시에 명사 their account를 목적어로 취할 수 있는 것은 동명사이므로 (B) accessing이 정답이다.
| 어휘 | personal 개인의 details 세부사항, 상세 정보 account 계좌 access v. 접근하다 n. 접근(권)

9. (C)
| 해석 |
사무실의 파일 관리 시스템을 더 잘 정리하기 위한 노력의 일환으로, Larson 씨는 날짜에 따라 모든 문서에 대해 라벨 작업을 했다.
| 해설 |
빈칸 뒤 to부정사 to organize의 수식을 받을 수 있으며 의미상으로도 적합한 (C) effort가 정답이다.
| 어휘 | in an effort to do ~하기 위한 노력의 일환으로 organize ~을 정리하다 filing 파일 정리 label ~에 라벨을 붙이다 according to ~에 따라 idealism 이상주의 impression 인상, 감명

10. (C)
| 해석 |
Howard 다리의 건설 공사를 총괄하는 것뿐만 아니라, Orlando Consultants는 Diamond Street 공원의 개조 공사에도 공동으로 작업하고 있다.
| 해설 |
빈칸 뒤에 위치한 동명사 supervising을 목적어로 취할 수 있는 것은 전치사인데, 문맥상 한 업체가 맡고 있는 일을 추가로 언급하는 의미가 되어야 알맞으므로 '~뿐만 아니라, ~ 외에도'를 뜻하는 (C) In addition to가 정답이다. (A) Such as도 전치사이지만 예를 들 때 사용하며, (B) Moreover는 부사, (D) As soon as는 접속사이다.

| 어휘 | supervise ~을 총괄하다, 감독하다 collaborate 공동 작업하다, 협력하다 renovation 개조, 보수 such as ~와 같은 moreover 더욱이, 게다가 as soon as ~하자마자

11. (A)
| 해석 |
Jackson 사는 제조 시설을 먼저 방문하지 않고는 공급업체들과 새로운 계약을 맺지 않는다.
| 해설 |
빈칸 뒤의 visiting이 이끄는 동명사구를 목적어로 취할 전치사가 필요하므로 (A) without이 정답이다. 나머지 보기는 모두 부사이므로 알맞은 문장 구조를 만들 수 없다.
| 어휘 | make a contract with ~와 계약을 맺다 supplier 공급업체 manufacturing 제조 facility 시설(물) instead 대신에 without -ing ~하지 않고

12. (B)
| 해석 |
Sandersville에 30일 이상 거주한 사람은 누구든지 도서관 이용 카드를 신청할 자격이 있다.
| 해설 |
빈칸 앞뒤에 각각 위치한 be 동사 is, to부정사와 어울리는 형용사가 필요하므로 이 둘과 함께 '~할 자격이 있다'라는 의미를 나타낼 때 사용하는 (B) eligible이 정답이다. (A) possible은 가주어/진주어 구문인 'It is ~ to do'의 구조일 때 적절하다.
| 어휘 | reside in ~에 거주하다 be eligible to do ~할 자격이 있다 apply for ~을 신청하다, ~에 지원하다 considerable 상당한, 많은 flexible 유연한, 탄력적인

13. (C)
| 해석 |
저희 Star 호텔 고객에게 합리적인 가격에 집과 같은 편안함을 제공해 드리기를 고대합니다.
| 해설 |
look forward to에서 to는 전치사이므로 동명사를 목적어로 취해야 한다. 따라서 (C) providing이 정답이다.
| 어휘 | look forward to -ing ~하기를 고대하다 comfort 편안함 reasonable 합리적인, 타당한

14. (B)
| 해석 |
사무용품 주문의 새로운 마감시한이 11월 30일이라는 점을 알려 드리기 위해 메일을 씁니다.
| 해설 |
전치사 for의 목적어 역할을 함과 동시에 명사구 office supplies를 목적어로 취할 수 있는 것은 동명사이므로 (B) ordering이 정답이다.
| 어휘 | let A know A에게 알리다 deadline 마감시한 supplies 용품, 물품 order ~을 주문하다

15. (B)
| 해석 |
더 큰 규모의 단체 손님들을 수용하기 위해, Fredo's Italian Restaurant은 최대 20명까지 앉을 수 있는 전용 공간을 보유하고 있다.
| 해설 |
in order to는 동사 원형과 결합해 목적의 의미를 나타낼 때 사용하므로 동사 원형인 (B) accommodate이 정답이다.
| 어휘 | private 전용의, 사적인 seat ~을 앉히다 up to 최대 ~까지 accommodate ~을 수용하다 accommodation 숙박 시설

16. (B)
| 해석 |
그 책임자는 마케팅 학위를 소유하고 있는 한 경력이 없는 후보자들도 기

꺼이 고려하고자 한다.

| 해설 |
빈칸 앞뒤에 각각 위치한 be 동사 is, to부정사와 어울리는 형용사가 필요하므로 이 둘과 함께 '기꺼이 ~하다, ~할 의향이 있다'라는 의미를 나타낼 때 사용하는 (B) willing이 정답이다. (C) necessary와 (D) possible은 가주어/진주어 구문인 'It is ~ to do' 구조와 어울린다.

| 어휘 | consider ~을 고려하다 candidate 후보자 as long as ~하는 한 degree 학위 useful 유용한 necessary 필요한, 필수의

17-20번 문제는 다음 이메일을 참조하시오.

발신: peter.black@goodliving.com
수신: russell@handcrafted.com
제목: 체리 나무 책장

Russell 씨께,

저는 Seattle의 가정용 가구 매장인 Good Living을 대표해 이메일을 보냅니다. 저희는 귀하께서 만드신 것과 같은 장인 제작 가구로 저희 재고 범위를 **17** 확장하는 데 관심이 있습니다. 저희는 특히 귀하께서 체리 나무로 제작하신 책장에 관심이 있습니다. 저희 책임자들 중 한 사람이 지난 봄에 열린 Design Expo에서 이 **18** 제품을 보았으며, 즉시 귀하께 연락 드려야 한다고 주장했습니다. 귀하의 웹 사이트에 따르면, 해당 제품이 판매용이기는 하지만, 가격이 기재되어 있지 않습니다. 해당 책장을 구입하는 것이 **19** 실제로 가능할 경우, 저희는 그 가격을 알고 싶습니다. 현재로서는, 저희는 오직 몇몇 제품들만 구입하는 데 관심이 있습니다. **20** 하지만, 고객들이 좋은 반응을 보일 경우에 추가로 구입할 수도 있습니다.

귀하로부터 소식 들을 수 있기를 고대합니다.

안녕히 계십시오.
Peter Black
Good Living

| 어휘 | on behalf of ~을 대표해 home furnishings 가정용 가구 be interested in ~하는 데 관심이 있다 stock 재고 artisan 장인, 공예가 piece 제품, 작품 create ~을 만들어 내다 particularly 특히 insist (that) ~하도록 주장하다 contact ~에게 연락하다 immediately 즉시 according to ~에 따르면 for sale 판매용인 value (비용) 가치 listed 기재된 acquire ~을 얻다 look forward to -ing ~하는 것을 고대하다

17. (D)

| 해설 |
our stock을 목적어로 취함과 동시에 전치사 in의 목적어 역할을 할 수 있는 것은 동명사이므로 (D) expanding이 정답이다.

18. (D)

| 해설 |
빈칸 앞에 위치한 this는 앞 문장에 언급된 the bookcase를 가리키므로 이를 대신할 수 있는 명사로 '제품, 물품'을 뜻하는 (D) item이 정답이다.

| 어휘 | invoice 거래 내역서 method 방법 portion 부분, 일부

19. (A)

| 해설 |
형용사 possible을 수식해 제품 구입과 관련된 실제적인 가능성을 나타내는 맥락이 되어야 하므로 '실제로, 정말로'를 뜻하는 부사 (A) indeed가 정답이다.

| 어휘 | quite 상당히, 꽤 likewise 마찬가지로

20. (B)

(A) 저희 매장은 또한 실내 디자인에 관해 전문적인 조언을 해드립니다.
(C) 안타깝게도, 저희가 보유한 구매 가능한 다른 제품과 유사합니다.
(D) 그러시다면, 귀하의 성함과 주소를 포함해 저희에게 이메일을 보내 주

시기만 하면 됩니다.

| 해설 |
앞 문장에 몇몇 제품들만 구입하는 데 관심이 있다는 말이 있으므로 그와 관련된 향후의 구입 방침을 알리는 의미로 쓰인 (B)가 정답이다.

| 어휘 | expert 전문적인 purchase ~을 구입하다 respond 반응하다 unfortunately 안타깝게도 similar to ~와 유사한 have A available 이용 가능한 A가 있다

DAY 08 | 분사

◆ 출제 포인트 1   분사의 역할
본책 p.191

1. limited

| 해석 |
Maldives로 향하는 항공편들은 한정되어 있으므로 미리 항공권을 예약하십시오.

| 해설 |
because절의 주어인 flights to the Maldives에 대한 보어로서 해당 항공편의 상태를 나타낼 분사가 쓰여야 알맞으므로 limited가 정답이다. 명사 limitation은 주어와 동격이 아니므로 오답이다.

| 어휘 | book ~을 예약하다 in advance 미리 limitation 한정 limited 제한된

2. preferred

| 해석 |
모든 회원들께서는 각자의 사용자 프로필에 선호하는 연락 방법을 업데이트하셔야 합니다.

| 해설 |
뒤에 위치한 명사 method를 수식할 형용사가 필요하므로 분사 preferred가 정답이다.

| 어휘 | preferred 선호되는, 우선의 preference 선호(하는 것) method 방법 contact 연락, 접촉

3. originating

| 해석 |
중국 남부 지역에서 유래된 조리법들은 매운 맛을 내는 재료들을 특징으로 한다.

| 해설 |
이미 문장의 동사 feature가 있으므로 동사는 올 수 없고 주어 Recipes를 뒤에서 수식하는 구조를 만들 수 있는 분사 originating이 정답이다.

| 어휘 | originate from ~에서 유래되다 feature ~을 특징으로 하다 ingredient (음식) 재료

◆ 출제 포인트 2   현재분사(-ing) vs. 과거 분사(p.p.)
본책 p.191

1. leading

| 해석 |
David James는 패션의 역사에서 선도적인 전문가들 중 한 사람이다.

| 해설 |
수식 받는 명사 experts가 이끌어 가는 주체로서 lead와 능동 관계를 형성하므로 현재분사 leading이 정답이다.

| 어휘 | leading 선도적인 expert 전문가

2. assigned

| 해설 |
모든 야영객들은 반드시 매일 밤 10시까지 각자 배정된 방에 있어야 한다.

| 해설 |
수식을 받는 명사 room은 배정되는 대상으로서 assign과 수동 관계를 형성하므로 과거 분사 assigned가 정답이다.
| 어휘 | assign ~을 배정하다   by (기한) ~까지

3. submitted

| 해석 |
Jenkins 씨는 각 부서에서 제출한 구매 주문서를 검토할 것이다.

| 해설 |
수식 받는 명사 purchase orders는 제출되는 대상으로서 submit과 수동 관계를 형성하므로 과거 분사 submitted가 정답이다.
| 어휘 | review 검토하다   purchase order 구매 주문(서)   submit 제출하다   department 부서

✦ 출제 포인트 3   -ing와 p.p.의 구별이 모호한 분사
본책 p.191

1. detailed

| 해석 |
각 직원은 경력상의 목표를 서술하는 상세한 개발 계획서를 작성할 것이다.

| 해설 |
뒤에 위치한 development plan을 수식해 '상세한 개발 계획서'라는 의미가 되어야 알맞으므로 '상세한, 자세한'을 뜻하는 detailed가 정답이다.
| 어휘 | detail ~을 상세히 설명하다   development 계발, 개발   outline 개요를 서술하다

2. challenging

| 해석 |
Patel 씨는 힘든 직책인 Cliffton Advertising의 미술 책임자로서 탁월한 능력을 보이고 있다.

| 해설 |
뒤에 위치한 position을 수식해 '힘든 직책'이라는 의미가 되어야 알맞으므로 '힘든, 어려운' 등을 뜻하는 challenging이 정답이다.
| 어휘 | excel in ~에서 탁월하다   challenger 도전자   position 직책, 직위, 자리

3. established

| 해석 |
Boston에 본사를 둔 인정받는 회사인 Langston Dynamics는 규칙적으로 운동하는 직원들에게 장려금을 준다.

| 해설 |
뒤에 위치한 Boston-based company를 수식해 '인정 받는 회사'라는 의미가 되어야 알맞으므로 '인정 받는, 자리를 잡은' 등을 뜻하는 established가 정답이다.
| 어휘 | establish ~을 확립하다   incentive 장려 정책, 인센티브   exercise 운동하다   regularly 주기적으로

✦ 출제 포인트 4   감정 동사의 -ing / p.p.
본책 p.192

1. fascinating

| 해석 |
Haruki Ishiguro 씨는 곧 출간될 자신의 자서전에서 발췌한 매력적인 부분을 읽어 주었다.

| 해설 |
뒤에 위치한 excerpt가 매력적으로 느끼게 만드는 주체에 해당되므로 -ing 형태인 fascinating이 정답이다. -ed 형태인 fascinated는 그와 같은 감정을 느끼는 주체에 대해 사용한다.
| 어휘 | fascinating 매력적인   fascinated 매료된   excerpt 발췌 내용   autobiography 자서전

2. interested

| 해석 |
Marietta Fire Department는 응급 처치를 배우는 데 관심이 있는 모든 이에게 강좌를 제공할 것이다.

| 해설 |
수식 받는 대명사 anyone이 관심을 느끼는 사람에 해당되므로 -ed 형태인 interested가 정답이다
| 어휘 | interesting 흥미로운   interested in ~에 관심 있는   first aid 응급 처치

3. exciting

| 해석 |
Bob Forte 씨는 전문 사진 작가로서 흥미로운 경력을 추구하기로 결정했다.

| 해설 |
뒤에 위치한 career가 흥미를 느끼게 만드는 주체에 해당되므로 -ing 형태인 exciting이 정답이다.
| 어휘 | decide to do ~하기로 결정하다   pursue ~을 추구하다   exciting 흥미진진한   excited 흥분한, 신이 난   professional 전문적인   photographer 사진 작가

✦ 출제 포인트 5   자동사의 분사 : -ing형 형용사
본책 p.192

1. rising

| 해석 |
증가하고 있는 연료비로 인해, Fox Shipping은 현재의 요금을 인상할 것이다.

| 해설 |
fuel costs를 수식할 분사가 필요한데, 동사 rise가 자동사이므로 현재분사의 형태만 가능하다. 따라서 rising이 정답이다.
| 어휘 | due to ~로 인해   increase ~을 인상하다   current 현재의   rate 요금

2. growing

| 해석 |
점점 증가하는 Westport의 인구가 여러 위성 도시의 개발로 이어졌다.

| 해설 |
뒤에 위치한 population을 수식할 분사를 골라야 하는데, 동사 grow가 '증가'의 의미를 나타낼 때는 자동사로 쓰이므로 현재분사 growing이 정답이다.
| 어휘 | population 인구   lead to ~로 이어지다   satellite 위성

3. remaining

| 해석 |
고객들이 자신의 회원 포인트를 사용하는 일을 기억할 것인지가 유일하게 남아 있는 문제점이다.

| 해설 |
problem을 수식할 분사가 필요한데, remain이 자동사이므로 현재분사의 형태인 remaining이 정답이다.
| 어휘 | whether ~인지 (아닌지)   remember to do ~하는 것을 기억하다

✦ 출제 포인트 6   분사구문
본책 p.193

1. Being

| 해석 |
주요 투자자여서, Alkire 씨는 그 레스토랑의 형편없는 후기에 대해 우려했다.

| 해설 |
명사구 a main investor와 함께 분사구문을 만들 수 있는 분사 Being이 정답이다. Has been은 동사의 형태이므로 접속사와 주어 없이 쓸 수 없다.
| 어휘 | investor 투자자   be concerned about ~에 대해 우려하다, 걱정하다   poor 형편 없는, 저조한   review 후기, 평가

2. confirming

| 해석 |
Dylarama 사는 어제 새로운 태블릿 제품을 발표했는데, 이는 이미 경쟁적인 시장에 진입하겠다는 의도를 확인해 주는 것이다.
| 해설 |
문장의 주어 Dylarama가 경쟁적인 시장에 진입하겠다는 의도를 확인해 주는 주체에 해당되므로 능동의 의미를 나타내는 분사구문을 만들 수 있는 현재분사 confirming이 정답이다.
| 어휘 | announce ~을 발표하다   confirm ~을 확인해 주다   intent to do ~하겠다는 의도   enter ~에 진입하다   competitive 경쟁적인

3. thereby

| 해석 |
우리는 더 큰 곳으로 이사해서 더 많은 상품을 구비할 수 있게 되었다.
| 해설 |
완전한 문장 뒤에 콤마와 함께 이어지는 분사 구문의 구조인데, 빈칸 뒤의 현재분사 allowing을 수식하기에 의미상 적합한 부사인 thereby(그러므로)를 정답으로 선택한다.
| 어휘 | location 장소   stock 재고로 갖고 있다   a wider selection of ~의 더욱 다양한 구비   merchandise 상품

DAY 08 | 실전문제   본책 p.194

정답 1 (C)   2 (C)   3 (D)   4 (B)   5 (B)   6 (B)
      7 (C)   8 (B)   9 (D)   10 (C) 11 (B) 12 (D)
      13 (C) 14 (A) 15 (C) 16 (D) 17 (D) 18 (A)
      19 (D) 20 (B)

---

1. (C)

| 해석 |
자격을 갖춘 지원자는 최소 10년 동안 비용 청구 시스템을 이용해 근무한 경력을 지닌 분이어야 합니다.
| 해설 |
명사 candidate 앞은 형용사 자리이므로 형용사를 대신할 수 있는 과거 분사 (C) qualified가 정답이다.
| 어휘 | candidate 지원자   at least 최소한   experience 경력   billing system 비용 청구 시스템   qualify 자격을 얻다, ~에게 자격을 주다   qualifier 예선 경기, 예선 통과자   qualified 자격이 있는, 적격인   qualification 자격(증)

2. (C)

| 해석 |
주방 초보자용 세트에는 냄비 2개, 큰 부엌칼, 그리고 다양한 크기의 그릇 5개가 딸려 있습니다.
| 해설 |
명사 sizes를 앞에서 수식할 수 있는 단어가 들어갈 자리이므로 명사를 수식할 수 있는 현재분사 (C) varying이 정답이다. 명사인 (D) variation은 sizes와 복합 명사를 구성하기에 의미가 적합하지 않으므로 오답이다.
| 어휘 | starter 초보자(의)   come with ~가 딸려 있다   pot 냄비   bowl (움푹한) 그릇   vary 다양하다, 서로 다르다   varying 다양한, 서로 다른   variation 변형(된 것)

3. (D)

| 해석 |
욕실과 주방 싱크대는 스페인에서 수입된 고급 자재로 만들어져 있다.
| 해설 |
이미 문장의 동사 are made가 있으므로 빈칸에는 high quality materials를 수식해줄 말이 와야 한다. high quality materials는 사람에 의해 수입되는 것이므로 수동의 의미를 나타내는 과거 분사 (D) imported가 정답이다.
| 어휘 | high quality 고급의, 고품질의   material 재료, 자재   import ~을 수입하다

4. (B)

| 해석 |
동봉된 전단에는 우리 Fredericktown 지점의 할인판매가 기재되어 있는데, 그곳은 3월 말에 문을 닫을 예정이다.
| 해설 |
flyer 앞의 빈칸에는 명사를 수식할 수 있는 분사가 와야 하는데, flyer는 사람에 의해 동봉되는 대상이므로 수동의 의미를 나타내는 과거 분사 (B) enclosed가 정답이다.
| 어휘 | sales 판매(량), 매출   branch 지점, 지사   enclosure 동봉(된 것)   enclosed 동봉된   enclose ~을 동봉하다

5. (B)

| 해석 |
시의회는 이번 주에 Lucca 강 아래 터널 건설안을 논의하기 위해 만날 것이다.
| 해설 |
명사 construction을 수식할 수 있는 단어가 필요하므로 형용사 역할을 수행하는 과거 분사 (B) proposed가 정답이다.
| 어휘 | city council 시의회   discuss 논의하다   propose 제안하다   proposed 제안된   proposal 제안, 제의

6. (B)

| 해석 |
회사의 소프트볼 팀 가입에 관심이 있는 직원들은 인사부의 Valerie Dixon 씨에게 이메일을 보내야 한다.
| 해설 |
이미 문장의 동사 should send가 있으므로 빈칸에는 Employees를 뒤에서 수식하는 분사구를 이끌 분사가 와야 한다. 따라서 전치사 in과 결합해 '~에 관심이 있는'을 의미하는 (B) interested가 정답이다.
| 어휘 | join ~에 가입하다   interest ~의 관심을 끌다

7. (C)

| 해석 |
시의 규정에 따르면, 기존의 모든 구조물들은 반드시 지역 문화 역사를 보존하기 위해 특정한 외관을 유지해야 한다.
| 해설 |
빈칸은 명사를 수식할 분사 자리인데 자동사 exist는 현재분사 형태로만 명사를 수식할 수 있으므로 (C) existing이 정답이다. 명사 (B) existence는 structures와 복합 명사를 구성하기에 의미가 적합하지 않으므로 답이 될 수 없다.
| 어휘 | according to ~에 따르면   regulation 규제, 규정   structure 구조(물)   maintain ~을 유지하다   certain 특정한   appearance 외관   preserve ~을 보존하다   local 지역의, 현지의   exist 존재하다   existence 존재(감)   existing 기존의

8. (B)

| 해석 |
회의 참석자들은 각자 수정된 계약서의 디지털 버전 뿐만 아니라 인쇄본도 제공 받았다.
| 해설 |
빈칸에는 명사 agreement를 수식할 형용사가 와야 하는데, '계약(서)'를 의미하는 agreement는 사람에 의해 수정되는 대상이므로 수동의 의미를 나타내는 과거 분사 (B) revised가 정답이다.
| 어휘 | attendee 참석자   be provided with ~을 제공 받다   as well as ~뿐만 아니라   revision 수정   revise ~을 수정하다

9. (D)

| 해석 |
여름 퍼레이드 행사로 인해, 이번 주 토요일에 Wayzata 시내와 인근 지역에 주차를 하는 것이 어려울 것 같다.

| 해설 |
빈칸 뒤에 위치한 명사 area를 수식해 '인근 지역'이라는 의미가 되어야 자연스러우므로 '인근의, 주변의'를 뜻하는 (D) surrounding이 정답이다. (C) surrounded는 '둘러싸인'이라는 의미로 하나의 경계 내에 해당되는 공간을 가리키므로 의미상 알맞지 않다.
| 어휘 | due to ~로 인해, ~ 때문에   be likely to do ~할 가능성이 있다   surround ~을 둘러싸다

10. (C)
폭우에도 불구하고, Martinez 씨의 항공편은 예정된 출발 시간에 떠날 수 있었다.
| 해설 |
departure time은 사람에 의해 일정이 잡히는 대상이므로 수동의 의미를 갖는 과거 분사 (C) scheduled가 정답이다.
| 어휘 | despite ~에도 불구하고   heavy rain 폭우   scheduled 예정된

11. (B)
| 해설 |
많은 다른 제품들과는 달리, Orange Power는 표면을 세척해 줄 뿐만 아니라 기분 좋은 향기도 납니다.
| 해설 |
명사 scent를 수식할 분사로 알맞은 것을 찾아야 하는데, scent가 좋은 기분을 느끼게 만드는 주체이므로 현재분사 (B) pleasing이 정답이다. (D) pleased는 주체가 좋은 기분을 느낄 때 사용한다.
| 어휘 | unlike ~와 달리   not only A but (also) B A뿐만 아니라 B도   scent 향기   please 기쁘게 하다   pleasing 기분 좋게 만드는   pleased 기뻐하는

12. (D)
| 해설 |
새로 칠한 페인트가 낡은 건물을 매력으로 가득하여 사람의 마음을 끄는 건물로 변모시켰다.
| 해설 |
명사 property를 수식하기에 적합한 분사를 골라야 하므로 '매력적인, 마음을 끄는'이란 의미를 가진 (D) inviting이 정답이다. 과거 분사인 (B) invited는 '초대된, 요청 받은' 등을 의미하므로 의미상 적합하지 않다.
| 어휘 | coat (페인트 등의) 칠   property 건물, 부동산   be full of ~로 가득하다   charm 매력   invite ~을 초대하다   invitation 초대(장)   inviting 마음을 끄는

13. (C)
| 해설 |
Ackerman 씨는 자신이 먹는 모든 것을 기록하여 반드시 칼로리 섭취량이 합당한 수준으로 유지되도록 하려고 한다.
| 해설 |
이미 문장의 동사 keeps가 있으므로 빈칸에는 준동사가 와야 한다. 주어 Mr. Ackerman이 칼로리 유지를 하는 주체이므로 능동의 의미를 나타내는 현재분사 (C) ensuring이 정답이다.
| 어휘 | keep a record of ~을 기록하다   ensure that ~하는 것을 확실히 하다, 반드시 ~하도록 하다   intake 섭취(량)   remain 유지되다   reasonable 합당한

14. (A)
| 해설 |
마지막 순간에 1만 달러의 후한 기부가 접수되었는데, 그 결과 박물관이 운영을 계속할 수 있게 되었다.
| 해설 |
빈칸 뒤에 allowing이 이끄는 분사구문이 이어지고 있는데, -ing 분사와 잘 어울리며 의미상으로도 '그러므로 ~하다'가 적합하므로 이에 해당하는 부사인 (A) thereby가 정답이다.
| 어휘 | generous 후한   donation 기부   receive 수령하다   at the last minute 임박해서, 마지막 순간에   museum 박물관   operation 운영

15. (C)
| 해석 |
직원들은 30년 동안 재직한 끝에 은퇴할 예정인 Justin Shaffer 씨를 기리는 연회에 초대되었다.
| 해설 |
이미 문장의 동사 are invited가 있으므로 빈칸에는 명사 banquet을 뒤에서 수식하는 분사가 와야 알맞다. banquet이 Justin Shaffer를 기리는 주체이므로 현재분사 (C) honoring이 정답이다
| 어휘 | banquet 연회   retire 은퇴하다   honor ~을 기리다, ~에게 영예를 주다

16. (D)
| 해설 |
새롭게 만들어진 테스트가 의사들이 환자의 통증 수준을 더 잘 평가하는 데 도움이 될 것이다.
| 해설 |
빈칸 앞의 부사 newly의 수식을 받음과 동시에 그 뒤의 명사 test를 수식할 수 있는 것은 형용사이다. 따라서 형용사 역할을 하는 과거 분사 (D) created가 정답이다.
| 어휘 | assist A in -ing A가 ~하는 데 도움을 주다   assess ~을 평가하다, 가늠하다   discomfort 통증, (신체적) 불편함   create ~을 만들어 내다   creation 창작(물)

17-20번 문제는 다음 이메일을 참조하시오.

수신: 전 직원
발신: Minjune Park
날짜: 7월 4일
제목: 전기 안전 프로그램

7월 20일부터 25일에 해당되는 기간에, Metro Power에서 전기 안전 프로그램을 **17** 시작합니다. 이 운동에 대한 관심을 불러일으키기 위해, 해당 주에 다양한 행사가 계획되어 있습니다. **18** 여기에는 경품 추첨과 안전 조치에 관한 발표가 포함되어 있습니다.

홍보 활동의 일환으로 많은 **19** 포스터들도 준비되어 있습니다. 이 포스터에는 안전하게 전기를 이용하기 위한 간단한 팁뿐만 아니라 해당 주에 열리는 행사들이 기재되어 있습니다.

이 정보는 **20** 행사에 참가하는 공공 시설들의 게시판에 부착될 것입니다. 또한 우리 웹사이트에도 게시될 것이며, 다운로드도 가능합니다. 이 중요한 지역 복지 활동에 관해 입소문을 내는 데 여러분의 도움을 요청드립니다.

| 어휘 | electric safety 전기 안전   bring attention to ~에 대한 관심을 불러일으키다   initiative (조직적) 계획, 운동   a variety of 다양한   a number of 많은 (수의)   as part of ~의 일환으로   publicity campaign 홍보 활동   list ~을 기재하다   B as well as A A뿐만 아니라 B도   affix A to B A를 B에 부착하다   notice board 게시판   public facility 공공 시설   post ~을 게시하다   available 이용 가능한   ask for ~을 요청하다   assistance in ~에 대한 도움   spread the word 입소문을 내다   outreach 복지, 봉사   effort (조직적) 운동, 활동

17. (D)
| 해설 |
빈칸 앞에 전기 안전 프로그램 실시 기간으로 쓰여 있는 July 20-25는 상단의 이메일 작성 날짜보다 미래 시점에 해당되므로 미래 시제인 (D) will be launching이 정답이다. 미래 완료 시제인 (C) will have launched는 특정 미래 시점 표현과 함께 사용하며, 해당 시점 이전에 완료되는 일을 나타낸다.
| 어휘 | launch ~을 시작하다

18. (A)
(B) Metro Power는 30년 동안 가정에 전기를 제공해 오고 있습니다.

(C) 그런 행사는 기상 상태가 좋지 못할 경우에 취소될 가능성이 있습니다.
(D) 전기 기기 및 콘센트와 관련된 사고는 흔히 예방 가능한 것들입니다.
| 해설 |
앞 문장에 다양한 행사(a variety of events)가 계획된 사실이 언급되어 있으므로 이 행사들을 These로 지칭해 두 가지 행사를 예로 들어 알리는 (A)가 정답이다.
| 어휘 | include ~을 포함하다   prize drawing 경품 추첨 행사   measure 조치   provide A with B A에게 B를 제공하다   decade 10년   be subject to ~ 당하기 쉽다, ~에 취약하다   cancellation 취소   poor 좋지 못한   involving ~와 관련된   appliance (가전) 기기   outlet 콘센트   preventable 예방 가능한

19. (D)
| 해설 |
빈칸에 들어갈 명사에 대해 부연 설명하는 이후의 내용에서 '행사 관련 정보들이 들어 있다'는 말과 '게시판에 부착될 것이다'라는 내용이 있으므로 (D) posters가 정답임을 알 수 있다.
| 어휘 | opinion 의견   payment 지불(액)

20. (B)
| 해설 |
빈칸은 전치사 in의 목적어인 public facilities를 수식할 형용사 자리이며, 분사가 그 역할을 대신할 수 있다. 자동사 participate은 현재분사의 형태로만 명사를 수식할 수 있으므로 (B) participating이 정답이다.
| 어휘 | participate 참가하다   participant 참가자

DAY 09 전치사

◆ 출제 포인트 1   시간 전치사 (1)   본책 p.197

1. on
| 해석 |
그 강연 시리즈는 2월 15일에 시작되어 그 다음 금요일까지 지속될 것이다.
| 해설 |
날짜 표현 앞에는 전치사 on을 쓴다.
| 어휘 | continue 지속되다, 계속되다   following 그 다음의

2. at
| 해석 |
올해 화재 예방 점검이 계획대로 오늘 오후 1시에 시작될 것이다.
| 해설 |
시각을 나타내는 숫자 앞에는 전치사 at을 쓴다.
| 어휘 | fire inspection 화재 예방 점검   as planned 계획대로

3. after
| 해석 |
오직 오후 6시 이후에만 오실 수 있는 환자들을 위해 저녁 시간 예약이 가능합니다.
| 해설 |
6:00 P.M.이라는 하나의 기준 시점과 어울릴 수 있는 전치사 after가 정답이다. between은 두 개의 기준 시점과 함께 'between A and B'의 구조로 사용한다.
| 어휘 | appointment 예약, 약속   available 시간이 있는   patient 환자

◆ 출제 포인트 2   시간 전치사 (2) : 시점 vs. 기간   본책 p.197

1. by
| 해설 |
지출 품의서는 반드시 금요일 오후까지 회계부로 제출되어야 한다.

| 해설 |
Friday afternoon이 제출 기한, 즉 시점에 해당되므로 '~까지'라는 의미로 시점 명사와 어울리는 전치사 by가 정답이다.
| 어휘 | expense 지출 (비용)   submit ~을 제출하다   Accounting 회계부

2. within
| 해석 |
이사 후 14일 이내에 주소 변경 사실을 시청에 알리시기 바랍니다.
| 해설 |
기간을 나타내는 14 days를 목적어로 취해야 하므로 기간 표현과 함께 사용하는 전치사 within이 정답이다.
| 어휘 | notify A of B A에게 B를 알리다

3. During
| 해석 |
회의 중에, Han 씨는 새로운 연구 부서의 목적을 설명했다.
| 해설 |
the meeting은 기간을 나타내는 명사이므로 ' ~ 중에, ~ 동안'을 뜻하는 전치사 During이 정답이다.
| 어휘 | explain ~을 설명하다   purpose 목적

◆ 출제 포인트 3   장소 전치사   본책 p.198

1. near
| 해석 |
선물은 안내 데스크 근처에 있는 카운터에 놓아 두시면 됩니다.
| 해설 |
the information desk는 장소를 나타내는 명사구이므로 장소 명사와 함께 사용하는 전치사 near가 정답이다.
| 어휘 | be left on ~에 놓이다, 남겨지다

2. in
| 해석 |
호텔 1층 로비에는 여러 개의 식당이 편리하게 위치하고 있습니다.
| 해설 |
lobby는 넓은 장소를 나타내는 명사이므로 전치사 in이 정답이다.
| 어휘 | several 몇몇의   conveniently 편리하게   be located 위치하다

3. throughout
| 해석 |
무료 와이파이 연결 서비스는 그 병원의 많은 건물 전역에서 손쉽게 이용 가능하다.
| 해설 |
문장 전체의 의미상 '많은 건물에 걸쳐'라는 의미가 적합하므로 이러한 의미를 갖는 전치사 throughout이 정답이다.
| 어휘 | free 무료의   connection 연결   readily 손쉽게, 즉시   numerous 많은, 다수의

◆ 출제 포인트 4   방향/이유/양보/목적/범위/관련 전치사   본책 p.198

1. to
| 해석 |
고려되기 위해서는 디자인은 반드시 점심 시간까지 Boice 씨에게 제출되어야 한다.
| 해설 |
Mr. Boice는 제출되는 디자인을 받는 사람이어야 하므로 '~에게, ~ 쪽으로' 등의 의미로 방향을 나타내는 전치사 to가 정답이다.
| 어휘 | submit ~을 제출하다   consider ~을 고려하다

2. due to

| 해석 |
경기장의 배관 시설 문제로 인해 경기가 다른 장소로 옮겨졌다.

| 해설 |
problems 이하 부분은 경기 장소가 바뀐 이유에 해당되므로 '~로 인해'라는 의미로 이유를 나타내는 전치사 due to가 정답이다.

| 어휘 | relocate ~을 옮기다, 이전하다 plumbing 배관 (시설)

3. despite

| 해석 |
고객 주차와 관련된 업주들의 우려에도 불구하고 그 건설 공사가 지속될 것이다.

| 해설 |
concern은 '우려, 걱정'을 의미하므로 '~에도 불구하고 공사가 지속된다'는 의미가 되어야 자연스럽다. 따라서 '~에도 불구하고'라는 의미로 양보를 나타내는 전치사 despite이 정답이다.

| 어휘 | construction 건설 공사 regarding ~에 관한

◆ 출제 포인트 5 | 기타 빈출 전치사
본책 p.199

1. with

| 해석 |
반려 동물이 있는 아파트 세입자들은 이사 나갈 때 전문 청소 서비스 일정을 잡아야 한다.

| 해설 |
아파트 세입자와 반려 동물은 소유 관계로 볼 수 있으므로 '~가 있는, ~을 갖고 있는'이라는 의미의 전치사 with가 정답이다.

| 어휘 | tenant 세입자 be required to do ~해야 하다 arrange ~의 일정을 잡다 move out 이사 나가다

2. except

| 해석 |
마케팅부를 제외한 모든 직원들이 설문 조사에 참여할 것이다.

| 해설 |
앞에 '모든 직원들'이라는 말이 쓰여 있는데, 뒤에 마케팅부의 사람들이 따로 언급되어 있으므로 제외 대상이 되어야 의미상 알맞다. 따라서 '~을 제외하고'를 의미하는 전치사 except가 정답이다.

| 어휘 | those (수식어구와 함께) ~하는 사람들 participate in ~에 참여하다 survey 설문 조사(지)

3. According to

| 해석 |
계약서에 따르면, Matterhorn Studios가 그 영화에 대한 독점 배급 권리를 가진다.

| 해설 |
계약서(agreement)는 독점 배급 권리라는 자격을 확인할 수 있는 근거에 해당된다. 따라서 '~에 따르면'이라는 의미로 출처 또는 근거 등을 나타내는 전치사 According to가 정답이다.

| 어휘 | exclusive 독점적인, 전용의 distribution 유통, 배급, 배부 right 권리 film 영화

◆ 출제 포인트 6 | 용법에 주의해야 하는 유사 의미 전치사
본책 p.199

1. between

| 해석 |
Halifax로 가는 급행 열차는 오후 5시와 7시 사이에 가장 빈번히 운행한다.

| 해설 |
뒤에 두 개의 시각이 'A and B'의 구조로 쓰여 있으므로 between이 정답이다.

| 어휘 | express 급행의, 특송의 run 운행되다, 운영되다 frequently 빈번히, 자주

2. by

| 해석 |
다리 보수 공사는 다음 주 수요일까지 완료될 예정이다.

| 해설 |
next Wednesday는 공사가 완료되는 시점을 나타내므로 완료의 개념을 가진 by가 정답이다. until은 상태 등의 지속 개념을 나타낼 때 사용한다.

| 어휘 | renovation 보수, 개조 complete ~을 완료하다

3. during

| 해석 |
회사의 정책에 따라, 업무 시간 동안 개인 전화의 사용은 금지된다.

| 해설 |
business hours는 기간을 함축하는 명사이므로 '~ 동안'이라는 의미의 during이 정답이다. for는 숫자 표현이 포함된 명사구와 함께 사용한다.

| 어휘 | under (영향) ~에 따라, ~ 하에서 policy 정책, 방침 prohibit ~을 금지하다

DAY 09 | 실전문제
본책 p.200

정답 | 1 (C) | 2 (B) | 3 (D) | 4 (A) | 5 (B) | 6 (B) |
7 (C)	8 (D)	9 (C)	10 (B)	11 (B)	12 (C)
13 (D)	14 (B)	15 (A)	16 (C)	17 (B)	18 (D)
19 (D)	20 (C)

1. (C)

| 해석 |
공연 시작 최대 24시간 전까지 전액 환불을 위한 취소가 수용될 것입니다.

| 해설 |
빈칸에는 앞뒤에 있는 명사를 연결할 전치사가 필요하므로 유일한 전치사인 (C) prior to가 정답이다. (A) previous와 (B) advanced는 형용사이며, (D) in fact는 부사의 역할을 한다.

| 어휘 | cancellation 취소 accept ~을 받아들이다, 수용하다 full refund 전액 환불 up to 최대 ~까지 previous 이전의, 과거의 advanced 발전된, 진보한 prior to ~ 전에, ~에 앞서 in fact 사실은, 실제로

2. (B)

| 해석 |
3월 10일부터 개조 공사로 인해 레스토랑이 문을 닫는다는 점에 유의하시기 바랍니다.

| 해설 |
renovations는 '개조, 보수' 등을 의미하며, 레스토랑이 문을 닫는 이유로 판단할 수 있으므로 '~ 때문에, ~을 위해' 등의 의미로 이유나 목적을 나타낼 때 사용하는 전치사 (B) for가 정답이다.

| 어휘 | Please be advised that ~라는 점에 유의하십시오, ~임을 알려 드립니다 starting on + 날짜 ~부터, ~부로

3. (D)

| 해석 |
지역 주민들이 가장 좋아하는 곳인 Mickey's Diner는 새벽 2시까지 영업하며, 무료 커피 리필 서비스를 제공한다.

| 해설 |
2 A.M.이라는 시점 명사와 함께 쓰이면서 동시에 stay open과 어울려 '~까지'라는 지속 상태를 나타내는 전치사 (D) until이 정답이다.

| 어휘 | favorite 가장 좋아하는 것 resident 주민 stay open 영업하다, 문을 열다 free 무료의

4. (A)

| 해석 |
계약서가 효력을 발휘하기 위해서는, 반드시 서명되어 5월 31일 이전에 저

희 사무실에서 받아야 합니다.
| 해설 |
May 31는 서명된 계약서를 받는 미래의 기준 시점이다. 따라서 '~ 이전에'를 의미하는 (A) before가 정답이다. (B) since는 과거의 시작 시점을 의미할 때 사용한다.
| 어휘 | for A to do A가 ~하기 위해, A가 ~할 수 있도록 contract 계약(서) go into effect 효력을 발휘하다, 발효되다 sign ~에 서명하다 receive ~을 받다

5. (B)
| 해석 |
Walker Institute는 캠페인을 시작한 후 30일 이내에 모금 목표액에 도달할 수 있었다.
| 해설 |
30 days는 기간을 나타내므로 기간 명사와 함께 사용하는 (B) within이 정답이다. (A) during은 지속 시간의 의미를 내포하는 명사와 함께 사용한다.
| 어휘 | reach ~에 도달하다, 이르다 fundraising 모금 (행사), 기금 마련 (행사) launch ~을 시작하다, ~에 착수하다

6. (B)
| 해석 |
유해 배출 물질로부터 보호하기 위하여, 테스트가 지속되는 내내 반드시 보호 안경을 착용하셔야 합니다.
| 해설 |
빈칸 뒤에 위치한 the duration은 지속 시간을 의미하는 명사이므로 '~ 동안 내내'라는 의미로 지속 시간 전체를 가리킬 때 사용하는 (B) throughout이 정답이다.
| 어휘 | protect against ~로부터 보호하다 harmful 유해한 emission 배출 물질

7. (C)
| 해석 |
Felicia Jones 씨가 진행하는 세미나는 Emerald Room의 기술적인 문제로 인해 다른 방으로 옮겨졌다.
| 해설 |
technical issues는 '기술적인 문제'를 의미하므로 세미나가 다른 곳으로 옮겨진 이유로 판단할 수 있다. 따라서 이유를 나타내는 전치사 (C) because of가 정답이다.
| 어휘 | led by ~가 진행하는, 이끄는 be moved to ~로 옮겨지다 instead of ~ 대신에 as a result 결과적으로 in order to (do) ~하기 위해

8. (D)
| 해석 |
The Vineyard는 향후 3년에 걸쳐 전국에 10개의 새로운 지사를 개설하는 계획을 발표했다.
| 해설 |
the nation은 그 앞에 언급된 '10개의 새로운 지사들'이 위치할 넓은 장소에 해당된다. 따라서 '~ 전역에서'라는 의미로 장소 범위를 나타낼 때 사용하는 (D) across가 정답이다.
| 어휘 | announce ~을 발표하다 branch office 지사, 지점 over ~ 동안에 걸쳐 beside ~ 옆에 regarding ~와 관련해

9. (C)
| 해석 |
Ranker 씨는 교육 분야에 대한 헌신으로 인해 올해의 최고 교사 후보로 지명되었다.
| 해설 |
빈칸 뒤의 명사구는 '교육 분야에 대한 헌신'을 의미하며, Ranker 씨가 최고의 교사 후보로 지명된 이유에 해당한다. 따라서 이유를 나타내는 전치사 (C) for가 정답이다.
| 어휘 | be nominated as ~의 후보로 지명되다 commitment 헌신 field 분야 education 교육

10. (B)
| 해석 |
회의장에서 걸어갈 수 있는 거리에 별 다섯 개짜리 식당들이 몇 개 있다.
| 해설 |
walking distance와 함께 쓰여 '걸을 수 있는 거리에'라는 표현을 구성할 수 있는 전치사인 (B) within이 정답이다.
| 어휘 | several 몇몇의, 여럿의 be located 위치하다 nearby a. 근처의 ad. 근처에

11. (B)
| 해석 |
Treetop Greenhouse는 스페인 분홍 장미나 허스턴 백합 같이 선택 가능한 아주 다양한 꽃들을 제공하고 있다.
| 해설 |
빈칸 뒤에 위치한 두 가지 꽃들은 앞서 언급된 다양한 종류의 꽃들에 대한 예시에 해당되므로 '~와 같은'이라는 의미의 전치사 (B) such as가 정답이다.
| 어휘 | offer ~을 제공하다 a wide range of 아주 다양한 choose from ~에서 선택하다 in addition 추가로, 게다가 while ~하는 동안, ~인 반면 even if 설사 ~한다 하더라도

12. (C)
| 해석 |
소득 수준에 상관없이 Virginia의 New Hope 지역 내 모든 시민들이 교육비에 대한 세금 혜택을 이용할 수 있다.
| 해설 |
'모든 시민들이 이용할 수 있다'는 말이 있으므로 빈칸 뒤에 언급된 '소득 수준'은 이용 조건이 아님을 알 수 있다. 따라서 '~에 상관없이'라는 의미의 (C) regardless of가 정답이다.
| 어휘 | tax 세금 benefit 혜택, 이점 expense 지출 (비용) citizen 시민 income 소득, 수입 prior to ~ 전에 along with ~와 함께

13. (D)
| 해석 |
많은 업적들 중에서, Oswald Trent 씨는 혁신적인 진공 청소기를 발명한 것으로 가장 잘 알려져 있다.
| 해설 |
his numerous achievements는 '혁신적인 진공 청소기의 발명'이라는 업적이 포함되는 범위에 해당된다. 따라서 '~ 중에서, ~에 포함된'이라는 의미의 전치사 (D) Among이 정답이다.
| 어휘 | numerous 많은, 다수의 achievement 업적, 성취 be best known for ~로 가장 잘 알려져 있다 invent ~을 발명하다 revolutionary 혁신적인

14. (B)
| 해석 |
Sinter Corp.는 전문적인 분위기를 유지하고 있지만, 대부분의 다른 회사들과는 달리 옷을 편하게 입어도 되는 근무 복장 규정이 있다.
| 해설 |
평상복을 입어도 되는 복장 규정은 빈칸 뒤에 위치한 '대부분의 다른 회사들(most other companies)'과 비교되는 부분에 해당된다. 따라서 '~와 달리'라는 의미의 전치사 (B) unlike가 정답이다.
| 어휘 | maintain ~을 유지하다 atmosphere 분위기 contrary 대조적인 aside 한쪽으로 except ~을 제외하고

15. (A)
| 해석 |
모든 방문객들은 입구 옆에 위치한 걸이에 걸려 있는 실험실 가운들 중 하나를 착용해야 한다.
| 해설 |
분사로 쓰인 동사 hang과 어울리는 위치 전치사로 '~에 걸려 있다'라는 의미를 나타낼 때 함께 사용하는 (A) on이 정답이다.

| 어휘 | be required to do ~해야 하다 put on ~을 착용하다, 입다 lab coat 실험실 가운 hang on ~에 걸려 있다 hook 고리, 걸이 entrance 입구

16. (C)

| 해석 |
여러 매장들이 새로운 라인의 믹서기 제품과 관련해 우리에게 연락해 오고 있는데, 고객들이 더 새로운 모델을 요청하고 있기 때문이다.

| 해설 |
a new line of mixers는 '새로운 라인의 믹서기'를 의미하며, 여러 매장들이 연락하는 목적이나 연락을 통한 대화 주제에 해당되므로 '~에 관련해' 등의 의미로 주제를 나타낼 때 사용하는 (C) regarding이 정답이다.

| 어휘 | contact ~에게 연락하다 as ~ 때문에 request ~을 요청하다, 요구하다 through ~을 통해서

17-20번 문제는 다음 기사를 참고하시오.

냉동 디저트 식품 시장에 진출하는 Tasty Plate

CHICAGO (6월 15일) – Chicago에 본사를 둔 냉동 식품 17 생산업체 Tasty Plate가 새로운 라인의 디저트 제품을 출시할 예정입니다. 이 회사는 냉동 식품 부문에 맛있는 중국 음식을 들여놓기를 원했던 요리사 Diana Wong 씨에 의해 30년도 더 이전에 설립되었습니다. 그 이후로, 이 업체의 제공 서비스는 성장을 거듭해 인도 요리와 멕시코 요리를 포함해 아주 다양한 종류의 요리를 포함하기에 이르렀습니다. 18 여러 다른 요리들 또한 이 업체에 의해 개발 중에 있습니다.

Tasty Plate는 올 19 연말까지 자사의 첫 디저트 제품을 출시할 계획이지만, 아직 최종 조리법을 개발하지 못했습니다. Tasty Plate의 수석 요리사인 Blaine Morris 씨는 냉동과 재가열이 잘되는 재료와 맛을 회사에서 찾아낼 수 있을 것이라고 계속 확신하고 있습니다. "디저트가 저희에게는 처음이기 때문에 이 일은 수많은 20 도전 과제를 제시하겠지만, 냉동 식품이 좋은 맛을 내도록 만드는 일은 저희 Tasty Plate가 전문으로 하는 것입니다."라고 그는 말했습니다.

| 어휘 | frozen 냉동된 Chicago-based Chicago에 본사를 둔 launch ~을 출시하다 line 제품 라인 more than ~가 넘는 section 부문, 영역 since then 그때 이후로 offering 제공(되는 것) grow to do 성장해서 ~하게 되다 include ~을 포함하다 a wide range of 아주 다양한 종류의 plan to do ~할 계획이다 release ~을 출시하다 have yet to do 아직 ~하지 못하다 develop ~을 개발하다 recipe 조리법 remain + 형용사 계속 ~한 상태로 있다, 여전히 ~한 상태이다 be able to do ~할 수 있다 ingredient (음식) 재료 flavor 맛 freeze 얼다, 얼리다 reheat 다시 데우다 present ~을 제시하다 numerous 수많은 specialize in ~을 전문으로 하다

17. (B)

| 해설 |
회사명에 해당되는 주어 Tasty Plate를 설명하는 삽입구에 빈칸이 속해 있으므로 Tasty Plate와 동격을 이룰 수 있는 '생산업체'라는 뜻의 명사 (B) producer가 정답이다.

18. (D)
(A) 모든 냉동 식품에는 반드시 유통 기한이 찍혀 있어야 합니다.
(B) 짐바브웨와 아르헨티나에도 제조 시설을 보유하고 있습니다.
(C) 그 레스토랑은 전 세계의 대부분의 주요 국가에 지점이 있습니다.

| 해설 |
앞 문장에 회사가 성장해 인도 요리와 멕시코 요리를 포함해 다양한 요리를 제공하게 되었다고 쓰여 있다. 따라서 그 외에 개발 중인 다른 요리들이 있다는 사실을 언급한 (D)가 정답이다.

| 어휘 | be stamped with ~가 찍혀 있다 expiration date 유통 기한, 만기일 manufacturing 제조 facility 시설물 as well ~도, 또한 location 지점, 위치 worldwide 전 세계에 cuisine 요리 develop ~을 개발하다

19. (D)

| 해설 |
빈칸 뒤에 위치한 the end of this year는 제품 출시 기한을 나타내는 시점 표현에 해당되므로 시점 명사와 함께 '~까지'라는 의미로 쓰이는 (D) by가 정답이다.

20. (C)

| 해설 |
주어 This는 앞 문장에서 말한 적합한 재료와 맛을 찾는 일을 가리키며, 빈칸 뒤에는 디저트 제품이 처음이라는 말이 쓰여 있다. 따라서 처음 개발하는 디저트에 필요한 재료와 맛을 찾는 과정에서 발생 가능한 일을 나타낼 명사가 필요하므로 '도전 과제, 힘든 일'을 뜻하는 (C) challenges가 정답이다.

| 어휘 | occasion 때, 경우, 행사

DAY 10 부사절 접속사/등위·상관 접속사

◆ 출제 포인트 1 부사절 접속사 자리 본책 p.203

1. Unless

| 해석 |
비가 곧 멈추지 않는다면, 경기는 나중에 다시 열릴 것이다.

| 해설 |
콤마 앞뒤에 각각 완전한 절이 왔으므로, 이 두 절을 연결할 수 있는 접속사인 Unless가 정답이다. Despite은 전치사이므로 답이 될 수 없다.

| 어휘 | reschedule 일정을 변경하다 later 나중의, 나중에

2. because

| 해설 |
여러 직원이 예기치 못하게 그만두는 바람에 레스토랑 개업식이 연기되었다.

| 해설 |
앞뒤에 각각 주어와 동사가 포함된 절이 하나씩 위치한 구조이므로 이 두 절을 연결하는 역할을 하는 접속사인 because가 정답이다.

| 어휘 | delay 연기하다 moreover 게다가 several 여럿의, 몇몇의 leave (회사 등을) 그만두다, 떠나다 unexpectedly 예기치 못하게

3. Once

| 해설 |
그 제품이 구매 가능하게 되는 대로, 저희가 이메일 통보를 드리겠습니다.

| 해설 |
콤마 앞뒤에 각각 완전한 절이 왔으므로, 이 두 절을 연결할 수 있는 접속사인 Once가 정답이다. Then은 부사이므로 답이 될 수 없다.

| 어휘 | notification 통보, 통지(서)

◆ 출제 포인트 2 부사절 접속사 (1) 이유/양보 본책 p.203

1. even though

| 해설 |
Whiteflower는 고급 호텔이기는 하지만 저렴한 객실 요금을 제공한다.

| 해설 |
'고급 호텔이지만 저렴한 요금을 제공한다'와 같은 의미가 되어야 자연스러우므로 '~이기는 하지만'이라는 뜻으로 양보를 나타내는 접속사 even though가 정답이다.

| 어휘 | rate 요금 luxurious 고급의, 호화로운

2. Since

| 해석 |
회사에 새로 입사한 직원이기 때문에, Farewell 씨는 회사 정책에 익숙하지 않다.

| 해설 |
회사에 새로 입사한 직원이라는 사실이 회사 정책에 익숙하지 않은 이유로 판단할 수 있으므로 이유를 나타내는 접속사인 Since가 정답이다.

| 어휘 | be familiar with ~에 익숙하다, 친숙하다 policy 정책, 방침

3. Although

| 해석 |
회사의 차량들이 출장용으로 이용 가능하기는 하지만, 대부분의 직원들은 개인 차량을 이용한다.

| 해설 |
'회사 차량을 이용할 수 있지만 직원들이 개인 차량을 이용한다'와 같은 의미가 되는 것이 가장 자연스러우므로 '~이기는 하지만'이라는 의미로 양보를 나타내는 접속사 Although가 정답이다.

| 어휘 | vehicle 차량

✦ 출제 포인트 3   부사절 접속사 (2) 시간/조건   본책 p.204

1. Before

| 해석 |
협상이 시작되기 전에, 대표이사는 어떤 일자리도 없어지지 않을 것이라고 보장했다.

| 해설 |
문맥상 '협상이 시작되도록'이라는 의미보다는 '협상 전에'라는 뜻이 되어야 적절하므로 Before가 정답이다.

| 어휘 | negotiation 협상, 협의 guarantee (that) ~임을 보장하다

2. if

| 해석 |
악천후가 발생될 경우에 음악 콘서트가 실내로 옮겨질 것입니다.

| 해설 |
악천후가 발생되는 것은 콘서트가 실내로 옮겨지는 조건에 해당되므로 조건을 나타내는 접속사 if가 정답이다.

| 어휘 | indoors 실내로 inclement weather 악천후

3. as soon as

| 해석 |
Rodriguez 씨가 편집을 완료하자마자 직원 사진이 온라인상에 업로드될 것이다.

| 해설 |
편집이 완료되어야 사진이 온라인으로 업로드될 수 있는 것이므로 '~하자마자'라는 의미의 접속사 as soon as가 정답이다.

| 어휘 | edit ~을 편집하다

✦ 출제 포인트 4   부사절 접속사 (3) 목적/결과   본책 p.204

1. so that

| 해석 |
저희가 좌석을 마련할 수 있도록 귀하께서 참가 가능하신지를 11월 1일까지 제게 알려 주시기 바랍니다.

| 해설 |
좌석을 마련하는 일이 11월 1일까지 참가 여부를 통보 받아야 하는 목적에 해당되므로 '~하기 위해서'를 의미하는 so that이 정답이다.

| 어휘 | whether ~인지 (아닌지) participate 참가하다 arrange ~을 마련하다, 조치하다 seating 좌석(의 설비)

2. that

| 해석 |
낮춰진 속도 제한이 매우 효과적이어서 연간 사고가 50퍼센트 감소되었다.

| 해설 |
앞에 위치한 'so + 형용사'와 결합될 수 있는 것으로서 '너무 ~해서 …하게 되다'라는 의미를 구성할 때 사용하는 that이 정답이다.

| 어휘 | reduced 낮춰진, 감소된 effective 효과적인 annual 연간의, 해마다의 drop 감소하다, 줄어들다 by (차이) ~만큼

3. so

| 해석 |
귀하의 서비스가 중단되지 않고 지속될 수 있도록 기한이 지난 고지서 비용을 즉시 납부하시기 바랍니다.

| 해설 |
서비스를 중단하지 않고 지속시키는 일은 밀린 비용을 납부하는 목적에 해당되므로 목적을 나타낼 때 사용하는 접속사 so가 정답이다. so that에서 that은 이와 같이 생략 가능하다.

| 어휘 | overdue 기한이 지난 bill 청구서 immediately 즉시 continue uninterrupted 중단되지 않고 지속되다

✦ 출제 포인트 5   부사절의 축약   본책 p.205

1. speaking

| 해석 |
기자에게 얘기할 때, Sara Baker 씨는 합병의 중요성을 강조했다.

| 해설 |
주절의 주어 Sara Baker가 기자에게 말하는 주체에 해당되므로 능동태 구문이 축약된 구조가 되어야 알맞다. 따라서 speaking이 정답이다.

| 어휘 | emphasize ~을 강조하다 importance 중요(성) merger 합병

2. before

| 해석 |
여객선의 모든 탑승객들은 승선하기 전에 각자의 수하물을 확인하도록 권고됩니다.

| 해설 |
부사절을 축약하여 '부사절 접속사 + -ing' 형태로 사용 가능한 접속사가 필요하므로 before가 정답이다.

| 어휘 | be encouraged to do ~하도록 권장되다 luggage 수하물 board ~에 탑승하다

3. As

| 해석 |
보고서에 나타난 바와 같이, 오디오북에 대한 소비자들의 관심이 상당히 증가되었다.

| 해설 |
'보고서에 나타난 바와 같이'라는 의미가 되어야 적절하므로 '~한 대로, ~한 것과 같이' 등의 의미로 출처나 근거 내용을 나타낼 때 사용하는 접속사 As가 정답이다.

| 어휘 | indicate ~을 나타내다, 가리키다 consumer 소비자 interest in ~에 대한 관심 increase 증가되다 significantly 상당히, 많이

✦ 출제 포인트 6   등위 접속사 / 상관 접속사   본책 p.205

1. and

| 해석 |
그 기사는 저희 웹 사이트에서 삭제되었고, 저희는 그 기사의 부정확성에 대해 사과 드립니다.

| 해설 |
과거 시점에 취해진 조치와 현재 시점의 사과를 나타내는 절들이 앞뒤에 나열되어 있으므로 순차적으로 발생된 일을 연결할 수 있는 and가 정답이

다. or는 선택 사항이나 부정적인 결과를 제시할 때 쓰이므로 맞지 않다.
| 어휘 | remove ~을 없애다   apologize for ~에 대해 사과하다   inaccuracy 부정확(성)

2. or
| 해석 |
이번 주말에 구매하시는 영화 입장권에는 무료 팝콘 또는 탄산 음료 중의 하나가 포함됩니다.
| 해설 |
앞에 위치한 either와 짝을 이뤄 'A 또는 B 둘 중의 하나'라는 의미를 나타내는 or가 정답이다. and는 both와 함께 'both A and B'의 구조를 이룰 때 사용한다.
| 어휘 | purchase 구매(품)   include ~을 포함하다   free 무료의

3. so
| 해석 |
도쿄에서 운전하는 것은 혼란스러울 수 있으므로, 네비게이션 시스템을 이용하는 것이 도움이 된다.
| 해설 |
도쿄에서 운전하는 일이 혼란스럽다는 사실은 네비게이션이 도움이 된다는 점의 원인으로 볼 수 있으므로 '그러므로, 그래서' 등의 의미로 결과를 나타낼 때 사용하는 등위 접속사 so가 정답이다.
| 어휘 | confusing 혼란스러운

DAY 10 | 실전문제   본책 p.206

정답
1	(B)	2	(C)	3	(C)	4	(B)	5	(D)	6	(B)
7	(C)	8	(B)	9	(D)	10	(C)	11	(A)	12	(C)
13	(D)	14	(A)	15	(D)	16	(B)	17	(D)	18	(B)
19	(B)	20	(A)								

1. (B)
| 해석 |
시에서 허가증을 승인할 때까지, 97번가 현장의 공사 작업은 보류 상태로 유지될 것이다.
| 해설 |
콤마 앞뒤에 각각 완전한 절이 있으므로 이 절들을 연결할 수 있는 접속사 (B) Until이 정답이다.
| 어휘 | approve ~을 승인하다   permit 허가증   site 현장   remain + 형용사 ~한 상태로 남아 있다   suspended 보류된, 유예된

2. (C)
| 해석 |
추적 번호와 배송 물품의 중량이 컴퓨터에 입력 완료된 후에 상자들이 적재되어야 한다.
| 해설 |
빈칸 뒤에 after절의 주어가 'A and B'의 구조로 쓰여 있으므로 이 구조와 함께 상관 접속사를 이룰 수 있는 (C) both가 정답이다. (A) nor는 neither와 함께, (B) either는 'A or B'의 구조와 함께 사용된다.
| 어휘 | load ~을 적재하다, 싣다   tracking number 추적 번호   enter A into B A를 B에 입력하다

3. (C)
| 해석 |
인사부장이 모든 면접을 완료한 후에 채용 결정을 내릴 것이다.
| 해설 |
빈칸 앞뒤에 각각 완전한 절이 있으므로 빈칸은 이 절들을 연결할 접속사 자리이다. 따라서 유일한 접속사인 (C) after가 정답이다. (A) then은 부사, (B) with와 (D) from은 전치사이다.
| 어휘 | human resources manager 인사부장   make a decision 결정을

내리다   hiring 고용   complete ~을 완료하다

4. (B)
| 해석 |
Yolanda Gates 씨는 오늘 아침에 시장 선거 운동을 공언했지만, 아직 모금 활동을 시작하지 못했다.
| 해설 |
빈칸 앞뒤의 두 절을 역접 관계로 연결할 수 있는 접속사 (B) but이 정답이다. (A) likewise는 부사이며, (C) whether는 접속사이지만 의미가 맞지 않고, (D) next는 형용사이다.
| 어휘 | announce ~을 발표하다   campaign 선거 운동, 유세 활동   have yet to do 아직 ~하지 못하다   fundraising 모금 (활동), 자금 마련   likewise 마찬가지로   whether ~인지 (아닌지)

5. (D)
| 해석 |
직원들이 컬러 복사를 하도록 허용되기는 하지만, 경영진에서는 가급적이면 흑색 잉크를 사용하도록 요청하고 있다.
| 해설 |
콤마 앞뒤의 두 절을 '~이기는 하지만'이라는 의미로 연결할 수 있는 양보의 접속사 (D) Although가 정답이다.
| 어휘 | be allowed to do ~하도록 허용되다   make a copy 복사하다   management 경영(진)   request that ~하도록 요청하다, 요구하다   whenever possible 가급적이면, 가능한 한   despite ~에도 불구하고

6. (B)
| 해석 |
우리가 계약서 세부 사항을 최종 확정할 수 있도록 Bradford 씨가 내일 우리 사무실을 방문할 예정이다.
| 해설 |
빈칸 뒤에 위치한 that과 결합하여 목적의 의미를 나타낼 수 있는 (B) so가 정답이다.
| 어휘 | finalize ~을 최종 확정하다   contract 계약(서)   details 세부 사항

7. (C)
| 해석 |
Kenny 박사의 강연은 언제나 호평을 받고 있는데, 그가 중요한 정보를 명확하게 설명하는 능력을 지니고 있기 때문이다.
| 해설 |
빈칸 앞뒤에 각각 위치한 두 절을 연결할 접속사 자리이다. 명확하게 설명하는 능력이 강연에 대해 호평을 받는 이유이므로 (C) because가 정답이다.
| 어휘 | well received 호평을 받는   ability to do ~할 수 있는 능력   clearly 명확하게, 분명하게

8. (B)
| 해석 |
일부 오래된 파일들을 살펴보는 동안, 우리는 창업주가 이전 사장님과 촬영한 사진 한 장을 발견했다.
| 해설 |
동사의 -ing형과 결합할 수 있는 접속사를 찾아야 한다. '오래된 파일을 살펴보는 동안'이라는 의미가 되어야 적절하므로 (B) While이 정답이다. (A) In addition은 부사구의 역할을 하며, (C) Because of는 전치사이다. (D) As though도 부사절 접속사이지만 의미가 어울리지 않는다.
| 어휘 | sort through (정리 등을 위해) ~을 자세히 살펴보다   discover ~을 발견하다   founder 창업주, 설립자   former 이전의   in addition 추가로

9. (B)
| 해석 |
개조 공사가 완료되는 대로 보험사 직원이 그 주택의 가치를 다시 평가할 것이다.

| 해설 |
빈칸 앞뒤에 위치한 두 절을 '~하는 대로'라는 의미로 연결할 접속사 (B) once가 정답이다. (A) still과 (C) later는 부사이고, (D) while도 접속사이지만 문장의 의미에 어울리지 않는다.
| 어휘 | insurance agent 보험사 직원 assess ~을 평가하다 value 가치 renovation 개조, 보수

10. (C)
| 해설 |
Madison Aquarium을 둘러보실 때, 유리 벽을 손으로 두드리거나 동물에게 먹이를 주는 일을 삼가도록 요청 드립니다.
| 해설 |
exploring과 결합해 '수족관을 둘러볼 때'라는 의미가 되어야 자연스러우므로 '~할 때'를 뜻하는 부사절 접속사 (C) When이 정답이다. (A) During은 전치사이며, (B) So that은 접속사이지만 '접속사 + -ing' 구조로 쓰이지 않는다. (D) In order to는 동사 원형과 함께 사용한다.
| 어휘 | explore ~을 둘러보다 ask that ~하도록 요청하다 refrain from -ing ~하는 것을 삼가다 tap on (손으로) ~을 두드리다 feed ~에게 먹이를 주다 in order to do ~할 수 있도록

11. (A)
| 해설 |
Jeff Thomas 씨께서 회의에 직접 참석하실 수는 없지만, 화상 회의를 통해 참여하실 것입니다.
| 해설 |
콤마 앞뒤에 각각 위치한 두 절을 '비록 ~이지만'이라는 의미로 연결할 수 있는 양보의 접속사 (A) While이 정답이다. (B) As if와 (D) Whether도 접속사이지만 의미상 부적합하고, (C) Immediately는 부사이다.
| 어휘 | be unable to do ~할 수 없다 in person 직접 (가서) via ~을 통해 video conference 화상 회의 immediately 즉시

12. (C)
| 해설 |
이제 성수기가 시작되었으므로, Virginia Beach 구역 내의 호텔과 레스토랑들은 평소보다 더 바쁘다.
| 해설 |
콤마 앞뒤에 각각 위치한 두 절을 연결할 접속사로 '이제 성수기가 시작되었으므로 평소보다 더 바쁘다'와 같이 이유를 나타낼 수 있는 (C) Now that이 정답이다.
| 어휘 | peak season 성수기 than normal 평소보다 in particular 특히

13. (D)
| 해설 |
Draper 씨는 신규 고객과 만날 때, 항상 자신의 명함 한 장을 반드시 남겨 놓는다.
| 해설 |
콤마 앞뒤의 두 절을 '~할 때'라는 의미로 연결할 수 있는 접속사 (D) When이 정답이다. 나머지 선택지의 접속사는 의미상 적절하지 않다.
| 어휘 | make sure to do 반드시 ~하다 leave ~을 남겨 놓다

14. (A)
| 해설 |
기계 담당 기사들은 책임자에 의해 별도로 지시를 받지 않는 한 항상 각자의 장비 옆에서 자리를 지키고 있어야 한다.
| 해설 |
빈칸 뒤에 주어 없이 부사 otherwise와 과거 분사 instructed만 있으므로 '부사절 접속사 + p.p.' 축약 구조가 되어야 한다. 따라서 부사 otherwise, 과거 분사 instructed와 함께 '별도의 지시가 없으면'이라는 부정 조건을 나타내는 접속사 (A) unless가 정답이다.
| 어휘 | operator (기계 등의) 기사, 운전자 equipment 장비 at all times 항상

15. (D)
| 해설 |
Heaven's 카페의 출장 요리 책임자는 특별 요청 사항이 최소 48시간 전에 미리 이뤄지기만 하면 그것을 수용할 수 있다.
| 해설 |
빈칸 앞뒤의 두 절을 연결할 접속사가 필요한데, 48시간 전에 요청하는 것이 요청 수용의 조건이므로 조건 접속사 (D) as long as가 정답이다. (A) prior to와 (C) according to는 전치사이며, (B) unless는 접속사이지만 의미가 맞지 않는다.
| 어휘 | caterer 출장 요리업자, 출장 요리업체 accommodate ~을 수용하다 make a request 요청하다, 요구하다 at least 최소한 in advance 미리 prior to ~에 앞서 according to ~에 따르면

16. (B)
| 해설 |
지원서는 금요일 업무 시간 종료 시점까지 접수된다는 조건 하에 받아들여질 것이다.
| 해설 |
빈칸 앞뒤의 두 절을 연결할 접속사가 필요하므로 유일한 접속사인 (B) provided that이 정답이다. (A) regardless of와 (C) as a result of는 전치사이며, (D) rather than은 각각 주어와 동사가 포함된 두 절을 연결하는 접속사로 쓰이지 않는다.
| 어휘 | application 지원(서), 신청(서) accept ~을 받아들이다 by (기한) ~까지 regardless of ~에 상관 없이 provided that ~을 조건으로 as a result of ~의 결과로서

17-20번 문제는 다음 공지를 참고하시오.

전 직원에게 알립니다.

저희는 <Risen from Waste>라는 제목으로 지역 미술가인 Cathy Krum 씨의 작품을 볼 수 있는 특별 미술 공개 행사에 여러분 모두를 초대하고자 합니다. 이 행사는 우리의 Art in the Square 시리즈의 일환으로 8월 17일에서 29일까지 중앙 아트리움에서 개최될 것입니다. 이 전시회가 300곳이 넘는 도시를 순회해 **17** 오긴 했지만, 이번 행사는 Greensboro에서 처음 열리는 것입니다.

<Risen from Waste>는 낡은 타이어나 버려진 가구 등과 같은 **18** 재활용 물품들만 전적으로 활용해 만든 작품들을 특징으로 합니다. Krum 씨는 이 물품들을 활용하는 것이 환경 보존의 중요성에 관한 메시지를 전하는 데 도움이 될 것으로 생각하고 있습니다.

이번 전시회를 방문하는 것은 당연히 **19** 선택적이기는 하지만, 저희는 모든 직원들께 잠시 시간 내어 들러 보시기를 권합니다. Krum 씨의 작품은 독보적인 것이며, 우리 도시에서 오직 잠시 동안만 개최될 것입니다. **20** 이 전시회를 보는 것이 여러분의 하루에 잠깐이나마 휴식을 가져다 주리라 생각합니다.

| 어휘 | invite A to B A를 B로 초대하다 showcase 공개 행사 entitled A A라는 제목의 hold ~을 개최하다 atrium 아트리움, 안뜰 as part of ~의 일환으로 exhibition 전시회 feature ~을 특징으로 하다 piece 작품 entirely 전적으로 made of ~로 만들어진 material 물품, 재료 discarded 버려진 help do ~하는 데 도움이 되다 spread ~을 전하다, 퍼뜨리다 conservation 보존 encourage A to do A에게 ~하도록 권하다 take a few moments to do 잠시 시간 내어 ~하다 stop by 들르다 one-of-a-kind 독보적인

17. (D)
| 해설 |
빈칸 뒤에 두 개의 절이 있으므로 빈칸은 접속사 자리이다. '300곳이 넘는 도시를 다녔지만, Greensboro는 처음이다'와 같은 양보의 의미가 되어야 적절하므로 '비록 ~이기는 하지만'을 뜻하는 접속사 (D) Although가 정답이다.

| 어휘 | besides 게다가 therefore 따라서

18. (B)
| 해설 |
빈칸은 전치사 of의 목적어인 materials를 수식할 형용사 자리이며, 분사가 그 역할을 대신할 수 있다. 물품은 사람에 의해 재활용되는 대상이므로 수동의 의미를 나타내는 과거 분사 (B) recycled가 정답이다.

19. (B)
| 해설 |
앞부분과 대조적인 내용이 이어지는 but절에 꼭 가보도록 당부하는 내용이 나온다. 따라서 주절은 꼭 가보지 않아도 된다는 의미가 되어야 알맞으므로 필수가 아님을 나타내는 형용사로서 '선택적인'을 의미하는 (B) optional이 정답이다.
| 어휘 | accessible 접근할 수 있는, 이용할 수 있는 irrelevant 무관한

20. (A)
(B) 행사가 끝날 때 모든 작품이 구매 가능했습니다.
(C) 플라스틱 병과 깨진 유리, 그리고 신문지도 사용되었습니다.
(D) 이것이 바로 우리가 살고 있는 세상을 보호하는 것이 필수인 이유입니다.
| 해설 |
앞서 꼭 가보도록 당부하는 말과 함께 훌륭한 전시회임을 강조했다. 따라서 해당 전시회를 it으로 지칭해 그곳을 방문하는 것에 따른 긍정적인 영향을 알리는 (A)가 정답이다.
| 어휘 | view ~을 보다 relaxation 휴식 necessary 필수인, 필요한 protect ~을 보호하다 planet 세상, 행성

DAY 11 명사절 접속사/형용사절 접속사(=관계대명사)

◆ 출제 포인트 1 명사절의 위치
본책 p.209

1. That
| 해석 |
Mitchell 씨의 제안이 위원회의 승인을 받지 못했다는 것은 놀라운 일이었다.
| 해설 |
빈칸 이하부터 동사(was) 앞 까지의 주어 역할을 하는 명사절을 이끌어야 하므로 명사절 접속사인 That이 정답이다.
| 어휘 | proposal 제안 approve 승인하다 committee 위원회 surprising 놀라운

2. whether
| 해석 |
많은 고객들이 서비스가 곧 복구될 것인지를 묻기 위해 오늘 아침에 회사로 전화했다.
| 해설 |
타동사 ask의 목적어 역할을 할 명사절을 이끌어야 하므로 명사절 접속사인 whether가 정답이다.
| 어휘 | ask whether ~인지 (아닌지) 묻다 restore ~을 복구하다, 회수시키다

3. whether
| 해석 |
우천 여부에 상관없이, Chester Park에서 단체 사진 촬영이 있을 것이다.
| 해설 |
전치사 Regardless of의 목적어 역할을 할 명사절을 이끌 접속사가 필요하므로 whether가 정답이다. even은 부사이다.
| 어휘 | regardless of ~에 상관 없이 take a photograph 사진을 찍다

◆ 출제 포인트 2 명사절 접속사 (1) that/whether/how
본책 p.209

1. that
| 해석 |
그 자선 행사의 진행 책임자는 10,000달러가 넘는 금액을 모금할 것으로 추정하고 있다.
| 해설 |
빈칸 뒤의 완전한 절과 어울리며 의미상으로도 '~하는 것'이 적합하므로 이러한 기능을 가진 명사절 접속사 that이 정답이다.
| 어휘 | coordinator (행사 등의) 진행 책임자 charity 자선 (활동) raise ~을 모금하다 over ~가 넘는

2. how
| 해석 |
보너스는 직원이 얼마나 많은 휴가를 사용했는지에 따라 다를 것이다.
| 해설 |
on의 목적어 역할을 할 명사절을 이끌 접속사로 쓰이면서 바로 뒤에 위치한 형용사 many와 결합 가능한 how가 정답이다.
| 어휘 | differ 다르다, 차이가 나다 depending on ~에 따라 다른

3. whether
| 해석 |
사건 보고서가 Gyatt 씨의 최신 승용차가 리콜되어야 하는지를 결정할 것이다.
| 해설 |
타동사 determine의 목적어 역할을 할 명사절을 이끌어야 하므로 명사절 접속사인 whether가 정답이다.
| 어휘 | incident 사건 determine ~을 결정하다 recall (결함 제품 등) ~을 리콜하다, 회수하다

◆ 출제 포인트 3 명사절 접속사 (2) who/what/which
본책 p.210

1. which
| 해석 |
이번 홍보 행사 중에, 고객들이 어느 아이스크림 맛이 가장 좋은지를 결정할 것이다.
| 해설 |
바로 뒤의 명사구 ice cream flavor를 수식해 선택과 관련된 의미를 나타내야 하므로 which가 정답이다.
| 어휘 | promotion 홍보 (행사) decide ~을 결정하다 flavor 맛

2. what
| 해석 |
무엇이 놀라운 선거 결과를 초래했는지를 분석가들이 아마도 정확히 밝혀낼 것이다.
| 해설 |
determine의 목적어절에 주어가 없으므로, 목적어절을 이끄는 접속사의 역할과 동사 caused의 주어의 역할을 동시에 할 수 있는 what이 정답이다.
| 어휘 | analyst 분석가 likely 아마도 determine ~을 밝혀내다 exactly 정확히 cause ~을 초래하다 election 선거

3. who
| 해석 |
우리는 숙박 시설을 예약하기 전에 누가 콘퍼런스에 참석할지를 결정해야 한다.
| 해설 |
decide의 목적어에 해당되는 명사절 내에서 동사 will be attending의 주어가 필요하므로 주어 역할이 가능한 who가 정답이다.
| 어휘 | book ~을 예약하다 accommodations 숙박 시설

◆ 출제 포인트 4 명사절 접속사+to부정사

1. whether
| 해석 |
다양한 저희 휴가 패키지를 통해 모험 또는 휴식 중에 어느 것을 추구할지 선택하실 수 있습니다.
| 해설 |
뒤에 위치한 or와 결합 가능한 접속사가 필요하므로 whether가 정답이다.
| 어휘 | whether to do A or B A 또는 B 중에서 어느 것을 할지   pursue ~을 추구하다   adventure 모험   relaxation 휴식

2. how
| 해석 |
Nolan Communications는 다양한 프로그래밍 언어 사용법을 아는 기술자를 채용하는 중이다.
| 해설 |
바로 뒤의 to부정사와 결합 가능한 접속사가 필요하므로 how가 정답이다.
| 어휘 | programming language 프로그래밍 언어

3. which
| 해석 |
저희 스타일리스트가 귀하의 의상에 맞춰 어떤 신발을 선택해야 할지 결정하는 데 도움을 드릴 것입니다.
| 해설 |
바로 뒤에 위치한 명사 shoes를 수식해 선택의 의미를 나타내야 알맞으므로 which가 정답이다.
| 어휘 | help A do A가 ~하는 것을 돕다   determine ~을 결정하다   outfit 의상

◆ 출제 포인트 5 형용사절 접속사(관계대명사)의 종류 (1)

1. who
| 해석 |
해당 라디오 광고를 언급하는 어느 고객이든 막대 빵을 무료로 받으시게 됩니다.
| 해설 |
동사 mentions의 주어 역할을 함과 동시에 사람 선행사 Any customer를 수식해야 하므로 주격 관계대명사 who가 정답이다.
| 어휘 | mention ~을 언급하다   advertisement 광고   order 주문(품)

2. that
| 해석 |
Trent Elliot 씨는 풍력 에너지의 분배를 용이하게 해 주는 사업을 시작하기를 바라고 있다.
| 해설 |
동사 facilitates의 주어 역할을 함과 동시에 사물 선행사 business를 수식해야 하므로 주격 관계대명사 that이 정답이다.
| 어휘 | facilitate ~을 용이하게 하다   distribution 유통, 분배

3. which
| 해석 |
Nashville Chicken은 다섯 곳의 지점을 보유하고 있는데, 그중 하나는 현재 개조 공사로 인해 문을 닫은 상태이다.
| 해설 |
전치사 of와 결합 가능한 관계대명사가 필요한데, 사물 선행사 five locations를 수식해야 하므로 which가 정답이다.
| 어휘 | location 지점, 위치   currently 현재   renovation 개조 (공사)

◆ 출제 포인트 6 형용사절 접속사(관계대명사)의 종류 (2)

1. whose
| 해석 |
우리는 전문지식이 우리의 요구에 더 잘 맞는 다른 후보로 결정했다.
| 해설 |
사람 선행사와 (candidate) 함께 쓰이며 동시에 뒤의 명사 expertise를 수식할 수 있는 것은 소유격 관계대명사 whose이다.
| 어휘 | candidate 지원자, 후보자   expertise 전문지식   suit one's needs ~의 요구에 부합하다

2. whose
| 해석 |
팀원들이 서로 다른 교대 근무를 하는 팀들은 자체 회의 시간을 마련해야 한다.
| 해설 |
사물 선행사 teams를 수식함과 동시에 바로 뒤의 명사 members도 수식할 수 있는 것은 소유격 관계대명사 whose이다.
| 어휘 | shift 교대 근무(조)   arrange ~을 마련하다, 조정하다

3. who
| 해석 |
1년 구독을 구입하는 고객분들에게 30%의 할인이 이용 가능합니다.
| 해설 |
동사 purchase의 주어 역할을 함과 동시에 사람 선행사 customers를 수식해야 하므로 주격 관계대명사 who가 정답이다.
| 어휘 | available 이용 가능한   purchase 구매하다   subscription 정기 구독

DAY 11 | 실전문제

정답 1 (B) 2 (C) 3 (D) 4 (A) 5 (B) 6 (B)
      7 (D) 8 (B) 9 (D) 10 (D) 11 (D) 12 (B)
      13 (B) 14 (B) 15 (D) 16 (D) 17 (D) 18 (D)
      19 (D) 20 (C)

1. (B)
| 해석 |
그 회사는 거래 계약이 확정될 때까지 Eclectic Motors와 협상된 계약 조항을 논의하지 않을 것이다.
| 해설 |
빈칸 뒤의 동사 were의 주어이자 사물 선행사 contract terms를 수식할 관계대명사가 필요하므로 (B) that이 정답이다.
| 어휘 | discuss ~을 논의하다   contract terms 계약 조항, 약관   negotiate ~을 협상하다   deal 거래   final (최종) 확정적인

2. (C)
| 해석 |
<Toronto Daily> 디지털 패키지를 신청한 구독자들은 온라인 기사에 대한 무제한 이용 권한이 있다.
| 해설 |
빈칸 뒤의 동사 have signed up의 주어이자 사람 선행사 subscribers를 수식할 관계대명사가 필요하므로 (C) who가 정답이다.
| 어휘 | subscriber 구독자   sign up for ~을 신청하다   unlimited 무제한의   access to ~에 대한 이용 (권한)

3. (D)
| 해석 |
그 회사는 해외 투자를 기술한 작년 예산 보고서를 아직 발표해야 한다.

| 해설 |
선행사가 사물(report)이며 빈칸 뒤의 동사 describes의 주어 역할을 해야 하므로 사물 주격 관계대명사 (D) which가 정답이다.
| 어휘 | still 여전히   release 발표하다   budget 예산   describe 설명하다, 기술하다   overseas 해외의   investment 투자

4. (A)
| 해석 |
과학자들은 수질 오염이 지역 사회에서 높은 발생 비율을 보이고 있는 피부 질환의 원인인지를 밝혀내기를 원한다.
| 해설 |
find out은 목적어를 필요로 하는 동사구이므로 빈칸 이하는 명사절이 되어야 알맞다. 따라서 유일한 명사절 접속사인 (A) whether가 정답이다.
| 어휘 | find out ~을 밝혀내다   pollution 오염   be responsible for ~에 대한 원인이다   rate 비율   disease 질환   either 둘 중 하나

5. (B)
| 해석 |
Kirking 호텔의 Bella Johnson 대표이사는 새로운 고급 숙박 시설 체인을 개장할 예정이라고 발표했다.
| 해설 |
빈칸 앞에 위치한 동사 announced의 목적어 역할을 할 명사절을 이끌며 접속사로서, 뒤에 완전한 절이 이어지는 명사절 접속사인 (B) that이 정답이다.
| 어휘 | announce that ~라고 발표하다

6. (B)
| 해설 |
Baritone 사는 Waters Building 3층에 사무실이 위치해 있는 회계 법인을 인수했다.
| 해설 |
빈칸 바로 뒤의 명사 office를 수식함과 동시에 사물 선행사 accounting firm을 수식할 수 있는 것은 소유격 관계대명사이므로 (B) whose가 정답이다.
| 어휘 | purchase ~을 매입하다   accounting firm 회계 법인   floor 층

7. (D)
| 해석 |
그 요리사는 감자를 곁들인 닭고기 요리를 제공할 것인지 아니면 구운 생선과 채소를 제공할 것인지를 결정해야 한다.
| 해설 |
빈칸 바로 뒤의 to부정사와 결합 가능하면서 동사 decide의 목적어로 쓰일 명사절을 이끌 접속사가 필요하다. or와도 어울리는 (D) whether가 정답이다.
| 어휘 | serve (음식 등) ~을 제공하다   baked 구운

8. (B)
| 해석 |
대부분의 Morris City 주민들은 지역 경제의 약 30퍼센트를 차지하고 있는 철강 산업에서 일한다.
| 해설 |
선행사가 사물(steel industry)이며 주어 없는 절을 이끌 관계대명사가 필요하므로 이 역할이 가능한 (B) which가 정답이다.
| 어휘 | resident 주민   steel 철강   industry 산업   account for ~을 차지하다   local economy 지역 경제

9. (D)
| 해석 |
의제에 따르면, 우리는 현재 사무실의 특징들이 회사에서 필요로 하는 부분에 얼마나 잘 부합하는지를 논의할 것이다.
| 해설 |
빈칸 바로 뒤의 부사 well과 결합 가능하면서 동사 discuss의 목적어로 쓰일 명사절을 이끌 접속사가 필요하므로 (D) how가 정답이다.
| 어휘 | according to ~에 따르면   agenda 의제   current 현재의   feature 특징   suit ~에 어울리다

10. (D)
| 해석 |
배우들이 오늘 저녁 7시에 초연될 예정인 연극 공연을 위한 최종 리허설을 진행 중이다.
| 해설 |
콤마 뒤에 위치할 수 있으면서 그 뒤에 위치한 과거 분사 set과 결합 가능한 형태가 필요하므로 관계대명사 which와 be 동사가 결합된 (D) which is가 정답이다. 관계대명사 that은 콤마 뒤에 오지 못한다.
| 어휘 | rehearsal 리허설, 예행 연습   be set to do ~할 예정이다   debut (공연 등이) 초연되다

11. (D)
| 해석 |
Right Start는 교육 프로그램으로서 고등학생들이 어느 진로를 추구해야 하는지를 선택하는 데 도움을 준다.
| 해설 |
빈칸 바로 뒤의 '명사 + to부정사'와 결합 가능한 접속사가 필요하므로 (D) which가 정답이다.
| 어휘 | career path 진로   pursue ~을 추구하다

12. (B)
| 해석 |
저희 투자자들이 시제품 작업이 어떻게 진척되고 있는지 확인하기 위해 New Haven 시설을 방문할 예정입니다.
| 해설 |
빈칸에 동사 see의 목적어 역할을 할 명사절을 이끌 접속사가 필요하므로 유일한 명사절 접속사인 (B) how가 정답이다.
| 어휘 | facility 시설(물)   prototype 시제품   progress 진척되다   upon (-ing) ~하자마자

13. (B)
| 해석 |
Moreno 씨의 Perth로의 전근 요청이 승인될 것인지는 두고 봐야 한다.
| 해설 |
맨 앞의 it은 가주어이므로 빈칸 이하의 절이 진주어인 명사절이다. 따라서 유일한 명사절 접속사인 (B) whether가 정답이다. It remains to be seen은 whether가 이끄는 절과 결합해 '~인지 (아닌지) 두고 봐야 한다'라는 의미를 나타낸다.
| 어휘 | request 요청(서)   transfer ~을 전근시키다   approve ~을 승인하다   as if 마치 ~인 것처럼   whereas ~인 반면

14. (B)
| 해석 |
승객들이 무료로 각자의 예약을 취소할 수 있는지는 그들이 구입한 티켓 유형에 달려 있다.
| 해설 |
빈칸 뒤로 동사가 두 개(are와 depends) 쓰여 있으므로 depends 앞까지는 문장의 주어 역할을 하는 명사절이 되어야 알맞다. 따라서 명사절 접속사인 (B) Whether가 정답이다.
| 어휘 | depend on ~에 달려 있다   purchase ~을 구입하다   thus 따라서   additionally 추가로   even if 설사 ~라 하더라도

15. (D)
| 해석 |
Malcolm Engineering은 서른 명의 신입 사원을 고용했는데, 이들 대부분은 최근 졸업생들이다.
| 해설 |
바로 뒤에 위치한 동사 are의 주어 역할을 하면서, 절과 절을 연결할 접속

사가 필요하므로 관계대명사와 결합되어 주어 역할을 할 수 있는 형태인 most of whom이 정답이다.
| 어휘 | recent 최근의   graduate 졸업생

16. (D)
| 해석 |
직원 생산성과 관련된 통찰을 얻기 위해, 신임 부서장은 직원들에게 각자의 일이 무엇을 포함하는지 설명하도록 요청했다.
| 해설 |
빈칸 이하 부분은 동사 describe의 목적어로 쓰일 명사절이 되어야 하는데, 이 절은 동사 involve의 목적어가 빠진 불완전한 구조이다. 따라서 불완전한 절을 이끄는 명사절 접속사 (D) what이 정답이다.
| 어휘 | insight 통찰(력)   productivity 생산성   describe ~을 설명하다   involve ~을 포함하다

17-20번 문제는 다음 기사를 참고하시오.

Phoenix의 스타 – 비즈니스 요약 기사

PHOENIX (2월 3일) — Otto G. Clancy가 Nile River Manufacturing의 최고 재무 이사(CFO)로 승진되었습니다. 이번 승진은 화요일에 발표된 보도 자료를 통해 **17** 확인되었습니다. **18** Clancy 씨는 5년간 수석 회계 책임자로 근무해 왔습니다. 최고 재무 이사로서, 그는 회사의 투자와 재무 관련 보고를 총괄할 것입니다. **19** 추가로, 회사의 어느 영역이 향후에 가장 수익성이 높을 가능성이 있는지를 결정하는 일도 맡게 될 것입니다. Clancy 씨는 또한 작년에 Nile River Manufacturing의 자선 기부 행사를 **20** 조직했던 직원이기도 했습니다.

| 어휘 | promote A to B A를 B로 승진시키다   chief financial officer 최고 재무 이사   promotion 승진   press release 보도 자료   oversee ~을 총괄하다   investment 투자(금)   financial 재무의   reporting 보고, 보도   be charged with ~을 맡다, 책임지다   be likely to do ~할 가능성이 있다   profitable 수익성이 있는   charitable 자선 활동의   contribution 기부(금)

17. (B)
| 해설 |
앞서 언급된 승진과 관련하여 보도 자료를 통해(through a press release) 할 수 있는 일을 나타내는 어휘가 필요하다. 따라서 was와 함께 '승진이 확인되었다'라는 의미를 나타낼 수 있는 (B) confirmed가 정답이다.
| 어휘 | deny ~을 거부하다   earn ~을 벌다, 얻다   request ~을 요청하다

18. (D)
(A) 이 회사는 또한 새로운 사원급 회계사를 구하고 있습니다.
(B) Nile River Manufacturing은 많은 가전 기기 업체들과 협업할 것입니다.
(C) 이사회가 Clancy 씨와 처음으로 만날 것입니다.
| 해설 |
빈칸 앞에는 Clancy 씨의 승진 사실을 알리는 내용이 왔고, 빈칸 뒤에는 최고 재무 이사로서 앞으로 할 일이 언급되었다. 따라서 빈칸에는 Clancy 씨가 그 동안 회사에서 해 온 일을 서술하는 내용의 (D)가 오는 것이 가장 적절하다.
| 어휘 | seek ~을 구하다, 찾다   entry-level 사원급의   accountant 회계사   a number of 많은 (수의)   appliance (가전) 기기   board of directors 이사회   for the first time 처음으로   senior accounting director 수석 회계 책임자

19. (D)
| 해설 |
빈칸 앞에는 투자 및 재무 관련 보고를 총괄하는 업무가, 빈칸 뒤에는 수익성 여부를 판단하는 업무가 언급되어 있다. 따라서 빈칸에는 '추가로'라는 의미로 정보를 덧붙여 말할 때 사용하는 (D) Additionally가 가장 적절하다.

| 어휘 | consequently 결과적으로   on the contrary 대조적으로

20. (C)
| 해설 |
빈칸 이하는 the employee를 수식하는 역할을 해야 하는데, last year라는 과거 시점 부사가 있으므로 주격 관계대명사와 과거 시제 동사가 결합된 구조인 (C) who coordinated가 정답이다.
| 어휘 | coordination 조직(화)   coordinate ~을 조직하다, 편성하다

DAY 12   비교

◆ 출제 포인트 1   원급

1. flexible
| 해석 |
판매업체들은 선호하는 부스 위치를 요청할 때 가능한 한 유연한 자세를 가져야 한다.
| 해설 |
as ~ as 구조로 원급 비교를 나타낼 때 원급 형용사 또는 부사가 그 사이에 위치하므로 형용사인 flexible이 정답이다.
| 어휘 | vendor 판매업체   flexible 유연한   flexibility 유연함   request ~을 요청하다   preferred 선호하는   booth 부스, 칸막이 공간   location 위치, 지점

2. safely
| 해석 |
Novak Chemicals는 자사의 폐기물을 가능한 한 안전하게 처분한다.
| 해설 |
as ~ as 구조로 원급 비교를 나타낼 때 원급 형용사 또는 부사가 그 사이에 위치하므로 원급 부사인 safely가 정답이다.
| 어휘 | dispose of ~을 처분하다   waste product 폐기물

3. responsive
| 해석 |
Camden 병원에 근무하는 간호사들만큼 환자들이 필요로 하는 것에 즉각 대응하는 간호사들은 거의 없다.
| 해설 |
as ~ as 구조로 원급 비교를 나타낼 형용사 또는 부사가 필요한데, be 동사 are 뒤에서 보어 역할을 해야 하므로 형용사인 responsive가 정답이다.
| 어휘 | responsive to ~에 즉각 대응하는   responsively 즉각 대응하여

◆ 출제 포인트 2   비교급 (1)

1. slimmer
| 해석 |
Bonfire Designs에서 나온 최신 전자 리더기는 이전의 모델들보다 더 얇다.
| 해설 |
than과 짝을 이뤄 비교를 나타내야 하므로 비교급 형용사의 형태인 slimmer가 정답이다.
| 어휘 | slim 얇은, 가는   previous 이전의

2. than
| 해석 |
월간 비즈니스 보고서를 준비하는 일은 주간 보고서를 준비하는 것보다 더 시간이 많이 소모된다.
| 해설 |
more time-consuming과 짝을 이뤄 비교를 나타내야 하므로 비교 대상

앞에 사용하는 than이 정답이다.
| 어휘 | time-consuming 시간이 소모되는

3. more carefully
| 해석 |
이 송별회는 다른 행사들보다 더 신중하게 계획되었습니다.
| 해설 |
동사 has been planned를 수식할 부사가 비교급으로 쓰여야 알맞으므로 more carefully가 정답이다.
| 어휘 | farewell gathering 송별회

◆ 출제 포인트 3   비교급 (2)

1. even
| 해석 |
Murillo 씨는 현재 전보다 훨씬 더 폭넓은 업무들을 수행해야 한다.
| 해설 |
비교급 wider를 수식해 그 의미를 강조할 부사가 필요하므로 even이 정답이다.
| 어휘 | be required to do ~해야 하다   perform ~을 수행하다   task 업무, 일

2. easier
| 해석 |
새롭게 지어진 고속도로는 도시 전역에서 운전하는 일을 훨씬 더 쉽게 만들어 준다.
| 해설 |
much가 앞에서 수식해 의미를 강조할 수 있는 것은 비교급 형용사이므로 easier가 정답이다.
| 어휘 | highway 고속도로   make it A to do ~하는 것을 A하게 만들다   across ~ 전역에서

3. superior
| 해석 |
Blue Moon의 분위기는 가격이 더 높은 식당들보다 뛰어나다.
| 해설 |
빈칸 뒤의 전치사 to와 어울리는 라틴계 비교급 표현 superior가 정답이다.
| 어휘 | atmosphere 분위기   superior to ~보다 뛰어난   expensive 비싼

◆ 출제 포인트 4   최상급 (1)

1. fullest
| 해석 |
그 영화를 가능한 한 최대 한도로 즐기실 수 있도록 극장에서 관람하십시오.
| 해설 |
정관사 the와 결합해 명사 extent를 수식할 수 있는 것은 최상급이므로 fullest가 정답이다.
| 어휘 | to the fullest extent possible 가능한 한 최대 한도로

2. greatest
| 해석 |
작년에, 고용 성장은 관광과 의료 서비스 분야에서 가장 높았다.
| 해설 |
정관사 the와 결합한 형태로 was 뒤에서 보어 역할을 할 수 있는 것은 형용사의 최상급이므로 greatest가 정답이다. 명사 greatness는 주어와 동격이 아니므로 오답이다.
| 어휘 | employment 고용   growth 성장   tourism 관광업   sector 분야

3. most comprehensive
| 해석 |
저희는 전국에서 가장 종합적인 교육 프로그램들 중의 하나를 제공합니다.
| 해설 |
명사구 training programs를 수식할 최상급 형용사가 필요하므로 most comprehensive가 정답이다.
| 어휘 | comprehensive 종합적인   comprehensively 종합적으로   training 교육

◆ 출제 포인트 5   최상급 (2)

1. strongest
| 해석 |
Sunbrella 캔버스는 보트용 덮개로 이용 가능한 가장 튼튼한 직물들 중의 하나이다.
| 해설 |
빈칸 뒤의 available과 어울리는 최상급 형용사 strongest가 정답이다.
| 어휘 | fabric 직물   cover 덮개

2. Of
| 해석 |
Dutton 교수가 가르치는 모든 과정들 중에서, 중세 문학이 가장 어렵다.
| 해설 |
최상급이 사용된 문장에서, 그 비교 범위를 나타낼 전치사가 필요하므로 Of가 정답이다.
| 어휘 | medieval 중세의   literature 문학   challenging 어려운, 힘든

3. yet
| 해석 |
<Precinct>의 최신 방영분은 지금까지 중에서 가장 흥미로운 것이며, 훌륭한 캐릭터 변화를 선보입니다.
| 해설 |
앞에 위치한 최상급 표현을 강조할 부사가 필요하므로 '지금까지 중에서'를 뜻하는 yet이 정답이다.
| 어휘 | episode (방송의) 방영분, 1회분   showcase ~을 선보이다   character development 인물[캐릭터] 변화

◆ 출제 포인트 6   관용 표현

1. no later
| 해석 |
참가자들은 늦어도 9월 29일까지는 각자 마음에 드는 이야기에 대해 투표해야 한다.
| 해설 |
than과 결합될 수 있는 것으로 특정 시점과 관련해 '늦어도 ~까지는'을 의미할 때 사용하는 no later가 정답이다.
| 어휘 | participant 참가자   vote for ~에 대해 투표하다

2. most frequently
| 해석 |
티라미수는 저희 디저트 메뉴에서 네 번째로 가장 자주 주문되는 제품입니다.
| 해설 |
the fourth와 결합 가능한 것은 최상급이므로 most frequently가 정답이다.
| 어휘 | frequently 흔히, 자주

3. ever
| 해석 |
Sadler Landscaping으로 인해 완벽한 잔디 상태를 유지하는 일이 그 어

느 때보다 더 쉬워졌습니다.
| 해설 |
비교를 나타낼 때 사용하는 than 뒤에 위치해 비교 대상으로 쓰일 수 있는 것이 필요하므로 '그 어느 때보다 더'라는 의미를 구성하는 ever가 정답이다.
| 어휘 | maintain ~을 유지하다   lawn 잔디(밭)   thanks to ~로 인해, ~ 덕분에

DAY 12 | 실전문제
본책 p.218

정답
1 (C)	2 (D)	3 (B)	4 (A)	5 (D)	6 (D)
7 (C)	8 (A)	9 (C)	10 (A)	11 (C)	12 (C)
13 (C)	14 (D)	15 (C)	16 (A)	17 (C)	18 (D)
19 (B)	20 (B)				

1. (C)
| 해석 |
테스트 결과에 따르면, 하이브리드 엔진은 전기 엔진보다 연비 측면에서 더 효율적이었다.
| 해설 |
비교를 나타내는 than과 결합 가능하면서 be 동사 뒤에서 보어 역할을 할 수 있는 것은 비교급 형용사이므로 (C) more efficient가 정답이다.
| 어휘 | according to ~에 따르면   in terms of ~의 측면에서   gas mileage 연비   efficiently 효율적으로   efficient 효율적인

2. (D)
| 해석 |
Garrison Dean의 새 사진 전시회가 좋기는 하지만, 그의 몇몇 이전 작품만큼 인상적이지는 않다.
| 해설 |
빈칸 앞에 위치한 'as + 형용사'와 결합해 원급 비교를 나타내는 구조가 되어야 알맞으므로 (D) as가 정답이다.
| 어휘 | exhibit 전시회   impressive 인상적인   work 작품

3. (B)
| 해석 |
투어가 일정대로 유지될 수 있도록 늦어도 오후 3시 15분까지는 버스에 승차하시기를 요청 드립니다.
| 해설 |
시점 표현 앞에서 no, than과 결합해 '늦어도 ~까지는'이라는 의미를 구성할 때 사용하는 (B) later가 정답이다.
| 어휘 | board ~에 탑승하다   so that (목적) ~할 수 있도록   stay on schedule 일정대로 유지되다   lately 최근에

4. (A)
| 해석 |
패널 참가자들이 극작가 Rachel Nunez뿐만 아니라 그 작가의 가장 인기 있는 연극 작품이 현대 사회에 미치는 영향을 논의할 것이다.
| 해설 |
소유격 대명사와 명사 사이에 위치할 수 있는 것은 최상급 형용사이므로 (A) most popular가 정답이다.
| 어휘 | panelist 패널 참가자, 토론자   playwright 극작가   impact of A on B A가 B에 미치는 영향   play 연극   popularity 인기   popularize ~을 대중화하다

5. (D)
| 해석 |
개정된 사용 설명서를 통해, 저희 고객들께서는 훨씬 더 쉽게 책장을 조립할 수 있으실 것입니다.
| 해설 |
빈칸 앞에 위치한 much의 수식을 받을 수 있는 것은 비교급이므로 부사의 비교급 형태인 (D) more easily가 정답이다.

| 어휘 | revised 개정된   instruction manual 사용 설명서   assemble ~을 조립하다

6. (D)
| 해석 |
Dallas 시내 한복판에 위치한 Fashion Bin은 50퍼센트가 넘는 할인액으로 디자이너 의류 제품을 판매한다.
| 해설 |
more와 결합해 숫자 표현 앞에 쓰일 수 있는 것이 필요하므로 '~가 넘는'이라는 의미로 사용하는 (D) than이 정답이다.
| 어휘 | located in ~에 위치한   clothing 의류

7. (C)
| 해석 |
폭풍우로 인해 전선이 심각하게 손상되었지만, Nikita Electric은 가능한 한 빨리 전원을 복구하겠다고 약속하고 있다.
| 해설 |
'as ~ as possible'의 구조로 비교를 나타낼 때 as와 as 사이에 원급 형용사나 부사가 쓰이므로 원급 부사인 (C) quickly가 정답이다.
| 어휘 | power line 전선   severely 심하게   damaged 손상된   restore ~을 복구하다

8. (A)
| 해석 |
이사회가 놀랄 정도로, Onestar 사와의 합병은 애초에 예상된 것보다 훨씬 더 이득이 많았다.
| 해설 |
빈칸 뒤의 비교급 형용사 more beneficial을 수식해 그 의미를 강조할 수 있는 부사가 필요하므로 (A) even이 정답이다.
| 어휘 | to one's surprise ~에게 놀랍게도   merger 합병   beneficial 이득이 되는, 유익한   originally 원래   predict 예상하다

9. (C)
| 해석 |
단점에도 불구하고, 분석가들은 주지사의 세금 관련 제안이 지금까지 단연코 가장 혁신적이라는 데 동의한다.
| 해설 |
정관사 the와 결합 가능하면서 so far라는 비교 범위와 어울리는 의미를 나타낼 수 있는 것은 최상급이다. 그런데 be 동사 is 뒤에서 보어 역할을 해야 하므로 최상급 형용사인 (C) most innovative가 정답이다.
| 어휘 | despite ~에도 불구하고   fault 단점, 결함   analyst 분석가   governor 주지사   proposal 제안(서)   by far 단연코   so far 지금까지   innovatively 혁신적으로   innovation 혁신   innovative 혁신적인

10. (A)
| 해석 |
그 고객들은 선호하는 위치에 있는 곳을 찾는 것보다 알맞은 크기의 주택을 구입하는 데 더 관심이 있다.
| 해설 |
동사 care 뒤에 위치한 more와 함께 빈칸 앞뒤에 위치한 두 동명사구를 비교해야 하므로 (A) than이 정답이다.
| 어휘 | care about ~에 관심을 갖다   preferred 선호하는   location 위치, 지점

11. (C)
| 해석 |
Desert Technologies는 Proton X5가 경량이며 현재 시중에서 가장 속도가 빠른 컴퓨터라는 점을 주장하고 있다.
| 해설 |
정관사 the와 결합해 바로 뒤에 위치한 명사 computer를 수식하려면 최상급 형용사가 적합하므로 (C) speediest가 정답이다.
| 어휘 | claim (that) ~라고 주장하다   lightweight 경량   on the market 시중에 (나온)

12. (C)

|해석|
회의에서 Kerry 씨는 새 프로젝트에서 팀으로 협력하는 것이 가장 중요하다고 강조했다.

|해설|
정관사 the와 결합하며 2형식 동사 is의 보어 역할을 하려면 최상급 형용사가 필요하므로 (C) most important가 정답이다.

|어휘| stress 강조하다   work together 협력하다   important 중요한   importance 중요성

13. (C)

|해석|
발표 중에 오직 10분밖에 남지 않은 상황에서, Webber 씨는 제조 과정을 가능한 한 가장 간략하게 설명할 것이다.

|해설|
정관사 the, 형용사 possible과 결합해 명사를 수식하는 최상급 표현을 구성해야 하므로 (C) briefest가 정답이다.

|어휘| explanation 설명   manufacturing 제조   process 과정   briefly 간략하게   brief 간략한

14. (D)

|해석|
예상보다 행사장 비용이 더 높기 때문에 그 프로젝트의 예산이 조정되어야 한다.

|해설|
빈칸 앞에 위치한 than과 결합해 "예상보다"라는 비교의 의미를 나타낼 때는 과거 분사를 사용하므로 (D) anticipated가 정답이다.

|어휘| budget 예산   adjust ~을 조정하다   venue 행사장   anticipate ~을 예상하다

15. (C)

|해석|
심포지엄에 참석한 모든 연설자들 중에서, Carl Bowman 씨가 가장 언변이 뛰어나다는 것이 만장일치된 의견이었다.

|해설|
be 동사 was 뒤에서 보어 역할을 할 형용사가 필요한데, 정관사 the와 결합해 최상급을 구성해야 하므로 (C) most eloquent가 정답이다.

|어휘| consensus 만장일치   eloquent 언변이 뛰어난   eloquently 뛰어난 언변으로

16. (A)

|해석|
Ventura 씨보다 더 활동적으로 더 나은 의료 서비스를 위해 캠페인을 벌인 사람은 없었지만, 그녀는 충분한 지지를 받을 수 없었다.

|해설|
동사 campaigned를 뒤에서 수식할 부사가 필요한데, 그 뒤에 위치한 than과 어울려 비교의 의미를 나타내야 하므로 비교급의 형태인 (A) more energetically가 정답이다.

|어휘| campaign 캠페인을 벌이다   health care 의료 서비스   support 지지   energetically 활동적으로   energetic 활동적인

17-20번 문제는 다음 웹페이지에 관한 문제입니다.

Fairstone Institute가 곧 탄수화물 섭취에 관해 지금까지 17 종합적인 연구를 시작할 것입니다. 18 참가자들의 절반에게는 무제한적으로 탄수화물을 먹는 것이 허용될 것입니다. 나머지 절반은 19 선별된 탄수화물 식품 목록에서 선택할 수 있을 것입니다. 참가자들은 또한 자신이 먹는 모든 음식을 기록하도록 요청받게 됩니다. 20 추가로, 참가자들은 매 식사 후에 각자의 에너지 수준을 평가하는 설문지를 작성해야 합니다. 이 실험은 30일 동안에 걸쳐 진행됩니다. 선임 연구원들이 여전히 자원 참가자들을 찾고 있으므로, 관심이 있으실 경우에 carbstudy@fairstone.com으로 저희에게 연락 주시기 바랍니다.

|어휘| study 연구   carbohydrate 탄수화물   consumption 소비   to date 지금까지   choose from ~에서 선택하다   be asked to do ~하도록 요청받다   keep a record of ~을 기록하다   complete ~을 작성 완료하다   survey 설문(지)   assess ~을 평가하다   experiment 실험   take place (일, 행사 등이) 발생되다, 일어나다   over ~ 동안에 걸쳐   lead researcher 선임 연구원   look for ~을 찾다   volunteer 자원 봉사자   contact ~에게 연락하다   if interested 관심이 있을 경우에

17. (C)

|해설|
빈칸은 바로 뒤에 위치한 명사 study를 수식할 형용사 자리이다. 빈칸 앞의 소유격과 함께 쓰이면서 '지금까지 (중에서)'라는 의미인 to date와 어울리려면 최상급 형용사가 되어야 하므로 (C) most comprehensive가 정답이다.

|어휘| comprehensively 종합적으로, 포괄적으로   compression 압축, 요약

18. (D)

(A) 일부 참가자들은 과도한 양의 탄수화물을 섭취했습니다.
(B) 적당량을 먹을 경우, 탄수화물은 균형 잡힌 식사의 일부가 됩니다.
(C) 참가자들은 18세에서 49세 사이의 남성과 여성들이 될 것입니다.

|해설|
빈칸 뒤에는 '나머지 절반'을 의미하는 The other half와 함께 이들이 실험 중에 할 수 있는 일이 제시되므로 다른 절반의 사람들이 할 일을 먼저 언급하는 (D)가 정답이다.

|어휘| consume ~을 소비하다   excessive 과도한   proper 적당한   balanced 균형 잡힌   be allowed to do ~하도록 허용되다   unlimited 무제한의

19. (B)

|해설|
부정 관사 a와 명사 list 사이에 위치한 빈칸은 형용사 자리인데, 분사가 그 역할을 대신할 수 있다. list는 사람에 의해 선별되는 대상이므로 수동의 의미를 나타내는 과거 분사 (B) selected가 정답이다.

|어휘| selection 선정(된 것)   select ~을 선정하다

20. (B)

|해설|
앞 문장에는 먹은 음식을 기록하는 일이, 빈칸 뒤에는 설문지를 작성하는 일이 쓰여 있다. 따라서 참가자들이 할 일을 나열하는 흐름임을 알 수 있으므로 '추가로'라는 의미로 정보를 추가할 때 사용하는 (B) In addition이 정답이다.

|어휘| in contrast 대조적으로   instead 그 대신에

DAY 13   어휘-동사/형용사/부사

◆ 출제 포인트 1   동사 어휘 (1)

1. enroll

|해석|
저희는 여러분께서 지역 문화 센터에서 제공되는 마케팅 입문 과정에 등록하시도록 권해 드립니다.

|해설|
전치사 in과 어울려 '~에 등록하다'라는 의미를 구성하는 enroll이 정답이다.

|어휘| recommend that ~하도록 권하다   introductory 입문의   community center 지역 문화 센터

2. comply

| 해석 |
건축가의 설계도가 지역 규정을 준수하지 않았기 때문에 공사가 중단되었다.

| 해설 |
전치사 with와 어울려 '~을 준수하다'라는 의미를 구성하는 comply가 정답이다.

| 어휘 | halt ~을 중단하다 architect 건축가 plans 설계도 assign ~을 할당하다, 배정하다 regulation 규정, 규제

3. address

| 해석 |
온라인에서 이용 가능한 설명서가 저희 소프트웨어에서 겪을 수도 있는 문제들을 처리해 줄 것입니다.

| 해설 |
'문제, 사안' 등을 뜻하는 목적어 issues와 어울리는 동사는 '~을 처리하다, 해결하다' 등을 의미하는 address이다.

| 어휘 | manual 설명서 install ~을 설치하다 encounter ~을 접하다, 마주하다

◆ 출제 포인트 2 동사 어휘 (2)
본책 p.220

1. ensure

| 해석 |
분기별 점검이 공장 내 기계가 훌륭한 상태로 유지되고 있는지 확실히 해 줄 것입니다.

| 해설 |
뒤에 이어지는 that절을 목적어로 취할 수 있는 동사 ensure가 정답이다.

| 어휘 | quarterly 분기의 inspection 점검 reserve ~을 예약하다 machinery 기계 remain ~하게 유지되다, 남아 있다

2. forwarded

| 해석 |
Jennifer 씨는 그 기사를 수정한 후에 최종 원고를 편집장에게 전송했다.

| 해설 |
빈칸 뒤에 위치한 'A to B'의 구조와 어울려 쓰이는 동사로 '~을 전송하다'라는 의미를 나타내는 forwarded가 정답이다.

| 어휘 | revise ~을 수정하다 exchange ~을 교환하다 final draft 최종 원고 editor 편집자

3. announced

| 해석 |
교통국이 Astoria 지하철 노선의 연장을 발표했다.

| 해설 |
사물 목적어 the extension을 목적어로 취할 수 있는 announced가 정답이다. inform은 inform A of B의 구조로 쓰이며 'A(사람)에게 B를 알려 주다'라는 의미이다.

| 어휘 | transportation 교통 extension 연장, 확장, 확대

최빈출 확인 문제
본책 p.221

정답 1 (B) 2 (B) 3 (C) 4 (A) 5 (B) 6 (B)
      7 (B) 8 (C) 9 (D) 10 (D) 11 (A) 12 (C)

1. (B)

| 해석 |
새로운 광고 회사들은 고객들이 필요로 하는 것에 대해 명확히 이해할 수 있도록 그들과 끈끈한 관계를 구축해야 한다.

| 해설 |
'관계'를 의미하는 명사 relationship과 어울리는 동사가 필요하므로 '~을 구축하다'를 뜻하는 (B) build가 정답이다.

| 어휘 | advertising 광고 firm 회사 build a relationship 관계를 구축하다 gain a clear understanding of ~을 명확히 이해하다 treat ~을 다루다, 처리하다 raise ~을 끌어 올리다 locate ~의 위치를 찾아내다

2. (B)

| 해석 |
Parkland Heights 주민들은 옥상 수영장에 대한 개선 작업이 반드시 이뤄져야 한다는 점에 동의한다.

| 해설 |
빈칸 뒤에 위치한 that절을 목적어로 취할 수 있는 (B) agree가 정답이다.

| 어휘 | resident 주민 make an improvement to ~을 개선하다 rooftop 옥상 contain ~을 포함하다 revise ~을 수정하다 defer ~을 미루다

3. (C)

| 해석 |
Shriner's 병원의 직원들은 아동과 젊은 사람들에 대한 건강 관리와 치료를 전문으로 한다.

| 해설 |
빈칸 뒤에 위치한 전치사 in과 어울려 쓰일 수 있는 자동사 (C) specializes가 정답이다.

| 어휘 | care 건강 관리, 돌봄 treatment 치료, 처치 identify ~을 확인하다, 식별하다 process ~을 처리하다 finalize ~을 최종 확정하다

4. (A)

| 해석 |
작가 Emma Kay 씨와 Mountaintop 출판사는 인세 지불 금액을 10퍼센트 인상하기로 합의에 도달했다.

| 해설 |
'합의, 동의'를 뜻하는 명사 agreement와 어울리는 동사가 필요하므로 '~에 도달하다'를 뜻하는 (A) reached가 정답이다.

| 어휘 | royalty payment 인세, 저작권 사용료 by (차이) ~만큼 notify ~에게 통보하다

5. (B)

| 해석 |
IT 부서의 보고서는 회사의 방화벽 프로그램을 업데이트하는 것이 컴퓨터 네트워크 오류를 방지할 수 있는 것이라 시사한다.

| 해설 |
방화벽 프로그램 업데이트의 목적과 관련된 동사가 필요한데, '오류, 고장' 등을 의미하는 failure와 어울려야 하므로 '~을 방지하다'라는 의미로 쓰이는 (B) prevent가 정답이다.

| 어휘 | suggest that ~임을 시사하다 firewall 방화벽 failure 오류, 실패 enhance ~을 강화하다 organize ~을 조직하다

6. (B)

| 해석 |
Streetlight Studios의 임원들은 제작을 진행하기에 앞서 그 영화의 대본에 대한 추가 변경을 요청했다.

| 해설 |
사물 명사로서 '변경'을 의미하는 changes와 어울리는 동사가 필요하므로 '~을 요청하다'를 뜻하는 (B) requested가 정답이다.

| 어휘 | executive 임원 additional 추가적인 script 대본 proceed with ~을 계속 진행하다 inform ~에게 알리다 comply (with) 준수하다

7. (B)

| 해석 |
Oberlin's 법학 대학원의 졸업생들은 최고의 법률 회사에서 경력을 추구함에 따라 서로를 상대로 지속적으로 경쟁할 것이다.

| 해설 |
빈칸 뒤에 위치한 전치사 against와 어울리는 자동사가 필요하므로 '~을 상대로 경쟁하다'라는 의미를 구성하는 (B) compete이 정답이다.

| 어휘 | graduate 졸업생 continue to do 지속적으로 ~하다 against ~을

상대로 pursue ~을 추구하다 associate ~와 연관 짓다 finance ~에 자금을 제공하다

8. (C)

| 해석 |
Hasan 씨는 오늘 오후 4시 30분까지 출판사에 자신의 소설 초안을 제출해야 한다.

| 해설 |
빈칸 뒤에 위치한 'A to B'의 구조와 어울려 전달의 의미를 나타낼 동사가 필요하므로 '~을 제출하다'를 뜻하는 (C) submit이 정답이다.

| 어휘 | first draft 초안 publisher 출판사 urge ~에게 촉구하다

9. (D)

| 해석 |
해마다 나오는 매 편집본에 대해, <Best American Poetry>의 편집 책임자는 어느 시를 포함시킬 것인지를 결정할 초청 편집자를 선임한다.

| 해설 |
빈칸 뒤에 위치한 사람 명사 a guest editor를 목적어로 취할 수 있는 동사로 '~을 선임하다'라는 의미로 쓰이는 (D) appoints가 정답이다.

| 어휘 | annual 해마다의 edition 편집본, ~판 editor 편집자 include ~을 포함하다 predict ~을 예측하다 operate ~을 운영하다, 가동하다

10. (D)

| 해석 |
Mellinger의 Southcoast Foods 인수는 식료품 매장 시장 점유율에 있어 15퍼센트의 증가라는 결과를 낳을 것이다.

| 해설 |
빈칸 뒤에 위치한 전치사 in과 어울리는 자동사가 필요하므로 '~라는 결과를 낳다'라는 의미를 구성하는 (D) result가 정답이다.

| 어휘 | acquisition 인수, 매입 increase in ~의 증가 grocer 식료 잡화상 market share 시장 점유(율)

11. (A)

| 해석 |
유권자 등록 정보를 담고 있는 어떠한 우편물이든지 반드시 4층에 있는 Larry Watson 씨에게 전달되어야 한다.

| 해설 |
빈칸 뒤에 위치한 'to + 사람 명사' 구조와 어울리는 동사가 필요하므로 '~가 전달되다'라는 의미를 구성할 수 있는 (A) delivered가 정답이다.

| 어휘 | contain ~을 담고 있다 voter 유권자 registration 등록 store ~을 저장하다 handle ~을 처리하다 respond 답변하다, 대응하다

12. (C)

| 해석 |
주 정부는 산업 공해 물질의 양을 감소시키기 위해 새 환경 정책을 시행했다.

| 해설 |
빈칸 뒤에 위치한 사물 명사 environmental policies와 의미가 어울리는 동사가 필요하므로 '~을 시행하다'라는 뜻으로 쓰이는 (C) implemented가 정답이다.

| 어휘 | state government 주 정부 policy 정책 reduce ~을 감소시키다 amount 양, 수량 industrial 산업의, 공업의 pollutant 공해 물질 convince ~을 설득하다 achieve ~을 달성하다 preserve ~을 보존하다

◆ 출제 포인트 3 **형용사 어휘 (1)** 본책 p.222

1. significant

| 해설 |
Air Tropico는 Hawaii로 가는 여러 직항로를 개설한 후에 상당한 성장을 경험했다.

| 해설 |
명사 growth를 수식해 성장 정도를 나타낼 형용사가 필요하므로 '상당한'을 뜻하는 significant가 정답이다.

| 어휘 | completed 완료된 several 여럿의 direct route 직항로

2. stable

| 해설 |
모바일 기술의 발전이 있다 하더라도, 데스크톱 컴퓨터에 대한 수요는 안정적인 상태로 유지되어 왔다.

| 해설 |
주어 demand(수요)의 상태를 나타낼 형용사 보어가 필요하므로 '안정적인'을 뜻하는 stable이 정답이다.

| 어휘 | even with ~가 있어도 rise 발전, 증가 demand for ~에 대한 수요 remain + 형용사 ~한 상태로 유지되다 casual 평상시의, 격식 없는

3. affordable

| 해설 |
기부금은 지역 사회의 주민들을 위해 프로그램 참가비를 저렴하게 유지하는 데 사용될 것입니다.

| 해설 |
동사 keep의 목적어 program fees의 상태를 나타낼 목적격 보어가 필요하므로 비용 수준과 관련해 '저렴한, 알맞은'이라는 뜻으로 쓰이는 affordable이 정답이다.

| 어휘 | donation 기부(금) resident 주민 community 지역사회

◆ 출제 포인트 4 **형용사 어휘 (2)** 본책 p.222

1. useful

| 해설 |
선임 디자이너는 그 피드백이 매우 유용하다고 생각했기 때문에 시제품을 변경할 것이다.

| 해설 |
동사 found의 목적어로 쓰인 사물 명사 feedback의 상태를 나타낼 목적격 보어가 필요하므로 '유용한'을 뜻하는 useful이 정답이다.

| 어휘 | modify ~을 변경하다, 수정하다 prototype 시제품

2. numerous

| 해설 |
제작 과정에서 맞닥뜨린 수많은 문제점들로 인해, 그 영화의 개봉이 연기되었다.

| 해설 |
복수 명사 problems를 수식할 형용사가 필요하므로 복수 명사와 함께 사용하는 numerous가 정답이다.

| 어휘 | due to ~로 인해 numerous 수많은, 다수의 supportive 지지하는 encounter ~와 맞닥뜨리다 premiere 개봉 delay 연기하다

3. previous

| 해설 |
귀하의 지원 서류 묶음에 이전의 고용주에게서 받은 추천서를 포함시켜 주시기 바랍니다.

| 해설 |
단수 명사 employer를 수식해야 하며 의미상으로도 어울리는 previous가 정답이다.

| 어휘 | a letter of recommendation 추천서 various 다양한 previous 이전의, 과거의 employer 고용주 application 지원(서) packet (서류 등의) 묶음

최빈출 확인 문제
본책 p.223

정답 1 (D) 2 (C) 3 (D) 4 (D) 5 (C) 6 (C)
　　　7 (A) 8 (D) 9 (A) 10 (B) 11 (B) 12 (D)

1. (D)
| 해석 |
Collin 출판의 <Intro to Geometry>는 다수의 사소한 오류들로 인해 다시 출간되어야 했다.
| 해설 |
errors(오류, 실수)를 수식해 책이 다시 출간되는 이유를 나타낼 형용사가 필요하므로 '사소한'을 의미하는 (D) minor가 정답이다.
| 어휘 | re-publish ~을 다시 출간하다 due to ~로 인해 reliable 신뢰할 만한 detailed 상세한 minor 사소한

2. (C)
| 해석 |
Bangkok은 합리적인 가격에 믿을 수 없을 정도의 요리들을 제공하는 수많은 고급 레스토랑의 본고장이다.
| 해설 |
prices를 수식해 가격 수준을 나타낼 형용사가 필요하므로 '합리적인'을 뜻하는 (C) reasonable이 정답이다.
| 어휘 | home 본고장, 본거지 gourmet <음식이> 고급의, 미식가를 위한 serve (음식 등) ~을 제공하다 incredible 믿을 수 없는 operational 운영 중인, 가동되는 willing 의향이 있는 valuable 소중한

3. (D)
| 해석 |
대출 상환 유예 기간에, 부분적인 납입 비용은 받아들여지겠지만, 이자는 지속적으로 늘어날 것입니다.
| 해설 |
payments를 수식해 상환되는 납입액의 정도와 관련된 의미를 나타낼 형용사가 필요하므로 '부분적인'을 뜻하는 (D) partial이 정답이다.
| 어휘 | loan 대출 deferment 유예 acceptable 받아 들일 수 있는 interest 이자 considerate 사려 깊은, 배려하는 sensible 분별 있는, 실용적인 desirable 바람직한

4. (D)
| 해석 |
기업 구조 조정이 6명의 영업 사원들이 전근을 신청하는 결과를 초래했으며, 이로 인해 그 자리들이 공석으로 남겨졌다.
| 해설 |
분사로 쓰인 동사 leave의 목적어 those positions의 상태를 나타낼 목적격 보어가 필요한데, 직원들이 전근한 것에 따른 결과와 관련되어야 하므로 '공석의'를 뜻하는 (D) vacant가 정답이다.
| 어휘 | restructuring 구조 조정 cause A to do A가 ~하는 결과를 초래하다 representative 직원 apply for ~을 신청하다 transfer 전근 potential 잠재적인 bright 밝은 hollow (속이) 비어 있는

5. (C)
| 해석 |
프로젝트 팀장들은 더욱 창의적인 일에 초점을 맞출 수 있도록 일일 운영 업무들을 위임하는 것이 유익하다고 생각했다.
| 해설 |
진목적어인 to delegate 이하에 제시된 일이 지니는 성격을 나타낼 목적격 보어가 필요하므로 업무 위임의 유익함을 의미할 수 있는 (C) beneficial이 정답이다.
| 어휘 | delegate ~을 위임하다 task 업무, 일 so that (목적) ~할 수 있도록 focus on ~에 초점을 맞추다 creative 창의적인 financial 재정의, 재무의 abundant 풍부한 legible (글씨체가) 알아 볼 수 있는

6. (C)
| 해석 |
연휴 기간 중의 많은 통화량으로 인해, 고객들이 우리 온라인 채팅 서비스를 이용하는 것을 선호할 수 있다.
| 해설 |
빈칸 뒤에 위치한 call volumes를 수식해 통화량의 정도를 나타낼 형용사가 필요하므로 '많은, 과도한'을 뜻하는 (C) heavy가 정답이다.
| 어휘 | due to ~로 인해 call volumes 통화량 prefer to do ~하는 것을 선호하다 steep 가파른, 급격한 wide 넓은

7. (A)
| 해석 |
저희 주차 안내원이 발생할 수 있는 어떠한 긴급 상황에 대해서도 도움을 드릴 수 있도록 자리하고 있습니다.
| 해설 |
주어인 사람 명사에 어울리며 빈칸 뒤 to부정사와도 함께 쓸 수 있는 형용사 (A) available이 정답이다. (B) obvious는 주로 가주어 it과 함께 사용한다.
| 어휘 | attendant 안내원, 종업원 assist with ~을 돕다 situation 상황 arise 발생되다 available (사람이) 시간이 나는 obvious 명백한 voluntary 자발적인 probable 있을 것 같은

8. (D)
| 해석 |
Universal 건축은 주거 비용이 비싸지 않고 환경적으로 지속 가능한 주택을 제공하기 위해 진보한 3차원 프린팅 기술을 활용하고 있다.
| 해설 |
사물 명사 3D printing technology를 수식해 그 기술력의 특징을 나타낼 형용사가 필요하므로 '진보한, 발전된'을 의미하는 (D) advanced가 정답이다.
| 어휘 | provide ~을 제공하다 inexpensive 비싸지 않은 sustainable 환경적으로 지속 가능한

9. (A)
| 해석 |
'21세기의 리더십'이라는 제목의 시간은 짧기는 했지만, 매우 유익했다.
| 해설 |
but 앞에 위치한 brief와 함께 한 강연의 특징을 나타낼 형용사가 필요하므로 '유익한'을 의미하는 (A) informative가 정답이다.
| 어휘 | session (특정 활동을 위한) 시간 entitled ~라는 제목의 brief 짧은 eventual 최종적인, 궁극적인 advisory 자문의

10. (B)
| 해석 |
Kate Schmidt 씨는 <The Simple Life>에서 보여준 우수한 연기로 인해 '여우 주연상' 부문의 후보로 지명되었다.
| 해설 |
performance를 수식해 해당 공연의 수준이나 특성을 나타낼 형용사가 필요하므로 '우수한, 특출한' 등을 의미하는 (B) exceptional이 정답이다.
| 어휘 | nominate ~을 후보로 지명하다 category 부문, 범주 performance 연기, 공연 responsive 즉각 반응하는 multiple 다수의 whole 전체적인

11. (B)
| 해석 |
업계 내의 심화된 경쟁에도 불구하고, Nova S 전화기는 일년 내내 한결 같은 판매량을 유지했다.
| 해설 |
sales를 수식해 매출이나 판매량의 정도와 관련된 의미를 나타낼 형용사가 필요하므로 '한결 같은, 꾸준한'을 뜻하는 (B) steady가 정답이다.
| 어휘 | despite ~에도 불구하고 competition 경쟁 industry 업계 maintain ~을 유지하다 sales 판매(량), 매출 throughout (기간) ~ 동안 내내

renewable 갱신 가능한   correct 정확한, 옳은

12. (D)

| 해석 |
병원 경영진은 24시간 교대 근무하는 직원들을 위해 휴게실이 더욱 편안해지도록 3개의 트윈 침대를 놓았다.

| 해설 |
동사 make의 목적어 it을 설명할 목적격 보어가 필요한데, it은 break room을 가리키므로 휴게실의 특성과 관련된 형용사로 '편안한'을 뜻하는 (D) comfortable이 정답이다.

| 어휘 | place ~을 놓다, 두다   break room 휴게실   shift 교대 근무(조)   capable 능력 있는, 할 수 있는   favorable 찬성하는, 호의적인

◆ 출제 포인트 5   부사 어휘 (1)

1. soon

| 해석 |
Hammer Studios는 모든 게임기에서 즐길 수 있는 <Dungeon Crawl 3>를 곧 출시할 것이다.

| 해설 |
미래 시제 동사 will release와 어울리는 부사 soon이 정답이다.

| 어휘 | once (과거의) 한때   release ~을 출시하다   game console 게임기

2. conveniently

| 해석 |
가장 최근에 문을 연 Anytime Health 지점들은 Waterford와 Vienna 지역의 편리한 곳에 위치해 있다.

| 해설 |
located와 어울려 '편리하게 위치한'이라는 의미를 사용할 때 사용하는 부사 conveniently가 정답이다.

| 어휘 | branch 지점, 지사   fluently 유창하게

3. recently

| 해석 |
결함이 있는 장비로 인해, Cleveland 공장은 최근 주간 할당량을 충족하지 못했다.

| 해설 |
현재 완료 시제 동사 has met과 어울리는 부사 recently가 정답이다.

| 어휘 | due to ~로 인해   faulty 결함이 있는   equipment 장비   meet ~을 충족하다   quota (작업 등의) 할당량   briefly 간단히, 잠깐   recently 최근에

◆ 출제 포인트 6   부사 어휘 (2)

1. highly

| 해석 |
Roman Academy의 3개월 집중 이탈리아어 강좌는 매우 효과적인 것으로 여겨지고 있다.

| 해설 |
형용사 effective를 수식해 효과적인 정도를 강조하는 highly가 정답이다.

| 어휘 | intensive 집중적인   be regarded as ~한 것으로 여겨지다   correctly 정확히, 올바르게   effective 효과적인

2. still

| 해석 |
10년 동안 Tokyo에 거주해 왔지만, Kellison 씨는 여전히 일본어를 이해하는 데 큰 어려움을 겪고 있다.

| 해설 |
10년 동안 거주했음에도 현재 어려움을 겪고 있는 상황을 강조할 부사가 필요하므로 '여전히'를 뜻하는 still이 정답이다.

| 어휘 | decade 10년   struggle to do ~하는 데 큰 어려움을 겪다

3. relatively

| 해석 |
다른 주요 도시들에 비해, Dallas 지역의 생활비는 상대적으로 낮다.

| 해설 |
형용사 low를 수식해 생활비의 낮은 정도를 나타낼 수 있는 부사 relatively가 정답이다.

| 어휘 | compared with ~에 비해, ~와 비교해   cost of living 생활비   efficiently 효율적으로

최빈출 확인 문제   본책 p.225

| 정답 | 1 (C) | 2 (D) | 3 (C) | 4 (A) | 5 (C) | 6 (B) |
| | 7 (A) | 8 (B) | 9 (A) | 10 (C) | 11 (C) | 12 (B) |

1. (C)

| 해석 |
일부 독자들이 내용에 대해 불만을 제기한 끝에 의견 칼럼은 웹 사이트에서 즉시 삭제되었다.

| 해설 |
일의 전후 관계를 나타내는 접속사 after와 어울려 삭제 조치를 취한 방식을 나타낼 부사가 필요하므로 '즉시, 지체 없이'를 의미하는 (C) promptly가 정답이다.

| 어휘 | column (신문 등의) 칼럼   remove ~을 제거하다   complain about ~에 대해 불만을 제기하다   content 내용(물)   equally 동등하게   randomly 무작위로   comparatively 비교적

2. (D)

| 해석 |
E-Crunch와 같은 인기 세무 준비 소프트웨어는 사용자들이 정확하게 소득세 환급액을 계산하는 데 도움을 준다.

| 해설 |
to부정사로 쓰인 동사 calculate을 수식해 계산하는 방식을 나타낼 부사가 필요하므로 '정확하게'를 의미하는 (D) precisely가 정답이다.

| 어휘 | preparation 준비, 대비   calculate ~을 계산하다   income tax return 소득세 환급(액)   relatively 비교적, 상대적으로   widely 널리, 폭넓게   indefinitely 무기한으로

3. (C)

| 해석 |
Tanaka 박사는 30년간의 재직 끝에 신문사에서 은퇴했으며, 현재 조용한 카페에서 시간제로 근무하고 있다.

| 해설 |
현재 시제 동사(works)와 어울리는 부사 (C) now가 정답이다.

| 어휘 | retire from ~에서 은퇴하다   work part-time 시간제로 근무하다

4. (A)

| 해석 |
장기 휴가 신청서는 부서장이 아니라 인사부의 Barbara Weiss 씨에게 곧바로 제출되어야 한다.

| 해설 |
전치사 to와 어울려 문서가 제출되는 방식을 나타낼 부사가 필요하므로 '곧바로, 곧장'을 뜻하는 (A) directly가 정답이다.

| 어휘 | extended 연장된, 장기간의   leave request 휴가 신청(서)   submit ~을 제출하다   HR 인사부   nearly 거의   basically 기본적으로

5. (C)

| 해석 |
오일 교환 작업이 Motor-Pro에서는 일반적으로 30달러가 들기는 하지만, 현재 3월 말까지 50퍼센트 할인된다.

| 해설 |
현재 시제 동사(costs)와 어울리는 부사 (C) typically가 정답이다.

| 어휘 | while ~이기는 하지만   cost ~의 비용이 들다   off 할인된   familiarly 친근하게, 익숙하게   typically 일반적으로   previously 이전에, 과거에

6. (B)
| 해석 |
Dunphy Tower 공사 작업은 시청에서 건축 허가를 승인한 직후에 시작될 수 있을 것이다.
| 해설 |
일의 전후 관계를 나타내는 after와 어울려 '~한 직후에'라는 의미를 구성하는 부사 (B) immediately가 정답이다.
| 어휘 | approve ~을 승인하다   permit 허가증   unevenly 고르지 않게, 불균형하게   habitually 습관적으로   currently 현재

7. (A)
| 해석 |
새 지하철 노선의 개통은 대부분의 우리 직원들에게 있어 통근 시간을 크게 줄여 주었다.
| 해설 |
'감소하다'를 뜻하는 동사 reduce를 수식해 그 정도를 나타낼 부사가 필요하므로 '급격히, 대폭' 등을 의미하는 (A) drastically가 정답이다.
| 어휘 | commute 통근 (시간)   the majority of 대부분의   necessarily 필수적으로   strictly 엄격히   formerly 이전에

8. (B)
| 해석 |
Jim Harrison 씨는 가장 어린 팀원으로, 이전에 5년 동안 싱가포르에서 근무했다.
| 해설 |
과거 시제 동사(worked)와 어울려 쓰이는 부사 (B) previously가 정답이다.
| 어휘 | previously 이전에   highly 매우

9. (A)
| 해석 |
직원들은 소기업들을 위한 소셜 미디어 활용에 관한 발표에 참석하도록 적극 권고됩니다.
| 해설 |
과거 분사 encouraged를 수식해 권고하는 정도를 나타낼 부사가 필요하므로 '적극적으로, 강력히' 등을 뜻하는 (A) strongly가 정답이다.
| 어휘 | extremely 극히   mutually 상호간에   closely 면밀히

10. (C)
| 해석 |
처음에 온라인 일정 관리 시스템에 대해 불만을 제기했던 사무실 직원들이 현재 과거의 방식보다 그것을 선호하고 있다.
| 해설 |
과거 시제 동사(complained)와 자주 어울려 쓰이는 부사 (C) initially가 정답이다.
| 어휘 | complain about ~에 대해 불만을 제기하다   prefer ~을 선호하다   over (비교) ~보다, ~에 비해   method 방식, 방법   favorably 찬성하여, 호의적으로   initially 처음에   annually 연례적으로, 해마다

11. (C)
| 해석 |
Toby Capparelle 씨를 부주방장으로 고용하면서, Acorn Bistro는 곧 이탈리안 요리들을 제공하기 시작할 것으로 예상된다.
| 해설 |
미래의 일에 대한 예상을 나타내는 be expected to do와 어울리는 부사로 '곧, 머지 않아'를 뜻하는 (C) shortly가 정답이다.
| 어휘 | hiring 고용   assistant 부 ~, 보조의   be expected to do ~할 것으로 예상되다   nearly 거의   recently 최근에

12. (B)
| 해석 |
Jonathan Davis 씨는 지속적으로 뛰어난 앨범과 라이브 공연으로 인해 포크 음악 명예의 전당의 일원이 되었다.
| 해설 |
'뛰어난, 훌륭한' 등을 뜻하는 형용사 outstanding을 수식할 만한 부사로 보기 중 가장 적합한 것은 어떤 상태나 동작의 지속성을 나타낼 때 사용하는 (B) consistently이다.
| 어휘 | Hall of Fame 명예의 전당   outstanding 뛰어난   jointly 공동으로   consistently 지속적으로   exactly 정확히   reluctantly 마지 못해, 꺼려하여

DAY 13 | 실전문제 본책 p.226

정답	1 (D)	2 (C)	3 (B)	4 (B)	5 (A)	6 (C)
	7 (C)	8 (B)	9 (A)	10 (D)	11 (C)	12 (C)
	13 (C)	14 (B)	15 (C)	16 (A)	17 (D)	18 (B)
	19 (A)	20 (B)				

1. (D)
| 해석 |
Delta 사의 Ariel Blackstone 대표이사는 어제 있었던 경축 행사에서 은퇴를 발표했으며, Sofia Lee 씨를 후계자로 지명했다.
| 해설 |
빈칸 뒤에 위치한 '사람 + as + 자격/신분' 구조와 어울리는 동사로 '~을 …로 지명하다'라는 의미를 구성할 때 사용하는 (D) named가 정답이다.
| 어휘 | announce ~을 발표하다   retirement 은퇴   gala 경축 행사   successor 후계자

2. (C)
| 해석 |
국제 항공편의 요금이 더욱 저렴해짐에 따라 점점 더 많은 관광객들이 다른 나라로 여행을 가기 시작했다.
| 해설 |
become과 어울리는 보어로서 국제 항공편의 특성을 나타낼 형용사가 필요한데, 더 많은 사람들이 여행을 가는 이유와 관련되어야 하므로 '가격이 저렴한'을 뜻하는 (C) affordable이 정답이다.
| 어휘 | comparable 비교할 만한   expressive 표현력이 있는   capable ~을 할 수 있는, 유능한

3. (B)
| 해석 |
새 용접 기계로 인해 공장이 생산을 가속화하게 될 것이며, 이는 회사가 증가하고 있는 수요를 충족하는 데 도움이 될 것이다.
| 해설 |
'생산'을 뜻하는 production과 어울리는 동사로 새 기계에 따른 긍정적인 변화와 관련된 것이 필요하므로 '~을 가속화하다'를 뜻하는 (B) accelerate가 정답이다.
| 어휘 | welding 용접   rising 증가하는   demand 수요   subscribe ~을 구독하다   inform ~에게 알리다   resist ~에 저항하다

4. (B)
| 해석 |
회사 업무가 지닌 민감한 성격으로 인해, Bio Labs는 자사의 시설에 대한 출입을 엄격히 통제하고 있다.
| 해설 |
동사 controls를 수식해 통제 방식을 나타낼 부사가 필요하므로 '엄격히'를 의미하는 (B) strictly가 정답이다.
| 어휘 | sensitive 민감한   nature 성격, 특성   control ~을 통제하다   entry to ~로의 출입   facility 시설   tensely 팽팽히, 긴장하여   hardly 거의 ~ 않다   merely 단지, 그저

5. (A)

| 해석 |
벽에 제대로 부착될 수 있도록 고리 뒷면의 접착제가 완전히 마를 수 있게 하십시오.

| 해설 |
빈칸 뒤에 위치한 전치사 to와 함께 '~에 달라붙다'라는 의미로 쓰이는 자동사 (A) adheres가 정답이다.

| 어휘 | glue 접착제   fully 완전히, 전적으로   so that (목적) ~할 수 있도록   properly 제대로, 적절히   adhere to ~에 부착되다   comply 준수하다   utilize ~을 활용하다

6. (C)

| 해석 |
면접 시간 중에, Suzuki 씨는 중장비로 작업했던 자신의 폭넓은 경험에 관해 상세히 말했다.

| 해설 |
명사 experience를 수식해 경험의 정도를 나타낼 형용사가 필요하므로 '폭넓은'을 의미하는 (C) extensive가 정답이다.

| 어휘 | elaborate on ~을 상세히 말하다   heavy machinery 중장비   prospective 장래의, 유망한   imperative 필수적인, 반드시 해야 하는   punctual 시간을 엄수하는

7. (C)

| 해석 |
<Deep Space>의 출연진과 스태프는 Critics' Awards에 대한 후보자 명단을 간절히 기다리고 있다.

| 해설 |
동사 are awaiting을 수식해 후보자 명단을 기다리는 정도를 나타낼 부사가 필요하므로 '간절히, 열망하여'를 뜻하는 (C) eagerly가 정답이다.

| 어휘 | cast 출연진   await ~을 기다리다   nominee 지명 후보자   greatly 대단히, 매우   accurately 정확히   commonly 흔히

8. (B)

| 해석 |
비즈니스 프로그램에 등록한 모든 학생들은 반드시 기초 작문 코스를 이수해야 졸업 자격을 얻을 수 있다.

| 해설 |
'강좌, 학업 과정' 등을 뜻하는 course와 어울리는 동사로 '~을 이수하다, 완료하다' 등을 의미하는 (B) complete이 정답이다.

| 어휘 | enroll in ~에 등록하다   qualify for ~에 대한 자격을 얻다   retire 은퇴하다   deserve ~을 받을 만한 자격이 있다   present ~을 발표하다, 제시하다

9. (A)

| 해석 |
Speedy Shipping의 혁신적인 GPS 추적 시스템으로 인해 고객들은 온라인에 접속해 배송 물품의 정확한 위치를 찾을 수 있다.

| 해설 |
GPS-tracking system을 수식해 이 시스템의 특징을 나타낼 형용사가 필요하므로 '혁신적인'을 뜻하는 (A) innovative가 정답이다.

| 어휘 | go online 온라인에 접속하다   exact 정확한   location 위치, 지점   alert 경계하는, 기민한   uncertain 불확실한   assorted 갖가지의

10. (D)

| 해석 |
Donaldson 씨는 Elstar Industries 와의 협상에 앞서 제안된 계약서를 철저히 검토하도록 우리에게 지시했다.

| 해설 |
to부정사로 쓰인 동사 review를 수식해 계약서를 검토하는 방식을 나타낼 부사가 필요하므로 '철저히'를 뜻하는 (D) thoroughly가 정답이다.

| 어휘 | instruct 지시하다   review ~을 검토하다   proposed 제안된   contract 계약(서)   negotiation 협상, 협의   previously 이전에   relatively 상대적으로   highly 매우, 많이

11. (C)

| 해석 |
Stone Tires는 제품 리콜과 관련해 넘쳐 나는 전화를 처리하기 위해 다수의 새로운 전화 상담원을 고용해야 했다.

| 해설 |
복수 명사 operators를 수식할 수 있으며 의미상으로도 적합한 (C) multiple이 정답이다.

| 어휘 | hire ~을 고용하다   operator 전화 상담원   handle ~을 처리하다   influx 밀려듦, 유입   related to ~와 관련된   recall (결함 제품의) 리콜, 회수   periodical 정기 간행의   fierce 극심한, 맹렬한   multiple 다수의

12. (C)

| 해석 |
암호화 소프트웨어로 민감한 데이터 파일들을 보호하면 그 파일에 해커들이 접근할 수 없도록 방지해 줄 것이다.

| 해설 |
빈칸 뒤에 위치한 '목적어 + from + -ing' 구조와 어울려 '~가 …하지 못하게 하다'라는 의미를 나타낼 때 사용하는 (C) prevent가 정답이다.

| 어휘 | protect ~을 보호하다   sensitive 민감한   encryption 암호화   access ~에 접근하다   ignore ~을 무시하다

13. (C)

| 해석 |
운전면허증을 취득하려면, 지원자들은 반드시 지역 내 거주자임을 입증해야 한다.

| 해설 |
driver's license와 관련된 자격 요건이 언급되어 있으므로 그 목적과 관련된 동사로 '~을 얻다, 획득하다'를 뜻하는 (C) obtain이 정답이다.

| 어휘 | in order to do ~하기 위해   applicant 지원자, 신청자   prove (that) ~임을 입증하다   resident 거주자, 주민   define (의미 등) ~을 정의하다

14. (B)

| 해석 |
5층에 위치한 회의실은 에어컨 설치 작업이 완료될 때까지 출입할 수 없을 것이다.

| 해설 |
주어 meeting room에 대한 보어로서 공사 작업 중일 때의 상태를 나타낼 형용사가 필요하므로 '접근할 수 없는'을 의미하는 (B) inaccessible이 정답이다.

| 어휘 | installation 설치   complete 완료된   irresponsible 무책임한   undeniable 부인할 수 없는   improbable 사실일 것 같지 않은

15. (C)

| 해석 |
Carson 주지사의 높은 지지율은 주로 지역 내 공해 감소에 대한 효율성에 기인해 왔다.

| 해설 |
'~에 기인하다'를 의미하는 be attributed to에서 원인을 이끄는 전치사 앞에 들어가 원인의 정도를 나타낼 부사가 필요하므로 '주로'를 의미하는 (C) primarily가 정답이다.

| 어휘 | governor 주지사   approval ratings 지지율   be attributed to ~에 기인하다   effectiveness 효율성   pollution 공해, 오염   extremely 극히, 극도로   diligently 근면하게

16. (A)

| 해석 |
금연 캠페인이 뚜렷하게 성공을 거둬 왔으며, 그로 인해 성인들 사이에서 흡연이 15퍼센트 넘게 감소되었다.

| 해설 |
형용사 successful을 수식해 성공적인 정도를 나타낼 부사가 필요하므로

'뚜렷하게, 현저하게'를 의미하는 (A) markedly가 정답이다.
| 어휘 | loosely 느슨하게   intimately 친밀하게   affordably (가격이) 알맞게, 감당할 수 있게

17-20번 문제는 다음 광고를 참조하시오.

Maury's 중고 자동차에서 다시 한번 연례 가을 세일 행사가 열릴 때가 되었습니다. 중고 자동차 구입에 관심이 있는 분이시라면, 행사장에 들르셔서 전혀 손해되지 않는 시험 운행을 해 보시기 바랍니다. **17** 비용을 지불하시거나 어떤 것에도 가입하시도록 요청 드리지 않습니다. 저희 영업 사원들은 여러분께서 문의하실 경우에 가격 정보만 말씀드립니다! 차량을 구입하시는 경우에는, 저희 Maury's가 180일이 **18** 넘는 기간에 대해 차량을 보증해 드릴 것입니다. 이 기간 중에 어떠한 기계적인 문제라도 겪으실 경우, 저희 전문 정비사들 중 한 명에게 **19** 그저 차량을 가져오셔서 무료 수리를 받으시기만 하면 됩니다. 오늘 저희 매장을 방문하시기 바라며, 반드시 유효한 운전면허증을 **20** 지참하시기 바랍니다!

| 어휘 | annual 연례의, 해마다의   be in the market for ~을 구입하는 데 관심이 있다   used 중고의   stop by 들르다   completely 전적으로   risk-free 안전한, 구입자에게 손해가 없는   sales associate 영업 사원   in the event (that) ~할 경우에   guarantee ~을 보증하다   mechanical 기계적인   expert 전문적인   mechanic 정비사   be sure to do 반드시 ~하다   valid 유효한

17. (D)
(A) maurysvehicles.com에서 새로운 저희 차량 제품 라인을 미리 확인해 보십시오.
(B) 모든 구매 제품에 대해 10퍼센트의 선금이 필수입니다.
(C) 더 작은 자동차들이 항상 연비가 더 좋은 것은 아닙니다.
| 해설 |
앞 문장에 risk-free라는 표현과 함께 행사장에 들러서 시험 운행을 해 보라고 권하는 말이 있으므로 어떠한 부담도 없을 것임을 약속하는 의미로 쓰인 (D)가 정답이다.
| 어휘 | preview ~을 미리 보다   down payment 선금, 착수금   required 필수인   fuel efficient 연비가 좋은

18. (B)
| 해설 |
숫자가 포함된 표현(180 days) 앞에 위치할 수 있는 것으로 '~가 넘는'이라는 의미를 나타내는 (B) over가 정답이다.

19. (A)
| 해설 |
빈칸 뒤의 명령문과 의미상 가장 잘 어울리는 부사인 (A) simply가 정답이다. simply는 명령문과 함께 쓰여 '그저 ~하기만 하면 된다'라는 의미로 사용된다.
| 어휘 | evenly 고르게, 균등하게   generally 일반적으로   justly 바르게, 공정하게

20. (B)
| 해설 |
빈칸 뒤에 위치한 a valid driver's license(유효한 운전면허증)는 행사장 방문 시에 가져와야 할 물품에 해당되므로 '~을 가져오다'를 뜻하는 (B) bring이 정답이다.
| 어휘 | achieve ~을 달성하다   renew ~을 갱신하다   initiate ~을 시작하다

DAY 14 어휘-명사/전치사

◆ 출제 포인트 1   명사 어휘 (1)
본책 p.228

1. estimates
| 해석 |
물류 관리팀은 모든 해외 주문품의 운송비에 대해 때맞춘 견적서를 제공합니다.
| 해설 |
운송비와 관련해 제때 제공해 주는 것으로 적절한 대상을 나타낼 명사가 필요하며 명사 cost와도 어울려야 하므로 '견적(서)'를 의미하는 estimates가 정답이다.
| 어휘 | logistics 물류 (관리)   provide ~을 제공하다   timely 때맞춘   transportation cost 운송비

2. addition
| 해석 |
NetCast의 모바일 서비스 약정에 무제한 영상 통화를 추가하는 것은 그 서비스를 더욱 매력적으로 만들 것이다.
| 해설 |
뒤에 이어지는 'A to B'의 구조와 어울리는 것으로서 '~에 대한 …의 추가'라는 의미를 구성할 수 있는 addition이 정답이다.
| 어휘 | content 내용(물)   unlimited 무제한의   mobile plan 모바일 서비스 약정   appealing 매력적인

3. alternative
| 해석 |
태양열 전지판은 석탄 및 천연 가스에 대한 더 깨끗하고 저렴한 대안으로 판명되었다.
| 해설 |
뒤에 위치한 'to + 명사구'의 구조와 어울리는 것으로서 '~의 대안'이라는 의미를 나타낼 때 사용하는 alternative가 정답이다.
| 어휘 | solar panel 태양열 전지판   prove ~으로 판명되다   option 선택권   coal 석탄

◆ 출제 포인트 2   명사 어휘 (2)
본책 p.228

1. priority
| 해석 |
최고재무관리자는 예산의 균형을 맞추는 것을 이번 회계 연도에서 최우선 순위로 삼았다.
| 해설 |
high와 어울려 '최우선 순위'라는 의미를 구성할 때 사용하는 priority가 정답이다.
| 어휘 | financial director 최고재무관리자   balance ~의 균형을 잡다   budget 예산   adjustment 조정, 조절   fiscal year 회계 연도

2. fact
| 해석 |
대부분의 시골 주민들에게 적절한 의료 서비스가 부족하다는 사실이 그 기사에서 강조되었다.
| 해설 |
동격의 that절과 함께 '~라는 사실'이라는 의미로 쓰이는 fact가 정답이다.
| 어휘 | gossip (사생활에 대한) 소문   rural 시골의   resident 주민   lack ~가 부족하다   adequate 적절한   highlight 강조하다

3. purpose
| 해석 |
이 연구의 목적은 주문 지연의 흔한 원인들을 확인하는 것이다.

| 해설 |
뒤에 위치한 'be to do' 구조와 어울려 '목적은 ~하는 것이다'라는 의미를 구성하는 purpose가 정답이다.
| 어휘 | indication 표시, 조짐 identify ~을 확인하다, 알아보다 common 흔한 cause 원인 delayed 지연된

최빈출 확인 문제
본책 p.229

정답 1 (B)   2 (C)   3 (C)   4 (D)   5 (B)   6 (C)
      7 (B)   8 (C)   9 (C)   10 (A) 11 (C) 12 (B)

1. (B)
| 해설 |
Hopeworks Charity는 공구와 페인트, 자재 및 기타 공사 중에 필요한 용품을 제공할 것이다.
| 해설 |
'A, B, C, and other' 구조에서 other의 수식을 받을 명사는 앞서 나열된 명사들을 아우를 수 있는 범주와 관련되어야 하므로 '용품, 물품'을 의미하는 (B) supplies가 정답이다.
| 어휘 | tool 공구 material 재료 required 필요한 capability 능력 attribute 자질, 속성 facility 시설

2. (C)
| 해설 |
Nationwide Home Insurance는 다른 업체들과는 달리 홍수로 인해 야기된 피해에 대해 모든 보상을 제공한다.
| 해설 |
홍수와 같은 재해로 인한 피해에 대해 제공되는 것을 나타낼 명사가 필요하므로 '보상 (범위)'을 의미하는 (C) coverage가 정답이다.
| 어휘 | unlike ~와 달리 agency 업체, 대행사 damage 피해, 손상 caused by ~에 의해 야기된 flooding 홍수 guarantee 보증, 보장 potential 잠재력

3. (C)
| 해설 |
Leanders 사는 지출 비용을 줄이기 위해 자사의 디지털 음악 재생기 제품 라인의 생산을 중단했다.
| 해설 |
특정 제품의 생산을 중단함으로써 줄일 수 있는 것을 나타낼 명사가 필요하므로 '지출 비용'을 의미하는 (C) expenses가 정답이다.
| 어휘 | line 제품 라인 reduce ~을 줄이다 credit 신용(도), 학점 custom 관습, 관례 value 가치

4. (D)
| 해설 |
회사 야유회에 참석할 수 없는 직원들은 소속 부서장으로부터 허가를 받아야 할 것이다.
| 해설 |
회사의 행사에 참석하지 못하는 사람들이 부서장으로부터 얻어야 하는 것을 나타낼 명사가 필요하므로 '허가'를 의미하는 (D) permission이 정답이다.
| 어휘 | attend ~에 참석하다 obtain ~을 얻다, 획득하다 registration 등록 commission 수수료, 위원회 suggestion 제안, 의견

5. (B)
| 해설 |
이 위원회의 목적은 다가오는 정보 기술 분야의 발전에 대비해 직원들을 준비시키는 것입니다.
| 해설 |
빈칸 뒤에 이어지는 'be to do' 구조와 어울려 '목적은 ~하는 것이다'라는 의미를 나타낼 때 사용하는 (B) aim이 정답이다.
| 어휘 | committee 위원회 prepare A for B B에 대비해 A를 준비시키다

workforce 직원들, 인력 upcoming 다가오는 advancement 발전, 진보 solution 해결책

6. (C)
| 해설 |
Chicago Marathon을 후원하는 데 관심 있는 기업들은 저희 웹 사이트에서 후원 신청서를 찾아보실 수 있습니다.
| 해설 |
목적을 나타내는 전치사 for와 함께 '~의 신청서'라는 의미를 나타내는 (C) application이 정답이다.
| 어휘 | interested in ~에 관심 있는 support ~을 후원하다 sponsorship 후원, 협찬 addition 추가(되는 것) impression 인상, 감명 entirety 전체, 전부

7. (B)
| 해설 |
디자인팀은 다음 주에 있을 컨벤션 행사의 시작에 앞서 시제품에 대한 모든 수정을 완료할 것이다.
| 해설 |
동사 finish의 목적어로서 완료될 수 있는 대상을 나타낼 명사가 필요한데, 빈칸 뒤의 전치사 to와 어울려야 하므로 '~에 대한 수정'을 의미하는 (B) revisions가 정답이다.
| 어휘 | prototype 시제품 provision 공급, 대비 nomination 후보 지명

8. (C)
| 해설 |
Greenhaven Heights는 명문 학교들과의 인접성으로 인해 가족들에게 이상적인 아파트 단지이다.
| 해설 |
빈칸 뒤의 전치사 to와 어울리는 명사로서 '~와의 인접성'을 의미하는 (C) proximity가 정답이다.
| 어휘 | ideal 이상적인 prestigious 명성 높은, 권위 있는 diligence 근면 competence 역량, 능력 achievement 업적, 달성

9. (C)
| 해설 |
대리석 조리대를 설치하는 과정이 쉬워 보이기는 하지만, 단 한번의 실수가 생겨도 큰 비용이 들 수 있다.
| 해설 |
빈칸 뒤의 for + -ing 구조와 어울리며 '~에 대한 과정, 절차'를 의미하는 (C) procedure가 정답이다.
| 어휘 | while ~이기는 하지만 install ~을 설치하다 countertop 조리대 appear to do ~하는 것 같다 costly 많은 비용이 드는 capacity 용량, 수용력 category 항목, 범주 likelihood 가능성

10. (A)
| 해설 |
Harris 시장이 가장 최근에 더 젊은 유권자들과 교류하기 위한 시도로 여러 인기 팟캐스트에 출연했다.
| 해설 |
빈칸 뒤의 to부정사와 함께 '~하기 위한 시도로'라는 의미를 구성할 때 사용하는 (A) attempt가 정답이다.
| 어휘 | appear 출연하다, 나타나다 recent 최근의 connect with ~와 교류하다, 연결되다 voter 유권자 omission 생략 evaluation 평가(서) conclusion 결론, 결말

11. (C)
| 해설 |
주주들은 회사의 실망스러운 실적에 대해 Mark Rafferty 대표이사의 공식적인 언급을 요구했다.
| 해설 |
빈칸 뒤에 위한 전치사 on과 함께 '~에 대한 언급, 의견'을 의미할 때 사용

하는 (C) comment가 정답이다.
| 어휘 | stockholder 주주   request ~을 요구하다   official 공식적인   disappointing 실망시키는   performance 실적, 성과   attraction 명소, 인기장소   preparation 준비, 대비

12. (B)
| 해석 |
탄탄한 부동산 시장은 경제가 불경기에서 회복되었음을 보여주는 좋은 징조이다.
| 해설 |
빈칸 뒤의 that절과 동격을 이루어 '~임을 보여주는 징조, 표시' 등을 의미할 때 사용하는 (B) indicator가 정답이다.
| 어휘 | real estate 부동산   recover 회복되다   recession 불경기   procedure 절차   reference 참조, 조회   objective 목적

◆ 출제 포인트 3 전치사 어휘 (1)   본책 p.230

1. as
| 해석 |
Jason 씨는 <Prism Magazine>에 입사하기 전에 <Metro Daily>에서 칼럼니스트로 근무했다.
| 해설 |
칼럼니스트는 직업에 해당되므로 자격이나 신분을 나타낼 때 사용하는 전치사 as가 정답이다.
| 어휘 | join ~에 입사하다, 합류하다

2. Upon
| 해석 |
Mercy 병원에서 은퇴하자마자, Smith 박사는 의대생들을 위한 온라인 세미나를 만들 것이다.
| 해설 |
retiring이 이끄는 동명사구를 목적어로 취해야 하므로 전치사인 Upon이 정답이다. Apart는 부사이다.
| 어휘 | apart 따로, 떨어져   retire from ~에서 은퇴하다

3. Given
| 해석 |
최근 지역 관광 산업의 급증을 감안하면, 주민들은 늘어나는 교통량에 대비해야 한다.
| 해설 |
'~을 감안해 늘어나는 교통량에 대비해야 한다'는 의미가 되어야 적절하므로 '~을 감안하면, ~을 고려해 볼 때'를 뜻하는 전치사 Given이 정답이다.
| 어휘 | recent 최근의   surge in ~의 급증   tourism 관광 산업   resident 주민   traffic 교통량

◆ 출제 포인트 4 전치사 어휘 (2)   본책 p.230

1. on behalf of
| 해석 |
Freeland 씨는 Canadian Steel을 대표해 교역 협상에 참석할 것이다.
| 해설 |
회사를 대표해 협상에 참석한다는 의미가 되어야 자연스러우므로 '~을 대표해'를 뜻하는 on behalf of가 정답이다.
| 어휘 | trade 교역, 무역   negotiation 협상, 협의

2. instead of
| 해석 |
악천후로 인해, 그 음악 축제는 이번 주 토요일 대신 다음 주말에 개최될 것이다.

| 해설 |
다음 주말에 행사가 열린다는 말이 있으므로 this Saturday는 개최 시점이 아님을 알 수 있다. 따라서 선택되지 않는 대상 앞에 쓰여 '~ 대신, ~가 아니라'를 의미하는 instead of가 정답이다.
| 어휘 | due to ~로 인해   take place (일, 행사 등이) 개최되다, 발생되다   aside from ~ 외에는

3. in addition to
| 해석 |
Omega 노트북 컴퓨터는 완전히 맞춤 제작 가능한 키보드뿐만 아니라 터치 바 인터페이스도 제공한다.
| 해설 |
두 가지 특정 기능이 제공된다는 의미가 되어야 적절하므로 '~뿐만 아니라'라는 의미로 추가 정보를 말할 때 사용하는 in addition to가 정답이다.
| 어휘 | along (길 등) ~을 따라   fully 완전히, 전적으로   customizable 맞춤 제작 가능한

최빈출 확인 문제   본책 p.231

정답	1 (A)	2 (C)	3 (C)	4 (C)	5 (A)	6 (B)
	7 (B)	8 (C)	9 (A)	10 (A)	11 (D)	12 (A)

1. (A)
| 해석 |
시설 관리 비용으로 인해, Oxbow Golf Club의 회비가 내년에 15퍼센트 인상될 것이다.
| 해설 |
15%와 같이 변화의 차이를 나타내는 수치는 '~만큼'을 뜻하는 전치사 by와 함께 사용하므로 (A) by가 정답이다.
| 어휘 | maintenance 시설 관리   increase 인상되다

2. (C)
| 해석 |
컨벤션에 무료로 입장하시려면, 정문에서 소속 회사 사원증과 함께 VIP 출입증을 제시해 주시기 바랍니다.
| 해설 |
빈칸 앞뒤에 위치한 명사구들은 제시해야 하는 두 가지 대상에 해당되므로 '~와 함께'를 의미하는 (C) along with가 정답이다.
| 어휘 | for free 무료로   additionally 추가로   on behalf of ~를 대신하여

3. (C)
| 해석 |
Turner Studios는 최대 8백만 달러의 가치에 달하는 거래 계약으로 <Midnight Monster>에 대한 영화 판권을 얻었다.
| 해설 |
비용을 나타내는 명사구와 결합 가능한 것으로 '~의 가치가 있는'을 의미할 때 사용하는 (C) worth가 정답이다.
| 어휘 | acquire ~을 얻다, 획득하다   film right 영화 판권   deal 거래 계약   up to 최대 ~의   in spite of ~에도 불구하고   except ~을 제외하고

4. (C)
| 해석 |
Praxis Inc.는 Delcor Appliances 인수에 따른 결과로 새로운 시장으로 사업을 확장할 수 있었다.
| 해설 |
사업 확장은 새로운 업체의 인수에 따른 결과로 판단할 수 있으므로 '~의 결과로'를 의미하는 (C) as a result of가 정답이다.
| 어휘 | expand into ~로 확장하다   acquisition 인수, 매입   moreover 더욱이

5. (A)

| 해석 |
그 대학교의 문학 축제는 Anita Davis 교수와 Jay Moss 교수를 포함해 소속 교수진들의 낭독 행사를 특징으로 할 것이다.
| 해설 |
빈칸 뒤에 위치한 'Anita Davis and Jay Moss'는 그 앞에 언급된 faculty members에 포함되는 사람들로 볼 수 있으므로 '~을 포함해'를 뜻하는 (A) including이 정답이다.
| 어휘 | feature ~을 특징으로 하다 reading 낭독, 낭송 faculty 교수진 pertaining ~에 관련된

6. (B)

| 해석 |
Vancouver 영화제에 참석하는 평론가들은 극장 개봉보다 2주 앞서 Tom Brautigan의 <Silver Suns>를 관람할 수 있다.
| 해설 |
'기간 명사 + 빈칸 + 시점 명사'의 구조에 어울리는 것으로서 '~보다 …만큼 앞서'라는 의미를 나타낼 때 사용하는 (B) ahead of가 정답이다.
| 어휘 | critic 평론가 theatrical release 극장 개봉(일)

7. (B)

| 해석 |
결함 있는 조향 장치에 대한 우려가 발생한 가운데, Takoma Motors는 자사의 최신 승용차를 리콜했다.
| 해설 |
'우려'를 의미하는 명사 concerns와 어울려 '우려가 있는 가운데'라는 의미를 나타낼 때 사용하는 (B) Amid가 정답이다.
| 어휘 | concern 우려 defective 결함이 있는 steering system 조향 장치 recall (결함 제품에 대해) ~을 리콜하다, 회수하다 apart 따로, 떨어져 atop ~ 꼭대기에 abroad 해외로

8. (C)

| 해석 |
항상 자신에게 요구되는 역할을 뛰어넘는 직무들을 기꺼이 맡으려 하는 Sager 씨는 종종 사무실에서 어쩔 줄 모른다.
| 해설 |
his required role과 같이 역할이나 능력 등을 나타내는 명사와 어울리는 전치사로서 '~을 넘어서는'을 의미할 때 사용하는 (C) beyond가 정답이다.
| 어휘 | willing to do 기꺼이 ~하려 하는 take on ~을 맡다 responsibility 직무, 책임 required 요구되는 overwhelmed 압도된 along (길 등) ~을 따라 towards ~쪽으로

9. (A)

| 해석 |
모든 차량들은 반드시 주의 규제에 따라 연례 점검을 거쳐야 한다.
| 해설 |
state regulations는 준수해야 하는 것에 해당되므로 '~에 따라'라는 의미로 준수 대상 앞에 사용하는 (A) in accordance with가 정답이다.
| 어휘 | vehicle 차량 undergo ~을 거치다, 겪다 yearly 연례의 inspection 점검 state (행정 구역) 주 regulation 규제, 규정 as opposed to ~와 대조적으로 on account of ~ 때문에 in advance of ~보다 앞서

10. (A)

| 해석 |
연결 상태가 약할 수도 있지만, 여객선에 승선한 모든 승객들에게 무료 와이파이가 이용 가능하다.
| 해설 |
'여객선'을 뜻하는 the ferry와 어울리는 전치사로 '~에 탑승한'을 의미하는 (A) aboard가 정답이다.
| 어휘 | connection 연결 weak 약한 past (이동) ~을 지나

11. (D)

| 해석 |
팬들의 요구에 대응해, 그 밴드는 그들과 직접 의사소통하기 위해 소셜 미디어 페이지를 만들었다.
| 해설 |
'요구, 수요'를 의미하는 명사 demand와 어울려 '요구에 대응해'라는 의미를 구성할 때 사용하는 (D) In response to가 정답이다.
| 어휘 | demand 요구, 수요 create ~을 만들다 communicate with ~와 의사소통하다 alongside of ~와 함께 in place of ~을 대신해서

12. (A)

| 해석 |
제품의 공식 출시에 앞서, 우리는 실험실에서 몇 가지 최종 테스트를 수행할 것이다.
| 해설 |
테스트는 제품 출시 전에 하는 일이므로 '~에 앞서'를 의미하는 (A) In advance of가 정답이다.
| 어휘 | official 공식적인 release 출시 conduct ~을 수행하다 last-minute 최종 순간의 lab 실험실 whether ~인지 (아닌지) as long as ~하는 한

✦ 출제 포인트 5 — 전치사를 포함한 숙어(1) 본책 p.232

1. compatible

| 해석 |
새로 나온 Tracer 앱은 대부분의 스마트폰 운영 시스템과 호환이 된다.
| 해설 |
전치사 with와 어울리는 형용사로서 '~와 호환이 되는'을 의미할 때 사용하는 compatible이 정답이다.
| 어휘 | reflective 반사하는, 반영하는 operating system 운영 시스템

2. for

| 해석 |
국제 개발부는 해외에 있는 우리의 사업 지분을 관리하는 일을 책임지고 있다.
| 해설 |
형용사 responsible과 어울리는 전치사로서 '~에 대한 책임이 있는'이라는 의미를 구성할 수 있는 for가 정답이다.
| 어휘 | business interests 사업 지분, 사업 이익 abroad 해외에

3. eligible

| 해석 |
그 클럽 회원에 대한 자격을 얻으려면 반드시 18세 이상이어야 한다.
| 해설 |
전치사 for와 어울리는 형용사로서 '~에 대한 자격이 있는'을 의미할 때 사용하는 eligible이 정답이다.
| 어휘 | considerate 사려 깊은

✦ 출제 포인트 6 — 전치사를 포함한 숙어(2) 본책 p.232

1. with

| 해석 |
개발팀은 일주일 단위로 책임자에게 경과 보고서를 제공한다.
| 해설 |
'provide + 사람 + with + 사물'의 구조가 되어야 하므로 with가 정답이다.
| 어휘 | development 개발 director 책임자, 부장, 이사 progress 경과, 진척 on a weekly basis 일주일 단위로

2. total

| 해석 |
어린이 병원 자선 행사는 기업 기부자들을 통해 총액 557,000달러를 벌어들였다.

| 해설 |
부정 관사 a와 괄호 뒤의 'of + 숫자'와 어울리는 명사로서 '총액'이라는 의미로 뒤에 오는 금액과 동격을 이루는 total이 정답이다.

| 어휘 | charity 자선 (활동)　earn ~을 벌다, 얻다　corporate 기업의　donor 기부자

3. array

| 해석 |
Harbrook 대학의 캠퍼스는 학생들을 위해 다양한 교통편 선택권을 제공한다.

| 해설 |
부정 관사 an, 전치사 of와 어울리는 명사로서 복수 명사 앞에서 '다양한'이라는 수식어구를 구성할 때 사용하는 array가 정답이다.

| 어휘 | transportation 교통편　entity 실재, 독립체

최빈출 확인 문제　　　　　　　　본책 p.233

정답　1 (B)　2 (B)　3 (D)　4 (D)　5 (B)　6 (C)
　　　7 (D)　8 (A)　9 (B)　10 (B)　11 (B)　12 (D)

---

1. (B)

| 해석 |
Mack's Supermarket은 추후 공지가 있을 때까지 Carolina Farms 산 고추를 갖춰 놓지 않을 것이다.

| 해설 |
빈칸 앞에 위치한 until further와 어울려 '추후 공지가 있을 때까지'라는 의미를 구성할 때 사용하는 (B) notice가 정답이다.

| 어휘 | stock (상품 등) ~을 갖춰 놓다, 재고로 보유하다　status 상태, 상황　concern 우려

2. (B)

| 해석 |
대부분의 운전자들은 Riverview Drive를 따라 줄어든 속도 제한에 대해 여전히 알지 못하고 있다.

| 해설 |
빈칸 앞뒤에 위치한 be 동사, 전치사 of와 어울리는 형용사로서 '~에 대해 알지 못하다'라는 의미를 구성하는 (B) unaware가 정답이다.

| 어휘 | reduced 줄어든, 감소된　competent 유능한, 능숙한　sensitive 민감한　willing 의향이 있는

3. (D)

| 해석 |
현재 여러 사람들이 휴가 중이므로, 마케팅팀은 분기 보고서를 완료하지 못한 상태이다.

| 해설 |
빈칸 앞에 위치한 be finished와 어울리는 전치사로서 완료 대상 앞에 사용하는 (D) with가 정답이다.

| 어휘 | currently 현재　on vacation 휴가 중인　be finished with ~을 완료하다　quarterly 분기의

4. (D)

| 해석 |
Cali Electronics는 고객들이 두 개의 중고 게임을 새로 출시된 제품과 교환할 수 있게 해 준다.

| 해설 |
빈칸 앞에 위치한 동사 exchange는 'exchange A for B'의 구조로 'A를 B로 교환하다'라는 의미로 쓰이므로 (D) for가 정답이다.

| 어휘 | exchange 교환하다　released 출시된　title (출판물 등의) 작품, 제품

5. (B)

| 해석 |
Bluth 부동산은 가격이 적당한 교외 주택에 대한 높은 수요에 대응해 Westchester 개발 프로젝트를 시작했다.

| 해설 |
빈칸 앞뒤의 형용사 high, 전치사 for와 어울리는 명사로 '~에 대한 높은 수요'라는 의미를 구성할 수 있는 (B) demand가 정답이다.

| 어휘 | initiate ~을 시작하다　development 개발　in response to ~에 대응해　affordable 가격이 알맞은　suburban 교외의　housing 주택 (공급)　population 인구　occurrence 발생

6. (C)

| 해석 |
놀랍게도, Burgerland의 포커스 그룹 참가자들은 두 가지 새로운 소스 맛 중 어느 한쪽에 대해서도 강한 선호도를 나타내지 않았다.

| 해설 |
빈칸 앞뒤의 형용사 strong, 전치사 for와 어울리는 명사로 '~에 대한 강한 선호도'라는 의미를 나타낼 때 사용하는 (C) preference가 정답이다.

| 어휘 | surprisingly 놀랍게도　focus group 포커스 그룹(시장 조사 등을 위한 그룹)　either of ~ 둘 중의 어느 하나　flavor 맛　courtesy 공손함

7. (D)

| 해석 |
Cosgrove Center의 연례 연회에서, 유명 화가 Amelia Kurst 씨가 예술에 대한 공헌으로 표창 받았다.

| 해설 |
빈칸 뒤의 'for + 업적/성과' 전치사구와 어울려 '~에 대해 표창 받다, 인정 받다'라는 의미를 구성할 수 있는 (D) recognized가 정답이다.

| 어휘 | annual 연례의　banquet 연회　renowned 유명한　contribution to ~에 대한 공헌, 기여　complete ~을 완료하다　resume ~을 재개하다　afford ~할 여유가 있다

8. (A)

| 해석 |
Nolan Athletics에서 생산되는 모든 헬멧 제품들은 내구성을 보장하기 위해 일련의 테스트를 거친다.

| 해설 |
빈칸 앞뒤에 각각 위치한 부정 관사 a, 전치사 of와 어울리는 명사로서 복수 명사 앞에서 '일련의'라는 수식어구를 구성할 때 사용하는 (A) series가 정답이다.

| 어휘 | put A through B A에게 B를 겪게 하다, 거치게 하다　guarantee ~을 보장하다　durability 내구성　shortage 부족　length 길이　presence 존재(감)

9. (B)

| 해석 |
장비의 이용가능 여부에 따라 대여가 불가할 수도 있으므로 개인 장비를 챙겨 오시는 것이 좋습니다.

| 해설 |
빈칸 뒤의 전치사 to와 함께 '~에 영향 받는, ~에 따라 좌우되는' 등을 의미로 쓰이는 (B) subject가 정답이다.

| 어휘 | It is recommended to do ~하는 것이 좋다, ~하도록 권고되다　gear 장비　rental 대여, 임대　availability 이용 가능성　equipment 장비　accountable 책임이 있는　public 공공의

10. (B)

| 해석 |
Murray 건설은 그 프로젝트에 약 1천만 달러를 소비했는데, 이는 예산의 70퍼센트 이상에 상당하는 것이다.

| 해설 |
빈칸 뒤의 전치사 to와 어울리는 형용사로서 '10 million dollars'라는 비

용이 예산에서 차지하는 비율을 나타내야 알맞으므로 to와 함께 '~에 상응하는, 맞먹는' 등을 의미하는 (B) equivalent가 정답이다.
| 어휘 | budget 예산   significant 상당한, 많은   appropriate 적절한   reasonable 합리적인

11. (B)
| 해석 |
주 요리를 구입할 때마다, Malcom Steakhouse 고객들은 목록에서 두 가지 곁들임 요리를 선택할 수 있다.
| 해설 |
빈칸 앞의 동사 select와 어울리는 전치사로 전체 범주에 해당되는 명사구 앞에 사용하는 (B) from이 정답이다.
| 어휘 | entrée 주 요리   purchase 구입(품)   select ~을 선택하다   side dish 곁들임 요리   following ~ 후에

12. (D)
| 해석 |
오토바이로 남미 지역을 걸쳐 여행한 적이 있는 Caron 씨는 그 지역에 대해 풍부한 지식을 갖고 있다.
| 해설 |
빈칸 앞뒤의 부정 관사 a, 전치사 of와 어울리는 명사로 불가산 명사 앞에서 '풍부한'이라는 수식어구를 구성할 때 사용하는 (D) wealth가 정답이다.
| 어휘 | through ~을 걸쳐, ~을 통해   fame 명예   labor 노동(력)   height 높이, 키

DAY 14 | 실전문제
본책 p.234

정답					
1 (C)	2 (C)	3 (C)	4 (D)	5 (C)	6 (A)
7 (B)	8 (B)	9 (B)	10 (A)	11 (B)	12 (C)
13 (B)	14 (B)	15 (D)	16 (D)	17 (B)	18 (A)
19 (D)	20 (D)				

1. (C)
| 해석 |
Carver 시는 이전에 오래된 식품 처리 공장이 있던 부지를 공원으로 변모시킬 것이다.
| 해설 |
빈칸 앞의 형용사 former와 어울리는 명사로서 용도 변경 전의 공장이 위치한 곳을 가리키는 말이 필요하므로 '부지'를 뜻하는 (C) site가 정답이다.
| 어휘 | turn A into B A를 B로 변모시키다, 전환하다   former 이전의   processing (가공) 처리   plant 공장   placement 취업 알선, 배치   arena 경기장, 공연장

2. (C)
| 해석 |
Natural Homes의 전문가들은 50달러의 저렴한 요금으로 배송 즉시 모든 가구를 조립해 줄 것이다.
| 해설 |
빈칸 뒤의 명사 delivery와 어울리는 전치사가 필요하므로 '배송 즉시'라는 의미를 구성해 배송 시점을 나타낼 때 사용하는 (C) upon이 정답이다.
| 어휘 | expert 전문가   assemble ~을 조립하다   delivery 배송   fee 요금, 수수료   afterward 그 후에, 나중에

3. (C)
| 해석 |
Leroy Varga 부장의 감독 하에, 영업팀은 지난 분기에 수익을 18퍼센트 증가시켰다.
| 해설 |
'under the ~ of + 사람'의 구조에 어울리는 명사로 '~의 감독하에, 지휘

하에' 등의 의미를 구성할 때 사용하는 (C) supervision이 정답이다.
| 어휘 | sales 영업, 판매(량)   profit 수익   quarter 분기   provision 공급   expansion 확장   attendance 참가(자의 수)

4. (D)
| 해석 |
안전 기준과 관련된 일부 부정적인 언론 보도에도 불구하고, 투자자들은 그 회사에 대해 지속적으로 신뢰를 나타내고 있다.
| 해설 |
빈칸은 express의 목적어가 될 감정 명사가 올 자리이며, 뒤의 전치사 in 과도 어울려야 하므로 in과 함께 '~에 대한 신뢰'를 의미할 때 사용하는 (D) confidence가 정답이다.
| 어휘 | despite ~에도 불구하고   negative 부정적인   publicity 언론 보도, 언론의 관심   regarding ~와 관련된   investor 투자자   continue to do 지속적으로 ~하다   exception 예외   gratitude 감사(의 마음)   sympathy 동정, 동조

5. (C)
| 해석 |
Ashley Center는 피트니스 센터나 영화관 같은 시설물을 갖추고 있다.
| 해설 |
예시를 나타내는 such as 앞에는 그 뒤에 위치한 명사들을 하나로 아우를 수 있는 명사가 쓰여야 한다. 피트니스 센터나 영화관은 모두 시설물에 해당되므로 '시설(물)'을 뜻하는 (C) facilities가 정답이다.
| 어휘 | be equipped with ~을 갖추고 있다   procedure 절차   facility 시설(물)

6. (A)
| 해석 |
오직 4월에 열린 교육 세미나에 참석한 직원들만 월요일에 열리는 세미나에서 제외된다.
| 해설 |
빈칸 앞뒤의 be 동사, 전치사 from과 어울리는 형용사로 '~에서 제외되다, 면제되다'를 의미할 때 사용하는 (A) exempt가 정답이다.
| 어휘 | hold ~을 열다, 개최하다   observe ~을 관찰하다, 준수하다   distinct 뚜렷한, 분명한

7. (B)
| 해석 |
기조 연설은 올해의 Xavier Award 수상자인 Valerie Gruber 씨에 의해 이뤄질 것이다.
| 해설 |
사람 이름인 Valerie Gruber와 동격을 이룰 수 있는 명사로 'of + 상 이름' 전치사구와 어울려 '~의 수령자, 수상자'라는 의미를 구성할 수 있는 (B) recipient가 정답이다.
| 어휘 | keynote speech 기조 연설   deliver (연설 등) ~을 하다

8. (B)
| 해석 |
정문에 있는 것 외에 동쪽 출입구에도 안내 부스가 마련되어 있다.
| 해설 |
빈칸 앞뒤에 각각 위치한 두 명사구를 연결할 전치사가 필요한데, 출입구 위치를 추가로 알리는 의미가 되어야 적절하므로 '~ 외에, ~뿐만 아니라'는 의미로 쓰이는 전치사 (B) in addition to가 정답이다.
| 어휘 | as if 마치 ~한 것처럼   regardless of ~에 상관 없이

9. (B)
| 해석 |
Braun 씨에게 시간이 제한되어 있으므로, 발표와 관련된 질문만 받을 것입니다.
| 해설 |
빈칸 앞뒤의 be 동사, 전치사 to와 어울리는 형용사로서 '~와 관련되다'라는 의미를 구성할 때 사용하는 (B) relevant가 정답이다.

| 어휘 | limited 제한된 make sure (that) 반드시 ~하도록 하다 definite 확실한, 분명한 potential 잠재적인

10. (A)
| 해석 |
안전상의 우려로 인해, 오직 수술을 수행하는 의료진만 그 환자의 병실에 대한 출입 권한을 얻을 수 있다.
| 해설 |
빈칸 앞뒤의 동사 gain, 전치사 to와 어울리는 명사로서 '~에 대한 출입 권한을 얻다'라는 의미를 구성할 수 있는 (A) access가 정답이다.
| 어휘 | concern 우려 perform ~을 수행하다 procedure 절차, 수술 gain ~을 얻다 solution 해결책 placement 취업 알선, 배치 direction 방향, 지시, 감독

11. (B)
| 해석 |
Yolanda's 카페는 종이컵 또는 플라스틱 컵 대신에 재사용 가능한 컵을 이용하는 모든 고객들에게 5퍼센트의 할인을 제공한다.
| 해설 |
빈칸 뒤의 명사구 'paper or plastic ones'는 할인 대상에 해당되지 않아야 의미가 자연스러우므로 '~ 대신에'라는 의미로 선택되지 않는 대상 앞에 사용하는 (B) instead of가 정답이다.
| 어휘 | reusable 재사용 가능한 as to ~에 관해 except ~을 제외하고

12. (C)
| 해석 |
세미나가 일정보다 앞서 진행되고 있으므로, 질의응답 시간에 10분이 추가될 것이다.
| 해설 |
빈칸 뒤의 schedule과 어울려 일정상의 진행 상태를 나타낼 전치사가 필요하므로 '~에 앞서'를 뜻하는 (C) ahead of가 정답이다.
| 어휘 | run 진행되다 extra 추가의 Q&A session 질의응답 시간

13. (B)
| 해석 |
Willem 씨의 업적에는 다수의 국제 콘퍼런스 행사들을 조직한 것이 포함되어 있었으며, 그중에서 가장 규모가 큰 것은 5,000명이 넘는 사람들이 참석했었다.
| 해설 |
빈칸 뒤의 동사 include는 범주를 나타내는 명사를 주어로, 세부 요소에 해당되는 명사를 목적어로 취한다. 따라서 여러 행사를 조직한 일이 포함될 수 있는 범주로서 적합한 단어를 보기에서 고르면, '업적'을 의미하는 (B) accomplishments가 정답이다.
| 어휘 | include ~을 포함하다 organize ~을 조직하다 multiple 다수의, 다양한 authorities 당국 capability 능력, 역량 proficiency 능숙, 숙달

14. (B)
| 해석 |
영수증이 구매의 증거로서 제시되지 못하는 경우에, 적립금으로 제공될 수 있습니다.
| 해설 |
빈칸 뒤에 위치한 proof of purchase는 영수증(receipt)의 역할에 해당되므로 '~로서'라는 의미로 역할이나 자격 등을 나타낼 때 사용하는 (B) as가 정답이다.
| 어휘 | in the event (that) ~하는 경우에 receipt 영수증 proof 증명(서) store credit 매장 포인트 through ~을 통해, ~에 걸쳐 except ~을 제외하고 along (길 등) ~을 따라

15. (D)
| 해석 |
모든 운동 경기에 대한 Farrah Hansen의 열정이 그렇게 성공적인 스포츠 기자가 된 이유이다.
| 해설 |
빈칸 뒤의 'for + 대상 분야' 전치사구와 가장 잘 어울리는 명사를 보기에서 찾으면, '~에 대한 열정'이라는 의미를 구성하는 (D) enthusiasm이 정답이다.
| 어휘 | athletics 운동 (경기) A is what makes B C A가 B를 C로 만든 이유이다 successful 성공적인 elevation 승진, 고도 assortment (같은 종류의 여러) 모음, 종합

16. (D)
| 해석 |
Lindberg & Nowak은 세부 요소까지 주의를 기울이는 것으로 얻은 명성 때문에 지역 내에서 손꼽히는 회계 서비스 제공업체가 되었다.
| 해설 |
빈칸 뒤의 'for + 특성/장점' 전치사구와 어울리는 명사로서 '~에 대한 명성, 평판'을 의미할 때 사용하는 (D) reputation이 정답이다.
| 어휘 | leading 손꼽히는, 선도적인 accounting 회계 attention to ~에 대한 주의, 관심 detail 세부 요소 preparation 준비, 대비 destination 목적지 confirmation 확인

17-20번 문제는 다음 기사를 참고하시오.

> 예산을 증대하는 Rainier 관광 위원회
>
> Rainier 관광 위원회는 지역 관광 산업을 홍보하기 위해 향후 3년에 걸쳐 5백만 달러가 넘는 금액을 지출할 예정입니다. 이 수치는 이 위원회의 17 과거 투자액보다 더 높은 것인데, 이것은 작년에는 85만 명이 넘는 관광객들을, 그리고 그 이전 해에는 60만 명이 넘는 사람들을 끌어들이는 데 도움이 되었습니다. 이와 같은 증가는 주로 지역 내의 아름다운 해변들로 떠나는 주말 여행과 관련된 것을 18 포함한, 강화된 마케팅 캠페인에 기인한 것입니다. Rainier 지역을 찾는 방문객들의 증가와 대조적으로, 기타 국내 지역들에 대한 여행은 최근 몇 년 동안 미약한 19 성장을 보여 왔습니다. 20 전문가들은 이것이 경기 침체에 일부 기인한다고 말합니다.
>
> | 어휘 | budget 예산 promote ~을 홍보하다 local 지역의, 현지의 figure 수치 board 위원회, 이사회 investment 투자(액) attract ~을 끌어들이다 gains 증가 primarily 주로 intensified 강화된 in contrast to ~와 대조적으로 rise in ~의 증가 domestic 국내의 recent 최근의

17. (B)
| 해설 |
빈칸 뒤의 investments를 부연 설명하는 which절의 내용을 보면, 과거의 상황을 설명하고 있다. 따라서 investments는 과거의 투자액을 의미해야 알맞으므로 '이전의, 과거의'를 뜻하는 (B) previous가 정답이다.
| 어휘 | prospective 유망한, 장차 ~가 될 current 현재의 following 다음의

18. (A)
| 해설 |
빈칸 앞에 이미 문장의 동사 are가 있으므로 접속사와 주어 없이는 또 다른 동사가 빈칸에 쓰일 수 없다. 따라서 명사구 the one을 목적어로 취할 수 있는 전치사 (A) including이 정답이다.

19. (D)
| 해설 |
대조를 나타내는 In contrast to 전치사구로 보아 콤마 앞뒤로 상반되는 내용이 이어져야 하므로 Rainier 지역 방문객의 증가와 달리 다른 지역은 관광 산업이 그다지 활발하지 못하다는 의미가 되어야 한다. 따라서 little과 함께 '미약한 성장'이라는 의미를 구성할 수 있는 (D) growth가 정답이다.
| 어휘 | effect 효과, 영향 value 가치 competition 경쟁, 경연 대회

20. (D)
(A) 위원회 위원들이 곧 이 사안에 대해 투표를 할 것입니다.
(B) 그 지역은 기차나 버스로 가장 쉽게 접근할 수 있습니다.
(C) 또 다른 캠페인은 지역 예술 축제들을 홍보했습니다.
| 해설 |
앞서 Rainier 지역과 대조되는 다른 국내 지역의 상황을 알리고 있으므로 그 상황을 this로 지칭해 전문가들이 분석한 원인을 말하는 내용인 (D)가 정답이다.
| 어휘 | vote on ~에 대해 투표하다   accessible 접근 가능한   attribute A to B A가 B에 기인한다고 말하다

DAY 15 PART 6

출제 포인트 1 대명사/지시어

기출 유형 맛보기

전 직원에게 알립니다.

우리의 2월 건강 운동을 시작하기 위해, 모든 분에게 에너지를 증가시킬 수 있는 몇몇 기본적인 방법을 상기시켜 드리고자 합니다.

올바르게 식사하고 활동적으로 지내는 것이 높은 에너지를 유지하는 가장 좋은 두 가지 방법들입니다. 간식으로 감자 칩 한 봉지를 먹는 대신, 신선한 과일이나 소량의 아몬드를 드셔 보시기 바랍니다. 또는 다음 번에 엘리베이터를 기다리실 때, 계단을 이용하는 것을 고려해 보십시오.

이 단순한 조치가 여러분의 전반적인 건강을 증진시켜 주고 하루종일 더 많은 에너지를 제공해 줄 것입니다.

PRACTICE | 기출 연습하기

정답 1 (A) 2 (D) 3 (B) 4 (C) 5 (C)

1. (A)
돌아오는 월요일부터, 한 기업 회계 법인의 직원들이 우리 사무실을 방문할 예정입니다. 지난주 회의에서 논의한 바와 같이, 우리 회사는 Birmingham과 Stafford 지역의 상업용 건물 매입 이후로 몇몇 회계 관련 문제들에 대처해 오고 있습니다.

이 어려운 일들을 처리하는 데 있어, 해당 회계사들이 다양한 서류를 요구할 수 있습니다. 우리는 여러분이 협조적인 태도를 유지하고 모든 필수 정보를 그분들에게 제공하도록 요청 드립니다.

| 해설 |
지시어 those가 있으므로 앞 문장에서 단서를 찾아야 한다. 앞 문장에서 언급된 몇몇 회계 문제들(some accounting problems)을 다르게 표현한 '어려운 일'이라는 의미의 (A) challenges가 정답이다.
| 어휘 | associate 직원   corporate 기업의   accounting firm 회계 법인   deal with ~에 대처하다, ~을 처리하다   acquisition 매입   commercial 상업의   property 건물, 부동산   accountant 회계사   require ~을 요구하다   a variety of 다양한   ask that ~하도록 요청하다   remain ~한 상태를 유지하다   cooperative 협조적인   provide A with B A에게 B를 제공하다   necessary 필수의   suggestion 제안   inquiry 문의 사항

2. (D)
Offerman 씨는 5월 19일까지 계속 다른 지역에 가 있을 것입니다. 자리를 비우신 동안, Randolph 씨가 구매 업무를 맡을 것입니다. 따라서, 구매와 관련된 모든 요청이나 문의 사항은 그분께 곧바로 전달되어야 합니다. Offerman 씨에게 보내진 모든 서신은 돌아오신 이후에나 처리될 것입니다.

| 해설 |
to의 목적어 자리인 빈칸은 요청이나 문의 사항을 전달받는 사람을 나타내는 말이어야 한다. 앞 문장에 Randolph 씨가 구매 업무를 대신 한다는 말이 있으므로 남성(Mr. Randolph)을 지칭하는 목적격 대명사 (D) him이 정답이다.
| 어휘 | be out of town 다른 지역에 가 있다   away 자리를 비운   in charge of ~을 맡고 있는   purchasing 구매   thus 따라서   inquiry 문의 사항   regarding ~와 관련된   directly 곧바로   correspondence 서신   not A until B B나 되어야 A하다   deal with ~을 처리하다, ~에 대처하다

3. (B)
Carol Kudrow 씨를 위해 이 추천서를 제공해 드리게 되어 기쁘게 생각합니다. Kudrow 씨는 저희 영업부에 해외 영업 부장으로 고용되어 있습니다. 이곳에서 Kudrow 씨의 주요 직무는 저희 제품을 해외에서 판매할 수 있도록 해외 고객들과의 관계를 유지하는 것입니다. 저희 회사를 위해 Kudrow 씨가 해 온 일을 바탕으로, 저는 Kudrow 씨가 귀하의 팀에 소중한 자산이 될 것이라 확신합니다.

| 해설 |
빈칸 뒤에 목적어가 없으므로 타동사 employ는 수동태로 쓰여야 한다. 또한, 다음 문장에 현재 시제 동사 is와 함께 현재 맡고 있는 주요 업무가 소개되어 있으므로 빈칸에 쓰일 동사도 현재의 고용 상태를 나타내야 알맞다. 따라서 현재 시제 수동태인 (B) is employed가 정답이다.
| 어휘 | letter of recommendation 추천서   sales 영업, 판매   head 부서장, 책임자   primary 주요한   responsibility 직무, 책임   maintain ~을 유지하다   relationship 관계   overseas 해외의   abroad 해외에서   based on ~을 바탕으로   valuable 소중한   asset 자산   employ ~을 고용하다

4. (C)
실내 개조 공사와 더불어, Burger Jack's의 경영진은 직원 유니폼에 몇 가지 변경 사항을 적용하기로 결정했습니다. 이는 1월 29일 토요일 오전 10시에 열리는 레스토랑 전 직원 대상 회의 시간에 공유될 것입니다. 새로운 메뉴 제품들 또한 이 회의에서 발표될 것이므로 모든 직원들의 참석이 필수입니다.

| 해설 |
빈칸 다음에 전 직원이 참석하는 회의 시간에 공유된다는 말이 있는데, 이는 앞 문장에서 결정 사항으로 언급한 몇몇 변경 사항(some changes)과 관련된 것이어야 알맞다. 따라서 이 복수 명사를 대신할 수 있는 대명사 (C) These가 정답이다.
| 어휘 | accompany ~와 더불어 일어나다   renovation 개조, 보수   management 경영진   make a change 변경하다   restaurant-wide 레스토랑 전체의   hold ~을 열다, 개최하다   present ~을 발표하다   attendance 참석   required 필수의

5. (C)
CHICAGO, 4월 27일 — 지역 가수 Lena Perkins 씨가 어젯밤 지역 내 삼림을 보호하기 위한 캠페인인 Save the Trees를 위한 행사장에 출연했습니다. 이 저녁 행사는 칵테일 제공 시간 및 5가지 코스 요리로 구성된 저녁 식사로 시작되었으며, Perkins 씨의 공연이 그 뒤를 이었습니다. 이 행사는 Delaware 호텔에서 개최되었습니다. 행사는 250명이 넘는 많은 손님들을 끌어들였습니다.

| 해설 |
빈칸 앞에 위치한 It은 앞서 언급된 행사(The event)를 가리키므로 동사 draw는 앞 문장의 동사 was held와 동일하게 과거 시제로 쓰여야 한다. 또한 빈칸 뒤에 목적어가 있어 능동태가 되어야 알맞으므로 이 조건들을 만족하는 형태인 (C) drew가 정답이다.

| 어휘 | local 지역의 appear 나타나다, 출연하다 protect ~을 보호하다 forest 숲림 kick off 시작되다 be followed by A A가 뒤따르다 performance 공연 a crowd of 많은 over ~가 넘는 draw ~을 끌어들이다

◆ 출제 포인트 2 시제   본책 p.238

기출 유형 맛보기

수신: r.tanner@fashionfactory.co.uk
발신: customerservice@ironfabrics.co.uk
제목: 귀하의 주문
날짜: 4월 15일

Tanner 씨께,

이전의 이메일에서 저희는 귀하에게 5월 1일의 창고 폐쇄에 관해 알려드렸습니다. 안타깝게도, 이는 그날 배송되도록 예정되어 있는 모든 제품의 배송이 지연될 것임을 의미합니다. 그 결과, Fashion Factory로 보내질 예정인 직물 선적은 5월 2일이나 되어야 보내질 것입니다.

저희는 이로 인해 야기될 수 있는 어떠한 불편함에 대해서도 사과 드립니다. 보상으로, 저희에게 다음 번에 주문하시는 제품에 대해 5퍼센트의 할인을 제공해 드리고자 합니다.

질문이 있으시면 즉시 저희에게 연락 주시기 바랍니다.

PRACTICE | 기출 연습하기   본책 p.239

정답 1 (C) 2 (C) 3 (C) 4 (D) 5 (B)

1. (C)

BANGKOK, 11월 11일 — 다음 달부터, WeTalk 사용자들께서는 모바일 기기의 WeTalk 애플리케이션을 통해 비용을 송금하실 수 있게 됩니다. 이 애플리케이션은 주로 채팅을 하고 미디어를 공유하는 데 사용됩니다. 이런 새로운 변화를 통해, 그것은 사용자들이 개인이나 사업체들에게도 돈을 이체하실 수 있게 해 줄 것입니다. 이 조치는 더욱 능률적인 모바일 이용 경험을 만들어 내기 위해 WeTalk가 기울이는 노력의 일환입니다.

| 해설 |
빈칸 앞에 쓰인 it은 앞서 언급된 The application을 가리키며, 첫 문장에 이 애플리케이션이 다음 달부터(Starting next month) 이용 가능한 것으로 나타나 있다. 따라서 빈칸에는 동사 allow를 미래 시제로 나타낸 (C) will allow가 알맞다.

| 어휘 | send a payment 송금하다 device 기기, 장치 mainly 주로 allow A to do A가 ~할 수 있게 해 주다 transfer money 돈을 이체하다 individual 개인, 사람 as well ~도, 또한 move 조치, 행동 effort 노력 create ~을 만들어 내다 streamlined 능률적인, 간소화된

2. (C)

어제 열린 회의에 대해 Patterson 씨가 그 내용을 기록했으며, 오늘 늦게 보내 드릴 것입니다. 회의에서 다뤄진 중요한 주제들 중에는 우리의 새 운동화 제품 라인의 개발 상황과 건물 내 주차 규정을 준수하기 위한 공지가 포함되어 있었습니다.

또한, 이번 달 매출 수치가 회의에서 공개되었습니다. 이 수치 자료는 요약되어 회의 기록과 함께 배부될 것입니다.

| 해설 |
빈칸 뒤에 제시된 회의와 관련해, 첫 문장에 '어제 열린 회의(yesterday's meeting)'라는 말이 있으므로 회의는 과거 시점에 열렸음을 알 수 있다. 따라서 매출 수치도 과거에 공개된 것이어야 맞으므로 과거 시제인 (C) were revealed가 정답이다.

| 어휘 | take notes 기록하다, 메모하다 cover (주제 등) ~을 다루다 include ~을 포함하다 development 개발 status (진행 등) 상황 line 제품 라인 reminder 공지, 상기시키는 것 follow ~을 준수하다, 따르다 regulation 규정 figure 수치 summarize ~을 요약하다 distribute ~을 배부하다 along with ~와 함께 reveal ~을 공개하다

3. (C)

Sunset Boulevard에 개장되는 새로운 역

8월 6일 — San Francisco Transit(SFT)은 남쪽 노선을 연장하기 위해 새로운 지하철역을 건설할 예정이라고 발표했습니다. 이 역에 대한 공사 작업은 다음 달에 시작될 것으로 예상됩니다. 현재, 이 남쪽 노선은 Montgomery Avenue에서 끝나지만, 새로운 종착역은 Sunset Boulevard의 버스 터미널이 될 것입니다. 50만 명이 넘는 사람들이 매일 SFT 열차를 이용하고 있으며, 남쪽 노선이 가장 붐빕니다.

| 해설 |
다음 문장에 공사 개시 시점으로 언급된 next month는 미래 시점에 해당되므로 지하철역이 미래에 건설된다는 것을 알 수 있다. 따라서 미래 시제인 (C) will be constructing이 정답이다.

| 어휘 | announce that ~라고 발표하다 extend ~을 연장하다, 확장하다 be expected to do ~할 것으로 예상되다 currently 현재 with A -ing A가 ~한 상태인, A가 ~하는 채로

4. (D)

전화 회의 중에 논의된 바와 같이, 우리는 매출을 증대할 수 있는 방법을 찾고 있습니다. Davenport 씨의 제안에 따라, 우리는 창가의 상품 진열을 다시 하고 신문에 전면 광고를 내기로 결정했습니다. 우리는 이와 같은 조치들이 더 많은 고객들을 끌어들일 것이라 믿습니다. 더욱이, 우리의 가을 제품 라인 출시 이전에 이 결정 사항들을 시행하는 것이 필수적입니다.

| 해설 |
앞 문장에 현재 완료 시제로 이제 막 결정된 사실을 알리는 have decided가 사용되었으므로 그 결정을 통해 더 많은 고객을 끌어 들이는 일은 미래에 발생되는 일이어야 알맞다. 따라서 미래 시제인 (D) will attract가 정답이다.

| 어휘 | conference call 전화 회의 look for ~을 찾다 way to do ~하는 방법 increase ~을 증가시키다 per ~에 따라 suggestion 제안, 의견 redo ~을 다시 하다 display 진열, 전시 full-paged 전면에 들어 가는 place an add 광고를 내다 measure 조치 furthermore 더욱이, 게다가 it is essential that ~하는 것이 필수적이다 implement ~을 시행하다 release 출시, 공개 attract ~을 끌어들이다

5. (B)

어제 인터뷰를 위해 시간을 내어 함께 자리해 주셔서 감사 드립니다. 기꺼이 질문에 답변해 주시려는 귀하의 마음이 감사했습니다. 저는 특히 귀하께서 제공해 주신 공장 견학 시간이 유익하게 느껴졌는데, 이로 인해 제가 귀사의 제품이 어떻게 조립되는지 더 면밀히 살펴볼 수 있었습니다. 인터뷰는 저희 잡지의 9월호에 실릴 것이며, 제가 곧 해당 잡지를 한 부 보내 드리겠습니다.

| 해설 |
첫 문장의 단서 yesterday와 다음 문장에 있는 과거 시제 동사 benefited와 함께 인터뷰가 과거에 이루어졌음을 알 수 있으므로 질문에 적극적으로 답변해 준 것에 대해 감사의 마음을 느낀 시점도 동일해야 한다. 따라서 과거 시제인 (B) was appreciated가 정답이다.
| 어휘 | take the time to do ~할 시간을 내다   willingness to do 기꺼이 ~하려는 마음   especially 특히   benefit from ~로부터 이득을 얻다   get a closer look at ~을 더 면밀히 보다   assemble ~을 조립하다   issue (잡지 등의) 호   appreciate ~에 대해 감사하다

◆ 출제 포인트 3 접속부사   본책 p.240

기출 유형 맛보기

> 편집자께,
>
> 귀사 잡지의 지난달 호에, 영화 감독 Stacey Moore의 영화 <Planets>에 대한 평론이 실려 있었습니다. 그 평론은 해당 영화가 독창성이 없고 지루하다고 설명했습니다. 또한 Moore 감독이 경험이 부족하기 때문에 이 영화가 실망스러웠다고 주장했습니다. 하지만 저는 이 영화를 즐겁게 보았으며, 많은 장점이 있다고 생각했습니다.
>
> 연기가 뛰어났고, 줄거리는 상당히 창의적이었습니다. 또한, 감독은 10년 동안 업계에서 일해 오고 있기 때문에, 자신이 무엇을 하고 있는지 압니다. 저는 이 영화를 모든 영화 팬들에게 적극 추천합니다.
>
> 진심을 담아,
> James Thatcher

PRACTICE | 기출 연습하기   본책 p.241
정답 1 (A)   2 (D)   3 (A)   4 (D)   5 (D)

1. (A)

> Grant 씨께,
>
> 3일 동안 진행되는 저희 Madrid 투어에 대한 귀하의 예약을 처리해 드릴 수 없다는 사실을 알려 드리게 되어 유감스럽게 생각합니다. 대규모 축구 토너먼트로 인해, 귀하께서 요청하신 기간에 그 도시에는 엄청난 방문객들이 유입될 것입니다. 그 결과, 그 도시에 위치한 대부분의 호텔들이 완전히 가득 차게 될 것입니다. 날짜가 유동적일 경우, 기꺼이 그 이후의 투어를 예약하실 수 있도록 도움을 드리고자 합니다.

| 해설 |
앞 문장에는 많은 방문객들이 찾을 것이라는 말이, 빈칸 뒤에는 대부분의 호텔들이 꽉 찰 것이라는 말이 쓰여 있다. 이는 원인과 결과에 해당되는 흐름이므로 '그 결과'를 뜻하는 접속부사 (A) As a result가 정답이다.
| 어휘 | regret to do ~해서 유감이다   inform A that A에게 ~라고 알리다   be unable to do ~할 수 없다   process ~을 처리하다   booking 예약   huge 엄청난   influx 유입   request ~을 요청하다   the majority of 대부분의   completely 완전히   flexible 유동적인   assist A in -ing A가 ~하도록 돕다

2. (D)

> Atlantic Airways는 모든 탑승객들께서 식사와 관련해 필요로 하시는 사항을 수용해 드리고자 합니다. 하지만 특별 식사는 명확히 요청되지 않은 한, 기내에서 이용하실 수 없습니다. 그러므로, 식사 제한이 있는 모든 탑승객들께서는 특별 식사를 요청하실 수 있도록 반드시 출발하기 최소 48시간 전에 직원에게 연락해 주시기 바랍니다.

| 해설 |
빈칸 앞에는 별도의 요청을 하지 않는 한 특별 식사를 이용할 수 없다는 말이, 빈칸 뒤에는 특별 식사를 원할 경우에 미리 연락하라고 당부하는 말이 쓰여 있다. 이는 원인과 결과의 흐름에 해당하므로 '그러므로'를 뜻하는 접속부사 (D) Therefore가 정답이다.
| 어휘 | accommodate ~을 수용하다   dietary 식사의, 음식물의   on board 탑승해 있는   unless ~하지 않는 한   specifically 분명히, 명확하게   restriction 제한   contact ~에게 연락하다   representative 직원   at least 최소한   in advance 미리

3. (A)

> Sunlake Dental에 예약하시려면, www.sunlakedental.com/book을 방문하시기 바랍니다. 또는, 952-555-6134번으로 저희 사무실에 전화하셔서 전화상으로 예약하실 수 있습니다. 저희를 처음 방문하실 경우, 예정된 예약 시간보다 최소 15분 먼저 도착하시도록 요청 드립니다. 또한 반드시 보험 가입 증명서를 지참하시기 바랍니다.

| 해설 |
빈칸 앞에는 온라인 예약 방법이, 빈칸 뒤에는 전화 예약 방법이 언급되어 있다. 이는 선택 가능한 또 다른 방법을 알리는 맥락이므로 '또는'이라는 의미로 대안을 나타내는 접속부사 (A) Alternatively가 정답이다.
| 어휘 | make an appointment 예약하다   over the phone 전화상으로   scheduled 예정된   make sure to do 반드시 ~하도록 하다   proof 증명(서)   insurance 보험

4. (D)

> 소박한 오두막 집들과 아름다운 호반 경치로 인해, Coopersville은 조용한 마을처럼 보일 수 있지만, 훨씬 그 이상입니다. 이곳에는 Montana 지역 최고의 등산로가 몇 개 있을 뿐만 아니라, 뛰어난 요리를 자랑하는 곳이며, 수상 경력이 있는 스파의 본고장이기도 합니다. 지난 몇 년에 걸쳐, 신혼 부부들을 위한 편안한 신혼 여행지로 인기를 얻어 왔습니다. 실제로, 이곳은 <Wedding> 지에 의해 최근 "올해의 신혼 여행지"로 지정되었습니다.

| 해설 |
빈칸 앞은 신혼 여행지로 인기를 얻고 있다는 내용이고, 빈칸 뒤에는 한 잡지에서 올해의 신혼 여행지로 선정된 사실이 언급되어 있다. 따라서 빈칸 뒤는 실제 예시에 해당하는 내용이므로 '실제로'라는 의미의 접속부사 (D) In fact가 정답이다.
| 어휘 | cabin 오두막집   not only A but (also) B A뿐만 아니라 B도   hiking trail 등산로   boast ~을 자랑하다   outstanding 뛰어난   cuisine 요리   home to ~의 본고장   award-winning 수상 경력이 있는   over ~ 동안에 걸쳐   popularity 인기   relaxing 편안하게 해 주는   destination 여행지   newlyweds 신혼 부부   recently 최근에   be named A A로 명명되다

5. (D)

> DETROIT, 9월 22일 — ChemZ Industries는 자사의 시설물이 안전하다고 여겨질 때까지 일시적으로 운영을 중단하라는 명령을 받았습니다. 이는 안전 절차의 실패로, 지난달에 공장에서 만들어지던 화학 물질이 누출된 데 따른 것입니다. 다량의 화학 물질이 잘못되어 인근의 강으로 배출되었습니다. 게다가, 분석 자료에 따르면 소량의 이 화학 물질이 강 하류에서 식물과 동물들에 의해 흡수되었던 것으로 나타났습니다.

| 해설 |
빈칸 앞에는 인근의 강으로 화학 물질이 흘러 들어간 사실이, 빈칸 뒤에는 식물과 동물들에게 그 화학 물질이 흡수된 사실이 쓰여 있다. 따라서 유해한 영향을 미친 사례와 관련해 추가 정보를 나열하는 흐름임을 알 수 있으므로 '게다가'라는 의미의 (D) In addition이 정답이다.
| 어휘 | be ordered to do ~하도록 명령을 받다   temporarily 일시적으로   suspend ~을 중단하다   operation 운영, 가동   facility 시설(물)   be deemed

+ 형용사 ~한 것으로 여겨지다   chemical 화학 물질   leak 누출되다   failure 실패, 하지 못함   mechanism 절차, 방법   large quantities of 다량의   accidentally 잘못하여, 뜻하지 않게   be released into ~로 배출되다   nearby 인근의   analysis 분석 (자료)   trace of 소량의   absorb ~을 흡수하다   downstream 강 하류에서

◆ 출제 포인트 4   어휘
본책 p.242

기출 유형 맛보기

수신: Kose Media 전 직원
발신: Linda Fernandez, 인사 전문가
날짜: 6월 30일
제목: 기회

우리 Rose Industries의 체육관은 경험 많은 개인 트레이너와 최신 장비를 제공하고 있습니다. 이와 같은 시설을 제공함으로써, 우리는 직원 복지를 향상시키기를 바랍니다.

많은 분들이 이 체육관이 일반인들도 이용할 수 있는 것인지를 문의해 오고 있습니다. 현재, 이 시설은 오직 내부용으로만 사용 가능합니다. 하지만 이와 같은 문의에 대한 대응으로, 우리는 직원들의 친구나 가족들에게 체육관을 개방하는 것을 고려하고 있습니다.

이 문제와 관련된 여러분의 의견은 소중하게 받아들여지므로, www.roseintranet.com/gymsurvey에서 찾아볼 수 있는 설문지를 작성해 주시기 바랍니다.

PRACTICE I 기출 연습하기
본책 p.243

정답 1 (C)   2 (C)   3 (A)   4 (B)   5 (B)

1. (C)

저희 서비스 담당 부서가 귀하의 이메일을 받았습니다. 이 이메일에 따르면, 귀하의 휴대 전화기 화면 전체에 걸쳐 금이 간 것으로 되어 있습니다. 해당 기기가 여전히 품질 보증 기간에 해당되고 저희를 통해 추가 보험 상품을 구입하신 점을 감안하면, 새 액정에 대한 비용은 무료가 됩니다. 손상된 제품을 저희 센터로 배송해 주시거나, 가까운 NexCom 지점에 가져다주시기 바랍니다.

| 해설 |
빈칸 뒤에 배송 대상으로 언급된 item은 글의 초반부에 제시된 화면에 금(crack)이 간 제품을 가리킨다. 따라서 그와 같은 상태를 나타낼 형용사로 '손상된'을 의미하는 (C) damaged가 정답이다.
| 어휘 | crack (깨지거나 갈라진) 금, 틈   across ~ 전체에   given that ~임을 감안하면   device 기기   under warranty 품질 보증 기간에 해당되는   additional 추가적인   drop A off at B A를 B에 갖다 놓다   harmful 유해한   incorrect 부정확한

2. (C)

Nelson 씨께,

8월 23일에 열리는 제12회 연례 Heroes of Perth Gala 행사에 초대해 주셔서 감사합니다. 참석하도록 요청 받은 것에 대해 영광으로 생각하고 있기는 하지만, 제가 행사 당일에 Moscow로 출장을 갑니다. 따라서, 귀하와 함께 할 수 없을 것입니다. 하지만 새 지역 문화 센터를 위한 모금 활동에 1,000달러를 기부하고 싶습니다. 제가 돈을 보내 드릴 수 있는 가장 좋은 방법을 알려 주시기 바랍니다.

| 해설 |
빈칸 앞뒤의 be 동사 및 to부정사와 결합 가능한 형용사가 필요한데, 출장을 가는 것으로 인한 결과(Therefore)와 관련된 의미도 나타내야 한다. 따라서 '~할 수 없다'라는 의미를 구성할 때 사용하는 (C) unable이 정답이다.
| 어휘 | invitation 초대(장)   be honored to do ~해서 영광스러워하다   be asked to do ~하도록 요청 받다   attend 참석하다   be on a business trip 출장을 가다   donate ~을 기부하다   fundraising 모금   effort (조직적인) 활동, 운동   the best way to do ~하는 가장 좋은 방법   doubtful 의심을 품은   expected 예상되는   prepared 준비된

3. (A)

Cape Town의 중심에 위치한 Safran Center는 악기를 구입하거나 판매할 때 찾아야 하는 곳입니다. 저희는 조심스럽게 사용된 기타와 드럼, 피아노, 바이올린을 비롯해 판매 가능한 많은 제품을 보유하고 있습니다. 그리고 약간의 여윳돈을 위해 뭔가를 판매할 생각이 있으시다면, 저희가 플루트에서부터 아코디언까지 무엇이든 매입합니다. 오늘 들르셔서 저희가 재고로 보유하고 있는 것을 확인해 보시기 바랍니다.

| 해설 |
다음 문장에 판매 제품으로 언급된 것이 기타와 드럼, 피아노, 바이올린이므로 이 물품들을 하나로 아우를 수 있는 명사로 '악기'를 의미하는 (A) instruments가 정답이다.
| 어휘 | located in ~에 위치한   extra 추가의, 별도의   stop by 들르다   have A in stock A를 재고로 보유하고 있다   instrument 악기   supplies 용품, 물품   cleaner 세제   appliance (가전) 기기

4. (B)

전 직원에게 알립니다

건물 내의 화재 경보기에 대한 정기 보수 작업이 오늘 오전 11시 30분에 시작될 것입니다. 우리는 업무 환경에 지장을 주지 않기 위해 1시간 내로 이 과정이 완료되기를 바라고 있습니다. 그럼에도 불구하고, 예기치 못한 문제가 발생될 경우, 약간 더 시간이 걸릴 수도 있습니다. 우리는 점심 시간 이후에도 기술자들이 여전히 이 부분에 대해 작업하고 있을 경우에 여러분의 양해와 인내를 당부 드립니다.

| 해설 |
빈칸 앞에 위치한 this는 앞 문장에서 말한 작업을 지칭하는 지시형용사이다. 앞 문장에 화재 경보기 정기 보수 작업이 시작된다고 했는데, 이는 하나의 작업 과정을 의미하므로 '과정'을 뜻하는 (B) process가 정답이다.
| 어휘 | routine 정례적인   maintenance (시설 등의) 유지 관리   fire alarm 화재 경보(기)   within ~ 이내에   so as not to do ~하지 않도록 하기 위해   disturb 방해하다, ~에 지장을 주다   nevertheless 그럼에도 불구하고   unforeseen 예기치 못한   arise 발생되다   ask for ~을 요청하다   patience 인내(심)   location 위치, 지점

5. (B)

Yamamoto 씨께,

분실된 귀하의 수하물이 회수되었다는 사실을 알려 드리게 되어 기쁩니다. 분실하신 가방들은 현재 Munich에 있는데, 이곳에서 그 가방들이 귀하의 연결 항공편에 실렸어야 했습니다. 이 가방들은 내일 아침 Berlin에 도착할 예정입니다. 가방들이 도착한 후에, 귀하의 분실물 신고서에 표기된 주소로 가능한 한 신속히 귀하의 물품들을 돌려보내 드리겠습니다.

| 해설 |
초반부에 언급된 상대방의 분실물(lost luggage, missing bags)을 되돌려 준다는 의미가 되어야 알맞다. 따라서 이 물품들을 대신할 명사로 '소유물'을 의미하는 (B) possessions가 정답이다.

| 어휘 | lost 분실한 luggage 수하물 recover ~을 회수하다, 되찾다 missing 빠진, 없는 currently 현재 be supposed to do ~하기로 되어 있다 be loaded onto ~로 실리다 transfer flight 연결 항공편 be scheduled to do ~할 예정이다 reach ~에 도달하다 as ~ as possible 가능한 한 ~하게 indicated on ~에 표기된 claim form 신고 양식 possession 소유물 payment 지불(금)

◆ 출제 포인트 5 빈칸에 알맞은 문장 넣기
본책 p.244

기출 유형 맛보기

날짜: 12월 2일
수신: 고객 서비스팀 <csteam@taloncorp.com>
발신: Peter North <peter.north@taloncorp.com>
제목: LV600 전원 코드

모든 고객 서비스 담당 직원들께,

우리는 최근 LV600 전자레인지와 관련해 다수의 불만 사항들을 접수해 오고 있습니다. 많은 고객들께서 이 기기가 사용 중에 갑자기 꺼진다고 알려 주셨습니다. 반품된 몇몇 전자레인지들을 점검해 본 끝에, 전원 코드에 결함이 있는 것으로 밝혀졌습니다. 이 결함이 갑작스러운 전원 차단의 원인입니다. 이 문제점이 안전 관련 위험을 야기하는 것은 아니므로 제품 리콜은 없을 것입니다. 대신, 이 문제를 겪고 있는 고객들은 무료로 새 전원 코드를 배송 받으시게 됩니다. 추가로, 결함이 있는 것들을 대체할 만큼의 충분한 코드가 생산될 때까지 LV600제품의 모든 배송은 중단된 상태입니다.

감사합니다.

Peter North
고객 서비스 팀장, Talon Corporation

(A) 예전 모델에는 동일한 고급 기능이 포함되어 있지 않습니다.
(B) 이 결함이 갑작스러운 전원 차단의 원인입니다.
(C) 이것은 저희 웹사이트의 FAQ 섹션에 설명되어 있습니다.
(D) 추가 비용으로 품질 보증 연장이 가능합니다.

PRACTICE | 기출 연습하기
본책 p.245

정답 1 (C)   2 (B)   3 (B)   4 (B)

1. (C)

조경 건축가 Nels Lindberg 씨에 의해 50년도 더 이전에 만들어진 Holmes 공원은 모든 연령대의 사람들을 위한 장소입니다. 이 공원은 5곳의 정원과 3개의 분수대, 그리고 많은 산책로를 자랑합니다. 또한 공원 중앙에 대형 호수가 위치해 있어, 온갖 색상과 크기의 야생 조류를 끌어 들이고 있습니다. 공원의 규모를 감안하면, 방문객들께서는 지도가 유용하다고 생각하실 수 있습니다. 공원의 어느 안내 센터에서든지 1부 가져가실 수 있습니다.

(A) 그들은 공원이 잘 알려지게 된 원인인 몇몇 새들을 볼 계획입니다.
(B) 가장 많은 사람들이 방문하는 정원은 Rose Garden입니다.
(D) 5세 미만의 아이들은 공원 입장이 허용되지 않습니다.
| 해설 |
앞 문장에 방문객들이 지도를 활용하면 유용할 것이라는 말이 있으므로 a map을 One으로 지칭해 그 지도를 받을 수 있는 장소를 알리는 문장인 (C)가 들어가는 것이 가장 자연스럽다.
| 어휘 | landscape 조경 architect 건축가 boast ~을 자랑하다 fountain 분수(대) walking trail 산책로 given (that) ~을 감안하면 find A + 형용사

A를 ~하다고 생각하다 be known for ~로 잘 알려지다 pick up ~을 가져가다 be allowed in ~로의 입장이 허용되다

2. (B)

관계자께,

지난봄에, 저는 Washington Coat Factory의 시즌 종료 세일 행사장에서 재킷을 하나 구입했습니다. 저는 이 재킷을 수납장에 넣어 뒀다가 최근에 날씨가 차가워지면서 꺼냈습니다. 그것을 착용해 보자마자, 저는 지퍼들 중 하나에 손상된 부분이 있다는 것을 알게 되었습니다. 현 시점에 이 제품을 반품하거나 교환하도록 해 주시는 일이 귀사의 반품 정책에 반하는 일이라는 것을 알고 있습니다. 그럼에도 불구하고, 저는 예외를 적용 받을 수 있기를 바라고 있습니다. 이 제품이 더 이상 재고가 없을 경우, 매장 포인트로 받아도 좋습니다. 어떻게 진행할지 제게 알려 주시기 바랍니다.

(A) 저는 여전히 그 제품이 배송되기를 기다리고 있습니다.
(C) 새로운 배송 정책이 이 문서에 설명되어 있습니다.
(D) 비용 지불이 현금으로 이뤄졌지만, 저는 영수증을 갖고 있습니다.
| 해설 |
앞 문장에 반품이나 교환이 불가능하다는 사실을 알고 있다는 말이 쓰여 있으므로 Nevertheless와 함께 대조적으로 자신은 예외를 적용 받을 수 있기를 바라는 마음을 나타내는 (B)가 정답이다.
| 어휘 | end-of-season sale 시즌 종료 세일 storage 수납장 upon -ing ~하자마자 try A on A를 한번 착용해 보다 damage 손상 allow A to do A가 ~할 수 있게 해 주다 return ~을 반품하다 exchange ~을 교환하다 at this point 현 시점에 against ~에 반대하는, 반대되는 policy 정책 no longer 더 이상 ~ 않다 in stock 재고가 있는 accept ~을 받아들이다 store credit 매장 포인트 how to do 어떻게 ~하는 것인지, ~하는 법 proceed 진행하다 nevertheless 그럼에도 불구하고 exception 예외 receipt 영수증

3. (B)

채용 담당자께,

저는 <Los Angeles Daily>의 부편집장 직책에 고려될 수 있도록 제 이력서를 제출하고자 합니다.

저는 출판 분야에서 일하면서 폭넓은 경력을 쌓았습니다. 지난 5년 동안, 저는 <Dallas Times>에서 예술 섹션의 콘텐츠 책임자 및 편집자로 근무해 왔습니다. 이에 앞서, 저는 <Chronicle News>에서 근무했으며, 이곳에서 많은 신문과 잡지에 기고했습니다. 제 경력이 귀 신문사가 인쇄물과 온라인에서 모두 성장하도록 돕는 데 도움이 될 것으로 생각합니다.

(A) 저는 또한 귀하의 단체에서 근무하는 인턴 자리에 지원하고자 합니다.
(C) 면접을 위해 시간을 내어 자리해 주셔서 감사 드립니다.
(D) 대부분의 신문들은 인터넷을 통해 독자를 확보하기 위해 노력하고 있습니다.
| 해설 |
빈칸 뒤에 이어지는 문장들은 지난 5년 동안 근무한 회사에서 한 일과 그에 앞서 다른 곳에서 했던 일을 설명하고 있다. 이는 자신의 경력을 강조하기 위한 것이므로 해당 업계에서 폭넓은 경험을 쌓았음을 나타내는 (B)가 정답이다.
| 어휘 | submit ~을 제출하다 résumé 이력서 consideration 고려 associate editor 부편집장 director 책임자, 이사, 부서장 prior to ~에 앞서 be employed at ~에서 근무하다 contribute to ~에 기여하다, 기고하다 a number of 많은 assist A in -ing A가 ~하는 데 도움이 되다 help A do A가 ~하도록 돕다 grow 성장하다 apply for ~에 지원하다 organization 단체, 기관 extensive 폭넓은 field 분야 take the time to do ~할 시간을 내다

4. (B)

Bandoo Industries는 여러분의 식료품 쇼핑을 더욱 손쉽게 만들어 드리기 위해 고안된 기능들을 갖춘 최신 냉장고 Quatro를 제조했습니다. 내장된 카메라는 여러분께서 문을 열지 않고도 냉장고의 내용물을 사진으로 찍으실 수 있게 해줍니다. **심지어 휴대 전화기의 카메라와 연결하실 수도 있습니다.** 이러한 방법으로, 깜빡 잊고 쇼핑 목록에 추가하지 못한 것이 있는지 손쉽게 확인해 보실 수 있습니다.

(A) 그 제품은 올해 열리는 Kitchen Expo에서 첫 선을 보였습니다.
(C) 또한 신선한 과일을 위해 온도 조절이 가능한 서랍들도 있습니다.
(D) 서비스 기사가 여러분의 자택을 방문해 냉장고를 설치해 드릴 것입니다.

| 해설 |
빈칸 뒤에 특정 방식을 가리키는 That way와 함께 쉽게 확인할 수 있는 일이 언급되어 있다. 따라서 앞서 언급한 내장 카메라를 이용한 냉장고의 편리한 기능을 설명하고 있는 (B)가 정답이다.

| 어휘 | fridge 냉장고 feature 기능, 특징 designed to do ~하도록 고안된 make A + 형용사 A를 ~하게 만들다 grocery shopping 식료품 쇼핑 built-in 내장된, 붙박이의 contents 내용(물) without -ing ~하지 않고 that way 그러한 방법으로, 그렇게 해서 see if ~인지 확인해 보다 forget to do ~하는 것을 잊다 add 추가하다 debut ~을 처음 선보이다 connect to ~에 연결되다 temperature-controlled 온도가 조절되는 drawer 서랍 install ~을 설치하다

DAY 15 | 실전문제
본책 p.246

정답 1 (C) 2 (A) 3 (B) 4 (D) 5 (D) 6 (B)
7 (C) 8 (A) 9 (A) 10 (B) 11 (C) 12 (D)
13 (D) 14 (B) 15 (A) 16 (C)

1–4번 문제는 다음 보도 자료를 참조하시오.

3월 28일에, Tristone 건설은 Sydney 국립 역사 박물관(NHMS)의 재설계 작업에 대한 계약을 따냈다. 이 박물관은 1975년에 처음 지어진 것으로서, 박물관의 시설을 현대화하고 더 잘 활용할 수 있도록 업그레이드될 것이다. **1 이 개선 작업에는 1층에 새 미술관을 짓는 공사가 포함되어 있다.** 추가로, 고급 공기 정화 장치나 온도 조절 시스템과 **2 같은** 특정 개선 사항들이 이 건물의 기반 시설을 더욱 효율적으로 만들어 줄 것이다. Tristone은 Melbourne의 현대미술관 **3 개조 공사**를 포함하여, 과거에 다른 유사 프로젝트들도 성공적으로 완료하였다. NHMS의 시설 관리 책임자인 Marissa Nguyen 씨가 Tristone의 직원들과 협력해 이 프로젝트를 **4 총괄할 것이다.**

| 어휘 | be awarded a contract 계약을 따내다 originally 처음에, 애초에 utilize ~을 활용하다 facility 시설(물) additionally 추가로 certain 특정한 improvement 개선, 향상 advanced 고급의 air filtration 공기 정화 장치 climate control 온도 조절 infrastructure 기반 시설 efficient 효율적인 complete ~을 완료하다 similar 유사한 including ~을 포함한 in cooperation with ~와 협력해 representative 직원

1. (C)
(A) Tristone은 지난봄에 개조 공사 프로젝트에 대한 예산 제안서를 제출했다.
(B) Nguyen 씨는 박물관 건물과 부지를 책임지고 있다.
(D) 센서로 조절되는 조명을 추가하는 것이 에너지 비용을 절약하는 흔한 방법이다.

| 해설 |
빈칸 앞에 특정 박물관 재설계 작업을 위해 시설물을 현대화하고 업그레이드한다는 내용이 있다. 따라서 이 작업을 The updates로 지칭해 그 작업에 포함되는 공사 세부 내용을 알리는 (C)가 정답이다.

| 어휘 | submit ~을 제출하다 budget 예산 proposal 제안(서) be responsible for ~에 대한 책임이 있다 grounds 부지, 구내 sensor-controlled 센서로 조절되는 common 흔한 method 방법 save on ~을 절약하다

2. (A)
| 해설 |
빈칸 뒤에 위치한 공기 정화 장치와 온도 조절 시스템은 빈칸 앞에 언급된 improvements의 구체적인 예시에 해당된다. 따라서 '~와 같은'이라는 의미로 예를 들 때 사용하는 (A) such as가 정답이다.

| 어휘 | in order 제대로 된, 알맞은 likewise 마찬가지로 in spite of ~에도 불구하고

3. (B)
| 해설 |
빈칸에 쓰일 명사는 바로 앞에서 언급한 '유사 프로젝트(similar projects)'에 해당되어야 한다. 따라서 앞서 언급된 박물관 업그레이드 작업과 유사한 일을 나타낼 수 있는 명사로 '개조, 보수' 등을 의미하는 (B) renovations가 정답이다.

| 어휘 | purchase 구매(품) promotion 승진, 홍보 revision 수정, 개정

4. (D)
| 해설 |
우선, 빈칸 앞뒤로 명사구와 전치사구만 있으므로 빈칸은 동사 자리임을 알 수 있다. 또한 Nguyen 씨가 프로젝트를 총괄하는 일은 초반부의 'The museum, originally built in 1975, will receive ~'에 나타난 것과 마찬가지로 미래의 일이 되어야 알맞으므로 동일하게 미래 시제 (D) will oversee가 정답이다.

| 어휘 | oversee ~을 총괄하다, 감독하다

5–8번 문제는 다음 기사를 참조하시오.

Walker Studios는 현재 전국의 극장에서 상영 중인 <Friday Night>의 속편을 제작할 계획이다. 이 스튜디오의 대표인 Henry Chen은 이 영화에 대한 입장권 **5 판매량**이 갑작스럽게 급증한 것을 바탕으로 이와 같은 결정을 내렸다. 속편에 대한 조치는 업계 전문가들에게 굉장한 놀라움으로 다가왔는데, 이 영화가 전문 평론가들로부터 **6 혹평**을 받은 바 있기 때문이다. **7 이 영화는** 또한 매표소 실적이 저조한 상태였다. 하지만 영화에 대한 관심이 소셜 미디어를 통해 젊은 관객들 사이에서 증가했다. 여러 인기 있는 온라인 블로그들이 젊은 세대가 마주하고 있는 문제점들을 탐구하는 이 영화를 **8 강력히 추천했다.**

| 어휘 | sequel 속편 currently 현재 make a decision 결정을 내리다 based on ~을 바탕으로 sudden 갑작스런 surge in ~의 급증 move 조치, 움직임 come as a surprise 놀라움으로 다가오다 quite a + 명사 굉장한 ~ industry 업계 expert 전문가 review 후기 critic 평론가 interest in ~에 대한 관심 audience members 관객, 청중 exploration 탐구, 탐험 faced by ~가 마주하고 있는 generation 세대

5. (D)
| 해설 |
빈칸 앞에 위치한 명사 ticket은 surge in과 어울려 급증되는 대상을 나타내기에 의미가 부족하다. 따라서 ticket과 복합 명사를 이뤄 전치사 in의 목적어로서 '입장권 판매량'이라는 의미를 구성할 수 있는 명사 (D) sales가 정답이다.

| 어휘 | salable 잘 팔리는, 수요가 있는

6. (B)
| 해설 |
'평가, 후기' 등을 의미하는 명사 reviews를 수식할 수 있는 형용사가 필요하므로 평가 방식이나 내용과 관련된 형용사로서 '가혹한' 등을 의미하는 (B) harsh가 정답이다.

| 어휘 | steep 급격한, 너무 비싼 brilliant 훌륭한, 멋진, 뛰어난

7. (C)
(A) 많은 극장들이 각자의 웹 사이트에서 구매용 입장권을 제공하고 있다.
(B) 그 감독이 영화 개봉일 밤 행사에 참석했다.
(D) 더욱이, 그것은 수상 경력이 있는 몇몇 배우들을 출연시켰다.

| 해설 |
앞서 속편을 제작하기로 결정한 것이 놀라움으로 다가왔다는(has come as quite a surprise) 내용이 왔으므로 추가 정보를 말하는 also와 함께 놀라움에 대한 원인으로서 또 다른 부정적인 상황을 말하는 문장인 (C)가 정답이다.

| 어휘 | director 영화 감독 perform poorly 저조한 성과를 내다 moreover 더욱이 feature ~을 주연시키다, 특징으로 하다 award-winning 수상 경력이 있는

8. (A)

| 해설 |
문장의 주어 Several popular online blogs와 동사 recommended 사이에 위치한 빈칸은 동사를 수식할 부사 자리이므로 (A) strongly가 정답이다.

| 어휘 | strengthen ~을 강화하다, 더 튼튼하게 하다

9-12번 문제는 다음 이메일을 참조하시오.

수신: staff@elementarypublishing.com
발신: s.lewis@elementarypublishing.com
날짜: 11월 16일
제목: 정책 변경

직원 여러분,

우리 Elementary 출판이 직원 근무 시간을 파악하기 위한 새로운 절차를 **9** 시행합니다. 1월부터, 모든 직원들은 각자의 도착 시간과 퇴근 시간을 기록해야 할 것입니다. 이는 여러분 모두에게 **10** 불편한 일이 될 수 있습니다. 하지만, 경영진은 반드시 모든 직원들의 소재가 확인되게 하고자 합니다. 1월 1일부터, 사무실에 도착하시면 곧장 자리로 가지 마시기 바랍니다. **11** 대신, 안내 데스크에서 여러분의 사원증을 스캔하는 것으로 하루를 시작해 주십시오. 일과를 마치고 퇴근하실 때 다시 한번 스캔하시기 바랍니다. 추가로, 첨부해 드린 양식에 서명하신 후 11월 30일, 수요일까지 제게 돌려보내 주시기 바랍니다. **12** 이는 여러분이 이 정책에 관해 통보받았음을 나타내기 위한 것입니다.

여러분의 협조에 감사드립니다.

Stan Lewis
인사부장

| 어휘 | policy 정책 procedure 절차 track ~을 파악하다, 추적하다 as of + 시점 ~부터 be required to do ~해야 하다 arrival 도착 departure 출발 ensure that ~하는 것을 확실히 해 두다 account for ~의 소재를 파악하다 reception desk 안내 데스크 leave for the day 일과를 마치고 퇴근하다 return ~을 돌려보내다 attached 첨부된 form 양식 cooperation 협조

9. (A)

| 해설 |
다음 문장에 정책 시행 시점으로 언급된 'As of January'는 이 이메일 작성 날짜로 상단에 표기된 'November 16'보다 미래 시점에 해당됩니다. 따라서 미래 시제를 대신할 수 있는 현재 진행 시제인 (A) is implementing이 정답이다.

| 어휘 | implement ~을 시행하다

10. (B)
| 해설 |
be 동사 뒤의 빈칸은 주어 This에 대한 보어 자리로, 부정 관사 an으로 보아 This를 보충 설명할 수 있는 명사가 쓰여야 한다. 여기서 This는 앞 문장에서 언급한 도착 시간과 퇴근 시간을 기록하는 일을 가리키므로, 이를 설명하기에 적절한 명사로 '불편함'을 의미하는 (B) inconvenience가 정답이다.

| 어휘 | alleviation 완화, 경감 exaggeration 과장 alternative 대안

11. (C)
| 해설 |
빈칸 앞 문장에는 곧장 자리로 가지 말라는 말이, 뒤에는 사원증을 먼저 스캔하라는 말이 쓰여 있습니다. 사원증을 스캔하는 것은 곧장 자리로 가는 대신 먼저 해야 할 일에 해당하므로 '대신'을 뜻하는 (C) Instead가 정답이다.

| 어휘 | depending on ~에 따라, ~에 달려 있는 if so 그렇다면, 그럴 경우

12. (D)
(A) 새로운 시스템에 몇몇 기술적인 문제들이 있습니다.
(B) 사원증에는 소형 전자 칩이 들어 있습니다.
(C) 우리 회사는 정규직 직원과 시간제 근무자를 모두 고용하고 있습니다.

| 해설 |
앞 문장에 첨부 양식을 작성해 11월 30일까지 돌려보내 달라고 요청하는 말이 쓰여 있으므로 이를 This로 지칭해 그 목적을 알리는 내용을 담은 (D)가 정답이다.

| 어휘 | technical 기술적인 contain ~을 담고 있다, 포함하다 be informed of ~에 관해 통보받다

13-16번 문제는 다음 기사를 참조하시오.

공장을 폐쇄하는 Ashford-Foley Industries

DALLAS ― 연례 투자자 회의에서, Ashford-Foley Industries(AFI)는 **13** 자사가 Texas의 Houston에 위치한 제조 공장을 폐쇄할 것이라고 발표했다. 이로써 회사는 1억 달러가 넘는 금액을 절약하게 될 것이다.

해당 공장이 문을 닫은 후에는 모든 주문이 AFI의 기존 생산 시설에 의해 처리될 것이다. **14** 네 곳도 모두 북미 지역에 위치해 있다. "Ashford-Foley 사는 전국에서 손꼽히는 타이어 회사입니다"라고 업계 분석가 Virgil Graves 씨는 말한다. "하지만 **15** 경쟁사들이 빠르게 시장 점유율을 확보하고 있습니다. 생산을 통합하는 것이 이 회사가 수익성을 유지하는 데 도움이 될 것입니다."

AFI는 향후 5년 동안에 걸쳐 Houston에 있는 시설의 운영을 점차적으로 줄여 나갈 것이다. **16** 그 이후에는, 해당 부지는 매각되거나 경매에 부쳐질 것이다.

| 어휘 | plant 공장 annual 연례의, 해마다의 investor 투자자 manufacturing 제조 handle ~을 처리하다 existing 기존의 leading 손꼽히는, 선도적인 industry 업계 analyst 분석가 market share 시장 점유(율) consolidate ~을 통합하다 profitable 수익성 있는 gradually 점차적으로 reduce ~을 줄이다 operation 운영, 가동 site 부지, 현장 be put up for auction 경매에 부쳐지다

13. (D)

| 해설 |
that절의 주어 자리인 빈칸은 공장을 폐쇄하는 주체로서 그 앞에 위치한 Ashford-Foley Industries를 대신할 수 있는 주격 대명사가 쓰여야 한다. 따라서 한 회사를 대신 지칭할 수 있는 (D) it이 정답이다.

14. (B)
(A) 해당 건물에 대한 제안이 거절되었다.
(C) 이 회사의 사옥도 Texas에 있다.

(D) 그 결정은 대체로 회사의 성공에 따른 결과이다.
| 해설 |
바로 앞 문장에 기존의 생산 시설들이(production facilities) 모든 주문을 처리한다는 말이 있으므로 이 시설들을 All four로 지칭해 위치를 알려 주는 (B)가 정답이다.
| 어휘 | property 건물, 부동산 decline ~을 거절하다 be located in ~에 위치해 있다 corporate office 사옥 decision 결정 largely 대체로, 주로

15. (A)
| 해설 |
빈칸에 쓰일 명사는 but절의 주어로서 시장 점유율을 빠르게 확보할 수 있는 주체를 나타내야 한다. 시장 점유율은 경쟁사들이 서로 많이 차지하려 애쓰는 것이므로 their와 함께 Ashford-Foley의 경쟁사를 가리키는 (A) competitors가 정답이다.
| 어휘 | participant 참가자 supplier 공급업체 advocate 지지자, 옹호자

16. (C)
| 해설 |
앞 문장에 앞으로 5년에 걸쳐 운영을 점차 줄인다는 내용이 있고, 빈칸 뒤에는 매각되거나 경매에 부쳐질 거라고 알리고 있다. 빈칸 뒤의 내용은 5년이 지난 후의 상황을 언급하는 것임을 알 수 있으므로 '그 이후에는'이라는 의미로 쓰이는 (C) After that time이 정답이다
| 어휘 | in summary 요약하자면 despite ~에도 불구하고 as a matter of fact 사실상, 사실은

DAY 16 주제, 목적 및 대상을 묻는 유형

기출 유형 맛보기   본책 p.250

> 수신: Oakridge Insurance 전 직원
> 발신: David Lester, 인사부장
> 날짜: 7월 15일
> 제목: 휴가 신청
> 8월 1일부터, 모든 직원들은 반드시 최소 2주 전에 미리 각자의 휴가 기간을 승인 받아야 합니다. 여러분께서 가져가셔서 작성 완료하셔야 하는 양식이 인사부에 있습니다. 소속 부서장님께서 그 후에 양식에 서명하셔야 합니다. 필요할 경우, 긴급 상황에는 갑작스러운 통보에도 휴가를 제공할 수 있다는 점을 알아두시기 바랍니다.
> 여러분의 협조에 감사드립니다.

Q. 회람은 왜 작성되었는가?
(A) 문의 사항에 대응하기 위해
(B) 새로운 정책을 설명하기 위해
(C) 직원 야유회를 공지하기 위해
(D) 부서장을 소개하기 위해

PRACTICE | 기출 연습하기   본책 p.251
정답 1 (C) 2 (C) 3 (C)

다음 초대장을 참조하시오.

> ~ 초대합니다 ~
> 분기별 전문 능력 개발 세미나
> 3월 3일 목요일 저녁 7시 Utica Hall

> 연설자: Theresa Synder 박사, Snyder Counseling 소속 심리학자
> 주제: "학생들의 동기 부여 촉진"
> 이 행사는 학생들을 가르치는 일과 직접적으로 관련되어 있는 Guerrero 대학 교원들로 한정됩니다. 이 세미나에 참석하시는 분들께서는 미리 웹 사이트 www.guerrerouni.edu에서 주제와 관련된 요점들을 검토하시어 행사를 준비해 주시기 바랍니다.
> 행사 기획자: Yvonne Stark

1. 이 초대장은 누구를 위한 것인가?
(A) 대학생들
(B) 인사부 직원들
(C) 교수들
(D) 심리학자들
| 해설 |
본문 첫 줄에, 학생들을 가르치는 일과 직접적으로 관련된 Guerrero 대학 교원들로 한정되는 행사라는(This event is limited to Guerrero University personnel who are directly involved in teaching students) 말이 쓰여 있습니다. 따라서 학생들을 가르치는 교수들이 대상임을 알 수 있으므로 (C)가 정답이다.
| 어휘 | quarterly 분기의 psychologist 심리학자 boost ~을 촉진하다 motivation 동기 부여 be limited to ~로 한정되다 personnel 직원들, 인력 directly 직접적으로 be involved in ~에 관련되다 attend ~에 참석하다 be advised to do ~하기 바랍니다, ~하는 것이 좋습니다 prepare for ~을 준비하다 go over ~을 검토하다 in advance 미리 intended 대상이 되는

다음 공지를 참조하시오.

> 복원 프로젝트
> Clarkston 역사 협회가 Clarkston 지역의 건축 프로젝트를 후원할 것입니다. 목표는 도시에 있는 낡은 건물들을 복구하는 데 도움을 주는 것입니다. 이 단체는 다섯 곳의 다른 부지에 대해 100,000달러의 보조금을 지급합니다. 50년 이상 된 주거용 또는 상업용 건물을 소유하고 계신 분들께서 신청하실 수 있습니다. 지급되는 금액은 반드시 건물 개선 작업을 하는 데 사용되어야 합니다. 추가 정보는 555-7003번으로 Rita Becker 씨에게 연락하십시오.

2. 공지는 왜 쓰여졌는가?
(A) 도심 투어에 대해 얘기하기 위해
(B) 개장식 행사를 알리기 위해
(C) 자금 조달 기회를 설명하기 위해
(D) 수상자들을 소개하기 위해
| 해설 |
첫 문장에 건축 프로젝트를 후원한다는(sponsor building projects) 목적과 함께 그 방법으로 100,000달러의 보조금을 지급한다는(issue a grant of $100,000) 사실이 제시되어 있다. 이는 자금을 지원받을 수 있는 기회를 의미하는 것이므로 (C)가 정답이다.
| 어휘 | sponsor ~을 후원하다 restore ~을 복구하다 issue ~을 지급하다, 발급하다 grant 보조금 site 부지, 위치 residential 주거의 commercial 상업의 more than ~가 넘는 apply 신청하다 make an improvement 개선하다 contact ~에게 연락하다 discuss ~을 이야기하다 explain ~을 설명하다 funding 자금 제공 opportunity 기회 introduce ~을 소개하다 award winner 수상자

다음 이메일을 참조하시오.

> 마케팅 직원 여러분께
> 지난 경영진 회의에서, Wong 씨께서 우리의 새 광고 캠페인과 관련

된 제안을 해 주셨습니다. Wong 씨는 소셜 미디어에서 광고를 활용하는 것이 좋은 아이디어라고 생각하셨습니다. 제가 다양한 소셜 미디어 사이트의 광고 비용을 조사해 보았습니다. 이 정보를 여러분께서 다음 회의에 앞서 검토해 보실 수 있도록 여기에 첨부해 드렸습니다.

안녕히 계십시오.

Sabrina Perez
마케팅 부장

Q. Perez 씨는 왜 이메일을 보냈는가?
(A) 광고 캠페인의 성공을 보고하기 위해
(B) 특별 방문객을 위한 도움을 요청하기 위해
(C) 회의에서 나온 제안에 대한 후속 조치를 취하기 위해
(D) 완료된 프로젝트를 위한 비용 지불을 요청하기 위해

| 해설 |
첫 문장에, 회의에서 Wong 씨가 소셜 미디어 광고를 제안한 사실이(At the last management meeting, Mr. Wong put forward a proposal ~ use ads on social media) 언급되어 있고, 그 뒤로 해당 광고 비용을 조사한 일이(I have researched the costs of advertising ~) 쓰여 있다. 이는 제안 사항과 관련해 후속적으로 조치한 일을 알리는 것에 해당되므로 (C)가 정답이다.

| 어휘 | management 경영진 put forward (의견) ~을 내다, 제기하다 proposal 제안(서) regarding ~와 관련해 ad 광고 research ~을 조사하다 advertising 광고 (활동) various 다양한 attach ~을 첨부하다 review ~을 검토하다 success 성공 request ~을 요청하다 follow up on ~에 대한 후속 조치를 취하다 ask for ~을 요청하다 completed 완료된

패러프레이징 연습

본책 p.253

A.
1. (C) 가격에서 20퍼센트를 할인하다 → 할인을 받다
2. (E) 손상된 의자들 → 망가진 가구
3. (A) 상당히 확장되다 → 상당히 성장하다
4. (B) 계약서 사본 → 법적 문서
5. (D) 매년 여름에 이용 가능한 → 계절 기준으로 제공되는

B.
6. 3월 15일까지 완료된 설문지를 저희에게 보내 주시면 감사하겠습니다.
Q. Rager 씨는 왜 Britt 씨에게 글을 썼는가?
(A) 테스트 결과를 설명하기 위해 **(B) 의견을 요청하기 위해**

7. 저희 보상 프로그램에 신청하고자 하시면 이 간단한 절차를 따르시기 바랍니다.
Q. 이메일은 왜 보내졌는가?
(A) 등록 방법을 설명하기 위해 (B) 예약 일정을 정하기 위해

8. 저희는 귀하를 다시 뵙고자 하니, 언제 시간이 되시는지 저희에게 알려 주시기 바랍니다.
Q. Hofuku 씨는 왜 Edwards 씨에게 이메일을 보내는가?
(A) 예약에 관해 문의하기 위해 **(B) 만남을 요청하기 위해**

9. 이것은 Maxi Dress에서 봄 세일 행사가 곧 시작된다는 것을 알려 드리는 공지입니다.
Q. 이메일은 주로 무엇을 이야기하고 있는가?
(A) 다가오는 행사 (B) 연례 매출 목표

10. 오늘 작업자들이 새로운 문을 설치하는 대신 다시 페인트칠을 하고 낡은 바닥재를 교체할 것입니다.
Q. 회람은 왜 작성되었는가?
(A) 개조 공사에 대한 일정 변경을 알리기 위해
(B) 공간 부족 문제에 관한 불만을 처리하기 위해

DAY 16 | 실전문제

본책 p.254

정답 1 (C) 2 (D) 3 (C) 4 (A) 5 (D) 6 (B)
     7 (D) 8 (C) 9 (A)

1-2번 문제는 다음 회람을 참조하시오.

수신: King Burger 전 직원
발신: Melanie Gibb, 레스토랑 주인
날짜: 12월 14일
제목: 직원 공지

1 직원들이 각자의 교대 근무 시간에 늦게 오는 경우가 점점 더 늘고 있는 상황에 비추어 볼 때, 우리는 모든 직원들에게 시간을 엄수하도록 상기시키는 것이 필수적이라고 생각합니다. 우리 레스토랑에서는, 일일 교대 근무 일정을 엄격히 준수하는 것이 매우 중요합니다. 한 직원이 예정된 시간에 나오지 않을 경우, 동료 직원들이 그 직원을 대신하기 위해 늦게까지 근무해야 할 것입니다. 이는 용납될 수 없는 일입니다. 추가로, 지각과 관련된 우리의 정책을 기억해 주시기 바랍니다. 여러분이 지체될 것으로 생각될 경우, 반드시 예정된 근무 시작 시간보다 최소 1시간 전에는 담당 교대 근무 관리자에게 전화하셔야 합니다. 이렇게 하지 못하시는 직원들은 10달러의 벌금을 지불해야 하며, 3개월의 기간 내에 이와 같은 일이 3회 발생될 경우에, 해당 직원은 징계 처분을 받게 될 것입니다. 이를 명심해 주시기 바랍니다. **2** 확실치 않은 부분이 있을 경우, 담당 교대 근무 관리자에게 질문하시면 됩니다.

| 어휘 | in light of ~에 비추어 볼 때 the rising number of 점점 증가하는 ~의 수 case 경우, 사례 individual 사람, 개인 shift 교대 근무(조) it is necessary to do ~하는 것이 필수이다 remind A to do A에게 ~하도록 상기시키다 punctual 시간을 엄수하는 it is critical that ~하는 것이 매우 중요하다 stick to ~을 준수하다 closely 면밀히 be supposed to do ~할 예정이다 coworker 동료 직원 cover for ~을 대신하다 acceptable 용납되는 in addition 추가로 policy 정책 regarding ~에 관해 delayed 지체된 at least 최소한 fail to do ~하지 못하다 face ~에 직면하다 disciplinary action 징계 조치 keep A in mind A를 명심하다 be unsure about ~에 대해 불확실하다

1. 회람의 목적은 무엇인가?
(A) 근무 일정의 변동 사항을 알리는 것
(B) 레스토랑 장비와 관련된 문제점을 이야기하는 것
(C) 직원들에게 제대 출근하는 것에 대해 상기시키는 것
(D) 자원 봉사자들에게 행사 중에 일하도록 요청하는 것

| 해설 |
지문 초반부에 늦게 출근하는 직원들이 늘고 있어 시간을 엄수하도록 상기시켜야 한다는 점을(~ individuals are coming in late for their shifts, we feel it is necessary to remind all workers to be punctual) 알리고 있으므로 (C)가 정답이다.

| 어휘 | equipment 장비 arrive at work 출근하다 on time 제때 request A to do A에게 ~하도록 요청하다 volunteer 자원 봉사자

2. 문의 사항이 있을 경우에 직원들은 무엇을 해야 하는가?
(A) 게시판 확인하기
(B) Gibb 씨와의 회의 일정 잡기
(C) 직무 안내서 검토하기

(D) 상사에게 연락하기
| 해설 |
지문 마지막 문장에, 확실치 않은 부분에 대해 교대 근무 관리자에게 물어보라고(If there is anything you are unsure about, simply ask your shift manager) 하고 있는데, 이는 상사에게 연락하라는 뜻이므로 (D)가 정답이다.
| 어휘 | query 문의   arrange ~의 일정을 잡다, 조정하다   review ~을 검토하다   employee handbook 직무 안내서   contact ~에게 연락하다   supervisor 상사, 책임자

3–5번 문제는 다음 편지를 참조하시오.

Not Another Cheap Imitation
345 South Audley, 25b
London WC 9309X10

Lynn Wellyn
Crafty Kid's Clothes Closet
27 Cawley Road, Brooklyn, Victoria 0384

8월 12일

Wellyn 씨께,

3 8월 1일에 보내신 귀하의 편지에서 독보적인 저희 의류 제품 라인에 대해 보여주신 관심에 감사드립니다. 아래의 정보가 귀하의 모든 질문을 해결해 줄 것입니다.

1. 저희는 아동용 야외 의류와 실내용 의류, 그리고 잠옷에 대한 자체 제품 라인을 디자인하고 제조합니다. 이 의류들은 화려하고 내구성이 뛰어나며, 세탁 가능합니다. 야외 의류는 유명 브랜드의 합성 의류 소재를 활용해 만들어지고 있으며, 통기성이 있고 따뜻합니다. 저희는 이 제품들이 구매 가능한 가장 뛰어난 품질을 지니고 있다고 생각합니다.

2. 사전에 알려주시면, 저희는 최소한의 추가 요금으로 어떠한 것이든 선택하신 이름과 디자인 또는 로고를 저희 의류에 수놓아 드릴 수 있습니다.

3. 4 대부분의 주문품들은 2주 내 배송을 보장합니다. 200벌이 넘는 주문 사항에 대해서는 추가 배송 시간이 필요합니다. 이 제품들은 일반적으로 3주 내에 배송됩니다.

추가 질문이 있으실 경우, 제게 연락 주시기 바랍니다. 5 업데이트된 가격 목록이 담긴 현 제품 카탈로그를 동봉해 드립니다. 이용 가능하게 되는 대로 귀하께 연휴용 카탈로그를 보내 드리겠습니다. 귀하의 관심에 대해 다시 한번 감사드립니다!

안녕히 계십시오.
Joey Singh

| 어휘 | interest in ~에 대한 관심   one-of-a-kind 독보적인   following 아래의, 다음의   address ~을 해결하다   manufacture ~을 제조하다   durable 내구성이 좋은   washable 세탁 가능한   brand-name 유명 브랜드의   synthetic 합성의   material 소재, 재료   breathable 통기성이 있는   quality 품질   available 구매 가능한   prior 사전의, 앞선   notice 통보   embroider ~을 수놓다   minimal 최소의   additional 추가적인   be guaranteed to do ~하도록 보장되다   more than ~가 넘는   unit (제품의) 1개, 1대   usually 일반적으로   contact ~에게 연락하다   enclose ~을 동봉하다   current 현재의   as soon as ~하자마자

3. 이 편지의 목적은 무엇인가?
(A) 최근 제품을 구매한 고객에게 감사하기 위해
(B) 의류 제품 라인에 관한 정보를 요청하기 위해
(C) 정보에 대한 요청에 답변하기 위해
(D) 늦은 배송에 대해 사과하기 위해

| 해설 |
첫 단락에 8월 1일에 상대방이 편지를 보낸 사실과 함께 상대방의 질문에 대해 답변해 주겠다고(~ in your letter of August 1. The following information should address all your questions) 알리고 있는데, 이는 특정 정보에 대한 상대방의 요청에 답변하는 것이므로 (C)가 정답이다.
| 어휘 | recent 최근의   purchase 구매(품)   ask for ~을 요청하다   respond to ~에 답변하다   apologize for ~에 대해 사과하다

4. 편지는 무엇을 보장하고 있는가?
(A) 특정 시간 이내의 배송
(B) 대량 주문에 대한 할인
(C) 빠지거나 손상된 배송에 대한 환불
(D) 즉각적인 고객 서비스

| 해설 |
'보장' 내용에 대해 언급된 3번 항목에서 대부분의 주문품들은 2주 내에 배송되도록 보장된다고(Most orders are guaranteed to ship within two weeks) 쓰여 있으므로 (A)가 정답이다.
| 어휘 | certain 특정한, 일정한   large order 대량 주문   refund 환불   missing 빠진, 없는   damaged 손상된   delivery 배송(품)   prompt 즉각적인

5. 발신인은 편지와 함께 무엇을 보냈는가?
(A) 주문서
(B) 이전의 주문품
(C) 연휴용 카탈로그
(D) 가격 목록

| 해설 |
함께 보낸 것이 언급된 마지막 단락에, 업데이트된 가격 목록이 담긴 제품 카탈로그를 동봉했다고(I have enclosed our current catalog with the updated price list) 알리고 있으므로 '가격 목록'을 의미하는 (D)가 정답이다.
| 어휘 | form 양식, 서식   previous 이전의   listing 목록, 명단

6–9번 문제는 다음 기사를 참조하시오.

전자 제품 제조사 Digiprompt의 기쁨

CAIRO (10월 7일) — 6 Digiprompt의 Robert Ennels 전무 이사는 오늘 이집트에 지을 새 유통 공장의 개장 계획을 발표했습니다. 공사는 약 6개월 정도 소요될 것으로 예상되며, 공장은 4월 2까지는 개장될 예정입니다. Ennels 이사는 이번 조치가 Digiprompt 사의 다양한 합리적인 가격의 노트북 컴퓨터 제품들이 아프리카 대륙 전역의 고객들에게 다가가도록 돕는 데 있어 핵심적일 것이라고 생각한다고 기자 회견에서 기자들에게 말했습니다. 7 Ennels 이사는 지난달에 해당 지역으로 떠난 휴가에서 영감을 받았고, 그 지역에서 많은 기업들과 학교들이 낡은 장비를 사용하고 있다는 사실을 알게 되었다고 말했습니다. Ennels 이사는 아프리카 시장에서 성공을 거두기 위한 조건을 확인했다고 생각하고 있습니다. "단순히 뛰어난 제품을 보유하는 것만으로는 충분하지 않습니다,"라고 그는 말했습니다. "광고가 특히 중요한 것도 아닙니다. 제게 있어, 8 핵심 요소는 유통에 소비되는 비용을 줄이는 데 있습니다. 이것이 바로 저희가 이 새로운 사업을 통해 달성하고자 하는 바입니다." Ennels 이사는 아마 세계적으로 유명한 회사인 Assistatec의 공동 이사 역할로 가장 잘 알려져 있을 것입니다. 하지만, 9 Ennels 이사는 Digiprompt 사를 설립하기 위해 자발적으로 이 자리에서 물러났습니다. "제 공동 경영자와는 어떠한 논쟁 같은 것도 없었습니다"라고 그는 알렸습니다. "실제로, 저희는 지금까지도 여전히 사이 좋게 지내고 있습니다. 9 저는 그저 전적으로 혼자 일하고 싶은 강한 욕구를 느꼈을 뿐입니다." 이 새로운 프로젝트의 또 다른 특징은 Ennels 이사가 여유 시간에 아프리카 대륙을 지속적으로 탐험해 볼 기회가 생긴다는 점입니다. "그건 분명 아주 훌륭한 보너스이긴 하지만, 제가 이곳에 온 주된 이유는 아닙니다"라고 말하며 Ennels 이사는 웃었습니다.

| 어휘 | managing director 전무 이사   announce ~을 발표하다   distribution 유통, 배급   plant 공장   be expected to do ~할 것으로 예상되다   approximately 약, 대략   due to do ~할 예정인   by (기한) ~까지   press conference 기자 회견   key 중요한, 핵심적인   one's range of 다양한   affordable 합리적인 가격의   reach ~에게 도달하다   consumer 소비자   throughout ~ 전역에 걸쳐   continent 대륙   claim that ~라고 말하다, 주장하다   be inspired by ~에 의해 영감을 받다   region 지역   realize (that) ~임을 알게 되다   outdated 낡은   equipment 장비   identify ~을 확인하다   nor (부정어와 함께) ~도 아니다   advertising 광고   particularly 특히   factor 요소   reduce ~을 줄이다   achieve ~을 달성하다   venture (모험) 사업   be best known for ~로 가장 잘 알려져 있다   joint director 공동 이사   renowned 유명한   firm 회사   voluntarily 자발적으로   in order to do ~하기 위해   found ~을 설립하다   argument 논쟁   or anything (부정문에서) ~ 같은 것   get on well 사이 좋게 지내다   to this day 지금까지도   strong urge to do ~하고 싶은 강한 욕구   entirely 전적으로   for oneself 혼자   feature 특징   allow A B A에게 B를 (가지도록) 허용하다   opportunity to do ~할 수 있는 기회   explore ~을 탐색하다

6. 기사는 주로 무엇에 관한 것인가?
(A) 아프리카 대륙의 관광 명소
(B) 일부 새로운 부지의 건설 공사
(C) 신 제품의 출시
(D) 두 동료들 간의 사업 관계

| 해설 |
첫 문장에 새로 유통 공장이 지어진다는 사실이 발표되었다고(~ today announced the opening of a new distribution plant in Egypt) 알리는 부분이 목적에 해당되므로 이 건설 공사를 가리키는 (B)가 정답이다.
| 어휘 | attraction 명소   premises (건물이 딸린) 부지   launch 시작, 착수   relationship 관계   colleague 동료

7. 기사에 따르면, Ennels 씨는 최근에 무엇을 했는가?
(A) 동료 직원과 이야기를 나눴다.
(B) 일부 새로운 IT 장비를 구입했다.
(C) 건설 회사를 설립했다.
(D) 휴가를 떠났다.

| 해설 |
최근 시점에 해당되는 the month before가 언급된 중반부에서 Ennels 이사가 지난달에 휴가를 떠난 사실을(he was inspired by a holiday to the region the month before) 알 수 있으므로 (D)가 정답이다.
| 어휘 | take a vacation 휴가를 떠나다

8. Ennels 씨는 아프리카에서의 성공을 위해 가장 중요한 고려 사항이 무엇이라고 말하는가?
(A) 지역 시장에 맞게 제품을 맞춤 제작하기
(B) 강력한 마케팅 캠페인 하기
(C) 유통 비용을 낮게 유지하기
(D) 다양한 고품질 제품 보유하기

| 해설 |
Ennels 씨의 인터뷰 내용이 나오는 중반부에 유통에 드는 비용을 줄이는 것이 핵심 요소로(the key factor is in reducing the money spent on distribution) 언급되어 있으므로 (C)가 정답이다.
| 어휘 | consideration 고려 (사항)   tailor A to B A를 B에 맞추다   keep A + 형용사 A를 ~하게 유지하다   a range of 다양한   high-quality 고품질의

9. Ennels 씨는 왜 Digiprompt를 설립했는가?
(A) 독립적으로 일하고 싶은 욕망이 있었다.
(B) 이전 직장에서 해고되었다.
(C) 아프리카의 풍경에 대한 애정을 발견했다.
(D) 자선 활동을 하기를 원했다.

| 해설 |
지문 후반부에 자발적으로 이전의 직장을 떠나 Digiprompt를 설립한 사실과 함께(he voluntarily left this post in order to found Digiprompt) 혼자 일하고 싶은 욕구가 있었다고(I just felt a strong urge to work entirely for myself) 알리는 내용이 나온다. 즉, 독립적으로 일하고 싶었다는 뜻이므로 (A)가 정답이다.
| 어휘 | desire to do ~하고 싶은 욕망   independently 독립적으로   fire ~을 해고하다   previous 이전의   discover ~을 발견하다   landscape 풍경   charitable 자선의

DAY 17 세부 사항을 묻는 유형

기출 유형 맛보기

수신: Diane Clark <diane.clark@westforddesigns.com>
발신: Alan Scofield <scofield.a@floreston.gov>
제목: 여름 자선 달리기 대회
날짜: 6월 4일

Clark 씨께,

시의회 구성원의 한 사람으로서, 저는 올해 열리는 여름 자선 달리기 행사 기획을 담당하고 있습니다. 지난주에, 저는 이 대회를 광고하는 데 필요한 전단 500장을 귀사에서 주문했습니다. 제 주문에 500장의 전단을 더 추가해야 합니다. 가능하다면, 모든 전단을 6월 11일까지 받았으면 합니다. 그 이유는 자원 봉사자들이 그 다음 날 전단을 배부하도록 도와줄 것이기 때문입니다. 새 전단에 대한 비용 지불을 위해 오늘 이따가 전화 드리겠습니다.

감사합니다,

Alan Scofield

Q. 전단은 언제 배부될 것인가?
(A) 6월 5일에
(B) 6월 11일에
(C) 6월 12일에
(D) 6월 21일에

PRACTICE | 기출 연습하기

정답 **1** (C) **2** (C) **3** (B)

다음 정보를 참조하시오.

긴급 인쇄 작업
www.lux-printing.com

저희 Lux 인쇄와 함께 하시면, 마지막 순간에 진행되는 인쇄 작업도 번거로운 상황이 될 필요가 없습니다. 사진/로고/글을 업로드하신 후, 선호하시는 사이즈와 배치 방식에 관한 메모를 주시고 '미리 보기' 버튼만 누르시면 됩니다. 전문가들로 구성된 저희 팀이 30분 내로 주문 사항에 맞춘 이미지를 만들어 드릴 것입니다. 인쇄된 물품은 2시간 정도의 짧은 시간 내에 배송될 수 있습니다. 디자인에 만족하지 못하실 경우, 추가 비용 없이 수정을 요청하실 수 있습니다. 귀하의 이미지는 6개월 동안 안전한 저희 웹 사이트에 저장될 것이며, 저희 직원이 제공해 드리는 5자리 비밀 번호를 이용해 언제든지 접속해서 보실 수 있습니다.

1. 5자리 비밀 번호는 무엇에 대해 사용될 수 있는가?
(A) 서비스 비용 지불하기
(B) 배송 상태 추적하기
(C) 온라인으로 이미지 보기
(D) 할인 요청하기

| 해설 |
5자리 비밀 번호가 언급되는 마지막 문장에, 웹 사이트에 저장되는 이미지를 볼 수 있는 방법으로(Your image will be saved on our secure Web site ~ you can access it at any time by using the 5-digit code ~) 제시되고 있으므로 (C)가 정답이다.

| 어휘 | in a hurry 급한, 서두르는 last-minute 마지막 순간의 hassle 번거로운 상황 text 글자, 문자 layout 배치, 구획 preference 선호(하는 것) preview 미리 보기 professional 전문가 create ~을 만들어 내다 made-to-order 주문에 맞춰 제작한 less than ~ 미만의 material 물품, 재료, 자재 within ~ 이내에 as A as B B만큼 A한 be satisfied with ~에 만족하다 request ~을 요청하다 at no extra charge 추가 비용 없이 secure 안전한 access ~에 접속하다, ~을 이용하다 5-digit 5자리의 provide ~을 제공하다 pay for ~에 대한 비용을 지불하다 track ~을 추적하다 view ~을 보다

다음 광고를 참조하시오.

훌륭한 경관을 보유한 현대적인 아파트!

새로운 Cicero Tower 건물의 방 2개짜리 아파트가 3월 1일부터 이용 가능합니다. 옥외 발코니는 아름다운 Cheshire 강을 내려다보고 있습니다. 이 아파트에는 오븐과 냉장고, 그리고 전자레인지가 딸려 있습니다. 소액 요금으로 지정 주차 공간도 얻으실 수 있습니다. 매달 지불하는 1,150달러의 임대료에는 추가 비용 없이 수도 요금과 쓰레기 처리 비용이 포함되어 있습니다. 추가 정보를 원하시는 분은 555-0497번으로 전화주시기 바랍니다.

---

2. 월간 임대료에 무엇이 포함되어 있는가?
(A) 전기 요금
(B) 주차 공간
(C) 쓰레기 처리 서비스
(D) 세탁기

| 해설 |
월간 임대료 관련 정보가 제시된 후반부에, 임대료에 추가 비용 없이 수도 요금과 쓰레기 처리 비용이 포함되어 있다고(The rental fee of $1,150 per month includes ~ trash removal at no extra cost) 쓰여 있으므로 (C)가 정답이다.

| 어휘 | view 경관, 전망 available 이용 가능한 overlook (건물 등이) ~을 내려다 보다 come with ~가 딸려 있다, ~을 포함하다 refrigerator 냉장고 microwave 전자레인지 assigned 지정된, 배정된 obtain ~을 얻다, 획득하다 for a small fee 소액 요금으로 rental fee 임대료, 대여료 include ~을 포함하다 removal 제거, 없앰 at no extra cost 추가 비용 없이 electricity bill 전기 요금 spot 위치, 지점

다음 이메일을 참조하시오.

수신: Culver Appliances 전 직원 <stafflist@culver-appliances.com>
발신: Leo Derosa<l_derosa@culver-furniture.com>
날짜: 10월 16일
제목: 주목해야 할 사항

10월 1일에, 우리 매장은 200달러를 초과하는 모든 주문에 대해 무료 배송 서비스를 제공하기 시작했습니다. 배송 서비스가 무료인 반면에 설치 작업에 대해서는 여전히 50달러의 요금이 청구된다는 점에 유의하시기 바랍니다. 이는 고객과 직원들 모두에게 혼란을 초래한 부분입니다. 무료 및 유료 서비스와 관련된 규정을 여러분이 완전히 이해하고 있어야 한다는 점과 구매 시에 고객들께 적용되는 요금을 간략히 설명해 드려야 한다는 점은 중요합니다. 우리의 기준 배송 구역 외의 지역으로 제품을 받아야 하는 분이 있으실 경우, Dale Schaff 씨에게 문의하게 하십시오.

여러분의 협조에 감사 드립니다.

Leo Derosa
총무부장, Culver Appliances

---

3. 이메일에 따르면, Schaff 씨는 무엇을 할 것인가?
(A) 대량 제품 구매 돕기
(B) 특별 요청 처리하기
(C) 설치비 환급해 주기
(D) 직원들에게 제품 세부 사항 보내기

| 해설 |
Schaff 씨의 이름이 제시되는 마지막 문장에, 기준 배송 구역 외의 배송에 대해 Schaff 씨에게 문의해야 한다고(If anyone needs to have items delivered outside of our standard delivery zone, please refer them to Dale Schaff) 쓰여 있다. 이는 Schaff 씨가 특별한 배송 요청을 처리한다는 의미이므로 (B)가 정답이다.

| 어휘 | attention 주목, 관심 provide ~을 제공하다 free 무료의 exceed ~을 초과하다 note that ~임에 유의하다 while ~인 반면에 charge 청구(액) installation 설치 cause ~을 초래하다 confusion 혼란 among ~ 사이에서 fully 완전히, 전적으로 regarding ~와 관련해 outline ~을 간략히 설명하다 applicable 적용되는 purchase 구매(품) have A p.p. A가 ~되게 하다 standard 기준의, 표준의 refer A to B A를 B에게 문의하게 하다 cooperation 협조 assist with ~을 돕다 bulk 대량의 handle ~을 처리하다 reimburse ~을 환급해 주다 details 세부 사항, 상세 설명

패러프레이징 연습

본책 p.261

A.
1. (B) 가장 인기 있는 식당들 → 매우 인기 있는 레스토랑들
2. (D) 모든 것은 한번 판매되면 취소가 안 됩니다. → 반품 또는 환불 불가
3. (A) 가능성을 탐구하다 → 실현 가능한지 밝혀내다
4. (C) 역에서 불과 몇 분 거리에 위치한 → 편리한 곳에 위치한
5. (E) 냉장고와 식기 세척기들 → 일부 가전 기기들

B.
6. 이번 분기의 소득과 수익에 관한 요약 문서를 첨부해 드렸으니 확인해 보시기 바랍니다.
Q. Bridges 씨는 이메일에 무엇을 포함했는가?
(A) 재무 관련 정보 (B) 잠재 구매 상품의 목록

7. Children's Fund를 위한 기부금은 안내 데스크에 있는 상자에 넣으시면 됩니다.
Q. 방문객들은 무엇을 하도록 요청 받는가?
(A) 프로그램에 더 많은 시간 할애하기 **(B) 모금함에 돈 넣어 두기**

8. 오직 사원증을 착용한 직원들만 시험 시설에 출입이 허용될 것입니다.
Q. 사원증은 무엇을 위해 사용될 수 있는가?
(A) 주차 요금 할인 받기 **(B) 제한 구역에 출입하기**

9. Downtown Tours에서 근무하는 가이드들은 반드시 도시 곳곳의 관광지에 익숙해야 합니다.

Q. 해당 직책에 필요한 자격 요건은 무엇인가?
(A) 지역 내 관광에 관한 지식 (B) 지역 역사에 관한 전문 지식

10. 청구서 발급이나 연락처에 대한 변경은 www.pricehouse.co.uk/myaccount에서 안전하게 이뤄질 수 있습니다.
Q. 어떻게 이메일 주소를 업데이트할 수 있는가?
(A) 전화 통화를 함으로써 (B) 웹 사이트를 방문함으로써

DAY 17 | 실전문제
본책 p.262

| 정답 | 1 (B) | 2 (A) | 3 (B) | 4 (D) | 5 (B) | 6 (C) |
| | 7 (B) | 8 (C) | 9 (D) | | | |

1-3번 문제는 다음 설명서를 참조하시오.

Shinn Electronics 믹서기를 구입해 주셔서 감사합니다. 구입하신 기기를 좋은 상태로 유지하기 위해 다음의 절차를 따라 주시기 바랍니다.

- 전기와 연결되는 아래 부분을 제외하고, 모든 부품은 식기세척기에 사용하실 수 있습니다. 칼날 세트를 다루실 때 주의하시기 바랍니다.
- 물이 고이는 것을 방지하기 위해 용기 부분을 분리한 채로 믹서기를 보관하십시오.
- **1** 절대로 요리용 스토브에서 곧바로 수프나 기타 가열된 액체를 믹서기에 넣지 마셔야 하는데, 이는 플라스틱으로 된 용기에 균열이 생기게 할 수 있기 때문입니다.
- 반드시 밀폐용 고무 부분과 뚜껑이 올바른 위치에 있도록 하셔야 믹서기가 새지 않습니다.
- 모든 부품은 정부 안전 테스트를 통과한 것들입니다. 하지만, **2** 장기간 전기 코드를 사용하시면 안전 문제를 초래할 수 있으므로, 몇 달에 한번씩은 점검되어야 합니다.
- **3** 믹서기가 배송될 때 제품이 들어있던 포장재를 버리지 마십시오. 저희 Shinn Electronics는 반품 요청 시에 믹서기 및 부품과 함께 그 포장재를 제조사에 보내야 합니다.

|어휘| purchase 구매(품) follow ~을 따르다 below 아래에 keep A in good condition A를 좋은 상태로 유지하다 appliance (가전) 기기 part 부품 except for ~을 제외하고 base 아래 부분 dishwasher-safe 식기세척기에 사용할 수 있는 use care 주의하다 handle ~을 다루다, 처리하다 blade 칼날 store ~을 보관하다 with A p.p. A가 ~된 채로 pitcher (주전자 같은) 용기 remove ~을 제거하다 prevent ~을 방지하다 trapped 고여 있는, 갇혀 있는 put A into B A를 B 안으로 넣다 liquid 액체 straight from ~에서부터 곧바로 cause A to do A가 ~하도록 초래하다 crack (깨진) 금, 균열 make sure (that) 반드시 ~하도록 하다 rubber seal 밀폐용 고무 lid 뚜껑 leak 새다, 누출되다 long-term 장기간의 result in ~을 초래하다 inspect ~을 점검하다 throw away ~을 버리다 packaging 포장재 require A to do A가 ~하도록 요구하다 manufacturer 제조사 along with ~와 함께 return 반품 request 요청

1. 믹서기를 손상시킬 수 있는 것으로 무엇이 언급되는가?
(A) 작동 중 헐거운 상태의 뚜껑
(B) 뜨거운 물질에 대한 노출
(C) 오랜 작동 시간
(D) 식기세척기의 사용

|해설|
손상과 관련된 것으로 'crack'이 언급된 세 번째 항목을 보면, 수프를 비롯한 가열된 액체를 넣으면 용기에 균열을 일으킬 수 있다는(Never put soups or other heated liquids ~ this may cause the plastic pitcher to crack) 내용이 있다. 이는 뜨거운 물체를 넣지 말라는 뜻이므로 (B)가 정답이다.

|어휘| damage ~을 손상시키다 loose 헐거운 in operation 작동 중인 exposure to ~에의 노출 substance 물체, 물질

2. 고객들은 믹서기에 대해 무엇을 주기적으로 하도록 권고 받는가?
(A) 전원 코드 확인하기
(B) 밀폐용 고무 교체하기
(C) 칼날 세트를 날카롭게 만들기
(D) 안전 기능 확인하기

|해설|
질문의 regularly에 해당하는 표현으로, once every few months라는 반복 주기가 언급된 다섯 번째 항목에, 안전 문제로 인해 전기 코드를 몇 달마다 한번씩 점검해야 한다고(~ the electric cord ~ it should be inspected once every few months) 쓰여 있으므로 (A)가 정답이다.

|어휘| regularly 주기적으로 replace ~을 교체하다 sharpen ~을 날카롭게 하다 review ~을 확인하다, 검토하다 feature 기능, 특징

3. 설명서에 따르면, 고객들은 왜 포장재를 보관하도록 권고되는가?
(A) 제품 세척과 관련된 정보를 담고 있다.
(B) 제품이 반품될 경우에 반드시 포함되어야 한다.
(C) 보관 중에 제품 손상을 방지해 준다.
(D) 제조사의 주소 정보를 제공해 준다.

|해설|
packaging 관련 정보가 언급된 마지막 항목에, 제품을 반품할 때 필요하기 때문에 포장재를 버리지 말라고(Do not throw away the packaging ~ Shinn Electronics requires it to be sent to the manufacturer ~ for return requests) 당부하고 있으므로 (B)가 정답이다.

|어휘| instructions 설명서 retain ~을 갖고 있다, 보유하다 include ~을 포함하다 storage 보관, 저장

4-6번 문제는 다음 웹페이지를 참조하시오.

http://www.faroniatheater.org
Faronia 극장

전 세계의 여러 음악에 대한 기념
다가오는 행사: 켈트 음악 콘서트

2월 19일 토요일 오후 7시에 Faronia 극장이 사상 처음으로 개최하는 켈트 음악 콘서트와 함께 또 다른 문화의 풍요로움을 누려보세요. **4** 행사 개막 공연은 취미로 음악을 연주하는 한 지역 그룹으로 시작되지만, 나머지 공연에는 네 팀의 전문 연주 그룹이 포함됩니다. 청중들께서는 반주에 사용되는 바이올린이나 주석 피리 등과 같은 악기들과 함께 두 세기에 걸친 음악을 들으실 수 있습니다.

이 콘서트 프로그램은 켈트 음악계를 꼼꼼히 조사한 Amelia Palen 씨에 의해 기획되었습니다. **5** 저희 극장의 기획팀에 합류하시기 앞서, Palen 씨는 유럽 전역을 돌아다니며, 다양한 그룹들의 음악적 유산을 조사했기 때문에, 이 일에 완벽하게 어울리는 분입니다.

행사 입장권은 현재 매표소에서 구입 가능하며, 콘서트 뿐만 아니라 공연 후에 이어지는 음악가들과의 질의응답 시간도 포함되어 있습니다.

6 일부 기본적인 켈트 댄스를 배우시는 데 관심이 있으신 분들께서는 콘서트 당일에 함께 진행되는 3시간 길이의 워크숍에도 참가 신청하실 수 있습니다. 이 특별 활동에 참가하시려면 1인당 8달러의 추가 요금을 지불하셔야 합니다.

|어휘| celebrate ~을 기념하다, 축하하다 upcoming 다가오는, 곧 있을 Celtic 켈트족의, 켈트어의 engage with ~에 관여하다, 참여하다 richness 풍요로움 first-ever 사상 처음의 opening act 개막 공연 the rest of ~의 나머지 include ~을 포함하다 audience members 관객, 청중 span ~의 기간에 걸치다 instrument 악기 fiddle 바이올린 tin whistle 주석 피리 accompaniment 반주 meticulously 꼼꼼하게 research ~을 조사하다 music scene 음악계 prior to ~에 앞서 join ~에 합류하다, 가입하다 throughout ~ 전역에서 heritage 유산

a variety of 다양한   perfect fit 완벽히 어울리는 사람   available 구매 가능한   following ~ 후에   interested in ~에 관심이 있는   sign up for ~을 신청하다   take place (행사, 일 등) 발생되다, 일어나다   extra 추가의, 별도의   charge 청구(액)   take part in ~에 참가하다   unique 특별한, 독특한

4. 켈트 음악 콘서트에 관해 사실인 것은 무엇인가?
(A) Faronia 극장에서 해마다 개최된다.
(B) 오직 두 가지 공연만 관람 가능하다.
(C) 오직 현대 음악만 포함한다.
(D) 전문 음악가와 아마추어 음악인들을 특징으로 한다.

| 해설 |
첫 단락에 취미로 음악을 하는 그룹과 전문 음악 그룹들이 모두 나온다는(The opening act will be a local group that plays music as a hobby, ~ will include four professional performance groups) 내용이 나오므로 이와 같은 특징을 언급한 (D)가 정답이다.

| 어휘 | hold ~을 개최하다   annually 해마다   exclusively 오로지   contemporary 현대의, 동시대의   feature ~을 특징으로 하다   amateur 아마추어의

5. Palen 씨는 누구인가?
(A) 역사가
(B) 극장 직원
(C) 가수
(D) 여행사 직원

| 해설 |
Palen 씨의 이름이 제시되는 두 번째 단락에, 극장의 기획팀에 합류하기에 앞서(Prior to joining the theater's planning team ~) Palen 씨가 한 일이 설명되어 있는데, 이 부분을 통해 현재 극장 소속 직원임을 알 수 있으므로 (B)가 정답이다.

6. 웹 페이지에 따르면, 추가 요금으로 이용 가능한 것은 무엇인가?
(A) 오리엔테이션 프로그램
(B) 콘서트 녹음
(C) 댄스 강습
(D) 질의응답 시간

| 해설 |
additional fee에 해당하는 표현인 extra charge가 언급된 마지막 단락을 보면, 해당 추가 비용은 켈트 댄스를 배우는 워크숍에 참가하기 위한 것이므로(Those interested in learning some basic Celtic dance moves may sign up for a three-hour workshop ~) '댄스 강습'을 의미하는 (C)가 정답이다.

| 어휘 | additional 추가적인

7-9번 문제는 다음 편지를 참조하시오.

241 Grey Road, Victoria, BC P4T 9E4

9월 6일

Greg Dubois 씨
Connect to All, 고객 서비스
65 Winston Center
Victoria, BC P3L 8A5

회신: 회원 계정: 207-83-69

Greg 씨께,

저는 현재 Connect to All의 기본 회원 패키지에 가입되어 있습니다. 이 가입 서비스 패키지를 통해 저는 국내 전화 통화와 발신자 표시, 그리고 통화 대기 서비스를 이용할 수 있습니다. **7** 이 패키지의 월 정규 요금이 27달러이기 때문에, 제 8월 고지서에 왜 40달러가 청구되었는지 궁금합니다. 저는 더 많은 요금은 오직 프리미엄 회원 패키지 가입자들에게만 적용되는 것으로 알고 있습니다.

9 저는 2년 전에 기본 회원으로 Connect to All에 가입했으며, 제 서비스를 한번도 변경해 본 적이 없습니다. 제 기록을 신중히 검토하시면 이를 확인하실 수 있습니다.

지금까지 계속, 저는 귀사의 전화 서비스가 만족스러웠다고 생각했으며, 계속 현재의 가입 서비스를 유지할 계획입니다. **8** 이 오류를 수정해서 새로운 8월 고지서를 제게 보내 주시면 대단히 감사하겠습니다. 이 문제와 관련해 어떠한 추가 정보든지 필요하실 경우, 제 번호 (716) 633-8021번으로 전화 주십시오.

귀하의 시간과 노력에 대단히 감사드립니다.

안녕히 계십시오.
Ellen Gibbs

| 어휘 | account 계정, 계좌   currently 현재   belong to ~에 속해 있다   subscription (서비스 등의) 가입, 이용, 구독   entitle A to B A가 B할 수 있게 해 주다, A에게 B에 대한 자격을 주다   regular 일반의, 정규의   rate 요금   wonder why 왜 ~인지 궁금하다   be charged A A의 비용이 청구되다   as indicated on ~에 나타난 바와 같이   bill 고지서, 청구서   apply to ~에 적용되다   subscriber 서비스 가입자, 구독자   make a change to ~을 변경하다   verify ~을 확인하다, 입증하다   look through ~을 훑어보다   carefully 신중히   up until now 지금까지 계속   find A + 형용사 A가 ~하다고 생각하다   satisfactory 만족스러운   intend to do ~할 계획이다   grateful 감사하는   correct ~을 바로잡다   require ~을 필요로 하다   regarding ~와 관련해   effort 수고, 노력

7. 이 편지는 왜 쓰여졌는가?
(A) 월간 요금 납부를 요청하기 위해
(B) 고지서의 오류를 알리기 위해
(C) 새로운 전화번호를 제공하기 위해
(D) 회원 요금에 관해 문의하기 위해

| 해설 |
첫 단락에서 편지 발신인이 원래 요금이 27달러인데 왜 8월 고지서에 40달러가 청구되었는지 궁금하다고(Since the regular monthly rate for this package is $27, I am wondering why I have been charged $40 as indicated on my August bill) 밝히는 부분이 목적에 해당한다. 이는 청구서의 오류를 알리는 것이므로 (B)가 정답이다.

| 어휘 | payment 납부(액), 지불(액)   provide ~을 제공하다   inquire about ~에 관해 문의하다

8. Gibbs 씨는 전화 회사에 무엇을 하도록 요청하는가?
(A) 자신의 전화선 수리하기
(B) 자신의 회원 약정 업그레이드하기
(C) 수정된 고지서를 자신에게 우송하기
(D) 자신의 발신자 표시 서비스를 취소하기

| 해설 |
편지 발신인인 Gibbs 씨의 요청 사항을 찾아야 하는데, 마지막 단락에 오류를 바로잡아 새 고지서를 보내 달라고(I would be very grateful if you could ~ send me a new bill for August) 요청하는 내용이 있으므로 이 요청 사항이 언급된 (C)가 정답이다.

| 어휘 | repair ~을 수리하다   mail ~을 우송하다   cancel ~을 취소하다

9. Gibbs 씨는 자신의 가입 서비스에 관해 무슨 말을 하는가?
(A) 매달 40달러의 비용이 든다.
(B) 프리미엄 회원이다.
(C) 갱신하지 않을 것이다.
(D) 2년이 된 상태이다.

| 해설 |
이용 중인 서비스와 관련해, 두 번째 단락에 2년 전에 가입했다고(I joined Connect to All two years ago as a basic member) 알리는 내용이 있으므로 (D)가 정답이다.
| 어휘 | cost ~의 비용이 들다 renew ~을 갱신하다

DAY 18 진위 확인 유형

기출 유형 맛보기
본책 p.266

Demko Dry Cleaning은 지난 10년간 자랑스럽게도 Oakway 지역 사회에 서비스를 제공해 왔으며, 저희는 이 중요한 사실을 기념하고자 합니다. 2월 7일이 있는 주에 언제든지, 이 쿠폰을 제출하시면 10퍼센트의 할인을 받으실 수 있습니다. 이는 오직 세탁물에만 적용되며, 배달 또는 수선 서비스에 대해서는 사용될 수 없다는 점에 유의하시기 바랍니다.

저희 Demko Dry Cleaning의 고객이 되어 주셔서 감사드립니다!

Q. 할인 제공 서비스에 관해 언급된 것은 무엇인가?
(A) 다른 할인 서비스와 함께 이용될 수 없다.
(B) 다수의 제품들이 세탁되어야 한다.
(C) 오직 일주일 동안만 유효하다.
(D) 고객들이 1회 이상 이용할 수 있다.

PRACTICE | 기출 연습하기
본책 p.267

정답 1 (C) 2 (D) 3 (B)

다음 정보를 참조하시오.

Shelby Oral Care의 Smilebright-360 전동 칫솔을 구입해 주셔서 감사합니다. 주기적인 관리 일정을 준수하시면 구입하신 기기의 수명을 연장하실 수 있습니다. 매번 사용하신 후에, 또는 최소 하루에 한번은 칫솔 머리 부분을 물로 헹구셔서 남아 있는 치약이나 끼어 있는 음식물 입자를 제거해 주시기 바랍니다. 매주 칫솔 머리 부분을 제거하신 후, 따뜻한 물을 손잡이 전체에 흐르게 하시고, 금속 막대 부분을 말끔히 닦으시는 방법으로 더욱 철저히 칫솔을 세척해 주십시오.

칫솔 머리 부분은 칫솔모가 최적의 기능을 할 수 있도록 3개월마다 한 번씩 교체해 주셔야 합니다. 일단 완전히 충전되고 나면, 양치질 빈도에 따라 약 2주간 사용할 수 있는 정도의 전력이 칫솔에 공급됩니다. 충전기는 전기 코드에 꽂아 두신 상태로 놓아 두실 수 있는데, 칫솔이 올려져 있지 않을 경우에 자동으로 꺼지기 때문입니다.

Smilebright-360: 우리는 당신이 계속해서 미소 짓도록 도와 드립니다!

| 어휘 | purchase ~을 구입하다 electric toothbrush 전동 칫솔 extend ~을 연장하다 lifespan 수명 device 기기, 장치 adhere to ~을 준수하다 maintenance 유지 관리 at least 최소한 rinse ~을 물로 헹구다 remove ~을 제거하다 excess 남아 있는 trapped 끼어 있는 particle 입자 give A a cleaning A를 세척하다 thorough 철저한 run (물 등) ~을 흐르게 하다 over ~에 걸쳐 wipe down ~을 말끔히 닦다 shaft 막대, 손잡이 replace ~을 교체하다 optimal 최적의 bristle 솔 performance 기능, 성능 once 일단 ~하면 fully charged 완전히 충전된 approximately 약, 대략 depending on ~에 따라 frequency 빈도 charging station 충전기 be left p.p. ~된 상태로 두다 turn off 꺼지다 keep -ing 계속 ~하다

1. 충전기에 관해 언급된 것은 무엇인가?
(A) 깨끗하게 유지하기 위해 말끔히 닦아야 한다.
(B) 매우 빠르게 기기를 완전히 충전할 수 있다.
(C) 사용하지 않을 때 전원 코드를 뽑을 필요가 없다.
(D) 보조 배터리를 이용해 전력을 공급 받을 수 있다.
| 해설 |
충전기 관련 정보가 제시된 두 번째 단락 끝부분에, 전기 코드에 꽂아 둔 상태로 놓아 둘 수 있고 칫솔이 올려져 있지 않을 경우에 자동으로 꺼진다고(The charging station can be left plugged in because it automatically turns off when there is no toothbrush on it) 쓰여 있으므로 (C)가 정답이다.
| 어휘 | unplug ~의 전원 코드를 뽑다 power ~에 전력을 공급하다

다음 회람을 참조하시오.

수신: Aragon Consulting 전 직원
발신: Kristin Lockhart
제목: Barbara Wilk
날짜: 11월 9일

우리 Aragon Consulting을 대표해, 저는 다음 주부터 Barbara Wilk 씨가 마케팅 부서를 책임지게 될 것이라는 사실을 알려 드리게 되어 기쁩니다. Wilk 씨는 경력 기간에 걸쳐 권위 있는 Desalvo Prize를 포함해 여러 상을 수상했습니다. 그녀의 오랜 경력은 우리 회사에 매우 소중한 자산이 될 것입니다. 현재, 마케팅 부서는 대부분 업계에 새로 발을 들인 직원들로 구성되어 있기 때문에, 그들을 이끌면서 조언해 줄 수 있는 훌륭한 능력의 소유자가 필요합니다.

우리는 11월 14일 월요일 오후 6시 30분에 열리는 저녁 만찬과 함께 팀에 합류하시는 Wilk 씨를 정식으로 환영할 것입니다. Safari Grill에 여러 테이블이 마련되어 있으니 1층으로 내려가시기만 하면 됩니다.

2. Wilk 씨에 관해 언급된 것은 무엇인가?
(A) 몇 권의 책을 썼다.
(B) 대학에서 강의한다.
(C) 여러 개의 상을 받았다.
(D) 전에 Lockhart 씨와 함께 일했다.
| 해설 |
두 번째 문장에 여러 개의 상을 받은 적이 있다는(Ms. Wilk has received several awards ~) 내용이 있으므로 (C)가 정답이다.
| 어휘 | on behalf of ~을 대표해, 대신해 express ~을 표현하다 excitement 흥분(감) in charge of ~을 책임지는 receive ~을 받다 several 여럿의 throughout ~ 동안에 걸쳐 including ~을 포함해 prestigious 권위 있는 invaluable 매우 소중한 asset 자산 currently 현재 be made up of ~로 구성되다 filed 업계 accomplished 뛰어난 능력을 지닌 mentor ~에게 조언해 주다 officially 정식으로 head down to ~가 있는 아래로 내려 가다 multiple 여럿의

다음 양식을 참조하시오.

Cleo Catering Company: 모든 특별 행사를 위한 최고의 음식

저희 Cleo Catering Company에서는 여러분께 서비스를 제공해 드릴 수 있기를 고대합니다. 잠시 시간 내셔서 아래의 정보를 작성해 주시기 바랍니다. 그 후에 여러분의 개별 요구 사항에 적합한 서비스를 추천해 드리기 위해 전화 드릴 수 있습니다.

고객 성명: _____ 전화 번호: _____
행사 날짜: _____

원하시는 식사 종류: [ ] 뷔페 스타일 [ ] 좌석 식사 [ ] 다과만 필요함

행사 유형: [ ] 비격식 행사 [ ] 일부 격식을 갖춘 행사 [ ] 격식을 갖춘 행사
손님 숫자: [ ] 최대 20명 [ ] 21-50명 [ ] 51-100명 [ ] 101명 이상
행사 개최 도시: [ ] Delmar [ ] Glenview [ ] Kendale [ ] Overton
장식물 요청 여부: [ ] 네 [ ] 아니오
음식물 수령 방식: [ ] 직접 가져 감 [ ] 배달

3. Cleo Catering Company에 관해 언급된 것은 무엇인가?
(A) 격식을 갖춘 행사에 음식을 공급하는 일을 전문으로 한다.
(B) 제공된 답변들을 바탕으로 서비스를 추천해 준다.
(C) 급한 통보에 대해서는 음식을 제공할 수 없다.
(D) 최대 100명의 사람들이 참석하는 행사에 서비스를 제공할 수 있다.

| 해설 |
첫 단락에 아래의 정보를 양식에 작성하고 나면 적합한 서비스를 추천해 준다는(Please take a moment to fill out the information below. We can then call you with recommendations ~) 말이 쓰여 있으므로 이에 해당되는 (B)가 정답이다.

| 어휘 | exquisite 최고의, 훌륭한   occasion 행사, 경우   look forward to -ing ~하기를 고대하다   take a moment to do 잠시 시간 내어 ~하다   fill out ~을 작성하다   below 아래에   suit ~에 적합하다, 알맞다   desire 요구, 바람, 희망   desired 원하는   sit-down 자리에 앉아서 하는   refreshments 다과   up to 최대 ~의   formal 격식을 갖춘   decorations 장식(물)   required 필요한, 필수의   receipt 수령, 받음   specialize in ~을 전문으로 하다   supply ~을 공급하다   based on ~을 바탕으로   be unable to do ~할 수 없다   on short notice 급히 통보해서, 예고 없이

패러프레이징 연습
본책 p.269

A.
1. (D) 의사와 간호사들 → 의료진
2. (C) 10년 동안 운영되고 있는 → 10년 전에 설립되다
3. (A) 운영 방식을 개선하다 → 절차를 개선하다
4. (E) 등산객들과 운전자들 모두 → 보행자들과 운전자들
5. (B) 새로운 종류의 신발 → 다른 곳에서 본 적이 없는 신발

B.
6. 고객들은 전국의 100곳이 넘는 지점에서 운동복 제품을 쇼핑하실 수 있습니다.
Q. 업체에 관해 언급된 것은 무엇인가?
(A) 다수의 매장을 운영하고 있다.   (B) 주말에 문을 연다.

7. Ford Bridge의 공사 책임자는 작업자들이 예상보다 더 많은 시간을 필요로 한다고 말한다.
Q. 프로젝트에 관해 언급된 것은 무엇인가?
(A) 예상보다 더 오래 걸릴 것이다.   (B) 현재 점검을 받고 있다.

8. Glanmire 카페의 감자 수프가 <Atlanta News> 독자들에 의해 '가장 인기 있는 새로운 요리'로 선정되었다.
Q. Glanmire 카페에 관해 암시된 것은 무엇인가?
(A) 인기 있는 메뉴 제품을 제공한다.
(B) 지역 내에 새로 생긴 레스토랑이다.

9. 저희 무료 시식 행사에 대한 예약은 보통 빠르게 채워지므로, 주저하지 마시고 예약하시기 바랍니다!
Q. 무료 시식 행사에 관해 언급된 것은 무엇인가?
(A) 일년 내내 제공된다.   **(B) 수요가 높을 가능성이 있다.**

10. 조경 건축가 Rodrigo Diego 씨가 주변 환경과 조화를 이룰 수 있도록 그 건물의 정원을 디자인했다.
Q. 정원에 관해 암시된 것은 무엇인가?
(A) 완공하는 데 오랜 시간이 걸렸다.   **(B) 자연 환경과 잘 조화된다.**

DAY 18 | 실전문제
본책 p.270

정답 **1** (B) **2** (D) **3** (C) **4** (B) **5** (C) **6** (B)
       7 (B) **8** (D) **9** (B)

1-2번 문제는 다음 송장을 참조하시오.

거래 내역서	Evergreen Movers	
고객: Jessie Bartz		
2(B) 작업 시 집합 장소: 658 Ashcroft Way		
1 물품 운송 장소: 1392 Rutherford Court		
시작 날짜 및 시간: 5월 10일 오전 8시		

내역	수량	단가	소계
중형 상자 **2(C)** (24″×18″×16″)	12	2.75달러	33.00달러
소형 상자 **2(C)** (18″×12″×12″)	12	1.95달러	23.40달러
발포 비닐 (80피트 롤)	1	8.99달러	8.99달러
스티커 라벨 (25개짜리 롤)	1	0.00달러	0.00달러
1 물품 포장 및 운송 담당 직원 (2명)	7.5시간 (점심 시간 제외)	55.00달러 (2인 1조당)	412.50달러
2(A) 저희 회계부의 Cynthia Glenn 씨에게 늦어도 5월 12일까지는 총 비용을 송금해 주십시오. Glenn 씨는 555-4113번으로 연락 가능합니다.			총계: 477.89달러

| 어휘 | invoice 거래 내역서   pickup point 집합 장소   description 설명   quantity 수량   price per unit 개당 단가   subtotal 소계   bubble wrap (완충용) 발포 비닐   pack (짐 등) ~을 싸다   transport ~을 운송하다   crew (함께 작업하는) 조, 팀   exclude ~을 제외하다   remit ~을 송금하다   no later than 늦어도 ~까지는   accounting 회계   reach ~에게 연락하다

1. Evergreen Movers는 어떤 종류의 회사인가?
(A) 포장재 공급업체
(B) 이삿짐 업체
(C) 조경 회사
(D) 가구점

| 해설 |
송장 초반부에 물품 운송 장소(Moving items to)가 나와 있고, 도표 하단에 물품 포장 및 운송 직원(Packing and Transport Crew)이 언급된 것으로 보아 (B)가 정답임을 알 수 있다.

| 어휘 | supplier 공급자, 공급업체   packing material 포장재   landscaping 조경

2. 거래 내역서에 언급되지 않은 것은 무엇인가?
(A) 지불되는 금액을 받는 사람
(B) 직원들이 처음 가야 하는 곳
(C) 사용되는 상자의 사이즈
(D) 점심 시간이 지속되는 시간

| 해설 |
도표 하단의 'Please remit the total payment ~ to Cynthia Glenn ~' 부분에 (A)에서 언급하는 비용 수납 담당자가 명시되었고, 지문 상단의 'Meeting at pickup point'에 (B)에서 말하는 직원들이 처음 가야 하는 장소가 제시되어 있다. 또한, 도표 상단의 (24″×18″×16″)와 (18″×12″×12″)에서 상자의 규격도 확인할 수 있다. 하지만 점심 시간의 길이는 제시되어 있지 않으므로 (D)가 정답이다.

| 어휘 | submit a payment 지불 금액을 내다   container 상자, 용기   last 지속되다

3-6번 문제는 다음 웹사이트를 참조하시오.

> **Educomp**
> **온라인 학습 완성**
>
> Educomp Foundation은 지금까지 10년 넘게 법조계에서 접하고 있는 **3** 중대한 사안들에 관해 학습자들을 교육해 오고 있습니다. 저희 세미나는 **4(C)** 오로지 온라인상에서만 시청하실 수 있으며, 학생들과 젊은 전문가들에게 모두 매우 인기 있는 것으로 드러났습니다. 현재까지, **4(A)** 150만 명의 구독자들이 동영상을 시청하셨으며, 많은 분들이 긍정적인 의견을 남겨 주셨습니다. 학습자들은 흔히 저희 세미나의 지속 시간이 가장 만족스러운 측면들 중 하나라고 언급하고 있습니다. **4(D)** 각 재생 시간이 최대 길이 45분이기 때문에, 일정이나 생활이 바쁘신 분들께도 이상적입니다.
>
> 앞으로 제공될 다양한 강연이나 세미나에 관해 알아보시려면, 성명과 주소를 이 웹 사이트의 "더 알려 주세요" 섹션에 입력하시기만 하면 됩니다. 그 후에 **5** 저희 직원들이 여러분께 연간 카탈로그를 발송해 드릴 것입니다. 때때로, **6** 저희는 일부 개인 및 기업들에게 저희 강연 DVD를 받아 소장하실 수 있게 해 드리고 있습니다. 이 부분에 관심이 있으신 분께서는, 25달러의 우편환 양식을 작성해 주셔야 합니다. 이는 저희 웹 사이트에서 다운로드 하실 수 있습니다. 인쇄하신 후에 상세 정보를 기입해 주시기 바랍니다. 작성하시고 나면, 은행으로 가져가셔서 주문을 완료하실 수 있습니다. 이 금액을 저희가 수령하면, 저희가 이용하는 택배업체에서 영업일로 10일 이내에 DVD를 배송해 드릴 것입니다.

| 어휘 | perfection 완성   critical 중대한   issue 사안, 문제   face ~을 접하다, 마주하다   law industry 법조계   over ~가 넘는   exclusively 오로지, 독점적으로   available 이용 가능한   view 보다   prove 형용사 ~한 것으로 드러나다   extremely 대단히, 극히   A and B alike A와 B에게 동일하게   to date 현재까지   subscriber 구독자, 가입자   positive 긍정적인   state ~을 언급하다, 말하다   duration 지속 시간   pleasing 만족스러운   aspect 측면   maximum 최대의   ideal 이상적인   find out about ~에 관해 알아 보다   upcoming 다가오는   one's range of 다양한   then 그 후에   annual 연간의, 연례의   on occasion 때때로   allow A to do A가 ~할 수 있게 해 주다   individual 사람, 개인   obtain ~을 얻다   fill out ~을 작성하다   money order 우편환   form 양식   details 상세 정보   once 일단 ~하고 나면   complete 완료된, ~을 완료하다   sum 금액, 합계   courier 택배업체   within ~ 이내에

3. 첫 번째 단락, 첫 번째 줄의 단어 "critical"과 의미가 가장 가까운 것은 무엇인가?
(A) 위험한
(B) 부정적인
(C) 중요한
(D) 불확실한

| 해설 |
해당 문장에서 critical은 학습 내용을 나타내는 전치사 on의 목적어 issues를 수식하고 있는데, 법조계에서 접하고 있는 문제라는 말이 이어지는 것을 볼 때 '중요한'이라는 뜻으로 쓰였음을 알 수 있다. 따라서 '중요한'을 뜻하는 또 다른 형용사 (C)가 정답이다.

4. Educomp의 세미나에 관해 언급되지 않은 것은 무엇인가?
(A) 1백만 명이 넘는 사람들이 시청했다.
(B) 오직 학생들만 참석할 수 있다.
(C) 오직 인터넷으로만 시청 가능하다.
(D) 1시간 미만으로 지속된다.

| 해설 |
첫 단락 초반부의 'exclusively available to view online'에서 (C)를, 그 뒤에 이어지는 'To date, 1.5 million subscribers ~'에서 (A)를, 그리고 같은 단락 마지막 문장의 'maximum length of 45 minutes'에서 (D)를 각각 확인할 수 있다. 하지만 같은 단락 중반부에 학생들과 직장인들에게 모두 인기가 있다고 했으므로 (B)가 정답이다.

| 어휘 | attend ~에 참석하다   last 지속되다

5. Educomp에 관해 언급된 것은 무엇인가?
(A) 15년 넘게 운영되어 오고 있다.
(B) 현재 다른 도시로 이전하는 중이다.
(C) 일 년에 한번 카탈로그를 만든다.
(D) 작년에 큰 수익을 기록했다.

| 해설 |
두 번째 단락 초반부에, 직원들이 연간 카탈로그(our annual catalog)를 발송해 준다는 말이 있는데, 이를 통해 일 년에 한번 카탈로그를 만드는 것을 알 수 있으므로 (C)가 정답이다.

| 어휘 | in business 운영 중인, 영업 중인   currently 현재   relocate to ~로 이전하다   profit 수익   previous 이전의, 과거의

6. 독자들은 어떻게 강연 자료 DVD를 받을 수 있는가?
(A) 웹 사이트에 정보를 제출함으로써
(B) 비용을 지불함으로써
(C) 동영상 파일을 다운로드함으로써
(D) 택배업체에 연락함으로써

| 해설 |
DVD를 구하는 방법이 언급된 두 번째 단락 후반부에, 25달러의 우편환 양식을 작성해 은행에 가져가서 주문하는 방법이(you will need to fill out a money order form for $25. ~ you can take this to your bank to complete the order ~) 언급되었는데, 이는 결국 비용 지불을 뜻하는 것이므로 (B)가 정답이다.

| 어휘 | material 자료, 재료   submit ~을 제출하다   contact ~에게 연락하다

7-9번 문제는 다음 광고를 참조하시오.

> **Lamont 조경**: 여러분의 건물 가치를 높이고 정원이 최상의 상태로 보이도록 유지하십시오!
>
> **7** Lamont 조경은 약 30년 전에 Jason Lamont 씨에 의해 설립되었으며, Lamont 씨는 지역 대학교를 다니기 위해 Meadowcreek으로 이사했지만, 나중에 이곳에서 개인 사업을 시작하기로 결심했습니다.
>
> **8** Lamont 조경은 가족 소유로 운영되는 업체로, 고객들을 위해 스타일과 기능성의 완벽한 조화를 만들어 내기 위해 애쓰고 있습니다. 처음 문을 열었을 당시, **9(C)** 팀은 오직 소규모 주거 프로젝트만 맡아서 진행했습니다. 하지만, 시간이 흘러, 업계 선두 주자로서의 입지를 확고히 해 오면서, 규모가 더 큰 프로젝트를 맡게 되었고, **9(D)** 상업용 건물에 대해서도 작업을 하게 되었습니다. **9(D)** 이제 Lamont 조경은 심지어 프로젝트에 필요한 꽃과 나무, 그리고 관목을 제공하기 위한

자체 비닐하우스까지 보유하고 있습니다. 또한 긴급 대응 서비스도 추가했는데, **9(A)** 이를 통해 관개 수로가 망가지거나 나무가 쓰러졌을 경우에 대비해 직원들이 24시간 긴급 전화에 대응하고 있습니다.

2년 전에, **8** Rachel Zager 씨가 회사의 운영을 맡았으며, 훌륭한 고객 서비스라는 전통을 이어가고 있습니다. Lamont 조경에 관해 더 많은 것을 알아보시려면, www.lamontlandscaping.com을 방문하시기 바랍니다.

| 어휘 | property 건물, 부동산 value 가치 keep A -ing A가 계속 ~하도록 하다 found ~을 설립하다 relocate to ~로 이사하다 decide to do ~하기로 결심하다 family-owned-and-operated 가족 소유로 운영되는 strive to do ~하기 위해 애쓰다 blend of ~의 조합, 혼합 functionality 기능성 residential 주거의 over time 시간이 흘러 establish oneself as ~로서의 입지를 확고히 하다 industry leader 업계 선두주자 take on ~을 맡다 commercial 상업용의 as well ~도, 또한 shrub 관목 add ~을 추가하다 emergency response 긴급 대응 respond to ~에 대응하다 around the clock 24시간으로 in case of ~의 경우에 (대비해) irrigation pipe 관개 수로 fallen 쓰러진 assume (책임 등) ~을 맡다 continue ~을 이어가다 tradition 전통

7. 이 광고는 어디에서 볼 수 있을 것 같은가?
(A) 여행 가이드에서
(B) 지역 신문에서
(C) 대학교에서
(D) 직업 박람회에서

| 해설 |
첫 단락에 Lamont Landscaping이라는 업체가 해당 지역을 'here(이곳)'이라는 말로 소개하며 회사의 광고를 위해 설립 배경부터 설명하고 있는데 이러한 내용은 지역 신문에서 찾아볼 수 있는 것이므로 (B)가 정답이다.

8. Zager 씨에 관해 무엇이 사실일 것 같은가?
(A) 고객 서비스 콜 센터를 열었다.
(B) Meadowcreek을 벗어나 이사했다.
(C) 사업 방향을 바꾸고 싶어 한다.
(D) Jason Lamont 씨의 친척이다.

| 해설 |
Zager 씨의 이름이 언급된 마지막 단락에 Rachel Zager 씨가 2년 전에 회사 운영을 맡았다고(Rachel Zager assumed control of the business) 쓰여 있고, 두 번째 단락에 가족 소유로 운영되는 업체라고(a family-owned-and-operated business) 밝혔다. 따라서 Zager 씨는 설립자로 언급된 Jason Lamont 씨와 친인척 관계에 있는 사람임을 알 수 있으므로 (D)가 정답이다.

| 어휘 | move out of ~에서 이사 가다 direction 방향 relative 인척, 친척

9. 업체가 변경된 방식으로 언급되지 않은 것은 무엇인가?
(A) 일부 서비스를 하루 24시간 이용 가능하게 만들었다.
(B) 정부 건물을 위한 프로젝트를 확보했다.
(C) 서비스를 제공하는 건물의 종류를 늘렸다.
(D) 일부 자체 자재를 공급하기 시작했다.

| 해설 |
두 번째 단락 마지막에 24시간 이용 가능한 서비스(respond to emergency calls around the clock)가 언급된 부분에서 (A)를, 같은 단락 초반부에 소규모 주거지 프로젝트에서 상업용 건물로 서비스가 확대된(only worked on small residential projects. ~ working at commercial properties as well) 사실이 언급된 부분에서 (C)를, 그리고 자체 비닐하우스를 통해 프로젝트에 필요한 식물 재배를(~ has its own greenhouse to provide ~) 언급한 부분에서 (D)도 확인할 수 있다. 하지만 정부 건물과 관련된 내용은 없으므로 (B)가 정답이다.

| 어휘 | make A available A를 이용 가능하게 만들다, 제공하다 secure ~을 확보하다 expand ~을 늘리다, 확대하다 supply ~을 공급하다 material 자재, 재료

DAY 19 문장 넣기/의도 파악/동의어 찾기 유형

01 문장 넣기 유형

기출 유형 맛보기   본책 p.274

[지시어가 단서인 경우]

> 그 레스토랑 지배인은 더 많은 고객들을 상대하기 위한 창의적인 방법을 필요로 했기 때문에, 건물 옥상을 깨끗이 치우고 테이블과 의자를 마련했습니다. —[1]—. 현재 이 업체는 봄과 여름에 거의 두 배에 달하는 수의 예약을 받고 있으며, 이로 인해 매출이 증대하고 기억에 남을 만한 경험을 만들어 드리고 있습니다. —[2]—.

Q. [1], [2]로 표시된 위치들 중에서, 다음 문장이 들어가기에 가장 적절한 곳은 어디인가?
"그 공간은 곧 식사 손님들에게 인기를 얻게 되었습니다."
(A) [1]
(B) [2]

[접속부사가 단서인 경우]

> 어제 열린 시의회 회의에서, 의원들은 시 자금에서 25,000달러가 넘는 금액을 지역 사회의 여러 단체에 제공하는 계획을 승인했습니다. 이는 500달러에서 1,000달러까지의 금액으로 지급될 것입니다. —[1]—. 단체들은 반드시 시에 등록된 상태여야 하며, 최소 10명의 활동 인원을 보유하고 있어야 합니다. 이 자금을 신청하기 위해서는, www.cottonwoodcity.gov/funding을 방문해 필수 영역들을 작성 완료해야 합니다. —[2]—

Q. [1], [2]로 표시된 위치들 중에서, 다음 문장이 들어가기에 가장 적절한 곳은 어디인가?
"또는, 시청에서 종이 문서로 된 신청서를 가져가시기 바랍니다."
(A) [1]
(B) [2]

PRACTICE | 기출 연습하기   본책 p.275

정답 **1** (C)   **2** (A)   **3** (D)

다음 이메일을 참조하시오.

> Molina 씨께,
>
> —[1]—. 저희 기록에 따르면 귀하의 <Home Decorating Monthly> 구독 기간이 8월 31일에 만료되는 것으로 나타납니다. —[2]—. 저희 잡지의 월간 간행물을 계속 받고자 하시면, 구독 서비스 갱신을 위해 동봉해 드린 신청서를 돌려 보내 주십시오. —[3]—. 단 한 권의 잡지도 놓치지 않기 위해, 이 문제를 처리하는 데 있어 지체하지 마시기 바랍니다. —[4]—.

1. [1], [2], [3], [4]로 표시된 위치들 중에서, 다음 문장이 들어가기에 가장 적절한 곳은 어디인가?
"계정 관리팀이 그 후에 귀하께 서비스에 대한 청구서를 발송해 드릴 것입니다."

(A) [1] (B) [2] **(C) [3]** (D) [4]

| 해설 |
제시된 문장은 부사 then으로 보아 함께 특정한 일 이후에 발생하는 것으로서 상대방에게 서비스 청구서를 발송해 준다는 의미를 나타낸다. 이는 상대방인 고객이 신청서를 돌려 보낸(send back the enclosed application) 이후에 발생되는 조치로 판단할 수 있으므로 [3]에 들어가야 앞 문장과의 흐름이 자연스럽다. 따라서 (C)가 정답이다.

| 어휘 | subscription 구독, 서비스 가입   expire 만료되다   continue -ing 계속 ~하다   receive ~을 받다   issue (잡지 등의) 호   enclosed 동봉된   application 신청(서)   renewal 갱신   ensure that 반드시 ~하도록 하다   miss ~을 놓치다   delay 지체하다   take care of ~을 처리하다   account 계정, 계좌   then 그 후에, 그런 다음   bill 고지서, 청구서

다음 편지를 참조하시오.

Nazario 씨께,

매년, 저희는 <Insider Monthly>의 모든 구독자분들께 저희 출판물의 어느 섹션을 즐겨 읽으시는지, 그리고 무슨 종류의 기사를 보기를 원하시는지 알기 위해 독자 설문지를 보내 드리고 있습니다. 귀하께서는 아직 설문 양식을 돌려 보내지 않으셨습니다. —[1]—. 귀하와 같은 독자로부터 얻는 의견을 통해, 저희는 채굴 장비와, 굴착 작업 안전, 그리고 광산 관련 규제에 관해 높은 평가를 받는 권위 있는 매체로 남을 수 있습니다. —[2]—. 귀하의 편의를 위해 설문지 1부를 다시 동봉해 드렸습니다. —[3]—. 작성을 완료하신 후에 뒷면에 인쇄되어 있는 주소로 돌려 보내 주시기 바랍니다. —[4]—. 그렇게 해 주시면, Walton Industries에서 제공하는 1,000달러 상당의 상품권을 받으실 수 있는 추첨 행사에 자동으로 참여하시게 될 것입니다.

안녕히 계십시오.

Darwin Alvez

---

2. [1], [2], [3], [4]로 표시된 위치들 중에서, 다음 문장이 들어가기에 가장 적절한 곳은 어디인가?

"이것이 단순히 실수일 경우, 여전히 참여할 시간이 있으므로 안심하시기 바랍니다."

(A) [1] (B) [2] (C) [3] (D) [4]

| 해설 |
제시된 문장은 앞서 언급된 것을 대신하는 this와 함께 그 일이 실수일 경우에 안심하도록 당부하는 내용이다. 따라서 [1]에 들어가 아직 설문 양식을 돌려 보내지 않았더라도(You have yet to return your survey form) 여전히 참여 가능하다는 사실을 알리는 흐름이 되어야 알맞으므로 (A)가 정답이다.

| 어휘 | survey 설문(지)   subscriber 구독자, 서비스 가입자   find out ~을 알아보다   publication 출판(물)   have yet to do 아직 ~하지 않았다   through ~을 통해   ensure that 꼭 ~하도록 하다   remain ~로 유지되다, 계속 남아 있다   respected 높은 평가를 받는   authority 권위자   extraction 채굴   equipment 장비   drilling 굴착   mine-related 광산과 관련된   regulation 규제   enclose ~을 동봉하다   convenience 편의   complete ~을 작성 완료하다   enter A into B A를 B에 참가시키다   drawing 추첨   gift certificate 상품권   oversight 실수, 간과   rest assured that ~이므로 안심하십시오   participate 참여하다

다음 공지를 참조하시오.

신청서를 받고 있습니다

Kenwood Nature Trust(KNT)에서는 지역 사회 정원 프로젝트를 개발할 수 있는 비영리 단체를 찾고 있습니다. —[1]—. 도시의 북쪽 끝자락에 위치한 4에이커의 부지가 시에 기부되었습니다. KNT는 이 부지를 개인 용도로 활용할 수 없는 소규모 토지로 전환하는 프로젝트에 자금을 제공할 것입니다. —[2]—. 이는 아파트 건물에서 생활하면서 화분 외에는 각자 원하는 꽃이나 채소를 심을 장소가 없는 대부분의 Kenwood 지역 주민들에게 원예를 즐거운 취미로서 이용할 수 있게 해 줄 것입니다.

관심 있는 분들께서는 KNT의 웹 사이트 www.kenwoodnature.org를 방문하시기 바랍니다. —[3]—. 소속 단체의 비영리성을 보여주는 증명서와 함께 제안하시고자 하는 정원의 디자인을 업로드해 주셔야 합니다. —[4]—.

---

3. [1], [2], [3], [4]로 표시된 위치들 중에서, 다음 문장이 들어가기에 가장 적절한 곳은 어디인가?

"예상 작업 진행표와 같은 추가 서류 또한 제공해 주시면 감사하겠습니다."

(A) [1] (B) [2] (C) [3] **(D) [4]**

| 해설 |
제시된 문장은 추가 사항을 말할 때 사용하는 also와 함께 추가로 필요한 서류를 언급하고 있다. 따라서 제출해야 하는 서류들이 언급되는 문장 (They should upload a design ~ along with a certificate showing ~) 뒤에 위치한 [4]에 들어가 서류와 관련된 추가 정보를 말하는 흐름이 되어야 알맞으므로 (D)가 정답이다.

| 어휘 | application 신청(서)   accept ~을 받아들이다   seek ~을 찾다, 구하다   nonprofit 비영리의   organization 단체, 기관   develop ~을 개발하다   donate A to B A를 B에게 기부하다   finance ~에 자금을 제공하다   convert A to B A를 B로 전환하다, 탈바꿈시키다   plot (작은) 땅, 토지   for individual use 개인 용도의   make A available A를 이용 가능하게 만들다   gardening 원예   resident 주민   the majority of 대부분의   with nowhere to do ~할 곳이 없는 채로   plant ~을 심다   except ~을 제외하고   party 사람, 당사자   proposed 제안된   along with ~와 함께   certificate 증명서, 인증서   status 상태, 상황   additional 추가의   estimated 예상된, 추정의   timeline 진행 상황표   appreciate ~에 대해 감사하다

02 의도 파악 유형

기출 유형 맛보기
본책 p.277

Charles Jensen [오전 9:26] 좋은 소식입니다! Stockton 사와의 계약이 체결되었습니다. 우리의 새 제휴 업체로서, 그곳에서 다음 달부터 북서 지역을 맡게 될 겁니다.

Ki-woo Choi [오전 9:27] 정말 잘됐네요! 그렇게 되면 고객들에게 제품을 배송하는 데 드는 시간이 줄어들 거예요.

Beth Saldivar [오전 9:28] 제 생각이 바로 그거예요.

Q. 오전 9시 28분에, Saldivar 씨가 "My thoughts exactly"라고 썼을 때 의미한 것은 무엇이겠는가?
(A) 회사는 사무실을 다른 지역으로 옮겨야 한다.
(B) 회사의 제품 배송이 더욱 신속히 이뤄질 것이다.

PRACTICE | 기출 연습하기
본책 p.278

정답 1 (B)   2 (C)

다음 온라인 채팅을 참조하시오.

Vineet Dhebar, 오전 8:32
Jieun, 거의 도착하셨나요? 발표가 약 90분 후에 시작됩니다.

Jieun Choi, 오전 8:33
가는 중이에요. Custer 다리에 사고가 나는 바람에, 차들이 밀려 있어요. 준비 작업을 시작해 주시겠어요?

Vineet Dhebar, 오전 8:34
알겠습니다. 마이크와 프로젝트를 연결해 드릴 수 있어요.

Jieun Choi, 오전 8:35
감사합니다. 필요하실 경우, 그 행사장에 있는 여분의 전선을 사용하실 수 있어요.

Vineet Dhebar, 오전 8:36
좋습니다. 와, 사람들이 이미 등록 테이블에 줄을 서고 있어요, 심지어 9시 30분이나 되어야 개방하는데요.

Jieun Choi, 오전 8:37
이럴 수가! 사람들이 앞쪽과 가까운 좋은 자리를 원하는 것 같아요.

1. 오전 8시 37분에, Choi 씨가 "No way"라고 썼을 때 의미한 것은 무엇이겠는가?
(A) 앞쪽과 가까운 자리를 이용할 수 없어서 실망하고 있다.
(B) 일부 사람들이 일찍 도착한 것에 대해 놀라고 있다.
(C) Dhebar 씨의 제안에 강력히 반대하고 있다.
(D) 행사장에 9시 30분까지 도착할 수 있을 것으로 생각하지 않는다.

| 해설 |
앞서 Dhebar 씨가 9시 30분이나 되어야 문을 여는데도 사람들이 벌써 줄을 서고 있다고(people are already lining up ~ which doesn't even open until nine thirty) 말한 것에 대한 반응으로 'No way'라고 답변하는 상황입니다. 따라서 사람들이 일찍 도착한 것에 대한 놀라움에 해당되는 말이라는 것을 알 수 있으므로 (B)가 정답이다.

| 어휘 | presentation 발표 in + 시간 ~ 후에 about 약, 대략 on one's way 가는 중인, 오는 중인 traffic 차량들, 교통 backed up 밀려 있는 get A ready A를 준비하다 hook up ~을 연결하다 venue 행사장 extra 여분의, 별도의 registration 등록 not A until B B나 되어야 A하다 near ~에 가까운 be disappointed that ~해서 실망하다 available 이용 가능한 be surprised that ~해서 놀라다 arrive 도착하다 disagree with ~에 반대하다 proposal 제안(서) get to ~로 가다 by (기한) ~까지

다음 문자 메시지 대화를 참조하시오.

Marco Malakian [오후 1:12]
Wendy 씨… Viscotti Fine Foods의 직원 한 분이 전화하셔서 내부 인원 문제로 인해 4월 8일에 있을 우리 제품 출시 행사에 출장 요리를 제공해 줄 수 없을 거라고 얘기하셨어요.

Wendy Partridge [오후 1:15]
흠… 우리가 어떻게 해야 하는지 제가 마케팅 부장님께 여쭤 볼까요?

Marco Malakian [오후 1:18]
저, Ramsay Road에 위치한 Primo Catering에 알아볼 수 있을 거예요. 비즈니스 관련 행사장으로 인기 있는 곳이기는 한데, 이미 일정이 꽉 차 있을지도 몰라요.

Wendy Partridge [오후 1:20]
제가 확인해 볼게요.

Marco Malakian [오후 1:24]
아주 좋습니다. 그리고 그곳이 너무 바쁠 경우에, 제가 마케팅 부장님과 만나서 대안을 마련해 볼게요.

Wendy Partridge [오후 1:27]
좋아요. 곧 다시 얘기해요.

2. 오후 1시 20분에, Partridge 씨가 "I'll check it out"이라고 썼을 때 의미한 것은 무엇이겠는가?
(A) 제품 출시 행사가 연기될 수 있는지 알아볼 것이다.
(B) Viscotti Fine Foods에서 제공하는 서비스의 상세 정보를 검토할 것이다.

이다.
(C) Primo Catering의 이용 가능 여부에 대해 문의할 것이다.
(D) Ramsay Road에 있는 행사장을 예약하려고 시도할 것이다.

| 해설 |
제시된 문장은 '확인해 보겠다'는 의미이며, 앞서 Malakian 씨가 Primo Catering에 알아볼 수는 있지만 일정이 꽉 차 있을 수도 있다고 말한 것에 대한 반응으로 쓰였다. 따라서 그 업체의 일정을 자신이 확인해 보겠다는 뜻으로 말한 문장임을 알 수 있으므로 Primo Catering의 이용 가능 여부에 대한 문의를 의미하는 (C)가 정답이다.

| 어휘 | representative 직원 be able to do ~할 수 있다 cater ~에 출장 요리를 제공하다 launch 출시, 공개 staffing 인원 운용, 직원 채용 want A to do A가 ~하기를 원하다 try ~에 한번 알아보다 check A out A를 확인해 보다 get together with ~와 만나다, 모이다 alternative 대안의, 대체하는 whether ~인지 (아닌지) postpone ~을 연기하다 review ~을 검토하다 details 상세 정보 inquire about ~에 대해 문의하다 availability 이용 가능 여부 attempt to do ~하도록 시도하다 reserve ~을 예약하다 venue 행사장

03 동의어 찾기 유형

기출 유형 맛보기
본책 p.280

그 사무용품점은 총 금액이 최소 200달러가 되는 용품의 주문에 대해 배송비를 부담할 것이다.

Q. 첫 번째 단락, 첫 번째 줄의 'cover'와 의미가 가장 가까운 것은?
(A) 설명하다
(B) 지불하다
(C) 보호하다
(D) 숨기다

PRACTICE | 기출 연습하기
본책 p.281

정답 1 (A)   2 (D)   3 (B)   4 (C)   5 (A)   6 (B)
      7 (D)   8 (D)   9 (C)   10 (C) 11 (A) 12 (D)

1. (A)
| 해석 |
3월 3일 행사를 취재하기 위해 초청된 기자 명단은 저희 웹사이트에서 찾을 수 있습니다.
(A) ~에 대해 보도하다
(B) 보호하다
(C) 창조하다
(D) 지불하다
| 해설 |
문장 속에서 cover the event는 journalists(언론인, 기자)가 행하는 행위이므로 '행사를 취재하다'라는 의미로 사용되었음을 알 수 있다. 따라서 '보도하다'라는 의미인 (A) report on이 정답이다.
| 어휘 | journalist 언론인, 기자 invite 초대하다

2. (D)
| 해설 |
단일 포커스 그룹으로부터 나온 결과가 반드시 대중들의 의견을 반영하는 것은 아니므로, 추가적인 시장 조사가 바람직하다.
(A) 참석하다
(B) ~에 대해 생각하다
(C) 기억하다
(D) 보여주다
| 해설 |
주어인 '포커스 그룹에서 나온 결과'는 목적어인 '대중들의 의견'을 보여주는 것이므로 reflect가 '반영하다, 보여주다'라는 의미로 사용되었음을 알

수 있다. 따라서 '보여주다'라는 의미의 (D) show가 정답이다.

| 어휘 | focus group 포커스 그룹(시장 조사를 위한 그룹)   not necessarily 반드시 ~은 아닌   public opinion 여론, 대중들의 의견   further 그 이상의   advisable 권장되는

3. (B)
| 해석 |
관광객과 사업가들이 이 지역에 끌리면서 도시는 경제 성장을 이룰 것으로 예상된다.
(A) 유발했다
(B) 끌었다
(C) 삽화를 넣었다
(D) 움직였다
| 해설 |
관광객들과 사업가들이 해당 지역에 끌린 것이므로 draw는 '끌어당기다'라는 의미로 사용되었음을 알 수 있다. 따라서 '끌다, 매료시키다'라는 의미의 (B) attracted가 정답이다.

| 어휘 | economic growth 경제 성장   tourist 관광객   business people 사업가

4. (C)
| 해석 |
우리는 회사에 중요한 공헌을 하는 사람들을 표창하기 위해 시상식을 개최할 것입니다.
(A) 깨닫다
(B) 받아들이다
(C) 명예를 주다
(D) 찬성하다
| 해설 |
목적어가 '회사에 중요한 공헌을 하는 사람들'이므로 recognize가 문장 속에서 '표창하다'라는 의미로 사용되었음을 알 수 있다. 따라서, 이와 의미상 가장 유사한 '(공로 등) 치하하다, 명예를 주다'라는 뜻을 가진 (C) honor를 정답으로 선택한다.

| 어휘 | ceremony 의식, 식   those who ~하는 사람들   make a contribution 기여하다   significant 상당한

5. (A)
| 해석 |
저희는 모든 소포를 완벽한 상태로 배송하기 위해 최선을 다하지만, 때때로 손상되기 쉬운 물건들은 깨질 수도 있습니다.
(A) 상태
(B) 제공
(C) 연습
(D) 규칙
| 해설 |
의미상 소포의 배송을 '완벽한 상태'로 하는 것이므로 condition이 '상태'라는 의미로 사용되었다. 따라서, 이와 같은 의미를 가진 (A) state가 정답이다.

| 어휘 | do one's best 최선을 다하다   package 소포   fragile 깨지기 쉬운, 불안정한

6. (B)
Brooks 씨가 지원서의 첫 절반을 검토할 것이며, Cooper 씨가 나머지를 처리할 것이다.
(A) 기초
(B) 나머지
(C) 상기시키는 것
(D) 정지, 멈춤
| 해설 |
the rest는 Cooper 씨가 처리할 분량을 나타내는데, 앞서 Brooks 씨가 절반을 맡는다는 말이 있으므로 나머지 절반을 의미한다는 것을 알 수 있

다. 따라서 '나머지'를 뜻하는 또 다른 명사인 (B)가 정답이다.

| 어휘 | look through ~을 검토하다   application 지원(서)   handle ~을 처리하다   rest 나머지

7. (D)
XL300 노트북 컴퓨터는 경량에 소형이며, 이로 인해 가격에 비해 뛰어난 가치를 지닌다.
(A) 지불 비용
(B) 견적(서)
(C) 원칙
(D) 싸게 사는 물건
| 해설 |
가격에 비해 뛰어난 가치를 지닌다는 특성을 말하고 있는데, 이와 같은 비용 가치는 싸게 산 물건에 해당되는 것이므로 (D)가 정답이다.

| 어휘 | lightweight 경량의   compact 소형의   make A B A를 B로 만들다   value 가치

8. (D)
귀하의 출품작인 <Children in the Rain>이 제7회 연례 Amateur Art Challenge의 수상 작품으로 선정되었습니다.
(A) 노력
(B) 잡지 구독
(C) 출입구
(D) 경연대회 제출 작품
| 해설 |
'be chosen as' 뒤에 위치하는 명사는 주어와 동격에 해당되므로 'Your entry'가 수상 작품(winner)임을 알 수 있다. 따라서 entry는 '출품작, 참가작'을 나타내므로 '경연대회 제출 작품'을 뜻하는 (D)가 정답이다.

| 어휘 | entry 출품작, 참가작   be chosen as ~로 선정되다   subscription 구독   submission 제출(되는 것)

9. (C)
그 교수는 화학 공학 분야의 손꼽히는 인물들과의 인터뷰를 특징으로 하는 교재를 선택했다.
(A) 아이디어
(B) 형태
(C) 사람들
(D) 숫자
| 해설 |
interviews와 함께 사용하는 전치사 with 뒤에는 인터뷰 대상자, 즉 사람 명사가 목적어로 쓰인다. 따라서 figures가 특정한 사람들을 가리킨다는 것을 알 수 있으므로 (C)가 정답이다.

| 어휘 | choose ~을 선택하다   feature ~을 특징으로 하다   leading 손꼽히는, 선도적인   field 분야   chemical engineering 화학 공학

10. (C)
Animal House는 여러분께서 휴가를 떠나신 동안 반려 동물을 극도로 주의해서 다룰 것을 약속 드립니다.
(A) 기쁘게 하다
(B) 고려하다
(C) 다루다
(D) 수리하다
| 해설 |
'극도로 주의해서'를 의미하는 'with the utmost care'는 반려 동물을 다루는 방식을 나타낸다. 따라서 treat이 '~을 다루다'라는 의미로 쓰였음을 알 수 있으므로 동일한 뜻으로 쓰이는 또 다른 동사인 (C) handle이 정답이다.

| 어휘 | promise to do ~하겠다고 약속하다   treat ~을 다루다   with care 주의해서, 조심스럽게   utmost 최고의, 극도의   while ~하는 동안   be away on vacation 휴가로 떠나 있는

11. (A)
여러분의 차량을 최상의 상태로 유지하시려면, 반드시 주기적으로 오일을 교환하고 타이어의 위치를 바꿔주셔야 합니다.
(A) 유지하다
(B) 배달하다
(C) 공표하다
(D) 테스트하다

| 해설 |
'최상의 상태로'를 의미하는 in top condition은 차량의 상태를 유지하는 방식에 해당되므로 maintain이 '~을 유지하다'라는 뜻으로 쓰였음을 알 수 있다. 따라서 이와 같은 의미로 사용되는 또 다른 동사인 (A) keep이 정답이다.

| 어휘 | maintain ~을 유지하다 vehicle 차량 be sure to do 반드시 ~하다 regularly 주기적으로 rotate ~을 교대시키다, 순환시키다

12. (D)
일정이 잠정적이기는 하지만, 현재로서는 Fox 씨께서 오후 2시에 발표를 하실 예정입니다.
(A) 가득 찬
(B) 실험적인
(C) 주저하는
(D) 분명하지 않은

| 해설 |
schedule의 보어로 쓰인 tentative는 일정상의 상황과 관련된 의미를 지닌다. 그런데 but절에 '지금으로선(for now)'이라는 말과 함께 현 상황에서만 알 수 있는 일정을 말하고 있으므로 확정된 상태가 아닌 것으로 판단할 수 있다. 따라서 '분명하지 않은'을 뜻하는 (D) indefinite이 정답이다.

| 어휘 | tentative 잠정적인 for now 현재로서는 be set to do ~할 예정이다

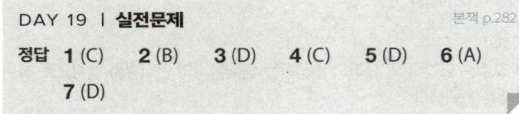

DAY 19 | 실전문제 본책 p.282
정답 1. (C) 2. (B) 3. (D) 4. (C) 5. (D) 6. (A)
      7. (D)

1-3번 문제는 다음 온라인 채팅을 참조하시오.

Roseanne Trantham [오전 9:13]
3월 17일에 있을 우리 기획 회의를 최대로 활용하기 위해, 여러분 모두가 준비를 좀 해주셨으면 합니다. 치열한 시장 경쟁이 우리의 수익에 악영향을 미쳐 왔습니다. 저는 사업을 확장해야 할 때라고 생각합니다.

Todd Connelly [오전 9:15]
생각해 두신 것이라도 있으신가요?

Roseanne Trantham [오전 9:16]
1 점점 더 많은 매장들이 미술용품을 구비하고 있기 때문에, 우리가 차별화될 수 있도록, 2 우리 재고에 더욱 다양한 제품을 추가해야 합니다.

Phil Kang [오전 9:17]
여러 다른 기법들과 관련된 참고 도서들을 갖춰 놓으면 우리 고객들에게 유용할 겁니다.

Santosh Munshif [오전 9:18]
좋은 생각입니다! 그렇게 하면 초보자들에게 우리 업체가 더욱 매력적으로 느껴질지도 몰라요.

Todd Connelly [오전 9:19]
맞아요! 그리고 유명한 그림을 인쇄한 커피 머그잔을 판매하는 것도 고려해 볼 수 있습니다. 이 제품들은 훌륭한 선물이 될 거예요.

Roseanne Trantham [오전 9:20]
유용한 아이디어를 제시해 주실 줄 알았어요. 3 그와 같은 제품을 도매로 구입하기에 가장 좋은 곳을 알아보신 다음에 회의에서 제게 다시 알려 주세요.

Phil Kang [오전 9:21]
3 좋습니다.

| 어휘 | make the most of ~을 최대한 이용하다 make a preparation 준비하다 fierce competition 치열한 경쟁 adversely affect ~에 악영향을 미치다 revenue 수익 branch out 사업을 확장하다 have A in mind A를 생각해 두다, 염두에 두다 stock (매장 등에서) ~을 구비하다, 갖춰 놓다 set A apart A를 차별화하다 a great variety of 아주 다양한 inventory 재고(품), 재고 목록 reference book 참고 도서 related to ~와 관련된 appealing to ~에게 매력적인 consider -ing ~하는 것을 고려하다 with A p.p. A가 ~된 채로 make ~이 되다 come up with (아이디어 등) ~을 제시하다, 생각해 내다 look into ~을 자세히 알아보다, 조사하다 wholesale 도매로

1. 메시지 작성자들의 회사는 현재 어떤 종류의 상품을 판매하고 있는가?
(A) 운동복
(B) 커피 머그잔
(C) 미술용품
(D) 참고 도서

| 해설 |
9시 16분 메시지에서, Trantham 씨가 경쟁 업체의 상황과 관련해 점점 더 많은 매장들이 미술용품을 구비하고 있다고(More and more stores are stocking art supplies) 알리는 것으로 보아 이들의 회사가 미술용품 판매업체임을 알 수 있으므로 (C)가 정답이다.

| 어휘 | currently 현재 apparel 의복, 의류

2. 오전 9시 13분에, Trantham 씨가 "I think it's time to branch out"이라고 썼을 때 의미한 것은 무엇이겠는가?
(A) 회사에서 더 많은 소매 판매점을 열어야 한다.
(B) 업체에서 더 많은 종류의 상품을 제공해야 한다.
(C) 회의 의제에 더 많은 논의 사항들이 있어야 한다.
(D) 그룹에 더 많은 일원들이 추가되어야 한다.

| 해설 |
해당 문장에 앞서 치열한 경쟁에 따른 부정적인 영향이 언급되어 있고, 뒤이어 9시 16분 메시지에서 더 다양한 제품을 추가해야 한다는(we need to add a greater variety of items) 방안을 말하고 있다. 따라서 상품 종류를 확장해야 한다는 의미임을 알 수 있으므로 (B)가 정답이다.

| 어휘 | retail store 소매 판매점 a wider selection of 더 많은 종류의, 더 다양한 agenda 의제 discussion point 논의 사항

3. Kang 씨는 무엇을 하는 데 동의하는가?
(A) 회의실 마련하기
(B) 이메일로 추천 사항 보내기
(C) 최종 보고서 교정 보기
(D) 일부 조사 작업 수행하기

| 해설 |
Kang 씨가 동의하는 말은 맨 마지막 메시지에 나타나 있는데, 이는 바로 앞서 Trantham 씨가 도매로 구입하기에 가장 좋은 곳을 알아본(Look into the best place ~) 다음에 자신에게 알려 달라고 요청한 것에 대한 동의이다. 즉 조사 작업을 하는 데 동의하는 것이므로 (D)가 정답이다.

| 어휘 | agree to do ~하는 데 동의하다 set up ~을 마련하다, 설치하다 proofread ~을 교정 보다 conduct ~을 수행하다 research 조사, 연구

4-7번 문제는 다음 기사를 참조하시오.

HENTHORN VALLEY – Caprea Gallery의 소유주 Desmond Alarcon 씨에게는 빛을 발하는 창의적인 면이 있지만, 그의 배경은 사람들이 예상할 수 있는 것과는 다릅니다. —[1]— Alarcon 씨는 세무 회계사로서 일하던 원래의 직업을 포기한 후에 미술계에 몸담기 시작했습니다. 젊었을 때부터 미술에 대한 열정을 지니고 있었지만, 그가 취미 생활을 정식 직업으로 ④ 변화시킨 것은 수십 년이 더 흐른 뒤였습니다.

Caprea Gallery는 3년 전에 개장했으며, 서서히 인기를 얻어 오고 있습니다. —[2]— Alarcon 씨는 초기에 큰 어려움에 직면했는데, ⑤ Henthorn Valley 지역의 미술 관련 활동과 행사에 대한 관심 수준이 매우 낮았기 때문이었습니다. "당시에, 사람들은 그림이나 조각품들을 직접 볼 기회가 전혀 없었습니다. 저는 그것을 바꾸기 위해 열심히 노력해 왔습니다."

Alarcon 씨의 부단한 노력이 결실을 맺고 있는 것처럼 보입니다. —[3]— 그의 미술관을 찾는 방문객들의 숫자는 지속적으로 증가해 왔으며, 미술을 바탕으로 하는 여러 지역 단체들이 생겨나기 시작했습니다. Alarcon 씨는 현장에서 다수의 강연과 기타 특별 행사들을 주최하고 있습니다. ⑦ 또한 더 많은 사람들에게 다가가기 위한 방법들도 찾고 있습니다. —[4]—

⑥ 다음 달부터, Caprea Gallery에서 소장하고 있는 일부 그림들이 시청과 Henthorn Valley 도서관, 그리고 시에서 소유하고 있는 기타 건물에 대여되어 로비와 복도 공간에서 전시될 것입니다.

| 어휘 | expect ~을 예상하다, 기대하다   field 분야   give up ~을 포기하다   original 원래의, 애초의   accountant 회계사   passion for ~에 대한 열정   since ~ 이후로   it is not until A that ~한 것은 A 이후이다, A 이후에나 ~하다   turn A into B A를 B로 바꾸다, 전환하다   gain in popularity 인기를 얻다   face ~와 맞닥뜨리다   obstacle 장애물   in the early days 초기에   interest in ~에 대한 관심   art-related 미술과 관련된   opportunity to do ~할 수 있는 기회   in person 직접 (가서)   It seems that ~한 것 같다   pay off 결실을 맺다, 성과가 있다   steadily 지속적으로   several 여럿의   art-based 미술을 바탕으로 하는   spring up 생겨나다, 솟아나다   numerous 다수의   on site 구내에, 현장에서   look for ~을 찾다   way to do ~하는 방법   reach ~에게 다가가다   on loan 대여되어   display 전시, 진열   corridor 복도

4. 첫 번째 단락, 다섯 번째 줄의 단어 "turned"와 의미가 가장 가까운 것은 무엇인가?
(A) 뒤집었다
(B) 가져왔다
(C) 변모시켰다
(D) 회전시켰다
| 해설 |
turned 뒤에 'A into B'의 구조로 '취미에서 정식 직업으로'라는 말이 쓰여 있다. 따라서 turned가 변화와 관련된 동사임을 알 수 있으므로 '변모시키다'라는 의미로 쓰이는 (C) transformed가 정답이다.

5. Alarcon 씨는 무엇이 해당 지역의 미술에 대한 관심 부족의 원인이 되었다고 생각하는가?
(A) 미술품 제작에 드는 높은 비용
(B) 미술 강좌의 감소
(C) 한 미술관의 폐업
(D) 미술에 대한 노출의 부족
| 해설 |
두 번째 단락에 미술 활동이나 행사에 대한 관심이 매우 낮았고 그림이나 조각품을 직접 볼 기회가 없었다는 점을(~ the level of interest in art-related activities ~ was very low. "At the time, people didn't have any opportunities to see paintings and sculptures in person) 이유로 언급하고 있다. 이는 결국 미술에 대한 노출이 부족했음을 의미하는 것이므로 (D)가 정답이다.
| 어휘 | contribute to ~에 대한 원인이 되다   lack of ~의 부족   reduction in ~의 감소   closure 폐업   exposure to ~에 대한 노출

6. Caprea Gallery에 관해 암시된 것은 무엇인가?
(A) 공공 건물에 미술품을 제공할 것이다.
(B) 미술 경연 대회를 주최할 것이다.
(C) 오직 지역 미술가들의 작품만 전시한다.
(D) 몇몇 새 가이드를 고용할 계획이다.
| 해설 |
마지막 단락에 시청과 도서관, 그리고 시 소유의 건물에 미술품을 대여해 전시할 수 있게 해 준다는 말이 있으므로(~ will be on loan to city hall, the Henthorn Valley library, and other city-owned buildings for display ~) 공공 건물에 미술품을 제공하는 일을 의미하는 (A)가 정답이다.
| 어휘 | host ~을 주최하다   competition 경연 대회   plan to do ~할 계획이다

7. [1], [2], [3], [4]로 표시된 위치들 중에서, 다음 문장이 들어가기에 가장 적절한 곳은 어디인가?
"사실, 그는 그렇게 하기 위해 특별한 해결책을 생각해 냈습니다."
(A) [1]
(B) [2]
(C) [3]
(D) [4]
| 해설 |
제시된 문장은 특정 행위를 가리키는 do so와 함께 그 일을 위한 해결책을 생각해 냈다는 의미이다. 따라서 더 많은 사람들에게 다가갈 방법을 찾고 있다는 문장 뒤에 위치한 [4]에 들어가야 그렇게 하기 위한 해결책을 설명하는 다음 단락과의 연결이 자연스러워지므로 (D)가 정답이다.
| 어휘 | in fact 사실, 실제로   come up with (아이디어 등) ~을 생각해 내다   unique 특별한, 독특한   solution 해결책

DAY 20   다중 지문 연계 유형

기출 유형 맛보기
본책 p.284

1. 이중 지문

Kirkland Aquarium: 입장료 정보

Kirkland Aquarium은 매일 오전 10시에서 오후 8시까지 개장합니다. 입장권 선택권은 다음과 같습니다.

입장권 종류	가격	제공 사항
베이직	8.00달러	모든 수조 전시물에 대한 이용
브론즈	12.00달러	베이직 서비스 + 가이드 동반 투어
실버	15.00달러	브론즈 서비스 + 펭귄 전시 구역 입장
골드	25.00달러	실버 서비스 + Shark Dive 라이브 공연 입장

수신: info@kirklandaqua.com
발신: b.davis@rightwayins.com
날짜: 4월 5일
제목: Kirkland Aquarium 방문

관계자께,

저는 Rightway 보험의 인사부장입니다. 저희 직원들은 매년 봄에 단체 여행을 하는데, 올해는 귀하의 수족관을 방문하기로 결정했습니다. 저희 일행은 총 25명이 될 것입니다. 따라서, 저희가 방문하는 동안 함께 다닐 수 있는지 확인해 두고자 합니다. 펭귄 전시 구역을 방문하는 특정 시간대를 예약하는 것이 가능한가요? 저희는 또한 Shark Dive 행사를 볼 수 있기를 고대하고 있습니다. 555-0479번으로 제게 전화 주시기 바랍니다.

안녕히 계십시오.

Barney Davis

Q. Davis 씨는 무슨 종류의 입장권을 구입할 것 같은가?
(A) 베이직   (B) 브론즈   (C) 실버   **(D) 골드**

2. 삼중 지문

---

http://www.lexingtoncommunityconnect.org/housing

임대할 아파트를 찾습니다

날짜: 9월 12일

저는 재정 자문가인데, 일 때문에 Lexington으로 이사할 예정입니다. 한 달에 약 1,600달러의 비용으로 도심 근처에 위치한 침실 2개짜리 아파트를 찾고자 합니다. 새로운 곳에서 처음 근무를 시작하는 날은 12월 1일입니다.

---

http://www.lexingtoncommunityconnect.org/housing

임대 가능한 훌륭한 침실 2개짜리 아파트

날짜: 9월 12일

시내의 Purcell Building에 위치한 이 아름다운 아파트는 Roland 공원이 내려다 보이는 곳입니다. 실내는 최근에 개조되었으며, 새 세입자는 11월 15일 또는 그 이후로 입주할 수 있습니다. 월 임대료는 1,500달러이며, 수도와 가스 요금이 포함되어 있습니다.

수신: Andres Watkins <andres@watkinsproperties.com>
발신: Virginia Spencer <v_spencer@yorkshire-inc.com>
날짜: 9월 13일
제목: 침실 2개짜리 아파트

Watkins 씨께,

Lexington Community Connect에서 Purcell Building 내의 아파트에 관해 귀하께서 게시하신 글을 봤습니다. 저는 그 아파트를 이용 가능한 첫날에 입주하고자 합니다. 가능할 경우, 9월 17일에 그 아파트를 둘러보고 싶은데, 제가 업무로 인해 그 도시에 갈 예정이기 때문입니다. 감사합니다!

Virginia Spencer
(638) 555-9926

Q. Spencer 씨는 어느 날짜에 Purcell Building에서 거주를 시작하기를 원하는가?
(A) 9월 11일
(B) 9월 17일
(C) 11월 15일
(D) 12월 1일

PRACTICE | 기출 연습하기   본책 p.286

정답 1 (B) 2 (B) 3 (C) 4 (A) 5 (B) 6 (B)

다음 두 이메일을 참조하시오.

수신: Dennis Seiler <seilerd@reinltd.com>
발신: Mina Nayar <nayarm@reinltd.com>
날짜: 1월 6일
제목: 직원 연회

Seiler 씨께,

기획 위원회에서는 3월 3일을 직원 연회 날짜로 선택했습니다. Timothy Almaraz 부사장님께서 행사에 참석하시기 위해 항공편으로 이곳 Houston으로 오시기로 동의하셨습니다. 우리가 선호하는 장소인 Sapphire Plaza는 우리 예산에 비해 너무 비용이 많이 듭니다. 하지만, 현재 비수기이기 때문에 이 행사장과 협의해 비용을 낮춰 보려고 합니다. 이렇게 하는 것이 효과가 없을 경우, 대신 Lanham Hall에 있는 장소를 예약해야 할 것입니다. 계속 소식 전해 드리겠습니다.

안녕히 계십시오.

Mina Nayar

수신: Timothy Almaraz <almarazt@reinltd.com>
발신: Mina Nayar <nayarm@reinltd.com>
날짜: 2월 27일
제목: Houston 지사 직원 연회

Almaraz 부사장님께,

비서를 통해 항공편 상세 정보를 전달 받았습니다. 저희는 부사장님께서 이곳 Houston의 직원 연회에 참석하실 수 있다는 사실에 매우 기쁩니다. 제 동료 직원인 John Herbert 씨가 부사장님을 공항에서 호텔까지 차로 모셔다 드릴 것입니다. 체크인하시고 짐을 옮겨 놓으신 후에, 연회가 열리는 Sapphire Plaza로 다시 모셔다 드릴 예정입니다. 부사장님의 방문을 더욱 즐겁게 만들어 드릴 수 있도록 제가 할 수 있는 일이 있을 경우, 알려 주시기 바랍니다.

안녕히 계십시오.

Mina Nayar

---

1. Nayar 씨에 관해 무엇이 사실일 것 같은가?
(A) 공항에서 Almaraz 씨를 만날 계획이다.
(B) 성공적으로 가격 인하를 협의했다.
(C) 선호하는 출장 요리 업체를 이용할 수 없었다.
(D) 행사가 연기되어야 했다.

| 해설 |
두 번째 지문 중반부에 행사장이 Sapphire Plaza라고 언급되어 있는데 (Sapphire Plaza for the banquet), 첫 지문에 이 행사장이 비싼 곳이기 때문에 비용을 협의해 보겠다고(The Sapphire Plaza ~ However, I will try to negotiate with the venue to get a lower price ~) 언급되어 있다. 따라서 비용 인하 문제가 잘 협의되었음을 알 수 있으므로 (B)가 정답이다.

| 어휘 |
banquet 연회 planning committee 기획 위원회 select ~을 선택하다 agree to do ~하기로 동의하다 attend ~에 참석하다 preferred 선호하는 budget 예산 negotiate with ~와 협의하다 venue 행사장 low season 비수기 work 효과가 있다 book ~을 예약하다 keep A updated A에게 계속 새로운 소식을 전하다

---

branch 지사 receive ~을 받다 details 상세 정보 assistant 비서, 조수 be pleased that ~해서 기쁘다 be able to do ~할 수 있다 take A to B A를 B로 데려가다 drop off ~을 갖다 놓다, 내려 놓다 make A + 형용사 A를 ~하게 만들다 let A know A에게 알리다

plan to do ~할 계획이다 successfully 성공적으로 decrease 인하, 감소
caterer 출장 요리 업체 available 이용 가능한 postpone ~을 연기하다

다음 회람과 이메일을 참조하시오.

날짜: 9월 16일
발신: Tony Stevens, 보안 책임자
수신: Valley 연구소 전 직원
제목: 보안 변동 사항

기술자들이 우리 Valley 건물을 방문해 모든 출입문에 전자 잠금 장치를 설치할 것입니다. 이는 우리 직원과 회사의 자산 모두를 보호하기 위한 방법입니다. 직원들은 소속 부서장들을 통해 출입증을 제공 받을 것입니다. 이 출입증을 이용해 필요한 공간에 출입할 수 있을 것입니다. 우리는 9월 25일에 새로운 시스템을 이용하기 시작할 예정입니다. 질문이나 의견이 있으신 분들은 tstevens@valley-lab.com으로 제게 연락 주시기 바랍니다.

수신: tstevens@valley-lab.com
발신: jmaguire@valley-lab.com
날짜: 9월 29일
제목: 출입증 문제

Stevens 씨께,

제 직원 출입증의 문제와 관련하여 알려드리고자 합니다. 제가 이 출입증을 갖다 댈 때마다 문이 열리지 않습니다. 오직 "오류" 메시지만 뜹니다. 제 출입증은 우리가 새 시스템을 이용하기 시작한 바로 다음 날에 작동을 멈췄습니다. 다행히도, 제 동료 직원들이 실험실로 들어갈 수 있게 해 주고 있습니다. 하지만, 제가 10월 3일에 일찍 출근해야 하기 때문에, 그 전에 이 문제를 바로잡고자 합니다. 제 출입증을 어떻게 교체 받을 수 있는지 알려 주시기 바랍니다.

감사합니다.

Jill Maguire

2. Maguire 씨는 언제 처음 자신의 출입증에 대한 문제를 인식했는가?
(A) 9월 16일에
(B) 9월 26일에
(C) 9월 29일에
(D) 10월 3일에

| 해설 |
두 번째 지문에서 Maguire 씨는 출입증이 새 시스템을 이용하기 시작한 바로 다음 날에 작동을 멈췄다고(~ stopped working the day after we started using the system) 알리고 있고, 첫 지문에는 9월 25일에 새로운 시스템 이용을 시작할 것이라고(~ start to use the new system on September 25) 나타나 있다. 따라서 9월 26일에 문제를 인식했음을 알 수 있으므로 (B)가 정답이다.

| 어휘 |
install ~을 설치하다 lock 잠금 장치 a way for A to do A가 ~하는 방법 property 자산, 건물 give A access to B A가 B에 출입할 수 있게 하다 comment 의견 contact ~에게 연락하다

inform A about B A에게 B에 관해 알리다 whenever ~할 때마다 swipe (판독기에) ~을 읽히다 fortunately 다행히도 coworker 동료 직원 let A into B A를 B에 들여보내다 fix ~을 바로잡다, 고치다 then 그때 let A know how A에게 어떻게 ~하는지 알리다 get A p.p. A를 ~되게 하다 replace ~을 교체하다

notice ~을 인식하다, 알아 차리다

다음 제품 설명과 고객 리뷰, 그리고 온라인 답변을 참조하시오.

Newport Home: 핸드 믹서기, 모델명 R85

이 다목적 주방 도구가 없다면 어떤 주방도 완전하지 않습니다! R85는 수프를 섞거나 스무디를 만드는 일을 비롯한 여러 용도에 안성맞춤인 제품입니다. 이 제품의 소형 사이즈는 보관 공간이 부족한 주방에 이상적입니다. 하지만 제품의 사이즈를 얕보지 마십시오. 강력한 모터가 아주 다양한 음식을 처리할 수 있습니다. 이 기기는 세 가지 다른 속도 설정과 경량 디자인을 특징으로 합니다.

소매가: 65.00달러 / **3** Newport 보상 프로그램 회원 특가: 55.00달러

www.newporthome.com/customerreviews/R85/0124

| 홈 | 카탈로그 | 이용 후기 | 연락처 |

R85 핸드 믹서기 이용 후기: 평점 4.5/5, 작성자 Christina Neville, 6월 4일

전반적으로, 저는 이 핸드 믹서기가 얼마나 강력한지에 대해 매우 깊은 인상을 받았는데, 특히 그 작은 사이즈를 감안하면 더욱 그렇습니다. **3** 저는 Newport 보상 프로그램 회원이기 때문에, 할인된 가격에 구입했습니다. 하지만, 그 성능을 보면, 기꺼이 정가를 지불했을 수도 있습니다. **4** 이 기기의 유일한 단점은 칼날을 손으로 씻어야 한다는 것입니다. 저는 모든 부품을 식기세척기에 넣을 수 있기를 기대했었습니다.

www.newporthome.com/customerreviews/R85/cs476

| 홈 | 카탈로그 | 이용 후기 | 연락처 |

Christina Neville 씨의 후기에 대한 Derrick Mason[Newport 고객 서비스]의 답변

R85 핸드 믹서기에 대한 귀하의 이용 후기를 공유해 주셔서 감사드립니다. 저희는 귀하께서 요리하시는 데 있어 이 제품의 다양한 용도를 알게 되신 것 같아 기쁩니다. 귀하의 의견과 관련해, **4** 저희 R83 모델 구매를 고려해 보시기 바랍니다. 이 제품은 R85만큼 가볍지는 않지만, 분명 귀하의 불만 사항을 해결해 줄 것입니다. 상단에 위치한 '카탈로그' 버튼을 클릭하시면 이 모델과 다른 유사 모델들을 찾아보실 수 있습니다. Newport Home 고객이 되어 주신 것에 감사드립니다!

| 어휘 |
complete 완전한 versatile 다목적의 blend ~을 섞다, 혼합하다 compact 소형의 ideal 이상적인 let A do A가 ~하게 하다 fool ~을 속이다 handle ~을 다루다 a wide variety of 아주 다양한 device 기기, 장치 feature ~을 특징으로 하다 lightweight 경량의 retail price 소매가

review 이용 후기 rate ~을 평가하다, 점수를 매기다 overall 전반적으로 be impressed by ~에 깊은 인상을 받다 especially 특히 considering ~을 감안하면 performance 성능 downside 단점 blade 칼날 expect to do ~할 것으로 기대하다 put A in B A를 B에 넣다 component 부품

reply to ~에 대답하다 be pleased that ~해서 기쁘다 regarding ~와 관련해 consider -ing ~하는 것을 고려하다 as A as B B만큼 A한 address ~을 해결하다 complaint 불만 similar 유사한 by (방법) ~함으로써 above 상단에, 위에

3. Neville 씨에 관해 암시된 것은 무엇인가?
(A) 주문에 대해 무료 배송 서비스를 받았다.
(B) 제품 구매를 위해 쿠폰을 사용했다.
(C) 해당 핸드 믹서기를 55.00달러에 구입했다.

(D) 선물로 핸드 믹서기를 받았다.

| 해설 |
두 번째 지문인 이용 후기의 작성자 Neville 씨는 Newport 보상 프로그램 회원이기 때문에 할인된 가격에 구입한 사실을 밝히고 있고(I am a Newport Rewards Member, so I got it at a discount), 첫 지문 마지막에 해당 프로그램 회원은 55.00달러에(Newport Rewards Members Special Price: $55.00) 구입할 수 있다고 쓰여 있다. 따라서 이와 같은 내용을 언급한 (C)가 정답이다.

| 어휘 | receive ~을 받다   make purchase 구입하다

4. Mason 씨는 왜 R83 모델을 Neville 씨에게 추천하는가?
(A) 부품을 식기세척기에 넣어 세척할 수 있다.
(B) 작은 공간에 맞게 넣을 수 있다.
(C) 경량 디자인으로 되어 있다.
(D) 배터리가 오랜 시간 지속된다.

| 해설 |
R83 모델이 언급되는 세 번째 지문에, 상대방의 불만 사항을 해결해 줄 것이라고(it does address your complaint) 알리면서 해당 제품을 추천하고 있다. 그런데 두 번째 지문 마지막에 Neville 씨는 식기세척기로 세척할 수 없다는 단점을(~ the blades have to be washed by hand. I was expecting to be able to put all components in the dishwasher) 언급하고 있으므로 R83 모델은 그것이 가능한 제품임을 알 수 있다. 따라서 (A)가 정답이다.

| 어휘 | part 부품   be able to do ~할 수 있다   fit into ~에 꼭 들어 맞다   last 지속되다

다음 온라인 양식과 이메일, 그리고 웹사이트를 참조하시오.

---

www.commerciallinens.com/contact
Commercial Linens 연락 양식

성명: Elizabeth Ralston
이메일 주소: ralston_e@seasidegrillrestaurant.com
의견: 저는 Cape Charles에 위치한 Seaside Grill의 매니저이며, 5 저희 레스토랑은 여러 해 동안 Patino 제품 라인의 테이블보를 구입해 오고 있습니다. 안타깝게도, 저희가 가장 최근에 주문한 제품은 실망 그 자체였습니다. 그 테이블보들은 훨씬 더 얇아 보이며, 불쾌한 왁스 성분의 질감으로 되어 있었습니다.

수신: ralston_e@seasidegrillrestaurant.com
발신: caleb@commerciallinens.com
날짜: 2월 18일
제목: 고객 의견에 대한 답변

Ralston 씨께,

귀하의 구매 제품에 대해 실망스러운 경험을 하셨다니 사과의 말씀드립니다. 5 일부 저희 제품에 대한 제조사가 폐업을 했는데, 대체 업체가 동일한 수준의 품질을 제공하지 못하는 것 같습니다. 저희는 이 상황을 해결하기 위해 노력하고 있습니다. 동시에, 귀하의 기준을 충족하지 못하는 어떠한 제품에 대한 반품이라도 기꺼이 수용하겠습니다. 저희는 또한 시범적으로 사용해 보실 수 있도록 저희 6 최신 제품인 E422의 무료 샘플도 제공해 드리고자 합니다. 귀하의 양해에 감사드립니다.

Caleb Escobar

---

www.commerciallinens.com/catalog/restaurant_supplies
저희 Commercial Linens의 카탈로그에 추가된 최신 제품입니다! 저희는 새로운 Cotton-Rich 제품 라인을 선보이게 되어 기쁘게 생각하며, 이 제품 라인은 내구성과 함께 고급스러운 느낌을 주는 두툼한 고급 면으로 만들어진 냅킨을 제공합니다.

제품 번호	사이즈	개당 단가
G348	16″×16″	0.75달러
6 E422	18″×18″	0.90달러
L197	20″×20″	1.05달러
A506	21″×21″	1.20달러

| 어휘 |
purchase ~을 구입하다   unfortunately 안타깝게도   recent 최근의   disappointment 실망(감)   seem to do ~하는 것 같다   much (비교급 수식) 훨씬   thin 얇은, 가는   unpleasant 불쾌한   waxy 왁스로 된   texture 질감

apologize that ~라는 점에 대해 사과하다   disappointing 실망시키는   manufacturer 제조사   go out of business 폐업하다   it seems that ~하는 것 같다   replacement 대체(하는 것)   offer ~을 제공하다   quality 품질   remedy ~을 해결하다   situation 상황   in the meantime 그와 동시에, 그 사이에   accept ~을 수용하다   return 반품   meet ~을 충족하다   free 무료의   try ~을 한번 사용해 보다

addition 추가(되는 것)   line 제품 라인   provide ~을 제공하다   made from ~로 만들어진   heavy cotton 두꺼운 면   durability 내구성

5. Patino 테이블보에 관해 암시된 것은 무엇인가?
(A) 가격이 최근에 인상되었다.
(B) 제조사가 변경되었다.
(C) 가장 인기 있는 제품 라인이다.
(D) 단종되었다.

| 해설 |
첫 지문에 Ralston 씨가 Patino 테이블보를 구입한 사실과(our restaurant has been purchasing the Patino line of tablecloths ~) 그에 대한 실망감을 언급하고 있고, Ralston 씨에게 사과하는 두 번째 지문에는 대체 업체가 동일한 수준의 품질을 제공하지 못하고 있다고(~ the replacement is not offering the same level of quality) 알리고 있다. 따라서 Patino 테이블보의 제조사가 변경되었음을 알 수 있으므로 이를 언급한 (B)가 정답이다.

| 어휘 | increase ~을 인상하다   discontinue ~을 단종하다

6. Ralston 씨에게 어느 냅킨 사이즈가 보내질 것인가?
(A) 16″×16″
(B) 18″×18″
(C) 20″×20″
(D) 21″×21″

| 해설 |
두 번째 지문 마지막에 최신 제품인 E422의 무료 샘플을 제공해 주겠다고(~ give you a free sample of our newest product, E422 ~) 알리고 있는데, 세 번째 지문에 이 제품의 규격이 18″×18″로 표기되어 있으므로 (B)가 정답이다.

DAY 20 | 실전문제   본책 p.290

| 정답 | 1 (B) | 2 (A) | 3 (D) | 4 (B) | 5 (B) | 6 (C) |
| | 7 (B) | 8 (A) | 9 (B) | 10 (B) | | |

1-5번 문제는 다음 광고와 이메일을 참조하시오.

Astro Educational Institute

워크숍 시리즈

저희 Astro Education 사는 학습자들이 각자의 능력을 업그레이드하고 경력 분야에서 발전을 이룰 수 있도록 도와 드리는 데 있어 전국에서 손꼽히는 시설들 중 한 곳이라고 여기고 있습니다. 저희 학습 과정은 모두 각자의 분야에서 **1(A)** 석사 학위 이상의 자격을 보유한 전문가들에 의해 제공되고 있으며, 매우 경쟁력 있게 수강료가 책정되어 있습니다. 더욱이, 저희는 **1(C)** New York과 California를 포함해 10개 주에 지사를 보유하고 있으며, 이는 분명 여러분께서 편리한 곳에서 학습하실 수 있다는 점을 의미합니다.

다음 학습 과정들은 10월 개강으로 등록 가능합니다.

강좌명	설명	1인당 수강료
온라인 광고	업계 전문가 Mark Pilate 씨를 통해 웹 광고의 비결을 배워 보십시오.	450.00달러
직원 관리	직원들로부터 최상의 업무 수행 능력을 이끌어 내는 방법을 확인해 보십시오.	550.00달러
2 영업의 비밀	마케팅 능력을 갈고 닦기를 원하시나요? 그러시다면 이 일주일 기간의 집중 강좌가 바로 여러분을 위한 것입니다!	**2** 400.00달러
성공적인 발표	자신감 있고 전문적으로 전달되는 발표를 통해 동료 직원과 고객들에게 깊은 인상을 남기는 법을 배워 보십시오.	425.00달러

4 특별 판촉 행사의 하나로, 동일한 회사에서 1명이 넘는 인원이 수강하실 경우에 10퍼센트 할인을 제공해 드립니다. 이 훌륭한 특가 서비스를 이용하시려면, **1(D)** 전화상으로 예약하실 때 참조 코드 SAVE10을 말씀해 주시기만 하면 됩니다.

수신: customerservice@astroed.com
발신: t.hurney@jjenterprises.net
날짜: 9월 25일
제목: 문의

관계자께,

4 저는 저와 저희 JJ Enterprises에서 함께 근무하는 5명의 다른 동료 직원들을 위해 귀사의 강좌들 중 하나에 대한 자리를 예약했습니다. 저는 저희가 '온라인 광고' 강좌에서 매우 큰 도움을 받을 것이라고 생각했지만, 예산상의 제약으로 인해 **2** 그 대신 가장 저렴한 것을 선택할 수밖에 없었습니다. 저희는 기억에 남을 만한 학습 경험이 될 것이라고 확신하는 강좌를 다음 주에 수강할 수 있기를 대단히 크게 고대하고 있습니다.

제가 여행 준비를 확정하기에 앞서 몇 가지 사항들을 명확하게 해 두고자 합니다. **3** 귀사의 무료 셔틀버스 서비스가 공항에서 얼마나 자주 운행되는지 궁금합니다. 이 부분이 제가 호텔을 어디로 예약해야 하는지를 결정하는 데 도움이 될 것입니다. 또한, 귀사의 직원을 통해 수강하기 전에 **5** 일부 유인물을 출력해야 한다고 들었는데, 귀사의 웹사이트에서 찾을 수 없는 것 같습니다. 이 자료가 어디에 있는지 알려 주시겠습니까?

귀하의 도움에 대해 미리 감사드립니다.

Thelma Hurney

| 어휘 |

consider A B A를 B로 여기다 leading 손꼽히는, 선도적인 facility 시설 help A do A가 ~하는 것을 돕다 enable A to do A가 ~할 수 있게 하다 advance 발전하다, 진보하다 expert 전문가 Master's Degree 석사 학위 respective 각각의 field 분야 competitively 경쟁력 있게 priced 가격이 책정된 furthermore 더욱이 including ~을 포함해 be sure to do 분명 ~하다 be able to do ~할 수 있다 convenient 편리한 following 다음의, 아래의 available 이용 가능한 enroll 등록하다 industry 업계 find out ~을 알아보다 how to do ~하는 법 get A from B B로부터 A를 이끌어 내다 performance 수행 능력 hone ~을 갈고 닦다, 연마하다 intensive 집중적인 wow ~에게 깊은 인상을 남기다 colleague 동료 직원 through ~을 통해 confidently 자신감 있게 promotion 판촉 행사 attend 참석하다 take advantage of ~을 이용하다 fabulous 훌륭한, 아주 멋진 offer 특가 서비스 quote (인용해서) ~을 말하다 reference 참조, 조회 book ~을 예약하다

---

benefit from ~로부터 혜택을 보다, 이득을 얻다 due to ~로 인해 budget 예산 constraint 제약 go for ~로 정하다 instead 그 대신 look forward to -ing ~하기를 고대하다 memorable 기억에 남을 만한 clarify ~을 분명히 해 두다 finalize ~을 최종 확정하다 arrangement 준비, 조정 complimentary 무료의 run 운행하다, 운영되다 decide ~을 결정하다 where to do ~할 곳 be told to do ~라는 얘기를 듣다 handout 유인물 in advance 미리

1. 광고에서 공지되지 않은 것은 무엇인가?
(A) 강좌 진행자들이 전문 자격 요건을 갖추고 있다.
(B) 많은 강좌들이 온라인으로 제공될 것이다.
(C) 해당 업체가 다양한 지점에 시설을 보유하고 있다.
(D) 강좌 자리는 전화로 예약될 수 있다.

| 해설 |
첫 지문 첫 단락의 'experts all with a Master's Degree or above' 부분에서 강좌 진행자들의 전문 자격 요건을 언급한 (A)를, 같은 단락의 'have offices in ten states, including New York and California'에서 다양한 지점을 언급한 (C)를, 그리고 마지막 단락의 'when booking over the phone'에서 전화 예약 방법을 언급한 (D)를 확인할 수 있다. 하지만 많은 강좌들이 온라인으로 제공된다는 정보는 제시되어 있지 않으므로 (B)가 정답이다.

| 어휘 | qualification 자격 요건 multiple 다양한, 다수의 reserve ~을 예약하다

2. Hurney 씨는 어느 강좌에 참석할 것 같은가?
(A) 영업의 비밀
(B) 성공적인 발표
(C) 온라인 광고
(D) 직원 관리

| 해설 |
두 번째 지문 첫 단락에 가장 저렴한 것을 선택할 수밖에 없었다고(~ we have had to go for your cheapest available option instead) 알리고 있는데, 첫 지문의 도표에서 가장 저렴한 400달러에 해당되는 강좌가 '영업의 비밀'이므로 (A)가 정답이다.

3. Astro Educational Institute은 다음 중 어느 것을 제공하는가?
(A) 할인된 호텔 요금
(B) 할인된 항공권
(C) 온라인 예약 시스템
(D) 무료 교통편 서비스

| 해설 |
두 번째 지문 두 번의 단락에 '귀사의 무료 셔틀버스 서비스(your complimentary shuttle service)'라는 언급을 통해 무료 교통편을 제공한다는 것을 알 수 있으므로 (D)가 정답이다.

| 어휘 | reduced 할인된(= discounted) rate 요금 booking 예약 free 무료의 transportation 교통편

4. Hurney 씨에 관해 암시된 것은 무엇인가?
(A) 예전에 강사로 일했었다.
(B) 자신의 예약에 대해 할인을 받을 것이다.
(C) 전에 Astro Educational Institute 강좌에 참석한 적이 있다.
(D) 온라인 영업 기술의 전문가이다.

| 해설 |
두 번째 지문 시작 부분에 자신 및 5명의 다른 동료 직원들을 위해 강좌 하나를 예약했다고(I booked a place ~ for myself and 5 other colleagues ~) 알리고 있고, 첫 지문 마지막 단락에 동일 회사에서 1인이 넘는 사람들이 수강하면 10퍼센트를 할인해 준다고(we will offer a 10% discount if more than one person attends from the same company) 쓰여 있으므로 (B)가 정답이다.

| 어휘 | previously 이전에, 과거에 receive ~을 받다

5. 이메일에 따르면, Hurney 씨는 무슨 정보를 찾고 있는가?
(A) 거래 내역서의 최종 합계 금액
(B) 일부 파일의 위치
(C) 한 지사로 가는 방법
(D) 한 강좌 진행자의 이름

| 해설 |
두 번째 지문 마지막 단락에, 출력해야 하는 유인물을 웹 사이트에서 찾을 수 없다며 어디에 있는지 알려 달라고(~ to print some handouts ~ but I can't seem to find them on your website. Could you tell me where these are?) 요청하고 있으므로 (B)가 정답이다.

| 어휘 | invoice 거래 내역서 directions to ~로 가는 방법, 길

6-10번 문제는 다음 기사 발췌문, 설명서와 이메일을 참조하시오.

<Health First Magazine>: 1월호

이 유익한 스마트폰 앱들과 함께 원하시는 건강 목표에 도달해 보십시오!

#1: Pro-Health
Pro-Health는 여러분의 운동 시간을 최대한 활용하실 수 있도록 도와 드리는 피트니스 앱입니다. 버튼 하나만 누르면, **6** 시간 경과에 따른 성취도를 측정하고 목표를 설정하실 수 있으며, 운동 관련 팁도 얻으실 수 있습니다.
Pro-Health 앱을 이용하시면, 걷거나 조깅을 하실 때 더 이상 그 경로를 측정하실 필요가 없습니다. 그저 앱을 켜 놓으시고 원하시는 경로로 이동하기만 하시면 됩니다. **7** 이 앱이 휴대 전화기의 GPS 기능을 이용해 이동하신 거리를 계산해 드립니다. 또한 평균 이동 속도와 소모된 칼로리를 파악해 얼마나 나아졌는지 확인하실 수 있도록 편리하게 이용 가능한 데이터베이스에 그 기록을 보관해 드릴 것입니다. 자택에서 운동하시나요? Pro-Health 동영상 라이브러리를 통해 장비를 거의 필요로 하지 않는 다양한 운동 동영상을 재생하실 수 있습니다. 일부 Pro-Health 패키지는 또한 여러분께서 특정 체형이나 운동 수준, 그리고 목표를 바탕으로 맞춤 운동을 만드실 수 있게 해 드립니다. **10** Novice 패키지에는 한 달에 불과 6달러의 비용으로 **6** 운동 데이터를 파악하시는 데 필요한 모든 기능뿐만 아니라 **10** 30개의 동영상이 담겨 있는 미니 라이브러리 이용 권한도 포함되어 있습니다. 운동 생활에 더욱 전념하시는 분들께서는 더 많은 동영상과 기능이 들어 있는 더 큰 패키지를 선택하실 수 있습니다.

Pro-Health 스마트폰 앱에 대한 귀하의 관심에 감사드립니다. 시작하시려면 아래의 정보를 작성해 주시기 바랍니다. 저희는 또한 Pro-Health 사용자들의 친구 또는 가족들께 할인을 제공해 드리고 있습니다. 친구를 통해 소개받으신 분이시라면, 반드시 아래에 추천인 코드를 입력하시기 바랍니다.

사용자 정보
8 성명: Ada Borelli
이메일: borellia@monteagleco.com
전화번호: 897-555-68820
Pro-Health에 대해 어떻게 알게 되셨나요? 잡지 기사
귀하의 운동 수준을 어떻게 설명하시겠습니까? 중급
Pro-Health 패키지
Novice: 6달러/월 [　]
Maintain: 10달러/월 [　]
8 Challenge: 12달러/월 [X]
Master: 15/월 [　]
추천인 코드: 해당 사항 없음

수신: borellia@monteagleco.com
발신: info@prohealthapp.com
날짜: 5월 9일
제목: 중요 업데이트

Pro-Health 사용자께,

저희 이용 계약 약관에 따라, Pro-Health는 일 년에 한번 어플리케이션의 패키지를 변경할 수 있는 권리를 지니고 있습니다. 저희는 **9(C)** 사용자의 수면 패턴을 추적하고 **9(A)** 영양분이 가득한 음식을 만드는 법을 가르쳐 드리는 섹션을 제공하는 새로운 기능을 추가하기 위해 일부 패키지 가격을 인상하기로 결정했습니다. 추가로, 모든 사용자 툴은 현재 제공되는 **9(D)** 영어뿐만 아니라 스페인어와 표준 중국어로도 이용 가능하게 될 것입니다. 아래에서 업데이트된 요금을 확인하시기 바라며, **10** 이는 7월 1일부터 적용됩니다.

패키지	동영상 라이브러리 이용	월간 청구 요금
10 Novice	20	6달러
Maintain	50	12달러
Challenge	80	15달러
Master	120	20달러

현 사용자들의 성원에 감사드리기 위한 방법으로, **8** Challenge 또는 Master 패키지를 이용하시는 분들께 무료 저항밴드를 보내 드립니다.

| 어휘 |
reach ~에 도달하다 help A do A가 ~하는 것을 돕다 make the most of ~을 최대한 활용하다 workout 운동 measure ~을 측정하다 achievement 성취, 달성 no longer 더 이상 ~ 않다 turn on ~을 켜다, 틀다 calculate ~을 계산하다 distance 거리 keep track of ~을 파악하다 calories burned 소모된 칼로리 improve 향상되다 exercise 운동하다 allow A to do A가 ~할 수 있게 하다 stream ~을 재생하다 a variety of 다양한 require little to no ~을 거의 필요로 하지 않다 equipment 장비 create ~을 만들어 내다 custom 맞춤의 based on ~을 바탕으로 specific 특정한, 구체적인 include ~을 포함하다 feature 기능, 특징 track ~을 파악하다, 추적하다 as well as ~뿐만 아니라 access to ~의 이용 devoted to ~에 전념하는 opt for ~을 선택하다

interest in ~에 대한 관심 complete ~을 작성 완료하다 below 아래에 get started 시작하다 offer ~을 제공하다 be referred by ~의 추천을 받다, 소개를 받다 be sure to do 꼭 ~하다 referral 추천인 describe ~을 설명하다 intermediate 중급의 N/A 해당 사항 없음

in line with ~에 따라 terms and conditions 조항, 약관 reserve the right to do ~할 권리를 지니다 packed with ~로 가득한 nutrition 영양분 additionally 추가로 not only A but also B A뿐만 아니라 B도 rate 요금

effective + 날짜 ~부터 시행되는 current 현재의 patronage 성원, 단골 이용
free 무료의 resistance band 저항 고무 밴드

6. 기사 발췌 내용에 따르면, 사용자들은 Pro-Health 앱으로 무엇을 할 수 있는가?
(A) 조깅 경로 추천받기
(B) 근처의 운동 시설 찾기
(C) 운동 진척 상황 파악하기
(D) 운동 장비 주문하기

| 해설 |
첫 지문의 첫 단락에 Pro-Health로 시간 경과에 따른 성취도를 측정할 수 있다는(measure your achievements over time) 말이 있고, 다음 단락 후반부에는 운동 데이터를 파악하는 데 필요한 기능이 있다고(all of the features for tracking your fitness data) 나타나 있다. 이는 운동에 따른 진척 상황을 파악하는 기능을 가리키므로 (C)가 정답이다.
| 어휘 | nearby 근처의 facility 시설 progress 진척, 진도

7. Pro-Health 스마트폰 앱에 관해 암시된 것은 무엇인가?
(A) 1월에 출시되었다.
(B) 전화기의 위치 기능을 이용한다.
(C) 반드시 항상 인터넷에 연결되어 있어야 한다.
(D) 3년 동안 베스트셀러 앱이었다.

| 해설 |
첫 지문 두 번째 단락에 휴대 전화기의 GPS 기능을 이용해 이동 거리를 계산해 준다고(The app will calculate the distance you traveled using your phone's GPS function) 쓰여 있으므로 위치 기능을 이용한다는 점을 언급한 (B)가 정답이다.
| 어휘 | release ~을 출시하다 make use of ~을 이용하다 be connected to ~에 연결되다

8. Borelli 씨는 왜 무료 저항 고무 밴드를 받을 것인가?
(A) Challenge 패키지를 구입했다.
(B) 친구에게 해당 서비스를 추천해 주었다.
(C) 고객 의견 설문지를 작성했다.
(D) 피트니스 대회에 참가했다.

| 해설 |
세 번째 지문 마지막에 Challenge 또는 Master 패키지를 이용하는 사람들이 무료 저항 고무 밴드를 받는다고(~ those with the Challenge or Master package will be sent a free resistance band) 쓰여 있는데 Borelli 씨가 작성한 양식인 두 번째 지문 하단에 Challenge 패키지에 표기되어 있으므로(Challenge: $12/month [X]) (A)가 정답이다.
| 어휘 | feedback 의견 survey 설문(지) participate in ~에 참가하다 competition 경기 대회, 경연 대회

9. 이메일에서 앱에 대해 계획된 개선 사항으로 언급되지 않은 것은 무엇인가?
(A) 일부 건강에 좋은 조리법 제공하기
(B) 다른 여러 국가의 등산로 지도 다운로드하기
(C) 수면 상태 추적 기능 추가하기
(D) 다른 언어로 콘텐츠 제공하기

| 해설 |
세 번째 지문 첫 단락의 'teaching you how to make dishes packed with nutrition'에서 건강에 좋은 조리법 제공을 뜻하는 (A)를, 'add a new function that will keep track of users' sleep patterns'에서 수면 상태 추적 기능을 언급한 (C)를, 그리고 'available not only in English as they are now, but also in Spanish and Mandarin'에서 다양한 언어를 언급한 (D)를 확인할 수 있다. 하지만 여러 국가의 등산로 지도 다운로드 기능은 언급되지 않으므로 (B)가 정답이다.
| 어휘 | recipe 조리법 trail map 길 안내도 content 콘텐츠, 내용(물)

10. Novice 패키지는 7월 1일부터 어떻게 변경될 것인가?
(A) 로그인 페이지의 기능들이 간소화될 것이다.
(B) 동영상 개수가 줄어들 것이다.
(C) 새로운 비용 지불 방식이 이용 가능해질 것이다.
(D) 월 이용 요금이 인상될 것이다.

| 해설 |
7월 1일이라는 날짜는 세 번째 지문 첫 단락 끝부분에 언급되었듯이 변동 사항이 적용되는 날짜이고(effective July 1) 해당 도표에 Novice 패키지의 동영상 개수가 '20'으로 표기되어 있다. 그런데 첫 지문 후반부에는 Novice 패키지를 통해 30개의 동영상을 이용할 수 있다고(The Novice package includes ~ access to a mini-library of 30 videos ~) 쓰여 있다. 따라서 7월 1일부터 Novice 패키지 가입자들이 이용 가능한 동영상 개수가 줄어든다는 것을 알 수 있으므로 이를 언급한 (B)가 정답이다.
| 어휘 | sign-in page 로그인 페이지 simplify ~을 간소화하다 method 방법 fee 요금, 수수료 raise ~을 인상하다, 증가시키다

Actual Test

본책 p.296

PART 1
1 (C) 2 (B) 3 (A) 4 (D) 5 (D) 6 (B)

PART 2
7 (A)　8 (B)　9 (A)　10 (B)　11 (A)　12 (C)
13 (B)　14 (B)　15 (C)　16 (A)　17 (A)　18 (C)
19 (B)　20 (B)　21 (A)　22 (A)　23 (A)　24 (A)
25 (A)　26 (C)　27 (A)　28 (A)　29 (C)　30 (A)
31 (C)

PART 3
32 (C)　33 (B)　34 (B)　35 (C)　36 (A)　37 (B)
38 (A)　39 (C)　40 (B)　41 (A)　42 (D)　43 (B)
44 (C)　45 (D)　46 (A)　47 (A)　48 (B)　49 (B)
50 (B)　51 (B)　52 (D)　53 (B)　54 (C)　55 (A)
56 (D)　57 (A)　58 (A)　59 (B)　60 (B)　61 (D)
62 (B)　63 (C)　64 (B)　65 (A)　66 (B)　67 (C)
68 (B)　69 (A)　70 (A)

PART 4
71 (A)　72 (B)　73 (C)　74 (C)　75 (A)　76 (D)
77 (C)　78 (A)　79 (D)　80 (B)　81 (C)　82 (D)
83 (B)　84 (D)　85 (B)　86 (C)　87 (A)　88 (D)
89 (C)　90 (C)　91 (B)　92 (D)　93 (C)　94 (B)
95 (D)　96 (D)　97 (C)　98 (C)　99 (D)　100 (A)

PART 5
101 (B)　102 (A)　103 (D)　104 (A)　105 (C)　106 (D)
107 (D)　108 (B)　109 (D)　110 (B)　111 (C)　112 (B)
113 (C)　114 (D)　115 (D)　116 (B)　117 (D)　118 (D)
119 (D)　120 (A)　121 (C)　122 (B)　123 (D)　124 (C)
125 (B)　126 (C)　127 (B)　128 (A)　129 (C)　130 (B)

PART 6
131 (A)　132 (B)　133 (C)　134 (C)　135 (B)　136 (B)
137 (C)　138 (D)　139 (C)　140 (C)　141 (B)　142 (B)
143 (B)　144 (A)　145 (C)　146 (B)

PART 7
147 (C)　148 (B)　149 (D)　150 (A)　151 (C)　152 (A)
153 (D)　154 (A)　155 (B)　156 (D)　157 (C)　158 (B)
159 (C)　160 (B)　161 (C)　162 (A)　163 (A)　164 (C)
165 (A)　166 (C)　167 (C)　168 (D)　169 (C)　170 (B)
171 (D)　172 (C)　173 (C)　174 (D)　175 (C)　176 (D)
177 (D)　178 (C)　179 (B)　180 (D)　181 (D)　182 (C)
183 (D)　184 (B)　185 (C)　186 (B)　187 (D)　188 (B)
189 (D)　190 (B)　191 (C)　192 (D)　193 (C)　194 (B)
195 (A)　196 (C)　197 (C)　198 (D)　199 (B)　200 (A)

Part 1

1.
(A) The woman is signing a piece of paper.
(B) The woman is plugging in a machine.
(C) The woman is copying a document.
(D) The woman is moving some office equipment.

(A) 여자가 종이 한 장에 서명하고 있다.
(B) 여자가 기계의 플러그를 꽂고 있다.
(C) 여자가 문서를 복사하고 있다.
(D) 여자가 일부 사무장비를 옮기고 있다.

| 해설 |
여자의 손동작과 시선 등으로 보아 복사기를 사용하고 있는 것으로 판단할 수 있으므로 이 동작에 초점을 맞춘 (C)가 정답이다. 서명하는 동작이나 플러그를 꽂는 동작, 그리고 장비를 옮기는 동작은 사진에서 볼 수 없다.

| 어휘 | sign ~에 서명하다　a piece of paper 종이 한 장　plug in ~의 플러그를 꽂다　equipment 장비

2.
(A) They are working at the airport.
(B) They are walking toward the plane.
(C) They are packing a backpack.
(D) They are buying an airline ticket.

(A) 사람들이 공항에서 일하고 있다.
(B) 사람들이 비행기를 향해 걸어가고 있다.
(C) 사람들이 배낭에 짐을 꾸리고 있다.
(D) 사람들이 항공권을 구입하고 있다.

| 해설 |
비행기를 향해 이동 중인 사람들의 동작에 초점을 맞춰 묘사한 (B)가 정답이다. 사람들의 옷차림과 배경 등으로 볼 때 일하는 것으로 보기 어려우며, 짐을 꾸리거나 항공권을 구입하는 동작도 보이지 않는다.

| 어휘 | toward ~을 향해, ~ 쪽으로　plane 비행기　pack ~에 짐을 꾸리다, 싸다, 포장하다

3.
(A) Some people are lifting a container.
(B) Some people are labeling the boxes.
(C) The man is polishing the glass door.
(D) The woman is wrapping up some items.

(A) 몇몇 사람들이 상자를 들어올리고 있다.
(B) 몇몇 사람들이 상자마다 라벨을 붙이고 있다.
(C) 남자가 유리문을 광이 나도록 닦고 있다.
(D) 여자가 몇몇 물품들을 포장하고 있다.

| 해설 |
두 사람이 함께 상자를 들어올리고 있는 동작에 초점을 맞춰 묘사한 (A)가 정답이다. 라벨 표기를 하는 동작과 유리문을 닦는 동작, 물품을 포장하는 동작은 사진에서 볼 수 없다.

| 어휘 | lift ~을 들어올리다　container 용기, 그릇, 상자　label ~을 라벨로 표기하다　polish ~을 광이 나도록 닦다　wrap up ~을 포장하다, 싸다

4.
(A) A worker is taking off a safety vest.
(B) The man is painting a rooftop.
(C) Some vehicles are being inspected.
(D) Some construction equipment is in use.

(A) 한 작업자가 안전 조끼를 벗고 있다.
(B) 남자가 옥상에 페인트칠을 하고 있다.
(C) 일부 차량들이 점검되는 중이다.
(D) 일부 공사 장비가 사용되고 있다.

| 해설 |
공사 장비가 사용되고 있는 상태에 초점을 맞춰 묘사한 (D)가 정답이다. 안전 조끼를 벗는 동작, 페인트칠을 하는 동작, 차량을 점검하는 동작은 사진에서 볼 수 없다.
| 어휘 | take off ~을 벗다 safety vest 안전 조끼 rooftop 옥상 vehicle 차량 inspect ~을 점검하다, 조사하다 equipment 장비 in use 사용 중인

5.
(A) Some sports gear is being handed out.
(B) Some fans are looking for their seats.
(C) The baseball stadium is being renovated.
(D) People are watching a sporting event.
(A) 일부 스포츠 장비가 지급되고 있다.
(B) 일부 팬들이 각자의 좌석을 찾고 있다.
(C) 야구 경기장이 개조되고 있다.
(D) 사람들이 스포츠 경기를 관람하고 있다.

| 해설 |
많은 사람들이 경기장에서 스포츠 경기를 관람하는 상황에 초점을 맞춰 묘사한 (D)가 정답이다. 장비가 지급되는 동작과 좌석을 찾는 동작, 그리고 개조 공사 중인 모습은 사진에서 볼 수 없다.
| 어휘 | sports gear 스포츠 장비 hand out ~을 나눠주다, 지급하다 look for ~을 찾다 seat 좌석 renovate ~을 개조하다, 보수하다

6.
(A) A picnic area is being cleared.
(B) Trees have been planted in lines.
(C) Some tables are being assembled.
(D) The park is crowded with visitors.
(A) 피크닉 공간이 청소되고 있다.
(B) 나무들이 줄지어 심어져 있다.
(C) 일부 탁자들이 조립되고 있다.
(D) 공원이 방문객들로 붐비고 있다.

| 해설 |
나무들이 줄지어 심어져 있는 상태에 초점을 맞춰 묘사한 (B)가 정답이다. 청소를 하는 사람의 동작과 탁자를 조립하는 사람의 동작, 방문객으로 보이는 사람의 모습은 모두 보이지 않는다.
| 어휘 | plant (식물 등) ~을 심다 in lines 줄지어, 줄을 서서 assemble ~을 조립하다 be crowded with ~로 붐비다

Part 2

7. Why did you buy a new car?
(A) Because this one is fuel efficient.
(B) A few months ago.
(C) At a local dealership.
왜 새 차를 사셨나요?
(A) 이것이 연비가 좋기 때문입니다.
(B) 몇 달 전에요.
(C) 지역 내 판매 대리점에서요.

| 해설 |
새 차를 산 이유를 묻는 Why 의문문에 대해 이유를 나타내는 Because와 함께 차량의 특성을 언급하는 (A)가 정답.
(B) 과거 시점 표현이므로 When 의문문에 어울리는 오답.
(C) 장소 표현이므로 Where 의문문에 어울리는 오답.
| 어휘 | fuel efficient 연비가 좋은 local 지역의, 현지의 dealership 판매 대리점

8. When's the medical journal releasing its next issue?
(A) For subscribers only.
(B) On April 5.
(C) A fascinating study.
그 의학 저널이 언제 다음 호를 출간하나요?
(A) 오직 구독자들만을 위한 것입니다.
(B) 4월 5일에요.
(C) 대단히 흥미로운 연구입니다.

| 해설 |
의학 저널이 다음 호를 출간하는 시점을 묻는 When 의문문에 대해 특정 날짜로 답변하는 (B)가 정답.
(A) 대상을 나타내는 For 전치사구로 답변하고 있으므로 질문의 핵심에서 벗어난 오답.
(C) 연구의 특성과 관련된 말이므로 질문의 핵심에서 벗어난 오답.
| 어휘 | medical 의학의, 의료의 release ~을 출시하다, 공개하다 issue (잡지 등의) 호 subscriber 구독자, 서비스 가입자 fascinating 대단히 흥미로운, 매력적인 study 연구, 조사

9. I think Martina Glenn's new novel will become a best-seller, don't you?
(A) Probably. She's really talented.
(B) At least two hundred pages.
(C) One of the local bookstores.
Martina Glenn의 신간 소설이 베스트셀러가 될 것 같아요. 그렇지 않나요?
(A) 아마도요. 그녀는 정말로 재능 있어요.
(B) 최소 200페이지요.
(C) 지역 내 서점들 중의 하나요.

| 해설 |
Martina Glenn의 신간 소설이 베스트셀러가 될 것 같지 않은지 확인하는 부가 의문문에 대해 가능성을 나타내는 Probably와 함께 그렇게 생각하는 이유를 언급하는 (A)가 정답.
(B) 책의 분량과 관련된 말이므로 질문의 핵심에서 벗어난 오답.
(C) 구입 장소를 알려 줄 때 할 수 있는 말이므로 베스트셀러 가능성과 관련 없는 오답.
| 어휘 | novel 소설 probably 아마 talented 재능 있는 at least 최소한, 적어도 local 지역의, 현지의

10. How many shipments should we expect to arrive?
(A) I'll be waiting for it.
(B) Two or three this afternoon.
(C) The shipment is coming by truck.
얼마나 많은 배송 물품이 도착할 것으로 우리가 예상해야 하나요?
(A) 제가 그것을 기다리고 있겠습니다.
(B) 오늘 오후에 2~3개요.
(C) 배송 물품이 트럭으로 옵니다.

| 해설 |
도착하는 배송 물품의 수를 묻는 How many 의문문에 대해 개수를 알려주는 말로 답변하는 (B)가 정답.
(A) it이 지칭하는 단수 명사가 무엇인지 알 수 없으므로 오답.
(C) 운송 수단을 알리는 답변이므로 방법을 묻는 How 의문문에 어울리는 오답.
| 어휘 | shipment 배송(품) expect to do ~할 것으로 예상하다, 기대하다 arrive 도착하다 by (수단) ~로, ~을 이용해

11. Who forgot to make copies of the report?
(A) Ms. Hampton did.
(B) I'll summarize what happened.
(C) Jenny would like some coffee.
누가 보고서를 복사하는 일을 잊었나요?
(A) Hampton 씨요.

(B) 무슨 일이 있었는지 제가 요약해 드리겠습니다.
(C) Jenny 씨가 커피를 마시고 싶어 합니다.

| 해설 |
보고서를 복사하는 일을 잊은 사람이 누구인지를 묻는 Who 의문문에 대해 forgot을 대신하는 did와 함께 직접 그 사람의 이름을 말하는 (A)가 정답.
(B) 질문에 언급된 과거 시제 동사(forgot)와 달리 미래 시제로 말하고 있어 시제 관계가 맞지 않는 오답.
(C) 질문에 쓰인 copies와 발음이 유사한 coffee를 활용한 오답.
| 어휘 | forget to do ~하는 것을 잊다   make copies of ~을 복사하다   report 보고(서)   summarize ~을 요약하다   would like ~하고 싶다, ~을 원하다

12. Where will this year's awards banquet be held?
(A) The last weekend in May.
(B) You did a great job.
(C) In Singapore, I think.
올해의 시상식 연회가 어디에서 개최되나요?
(A) 5월 마지막 주말입니다.
(B) 정말 잘해 주셨습니다.
(C) 싱가포르인 것 같아요.

| 해설 |
시상식 연회가 열리는 곳을 묻는 Where 의문문에 대해 장소를 나타내는 in 전치사구로 답변하는 (C)가 정답.
(A) 시점 표현이므로 When 의문문에 어울리는 오답.
(B) 칭찬을 할 때 사용하는 표현이므로 질문의 핵심에서 벗어난 오답.
| 어휘 | award 상   banquet 연회   hold ~을 개최하다, 열다

13. Isn't the utility payment due today?
(A) The price has increased significantly.
(B) Thank you for the reminder.
(C) He works as an accountant.
공과금 납부 기한이 오늘 아닌가요? (= ~ 오늘이죠?)
(A) 가격이 상당히 인상되었습니다.
(B) 알려 주셔서 감사합니다.
(C) 그는 회계사로 근무하고 있습니다.

| 해설 |
공과금 납부 기한이 오늘이 맞는지 확인하는 Isn't 부정 의문문에 대해 알려줘서 고맙다는 말로 상대방의 말이 맞다는 뜻을 나타낸 (B)가 정답.
(A) 공과금 납부 기한이 아닌 가격 인상을 언급하고 있어 질문의 핵심에서 벗어난 오답.
(C) 가리키는 대상을 알 수 없는 He를 언급한 오답.
| 어휘 | utility payment 공과금 납부(금)   due + 시점 ~가 기한인   increase 인상되다, 증가하다   significantly 상당히, 많이   reminder (말, 메시지 등) 알려 주는 것, 상기시키는 것   as (자격, 신분 등) ~로서   accountant 회계사

14. Please be careful about the icy road conditions.
(A) Only in the winter.
(B) All right, I'll watch out.
(C) Across the bridge.
빙판인 도로 상태에 주의하세요.
(A) 오직 겨울에만요.
(B) 알겠습니다, 조심할게요.
(C) 다리 건너편에요.

| 해설 |
빙판 도로에 주의하도록 당부하는 평서문에 대해 상대방의 의견을 수용하겠다는 의미의 All right과 함께 조심하겠다는 의지를 나타낸 (B)가 정답.
(A) 특정 기간을 알리는 말이므로 When 의문문에 어울리는 오답.
(C) 위치 표현이므로 Where 의문문에 어울리는 오답.

| 어휘 | be careful about ~에 대해 주의하다   icy 빙판의, 얼어 붙은   condition 상황, 상태   watch out 조심하다, 주의하다   across ~ 건너편에, 맞은편에

15. Who's leading the talks with the government?
(A) At ten tomorrow morning.
(B) In City Hall.
(C) Someone from the main office.
누가 정부와 나누는 담화를 진행하나요?
(A) 내일 오전 10시에요.
(B) 시청에서요.
(C) 본사에서 나오는 사람이요.

| 해설 |
담화 진행 책임자를 묻는 Who 의문문에 대해 그 담당자의 소속과 관련된 표현으로 답변하는 (C)가 정답.
(A) 시점 표현이므로 When 의문문에 어울리는 오답.
(B) 장소 표현이므로 Where 의문문에 어울리는 오답.
| 어휘 | lead ~을 진행하다, 이끌다   government 정부   main office 본사

16. You scanned the patient records from yesterday, didn't you?
(A) The medical clinic is nearby.
(B) We set a new sales record.
(C) I'm still working on it.
어제 오신 환자분의 기록을 살펴보셨죠, 그렇지 않나요?
(A) 진료소가 근처에 있어요.
(B) 우리는 매출 신기록을 세웠어요.
(C) 아직 그 일을 하는 중입니다.

| 해설 |
어제 온 환자의 기록을 살펴봤는지 확인하는 부가 의문문에 대해 그 일을 it으로 지칭해 아직 그 작업을 하는 과정 중임을 알리는 (C)가 정답.
(A) 진료소의 위치를 알려 주는 말이므로 질문의 핵심에서 벗어난 오답.
(B) 매출 신기록 달성 사실을 알리는 말이므로 환자 기록 확인 여부와 관련 없는 오답.
| 어휘 | patient 환자   medical clinic 진료소   nearby 근처에 있는   sales 매출, 판매(량), 영업   work on ~에 대한 일을 하다

17. When do you plan to visit Rome again?
(A) For about one week.
(B) At the Madison Hotel.
(C) Next month at the latest.
언제 다시 Rome을 방문하실 계획이신가요?
(A) 약 일주일 동안이요.
(B) Madison 호텔에서요.
(C) 늦어도 다음 달에요.

| 해설 |
상대방이 다시 Rome을 방문하는 시점을 묻는 When 의문문에 대해 대략적인 미래 시점 표현으로 답변하는 (C)가 정답.
(A) 기간을 나타내는 표현이므로 How long 의문문에 어울리는 오답.
(B) 장소 표현이므로 Where 의문문에 어울리는 오답.
| 어휘 | plan to do ~할 계획이다   about 약, 대략   at the latest 늦어도

18. Do you mind letting me borrow your printer?
(A) She borrowed it from the library.
(B) Erica will give you a ride.
(C) Sure, no problem.
당신 프린터를 제가 빌려 가도 괜찮을까요?
(A) 그녀는 도서관에서 그것을 빌렸습니다.
(B) Erica 씨가 당신을 차로 태워 드릴 겁니다.
(C) 그럼요, 문제없습니다.

| 해설 |
상대방의 프린터를 빌릴 수 있는지 묻는 Do you mind 일반 의문문에 대해 '문제없다'는 말로 빌려 가도 좋다는 뜻을 나타낸 (C)가 정답.
(A) 가리키는 대상을 알 수 없는 She를 언급한 오답.
(B) Erica 씨가 차로 태워 줄 예정임을 알리는 말이므로 프린터를 빌리는 일과 관련 없는 오답.

| 어휘 | borrow ~을 빌리다   give A a ride A를 차로 태워 주다

19. Is the conference room ready to be decorated?
(A) I learned a lot of useful information.
(B) Another group is still in there.
(C) The decorations are red and blue.

회의실이 장식될 준비가 되어 있나요?
(A) 저는 유용한 정보를 많이 알게 되었습니다.
(B) 또 다른 그룹이 여전히 그곳에 있습니다.
(C) 장식품이 빨간색과 파란색입니다.

| 해설 |
회의실이 장식될 준비가 되어 있는지 묻는 Is 일반 의문문에 대해 해당 장소를 there로 지칭해 다른 그룹이 아직 있다는 말로 준비된 상태가 아님을 알리는 (B)가 정답.
(A) 과거 시점에 자신이 한 일을 말하는 답변이므로 대회의실 준비 여부와 관련 없는 오답.
(C) 장식물의 색상을 언급하는 말이므로 질문의 핵심에서 벗어난 오답.

| 어휘 | be ready to do ~할 준비가 되다   decorate ~을 장식하다   useful 유용한   decoration 장식(물)

20. Should we have a picnic tomorrow for the team lunch?
(A) I'm not very hungry now.
(B) I think it's supposed to rain.
(C) To improve motivation.

우리가 내일 팀 점심 식사를 위해 피크닉을 가야 할까요?
(A) 저는 지금 그렇게 배가 고프지 않습니다.
(B) 비가 내릴 예정인 것 같아요.
(C) 동기를 증진하기 위해서요.

| 해설 |
내일 팀 점심 식사를 위해 피크닉을 가야 하는지 묻는 Should we 일반 의문문에 대해 비가 내릴 예정이라는 말로 갈 수 없음을 나타내는 (B)가 정답.
(A) 피크닉이 아닌 답변자 자신의 상태를 말하는 답변이므로 질문의 핵심에서 벗어난 오답.
(C) 목적을 나타내는 to부정사로 답변하고 있으므로 Why 의문문에 어울리는 오답.

| 어휘 | be supposed to do ~할 예정이다, ~하기로 되어 있다   improve ~을 증진하다, 향상시키다   motivation 동기 (부여)

21. How are sales at the Petersburg branch this year?
(A) They're better than ever.
(B) She sells all kinds of products.
(C) That brand is very popular.

올해 Petersburg 지점의 매출이 어떤가요?
(A) 그 어느 때보다 더 좋습니다.
(B) 그녀는 모든 종류의 제품을 판매합니다.
(C) 그 브랜드는 매우 인기가 높습니다.

| 해설 |
Petersburg 지점의 매출 수준을 묻는 How 의문문에 대해 sales를 They로 지칭해 어느 때보다 더 좋다는 말로 매출이 매우 높음을 나타내는 (A)가 정답.
(B) 가리키는 대상을 알 수 없는 She를 언급한 오답.
(C) 가리키는 대상을 알 수 없는 That brand와 그 특징을 언급한 오답.

| 어휘 | sales 매출, 판매(량), 영업   branch 지점, 지사   than ever 그 어느 때보다   popular 인기 있는

22. Do you want to work on budgets or inventory?
(A) Neither, I'm busy with something else.
(B) I'll find out for you.
(C) It worked out in the end.

예산 관련 작업과 재고 관련 작업 중에 어느 것을 하고 싶으세요?
(A) 둘 다 원치 않아요. 다른 일로 바쁘거든요.
(B) 제가 대신 알아봐 드릴게요.
(C) 결국엔 잘 되었어요.

| 해설 |
두 가지 업무를 놓고 묻는 선택 의문문에 대해 다른 일을 해야 하기 때문에 어느 것도 선택하지 않겠다는 뜻을 나타낸 (A)가 정답.
(B) 상대방을 대신 해 주겠다고 제안하는 말이므로 질문의 핵심에서 벗어난 오답.
(C) 과거 시점(worked)의 일에 대한 결과와 관련된 말이므로 앞으로 할 일을 묻는 질문에 맞지 않는 오답.

| 어휘 | budget 예산   inventory 재고(품), 재고 목록   neither 둘 다 아니다   in the end 결국에는

23. Where do I need to input my salary on this tax form?
(A) The accountant can answer that.
(B) No later than April 15.
(C) Yes, I've received it.

이 납세 신고서의 어디에 제 연봉을 기입해야 하나요?
(A) 회계사가 그 부분을 답변해 드릴 수 있습니다.
(B) 늦어도 4월 15일까지는요.
(C) 네, 저는 그것을 받았습니다.

| 해설 |
서식 내에 연봉을 기입하는 위치를 묻는 Where 의문문에 대해 그와 관련된 정보를 알 수 있는 방법으로서 회계사가 답변해 줄 수 있다고 말하는 (A)가 정답.
(B) 시점 표현이므로 When 의문문에 어울리는 오답.
(C) 의문사 의문문에 맞지 않는 Yes로 답변하는 오답.

| 어휘 | input ~을 기입하다, 입력하다   tax form 납세 신고서   accountant 회계사   no later than + 시점 늦어도 ~까지는   receive ~을 받다

24. Weren't the product samples supposed to arrive today?
(A) They're in these boxes.
(B) I have a late flight.
(C) Sure, let's give them a try.

제품 샘플들이 오늘 도착할 예정이지 않았나요? (= ~ 예정이죠?)
(A) 이 상자들 안에 들어 있습니다.
(B) 제 비행기는 늦은 시간에 있습니다.
(C) 물론이죠, 그것들을 한번 써봅시다.

| 해설 |
제품 샘플들이 오늘 도착할 예정이었던 것이 맞는지 확인하는 Weren't 부정 의문문에 대해 특정 상자에 들어 있다는 말로 이미 샘플들이 도착했음을 나타내는 (A)가 정답.
(B) 제품 샘플이 아닌 답변자 자신의 항공편 일정을 말하고 있어 질문의 핵심에서 벗어난 오답.
(C) 긍정을 뜻하는 Sure 뒤에 이어지는 말이 물품 도착 여부와 관련 없는 오답.

| 어휘 | be supposed to do ~할 예정이다, ~하기로 되어 있다   arrive 도착하다   flight 항공편   give A a try A를 시도해 보다, 경험해 보다

25. I'm planning on having my suit custom made.
(A) I can recommend a good tailor.
(B) No, it didn't really suit me.
(C) Aren't the plans well-organized?

저는 정장을 맞출 계획입니다.
(A) 제가 좋은 양복점을 추천해 드릴 수 있어요.
(B) 아뇨, 그건 제게 정말 맞지 않아요.
(C) 계획들이 잘 준비되어 있지 않나요?

| 해설 |
정장을 맞출 계획임을 밝히는 평서문에 대해 좋은 양복점을 추천해 주겠다는 말로 답변하는 (A)가 정답.
(B) 과거 시점의 일을 언급하고 있으므로 앞으로의 계획을 밝히는 말에 어울리지 않는 오답.
(C) 계획의 준비 상태를 확인하기 위해 되묻는 말이므로 핵심에서 벗어난 오답.

| 어휘 | custom made 맞춤 제작된   suit 정장   recommend ~을 추천하다   tailor 양복점   suit ~에게 맞다, 적합하다   well-organized 잘 준비된, 잘 정리된

26. What supplies should I request for the laboratory?
(A) Because I'm going there soon.
(B) Yes, just submit the form.
(C) Todd's worked in the lab a long time.

실험실용으로 무슨 물품을 신청해야 하나요?
(A) 제가 곧 그리로 가기 때문입니다.
(B) 네, 그냥 양식만 제출해 주세요.
(C) Todd 씨가 실험실에서 오랫동안 일해 왔습니다.

| 해설 |
신청해야 하는 용품이 무엇인지 묻는 What 의문문에 대해 Todd 씨가 실험실에서 오래 일했다는 말로 그 사람을 통해 확인할 수 있음을 알리는 (C)가 정답.
(A) 이유를 나타내는 Because절로 답변하고 있으므로 Why 의문문에 어울리는 오답.
(B) 의문사 의문문에 맞지 않는 Yes로 답변하는 오답.

| 어휘 | supplies 용품, 물품   request ~을 신청하다, 요청하다   laboratory 실험실, 연구실(= lab)   submit ~을 제출하다   form 양식, 서식

27. Are you considering a nonstop flight or one with a layover?
(A) I need to check my schedule.
(B) Leaving at noon tomorrow.
(C) No, that's not correct.

직항편과 경유지가 있는 것 중에 어느 것을 고려하고 계신가요?
(A) 제 일정을 확인해 봐야 합니다.
(B) 내일 정오에 떠납니다.
(C) 아뇨, 그건 맞지 않아요.

| 해설 |
이용할 항공편과 관련해 두 가지 종류를 언급하는 선택 의문문에 대해 일정을 확인해야 한다는 말로 선택을 위한 조건을 먼저 제시하는 (A)가 정답.
(B) 미래 시점에 출발한다고 답변하고 있으므로 When 의문문에 어울리는 오답.
(C) 선택 의문문에 맞지 않는 No로 답변하는 오답.

| 어휘 | consider ~을 고려하다   nonstop flight 직항편   layover 경유(지), 기착지   leave 떠나다, 출발하다   correct 맞은, 옳은, 정확한

28. Have you seen ticket prices for flights?
(A) All right, then let's take the train.
(B) She is a frequent flyer.
(C) I loved exploring the city.

항공권 가격을 확인해 보셨나요?
(A) 알았어요, 그럼 기차를 타죠.
(B) 그녀는 항공편 단골 이용 고객입니다.
(C) 그 도시를 탐방한 것이 아주 좋았어요.

| 해설 |
항공권 가격이 비싸다는 의도로 항공권 가격을 확인했는지 묻는 Have 일반 의문문에 대해 기차를 타자는 대안을 제시하는 (A)가 정답.
(B) 가리키는 대상을 알 수 없는 She를 언급한 오답.
(C) 자신이 과거에 한 일을 언급하는 말이므로 질문의 핵심에서 벗어난 오답.

| 어휘 | flight 항공편, 비행   then 그럼, 그렇다면   take (교통편) ~을 이용하다, 타다   frequent flyer 항공사 단골 고객   explore ~을 탐방하다, 둘러보다

29. We should make it easier for customers to see these sweaters.
(A) Yes, I'll review the contract.
(B) Four different sizes, I think.
(C) Aiden volunteered to set up a display.

우리는 고객들이 이 스웨터들을 더 쉽게 볼 수 있도록 해야 합니다.
(A) 네, 제가 계약서를 검토해 보겠습니다.
(B) 네 가지 다른 사이즈인 것 같아요.
(C) Aiden 씨가 진열품을 설치하겠다고 자원해 주셨어요.

| 해설 |
고객들이 스웨터들을 더 쉽게 볼 수 있도록 해야 한다고 알리는 평서문에 대해 Aiden 씨가 진열품을 설치하겠다고 자원한 사실을 밝힘으로써 이미 조치를 취한 상황임을 알리는 (C)가 정답.
(A) 답변자 자신이 계약서를 검토하겠다는 말이므로 핵심에서 벗어난 오답.
(B) 사이즈 종류를 알리는 말이므로 핵심에서 벗어난 오답.

| 어휘 | make it + 형용사 + for A to do A가 ~하는 것을 …하게 만들다   review ~을 검토하다   contract 계약(서)   volunteer to do ~하겠다고 자원하다   set up ~을 설치하다, 마련하다   display 진열(품), 전시(품)

30. The sample design portfolios must be mailed separately.
(A) I'll tell the job applicants.
(B) At least sixteen pages.
(C) I added some brighter colors.

샘플 디자인 포트폴리오는 반드시 따로 우송되어야 합니다.
(A) 제가 구직 지원자들에게 말하겠습니다.
(B) 최소 16페이지요.
(C) 제가 일부 더 밝은 색상들을 추가했습니다.

| 해설 |
샘플 디자인 포트폴리오가 따로 우송되어야 한다는 사실을 알리는 평서문에 대해 그와 같은 정보를 알아야 하는 사람인 구직 지원자들에게 알리겠다는 뜻을 나타낸 (A)가 정답.
(B) 문서의 분량에 해당되는 답변이므로 핵심에서 벗어난 오답.
(C) 과거 시점(added)의 일을 말하고 있으므로 앞으로 해야 하는 일을 언급하는 상황에 맞지 않는 오답.

| 어휘 | portfolio (구직 시에 제출하는 작업물들을 담은) 포트폴리오   mail 우송하다, 우편으로 보내다   separately 따로, 별도로, 나눠서   job applicant 구직 지원자   at least 최소한, 적어도   add ~을 추가하다   bright 밝은

31. Why has the staff meeting not been scheduled yet?
(A) Okay, I'll meet you tomorrow.
(B) A new employee on the staff.
(C) You didn't get the e-mail?

왜 직원 회의 일정이 아직 정해지지 않은 건가요?
(A) 좋아요, 내일 뵙겠습니다.
(B) 직원들 중에 신입 사원 한 명이요.

(C) 이메일 못 받으셨어요?

| 해설 |
직원 회의 일정이 아직 정해지지 않은 이유를 묻는 Why 의문문에 대해 이메일을 받지 못했는지 반문하는 것으로 관련 정보가 이미 제공된 상황임을 언급하는 (C)가 정답.
(A) Yes와 같은 역할을 하는 Okay로 답변하고 있으므로 이유를 묻는 의문사 Why에 맞지 않는 오답.
(B) 신입 직원을 언급하고 있으므로 질문의 핵심에서 벗어난 오답.

| 어휘 | schedule ~의 일정을 정하다

Part 3

Questions 32-34 refer to the following conversation.

> W: Good morning. **32** **I heard an ad about your hair salon on the radio**, and I'm wondering if I could book an appointment.
> M: Of course. We're located in the Ashford Building. **33** **We're the only hair salon in the business district. So, if you work around here, it's easy to stop by** on a lunch break or after work. What day did you have in mind?
> W: Are there any openings for Friday? **34** **I have a meeting with an important new client next week**, so I want to take care of this quickly.

32-34번 문제는 다음 대화를 참조하시오.

여: 안녕하세요. 제가 라디오에서 그쪽 미용실에 관한 광고를 들었는데, 예약을 할 수 있는지 궁금해요.
남: 물론입니다. 저희는 Ashford 빌딩에 위치해 있습니다. 저희가 상업 지구 내에서 유일한 미용실입니다. 그래서 이곳 근처에서 근무하고 계시면, 점심 식사 시간이나 퇴근 후에 들르시기 쉽습니다. 무슨 요일을 생각하고 계신가요?
여: 금요일에 빈 시간대가 있나요? 제가 다음 주에 중요한 신규 고객과 회의가 있어서, 이 일을 빨리 처리하고 싶어요.

| 어휘 | ad 광고   wonder if ~인지 궁금하다   book an appointment 예약하다   be located in ~에 위치해 있다   district 구역, 지구   stop by 들르다   have A in mind A를 마음에 두다, 염두에 두다   opening 빈 시간대   take care of ~을 처리하다, 다루다   quickly 빨리, 신속히

32. 여자는 해당 업체에 대해 어떻게 알게 되었는가?
(A) 친구와 이야기함으로써
(B) 잡지를 읽음으로써
(C) 라디오를 들음으로써
(D) 전단을 받음으로써

| 해설 |
대화 초반부에, 여자가 라디오에서 미용실 광고를 들었다는(I heard an ad about your hair salon on the radio ~) 말로 정보의 출처를 밝히고 있으므로 (C)가 정답이다.

33. 남자의 말에 따르면, 무엇이 해당 업체를 특별하게 만드는가?
(A) 합리적인 가격
(B) 편리한 위치
(C) 아는 것이 많은 직원들
(D) 환경 친화적인 상품

| 해설 |
업체의 특징이 언급되는 중반부에, 남자가 점심 식사 시간이나 퇴근 후에 들르기 쉽다는 점을(So, if you work around here, it's easy to stop by ~) 알리고 있는데, 이는 위치의 편리함을 말하는 것이므로 (B)가 정답

이다.

| 어휘 | reasonable (가격이) 적정한   convenient 편리한   knowledgeable 아는 것이 많은   environmentally friendly 환경 친화적인

34. 여자는 다음 주에 무엇을 할 계획인가?
(A) 휴가 가기
(B) 고객과 만나기
(C) 연설하기
(D) 사무실 이전하기

| 해설 |
'다음 주'라는 시점이 언급되는 후반부에 여자가 중요한 신규 고객과 회의가 있다고(I have a meeting with an important new client next week ~) 알리고 있으므로 (B)가 정답이다.

| 어휘 | relocate 이전하다

Questions 35-37 refer to the following conversation.

> W: Excuse me. **35** **I'm wondering if you could tell me the best way to get to the Tetrick Building in the historic district**. Is it close enough to walk?
> M: Not really. There's a subway station at the end of the block. You can take Line 3 northbound for three stops and get off at Fleming Station.
> W: Thanks. I hope it doesn't take a long time. **36** **I'm interviewing for a new job at two o'clock.**
> M: **37** **You should check the exact travel times on the Department of Transportation's homepage online** if you have a smartphone.

35-37번 문제는 다음 대화를 참조하시오.

여: 실례합니다. 유적지 구역 내에 있는 Tetrick 빌딩으로 가는 가장 좋은 방법을 저에게 알려 주실 수 있는지 궁금합니다. 걸어서 가기에 충분히 가까운가요?
남: 꼭 그렇지는 않습니다. 이 블록 끝에 지하철역이 하나 있어요. 3호선을 타시고 북쪽으로 세 정거장 가신 다음, Fleming 역에서 내리시면 됩니다.
여: 감사합니다. 시간이 오래 걸리지 않았으면 좋겠어요. 제가 새 직장 때문에 2시에 면접을 보거든요.
남: 스마트폰을 갖고 계시면 교통국 홈페이지에서 온라인으로 정확한 운행 시간을 확인해 보세요.

| 어휘 | wonder if ~인지 궁금하다   the best way to do ~하는 가장 좋은 방법   get to ~로 가다   historic 역사적인   district 구역, 지구   close 가까운   enough to do ~하기에 충분히   take (교통편) ~을 타다, 이용하다   northbound 북쪽으로 향하는   get off at ~에서 내리다   take a long time 시간이 오래 걸리다   exact 정확한   travel time 운행 시간, 이동 시간   Department of Transportation 교통국

35. 여자는 무엇에 관해 문의하는가?
(A) 지하철 요금
(B) 한 업체의 폐장 시간
(C) 한 장소로 가는 방법
(D) 교통 체증

| 해설 |
대화를 시작하면서 여자가 Tetrick Building으로 가는 가장 좋은 방법을 알려 줄 수 있는지(I'm wondering if you could tell me the best way to get to the Tetrick Building ~) 묻고 있으므로 (C)가 정답이다.

| 어휘 | fare (교통편) 요금   directions to ~로 가는 방법, 찾아가는 길   site 장소, 현장   traffic 교통편, 차량들   delay 지연, 지체

36. 여자는 오늘 오후에 무엇을 할 계획인가?
(A) 면접에 참석하기

(B) 콘서트에 가기
(C) 역사 여행 떠나기
(D) 전시회 방문하기

| 해설 |
대화 중반부에, 여자가 오후 시점에 해당되는 at two o'clock이라는 표현과 함께 면접을 본다(I'm interviewing for a new job ~) 알리고 있으므로 (A)가 정답이다.

| 어휘 | plan to do ~할 계획이다   attend ~에 참석하다   take a tour 여행하다   exhibit 전시(회)

37. 남자는 무엇을 하도록 권하는가?
(A) 택시 타기
(B) 웹 사이트 확인하기
(C) 사무실에 전화하기
(D) 지도 다운로드하기

| 해설 |
남자가 권하는 일이 언급되는 후반부에, 온라인으로 홈 페이지에서 정확한 운행 시간을 확인해 보도록(You should check the exact travel times on the Department of Transportation's homepage online ~) 권하고 있으므로 (B)가 정답이다.

Questions 38-40 refer to the following conversation.

W: Hello. **38** **My doctor called in a prescription for me, and the pharmacist said it would be ready** anytime after ten o'clock. My name is Latoya Hunt.
M: I'm really sorry, but I can't process any requests for medication at the moment. **39** **Unfortunately, our computer shut down unexpectedly.** A technician is looking into the issue, but it could take another hour or so.
W: Oh, I can't wait that long. I'm on my lunch break, and I need to get back to my office. I won't have time to stop by in person tomorrow either.
M: Well, **40** **I could send you your order through our delivery service. And since it's our fault, I'll waive the fee.**

38-40번 문제는 다음 대화를 참조하시오.
여: 안녕하세요. 의사 선생님께서 제 처방전을 내리셨고, 약사님께서 10시 이후에 언제든지 준비될 거라고 하셨어요. 제 이름은 Latoya Hunt입니다.
남: 정말 죄송하지만, 현재 의약품에 대한 어떤 요청도 처리해 드릴 수 없습니다. 안타깝게도, 저희 컴퓨터가 예기치 못하게 정지되었어요. 수리 기사가 그 문제를 조사해 보는 중인데, 앞으로 1시간 정도 더 걸릴 수도 있습니다.
여: 아, 저는 그렇게 오래 기다릴 수 없어요. 지금 점심 시간이라서, 사무실로 돌아가야 해요. 내일 직접 들를 시간도 나지 않습니다.
남: 저, 저희 배송 서비스를 통해서 주문품을 보내 드릴 수 있습니다. 그리고 저희 잘못이기 때문에, 그 요금은 받지 않겠습니다.

| 어휘 | call in 전화해 ~을 요청하다   prescription 처방전   pharmacist 약사   process ~을 처리하다   request 요청   medication 약, 약물   at the moment 현재   unfortunately 안타깝게도, 아쉽게도   shut down (시스템 등이) 정지되다, 중단되다   unexpectedly 예기치 못하게   look into ~을 조사하다   issue 문제, 사안   take ~의 시간이 걸리다   or so (숫자 표현 뒤에서) ~ 정도   that 그렇게, 그만큼   get back to ~로 돌아가다   stop by 들르다   in person 직접 (가서)   either (부정문에서) ~도   order 주문(품)   through ~을 통해   since ~이므로   fault 잘못, 실수   waive (비용 등) ~을 받지 않다, 철회하다   fee 요금, 수수료

38. 남자는 어디에서 근무할 것 같은가?
(A) 약국에서
(B) 의류 매장에서
(C) 카페에서
(D) 치과에서

| 해설 |
여자가 대화를 시작하면서 의사가 처방을 내렸고 약사가 10시 이후에 준비된다고 말했다면서(My doctor called in a prescription for me, and the pharmacist said it would be ready ~) 자신의 이름을 밝히고 있다. 따라서 처방약을 찾으러 약국에 간 상황임을 알 수 있으므로 (A)가 정답이다.

39. 남자는 무슨 문제점을 언급하는가?
(A) 한 팀에 직원이 부족하다.
(B) 한 가지 정책이 최근에 변경되었다.
(C) 컴퓨터가 작동되지 않고 있다.
(D) 주문 양식에 서명이 되지 않았다.

| 해설 |
대화 중반부에, 남자가 부정적인 얘기를 꺼낼 때 사용하는 Unfortunately와 함께 컴퓨터가 정지된 사실을(our computer shut down unexpectedly) 언급하고 있으므로 (C)가 정답이다.

| 어휘 | short-staffed 직원이 부족한   policy 정책, 방침   recently 최근에   work (기계 등이) 작동되다   order form 주문 양식   sign ~에 서명하다

40. 남자는 여자에게 무엇을 제안하는가?
(A) 업체 카탈로그
(B) 무료 배송 서비스
(C) 제품 샘플
(D) 할인 쿠폰

| 해설 |
남자의 제안 사항이 언급되는 후반부에, 배송 서비스를 통해서 주문품을 보내 줄 수 있다는 말과 함께 배송 요금을 받지 않겠다고(I could send you your order through our delivery service. And since it's our fault, I'll waive the fee) 알리고 있으므로 (B)가 정답이다.

| 어휘 | free 무료의

Questions 41-43 refer to the following conversation with three speakers.

W1: Welcome to Jenkins Realty, Mr. Hayes. I've asked Ms. Lang to join us. She's the one you spoke to on the phone.
M: Thanks for meeting with me. **41** **I'm looking for a new site for my catering business.** I plan to buy more ovens and refrigerators because we've been growing steadily, so I'll need at least 800 square feet.
W2: All right. And, you mentioned that **42** **you must have a building with a designated zone for loading goods?**
M: That's right. It'll make transporting our items much easier.
W2: That's understandable. We have a few buildings in mind that meet your needs.
M: Wonderful. And are they available by June 1? **43** **We absolutely must move on that date because our current building will be demolished to make room for a shopping center.**

41-43번 문제는 다음 세 명의 대화를 참조하시오.

여1: Jenkins Realty에 오신 것을 환영합니다, Hayes 씨. 제가 Lang 씨께 저희와 함께 하도록 요청 드렸습니다. 이 분이 전화상으로 이야기 나누셨던 분입니다.

남: 만나 주셔서 감사합니다. 제가 운영하는 출장 요리 업체에 필요한 새로운 장소를 찾는 중입니다. 저희가 지속적으로 성장해 오고 있기 때문에 추가 오븐과 냉장고를 구입할 계획이라서, 최소 800평방피트의 공간이 필요합니다.

여2: 알겠습니다. 그리고, 반드시 상품을 싣는 데 필요한 지정 구역이 있는 건물이어야 한다고 말씀하셨죠?

남: 맞습니다. 그래야 저희 제품을 운송하는 일이 훨씬 더 수월해질 겁니다.

여2: 이해가 됩니다. 그 필요 사항을 충족하는 몇몇 건물이 생각납니다.

남: 아주 좋습니다. 그리고 6월 1일까지 이용 가능한가요? 저희가 반드시 그 날짜에 이전해야 하는데, 현재 이용 중인 건물이 쇼핑 센터 건설에 필요한 자리를 확보하기 위해 철거될 것이기 때문입니다.

| 어휘 | ask A to do A에게 ~하도록 요청하다 join ~와 함께 하다 on the phone 전화상으로 meet with (약속하여) ~와 만나다 look for ~을 찾다 site 장소, 현장 catering 출장 요리 제공(업) business 업체, 회사 plan to do ~할 계획이다 refrigerator 냉장고 grow 성장하다 steadily 지속적으로, 꾸준히 at least 최소한 square feet 평방피트 mention that ~라고 말하다, 언급하다 designated 지정된 load ~을 싣다 goods 상품 make A + 형용사 A를 ~한 상태로 만들다 transport ~을 운송하다 much (비교급 수식) 훨씬 understandable 이해할 수 있는 have A in mind A를 생각해 두다 meet ~을 충족하다 available 구입 가능한, 이용 가능한 absolutely 반드시, 절대로 current 현재의 demolish ~을 철거하다 make room 공간을 확보하다

41. 남자는 자신의 업체에 대해 무엇을 암시하는가?
(A) 새로운 장비를 구할 것이다.
(B) 추가 직원을 고용할 것이다.
(C) 경쟁사를 매입할 것이다.
(D) 새로운 서비스를 추가할 것이다.

| 해설 |
대화 중반부에, 남자가 추가 오븐과 냉장고를 구입할 계획임을 알리고 있는데(I'm looking for a new site for my catering business. I plan to buy more ovens and refrigerators ~), 이는 새 장비를 구입하겠다는 말이므로 (A)가 정답이다.

| 어휘 | equipment 장비 competitor 경쟁사, 경쟁자 add ~을 추가하다

42. 남자에게 필수인 한 가지 특징은 무엇인가?
(A) 엄격한 보안
(B) 휴게실
(C) 지하 주차장
(D) 짐을 싣는 구역

| 해설 |
대화 중반부에, 남자가 상품을 싣는 데 필요한 지정 구역이 있는 건물을 필요로 한다는 사실을(~ you must have a building with a designated zone for loading goods) 언급하고 있으므로 (D)가 정답이다.

| 어휘 | essential 필수적인 tight 엄격한, 빠듯한

43. 남자의 말에 따르면, 왜 이전 날짜를 변경할 수 없는가?
(A) 개장 행사가 홍보되었다.
(B) 건물이 허물어질 것이다.
(C) 이사 서비스가 예약되었다.
(D) 임대 계약이 만료될 것이다.

| 해설 |
대화 마지막에, 남자가 6월 1일에 꼭 이전해야 한다는 말과 함께 현재 이용 중인 건물이 철거된다는(We absolutely must move on that date because our current building will be demolished ~) 사실을 알리고 있으므로 (B)가 정답이다.

| 어휘 | be unable to do ~할 수 없다 promote ~을 홍보하다 tear down (건물 등) ~을 허물다, 철거하다 book ~을 예약하다 lease agreement 임대 계약(서) expire 만료되다

Questions 44-46 refer to the following conversation.

M: Caroline, **44** do you know if the new curtains for Conference Room B will be delivered today? As you know, the current ones aren't dark enough for when we use the projector and screen.
W: I'm ready to place the order, but **45** don't forget that I need the manager to approve that cost. I'm still waiting for that. Can't you use Conference Room A in the meantime?
M: Well, I'm supposed to give a presentation at 2, and **46** Mr. Reeves already reserved the room for that time. I'll talk to him to find out if he's able to change rooms with me.

44-46번 문제는 다음 대화를 참조하시오.

남: Caroline 씨, 오늘 대회의실 B에 새로운 커튼이 배송되는지 알고 계세요? 아시다시피, 지금 사용 중인 것은 우리가 프로젝터와 스크린을 사용할 때 충분히 어둡지 않아요.

여: 주문할 준비가 되어 있기는 하지만, 부장님께서 그 비용을 승인해 주셔야 한다는 점을 잊지 마세요. 여전히 그것을 기다리고 있거든요. 그동안 대회의실 A를 사용하실 수는 없나요?

남: 저, 제가 2시에 발표를 할 예정인데, Reeves 씨가 이미 그 시간에 그 방을 예약하셨어요. 그 방들을 서로 맞바꿀 수 있는지 확인하기 위해 그 분에게 얘기해 볼게요.

| 어휘 | current 현재의 enough (형용사 뒤에서) 충분히 be ready to do ~할 준비가 되다 place an order 주문하다 forget that ~임을 잊다 need A to do A가 ~하기를 원하다 approve ~을 승인하다 in the meantime 그동안, 그 사이에 be supposed to do ~할 예정이다, ~하기로 되어 있다 give a presentation 발표하다 reserve ~을 예약하다 find out if ~인지 확인하다, 알아보다 be able to do ~할 수 있다

44. 대화의 주제는 무엇인가?
(A) 사업 계약
(B) 장비 수리
(C) 제품 배송
(D) 신입 직원

| 해설 |
대화를 시작하면서 남자가 새로운 커튼이 오늘 배송되는지 물었고(~ do you know if the new curtains for Conference Room B will be delivered today?) 이와 관련한 대화가 이어지고 있으므로 (C)가 정답이다.

| 어휘 | agreement 계약(서) repair 수리

45. 여자는 남자에게 무엇에 관해 상기시키는가?
(A) 나중에 남자를 만날 계획을 갖고 있다.
(B) 오늘 일찍 퇴근할 것이다.
(C) 외부 지역에서 열리는 콘퍼런스에 참석할 것이다.
(D) 예산 승인을 기다리고 있다.

| 해설 |
대화 중반부에 여자가 부장님이 비용을 승인해 주셔야 한다는 점을 잊지 말라고(~ don't forget that I need the manager to approve that cost) 당부하고 있으므로 예산 승인을 기다리고 있다는 의미로 쓰인 (D)가 정답이다.

| 어휘 | plan to do ~하려는 계획 leave the office 퇴근하다 attend ~에

참석하다   out-of-town 외부 지역의   await ~을 기다리다   budget 예산   approval 승인

46. 남자는 왜 Reeves 씨에게 이야기할 것인가?
(A) 예약 사항 변경을 요청하기 위해
(B) 새로운 배정 업무를 주기 위해
(C) 특별 행사에 초대하기 위해
(D) 한 문서에 관한 의견을 요청하기 위해

| 해설 |
Reeves 씨의 이름이 언급되는 마지막 부분에, Reeves 씨가 이미 예약한 방과 서로 맞바꿀 수 있는지 확인하기 위해 얘기하겠다고(Mr. Reeves already reserved the room for that time. I'll talk to him to find out if he's able to change rooms with me) 남자가 말하고 있다. 따라서 예약 변경 요청을 의미하는 (A)가 정답이다.

| 어휘 | request ~을 요청하다   reservation 예약   work assignment 배정 업무, 할당 업무   ask for ~을 요청하다   feedback 의견

Questions 47-49 refer to the following conversation.

> W: Hi, Manuel. Thanks again for all of your hard work with **47** the grand opening at the Langston branch last month.
> M: It was my pleasure. I'm glad that everything went smoothly. **48** A lot of people were impressed that they didn't have to wait a long time in the checkout aisle.
> W: I heard that, too. I'm glad we invested in high-tech scanners that help to keep the lines moving, and our sales clerks have been offering excellent customer service.
> M: We should do something for them to show our appreciation.
> W: What did you have in mind?
> M: **49** How about this—I'll call a local catering company and get them to bring in a selection of coffee and muffins?

47-49번 문제는 다음 대화를 참조하시오.
여: 안녕하세요, Manuel 씨. 지난달에 Langston 지점에서 있었던 개장식과 관련해 보여주신 모든 노고에 대해 다시 한번 감사드립니다.
남: 별 말씀을요. 모든 일이 순조롭게 진행되어서 기쁩니다. 많은 사람들이 계산대 통로에서 오랜 시간을 기다릴 필요가 없었던 것에 대해 깊은 인상을 받았어요.
여: 저도 그 얘기를 들었어요. 대기하는 줄이 계속 움직이게 하는 최신 스캐너에 우리가 투자한 것이 기쁘고, 우리 판매 점원들은 계속해서 훌륭한 고객 서비스를 제공하고 있어요.
남: 감사의 뜻을 전하기 위해 그 점원들에게 뭔가 해야 해요.
여: 생각해 두신 것이라도 있으세요?
남: 제가 지역 출장 요리 업체에 전화해서 다양한 커피와 머핀을 제공하도록 하는 건 어떨까요?

| 어휘 | branch 지점, 지사   go smoothly 순조롭게 진행되다   be impressed that ~라는 점에 대해 깊은 인상을 받다   checkout 계산(대)   aisle 통로, 복도   invest in ~에 투자하다   high-tech 최신의, 첨단의   keep A -ing A를 계속 ~하게 만들다   sales 판매, 영업   clerk 점원   offer ~을 제공하다   have A in mind A를 생각해 두다, 마음에 두다   How about A? A는 어떠세요?   local 지역의, 현지의   catering 출장 요리 제공(업)   get A to do A에게 ~하게 하다   bring in ~을 가져오다, 들여오다   a selection of 다양한

47. 지난달에 무슨 일이 있었는가?
(A) 건물 임대 계약이 만료되었다.

(B) 반품 정책이 업데이트되었다.
(C) 추가 지점이 개장했다.
(D) 신제품이 출시되었다.

| 해설 |
'지난달'이라는 시점이 언급되는 초반부에, 여자가 Langston 지점에서 있었던 개장식을(~ the grand opening at the Langston branch last month) 언급하고 있으므로 (C)가 정답이다.

| 어휘 | lease 임대 계약(서)   expire 만료되다   return 반품, 반납   policy 정책, 방침   additional 추가의   launch ~을 출시하다

48. 남자의 말에 따르면, 무슨 특징이 고객들에게 깊은 인상을 주었는가?
(A) 저렴한 배송 서비스
(B) 다양한 선택권
(C) 아는 것이 많은 직원들
(D) 빠른 계산 시간

| 해설 |
대화 중반부에, 남자가 많은 사람들이 계산대 통로에서 오랜 시간을 기다릴 필요가 없었던 것에 대해 깊은 인상을 받은(A lot of people were impressed that they didn't have to wait a long time ~) 사실을 언급하고 있다. 즉, 계산이 빨리 끝났다는 말이므로 (D)가 정답이다.

| 어휘 | affordable (가격이) 저렴한, 알맞은   selection 선택 (가능한 것)   knowledgeable 아는 것이 많은

49. 남자는 무엇을 할 것이라고 말하는가?
(A) 일부 문서 복사하기
(B) 출장 요리 업체와 이야기하기
(C) 한 직원을 승진시키기
(D) 디자인 한 가지를 선택하기

| 해설 |
대화 마지막에, 남자가 지역 출장 요리 업체에 전화하는 것을(How about this — I'll call a local catering company ~) 제안하고 있으므로 (B)가 정답이다.

| 어휘 | promote 승진시키다

Questions 50-52 refer to the following conversation.

> W: Hi, Stephen. I hope you had a good time at the **50** National Real Estate Convention.
> M: I'm really glad I went.
> W: That's great. Did you pick up any useful tips?
> M: Actually, yes. The keynote speaker, **51** Geraldo Sanz, suggested that **50** realtors like us **51** should enroll in a class on how to take photos.
> W: That makes sense. Potential customers are always browsing them on our Web site.
> M: Exactly. And he mentioned that the Cooper Institute is starting a new course on the topic next month.
> W: Maybe some of our employees would be interested in attending.
> M: Right. **52** I'm going to put up a paper in the break room for people to write down their name if they want to participate.

50-52번 문제는 다음 대화를 참조하시오.
여: 안녕하세요, Stephen 씨. 전국 부동산 회의에서 즐거운 시간 보내셨기를 바랍니다.
남: 그곳에 간 것이 정말 기뻤어요.
여: 잘됐네요. 유용한 팁이라도 배우셨나요?

남: 실은, 그랬어요. 기조 연설자이신 Geraldo Sanz 씨께서 우리 같은 부동산 중개업자들이 사진 촬영 방법에 관한 강좌에 등록해야 한다고 권해 주셨어요.
여: 이해가 되네요. 잠재 고객들이 항상 우리 웹 사이트에서 둘러보니까요.
남: 바로 그거예요. 그리고 Cooper Institute에서 다음달에 그 주제로 새로운 강좌를 시작한다는 말씀도 해주셨어요.
여: 아마 일부 우리 직원들이 참석하는 데 관심이 있을 거예요.
남: 맞아요. 참여하기를 원할 경우에 사람들이 각자의 이름을 적어 놓을 수 있도록 휴게실에 종이를 붙여 놓을 예정입니다.

| 어휘 | pick up (정보 등) ~을 배우다, 알게 되다   useful 유용한   actually 실은, 사실은   keynote speaker 기조 연설자   suggest that ~라고 권하다, 제안하다   realtor 부동산 중개업자   enroll in ~에 등록하다   how to do ~하는 법   make sense 말이 되다, 앞뒤가 맞다   potential 잠재적인   browse ~을 둘러보다   mention that ~라고 말하다, 언급하다   be interested in ~에 관심이 있다   attend 참석하다, 출석하다   put up ~을 붙여 놓다, 게시하다   break room 휴게실   participate 참여하다

50. 화자들은 어디에서 근무할 것 같은가?
(A) 마케팅 회사에서
(B) 부동산 중개업체에서
(C) 보험 회사에서
(D) 금융 기관에서

| 해설 |
대화 초반부에, National Real Estate Convention에 참석한 일을 언급하는 것과 중반부에 자신들을 us로 지칭해 realtors like us라고 말하는 것에서 이들이 부동산 중개 업무를 하는 사람들임을 알 수 있으므로 (B)가 정답이다.

| 어휘 | firm 회사   agency 회사, 대행사   insurance 보험   financial 금융의, 재무의   institution 기관, 협회

51. Geraldo Sanz 씨는 무엇을 권했는가?
(A) 경쟁 업체의 웹 사이트 둘러보기
(B) 새로 출간된 책 읽어보기
(C) 사진 촬영 강좌 수강하기
(D) 더 많은 직원 회의 개최하기

| 해설 |
Geraldo Sanz 씨의 이름이 제시되는 중반부에, 사진 촬영 방법에 관한 강좌에 등록해야 한다고 권했다는(~ should enroll in a class on how to take photos) 사실이 언급되고 있으므로 (C)가 정답이다.

| 어휘 | competitor 경쟁 업체   photography 사진 촬영   hold ~을 개최하다, 열다

52. 남자는 무엇을 할 계획인가?
(A) 더 짧은 휴식 일정 잡기
(B) 일부 소프트웨어 다운로드하기
(C) 가격 견적서 받아보기
(D) 서명 등록 용지 게시하기

| 해설 |
대화 마지막에, 남자가 사람들이 이름을 적어 놓을 수 있도록 휴게실에 종이를 붙여 놓을 것이라고(I'm going to put up a paper in the break room for people to write down their name ~) 알리고 있으므로 (D)가 정답이다.

| 어휘 | break 휴식   estimate 견적(서)   post ~을 게시하다   sign-up 서명 등록   sheet 종이, 용지

Questions 53-55 refer to the following conversation with three speakers.

M: Hello, my name is Bernard Fenway. I couldn't go to San Francisco 53 **on your airline** due to medical reasons, so I'd like to be reimbursed for my missed flight.
W1: All right, sir. You would receive the refund on May 1.
M: 54 **May 1? I thought it would be faster than that.**
W1: Well, 54 **it's our policy to issue refunds on the first of the month,** but let me double-check with my manager. Ms. Garrison, can we change the date that money is returned to passengers for a medical cancellation?
W2: It might be possible. 55 **What's the number of the credit card used to make the purchase?** We can look up the transaction in our system.
W1: 55 **I'll ask him now.**

53-55번 문제는 다음 세 명의 대화를 참조하시오.
남: 안녕하세요, 제 이름은 Bernard Fenway입니다. 제가 진료상의 이유로 인해 그쪽 항공사를 이용해 San Francisco로 갈 수 없었기 때문에, 타지 못한 항공편에 대해 비용 환불을 받고 싶습니다.
여1: 알겠습니다, 고객님. 5월 1일에 환불을 받으시게 될 겁니다.
남: 5월 1일이요? 저는 그것보다 더 빠를 것으로 생각했는데요.
여1: 저, 매달 1일에 환불 금액을 지급해 드리는 것이 저희 정책입니다만, 제 상사에게 다시 한번 확인해 보겠습니다. Garrison 씨, 진료 문제로 인한 취소에 대해 승객에게 금액을 돌려주는 날짜를 변경할 수 있나요?
여2: 가능할 수도 있어요. 그 티켓 구매에 사용된 신용카드 번호가 뭐죠? 우리 시스템에서 해당 거래 내역을 조회해 볼 수 있어요.
여1: 지금 그 승객에게 물어볼게요.

| 어휘 | due to ~로 인해   medical 의료의   would like to do ~하고 싶다   reimburse ~을 환불해 주다, 환급해 주다   missed 놓친, 지나친   receive ~을 받다   refund 환불(금)   policy 정책, 방침   issue ~을 지급하다, 발급하다   double-check ~을 다시 한번 확인하다, 이중으로 확인하다   cancellation 취소   make a purchase 구매하다   look up ~을 조회하다, 검색하다   transaction 거래

53. 여자들은 어디에서 근무할 것 같은가?
(A) 항공사에서
(B) 택시 회사에서
(C) 호텔에서
(D) 병원에서

| 해설 |
대화 시작 부분에, 남자가 여자들이 일하는 업체를 on your airline이라고 지칭하고 있으므로 (A)가 정답이다.

54. 남자는 무엇에 대해 놀라워하는가?
(A) 예약 수수료
(B) 늦은 출발
(C) 환불 정책
(D) 서비스 업그레이드

| 해설 |
대화 중반부에, 남자가 5월 1일이라는 날짜가 늦다는 점에 대해(May 1? I thought it would be faster than that) 놀라움을 나타내고 있다. 뒤이어 여자 한 명이 환불금 지급 날짜와 관련된 정책을(it's our policy to issue refunds on the first of the month) 설명하고 있으므로 (C)가 정답이다.

| 어휘 | booking 예약   fee 수수료, 요금   departure 출발

55. 여자들은 무엇을 필요로 하는가?
(A) 신용카드 번호

(B) 회원 가입 확인서
(C) 예약 날짜
(D) 쿠폰 코드

| 해설 |
대화 마지막에 여자 한 명이 티켓 구매에 사용된 신용카드 번호를 묻자(What's the number of the credit card used to make the purchase?), 다른 여자가 남자에게 물어보겠다고(I'll ask him now) 대답하고 있으므로 (A)가 정답이다.

| 어휘 | confirmation 확인(서)   reservation 예약   voucher 쿠폰, 상품권

Questions 56-58 refer to the following conversation.

> M: Lilian, I just spoke with our newest client, Mr. Palmer, about his kitchen renovations. He said that he doesn't like 56 the handles of the cabinet doors. He wants them to be twice as large.
> W: Hmm… but when he looked at the samples, he approved the overall plan.
> M: I understand that, but he's changed his mind. He's selected another type, and I've placed an order for those. 57 We'll have to take the current ones off.
> W: Well, we can't get a refund for those items.
> M: That's all right. 57 I've informed Mr. Palmer that he'll have to pay for both sets. 58 I'll make adjustments to our service contract with him to reflect this change.

56-58번 문제는 다음 대화를 참조하시오.

남: Lilian 씨, 우리의 새 고객인 Palmer 씨와 그분의 주방 개조 공사에 관해 막 이야기했어요. 그분께서는 찬장 문에 달린 손잡이들이 마음에 들지 않는다고 말씀하셨어요. 두 배 더 큰 것을 원하고 계세요.
여: 흠… 하지만 그분께서 샘플들 보셨을 때, 전반적인 계획을 승인해 주셨잖아요.
남: 그 점을 알고 있지만, 생각을 바꾸셨어요. 다른 종류를 선택하셔서 제가 그 주문을 해 두었습니다. 현재 달려 있는 것들을 떼어내야 할 겁니다.
여: 저, 그 제품들에 대해서는 환불을 받을 수 없습니다.
남: 그건 괜찮습니다. 제가 Palmer 씨에게 두 세트 모두에 대한 비용을 지불하셔야 한다고 알려 드렸습니다. 제가 그분과 우리 서비스 계약서를 수정해서 이 변동 사항을 반영하겠습니다.

| 어휘 | renovation 개조, 보수   cabinet 찬장   want A to do A가 ~하기를 원하다   twice as large 두 배 더 큰   approve ~을 승인하다   overall 전반적인   select ~을 선택하다   place an order 주문하다   take A off A를 떼어내다   current 현재   refund 환불(금)   inform A that A에게 ~라고 알리다   pay for ~에 대한 비용을 지불하다   make an adjustment to ~을 수정하다, 변경하다   contract 계약(서)   reflect ~을 반영하다

56. Palmer 씨는 찬장 문과 관련해 무엇을 바꾸고 싶어 하는가?
(A) 나무 종류
(B) 문의 두께
(C) 외관 색상
(D) 손잡이 크기

| 해설 |
Palmer 씨의 이름이 제시되는 초반부에, 그 사람을 He로 지칭하면서 찬장 문에 달린 손잡이들이 마음에 들지 않는다고(~ the handles of the cabinet doors. He wants them to be twice as large) 말한 사실이 언급되고 있으므로 (D)가 정답이다.

| 어휘 | thickness 두께   exterior 외관, 외부

57. 여자는 왜 "we can't get a refund for those items"라고 말하는가?
(A) 불필요한 지출을 걱정하고 있다.
(B) 다른 업체를 이용해야 한다고 생각한다.
(C) 요청하는 방법을 알지 못한다.
(D) 실수가 고쳐지기를 원하고 있다.

| 해설 |
중반부에, 남자가 현재 사용 중인 것을 떼어내야 한다고(We'll have to take the current ones off) 말하자, 여자가 "그것들에 대해 환불받을 수 없다"고 대답하는 흐름이다. 뒤이어 남자가 Palmer 씨가 비용을 지불할 것임을 알리고 있는 것으로 보아, 이는 고객 변심으로 인해 자신들이 비용을 추가로 부담하게 될 것을 걱정하는 마음에서 한 말임을 알 수 있으므로 (A)가 정답이다.

| 어휘 | be concerned about ~을 걱정하다   unnecessary 불필요한   spending 소비   how to do ~하는 법   make a request 요청하다

58. 남자는 무엇을 할 계획인가?
(A) 계약서 변경하기
(B) 치수 측정하기
(C) 작업팀 고용하기
(D) 비용 지불하기

| 해설 |
대화 마지막에 남자가 서비스 계약서를 수정해서 변동 사항을 반영하겠다고(I'll make adjustments to our service contract with him ~) 알리고 있으므로 (A)가 정답이다.

| 어휘 | adjust ~을 변경하다, 조정하다   take measurements 치수를 측정하다   crew (함께 일하는) 팀, 반   make a payment 비용을 지불하다

Questions 59-61 refer to the following conversation.

> M: Hi, Ms. Snyder. I'm performing the final changes to the file we're sending to the printer today. 59 Could I talk to you for a minute?
> W: I'm headed to a meeting with Mr. Calhoun. 59 Is it something urgent?
> M: 60 It's about the description of the new hiking boots. It says that the soles are made of plastic, but it should be rubber, right? The manufacturer changed to using high-quality materials.
> W: Oh, you're right. Yes, that should definitely be changed. 61 Thanks for your close attention to this project. 61 If no one had caught the mistake in time, we would have had to pay for a costly reprint later.
> M: I'm glad that won't be the case.

59-61번 문제는 다음 대화를 참조하시오.

남: 안녕하세요, Snyder 씨. 오늘 우리가 인쇄소에 보낼 파일에 최종 수정 작업을 하는 중입니다. 잠시 얘기하실 수 있으세요?
여: 제가 Calhoun 씨와의 회의에 가는 중입니다. 긴급한 일인가요?
남: 새 등산화에 대한 설명과 관련된 것입니다. 밑창이 플라스틱으로 만들어져 있다고 쓰여 있는데, 고무가 되어야 하지 않나요? 제조사에서 고품질 재료를 사용하는 것으로 변경되었어요.
여: 아, 맞아요. 네, 그 부분이 분명 수정되어야 합니다. 이 프로젝트에 대해 세심한 주의를 기울여 주셔서 감사합니다. 그 실수를 제때 찾아낸 사람이 아무도 없었다면, 나중에 비싼 재인쇄 비용을 지불했어야 했을 거예요.
남: 그런 경우가 발생하지 않게 되어서 기쁩니다.

| 어휘 | perform ~을 실시하다, 수행하다   for a minute 잠시, 잠깐   be headed to ~로 가다, 향하다   urgent 긴급한   description 설명, 묘사   say that (문서

등에) ~라고 쓰여 있다   sole (신발의) 밑창   be made of ~로 만들어지다
manufacturer 제조사   high-quality 고품질의   material 재료, 자재, 물품
definitely 분명히, 확실히   close attention 세심한 주의   in time 제때, 제
시간에   would have p.p. ~했을 것이다   pay for ~에 대한 비용을 지불하다
costly 비싼, 돈이 많이 드는   reprint 재인쇄   case 경우, 사례

59. 여자가 "I'm headed to a meeting with Mr. Calhoun"이라고 말할 때 무엇을 암시하는가?
(A) 잠깐 이야기만 할 수 있는 시간이 난다.
(B) 한 가지 문제가 해결될 것으로 예상하고 있다.
(C) 남자의 메시지를 받았다.
(D) 한 행사에 참석할 수 없다.

| 해설 |
대화 초반부에, 남자가 잠깐 얘기할 수 있는지 묻자(Could I talk to you for a minute?) 여자가 "Calhoun 씨와의 회의에 가는 길이다"라고 말하면서 급한 일인지(Is it something urgent?) 묻는 상황이다. 이는 오래 얘기할 수 없는 상황임을 나타내는 것이므로 (A)가 정답이다.

| 어휘 | available (사람이) 시간이 나는   brief 짧은, 잠깐의   expect A to do A가 ~할 것으로 예상하다   resolve ~을 해결하다   receive ~을 받다   be unable to do ~할 수 없다   attend ~에 참석하다

60. 남자는 무엇에 대해 우려된다고 말하는가?
(A) 인쇄소의 신뢰성
(B) 제품 설명의 정확성
(C) 계약 협상 마감 시한
(D) 일부 상품을 수입하는 비용

| 해설 |
대화 중반부에, 남자가 등산화에 대한 설명에 밑창이 플라스틱으로 만들어져 있다고 쓰여 있는데 고무가 되어야 한다는(It's about the description of the new hiking boots. It says that the soles are made of plastic, but it should be rubber, right?) 점을 지적하고 있다. 이는 제품 설명에 오류가 있다는 말이므로 (B)가 정답이다.

| 어휘 | dependability 신뢰성   accuracy 정확성   deadline 마감 시한   contract 계약(서)   negotiation 협상   import ~을 수입하다   goods 상품

61. 여자는 왜 남자에게 감사하는가?
(A) 추가 시간 동안 근무하겠다고 제안했다.
(B) 할당받은 업무를 빠르게 완료했다.
(C) 적격인 상담 전문가를 추천했다.
(D) 불필요한 비용 지불을 방지했다.

| 해설 |
후반부에, 여자가 감사 인사를 하면서 실수를 제때 찾아낸 사람이 아무도 없었다면 나중에 비싼 재인쇄 비용을 지불했어야 했을 것이라고(If no one had caught the mistake in time, we would have had to pay for a costly reprint later) 말리고 있다. 이는 남자로 인해 비용 문제를 막을 수 있었음을 의미하는 것이므로 (D)가 정답이다.

| 어휘 | offer to do ~하겠다고 제안하다   additional 추가의   complete ~을 완료하다   assignment 배정(된 일)   qualified 적격인, 자격이 있는   prevent ~을 방지하다, 막다   unnecessary 불필요한

Questions 62-64 refer to the following conversation and sign.

W: Hi, Sharad. It's Mayuka. Unfortunately, I'll be arriving late to the office today. I've just seen on the departure board that **62** the train I was planning on taking has been canceled. I'll have to take the one after that.
M: All right. But **63** aren't you supposed to present the progress report to the representative from Coral Investments?
W: This train will get me there early enough for that meeting, but **64** I won't have time to set up the projector and sound system in the meeting room.
M: **64** I can take care of that for you.
W: Thanks. I really appreciate that.

Departures to Hillside	
Departure Time	Platform
7:55 A.M.	7
8:35 A.M.	**62** CANCELED
9:10 A.M.	**62** 3
9:40 A.M.	DELAYED
10:05 A.M.	6
10:30 A.M.	2

62-64번 문제는 다음 대화와 표지판을 참조하시오.
여: 안녕하세요, Sharad 씨. 저는 Mayuka입니다. 안타깝게도, 제가 오늘 사무실에 늦게 도착합니다. 출발 시간 안내판에서 제가 타려고 계획했던 기차가 취소되었다는 사실을 막 확인했어요. 그 다음 것을 타야 할 거예요.
남: 알겠습니다. 하지만 Coral 투자에서 오는 직원에게 경과 보고서를 발표하기로 되어 있지 않으신가요?
여: 이 기차를 타면 그 회의에 맞춰 충분히 일찍 도착하겠지만, 제가 회의실에 프로젝터와 음향 시스템을 설치할 시간이 없을 거예요.
남: 제가 대신 그 일을 처리해 드릴 수 있습니다.
여: 고맙습니다. 그렇게 해주신다니 정말 감사합니다.

Hillside행 출발 정보	
출발 시각	승강장
오전 7:55	7
오전 8:35	취소
오전 9:10	3
오전 9:40	출발 지연
오전 10:05	6
오전 10:30	2

| 어휘 | unfortunately 안타깝게도, 아쉽게도   arrive 도착하다   departure 출발, 떠남   plan on -ing ~할 계획이다   cancel ~을 취소하다   take (교통편) ~을 타다, 이용하다   be supposed to do ~하기로 되어 있다, ~할 예정이다   present ~을 발표하다, 제시하다   progress 진행 (상황), 경과   representative 직원   get A there A를 그곳에 데려다주다   enough (형용사, 부사 뒤에서) 충분히   set up ~을 설치하다, 마련하다   take care of ~을 처리하다   appreciate ~에 대해 감사하다

62. 시각 자료를 보시오. 여자는 어느 승강장에서 출발할 것인가?
(A) 7번 승강장
(B) 3번 승강장
(C) 6번 승강장
(D) 2번 승강장

| 해설 |
대화 초반부에, 여자가 자신이 타려고 계획했던 기차가 취소된 사실과 함께 그 다음 것을 타야 할 한다고(~ the train I was planning on taking has been canceled. I'll have to take the one after that) 알리고 있다. 시각 자료에서 취소 표기된(CANCELED) 것의 다음 기차가 3번 승강장에서 출발할 것임을 알 수 있으므로 (B)가 정답이다.

Actual Test 213

63. 남자는 여자에게 무엇에 관해 묻는가?
(A) 일부 비용 환급 요청
(B) 일부 직원 평가
(C) 여자의 고객 대상 발표
(D) 한 가지 제안에 대한 여자의 승인

| 해설 |
중반부에, 남자가 Coral Investments에서 오는 직원에게 경과 보고서 내용을 발표하기로 되어 있지 않은지(~ aren't you supposed to present the progress report to the representative~) 여자에게 묻고 있으므로 (C)가 정답이다.

| 어휘 | reimbursement 비용 환급 request 요청(서) review 평가, 후기, 의견 presentation 발표 approval 승인 proposal 제안(서)

64. 남자는 무엇을 하겠다고 제안하는가?
(A) 행사 연기하기
(B) 일부 장비 설치하기
(C) 회의 녹화하기
(D) 회의실 예약하기

| 해설 |
후반부에, 여자가 회의실에 프로젝터와 음향 시스템을 설치할 시간이 없을 것이라고(I won't have time to set up the projector and sound system ~) 말하자, 남자가 자신이 처리해 주겠다고(I can take care of that for you) 답변하고 있다. 따라서 장비 설치를 의미하는 (B)가 정답이다.

| 어휘 | postpone ~을 연기하다 equipment 장비 reserve ~을 예약하다

Questions 65-67 refer to the following conversation and table.

M: Thanks for volunteering to help me plan the annual employee outing, Seoyeon. **65 I met with Mr. Cooper this morning, and he's confirmed the official date.** It'll be on Friday, June 19.
W: Wonderful! We've been waiting for that so we could book the boat for the group tour. Did you find a company that can accommodate us?
M: Yes. I have a brochure here from Bayside Boat Tours. We have about thirty employees, but some of them will bring their spouses, so **62 how about booking the largest boat?**
W: **66 That's a great idea.** And **67 I'll contact a caterer to coordinate the lunch** we will have after the boat ride.

Bayside Boat Tours

Boat Type	Max Passengers
Gudgeon	20
Davit	35
Ballaster	40
66 Scuttle	55

65-67번 문제는 다음 대화와 표를 참조하시오.
남: 연례 직원 야유회 계획을 자원해 도와주셔서 감사합니다, Seoyeon 씨. 제가 오늘 아침에 Cooper 씨를 만났는데, 공식적인 날짜를 확정해 주셨어요. 그 날짜는 6월 19일 금요일입니다.
여: 아주 잘됐네요! 그룹 투어에 필요한 보트를 예약하기 위해 그 날짜를 계속 기다려 왔잖아요. 우리를 수용할 수 있는 업체를 찾으셨나요?
남: 네. Bayside Boat Tours에서 받은 안내 책자가 여기 있습니다. 우리 직원들이 약 30명이지만, 일부는 직원들이 배우자를 동반할 것이기 때문에, 가장 큰 보트를 예약하는 게 어떨까요?
여: 아주 좋은 생각입니다. 그리고 보트 타기 이후에 우리가 먹을 점심 식사를 준비할 수 있도록 제가 출장 요리 업체에 연락할게요.

Bayside Boat Tours

보트 종류	최대 탑승객 수
Gudgeon	20
Davit	35
Ballaster	40
Scuttle	55

| 어휘 | volunteer to do 자원해서 ~하다 help A do A가 ~하는 데 도움을 주다 plan ~을 계획하다 annual 연례의, 해마다의 outing 야유회 confirm ~을 확정하다, 확인해주다 official 공식적인, 정식의 book ~을 예약하다 accommodate ~을 수용하다 brochure 안내 책자, 소책자 about 약, 대략 spouse 배우자 how about -ing? ~하는 게 어때요? contact ~에게 연락하다 caterer 출장 요리 업체 coordinate ~을 마련하다, 편성하다 max(= maximum) 최대의

65. 남자의 말에 따르면, 오늘 아침에 직원 야유회를 위해 무엇이 최종 확정되었는가?
(A) 그룹 규모
(B) 예산
(C) 행사 지속 시간
(D) 날짜

| 해설 |
'오늘 아침'이라는 시점이 언급되는 초반부에, Cooper 씨가 공식적인 날짜를 확정해 준 사실을(I met with Mr. Cooper this morning, and he's confirmed the official date) 알리고 있으므로 (D)가 정답이다.

| 어휘 | finalize ~을 최종 확정하다 budget 예산 duration 지속 시간

66. 시각 자료를 보시오. 화자들은 어느 보트 모델을 선택하는가?
(A) Gudgeon
(B) Davit
(C) Ballaster
(D) Scuttle

| 해설 |
대화 후반부에 남자가 가장 큰 보트를 예약하는 게 어떤지(how about booking the largest boat?) 제안하자 여자가 That's a great idea라는 말로 동의하고 있다. 시각 자료에서 가장 많은 인원인 55명을 수용할 수 있는 Scuttle이 가장 큰 보트이므로 (D)가 정답이다.

| 어휘 | select ~을 선택하다

67. 여자는 무엇을 할 것이라고 말하는가?
(A) 여행사에 연락하기
(B) 지도 출력하기
(C) 식사 준비하기
(D) 서명 등록 용지 게시하기

| 해설 |
대화 마지막에, 여자가 점심 식사를 준비할 수 있도록 출장 요리 업체에 연락하겠다고(I'll contact a caterer to coordinate the lunch ~) 알리고 있으므로 (C)가 정답이다.

| 어휘 | contact ~에게 연락하다 print out ~을 출력하다 arrange ~을 마련하다, 조정하다 post ~을 게시하다 sign-up 서명 등록

Questions 68-70 refer to the following conversation and invoice.

W: Hi, Mr. Etheridge. Thanks for stopping in to pick up your banners.
M: I'm glad they were ready so quickly. We're starting to sell the apartments in Abdella Tower, **68 so we wanted to use them to promote the building.**
W: I understand. I've got the invoice here for you.
M: Hmm … I think there's a mistake. We only ordered three banners. **69 The twelve-inch-by-eighteen-inch banner should not be on this invoice.**
W: Sorry about that. You're right. I'll correct that now and print a new invoice. In the meantime, **70 I'll have my coworker put labels on the boxes** so you know the size of the banner that's in each one.
M: Thanks, that would be helpful.

Invoice: Ace Printing	
69 12″×18″	$30
18″×24″	$35
24″×36″	$50
36″×48″	$75
TOTAL	$190

68-70번 문제는 다음 대화와 거래 내역서를 참조하시오.

여: 안녕하세요, Etheridge 씨. 현수막을 가져가시기 위해 들러 주셔서 감사합니다.
남: 이렇게 빨리 준비되어서 기쁩니다. 저희가 Abdella Tower에 있는 아파트들을 매각하기 시작하고 있기 때문에, 그 건물을 홍보하는 데 현수막을 사용하고 싶었거든요.
여: 그렇군요. 여기 거래 내역서입니다.
남: 흠… 제 생각에 실수가 있는 것 같아요. 저희는 세 개의 현수막만 주문했습니다. 폭 12인치에 길이가 18인치인 현수막은 이 거래 내역서에 포함되지 않아야 합니다.
여: 그 부분에 대해 사과드립니다. 맞는 말씀이에요. 지금 그 부분을 수정해서 새 내역서를 출력해 드리겠습니다. 그 사이에, 각 상자에 들어 있는 현수막의 크기를 아실 수 있도록 제 동료 직원에게 상자마다 라벨을 부착하게 하겠습니다.
남: 감사합니다, 그렇게 해 주시면 도움이 될 겁니다.

거래 내역서: Ace 인쇄	
12" x 18"	30달러
18" x 24"	35달러
24" x 36"	50달러
36" x 48"	75달러
총액	190달러

| 어휘 | stop in 들르다   pick up ~을 가져가다, 가져오다   banner 현수막   promote ~을 홍보하다   invoice 거래 내역서   order ~을 주문하다   A by B (크기를 나타낼 때) 폭이 A에 길이가 B인   correct ~을 수정하다, 바로잡다   in the meantime 그 사이에, 그 동안에   have A do A에게 ~하게 하다   put A on B A를 B에 붙이다   helpful 도움이 되는

68. 남자는 현수막으로 무엇을 할 계획인가?
(A) 잠재 직원들에게 길 안내하기

(B) 부동산 광고하기
(C) 새 기기 홍보하기
(D) 회사 투자자 환영하기

| 해설 |
현수막이 언급되는 초반부에, 남자가 아파트가 있는 건물을 홍보하는 데 현수막을 사용하고 싶었다고(~ so we wanted to use them to promote the building) 알리고 있으므로 (B)가 정답이다.
| 어휘 | direct ~에게 길을 안내하다   potential 잠재적인   advertise ~을 광고하다   property 건물, 부동산   device 기기, 장치   investor 투자자

69. 시각 자료를 보시오. 어느 금액이 거래 내역서에서 삭제되어야 하는가?
(A) 30달러
(B) 35달러
(C) 50달러
(D) 75달러

| 해설 |
대화 중반부에, 남자가 폭 12인치에 길이가 18인치인 현수막은 거래 내역서에 포함되지 말아야 한다고(The twelve-inch-by-eighteen-inch banner should not be on this invoice ~) 알리고 있다. 시각 자료에서 해당 수치인 12" x 18" 크기의 비용이 30달러이므로 (A)가 정답이다.
| 어휘 | amount 금액, 액수   delete ~을 삭제하다

70. 여자의 동료 직원은 곧이어 무엇을 할 것인가?
(A) 일부 용기에 라벨 부착하기
(B) 새 계산서 출력하기
(C) 책임자와 이야기하기
(D) 시연회 진행하기

| 해설 |
대화 후반부에, 여자가 동료 직원에게 상자마다 라벨을 부착하게 하겠다고 (I'll have my coworker put labels on the boxes ~) 하므로 (A)가 정답이다.
| 어휘 | colleague 동료 직원   label ~에 라벨을 부착하다   container 용기, 그릇   bill 계산서, 청구서   give a demonstration 시연하다, 시범 보이다

Part 4

Questions 71-73 refer to the following excerpt from a meeting.

W: Before we wrap up this meeting, I'd like to talk about a new project. **71 We've just finalized a contract to design a Web site for Wendell Publishing**, but the deadline is very tight because the client wants everything done by May 1. So, **72 I'd like to give each team an assignment to divide the work evenly.** I think this will help us to work more efficiently. I'll e-mail you details about the assignments right after this meeting. **73 Please review the information today** to make sure you understand what to do.

71-73번 문제는 다음 회의 발췌 내용을 참조하시오.

여: 이 회의를 마무리하기에 앞서, 새 프로젝트에 관해 이야기하고자 합니다. 우리가 Wendell 출판사를 위해 웹 사이트를 디자인하는 계약을 막 최종 확정하기는 했지만, 마감 시한이 매우 빡빡한데, 고객사에서 모든 작업이 5월 1일까지 완료되기를 원하기 때문입니다. 따라서, 업무를 균등하게 분배하기 위해 각 팀에 업무를 배정하려고 합니다. 저는 이렇게 하는 것이 우리가 더욱 효율적으로 일하는 데 도움이 된다고 생각합니다. 이 회의 직

후에 배정 업무와 관련된 세부 사항을 이메일로 보내 드리겠습니다. 무엇을 해야 하는지 반드시 이해하실 수 있도록 오늘 그 정보를 검토해 보시기 바랍니다.

| 어휘 | wrap up ~을 마무리하다   finalize ~을 최종 확정하다   contract 계약(서)   deadline 마감 시한   tight (일정, 비용 등이) 빡빡한   want A p.p. A가 ~되기를 원하다   by (기한) ~까지   assignment 배정(된 일), 할당(된 일)   divide ~을 분배하다, 나누다   evenly 균등하게, 고르게   efficiently 효율적으로   details 세부 사항, 상세 정보   right after ~ 직후에   review ~을 검토하다   make sure (that) 반드시 ~하도록 하다

71. 화자의 회사는 어떤 종류의 서비스를 제공하는가?
(A) 웹 디자인
(B) 제품 테스트
(C) 건물 개조 공사
(D) 재무 상담

| 해설 |
담화 초반부에, 화자가 Wendell Publishing 사를 위해 웹 사이트를 디자인하는 계약을 최종 확정한 사실을(We've just finalized a contract to design a Web site for Wendell Publishing ~) 알리고 있으므로 (A)가 정답이다.

| 어휘 | renovation 개조, 보수   financial 재무의, 재정의

72. 화자는 주로 무엇을 이야기하고 있는가?
(A) 예산 보고서
(B) 팀 배정 업무
(C) 신입 사원
(D) 배송 지연

| 해설 |
초반부의 배경 설명에 이어 중반부에서 업무를 균등하게 분배하기 위해 각 팀에 업무를 배정하려고 한다는(I'd like to give each team an assignment to divide the work evenly) 내용이 나오므로 (B)가 정답이다.

| 어휘 | budget 예산   delay 지연, 지체

73. 청자들은 오늘 무엇을 하도록 요청받는가?
(A) 일부 제안 사항을 이메일로 보내기
(B) 고객과 만나기
(C) 일부 정보 검토하기
(D) 제품 구매 권유하기

| 해설 |
'오늘'이라는 시점이 제시되는 후반부에, 오늘 정보를 검토해 보도록 (Please review the information today ~) 요청하고 있으므로 (C)가 정답이다.

| 어휘 | be asked to do ~하도록 요청받다   suggestion 제안, 의견   give a sales pitch 제품 구매를 권유하다

Questions 74-76 refer to the following recorded message.

M: You've reached the Holt City **74 Department of Transportation**. To report problems with any streets within the city limits, press 1 and leave a message. Please note that **75 the expansion of Wallace Street has been delayed due to the bad weather during the recent tropical storm**. Work will start again as soon as possible. To stay informed on this and other road closures, **76 don't forget to sign up for our mailing list**. You may do so by visiting our Web site.

74-76번 문제는 다음 녹음 메시지를 참조하시오.
남: Holt City 교통부입니다. 우리 시 경계 내의 어떤 거리와 관련된 문제든 신고하시려면, 1번을 누르신 후 메시지를 남겨 주십시오. Wallace Street 확장 공사는 최근의 열대성 폭풍우 기간 동안의 악천후로 인해 지연되었다는 점에 유의하시기 바랍니다. 가능한 한 빨리 작업이 다시 시작될 것입니다. 이를 비롯한 기타 도로 폐쇄에 관한 정보를 계속 얻으시려면, 저희 우편물 발송 대상자 명단에 등록하는 것을 잊지 마세요. 저희 웹 사이트를 방문하시면 그렇게 하실 수 있습니다.

| 어휘 | reach ~에 연락하다   department 부서, 부처   transportation 교통(편)   report ~을 신고하다, 알리다   within ~ 이내에   limit 경계, 한계   leave ~을 남기다   note that ~임에 유의하다, 주목하다   expansion 확장, 확대   delay ~을 지연시키다   due to ~로 인해   tropical storm 열대성 폭풍우   as soon as possible 가능한 한 빨리   stay + 형용사 ~인 상태를 유지하다, 계속 ~한 상태로 있다   informed 정보를 얻은   forget to do ~하는 것을 잊다   sign up for ~에 등록하다, ~을 신청하다   mailing list 우편물 발송 대상자 명단

74. 시의 어느 부서에 의해 메시지가 만들어졌는가?
(A) 노동부
(B) 보건부
(C) 교통부
(D) 에너지부

| 해설 |
담화 시작 부분에, 화자가 Department of Transportation에 연결되었다는 말로 소속 부서를 밝혔으므로 (C)가 정답이다.

75. 메시지 내용에 따르면, 프로젝트가 왜 지연되었는가?
(A) 지역 내에 악천후가 있었다.
(B) 예산에 여유가 충분하지 않았다.
(C) 일부 주민들이 몇몇 불만을 제기했다.
(D) 일부 자재가 배송되지 않았다.

| 해설 |
지연 문제가 언급되는 중반부에, 열대성 폭풍우 발생 기간 중의 악천후로 인해 지연되었다는(~ the expansion of Wallace Street has been delayed due to the bad weather during the recent tropical storm) 사실이 언급되고 있으므로 (A)가 정답이다.

| 어휘 | severe weather 악천후   room 여유, 여지   budget 예산   resident 주민   make a complaint 불만을 제기하다   material 자재, 재료, 물품

76. 청자들은 무엇을 하도록 상기되는가?
(A) 나중에 다시 전화하기
(B) 일정 업데이트하기
(C) 양식에 서명하기
(D) 우편물 발송 대상자 명단에 가입하기

| 해설 |
청자들에게 상기시키는 일이 언급되는 후반부에, 잊지 말고 우편물 발송 대상자 명단에 등록하도록(~ don't forget to sign up for our mailing list) 당부하고 있으므로 (D)가 정답이다.

| 어휘 | be reminded to do ~하도록 상기되다   form 양식, 서식   join ~에 가입하다, 참가하다

Questions 77-79 refer to the following announcement.

M: May I have your attention, please? I know **77 you'll leave soon to meet your group members**, but I have a quick announcement. **77 As tour guides, many of you** have expressed concern about people arriving late to the bus when you stop at a site. This creates a negative experience for everyone left waiting. **78 We couldn't do** much about this because no one wanted to give out their personal cell phone information to participants. Now, we've purchased several company phones. You'll each be given a phone to use while you are on duty, and **79** every Monday at the staff meeting, I'll inspect them to make sure they're still in good working order.

77-79번 문제는 다음 공지를 참조하시오.
남: 잠시 주목해 주시겠습니까? 여러분께서 그룹 인원들을 만나러 곧 나가신다는 점을 알고 있지만, 간단한 공지가 하나 있습니다. 투어 가이드로서, 여러분 중 많은 사람이 한 장소에 잠시 들렸을 때 버스에 늦게 도착하는 사람들에 관한 우려를 나타내 주셨습니다. 이는 대기하고 있는 나머지 모든 사람들에게 부정적인 경험을 만들어줍니다. 우리가 이 부분에 대해 할 수 있는 것이 많지 않았는데, 아무도 참가자들에게 개인 휴대전화 번호를 알려주기를 원하지 않았기 때문입니다. 이제, 우리는 여러 대의 회사 전화기를 구입했습니다. 여러분 각자가 근무 중에 사용할 전화기를 지급받게 될 것이며, 매주 월요일 직원 회의 시간에, 여전히 작동 상태가 양호한지 확실히 해두기 위해 제가 전화기들을 점검할 것입니다.

| 어휘 | attention 주목, 주의 leave 나가다, 떠나다 announcement 공지, 알림 express (감정, 생각 등) ~을 나타내다, 표현하다 concern 우려, 걱정 arrive 도착하다 stop at ~에 잠시 들르다 site 장소, 현장 create ~을 만들어내다 negative 부정적인 left waiting 남아서 기다리고 있는 give out ~을 알려주다, 나눠주다 participant 참가자 purchase ~을 구입하다 several 여럿의, 몇몇의 while ~하는 중에, ~하면서 on duty 근무 중인 inspect ~을 점검하다 make sure (that) ~임을 확실히 해 두다, 반드시 ~하도록 하다 in good working order 좋은 작동 상태로 있는

77. 청자들은 어디에서 근무하고 있을 것 같은가?
(A) 우체국에서
(B) 패션 스튜디오에서
(C) 여행사에서
(D) 사업 기관에서

| 해설 |
담화 초반부에, 청자들을 you로 지칭해 그룹 인원들을 만나는 일과(~ you'll leave soon to meet your group members) 함께 투어 가이드라고(As tour guides, many of you ~) 언급하는 부분이 있으므로 (C)가 정답이다.

| 어휘 | institute 기관, 협회

78. 화자가 "Now, we've purchased several company phones"라고 말할 때 암시하는 것은 무엇인가?
(A) 한 가지 문제가 해결되었다.
(B) 연락 정보 목록이 업데이트되었다.
(C) 한 제품이 적극 추천되었다.
(D) 일부 자금을 더 이상 이용할 수 없다.

| 해설 |
담화 중반부에, 참가자들에게 개인 휴대전화 번호를 알려주기 원하지 않았기 때문에 아무것도 할 수 없었다는(We couldn't do much about this because no one wanted to give out their personal cell phone information ~) 말 뒤에 "여러 대의 회사 전화기를 구입했다"고 말하는 상황이다. 이는 해당 문제를 해결하기 위한 조치가 취해졌음을 알리는 것이므로 (A)가 정답이다.

| 어휘 | resolve ~을 해결하다 directory (전화번호, 주소 등이 담긴) 연락 정보 목록 highly 매우, 대단히 fund 자금, 기금 no longer 더 이상 ~ 않다 available 이용 가능한

79. 화자는 매주 월요일에 무엇을 할 계획인가?
(A) 재무 상세 정보 제공하기
(B) 일부 의견 분석하기
(C) 일정 변경 사항 공지하기
(D) 일부 기기 확인하기

| 해설 |
'매주 월요일'이라는 시점이 언급되는 후반부에, 매주 월요일 직원 회의 시간에 전화기의 작동 상태를 점검할 것이라고(~ every Monday at the staff meeting, I'll inspect them ~) 알리고 있으므로 (D)가 정답이다.

| 어휘 | financial 재무의, 재정의 details 상세 정보 analyze ~을 분석하다 feedback 의견 device 기기, 장치

Questions 80-82 refer to the following talk.

M: Good morning, and **80** welcome to Ballico Orchard. We're pleased that you've signed up for this tour, which is available year-round. **80** This orchard is the only one in the area that uses traditional equipment to remove the juice from the apples. **81** We'll see that equipment first. **81** Then, we'll take a walk among the trees while I tell you more about the harvesting process. **81** Finally, we'll visit the underground storage area, where we have hundreds of bottles of juice ready for shipment. **82** There you will have a chance to taste all of our products, so make sure to sample them all.

80-82번 문제는 다음 담화를 참조하시오.
남: 안녕하세요, Ballico 과수원에 오신 것을 환영합니다. 일년 내내 이용 가능한 이 견학 행사를 신청해 주셔서 기쁘게 생각합니다. 저희 과수원은 사과에서 주스를 얻기 위해 전통적인 장비를 사용하는, 지역 내에서 유일한 곳입니다. 우리는 그 장비부터 볼 것입니다. 그런 다음, 여러분께 수확 과정에 대해 더 많은 말씀드리는 동안 나무들 사이를 산책할 것입니다. 마지막으로, 지하 저장 구역을 방문하게 될 텐데, 이곳에서 저희가 수백 개의 주스 병들을 배송 준비합니다. 그곳에서 모든 저희 제품들을 맛보실 기회를 가지시게 되므로, 반드시 그 제품들을 모두 시음해 보시기 바랍니다.

| 어휘 | orchard 과수원 signed up for ~을 신청하다, ~에 등록하다 available 이용 가능한 year-round 연중으로, 일 년 내내 traditional 전통적인 equipment 장비 remove A from B B에서 A를 제거하다 take a walk 걷다, 산책하다 among ~ 사이로 while ~하는 동안 harvesting 수확 process 과정 storage 저장, 보관 have A ready A를 준비하다 shipment 배송, 선적 have a chance to do ~할 기회를 갖다 make sure to do 반드시 ~하도록 하다 sample ~을 시음하다, 시식하다

80. 담화가 어디에서 이뤄지고 있는가?
(A) 슈퍼마켓에서
(B) 과수원에서
(C) 원예용품 매장에서
(D) 식당에서

| 해설 |
시작 부분의 인사 welcome to Ballico Orchard와 바로 뒤이어 제시되는 This orchard를 통해 과수원이 배경임을 알 수 있으므로 (B)가 정답이다.

81. 화자는 왜 담화를 하고 있는가?
(A) 실수를 바로잡기 위해
(B) 직무를 설명하기 위해
(C) 활동 개요를 전달하기 위해
(D) 안전 관련 조언을 제공하기 위해

| 해설 |
담화 중반부에, 장비를 먼저 본다고(We'll see that equipment first. Then ~) 알린 후에 산책과(Then, we'll take a walk ~) 저장 구역 방문

(Finally, we'll visit ~) 등 견학 중에 할 활동들을 순서대로 알리고 있으므로 (C)가 정답이다.
| 어휘 | correct ~을 바로잡다, 고치다 explain ~을 설명하다 job responsibilities 직무, 책무 overview 개요, 개관

82. 화자는 청자들에게 무엇을 하도록 권하는가?
(A) 질문 적어 놓기
(B) 카탈로그 가져가기
(C) 휴대전화 꺼 놓기
(D) 일부 제품 시식해 보기

| 해설 |
담화 마지막에, 화자는 모든 제품들을 맛볼 기회가 있기 때문에 반드시 모두 시음해 보도록(There you will have a chance to taste all of our products, so make sure to sample them all) 권하고 있으므로 (D)가 정답이다.
| 어휘 | encourage A to do A에게 ~하도록 권하다 pick up ~을 가져가다, 가져오다 turn off ~을 끄다 try ~을 한번 먹어보다

Questions 83-85 refer to the following broadcast.

W: Up next is the daily business news on WKRN Radio. At a press conference yesterday, **83 the president of the Mankato Corporation announced the company's plans to expand into the education market.** Mankato currently provides custom designs for ad campaigns, logos, and more. Later this year, it will start running workshops to train freelancers. This program will be led by **84 the firm's lead graphic designer, Greg McEvoy.** Instructors for several courses are still needed, so **85 the company will interview job candidates next month.** For more information, contact Mankato's HR office.

83-85번 문제는 다음 방송을 참조하시오.
여: 다음 순서는 WKRN 라디오 일일 비즈니스 뉴스입니다. 어제 있었던 기자 회견에서, Mankato Corporation 대표이사가 교육 시장으로 사업을 확장하는 계획을 발표했습니다. Mankato 사는 현재 광고 캠페인과 로고 등에 필요한 맞춤 제작 디자인을 제공하고 있습니다. 올해 후반기에, 프리랜서들을 교육하는 워크숍을 운영하기 시작할 것입니다. 이 프로그램은 회사의 선임 그래픽 디자이너인 Greg McEvoy 씨에 의해 진행될 것입니다. 여러 강좌를 맡을 강사들이 여전히 필요한 상태이기 때문에, 이 회사는 다음 달에 구직 지원자들을 대상으로 면접을 실시할 것입니다. 더 많은 정보를 원하시면, Mankato 사의 인사부에 연락하시기 바랍니다.
| 어휘 | Up next is A (방송에서) 다음 순서는 A입니다 press conference 기자 회견 announce ~을 발표하다, 공지하다 plan to do ~하려는 계획 expand into (사업 등을) ~로 확장하다, 확대하다 currently 현재 custom 맞춤 제작의, 주문 제작의 ad 광고 train ~을 교육하다 be led by ~에 의해 진행되다 instructor 강사 several 여럿의, 몇몇의 job candidate 구직 지원자 contact ~에게 연락하다

83. 화자는 주로 무엇에 관해 이야기하고 있는가?
(A) 주식 동향
(B) 사업 확장
(C) 기업 합병
(D) 업계에서 주는 상

| 해설 |
시작 부분에, 한 회사가 교육 시장으로 사업을 확장하는 계획을 발표한 사실을(~ the company's plans to expand into the education market) 언급한 뒤로 관련 정보를 전달하고 있으므로 (B)가 정답이다.
| 어휘 | stock 주식 trend 동향, 경향 expansion 확장, 확대 corporate 기업의 merger 합병 industry 업계

84. Greg McEvoy 씨는 누구인가?
(A) 대학 교수
(B) 회사 대표이사
(C) 재무 전문가
(D) 그래픽 디자이너

| 해설 |
Greg McEvoy 씨의 이름이 언급되는 중반부에, the firm's lead graphic designer, Greg McEvoy라고 소개하고 있으므로 (D)가 정답이다.
| 어휘 | financial 재무의, 재정의 expert 전문가

85. Mankato Corporation은 다음 달에 무엇을 할 계획인가?
(A) 기부금 내기
(B) 구인 면접 개최하기
(C) 건축 프로젝트 시작하기
(D) 컨벤션 주최하기

| 해설 |
'다음 달'이라는 시점이 언급되는 후반부에, 다음 달에 구직 지원자들을 대상으로 면접을 실시한다고(~ the company will interview job candidates next month) 알리고 있으므로 (B)가 정답이다.
| 어휘 | make a donation 기부하다 hold ~을 개최하다, 열다 host ~을 주최하다

Questions 86-88 refer to the following announcement.

M: Good morning, everyone. I wanted to announce that **86 five new projectors will be delivered to our office tomorrow.** Originally, we were only going to buy one for the main conference room only. **87 Fortunately, they were so inexpensive** that I was able to get one for each meeting room while staying within the budget. These devices attach to the ceiling. Instructions will be provided on our company Web site about how to connect your laptop to the device. **88 If you really need help, you can contact the IT team,** but they are short-staffed. In most cases, **88 it's better to figure it out using the instructions.**

86-88번 문제는 다음 공지를 참조하시오.
남: 안녕하세요, 여러분. 5대의 새 프로젝터가 내일 우리 사무실로 배송된다는 사실을 알려 드리고자 합니다. 원래, 우리는 오직 대회의실을 위해 1대만 구입하려고 했습니다. 다행히도, 그 제품들이 그렇게 비싸지 않아서 예산 범위 내에서 각 회의실에 1대씩 구입할 수 있었습니다. 이 기기들은 천장에 부착됩니다. 여러분의 노트북 컴퓨터를 이 기기에 연결하는 방법과 관련해 우리 회사 웹 사이트에 사용 설명서가 제공될 것입니다. 정말로 도움이 필요하실 경우, IT 팀에 연락하실 수 있지만, 그곳은 직원이 부족한 상태입니다. 대부분의 경우, 사용 설명서를 이용해 알아보시는 것이 더 좋습니다.
| 어휘 | announce that ~임을 알리다, 공지하다 originally 원래, 애초에 fortunately 다행히도 so A that B 너무 A해서 B하다 inexpensive 비싸지 않은 be able to do ~할 수 있다 while ~하면서, ~하는 동안 stay within ~ 범위 내에서 유지하다 budget 예산 device 기기, 장치 attach to ~에 부착되다 ceiling 천장 instructions 설명, 안내, 지시 how to do ~하는 방법 connect A to B A를 B에 연결하다 contact ~에게 연락하다 short-staffed 직원이 부족한 case 경우, 사례 figure A out A를 알아내다, 확인하다

86. 어떤 종류의 장비가 내일 배송될 것인가?
(A) 복사기
(B) 보안 카메라
(C) 프로젝터
(D) 파쇄기

| 해설 |
'내일'이라는 시점이 제시되는 초반부에, 5대의 새 프로젝터가 내일 배송된다는(~ five new projectors will be delivered to our office tomorrow) 사실을 알리고 있으므로 (C)가 정답이다.

| 어휘 | shredder 파쇄기

87. 화자는 장비의 무슨 특징에 대해 만족하는가?
(A) 가격이 저렴하다.
(B) 무선으로 연결된다.
(C) 조용하게 작동된다.
(D) 무게가 가볍다.

| 해설 |
담화 중반부에, 화자는 프로젝터를 they로 지칭해 비싸지 않다는 (Fortunately, they were so inexpensive ~) 특징을 언급하고 있으므로 (A)가 정답이다.

| 어휘 | feature 특징   equipment 장비   be pleased about ~에 만족하다   operate 작동되다, 가동되다   quietly 조용하게   lightweight 무게가 가벼운, 경량의

88. 화자는 왜 "but they are short-staffed"라고 말하는가?
(A) 지연 이유를 설명하기 위해
(B) 프로젝트에 자원할 사람을 요청하기 위해
(C) 추가 직원 고용에 대한 지지를 나타내기 위해
(D) 도움 없이 일을 완수하도록 권하기 위해

| 해설 |
담화 후반부에, 도움이 필요하면 IT팀에 연락할 수 있다고(If you really need help, you can contact the IT team) 말한 뒤로 "그곳에 직원이 부족하다"고 알리는 상황이다. 뒤이어 설명서를 이용해 알아보도록(it's better to figure it out using the instructions) 권하고 있는데, 이는 IT팀의 도움을 받지 않고 해결하도록 권하는 말이므로 (D)가 정답이다.

| 어휘 | explain ~을 설명하다   delay 지연, 지체   ask for ~을 요청하다   volunteer 자원 봉사자   support 지지, 후원   hire ~을 고용하다   task 일, 업무

Questions 89-91 refer to the following introduction.

M: Thank you all for coming to this workshop today, and I'm pleased that we've got such a great turnout. **89 I see that we do have some people standing in the back. Please accept my apologies for the lack of seating.** Now I'd like to introduce your instructor, **90 Alicia Marshall. Ms. Marshall is a best-selling author of several books on business life.** During this workshop, **91 she will cover some tips on how to manage your time well.** There are handouts that accompany this workshop, but I encourage you to take notes too. Ms. Marshall has a lot of useful information to share, so let's get started.

89-91번 문제는 다음 소개를 참조하시오.

남: 오늘 이 워크숍에 와 주신 여러분 모두에게 감사드리며, 이렇게 많은 참석자가 자리해 주신 것을 보니 기쁩니다. 몇몇 분들이 뒤쪽에 서 계신 것이 보입니다. 좌석 부족 문제에 대해 사과드립니다. 이제, 여러분의 강사 Alicia Marshall 씨를 소개해 드리고자 합니다. Marshall 씨는 비즈니스 생활에 관한 책을 여러 권 쓴 베스트셀러 저자이십니다. 이번 워크숍 시간 중에 시간을 잘 관리하는 방법에 관한 몇몇 팁을 다루실 것입니다. 이 워크숍에 딸려 있는 유인물이 있기는 하지만, 저는 여러분께 필기도 함께 할 것을 권해 드립니다. Marshall 씨께서 공유할 유용한 정보가 많이 있으니 시작해 보겠습니다.

| 어휘 | turnout 참석자의 수   in the back 뒤쪽에   Please accept my apologies for ~에 대해 사과드립니다   introduce ~을 소개하다   instructor 강사   author 저자, 작가   several 여럿의, 몇몇의   cover (주제 등) ~을 다루다   how to do ~하는 법   handout 유인물   accompany ~에 동반되다   encourage A to do A에게 ~하도록 권하다, 장려하다   take notes 필기하다   useful 유용한   share ~을 공유하다   get started 시작하다

89. 화자는 청자들에게 왜 사과하는가?
(A) 발표자가 참석할 수 없다.
(B) 등록 과정이 복잡했다.
(C) 좌석이 충분하지 않다.
(D) 시작 시간이 변경되었다.

| 해설 |
초반부에, 서 있는 사람들에게 사과하면서 그 이유로 좌석 부족(I see that we do have some people standing in the back. Please accept my apologies for the lack of seating)을 언급하고 있으므로 (C)가 정답이다.

| 어휘 | presenter 발표자   available (사람이) 참석할 수 없는, 시간이 나지 않는   registration 등록   process 과정   complicated 복잡한

90. Alicia Marshall은 누구인가?
(A) 뉴스 방송 진행자
(B) 사업가
(C) 베스트셀러 저자
(D) 시 공무원

| 해설 |
Alicia Marshall 씨의 이름이 제시되는 중반부에, Ms. Marshall is a best-selling author of several books라는 말로 베스트셀러 도서의 저자임을 알리고 있으므로 (C)가 정답이다.

| 어휘 | official 공무원, 당국자

91. Alicia Marshall의 워크숍 주제는 무엇이 될 것인가?
(A) 마케팅 기술
(B) 시간 관리
(C) 효과적인 팀워크
(D) 해외 투자

| 해설 |
Alicia Marshall 씨를 she로 지칭하면서 시간을 잘 관리하는 방법에 관한 팁을 다룰 것이라고(~ she will cover some tips on how to manage your time well) 알리고 있으므로 (B)가 정답이다.

| 어휘 | effective 효과적인   overseas 해외의   investment 투자(금)

Questions 92-94 refer to the following excerpt from a meeting.

M: All right, everyone, now that you've been introduced to our computer system, I hope that you all feel comfortable **92 searching for properties** and adding new information. **92 Prior to showing a home to a potential buyer, 93 you can search for the property's file to view that information.** Most people have a lot of questions during the visit. **93 It makes a good impression if you know all of the details.** We know that efficiency is key in today's market. So, **94 don't forget to reply to e-mails** from customers as quickly as possible. That's your top priority.

92-94번 문제는 다음 회의 발췌문 내용을 참조하시오.
남: 좋습니다, 여러분, 이제 여러분에게 우리 컴퓨터 시스템을 소개했으니, 부동산을 검색하고 새로운 정보를 추가하는 일을 여러분 모두가 편하게 느끼시기 바랍니다. 잠재 구매자에게 주택을 보여주기에 앞서, 그 정보를 확인해 보실 수 있도록 해당 건물의 파일을 검색하실 수 있습니다. 대부분의 사람들이 방문 중에 많은 질문을 합니다. 여러분이 모든 상세 정보를 알고 있다면 좋은 인상을 남기게 됩니다. 우리는 오늘날의 시장에서 효율성이 핵심이라는 점을 알고 있습니다. 따라서, 잊지 마시고 가능한 한 신속히 고객들의 이메일에 답변해 주십시오. 그것이 여러분이 해야 하는 최우선 사항입니다.

| 어휘 | be introduced to ~을 소개받다, 안내받다   comfortable 편안한, 편한   search for ~을 검색하다, 찾다   property 부동산, 건물   add ~을 추가하다   prior to ~에 앞서, ~ 전에   potential 잠재적인   view ~을 보다   during ~ 중에, ~ 동안   make a good impression 좋은 인상을 남기다   details 상세 정보, 세부 사항   efficiency 효율성   forget to do ~하는 것을 잊다   reply to ~에 답변하다   as quickly as possible 가능한 한 신속히   top priority 최우선 사항

92. 청자들은 누구일 것 같은가?
(A) 공사장 작업자
(B) 은행 창구 직원
(C) 부동산 중개소 직원
(D) 실험실 기사

| 해설 |
담화 초반부에, 건물을 검색하는 일(searching for properties)과 집을 구매자에게 보여주는 일(showing a home to a potential buyer)이 언급되어 있는데, 이와 같은 일을 할 수 있는 사람은 부동산 중개소 직원이므로 (C)가 정답이다.

| 어휘 | real estate 부동산   agent 직원, 대리인   laboratory 실험실

93. 화자가 "Most people have a lot of questions during the visit"이라고 말할 때 무엇을 암시하는가?
(A) 일부 설명이 충분히 명확하지 않다.
(B) 더 많은 정보가 온라인으로 게시되어야 한다.
(C) 활동에 예상보다 더 오래 걸릴 수 있다.
(D) 정보 파일을 신중히 읽어야 한다.

| 해설 |
담화 중반부에, 건물의 파일을 검색할 수 있다는(~ you can search for the property's file to view that information) 말에 이어 "사람들이 방문 중에 많은 질문을 한다"고 말하는 상황이다. 그리고 뒤이어 정보를 잘 아는 것이 좋은 인상을 남기는 방법임을(It makes a good impression if you know all of the details) 알리고 있는데, 이는 건물 파일을 잘 읽어보도록 당부하는 말에 해당되므로 (D)가 정답이다.

| 어휘 | instructions 설명, 안내, 지시   post ~을 게시하다   take longer 시간이 더 오래 걸리다   than expected 예상보다   carefully 신중히

94. 화자의 말에 따르면, 무엇이 최우선 사항인가?
(A) 팀으로서 함께 일하기
(B) 메시지에 신속히 답변하기
(C) 안전한 이메일 비밀번호 사용하기
(D) 규제 사항 준수하기

| 해설 |
담화 후반부에 가능한 한 신속히 고객들의 이메일에 답변하라는 말과 함께 그것이 최우선 사항이라고(~ don't forget to reply to e-mails from customers as quickly as possible. That's your top priority) 알리고 있으므로 (B)가 정답이다.

| 어휘 | respond to ~에 답변하다, 반응하다   secure 안전한   comply with ~을 준수하다   regulation 규제, 규정

Questions 95-97 refer to the following telephone message and floor plan.

M: Hello, this is Ravi Dayal. **95** **I'm organizing the trade show** next month at Coburn Plaza. There have been a few adjustments to the floor plan for the space you are renting. I've e-mailed you the latest copy. You'll see that we still have the shelves in the same place. **96** **So, you can display your tablet computers right near the entrance.** **97** **I've added a small section of chairs.** I think this would be a good place for customers to wait if you are busy.

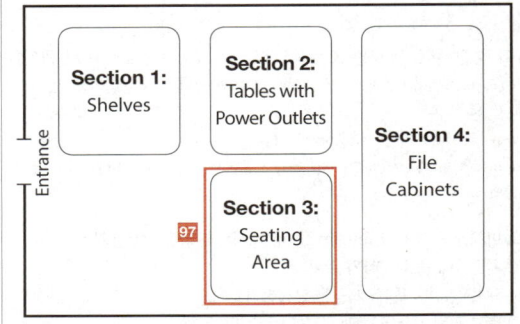

95-97번 문제는 다음 전화 메시지와 평면도를 참조하시오.
남: 안녕하세요, 저는 Ravi Dayal입니다. 제가 다음 달에 Coburn Plaza에서 열리는 무역 박람회 행사를 준비하고 있습니다. 귀사에서 임대하는 공간에 대해 평면도상에서 몇몇 조정 사항이 있습니다. 제가 최신 사본을 이메일로 보내 드렸습니다. 동일한 위치에 여전히 진열대들이 있다는 것이 보이실 겁니다. 따라서, 출입구 바로 근처에 귀사의 태블릿 컴퓨터들을 진열하실 수 있습니다. 의자를 놓을 수 있는 작은 구역을 추가해 드렸습니다. 이는 바쁘실 경우에 고객들이 대기하기에 아주 좋은 곳이 될 것으로 생각합니다.

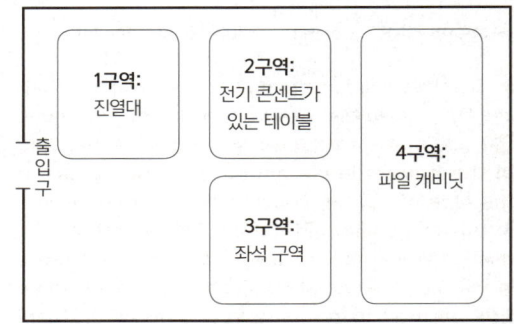

| 어휘 | organize ~을 준비하다, 조직하다   adjustment 조정, 조절   floor plan 평면도   rent ~을 임대하다, 대여하다   latest 최신의   copy 사본   shelf 진열대, 선반   display ~을 진열하다, 전시하다   right near ~ 바로 근처에   add ~을 추가하다   power outlet 전기 콘센트   seating 좌석

95. 화자는 누구일 것 같은가?
(A) 컴퓨터 프로그래머
(B) 백화점 매니저
(C) 건물 소유주

(D) 무역 박람회 조직 담당자

| 해설 |
담화 시작 부분에, 화자가 무역 박람회 행사를 준비하고 있다고(I'm organizing the trade show ~) 알리고 있으므로 (D)가 정답이다.
| 어휘 | owner 소유주 organizer 조직 담당자, 주최자

96. 화자는 일부 태블릿 컴퓨터에 관해 무엇이라고 언급하는가?
(A) 합리적인 가격에 제공된다.
(B) 곧 배송될 것이다.
(C) 고객들에게 계속 인기가 있다.
(D) 출입구 근처에 놓을 수 있다.

| 해설 |
태블릿 컴퓨터가 언급되는 중반부에, 출입구 바로 근처에 태블릿 컴퓨터들을 진열할 수 있다고(So, you can display your tablet computers right near the entrance) 알리고 있으므로 (D)가 정답이다.
| 어휘 | reasonable (가격이) 합리적인, 저렴한 ship ~을 배송하다 be popular with ~에게 인기 있다 position ~을 놓다, 두다

97. 시각 자료를 보시오. 어느 구역이 추가되었는가?
(A) 구역 1
(B) 구역 2
(C) 구역 3
(D) 구역 4

| 해설 |
추가된 구역이 언급되는 후반부에, 의자를 놓을 수 있는 작은 구역을 추가했다고(I've added a small section of chairs) 알리고 있다. 시각 자료에서 좌석 공간(Seating Area)에 해당되는 곳이 Section 3이므로 (C)가 정답이다.

Questions 98-100 refer to the following excerpt from a meeting and graph.

W: I've checked the most recent sales figures for 98 **our retail clothing stores.** You can see on this chart here that 99 **the highest sales category reached nine million euros.** We would like to take advantage of this trend. We will keep about the same amount of display space for each of the four products. However, we want to make the popular items easier for customers to find. So, 99 **we'll move the best-selling product near the entrances.** 100 **I'll e-mail the supervisors** of each store to ask them to make this change right away. I hope this will help us to boost profits further.

Annual Sales in Millions of Euros

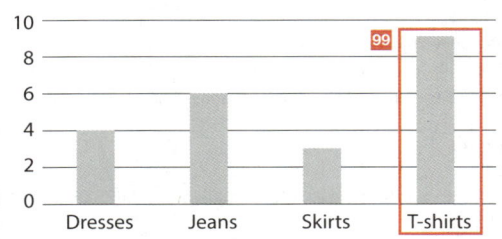

98-100번 문제는 다음 회의 발췌 내용과 그래프를 참조하시오.
여: 제가 우리 소매 의류 매장들에 대한 가장 최근의 매출 수치를 확인해 봤습니다. 여기 이 차트에서 가장 높은 매출 항목이 9백만 유로에 달했다는 것을 보실 수 있습니다. 우리는 이와 같은 추세를 활용하고자 합니다. 우리는 네 가지 제품 각각에 대해 거의 동일한 수준의 진열 공간을 유지할 것입니다. 하지만, 인기 있는 제품을 고객들이 더 쉽게 찾을 수 있게 하기를 원합니다. 따라서, 베스트셀러 제품을 입구 근처로 옮길 것입니다. 즉시 이렇게 변경하도록 요청하는 이메일을 각 매장의 운영 책임자들에게 보낼 것입니다. 저는 이 방법이 수익을 한층 더 증대하는 데 있어 우리에게 도움이 되기를 바랍니다.

연간 매출, 백만 유로 단위

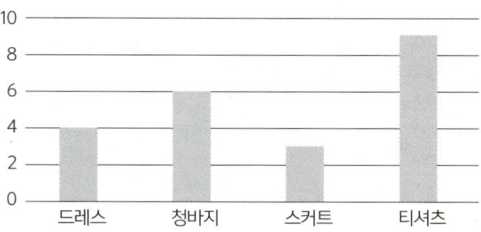

| 어휘 | recent 최근의 sales 매출, 판매(량), 영업 figure 수치, 숫자 retail store 소매점 category 항목, 범주 reach ~에 달하다, 도달하다 take advantage of ~을 활용하다, 이용하다 trend 추세, 경향 about the same 거의 동일한 amount 수준, 양, 분량 display 전시, 진열 make A + 형용사 A를 ~한 상태로 만들다 near ~ 근처에 supervisor 책임자, 부서장, 감독 ask A to do A에게 ~하도록 요청하다 make a change 변경하다 right away 즉시 boost ~을 증대하다, 촉진하다 profit 수익 further 한층 더, 더욱

98. 청자들은 무슨 종류의 업체에서 근무하는가?
(A) 의류 제조사
(B) 회계 법인
(C) 소매점 체인
(D) 패션 잡지사

| 해설 |
담화를 시작하면서 화자가 소속 회사를 our retail clothing stores로 언급하고 있으므로 (C)가 정답이다.

99. 시각 자료를 보시오. 화자의 말에 따르면, 무슨 제품이 입구 근처로 옮겨질 것인가?
(A) 드레스
(B) 청바지
(C) 스커트
(D) 티셔츠

| 해설 |
담화 초반부에, 가장 높은 매출 항목이 9백만 유로에 달했다는 점과(~ the highest sales category reached nine million euros) 베스트셀러 제품을 입구 근처로 옮길 것이라고(~ we'll move the best-selling product near the entrances) 알리고 있다. 시각 자료에서 9백만 유로에 해당되는 항목이 T-shirts이므로 (D)가 정답이다.

100. 화자는 무엇을 할 계획인가?
(A) 일부 책임자들에게 연락하기
(B) 일부 매장 견학하기
(C) 설문 조사지 배부하기
(D) 직원 승진 공지하기

| 해설 |
담화 마지막에, 화자가 책임자들에게 이메일을 보내겠다고(I'll e-mail the supervisors ~) 알리고 있으므로 (A)가 정답이다.
| 어휘 | contact ~에게 연락하다 tour ~을 견학하다, 둘러보다 distribute ~을 배부하다, 나눠주다 survey 설문 조사(지) promotion 승진

Part 5

101. (B)
| 해석 |
그 작가가 너무 늦었기 때문에, 오직 소규모 팬들로 이뤄진 사람들만이 도서 사인회 행사에 남아 있었다.
| 해설 |
형용사 small과 전치사 of 사이에 위치한 빈칸은 형용사의 수식을 받을 명사 자리인데, 부정 관사 a와 어울리려면 단수 명사가 쓰여야 하므로 단수 명사의 형태인 (B) crowd가 정답이다.
| 어휘 | author 작가, 저자   remain 남아 있다, 그대로 있다   book signing 도서 사인회   crowded 붐비는, 사람들로 복잡한   crowd n. 사람들, 군중 v. (사람들이) ~을 가득 메우다

102. (A)
| 해석 |
모든 부서의 직원들은 금요일 오후까지 각자의 정식 근무 시간표를 제출해야 한다.
| 해설 |
to부정사로 쓰인 동사 submit과 목적어인 명사 timesheets 사이에 위치한 빈칸은 형용사 official과 함께 목적어를 수식하는 역할을 해야 한다. 따라서 명사 수식이 가능한 소유격 대명사 (A) their가 정답이다.
| 어휘 | department 부서   be requested to do ~해야 하다   submit ~을 제출하다   official 정식의, 공식적인   timesheet 근무 시간표   by (기한) ~까지

103. (D)
| 해석 |
계약서는 그 건물의 4층 전체를 사무 공간으로 사용하기 위한 임대 관련 사항을 다루고 있다.
| 해설 |
빈칸 뒤에 쓰인 rental(임대)은 contract(계약서)에 기재된 주요 내용으로 볼 수 있다. 따라서 둘 사이의 의미 관계를 나타낼 동사로 '(주제 등) ~을 다루다, 포함하다'를 뜻하는 (D) covers가 정답이다.
| 어휘 | contract 계약(서)   rental 임대, 대여   entire 전체의   apply 신청하다, 지원하다, ~을 적용하다   wrap ~을 포장하다, 싸다   cover (주제 등) ~을 다루다

104. (A)
| 해석 |
Reynolds 씨는 가벼운 건강 관련 문제를 겪고 있기 때문에 일을 조금 쉬고 있다.
| 해설 |
빈칸 앞뒤로 주어와 동사가 각각 포함된 두 개의 절이 쓰여 있으므로 빈칸은 이 절을 연결할 접속사 자리이다. 건강 문제가 있는 것이 일을 쉬는 이유에 해당되므로 이유 접속사 (A) because가 정답이다. (B) concerning과 (D) despite은 전치사이고, (C) whether는 접속사이지만 의미가 맞지 않는다.
| 어휘 | take A off A의 시간만큼 일을 쉬다, 휴무하다   suffer from (질병 등) ~을 겪다, 앓다   minor (정도 등) 가벼운, 미미한   issue 문제, 사안   concerning ~와 관련해   whether ~인지 (아닌지), ~에 상관없이   despite ~에도 불구하고

105. (C)
| 해석 |
창고에 있는 상자들은 내용물 손상을 예방할 수 있도록 반드시 신중하게 옮겨져야 한다.
| 해설 |
in order to와 결합해 목적을 나타낼 동사가 필요한데, 목적어에 해당되는 damage가 '손상, 피해'를 의미하므로 이에 대한 조치와 관련된 동사로 '~을 예방하다'를 뜻하는 (C) prevent가 정답이다.
| 어휘 | warehouse 창고   carefully 신중하게, 조심스럽게   in order to do ~할 수 있도록   damage to ~에 대한 손상, 피해   content 내용(물)   ignore ~을 무시하다   postpone ~을 연기하다   prevent ~을 예방하다   interrupt ~을 방해하다, 중단시키다

106. (D)
| 해석 |
Jones 씨는 신규 매장의 개장을 위해 개최되는 기념식에 대한 책임을 맡았다.
| 해설 |
정관사 the의 수식을 받음과 동시에 전치사 for의 목적어 역할을 할 명사가 빈칸에 필요한데, 행사 개최의 목적과 관련되어야 하므로 '매장의 개장'이라는 의미를 구성할 수 있는 (D) opening이 정답이다.
| 어휘 | be placed in charge of ~에 대한 책임을 맡다   ceremony 기념식   hold ~을 개최하다   openly 공공연히, 드러내 놓고   openness 개방성, 솔직함   opening 개장, 개점, 개막

107. (D)
| 해석 |
오직 그 극단의 회원에 한해 공연 시작에 앞서 무대 뒤쪽 구역에 대한 출입이 허용된다.
| 해설 |
빈칸 다음을 보면 주어(members)와 동사(are permitted), 그리고 전치사구들로 구성된 절이 하나만 존재한다. 따라서 부사인 (A) Easily와 (D) Only 중에서 정답을 골라야 하는데, 명사를 수식해 강조의 의미를 나타내는 역할이 가능한 (D) Only가 정답이다. (B) Provided와 (C) Until은 접속사이므로 두 개의 절을 연결해야 한다.
| 어휘 | theatrical organization 극단   permit A B A에게 B를 허용하다   backstage 무대 뒤쪽 구역   prior to ~에 앞서, ~ 전에   easily 쉽게, 편리하게   provided (that) (만일) ~라면   until (지속) ~까지

108. (B)
| 해석 |
Davidson Motors는 20대 구매자들을 대상으로 더욱 경쟁력을 갖추기 위해 추가 차량들을 소개할 계획이다.
| 해설 |
to부정사로 쓰인 be 동사와 결합할 보어가 필요한데, 새로운 차량을 소개하는 목적과 관련되어야 하므로 '경쟁력 있는'을 뜻하는 형용사 (B) competitive가 정답이다.
| 어휘 | plan to do ~할 계획이다   introduce ~을 소개하다, 도입하다   additional 추가적인   vehicle 차량   in one's twenties 20대인   competitively 경쟁적으로   competitive 경쟁력 있는, 경쟁적인   competition 경쟁, 대회, 시합   compete 경쟁하다

109. (D)
| 해석 |
모든 콘서트 관람객들은 극장 출입 자격을 얻을 수 있도록 유효한 입장권을 제시해야 한다.
| 해설 |
빈칸에 쓰일 형용사는 ticket을 수식해 그 특성을 나타내야 하는데, 극장에 출입할 수 있도록 제시하는 입장권은 '유효한' 것이어야 하므로 (D) valid가 정답이다.
| 어휘 | concertgoer 콘서트 관람객   be required to do ~해야 하다   present ~을 제시하다   gain admission to ~에 대한 출입 자격을 얻다   direct 직접적인, 직행의, 솔직한   varied 다양한   prompt 즉각적인, 지체 없는   valid 유효한

110. (B)
| 해석 |
지역 주민인 Norris 박사는 치과 의학 분야에서의 혁신적인 업적으로 인정 받았다.
| 해설 |
빈칸은 형용사 innovative의 수식을 받음과 동시에 전치사 for의 목적어 역할을 할 명사 자리이므로 명사인 (B) achievement가 정답이다. 동명사인 (C) achieving은 형용사의 수식을 받지 못한다.

| 어휘 | local 지역의, 현지의   resident 주민   be recognized for ~에 대해 인정받다, 표창 받다   innovative 혁신적인   field 분야   dentistry 치과 의학   achievable 달성할 수 있는, 성취할 수 있는   achievement 업적, 달성, 성취   achieve ~을 달성하다, 성취하다

111. (C)

| 해석 |
Harold's 제약에서 제공하는 가격은 전체 의학 제품 라인에 걸쳐 변함없는 상태로 유지되어 왔다.

| 해설 |
빈칸 뒤에 위치한 명사구는 가격이 변함없이 유지되는 제품에 해당되므로 대상 범위를 나타내 '~에 걸쳐'라는 의미로 쓰이는 전치사 (C) across가 정답이다.

| 어휘 | pharmaceutical a. 약학의, 제약의 n. 약, 제약   remain 형용사 ~한 상태로 유지되다, 남아 있다   constant 변함없는, 일정한   entire 전체의   line (제품) 라인, 종류   healthcare 의료, 건강 관리   onto ~ 위로   beside ~ 옆에   across (대상 범위) ~에 걸쳐   between (A and B) (A와 B) 사이에

112. (B)

| 해석 |
그 책임자 직책에 대한 5명의 지원자들이 지닌 자격은 학력과 경력에서 크게 차이가 난다.

| 해설 |
자동사 differ와 전치사 by 사이에 위치한 빈칸은 differ를 수식할 부사 자리이므로 부사인 (B) greatly가 정답이다.

| 어휘 | qualification 자격 (요건)   applicant 지원자   supervisor 책임자, 상사, 부서장   position 직책, 일자리   differ 차이가 나다, 다르다   by (원인, 기준 등) ~에 따라, ~에 의해   greatly 크게, 대단히, 매우

113. (C)

| 해석 |
Tanaka 씨가 그 시설물에 도착하는 대로, 꼭 대회의실로 모셔 가시기 바랍니다.

| 해설 |
콤마 앞뒤로 주어와 동사가 각각 포함된 두 개의 절이 위치해 있으므로 빈칸은 이 절을 연결할 접속사 자리이다. 'Tanaka 씨가 도착하는 대로 ~로 모셔 가세요'라는 의미가 되어야 적절하므로 '~하는 대로'를 뜻하는 접속사 (C) As soon as가 정답이다. (A) As well as와 (B) Not only는 두 절을 연결하는 접속사로 쓰이지 않으며, (D) So that은 의미가 맞지 않는다.

| 어휘 | arrive at ~에 도착하다   facility 시설(물)   be sure to do 꼭 ~하다   take A to B A를 B로 데려가다   as well as ~뿐만 아니라 …도   not only A (but also B) A뿐만 아니라 (B도)   as soon as ~하는 대로, ~하자마자   so that (목적) ~할 수 있도록, (결과) 그 결과, 그래서

114. (D)

| 해석 |
지역 뉴스 방송국 기자가 Blueline Bay를 가로지르는 제안된 현수교 공사에 관해 보도했다.

| 해설 |
정관사 the와 명사 construction 사이에 위치한 빈칸은 명사를 수식해야 하므로 이 역할이 가능한 분사 중 하나를 골라야 한다. construction(공사)은 사람에 의해 제안되는 것이므로 수동의 의미를 나타내는 과거 분사 (D) proposed가 정답이다.

| 어휘 | local 지역의, 현지의   news station 방송국   report on ~에 관해 보도하다   construction 공사, 건설   suspension bridge 현수교   across ~을 가로질러   propose ~을 제안하다   proposal 제안(서)

115. (D)

| 해석 |
전통적으로 3일 동안 진행되어 왔지만, 올여름에는 Emerson County Fair가 일주일 동안 개최될 것이다.

| 해설 |
과거에 3일 동안 진행되었던 것과 달리 올여름에는 일주일 동안 개최된다는 의미를 나타내는 문장이다. 따라서 과거에 3일 동안 진행되었던 것은 그 동안 지속된 일반적인 관례로 판단할 수 있으므로 이러한 의미를 나타낼 부사로 '전통적으로, 일반적으로'를 뜻하는 (D) traditionally가 정답이다.

| 어휘 | while ~이지만, ~인 반면   last 지속되다   hold ~을 개최하다   exceptionally 예외적으로, 특별히   financially 재정적으로   positively 긍정적으로   traditionally 전통적으로, 일반적으로

116. (D)

| 해석 |
중대한 배송 문제로 인해, MacGregor 사의 어떤 제품도 몇 주 동안 도착하지 않을 예정이다.

| 해설 |
빈칸 뒤에 위치한 복수 명사 weeks를 수식하기에 적합하며, 문맥상 '몇 주'라는 의미를 구성하는 (D) several이 정답이다.

| 어휘 | because of ~로 인해, ~ 때문에   major 중대한, 주요한   shipping 배송, 선적   be due to do ~할 예정이다   arrive 도착하다   another 또 다른 하나의   variable 가변적인, 변동이 심한   plentiful 풍부한   several 몇몇의, 여럿의

117. (B)

| 해석 |
일단 양측에 의해 계약서에 서명이 되면, 계약 조항에 대한 어떠한 추가적인 조정도 이뤄질 수 없다.

| 해설 |
서명이 된 시점 이후로 계약 조항과 관련해 추가적으로 이뤄질 수 없는 일을 나타낼 명사가 필요하므로 '조정'을 의미하는 (B) adjustments가 정답이다.

| 어휘 | once 일단 ~하면, ~하는 대로   contract 계약(서)   party 당사자, 사람   further 추가적인   conditions (계약 등의) 조항, 조건, 약관   make adjustments 조정하다   commitment 전념, 헌신   conversion 전환, 개조   selection 선택(된 것)

118. (D)

| 해석 |
Harper Media의 직원들을 대상으로 하는 모든 명함은 각 개인의 개성을 반영할 수 있도록 주문 제작되었다.

| 해설 |
has been과 결합 가능한 것은 현재 분사 또는 과거 분사이다. 그런데 빈칸 뒤에 목적어 없이 to부정사구가 이어지고 있으므로 타동사 customize의 과거 분사가 쓰여 수동태가 되어야 알맞다. 따라서 과거 분사인 (D) customized가 정답이다.

| 어휘 | business card 명함   reflect ~을 반영하다   individual 개인, 사람   personality 개성, 성격   customize ~을 주문 제작하다, 맞춤 제작하다

119. (D)

| 해석 |
Watts 씨가 오전 11시에는 회사로 돌아가긴 하지만, 그 이후에는 언제든지 만날 시간이 난다.

| 해설 |
주절에 오전 11시나 되어야 회사로 돌아간다는 말이 있으므로 but절에서 말하는 '시간이 나는' 시점은 그 이후가 되어야 알맞다. 따라서 11 A.M.을 대신하는 that과 함께 '그 이후에'라는 의미를 구성할 수 있는 전치사 (D) after가 정답이다.

| 어휘 | not A until B B나 되어야 A하다   return to ~로 돌아가다   available (사람이) 시간이 나는   anytime 언제든지   behind ~ 뒤에, ~ 이면에   along (길 등) ~을 따라   during ~ 중에, ~ 동안

120. (A)

| 해설 |
그 매장은 고급 주택 지역에 위치한 지점임에도 불구하고 약간 할인된 가격에 장신구를 판매한다.

| 해설 |
전치사 at의 목적어 prices를 수식하는 과거 분사 reduced를 수식해 할인된 정도를 나타낼 부사가 필요하므로 (A) slightly가 정답이다.
| 어휘 | jewelry 장신구, 보석 제품   reduced 할인된   despite ~에도 불구하고   location 지점, 위치   exclusive 고급의, 고가의   neighborhood 지역, 인근   slightly 약간, 조금   slight 약간의, 조금의   slighting 깔보는, 무시하는

121. (C)
| 해석 |
프런트 데스크의 안내 담당 직원이 외부 사람들에 의해 걸려 온 모든 전화를 해당 부서로 돌려줄 수 있다.
| 해설 |
전치사 to의 목적어로서 외부의 전화를 받는 부서를 나타내는 department를 수식할 형용사가 필요한데, 의미상 전화의 목적에 따라 관련 부서가 전화를 받아야 한다. 따라서 '해당되는, 적절한'이라는 의미로 쓰이는 (C) appropriate이 정답이다.
| 어휘 | receptionist 안내 담당 직원   transfer A to B A를 B로 옮기다, 넘기다   make a call 전화하다   outside 외부의   party 사람, 당사자   department 부서   intentional 고의의   subsequent 그 다음의, 이후의   appropriate 해당되는, 적절한   significant 상당한, 많은

122. (C)
| 해석 |
인사부의 Prentice 씨가 내일 오후에 있을 회의에서 고객 응대에 대한 회사의 새 지침을 발표할 예정이다.
| 해설 |
빈칸 뒤에 목적어 역할을 하는 명사구 the firm's new guidelines가 있으므로 타동사 present가 능동태로 쓰여야 한다. 또한 미래 시점 표현 tomorrow afternoon과 어울려야 하므로 이 조건들을 모두 만족하는 것으로서 미래를 대신하는 현재 진행 시제인 (C) is presenting이 정답이다.
| 어휘 | HR 인사(부)   firm 회사   deal with ~을 대하다, ~에 대처하다   present ~을 발표하다, 제시하다

123. (D)
| 해석 |
비록 그 보고서의 오류들이 거의 눈에 잘 띄지 않지만, 부서장은 완전히 다시 작성되도록 요청했다.
| 해설 |
'오류가 눈에 띄지 않지만, 다시 작성되도록 요청했다'와 같은 의미가 되어야 자연스러우므로 빈칸이 속한 Although절은 부정의 의미가 포함되어야 한다. 따라서 '거의 ~ 않다'라는 뜻으로 부정을 나타내는 부사 (D) barely가 정답이다.
| 어휘 | although 비록 ~이기는 하지만   noticeable 눈에 잘 띄는, 두드러진   ask A to do A가 ~하도록 요청하다   completely 완전히, 전적으로   rewrite ~을 다시 작성하다   preferably 가급적이면   correctly 정확히, 올바르게   carefully 조심스럽게, 신중하게   barely 거의 ~ 않다

124. (A)
| 해석 |
어떠한 가격 할인도 반드시 해당 분기에 대한 회사의 목표 수익 수치에 영향을 미치지 않도록 해야 한다.
| 해설 |
'가격'을 뜻하는 명사 price와 복합 명사를 이루기에 적절한 명사가 필요하므로 '가격 할인'이라는 의미를 구성할 수 있는 (A) reductions가 정답이다.
| 어휘 | It is imperative that 반드시 ~해야 한다   affect ~에 영향을 미치다   targeted 목표로 설정된   revenue 수익, 세입   quarter 분기   reduction 할인, 감소   sensation 느낌, 감각, 선풍   institution 기관, 단체, 협회   reservation 예약

125. (B)
| 해석 |
Benson 씨는 정확성을 떨어뜨리지 않으면서 속도를 높여 자신의 할당 업무를 완료했다.
| 해설 |
빈칸 앞에 '전치사 + 명사'가 있으므로 빈칸에는 명사의 목적어 역할을 하는 명사 또는 동명사를 수식하는 부사 중의 하나가 필요하다. '명확성을 떨어뜨리지 않은 채로 속도를 높여 완료했다'와 같은 의미가 되어야 알맞으므로 '명확성'을 뜻하는 명사 (B) clarity가 정답이다.
| 어휘 | increase ~을 높이다, 증가시키다   complete ~을 완료하다   assignment 할당 업무, 배정된 일   without ~하지 않고, ~하지 않은 채   compromise (질, 수준 등) ~을 떨어뜨리다, ~에 누를 끼치다   clearly 명확히, 분명히   clarity 명확성   clear a. 명확한, 분명한, 투명한, 한산한 v. ~을 치우다, 깨끗하게 하다

126. (A)
| 해석 |
Weston 호텔에는 이번 달에 빈 객실이 없기 때문에, Jenkins 씨는 반드시 다른 곳에 객실을 예약해야 한다.
| 해설 |
Weston Hotel에 빈 방이 없다는 것이 Because절에 이유로 제시되어 있다. 따라서 다른 숙박 시설에 있는 객실을 예약해야 하므로 '다른 곳에'를 뜻하는 부사 (A) elsewhere가 정답이다.
| 어휘 | vacancy 빈 방   book ~을 예약하다   elsewhere 다른 곳에   somewhat 다소, 약간   furthermore 게다가, 더욱이

127. (B)
| 해석 |
Tyler Institute의 연례 우수 성과 표창을 위한 기념식이 개최될 예정이다.
| 해설 |
빈칸에 쓰일 명사는 전치사 for의 목적어로서 우수한 성과와 관련해 행사를 개최하는 목적을 나타내야 한다. 따라서 성과나 공로 등을 인정하는 행사로 판단할 수 있으므로 '표창, 인정' 등을 뜻하는 (B) recognition이 정답이다.
| 어휘 | ceremony 기념식   hold ~을 개최하다   annual 연례적인, 해마다의   outstanding 우수한, 뛰어난   performance 성과, 실적, 수행 능력   omission 생략   recognition 표창, 인정   standard 표준, 기준   exception 예외

128. (A)
| 해석 |
사람들 앞에서 말하는 것을 좋아하지 않기 때문에, Turner 씨는 콘퍼런스에서 자신의 작업물을 발표하기를 꺼린다.
| 해설 |
빈칸 앞쪽에 위치한 be 동사 뒤에 보어가 필요하므로 형용사 (A) reluctant가 정답이다.
| 어휘 | in public 사람들이 있는 데서, 공개적으로   be reluctant to do ~하기를 꺼리다, 주저하다   present ~을 발표하다, 제시하다   work 작업물, 작품   reluctance 꺼림, 내키지 않음   reluctantly 꺼려하여, 마지못해

129. (C)
| 해석 |
항공권을 구입하기에 앞서, Vernon 씨는 그것이 구매 가능한 가장 저렴한 것임을 확인했다.
| 해설 |
purchasing이 이끄는 동명사구를 목적어로 취해야 하므로 빈칸은 전치사 자리이다. 항공권을 구입하기 전에 가격 수준을 확인해야 하므로 '~에 앞서, ~ 전에'라는 의미로 쓰이는 전치사 (C) Prior to가 정답이다. (A) Owing to는 전치사이지만 의미가 맞지 않으며, (B) Provided that은 접속사, (D) Instead는 부사이므로 오답이다.
| 어휘 | purchase ~을 구입하다   confirm that ~임을 확인하다   available 구매 가능한   owing to ~ 때문에   provided that 만약 ~라면   prior to ~에

앞서, ~ 전에   instead 대신에

130. (D)

| 해석 |
다리 수리 작업이 완료되었을 때쯤, 통행 차량들이 이미 여러 차례 그 위로 가로질러 지나갔다.

| 해설 |
콤마 앞뒤로 각각 주어와 동사가 포함된 두 절이 있으므로 빈칸은 이들을 연결할 접속사 자리이다. 그런데 두 절의 시제가 각각 과거 시제(were finished)와 과거 완료 시제(had crossed)이므로 이와 같은 시제로 구성된 문장에서 과거 시제가 쓰인 절을 이끄는 접속사 (D) By the time이 정답이다. (A) Due to는 전치사이며, (B) Unless와 (C) Whenever는 접속사이지만 두 동사의 시제 관계를 적절히 나타내지 못한다.

| 어휘 | repair 수리   vehicular traffic 통행 차량들, 차량 통행   cross over ~ 위로 가로질러 건너다   on numerous occasions 여러 차례   due to ~로 인해   unless ~하지 않는다면, ~가 아니라면   whenever ~할 때마다, ~할 때는 언제든지   by the time ~할 때 즈음에는

Part 6

131-134번 문제는 다음 이메일을 참조하시오.

수신: Sylvia Bannister
발신: Carl Jepson
날짜: 3월 12일
제목: 인테리어 작업

Bannister 씨께,

저희는 귀하께서 새 주택에 대해 요청하신 인테리어 작업으로 바빴습니다. 가장 먼저, 저희는 볼리비아에서 디자인 품질로 유명한 한 제조사로부터 일부 타일 제품을 131 구입했습니다. 만약을 대비해서, 저희는 132 다소 적은 수량의 타일을 주문했습니다. 하지만, 그 제품을 받아 테스트하자마자 품질을 확인했으며 주방과 욕실에 사용할 만큼 충분한 수량을 주문했습니다. 저희는 또한 벽에 페인트 칠을 하는 대신 벽지를 사용하기로 결정했으며, 그렇게 함으로써 저희 작업자들이 더 빨리 일을 할 수 있었습니다. 133 이로 인해 저희가 2주 내에 모든 일을 완료할 수 있을 것입니다.

저희는 주택의 외관에 134 대해 만족스럽게 생각하고 있으며, 언제든지 방문하셔서 저희 작업 진행 상황을 확인해 보시도록 요청 드립니다.

안녕히 계십시오.

Carl Jepson
Jepson Home Interior

| 어휘 | be busy with ~로 바쁘다   request ~을 요청하다   manufacturer 제조사   renowned for ~로 유명한   quality 질, 품질   precaution 예방 조치   a small number of 적은 수량의   upon -ing ~하자마자   receive ~을 받다   confirm ~을 확인하다   enough for ~하기에 충분한 수량   decide to do ~하기로 결정하다   wallpaper 벽지   rather than ~하는 대신, ~하지 않고   thereby 그렇게 함으로써   be delighted with ~에 대해 만족하다, 기뻐하다   appearance 외관, 겉모습   invite A to do A에게 ~하도록 요청하다   anytime 언제든지   progress 진행 상황, 진척

131. (A)

| 해설 |
각 보기가 모두 능동태 동사의 형태이고 시제가 다르므로 시제 관련 단서를 찾아야 한다. 빈칸의 문장은 앞 문장에서 언급된 그 동안 바빴던 것에 대한 이유를 설명하는 문장이며, 뒤에 이어지는 문장에서도 타일 제품 구입과 관련해 과거 시점에 주문한(ordered) 사실이 쓰여 있으므로 동일한 과거 시제인 (A) purchased가 정답이다.

| 어휘 | purchase ~을 구입하다

132. (A)

| 해설 |
원급 형용사 small을 앞에서 수식하며 의미상으로도 적합한 '다소, 좀, 약간'이란 의미의 (A) rather가 정답이다. (C) much는 비교급을 수식한다.

133. (C)

(A) 주방이 주택 내에서 가장 큰 공간 중 하나입니다.
(B) 이것이 저희가 귀하의 주택 외부에서 하고 있는 작업입니다.
(D) 저희에게 더 많은 예산이 제공되도록 소유주를 설득할 수 있기를 바랍니다.

| 해설 |
앞 문장에 벽지 작업을 하기로 결정한 것으로 인해 작업자들이 더 빨리 일을 할 수 있었다고 알리고 있다. 따라서 그 결과로서 작업 일정상의 완료 시점을 언급하는 (C)가 정답이다. 나머지 보기들은 모두 앞 문장에 언급된 작업 속도와 관련이 없어 자연스럽게 연결되지 않는다.

| 어휘 | outside 외부, 바깥   allow A to do A가 ~할 수 있게 해주다   within ~ 이내에   hope to do ~하기를 바라다   convince A to do ~하도록 A를 설득하다   owner 소유주   budget 예산

134. (C)

| 해설 |
빈칸 앞에 위치한 be delighted는 전치사 with와 결합해 '~에 대해 만족하다, 기뻐하다'라는 의미를 나타내므로 (C) with가 정답이다.

| 어휘 | beyond (위치) ~ 너머에, (시간) ~을 지나, (능력 등) ~을 능가하는   over (위치) ~ 위로 가로질러, (수량 등) ~을 넘는, (기간) ~ 동안에 걸쳐, (비교) ~보다, (대상) ~에 대해

135-138번 문제는 다음 기사를 참조하시오.

Donald Kern 씨 측의 한 변호사는 이 사업가가 시에 큰 액수의 금액을 기부했다고 135 발표했습니다. 이 금액은 Hamburg 공원 인근에 지어지고 있는 지역 문화 센터 공사를 완료하는 데 사용될 것입니다. "저희는 Kern 씨의 넓은 마음에 감사드리며, 특히 우리 시에 재정적 어려움이 존재하는 지금과 같은 시기에 더욱 그렇게 느껴집니다"라고 Elliot Stevens 시장님께서 말씀하셨습니다.

136 이 센터의 공사는 자금 부족 문제로 인해 중단된 바 있습니다. 이제 Kern 씨 덕분에 두 번째 건물이 137 기존의 건물 옆에 지어질 수 있습니다. 이 센터에 강좌와 체육 행사, 그리고 세미나를 개최할 더 많은 공간이 생길 것입니다. 추가로, 새 수영장이 센터 주차장과 138 인접한 곳에 위치하게 될 것입니다.

| 어휘 | lawyer 변호사   associated with ~와 관련된   make a donation 기부하다, 기부금을 내다   fund 자금, 기금   complete ~을 완료하다   construction 공사, 건설   community center 지역 문화 센터   near ~ 인근에, 근처에   appreciate ~에 대해 감사하다   generosity 넓은 마음, 아량   mayor 시장   especially 특히   financial 재정적인, 재무의   thanks to ~ 덕분에   beside ~ 옆에   room (관사 없이) 공간   athletic 체육의, 운동의   in addition 추가로   be located 위치해 있다   parking lot 주차장

135. (B)

| 해설 |
빈칸 앞뒤로 각각 명사구와 that절만 있으므로 빈칸은 문장의 동사 자리이다. 따라서 (A)와 (B) 중에서 적절한 시제를 고르는 문제인데, 변호사가 해당 내용을 발표한 시점은 관련 내용을 언급하는 첫 단락 마지막 문장의 동사 'said'에서 알 수 있듯이 과거의 일이므로 현재 완료 시제 (B) has announced가 정답이다. 현재 완료가 이처럼 이미 '완료'된 행위에 사용할 수 있다는 점을 기억한다.

| 어휘 | announce ~을 발표하다, 알리다   announcement 발표, 공지

136. (B)

(A) Kern 씨는 성공을 거둔 여러 업체를 시에 소유하고 있습니다.

(C) 그 지역 문화 센터는 지역 내 여러 가정에게 인기 있는 장소입니다.
(D) Stevens 시장은 다가오는 가을에 재선에 출마할 예정입니다.

| 해설 |
첫 번째 문장에서 기부한 사실이 과거 시제(made a large donation)로 나타나 있는데, 그보다 이전에 자금 부족의 문제가 있었다는 의미가 되어야 자연스러우므로 대과거 시제(had + p.p.)로 표현한 (B)가 정답이다. 대과거는 과거보다 이전의 사건을 표현하는 시제라는 점을 기억한다.

| 어휘 | several 여럿의, 몇몇의   successful 성공적인   halt ~을 중단시키다   due to ~로 인해   lack of ~의 부족   popular 인기 있는   local 지역의, 현지의   run for reelection 재선에 출마하다

137. (C)

| 해설 |
두 번째 건물(second building)이 지어질 수 있다는 말이 있으므로 building을 대신하는 대명사 one을 수식할 형용사로 첫 번째 건물을 가리키는 것이 필요하다. 따라서 '기존의, 존재하는'을 의미하는 (C) existing이 정답이다.

| 어휘 | notice ~을 알아차리다, 인식하다   conserved 보존된   existing 기존의, 존재하는   tangible 만질 수 있는, 유형의

138. (D)

| 해설 |
빈칸 앞에 위치한 be located와 결합해 위치 정보를 나타낼 전치사가 필요하므로 '~에 인접한, ~와 가까운'을 뜻하는 (D) adjacent to가 정답이다.

| 어휘 | such as ~와 같은   except for ~을 제외하고   even though 비록 ~이기는 하지만   adjacent to ~에 인접한, ~와 가까운

139-142번 문제는 다음 광고를 참조하시오.

자택을 재단장하는 데 관심이 있으신가요?

여러분의 자택을 현대적으로 보이도록 만들고 싶지만, 비용 문제가 걱정되시나요? 그러시다면, 저희 Morrison Home Decorating에 연락해 보십시오. **139** 저희는 여러분의 예산을 초과하지 않는 모든 종류의 장식용품을 보유하고 있습니다. 이 제품들에는 예술 작품과 가구, 그리고 가전제품이 포함되어 있습니다. 엄선된 저희 제품이 아주 마음에 드실 것입니다.

저희 Morrison Home Decorating은 고객 여러분을 **140** 아낍니다. 그것이 바로 저희가 여러분께서 원하시는 것을 귀 기울여 들은 다음, 여러분의 자택이 어떤 모습을 갖춰야 하는지와 관련해 올바른 결정을 내리시도록 도와 드리는 **141** 이유입니다. 저희가 보유하고 있는 **142** 모든 제품들을 확인해 보시려면, www.morrisonhd.com을 통해 온라인으로 저희 매장을 방문하시기 바랍니다.

| 어휘 | be interested in ~에 관심이 있다   have A p.p. A가 ~되게 하다   redecorate ~을 재단장하다   Would you like to do? ~하고 싶으신가요?   make A do A가 ~하도록 만들다   look + 형용사 ~한 것처럼 보이다   be worried about ~을 걱정하다   contact ~에게 연락하다   include ~을 포함하다   work 작품, 작업물   appliances 가전 제품   selection 엄선(된 것), 선택(할 수 있는 것)   care about ~에게 관심을 갖다, 신경 써 주다   carefully 주의하여, 신중히   help A do A가 ~하도록 돕다   make a decision 결정하다   right 올바른, 맞는   regarding ~와 관련해   one's collection of 보유하고 있는, 소장하고 있는

139. (C)
(A) 저희 사무실은 West Haven Street 985번지에 위치해 있습니다.
(B) 저희가 이번 달에 제공해 드리는 특별 할인에 관해 꼭 물어보십시오.
(D) 저희 전문가들이 여러분의 모든 질문에 답변해 드리기 위해 대기하고 있습니다.

| 해설 |
앞서 집을 현대적으로 보이도록 만드는 일과 관련해 비용 문제가 걱정되는지 물은 후에 해당 업체에 연락하도록 권유하고 있다. 따라서 비용 문제를 해결해 줄 수 있는 업체로 볼 수 있으므로 이와 관련된 정보를 담은 것으로 예산을 초과하지 않고 제품을 구입할 수 있다는 의미를 담은 (C)가 정답이다. 또한, 빈칸 뒤의 대명사 'These'는 (C)에 언급된 복수 명사 decorations를 지칭하고 있다.

| 어휘 | be located at ~에 위치해 있다   be sure to do 꼭 ~하다   offer ~을 제공하다   sort 종류   decoration 장식(품)   exceed ~을 초과하다   budget 예산   expert 전문가   stand by 대기하다

140. (C)

| 해설 |
빈칸 앞에 위치한 동사 care는 전치사 about과 결합해 '~에게 관심을 갖다, 신경 써 주다' 등의 의미를 나타내므로 (C) about이 정답이다.

| 어휘 | around ~ 주위에, ~의 곳곳에, ~을 돈 곳에   onto ~ 위로

141. (B)

| 해설 |
빈칸 앞에 쓰인 That은 고객들에게 신경 쓰는 업체임을 밝히는 앞 문장 전체를 가리킨다. 그리고 빈칸 뒤에는 고객들의 말에 귀 기울이고 도움을 준다는 말이 쓰여 있으므로 원인과 결과에 해당되는 의미 관계로 판단할 수 있다. 따라서 이유를 나타내는 의문사 (B) why가 정답이다.

142. (D)

| 해설 |
소유격 대명사 our와 명사 collection 사이에 위치한 빈칸은 명사를 수식할 형용사 자리이므로 (D) complete이 정답이다. 또 다른 명사 (B) completion의 경우 collection과 복합 명사를 구성하기에 의미상 적합하지 않으므로 오답이다.

| 어휘 | complete a. 완전한, 완벽한 v. ~을 완료하다   completion 완료, 완수   completely 완전히, 전적으로

143-146번 문제는 다음 기사를 참조하시오.

Nashville 채용 박람회, 4월 11일 — 연례 Nashville 채용 박람회가 4월 9일 토요일에 시에서 개최되었습니다. **143** 이 박람회는 동남부 지역 전역에 위치한 사업체들을 유치하는 행사입니다. 매년 그랬던 것처럼, 기술 및 제조 분야의 업체마다 대표자들이 **144** 많이 파견되었습니다. **145** 게다가, 올해 평소보다 훨씬 더 많은 엔지니어링 회사들이 참가했습니다. 행사 참관인들은 높은 교육을 받은 Nashville 지역 학생들의 숫자로 인해 그 업체들이 이번 **146** 행사에 참석하기로 결정한 것으로 추정했습니다.

| 어휘 | annual 연례적인, 해마다의   be held in ~에서 개최되다   manufacturing 제조   firm 업체, 회사   represent ~을 대표하다   much (비교급 수식) 훨씬   than normal 평소보다   present 참석한, 출석한   observer 참관인, 관측자   speculate that ~라고 추측하다   choose to do ~하기로 결정하다   attend ~에 참석하다   due to ~로 인해   the number of ~의 수, 숫자   highly educated 높은 교육을 받은, 고등 교육을 받은

143. (B)
(A) 기조 연설자가 또한 올해의 주제를 강조할 것입니다.
(C) 여러 직원들이 자원 봉사자들의 노고를 인정했습니다.
(D) 참가자 수가 과거의 여러 해에 그랬던 것만큼 높지 않았습니다.

| 해설 |
앞 문장에는 과거 시점에 행사가 개최된(was held) 사실이, 바로 다음 문장에는 행사 참가 업체가 속한 분야가 소개되어 있다. 따라서 현재 시제 동사와 함께 참가 업체와 관련해 이 행사가 지니는 일반적인 성향을 언급하는 (B)가 정답이다. (A)는 미래의 일을 말하고 있어 시제 관계가 맞지 않으며, (D)의 경우 뒤에 더 많은 회사들이(much more) 참석했다고 알린 사실과 어울리지 않는다.

| 어휘 | keynote speaker 기조 연설자   highlight ~을 강조하다, 집중 조명하다

theme 주제 fair 박람회 attract ~을 유치하다, 끌어들이다 entire 전체의
several 여럿의, 몇몇의 recognize ~을 인정하다, 표창하다 volunteer 자원
봉사자 attendance 참석, 참석자 수 as A as B B만큼 A한 previous 이전의,
과거의

144. (A)

| 해설 |
수동태를 구성하는 be 동사와 과거 분사 사이에 위치한 빈칸은 과거 분사
를 수식할 부사 자리이므로 부사인 (A) heavily가 정답이다.

| 어휘 | heavily (정도, 양 등) 크게, 많이, 심하게 heaviness 무게(감), 중량,
중압감

145. (D)

| 해설 |
빈칸 앞 문장에는 많은 기술 및 제조 업체 대표자들이 온 사실이 언급되어
있고, 빈칸 뒤에는 많은 엔지니어링 회사들이 올해 참석한 사실이 쓰여 있
다. 따라서, 유사한 내용을 덧붙일 때 사용하는 접속부사 (D) Moreover가
정답이다.

| 어휘 | therefore 그 결과, 따라서 instead 대신 for example 예를 들면
moreover 더욱이, 게다가

146. (B)

| 해설 |
빈칸에 쓰일 명사는 attend의 목적어 자리인데, 지문에서 말하는
Nashville Job Fair를 가리키는 this의 수식을 받아야 하므로 Nashville
Job Fair를 대신할 명사가 필요하다는 것을 알 수 있다. 따라서 '행사'를 의
미하는 (B) event가 정답이다.

| 어휘 | happening 우연한 일, 우발 사건 display 진열(품), 전시(품)

Part 7

147–148번 문제는 다음 공지를 참조하시오.

> 147 저희 Halifax Jewelry에서
> 연중 가장 저렴한 가격을 이용해 보세요!
>
> 147 저희는 148 도심에 위치한 지점에 제품 선택 범위를 확대했으
> 며, 다음 거래 제품을 구입하실 수 있습니다:
> 모든 목걸이: 30% 할인·모든 반지: 40% 할인·모든 팔찌: 50% 할인
> 온라인을 비롯해 다른 어떤 곳에서도 이와 같은 가격을 찾아보실 수 없
> 을 것입니다!
> 저희는 또한 제조사에서 제공하는 2년 품질 보증 기간 외에 5년간의
> 품질 보증 서비스도 제공합니다.
> 오직 10%만 할인되는 고급 제품에 대한 금융 지원 서비스도 이용 가능
> 합니다!
> 이번 세일 행사는 8월 5일부터 8월 8일까지 진행됩니다.
>
> | 어휘 | expand ~을 확대하다, 확장하다 selection 선택 (가능 제품들)
> location 지점, 위치 pick up ~을 구입하다 deal 거래 제품, 거래 조건
> anywhere else 다른 어떤 곳에서도 offer ~을 제공하다(= provide)
> warranty 품질 보증(서) on top of ~ 외에, ~뿐만 아니라 manufacturer
> 제조사 financing 재정 지원, 자금 조달 available 이용 가능한 select
> 고급의, 엄선된 down 할인된 run 진행되다, 운영되다

147. 이 공지는 누구에 의해 발표되었는가?
(A) 마케팅 임원
(B) 재정 자문
(C) 매장 책임자
(D) 제조 담당 기술자

| 해설 |
지문 초반부에, 소속 업체를 our와 We 등의 대명사로 지칭해 가장 저렴한
가격을 이용하도록 권하는 말과(Get our lowest prices ~) 제품 범위를

확대한 사실을(We've expanded our selection ~) 알리는 내용으로 볼
때 해당 매장의 운영 책임자가 공지 발표의 주체임을 알 수 있으므로 (C)가
정답이다.

| 어휘 | executive (기업이나 조직의) 간부, 이사 financial 금융의, 재정의
advisor 고문, 조언자 manufacturing 제조업

148. Halifax Jewelry에 관해 암시된 것은 무엇인가?
(A) 오직 일 년에 한번 세일을 개최한다.
(B) 시내 지역에 지점이 있다.
(C) 2년 동안 운영되어 왔다.
(D) 최근 자사의 건물을 확장했다.

| 해설 |
지문 초반부에, 도심에 위치한 지점이(our city center location) 있다는
정보로 보아 시내 지역에 지점이 있음을 알 수 있으므로 (B)가 정답이다.

| 어휘 | downtown 도심지의 in operation 운영[가동] 중인 recently 최근에

149–150번 문제는 다음 웹 페이지를 참조하시오.

> http://www.auroratech.com.au
>
> | 홈 | 제품 소개 | 이용 후기 | **회사 소개** | 연락처 |
>
> 우리 Aurora Tech는 호주의 선도적인 기술 제품 생산업체입니다. 우
> 리의 품질에 대한 명성은 회사의 성장에 지속적인 동력이 되고 있습
> 니다.
>
> 우리는 다양한 업계에 속한 분들을 위해 해결책을 개발하는 데 크게 힘
> 쏟고 있습니다. 149 우리의 제품은 직원들의 상상력에 의해 힘을 얻습
> 니다. 우리는 최근 150 Blue Skies Program을 시작했습니다. 이 프
> 로그램은 Michael Molnar 씨께서 진두 지휘해 개발된 것으로, 150
> Sydney와 Melbourne, 그리고 Perth 지역 사무실의 직원들이 서
> 로 협업할 수 있게 해주는 것입니다.
>
> 우리는 언제나 기꺼이 우리의 제품과 업무 환경에 관한 의견을 모으고
> 있습니다. 여기를 클릭해 여러분의 의견을 공유해 주십시오.
>
> | 어휘 | review 후기, 평가, 의견 leading 선도적인, 앞서 가는
> technological 기술의 goods 상품 reputation for ~에 대한 명성, 평판
> quality 품질 constantly 지속적으로 drive ~을 추진시키다, 밀어붙이다
> growth 성장 develop ~을 개발하다 solution 해결책 a variety of
> 다양한 industry 업계 be powered by ~에 의해 힘을 얻다, 움직이다
> imagination 상상(력) recently 최근에 launch ~을 시작하다, 출시하다
> spearheaded by ~가 진두 지휘한, 선봉에 선 allow A to do A가 ~할 수
> 있게 해주다 collaborate with ~와 협업하다 gather ~을 모으다
> feedback 의견 work environment 업무 환경 share ~을 공유하다

149. Aurora Tech의 직원들에 관해 암시된 것은 무엇인가?
(A) 경쟁력 있는 급여를 받는다.
(B) 여러 다른 업계에서 근무했었다.
(C) 효율적인 거래 관행을 발전시켰다.
(D) 창의적으로 생각할 수 있다.

| 해설 |
두 번째 단락에, 회사의 제품이 직원들의 상상력에 의해 만들어진다는 (~
powered by the imagination of our employees) 말이 있는데, 이는
직원들이 창의적이라는 말과 같으므로 (D)가 정답이다.

| 어휘 | competitive 경쟁력 있는 compensation 보상 efficient 효율적인
trading (상)거래, 영업 practice 관행 creatively 창의적으로

150. Aurora Tech는 왜 Blue Skies Program을 만들었는가?
(A) 서로 다른 지사에 있는 직원들을 연결시키기 위해
(B) 현재의 고객들로부터 의견을 받기 위해
(C) 사람들에게 기술 장비 이용 방법을 가르치기 위해
(D) 호주 내의 여러 도시에 매장을 개장하기 위해

| 해설 |
Blue Skies Program이 소개되는 두 번째 단락에, 그 프로그램이 Sydney와 Melbourne, 그리고 Perth 지역의 사무실에서 근무하는 직원들이 서로 협업할 수 있게 해준다고(~ allows employees at offices in Sydney, Melbourne, and Perth to collaborate with each other) 알리고 있다. 이는 서로 다른 곳에 있는 직원들을 연결해 주는 것을 뜻하므로 (A)가 정답이다.

| 어휘 | branch 지사 device 장치

151-152번 문제는 다음 온라인 채팅을 참조하시오.

Ryan Maranto [오후 1:38]
Colson 통신에 연락 주셔서 감사합니다. 무엇을 도와 드릴까요?

Wanda Hester [오후 1:39]
제가 방금 제 9월 고지서를 받았는데, **152** 비용이 과다 청구된 것 같아요. 저희 업체는 기업용 기본 패키지에만 가입되어 있거든요.

Ryan Maranto [오후 1:40]
그 고지서 상단에 나와 있는 고객 ID 코드를 알려 주시겠습니까?

Wanda Hester [오후 1:42]
네, TL-93849입니다.

Ryan Maranto [오후 1:43]
감사합니다. **151** 저희 기록에 따르면, Sungate 사가 3주 전에 주소지를 변경했습니다. **152** 그 새 건물에는 광대역 인터넷 선이 없었기 때문에, 1회에 한하는 설치비가 청구되신 겁니다.

Wanda Hester [오후 1:44]
이제 이해가 되네요. **152** 기사 한 분께서 방문하셨던 게 기억이 나요. 질문에 답변해 주셔서 감사합니다.

| 어휘 | contact ~에게 연락하다 receive ~을 받다 bill 고지서, 청구서 it seems that ~인 것 같다 overcharge ~에게 비용을 과다 청구하다 sign up for ~에 가입하다, ~을 신청하다 corporate 기업의 appear 나타나다, 보이다 according to ~에 따르면 broadband 광대역의 charge A B A에게 B를 청구하다, 부과하다 installation 설치 fee 요금, 수수료 make sense 이해가 되다, 앞뒤가 맞다 have A do A에게 ~하게 하다

151. Sungate에 관해 암시된 것은 무엇인가?
(A) 인터넷 서비스 공급업체이다.
(B) Maranto 씨가 속한 회사이다.
(C) 최근 위치 이전 과정을 거쳤다.
(D) 월 서비스 패키지를 업그레이드했다.

| 해설 |
Sungate가 언급되는 1시 43분 메시지에 Sungate가 3주 전에 주소지를 변경했다고(~ Sungate changed its address three weeks ago) 나타나 있으므로 이와 같은 위치 이전을 언급한 (C)가 정답이다.

| 어휘 | provider 공급자, 공급업체 employer 고용주, 고용인 undergo (변화 등을) 겪다, 경험하다 relocation 재배치, 전근

152. 오후 1시 44분에, Hester 씨가 "That makes sense"라고 썼을 때 의미한 것은 무엇이겠는가?
(A) 고지서 요금이 예상보다 더 높았던 이유가 이해된다.
(B) 회사에서 월 이용 요금을 인상한 사실을 기억했다.
(C) 고객 ID 코드를 찾을 수 있었다.
(D) 해당 프로그램을 설명하는 과거의 이메일을 찾았다.

| 해설 |
"That makes sense"는 앞서 1시 43분에 Maranto 씨가 광대역 인터넷 선에 대한 설치비가 청구되었다고(~ so you were charged a one-time installation fee) 말한 것에 대한 반응이며, 바로 뒤에 그 일이 기억난다고(I remember ~) 말하는 것으로 보아 요금 청구를 수긍하고 있다. 이는 1시 39분에 Hester 씨가 문의한 과다 청구 요금의(~ I've been

overcharged) 이유를 이해한다는 뜻이므로 (A)가 정답이다.

| 어휘 | than expected 예상보다 locate ~의 정확한 위치를 찾아내다

153-154번 문제는 다음 이메일을 참조하시오.

수신: Frieda Orlando
발신: Jin-hee Cheong
날짜: 10월 4일
제목: 할 일
첨부: 9월.dox

안녕하세요 Frieda 씨,

153 제가 첨부해 드린 수치와 함께 예산 요약서를 업데이트해 주시기 바랍니다. Warner 씨가 몇몇 장비 구매 내역을 빠트리셨다는 것을 알게 되었기 때문에, 그 부분이 수정되어야 합니다. 위원회가 다음 번에 언제 모일지 확실치 않기 때문에, 아직 최종 문서를 출력하지 않도록 합시다.

우리는 또한 Delway Inc.의 직물 샘플에 대한 평가를 마친 후에 그 가격 정보도 추가해야 합니다. 이 샘플들이 현재 준비되어 있기는 하지만, 그쪽 택배업체에서 내일이나 되어야 배송할 수 있을 겁니다. 불필요한 지연을 피하기 위해, **154** 대신 당신이 점심 식사 직후에 직접 Delway Inc. 사를 방문해 그 샘플들을 받아오셨으면 합니다. 필요하실 경우에 찾아 가는 길을 알려 드릴 수 있습니다. 감사합니다!

Jin-hee

| 어휘 | budget 예산 summary 요약(서) attach ~을 첨부하다, 덧붙이다 figure 수치, 숫자 discover that ~임을 알게 되다, 발견하다 miss ~을 빠트리다, 놓치다 equipment 장비 purchase 구매(품) correct ~을 고치다, 바로잡다 committee 위원회 print out ~을 출력하다 add ~을 추가하다 pricing 가격 (책정) fabric 직물, 천 assess ~을 평가하다 courier 택배업체, 택배기사 not A until B B나 되어야 A하다 be able to do ~할 수 있다 avoid ~을 피하다 unnecessary 불필요한 delay 지연, 지체 need A to do A가 ~하기를 원하다 retrieve ~을 되찾아오다, 회수하다 in person 직접 (가서) instead 대신 directions 찾아 가는 길, 방법

153. 이메일의 목적은 무엇인가?
(A) 예산을 승인하는 것
(B) 위원회 회의를 연기하는 것
(C) 일부 장비를 주문하는 것
(D) 보고서를 업데이트하는 것

| 해설 |
첫 단락 시작 부분에, 첨부한 수치와 함께 예산 요약서를 업데이트하도록 이메일 수신인에게 요청하고 있으므로(Please update the budget summary with the attached figures) 이를 보고서 업데이트로 표현한 (D)가 정답이다.

| 어휘 | approve 승인하다 postpone 연기하다 update 가장 최근의 정보를 알려주다, 갱신하다

154. Cheong 씨는 Orlando 씨에게 무엇을 하도록 요청하는가?
(A) 일부 물품 가져오기
(B) Delway Inc.에 전화하기
(C) 일부 문서 출력하기
(D) 가격 목록 준비하기

| 해설 |
두 번째 단락에, 상대방에게 점심 식사 직후에 직접 Delway Inc. 사를 방문해 샘플들을 받아오도록(I need you to visit Delway Inc. right after lunch to retrieve them ~) 요청하는 내용이 있으므로 이를 언급한 (A)가 정답이다.

| 어휘 | prepare 준비하다

155-157번 문제는 다음 이메일을 참조하시오.

수신: Aberdeen Realty 판매팀 <saleslist@aberdeenrty.com>
발신: Gwen Reyes <reyesg@aberdeenrty.com>
날짜: 7월 16일

안녕하세요, 여러분.

우리 Aberdeen Realty의 최근 예산 감축으로 인해 **155** 세 명의 정규직 그래픽 디자이너들 중 두 명을 해고할 수밖에 없게 되었습니다. 결과적으로, 영업사원들이 오픈 하우스 행사에 필요한 안내 책자를 만드는 일과 같은 몇몇 추가적인 업무를 맡아야 할 것입니다. 따라서, 우리는 여러분이 더욱 손쉽게 업무를 수행할 수 있도록 이 능력을 향상시키는 데 도움이 되는 그래픽 디자인 강좌를 제공할 예정입니다.

이 강좌는 우리 대회의실에서 개최될 것이며, **157(B)** 강사는 권위 있는 Kappa Institute 소속의 Edward Stokes 씨입니다. 각 레벨에 대해 총 다섯 번의 시간이 있을 것이며, 일주일에 한번씩 **157(D)** 5주 동안 진행됩니다. **157(A)** 이 강좌는 점심 식사 시간 동안 진행될 것이므로 늦게까지 회사에 남아 있으실 필요가 없습니다. **156** 계획된 일정은 다음과 같습니다: 매주 화요일 – 초급 레벨, 매주 수요일 – 중급 레벨, 매주 금요일 – 고급 레벨. 여러분에게 가장 적합한 레벨을 선택하시기 바랍니다.

여러분의 업무와 관련해 유연성을 발휘해 주셔서 감사드리며, 영업 활동을 성공적으로 만드는 데 필요한 방법을 제공해 드리기 위해 지속적으로 최선을 다하겠습니다.

안녕히 계십시오.

Gwen Reyes

| 어휘 | recent 최근의 budget 예산 cut 감축, 삭감 result in ~을 결과가 발생되다 lay off ~을 해고하다 as a result 결과적으로, 그 결과 salespeople 영업사원들 be expected to do (기대되는 것으로서) ~해야 하다 take on ~을 맡다 additional 추가적인 task 업무, 일 create ~을 만들어내다 brochure 안내 책자 therefore 따라서, 그러므로 help A do A가 ~하는 것을 돕다 improve ~을 향상시키다, 개선하다 skill 능력, 기술 so that (목적) ~할 수 있도록 carry out ~을 수행하다 be held in ~에서 개최되다 instructor 강사 prestigious 권위 있는 session (특정 활동을 위한) 시간 in total 총, 모두 합쳐 run 진행되다, 운영되다 take place (일, 행사 등) 발생되다, 일어나다 over ~ 동안에 걸쳐 noon break 점심 시간 A is as follows A는 다음과 같다 intermediate 중급의 advanced 고급의 select ~을 선택하다 suit ~에게 적합하다 flexibility 유연(성), 탄력적임 continue to do 지속적으로 ~하다 provide A with B A에게 B를 제공하다 tool 방법, 수단, 도구 make A B A를 B로 만들다 sales 영업, 판매 effort (조직적) 활동, 노력 success 성공

155. Aberdeen Realty는 왜 강좌를 제공하는가?
(A) 직원들이 지속적인 직업 능력 개발을 요청했다.
(B) 그 회사의 한 팀이 규모가 줄어들었다.
(C) 그 회사가 곧 웹 사이트를 공개할 것이다.
(D) 한 기관에서 무료 체험 서비스를 제공한다.

| 해설 |
첫 단락 시작 부분에, 세 명의 정규직 그래픽 디자이너들 중 두 명을 해고할 수밖에 없었던 사실을(~ having to lay off two of our three full-time graphic designers) 전하면서 추가 업무를 맡게 될 직원들에게 필요한 강좌를 제공한다고 알리고 있다. 이는 그래픽 디자인 부서의 인원이 줄어 든 것을 의미하므로 (B)가 정답이다.
| 어휘 | ongoing 계속 진행 중인 professional 직업의, 직종의, 전문적인 downsize 줄이다, 축소하다 launch 출시하다, 시작하다, 착수하다 trial (최종 결정을 내리기 전의) 시험[실험]

156. Aberdeen Realty의 일부 영업사원들에 관해 암시된 것은 무엇인가?
(A) 함께 Kappa Institute를 방문할 것이다.
(B) 보통 다른 직원들보다 더 늦게까지 근무한다.
(C) 추가 고객들을 맡도록 요청받았다.
(D) 이미 약간의 그래픽 디자인 업무 경험을 지니고 있다.

| 해설 |
두 번째 단락에, 초급 레벨에서부터 고급 레벨까지 제공한다는(~ Tuesdays-Beginner Level, Wednesdays-Intermediate Level, and Fridays-Advanced Level) 말과 함께 자신에게 적합한 것을 선택하도록 권하고 있다. 이는 높은 수준의 강좌를 선택하는 일부 직원들은 이미 그래픽 디자인 경험이 있음을 암시하는 것이므로 (D)가 정답이다.
| 어휘 | imply 암시하다 experience 경험

157. 해당 강좌에 관해 언급되지 않은 것은 무엇인가?
(A) 점심 시간에 개최될 것이다.
(B) 외부의 강사가 가르칠 것이다.
(C) 참가하는 데 테스트가 필요할 것이다.
(D) 5주 동안 개최될 것이다.

| 해설 |
두 번째 단락의 'take place over the noon break' 부분에서 점심 시간 개최를 언급한 (A)를, 'the instructor will be Edward Stokes of the prestigious Kappa Institute' 부분에서 외부 강사를 언급한 (B)를, 그리고 'for five weeks'에서 5주라는 기간을 언급한 (D)를 각각 확인할 수 있다. 하지만 참가를 위한 테스트는 지문에 제시되어 있지 않으므로 (C)가 정답이다.
| 어휘 | indicate 나타내다, 보여 주다 outside 외부의 entry 들어감, 입장

158-160번 문제는 다음 사내 소식지를 참조하시오.

싱가포르 관련 소식 요약

디자인팀의 복귀를 알려 드리게 되어 기쁘게 생각하며, **158** 이 팀의 직원 6명이 싱가포르에서 정확히 4일의 시간을 보내고 왔습니다. —[1]— Carrie Eagan 씨께서 이끄는 이 팀은 **158** 국제 디자인 대회의 대화형 미디어 부문 참가에 필요한 프로젝트 작업을 했습니다.

160 우리 회사가 매우 경쟁이 치열한 이 업계 행사에 참가작을 제출한 것은 이번이 처음입니다. —[2]— 비록 우리 디자인팀이 최종 결선 라운드까지 진출하지는 못했지만, 팀원들은 다른 창의적인 전문가들과의 교류를 즐겼습니다. **159** Carrie 씨는 이미 팀이 고유의 정체성을 발전시키고 내년 참가작을 돋보이게 만드는 데 도움이 될 만한 몇몇 아이디어를 갖고 있습니다. —[3]— 우리는 그 작품을 볼 수 있기를 고대합니다! —[4]—

| 어휘 | summary 요약(서) announce ~을 알리다, 공지하다 return 복귀, 반품, 반납 be led by A A가 이끌다 work on ~에 대한 작업을 하다 submit ~을 제출하다 entry 참가(작) highly-competitive 매우 경쟁이 치열한 industry 업계 although 비록 ~이기는 하지만 advance to ~로 진출하다, 나아가다 network with ~와 교류하다 creative 창의적인 professional 전문가 help A do A가 ~하도록 돕다 develop ~을 발전시키다, 개발하다 distinctive 고유의, 독특한 identity 정체(성) make A do A가 ~하도록 만들다 stand out 두드러지다, 눈에 띄다 look forward to -ing ~하기를 고대하다

158. 기사가 왜 쓰여졌는가?
(A) 회사의 반품 정책을 설명하기 위해
(B) 한 팀의 행사 참가를 조명하기 위해
(C) 한 프로젝트에 필요한 아이디어를 만들어 내기 위해
(D) 여러 팀의 구조 조정을 알리기 위해

| 해설 |
첫 단락에, 디자인팀 직원들이 싱가포르에서 4일의 시간을 보내고 돌아온

사실과 함께 International Design Competition의 Interactive Media 부문 참가에 필요한 프로젝트 작업을 한 일을(~ worked on a project for the Interactive Media category of the International Design Competition) 알리고 있다. 따라서 이 행사에 참가했음을 알 수 있으므로 (B)가 정답이다.

| 어휘 | return policy 환불 정책   highlight 강조하다   participation 참가, 참여   generate 발생시키다, 만들어 내다   restructure 구조를 조정하다, 개혁하다

159. Eagan 씨에 관해 언급된 것은 무엇인가?
(A) 업계에서 주는 상을 수상했다.
(B) 독특한 스타일로 알려져 있다.
(C) 한 콘테스트에 다시 참가할 계획이다.
(D) 최근에 팀에 합류했다.

| 해설 |
두 번째 단락에, Carrie 씨가 이미 내년 참가작을 돋보이게 만드는 데(~ make their entry for next year stand out) 도움이 될 아이디어를 갖고 있다고 알리는 부분을 통해 내년에도 행사에 참가할 것임을 알 수 있으므로 이를 언급한 (C)가 정답이다.

| 어휘 | be known for ~로 알려져 있다   enter (대회 등에) 출전[참가]하다

160. [1], [2], [3], [4]로 표시된 위치들 중에서, 다음 문장이 들어가기에 가장 적절한 곳은 어디인가?
"올해는, 전 세계에 있는 최고의 회사에 소속된 직원들이 포함되었습니다."
(A) [1]
(B) [2]
(C) [3]
(D) [4]

| 해설 |
제시된 문장은 특정 대상을 지칭하는 it과 함께 최고의 회사에 속한 직원들이 포함된 사실을 언급하고 있다. 이는 행사 참가자들에 관한 내용이므로 그 행사가 직접적으로 언급된(this highly-competitive industry event) 문장 뒤에 위치한 [2]에 들어가 참가자들의 특징을 소개하는 흐름이 되어야 알맞으므로 (B)가 정답이다.

| 어휘 | include ~을 포함하다   representative 직원, 대표(자), 대리인

161-163번 문제는 다음 이메일을 참조하시오.

발신: cdiaz@diazuniforms.com
수신: dmartinez@evebistro.com
제목: 8월 19일 주문
날짜: 8월 21일

Martinez 씨께,

161 귀하께서 8월 19일에 주문하신 다음 제품들이 배송 준비가 되어 있음을 알려 드리게 되어 기쁩니다.

흰색 요리사 가운 3벌, 미디엄 1벌, 라지 2벌
Trenton 종업원용 조끼 10벌, 스몰 3벌, 미디엄 4벌, 라지 3벌, 회색
Rushmore 타이 10개, 회색

161 재고 수량이 적은 탓에, 아래 기재된 제품들은 지연 주문 처리되어 있으며, 약 10일 후에 구매 가능할 것입니다.
Trenton 종업원용 셔츠 10벌, 스몰 3벌, 미디엄 4벌, 라지 3벌, 검정색
162 Marico 허리 앞치마 10개, 28센티미터 길이, 검정색

162 Marico 허리 앞치마는 25센티미터 길이의 제품만 개당 5.50달러에 구매 가능하며, Rushmore 셔츠는 개당 28달러에 귀하께서 원하신 사이즈를 보유하고 있습니다. 지연 문제에 대해 사과 드리며, 163 위 제품들을 기다렸다가 10일 후에 모두 함께 받기를 원하시는지, 또는 지금 일부 주문만 받으시고 10일 후에 한번 더 받기를 원하시는지, 아니면 일부 제품을 다른 것으로 대체해 즉시 주문을 모두 받기를 원하시는지 제게 알려 주시기 바랍니다.

귀하로부터 답변을 들을 때까지, 주문 사항을 대기 상태로 처리해 귀하의 고객 계정에 어떤 비용도 청구하지 않을 것입니다.

귀하의 성원에 감사드립니다!

Craig Diaz
Diaz Uniforms

| 어휘 | order n. 주문(품) v. ~을 주문하다   inform A that A에게 ~라고 알리다   following 다음의, 아래의   be ready for ~에 대한 준비가 되다   shipping 배송   wait staff 종업원   vest 조끼   due to ~로 인해   stock 재고(품)   listed 기재된, 나열된   below 아래에, 밑에   on back order 지연 주문 처리된, 이월 주문된   available 구입 가능한, 이용 가능한   approximately 약, 대략   in 기간 ~ 후에   apron 앞치마   variety 제품(종류), 품종   Please accept our apologies for ~에 대해 사과 드립니다.   delay 지연, 지체   whether A, B, or C A 또는 B인지 아니면 C인지   receive ~을 받다   partial 일부의, 부분적인   substitute ~을 대체하다   immediately 즉시   until (지속) ~할 때까지   hear back from ~로부터 답변을 듣다   place A on hold A를 대기 처리하다   charge A to B A를 B에 청구하다, 부과하다   account 계정   appreciate ~에 대해 감사하다   patronage (고객의) 성원, 애용

161. 이메일의 목적은 무엇인가?
(A) 지불 금액이 수납되었음을 확인해 주는 것
(B) 긴급 배송 서비스를 이용하도록 권하는 것
(C) 고객에게 주문 사항에 관한 정보를 알리는 것
(D) 결함이 있는 상품을 보낸 것에 대해 사과하는 것

| 해설 |
지문 초반부와 중반부에 각각 배송 준비가 된(~ are ready for shipping) 제품과 그렇지 않은 제품을(~ will be available in approximately 10 days) 알리는 내용으로 구성되어 있는데, 이는 고객의 주문품과 관련된 정보를 전달하는 것이므로 (C)가 정답이다.

| 어휘 | confirm 확인해 주다, 확정하다   expedited shipping 긴급 배송   faulty 결함이 있는

162. Marico 허리 앞치마에 관해 언급된 것은 무엇인가?
(A) 다양한 색상으로 구매 가능하다.
(B) 개당 28달러의 비용이 든다.
(C) 제품의 길이가 다르게 나온다.
(D) Diaz Uniforms로 반품될 것이다.

| 해설 |
지문 중반부에, 배송 지연된 제품으로 28센티미터짜리 Marico 허리 앞치마(Marico Waist Apron, 28-centimeter length)가 언급되어 있는데, 바로 다음 단락에 현재 25센티미터 길이의 제품만(25-centimeter variety) 이용 가능한 상태라고 알리고 있다. 이를 통해 길이가 다르게 나온다는 사실을 알 수 있으므로 (C)가 정답이다.

| 어휘 | multiple 많은, 다수의   come in (물건, 상품) ~로 나오다

163. Martinez 씨는 무엇을 하도록 요청받는가?
(A) Diaz 씨에게 어떻게 일을 진행하기를 원하는지 알리기
(B) 제품 카탈로그에서 일부 제품 확인해 보기
(C) 고객 계정을 이용해 비용 지불하기
(D) 선호하는 배송 회사 말하기

| 해설 |
지문 후반부에, 제품들을 기다렸다가 함께 받는 방법과 일부 주문품만 먼저 받고 10일 후에 한번 더 받는 방법, 그리고 일부 제품을 다른 것으로 대체해 즉시 모두 받는 방법을 언급하면서 원하는 방법을 알려 달라고 요청하는 부분이(~ inform me whether you would like to wait and receive ~) 있다. 이는 배송 업무를 어떻게 진행하기를 원하는지 말해 달라는 것이므로 (A)가 정답이다.

| 어휘 | proceed 진행하다   make a payment 결제하다, 대금을 지불하다

preferred 선호되는

164-167번 문제는 다음 온라인 채팅을 참조하시오.

Patricia Way [오후 3:26]
Ian 씨, **164** 혹시 직원 야유회 일정을 사람들에게 발송하셨나요?

Ian Cheng [오후 3:30]
아직이요. **165** Susan 씨가 월요일 아침에 보낼 예정이셨는데, 이번 주에 병가를 내셨어요.

Patricia Way [오후 3:31]
166 야유회가 여전히 계획대로 목요일에 진행될까요?

Alistair Bruce [오후 3:35]
꼭 그랬으면 좋겠어요. 행사장에 필요한 선금이 이미 지불된 상태이고, 참가하는 직원들을 수용하기 위해 중요한 사업 회의 하나를 금요일로 옮겨야 했거든요.

Ian Cheng [오후 3:41]
그건 걱정하지 마세요. **166** 제가 Susan 씨 비서에게 얘기해서 내일 아침까지 발송되도록 하겠습니다. 모든 일이 잘 처리될 겁니다.

Patricia Way [오후 3:45]
아주 좋습니다. 일정표를 받는 게 정말 기대되네요. 행사장 직원들이 저녁에 있을 우리 팀워크 향상 활동에 필요한 예약 사항을 확인해 주었나요?

Ian Cheng [오후 3:49]
아직 답변을 듣지 못했습니다. **167** 제가 전화를 걸어서 반드시 예약 사항을 확인받도록 하겠습니다.

Alistair Bruce [오후 3:52]
도와주셔서 정말 감사합니다, Ian 씨. 모든 직원들이 올해의 야유회를 정말로 고대하고 있는 것으로 알고 있거든요.

| 어휘 | retreat 야유회 send around (여기저기) ~을 발송하다 be supposed to do ~할 예정이다, ~하기로 되어 있다 send out ~을 발송하다 be off sick 병가를 낸 상태이다 go ahead 진행되다 as planned 계획대로 deposit 선금, 예치금 venue 행사장 move A to B A를 B로 옮기다 in order to do ~하기 위해 accommodate ~을 수용하다 assistant 비서, 조수 get A p.p. A가 ~되게 하다 take care of ~을 처리하다, 다루다 look forward to -ing[명사] ~을 고대하다 receive ~을 받다 itinerary 일정(표) confirm ~을 확인해 주다 booking 예약 hear back from ~로부터 답변을 듣다 phone ~에게 전화하다 make sure (that) 반드시 ~하도록 하다 reservation 예약

164. 논의의 목적은 무엇인가?
(A) 행사에 대한 환불을 요청하는 것
(B) 사업 회의 일정을 잡는 것
(C) 행사의 세부 사항을 이야기하는 것
(D) 회사의 병가 정책을 검토하는 것

| 해설 |
첫 메시지에서, 사람들에게 직원 야유회 일정을 보냈는지(has the schedule for the company retreat been sent around yet?) 물은 뒤로 이 행사의 준비 상황을 공유하는 것으로 채팅이 전개되고 있으므로 행사 세부 사항에 관한 이야기인 (C)가 정답이다.
| 어휘 | request 요청하다 refund 환불 schedule 일정을 잡다 details 세부 사항 sick leave 병가

165. 논의 내용에 따르면, 언제 일정표가 발송됐어야 했는가?
(A) 월요일
(B) 화요일
(C) 수요일
(D) 금요일

| 해설 |
질문의 동사가 'should have p.p.' 형태이므로 원래 일정표가 보내졌어야 하는 시점을 찾아야 한다. 3시 30분 메시지에 Susan 씨가 월요일 아침에 보낼 예정이었다는(Susan was supposed to send it out on Monday morning) 말이 있으므로 (A)가 정답이다.

166. 오후 3시 41분에, Cheng 씨가 "Don't worry about it"라고 썼을 때 의미한 것은 무엇이겠는가?
(A) 일정표를 배포할 수 있다.
(B) 행사장으로 가는 길을 알아낼 수 있다.
(C) 일부 오락 시간을 예약할 수 있다.
(D) 사업 회의에 참석할 수 있다.

| 해설 |
3시 41분 메시지에 Cheng 씨는 '걱정하지 말라'는 말 다음에 Susan 씨의 비서에게 말해 내일 오전까지 발송되도록 하겠다고(I'll speak to Susan's assistant and get it sent out by tomorrow morning) 알리고 있다. 이는 앞서 3시 31분에 Way 씨가 야유회가 계획대로 진행될 수 있는지 묻는 것에 대해 일정표가 문제없이 발송되어 야유회를 진행할 수 있으니 걱정하지 말라는 뜻이므로 (A)가 정답이다.
| 어휘 | circulate 유포하다, 순환시키다 directions 길 안내 entertainment 오락(물), 여흥 attend 참석하다

167. Cheng 씨는 곧이어 무엇을 할 것 같은가?
(A) 일부 발표 슬라이드 자료 준비하기
(B) 병가를 내고 휴식하기
(C) 전화 걸기
(D) 일부 비용 송금하기
| 해설 |
3시 49분에 Cheng 씨가 전화를 걸어서 반드시 예약 사항을 확인받겠다고(I'll phone ~ make sure the reservation is confirmed) 말하고 있으므로 (C)가 정답이다.
| 어휘 | prepare 준비하다 transfer 옮기다, 이동하다

168-171번 문제는 다음 기사를 참조하시오.

회의 – 득보다 실이 더 많다?
Ellen Perna 작성
일반적인 사무직 직장인들은 매달 30회가 넘는 회의에 참석하고 있으며, 이 수치는 관리자 직급에 있는 사람들에게 훨씬 더 높게 나타납니다. —[1]— 많은 회사들이 시험 삼아 일주일에 한번씩 회의 없는 날을 시행하고 있으며, 여기에는 지정 요일에 모든 그룹 회의를 금지하는 것이 포함됩니다. —[2]— **168** 이 시스템을 이용해 본 적이 있는 고용주들은 **169(B)** 업무 생산성의 증대를 경험한 바 있습니다. 이는 직원들이 **169(D)** 각자 배정된 프로젝트에 더욱 쉽게 집중할 수 있기 때문입니다. 직원들은 또한 **169(A)** 회사에 대해 더욱 호의적인 관점을 갖게 된다고 전합니다.

168 이와 같은 정책을 시행하는 고용주들은 해당 정책을 실시하는 데 있어 엄격해야 합니다. —[3]— 그렇지 않으면, 기존의 습관들이 회사 문화에 조금씩 다시 스며들 가능성이 있으며, 직원들은 곧 다시 불필요한 회의로 인해 일이 너무 많아지게 됩니다. **171** 회사의 특성에 따라, 일부 예외가 적용되어야 할 수도 있습니다. —[4]—

회의 없는 날이 반드시 회사에 알맞은 조치가 되도록 하려면, **170** 고용주들은 최소 두 달에 한번씩 직원이 필요로 하는 것을 평가해 필요에 따라 정책에 어떤 조정 사항이 이뤄져야 하는지 결정해야 합니다.

| 어휘 | more harm than good 득보다 실이 더 많은 average 일반적인, 평균적인 attend ~에 참석하다 over ~가 넘는 figure 수치, 숫자 even (비교급 수식) 훨씬 those (수식어구와 함께) ~하는 사람들 at the management level 관리자 직급에 있는 experiment 시험 삼아 ~을 하다, ~을 실험하다 implement ~을 시행하다 meeting-free 회의 없는

involve ~을 포함하다, 수반하다   ban ~을 금지하다   selected 지정된   increase in ~의 증대, 증가   output 생산량   focus on ~에 집중하다, 초점을 맞추다   assigned 배정된, 할당된   favorable 호의적인   view 관점, 시각   policy 정책   strict 엄격한   enforce ~을 실시하다, 시행하다   be likely to do ~할 가능성이 있다   creep back into ~로 조금씩 되돌아가다   be overloaded with ~로 일이 너무 많다   unnecessary 불필요한   depending on ~에 따라, ~에 달려 있는   nature 특성   make an exception 예외를 두다   ensure that 반드시 ~하도록 하다   move 조치, 움직임   evaluate ~을 평가하다   at least 최소한, 적어도   every other month 두 달에 한번씩   determine ~을 결정하다   make an adjustment to ~을 조정하다   if any 필요할 경우에

168. 이 기사의 대상자는 누구일 것 같은가?
(A) 행사 기획자들
(B) 직원 교육 담당자들
(C) 업체 소유주들
(D) 시장 분석가들
| 해설 |
회의 없는 날을 시행하는 일과 관련해, 첫 단락에는 이 시스템을 이용해 본 적이 있는 고용주들이(Employers who have used this system ~) 경험한 장점이, 두 번째 단락에는 그 고용주들이 해당 정책을 실시하는 데 있어(Employers who implement such a policy ~) 엄격해야 한다는 주의 사항을 언급하고 있다. 따라서 회사 소유주들을 대상으로 쓰여진 글임을 알 수 있으므로 (C)가 정답이다.
| 어휘 | analyst 분석가

169. 회의 없는 날의 이점으로 기사에 언급되지 않은 것은 무엇인가?
(A) 직원들이 회사에 대해 더욱 긍정적으로 느끼게 만든다.
(B) 직원들의 효율성을 향상시킬 수 있다.
(C) 직원들이 서로 더 잘 알게 되는 데 도움을 준다.
(D) 직원들이 각자의 업무에 집중할 수 있게 해준다.
| 해설 |
회의 없는 날의 이점이 언급된 첫 단락의 'increase in work output'에서 (B)를, 'staff members can focus on their assigned projects'에서 (D)를, 그리고 'having a more favorable view of the company'에서 (A)를 각각 확인할 수 있다. 하지만 서로 더 잘 알게 되는 것과 관련된 정보는 없으므로 (C)가 정답이다.
| 어휘 | benefit 혜택, 이득   positive 긍정적인   improve 향상시키다, 개선시키다   efficiency 효율성   get to know 알게 되다   concentrate on ~에 집중하다

170. 기사는 무엇을 주기적으로 하도록 권하는가?
(A) 일부 소프트웨어 업데이트하기
(B) 직원들의 필요 사항 재평가하기
(C) 직원 야유회 계획하기
(D) 출장 일정 조정하기
| 해설 |
마지막 단락에 고용주들이 최소 두 달에 한번씩 직원이 필요로 하는 것을 평가해야 한다는(~ employers should evaluate the needs of the staff at least every other month ~) 말이 있으므로 (B)가 정답이다.
| 어휘 | regularly 정기적으로   reassess 재평가하다   outing 야유회   adjust 조정하다, 조절하다

171. [1], [2], [3], [4]로 표시된 위치들 중에서, 다음 문장이 들어가기에 가장 적절한 곳은 어디인가?
"예를 들어, 고객 회의는 주중의 모든 요일에 여전히 열릴 수 있습니다."
(A) [1]
(B) [2]
(C) [3]
(D) [4]

| 해설 |
제시된 문장이 For instance로 시작되고 있어 예시에 해당한다는 것을 알 수 있으며, 고객 회의를 주중 모든 요일에 열 수 있다는 의미이므로 회의 개최 일정과 관련된 예시인 것으로 판단할 수 있다. 따라서 회사의 특성에 따라 예외가 필요하다는 점을 말하는 문장 뒤에 위치한 [4]에 들어가 주중 매일 회의가 필요한 예외적인 경우를 언급하는 흐름이 되어야 적절하므로 (D)가 정답이다.

172-175번 문제는 다음 행사 일정표를 참조하시오.

Winnipeg 창조적 글쓰기 축제(WCWF)
1월 14일-16일, 캐나다 Winnipeg, Vanderbilt Plaza

1월 14일 행사 진행 순서

작가의 방해 요소: 벗어나는 방법   **172** 오전 12:30 – 오후 1:15
Bison Hall
수년 동안의 글쓰기 워크숍과 의견 수렴 시간을 통해, 소설가 Alan Cruz 씨께서는 창의성에 가장 흔히 장애가 되는 요소에 관한 정보를 수집해 오셨습니다. 이 유익한 발표 시간을 통해, Cruz 씨께서 작가들이 지속적으로 아이디어를 샘솟게 하는 방법에 관한 팁을 제공해 주실 것입니다.

영향력 미치기   **172** 오후 1:30 – 오후 2:30
173 Marten Room
Rasmussen 대학의 Arjuna Parikh 글쓰기 교수님께서 미숙한 작가들이 흔히 저지를 수 있는 실수를 공유해 주실 것입니다. 그런 다음, **173** 청중들께 각자의 작품 발췌본을 공개하도록 요청 드려 Parikh 교수님과 경험 많은 동료 교수님들로부터 반응을 들어 볼 것입니다.

문학 평론   **172** 오후 2:45 – 오후 3:15
Gannett Hall
전문가들로 구성된 패널 위원들이 저명한 작가 Melinda Sanchez의 단편 소설에 관한 의견을 제시하는 시간을 지켜보시기 바랍니다.

저술에서부터 구매까지: 작품 출판하기   **172** 오후 3:30 – 오후 5:30
Eider Room
출판 과정을 진행하는 일은 초보 작가들에게 힘들고 혼란스러울 수 있습니다. Maxwell 출판사의 위촉 편집자 Glenda Cordero 씨께서 첫 원고를 준비하는 일에서부터 서점의 선반에 진열된 도서를 확인하기까지의 과정을 하나하나 설명해 드릴 것입니다.

모든 시간에 대한 좌석은 선착순으로 이용 가능합니다.

• **174** 올해는 사전에 유인물의 형태로 보충 자료를 배부해 드리는 대신, 저희 웹 사이트 www.wcwf.org에서 다운로드해 이용하실 수 있습니다. 행사장 전역에서 무료 와이파이 연결 서비스가 이용 가능하며, 비즈니스 센터에서 인쇄도 하실 수 있습니다.

• WCWF의 적은 운영 예산으로 인해, 저희는 **175** 여러분의 입소문에 의존해 다른 분들의 참여를 이끌어 내야 하므로, 많은 홍보 부탁 드립니다.

| 어휘 | creative 창의적인   writing 작문, 저술   block 방해, 장애   path out 빠져나오는 길   through ~을 통해   session (특정 활동을 위한) 시간   novelist 소설가   gather ~을 모으다   obstacle 장애(물)   creativity 창의(성)   informative 유익한   keep A -ing A가 계속 ~하도록 유지하다   flow 흐르다, 흘러나오다   make an impact 영향을 미치다   make a pitfall 실수를 저지르다   inexperienced 미숙한, 경험이 없는   audience members 청중, 관객   be invited to do ~하도록 요청 받다   excerpt 발췌(본)   work 작품, 작업물   receive response from ~로부터 반응을 듣다   colleague 동료   literary review 문학 평론   watch A do A가 ~하는 것을 보다   expert 전문가   short story 단편 소설   established 저명한   get A p.p. A가 ~되게 하다   publish ~을 출판하다   navigate ~을 진행시키다, 처리하다   process 과정   challenging 힘든, 어려운   confusing 혼란스러운   first-time 처음 하는   commissioning editor 위촉 편집자   walk A through B A에게 B를 차례차례 설명하다   prepare ~을 준비하다   manuscript 원고   available 이용 가능한   on a first-come, first-served basis 선착순으로   rather than

~하는 대신, ~하지 않고 distribute ~을 배부하다 supplementary 보충의
material 자료, 재료 handout 유인물 in advance 사전에, 미리 free
무료의 connection 연결 venue 행사장 owing to ~로 인해 operational
운영의 budget 예산 rely on A to do A가 ~하는 것에 의존하다 spread
the word 입소문을 내다 get A involved A를 참여시키다, 관여시키다

172. Winnipeg 창조적 글쓰기 축제에 관해 사실인 것은 무엇인가?
(A) 활동들이 오전과 오후에 진행될 것이다.
(B) 항상 Vanderbilt Plaza에서 주최한다.
(C) 각 시간의 소요 시간이 서로 다르다.
(D) 일부 시간들은 서로 부분적으로 겹친다.

| 해설 |
각 활동 항목별로 지속 시간이 45분(12:30 A.M.–1:15 P.M.), 1시간(1:30 P.M.–2:30 P.M.), 30분(2:45 P.M.–3:15 P.M.), 2시간(3:30 P.M.–5:30 P.M.)으로 다르게 정해져 있으므로 이와 같은 차이점을 언급한 (C)가 정답이다.

| 어휘 | host 주최하다 duration 지속 (기간) partially 부분적으로 overlap 겹치다, 겹쳐지다

173. 참석자들은 어디에서 각자의 글에 관한 의견을 들을 수 있는가?
(A) Bison Hall에서
(B) Eider Room에서
(C) Gannett Hall에서
(D) Marten Room에서

| 해설 |
각자의 글에 관한 의견을 들을 수 있는 활동은 청중들에게 각자의 작품 발췌본을 공개하도록 요청한 다음에 교수들로부터 반응을 들어 보는(~ show excerpts from their own work to receive responses from Mr. Parikh ~) 두 번째 시간에 해당한다. 이 시간이 진행되는 장소가 Marten Room이므로 (D)가 정답이다.

| 어휘 | attendee 참석자

174. 보충 자료에 관해 언급된 것은 무엇인가?
(A) 첫 번째 시간 중에 배부될 것이다.
(B) 참가자들이 다운로드해야 한다.
(C) 사전에 참석자들에게 우송될 것이다.
(D) 비즈니스 센터에서 구입해야 한다.

| 해설 |
보충 자료가 언급된 가장 아래의 항목에 유인물의 형태로 보충 자료를 배부하지 않고 웹 사이트 www.wcwf.org에서 다운로드해 이용할 수 있다는(~ they will be available for download on our Web site ~) 알리고 있으므로 (B)가 정답이다.

| 어휘 | supplemental 보충의, 추가의 participant 참가자 in advance 미리

175. 사람들은 무엇을 하도록 요청 받는가?
(A) 온라인으로 각자의 좌석 선택하기
(B) 예산을 위해 기부금 내기
(C) 다른 이들에게 행사에 관해 말하기
(D) 종료 시까지 질문하지 않기

| 해설 |
요청 사항이 언급된 마지막 항목에, 입소문에 의존해 다른 사람들이 참여하도록 만들어야 한다고 알리면서 소문을 내 달라고(~ we rely on you to spread the word to get others involved, so please do so) 요청하고 있으므로 이를 언급한 (C)가 정답이다.

| 어휘 | make a donation 기부[기증]하다

176–180번 문제는 다음 웹 페이지와 이메일을 참조하시오.

http://www.petstock.com

| 홈 | 온라인 카탈로그 | 고객 이용 후기 | **안내 정보** | 연락처 |

Pet Stock
행복하고 건강한 반려 동물을 위해 필요한 용품!

저희는 전화상으로 또는 온라인으로 주문을 **176** 받을 수 있습니다. 저희는 여러분의 주문품을 정확한 시간에 안전하게 배송해 드리기 위해 최선을 다하고 있습니다. **177** 깨지거나 찢긴 제품, 또는 찌그러진 제품을 받으실 경우, 반송하셔서 전액 환불을 받으실 수 있습니다. 이 경우, 발생되는 모든 배송 요금에 대해서도 비용을 환급해 드릴 것입니다.

배송 요금

배송지	익일 배송, 배송 추적 서비스 포함	일반 배송, 배송 추적 서비스 포함	일반 배송, 배송 추적 서비스 미포함
179 국내 (미국 내)	12.95달러	9.95달러	8.45달러
캐나다/멕시코	29.95달러	19.95달러	17.95달러
북미 이외의 지역	이용 불가능	49.95달러	47.95달러

| 어휘 | review 이용 후기, 평가, 의견 supplies 용품, 물품 take an order 주문을 받다 over the phone 전화상으로 promptly 정확히 제시간에, 지체 없이 receive ~을 받다 broken 깨진, 망가진 torn 찢긴 bent 구부러진 merchandise 상품 full refund 전액 환불 reimburse ~에게 비용을 환급하다 shipping 배송 incur (비용) ~을 발생시키다 destination 도착지, 목적지 overnight 하룻밤 사이의, 야간의 tracking 추적 domestic 국내의 unavailable 이용 불가능한

수신: Pet Stock <customerservice@petstock.com>
발신: Lillian Castleberry <lcastleberry@kearneymail.com>
180 날짜: 3월 13일
제목: Pet Stock 주문

관계자께,

저는 온라인으로 귀사의 매장에서 Kiko 브랜드의 애견 사료를 **179** 국내 배송으로 구입했으며, 이 제품이 어제 **179** 익일 배송으로 도착했습니다. **178** 저는 이 사료를 쓸 수 없다는 것을 알게 되어 대단히 실망스러웠습니다. Kiko 사에서 그 조리법을 변경한 것으로 보이며, 제 강아지가 지금 그것을 먹으려 하지 않습니다. 처음에는, 제가 받은 그 특정 제품에 문제가 있다고 생각해서 **180** 조리 방식이 실제로 변경되었는지를 확인하기 위해 오늘 아침에 지역 매장에 갔었습니다. 귀사의 웹 사이트에는 새로운 조리법에 대한 언급이 없었는데, 저는 이것이 큰 실수라고 생각합니다. 다른 고객들이 동일한 문제를 겪지 않도록 적절히 업데이트해 주시기 바랍니다.

안녕히 계십시오.

Lillian Castleberry

| 어휘 | domestically 국내에서 arrive 도착하다 extremely 대단히, 매우 be disappointed to do ~해서 실망하다 discover that ~임을 알게 되다, 발견하다 unusable 사용할 수 없는 It seems that ~인 것 같다 recipe 조리법 at first 처음에는 specific 특정한, 구체적인 bag 봉지, 포대, 자루 local 지역의, 현지의 whether or not ~인지 아닌지 indeed 실제로, 사실은 adjust ~을 변경하다, 조정하다 mention 언급, 말 significant 큰, 상당한 oversight 실수, 간과 appropriate 적절한 so that (목적) ~할 수 있도록

Actual Test 233

176. 웹 페이지에서 첫 번째 단락, 첫 번째 줄의 단어 "take"와 의미가 가장 가까운 것은 무엇인가?
(A) 선택하다
(B) 붙잡다
(C) 받다
(D) 제거하다
| 해설 |
take의 목적어로 orders가 쓰여 있고, 그 방식으로 전화(over the phone)와 온라인(online)이 언급되어 있다. 따라서 업체가 주문을 받는 방식을 알리는 문장임을 알 수 있으므로 '~을 받다'라는 의미로 쓰이는 (C) accept가 정답이다.

177. Pet Stock에 관해 언급된 것은 무엇인가?
(A) 캐나다로 가는 익일 배송 서비스를 제공하지 않는다.
(B) 대량 구매에 대해서는 더 적은 배송 요금을 부과한다.
(C) 최근에 온라인으로 자사의 제품을 제공하기 시작했다.
(D) 손상된 제품을 반품하는 데 대한 경비를 지불해준다.
| 해설 |
첫 지문 첫 단락에, 깨지거나 찢긴 제품, 또는 찌그러진 제품에 대해 전액 환불을 받을 수 있다는 말과 함께 그럴 경우에는 모든 배송 요금도 환급해준다고 알리고 있으므로(Should you receive broken, torn, or bent merchandise ~ we will also reimburse you for any shipping costs you incur) 이와 같은 비용 환급 내용을 담은 (D)가 정답이다.
| 어휘 | charge (대가, 요금을) 청구하다   large purchase 대량 구매   expense 비용   damaged 손상된, 파손된

178. Castleberry 씨는 왜 이메일을 보냈는가?
(A) 환불을 요청하기 위해
(B) 배송 상태를 확인하기 위해
(C) 불만을 제기하기 위해
(D) 주문을 취소하기 위해
| 해설 |
Castleberry 씨가 쓴 이메일인 두 번째 지문 시작 부분에, 자신이 배송 받은 사료를 사용할 수 없다는 사실에 대단히 실망했다고(I was extremely disappointed to discover that the food was unusable) 알리면서 그 이유를 설명하고 있다. 이는 구매 제품에 대한 불만을 제기하는 것이므로 (C)가 정답이다.
| 어휘 | status 상태, 사정, 상태   complaint 불평, 항의   cancel 취소하다

179. Castleberry 씨는 배송에 대해 얼마를 청구 받았을 것 같은가?
(A) 9.95달러
(B) 12.95달러
(C) 19.95달러
(D) 29.95달러
| 해설 |
두 번째 지문 시작 부분에, Castleberry 씨가 배송받은 방법으로 국내 배송과 익일 배송이 언급되었다(~ to be sent domestically, and it arrived yesterday by overnight shipping). 첫 번째 지문의 도표에서 이 두 가지 항목에 해당되는(Domestic/Overnight with Tracking) 비용이 $12.95로 되어 있으므로 (B)가 정답이다.

180. 이메일에 따르면, Castleberry 씨는 3월 13일에 왜 지역 매장을 방문했는가?
(A) 제품 가격을 비교해 볼 계획이었다.
(B) 대체 물품을 구입해야 했다.
(C) 일부 제품을 교환하고 싶어 했다.
(D) 변경 사항을 확인하기로 결정했다.
| 해설 |
3월 13일이라는 날짜는 이메일 작성 날짜인데, 이메일의 중간 부분에 '오늘 아침(this morning)', 즉 같은 날에 조리 방식이 실제로 변경되었는지를

확인하기 위해 지역 매장에 갔다고(~ so I went to a local shop this morning to check whether or not the recipe had indeed been adjusted) 알리고 있으므로 (D)가 정답이다.
| 어휘 | plan to do ~할 계획이다   replacement 교체, 대체, 교체[대체]물
exchange 교환하다   confirm 확인해 주다, 확정하다

181-185번 문제는 다음 일정표와 이메일을 참조하시오.

국제 지속 가능성 콘퍼런스(ICS)
스웨덴, Stockholm, Atwater 콘퍼런스 센터
181 8월 7일-9일
181 행사 2일차 임시 일정 / 3월 27일에 업데이트됨

오전 8:30-오전 9:30	조찬 연회 및 일일 행사 등록
오전 9:30-오전 10:00	"책임감 있는 사업 확장" Craig Kerr, Vantaa Industries 총무부장 / 핀란드 Helsinki
오전 10:00-오전 11:00	**184** "새로운 풍력 발전 기술" Amrit Chopade, WHB Wind 선임 프로젝트 엔지니어 / 인도 Kolkata
오전 11:00-오후 12:30	"변화 추진하기: 정부 vs. 민간 부문" GebreAdonay, Vancouver Dahlia Research Institute / 캐나다
오후 12:30-오후 1:30	Clover Room에서의 점심 뷔페 식사
오후 1:30-오후 2:30	"주주들의 기대치 관리하기" **181** Celine Blanc, Malquin Industries / 호주 Melbourne
오후 2:30-오후 4:00	이 시간대의 발표자는 아직 확정되지 않았습니다. 행사 기획자인 Raquel Lagesse 씨와 Ignazio Cetta 씨에게 연락해 제안해 주세요.
182 오후 4:00-오후 5:00	**182** "민간 기업들과의 효과적인 제휴 관계 발전시키기" Halima Palomino, Cheron Co., / 이탈리아 Florence

| 어휘 | tentative 임시의, 잠정적인   reception 연회, 만찬   sign-in 등록, 신청   responsible 책임감 있는   expansion 확장, 확대   wind power 풍력   drive ~을 추진하다   private sector 민간 부문   shareholder 주주   expectation 기대(치)   presenter 발표자   time slot 시간대   confirm ~을 확정하다   contact ~에게 연락하다   suggestion 의견, 제안   develop ~을 발전시키다, 개발하다   effective 효과적인   partnership 제휴, 협력

수신: Raquel Lagesse <raquellegesse@icsustainability.org>
발신: Ignazio Cetta <cetta_ignozio@westchesteruni.edu>
날짜: 4월 20일
제목: 일정 업데이트

Raquel 씨께,

요청하신 바와 같이, 분야 내의 여러 저명한 분들께 콘퍼런스 연설 초청장을 **183** 발송해 드렸습니다. 다행히도, 브라질, Sao Paulo에 있는 Bahia Co. 사의 Manuela Gomes 씨께서 Blanc 씨의 발표 다음에 비어 있는 시간대를 자원해서 맡아 주시기로 하셨습니다. 작년에 브라질에서 열린 에너지 정상 회담에서, Gomes 씨는 주거용 태양열 전지판의 비용 효율성에 관해 연설을 하셨습니다. Gomes 씨께서 우리 콘퍼런스를 위해 이 발표의 수정 버전을 준비해 주실 것입니다.

추가로, **184** Amrit Chopade 씨로부터 연락을 받았는데, 이분께서는 질병 문제로 인해 행사 참가를 취소해야 합니다. **185** 이분의 동료이신 Kumari Dheer 씨께서 그 시간대를 맡는 데 동의해 주셨습니

다. 그녀의 전문 분야는 Chopade 씨와 다르기 때문에, 이번 주 후반에 어떤 주제를 다루실 계획인지 제게 알려주실 것입니다. 추가 사항을 확인하는 대로 이메일 보내 드리겠습니다.

안녕히 계십시오.

Ignazio

| 어휘 | extend an invitation 초청장을 발송하다 a number of 많은 (수의) prominent 저명한 figure 인물 field 분야 fortunately 다행히도 volunteer to do 자원하여 ~하다 take ~을 맡다 summit 정상 회담 cost-effectiveness 비용 효율성 residential 주거의 solar panels 태양열 전지판 prepare ~을 준비하다 modified 수정된 additionally 추가로 withdraw from ~을 취소하다, 철회하다 due to ~로 인해 medical ailment 질병 colleague 동료 agree to do ~하는 데 동의하다 one's area of expertise ~의 전문 분야 differ from ~와 다르다 let A know B A에게 B를 알리다 subject 주제 plan to do ~할 계획이다 cover (주제 등) ~을 다루다 find out ~을 확인하다, 알아 내다

181. Blanc 씨에 관해 사실인 것은 무엇인가?
(A) 아침에 연설하도록 요청했다.
(B) 현재 스웨덴의 Stockholm에 거주하고 있다.
(C) 8월 8일에 발표할 예정이다.
(D) 정부의 지원이라는 주제를 다룰 것이다.

| 해설 |
Blanc 씨의 이름은 첫 지문 도표에서 1시 30분에 시작되는(1:30 P.M.-2:30 P.M.) 행사의 발표자로 제시되어 있다. 그리고 상단에 이 도표가 행사 2일차 일정이라는(Tentative Schedule for DAY 2) 정보와 함께 행사 기간이 8월 7일부터 9일인 것으로(August 7-9) 표기되어 있으므로 Blanc 씨는 8월 8일 발표자들 중의 한 명임을 알 수 있다. 따라서 이 사실을 언급한 (C)가 정답이다.

| 어휘 | request 요청하다 currently 현재 reside (특정한 곳에) 살다 be scheduled to do ~할 예정이다 assistance 도움, 원조, 지원

182. 콘퍼런스 참석자들은 언제 사업 관계 형성에 관해 배울 것인가?
(A) 오전 9시 30분에
(B) 오전 11시에
(C) 오후 1시 30분에
(D) 오후 4시에

| 해설 |
질문의 'forming business relationships'는 '사업 관계 형성'을 의미하는데, 첫 지문 도표에서 이에 해당되는 주제의 연설을 찾으면 가장 아래에 쓰여 있는 '효과적인 제휴 관계 발전시키기(Developing Effective Partnerships ~)'이다. 이 발표의 시작 시간이 오후 4시(4:00 P.M.)이므로 (D)가 정답이다.

| 어휘 | attendee 참석자 relationship 관계

183. 이메일에서 첫 번째 단락, 첫 번째 줄의 단어 "extended"와 의미가 가장 가까운 것은 무엇인가?
(A) 개발되었다
(B) 연장시켰다
(C) 확대했다
(D) 제공했다

| 해설 |
동사 extend의 목적어로 '초대장'을 뜻하는 invitation이 쓰이면 '초대장을 발송하다'라는 의미를 나타낸다. 이는 초대장을 제공하는 것과 같으므로 (D)가 정답이다.

184. 어느 연설이 취소되었는가?
(A) 책임감 있는 사업 확장
(B) 새로운 풍력 발전 기술
(C) 변화 추진하기: 정부 vs. 민간 부문
(D) 주주들의 기대치 관리하기

| 해설 |
연설 취소와 관련된 정보는 두 번째 지문 두 번째 단락에 Amrit Chopade 씨로부터 질병 문제로 인해 행사 참가를 취소해야 한다는 연락을 받은 사실이(~ I've been contacted by Amrit Chopade, who must withdraw from the event due to a medical ailment) 언급되는 부분에 나타나 있다. 첫 지문 도표에 Amrit Chopade의 연설이 'New Technologies in Wind Power'로 쓰여 있으므로 (B)가 정답이다.

185. Cetta 씨는 Dheer 씨가 무엇을 할 것으로 예상하는가?
(A) 자신의 행사 출장 경비 부담하기
(B) 조만간 자신에게 선정된 주제 알려주기
(C) 기존의 발표 조정하기
(D) 이번 주에 대체 연설자 고용하기

| 해설 |
Dheer 씨의 이름은 두 번째 지문 두 번째 단락에 언급되는데, Kumari Dheer 씨가 발표자 한 명을 대신하는 데 동의한 사실과 함께 이번 주 후반에 어떤 주제를 다룰 계획인지 알려줄 것이라고(Kumari Dheer, ~ she will let me know what subject she plans to cover) 하는 것으로 보아 곧 선정한 주제를 알려줄 것임을 알 수 있으므로 쓰인 (B)가 정답이다.

| 어휘 | expect A to do A가 ~할 것으로 기대하다 travel expenses 여행[출장] 경비 inform A of B A에게 B를 알리다 recruit (신입 사원 등을) 모집하다 replacement 교체, 대체

186-190번 문제는 다음 두 이메일과 보도 자료를 참조하시오.

수신: Amalia Franco <a.franco@tehama.com>
발신: Randy Wallace <r.wallace@tehama.com>
날짜: 9월 4일 오전 10:24
제목: 독감 예방 주사

안녕하세요, Amalia 씨,

Birmingham 사무소의 프로젝트 책임자이신 Lena Boesen 씨께서 **190** 이곳 본사로 제게 막 전화 주셨습니다. 그분께서 Tehama로부터 후원 받는 One Stop Shot Program과 관련된 **187** 보도 자료 초안을 갖고 계신데, 어떤 질문에 대해서든 사람들이 우리에게 연락할 수 있도록 우리 고객 서비스 전화번호를 추가하도록 권해 주셨습니다. **186** 그분은 무료 진료소들을 이 프로그램에 참여하도록 하는 것이 필수적이라고 말씀하셨는데, 무료 진료소들은 흔히 백신 부족 문제를 겪으면서 어린아이들이나 임산부들로 그 사용을 국한하는 경향이 있기 때문입니다. Boesen 씨의 말씀에 따르면, 이는 노인들을 독감 바이러스에 특히 취약하게 만드는 것입니다. 저는 당신이 오늘 이 일을 처리할 시간이 있기를 바랍니다. 어떠한 문제라도 생기면 제게 알려 주시기 바랍니다.

안녕히 계십시오.

Randy

| 어휘 | flu 독감 shot 주사 headquarters 본사 draft 초안 press release 보도 자료 regarding ~와 관련해 sponsor ~을 후원하다 add ~을 추가하다 customer service line 고객 서비스 전화번호 so that (목적) ~할 수 있도록 contact ~에게 연락하다 It is vital to do ~하는 것이 필수이다 get A to do A를 ~하게 만들다 free 무료의 participate in ~에 참여하다 vaccine 백신 shortage 부족 have a tendency to do ~하는 경향이 있다 limit A to B A를 B로 제한하다 pregnant 임신한 according to ~에 따르면 leave A + 형용사 A를 ~한 상태로 만들다 the elderly 노인들 particularly 특히 vulnerable to ~에 취약한 deal with ~을 처리하다 run into ~을 겪다, ~와 마주치다

수신: Randy Wallace <r.wallace@tehamapharm.com>
발신: Amalia Franco <a.franco@tehamapharm.com>
날짜: 9월 4일 오후 3:19
제목: 회신: 독감 예방 주사
첨부: 보도 자료.doc

안녕하세요, Randy 씨,

187 Boesen 씨의 안내를 바탕으로 보도 자료를 업데이트했으며, 현재 발표 준비가 되어 있습니다. 당신께서 이 프로그램의 중요성을 강조하셨기 때문에, 정확히 올바른 접근 방식으로 되어 있는지를 확실히 해 둘 수 있도록 다시 한번 첨부 파일을 확인해 주시면 감사하겠습니다. Boesen 씨가 또한 이 메시지를 배포하기 위해 언론 매체들과 접촉하기 전에 한번 더 확인해 보기를 원하실 수도 있습니다.

감사합니다.

Amalia

| 어휘 | based on ~을 바탕으로, ~에 기반해 guidance 안내, 지도 publication 발표, 공개 stress ~을 강조하다 I would appreciate it if ~라면 감사하겠습니다 attached 첨부된 ensure that ~임을 확실히 해 두다, 반드시 ~하도록 하다 exactly 정확히 right 올바른, 맞는 approach 접근 방식 have a second look 다시 한번 확인하다 contact ~와 접촉하다 press outlet 언론 매체 distribute ~을 배포하다

즉시 보도용

Tehama가 독감 예방 접종 비율 향상을 위해 노력하고 있습니다

저희 Tehama에서 One Stop Shot Program에 관해서 알려 드립니다. 이 프로그램을 통해, 저희 단체는 여러 주요 도시 내의 무료 진료소를 통해 저소득층 사람들에게 무료로 180만 개의 독감 백신을 제공할 것입니다. 이 프로그램은 또한 과도한 부담을 겪고 있는 진료소에서 자원을 더욱 잘 관리하는 데 도움을 드릴 수 있도록 188 의사와 간호사들을 위해 무료로 하루 동안 참여하실 수 있는 워크숍도 제공해 드립니다. 이 워크숍은 190 St. Louis에 위치한 저희 단체의 본사뿐만 아니라, Detroit와 Cleveland, 그리고 Birmingham에 있는 지사에서도 열릴 것입니다. 이 프로그램에 관한 문의 사항은 1-800-555-7733번을 통해 전달해 주시기 바랍니다.

Tehama에 관해: Tehama는 국내 보건 수준을 향상시키는 데 전념하는 비영리 단체입니다. 189 저희는 기업과 개인의 기부금을 통해 재정적으로 후원 받고 있습니다.

| 어휘 | seek to do ~하기 위해 노력하다, 시도하다 improve ~을 향상시키다, 개선하다 rate 비율 announce ~을 알리다, 공지하다 through ~을 통해 organization 단체, 기관 dose 약의 1회분, 투여(량) available 이용 가능한 for free 무료로 low-income 저소득층 individual 사람, 개인 make A available A를 제공하다 help A do A가 ~하도록 돕다 resource 자원, 재원 overburden ~에게 과도한 부담을 주다 take place (일, 행사) 개최되다, 발생되다 as well as ~뿐만 아니라 branch office 지사 inquiry 문의 be directed to (질문 등이) ~로 전달되다 nonprofit 비영리의 dedicate to -ing ~하는 데 전념하다 financially 재정적으로 donation 기부(금) corporation 기업

---

186. Boesen 씨에 관해 암시된 것은 무엇인가?
(A) Franco 씨와 전화 회의 일정을 잡고 싶어 한다.
(B) 곧 새 지사로 전근될 것이다.
(C) 의료 진료소 운영에 정통한 사람이다.
(D) 작년에 One Stop Shot Program을 총괄했다.

| 해설 |
Boesen 씨로부터 들은 내용이 제시되는 첫 지문에, 그 사람이 무료 진료소의 참여가 필수적이라고 말한 사실, 무료 진료소의 백신 부족 문제를 지적한 부분, 그로 인해 백신 사용을 제한할 수밖에 없는 현실 등이 언급되었다. 이는 전반적인 진료소 운영 현실을 잘 알고 있는 사람이 할 수 있는 말들이므로 (C)가 정답이다.

| 어휘 | transfer to ~로 옮기다, 전근 가다 acquainted with ~를 알고 있는, ~와 친분이 있는 operation 운영 oversee 감독하다

187. Franco 씨는 최근에 무엇을 했는가?
(A) 고객 서비스 교육 실시하기
(B) 웹 사이트에 일부 정보 업로드하기
(C) 회사를 위해 기자 회견 진행하기
(D) 문서에 연락처 추가하기

| 해설 |
Franco 씨의 이름은 두 번째 지문의 발신인 항목에서 찾아볼 수 있으며, 이 지문 첫 문장에 Boesen 씨의 안내를 바탕으로 보도 자료를 업데이트했다고(I have updated the press release ~) 알리고 있다. 첫 지문에서 Boesen 씨가 보도 자료에 고객 서비스 전화번호를 추가하도록 권했다는 것으로 보아(~ she recommended adding the number for our customer service line ~) Franco 씨가 보도자료에 연락처를 추가했다는 것을 알 수 있으므로 (D)가 정답이다.

| 어휘 | conduct (특정한 활동을) 하다 contact details 연락처

188. One Stop Shot Program의 한 가지 목적은 무엇인가?
(A) 소득이 낮은 사람들에게 건강 검진 제공하기
(B) 의료인들에게 교육 제공하기
(C) 학교에 백신 배포하기
(D) 주요 도시들마다 무료 진료소 세우기

| 해설 |
One Stop Shot Program의 목적이 설명되어 있는 세 번째 지문 첫 단락에, 의사와 간호사들을 위해 무료로 하루 동안 참여할 수 있는 워크숍을 제공한다고(~ free one-day workshops for doctors and nurses ~) 알리는 내용이 있으므로 이를 언급한 (B)가 정답이다.

| 어휘 | health checkup 건강검진 medical personnel 의료 인력 distribute 나누어 주다, 분배하다

189. 보도 자료에 무슨 정보가 제공되는가?
(A) 독감 백신 접종의 이점
(B) 진료소들이 충족해야 하는 요건들
(C) 백신 신청에 대한 마감시한
(D) Tehama의 자금 공급원

| 해설 |
보도 자료인 세 번째 지문 하단에 Tehama가 기업과 개인의 기부금을 통해 재정적으로 후원 받고 있다는(It is financially supported by donations from corporations and individuals) 말이 있는데, 이는 Tehama의 운영 자금 공급원을 밝히는 내용이므로 (D)가 정답이다.

| 어휘 | benefit 혜택, 이득 requirement 필요조건, 요건 apply for ~를 신청하다

190. Wallace 씨는 어디에서 근무하는가?
(A) Birmingham
(B) Cleveland
(C) Detroit
(D) St. Louis

| 해설 |
Wallace 씨의 이름은 첫 지문 상단의 발신인 항목에서 찾아볼 수 있으며, 이 지문 시작 부분에 자신이 본사에 근무하고 있음을(~ called me here at the headquarters) 밝히고 있다. 그리고 세 번째 지문 첫 단락에 본사가 St. Louis에 있다고(the organization's head office in St. Louis) 하므로 (D)가 정답이다.

191-195번 문제는 다음 웹 페이지와 이메일, 그리고 공지를 참조하시오.

www.ohlenrentals.com

| 홈 | 차량 예약 | 여행 관련 팁 | 연락처 |

저희 Ohlen Rentals는 차량 대여 서비스에 있어 신뢰할 수 있는 브랜드이며, 전국에 걸쳐 편리하게 이용할 수 있는 지점들이 있습니다. 거의 250만 대에 달하는 규모의 차량들을 보유하고 있지만, 사전 예약이 실망하는 일이 없는 유일한 방법인데, **191** 개별 지점들마다 차량들이 빠르게 소진되는 일이 매우 흔하기 때문입니다.

2월 한 달 내내, 저희는 고객 여러분께 감사의 뜻을 전하기 위해 특별 판촉 행사를 열 예정입니다. 2월 중에 차량을 대여하시는 모든 고객들께서는 대여 차량의 종류에 따라 경품 추첨 행사에 참여하시게 되는데, 소형차 및 경차 대여에 대해서는 100달러 상당의 Ohlen Rentals 상품권을, **193** 중대형 승용차와 SUV 대여에 대해서는 Indigo 호텔 1일 무료 숙박권을, 그리고 운반용 승합차 대여에 대해서는 무료 주말 대여 서비스를 제공해 드립니다. 추가로, 저희 월간 소식지를 신청하시는 모든 고객들께는 휴대용 머그잔이 제공됩니다.

여기를 클릭하셔서 예약 과정을 시작해 주시기 바랍니다.

| 어휘 | trusted 신뢰받는 vehicle 차량 rental 대여, 임대 convenient 편리한 location 지점, 위치 fleet (한 단체가 소유한 차량, 버스 등의) 무리 nearly 거의 book 예약하다 in advance 사전에, 미리 avoid ~을 피하다 disappointment 실망(감) individual 개별적인 branch 지점, 지사 run out of ~가 부족해지다, 다 떨어지다 throughout ~ 동안 내내 hold (행사 등) ~을 개최하다 promotion 판촉, 홍보 show appreciation to ~에게 감사의 뜻을 전하다 rent ~을 대여하다, 임대하다 be entered into ~에 참여하게 되다 prize drawing 경품 추첨 according to ~에 따라 gift certificate 상품권 compact 소형의 free 무료의 moving van 운반용 승합차 in addition 추가로 sign up for ~을 신청하다, ~에 등록하다 reservation 예약 process 과정

수신: Brianna Archambault <archambault_b@gladstone.net>
발신: Ohlen Rentals <bookings@ohlenrentals.com>
날짜: 2월 4일
제목: 예약 확인서

Archambault 씨께,

저희 Ohlen Rentals에서 차량 대여를 예약해 주셔서 감사드립니다. 예약 상세 정보는 다음과 같습니다.

192 대여 날짜/지점	2월 16일/Chicago O'Hare 국제 공항
반납 날짜/지점	2월 21일/Chicago O'Hare 국제 공항
195 패키지 유형	일반
193 차종	대형 SUV
일일 이용 요금	79.99달러
추가 요청 서비스	없음
소식지 신청	신청함
예약 확인 번호	TL49502R7

100달러의 선금이 8861번으로 끝나는 귀하의 신용카드로 청구되었습니다. **192** 차량을 가져가실 때, 반드시 예약에 사용하신 것과 동일한 신용카드를 제시해 주셔야 합니다. 하지만, 잔금은 차량을 반납하신 후에 지불하시면 됩니다. GPS 장치나 유아용 시트 등과 같은 특별 부대용품이 필요하실 경우, 최소 48시간 전에 미리 저희에게 알려 주시기 바랍니다.

| 어휘 | confirmation 확인(서) reserve ~을 예약하다 details 상세 정보, 세부 사항 A is as follows A는 다음과 같다 pick-up 가져가기, 가져오기 drop-off 갖다 놓기, 내려 놓기 rate 요금 requested 요청된 add-on 추가되는 것 deposit 선금 be charged to ~로 청구되다 however 하지만 not A until B B한 후에야 A하다 remaining 남아 있는 balance 잔금, 잔액 accessories 부대용품 device 장치, 기기 inform ~에게 알리다 at least 최소한, 적어도

Ohlen Rentals 고객 여러분께 알립니다.

다음 정보는 모든 Ohlen Rentals 지점에 적용됩니다.

1. 모든 차량 대여에는 제3의 차량과 운전자/동승자의 부상 및 손상에 대한 보상 서비스를 제공하는 **194** 기본 보험이 포함되어 있지만, 추가적인 법적 책임 보호 서비스는 별도의 요금을 통해 이용 가능합니다. 차량 열쇠를 가져가시는 서비스 카운터에서, 여러분의 필요 사항에 더 적합할 수 있는 기타 옵션 구입 방법에 관해 문의하시기 바랍니다.

2. 저희 Ohlen 보상 프로그램이 2월 22일에 종료됩니다. 포인트는 이 시점 이후에도 여전히 사용하실 수 있지만, 새로운 포인트는 쌓으실 수 없습니다.

3. **195** 저희는 더 이상 일반 패키지를 이용하시는 고객들께 두 번째 운전자를 추가하도록 허용하지 않습니다. 이를 원하실 경우에 반드시 프리미엄 패키지로 업그레이드하셔야 합니다.

| 어휘 | apply to ~에 적용되다 come with ~가 포함되다, 딸려 있다 insurance 보험 cover (보험 등이) ~을 보상해 주다 injury 부상 damage 손상, 피해 third-party 제3의 supplemental 추가적인, 보충의 liability 법적 책임 additional 추가의 fee 요금, 수수료 inquire about ~에 관해 문의하다 method 방법 suit ~에 적합하다 earn ~을 받다, 얻다 no longer 더 이상 ~ 않다 allow A to do A에게 ~하도록 허용하다, ~하게 해주다 add ~을 추가하다

191. Ohlen Rentals에 관해 웹 페이지에 암시된 것은 무엇인가?
(A) 국내 및 해외 지사를 보유하고 있다.
(B) 더 많은 차량을 구입할 것이다.
(C) 온라인 예약에 대해 할인을 제공한다.
(D) 서비스에 대한 수요가 높다.

| 해설 |
웹 페이지인 첫 지문 첫 단락에, 개별 지점들마다 차량들이 빠르게 소진되는 일이 매우 흔하다는(it is very common for individual branches to run out of vehicles quickly) 것으로 보아 이 업체의 차량 대여 서비스에 대한 수요가 높다는 것을 알 수 있으므로 (D)가 정답이다.

| 어휘 | domestic 국내의 give a discount 할인해 주다 in demand 수요가 많은

192. Archambault 씨는 2월 16일에 무엇을 할 것으로 예상되는가?
(A) 신용카드 제시하기
(B) 특별 부대용품 요청하기
(C) 비용 지불하기
(D) 항공권 보여주기

| 해설 |
2월 16일이라는 날짜는 두 번째 단락 도표 상단에 차량을 대여해 가는 날짜(Pick-up date, February 16)로 쓰여 있다. 이와 관련해, 도표 아래에 차량을 가져갈 때 예약 시 사용한 것과 동일한 신용카드를 제시해야 한다는(When you pick up the vehicle, you must show the same credit card you used to make the reservation) 말이 있으므로 (A)가 정답이다.

| 어휘 | present 제시하다, 보여 주다

193. Archambault 씨는 추첨 행사에서 무슨 상품을 탈 수도 있는가?
(A) 상품권
(B) 호텔 무료 숙박권

Actual Test   237

(C) 무료 주말 대여 서비스
(D) 휴대용 머그잔
| 해설 |
두 번째 지문 도표 중간에 Archambault 씨가 대여한 차량 종류가 대형 SUV로(Vehicle type, Full-size SUV) 표기되어 있다. 그리고 추천 행사 관련 정보가 제시된 첫 지문 두 번째 단락에 SUV 대여에 대해서는 Indigo Hotel 1일 무료 숙박권을 받을 수 있는(a free one-night stay at Indigo Hotel for full-size and SUV rentals) 경품 행사에 참여하게 된다고 하므로 (B)가 정답이다.

194. 공지에 따르면, 고객들은 차량 출고 카운터에서 무엇에 관해 문의해야 하는가?
(A) 언제 차량을 반납해야 하는지
(B) 어디에서 업데이트된 주행 경로 정보를 얻는지
(C) 차량 유지 관리를 위해 무엇을 해야 하는지
(D) 어떻게 보험 서비스를 구입하는지
| 해설 |
질문에 제시된 pick-up counter는 공지인 세 번째 지문 1번 항목의 'At the service counter where you pick up your keys'에서 찾아 볼 수 있다. 여기서, 기본 보험(basic insurance) 외에 이 차량 대여자에게 더 적합한 기타 옵션 구입 방법에 관해 문의하는 곳으로(~ please inquire about the method for purchasing other options) 이 카운터가 언급되어 있으므로 보험 서비스 구입 방식을 의미하는 (D)가 정답이다.
| 어휘 | maintenance 유지, 보수 관리 policy 정책, 방침

195. Archambault 씨에 관해 사실인 것은 무엇인가?
(A) 대여 차량을 운행하는 것이 허용된 유일한 사람이다.
(B) 자신의 예약에 대해 업그레이드를 요청했다.
(C) 다른 지점으로 차량을 반납할 계획이다.
(D) 대여 서비스에 대해 포인트를 쌓을 수 없을 것이다.
| 해설 |
세 번째 지문 3번 항목에 일반 패키지를 이용하는 사람은 운전자 추가가 허용되지 않는다고(We no longer allow customers to add a second driver with our standard package) 쓰여 있는데, Archambault 씨와 관련된 정보가 제시된 두 번째 지문 도표에 패키지 유형이 '일반'으로(Package type, Standard) 기재되어 있다. 따라서 Archambault 씨가 해당 대여 차량을 운전할 수 있는 유일한 사람임을 알 수 있으므로 이를 언급한 (A)가 정답이다.
| 어휘 | allow A to do A가 ~하는 것을 허용하다 operate 운행(운영)하다

196-200번 문제는 다음 회람과 광고, 그리고 이메일을 참조하시오.

수신: Lawrence Aquarium 전 직원
발신: Evelyn Gibbons, 현장 관리 책임자
제목: 곧 있을 변화
날짜: 2월 25일

여러분, 안녕하세요,

Lawrence Aquarium은 우리 시설로 더 많은 방문객들을 유치하고 더 나은 서비스를 제공하기 위해 많은 변화를 거치게 됩니다. 봄철은 학교마다 현장 학습 행사를 개최하는 일반적인 시기이므로, 우리는 이곳에서 견학을 하도록 장려하기 위해 학교의 단체 방문객들을 위한 특별 판촉 행사를 운영할 것입니다. 경영진에서는 다음과 같은 계획을 마련했습니다. **198** 4월 한 달 내내, 초등학교 학생들은 3달러에 수족관 견학을 할 수 있을 것이며, 이는 평소의 입장료에서 75%가 할인된 요금입니다. 학교의 단체 방문객들과 동행하는 성인은 또한 최대 5명까지 무료로 입장할 수 있습니다.

Darlene Keller 씨께서 우리 시설 전역의 방문객 이동 현황에 대한 평가를 완료하셨습니다. **196** 여기에는 사람들이 가장 많이 방문하는 전시회와 각 지점에서 사람들이 소비하는 평균 시간이 포함되어 있습

니다. 이 평가의 결과물을 검토한 끝에, 우리는 3월 1일부터 Marine Plants 전시회를 폐쇄하기로 결정했습니다. 이로 인해 서쪽 동에 크게 필요했던 일부 공간을 확보하게 될 것이며, **197** 기념품 매장 또는 카페 중 하나를 그 공간으로 이동시킬 예정입니다. 이 결정을 내리기 전에 여러분이 의견을 주시면 감사하겠으니, 이번 주중으로 제게 이메일을 보내 주시기 바랍니다. 카페를 확장할 경우, 현재 우리가 하는 방식대로 제품 포장 옵션만 제공하는 대신 좌석 공간에 필요한 탁자와 의자를 주문할 것입니다.

| 어휘 | ahead (시간상) 앞으로 undergo ~을 거치다, 겪다 a number of 많은 attract ~을 끌어들이다 facility 시설(물) hold (행사 등)을 개최하다 field trip 현장 학습 run ~을 운영하다, 진행하다 promotion 판촉 행사, 홍보 in order to do ~하기 위해 encourage A to do A에게 ~하도록 장려하다, 권하다 come up with (아이디어 등) ~을 생각해내다, 제안하다 following 다음의, 아래의 throughout ~ 동안 내내 be able to do ~할 수 있다 aquarium 수족관 reduction 할인, 감소 admission fee 입장료 up to 최대 ~까지 accompany ~와 동행하다 admit ~을 입장시키다 for free 무료로 complete ~을 완료하다 assessment 평가 flow 이동, 흐름 site 부지, 장소 including ~을 포함해 exhibit 전시회 point 한 지점 review ~을 검토하다, 살펴보다 result 결과(물) decide to do ~하기로 결정하다 close down ~을 폐쇄하다 free up space 공간을 확보하다 much-needed 크게 필요로 하는 wing (건물의) 동, 부속 건물 either A or B A 또는 B 중의 하나 appreciate ~에 대해 감사하다 feedback 의견 make a decision 결정을 내리다 expand ~을 확장하다 instead of ~하는 대신 to-go 포장용의 currently 현재

Lawrence Aquarium 현장 학습 프로그램!

198 4월 1일부터 5월 15일까지, 저희 Lawrence Aquarium은 초등학교 단체 방문객에게 입장료 할인을 제공합니다. 학생들에게는 1인당 불과 3달러의 요금만 청구할 것이며, 해당 단체 고객의 인솔자들은(최대 5명) 무료로 입장하실 수 있습니다. **199** 저희는 또한 방문하는 각 학급에 24″X36″ 사이즈의 고품질 해양 동물 포스터 2장을 제공해 드립니다. 추가 포스터 및 기타 기념품들은 저희 기념품 매장에서 판매되고 있으며, 이 매장은 건물 서쪽 동으로 이전되어 해양을 주제로 한 더욱 다양한 선물 상품 옵션에서 선택하실 수 있게 되었습니다. 555-9931번으로 전화 주셔서 입장권을 예약하시기 바랍니다.

| 어휘 | deal 거래 상품, 거래 조건 offer ~을 제공하다 discounted 할인된 admission 입장(료) charge A B A에게 B를 청구하다, 부과하다 chaperone 인솔자 at no cost 무료로 provide ~을 제공하다 high-quality 고품질의 marine 해양의 additional 추가의, 별도의 souvenir 기념품 on sale 판매 중인 end (한 장소의 중심에서 가장 먼) 끝 an extended selection of 더욱 다양한 marine-themed 해양을 주제로 한 choose from ~에서 선택하다 book ~을 예약하다

수신: Evelyn Gibbons <gibobnse@lawrenceaqua.com>
발신: Cecelia Chavez <chavezc@lawrenceaqua.com>
날짜: 5월 31일
제목: 학교 견학

Gibbons 씨께,

제가 지난 두 달 동안의 수치 자료를 살펴보았는데, 초등학교 학생들에게 다가가기 위한 우리의 결정이 성공적이었다는 사실을 말씀 드리게 되어 기쁩니다. **199** 판촉 행사 기간에 30개의 학급이 우리 시설을 방문했으며, 아이들이 아주 즐거운 시간을 보낸 것 같습니다. 학급용 포스터뿐만 아니라, 우리는 각 아이들에게 전단을 제공해 집으로 돌려 보냈습니다. 한쪽 면에는 해양 동물들의 실태에 관한 내용이 담겨 있고, 다른 한쪽 면에는 학부모들을 위한 연간 회원 정보가 들어 있었습니다. 우리는 이것이 일부 학부모들을 수족관 회원으로 만드는 계기가 될 수 있기를 바라고 있습니다.

200 Ambry 놀이공원과 제휴 관계를 맺기 위한 합의가 최종 확정되었습니다. 다음 달에, 그쪽에서 우리 수족관이 후원하는 작은 수조를 부지 내에 설치할 것이며, 그 목적은 우리 시설에 대한 관심을 이끌어내는 것입니다. 제가 다음 번 기획 회의에서 이 부분에 대한 내용을 더욱 자세히 설명해 드리겠습니다.

안녕히 계십시오.

Cecelia

| 어휘 | figure 수치, 숫자 decision to do ~하기로 한 결정 reach out to ~에게 다가가다 success 성공 have A do A가 ~하게 하다 in addition to ~뿐만 아니라 flyer 전단 fact 사실, 실태 agreement 합의, 동의 partner with ~와 제휴 관계를 맺다 finalize ~을 최종 확정하다 install ~을 설치하다 on-premises 부지 내의, 구내의 fish tank 수조 sponsored by ~가 후원하는 aim 목적 generate interest in ~에 대한 관심을 이끌어내다 explain ~을 설명하다 in greater detail 더욱 자세히 planning 기획

196. Marine Plants 전시회에 관해 암시된 것은 무엇인가?
(A) 건물 내에서 가장 넓은 공간이다.
(B) 그곳의 장비가 수리하기에는 너무 비싸다.
(C) 많은 방문객들이 찾지 않았다.
(D) 한때 견학 행사의 출발 지점이었다.

| 해설 |
Marine Plants 전시회가 언급된 첫 지문 두 번째 단락에, 가장 많이 방문하는 전시회와 각 지점의 평균 방문 시간 자료를 검토한 결과로 3월 1일부터 Marine Plants 전시회를 폐쇄한다는(~ which exhibits get the most visits ~ we have decided to close down the Marine Plants exhibit ~) 내용이 있다. 이는 Marine Plants 전시회를 관람하는 사람이 많지 않았음을 의미하는 것이므로 (C)가 정답이다.

| 어휘 | room 공간 equipment 장비

197. Gibbons 씨는 회람 수신자들에게 무엇을 하도록 요청했는가?
(A) 단체 활동을 위한 의견 제공하기
(B) 추가 견학 행사를 이끌도록 자원하기
(C) 특가 상품에 관한 정보 검토하기
(D) 두 가지 선택 사항에 관한 의견 공유하기

| 해설 |
Gibbons 씨의 이름은 첫 번째 지문 상단의 발신인 항목에서 찾아볼 수 있으며, 이 지문 두 번째 단락에 기념품 매장 또는 카페 중의 하나를 옮기는 일과 관련해 수신자들의 의견을 들어볼 수 있도록 이메일을 보내라고(~ we will move either the gift shop or the café ~ We would appreciate your feedback ~) 요청하고 있다. 따라서 이와 같은 의견 공유 내용을 언급한 (D)가 정답이다.

| 어휘 | recipient 받는 사람, 수령인 suggestion 제안, 제의 volunteer to do 자원해서 ~하다 share 공유하다 opinion 의견

198. 초등학교를 대상으로 하는 애초의 계획이 어떻게 변경되었는가?
(A) 운영 시간이 연장되었다.
(B) 어린이 입장권이 더 할인되었다.
(C) 할인 기간이 연장되었다.
(D) 성인 대상 입장료가 면제되었다.

| 해설 |
첫 지문 첫 단락에는 4월 한 달 내내 초등학교 학생들이 3달러에 수족관 견학을 할 수 있다고(~ throughout the month of April, elementary school students will ~) 쓰여 있는데, 두 번째 지문에는 4월 1일부터 5월 15일까지 초등학교 단체 방문객들에게 할인 입장료를 제공한다고(From April 1 to May 15, ~ offer discounted admission for elementary school groups) 알리고 있다. 따라서 할인 기간이 늘어났음을 알 수 있으므로 (C)가 정답이다.

| 어휘 | original 원래의 extend 연장하다, 확대하다 waive (권리 등을) 포기하다

199. Lawrence Aquarium에 관해 암시된 것은 무엇인가?
(A) 카페 좌석 공간에 필요한 가구를 구입했다.
(B) 60개의 해양 동물 포스터를 배부했다.
(C) 아이들을 위한 포스터 디자인 콘테스트를 개최했다.
(D) 학부모들에게 일부 신규 회원권을 판매했다.

| 해설 |
두 번째 지문에 각 학급에게 24"X36" 사이즈의 고품질 해양 동물 포스터 2장을 제공한다고(We will also provide two high-quality 24' X 36' posters ~) 쓰여 있는데, 세 번째 지문 첫 번째 단락에 판촉 행사 기간에 30개의 학급이 방문한 사실(We had thirty classes visit our site ~) 언급되어 있다. 따라서 총 60개의 포스터를 제공한 것으로 생각할 수 있으므로 (B)가 정답이다.

| 어휘 | distribute ~을 배포하다

200. Chavez 씨는 왜 Ambry 놀이공원을 언급하는가?
(A) 해당 수족관과 사업 관계를 형성했다.
(B) 초등학교에 유사한 견학 할인 서비스를 제공하고 있다.
(C) 현재 해당 수족관의 가장 큰 경쟁업체들 중 하나이다.
(D) 자선 기금 마련 행사를 후원할 계획을 갖고 있다.

| 해설 |
Ambry Amusement Park가 언급되는 세 번째 지문 두 번째 단락에, 이곳과 제휴 관계를 맺기 위한 합의가 최종 확정되었다고(The agreement to partner with Ambry Amusement Park has been finalized) 알리고 있으므로 이와 같은 사업 관계를 언급한 (A)가 정답이다.

| 어휘 | relationship 관계 similar 유사한 competitor 경쟁자, 경쟁 업체 sponsor 후원하다 charity 자선 (단체) fundraising 모금 활동(의)

필요한 내용만 알차게 담은
똑똑한 기본서

1. 20일 커리큘럼으로 LC와 RC를 한 번에!
   두께가 부담스러운 기본서 대신 700~800점 달성에
   최적화된 컴팩트한 분량의 20일 커리큘럼

2. 철저한 데이터 분석을 바탕으로 한 출제빈도 수록
   최소한의 학습과 시간으로 목표 점수에 도달할 수 있도록
   출제 빈도가 높은 문제만 수록

3. 다양한 무료 학습자료 제공
   다양한 버전의 무료 MP3 다운로드(LC)
   실전 시험과 비슷한 난이도의 Actual Test 2회 제공 (교재 1회 + 온라인 1회)